Pro Spring 3

Clarence Ho

Apress®

Pro Spring 3

ISBN-13 (pbk): 978-1-4302-4107-2

ISBN-13 (electronic): 978-1-4302-4109-6

President and Publisher: Paul Manning
Lead Editor: Steve Anglin
Developmental Editor: Chris Nelson
Technical Reviewer: Manuel Jordan Elera
Editorial Board: Steve Anglin, Ewan Buckingham, Gary Cornell, Louise Corrigan, Morgan Ertel, Jonathan Gennick, Jonathan Hassell, Robert Hutchinson, Michelle Lowman, James Markham, Matthew Moodie, Jeff Olson, Jeffrey Pepper, Douglas Pundick, Ben Renow-Clarke, Dominic Shakeshaft, Gwenan Spearing, Matt Wade, Tom Welsh
Coordinating Editor: Brent Dubi
Copy Editor: Kim Wimpsett
Compositor: Mary Sudul
Indexer: SPi Global
Cover Designer: Anna Ishchenko

Distributed to the book trade worldwide by Springer Science+Business Media New York, 233 Spring Street, 6th Floor, New York, NY 10013. Phone 1-800-SPRINGER, fax (201) 348-4505, e-mail orders-ny@springer-sbm.com, or visit www.springeronline.com.

For information on translations, please e-mail rights@apress.com, or visit www.apress.com.

Apress and friends of ED books may be purchased in bulk for academic, corporate, or promotional use. eBook versions and licenses are also available for most titles. For more information, reference our Special Bulk Sales–eBook Licensing web page at www.apress.com/bulk-sales.

Any source code or other supplementary materials referenced by the author in this text is available to readers at www.apress.com. For detailed information about how to locate your book's source code, go to http://www.apress.com/source-code/.

To all my friends and colleagues that I worked with for giving me invaluable support, advice and wonderful working experience. To my family, especially my mom, Yeung, for their true love and warmest support on all of my decisions. Also to the authoring team, including Chris, Manuel and Brent, in providing me extraordinary support in writing this book.

—*Clarence Ho*

Contents at a Glance

Contents

About the Authors

 **Clarence Ho** is the Senior Java Architect of a HK-based software consultancy firm, SkywideSoft Technology Limited (www.skywidesoft.com). Working in IT for over 20 years, Clarence has been the team leader on many in-house application development projects, as well as providing consultancy services on enterprise solutions to clients. Clarence started programming with Java in 2001, and then was heavily involved in the design and development of JEE applications with technologies including EJB, Spring Framework, Hibernate, JMS, WS, etc., beginning from 2005. Since then, Clarence has performed as a Java Enterprise Architect.

Currently Clarence is working as a consultant for an international financial institution, contributing in various areas including Java EE architectural design, education, providing recommendations on technology solutions as well as application development best practices.

When he has spare time, Clarence enjoys playing sports (jogging, swimming, soccer, hiking, etc.), reading, watching movies, hanging out with friends, etc.

Rob Harrop is a co-founder of SpringSource, the software company behind the wildly-successful Spring Framework. Currently, he is CTO at First Banco. Prior to SpringSource, Rob was co-founder and CTO at Cake Solutions, a boutique consultancy in Manchester, UK. He specializes in high-volume, high-scale enterprise systems.

Rob is the author and co-author of 5+ books. You can follow him on Twitter at @robertharrop

About the Technical Reviewer

Manuel Jordan Elera is an autodidactic developer and researcher who enjoys learning new technologies for his own experiments and creating new integrations.

Manuel won the 2010 Springy Award – Community Champion. In his little free time, he reads the Bible and composes music on his guitar. Manuel is a Senior Member in the Spring Community Forums known as *dr_pompeii*.

Technical Reviewer for these books (All published by Apress):

- Pro SpringSource dm Server (2009)
- Spring Enterprise Recipes (2009)
- Spring Recipes (Second Edition) (2010)
- Pro Spring Integration (2011)
- Pro Spring Batch (2011)
- Pro Spring MVC: With Web Flow (2012)

Read and contact him through his blog at `http://manueljordan.wordpress.com/` and follow him on his Twitter account, @dr_pompeii.

CHAPTER 1

Introducing Spring

When we think of the community of Java developers, we are reminded of the hordes of gold rush prospectors of the late 1840s, frantically panning the rivers of North America looking for fragments of gold. As Java developers, our rivers run rife with open source projects, but, like the prospectors, finding a useful project can be time-consuming and arduous.

A common gripe with many open source Java projects is that they are conceived merely out of the need to fill the gap in the implementation of the latest buzzword-heavy technology or pattern. Having said that, many high-quality, usable projects meet and address a real need for real applications, and during the course of this book, you will meet a subset of these projects. You will get to know one in particular rather well—Spring.

Throughout this book, you will see many applications of different open source technologies, all of which are unified under the Spring Framework. When working with Spring, an application developer can use a large variety of open source tools, without needing to write reams of code and without coupling his application too closely to any particular tool.

In this chapter, as its title implies, we introduce you to the Spring Framework, rather than looking at any solid examples or explanations. If you are already familiar with the Spring project, then you might want to skip this chapter and proceed straight to Chapter 2.

What Is Spring?

Perhaps one the hardest parts of actually explaining Spring as a technology is classifying exactly what it is. Typically, Spring is described as a lightweight framework for building Java applications, but that statement brings up two interesting points. First, you can use Spring to build any application in Java (e.g., stand-alone, Web, JEE applications, etc.), unlike many other frameworks such as Apache Struts, which is limited to web applications. Second, the lightweight part of the description doesn't really refer to the number of classes or the size of the distribution, but rather, it defines the principle of the Spring philosophy as a whole—that is, minimal impact. Spring is lightweight in the sense that you have to make few, if any, changes to your application code to gain the benefits of the Spring core, and should you choose to discontinue using Spring at any point, you will find doing so quite simple. Notice that we qualified that last statement to refer to the Spring core only—many of the extra Spring components, such as data access, require a much closer coupling to the Spring Framework. However, the benefits of this coupling are quite clear, and throughout the book we present techniques for minimizing the impact this has on your application.

Inverting Control or Injecting Dependencies?

The core of the Spring Framework is based on the principle of Inversion of Control (IoC).. IoC is a technique that externalizes the creation and management of component dependencies. Consider an example where class Foo depends on an instance of class Bar to perform some kind of processing. Traditionally, Foo creates an instance of Bar using the new operator or obtains one from some kind of factory class. Using the IoC approach, an instance of Bar (or a subclass) is provided to Foo at runtime by some external process. This behavior, the injection of dependencies at runtime, leads to IoC being renamed by Martin Fowler to the much more descriptive Dependency Injection (DI). The precise nature of the dependencies managed by DI is discussed in Chapter 4.

■ **Note** As you will see in Chapter 4, using the term *Dependency Injection* when referring to Inversion of Control is always correct. In the context of Spring, you can use the terms interchangeably, without any loss of meaning.

Spring's DI implementation is based around two core Java concepts: JavaBeans and interfaces. When you use Spring as the DI provider, you gain the flexibility of defining dependency configuration within your applications in different ways (e.g., externally in XML files, Spring Java configuration classes, or Java annotations within your code). JavaBeans (also known as POJOs, for Plain Old Java Objects) provide a standard mechanism for creating Java resources that are configurable in a number of ways. In Chapter 4, you will see how Spring uses the JavaBean specification to form the core of its DI configuration model; in fact, any Spring-managed resource is referred to as a *bean*. If you are unfamiliar with JavaBeans, then refer to the quick primer we present at the beginning of Chapter 4.

Interfaces and DI are technologies that are mutually beneficial. We are sure that no one reading this book will disagree that designing and coding an application to interfaces makes for a flexible application, but the complexity of wiring together an application that is designed using interfaces is quite high and places an additional coding burden on developers. By using DI, you reduce the amount of code you need to utilize an interface-based design in your application to almost zero. Likewise, by using interfaces, you can get the most out of DI because your beans can utilize any interface implementation to satisfy their dependency.

In the context of DI, Spring acts more like a container than a framework—providing instances of your application classes with all the dependencies they need—but it does so in a much less intrusive way. Using Spring for DI relies on nothing more than following the JavaBeans naming conventions (a requirement that, as you will see in Chapter 5, you can bypass using Spring's method injection support) within your classes—there are no special classes from which to inherit or proprietary naming schemes to follow. If anything, the only change you make in an application that uses DI is to expose more properties on your JavaBeans, thus allowing more dependencies to be injected at runtime.

■ **Note** Spring Framework version 3.0 (and newer) has support for Java-based bean metadata in addition to XML configuration files.

Evolution of Dependency Injection

In the past few years, thanks to the popularity gained by Spring and other DI frameworks, DI has gained wide acceptance among the Java developer communities. At the same time, developers were convinced that using DI was a best practice in application development, and the benefits of using DI were also well understood.

Widespread DI practice also influenced the development of the Java Community Process (JCP) led by Sun Microsystems (acquired by Oracle in 2009). In 2009, "Dependency Injection for Java" become a formal Java Specification Request (JSR-330), and as you might expect, one of the specification leads was Rod Johnson—the founder of the Spring Framework.

In Java Enterprise Edition version 6 (referred to as JEE 6), JSR-330 became one of the included specifications of the entire technology stack. In the meantime, the Enterprise JavaBeans (EJB) architecture (starting from version 3.0) was also revamped dramatically; it adopted the DI model in order to ease the development of various Enterprise JavaBeans apps.

Although we leave the full discussion of DI until Chapter 4, it is worth taking a look at the benefits of using DI rather than a more traditional approach:

- *Reduced glue code*: One of the biggest plus points of DI is its ability to reduce dramatically the amount of code you have to write to glue the different components of your application together. Often this code is trivial—where creating a dependency involves simply creating a new instance of an object. However, the glue code can get quite complex when you need to look up dependencies in a JNDI repository or when the dependencies cannot be invoked directly, as is the case with remote resources. In these cases, DI can really simplify the glue code by providing automatic JNDI lookup and automatic proxying of remote resources.

- *Simplified application configuration*: By adopting DI, the process of configuring an application was greatly simplified. You can use annotations or XML to configure those classes that were injectable to other classes. You can use the same technique to express the dependency requirements to the "injector" for injecting the appropriate bean instance or property. In addition, DI makes it much simpler to swap one implementation of a dependency for another. Consider the case where you have a data access object (DAO) component that performs data operations against a PostgreSQL database and you want to upgrade to Oracle. Using DI, you can simply reconfigure the appropriate dependency on your business objects to use the Oracle implementation rather than the PostgreSQL one.

- *The ability to manage common dependencies in a single repository*: Using a traditional approach to dependency management of common services, for example, data source connection, transaction, remote services, etc., you create instances (or lookup from some factory classes) of your dependencies where they are needed—within the dependent class. This will cause the dependencies to spread across the classes in your application, and changing them can prove problematic. When you use DI, all the information about those common dependencies is contained in a single repository (with Spring, you have the choice of storing the information in XML files or Java classes), making the management of dependencies much simpler and less error prone.

- *Improved testability*: When you design your classes for DI, you make it possible to replace dependencies easily. This is especially handy when you are testing your application. Consider a business object that performs some complex processing; for part of this, it uses a DAO to access data stored in a relational database. For your test, you are not interested in testing the DAO; you simply want to test the business object with various sets of data. In a traditional approach, where the business object is responsible for obtaining an instance of the DAO itself, you have a hard time testing this, because you are unable to replace the DAO implementation easily with a mock implementation that returns your test data sets. Instead, you need to make sure your test database contains the correct data and uses the full DAO implementation for your tests. Using DI, you can create a mock implementation of the DAO object that returns the test data sets, and then you can pass this to your business object for testing. This mechanism can be extended for testing any tier of your application and is especially useful for testing web components where you can create mock implementations of `HttpServletRequest` and `HttpServletResponse`.

- *Fostering good application design*: Designing for DI means, in general, designing against interfaces. A typical injection-oriented application is designed so that all major components are defined as interfaces, and then concrete implementations of these interfaces are created and hooked together using the DI container. This kind of design was possible in Java before the advent of DI and DI-based containers such as Spring, but by using Spring, you get a whole host of DI features for free, and you are able to concentrate on building your application logic, not a framework to support it.

As you can see from this list, DI provides a lot of benefits for your application, but it is not without its drawbacks. In particular, DI can make it difficult for someone not intimately familiar with the code to see just what implementation of a particular dependency is being hooked into which objects. Typically, this is only a problem when developers are inexperienced with DI; after becoming more experienced and following good DI coding practice (e.g., putting all injectable classes within each application layer into the same package), developers will be able to discover the whole picture easily. For the most part, the massive benefits far outweigh this small drawback, but you should consider this when planning your application.

Beyond Dependency Injection

The Spring core alone, with its advanced DI capabilities, is a worthy tool, but where Spring really excels is in its myriad of additional features, all elegantly designed and built using the principles of DI. Spring provides features for all layers of an application, from helper application programming interfaces (APIs) for data access right through to advanced Model View Controller (MVC) capabilities. What is great about these features in Spring is that, although Spring often provides its own approach, you can easily integrate them with other tools in Spring, making these tools first-class members of the Spring family.

Aspect-Oriented Programming with Spring

Aspect-oriented programming (AOP) is one of the "programming models of the moment" in the Java space. AOP provides the ability to implement crosscutting logic—that is, logic that applies to many parts of your application—in a single place and to have that logic applied across your application automatically. AOP is enjoying an immense amount of time in the limelight at the moment; however, behind all the hype is a truly useful technology that has a place in any Java developer's toolbox.

Spring's approach to AOP is creating "dynamic proxies" to the target objects and "weaving" the objects with the configured advice to execute the crosscutting logic.

Another popular AOP library is the Eclipse AspectJ project (`www.eclipse.org/aspectj`), which provides more powerful features including object construction, class loading, and stronger crosscutting capability.

However, the good news for Spring and AOP developers is that starting from version 2.0, Spring provides much tighter integration with AspectJ. The following are some highlights:

- Support for AspectJ-style pointcut expressions

- Support for `@AspectJ` annotation style, while still using Spring AOP for weaving

- Support for aspects implemented in AspectJ for DI

- Support of for load-time weaving within the Spring `ApplicationContext`

Both kinds of AOP have their place, and in most cases, Spring AOP is sufficient in addressing an application's crosscutting requirements. However, for more complicated requirements, AspectJ can be used, and both Spring AOP and AspectJ can be mixed in the same Spring-powered application.

AOP has many applications. A typical one given in many of the traditional AOP examples involves performing some kind of logging, but AOP has found uses well beyond the trivial logging applications. Indeed, within the Spring Framework itself, AOP is used for many purposes, particularly in transaction management. Spring AOP is covered in full detail in Chapters 6 and 7, where we show you typical uses of AOP within the Spring Framework and your own applications, as well as AOP performance and areas where traditional technologies are better suited than AOP.

Spring Expression Language (SpEL)

Expression Language (EL) is a technology to allow an application to manipulate Java objects at runtime. However, the problem with EL is that different technologies provide their own EL implementations and syntaxes. For example, Java Server Pages (JSP) and Java Server Faces (JSF) both have their own EL, and their syntaxes are different. To solve the problem, the Unified Expression Language (EL) was created.

Because the Spring Framework is evolving so quickly, there is a need for a standard expression language that can be shared among all the Spring Framework modules as well as other Spring projects. Consequently, starting in version 3.0, Spring introduced the Spring Expression Language (SpEL). SpEL provides powerful features for evaluating expressions and for accessing Java objects and Spring beans at runtime. The result can be used in the application or injected into other JavaBeans.

In this book, you won't find a chapter dedicated to SpEL. However, throughout the book, we will use SpEL where appropriate with detailed explanations.

Validation in Spring

Validation is another large topic in any kind of application. The ideal scenario is that the validation rules of the attributes within JavaBeans containing business data can be applied in a consistent way, regardless of whether the data manipulation request is initiated from the frontend, a batch job, or remotely (e.g., Web Services, RESTful Web Services, RPC, etc.).

Driven by need, the JCP developed the Bean Validation API specification (JSR-303). The Bean Validation API provides a standard way for defining bean validation rules. For example, when applying the `@NotNull` annotation to a bean's property, it means that the attribute shouldn't contain a null value before being able to persist into the database.

Starting in version 3.0, Spring provides out-of-the-box support for JSR-303. To use the API, just declare a `ValidatorFactoryBean` and inject the `Validator` interface into any Spring-managed beans. Spring will resolve the underlying implementation for you. By default, Spring will first look for the

Hibernate Validator (`hibernate.org/subprojects/validator`), which is a popular JSR-303 implementation. Many frontend technologies (e.g., JSF 2, Google Web Toolkit), including Spring MVC, also support the application of JSR-303 validation in the user interface. The time when developers need to program the same validation logic in both the user interface and the backend layer is gone. The details will be discussed in Chapter 14.

Accessing Data in Spring

Data access and persistence seem to be the most discussed topics in the Java world. It seems that you cannot visit a community site such as `www.theserverside.com` without being bombarded with articles and blog entries for the latest, greatest data access tool. Spring provides excellent integration with a choice selection of these data access tools. In addition to this, Spring makes plain vanilla Java Database Connectivity (JDBC) a viable option for many projects with its simplified wrapper APIs around the standard API.

As of version 3.*x*, Spring's data access module provides out-of-the-box support for JDBC, Hibernate, MyBatis (formerly iBATIS), Java Data Object (JDO), and the Java Persistence API (JPA).

However, in the past few years, because of the explosive growth of the Internet and cloud computing, besides relational database, a lot of other "special-purpose" databases were developed. Examples include databases based on key-value pairs to handle extremely large volumes of data (generally referred to as NoSQL), graph databases, document databases, and so on. To help developers support those databases and to not complicate the Spring's data access module, a separate project called Spring Data (`www.springsource.org/spring-data`) was created. The project was further split into different categories to support more specific database access requirements.

■ **Note**   The support of nonrelational databases in Spring will not be covered in this book. For those who are interested in this topic, the Spring Data project mentioned earlier is a good place to look. The project page details the nonrelational databases that it supports, with links to those databases' home pages.

The JDBC support in Spring makes building an application on top of JDBC realistic, even for more complex applications. The support for Hibernate, MyBatis, JDO, and JPA makes already simple APIs even simpler, thus easing the burden on developers. When using the Spring APIs to access data via any tool, you are able to take advantage of Spring's excellent transaction support. You'll find a full discussion of this in Chapter 13.

One of the nicest features in Spring is the ability to mix and match data access technologies easily within an application. For instance, you may be running an application with Oracle, using Hibernate for much of your data access logic. However, if you want to take advantage of some Oracle-specific features, then it is simple to implement that part of your data access tier using Spring's JDBC APIs.

Object/XML Mapping (OXM) in Spring in Spring

Most applications need to integrate or provide services to other applications. One common requirement is to exchange data with other systems, either on a regular basis or in real time. In terms of data format, XML is the most commonly used format. As a result, there exists a common need to transform a JavaBean into XML format, and vice versa.

Spring supports many common Java-to-XML mapping frameworks and, as usual, eliminates the needs for directly coupling to any specific implementation. Spring provides common interfaces for marshaling (transforming JavaBeans into XML) and unmarshaling (transforming XML into Java objects) for DI into any Spring beans. Common libraries such as the Java API for XML Binding (JAXB), Castor, XStream, and XMLBeans are supported. In Chapter 16, when we discuss remotely accessing a Spring application for business data in XML format, you will see how to use Spring's Object to XML Mapping (OXM) support in your application.

Managing Transactions

Spring provides an excellent abstraction layer for transaction management, allowing for programmatic and declarative transaction control. By using the Spring abstraction layer for transactions, you can make changing the underlying transaction protocol and resource managers simple. You can start with simple, local, resource-specific transactions and move to global, multiresource transactions without having to change your code.

Transactions are covered in full detail in Chapter 13.

Simplifying and Integrating with JEE

As stated earlier, in the past few years, DI frameworks like Spring have gained wide acceptance, and a lot of developers choose to construct applications using DI frameworks in favor of the JEE's EJB approach. As a result, the JCP communities also realize the complexity of EJB, and in versions 3.0 and 3.1 of the EJB specification, the API was simplified, and it now embraces many of the concepts from DI.

However, for those applications that were built on EJB or need to deploy the Spring-based applications in a JEE container and utilize the application server's enterprise services (e.g., JTA Transaction Manager, data source connection pooling, JMS connection factories, etc.), Spring also provides simplified support for those technologies. For EJB, Spring provides a simple declaration to perform the JNDI lookup and inject into Spring beans. On the reverse side, Spring also provides simple annotation for injecting Spring beans into EJBs.

For any resources stored in a JNDI-accessible location, Spring allows you to do away with the complex lookup code and have JNDI-managed resources injected as dependencies into other objects at runtime. As a side effect of this, your application becomes decoupled from JNDI, allowing you more scope for code reuse in the future.

MVC in the Web Tier

Although Spring can be used in almost any setting from the desktop to the Web, it provides a rich array of classes to support the creation of web-based applications. Using Spring, you have maximum flexibility when you are choosing how to implement your web frontend.

For developing web applications, the MVC pattern is the most popular practice. In recent versions, Spring has gradually evolved from a simple web framework into a full-blown MVC implementation.

First, view support in Spring MVC is extensive. In addition to standard support for JSP, which is greatly bolstered by the Spring tag libraries, you can take advantage of fully integrated support for Apache Velocity, FreeMarker, Apache Tiles, and XSLT. In addition to this, you will find a set of base view classes that make it simple to add Excel and PDF output to your applications.

In many cases, you will find Spring MVC sufficient in fulfilling your web application development needs. However, Spring can also integrate with other popular web frameworks such as Struts, JSF, Google Web Toolkit (GWT), and so on.

In the past few years, the technology of web frameworks has evolved quickly. Users have required more responsive and interactive experiences, and that has resulted in the arise of Ajax as a widely adopted technology in developing Rich Internet Applications (RIAs). On the other hand, users also want to be able to access their applications from any device, including smartphones and tablets. This results in the requirements of web frameworks that support HTML5, JavaScript, and CSS3 to fulfill the requirements. In Chapter 17, we will discuss developing web applications using Spring MVC with jQuery (a popular JavaScript library supporting Ajax and many other features) and JSP.

Another Spring project for web application development that's worth mentioning is the Spring Web Flow project (`www.springframework.org/webflow`). The project was developed to address the needs of controlling the page flow, as well as provide more fine-grained control on web application–based data that needs to be maintain across a series of pages (called *conversational scope*). In Chapter 18, we will take a look on Spring Web Flow project and its integration with PrimeFaces (`www.primefaces.org`), a popular JSF framework.

Remoting Support

Accessing or exposing remote components in Java has never been the simplest of jobs. Using Spring, you can take advantage of extensive support for a wide range of remoting techniques to quickly expose and access remote services.

Spring provides support for a variety of remote access mechanisms, including Java RMI, JAXRPC, Caucho Hessian, and Caucho Burlap. In addition to these remoting protocols, Spring also provides its own HTTP-based invoker that is based on standard Java serialization. By applying Spring's dynamic proxying capabilities, you can have a proxy to a remote resource injected as a dependency into one of your classes, thus removing the need to couple your application to a specific remoting implementation and also reducing the amount of code you need to write for your application.

Another remote technology that has gained wide acceptance these days is the RESTful Web Services (RESTful-WS). RESTful-WS is designed around HTTP and greatly simplifies the mechanism in invoking services and getting the result. For example, when a client issues an HTTP GET request to the URL `http://somedomain.com/someapp/customer/123`, it means that the client wants to retrieve the information for customer information with an ID (or customer number) that equals 123. The return value can be either in XML, in JavaScript Object Notation (JSON), or in other formats supported by the clients as stated in its HTTP request header. Starting in version 3.0, the Spring MVC module provides comprehensive support for RESTful-WS. We will discuss remote support in Spring in Chapter 16.

■ **Note** The JCP has also formalized the standard of RESTful-WS as JAX-RS, the Java API for Restful Web Services (JSR 311).

Mail Support

Sending e-mail is a typical requirement for many different kinds of application and is given first-class treatment within the Spring Framework. Spring provides a simplified API for sending e-mail messages that fits nicely with the Spring DI capabilities. Spring supports the standard Java Mail API.

Spring provides the ability to create a prototype message in the DI container and use this as the base for all messages sent from your application. This allows for easy customization of mail parameters such as the subject and sender address. In addition, for customizing the message body, Spring integrates with templating engines, such as Apache Velocity, which allows the mail content to be externalized from the Java code.

Job Scheduling Support

Most nontrivial applications require some kind of scheduling capability. Whether this is for sending updates to customers or performing housekeeping tasks, the ability to schedule code to run at a predefined point in time is an invaluable tool for developers.

Spring provides its own scheduling support that can fulfill most common scenarios. A task can be scheduled either for a fixed interval or by using a Unix cron expression.

On the other hand, for task execution and scheduling, Spring integrates with other scheduling libraries as well. For example, in the application server environment, Spring can delegate the execution to the CommonJ library being used by many commonly used application servers. For job scheduling, Spring also supports libraries including the JDK Timer API and Quartz, a commonly used open source scheduling library.

The scheduling support in Spring is covered in full in Chapter 15.

Dynamic Scripting Support

Starting from JDK 6, Java had introduced the dynamic language support, in which you can execute scripts written in other languages in a JVM environment. Examples include Groovy, JRuby, JavaScript, and so on.

Spring also supports the execution of dynamic scripts in a Spring powered application, or you can define a Spring bean that was written in a dynamic scripting language and injected into other JavaBeans. Spring supported dynamic scripting languages include Groovy, JRuby, and BeanShell. In Chapter 22, we will discuss the support of dynamic scripting in Spring in detail.

Simplified Exception Handling

One area where Spring really helps reduce the amount of repetitive, boilerplate code you need to write is in exception handling. The core of the Spring philosophy in this respect is that checked exceptions are overused in Java and that a framework should not force you to catch any exception from which you are unlikely to be able to recover—a point of view that we agree with wholeheartedly.

In reality, many frameworks are designed to reduce the impact of having to write code to handle checked exceptions. However, many of these frameworks take the approach of sticking with checked exceptions but artificially reducing the granularity of the exception class hierarchy. One thing you will notice with Spring is that because of the convenience afforded to the developer from using unchecked exceptions, the exception hierarchy is remarkably granular.

Throughout the book you will see examples of where the Spring exception handling mechanisms can reduce the amount of code you have to write and, at the same time, improve your ability to identify, classify, and diagnose errors within your application.

The Spring Project

One of the most endearing things about the Spring project is the level of activity currently present in the community and the amount of cross-pollination between other projects such as CGLIB, Apache Geronimo, and AspectJ. One of the most touted benefits of open source is that if the project folded tomorrow, you would be left with the code; but let's face it—you do not want to be left with a codebase the size of Spring to support and improve upon. For this reason, it is comforting to know how well established and active the Spring community is.

Origins of Spring

The origins of Spring can be traced back to the book *Expert One-to-One J2EE Design and Development* by Rod Johnson (Wrox, 2002). In this book, Rod presented his own framework called the Interface 21 Framework, a framework he developed to use in his own applications. Released into the open source world, this framework formed the foundation of the Spring Framework as we know it today.

Spring proceeded quickly through the early beta and release candidate stages, and the first official 1.0 release was made available March 24, 2004. Since then, Spring has undergone dramatic growth, and at the time of writing, the latest version of Spring Framework is 3.1.

The Spring Community

The Spring community is one of the best in any open source project we have encountered. The mailing lists and forums are always active, and progress on new features is usually rapid. The development team is truly dedicated to making Spring the most successful of all the Java application frameworks, and this shows in the quality of the code that is reproduced. Much of the ongoing development in Spring is in reworking existing code to be faster, smaller, neater, or all three.

As we mentioned already, Spring also benefits from excellent relationships with other open source projects, a fact that is extremely beneficial when you consider the large amount of dependency the full Spring distribution has.

From a user's perspective, perhaps one of the best features of Spring is the excellent documentation and test suite that accompany the distribution. Documentation is provided for almost all the features of Spring, making picking up the framework simple for new users. The test suite Spring provides is impressively comprehensive—the development team writes tests for everything. If they discover a bug, they fix that bug by first writing a test that highlights the bug and then getting the test to pass.

What does all this mean to you? Well, put simply, it means you can be confident in the quality of the Spring Framework and confident that, for the foreseeable future, the Spring development team will continue to improve upon what is already an excellent framework.

Spring for Microsoft .NET

The main Spring Framework project is 100 percent Java based. However, because of the success of the Java version, developers in the .NET world started to feel a little bit left out; thus, Mark Pollack and Rod Johnson started the Spring .NET project. Aside from Rod, both projects have completely different development teams, so the .NET project should have minimal impact on the Spring Java. In fact, the authors believe this is excellent news. Contrary to popular belief in the Java world, .NET is not a load of garbage produced by the Beast, a fact that we can attest to, having delivered several successful .NET applications to our clients. This project opens up whole new avenues for cross-pollination, especially since .NET already has the lead in some areas, such as source-level metadata, and should lead to a better product on both fronts. Another side effect of this project is that it makes the move between platforms much easier for developers, because you can use Spring on both sides. This is given even more weight by the fact that other projects such as Hibernate and MyBATIS now have .NET equivalents. You can find more information on Spring .NET at `www.springframework.net`.

The SpringSource Tool Suite/Spring IDE

To ease the development of Spring-based applications in Eclipse (the most commonly used IDE for Java application development), Spring created the Spring IDE project. Soon after that, SpringSource, the company behind Spring founded by Rod Johnson, created an integrated tool called the SpringSource Tool Suite (STS). Although it used to be a paid product, the tool is now freely available. The tool integrates the Eclipse IDE, Spring IDE, Mylyn (a task-based development environment in Eclipse), Maven for Eclipse, AspectJ Development Tool, and many other useful Eclipse plug-ins into a single package. In each new version, more features are being added, such as Groovy scripting language support, Spring Roo support, and SpringSource tcServer (an application server with paid support offered by SpringSource that was built on top of the Tomcat server) support. The sample source code in this book for each chapter, as well as the code for the sample application, will all be developed in STS, so you need to download STS and import the projects. (STS will be discussed in detail in Appendix A.) In case you want to know more about using STS for Spring application development immediately, feel free to jump ahead to Appendix A.

The Spring Security Project

The Spring Security project (`http://static.springsource.org/spring-security/site/index.html`), formerly known as the Acegi Security System for Spring, is another important project within the Spring portfolio. Spring Security provides comprehensive support for both web application and method-level security. It tightly integrates with the Spring Framework and other commonly used authentication mechanisms, such as HTTP basic authentication, form-based login, X.509 certificate, SSO product (e.g., SiteMinder), and so on. It provides role-based access control to application resources, and in applications with more complicated security requirements (e.g., data segregations), Access Control List (ACL) is supported. However, Spring Security is mostly used in securing web applications, which we will discuss in detail in Chapter 17.

Spring Batch and Integration

Needless to say, batch job execution and integration are common use cases in applications. To cope with this need and to make it easy for developers in these areas, Spring created the Spring Batch and Spring Integration projects. Spring Batch provides a common framework and various policies for batch job implementation, reducing a lot of boilerplate code. By implementing the Enterprise Integration Pattern (EIP), Spring Integration can make integrating Spring applications with external systems easy. We'll discuss the details in Chapter 20.

Many Other Projects

We've covered the core modules of Spring and some of the major projects within the Spring portfolio, but there still many other projects that have been driven by the need of the community for different requirements. Some examples include Spring BlazeDS for Flex integration, Spring Mobile, Spring Dynamic Modules, Spring Social, Spring AMQP, and so on. Those projects will not be covered in this book. For details, you can refer to the SpringSource web site (`www.springsource.org/projects`).

Alternatives to Spring

Going back to our previous comments on the number of open source projects, you should not be surprised to learn that Spring is not the only framework offering Dependency Injection features or full end-to-end solutions for building applications. In fact, there are almost too many projects to mention. In the spirit of being open, we include a brief discussion of several of these frameworks here, but it is our belief that none of these platforms offers quite as comprehensive a solution as that available in Spring.

JBoss Seam Framework

Founded by Gavin King (the creator of the Hibernate ORM library), the Seam Framework (www.seamframework.org) is another full-blown DI-based framework; it contains layers from web application front-end (JSF), the business logic layer (EJB 3), and JPA for persistence. As you can see, the main difference between Seam and Spring is that the Seam framework is built entirely on JEE standards. JBoss also contributes the ideas in the Seam framework back to the JCP and becomes JSR-299 ("Contexts and Dependency Injection for the Java EE Platform").

Google Guice

Another popular DI framework is Google Guice (http://code.google.com/p/google-guice). Led by the search engine giant Google, Guice is a lightweight framework that focuses on providing DI for application configuration management. It was also the reference implementation of the JSR-330 specification ("Dependency Injection for Java").

PicoContainer

PicoContainer (www.picocontainer.org) is an exceptionally small (around 300KB) DI container that allows you to use DI for your application without introducing any dependencies other than PicoContainer. Because PicoContainer is nothing more than a DI container, you may find that as your application grows, you need to introduce another framework, such as Spring, in which case you would have been better off using Spring from the start. However, if all you need is a tiny DI container, then PicoContainer is a good choice, but since Spring packages the DI container separate from the rest of the framework, you can just as easily use that and keep the flexibility for the future.

JEE 6 Container

As discussed previously, the concept of DI was widely adopted and also realized by JCP. As a result, in JEE 6, the technology stack (EJB 3.1, JPA 2.1, JSR-299, JSR-330, etc.) was mostly revamped to adopt DI and simplify the development of JEE applications. So, when you are developing an application for JEE 6–compliant application servers, you can use standard DI techniques across all layers. At the time of writing, popular JEE 6–compliant application servers include JBoss AS 7, Oracle Glassfish 3.1, and WebSphere 8.

Summary

In this chapter, we presented you with a high-level view of the Spring Framework complete with discussions of all the major features, and we guided you to the relevant sections of the book where these features are discussed in detail. After reading this chapter, you should have some kind of idea about what Spring can do for you; all that remains is to see *how* it can do it. On that note, it is time to proceed.

In the next chapter, we discuss all the information you need to know to get up and running with a basic Spring application. We show you how to obtain the Spring Framework and discuss the packaging options, the test suite, and the documentation. Also, Chapter 2 introduces some basic Spring code, including the time-honored "Hello World!" example in all its DI-based glory.

CHAPTER 2

Getting Started

Often the hardest part of coming to grips with any new development tool is knowing where to begin. Typically, this problem is worse when the tool offers as many choices as Spring. Fortunately, getting started with Spring isn't actually that hard if you know where to look first. In this chapter, we present you with all the basic knowledge you need to get off to a flying start. Specifically, we will look at the following:

- *Obtaining Spring:* The first logical step is to obtain or build the Spring JAR files. If you want to get up and running quickly with the standard Spring distribution, simply download the latest Spring distribution from the Spring web site at www.springframework.org. However, if you want to be on the cutting edge of Spring developments, check out the latest version of the source code from Spring's GitHub repository. If you use Maven for application development, you can simply add the dependencies for Spring into the project's pom.xml (project object model) file, and Maven will download the JAR files for you. Please refer to the section "Spring Modules on the Maven Repository" for details.

- *Spring packaging options:* Spring packaging is modular; it allows you to pick and choose which components you want to use in your application and to include only those components when you are distributing your application.

- *Spring dependencies:* The full distribution of Spring includes a voluminous set of dependencies, but in many cases, you need only a subset of these dependencies. In this section, we look at which Spring features require which dependencies; this information helps you reduce the size of your application to the absolute minimum.

- *Spring samples:* Spring comes with a large selection of sample applications that make ideal reference points for building your own applications. In this section, we will take a look inside the sample applications to give you a feel for the amount of sample code that is available. If you couple this with the sample application you build during the course of this book, you should have more than enough of a codebase from which to start building your own applications.

- *Test suite and documentation:* One of the things members of the Spring community are most proud of is their comprehensive test suite and documentation set. Testing is a big part of what the team does. By using Clover (www.atlassian.com/software/clover), the team actively monitors the percentage of test coverage and is constantly striving to push this percentage higher. The documentation set provided with the standard distribution is also excellent.

- *Putting a spring into "Hello World!":* All bad punning aside, we think the best way to get started with any new programming tool is to dive right in and write some code.

We are going to look at some simple examples, including a full DI-based implementation of everyone's favorite, "Hello World!" Don't be alarmed if you don't understand all the code examples right away; full discussions follow later in the book.

If you are already familiar with the basics of the Spring Framework, feel free to proceed straight to Chapter 3 for a discussion of the sample application that you will be building during the course of this book. However, even if you are familiar with the basics of Spring, you may find some of the discussions in this chapter interesting, especially those on packaging and dependencies.

Obtaining the Spring Framework

Before you can get started with any Spring coding, you need to obtain the Spring code. You have a few options for retrieving the code: you can download a packaged distribution from the Spring web site, or you can check out the code from the Spring GitHub repository. Another option is to use an application dependency management tool such as Maven or Ivy, declare the dependency in the configuration file, and let the tool obtain the required libraries for you.

Downloading a Standard Distribution

Spring hosts its development on the SpringSource download center at `www.springsource.org/download`. Visit this page to download the latest release of Spring (version 3.1 at the time of writing). You can also download milestones/nightly snapshots for upcoming releases or previous versions from the download center.

Starting with release 3.0, the Spring Framework release comes in two flavors: one with the documentation included and one without. Prior to version 3.0, Spring used to provide another package that included all the third-party libraries (e.g., `commons-logging`, `hibernate`, etc.). However, Spring now relies on dependency management tools like Maven and Ivy to express its dependency to third-party libraries on each of its module. So when you declare your project to depend on any Spring module (e.g., `spring-context`), all the required dependencies will be automatically included. More about this will be discussed later in this chapter.

Checking Spring Out of GitHub

In case you want to get a grip on new features before they make their way even into the snapshots, you can check out the source code directly from SpringSource's GitHub repository.

To check out the latest version of the Spring code, first install GitHub, which you can download from `http://git-scm.com/`, and then open the Git Bash tool, and run the following command:

```
git clone git://github.com/SpringSource/spring-framework.git
```

Understanding Spring Packaging

After you download the package and extract it, under the `dist` folder, you will find a list of JAR files that represent each Spring module. After you understand the purpose of each module, you can then select the modules required in your project and include them in your code. Figure 2-1 shows the `dist` folder's content after extracting the downloaded Spring Framework package.

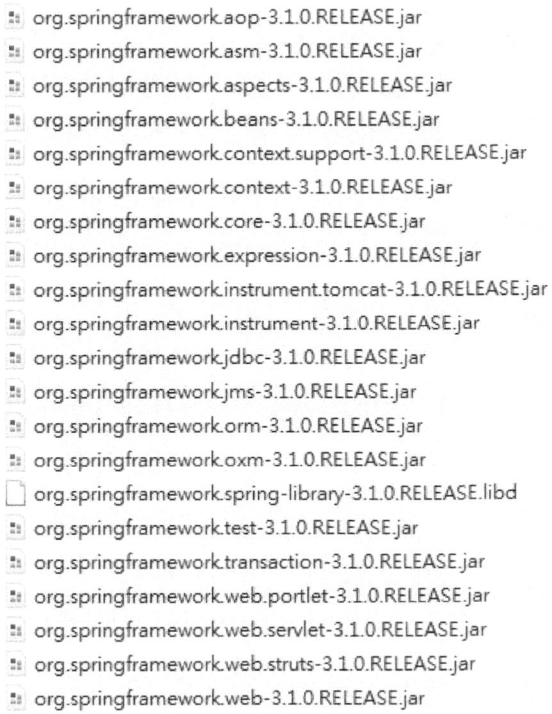

- org.springframework.aop-3.1.0.RELEASE.jar
- org.springframework.asm-3.1.0.RELEASE.jar
- org.springframework.aspects-3.1.0.RELEASE.jar
- org.springframework.beans-3.1.0.RELEASE.jar
- org.springframework.context.support-3.1.0.RELEASE.jar
- org.springframework.context-3.1.0.RELEASE.jar
- org.springframework.core-3.1.0.RELEASE.jar
- org.springframework.expression-3.1.0.RELEASE.jar
- org.springframework.instrument.tomcat-3.1.0.RELEASE.jar
- org.springframework.instrument-3.1.0.RELEASE.jar
- org.springframework.jdbc-3.1.0.RELEASE.jar
- org.springframework.jms-3.1.0.RELEASE.jar
- org.springframework.orm-3.1.0.RELEASE.jar
- org.springframework.oxm-3.1.0.RELEASE.jar
- org.springframework.spring-library-3.1.0.RELEASE.libd
- org.springframework.test-3.1.0.RELEASE.jar
- org.springframework.transaction-3.1.0.RELEASE.jar
- org.springframework.web.portlet-3.1.0.RELEASE.jar
- org.springframework.web.servlet-3.1.0.RELEASE.jar
- org.springframework.web.struts-3.1.0.RELEASE.jar
- org.springframework.web-3.1.0.RELEASE.jar

Figure 2-1. Spring Framework libraries upon extraction

Spring Modules

As of Spring version 3.1, Spring comes with 20 modules, packaged into 20 JAR files. Table 2-1 describes these JAR files and their corresponding modules. The actual JAR file format is, for example, `org.springframework.aop-3.1.0.RELEASE.jar`, though we have included only the specific module portion for simplicity (as in aop, for example).

Table 2-1. Spring Modules

JAR File	Description
aop	This module contains all the classes you need to use Spring's AOP features within your application. You also need to include this JAR in your application if you plan to use other features in Spring that use AOP, such as declarative transaction management. Moreover, classes that support integration with AspectJ are packed in this module too.
asm	ASM (`asm.ow2.org`) is a Java bytecode manipulation framework. Spring depends on this library to analyze the bytecode of Spring beans, dynamically modify them, and generate new bytecode during runtime.

JAR File	Description
aspects	This module contains all the classes for advanced integration with the AspectJ AOP library. For example, if you are using Java classes for your Spring configuration and need AspectJ-style annotation-driven transaction management, you will need this module.
beans	This module contains all the classes for supporting Spring's manipulation of Spring beans. Most of the classes here support Spring's bean factory implementation. For example, the classes required to parse the Spring's XML configuration file and Java annotations were packed into this module.
context	This module contains classes that provide many extensions to the Spring core. You will find that all classes need to use Spring's ApplicationContext feature (covered in Chapter 5), along with classes for EJB, Java Naming and Directory Interface (JNDI), and Java Management Extensions (JMX) integration. Also contained in this module are the Spring remoting classes, classes for integration with dynamic scripting languages (e.g., JRuby, Groovy, BeanShell), the Beans Validation (JSR-303) API, scheduling and task execution, and so on.
context.support	This module contains further extensions to the spring-context module. On the user interface side, there are classes for mail support and integration with templating engines such as Velocity, FreeMarker, and JasperReports. Also, integration with various task execution and scheduling libraries including CommonJ and Quartz are packaged here.
core	This is the core module that you will need for every Spring application. In this JAR file, you will find all the classes that are shared among all other Spring modules, for example, classes for accessing configuration files. Also, in this JAR, you will find a selection of extremely useful utility classes that are used throughout the Spring codebase and that you can use in your own application.
expression	This module contains all support classes for Spring Expression Language (SpEL).
instrument	This module includes Spring's instrumentation agent for Java Virtual Machine (JVM) bootstrapping. This JAR file is required for using load-time weaving with AspectJ in a Spring application.
instrument.tomcat	This module includes Spring's instrumentation agent for JVM bootstrapping in the Tomcat server.
jdbc	This module includes all classes for JDBC support. You will need this module for all applications that require database access. Classes for supporting data sources, JDBC data types, JDBC templates, native JDBC connections, and so on, are packed in this module.
jms	This module includes all classes for JMS support.
orm	This module extends Spring's standard JDBC feature set with support for popular ORM tools including Hibernate, iBATIS (but not MyBatis), JDO, and JPA. Many of the classes in this JAR depend on classes contained in spring-jdbc.jar, so you definitely need to include that in your application as well.

JAR File	Description
oxm	This modules provide support for OXM (object to XML mapping). Classes for abstraction of XML marshaling and unmarshaling and support for popular tools like Castor, JAXB, XMLBeans, XStream, and so on, are packed into this module.
web.struts	This module include all classes for integration between Spring and the Struts web framework.
test	As we mentioned earlier, Spring provides a set of mock classes to aid in testing your applications. Many of these mock classes are used within the Spring test suite, so they are well-tested and make testing your applications much simpler. Certainly we have found great use for the mock HttpServletRequest and HttpServletResponse classes in unit tests for our web applications. On the other hand, Spring provides a tight integration with the JUnit unit testing framework, and many classes that support the development of JUnit test cases are provided in this module; for example, the SpringJUnit4ClassRunner provides a simple way to bootstrap the Spring ApplicationContext in a unit test environment.
transaction	This module provides all classes for supporting Spring's transaction infrastructure. You will find classes from the transaction abstraction layer to support of the Java Transaction API (JTA) and integration with application servers from major vendors.
web	This module contains the core classes for using Spring in your web applications, including classes for loading an ApplicationContext feature automatically, file upload support classes, and a bunch of useful classes for performing repetitive tasks such as parsing int values from the query string.
web.servlet	This module contains all the classes for Spring's own MVC framework. If you are using a separate MVC framework for your application, then you won't need any of the classes from this JAR file. Spring MVC is covered in more detail in Chapters 17 and 18.
web.portlet	This module provides support for using Spring MVC in developing portlets for deployment to a portal server environment.

Choosing Modules for Your Application

Without an IDE such as Eclipse or a dependency management tool like Maven or Ivy, choosing which modules to use in your application may be a bit tricky. For example, if you require Spring's bean factory and DI support only, you still need several modules including spring-core, spring-beans, spring-context, spring-aop, and spring-asm. If you need Spring's web application support, you then need to further add spring-web. For integration with Struts, you'll need spring-struts, and so on.

However, when using an IDE, especially SpringSource Tool Suite (STS), which will be used as the default IDE for all examples in this book, managing/visualize those dependencies becomes much easier. In STS, you have the option to create a Spring template project and choose from a number of project templates that suit your application. A Spring template project uses Maven for dependency management, and STS also is bundled with m2e, an Eclipse plug-in project for Maven integration. When you select the project template, Spring will create the project with the appropriate dependencies declared for you. Thanks to Maven's transitive dependencies support, all required third-party libraries will also be included automatically.

Figure 2-2 shows STS with a simple Spring utility project. The screen comes from the project's pom.xml (Maven Project Object Model) file and m2e plug-in's dependency hierarchy viewer, which is displaying all the dependencies required for the project. From the dependency hierarchy diagram, you can see that the project depends on spring-context, which in turns requires spring-aop, spring-beans, spring-core, spring-expression, and spring-asm. Also, spring-aop further depends on aopalliance, while spring-core depends on commons-logging. By default, the Spring project use log4j for logging purposes. Finally, you can see other testing dependencies (spring-test, junit).

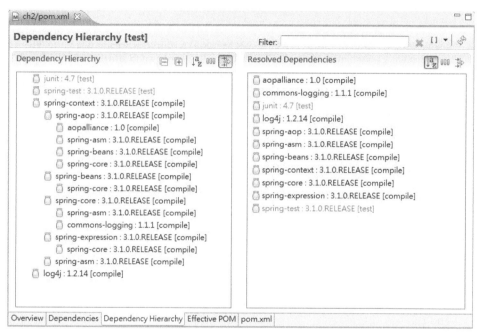

Figure 2-2. *Spring's dependency hierarchy for a simple Spring utility project that utilizes Spring's bean factory and DI features*

Spring Modules on the Maven Repository

Besides downloading them from the Internet, you also can manage Spring libraries via an application dependency management tool, such as Ivy and Maven. In this section, we will take a look at the Spring modules on the Maven repository.

Founded by Apache Software Foundation, Maven (http://maven.apache.org) has become one of the most popular tools in managing the dependencies for Java applications, from open source to enterprise environments.

Maven is a powerful application building, packaging, and dependency management tool. It manages the entire build cycle of an application, from resource processing and compiling to testing and packaging. There also exists a large number of Maven plug-ins for various tasks, such as updating databases and deploying a packaged application to a specific server (e.g., Tomcat, JBoss, WebSphere, etc.).

Almost all open source projects support distribution of their library via the Maven repository. The most popular one is the Maven Central repository hosted on Apache, and you can access and search for the existence and related information of an artifact on the Maven Central web site (http://search.maven.org). If you download and install Maven into your development machine, you automatically gain access to the Maven Central repository. Some other open source communities (e.g., JBoss, SpringSource, etc.) also provide their own Maven repository for their users. However, in order to be able to access those repositories, you need to add the repository into your Maven's setting file.

A detailed discussion on Maven is not in the scope of this book, and you can always refer to the online documentation or books that give you a detailed reference to Maven. However, since Maven is being widely adopted, it's worth mentioning the structure of Spring's packaging on the Maven repository.

Each Maven artifact is identified by a group ID, artifact ID, packaging type, and version. For example, for log4j, the group ID is log4j, the artifact ID is log4j, and the packaging type is jar. Under that, different versions are defined. For example, for version 1.2.16, the artifact's file name becomes log4j-1.2.16.jar under the group ID, artifact ID, and version folder.

Like other open source libraries, Spring's Maven artifacts can be found on Apache's Maven Central. However, SpringSource also hosts its own Maven repository and provides Spring libraries in the form of Enterprise Bundle Repositories (EBRs), which are OSGi compatible. The naming conversion of a Spring EBR is different from Maven Central.

To ease your confusion, it's worth mentioning the naming difference between Spring's artifacts in Maven Central and its own Maven repository, because your development team should standardize on one of them. Generally, using the artifacts from Maven Central is preferred. However, if you plan to deploy your application in an OSGi container (e.g., Spring dynamic modules), then use Spring EBR. Table 2-2 shows the respective naming of Spring's artifacts on Maven Central and SpringSource EBRs. From both repositories, the group ID is the same; just the artifact ID is different. As in Table 2-1, we will include only the module portion of the JAR file names.

Table 2-2. Spring Modules

Spring Module JAR File	Group ID	Artifact ID (Maven Central)	Artifact ID (Spring EBR)
aop	org.springframework	spring-aop	org.springframework.aop
asm	org.springframework	spring-asm	org.springframework.asm
aspects	org.springframework	spring-aspects	org.springframework.aspects
beans	org.springframework	spring-beans	org.springframework.beans
context	org.springframework	spring-context	org.springframework.context
context.support	org.springframework	spring-context -support	org.springframework.context.support
core	org.springframework	spring-core	org.springframework.core
expression	org.springframework	spring-expression	org.springframework.expression
instrument	org.springframework	spring-instrument	org.springframework.instrument
instrument.tomcat	org.springframework	spring-instrument -tomcat	org.springframework.instrument.tomcat
jdbc	org.springframework	spring-jdbc	org.springframework.jdbc

Spring Module JAR File	Group ID	Artifact ID (Maven Central)	Artifact ID (Spring EBR)
jms	org.springframework	spring-jms	org.springframework.jms
orm	org.springframework	spring-orm	org.springframework.orm
oxm	org.springframework	spring-oxm	org.springframework.oxm
web.struts	org.springframework	spring-struts	org.springframework.struts
test	org.springframework	spring-test	org.springframework.test
transaction	org.springframework	spring-tx	org.springframework.transaction
web	org.springframework	spring-web	org.springframework.web
web.servlet	org.springframework	spring-webmvc	org.springframework.web.servlet
web.portlet	org.springframework	spring-webmvc-portlet	org.springframework.web.portlet

Analyzing Spring Dependencies

Spring has numerous third-party library dependencies. If you are building Spring from source, then you are going to need all of these dependencies. However, at runtime, most likely you will require only a subset of the dependencies, and you can really minimize the size of your distribution by including only the necessary dependencies.

Because of the large number of dependencies, Spring groups them together to make working with them easier. Table 2-3 describes these groups; it also lists the JAR files in each group and defines what the dependencies are used for.

Table 2-3 reflects only the basic and common dependencies that the Spring framework's modules depend on. In your application, you will probably require additional dependencies. For example, for Spring XML support (i.e., the oxm module), if you are using Castor as the underlying object-to-XML mapping library, you need to add Castor's library. If you use XStream, then you need to add XStream's library, and so on. As we move on to later chapters and discussing each specific topic, we'll mention additional third-party libraries that are being used. So, please refer to the table as a general overview, instead of a complete reference.

Table 2-3. Spring Framework Third-Party Library Dependencies

Dependency Group	JAR Files	Description
aopalliance	aopalliance-1.0.jar	The AOP Alliance (http://aopalliance.sourceforge.net) is a combined, open source collaboration between many projects to provide a standard set of interfaces for AOP in Java. Spring's AOP implementation is based on the standard AOP Alliance APIs. You need this JAR file only if you plan to use any of Spring's AOP or AOP-based features.

Dependency Group	JAR Files	Description
aspectj	aspectjweaver-1.6.8.jar	Spring tightly integrates with AspectJ for more powerful AOP features. Whenever you use AspectJ, you will need this library.
caucho	com.springsource.com.caucho-3.2.1.jar	Spring remoting provides support for a wide variety of different protocols, including Caucho's Burlap and Hessian. You need the JAR in this group only if you are using the corresponding protocols in your application.
cglib	cglib-2.2.jar	CGLIB is a code generation library that Spring's aop module depends on. CGLIB is capable of generating proxy for both Java classes and interfaces.
dom4j	dom4j-1.6.1.jar	You must have dom4j when you are using Hibernate, so you need to include this JAR file if you plan to use Hibernate for ORM in your application.
easymock	easymock-2.5.1.jar	EasyMock is used in the Spring test suite, so you need to use this JAR only for building and running the test suite; you do not need to distribute this with your application.
freemarker	freemarker-2.3.15.jar	Spring provides wrapper classes around the FreeMarker templating engine and also provides support for using FreeMarker templates as views for your web applications. This is required whenever you are using FreeMarker.
hibernate	hibernate-core-3.6.10.Final.jar, hibernate-commons-annotations-3.2.0.Final.jar, hibernate-entitymanager-3.6.10.Final.jar, hibernate-jpa-2.0-api-1.0.1.Final.jar, hibernate-validator-4.1.0.GA.jar	These JAR files are required when you are using Spring's Hibernate integration and support classes. If you are using a different ORM tool, such as MyBatis, you can leave these JARs out of your application. When you are using Hibernate, you must also include the javassist.jar file in your application. The entity manager and JPA library are required when you use JPA and Hibernate as the persistence provider. The Hibernate validator is also required when you need JSR-303 Beans Validation API or JPA 2.0.
javassist	javassist-3.12.0.GA.jar	This is a library for bytecode manipulation.
mybatis	mybatis-3.0.6.jar, mybatis-spring-1.0.2.jar	These files are required when you are using MyBatis.

Dependency Group	JAR Files	Description
itext	itextpdf-5.1.2.jar	Spring uses iText to provide PDF support in the web tier. Include this JAR only if your web applications need to generate PDF output.
jee	activation-1.1.0.jar, connector-api-1.5.jar, jaxws-api-2.2.6.jar, ejb-api-3.0.jar, jms-1.1.jar, jstl-1.2.jar, jta-1.1.jar, mail-1.4.4.jar, servlet-2.5.jar, xml-apis-2.0.2.jar	As you can see, there is a large array of different JEE-related JAR files. You need the activation.jar and mail.jar files if you want to use the JavaMail implementation of Spring's mail support. You need connector-api.jar to use the JCA Connector for Hibernate, ejb.jar to use Spring's EJB support, and jms.jar for Spring's JMS support. For web applications you need servlet.jar and jstl.jar if you want to use Spring's JSTL support. The jaxws-api.jar file is required for JAX-WS support in Spring remoting, and jta.jar is used for JTA transaction support.
apache-commons	commons-attributes-api-2.1.jar, commons-attributes-compiler-2.2.jar, commons-beanutils-1.8.3.jar, commons-collections-3.2.0.jar, commons-dbcp-1.4.jar, commons-digester-2.1.jar, commons-discovery-0.5.jar, commons-fileupload-1.2.0.jar, commons-lang-2.5.jar, commons-logging-1.1.1.jar, commons-pool-1.5.4.jar, httpclient-4.1.1.jar,	Many of the components from the Apache Commons project are used by Spring. You need the commons-attributes-api.jar if you want to use source-level metadata in your application, plus you need the compiler JAR file to compile the attributes into your application. The BeanUtils, Collections, Digester, and Discovery JAR files are used by Struts, and Hibernate uses Collections as well. DBCP is used by Spring's JDBC support when you are using DBCP connection pools, and pooling is required by some of the sample applications. FileUpload is required if you want to use the corresponding Spring wrapper to handle file uploads in your web applications. Finally, logging is used throughout Spring, so you need to include it in every Spring-based application.
junit	junit-4.9.jar	JUnit is not required at all at runtime; it is used only for building and running the test suite.
log4j	log4j-1.2.14.jar	This is required when you want to use Spring to configure log4j logging.
poi	poi-3.6.jar	This adds support for Microsoft Excel output to Spring's MVC framework.
quartz	quartz-1.6.2.jar	This is used for Spring Quartz-based scheduling support.
struts	struts-1.2.9.jar	The Struts JAR is required whenever you want to use Struts in conjunction with Spring to build a web application.

Dependency Group	JAR Files	Description
velocity	velocity-1.5.0.jar	Spring provides wrapper classes around Velocity to DI-enable it and also to reduce the amount of code you need to write to use Velocity in your application. In addition to this, Spring provides classes to support the use of Velocity as the view provider in the web tier. If you are using any of these features, you need to include the Velocity JAR file in your distribution.

As you can see, Spring's dependencies are quite varied, and for most applications, you need only a fraction of the full dependency set. It is worthwhile spending the time to pick out exactly what dependencies you need and only adding those to your application. In this way, you can keep the size of your application down; this is a particular benefit to those of you who frequently need to deploy to remote locations. Keeping the size of your application as small as possible is especially important if you plan to distribute your application over the Web to people who may be downloading with a slow Internet connection.

The Sample Applications

An area where many open source, and indeed commercial, products fail is in providing enough well-documented sample code to make it easy for people to get started. Thankfully, Spring comes with a complete set of nifty sample applications that demonstrate a wide selection of the features in Spring. The sample applications are treated as first-class citizens of the framework by the development team, and they are constantly being improved and worked on by the team. For this reason, you will generally find that, after you get what you can from the test suite, the samples are a great place to get started when you are looking at new features.

Obtaining Spring Samples Source Code

All Spring samples source code (except the spring-mvc-showcase project) are hosted on SpringSource's SVN repository. To get the source code, invoke the following command in any empty directory:

svn co https://src.springframework.org/svn/spring-samples/

Figure 2-3 shows a sample applications folder upon checkout from this link.

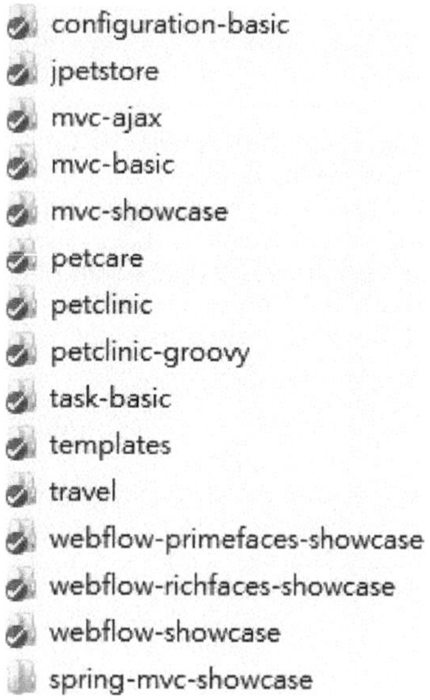

- configuration-basic
- jpetstore
- mvc-ajax
- mvc-basic
- mvc-showcase
- petcare
- petclinic
- petclinic-groovy
- task-basic
- templates
- travel
- webflow-primefaces-showcase
- webflow-richfaces-showcase
- webflow-showcase
- spring-mvc-showcase

Figure 2-3. *Spring sample applications*

The Petclinic Application

Petclinic (under the folder petclinic) is an interesting sample application that was built to showcase Spring's data access support. In it, you find a web-based application for querying and updating the database of a fictional veterinary office. The interesting thing about this application is that it comes with a selection of interchangeable DAO implementations that highlight how easy it is to decouple your application from the data access logic when you are using Spring.

The Hibernate DAO implementation really shows off Spring's Hibernate support by implementing each of the eight DAO methods with a single line or two. The JDBC implementation is equally as interesting. First, it showcases the use of SimpleJdbcTemplate and SimpleJdbcInsert to eliminate the needs of redundant code for common JDBC operations. On the other hand, it is very interesting to see how data access is handled in a much more object-oriented way. By using the RowMapper interface and its various implementations, the query result set can be directly mapped into value objects and returned to the caller.

This project also contains a very solid example of how to build a web application using Spring's MVC support, so if you are planning to use Spring MVC for one of your own applications, make sure you take a look at this sample first.

We cover JDBC support in Chapter 8, Hibernate in Chapter 9, and Spring MVC in Chapter 17.

The Petclinic Groovy Application

The Petclinic Groovy sample (under the folder petclinic-groovy) showcases the implementation of the same Petclinic application using Groovy and Grails. Groovy is a dynamic scripting language that runs on JVM, and Grails is a rapid development framework that enables the development of Groovy-based web applications. The controllers in the Spring MVC layer were all developed in the Groovy language.

A discussion of Grails is out of scope in this book, but the integration of Spring and Groovy will be covered in Chapter 22.

The jPetStore Application

The jPetStore sample (under the folder `jpetstore`) is based on the jPetStore sample created by Clinton Begin for iBATIS. As far as sample applications go, this one is huge. It contains a full DAO layer, created using Spring and iBATIS, with implementations for Oracle, Microsoft SQL Server, MySQL, and PostgreSQL. The business tier is fully Spring managed, and coupled with the DAO layer, it presents a good example of Spring-managed transactions.

Also included with this application is a solid example of how to use both Spring MVC and Struts. This application also highlights how to use Spring remoting using JAXRPC.

Spring MVC is covered in Chapter 17, iBATIS (MyBatis) is covered in Chapter 11, and Spring remoting is covered in Chapter 16.

Spring Configuration Basic Application

The configuration-basic project (under the folder `configuration-basic`) demonstrates how to define Spring's application configuration using Java classes, which is a new feature starting with Spring 3.0. In the project, there are no XML files; all the Spring-related configuration is declared in a Java class (`AppConfig.java`) with various annotations.

Spring configuration using Java classes is covered in Chapter 5.

Spring Task and Scheduling Application

The task-basic project (under the folder `task-basic`) demonstrates the use of Spring's task executor and scheduling support.

Spring's scheduling support will be covered in Chapter 15.

The Spring MVC Showcase Application

The Spring MVC Showcase project (under the folder `spring-mvc-showcase`) demonstrates the capabilities of the Spring MVC Web Framework through a number of small and simple samples. It was built upon Spring MVC 3 and showcases major Spring MVC 3 features such as the following:

- The use of the `@Controller` annotation to declare Spring MVC controllers

- Mapping request, obtaining request data, and generating response

- Message converters and view rendering

- Forms, type validation, file upload, and exception handling

We cover Spring MVC in detail in Chapter 17.

■ **Note** Unlike other Spring sample projects, the spring-mvc-showcase project is hosted at GitHub (`www.github.com`), which is a very popular social-coding web site. To obtain the source code from GitHub, first get the Git tool (`http://git-scm.com`). After Git is installed, issue the following command to clone the project repository from GitHub to your desktop: `git clone https://github.com/SpringSource/spring-mvc-showcase`.

The Spring MVC Basic and Ajax Application

Besides the spring-mvc-showcase project, Spring provides two other projects to demonstrate the various usage scenarios of Spring MVC 3. The project mvc-basic (under the folder mvc-basic) is a very simple Spring MVC project with a single controller. The mvc-ajax project (under the folder mvc-ajax) demonstrates how to use Spring MVC to build web applications with Ajax support. The server side was built using Spring MVC, and using its build-in RESTful-WS support, requests were mapped and data was returned in JSON format. On the client side, jQuery, a popular JavaScript library with Ajax support, was used to interact with Spring MVC to provide a rich user experience.

The Spring Petcare Application

The petcare sample (under the folder petcare) is another interesting project. It is a full-blown web application that showcase a lot of different features of the Spring Framework and other Spring projects. On the web side, it uses Spring MVC with Spring Security for securing those protected resources. For views, it integrates with Tiles for templating support. Mailing support can also be found here.

Another interesting feature is the integration with the Spring Integration project in broadcasting application messages. Another Spring project, Spring Roo, was used to generate the JavaBeans base on the backend database schema.

Protecting web application resources using Spring Security will be covered in Chapter 17, while a high-level overview on using Spring Framework with other Spring projects, including Spring Integration and Spring Roo, will be covered in Chapter 20.

Spring Webflow Sample Applications

Several sample projects showcase the features of Spring and Spring Webflow. The travel application (under the folder travel) is a reference for Spring Framework 3 with Spring Webflow 2.1.

Spring Webflow integrates with many view technologies; one of them is Java Server Faces (JSF). Spring Faces is a module in Spring Webflow that provides tight integration with JSF. There are two sample applications to demonstrate this feature. The webflow-primefaces-showcase sample (under the folder webflow-primefaces-showcase) shows the integration with Primefaces, while the webflow-richfaces-showcase sample (under the folder webflow-richfaces-showcase) shows the integration with JBoss Richfaces. Both Primefaces and JBoss Richfaces are popular JSF libraries, and their latest versions comply with JSF 2.0 standards.

Web application development using Spring Webflow, with Primefaces as an example, will be covered in Chapter 18.

Spring Documentation

One of the aspects of Spring that makes it such a useful framework for real developers who are building real applications is its wealth of well-written, accurate documentation. In every release, the Spring Framework's documentation team works hard to ensure that all the documentation is finished and polished by the development team. This means that every feature of Spring is not only fully documented in the JavaDoc but is also covered in the Spring reference manual included in every distribution. If you haven't yet familiarized yourself with the Spring JavaDoc and the reference manual, do so now. This book does not aim to be a replacement for either of these resources; rather, it aims to be a complementary reference, demonstrating how to build a Spring-based application from the ground up.

Putting a Spring into "Hello World!"

We hope by this point in the book you appreciate that Spring is a solid, well-supported project that has all the makings of a great tool for application development. However, one thing is missing—we haven't shown you any code yet. We are sure you are dying to see Spring in action, and because we cannot go any longer without getting into the code, let's do just that. Do not worry if you do not fully understand all the code in this section; we go into much more detail on all the topics as we proceed through the book.

Building the Sample "Hello World!" Application

Now, we are sure you are familiar with the traditional "Hello World!" example, but just in case you have been living on the moon for the past 30 years, Listing 2-1 shows the Java version in all its glory.

Listing 2-1. Typical "Hello World!" Example

```
package com.apress.prospring3.ch2;

public class HelloWorld {

    public static void main(String[] args) {
        System.out.println("Hello World!");
    }
}
```

As far as examples go, this one is pretty simple—it does the job, but it is not very extensible. What if we want to change the message? What if we want to output the message differently, maybe to stderr instead of stdout or enclosed in HTML tags rather than as plain text?

We are going to redefine the requirements for the sample application and say that it must support a simple, flexible mechanism for changing the message, and it must be simple to change the rendering behavior. In the basic "Hello World!" example, you can make both of these changes quickly and easily by just changing the code as appropriate. However, in a bigger application, recompiling takes time, and it requires the application to be fully tested again. No, a better solution is to externalize the message content and read it in at runtime, perhaps from the command-line arguments shown in Listing 2-2.

Listing 2-2. Using Command-Line Arguments with "Hello World!"

```
package com.apress.prospring3.ch2;

public class HelloWorldWithCommandLine {

    public static void main(String[] args) {
        if(args.length > 0) {
            System.out.println(args[0]);
        } else {
            System.out.println("Hello World!");
        }
    }
}
```

This example accomplishes what we wanted—we can now change the message without changing the code. However, there is still a problem with this application: the component responsible for rendering the message is also responsible for obtaining the message. Changing how the message is obtained means changing the code in the renderer. Add to this the fact that we still cannot change the renderer easily; doing so means changing the class that launches the application.

If we take this application a step further, away from the basics of "Hello World!" a better solution is to refactor the rendering and message retrieval logic into separate components. Plus, if we really want to make our application flexible, we should have these components implement interfaces and define the interdependencies between the components and the launcher using these interfaces.

By refactoring the message retrieval logic, we can define a simple MessageProvider interface with a single method, getMessage(), as shown in Listing 2-3.

Listing 2-3. The MessageProvider Interface

```
package com.apress.prospring3.ch2;

public interface MessageProvider {

    public String getMessage();
}
```

As you can see in Listing 2-4, the MessageRenderer interface is implemented by all components that can render messages.

Listing 2-4. The MessageRenderer Interface

```
package com.apress.prospring3.ch2;

public interface MessageRenderer {

    public void render();
    public void setMessageProvider(MessageProvider provider);
    public MessageProvider getMessageProvider();
}
```

As you can see, the MessageRenderer interface has a method, render(), and also a JavaBean-style property, MessageProvider. Any MessageRenderer implementations are decoupled from message retrieval and delegate it instead to the MessageProvider with which they are supplied. Here, MessageProvider is a dependency of MessageRenderer. Creating simple implementations of these interfaces is easy (see Listing 2-5).

Listing 2-5. The HelloWorldMessageProvider Class

```
package com.apress.prospring3.ch2;

public class HelloWorldMessageProvider implements MessageProvider {

    public String getMessage() {
        return "Hello World!";
    }
}
```

In Listing 2-5, you can see that we have created a simple MessageProvider that always returns "Hello World!" as the message. The StandardOutMessageRenderer class (shown in Listing 2-6) is just as simple.

Listing 2-6. The StandardOutMessageRenderer Class

```
package com.apress.prospring3.ch2;

public class StandardOutMessageRenderer implements MessageRenderer {

    private MessageProvider messageProvider = null;

    public void render() {
        if (messageProvider == null) {
            throw new RuntimeException(
                "You must set the property messageProvider of class:"
                + StandardOutMessageRenderer.class.getName());
        }
        System.out.println(messageProvider.getMessage());
    }

    public void setMessageProvider(MessageProvider provider) {
        this.messageProvider = provider;
    }

    public MessageProvider getMessageProvider() {
        return this.messageProvider;
    }
}
```

Now all that remains is to rewrite the main() of our entry class, as shown in Listing 2-7.

Listing 2-7. Refactored "Hello World!"

```
package com.apress.prospring3.ch2;

public class HelloWorldDecoupled {

    public static void main(String[] args) {
        MessageRenderer mr = new StandardOutMessageRenderer();
        MessageProvider mp = new HelloWorldMessageProvider();
        mr.setMessageProvider(mp);
        mr.render();
    }
}
```

The code here is fairly simple: we instantiate instances of HelloWorldMessageProvider and StandardOutMessageRenderer, although the declared types are MessageProvider and MessageRenderer, respectively. This is because we need to interact only with the methods provided by the interface in the programming logic, and those interfaces were already implemented by HelloWorldMessageProvider and StandardOutMessageRenderer, respectively. Then, we pass the MessageProvider to the MessageRenderer and invoke MessageRenderer.render(). Figure 2-4 shows the output from this example, as expected.

Figure 2-4 *Output of* HelloWorldDecoupled

Now this example is more like what we are looking for, but there is one small problem. Changing the implementation of either the MessageRenderer or MessageProvider interface means a change to the code. To get around this, we can create a simple factory class that reads the implementation class names from a properties file and instantiates them on behalf of the application (see Listing 2-8).

Listing 2-8. *The* MessageSupportFactory *Class*

```java
package com.apress.prospring3.ch2;

import java.io.FileInputStream;
import java.util.Properties;

public class MessageSupportFactory {

    private static MessageSupportFactory instance = null;
    private Properties props = null;
    private MessageRenderer renderer = null;
    private MessageProvider provider = null;

    private MessageSupportFactory() {
        props = new Properties();

        try {
            props.load(new FileInputStream("ch2/src/conf/msf.properties"));

            // get the implementation classes
            String rendererClass = props.getProperty("renderer.class");
            String providerClass = props.getProperty("provider.class");
            renderer = (MessageRenderer) Class.forName(rendererClass).newInstance();
            provider = (MessageProvider) Class.forName(providerClass).newInstance();
        } catch (Exception ex) {
            ex.printStackTrace();
        }
    }

    static {
        instance = new MessageSupportFactory();
    }

    public static MessageSupportFactory getInstance() {
        return instance;
    }

    public MessageRenderer getMessageRenderer() {
```

```
        return renderer;
    }

    public MessageProvider getMessageProvider() {
        return provider;
    }

}
```

The implementation here is trivial and naïve, the error handling is simplistic, and the name of the configuration file is hard-coded, but we already have a substantial amount of code. The configuration file for this class is quite simple:

```
renderer.class=com.apress.prospring3.ch2.StandardOutMessageRenderer
provider.class=com.apress.prospring3.ch2.HelloWorldMessageProvider
```

Make a simple modification to the main() method (as shown in Listing 2-9), and we are in business.

Listing 2-9. Using MessageSupportFactory

```
package com.apress.prospring3.ch2;

public class HelloWorldDecoupledWithFactory {

    public static void main(String[] args) {
        MessageRenderer mr = MessageSupportFactory.getInstance().getMessageRenderer();
        MessageProvider mp = MessageSupportFactory.getInstance().getMessageProvider();
        mr.setMessageProvider(mp);
        mr.render();
    }
}
```

Before we move on to see how we can introduce Spring into this application, let's quickly recap what we have done. Starting with the simple "Hello World!" application, we defined two additional requirements that the application must fulfill. The first was that changing the message should be simple, and the second was that changing the rendering mechanism should also be simple. To meet these requirements, we introduced two interfaces: MessageProvider and MessageRenderer. The MessageRenderer interface depends on an implementation of the MessageProvider interface to be able to retrieve a message to render. Finally, we added a simple factory class to retrieve the names of the implementation classes and instantiate them as applicable.

Create Spring Project in STS

Before we discuss how to refactor the "Hello World!" application with Spring, we'll show you how to use STS for Spring-based application development. STS can save you a lot of time when creating Spring projects of different types (e.g., simple Spring DI applications, Web applications, JPA applications, etc.), and STS will create a project with all required dependencies declared for you. So, let's download and install STS first and create the project for refactoring the "Hello World!" application.

First, download STS from the SpringSource web site (www.springsource.com/downloads/sts), select your development environment, and install it. At the time of writing, the version is 2.8.1. This is also the version we used for developing all the example code presented in this book, as well as the sample application.

Next, after installation, start STS, and create a new Spring template project. For template selection, choose Simple Spring Utility Project (see Figure 2-5).

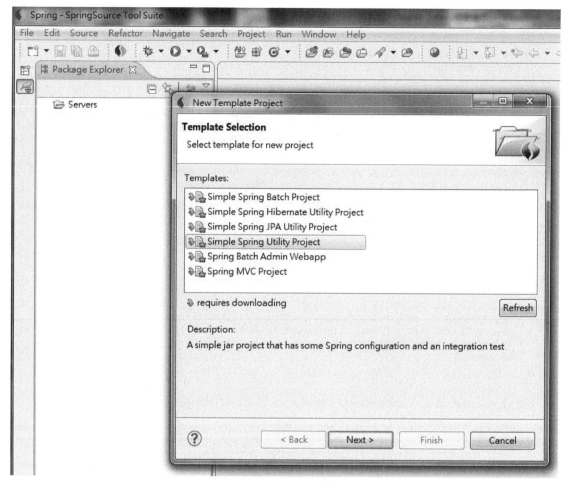

Figure 2-5. *Creating a simple Spring utility project in STS*

Afterward, STS will ask you for the basic project information, such as project name, base package name, and so on (see Figure 2-6).

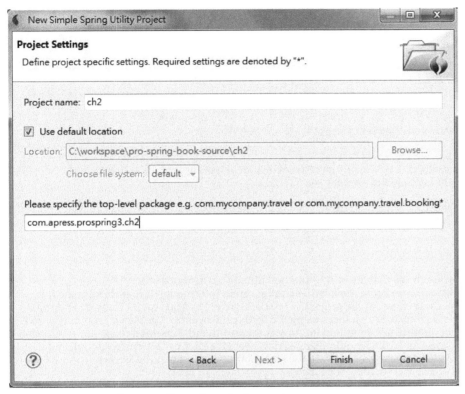

Figure 2-6. Defining basic attributes for a Spring project

STS will then create the project with Maven dependencies support enabled. The required dependencies (spring-context, spring-test, log4j, etc.) will be declared and included automatically. You don't need to include the Spring libraries manually for the project.

Now we are ready to refactor the previous "Hello World!" application in Spring.

Refactoring with Spring

The final example shown earlier met the goals we laid out for our sample application, but there are still problems with it. The first problem is that we had to write a lot of glue code to piece the application together, while at the same time keeping the components loosely coupled. The second problem was that we still had to provide the implementation of MessageRenderer with an instance of MessageProvider manually. We can solve both of these problems using Spring.

To solve the problem of too much glue code, we can completely remove the MessageSupportFactory class from the application and replace it with a Spring interface, ApplicationContext. Don't worry too much about this interface; for now it is enough to know that this interface is used by Spring for storing all the environmental information with regard to an application being managed by Spring. This interface extends another interface, ListableBeanFactory, which acts as the provider for any Spring-managed beans instance (see Listing 2-10).

Listing 2-10. Using Spring's ApplicationContext

```
package com.apress.prospring3.ch2;

import org.springframework.context.ApplicationContext;
import org.springframework.context.support.ClassPathXmlApplicationContext;

public class HelloWorldSpringDI {

    public static void main(String[] args) {

        // Initialize Spring ApplicationContext
        ApplicationContext ctx = new ClassPathXmlApplicationContext
            ("META-INF/spring/app-context.xml");

        MessageRenderer mr = ctx.getBean("renderer", MessageRenderer.class);
        mr.render();
    }

}
```

In Listing 2-10, you can see that the main() method obtains an instance of
ClassPathXmlApplicationContext (the application configuration information is loaded from the file
META-INF/spring/app-context.xml in the project's classpath), typed as ApplicationContext, and from
this, it obtains the MessageRenderer instances using the ApplicationContext.getBean() method. Don't
worry too much about the getBean() method for now; just know that this method reads the application
configuration (in this case an XML file), initializes Spring's ApplicationContext environment, and then
returns the configured bean instance. This XML file (app-context.xml) serves the same purpose as the
one we used for MessageSupportFactory (see Listing 2-11).

Listing 2-11. Spring XML Application Configuration

```
<?xml version="1.0" encoding="UTF-8"?>
<beans xmlns="http://www.springframework.org/schema/beans"
    xmlns:xsi=http://www.w3.org/2001/XMLSchema-instance
    xmlns:p="http://www.springframework.org/schema/p"
     xmlns:context="http://www.springframework.org/schema/context"
     xsi:schemaLocation="http://www.springframework.org/schema/beans
         http://www.springframework.org/schema/beans/spring-beans-3.0.xsd
         http://www.springframework.org/schema/context
         http://www.springframework.org/schema/context/spring-context-3.0.xsd">

    <bean id="provider" class="com.apress.prospring3.ch2.HelloWorldMessageProvider"/>

    <bean id="renderer" class="com.apress.prospring3.ch2.StandardOutMessageRenderer"
        p:messageProvider-ref="provider"/>

</beans>
```

The previous file shows a typical Spring ApplicationContext configuration file. First, Spring's
namespaces are declared, and the default namespace is beans, which is used to declare the beans that
need to be managed by Spring, and its dependency requirements (for the above example, the renderer
bean's messageProvider property is referencing the provider bean) for Spring to resolve and inject those
dependencies.

Afterward, we declare the bean with the ID "provider" and the corresponding implementation class. When Spring sees this bean definition during ApplicationContext initialization, it will instantiate the class and store it with the specified ID.

Then the "renderer" bean is declared, with the corresponding implementation class. Remember that this bean depends on the MessageProvider interface for getting the message to render. To inform Spring about the DI requirement, we use the p namespace attribute. The tag attribute p:messageProvider-ref="provider" tells Spring that the bean's property, messageProvider, should be injected with another bean. The bean to be injected into the property should reference a bean with the ID "provider". When Spring sees this definition, it will instantiate the class, look up the bean's property named messageProvider, and inject it with the bean instance with the ID "provider".

As you can see, upon the initialization of Spring's ApplicationContext, the main() method now just obtains the MessageRenderer bean by using its type-safe getBean() method (passing in the ID and the expected return type, which is the MessageRenderer interface) and calls render(); Spring has created the MessageProvider implementation and injected it into the MessageRenderer implementation. Notice that we didn't have to make any changes to the classes that are being wired together using Spring. In fact, these classes have no reference to Spring whatsoever and are completely oblivious to its existence. However, this isn't always the case. Your classes can implement Spring-specified interfaces to interact in a variety of ways with the DI container.

Now let's see the Spring DI–powered "Hello World!" application in action. In STS, just right-click the class HelloWorldSpringDI and choose Run As and then Java Application. The execution result will be displayed on the Console tab (see Figure 2-7).

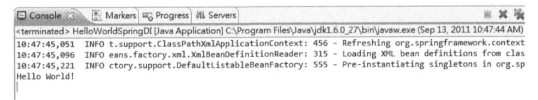

Figure 2-7. Execution output of HelloWorldSpringDI

Summary

In this chapter, we presented you with all the background information you need to get up and running with Spring. We showed you how to obtain both the Spring release distribution and the current development version directly from GitHub. We described how Spring is packaged and the dependencies you need for each of Spring's features. Using this information, you can make informed decisions about which of the Spring JAR files your application needs and which dependencies you need to distribute with your application. Spring's documentation, sample applications, and test suite provide Spring users with an ideal base from which to start their Spring development, so we took some time to investigate what is available in the Spring distribution. Finally, we presented an example of how, using Spring DI, it is possible to make the traditional "Hello World!" a loosely coupled, extendable message-rendering application.

The important thing to realize is that we only scratched the surface of Spring DI in this chapter, and we barely made a dent in Spring as a whole. In the next chapter, we take an in-depth look at the sample application that we will be building, paying particular attention to how we can use Spring to solve common design issues and how we have made our application simpler and more manageable using Spring.

CHAPTER 3

The Sample Application

The examples in each chapter of this book are tailored to the current discussion and are designed to elaborate on the implementation of each feature in an easy-to-understand manner. For the most part, these examples provide a sufficient explanation for the topic they are demonstrating. That said, the examples appear in isolation and are not based on a real-world scenario, which can make understanding how the different Spring features work together difficult. To overcome this, we have built a basic blog application, SpringBlog, that highlights most of the topics discussed in this book and shows how the different Spring features work together.

You should note that this application is purposely very simple, and indeed, many of its features were conceived so we could highlight a particular piece of Spring functionality. Despite its simplicity, the SpringBlog application demonstrates how a Spring-based application is constructed and how the components are glued together.

In this chapter, you get to take a peek at the finished SpringBlog application. We then discuss the Spring features used to implement different parts of the application. This chapter also highlights some of the decisions we made when designing the SpringBlog application and why we made them. More than anything, this chapter serves as a road map to the rest of the book, allowing you to highlight an area that is important to your own application and immediately identify where that area is covered in the book.

Specifically, this chapter covers two main topics:

- *Requirements of the SpringBlog application*: In this section, we discuss the requirements of the SpringBlog application and sneak a peek at the finished product of these requirements. We also discuss why we chose to include certain requirements and why we ignored others when we built the sample application.

- *Implementing the SpringBlog application*: In this section, we take a high-level look at how the requirements discussed in the previous section are implemented using Spring. This section does not go into any detail on the individual Spring features; instead, it discusses the features generally and points you to other chapters that contain more complete descriptions.

If you are already comfortable with the design of Spring applications or you already know which topics are most important to your application, feel free to skip this chapter. If you are completely new to Spring, reading this chapter will give you a good idea of where the different Spring components fit into your applications.

Requirements of the SpringBlog Application

When defining the requirements for the SpringBlog application, our main goal was to highlight certain Spring Framework features in the context of a full application. For this reason, we included a few features, such as auditing and obscenity filtering, that you would not expect to see in a traditional blog application but that are useful features nonetheless and provide a way to highlight certain features of the Spring Framework.

This section provides a full rundown of the features included in the SpringBlog application.

Security and Authentication

Like most other blog applications, the SpringBlog application provides security controls that prevent unauthorized users from creating and editing blog entries.

As you can see in Figure 3-1, the SpringBlog application provides a login form for users to sign in and identify themselves as valid and registered users of the application.

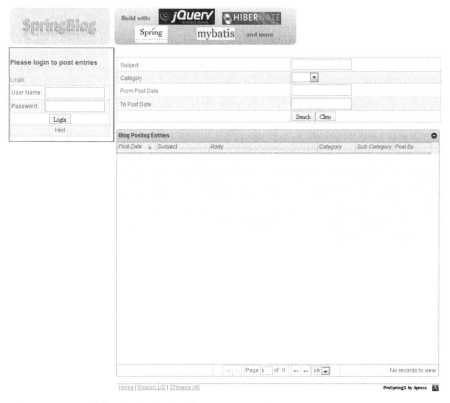

Figure 3-1. *User identity in SpringBlog*

However, login is not required for viewing blog entries. In SpringBlog, you are assigned the Anonymous identity automatically. Using the login function, you can validate your details against the user list in the database and assign yourself a different identity. Internally, SpringBlog uses this identity for security access control, and the user information will also be used in the audit process.

The security control requirements are as follows:

- Anonymous users are allowed only to view blog entries.

- There are two user roles within the application, namely, a user (ROLE_USER) and an admin (ROLE_ADMIN).

- Users with the user role (ROLE_USER) assigned can perform the following actions:

  - Post a blog entry or comment on an existing entry

  - Edit a blog entry or comment they have created

- Users with the admin role (ROLE_ADMIN) assigned can perform the following actions:

  - View audit data

  - Perform user maintenance

Viewing Blog Entries

An obvious requirement for any blog system is that it can display blog entries to users. As Figure 3-2 shows, the SpringBlog application displays all postings to the blog on the home page, in reverse chronological order. The blog entries will be displayed in table format.

Figure 3-2. Viewing recent blog entries

Users can configure the number of entries per page to be displayed; filter the blog entries by subject, category, and post date; and control the display order of the blog entries.

Clicking a particular blog entry displays just that entry, along with the list of comments posted for that entry and the files that have been attached to it, as shown in Figure 3-3.

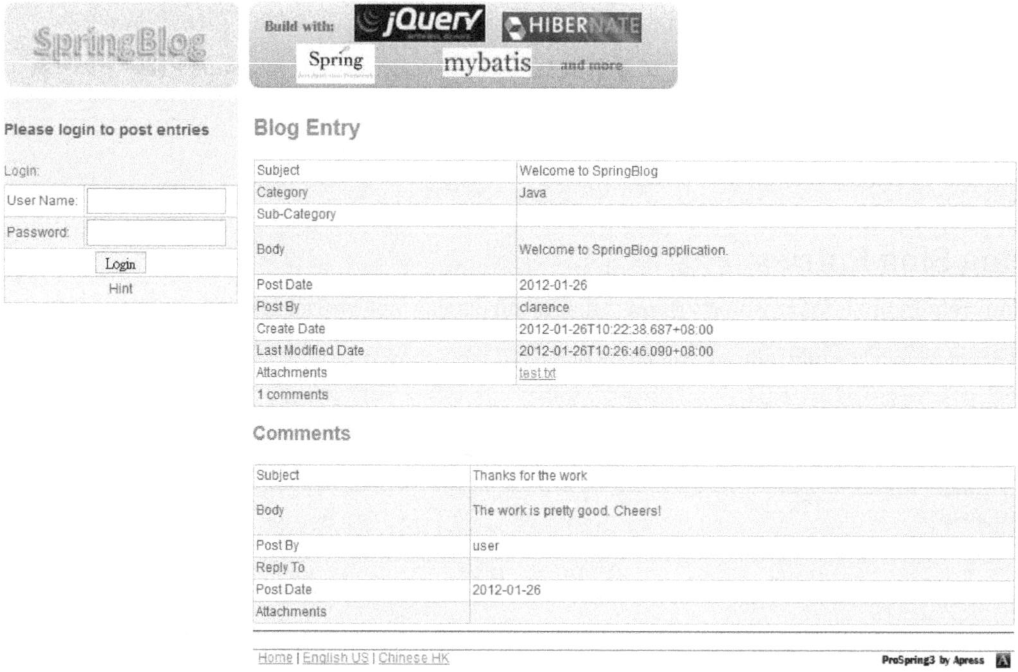

Figure 3-3. *Viewing a blog entry*

Posting Blog Entries

Without the ability to post blog entries, there would be nothing to display. After logging in as a valid user, you can post a new blog entry using the entry form shown in Figure 3-4, which you can access using the New Blog Posting link on the home page.

When posting/editing a blog entry, you can enter the details, as well as select the category and subcategory of the blog entry so visitors can easily filter out those blog entries that they don't want to see. In addition, validation rules will be applied to the blog entry during posting.

Once you have created a blog entry, you can edit it by clicking the Edit link on the entry's detail page (a blog entry can be edited only by the user who posted it). Behind the scenes, SpringBlog uses the same HTML form both for creating and for editing a blog entry, but it uses different Spring Controller methods to handle each action.

Figure 3-4. Posting a blog entry

Commenting on a Blog Entry

As with most blog applications, SpringBlog allows users to express their opinions about particular entries by posting comments (login is also required for posting comments). Users can post comments, as shown in Figure 3-5, using the "Post a comment" link on an entry's detail page.

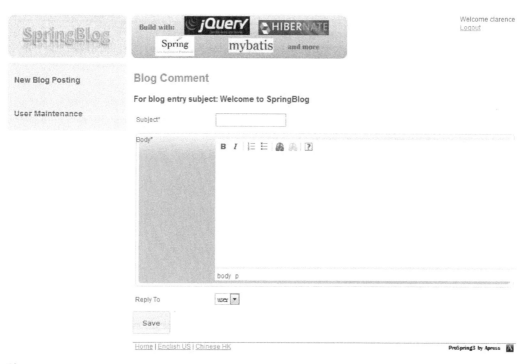

Figure 3-5. *Posting a comment*

As is the case with the entry posting functionality, this functionality also allows you to edit comments.

Filtering Out Obscenities

One of the features of the Spring Framework we really wanted to highlight in SpringBlog was AOP, but we did not want to use the traditional example of logging, and AOP-based transaction management is already built into the Spring Framework. Although most blogs do not use any kind of obscenity filter, we decided that ours would. During design, it seemed that using AOP was the best way to apply this feature across the application.

With this functionality in place, when you try to post an entry such as that shown in Figure 3-6, you actually get a posting like the one in Figure 3-7. The ROT13 algorithm is used to perform filtering and will be discussed in detail in Chapter 21.

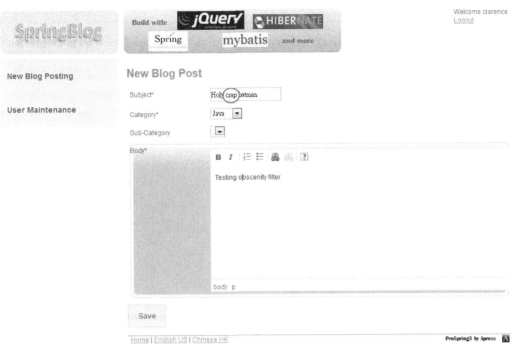

Figure 3-6. Attempting to post an obscenity

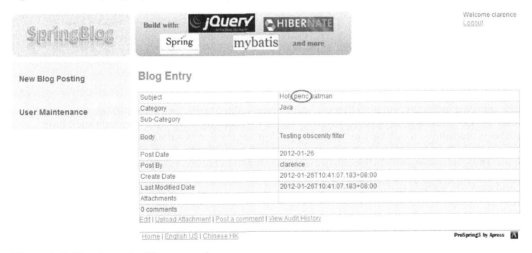

Figure 3-7. The obscenity filter at work

Attaching Files to a Blog Entry or Comment

Unlike many blog applications used on the World Wide Web, SpringBlog allows files to be uploaded with blog entries and comments. In reality, this feature poses quite a large security risk, but it does allow us to demonstrate Spring Framework's excellent file upload handling. Figure 3-8 shows a file being uploaded for an existing entry.

Figure 3-8. Uploading a file to SpringBlog

Auditing Blog Actions

One feature that we included purely to demonstrate a particular Spring feature is auditing. By introducing the need for all blog operations to be logged for auditing purposes, we made each blog operation require multiple database operations; this requires the use of a database transaction that, obviously, we manage using Spring's transaction management features.

You can view the audit history of a blog posting, as shown in Figure 3-9, by clicking the View Audit History link on the blog entry detail page. As discussed, only users with the administrator role can see the link and view the audit history.

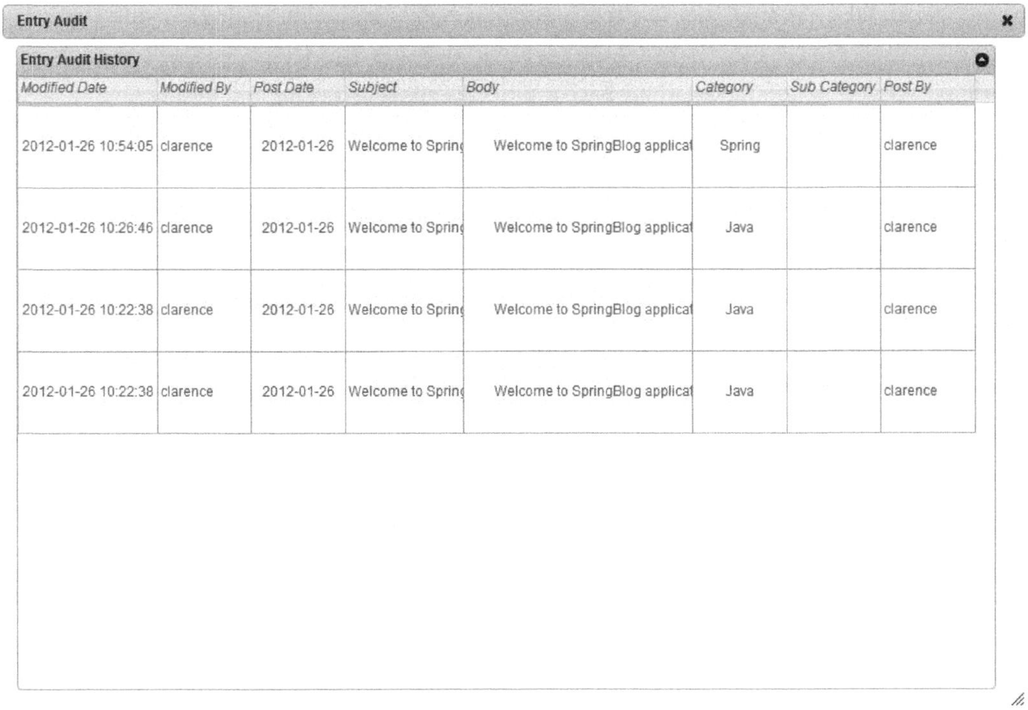

Entry Audit								✕
Entry Audit History								●
Modified Date	Modified By	Post Date	Subject	Body	Category	Sub Category	Post By	
2012-01-26 10:54:05	clarence	2012-01-26	Welcome to Spring	Welcome to SpringBlog applicat	Spring		clarence	
2012-01-26 10:26:46	clarence	2012-01-26	Welcome to Spring	Welcome to SpringBlog applicat	Java		clarence	
2012-01-26 10:22:38	clarence	2012-01-26	Welcome to Spring	Welcome to SpringBlog applicat	Java		clarence	
2012-01-26 10:22:38	clarence	2012-01-26	Welcome to Spring	Welcome to SpringBlog applicat	Java		clarence	

Figure 3-9. Viewing audit data

RSS Feed

Instead of visiting the site regularly, some users may want to receive Really Simple Syndication (RSS) feeds from their self-developed web application or via their own personalized portal site (for example, from iGoogle). The SpringBlog application will provide the blog entries via RESTful-WS. Because of this service, consumers are able to retrieve the blog entries in XML or JSON format.

Upload Blog from an XML File

Some users may want to write their blogs offline and then submit them to SpringBlog. SpringBlog provides this service too. Users can write their blogs, save them in an XML file with predefined tags, and upload the file to a particular location on the server. SpringBlog will poll the folder regularly and import them when new files are found.

Implementing SpringBlog

One of the best reasons for using Spring is that it makes designing and building an application using traditional OOP practices much simpler. Moreover, recently Spring's maturity and comprehensive feature set has made it a strong backbone for a JEE application. With Spring, you are free to design your applications as you see fit and have Spring worry about wiring the different components together. Spring removes the need for false patterns, such as Factory and Singleton, that hinder testing and only partially solve the problem for which they are designed.

In this section, we present a high-level overview of the design and implementation decisions of the SpringBlog application with pointers to where each topic is discussed in detail.

Development Tool and Dependency Management

Before going into the design, let's decide how we are going to implement the SpringBlog application. For developing Spring-based applications, the most appropriate tool is SpringSource Tool Suite (STS). STS bundles Eclipse IDE, Spring IDE, and a lot of useful tools (such as the Maven plug-in for Eclipse, Mylyn, AspectJ Development Tool for Eclipse, and so on) into a single package. If you already have a version of Eclipse installed on your development machine, you can also install STS plug-ins via the STS Eclipse update site (www.springsource.com/downloads/sts). The SpringBlog application will be developed using STS. Details on STS will be provided in Appendix A.

As discussed previously, the entire Spring Framework is composed of many modules, and each module depends on other Java libraries as well. Although you can sort out the required Spring modules and third-party dependencies and include them into your project manually, it's much easier to use a dependency management tool to handle it for you. STS comes with out-of-the-box support with Maven, a popular application dependency management tool. The SpringBlog application will use Maven to manage the dependencies, as well as the build life cycle. For version control, Git will be used, and besides downloading the source code of the sample application from the book's page, you can also check out the latest version of the application from GitHub (http://github.com).

Application Design

The design of SpringBlog is very simple, with each tier defined in terms of interfaces rather than concrete classes. In each tier, the interfaces that correspond to that tier define only the methods exposed by that tier to other tiers classified as client tiers. Parameters for configuring SpringBlog will not be hard-coded in the application. Instead, the configuration methods are declared on the classes that implement the interfaces in each tier, and configuration data is injected using Spring's IoC-based configuration mechanisms. Chapter 21 presents a full discussion of the different interfaces that make up SpringBlog, how they are wired together using Spring, and factors affecting interface granularity.

The SpringBlog application also contains a basic Domain Object Model (DOM) that encapsulates both data and behavior. In Chapter 12, we take the time to look at the different flavors of the DOM you may have seen in projects that you have worked on, and we discuss the factors you must consider when deciding whether to encapsulate behavior in the DOM or in separate service objects.

Application Configuration Management

In the SpringBlog application, we will use the latest Spring Framework (at the time of writing, version 3.1) for DI configuration. Starting from version 3.0, Spring supports the configuration management via either XML files or Java annotations.

For SpringBlog, we will take a mixed approach. First, all the infrastructure setup (for example, the data source, transaction manager, and so on) will be defined in various XML configuration files for easier maintenance. For those injectable beans and beans that require DI, we will use Java annotations to express the DI requirements. Second, the requirements of transaction support will be defined using Java annotations too. We will then rely on Spring's component scan and autowire features for scanning those classes for those annotations and manage the beans and their requirements on various resources under the cover.

Details of Spring configuration topics will be covered in Chapters 4 and 5.

SpringBlog's Layered Application Architecture

Before we dive into the implementation of each layer, let's take a higher-level look of the layers that we are going to implement in SpringBlog. Figure 3-10 depicts the SpringBlog application's layered architecture, and the following list describes the layers within SpringBlog application (from backend to frontend):

Persistence layer: This layer interacts directly with the underlying persistence data store (RDBMS in this case) and transforms the retrieved data into Java domain objects for service layer use. For the backend database, an embedded H2 database (www.h2database.com) will be used for easy deployment. However, MySQL will be supported too, and instructions will be provided in the sample application in case you want to use MySQL as the backend database.

Service layer: This layer is the core layer within the application. All business logic will be implemented in this layer. Any application service request, no matter from which channel it comes (for example, browser interface, RESTful-WS request, batch job, and so on) should route through this layer to perform the required business processing. For example, the validation of bean attributes will happen here. Also, this layer relies on the persistence layer via DI for database access.

Batch job and integration layer: This layer provides integration with external parties. For example, it will poll for XML files (from a configurable folder location) that contain blog entries from users and import them into SpringBlog via batch processing. It interacts with the service layer for uploading blog entries.

Presentation layer: This is the layer for the web application, which provides the frontend for SpringBlog users. It also handles the RSS feed to generate XML data to consumers. It interacts with the service layer for data processing and business logic execution.

Security layer: The security layer protects those secure resources. For example, anonymous users are allowed only to view blog entries. Login functions will be provided, and role-based access will then be given to the users to ensure that they can only access the functions assigned to the roles to which they belong.

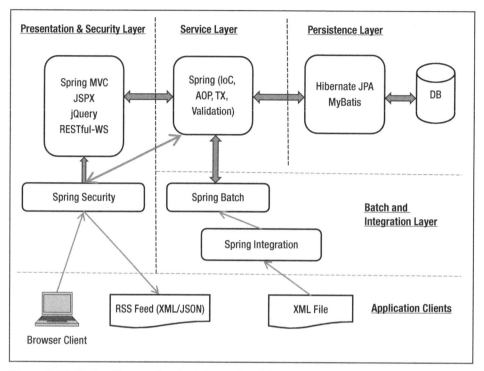

Figure 3-10. *SpringBlog application's layered architecture*

Having discussed the layered architecture, let's look at how each layer will be implemented in the SpringBlog application.

Implementing the Persistence Layer

Data access is a topic close to many developers' hearts, and it is often the subject of many heated discussions on developer forums across the Internet. In recent times, the focus in the Java world has been on object-relational mapping (ORM) tools as a replacement for JDBC, which many see as an overcomplicated mess. A big part of Spring's feature set lies in its support for data access technologies. All in all, Spring supports several different data access mechanisms: plain JDBC, Hibernate, MyBatis (iBATIS), Java Data Objects (JDO), and JPA.

With the SpringBlog application, we wanted to show how easy it is to switch between data access implementations, so we built two different implementations of the persistence layer, one using JPA (using Hibernate as the underlying persistence service provider) and the other using MyBatis.

Hibernate is perhaps the most well-known ORM tool in the Java world, and it has enjoyed a great success because of the ease with which it can be used to develop high-performance persistence logic. Although Hibernate has quite a simple API, the error-handling code you need to use Hibernate is quite verbose; Spring simplifies this greatly, reducing most Hibernate operations to just a single line of code. Also, because of the significant success ORM tools like Hibernate have achieved and Hibernate's wide acceptance by developers for data access, JCP has formulized the technology into JEE's technology stack. Starting from EJB 3.0, the entity bean specification has been replaced by the Java Persistence API (JPA). Currently at version 2.0, JPA is part of the JEE 6 standard and has incorporated many ideas from popular

ORM frameworks. JPA defines a common ORM pattern for object to relational mapping for Java application to access RDBMS, while leaving the implementation (called the *persistence provider*) to the open source communities and commercial vendors. Some popular JPA persistence providers include Hibernate, Eclipselink, and OpenJPA. Chapter 9 discusses Spring's support for Hibernate, and Chapter 10 discusses Spring's support for JPA. These two chapters combined show how we use Spring and JPA 2, using Hibernate as the persistence service provider, to build the implementation of our data access tier. For Spring with JPA and Hibernate, we will also discuss how to use the Spring Data JPA to implement logging for users who create blogs or comment and how to use Hibernate's Envers (Entity Versioning System) to implement the audit log function.

Strictly speaking, MyBatis is not an ORM tool but a DataMapper framework that does not remove all responsibility from the developer for creating the SQL statements needed to map Java objects to data in the RDMBS. MyBatis introduces the concept of a SQL map, allowing you to specify a variety of SQL queries and how these queries map to both input and output parameters. MyBatis is quite powerful in some aspects of data access. Chapter 11 discusses MyBatis in detail and shows how we built the second data access implementation.

In all cases, we use Spring's infrastructure classes for each data access tool. These classes integrate with Spring's transaction architecture, which allows transactions to be managed in a platform- and resource-provider-independent way in the service layer of the SpringBlog application.

Implementing the Service Layer

The SpringBlog application is fairly simple, and aside from the basic storage and retrieval of blog data, there are very few business rules in the system. However, there are two particular business functions in the SpringBlog application that exploit two of the most interesting Spring features: the AOP-based obscenity filter and the audit log.

Using AOP for Obscenity Filtering

AOP is a hot topic in the Java world at the moment, and as a result, Java developers are fortunate to have a wide range of AOP implementations available to them. Spring AOP support comes in two forms: the Spring native AOP framework and integration with the AspectJ AOP framework. Chapters 6 and 7 discuss both Spring AOP and AspectJ integration in detail.

For the SpringBlog application, we wanted to provide a practical example of AOP usage rather than the traditional (and boring) logging example. One of the features that we were working on for the sample application was an obscenity filter, and during design, it became apparent that AOP was the ideal mechanism for implementing this filter. In Chapter 21, you will see how we built the obscenity filter and how we used AOP to apply the filter selectively to the relevant methods.

Using Spring Transaction Support

As developers, one of the features of Spring that we found most impressive was the transaction support. Spring's transaction support provides a simple mechanism to control transactions across one or more resource providers, either programmatically or declaratively. Chapter 13 discusses the transaction framework in detail, focusing specifically on database transactions using both local and distributed transactions.

For the SpringBlog application, we defined a requirement that all operations in the blog be audited and logged to the database. To ensure that an operation is rolled back if the audit process fails, we used the Spring transaction framework to encapsulate each operation and its audit process in a single transaction. We will discuss this in Chapter 13.

Bean Validation

One thing developers want the most is a centralized validation rules engine, in which all the validation rules are applied and checked against the data, no matter where the data comes from (e.g., a user enters the information via the web application or from an XML file during batch job processing). The ideal case is that those validation rules need to be defined only once, and then the data can be validated against those rules on any layer when required. The Bean Validation API (JSR-303) was created to serve this purpose. In SpringBlog, we will use Bean Validation API for centralized validation check. The details of Spring's Bean Validation API support will be discussed in Chapter 13.

In SpringBlog, we will use Hibernate Validator (`http://hibernate.org/subprojects/validator`), a popular implementation of the Bean Validation API.

Two Different Service Layers Implementation

Traditionally, in the data access layer, developers will implement data access objects (DAOs) to separate the data access logic from the business logic. Those DAOs will be injected into the objects within the service layer. The intention is to make the switch from one data access implementation to another easier. However, the DAO pattern introduces one more layer between the service layer and backend database, which has proven to be quite cumbersome in most scenarios. In addition, by using standards like JPA, the persistence context can be injected directly into the service layer for data access, using the standard API as defined by JPA. You then have the flexibility to switch from one JPA persistence provider to another (such as from Hibernate to Eclipselink) easily. As a result, most applications these days do not use DAO, and all the business and data access logic is encapsulated into the service layer.

For the SpringBlog application, the service layer includes a number of interfaces that reflect the business services that the layer can provide. And as discussed earlier, we will provide two different implementations of the service layer using different persistence technologies; one uses JPA and Hibernate, while the other uses MyBatis.

We will also show you how to specify which service implementation to use in the application by using a new configuration feature in Spring 3.1 called *profiles*. Configuration and profiles will be discussed in Chapter 5.

Implementing the Batch and Integration Layer

Most applications need to integrate with other systems for exchanging information, either through a batch or on a real-time basis. Two Spring projects, Spring Batch and Spring Integration, can work together and provide a powerful and standard platform for the implementation of batch jobs and basic Enterprise Integration Pattern (EIP).

We will use the two Spring projects to implement a batch job to import blog entries from an XML file. We will use Spring Integration's file polling support to trigger the batch job whenever a file arrives into the specific folder. A brief introduction to Spring Batch and Spring Integration will be provided in Chapter 20.

Implementing the Presentation Layer

As with support for data access technologies, Spring is well known for its support of a wide range of different web application frameworks and tools. Chapters 17 and 18 provide a detailed discussion of the Spring MVC framework and some common view technologies supported by Spring, including Java Server Pages (JSP) and Java Server Faces (JSF).

Spring MVC

Currently there are many web frameworks on the market, and each has its pros and cons. Standardizing on a single framework and hoping it can address all the requirements of web applications with different natures and business purposes is almost impossible.

In SpringBlog, we will implement the web layer using a more common and simple approach. The MVC pattern will be adopted, and Spring MVC will be used as the framework. On the view side, we will use standard JSP pages. For Ajax features, we will use jQuery JavaScript library and Spring MVC's comprehensive RESTful-WS support for implementation. Details will be covered in Chapter 17.

Using Tiles

With most web applications, only a portion of the screen changes each time a new request is processed, and common elements such as the header and navigation bar remain the same. Using Tiles, you can assemble your pages from individual parts called *tiles*, enabling common elements to be defined once and reused across the application. Chapter 17 looks at using Tiles with a Spring application and shows how we used Tiles to build the sample application.

RESTful-WS and OXM

Another feature that Spring provides is an RSS feed in XML format. To accomplish this, we will use Spring MVC's RESTful-WS and Object to XML Mapping (OXM) support. For XML marshaling and unmarshaling, we will use Castor (`www.castor.org`). Other XML binding frameworks that Spring supports include JAXB, XStream, and XMLBeans. This will also be covered in Chapter 16.

Implementing the Security Layer

Security is another major concern for any application, especially web applications. Without a proper security control, your web application may suffer from web attacks and loss of important business data.

The Spring Security (formerly called Acegi Security Framework for Spring) is almost the default security framework for Spring-powered applications. Its comprehensive support for both declarative and programmatic security access control and tight integration with Spring greatly simplifies the code developers need to implement. For the SpringBlog application, we will use Spring Security 3.1 to protect the web application and ensure that users are only allowed to do what they are granted to do based on the roles assigned. We will cover Spring Security in Chapter 16 and 17.

As the user information and their roles assigned are stored in SpringBlog database, we will implement a user detail service class for Spring Security to retrieve the information and apply the security measures accordingly.

Summary

In this chapter, you looked at the SpringBlog application that we discuss throughout the book, and you were introduced to various features of SpringBlog, how they are implemented, and where in the book they are discussed.

In the next chapter, we will discuss the core of the Spring Framework—its Inversion of Control (IoC) container. Chapter 4 extends the examples we covered in Chapter 2 and discusses the different kinds of IoC and how they are supported in Spring.

CHAPTER 4

Introducing IoC and DI in Spring

In Chapter 1, we covered the basic principles of Inversion of Control (IoC) and Dependency Injection (DI). Practically, DI is a specialized form of IoC, although you will often find that the two terms are used interchangeably. In this chapter, we take a much more detailed look at IoC and DI, formalizing the relationship between the two concepts and looking in great detail at how Spring fits into the picture.

After defining both and looking at Spring's relationship with them, we will explore the concepts that are essential to Spring's implementation of DI. This chapter covers only the basics of Spring's DI implementation; we discuss more advanced DI features in Chapter 5 and look at DI in the context of application design in both Chapters 5 and 12. More specifically, this chapter will cover the following topics:

Inversion of Control concepts: In this section, we discuss the various kinds of IoC including Dependency Injection and Dependency Lookup. This section looks at the differences between the various IoC approaches and presents the pros and cons of each.

Inversion of Control in Spring: This section looks at IoC capabilities available in Spring and how these capabilities are implemented. In particular, this section looks at the Dependency Injection services that Spring offers, including Setter Injection, Constructor Injection, and Method Injection.

Dependency Injection in Spring: This section looks at Spring's implementation of the IoC container. For bean definition and DI requirements, BeanFactory is the main interface an application interacts with. However, other than the first few samples, all the rest of the sample codes provided in this chapter will focus on using Spring's ApplicationContext interface, which is an extension of BeanFactory and provides much more powerful features than enterprise applications would require. We will cover the difference between BeanFactory and ApplicationContext in later sections.

Configuring Spring application context: The final part of this chapter focuses on using both the XML-based configuration and the Java annotation approach for the ApplicationContext configuration. This section starts with a discussion of DI configuration and moves on to look at additional services provided by BeanFactory (part of Spring's ApplicationContext) such as bean inheritance, life-cycle management, and autowiring.

Inversion of Control and Dependency Injection

At its core, IoC, and therefore DI, aims to offer a simpler mechanism for provisioning component dependencies (often referred to as an object's *collaborators*) and managing these dependencies throughout their life cycles. A component that requires certain dependencies is often referred to as the *dependent object* or, in the case of IoC, the target. This is a rather grand way of saying that IoC provides services through which a component can access its dependencies and services for interacting with the dependencies throughout their life. In general, IoC can be decomposed into two subtypes: Dependency Injection and Dependency Lookup. These subtypes are further decomposed into concrete implementations of the IoC services. From this definition, you can clearly see that when we are talking about DI, we are always talking about IoC, but when we are talking about IoC, we are not always talking about DI (for example, Dependency Lookup is also a form of IoC).

Types of Inversion of Control

You may be wondering why there are two different types of IoC and why these types are split further into different implementations. There seems to be no clear answer to this question; certainly the different types provide a level of flexibility, but to us, it seems that IoC is more of a mixture of old and new ideas; the two different types of IoC represent this.

Dependency Lookup is a much more traditional approach, and at first glance, it seems more familiar to Java programmers. Dependency Injection is a newer, less well-established approach that, although it appears counterintuitive at first, is actually much more flexible and usable than Dependency Lookup.

With Dependency Lookup–style IoC, a component must acquire a reference to a dependency, whereas with Dependency Injection, the dependencies are injected into the component by the IoC container. Dependency Lookup comes in two types: Dependency Pull and Contextualized Dependency Lookup (CDL). Dependency Injection also has two common flavors: Constructor Dependency Injection and Setter Dependency Injection.

■ **Note** For the discussions in this section, we are not concerned with how the fictional IoC container comes to know about all the different dependencies, just that at some point, it performs the actions described for each mechanism.

Dependency Pull

To a Java developer, Dependency Pull is the most familiar type of IoC. In Dependency Pull, dependencies are pulled from a registry as required. Anyone who has ever written code to access an EJB (2.1 or prior versions) has used Dependency Pull (i.e., via the JNDI API to look up an EJB component). Figure 4-1 shows the scenario of Dependency Pull via the lookup mechanism.

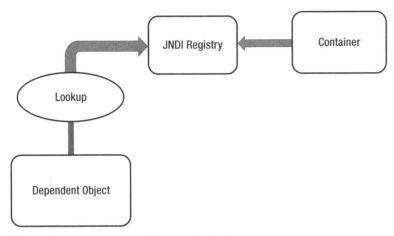

Figure 4-1. Dependency Pull via JNDI lookup

Spring also offers Dependency Pull as a mechanism for retrieving the components that the framework manages; you saw this in action in Chapter 2. Listing 4-1 shows a typical Dependency Pull lookup in a Spring-based application.

Listing 4-1. Dependency Pull in Spring

```
public static void main(String[] args) throws Exception {

    // get the bean factory
    BeanFactory factory = getBeanFactory();

    MessageRenderer mr = (MessageRenderer) factory.getBean("renderer");
    mr.render();
}
```

Not only is this kind of IoC prevalent in JEE-based applications (using EJB 2.1 or prior versions), which make extensive use of JNDI lookups to obtain dependencies from a registry, but it is also pivotal to working with Spring in many environments.

Contextualized Dependency Lookup

Contextualized Dependency Lookup (CDL) is similar, in some respects, to Dependency Pull, but in CDL, lookup is performed against the container that is managing the resource, not from some central registry, and it is usually performed at some set point. Figure 4-2 shows the CDL mechanism.

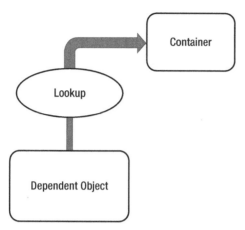

Figure 4-2. *Contextualized Dependency lookup*

CDL works by having the component implement an interface similar to that in Listing 4-2.

Listing 4-2. *Component Interface for CDL*

```
package com.apress.prospring3.ch4;

public interface ManagedComponent {
    public void performLookup(Container container);
}
```

By implementing this interface, a component is signaling to the container that it wants to obtain a dependency. The Container is usually provided by the underlying application server (e.g., Tomcat, JBoss) or framework (e.g., Spring). Listing 4-3 shows a simple Container interface that provides a Dependency Lookup service.

Listing 4-3. *A Simple Container Interface*

```
package com.apress.prospring3.ch4;

public interface Container {

    public Object getDependency(String key);
}
```

When the container is ready to pass dependencies to a component, it calls performLookup() on each component in turn. The component can then look up its dependencies using the Container interface, as shown in Listing 4-4.

Listing 4-4. *Obtaining Dependencies in CDL*

```
package com.apress.prospring3.ch4;

public class ContextualizedDependencyLookup implements ManagedComponent {
```

```
    private Dependency dependency;

    public void performLookup(Container container) {
        this.dependency = (Dependency) container.getDependency("myDependency");
    }
}
```

Note that in Listing 4-4, Dependency is an empty class.

Constructor Dependency Injection

Constructor Dependency Injection is Dependency Injection where a component's dependencies are
provided to it in its constructor(s). The component declares a constructor or a set of constructors taking
as arguments its dependencies, and the IoC container passes the dependencies to the component when
it instantiates it, as shown in Listing 4-5.

Listing 4-5. *Constructor Dependency Injection*

```
package com.apress.prospring3.ch4;

public class ConstructorInjection {

    private Dependency dependency;

    public ConstructorInjection(Dependency dependency) {
        this.dependency = dependency;
    }
}
```

Setter Dependency Injection

In Setter Dependency Injection, the IoC container injects a component's dependencies into the
component via JavaBean-style setter methods. A component's setters expose the set of dependencies the
IoC container can manage. Listing 4-6 shows a typical Setter Dependency Injection–based component.

Listing 4-6. *Setter Dependency Injection*

```
package com.apress.prospring3.ch4;

public class SetterInjection {

    private Dependency dependency;

    public void setDependency(Dependency dependency) {
        this.dependency = dependency;
    }
}
```

Within the container, the dependency requirement exposed by the setDependency() method is
referred to by the JavaBeans-style name, *dependency*. In practice, Setter Injection is the most widely used
injection mechanism, and it is one of the simplest IoC mechanisms to implement.

Injection vs. Lookup

Choosing which style of IoC to use—injection or lookup—is not usually a difficult decision. In many cases, the type of IoC you use is mandated by the container you are using. For instance, if you are using EJB 2.1 or prior versions, then you must use lookup-style IoC (via JNDI) to obtain the EJB from the JEE container. In Spring, aside from initial bean lookups, your components and their dependencies are always wired together using injection-style IoC.

■ **Note**   When you are using Spring, you can access EJB resources without needing to perform an explicit lookup. Spring can act as an adapter between lookup and injection-style IoC systems, thus allowing you to manage all resources using injection.

The real question is this: given the choice, which method should you use, injection or lookup? The answer to this is most definitely injection. If you look at the code in Listings 4-4 and 4-5, you can clearly see that using injection has zero impact on your components' code. The Dependency Pull code, on the other hand, must actively obtain a reference to the registry and interact with it to obtain the dependencies, and using CDL requires your classes to implement a specific interface and look up all dependencies manually. When you are using injection, the most your classes have to do is allow dependencies to be injected using either constructors or setters.

Using injection, you are free to use your classes completely decoupled from the IoC container that is supplying dependent objects with their collaborators manually, whereas with lookup, your classes are always dependent on the classes and interfaces defined by the container. Another drawback with lookup is that it becomes very difficult to test your classes in isolation from the container. Using injection, testing your components is trivial, because you can simply provide the dependencies yourself using the appropriate constructor or setter.

■ **Note**   For a more complete discussion of testing using Dependency Injection and Spring, refer to Chapter 19.

Lookup-based solutions are, by necessity, more complex than injection-based ones. Although complexity is nothing to be afraid of, we question the validity of adding unneeded complexity to a process as core to your application as dependency management.

All of these reasons aside, the biggest reason to choose injection over lookup is that it makes your life easier. You write substantially less code when you are using injection, and the code that you do write is simple and can, in general, be automated by a good IDE. You will notice that all of the code in the injection samples is passive, in that it doesn't actively try to accomplish a task. The most exciting thing you see in injection code is objects getting stored in a field only; no other codes were involved in pulling the dependency from any registry or container. Therefore, the code is much simpler and less error prone. Passive code is much simpler to maintain than active code, because there is very little that can go wrong. Consider the following code taken from Listing 4-4:

```
public void performLookup(Container container) {
    this.dependency = (Dependency) container.getDependency("myDependency");
}
```

In this code, plenty could go wrong: the dependency key could change, the container instance could be null, or the returned dependency might be the incorrect type. We refer to this code as having a lot of moving parts because plenty of things can break. Using Lookup might decouple the components of your application, but it adds complexity in the additional code required to couple these components back together in order to perform any useful tasks.

Setter Injection vs. Constructor Injection

Now that we have established which method of IoC is preferable, you still need to choose whether to use Setter Injection or Constructor Injection. Constructor Injection is particularly useful when you absolutely must have an instance of the dependency class before your component is used. Many containers, Spring included, provide a mechanism for ensuring that all dependencies are defined when you use Setter Injection, but by using Constructor Injection, you assert the requirement for the dependency in a container-agnostic manner.

Setter Injection is useful in a variety of cases. If the component is exposing its dependencies to the container but is happy to provide its own defaults, then Setter Injection is usually the best way to accomplish this. Another benefit of Setter Injection is that it allows dependencies to be declared on an interface, although this is not as useful as you might first think. Consider a typical business interface with one business method, defineMeaningOfLife(). If, in addition to this method, you define a setter for injection such as setEncylopedia(), then you are mandating that all implementations must use or at least be aware of the encyclopedia dependency. However, you don't need to define setEncylopedia() in the business interface. Instead, you can define the method in the classes implementing the business interface. While programming in this way, all recent IoC containers, Spring included, can work with the component in terms of the business interface but still provide the dependencies of the implementing class. An example of this may clarify this matter slightly. Consider the business interface in Listing 4-7.

Listing 4-7. The Oracle Interface

```
package com.apress.prospring3.ch4;

public interface Oracle {

    public String defineMeaningOfLife();
}
```

Notice that the business interface does not define any setters for Dependency Injection. This interface could be implemented as shown in Listing 4-8.

Listing 4-8. Implementing the Oracle Interface

```
package com.apress.prospring3.ch4;

public class BookwormOracle implements Oracle {

    private Encyclopedia encyclopedia;

    public void setEncyclopedia(Encyclopedia encyclopedia) {
        this. encyclopedia = encyclopedia;
    }

    public String defineMeaningOfLife() {
        return "Encyclopedias are a waste of money - use the Internet";
    }
}
```

As you can see, the BookwormOracle class not only implements the Oracle interface but also defines the setter for Dependency Injection. Spring is more than comfortable dealing with a structure like this—there is absolutely no need to define the dependencies on the business interface. The ability to use interfaces to define dependencies is an often-touted benefit of Setter Injection, but in actuality, you should strive to keep setters used solely for injection out of your business and DAO interfaces. Unless you are absolutely sure that all implementations of a particular business interface require a particular dependency, let each implementation class define its own dependencies and keep the business interface for business methods.

Although you shouldn't always place setters for dependencies in a business interface, placing setters and getters for configuration parameters in the business interface is a good idea and makes Setter Injection a valuable tool. We consider configuration parameters to be a special case for dependencies. Certainly your components depend on the configuration data, but configuration data is significantly different from the types of dependency you have seen so far. We will discuss the differences shortly, but for now, consider the business interface shown in Listing 4-9.

Listing 4-9. The NewsletterSender Interface

```
package com.apress.prospring3.ch4;

public interface NewsletterSender {

    public void setSmtpServer(String smtpServer);
    public String getSmtpServer();

    public void setFromAddress(String fromAddress);
    public String getFromAddress();

    public void send();
}
```

The NewsletterSender interface is implemented by classes that send a set of newsletters via e-mail. The send() method is the only business method, but notice that we have defined two JavaBean properties on the interface. Why are we doing this when we just said that you shouldn't define dependencies in the business interface? The reason is that these values, the SMTP server address and the address the e-mails are sent from, are not dependencies in the practical sense; rather, they are configuration details that affect how all implementations of the NewsletterSender interface function. Spring's Dependency Injection capabilities form the ideal solution to the external configuration of application components, not for dependency provision but as a mechanism for externalizing component configuration settings. The question here then is this: what is the difference between a configuration parameter and any other kind of dependency? In most cases, you can clearly see whether a dependency should be classed as a configuration parameter, but if you are not sure, look for the following three characteristics that point to a configuration parameter:

- Configuration parameters are passive. In the NewsletterSender example shown in Listing 4-8, the SMTP server parameter is an example of a passive dependency. Passive dependencies are not used directly to perform an action; instead, they are used internally or by another dependency to perform their actions. In the MessageRenderer example from Chapter 2, the MessageProvider dependency was not passive—it performed a function that was necessary for the MessageRenderer to complete its task.

- Configuration parameters are usually information, not other components. By this we mean that a configuration parameter is usually some piece of information that a component needs to complete its work. Clearly, the SMTP server is a piece of information required by the NewsletterSender, but the MessageProvider is really another component that the MessageRenderer needs to function correctly.

- Configuration parameters are usually simple values or collections of simple values. This is really a by-product of the previous two points, but configuration parameters are usually simple values. In Java this means they are a primitive (or the corresponding wrapper class) or a String or collections of these values. Simple values are generally passive. This means you can't do much with a String other than manipulate the data it represents; and you almost always use these values for information purposes—for example, an int value that represents the port number that a network socket should listen on, or a String that represents the SMTP server through which an e-mail program should send messages.

When considering whether to define configuration options in the business interface, also consider whether the configuration parameter is applicable to all implementations of the business interface or just one. For instance, in the case of implementations of NewsletterSender, it is obvious that all implementations need to know which SMTP server to use when sending e-mails. However, we would probably choose to leave the configuration option that flags whether to send secure e-mail off the business interface, because not all e-mail APIs are capable of this, and it is correct to assume that many implementations will not take security into consideration at all.

▓ **Note** Recall that in Chapter 2, we chose to define the dependencies in the business purposes. This was for illustration purposes and should not be treated in any way as a best practice.

Setter injection also allows you to swap dependencies for a different implementation on the fly without creating a new instance of the parent component. Spring's JMX support makes this possible. Perhaps the biggest benefit of Setter Injection is that it is the least intrusive of the injection mechanisms.

If you are defining constructors for injection on a class that would otherwise just have the default constructor, then you are affecting all code that uses that class in a non-IoC environment. Extra setters that are defined on a class for IoC purposes do not affect the ability of other classes to interact with it.

In general, setter-based injection is the best choice, because it has the least effect on your code's usability in non-IoC settings. Constructor injection is a good choice when you want to ensure that dependencies are being passed to a component, but bear in mind that many containers provide their own mechanism for doing this with Setter Injection. Most of the code in the sample application uses Setter Injection, although there are a few examples of Constructor Injection.

Inversion of Control in Spring

As we mentioned earlier, Inversion of Control is a big part of what Spring does, and the core of Spring's implementation is based on Dependency Injection, although Dependency Lookup features are provided as well. When Spring provides collaborators to a dependent object automatically, it does so using Dependency Injection. In a Spring-based application, it is always preferable to use Dependency Injection to pass collaborators to dependent objects rather than have the dependent objects obtain the collaborators via lookup. Figure 4-3 shows Spring's Dependency Injection mechanism (for Dependency Lookup, please refer to Figure 4-2).

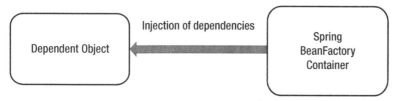

Figure 4-3. *Spring's Dependency Injection mechanism*

Although Dependency Injection is the preferred mechanism for wiring together collaborators and dependent objects, you need Dependency Lookup to access the dependent objects. In many environments, Spring cannot automatically wire up all of your application components using Dependency Injection, and you must use Dependency Lookup to access the initial set of components. For example, in stand-alone Java applications, you need to bootstrap Spring's container in the main() method and obtain the dependencies (via the ApplicationContext interface) for processing programmatically. However, when you are building web applications using Spring's MVC support, Spring can avoid this by gluing your entire application together automatically. Wherever it is possible to use Dependency Injection with Spring, you should do so; otherwise, you can fall back on the Dependency Lookup capabilities. You will see examples of both in action during the course of this chapter, and we will point them out when they first arise.

An interesting feature of Spring's IoC container is that it has the ability to act as an adaptor between its own Dependency Injection container and external Dependency Lookup containers. We will discuss this feature later in this chapter.

Spring supports both Constructor and Setter Injection and bolsters the standard IoC feature set with a whole host of useful additions to make your life easier.

The rest of this chapter introduces the basics of Spring's DI container complete with plenty of examples.

Dependency Injection with Spring

Spring's support for Dependency Injection is comprehensive and, as you will see in Chapter 5, goes beyond the standard IoC feature set we have discussed so far. The rest of this chapter addresses the basics of Spring's Dependency Injection container, looking at Setter, Constructor, and Method Injection, along with a detailed look at how Dependency Injection is configured in Spring.

Beans and BeanFactories

The core of Spring's Dependency Injection container is the BeanFactory interface. A BeanFactory is responsible for managing components, including their dependencies as well as their life cycles. In Spring, the term *bean* is used to refer to any component managed by the container. Typically your beans adhere, at some level, to the JavaBeans specification, but this is not required, especially if you plan to use Constructor Injection to wire your beans together.

If your application needs only DI support, you can interact with the Spring DI container via the BeanFactory interface. In this case, your application must create an instance of a class that implements the BeanFactory interface and configures it with bean and dependency information. After this is complete, your application can access the beans via the BeanFactory and get on with its processing. In some cases, all of this setup is handled automatically (for example, in a web application, Spring's ApplicationContext will be bootstrapped by the web container during application startup via a Spring-provided ContextLoaderListener class declared in the web.xml descriptor file). But in many cases, you need to code the setup yourself. All of the examples in this chapter require manual setup of the BeanFactory implementation.

Although a BeanFactory can be configured programmatically, it is more common to see it configured externally using some kind of configuration file. Internally, bean configuration is represented by instances of classes that implement the BeanDefinition interface. The bean configuration stores not only information about a bean itself but also about the beans that it depends on. For any BeanFactory implementation classes that also implement the BeanDefinitionRegistry interface, you can read the BeanDefinition data from a configuration file, using either PropertiesBeanDefinitionReader or XmlBeanDefinitionReader. The two main BeanFactory implementations that come with Spring implement BeanDefinitionRegistry. The PropertiesBeanDefinitionReader reads the bean definition from properties files, while XmlBeanDefinitionReader reads from XML files.

So you can identify your beans within the BeanFactory, each bean can be assigned either an ID or a name, or both. A bean can also be instantiated without any ID and name (known as an *anonymous* bean) or as an inner bean within a specific bean. Each bean has at least one name but can have any number (additional names are separated by commas). Any names after the first are considered aliases for the same bean. You use bean IDs or names to retrieve a bean from the BeanFactory and also to establish dependency relationships—that is, bean X depends on bean Y.

BeanFactory Implementations

The description of the BeanFactory might make using it seem overly complex, but in practice, this is not the case. Take a look at a simple example.

Let's say you have an implementation that mimics an oracle that can tell you the meaning of life. Listings 4-10 and 4-11 define the interface and a simple implementation, respectively.

Listing 4-10. The Oracle Interface

```
package com.apress.prospring3.ch4;

public interface Oracle {

    public String defineMeaningOfLife();
}
```

Listing 4-11. A Simple Oracle Interface Implementation

```
package com.apress.prospring3.ch4;

public class BookwormOracle implements Oracle {

    public String defineMeaningOfLife() {
        return "Encyclopedias are a waste of money - use the Internet";
    }
}
```

Now let's see, in a stand-alone Java program, how we can initialize Spring's BeanFactory and obtain the oracle bean for processing (see Listing 4-12).

Listing 4-12. Using the Bean Factory

```
package com.apress.prospring3.ch4;
import org.springframework.beans.factory.support.DefaultListableBeanFactory;
```

```
import org.springframework.beans.factory.xml.XmlBeanDefinitionReader;
import org.springframework.core.io.FileSystemResource;

public class XmlConfigWithBeanFactory {

    public static void main(String[] args) {

        DefaultListableBeanFactory factory = new DefaultListableBeanFactory();

        XmlBeanDefinitionReader rdr = new XmlBeanDefinitionReader(factory);
        rdr.loadBeanDefinitions(new
        FileSystemResource("src/main/resources/xmlBeanFactory.xml"));

        Oracle oracle = (Oracle)factory.getBean("oracle");
            System.out.println(oracle.defineMeaningOfLife());
    }
}
```

In Listing 4-12, you can see that we are using the DefaultListableBeanFactory—one of the two main BeanFactory implementations supplied with Spring—and that we are reading in the BeanDefinition information from an XML file using the XmlBeanDefinitionReader. Once the BeanFactory implementation is created and configured, we retrieve the Oracle bean using its name, oracle, which is configured in the XML configuration file. Listing 4-13 is the content of the XML for bootstrapping Spring's BeanFactory (xmlBeanFactory.xml).

Listing 4-13. Simple Spring XML Configuration

```
<?xml version="1.0" encoding="UTF-8"?>
<beans xmlns="http://www.springframework.org/schema/beans"
    xmlns:xsi="http://www.w3.org/2001/XMLSchema-instance"
    xsi:schemaLocation="http://www.springframework.org/schema/beans
        http://www.springframework.org/schema/beans/spring-beans-3.1.xsd">

    <!-- oracle bean used for a few examples -->
    <bean id="oracle" name="wiseworm" class="com.apress.prospring3.ch4.BookwormOracle"/>

</beans>
```

The previous file declares a Spring bean, gives it an ID of "oracle" and a name "wiseworm", and tells Spring that the underlying implementation class is com.apress.prospring3.ch4.BookwormOracle. Don't worry too much about the configuration at the moment; we will discuss the details in later sections.

Having the configuration defined, run the program in Listing 4-12, and you will see the phrase returned by the defineMeaningOfLife() method in the console output in STS.

In addition to XmlBeanDefinitionReader, Spring also provides PropertiesBeanDefinitionReader, which allows you to manage your bean configuration using properties rather than XML. Although properties are ideal for small, simple applications, they can quickly become cumbersome when you are dealing with a large number of beans. For this reason, it is preferable to use the XML configuration format for all but the most trivial of applications.

Of course, you are free to define your own BeanFactory implementations, although be aware that doing so is quite involved; you need to implement a lot more interfaces than just BeanFactory to get the same level of functionality you have with the supplied BeanFactory implementations. If all you want to do is define a new configuration mechanism, then create your definition reader by developing a class that extends the DefaultListableBeanFactory class, which has the BeanFactory interface implemented.

ApplicationContext

In Spring, the ApplicationContext interface is an extension to BeanFactory. In addition to DI services, the ApplicationContext also provides other services, such as transaction and AOP service, message source for internationalization (i18n), and application event handling, to name a few.

In developing Spring-based application, it's recommended that you interact with Spring via the ApplicationContext interface. Spring supports the bootstrapping of ApplicationContext by manual coding (instantiate it manually and load the appropriate configuration) or in a web container environment via the ContextLoaderListener. From this point onward, all the sample code in this book will use ApplicationContext.

Configuring ApplicationContext

Having discussed the basic concepts of IoC and DI and gone through a simple example of using Spring's BeanFactory interface, let's dive into the details on how to configure a Spring application.

In the following sections, we will go through various aspects of configuring Spring applications. Specifically, we will focus our attention on the ApplicationContext interface, which provides many more configuration options than the traditional BeanFactory interface.

Spring Configuration Options (XML and Java Annotations)

Before we dive into the details of configuring Spring's ApplicationContext, let's take a look at the options that are available for defining an application's configuration within Spring.

Originally, Spring supports defining beans either through properties or an XML file, and the XML file was used by most Spring application developers for quite some time. Since the release of JDK 5 and Spring's support of Java annotations, Spring (starting from Spring 2.5) also supports using Java annotations when configuring ApplicationContext.

So, which one is better, XML or annotations? There have been lots of debates on this topic, and you can find numerous discussions about this topic on the Internet (for example, try the Spring Community Forum at http://forum.springsource.org). There is no definite answer, and each approach has its pros and cons. Using XML file can externalize all configuration from Java code, while annotations allow the developer to define and view the DI setup from within the code. Spring also supports a mix of the two approaches in a single ApplicationContext (the XML file configuration will override the annotation ones). One common approach nowadays is to define the application infrastructure (e.g., data source, transaction manager, JMS connection factory, JMX, etc.) in XML file, while defining the DI configuration (injectable beans and beans' dependencies) in annotations. However, no matter which option you choose, stick to it and deliver the message clearly across the entire development team. Agreeing on the style to use and keeping it consistent across the application will make ongoing development and the maintenance activities much easier.

To facilitate your understanding of both the XML and annotation configuration, we'll provide sample code for XML and annotations side by side whenever appropriate.

Basic Configuration Overview

For XML configuration, you need to declare the required namespace base provided by Spring that your application requires. Listing 4-13 shows the most basic sample, which declares only the beans namespace for you to define the Spring beans.

Besides beans, Spring provides a large number of other namespaces for different purposes. Listing 4-14 is the namespace declaration for the Spring configuration that will be used by the samples in this chapter. In the section on Spring configuration, we will prepare two configuration files throughout the samples. One is `app-context-xml.xml` for the XML-style configuration, and the other is `app-context-annotation.xml` for the annotation-style configuration.

Listing 4-14. Spring XML Configuration

```
<?xml version="1.0" encoding="UTF-8"?>
<beans xmlns="http://www.springframework.org/schema/beans"
    xmlns:xsi="http://www.w3.org/2001/XMLSchema-instance"
    xmlns:context="http://www.springframework.org/schema/context"
    xmlns:p="http://www.springframework.org/schema/p"
    xmlns:c="http://www.springframework.org/schema/c"
    xmlns:util="http://www.springframework.org/schema/util"
    xsi:schemaLocation="http://www.springframework.org/schema/beans
        http://www.springframework.org/schema/beans/spring-beans-3.1.xsd
        http://www.springframework.org/schema/context
        http://www.springframework.org/schema/context/spring-context-3.1.xsd
        http://www.springframework.org/schema/util
        http://www.springframework.org/schema/util/spring-util-3.1.xsd">

</beans>
```

From the previous namespace declaration, we have made beans the default namespace. The following namespaces were also declared:

> context: The `context` namespace provides support for configuring Spring's `ApplicationContext`.

> p: The p namespace provides a simpler DI configuration for Setter Injection.

> c: New in Spring 3.1, the c namespace provides a more simple DI configuration for Constructor Injection.

> util: The `util` namespace provides some useful utilities for DI configuration.

Spring also provides a lot of namespace for various purpose, such as aop for AOP support, tx for transaction support, and so on. Those namespaces will be covered in the appropriate chapters.

To use Spring's annotation support in your application, you need to declare the tags shown in Listing 4-15 in your XML configuration (`app-context-annotation.xml`).

Listing 4-15. Spring XML Configuration with Annotation Support

```
// Namespace declarations skipped

<context:annotation-config/>

<context:component-scan base-package="com.apress.prospring3.ch4.annotation" />
```

The `<context:annotation-config>` tag tells Spring to scan the codebase for dependency requirements, while the `<context:component-scan>` tag tells Spring to scan the code for injectable beans under the package (and all its subpackages) specified. In the `<context:component-scan>` tag, multiple packages can be defined by using either a comma, a semicolon, or a space as the delimiter. Moreover, the tag support inclusion and exclusion of components scan for more fine-grained control. For example, consider the configuration in Listing 4-16.

Listing 4-16. Spring XML Configuration Component Scan

```
<context:component-scan base-package="com.apress.prospring3.ch4.annotation" >
    <context:exclude-filter type="assignable" expression="com.example.NotAService"/>
</ context:component-scan>
```

The previous tag tells Spring to scan the package as specified but omit the classes that were assignable to the type as specified in the expression (can be either a class or an interface). Besides the exclude filter, you can also use an include filter. And for the type, you can use annotation, regex, assignable, AspectJ, or custom (with your own filter class that implements org.springframework.core.type.filter.TypeFilter) as the filter criteria. The expression format depends on the type you specified.

Declare Spring Components

After you develop some kind of service classes and want to use it in a Spring base application, you need to tell Spring that those beans are eligible for injection to other beans and have Spring manage them for you. Consider the sample in Chapter 2, where the MessageRender outputs the message and depends on the MessageProvider to provide the message to render. Listing 4-17 recaps the interfaces and implementations of the two services.

Listing 4-17. MessageRenderer and MessageProvider

```
package com.apress.prospring3.ch4;

public interface MessageRenderer {

    public void render();

    public void setMessageProvider(MessageProvider provider);

    public MessageProvider getMessageProvider();

}

package com.apress.prospring3.ch4.xml;

import com.apress.prospring3.ch4.MessageProvider;
import com.apress.prospring3.ch4.MessageRenderer;

public class StandardOutMessageRenderer implements MessageRenderer {

    private MessageProvider messageProvider = null;

    public void render() {
        if (messageProvider == null) {
            throw new RuntimeException(
            "You must set the property messageProvider of class:"
            + StandardOutMessageRenderer.class.getName());
        }

        System.out.println(messageProvider.getMessage());
    }
```

```
    public void setMessageProvider(MessageProvider provider) {
        this.messageProvider = provider;
    }

    public MessageProvider getMessageProvider() {
        return this.messageProvider;
    }

}

package com.apress.prospring3.ch4;

public interface MessageProvider {

    public String getMessage();

}

package com.apress.prospring3.ch4.xml;

import com.apress.prospring3.ch4.MessageProvider;

public class HelloWorldMessageProvider implements MessageProvider {

    public String getMessage() {
        return "Hello World!";
    }

}
```

To declare the beans in XML file, on top of the basic configuration (as stated earlier in Listing 4-14), you add the <bean> tags in Listing 4-18 to the file app-context-xml.xml.

Listing 4-18. Declare Spring Beans (XML)

```
<bean id="messageRenderer" class="com.apress.prospring3.ch4.xml.StandardOutMessageRenderer"/>

<bean id="messageProvider" class="com.apress.prospring3.ch4.xml.HelloWorldMessageProvider"/>
```

The previous tags declare two beans, one with an ID of "messageProvider" with the HelloWorldMessageProvider implementation and the other with an ID of "messageRenderer" with the StandardOutMessageRenderer implementation.

To define the Spring beans via annotation, you don't need to modify the XML configuration file (app-context-annotation.xml) anymore; you just need to add the corresponding annotation to the service implementation classes under the package com.apress.prospring3.ch4.annotation (see Listing 4-19).

Listing 4-19. Declare Spring Beans (Annotation)

```
package com.apress.prospring3.ch4.annotation;

import org.springframework.stereotype.Service;

// Rest of codes omitted
@Service("messageRenderer")
```

```
public class StandardOutMessageRenderer implements MessageRenderer {

package com.apress.prospring3.ch4.annotation;

import org.springframework.stereotype.Service;

// Rest of codes omitted
@Service("messageProvider")
public class HelloWorldMessageProvider implements MessageProvider {
```

From the previous code sample, you use Spring's @Service annotation to specify that the bean provides services that other beans may require, passing in the bean name as the parameter. When bootstrapping Spring's ApplicationContext with the XML configuration in Listing 4-15, Spring will seek out those components and instantiate the beans with the specified names.

Using either approach doesn't affect the way you obtain the beans from ApplicationContext. Listing 4-20 shows the example code to obtain the message provider.

Listing 4-20. Declare Spring Beans (Testing)

```
package com.apress.prospring3.ch4;

import org.springframework.context.support.GenericXmlApplicationContext;

public class DeclareSpringComponents {

    public static void main(String[] args) {

        GenericXmlApplicationContext ctx = new GenericXmlApplicationContext();
        ctx.load("classpath:app-context-xml.xml");
        ctx.refresh();

        MessageProvider messageProvider = ctx.getBean("messageProvider",
            MessageProvider.class);

        System.out.println(messageProvider.getMessage());
    }

}
```

From Listing 4-20, instead of the DefaultListableBeanFactory, an instance of GenericXmlApplicationContext was instantiated. The GenericXmlApplicationContext class implements the ApplicationContext interface and is able to bootstrap Spring's ApplicationContext from the configurations defined in XML files.

You can swap the app-context-xml.xml file with app-context-annotation.xml in the provided source code for this chapter, and you will find that both cases produce the same result; i.e., "Hello World!" is printed.

Listing 4-21 (app-context-xml.xml) and Listing 4-22 (app-context-annotation.xml) recap the configuration files content for both XML and annotation-style configuration that we have discussed so far.

Listing 4-21. XML Configuration (app-context-xml.xml)

```
<?xml version="1.0" encoding="UTF-8"?>
<beans xmlns="http://www.springframework.org/schema/beans"
       xmlns:xsi="http://www.w3.org/2001/XMLSchema-instance"
```

```
        xmlns:context="http://www.springframework.org/schema/context"
        xmlns:p="http://www.springframework.org/schema/p"
        xmlns:c="http://www.springframework.org/schema/c"
        xmlns:util="http://www.springframework.org/schema/util"
        xsi:schemaLocation="http://www.springframework.org/schema/beans
            http://www.springframework.org/schema/beans/spring-beans-3.1.xsd
            http://www.springframework.org/schema/context
            http://www.springframework.org/schema/context/spring-context-3.1.xsd
            http://www.springframework.org/schema/util
            http://www.springframework.org/schema/util/spring-util-3.1.xsd">

    <bean id="messageProvider"
          class="com.apress.prospring3.ch4.xml.HelloWorldMessageProvider"/>

</beans>
```

Listing 4-22. Annotation Configuration (app-context-annotation.xml)

```
<?xml version="1.0" encoding="UTF-8"?>
<beans xmlns="http://www.springframework.org/schema/beans"
       xmlns:xsi="http://www.w3.org/2001/XMLSchema-instance"
       xmlns:context="http://www.springframework.org/schema/context"
       xmlns:p="http://www.springframework.org/schema/p"
       xmlns:c="http://www.springframework.org/schema/c"
       xmlns:util="http://www.springframework.org/schema/util"
       xsi:schemaLocation="http://www.springframework.org/schema/beans
           http://www.springframework.org/schema/beans/spring-beans-3.1.xsd
           http://www.springframework.org/schema/context
           http://www.springframework.org/schema/context/spring-context-3.1.xsd
           http://www.springframework.org/schema/util
           http://www.springframework.org/schema/util/spring-util-3.1.xsd">

    <context:annotation-config/>

    <context:component-scan
        base-package="com.apress.prospring3.ch4.annotation"/>

</beans>
```

Using Setter Injection

To configure Setter Injection using XML configuration, you need to specify <property> tags under the
<bean> tag for each <property> into which you want to inject a dependency. For example, to assign the
message provider bean to the messageProvider property of the messageRenderer bean, you simply change
the <bean> tag for the messageRenderer bean, as shown in Listing 4-23.

Listing 4-23. Setter Injection (XML)

```
<bean id="messageRenderer" class="com.apress.prospring3.ch4.xml.StandardOutMessageRenderer">
    <property name="messageProvider">
        <ref bean="messageProvider"/>
    </property>
</bean>
```

From this code, you can see that we are assigning the messageProvider bean to the messageProvider property. You can use the <ref> tag to assign a bean reference to a property (discussed in more detail shortly).

If you are using Spring 2.5 or later and have the p namespace declared in your XML configuration file, you can declare the injection as shown here:

```
<bean id="messageRenderer" class="com.apress.prospring3.ch4.xml.StandardOutMessageRenderer"
    p:messageProvider-ref="messageProvider"/>
```

The p namespace provides a simplified way for defining Setter Injection.

For annotation, it's even simpler. You just need to add an @Autowired annotation to the setter method, as shown in Listing 4-24.

Listing 4-24. Setter Injection (Annotation)

```
package com.apress.prospring3.ch4.annotation;

import org.springframework.beans.factory.annotation.Autowired;

// Rest of the codes omitted
@Service("messageRenderer")
public class StandardOutMessageRenderer implements MessageRenderer {

    ...
    @Autowired
    public void setMessageProvider(MessageProvider provider) {
        this.messageProvider = provider;
    }
    ...
}
```

Since we declared the <context:annotation-config> tag in the XML configuration file, during the initialization of Spring's ApplicationContext, Spring will discover those @Autowired annotations and inject the dependency (discovered via the <context:component-scan> tag) as required.

■ **Note** Instead of the @Autowired, you can also use the @Resource(name="messageProvider") to achieve the same result. The @Resource is one of the annotations in the JSR-250 standard that defines a common set of Java annotations for use on both JSE and JEE platforms. Different from @Autowired, the @Resource annotation supports the name parameter for more fine-grained DI requirements.

Now let's verify the result by using the code in Listing 4-25.

Listing 4-25. Using Setter Injection (Testing)

```
package com.apress.prospring3.ch4;

import org.springframework.context.support.GenericXmlApplicationContext;

public class UsingSetterInjection {
```

```
    public static void main(String[] args) {

        GenericXmlApplicationContext ctx = new GenericXmlApplicationContext();
        ctx.load("classpath:app-context-xml.xml");
        ctx.refresh();

        MessageRenderer messageRenderer = ctx.getBean("messageRenderer",
            MessageRenderer.class);
        messageRenderer.render();
    }

}
```

Like the previous section, you can swap the app-context-xml.xml file with app-context-annotation.xml in the provided source code for this chapter, and you will find that both cases produce the same result; i.e., "Hello World!" is printed.

Using Constructor Injection

In the previous example, the MessageProvider implementation, HelloWorldMessageProvider, returned the same hard-coded message for each call of the getMessage() method. In the Spring configuration file, you can easily create a configurable MessageProvider that allows the message to be defined externally, as shown in Listing 4-26.

Listing 4-26. The ConfigurableMessageProvider Class (XML)

```
package com.apress.prospring3.ch4.xml;

import com.apress.prospring3.ch4.MessageProvider;

public class ConfigurableMessageProvider implements MessageProvider {

    private String message;

    public ConfigurableMessageProvider(String message) {
        this.message = message;
    }

    public String getMessage() {
        return message;
    }
}
```

As you can see, it is impossible to create an instance of ConfigurableMessageProvider without providing a value for the message (unless you supply null). This is exactly what we want, and this class is ideally suited for use with Constructor Injection. Listing 4-27 shows how you can redefine the messageProvider bean definition to create an instance of ConfigurableMessageProvider, injecting the message using Constructor Injection.

Listing 4-27. Using Constructor Injection (XML)

```
<bean id="messageProvider" class="com.apress.prospring3.ch4.xml.ConfigurableMessageProvider">
    <constructor-arg>
```

```
        <value>This is a configurable message</value>
    </constructor-arg>
</bean>
```

In this code, instead of using a `<property>` tag, we used a `<constructor-arg>` tag. Because we are not passing in another bean this time, just a `String` literal, we use the `<value>` tag instead of the `<ref>` to specify the value for the constructor argument.

When you have more than one constructor argument or your class has more than one constructor, you need to give each `<constructor-arg>` tag an `index` attribute to specify the index of the argument, starting at 0, in the constructor signature. It is always best to use the `index` attribute whenever you are dealing with constructors that have multiple arguments to avoid confusion between the parameters and ensure that Spring picks the correct constructor.

Like the p namespace, in Spring 3.1, you can also use the c namespace, as shown here:

```
<bean id="messageProvider"
class="com.apress.prospring3.ch4.xml.ConfigurableMessageProvider"
        c:message="This is a configurable message"/>
```

To use an annotation for Constructor Injection, we also use the `@Autowired` annotation in the target bean's constructor method, as shown in Listing 4-28, which is an alternative option to the one using Setter Injection, as shown in Listing 4-24.

Listing 4-28. Using Constructor Injection (Annotation)

```
package com.apress.prospring3.ch4.annotation;

import org.springframework.beans.factory.annotation.Value;

...
@Service("messageProvider")
public class ConfigurableMessageProvider implements MessageProvider {

    private String message;

    @Autowired
    public ConfigurableMessageProvider(@Value("This is a configurable message") String↵
message) {
        this.message = message;
    }
...
}
```

From the previous listing, you can see that we use another annotation, `@Value`, to define the value to be injected into the constructor. This is the way in Spring you inject values into a bean. Besides simple strings, you can also use the powerful SpEL for dynamic value injection (more on this later in this chapter).

However, hard-coding the value in the code is not a good idea, since to change it, you would need to recompile the program. Even if you choose annotation-style DI, a good practice is to externalize those values for injection. To externalize the message, let's define the message as a Spring bean in the annotation configuration file, as in Listing 4-29.

Listing 4-29. Using Constructor Injection (Annotation)

```
<bean id="message" class="java.lang.String"
        c:_0="This is a configurable message"/>
```

Here we defined a bean with an ID of "message", type java.lang.String. Notice that we also used the c namespace for Constructor Injection to set the string value, and _0 indicates the index for constructor argument.

Have the bean declared, we can take away the @Value annotation from the target bean, as in Listing 4-30.

Listing 4-30. Using Constructor Injection (Annotation)

```
package com.apress.prospring3.ch4.annotation;
...
@Service("messageProvider")
public class ConfigurableMessageProvider implements MessageProvider {

    private String message;

    @Autowired
    public ConfigurableMessageProvider(String message) {
        this.message = message;
    }
...
}
```

Since we declared the message bean and its ID are the same as the name of the argument specified in the constructor, Spring will detect the annotation and inject the value into the constructor method.

Now run the test (the UsingSetterInjection class shown in Listing 4-25) against both the XML (app-context.xml.xml) and annotation configurations (app-context-annotation.xml), and the configured message will be displayed in both cases. The following is the sample output:

```
This is a configurable message
```

Avoiding Constructor Confusion

In some cases, Spring finds it impossible to tell which constructor you want it to use for Constructor Injection. This usually arises when you have two constructors with the same number of arguments and the types used in the arguments are represented in exactly the same way. Consider the code in Listing 4-31.

Listing 4-31. Constructor Confusion

```
package com.apress.prospring3.ch4.xml;

import org.springframework.context.support.GenericXmlApplicationContext;

public class ConstructorConfusion {

    private String someValue;

    public ConstructorConfusion(String someValue) {
        System.out.println("ConstructorConfusion(String) called");
        this.someValue = someValue;
    }

    public ConstructorConfusion(int someValue) {
        System.out.println("ConstructorConfusion(int) called");
```

```
      this.someValue = "Number: " + Integer.toString(someValue);
   }

   public static void main(String[] args) {

      GenericXmlApplicationContext ctx = new GenericXmlApplicationContext();
      ctx.load("classpath:app-context-xml.xml");
      ctx.refresh();

      ConstructorConfusion cc = (ConstructorConfusion) ctx.getBean("constructorConfusion");
      System.out.println(cc);
   }

   public String toString() {
      return someValue;
   }
}
```

Here, you can clearly see what this code does—it simply retrieves a bean of type ConstructorConfusion from ApplicationContext and writes the value to console output. Now look at the configuration code in Listing 4-32 (app-context-xml.xml).

Listing 4-32. Confused Constructors

```
<bean id="constructorConfusion"
   class="com.apress.prospring3.ch4.xml.ConstructorConfusion">
   <constructor-arg>
      <value>90</value>
   </constructor-arg>
</bean>
```

Which of the constructors is called in this case? Running the example yields the following output:

```
ConstructorConfusion(String) called
90
```

This shows that the constructor with the String argument was called. This is not the desired effect, since we want to prefix any integer values passed in using Constructor Injection with Number:, as shown in the int constructor. To get around this, we need to make a small modification to the configuration, shown in Listing 4-33 (app-context-xml.xml).

Listing 4-33. Overcoming Constructor Confusion

```
<bean id="constructorConfusion"
   class="com.apress.prospring3.ch4.xml.ConstructorConfusion">
   <constructor-arg type="int">
      <value>90</value>
   </constructor-arg>
</bean>
```

Notice now that the <constructor-arg> tag has an additional attribute, type, that specifies the type of argument Spring should look for. Running the example again with the corrected configuration yields the correct output:

```
ConstructorConfusion(int) called
Number: 90
```

For annotation-style Construction Injection, the confusion can be avoided by applying the annotation directly to the target constructor method, as we've done in Listing 4-34.

Listing 4-34. Constructor Confusion (Annotation)

```
package com.apress.prospring3.ch4.annotation;

// Codes omitted

@Service("constructorConfusion")
public class ConstructorConfusion {

    private String someValue;

    public ConstructorConfusion(String someValue) {
        System.out.println("ConstructorConfusion(String) called");
        this.someValue = someValue;
    }

    @Autowired
    public ConstructorConfusion(@Value("90") int someValue) {
        System.out.println("ConstructorConfusion(int) called");
        this.someValue = "Number: " + Integer.toString(someValue);
    }

// Codes omitted

}
```

By applying the @Autowired annotation to the desired constructor method, Spring will use that method to instantiate the bean and inject the value as specified. Like before, you should externalize the value into the configuration.

■ **Note** You can apply the @Autowired annotation to only one of the constructor methods. If you apply the annotation to more than one constructor method, Spring will complain during bootstrapping the ApplicationContext.

Injection Parameters

In the two previous examples, you saw how to inject other components and values into a bean using both Setter Injection and Constructor Injection. Spring supports a myriad of options for injection parameters, allowing you to inject not only other components and simple values but also Java Collections, externally defined properties, and even beans in another factory. You can use all of these injection parameter types for both Setter Injection and Constructor Injection by using the corresponding tag under the <property> and <constructor-args> tags, respectively.

Injecting Simple Values

Injecting simple values into your beans is easy. To do so, simply specify the value in the configuration tag, wrapped inside a <value> tag. By default, not only can the <value> tag read String values, but it can also convert these values to any primitive or primitive wrapper class. Listing 4-35 shows a simple bean that has a variety of properties exposed for injection.

Listing 4-35. Injecting Simple Values (XML)

```
package com.apress.prospring3.ch4.xml;

import org.springframework.context.support.GenericXmlApplicationContext;

public class InjectSimple {

    private String name;

    private int age;

    private float height;

    private boolean programmer;

    private Long ageInSeconds;

    public static void main(String[] args) {

        GenericXmlApplicationContext ctx = new GenericXmlApplicationContext();
        ctx.load("classpath:app-context-xml.xml");
        ctx.refresh();

        InjectSimple simple = (InjectSimple)ctx.getBean("injectSimple");
        System.out.println(simple);
    }
    public void setAgeInSeconds(Long ageInSeconds) {
        this.ageInSeconds = ageInSeconds;
    }

    public void setProgrammer(boolean programmer) {
        this.programmer = programmer;
    }

    public void setAge(int age) {
        this.age = age;
    }

    public void setHeight(float height) {
        this.height = height;
    }

    public void setName(String name) {
        this.name = name;
    }

    public String toString() {
        return    "Name :" + name + "\n"
```

```
              + "Age:" + age + "\n"
              + "Age in Seconds: " + ageInSeconds + "\n"
              + "Height: " + height + "\n"
              + "Is Programmer?: " + programmer;
    }
}
```

In addition to the properties, the InjectSimple class also defines the main() method that creates an ApplicationContext and then retrieves an InjectSimple bean from Spring. The property values of this bean are then written to the console output. Listing 4-36 shows the configuration (app-context-xml.xml) for this bean.

Listing 4-36. Configuring Simple Value Injection

```
<bean id="injectSimple" class="com.apress.prospring3.ch4.xml.InjectSimple">
    <property name="name">
        <value>John Smith</value>
    </property>
    <property name="age">
        <value>35</value>
    </property>
    <property name="height">
        <value>1.78</value>
    </property>
    <property name="programmer">
        <value>true</value>
    </property>
    <property name="ageInSeconds">
        <value>1103760000</value>
    </property>
</bean>
```

You can see from Listings 4-35 and 4-36 that it is possible to define properties on your bean that accept String values, primitive values, or primitive wrapper values and then inject values for these properties using the <value> tag. Here is the output created by running this example as expected:

```
Name: John Smith
Age: 35
Age in Seconds: 1103760000
Height: 1.78
Is Programmer?: true
```

For annotation-style simple value injection, we can apply the @Value annotation to the bean properties. This time, instead of the setter method, we apply the annotation to the property declaration statement, as you can see in Listing 4-37. (Spring supports the annotation either at the setter method or in the properties.)

Listing 4-37. Injecting Simple Values (Annotation)

```
package com.apress.prospring3.ch4.annotation;

import org.springframework.beans.factory.annotation.Value;
import org.springframework.context.support.GenericXmlApplicationContext;
import org.springframework.stereotype.Service;
```

```java
@Service("injectSimple")
public class InjectSimple {

    @Value("John Smith")
    private String name;

    @Value("35")
    private int age;

    @Value("1.78")
    private float height;

    @Value("true")
    private boolean programmer;

    @Value("1103760000")
    private Long ageInSeconds;

    public static void main(String[] args) {

        GenericXmlApplicationContext ctx = new GenericXmlApplicationContext();
        ctx.load("classpath:app-context-annotation.xml");
        ctx.refresh();

        InjectSimple simple = (InjectSimple)ctx.getBean("injectSimple");
        ctx.getBean("injectRef");
        System.out.println(simple);
    }

    // Getter/setter methods omitted

    public String toString() {
        return    "Name :" + name + "\n"
                + "Age:" + age + "\n"
                + "Age in Seconds: " + ageInSeconds + "\n"
                + "Height: " + height + "\n"
                + "Is Programmer?: " + programmer;
    }

}
```

This achieves the same result as the XML configuration.

Injecting Values Using SpEL

One powerful feature introduced into Spring 3 is the Spring Expression Language(SpEL). SpEL enables you to evaluate an expression dynamically and then use it in Spring's ApplicationContext. One use case is to use the result for injection into Spring beans. In this section, we take a look at how to use SpEL to inject properties from other beans, by using the example presented in the previous sample.

Suppose now we want to externalize the values to be injected into a Spring bean in a configuration class, as in Listing 4-38.

Listing 4-38. Injecting Values Using SpEL (XML)

```
package com.apress.prospring3.ch4.xml;

public class InjectSimpleConfig {

    private String name = "John Smith";

    private int age = 35;

    private float height = 1.78f;

    private boolean programmer = true;

    private Long ageInSeconds = 1103760000L;

    // Getter/setter method omitted
}
```

We can then define the bean in the XML configuration and use SpEL to inject the bean's properties into the dependent bean, as we have done in Listing 4-39 (app-context-xml.xml).

Listing 4-39. Injecting Values Using SpEL (XML)

```
<bean id="injectSimpleConfig" class="com.apress.prospring3.ch4.xml.InjectSimpleConfig"/>

<bean id="injectSimpleSpel" class="com.apress.prospring3.ch4.xml.InjectSimpleSpel">
    <property name="name">
        <value>#{injectSimpleConfig.name}</value>
    </property>
    <property name="age">
        <value>#{injectSimpleConfig.age + 1}</value>
    </property>
    <property name="height">
        <value>#{injectSimpleConfig.height}</value>
    </property>
    <property name="isProgrammer">
        <value>#{injectSimpleConfig.programmer}</value>
    </property>
    <property name="ageInSeconds">
        <value>#{injectSimpleConfig.ageInSeconds}</value>
    </property>
</bean>
```

Notice that we use the SpEL #{injectSimpleConfig.name} in referencing the property of the other bean. For the age, we add 1 to the value from the bean to indicate that we can use SpEL to manipulate the property as we see fit and inject into the dependent bean. Now we can test the configuration with the program in Listing 4-40.

Listing 4-40. Injecting Values Using SpEL (XML)

```
package com.apress.prospring3.ch4.xml;

import org.springframework.context.support.GenericXmlApplicationContext;
```

```
public class InjectSimpleSpel {

    private String name;

    private int age;

    private float height;

    private boolean programmer;

    private Long ageInSeconds;

    public static void main(String[] args) {

        GenericXmlApplicationContext ctx = new GenericXmlApplicationContext();
        ctx.load("classpath:app-context-xml.xml");
        ctx.refresh();

        InjectSimpleSpel simple = (InjectSimpleSpel)ctx.getBean("injectSimpleSpel");
        System.out.println(simple);
    }
// Other codes omitted
}
```

The following is the output of the program:

```
Name: John Smith
Age:36
Age in Seconds: 1103760000
Height: 1.78
Is Programmer?: true
```

When using annotation-style value injection, we just need to substitute the value annotations with the SpEL expressions (see Listing 4-41).

Listing 4-41. Injecting Values Using SpEL (Annotation)

```
package com.apress.prospring3.ch4.annotation;

import org.springframework.beans.factory.annotation.Value;
import org.springframework.context.support.GenericXmlApplicationContext;
import org.springframework.stereotype.Service;

@Service("injectSimpleSpel")
public class InjectSimpleSpel {

    @Value("#{injectSimpleConfig.name}")
    private String name;

    @Value("#{injectSimpleConfig.age + 1}")
    private int age;

    @Value("#{injectSimpleConfig.height}")
    private float height;
```

```
    @Value("#{injectSimpleConfig.programmer}")
    private boolean programmer;

    @Value("#{injectSimpleConfig.ageInSeconds}")
    private Long ageInSeconds;
// Other codes omitted
}
```

Listing 4-42 shows the annotation version of the InjectSimpleConfig class.

Listing 4-42. *InjectSimpleConfig Class (Annotation)*

```
package com.apress.prospring3.ch4.annotation;

import org.springframework.stereotype.Component;

@Component("injectSimpleConfig")
public class InjectSimpleConfig {

    private String name = "John Smith";

    private int age = 35;

    private float height = 1.78f;

    private boolean programmer = true;

    private Long ageInSeconds = 1103760000L;

    // Getter/setter methods omitted
}
```

From Listing 4-42, instead of the @Service annotation, @Component was used. Basically, using @Component has the same effect as @Service. Both annotations were instructing Spring that the annotated class is a candidate for autodetection using annotation-based configuration and classpath scanning. However, since the InjectSimpleConfig class is storing the application configuration, rather than providing a business service, using @Component makes more sense. Practically, @Service is a specialization of @Component, which indicates that the annotated class is providing a business service to other layers within the application.

Testing the program will produce the same result. Using SpEL, you can access any Spring-managed beans and properties and manipulate them for application use by Spring's support of sophisticated language features and syntax.

Injecting Beans in the Same XML Unit

As you have already seen, it is possible to inject one bean into another using the <ref> tag. Listing 4-43 shows a class that exposes a setter to allow a bean to be injected.

Listing 4-43. *Injecting Beans*

```
package com.apress.prospring3.ch4.xml;

import org.springframework.context.support.GenericXmlApplicationContext;
```

```
import com.apress.prospring3.ch4.Oracle;

public class InjectRef {

    private Oracle oracle;

    public void setOracle(Oracle oracle) {
        this.oracle = oracle;
    }

    public static void main(String[] args) {

        GenericXmlApplicationContext ctx = new GenericXmlApplicationContext();
        ctx.load("classpath:app-context-xml.xml");
        ctx.refresh();

        InjectRef injectRef = (InjectRef) ctx.getBean("injectRef");
        System.out.println(injectRef);
    }

    public String toString() {
        return oracle.defineMeaningOfLife();
    }
}
```

To configure Spring to inject one bean into another, you first need to configure two beans: one to be injected and one to be the target of the injection. Once this is done, you simply configure the injection using the <ref> tag on the target bean. Remember that <ref> must come under either <property> or <constructor-arg> depending on whether you are using Setter or Constructor Injection. Listing 4-44 shows an example of this configuration (app-context-xml.xml).

Listing 4-44. Configuring Bean Injection

```
<bean id="oracle" name="wiseworm" class="com.apress.prospring3.ch4.BookwormOracle"/>

<bean id="injectRef" class="com.apress.prospring3.ch4.xml.InjectRef">
    <property name="oracle">
        <ref local="oracle"/>
    </property>
</bean>
```

Running the class in Listing 4-43 will produce the following output:

```
Encyclopedias are a waste of money - use the Internet
```

An important point to note is that the type being injected does not have to be the exact type defined on the target; the types just need to be compatible. *Compatible* means that if the declared type on the target is an interface, then the injected type must implement this interface. If the declared type is a class, then the injected type must be either the same type or a subtype. In this example, the InjectRef class defines the setOracle() method to receive an instance of Oracle, which is an interface, and the injected type is BookwormOracle, a class that implements Oracle. This is a point that causes confusion for some developers, but it is really quite simple. Injection is subject to the same typing rules as any Java code, so as long as you are familiar with how Java typing works, then understanding typing in injection is easy.

In the previous example, the id of the bean to inject was specified using the local attribute of the <ref> tag. As you will see later, in the section "Understanding Bean Naming," you can give a bean more than one name so that you can refer to it using a variety of aliases. When you use the local attribute, it means that the <ref> tag only ever looks at the bean's id and never at any of its aliases. Moreover, the bean definition should exist in the same XML configuration file. To inject a bean by any name or import one from other XML configuration files, use the bean attribute of the <ref> tag instead of the local attribute. Listing 4-45 shows an alternative configuration for the previous example using an alternative name for the injected bean.

Listing 4-45. Injecting Using Bean Aliases

```
<bean id="oracle" name="wiseworm" class="com.apress.prospring.ch4.BookwormOracle"/>

<bean id="injectRef" class="com.apress.prospring3.ch4.xml.InjectRef">
   <property name="oracle">
      <ref bean="wiseworm"/>
   </property>
</bean>
```

In this example, the oracle bean is given an alias using the name attribute, and then it is injected into the injectRef bean by using this alias in conjunction with the bean attribute of the <ref> tag. Don't worry too much about the naming semantics at this point—we discuss this in much more detail later in the chapter. Running the InjectRef class again (Listing 4-43) will produce the same result as the previous example.

Injection and ApplicationContext Nesting

So far, the beans we have been injecting have been located in the same ApplicationContext (and hence the same BeanFactory) as the beans they are injected into. However, Spring supports a hierarchical structure for ApplicationContext so that one context (and hence the associating BeanFactory) is considered the parent of another. By allowing ApplicationContexts to be nested, Spring allows you to split your configuration into different files—a godsend on larger projects with lots of beans.

When nesting ApplicationContexts, Spring allows beans in what is considered the child context to reference beans in the parent context. ApplicationContext nesting using the GenericXmlApplicationContext is very simple to get a grip on. To nest one GenericXmlApplicationContext inside another, simply call the setParent() method in the child ApplicationContext, as shown in Listing 4-46.

Listing 4-46. Nesting GenericXmlApplicationContext

```
package com.apress.prospring3.ch4;

import org.springframework.context.support.GenericXmlApplicationContext;

public class HierarchicalAppContextUsage {

  public static void main(String[] args) {

        GenericXmlApplicationContext parent = new GenericXmlApplicationContext();
        parent.load("classpath:parent.xml");
        parent.refresh();

        GenericXmlApplicationContext child = new GenericXmlApplicationContext();
        child.load("classpath:app-context-xml.xml");
        child.setParent(parent);
```

```
        child.refresh();

        SimpleTarget target1 = (SimpleTarget) child.getBean("target1");
        SimpleTarget target2 = (SimpleTarget) child.getBean("target2");
        SimpleTarget target3 = (SimpleTarget) child.getBean("target3");

        System.out.println(target1.getVal());
        System.out.println(target2.getVal());
        System.out.println(target3.getVal());

    }

}
```

Listing 4-47 shows the SimpleTarget class.

Listing 4-47. The SimpleTarget Class

```
package com.apress.prospring3.ch4;

public class SimpleTarget {

    private String val;

    public void setVal(String val) {
        this.val = val;
    }

    public String getVal() {
        return val;
    }

}
```

Inside the configuration file for the child ApplicationContext, referencing a bean in the parent ApplicationContext works exactly like referencing a bean in the child ApplicationContext, unless you have a bean in the child ApplicationContext that shares the same name. In that case, you simply replace the bean attribute of the <ref> tag with parent, and you are on your way. Listing 4-48 shows a sample configuration file for the parent BeanFactory (parent.xml).

Listing 4-48. Parent ApplicationContext Configuration

```
<bean id="injectBean" class="java.lang.String">
    <constructor-arg>
        <value>Bean In Parent</value>
    </constructor-arg>
</bean>
<bean id="injectBeanParent" class="java.lang.String">
    <constructor-arg>
        <value>Bean In Parent</value>
    </constructor-arg>
</bean>
```

As you can see, this configuration simply defines two beans: injectBean and injectBeanParent. Both are String objects with the value Bean In Parent. Listing 4-49 shows a sample configuration for the child ApplicationContext (app-context-xml.xml).

Listing 4-49. Child ApplicationContext Configuration

```
<bean id="target1" class="com.apress.prospring3.ch4.SimpleTarget">
    <property name="val">
        <ref bean="injectBeanParent"/>
    </property>
</bean>

<bean id="target2" class="com.apress.prospring3.ch4.SimpleTarget">
    <property name="val">
        <ref bean="injectBean"/>
    </property>
</bean>

<bean id="target3" class="com.apress.prospring3.ch4.SimpleTarget">
    <property name="val">
        <ref parent="injectBean"/>
    </property>
</bean>

<bean id="injectBean" class="java.lang.String">
    <constructor-arg>
        <value>Bean In Child</value>
    </constructor-arg>
</bean>
```

Notice that we have defined four beans here. The injectBean in this listing is similar to the injectBean in the parent except that the String it represents has a different value, indicating that it is located in the child ApplicationContext.

The target1 bean is using the bean attribute of the <ref> tag to reference the bean named injectBeanParent. Because this bean exists only in the parent BeanFactory, target1 receives a reference to that bean. There are two points of interest here. First, you can use the bean attribute to reference beans in both the child and the parent ApplicationContexts. This makes it easy to reference the beans transparently, allowing you to move beans between configuration files as your application grows. The second point of interest is that you can't use the local attribute to refer to beans in the parent ApplicationContext. The XML parser checks to see that the value of the local attribute exists as a valid element in the same file, preventing it from being used to reference beans in the parent context.

The target2 bean is using the bean attribute of the <ref> tag to reference the injectBean. Because that bean is defined in both ApplicationContexts, the target2 bean receives a reference to the injectBean in its own ApplicationContext.

The target3 bean is using the parent attribute of the <ref> tag to reference the injectBean directly in the parent ApplicationContext. Because target3 is using the parent attribute of the <ref> tag, the injectBean declared in the child ApplicationContext is ignored completely.

The code in Listing 4-46 also demonstrates the semantics discussed here by retrieving each of the three targetX beans from the child BeanFactory and outputting the value of the val property in each case.

Here is the output from running the HierarchicalAppContextUsage class (Listing 4-46):

```
Bean In Parent
Bean In Child
Bean In Parent
```

As expected, the target1 and target3 beans both get a reference to beans in the parent ApplicationContext, whereas the target2 bean gets a reference to a bean in the child ApplicationContext.

Using Collections for Injection

Often your beans need access to collections of objects rather than just individual beans or values. Therefore, it should come as no surprise that Spring allows you to inject a collection of objects into one of your beans. Using the collection is simple: you choose either <list>, <map>, <set>, or <props> to represent a List, Map, Set, or Properties instance, and then you pass in the individual items just as you would with any other injection. The <props> tag only allows for Strings to be passed in as the value because the Properties class allows only for property values to be Strings. When using <list>, <map>, or <set>, you can use any tag you want when injecting into a property, even another collection tag. This allows you to pass in a List of Maps, a Map of Sets, or even a List of Maps of Sets of Lists! Listing 4-50 shows a class that can have all four collection types injected into it.

Listing 4-50. Collection Injection (XML)

```
package com.apress.prospring3.ch4.xml;

import java.util.List;
import java.util.Map;
import java.util.Properties;
import java.util.Set;

import org.springframework.context.support.GenericXmlApplicationContext;
public class CollectionInjection {

    private Map<String, Object> map;

    private Properties props;

    private Set set;

    private List list;

    public static void main(String[] args) {
        GenericXmlApplicationContext ctx = new GenericXmlApplicationContext();
        ctx.load("classpath:app-context-xml.xml");
        ctx.refresh();

        CollectionInjection instance = (CollectionInjection) ctx.getBean("injectCollection");
        instance.displayInfo();
    }

    public void setList(List list) {
        this.list = list;
    }

    public void setSet(Set set) {
        this.set = set;
    }
```

```java
    public void setMap(Map <String, Object> map) {
        this.map = map;
    }

    public void setProps(Properties props) {
        this.props = props;
    }

    public void displayInfo() {

        // display the Map
        System.out.println("Map contents:\n");
        for (Map.Entry<String, Object> entry: map.entrySet()) {
            System.out.println("Key: " + entry.getKey() + " - Value: " + entry.getValue());
        }

        // display the properties
        System.out.println("\nProperties contents:\n");
        for (Map.Entry<Object, Object> entry: props.entrySet()) {
            System.out.println("Key: " + entry.getKey() + " - Value: " + entry.getValue());
        }

        // display the set
        System.out.println("\nSet contents:\n");
        for (Object obj: set) {
            System.out.println("Value: " + obj);
        }

        // display the list
        System.out.println("\nList contents:\n");
        for (Object obj: list) {
            System.out.println("Value: " + obj);
        }
    }
}
```

That is quite a lot of code, but it actually does very little. The main() method retrieves a CollectionInjection bean from Spring and then calls the displayInfo() method. This method just outputs the contents of the Map, Properties, Set, and List instances that will be injected from Spring. In Listing 4-51, you can see the configuration required to inject values for each of the properties on the CollectionInjection class.

Also notice the declaration of the Map<String,Object> property. For JDK 5 and newer versions, Spring also supports the strongly typed Collection declaration and will perform the conversion from the XML configuration to the corresponding type specified accordingly (app-context-xml.xml).

Listing 4-51. *Configuring Collection Injection (XML)*

```xml
<bean id="oracle" name="wiseworm" class="com.apress.prospring3.ch4.BookwormOracle"/>

<bean id="injectCollection" class="com.apress.prospring3.ch4.xml.CollectionInjection">
    <property name="map">
        <map>
            <entry key="someValue">
                <value>Hello World!</value>
```

```
                </entry>
                <entry key="someBean">
                    <ref local="oracle"/>
                </entry>
            </map>
        </property>
        <property name="props">
            <props>
                <prop key="firstName">Clarence</prop>
                <prop key="secondName">Ho</prop>
            </props>
        </property>
        <property name="set">
            <set>
                <value>Hello World!</value>
                <ref local="oracle"/>
            </set>
        </property>
        <property name="list">
            <list>
                <value>Hello World!</value>
                <ref local="oracle"/>
            </list>
        </property>
    </bean>
```

In this code, you can see that we have injected value into all four setters exposed on the CollectionInjection class. For the map property, we have injected a Map instance using the <map> tag. Notice that each entry is specified using an <entry> tag, and each has a String key and then an entry value. This entry value can be any value you can inject into a property separately; this example shows the use of the <value> and <ref> tags to add a String value and a bean reference to the Map. For the props property, we use the <props> tag to create an instance of java.util.Properties and populate it using <prop> tags. Notice that although the <prop> tag is keyed in a similar manner to the <entry> tag, you can specify a String value only for each property that goes in the Properties instance.

Both the <list> and <set> tags work in exactly the same way: you specify each element using any of the individual value tags such as <value> and <ref> that are used to inject a single value into a property. In Listing 4-51, you can see that we have added a String value and a bean reference to both the List and the Set.

Here is the output generated by Listing 4-50. As expected, it simply lists the elements added to the collections in the configuration file.

```
Map contents:

Key: someValue - Value: Hello World!
Key: someBean - Value: com.apress.prospring3.ch4.xml.BookwormOracle@2a0ab444

Properties contents:

Key: secondName - Value: Ho
Key: firstName - Value: Clarence

Set contents:

Value: Hello World!
```

Value: com.apress.prospring3.ch4.xml.BookwormOracle@2a0ab444

List contents:

Value: Hello World!
Value: com.apress.prospring3.ch4.xml.BookwormOracle@2a0ab444

Remember, with the <list>, <map>, and <set> elements, you can employ any of the tags used to set the value of noncollection properties to specify the value of one of the entries in the collection. This is quite a powerful concept because you are not limited just to injecting collections of primitive values; you can also inject collections of beans or other collections.

Using this functionality, it is much easier to modularize your application and provide different, user-selectable implementations of key pieces of application logic. Consider a system that allows corporate staff to create, proofread, and order their personalized business stationery online. In this system, the finished artwork for each order is sent to the appropriate printer when it is ready for production. The only complication is that some printers want to receive the artwork via e-mail, some via FTP, and still more using Secure Copy Protocol (SCP). Using Spring's collection injection, you can create a standard interface for this functionality, as shown in Listing 4-52.

Listing 4-52. The ArtworkSender Interface

```
package com.apress.prospring3.ch4;

public interface ArtworkSender {

    public void sendArtwork(String artworkPath, Recipient recipient);

    public String getFriendlyName();

    public String getShortName();
}
```

In Listing 4-52, the Recipient class is an empty class. From this interface, you can create multiple implementations, each of which is capable of describing itself to a human, such as the ones shown in Listing 4-53.

Listing 4-53. The FtpArtworkSender Class

```
package com.apress.prospring3.ch4;

public class FtpArtworkSender implements ArtworkSender {

    public void sendArtwork(String artworkPath, Recipient recipient) {

        // ftp logic here...
    }

    public String getFriendlyName() {
        return "File Transfer Protocol";
    }

    public String getShortName() {
        return "ftp";
    }
}
```

Imagine that you then develop an ArtworkManager class that supports all available implementations of the ArtworkSender interface. With the implementations in place, you simply pass a List to your ArtworkManager class, and you are on your way. Using the getFriendlyName() method, you can display a list of delivery options for the system administrator to choose from when you are configuring each stationery template. In addition, your application can remain fully decoupled from the individual implementations if you just code to the ArtworkSender interface. We will leave the implementation of the ArtworkManager class as an exercise for you.

Besides the XML configuration, we can also use annotation for collections injection. However, we would also like to externalize the values of the collections into the configuration file for easy maintenance. Listing 4-54 is the configuration of four different Spring beans that mimic the same collection properties of the previous sample (app-context-annotation.xml).

Listing 4-54. Configuring Collection Injection (Annotation)

```
<util:map id="map" map-class="java.util.HashMap">
    <entry key="someValue">
        <value>Hello World!</value>
    </entry>
    <entry key="someBean">
        <ref bean="oracle"/>
    </entry>
</util:map>

<util:properties id="props">
        <prop key="firstName">Clarence</prop>
        <prop key="secondName">Ho</prop>
</util:properties>

<util:set id="set">
        <value>Hello World!</value>
        <ref bean="oracle"/>
</util:set>

<util:list id="list">
        <value>Hello World!</value>
        <ref bean="oracle"/>
</util:list>
```

Let's also develop an annotation version of the BookwormOracle class. Listing 4-55 shows the class content.

Listing 4-55. The BookwormOracle Class (Annotation)

```
package com.apress.prospring3.ch4.annotation;

import org.springframework.stereotype.Service;

import com.apress.prospring3.ch4.Oracle;

@Service("oracle")
public class BookwormOracle implements Oracle {

    public String defineMeaningOfLife() {
```

```
                    return "Encyclopedias are a waste of money - use the Internet";
        }

}
```

In the configuration in Listing 4-54, we make use of the util namespace provided by Spring to declare our beans for storing collection properties. It greatly simplifies the configuration when comparing to previous versions of Spring. In the testing class, we inject the previous beans and use the JSR-250 @Resource annotation with the name specified, as in Listing 4-56.

Listing 4-56. Configuring Collection Injection (Annotation)

```
package com.apress.prospring3.ch4.annotation;

// Other codes omitted
@Service("injectCollection")
public class CollectionInjection {

    @Resource(name="map")
    private Map<String, Object> map;

    @Resource(name="props")
    private Properties props;

    @Resource(name="set")
    private Set set;

    @Resource(name="list")
    private List list;

// Other codes omitted
}
```

Run the test program, and you will get the same result as the sample using XML configuration.

■ **Note** You may wonder why the annotation @Resource was used instead of @Autowired. It's because the @Autowired annotation is semantically defined in a way that it always treats arrays, collections, and maps as sets of corresponding beans, with the target bean type derived from the declared collection value type. So, for example, if a class has an attribute of type List<Oracle> and has the @Autowired annotation defined, Spring will try to inject all beans of type Oracle within the current ApplicationContext into that attribute (instead of the <util:list> declared in the configuration file), which will result in either the unexpected dependencies being injected or Spring throwing an exception if no bean of type Oracle was defined. So, for collection type injection, we have to explicitly instruct Spring to perform injection by specifying the bean name, which the @Resource annotation supports.

Using Method Injection

Besides Constructor and Setter Injection, another less frequently used DI feature that Spring provides is Method Injection. Spring's Method Injection capabilities come in two loosely related forms, Lookup Method Injection and Method Replacement. Lookup Method Injection provides another mechanism by which a bean can obtain one of its dependencies, and Method Replacement allows you to replace the implementation of any method on a bean arbitrarily, without having to change the original source code.

To provide these two features, Spring uses the dynamic bytecode enhancement capabilities of CGLIB. If you want to use Lookup Method Injection or Method Replacement in your application, make sure you have the CGLIB JAR file on your classpath.

Lookup Method Injection

Lookup Method Injection was added to Spring since version 1.1 to overcome the problems encountered when a bean depends on another bean with a different life cycle—specifically, when a singleton depends on a nonsingleton. In this situation, both Setter and Constructor Injection result in the singleton maintaining a single instance of what should be a nonsingleton bean. In some cases, you will want to have the singleton bean obtain a new instance of the nonsingleton every time it requires the bean in question.

Consider a scenario where there is a LockOpener class that provides the service of opening any locker. The LockOpener class relies on a KeyHelper class for opening the locker, which was injected into LockOpener. However, the design of KeyHelper class involves some internal states that make it not suitable for reuse. Every time the openLock() method is called, a new KeyHelper instance is required. In this case, LockOpener will be a singleton. However, if we inject the KeyHelper class using the normal mechanism, the same instance of the KeyHelper class (that was instantiated when Spring performed the injection the first time) will be reused. To make sure that a new instance of the KeyHelper instance was passed into the openLock() method every time it was invoked, we need to use a Lookup Method Injection.

Typically, you can achieve this by having the singleton bean implement the ApplicationContextAware interface (we will discuss this interface in next chapter). Then, using the ApplicationContext instance, the singleton bean can look up a new instance of the nonsingleton dependency every time it needs it. Lookup Method Injection allows the singleton bean to declare that it requires a nonsingleton dependency and that it receive a new instance of the nonsingleton bean each time it needs to interact with it, without needing to implement any Spring-specific interfaces.

Lookup Method Injection works by having your singleton declare a method, the lookup method, which returns an instance of the nonsingleton bean. When you obtain a reference to the singleton in your application, you are actually receiving a reference to a dynamically created subclass on which Spring has implemented the lookup method. A typical implementation involves defining the lookup method, and thus the bean class, as abstract. This prevents any strange errors from creeping in when you forget to configure the Method Injection and you are working directly against the bean class with the empty method implementation instead of the Spring-enhanced subclass. This topic is quite complex and is best shown by example.

In this example, we create one nonsingleton bean and two singleton beans that both implement the same interface. One of the singletons obtains an instance of the nonsingleton bean using "traditional" Setter Injection; the other uses Method Injection. Listing 4-57 shows the MyHelper bean, which in our example is the nonsingleton bean.

Listing 4-57. The MyHelper Bean

```
package com.apress.prospring3.ch4.mi;

public class MyHelper {

    public void doSomethingHelpful() {
```

```
        // do something!
    }
}
```

This bean is decidedly unexciting, but it serves the purposes of this example perfectly. In Listing 4-58, you can see the DemoBean interface, which is implemented by both of the singleton beans.

Listing 4-58. The DemoBean Interface

```
package com.apress.prospring3.ch4.mi;

public interface DemoBean {

    public MyHelper getMyHelper();

    public void someOperation();
}
```

This bean has two methods: getMyHelper() and someOperation(). The sample application uses the getMyHelper() method to get a reference to the MyHelper instance and, in the case of the method lookup bean, to perform the actual method lookup. The someOperation() method is a simple method that depends on the MyHelper class to do its processing.

Listing 4-59 shows the StandardLookupDemoBean class, which uses Setter Injection to obtain an instance of the MyHelper class.

Listing 4-59. The StandardLookupDemoBean Class

```
package com.apress.prospring3.ch4.mi;

public class StandardLookupDemoBean implements DemoBean {

    private MyHelper myHelper;

    public void setMyHelper(MyHelper myHelper) {
        this.myHelper = myHelper;
    }

    public MyHelper getMyHelper() {
        return this.myHelper;
    }

    public void someOperation() {
        myHelper.doSomethingHelpful();
    }
}
```

This code should all look familiar, but notice that the someOperation() method uses the stored instance of MyHelper to complete its processing. In Listing 4-60, you can see the AbstractLookupDemoBean class, which uses Method Injection to obtain an instance of the MyHelper class.

Listing 4-60. The AbstractLookupDemoBean Class

```
package com.apress.prospring3.ch4.mi;

public abstract class AbstractLookupDemoBean implements DemoBean {

    public abstract MyHelper getMyHelper();

    public void someOperation() {
        getMyHelper().doSomethingHelpful();
    }
}
```

Notice that the getMyHelper() method is declared as abstract and that this method is called by the someOperation() method to obtain a MyHelper instance. In Listing 4-61, you can see the configuration code required for this example (lookup.xml).

Listing 4-61. Configuring Method Lookup Injection

```
<?xml version="1.0" encoding="UTF-8"?>
<beans xmlns="http://www.springframework.org/schema/beans"
    xmlns:xsi="http://www.w3.org/2001/XMLSchema-instance"
    xsi:schemaLocation="http://www.springframework.org/schema/beans
        http://www.springframework.org/schema/beans/spring-beans-3.1.xsd">

    <bean id="helper" class="com.apress.prospring3.ch4.mi.MyHelper" scope="prototype"/>

    <bean id="abstractLookupBean" class="com.apress.prospring3.ch4.mi.AbstractLookupDemoBean">
        <lookup-method name="getMyHelper" bean="helper"/>
    </bean>

    <bean id="standardLookupBean" class="com.apress.prospring3.ch4.mi.StandardLookupDemoBean">
        <property name="myHelper">
            <ref local="helper"/>
        </property>
    </bean>
</beans>
```

The configuration for the helper and standardLookupBean beans should look familiar to you by now. For the abstractLookupBean, you need to configure the lookup method using the <lookup-method> tag. The name attribute of the <lookup-method> tag tells Spring the name of the method on the bean that it should override. This method must not accept any arguments, and the return type should be that of the bean you want to return from the method. In this case, the method should return a class of type MyHelper, or its subclasses. The bean attribute tells Spring which bean the lookup method should return.

Listing 4-62 shows the final piece of code for this example.

Listing 4-62. The LookupDemo Class

```
package com.apress.prospring3.ch4.mi;

import org.springframework.context.support.GenericXmlApplicationContext;
import org.springframework.util.StopWatch;
```

```
public class LookupDemo {

    public static void main(String[] args) {

        GenericXmlApplicationContext ctx = new GenericXmlApplicationContext();
        ctx.load("classpath:lookup.xml");

        DemoBean abstractBean = (DemoBean) ctx.getBean("abstractLookupBean");
        DemoBean standardBean = (DemoBean) ctx.getBean("standardLookupBean");

        displayInfo(standardBean);
        displayInfo(abstractBean);
    }

    public static void displayInfo(DemoBean bean) {
        MyHelper helper1 = bean.getMyHelper();
        MyHelper helper2 = bean.getMyHelper();

        System.out.println("Helper Instances the Same?: "
                + (helper1 == helper2));

        StopWatch stopWatch = new StopWatch();
        stopWatch.start("lookupDemo");

        for (int x = 0; x < 100000; x++) {
            MyHelper helper = bean.getMyHelper();
            helper.doSomethingHelpful();
        }

        stopWatch.stop();

        System.out.println("100000 gets took " + stopWatch.getTotalTimeMillis() + " ms");
    }
}
```

In this code, you can see that we retrieve the abstractLookupBean (the instantiation of the abstract class is supported only when using method lookup injection, in which Spring will use CGLIB to generate a subclass of the AbstractLookupDemoBean class that overrides the method dynamically) and the standardLookupBean from the GenericXMLApplicationContext and pass each reference to the displayInfo() method. The first part of the displayInfo() method creates two local variables of MyHelper and assigns them each a value by calling getMyHelper() on the bean passed to it. Using these two variables, it writes a message to stdout indicating whether the two references point to the same object. For the abstractLookupBean class, a new instance of MyHelper should be retrieved for each call to getMyHelper(), so the references should not be the same. For standardLookupBean, a single instance of MyHelper is passed to the bean by Setter Injection, and this instance is stored and returned for every call to getMyHelper(), so the two references should be the same.

───

■ **Note** The StopWatch class used in the previous example is a utility class available with Spring. You'll find StopWatch very useful when you need to perform simple performance tests and when you are testing your applications.

───

The final part of the `displayInfo()` method runs a simple performance test to see which bean is faster. Clearly, the `standardLookupBean` should be faster because it returns the same instance each time, but it is interesting to see the difference.

Before we can run the example, we need to add the CGLIB dependency into the project, which is shown in Table 4-1. For details in adding project dependencies in STS, please refer to Appendix A.

Table 4-1. Dependency for Method Injection

Group ID	Artifact ID	Version	Description
cglib	cglib	2.2.2	Code generation library required by Spring for Method Injection

We can now run the `LookupDemo` class (Listing 4-62) for testing. Here is the output we received from this example:

```
Helper Instances the Same?: true
100000 gets took 3 ms
Helper Instances the Same?: false
100000 gets took 367 ms
```

As you can see, the helper instances are, as expected, the same when we use `standardLookupBean` and different when we use `abstractLookupBean`. There is a noticeable performance difference when we use the `standardLookupBean`, but that is to be expected.

Considerations for Method Lookup Injection

Method Lookup Injection is intended for use when you want to work with two beans of different life cycles. Avoid the temptation to use Method Lookup Injection when the beans share the same life cycle, especially if they are singletons. Listing 4-62 shows a noticeable difference in performance between using Method Injection to obtain new instances of a dependency and using standard DI to obtain a single instance of a dependency. Also, make sure you don't use Method Lookup Injection needlessly, even when you have beans of different life cycles.

Consider a situation in which you have three singletons that share a dependency in common. You want each singleton to have its own instance of the dependency, so you create the dependency as a nonsingleton, but you are happy with each singleton using the same instance of the collaborator throughout its life. In this case, Setter Injection is the ideal solution; Method Lookup Injection just adds unnecessary overhead.

When you are using Method Lookup Injection, there are a few design guidelines that you should bear in mind when building your classes. In the earlier examples, we declared the lookup method in an interface. The only reason we did this was we did not have to duplicate the `displayInfo()` method twice for two different bean types. As we mentioned earlier, generally you do not need to pollute a business interface with unnecessary definitions that are used solely for IoC purposes. Another point to bear in mind is that although you don't have to make your lookup method abstract, doing so prevents you from forgetting to configure the lookup method and then using a blank implementation by accident.

Method Replacement

Although the Spring documentation classifies method replacement as a form of injection, it is very different from what you have seen so far. So far, we have used injection purely to supply beans with their collaborators. Using method replacement, you can replace the implementation of any method on any beans arbitrarily without having to change the source of the bean you are modifying. For example, you have a third-party library that you use in your Spring application, and you need to change the logic of a certain method. However, since you are not able to change the source code because it was provided by that third party, one solution is to use method replacement to just replace the logic for that method with your own implementation.

Internally you achieve this by creating a subclass of the bean class dynamically. You use CGLIB and redirect calls to the method you want to replace to another bean that implements the MethodReplacer interface.

In Listing 4-63 you can see a simple bean that declares two overloads of a formatMessage() method.

Listing 4-63. The ReplacementTarget Class

```
package com.apress.prospring3.ch4.mi;

public class ReplacementTarget {

    public String formatMessage(String msg) {
        return "<h1>" + msg + "</h1>";
    }

    public String formatMessage(Object msg) {
        return "<h1>" + msg + "</h1>";
    }
}
```

You can replace any of the methods on the ReplacementTarget class using Spring's method replacement functionality. In this example, we show you how to replace the formatMessage(String) method, and we also compare the performance of the replaced method with that of the original.

To replace a method, you first need to create an implementation of the MethodReplacer interface; this is shown in Listing 4-64.

Listing 4-64. Implementing MethodReplacer

```
package com.apress.prospring3.ch4.mi;

import java.lang.reflect.Method;

import org.springframework.beans.factory.support.MethodReplacer;

public class FormatMessageReplacer implements MethodReplacer {

    public Object reimplement(Object arg0, Method method, Object[] args)
            throws Throwable {

        if (isFormatMessageMethod(method)) {

            String msg = (String) args[0];

            return "<h2>" + msg + "</h2>";
        } else {
            throw new IllegalArgumentException("Unable to reimplement method "
                    + method.getName());
        }
    }
```

```java
    private boolean isFormatMessageMethod(Method method) {

        // check correct number of params
        if (method.getParameterTypes().length != 1) {
            return false;
        }

        // check method name
        if (!("formatMessage".equals(method.getName()))) {
            return false;
        }

        // check return type
        if (method.getReturnType() != String.class) {
            return false;
        }

        // check parameter type is correct
        if (method.getParameterTypes()[0] != String.class) {
            return false;
        }

        return true;
    }
}
```

The MethodReplacer interface has a single method, reimplement(), that you must implement. Three arguments are passed to reimplement(): the bean on which the original method was invoked, a Method instance that represents the method that is being overridden, and the array of arguments passed to the method. The reimplement() method should return the result of your reimplemented logic, and, obviously, the type of the return value should be compatible with the return type of the method you are replacing. In Listing 4-64, the FormatMessageReplacer first checks to see whether the method that is being overridden is the formatMessage(String) method; if so, it executes the replacement logic—in this case, surrounding the message with <h2> and </h2>—and returns the formatted message to the caller. It is not necessary to check to see whether the message is correct, but this can be useful if you are using a few MethodReplacers with similar arguments. Using a check helps prevent a situation where a different MethodReplacer with compatible arguments and return types is used accidentally.

Listing 4-65 shows an ApplicationContext that defines two beans of type ReplacementTarget—one has the formatMessage(String) method replaced, and the other does not (replacement.xml).

Listing 4-65. Configuring Method Replacement

```xml
<?xml version="1.0" encoding="UTF-8"?>
<beans xmlns="http://www.springframework.org/schema/beans"
    xmlns:xsi="http://www.w3.org/2001/XMLSchema-instance"
    xsi:schemaLocation="http://www.springframework.org/schema/beans
        http://www.springframework.org/schema/beans/spring-beans-3.1.xsd">

    <bean id="methodReplacer" class="com.apress.prospring3.ch4.mi.FormatMessageReplacer"/>

    <bean id="replacementTarget" class="com.apress.prospring3.ch4.mi.ReplacementTarget">
        <replaced-method name="formatMessage" replacer="methodReplacer">
            <arg-type>String</arg-type>
```

```
        </replaced-method>
    </bean>

    <bean id="standardTarget" class="com.apress.prospring3.ch4.mi.ReplacementTarget"/>

</beans>
```

As you can see from Listing 4-65, the MethodReplacer implementation is declared as a bean in the ApplicationContext. We then used the <replaced-method> tag to replace the formatMessage(String) method on the replacementTargetBean. The name attribute of the <replaced-method> tag specifies the name of the method to replace, and the replacer attribute is used to specify the name of the MethodReplacer bean that we want to replace the method implementation. In cases where there are overloaded methods such as in the ReplacementTarget class, you can use the <arg-type> tag to specify the method signature to match. The <arg-type> supports pattern matching, so String is matched to java.lang.String and also to java.lang.StringBuffer.

Listing 4-66 shows a simple demo application that retrieves both the standardTarget and replacementTarget beans from the ApplicationContext, executes their formatMessage(String) methods, and then runs a simple performance test to see which is faster.

Listing 4-66. Method Replacement in Action

```java
package com.apress.prospring3.ch4.mi;

import org.springframework.context.support.GenericXmlApplicationContext;
import org.springframework.util.StopWatch;

public class MethodReplacementExample {

    public static void main(String[] args) {

        GenericXmlApplicationContext ctx = new GenericXmlApplicationContext();
        ctx.load("classpath:replacement.xml");
        ctx.refresh();

        ReplacementTarget replacementTarget = (ReplacementTarget) ctx
                .getBean("replacementTarget");
        ReplacementTarget standardTarget = (ReplacementTarget) ctx
                .getBean("standardTarget");

        displayInfo(replacementTarget);
        displayInfo(standardTarget);
    }

    private static void displayInfo(ReplacementTarget target) {
        System.out.println(target.formatMessage("Hello World!"));

        StopWatch stopWatch = new StopWatch();
        stopWatch.start("perfTest");

        for (int x = 0; x < 1000000; x++) {
            String out = target.formatMessage("foo");
        }
```

```
        stopWatch.stop();

        System.out.println("1000000 invocations took: "
                + stopWatch.getTotalTimeMillis() + " ms");
    }
}
```

You should be very familiar with this code by now, so we won't go into any detail on it. On our machine, running this example yields the following output:

```
<h2>Hello World!</h2>
1000000 invocations took: 363 ms
<h1>Hello World!</h1>
1000000 invocations took: 107 ms
```

As expected, the output from the replacementTarget bean reflects the overridden implementation that the MethodReplacer provides. Interestingly, though, the dynamically replaced method is more than three times slower than the statically defined method. Removing the check for a valid method in the MethodReplacer made a negligible difference across a number of executions, so we can conclude that most of the overhead is in the CGLIB subclass.

When to Use Method Replacement

Method replacement can prove quite useful in a variety of circumstances, especially when you want to override only a particular method for a single bean rather than all beans of the same type. That said, we still prefer using standard Java mechanisms for overriding methods rather than depending on runtime bytecode enhancement.

If you are going to use method replacement as part of your application, we recommend you use one MethodReplacer per method or group of overloaded methods. Avoid the temptation to use a single MethodReplacer for lots of unrelated methods; this results in lots of unnecessary String comparisons while your code works out which method it should reimplement. We have found that performing simple checks to ensure that the MethodReplacer is working with the correct method is useful and doesn't add too much overhead to your code. If you are really concerned about performance, you can simply add a boolean property to your MethodReplacer, which allows you to turn the check on and off using Dependency Injection.

Understanding Bean Naming

Spring supports quite a complex bean naming structure that allows you the flexibility to handle many different situations. Every bean must have at least one name that is unique within the containing ApplicationContext. Spring follows a simple resolution process to determine what name is used for the bean. If you give the <bean> tag an id attribute, then the value of that attribute is used as the name. If no id attribute is specified, Spring looks for a name attribute, and if one is defined, it uses the first name defined in the name attribute. (We say the first name because it is possible to define multiple names within the name attribute; this is covered in more detail shortly.) If neither the id nor the name attribute is specified, Spring uses the bean's class name as the name, provided, of course, that no other bean is using the same class name. In case multiple beans without an ID or the name defined are using the same class name, Spring will throw an exception (of type org.springframework.beans.factory.NoSuchBean DefinitionException) on injection during ApplicationContext initialization. Listing 4-67 shows a sample configuration that uses all three naming schemes.

Listing 4-67. Bean Naming

```
<bean id="string1" class="java.lang.String"/>
<bean name="string2" class="java.lang.String"/>
<bean class="java.lang.String"/>
```

Each of these approaches is equally valid from a technical point of view, but which is the best choice for your application? To start with, avoid using the automatic name by class behavior. This doesn't allow you much flexibility to define multiple beans of the same type, and it is much better to define your own names. That way, if Spring changes the default behavior in the future, your application continues to work. When choosing whether to use id or name, always use id to specify the bean's default name. Prior to Spring 3.1, the id attribute is the same as the XML identity (i.e., xsd:ID), which posts a restriction in the characters that you can use. As of Spring 3.1, Spring uses xsd:String for the id attribute, so the previous restriction on the characters that you can use is gone. However, Spring will continue to ensure that the id is unique across the entire ApplicationContext. As a general practice, you should give your bean a name using id and then associate the bean with other names using name aliasing, as discussed in the next section.

Bean Name Aliasing

Spring allows a bean to have more than one name. You can achieve this by specifying a space-, comma-, or semicolon-separated list of names in the name attribute of the bean's <bean> tag. You can do this in place of, or in conjunction with, using the id attribute.

Besides using the name attribute, you can also use the <alias> tag for defining aliases for Spring bean names. Listing 4-68 shows a simple <bean> configuration that defines multiple names for a single bean (app-context-xml.xml).

Listing 4-68. Configuring Multiple Bean Names

```
<bean id="name1" name="name2 name3,name4;name5" class="java.lang.String"/>
<alias name="name1" alias="name6"/>
```

As you can see, we have defined six names: one using the id attribute and the other four as a list using all allowed bean name delimiters in the name attribute (this is just for demonstration purposes and is not recommended for real-life development). In real-life development, it's recommended you standardize on the delimiter to use for separating bean names' declarations within your application. One more alias was defined using the <alias> tag. Listing 4-69 shows a sample Java routine that grabs the same bean from the ApplicationContext six times using different names and verifies that they are the same bean.

Listing 4-69. Accessing Beans Using Aliases

```
package com.apress.prospring3.ch4.xml;

import org.springframework.context.support.GenericXmlApplicationContext;

public class BeanNameAliasing {

    public static void main(String[] args) {

        GenericXmlApplicationContext ctx = new GenericXmlApplicationContext();
        ctx.load("classpath:app-context-xml.xml");
        ctx.refresh();
```

```
        String s1 = (String) ctx.getBean("name1");
        String s2 = (String) ctx.getBean("name2");
        String s3 = (String) ctx.getBean("name3");
        String s4 = (String) ctx.getBean("name4");
        String s5 = (String) ctx.getBean("name5");
        String s6 = (String) ctx.getBean("name6");

        System.out.println((s1 == s2));
        System.out.println((s2 == s3));
        System.out.println((s3 == s4));
        System.out.println((s4 == s5));
        System.out.println((s5 == s6));
    }
}
```

This code prints true five times to the console output for the configuration contained in Listing 4-68, verifying that the beans accessed using different names are in fact the same bean.

You can retrieve a list of the bean aliases by calling ApplicationContext.getAliases(String) and passing in any one of the bean's names or ID. The list of aliases, other than the one you specified, will then be returned as a String array.

Bean name aliasing is a strange beast because it is not something you tend to use when you are building a new application. If you are going to have many other beans inject another bean, then they may as well use the same name to access that bean. However, as your application goes into production and maintenance work gets carried out, modifications are made, and so on, bean name aliasing becomes more useful.

Consider the following scenario: you have an application in which 50 different beans, configured using Spring, all require an implementation of the Foo interface. Twenty-five of the beans use the StandardFoo implementation with the bean name standardFoo, and the other 25 use the SuperFoo implementation with the superFoo bean name. Six months after you put the application into production, you decide to move the first 25 beans to the SuperFoo implementation. To do this, you have three options:

- The first is to change the implementation class of the standardFoo bean to SuperFoo. The drawback of this approach is that you have two instances of the SuperFoo class lying around when you really need only one. In addition, you now have two beans to make changes to when the configuration changes.

- The second option is to update the injection configuration for the 25 beans that are changing, which changes the beans' names from standardFoo to superFoo. This approach is not the most elegant way to proceed—you could perform a find and replace, but then rolling back your changes when management isn't happy means retrieving an old version of your configuration from your version control system.

- The third, and most ideal, approach is to remove (or comment out) the definition for the standardFoo bean and make standardFoo an alias to the superFoo. This change requires minimal effort, and restoring the system to its previous configuration is just as simple.

Bean Instantiation Mode

By default, all beans in Spring are singletons. This means Spring maintains a single instance of the bean, all dependent objects use the same instance, and all calls to ApplicationContext.getBean() return the same instance. We demonstrated this in the previous example shown in Listing 4-64, where we were able to use identity comparison (==) rather than the equals() comparison to check whether the beans were the same.

The term *singleton* is used interchangeably in Java to refer to two distinct concepts: an object that has a single instance within the application, and the Singleton design pattern. We refer to the first concept as singleton and to the Singleton pattern as Singleton. The Singleton design pattern was popularized in the seminal *Design Patterns: Elements of Reusable Object Oriented Software* by Erich Gamma, et al. (Addison-Wesley, 1995). The problem arises when people confuse the need for singleton instances with the need to apply the Singleton pattern. Listing 4-70 shows a typical implementation of the Singleton pattern in Java.

Listing 4-70. *The Singleton Design Pattern*

```
package com.apress.prospring3.ch4;

public class Singleton {

    private static Singleton instance;

    static {
        instance = new Singleton();
    }

    public static Singleton getInstance() {
        return instance;
    }
}
```

This pattern achieves its goal of allowing you to maintain and access a single instance of a class throughout your application, but it does so at the expense of increased coupling. Your application code must always have explicit knowledge of the Singleton class in order to obtain the instance—completely removing the ability to code to interfaces. In reality, the Singleton pattern is actually two patterns in one. The first, and desired, pattern involves maintenance of a single instance of an object. The second, and less desirable, is a pattern for object lookup that completely removes the possibility of using interfaces. Using the Singleton pattern also makes it very difficult to swap out implementations arbitrarily, because most objects that require the Singleton instance access the Singleton object directly. This can cause all kinds of headaches when you are trying to unit test your application because you are unable to replace the Singleton with a mock for testing purposes.

Fortunately, with Spring you can take advantage of the singleton instantiation model without having to work around the Singleton design pattern. All beans in Spring are, by default, created as Singleton instances, and Spring uses the same instances to fulfill all requests for that bean. Of course, Spring is not just limited to use of the singleton instance; it can still create a new instance of the bean to satisfy every dependency and every call to getBean(). It does all of this without any impact on your application code, and for this reason, we like to refer to Spring as being *instantiation mode agnostic*. This is a very powerful concept. If you start off with an object that is a singleton but then discover it is not really suited to multithread access, you can change it to a nonsingleton without affecting any of your application code.

■ **Note** Although changing the instantiation mode of your bean won't affect your application code, it does cause some problems if you rely on Spring's life-cycle interfaces. We cover this in more detail in Chapter 5.

Changing the instantiation mode from singleton to nonsingleton is simple (see Listing 4-71, the app-context-xml.xml file).

Listing 4-71. Nonsingleton Bean Configuration

```
<bean id="nonSingleton" class="java.lang.String" scope="prototype">
   <constructor-arg>
      <value>Clarence Ho</value>
   </constructor-arg>
</bean>
```

As you can see, the only difference between this bean declaration and any of the declarations you have seen so far is that we added the scope attribute and set the value to prototype. Spring defaults the scope to value singleton. The prototype scope instructs Spring to instantiate a new instance of the bean every time a bean instance was requested by the application. Listing 4-72 shows the effect this setting has on your application.

Listing 4-72. Nonsingleton Beans in Action

```
package com.apress.prospring3.ch4;

import org.springframework.context.support.GenericXmlApplicationContext;

public class NonSingleton {

    public static void main(String[] args) {

            GenericXmlApplicationContext ctx = new GenericXmlApplicationContext();
            ctx.load("classpath:app-context-xml.xml");
            ctx.refresh();

            String s1 = (String) ctx.getBean("nonSingleton");
            String s2 = (String) ctx.getBean("nonSingleton");

            System.out.println("Identity Equal?: " + (s1 ==s2));
            System.out.println("Value Equal:? " + s1.equals(s2));
            System.out.println(s1);
            System.out.println(s2);
    }
}
```

Running this example gives you the following output:

```
Identity Equal?:  false
Value Equal:? true
Clarence Ho
Clarence Ho
```

You can see from this that although the values of the two String objects are clearly equal, the identities are not, despite that both instances were retrieved using the same bean name.

Choosing an Instantiation Mode

In most scenarios, it is quite easy to see which instantiation mode is suitable. Typically we find that singleton is the default mode for our beans. In general, singletons should be used in the following scenarios:

- *Shared objects with no state*: When you have an object that maintains no state and has many dependent objects. Because you do not need synchronization if there is no state, you do not really need to create a new instance of the bean each time a dependent object needs to use it for some processing.

- *Shared object with read-only state*: This is similar to the previous point, but you have some read-only state. In this case, you still do not need synchronization, so creating an instance to satisfy each request for the bean is just adding additional overhead.

- *Shared object with shared state*: If you have a bean that has state that must be shared, then singleton is the ideal choice. In this case, ensure that your synchronization for state writes is as granular as possible.

- *High throughput objects with writable state*: If you have a bean that is used a great deal in your application, then you may find that keeping a singleton and synchronizing all write access to the bean state allows for better performance than constantly creating hundreds of instances of the bean. When using this approach, try to keep the synchronization as granular as possible without sacrificing consistency. You will find that this approach is particularly useful when your application creates a large number of instances over a long period of time, when your shared object has only a small amount of writable state, or when the instantiation of a new instance is expensive.

You should consider using nonsingletons in the following scenarios:

- *Objects with writable state*: If you have a bean that has a lot of writable state, then you may find that the cost of synchronization is greater than the cost of creating a new instance to handle each request from a dependent object.

- *Objects with private state*: In some cases, your dependent objects need a bean that has private state so that they can conduct their processing separately from other objects that depend on that bean. In this case, singleton is clearly not suitable, and you should use nonsingleton.

The main benefit you gain from Spring's instantiation management is that your applications can immediately benefit from the lower memory usage associated with singletons, with very little effort on your part. Then, if you find that singleton does not meet the needs of your application, it is a trivial task to modify your configuration to use nonsingleton mode.

Bean Scopes

In addition to the singleton and prototype scopes, other scopes also exist when defining a Spring bean for more specific purposes. You can also implement your own custom scope and register it in Spring's ApplicationContext. The following are the bean scopes that are supported as of version 3.1:

- *Singleton:* The default singleton scope.

- *Prototype:* A new instance will be created by Spring when requested by application.

- *Request:* For web application use. When using Spring MVC for web application, beans with request scope will be instantiated for every HTTP request and then destroyed when the request is completed.

- *Session:* For web application use. When using Spring MVC for web applications, beans with session scope will be instantiated for every HTTP session and then destroyed when the session is over.

- *Global session:* For portlet-based web applications. The global session scope beans can be shared among all portlets within the same Spring MVC–powered portal application.

- *Thread*: A new bean instance will be created by Spring when requested by a new thread, while for the same thread, the same bean instance will be returned. Note that this scope is not registered by default.

- *Custom:* Custom bean scope that can be created by implementing the interface org.springframework.beans.factory.config.Scope and registering the custom scope in Spring's configuration (for XML, use the class org.springframework.beans .factory.config.CustomScopeConfigurer).

Resolving Dependencies

During normal operation, Spring is able to resolve dependencies by simply looking at your configuration file or annotations in your classes. In this way, Spring can ensure that each bean is configured in the correct order so that each bean has its dependencies correctly configured. If Spring did not perform this and just created the beans and configured them in any order, a bean could be created and configured before its dependencies. This is obviously not what you want and would cause all sorts of problems within your application.

Unfortunately, Spring is not aware of any dependencies that exist between beans in your code. For instance, take one one bean, called bean A, which obtains an instance of another bean, called bean B, in the constructor via a call to getBean(). For example, in the constructor of BeanA, you get an instance of BeanB by calling ctx.getBean("beanB"), without asking Spring to inject the dependency for you. In this case, Spring is unaware that bean A depends on bean B, and, as a result, it may instantiate bean A before bean B. You can provide Spring with additional information about your bean dependencies using the depends-on attribute of the <bean> tag. Listing 4-73 shows how the scenario for bean A and bean B would be configured.

Listing 4-73. Manually Defining Dependencies

```
<bean id="beanA" class="com.apress.prospring.ch4.BeanA" depends-on="beanB"/>
<bean id="beanB" class="com.apress.prospring.ch4.BeanB"/>
```

In this configuration, we are asserting that bean beanA depends on bean beanB. Spring takes this into consideration when instantiating the beans and ensures that beanB is created before beanA.

When developing your applications, avoid designing your applications to use this feature; instead, define your dependencies by means of Setter and Constructor Injection contracts. However, if you are integrating Spring with legacy code, then you may find that the dependencies defined in the code require you to provide extra information to the Spring Framework.

Autowiring Your Bean

In all the examples so far, we have had to define explicitly, via the configuration file, how the individual beans are wired together. If you don't like having to wire all your components together, then you can have Spring attempt to do so automatically. By default, autowiring is disabled. To enable it, you specify which method of autowiring you want to use by using the autowire attribute of the bean you want to autowire.

Different Modes of Autowiring

Spring supports four modes for autowiring: byName, byType, constructor, default, and no (which is the default). When using byName autowiring, Spring attempts to wire each property to a bean of the same name. So, if the target bean has a property named foo and a foo bean is defined in the ApplicationContext, the foo bean is assigned to the foo property of the target.

When using byType autowiring, Spring attempts to wire each of the properties on the target bean automatically using a bean of the same type in the ApplicationContext. So, if you have a property of type String on the target bean and a bean of type String in the ApplicationContext, then Spring wires the String bean to the target bean's String property. If you have more than one bean of the same type, in this case String, in the same ApplicationContext, then Spring is unable to decide which one to use for the autowiring and throws an exception (of type org.springframework.beans.factory.NoSuchBeanDefinitionException).

The constructor autowiring mode functions just like byType wiring, except that it uses constructors rather than setters to perform the injection. Spring attempts to match the greatest numbers of arguments it can in the constructor. So, if your bean has two constructors, one that accepts a String and one that accepts a String and an Integer, and you have both a String and an Integer bean in your ApplicationContext, Spring uses the two-argument constructor.

In default mode, Spring will choose between constructor and byType modes automatically. If your bean has a default (no-arguments) constructor, then Spring uses byType; otherwise, it uses constructor.

Listing 4-74 shows a simple configuration that autowires three beans of the same type using each of the different modes (autowiring.xml).

Listing 4-74. Configuring Autowiring

```
<bean id="foo" class="com.apress.prospring3.ch4.autowiring.Foo"/>
<bean id="bar1" class="com.apress.prospring3.ch4.autowiring.Bar"/>

<bean id="targetByName" autowire="byName"
class="com.apress.prospring3.ch4.autowiring.Target"
      lazy-init="true"/>
<bean id="targetByType" autowire="byType"
class="com.apress.prospring3.ch4.autowiring.Target"
      lazy-init="true"/>
<bean id="targetConstructor" autowire="constructor"
class="com.apress.prospring3.ch4.autowiring.Target"
      lazy-init="true"/>
```

This configuration should look very familiar to you now. Foo and Bar are empty classes. Notice that each of the Target beans has a different value for the autowire attribute. Moreover, the lazy-init attribute was set to true to inform Spring to instantiate the bean only when it is first requested, rather than at startup, so that we can output the result in the correct place in the testing program. Listing 4-75 shows a simple Java application that retrieves each of the Target beans from the ApplicationContext.

Listing 4-75. Autowiring Collaborators

```
package com.apress.prospring3.ch4.autowiring;

import org.springframework.context.support.GenericXmlApplicationContext;

public class Target {

    private Foo foo;
```

```java
    private Foo foo2;

    private Bar bar;

    public Target() {
    }

    public Target(Foo foo) {
        System.out.println("Target(Foo) called");
    }

    public Target(Foo foo, Bar bar) {
        System.out.println("Target(Foo, Bar) called");
    }

    public void setFoo(Foo foo) {
        this.foo = foo;
        System.out.println("Property foo set");
    }

    public void setFoo2(Foo foo) {
        this.foo2 = foo;
        System.out.println("Property foo2 set");
    }

    public void setBar(Bar bar) {
        this.bar = bar;
        System.out.println("Property bar set");
    }

    public static void main(String[] args) {
        GenericXmlApplicationContext ctx = new GenericXmlApplicationContext();
        ctx.load("classpath:autowiring.xml");
        ctx.refresh();

        Target t = null;

        System.out.println("Using byName:\n");
        t = (Target) ctx.getBean("targetByName");

        System.out.println("\nUsing byType:\n");
        t = (Target) ctx.getBean("targetByType");

        System.out.println("\nUsing constructor:\n");
        t = (Target) ctx.getBean("targetConstructor");

    }
}
```

In this code, you can see that the Target class has three constructors: a no-argument constructor, a constructor that accepts a Foo instance, and a constructor that accepts a Foo and a Bar instance. In addition to these constructors, the Target bean has three properties: two of type Foo and one of type Bar. Each of these properties and constructors writes a message to console output when it is called. The main method simply retrieves each of the `Target` beans declared in the `ApplicationContext`, triggering the autowire process. Here is the output from running this example:

```
Using byName:

Property foo set

Using byType:

Property bar set
Property foo set
Property foo2 set

Using constructor:

Target(Foo, Bar) called
```

From the output, you can see that when Spring uses `byName`, the only property that is set is the `foo` property, because this is the only property with a corresponding bean entry in the configuration file. When using `byType`, Spring sets the value of all three properties. The `foo` and `foo2` properties are set by the `foo` bean, and the `bar` property is set by the `bar1` bean. When using `constructor`, Spring uses the two-argument constructor, because Spring can provide beans for both arguments and does not need to fall back to another constructor.

When to Use Autowiring

In most cases, the answer to the question of whether you should use autowiring is definitely "no!" Autowiring can save you time in small applications, but in many cases, it leads to bad practices and is inflexible in large applications. Using `byName` seems like a good idea, but it may lead you to give your classes artificial property names so that you can take advantage of the autowiring functionality. The whole idea behind Spring is that you can create your classes how you like and have Spring work for you, not the other way around. You may be tempted to use `byType` until you realize that you can have only one bean for each type in your `ApplicationContext`—a restriction that is problematic when you need to maintain beans with different configurations of the same type. The same argument applies to the use of `constructor` autowiring.

In some cases, autowiring can save you time, but it does not really take that much extra effort to define your wiring explicitly, and you benefit from explicit semantics and full flexibility on property naming and on how many instances of the same type you manage. For any nontrivial application, steer clear of autowiring at all costs.

Bean Inheritance

In some cases, you many need multiple definitions of beans that are the same type or implement a shared interface. This can become problematic if you want these beans to share some configuration settings but not others. The process of keeping the shared configuration settings in sync is quite error-prone, and on large projects, doing so can be quite time-consuming. To get around this, Spring allows you to define a `<bean>` definition that inherits its property settings from another bean in the same `ApplicationContext`. You can override the values of any properties on the child bean as required, which allows you to have full control, but the parent bean can provide each of your beans with a base configuration. Listing 4-76 shows a simple configuration with two beans, one of which is the child of the other (`app-context-xml.xml`).

Listing 4-76. Configuring Bean Inheritance

```
<bean id="inheritParent" class="com.apress.prospring3.ch4.inheritance.SimpleBean">
    <property name="name">
        <value>Clarence Ho</value>
    </property>
    <property name="age">
        <value>22</value>
    </property>
</bean>

<bean id="inheritChild" class="com.apress.prospring3.ch4.inheritance.SimpleBean"
    parent="inheritParent">
    <property name="age">
        <value>35</value>
    </property>
</bean>
```

In this code, you can see that the `<bean>` tag for the inheritChild bean has an extra attribute, parent, which indicates that Spring should consider the inheritParent bean the parent of the bean. In case you don't want a parent bean definition to become available for lookup from the ApplicationContext, you can add the attribute abstract="true" in the `<bean>` tag when declaring the parent bean. Because the inheritChild bean has its own value for the age property, Spring passes this value to the bean. However, inheritChild has no value for the name property, so Spring uses the value given to the inheritParent bean. Listing 4-77 shows the code for the SimpleBean class used in a previous configuration.

Listing 4-77. The SimpleBean Class

```java
package com.apress.prospring3.ch4.inheritance;

import org.springframework.context.support.GenericXmlApplicationContext;

public class SimpleBean {

    public String name;

    public int age;

    public static void main(String[] args) {

        GenericXmlApplicationContext ctx = new GenericXmlApplicationContext();
        ctx.load("classpath:app-context-xml.xml");

        SimpleBean parent = (SimpleBean) ctx.getBean("inheritParent");
        SimpleBean child = (SimpleBean) ctx.getBean("inheritChild");

        System.out.println("Parent:\n" + parent);
        System.out.println("Child:\n" + child);
    }

    public void setName(String name) {
        this.name = name;
    }
```

```
    public void setAge(int age) {
        this.age = age;
    }

    public String toString() {
        return    "Name: " + name + "\n"
                + "Age: " + age;
    }
}
```

As you can see, the main() method of the SimpleBean class grabs both the inheritChild and inheritParent beans from the ApplicationContext and writes the contents of their properties to stdout. Here is the output from this example:

```
Parent:
Name: Clarence Ho
Age: 22
Child:
Name: Clarence Ho
Age: 35
```

As expected, the inheritChild bean inherited the value for its name property from the inheritParent bean but was able to provide its own value for the age property.

Child beans inherit both constructor arguments and property values from the parent beans, so you can use both styles of injection with bean inheritance. This level of flexibility makes bean inheritance a powerful tool for building applications with more than a handful of bean definitions. If you are declaring a lot of beans of the same value with shared property values, then avoid the temptation to use copy and paste to share the values; instead, set up an inheritance hierarchy in your configuration.

When you are using inheritance, remember that bean inheritance does not have to match a Java inheritance hierarchy. It is perfectly acceptable to use bean inheritance on five beans of the same type. Think of bean inheritance as more like a templating feature than an inheritance feature. Be aware, however, that if you are changing the type of the child bean, then that type must be compatible with the type of the parent bean.

Summary

In this chapter, we covered a lot of ground with both the Spring core and IoC in general. We showed you examples of the different types of IoC and presented a discussion of the pros and cons of using each mechanism in your applications. We looked at which IoC mechanisms Spring provides and when and when not to use each within your applications. While exploring IoC, we introduced the Spring BeanFactory, which is the core component for Spring's IoC capabilities, and then the ApplicationContext, which extends BeanFactory and provide additional functionalities. For ApplicationContext, we focused on the GenericXmlApplicationContext that allows external configuration of Spring using XML. Another method to declare DI requirements for ApplicationContext, that is, using Java annotations, was also discussed.

This chapter also introduced you to the basics of Spring's IoC feature set including Setter Injection, Constructor Injection, Method Injection, autowiring, and bean inheritance. In the discussion of configuration, we demonstrated how you can configure your bean properties with a wide variety of different values, including other beans, using both XML and annotation type configurations and the GenericXmlApplicationContext.

This chapter only scratched the surface of Spring and Spring's IoC container. In the next chapter, we look at some IoC-related features specific to Spring, and we take a more detailed look at other functionality available in the Spring core.

CHAPTER 5

Spring Configuration in Detail

In the previous chapter, we took a detailed look at the concept of Inversion of Control (IoC) and how it fits into the Spring Framework. However, as we said at the end of the previous chapter, we have really only scratched the surface of what the Spring core can do.

Spring provides a wide array of services that supplement and extend the basic IoC capabilities. A number of projects provide IoC containers, but none so far provides the same comprehensive feature set Spring provides. In this chapter, we are going to look in detail at some additional IoC-related features offered in Spring along with other functionality offered by the Spring core. In addition, we will look at using Java classes when configuring Spring's ApplicationContext, together with some new features that exist in 3.0 and 3.1 for more advanced configuration options. Specifically, we will be looking at the following:

- *Managing the bean life cycle:* So far, all the beans you have seen have been fairly simple and completely decoupled from the Spring container. In this section, we look at some strategies you can employ to enable your beans to receive notifications from the Spring container at various points throughout their life cycle. You can do this either by implementing specific interfaces laid out by Spring, by specifying methods that Spring can call via reflection, or by using JSR-250 JavaBeans life-cycle annotations.

- *Making your beans "Spring aware":* In some cases, you want a bean to be able to interact with the ApplicationContext that configured it. For this reason, Spring offers two interfaces, BeanNameAware and ApplicationContextAware, that allow your bean to obtain its assigned name (i.e., the id or name attribute in the <bean> tag, with the id attribute having higher preference) and reference its ApplicationContext, respectively. This section of the chapter looks at implementing these interfaces and gives some practical considerations for using them in your application.

- *Using FactoryBeans:* As its name implies, the FactoryBean interface is intended to be implemented by any bean that acts as a factory for other beans. The FactoryBean interface provides a mechanism by which you can easily integrate your own factories with the Spring BeanFactory.

- *Working with JavaBeans PropertyEditors:* The PropertyEditor interface is a standard interface provided in the java.beans package. PropertyEditors are used to convert property values to and from String representations. Spring uses PropertyEditors extensively, mainly to read values specified in the BeanFactory configuration and convert them into the correct types. In this section of the chapter, we discuss the set of PropertyEditors supplied with Spring and how you can use them within your application. We also take a look at implementing custom PropertyEditors.

- *Learn more about the Spring ApplicationContext:* As discussed in the previous chapter, the ApplicationContext is an extension of the BeanFactory intended for use in full applications. The ApplicationContext interface provides a useful set of additional functionality, including internationalized message provision, resource loading, and event publishing. In this chapter, we take a detailed look at the features in addition to IoC that the ApplicationContext offers. We also jump ahead of ourselves a little and look at how the ApplicationContext simplifies the use of Spring when you are building web applications.

- *Configuration using Java classes:* Prior to 3.0, Spring supported only the XML base configuration with annotations for beans and dependency configuration. Starting with 3.0, Spring offers another option for developers to configure the Spring ApplicationContext using Java classes. We take a look at this new option in Spring application configuration.

- *New features in the Spring 3.1 configuration:* Spring 3.1 provides some useful new features specific to configuration, such as profiles management, environment and property source abstraction, and so on. In this section, we take a look at those features and show how to use them to address specific configuration needs.

Spring's Impact on Application Portability

Most of the features discussed in this chapter are specific to Spring and, in many cases, are not available in other IoC containers. Although many IoC containers offer life-cycle management functionality, they probably do so through a different set of interfaces than Spring. If the portability of your application between different IoC containers is truly important, then you might want to avoid using some of the features that couple your application to Spring.

Remember, however, that by setting a constraint—that your application is portable between IoC containers—you are losing out on the wealth of functionality Spring offers. Because you are likely to be making a strategic choice to use Spring, it makes sense that you use it to the best of its ability.

Be careful not to create a requirement for portability out of thin air. In many cases, the end users of your application do not care if the application can run on three different IoC containers; they just want it to run. In our experience, it is often a mistake to try to build an application on the lowest common denominator of features available in your chosen technology. Doing so often sets your application at a disadvantage right from the get-go. However, if your application requires IoC container portability, then do not see this as a drawback—it is a true requirement and, therefore, one your application should fulfill. In *Expert One-on-One: J2EE Development without EJB* (Wrox, 2004), Rod Johnson and Jürgen Höller describe these types of requirement as phantom requirements and provide a much more detailed discussion of them and how they can affect your project.

Although using these features may couple your application to the Spring Framework, in reality you are increasing the portability of your application in the wider scope. Consider that you are using a freely available, open source framework that has no particular vendor affiliation. An application built using Spring's IoC container runs anywhere Java runs. For Java enterprise applications, Spring opens up new possibilities for portability. Spring provides many of the same capabilities as JEE and also provides classes to abstract and simplify many other aspects of JEE. In many cases, it is possible to build a web application using Spring that runs in a simple servlet container but with the same level of sophistication as an application targeted at a full-blown JEE application server. By coupling to Spring, you can increase your application's portability by replacing many features that either are vendor-specific or rely on vendor-specific configuration with equivalent features in Spring.

Bean Life-Cycle Management

An important part of any IoC container, Spring included, is that beans can be constructed in such a way that they receive notifications at certain points in their life cycle. This enables your beans to perform relevant processing at certain points throughout their life. In general, two life-cycle events are particularly relevant to a bean: post-initialization and pre-destruction.

In the context of Spring, the post-initialization event is raised as soon as Spring finishes setting all the property values on the bean and finishes any dependency checks that you configured it to perform. The pre-destruction event is fired just before Spring destroys the bean instance. However, for beans with prototype scope, the pre-destruction event will not be fired by Spring. The design of Spring is that the initialization life-cycle callback methods will be called on objects regardless of bean scope, while for beans with prototype scope, the destruction life-cycle callback methods will not be called. Spring provides three mechanisms a bean can use to hook into each of these events and perform some additional processing: interface-based, method-based, and annotation-based mechanisms.

Using the interface-based mechanism, your bean implements an interface specific to the type of notification it wants to receive, and Spring notifies the bean via a callback method defined in the interface. For the method-based mechanism, Spring allows you to specify, in your ApplicationContext configuration, the name of a method to call when the bean is initialized and the name of a method to call when the bean is destroyed. For the annotation mechanism, you can use JSR-250 annotations to specify the method that Spring should call after construction or before destruction.

In the case of both events, the mechanisms achieve exactly the same goal. The interface mechanism is used extensively throughout Spring so that you don't have to remember to specify the initialization or destruction each time you use one of Spring's components. However, in your own beans, you may be better served using the method-based or annotation mechanism because your beans do not need to implement any Spring-specific interfaces. Although we stated that portability often isn't as important a requirement as many books lead you to believe, this does not mean you should sacrifice portability when a perfectly good alternative exists. That said, if you are coupling your application to Spring in other ways, using the interface method allows you to specify the callback once and then forget about it. If you are defining a lot of beans of the same type that need to take advantage of the life-cycle notifications, then using the interface mechanism can avoid the need for specifying the life-cycle callback methods for every bean in the XML configuration file. Using JSR-250 annotations is also another viable option, since it's a standard defined by the JCP and you are also not coupled to Spring's specific annotations. Just make sure that the IoC container you are running your application on supports the JSR-250 standard.

Overall, the choice of which mechanism you use for receiving life-cycle notifications depends on your application requirements. If you are concerned about portability or you are just defining one or two beans of a particular type that need the callbacks, then use the method-based mechanism. If you use annotation-type configuration and certain that you are using an IoC container that supports JSR-250, then use the annotation mechanism. If you are not too concerned about portability or you are defining many beans of the same type that need the life-cycle notifications, then using the interface-based mechanism is the best way to ensure that your beans always receive the notifications they are expecting. If you plan to use a bean across many different Spring projects, then you almost certainly want the functionality of that bean to be as self-contained as possible, so you should definitely use the interface-based mechanism.

Figure 5-1 shows a high-level overview of how Spring manages the life cycle of the beans within its container.

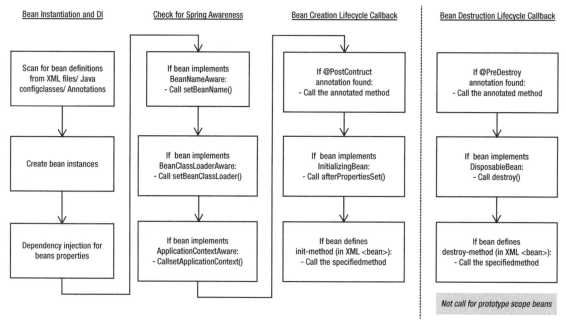

Figure 5-1. *Spring beans life cycle*

Hooking into Bean Creation

By being aware of when it is initialized, a bean can check to see whether all its required dependencies are satisfied. Although Spring can check dependencies for you, it is pretty much an all-or-nothing approach, and it doesn't offer any opportunities for applying additional logic to the dependency resolution procedure. Consider a bean that has four dependencies declared as setters, two of which are required and one of which has a suitable default in the event that no dependency is provided. Using an initialization callback, your bean can check for the dependencies it requires, throwing an exception or providing a default as needed.

A bean cannot perform these checks in its constructor because at this point, Spring has not had an opportunity to provide values for the dependencies it can satisfy. The initialization callback in Spring is called after Spring finishes providing the dependencies that it can and performs any dependency checks that you ask of it.

You are not limited to using the initialization callback just to check dependencies; you can do anything you want in the callback, but it is most useful for the purpose we have described. In many cases, the initialization callback is also the place to trigger any actions that your bean must take automatically in response to its configuration. For instance, if you build a bean to run scheduled tasks, the initialization callback provides the ideal place to start the scheduler—after all, the configuration data is set on the bean.

■ **Note**   You will not have to write a bean to run scheduled tasks because this is something Spring can do automatically through its built-in scheduling feature or via integration with the Quartz scheduler. We cover this in more detail in Chapter 15.

Execute a Method When a Bean Is Created

As we mentioned previously, one way to receive the initialization callback is to designate a method on your bean as an initialization method and tell Spring to use this method as an initialization method. As discussed, this callback mechanism is useful when you have only a few beans of the same type or when you want to keep your application decoupled from Spring. Another reason for using this mechanism is to enable your Spring application to work with beans that were built previously or were provided by third-party vendors.

Specifying a callback method is simply a case of specifying the name in the init-method attribute of a bean's <bean> tag. Listing 5-1 shows a basic bean with two dependencies.:

Listing 5-1. The SimpleBean Class

```
package com.apress.prospring3.ch5.lifecycle;

import org.springframework.beans.factory.BeanCreationException;
import org.springframework.context.ApplicationContext;
import org.springframework.context.support.GenericXmlApplicationContext;

public class SimpleBean {

    private static final String DEFAULT_NAME = "Luke Skywalker";

    private String name = null;

    private int age = Integer.MIN_VALUE;

    public void setName(String name) {
        this.name = name;
    }

    public void setAge(int age) {
        this.age = age;
    }

    public void init() {
        System.out.println("Initializing bean");

      if (name == null) {
            System.out.println("Using default name");
            name = DEFAULT_NAME;
        }

        if (age == Integer.MIN_VALUE) {
            throw new IllegalArgumentException(
                    "You must set the age property of any beans of type " + SimpleBean.class);
        }
    }

    public String toString() {
        return "Name: " + name + "\nAge: " + age;
    }
```

```java
public static void main(String[] args) {

    GenericXmlApplicationContext ctx = new GenericXmlApplicationContext();
    ctx.load("classpath:lifecycle/initMethod.xml");
    ctx.refresh(); // Refresh the ApplicationContext after XML config file loaded

    SimpleBean simpleBean1 = getBean("simpleBean1", ctx);
    SimpleBean simpleBean2 = getBean("simpleBean2", ctx);
    SimpleBean simpleBean3 = getBean("simpleBean3", ctx);
}

private static SimpleBean getBean(String beanName, ApplicationContext ctx) {
    try {
        SimpleBean bean =(SimpleBean) ctx.getBean(beanName);
        System.out.println(bean);
        return bean;
    } catch (BeanCreationException ex) {
        System.out.println("An error occured in bean configuration: "
                + ex.getMessage());
        return null;
    }
}
}
```

Notice that we have defined a method, init(), to act as the initialization callback. The init() method checks to see whether the name property has been set, and if it has not, it uses the default value stored in the DEFAULT_NAME constant. The init() method also checks to see whether the age property is set and throws an IllegalArgumentException if it is not.

The main() method of the SimpleBean class attempts to obtain three beans from the GenericXmlApplicationContext, all of type SimpleBean, using its own getBean() method. Notice that in the getBean() method, if the bean is obtained successfully, then its details are written to console output. If an exception is thrown in the init() method, as will occur in this case if the age property is not set, then Spring wraps that exception in a BeanCreationException. The getBean() method catches these exceptions and writes a message to the console output informing us of the error, as well as returns a null value.

Listing 5-2 shows an ApplicationContext configuration that defines the beans used in Listing 5-1 (lifecycle/initMethod.xml).

Listing 5-2. *Configuring the SimpleBeans*

```xml
<?xml version="1.0" encoding="UTF-8"?>
<beans xmlns="http://www.springframework.org/schema/beans"
    xmlns:xsi="http://www.w3.org/2001/XMLSchema-instance"
    xsi:schemaLocation="http://www.springframework.org/schema/beans
        http://www.springframework.org/schema/beans/spring-beans-3.1.xsd"
        default-lazy-init="true">

    <bean id="simpleBean1"
        class="com.apress.prospring3.ch5.lifecycle.SimpleBean"
        init-method="init">
        <property name="name">
            <value>Clarence Ho</value>
        </property>
        <property name="age">
            <value>100</value>
```

```
        </property>
    </bean>
    <bean id="simpleBean2"
        class="com.apress.prospring3.ch5.lifecycle.SimpleBean"
         init-method="init">
        <property name="age">
            <value>100</value>
        </property>
    </bean>
    <bean id="simpleBean3"
        class="com.apress.prospring3.ch5.lifecycle.SimpleBean"
        init-method="init">
        <property name="name">
            <value>Clarence Ho</value>
        </property>
    </bean>
</beans>
```

As you can see, the <bean> tag for each of the three beans has an init-method attribute that tells Spring that it should invoke the init() method as soon as it finishes configuring the bean. The simpleBean1 bean has values for both the name and age properties, so it passes through the init() method with absolutely no changes. The simpleBean2 bean has no value for the name property, meaning that in the init() method, the name property is given the default value. Finally, the simpleBean3 bean has no value for the age property. The logic defined in the init() method treats this as an error, so an IllegalArgumentException is thrown. Also note that in the <beans> tag, we added the attribute default-lazy-init="true" to instruct Spring to instantiate the beans defined in the configuration file only when the bean was requested from application. If we do not specify it, Spring will try to initialize all the beans during the bootstrapping of the ApplicationContext, and it will fail during the initialization of simpleBean3. Running the previous example yields the following output:

```
Initializing bean
Name: Clarence Ho
Age: 100
Initializing bean
Using default name
Name: Luke Skywalker
Age: 100
Initializing bean
An error occured in bean configuration: Error creating bean with name 'simpleBean3' defined in
class path resource [lifecycle/initMethod.xml]: Invocation of init method failed; nested
exception is java.lang.IllegalArgumentException: You must set the age property of any beans of
type class com.apress.prospring3.ch5.lifecycle.SimpleBean
```

From this output you can see that simpleBean1 was configured correctly with the values that we specified in the configuration file. For simpleBean2, the default value for the name property was used because no value was specified in the configuration. Finally, for simpleBean3, no bean instance was created because the init() method raised an error because of the lack of a value for the age property.

As you can see, using the initialization method is an ideal way to ensure that your beans are configured correctly. By using this mechanism, you can take full advantage of the benefits of IoC without losing any of the control you get from manually defining dependencies. The only constraint on your initialization method is that it cannot accept any arguments. You can define any return type, although it is ignored by Spring, and you can even use a static method, but the method must accept no arguments.

The benefits of this mechanism are negated when using a static initialization method, because you cannot access any of the bean's state to validate it. If your bean is using static state as a mechanism for saving memory and you are using a static initialization method to validate this state, then you should consider moving the static state to instance state and using a nonstatic initialization method. If you use Spring's singleton management capabilities, the end effect is the same, but you have a bean that is much simpler to test, and you also have the increased effect of being able to create multiple instances of the bean with their own state when necessary. Of course, there are instances in which you need to use static state shared across multiple instances of a bean, in which case you can always use a static initialization method.

Implementing the InitializingBean Interface

The InitializingBean interface defined in Spring allows you to define inside your bean code that you want the bean to receive notification that Spring has finished configuring it. In the same way as when you are using an initialization method, this gives you the opportunity to check the bean configuration to ensure that it is valid, providing any default values along the way. The InitializingBean interface defines a single method, afterPropertiesSet(), that serves the same purpose as the init() method in Listing 5-1. Listing 5-3 shows a reimplementation of the previous example using the InitializingBean interface in place of the initialization method.

Listing 5-3. Using the InitializingBean Interface

```
package com.apress.prospring3.ch5.lifecycle;

import org.springframework.beans.factory.BeanCreationException;
import org.springframework.beans.factory.InitializingBean;
import org.springframework.context.ApplicationContext;
import org.springframework.context.support.GenericXmlApplicationContext;

public class SimpleBeanWithInterface implements InitializingBean {

    private static final String DEFAULT_NAME = "Luke Skywalker";

    private String name = null;

    private int age = Integer.MIN_VALUE;

    public void setName(String name) {
        this.name = name;
    }

    public void setAge(int age) {
        this.age = age;
    }

    public void myInit() {
        System.out.println("My Init");
    }
    public void afterPropertiesSet() throws Exception {
        System.out.println("Initializing bean");

        if (name == null) {
            System.out.println("Using default name");
            name = DEFAULT_NAME;
```

```
            }

        if (age == Integer.MIN_VALUE) {
            throw new IllegalArgumentException(
                    "You must set the age property of any beans of type " + SimpleBean.class);
        }
    }

    public String toString() {
        return "Name: " + name + "\nAge: " + age;
    }

    public static void main(String[] args) {
        GenericXmlApplicationContext ctx = new GenericXmlApplicationContext();
        ctx.load("classpath:lifecycle/initInterface.xml");
        ctx.refresh();

        SimpleBeanWithInterface simpleBean1 = getBean("simpleBean1", ctx);
        SimpleBeanWithInterface simpleBean2 = getBean("simpleBean2", ctx);
        SimpleBeanWithInterface simpleBean3 = getBean("simpleBean3", ctx);
    }

    private static SimpleBeanWithInterface getBean(String beanName,
            ApplicationContext ctx) {
        try {
            SimpleBeanWithInterface bean = (SimpleBeanWithInterface) ctx.getBean(beanName);
            System.out.println(bean);
            return bean;
        } catch (BeanCreationException ex) {
            System.out.println("An error occured in bean configuration: "
                    + ex.getMessage());
            return null;
        }
    }
}
```

As you can see, not much in this example has changed (the changed codes are highlighted in bold). Aside from the obvious class name change, the only differences are that this class implements InitializingBean and the initialization logic has moved into the InitializingBean.afterPropertiesSet() method.

In Listing 5-4, you can see the configuration for this example (lifecycle/initInterface.xml).

Listing 5-4. Configuration Using InitializingBean

```xml
<?xml version="1.0" encoding="UTF-8"?>
<beans xmlns="http://www.springframework.org/schema/beans"
    xmlns:xsi="http://www.w3.org/2001/XMLSchema-instance"
    xsi:schemaLocation="http://www.springframework.org/schema/beans
        http://www.springframework.org/schema/beans/spring-beans-3.1.xsd"
        default-lazy-init="true">

    <bean id="simpleBean1"
        class="com.apress.prospring3.ch5.lifecycle.SimpleBeanWithInterface">
        <property name="name">
```

```
                <value>Clarence Ho</value>
            </property>
            <property name="age">
                <value>100</value>
            </property>
        </bean>

        <bean id="simpleBean2"
            class="com.apress.prospring3.ch5.lifecycle.SimpleBeanWithInterface">
            <property name="age">
                <value>100</value>
            </property>
        </bean>

        <bean id="simpleBean3"
            class="com.apress.prospring3.ch5.lifecycle.SimpleBeanWithInterface">
            <property name="name">
                <value>Clarence Ho</value>
            </property>
        </bean>
    </beans>
```

Again, there's not much difference between the configuration code in Listing 5-4 and the configuration code from Listing 5-2. The noticeable difference is the omission of the init-method attribute. Because the SimpleBeanWithInterface class implements the InitializingBean interface, Spring knows which method to call as the initialization callback, thus removing the need for any additional configuration. The output from this example is shown here:

```
Initializing bean
Name: Clarence Ho
Age: 100
Initializing bean
Using default name
Name: Luke Skywalker
Age: 100
Initializing bean
An error occured in bean configuration: Error creating bean with name 'simpleBean3' defined in
class path resource [lifecycle/initInterface.xml]: Invocation of init method failed; nested
exception is java.lang.IllegalArgumentException: You must set the age property of any beans of
type class com.apress.prospring3.ch5.lifecycle.SimpleBean
```

As you can see, the output is the same as the method mechanism.

Using JSR-250 @PostConstruct Annotation

Another method that can achieve the same purpose is to use the JSR-250 life-cycle annotation, @PostConstruct. Starting from Spring 2.5, Spring also supports JSR-250 annotations to specify the method that Spring should call if the corresponding annotation relating to the bean's life cycle exists in the class. Listing 5-5 shows the program with the @PostConstruct annotation applied.

Listing 5-5. Using JSR-250 @PostConstruct Annotation

```
package com.apress.prospring3.ch5.lifecycle;

import javax.annotation.PostConstruct;
// Other import statements omitted
public class SimpleBeanWithJSR250 {

    // Codes omitted
    @PostConstruct
    public void init() throws Exception {

    // Rest of codes omitted
    }
}
```

The program is exactly the same as the SimpleBean; just apply the @PostConstruct annotation before the init() method. Note that you can assign any name to the method.

For the configuration, we can use the one used by the interface mechanism (Listing 5-4). However, since we are using annotation, we need to add the context namespace and the <context:annotation-driven> tag into the configuration file.

Afterward, run the program, and you will see the same output as other mechanisms.

As we discussed earlier, all three approaches have their benefits and drawbacks. Using an initialization method, you have the benefit of keeping your application decoupled from Spring, but you have to remember to configure the initialization method for every bean that needs it. Using InitializingBean, you have the benefit of being able to specify the initialization callback once for all instances of your bean class, but you have to couple your application to do so. Using annotations, you need to apply the annotation to the method and make sure that the IoC container supports JSR-250. In the end, you should let the requirements of your application drive the decision about which approach to use. If portability is an issue, then use the initialization or annotation method; otherwise, use the InitializingBean interface to reduce the amount of configuration your application needs and the chance of errors creeping into your application because of misconfiguration.

Order of Resolution

You can use all mechanisms on the same bean instance. In this case, Spring invokes the method annotated with @PostConstruct first and then InitializingBean.afterPropertiesSet(), followed by your initialization method. This can be useful if you have an existing bean that performs some initialization in a specific method but you need to add some more initialization code when you use Spring.

Hooking into Bean Destruction

When using an ApplicationContext implementation that wraps the DefaultListableBeanFactory interface (such as GenericXmlApplicationContext, via the GenericApplicationContext.getDefaultListableBeanFactory() method), you can signal to the BeanFactory that you want to destroy all singleton instances with a call to ConfigurableBeanFactory.destroySingletons(). Typically, you do this when your application shuts down, and it allows you to clean up any resources that your beans might be holding open, thus allowing your application to shut down gracefully. This callback also provides the perfect place to flush any data you are storing in memory to persistent storage and to allow your beans to end any long-running processes they may have started.

To allow your beans to receive notification that destroySingletons() has been called, you have three options, all similar to the mechanisms available for receiving an initialization callback. The destruction callback is often used in conjunction with the initialization callback. In many cases, you create and configure a resource in the initialization callback and then release the resource in the destruction callback.

Executing a Method When a Bean Is Destroyed

To designate a method to be called when a bean is destroyed, you simply specify the name of the method in the destroy-method attribute of the bean's <bean> tag. Spring calls it just before it destroys the singleton instance of the bean (as stated before, Spring will not call this method for those beans with prototype scope). Listing 5-6 shows a simple class that implements InitializingBean, and in the afterPropertiesSet() method, it creates an instance of FileInputStream and stores this in a private field.

Listing 5-6. Using a destroy-method Callback

```
package com.apress.prospring3.ch5.lifecycle;

import java.io.FileInputStream;
import java.io.IOException;
import java.io.InputStream;

import org.springframework.beans.factory.InitializingBean;
import org.springframework.context.support.GenericXmlApplicationContext;

public class DestructiveBean implements InitializingBean {

    private InputStream is = null;

    public String filePath = null;

    public void afterPropertiesSet() throws Exception {

        System.out.println("Initializing Bean");

        if (filePath == null) {
            throw new IllegalArgumentException(
                    "You must specify the filePath property of " + DestructiveBean.class);
        }

        is = new FileInputStream(filePath);
    }

    public void destroy() {

        System.out.println("Destroying Bean");

        if (is != null) {
            try {
                is.close();
                is = null;
            } catch (IOException ex) {
                System.err.println("WARN: An IOException occured"
                        + " trying to close the InputStream");
```

```
            }
        }
    }

    public void setFilePath(String filePath) {
        this.filePath = filePath;
    }

    public static void main(String[] args) throws Exception {

        GenericXmlApplicationContext ctx = new GenericXmlApplicationContext();
        ctx.load("classpath:lifecycle/disposeMethod.xml");
        ctx.refresh(); // Refresh the ApplicationContext after XML config file loaded

        DestructiveBean bean = (DestructiveBean) ctx.getBean("destructiveBean");

        System.out.println("Calling destroy()");
        ctx.destroy();
        System.out.println("Called destroy()");
    }
}
```

This code also defines a destroy() method, in which the FileInputStream is closed and set to null, releasing the resource and allowing it to be garbage collected. The main() method retrieves a bean of type DestructiveBean from the GenericXmlApplicationContext and then invokes its destroy() (which will in turn invoke the ConfigurableBeanFactory.destroySingletons() that was wrapped by the ApplicationContext), instructing Spring to destroy all the singletons it is managing. Both the initialization and destruction callbacks write a message to console output informing us that they have been called. In Listing 5-7, you can see the configuration for the destructiveBean bean (lifecycle/disposeMethod.xml).

Listing 5-7. Configuring a destroy-method Callback

```xml
<?xml version="1.0" encoding="UTF-8"?>
<beans xmlns="http://www.springframework.org/schema/beans"
    xmlns:xsi="http://www.w3.org/2001/XMLSchema-instance"
    xsi:schemaLocation="http://www.springframework.org/schema/beans
        http://www.springframework.org/schema/beans/spring-beans-3.1.xsd">

    <bean id="destructiveBean"
        class="com.apress.prospring3.ch5.lifecycle.DestructiveBean"
        destroy-method="destroy">
        <property name="filePath">
            <value>d:/temp/test.txt</value>
        </property>
    </bean>

</beans>
```

Notice that we have specified the destroy() method as the destruction callback using the destroy-method attribute. Running this example yields the following output:

```
Initializing Bean
Calling destroy()
Destroying Bean
Called destroy()
```

As you can see, Spring first invokes the initialization callback, and the DestructiveBean instance creates the FileInputStream instance and stores it. Next, during the call to destroy(), Spring iterates over the set of singletons it is managing, in this case just one, and invokes any destruction callbacks that are specified. This is where the DestructiveBean instance closes the FileInputStream and sets the reference to null.

Implementing the DisposableBean Interface

As with initialization callbacks, Spring provides an interface, in this case DisposableBean, that can be implemented by your beans as a mechanism for receiving destruction callbacks. The DisposableBean interface defines a single method, destroy(), which is called just before the bean is destroyed. Using this mechanism is orthogonal to using the InitializingBean interface to receive initialization callbacks. Listing 5-8 shows a modified implementation of the DestructiveBean class that implements the DisposableBean interface.

Listing 5-8. Implementing DisposableBean

```
package com.apress.prospring3.ch5.lifecycle;

import java.io.FileInputStream;
import java.io.IOException;
import java.io.InputStream;

import org.springframework.beans.factory.DisposableBean;
import org.springframework.beans.factory.InitializingBean;
import org.springframework.context.support.GenericXmlApplicationContext;

public class DestructiveBeanWithInterface implements InitializingBean,
        DisposableBean {

    private InputStream is = null;

    public String filePath = null;

    public void afterPropertiesSet() throws Exception {

        System.out.println("Initializing Bean");

        if (filePath == null) {
            throw new IllegalArgumentException(
                    "You must specify the filePath property of " + DestructiveBean.class);
        }

        is = new FileInputStream(filePath);
    }

    public void destroy() {

        System.out.println("Destroying Bean");

        if (is != null) {
            try {
```

```
                is.close();
                is = null;
            } catch (IOException ex) {
                System.err.println("WARN: An IOException occured"
                        + " trying to close the InputStream");
            }
        }
    }

    public void setFilePath(String filePath) {
        this.filePath = filePath;
    }

    public static void main(String[] args) throws Exception {
        GenericXmlApplicationContext ctx = new GenericXmlApplicationContext();
        ctx.load("classpath:lifecycle/disposeInterface.xml");
        ctx.refresh();

        DestructiveBeanWithInterface bean = (DestructiveBeanWithInterface)
            ctx.getBean("destructiveBean");

        System.out.println("Calling destroySingletons()");
        ctx.destroy();
        System.out.println("Called destroySingletons()");

    }
}
```

Again, there is not much difference between the code (highlighted in bold) that uses the callback method mechanism and the code that uses the callback interface mechanism. In this case, we even used the same method names. Listing 5-9 shows an amended configuration for this example (lifecycle/disposeInterface.xml).

Listing 5-9. Configuration Using the DisposableBean Interface

```xml
<?xml version="1.0" encoding="UTF-8"?>
<beans xmlns="http://www.springframework.org/schema/beans"
    xmlns:xsi="http://www.w3.org/2001/XMLSchema-instance"
    xsi:schemaLocation="http://www.springframework.org/schema/beans
        http://www.springframework.org/schema/beans/spring-beans-3.1.xsd">

    <bean id="destructiveBean"
        class="com.apress.prospring3.ch5.lifecycle.DestructiveBeanWithInterface">
        <property name="filePath">
            <value>d:/temp/test.txt</value>
        </property>
    </bean>

</beans>
```

As you can see, aside from the different class name; the only difference is the omission of the destroy-method attribute.

Running this example yields the following output:

```
Initializing Bean
Calling destroy()
Destroying Bean
Called destroy()
```

Again, the output from the two different mechanisms is exactly the same.

Using JSR-250 @PreDestroy Annotation

The third way is to use the JSR-250 life-cycle @PreDestroy annotation, which corresponds to the @PostConstruct annotation. Listing 5-10 is the version of the DestructiveBean that uses both @PostConstruct and @PreDestroy in the same class to perform program initialization and destroy actions.

Listing 5-10. Implementing DisposableBean Using @PreDestroy

```
package com.apress.prospring3.ch5.lifecycle;

import java.io.FileInputStream;
import java.io.IOException;
import java.io.InputStream;

import javax.annotation.PostConstruct;
import javax.annotation.PreDestroy;

import org.springframework.context.support.GenericXmlApplicationContext;

public class DestructiveBeanWithJSR250 {

    private InputStream is = null;

    public String filePath = null;

    @PostConstruct
    public void afterPropertiesSet() throws Exception {

        System.out.println("Initializing Bean");

        if (filePath == null) {
            throw new IllegalArgumentException(
                    "You must specify the filePath property of " + DestructiveBean.class);
        }

        is = new FileInputStream(filePath);
    }

    @PreDestroy
    public void destroy() {

        System.out.println("Destroying Bean");

        if (is != null) {
```

```
            try {
                is.close();
                is = null;
            } catch (IOException ex) {
                System.err.println("WARN: An IOException occured"
                        + " trying to close the InputStream");
            }
        }
    }

    public void setFilePath(String filePath) {
        this.filePath = filePath;
    }

    public static void main(String[] args) throws Exception {

        GenericXmlApplicationContext ctx = new GenericXmlApplicationContext();
        ctx.load("classpath:lifecycle/disposeJSR250.xml");
        ctx.refresh();

        DestructiveBeanWithJSR250 bean = (DestructiveBeanWithJSR250)
            ctx.getBean("destructiveBean");

        System.out.println("Calling destroy()");
        ctx.destroy();
        System.out.println("Called destroy()");
    }
}
```

Listing 5-11 is the XML configuration for the bean, which adds the <context:annotation-config> tag (lifecycle/disposeJSR250.xml).

Listing 5-11. Configuration Using the DisposableBean with JSR-250 Annotation

```xml
<?xml version="1.0" encoding="UTF-8"?>
<beans xmlns="http://www.springframework.org/schema/beans"
    xmlns:xsi="http://www.w3.org/2001/XMLSchema-instance"
    xmlns:context="http://www.springframework.org/schema/context"
    xsi:schemaLocation="http://www.springframework.org/schema/beans
        http://www.springframework.org/schema/beans/spring-beans-3.1.xsd
        http://www.springframework.org/schema/context
        http://www.springframework.org/schema/context/spring-context-3.1.xsd">

    <context:annotation-config/>

    <bean id="destructiveBean"
        class="com.apress.prospring3.ch5.lifecycle.DestructiveBeanWithJSR250">
        <property name="filePath">
            <value>d:/temp/test.txt</value>
        </property>
    </bean>

</beans>
```

Running the program will give the same output as the other two mechanisms.

The destruction callback is an ideal mechanism for ensuring that your applications shut down gracefully and do not leave resources open or in an inconsistent state. However, you still have to decide whether to use the destruction method callback, the DisposableBean interface, or the @PreDestroy annotation. Again, let the requirements of your application drive your decision in this respect; use the method callback where portability is an issue, and use the DisposableBean interface or a JSR-250 annotation to reduce the amount of configuration required.

Order of Resolution

As with the case of bean creation, you can use all mechanisms on the same bean instance for bean destruction. In this case, Spring invokes the method annotated with @PreDestroy first and then DisposableBean.destroy(), followed by your destroy method.

Using a Shutdown Hook

The only drawback of the destruction callbacks in Spring is that they are not fired automatically; you need to remember to call AbstractApplicationContext.destroy() before your application is closed. When your application runs as a servlet, you can simply call destroy() in the servlet's destroy() method. However, in a stand-alone application, things are not quite so simple, especially if you have multiple exit points out of your application. Fortunately, there is a solution. Java allows you to create a shutdown hook, a thread that is executed just before the application shuts down. This is the perfect way to invoke the destroy() method of your AbstractApplicationContext (which was being extended by all concrete ApplicationContext implementations). The easiest way to take advantage of this mechanism is to use the AbstractApplicationContext's registerShutdownHook() method. The method automatically instructs Spring to register a shutdown hook of the underlying JVM runtime. This is shown in Listing 5-12.

Listing 5-12. Registering a Shutdown Hook

```
package com.apress.prospring3.ch5.lifecycle;

import org.springframework.context.support.GenericXmlApplicationContext;

public class ShutdownHookExample {

    public static void main(String[] args) {
        GenericXmlApplicationContext ctx = new GenericXmlApplicationContext();
        ctx.load("classpath:lifecycle/disposeInterface.xml");
        ctx.registerShutdownHook();
        ctx.refresh();

        DestructiveBeanWithInterface bean = (DestructiveBeanWithInterface)
            ctx.getBean("destructiveBean");
    }
}
```

Running this example results in the following output:

```
Initializing Bean
Destroying Bean
```

As you can see, the destroy() method is invoked, even though we didn't write any code to invoke it explicitly as the application was shutting down.

Making Your Beans "Spring Aware"

One of the biggest selling points of Dependency Injection over Dependency Lookup as a mechanism for achieving Inversion of Control is that your beans do not need to be aware of the implementation of the container that is managing them. To a bean that uses constructor or setter injection, the Spring container is the same as the container provided by Google Guice or PicoContainer. However, in certain circumstances, you may need a bean that is using Dependency Injection to obtain its dependencies so it can interact with the container for some other reason. An example of this may be a bean that automatically configures a shutdown hook for you, and thus it needs access to the ApplicationContext. In other cases, a bean may want to know what its name (i.e., the bean name that was assigned within the current ApplicationContext) is so it can perform some additional processing based on this name.

That said, this feature is really intended for internal Spring use. Giving the name some kind of business meaning is generally a bad idea and can lead to configuration problems where bean names have to be artificially manipulated to support their business meaning. However, we have found that being able to have a bean find out its name at runtime is really useful for logging. Consider a situation where you have many beans of the same type running under different configurations. The bean name can be included in log messages to help you differentiate between which one is generating errors and which ones are working fine when something goes wrong.

Using the BeanNameAware Interface

The BeanNameAware interface, which can be implemented by a bean that wants to obtain its own name, has a single method: setBeanName(String). Spring calls the setBeanName() method after it has finished configuring your bean but before any life-cycle callbacks (initialization or destroy) are called (refer to Figure 5-1). In most cases, the implementation of the setBeanName() interface is just a single line that stores the value passed in by the container in a field for use later. Listing 5-13 shows a simple bean that obtains its name using BeanNameAware and then later uses this bean name when writing log messages.

Listing 5-13. Implementing BeanNameAware

```
package com.apress.prospring3.ch5.interaction;

import org.apache.commons.logging.Log;
import org.apache.commons.logging.LogFactory;
import org.springframework.beans.factory.BeanNameAware;

public class LoggingBean implements BeanNameAware {

    private static final Log log = LogFactory.getLog(LoggingBean.class);

    private String beanName = null;

    public void setBeanName(String beanName) {
        this.beanName = beanName;
    }

    public void someOperation() {
        if(log.isInfoEnabled()) {
            log.info("Bean [" + beanName + "] - someOperation()");
        }
    }
}
```

This implementation is fairly trivial. Remember that BeanNameAware.setBeanName() is called before the first instance of the bean is returned to your application via a call to ApplicationContext.getBean(), so there is no need to check to see whether the bean name is available in the someOperation() method. Listing 5-14 shows a simple configuration for this example (interaction/logging.xml).

Listing 5-14. Configuring the LoggingBean Example

```
<?xml version="1.0" encoding="UTF-8"?>
<beans xmlns="http://www.springframework.org/schema/beans"
    xmlns:xsi="http://www.w3.org/2001/XMLSchema-instance"
    xsi:schemaLocation="http://www.springframework.org/schema/beans
        http://www.springframework.org/schema/beans/spring-beans-3.1.xsd">

    <bean id="loggingBean" class="com.apress.prospring3.ch5.interaction.LoggingBean"/>
</beans>
```

As you can see, no special configuration is required to take advantage of the BeanNameAware interface. In Listing 5-15 you can see a simple example application that retrieves the LoggingBean instance from the ApplicationContext and then calls the someOperation() method (interaction/logging.xml). class

Listing 5-15. The LoggingBeanExample Class

```
package com.apress.prospring3.ch5.interaction;

import org.springframework.context.support.GenericXmlApplicationContext;

public class LoggingBeanExample {

    public static void main(String[] args) {
        GenericXmlApplicationContext ctx = new GenericXmlApplicationContext();
        ctx.load("classpath:interaction/logging.xml");
        ctx.refresh();

        LoggingBean bean = (LoggingBean) ctx.getBean("loggingBean");
        bean.someOperation();
    }
}
```

This example generates the following log output—notice the inclusion of the bean name in the log message for the call to someOperation():

```
Loading XML bean definitions from class path resource [interaction/logging.xml]
Refreshing org.springframework.context.support.GenericXmlApplicationContext@5dccce3c: startup
date [Sun Sep 25 13:40:04 CST 2011]; root of context hierarchy
Pre-instantiating singletons in
org.springframework.beans.factory.support.DefaultListableBeanFactory@7ec5495e: defining beans
[loggingBean]; root of factory hierarchy
Bean [loggingBean] - someOperation()
```

Using the BeanNameAware interface is really quite simple, and it is put to good use when you are improving the quality of your log messages. Avoid being tempted to give your bean names business meaning just because you can access them; by doing so, you are coupling your classes to Spring for a feature that brings negligible benefit. If your beans need some kind of name internally, then have them implement an interface such as Nameable (which is specific to your application) with a method setName()

and then give each bean a name using Dependency Injection. This way, you can keep the names you use for configuration concise, and you won't need to manipulate your configuration unnecessarily to give your beans names with business meaning.

Using the ApplicationContextAware Interface

Using the ApplicationContextAware interface, it is possible for your beans to get a reference to the ApplicationContext that configured them. The main reason this interface was created was to allow a bean to access Spring's ApplicationContext in your application, such as acquire other Spring beans programmatically, using getBean(). You should, however, avoid this practice and use Dependency Injection to provide your beans with their collaborators. If you use the lookup-based getBean() approach to obtain dependencies when you can use Dependency Injection, you are adding unnecessary complexity to your beans and coupling them to the Spring Framework without good reason.

Of course, the ApplicationContext isn't just used to look up beans; it performs a great many other tasks. As you saw previously, one of these tasks is to destroy all singletons, notifying each of them in turn before doing so. In the previous section, you saw how to create a shutdown hook to ensure that the ApplicationContext is instructed to destroy all singletons before the application shuts down. By using the ApplicationContextAware interface, you can build a bean that can be configured in an ApplicationContext to create and configure a shutdown hook bean automatically. Listing 5-16 shows the code for this bean.

Listing 5-16. The ShutdownHookBean Class

```
package com.apress.prospring3.ch5.interaction;

import org.springframework.beans.BeansException;
import org.springframework.context.ApplicationContext;
import org.springframework.context.ApplicationContextAware;
import org.springframework.context.support.GenericApplicationContext;

public class ShutdownHookBean implements ApplicationContextAware {

    private ApplicationContext ctx;

    public void setApplicationContext(ApplicationContext ctx)
        throws BeansException {

        if (ctx instanceof GenericApplicationContext) {
            ((GenericApplicationContext) ctx).registerShutdownHook();
        }

    }
}
```

Most of this code should seem familiar to you by now. The ApplicationContextAware interface defines a single method, setApplicationContext(ApplicationContext), which Spring calls to pass your bean a reference to its ApplicationContext. In Listing 5-16, the ShutdownHookBean class checks to see whether the ApplicationContext is of type GenericApplicationContext, meaning it supports the registerShutdownHook() method; if it does, it will register a shutdown hook to the ApplicationContext. Listing 5-17 shows how to configure this bean to work with the DestructiveBeanWithInterface bean used in the previous section (interaction/shutdownHook.xml).

Listing 5-17. Configuring the ShutdownHookBean

```xml
<?xml version="1.0" encoding="UTF-8"?>
<beans xmlns="http://www.springframework.org/schema/beans"
    xmlns:xsi="http://www.w3.org/2001/XMLSchema-instance"
    xsi:schemaLocation="http://www.springframework.org/schema/beans
        http://www.springframework.org/schema/beans/spring-beans-3.1.xsd">

    <bean id="destructiveBean"
        class="com.apress.prospring3.ch5.lifecycle.DestructiveBeanWithInterface">
        <property name="filePath">
            <value>d:/temp/test.txt</value>
        </property>
    </bean>

    <bean id="shutdownHook"
        class="com.apress.prospring3.ch5.interaction.ShutdownHookBean"/>
</beans>
```

Notice that no special configuration is required. Listing 5-18 shows a simple example application that uses the ShutdownHookBean to manage the destruction of singleton beans.

Listing 5-18. Using ShutdownHookBean

```java
package com.apress.prospring3.ch5.interaction;

import org.springframework.context.support.GenericXmlApplicationContext;

import com.apress.prospring3.ch5.lifecycle.DestructiveBeanWithInterface;

public class ShutdownHookBeanExample {

    public static void main(String[] args) {

        GenericXmlApplicationContext ctx = new GenericXmlApplicationContext();
        ctx.load("interaction/shutdownHook.xml");
        ctx.refresh();

        DestructiveBeanWithInterface bean =
            (DestructiveBeanWithInterface) ctx.getBean("destructiveBean");
    }
}
```

This code should seem quite familiar to you. When Spring bootstraps the ApplicationContext and the destructiveBean defined in the configuration (since the bean implemented the ApplicationContextAware interface), Spring passes the reference of the ApplicationContext to the shutdownHook bean for registering the shutdown hook. Running this example yields the following output, as expected:

```
Initializing Bean
Destroying Bean
```

As you can see, even though no calls to destroy() are in the main application, the ShutdownHookBean is registered as a shutdown hook, and it calls destroy() just before the application shuts down.

Use FactoryBeans

One of the problems that you will face when using Spring is how to create and then inject dependencies that cannot be created simply by using the new operator. To overcome this problem, Spring provides the FactoryBean interface that acts as an adaptor for objects that cannot be created and managed using the standard Spring semantics. Typically, you use FactoryBeans to create beans that you cannot use the new operator to create such as those you access through static factory methods, although this is not always the case. Simply put, a FactoryBean is a bean that acts as a factory for other beans. FactoryBeans are configured within your ApplicationContext like any normal bean, but when Spring uses the FactoryBean interface to satisfy a dependency or lookup request, it does not return the FactoryBean; instead, it invokes the FactoryBean.getObject() method and returns the result of that invocation.

FactoryBeans are used to great effect in Spring; the most noticeable uses are the creation of transactional proxies, which we cover in Chapter 13, and the automatic retrieval of resources from a JNDI context. However, FactoryBeans are useful not just for building the internals of Spring; you'll find them really useful when you build your own applications, because they allow you to manage many more resources using IoC than would otherwise be available.

Custom FactoryBean Example: The MessageDigestFactoryBean

Often the projects that we work on require some kind of cryptographic processing; typically, this involves generating a message digest or hash of a user's password to be stored in a database. In Java, the MessageDigest class provides functionality for creating a digest of any arbitrary data. MessageDigest itself is abstract, and you obtain concrete implementations by calling MessageDigest.getInstance() and passing in the name of the digest algorithm you want to use. For instance, if we want to use the MD5 algorithm to create a digest, we use the following code to create the MessageDigest instance:

```
MessageDigest md5 = MessageDigest.getInstance("MD5");
```

If we want to use Spring to manage the creation of the MessageDigest object, the best we can do without a FactoryBean is have a property, algorithmName, on our bean and then use an initialization callback to call MessageDigest.getInstance(). Using a FactoryBean, we can encapsulate this logic inside a bean. Then any beans that require a MessageDigest instance can simply declare a property, messageDigest, and use the FactoryBean to obtain the instance. Listing 5-19 shows an implementation of FactoryBean that does just this.

Listing 5-19. *The MessageDigestFactoryBean Class*

```
package com.apress.prospring3.ch5.factory;

import java.security.MessageDigest;

import org.springframework.beans.factory.FactoryBean;
import org.springframework.beans.factory.InitializingBean;

public class MessageDigestFactoryBean implements
        FactoryBean<MessageDigest>, InitializingBean {

    private String algorithmName = "MD5";

    private MessageDigest messageDigest = null;

    public MessageDigest getObject() throws Exception {
```

```
        return messageDigest;
    }


    public Class<MessageDigest> getObjectType() {
        return MessageDigest.class;
    }


    public boolean isSingleton() {
        return true;
    }

    public void afterPropertiesSet() throws Exception {
        messageDigest = MessageDigest.getInstance(algorithmName);
    }

    public void setAlgorithmName(String algorithmName) {
        this.algorithmName = algorithmName;
    }
}
```

The FactoryBean interface declares three methods: getObject(), getObjectType(), and isSingleton(). Spring calls the getObject() method to retrieve the object created by the FactoryBean. This is the actual object that is passed to other beans that use the FactoryBean as a collaborator. In Listing 5-19, you can see that the MessageDigestFactoryBean passes a clone of the stored MessageDigest instance that is created in the InitializingBean.afterPropertiesSet() callback.

The getObjectType() method allows you to tell Spring what type of object your FactoryBean will return. This can be null if the return type is unknown in advance (for example, the FactoryBean creates different types of objects depending on the configuration, which will be determined only after the FactoryBean is initialized), but if you specify a type, Spring can use it for autowiring purposes. We return MessageDigest as our type (in this case a class, but try to return an interface type and have the FactoryBean instantiate the concrete implementation class, unless necessary). The reason is that we do not know what concrete type will be returned (not that it matters because all beans will define their dependencies using MessageDigest anyway).

The isSingleton() property allows you to inform Spring whether the FactoryBean is managing a singleton instance. Remember that by setting the singleton attribute of the FactoryBean's <bean> tag, you tell Spring about the singleton status of the FactoryBean itself, not the objects it is returning.

Now let's see how the FactoryBean is employed in an application. In Listing 5-20, you can see a simple bean that maintains two MessageDigest instances and then displays the digests of a message passed to its digest() method.

Listing 5-20. The MessageDigester Class

```
package com.apress.prospring3.ch5.factory;

import java.security.MessageDigest;

public class MessageDigester {

    private MessageDigest digest1 = null;
    private MessageDigest digest2 = null;
```

```
    public void setDigest1(MessageDigest digest1) {
        this.digest1 = digest1;
    }

    public void setDigest2(MessageDigest digest2) {
        this.digest2 = digest2;
    }

    public void digest(String msg) {
        System.out.println("Using digest1");
        digest(msg, digest1);

        System.out.println("Using digest2");
        digest(msg, digest2);
    }

    private void digest(String msg, MessageDigest digest) {
        System.out.println("Using alogrithm: " + digest.getAlgorithm());
        digest.reset();
        byte[] bytes = msg.getBytes();
        byte[] out = digest.digest(bytes);
        System.out.println(out);
    }
}
```

Listing 5-21 shows a simple BeanFactory configuration that configures two
MessageDigestFactoryBeans, one for the SHA1 algorithm and the other using the default (MD5)
algorithm (factory/factory.xml).

Listing 5-21. Configuring FactoryBeans

```xml
<?xml version="1.0" encoding="UTF-8"?>
<beans xmlns="http://www.springframework.org/schema/beans"
    xmlns:xsi="http://www.w3.org/2001/XMLSchema-instance"
    xsi:schemaLocation="http://www.springframework.org/schema/beans
        http://www.springframework.org/schema/beans/spring-beans-3.1.xsd">

    <bean id="shaDigest" class="com.apress.prospring3.ch5.factory.MessageDigestFactoryBean">
        <property name="algorithmName">
            <value>SHA1</value>
        </property>
    </bean>

    <bean id="defaultDigest"
        class="com.apress.prospring3.ch5.factory.MessageDigestFactoryBean"/>

    <bean id="digester"
        class="com.apress.prospring3.ch5.factory.MessageDigester">
        <property name="digest1">
            <ref local="shaDigest"/>
        </property>
        <property name="digest2">
            <ref local="defaultDigest"/>
        </property>
```

```
    </bean>
</beans>
```

As you can see, not only have we configured the two MessageDigestFactoryBeans, but we have also configured a MessageDigester, using the two MessageDigestFactoryBeans, to provide values for the digest1 and digest2 properties. For the defaultDigest bean, since the algorithmName property was not specified, no injection will happen, and the default algorithm (i.e., MD5) that was coded in the class will be used. In Listing 5-22, you see a basic example class that retrieves the MessageDigester bean from the BeanFactory and creates the digest of a simple message.

Listing 5-22. Using MessageDigester

```
package com.apress.prospring3.ch5.factory;

import org.springframework.context.support.GenericXmlApplicationContext;

public class MessageDigestExample {

    public static void main(String[] args) {
        GenericXmlApplicationContext ctx = new GenericXmlApplicationContext();
        ctx.load("classpath:factory/factory.xml");
        ctx.refresh();

        MessageDigester digester = (MessageDigester) ctx.getBean("digester");
        digester.digest("Hello World!");

    }
}
```

Running this example gives the following output:

```
Using digest1
Using alogrithm: SHA1
[B@786c730
Using digest2
Using alogrithm: MD5
[B@217f242c
```

As you can see, the MessageDigest bean is provided with two MessageDigest implementations, SHA1 and MD5, despite that no MessageDigest beans are configured in the BeanFactory. This is the FactoryBean at work.

FactoryBeans are the perfect solution when you are working with classes that cannot be created using the new operator. If you work with objects that are created using a factory method and you want to use these classes in a Spring application, then create a FactoryBean to act as an adaptor, allowing your classes to take full advantage of Spring's IoC capabilities.

Accessing a FactoryBean Directly

Given that Spring automatically satisfies any references to a FactoryBean by the objects produced by that FactoryBean, you may be wondering whether you can actually access the FactoryBean directly. The answer is "yes."

Accessing the FactoryBean is actually very simple: you simply prefix the bean name with an ampersand in the call to getBean(), as shown in Listing 5-23.

Listing 5-23. *Accessing FactoryBeans Directly*

```
package com.apress.prospring3.ch5.factory;

import java.security.MessageDigest;

import org.springframework.context.support.GenericXmlApplicationContext;

public class AccessingFactoryBeans {

    public static void main(String[] args) {
        GenericXmlApplicationContext ctx = new GenericXmlApplicationContext();
        ctx.load("classpath:factory/factory.xml");
        ctx.refresh();

        MessageDigest digest = (MessageDigest) ctx.getBean("shaDigest");

        MessageDigestFactoryBean factoryBean =
            (MessageDigestFactoryBean) ctx.getBean("&shaDigest");

      try {
        MessageDigest shaDigest = factoryBean.getObject();
        System.out.println(shaDigest.digest("Hello world".getBytes()));
      } catch (Exception ex) {
        ex.printStackTrace();
      }
    }
}
```

This feature is used in a few places in the Spring code, but your application should really have no reason to use it. The FactoryBean interface is intended to be used as a piece of supporting infrastructure to allow you to use more of your application's classes in an IoC setting. Avoid accessing the FactoryBean directly and then invoking its getObject() manually, and let Spring do it for you; if you do this manually, you are making extra work for yourself and are unnecessarily coupling your application to a specific implementation detail that could quite easily change in the future.

Using the factory-bean and factory-method Attributes

Sometimes you need to instantiate JavaBeans that were provided by a non-Spring-powered third-party application. You don't know how to instantiate that class, but you know that the third-party application did provide a class that can be used to get an instance of the JavaBean that your Spring application required. In this case, Spring bean's factory-bean and factory-method attributes in the <bean> tag can be used.

To take a look at how it works, Listing 5-24 shows another version of the MessageDigestFactory that provides a method to return a MessageDigest bean.

Listing 5-24. *The MessageDigestFactory Class*

```
package com.apress.prospring3.ch5.factory;

import java.security.MessageDigest;
```

```
public class MessageDigestFactory {

    private String algorithmName = "MD5";

    public MessageDigest createInstance() throws Exception {
        return MessageDigest.getInstance(algorithmName);
    }

    public void setAlgorithmName(String algorithmName) {
        this.algorithmName = algorithmName;
    }
}
```

Listing 5-25 shows how to configure the factory method for getting the corresponding MessageDigest bean instance (factory/factoryMethod.xml).

Listing 5-25. Configuring MessageDigestFactory

```
<?xml version="1.0" encoding="UTF-8"?>
<beans xmlns="http://www.springframework.org/schema/beans"
    xmlns:xsi="http://www.w3.org/2001/XMLSchema-instance"
    xsi:schemaLocation="http://www.springframework.org/schema/beans
        http://www.springframework.org/schema/beans/spring-beans-3.1.xsd">

    <bean id="shaDigestFactory"
        class="com.apress.prospring3.ch5.factory.MessageDigestFactory">
        <property name="algorithmName">
            <value>SHA1</value>
        </property>
    </bean>

    <bean id="defaultDigestFactory"
        class="com.apress.prospring3.ch5.factory.MessageDigestFactory"/>

    <bean id="shaDigest"
        factory-bean="shaDigestFactory"
        factory-method="createInstance">
    </bean>

    <bean id="defaultDigest"
        factory-bean="defaultDigestFactory"
        factory-method="createInstance"/>

    <bean id="digester"
        class="com.apress.prospring3.ch5.factory.MessageDigester">
        <property name="digest1">
            <ref local="shaDigest"/>
        </property>
        <property name="digest2">
            <ref local="defaultDigest"/>
        </property>
    </bean>
</beans>
```

Notice that two digest factory beans were defined, one using SHA1 and the other using the default algorithm. Then for the beans shaDigest and defaultDigest, we instructed Spring to instantiate the beans by using the corresponding message digest factory bean (factory-bean), and we specified the method to use to obtain the bean instance (factory-method). Listing 5-26 shows the testing class.

Listing 5-26. MessageDigestFactory in Action

```
package com.apress.prospring3.ch5.factory;

import org.springframework.context.support.GenericXmlApplicationContext;

public class MessageDigestFactoryExample {

    public static void main(String[] args) {
        GenericXmlApplicationContext ctx = new GenericXmlApplicationContext();
        ctx.load("classpath:factory/factoryMethod.xml");
        ctx.refresh();

        MessageDigester digester = (MessageDigester) ctx.getBean("digester");
        digester.digest("Hello World!");

    }
}
```

Running the program will generate the following output:

```
Using digest1
Using alogrithm: SHA1
[B@877ef83
Using digest2
Using alogrithm: MD5
[B@7a0d85cc
```

JavaBeans PropertyEditors

For those of you not entirely familiar with JavaBeans concepts, a PropertyEditor is an interface that converts a property's value to and from its native type representation into a String. Originally, this was conceived as a way to allow property values to be entered, as String values, into an editor and have them transformed into the correct type. However, because PropertyEditors are inherently lightweight classes, they have found uses in many different settings, including Spring.

Because a good portion of property values in a Spring-based application start life in the BeanFactory configuration file, they are essentially Strings. However, the property that these values are set on may not be String-typed. So, to save you from having to create a load of String-typed properties artificially, Spring allows you to define PropertyEditors to manage the conversion of String-based property values into the correct types.

The Built-in PropertyEditors

As of version 3.1, Spring comes with 13 built-in PropertyEditor implementations that are preregistered with the BeanFactory. Listing 5-27 shows a simple bean that declares 13 properties, one for each of the types supported by the built-in PropertyEditors.

Listing 5-27. Using the Built-in PropertyEditors

```
package com.apress.prospring3.ch5.pe;

import java.io.File;
import java.io.InputStream;
import java.net.URL;
import java.util.Date;
import java.util.List;
import java.util.Locale;
import java.util.Properties;
import java.util.regex.Pattern;

import org.springframework.context.support.GenericXmlApplicationContext;

public class PropertyEditorBean {

    private byte[] bytes;                // ByteArrayPropertyEditor

    private Class cls;                   // ClassEditor

    private Boolean trueOrFalse;         // CustomBooleanEditor

    private List<String> stringList;     // CustomCollectionEditor

    private Date date;                   // CustomDateEditor

    private Float floatValue;            // CustomNumberEditor

    private File file;                   // FileEditor

    private InputStream stream;          // InputStreamEditor

    private Locale locale;               // LocaleEditor

    private Pattern pattern;             // PatternEditor

    private Properties properties;       // PropertiesEditor

    private String trimString;           // StringTrimmerEditor

    private URL url;                     // URLEditor

    public void setCls(Class cls) {
        System.out.println("Setting class: " + cls.getName());
        this.cls = cls;
    }

    public void setFile(File file) {
        System.out.println("Setting file: " + file.getName());
        this.file = file;
    }

    public void setLocale(Locale locale) {
```

```java
        System.out.println("Setting locale: " + locale.getDisplayName());
        this.locale = locale;
    }

    public void setProperties(Properties properties) {
        System.out.println("Loaded " + properties.size() + " properties");
        this.properties = properties;
    }

    public void setUrl(URL url) {
        System.out.println("Setting URL: " + url.toExternalForm());
        this.url = url;
    }

    public void setBytes(byte[] bytes) {
        System.out.println("Adding " + bytes.length + " bytes");
        this.bytes = bytes;
    }

    public void setTrueOrFalse(Boolean trueOrFalse) {
        System.out.println("Setting Boolean: " + trueOrFalse);
        this.trueOrFalse = trueOrFalse;
    }

    public void setStringList(List<String> stringList) {
        System.out.println("Setting string list with size: "
            + stringList.size());
        this.stringList = stringList;
        for (String string: stringList) {
            System.out.println("String member: " + string);
        }
    }

    public void setDate(Date date) {
        System.out.println("Setting date: " + date);
        this.date = date;
    }

    public void setFloatValue(Float floatValue) {
        System.out.println("Setting float value: " + floatValue);
        this.floatValue = floatValue;
    }

    public void setStream(InputStream stream) {
        System.out.println("Setting stream: " + stream);
        this.stream = stream;
    }

    public void setPattern(Pattern pattern) {
        System.out.println("Setting pattern: " + pattern);
        this.pattern = pattern;
    }

    public void setTrimString(String trimString) {
```

```
        System.out.println("Setting trim string: " + trimString);
        this.trimString = trimString;
    }

    public static void main(String[] args) {
        GenericXmlApplicationContext ctx = new GenericXmlApplicationContext();
        ctx.load("classpath:pe/builtin.xml");
        ctx.refresh();

        PropertyEditorBean bean =
            (PropertyEditorBean) ctx.getBean("builtInSample");
    }
}
```

In Listing 5-27, you can see that `PropertyEditorBean` has 13 properties, each corresponding to one of the built-in `PropertyEditors`. In Listing 5-28, you can see a simple `BeanFactory` configuration specifying values for all of these properties (`pe/builtin.xml`).

Listing 5-28. Configuration Using PropertyEditors

```xml
<?xml version="1.0" encoding="UTF-8"?>
<beans xmlns="http://www.springframework.org/schema/beans"
    xmlns:xsi="http://www.w3.org/2001/XMLSchema-instance"
    xmlns:util="http://www.springframework.org/schema/util"
    xsi:schemaLocation="http://www.springframework.org/schema/beans
        http://www.springframework.org/schema/beans/spring-beans-3.1.xsd
        http://www.springframework.org/schema/util
        http://www.springframework.org/schema/util/spring-util-3.1.xsd">

    <bean class="org.springframework.beans.factory.config.CustomEditorConfigurer">
        <property name="customEditors">
            <map>
                <entry key="java.util.Date">
                    <bean class="org.springframework.beans.propertyeditors.CustomDateEditor">
                        <constructor-arg>
                            <bean class="java.text.SimpleDateFormat">
                                <constructor-arg value="yyyy-MM-dd" />
                            </bean>
                        </constructor-arg>
                        <constructor-arg value="true" />
                    </bean>
                </entry>
                <entry key="java.lang.String">
                    <bean
class="org.springframework.beans.propertyeditors.StringTrimmerEditor">
                        <constructor-arg value="true" />
                    </bean>
                </entry>
            </map>
        </property>
    </bean>

    <bean id="builtInSample" class="com.apress.prospring3.ch5.pe.PropertyEditorBean">
        <property name="bytes">
```

```xml
                    <value>Hello World</value>
                </property>
                <property name="cls">
                    <value>java.lang.String</value>
                </property>
                <property name="trueOrFalse">
                    <value>true</value>
                </property>
                <property name="stringList">
                    <util:list>
                        <value>String member 1</value>
                        <value>String member 2</value>
                    </util:list>
                </property>
                <property name="date">
                    <value>2011-12-29</value>
                </property>
                <property name="floatValue">
                    <value>123.45678</value>
                </property>
                <property name="file">
                    <value>classpath:test.txt</value>
                </property>
                <property name="stream">
                    <value>classpath:test.txt</value>
                </property>
                <property name="locale">
                    <value>en_US</value>
                </property>
                <property name="pattern">
                    <value>a*b</value>
                </property>
                <property name="properties">
                    <value>
                        name=foo
                        age=19
                    </value>
                </property>
                <property name="trimString">
                    <value>   String need trimming   </value>
                </property>
                <property name="url">
                    <value>http://www.springframework.org</value>
                </property>
            </bean>
</beans>
```

As you can see, although all the properties on the PropertyEditorBean are not Strings, the values for the properties are specified as simple Strings. Also note that we registered the CustomDateEditor and StringTrimmerEditor, since those two editors were not registered by default in Spring. Running this example yields the following output:

```
Adding 11 bytes
Setting class: java.lang.String
Setting Boolean: true
Setting string list with size: 2
String member: String member 1
String member: String member 2
Setting date: Thu Dec 29 00:00:00 CST 2011
Setting float value: 123.45678
Setting file: test.txt
Setting stream: java.io.BufferedInputStream@6490832e
Setting locale: English (US)
Setting pattern: a*b
Loaded 2 properties
Setting trim string: String need trimming
Setting URL: http://www.springframework.org
```

As you can see, Spring has, using the built-in PropertyEditors, converted the String representations of the various properties to the correct types. Table 5-1 summarizes the built-in PropertyEditors available in Spring.

Table 5-1. Spring PropertyEditors

PropertyEditor	Description
ByteArrayPropertyEditor	This PropertyEditor converts a String value into an array of bytes.
ClassEditor	The ClassEditor converts from a fully qualified class name into a Class instance. When using this PropertyEditor, be careful not to include any extraneous spaces on either side of the class name when using GenericXmlApplicationContext, because this results in a ClassNotFoundException.
CustomBooleanEditor	Convert a string into Java Boolean type.
CustomCollectionEditor	Converting a source collection (e.g., represent by the util namespace in Spring) into the target Collection type.
CustomDateEditor	Convert a string representation of date into a java.util.Date value. You need to register the CustomDateEditor in Spring's ApplicationContext with the desired date format.
CustomNumberEditor	Convert a string into the target number value, which can be Integer, Long, Float, and Double.
FileEditor	The FileEditor converts a String file path into a File instance. Spring does not check to see whether the file exists.
InputStreamEditor	Convert a string representation of a resource (e.g., file resource using file:D:/temp/test.txt or classpath:test.txt) into an input stream property.

PropertyEditor	Description
LocaleEditor	The LocaleEditor converts the String representation of a locale, such as en-GB, into a java.util.Locale instance.
Pattern	Converts a string into the JDK Pattern object or the other way round.
PropertiesEditor	PropertiesEditor converts a String in the format key1=value1 key2=value2 keyn=valuen into an instance of java.util.Properties with the corresponding properties configured.
StringTrimmerEditor	Performs trimming on the string values before injection. You need to explicitly register this editor.
URLEditor	The URLEditor converts a String representation of a URL into an instance of java.net.URL.

This set of PropertyEditors provides a good base for working with Spring and makes configuring your application with common components such as files and URLs much simpler.

Creating a Custom PropertyEditor

Although the built-in PropertyEditors cover some of the standard cases of property type conversion, there may come a time when you need to create your own PropertyEditor to support a class or a set of classes you are using in your application.

Spring has full support for registering custom PropertyEditors; the only downside is that the java.beans.PropertyEditor interface has a lot of methods, many of which are irrelevant to the task at hand—converting property types. Thankfully, JDK 5 or newer provides the PropertyEditorSupport class, which your own PropertyEditors can extend, leaving you to implement only a single method: setAsText().

Let's take a simple example to see implementing custom property editor in action. Suppose we have a Name class with just two properties, first name and last name. Listing 5-29 shows the class.

Listing 5-29. The Name Class

```
package com.apress.prospring3.ch5.pe;

public class Name {

    private String firstName;

    private String lastName;

    public Name() {
    }

    public Name(String firstName, String lastName) {
        this.firstName = firstName;
        this.lastName = lastName;
```

```
    }

    public String getFirstName() {
        return firstName;
    }

    public void setFirstName(String firstName) {
        this.firstName = firstName;
    }

    public String getLastName() {
        return lastName;
    }

    public void setLastName(String lastName) {
        this.lastName = lastName;
    }

    public String toString() {
        return "First name: " + firstName + " - Last name: " + lastName;
    }
}
```

To simplify the application configuration, let's develop a custom editor that converts a string with a space separator into the Name class's first name and last name, respectively. Listing 5-30 shows the custom property editor.

Listing 5-30. The NamePropertyEditor Class

```
package com.apress.prospring3.ch5.pe;

import java.beans.PropertyEditorSupport;

public class NamePropertyEditor extends PropertyEditorSupport {

    public void setAsText(String text) throws IllegalArgumentException {

        String[] name = text.split("\\s");

        Name result = new Name(name[0], name[1]);

        setValue(result);
    }
}
```

The editor is very simple. It extends JDK's PropertyEditorSupport class and implements the setAsText() method. In the method, we simply split the String into a string array with a space as the delimiter. Afterwards, an instance of Name class is instantiated, passing in the String before the space character as the first name and passing the String after the space character as the last name. Finally, the converted value is returned by calling the setValue() method with the result.

To use the NamePropertyEditor in our application, we need to register the editor in Spring's ApplicationContext. Listing 5-31 shows an ApplicationContext configuration that configures a CustomEditorConfigurer and the NamePropertyEditor (pe/custom.xml).

Listing 5-31. Using CustomEditorConfigurer

```xml
<?xml version="1.0" encoding="UTF-8"?>
<beans xmlns="http://www.springframework.org/schema/beans"
    xmlns:xsi="http://www.w3.org/2001/XMLSchema-instance"
    xsi:schemaLocation="http://www.springframework.org/schema/beans
        http://www.springframework.org/schema/beans/spring-beans-3.1.xsd">

    <bean name="customEditorConfigurer"
class="org.springframework.beans.factory.config.CustomEditorConfigurer">
        <property name="customEditors">
            <map>
                <entry key="com.apress.prospring3.ch5.pe.Name">
                    <bean class="com.apress.prospring3.ch5.pe.NamePropertyEditor"/>
                </entry>
            </map>
        </property>
    </bean>
    <bean id="exampleBean" class="com.apress.prospring3.ch5.pe.CustomEditorExample">
        <property name="name">
            <value>Clarence Ho</value>
        </property>
    </bean>
</beans>
```

You should notice three points in this configuration. The first is that the custom PropertyEditors are injected into the CustomEditorConfigurer class using the Map-typed customEditors property. The second point is that each entry in the Map represents a single PropertyEditor with the key of the entry being the name of the class for which the PropertyEditor is used. As you can see, the key for the NamePropertyEditor is com.apress.prospring3.ch5.pe.Name, which signifies that this is the class for which the editor should be used. The final point of interest here is that we used an anonymous bean declaration as the value of the single Map entry. No other bean needs to access this bean, so it needs no name, and as a result, you can declare it inside the <entry> tag.

Listing 5-32 shows the code for the CustomEditorExample class that is registered as a bean in Listing 5-31.

Listing 5-32. The CustomEditorExample Class

```java
package com.apress.prospring3.ch5.pe;

import org.springframework.context.support.GenericXmlApplicationContext;

public class CustomEditorExample {

    private Name name;

    public static void main(String[] args) {
        GenericXmlApplicationContext ctx = new GenericXmlApplicationContext();
        ctx.load("classpath:pe/custom.xml");
        ctx.refresh();

        CustomEditorExample bean =
          (CustomEditorExample) ctx.getBean("exampleBean");
```

```
        System.out.println(bean.getName());
    }

    public Name getName() {
        return name;
    }

    public void setName(Name name) {
        this.name = name;
    }
}
```

The previous code is nothing special. Run the example, and you will see the following output:

```
First name: Clarence - Last name: Ho
```

This is the output from the toString() method we implemented in the Name class, and you can see that the first name and last name of the Name object were correctly populated by Spring by using the configured NamePropertyEditor.

Starting from version 3, Spring introduced the Type Conversion and Field Formatting SPI, which provide a simpler and well-structured API in performing type conversion and field formatting. It's especially useful for web application development. Both the Type Conversion SPI and the Field Formatting API will be discussed in detail in Chapter 14.

More Spring ApplicationContext Configuration

So far, although we are discussing Spring's ApplicationContext, most of the features that we covered were mainly surrounding the BeanFactory interface wrapped by the ApplicationContext. In Spring, various implementations of the BeanFactory interface are responsible for bean instantiation, providing Dependency Injection and life-cycle support for beans managed by Spring. However, as stated, being an extension of the BeanFactory, ApplicationContext provides other useful functionalities as well.

The main function of the ApplicationContext is to provide a much richer framework on which to build your applications. An ApplicationContext is much more aware of the beans (compared with BeanFactory) that you configure within it, and in the case of many of the Spring infrastructure classes and interfaces, such as BeanFactoryPostProcessor, it interacts with them on your behalf, reducing the amount of code you need to write in order to use Spring.

The biggest benefit of using ApplicationContext is that it allows you to configure and manage Spring and Spring-managed resources in a completely declarative way. This means that wherever possible, Spring provides support classes to load an ApplicationContext into your application automatically, thus removing the need for you to write any code to access the ApplicationContext. In practice, this feature is currently available only when you are building web applications with Spring, which allows you to initialize Spring's ApplicationContext in the web application deployment descriptor. When using a stand-alone application, you can also initialize Spring's ApplicationContext by simple coding.

In addition to providing a model that is focused more on declarative configuration, the ApplicationContext supports the following additional features:

- Internationalization

- Event publication

- Resource management and access

- Additional life-cycle interfaces

- Improved automatic configuration of infrastructure components

In the following sections, we will discuss some of the most important features in `ApplicationContext` besides DI.

Internationalization with MessageSource

One area where Spring really excels is in support for internationalization (i18n). Using the `MessageSource` interface, your application can access String resources, called *messages*, stored in a variety of different languages. For each language you want to support in your application, you maintain a list of messages that are keyed to correspond to messages in other languages. For instance, if I wanted to display "The quick brown fox jumped over the lazy dog" in English and in Czech, I would create two messages, both keyed as `msg`; the one for English would say "The quick brown fox jumped over the lazy dog," and the one for Czech would say "Príšerne žlutoucký kun úpel dábelské ódy."

Although you don't need to use `ApplicationContext` to use `MessageSource`, the `ApplicationContext` interface actually extends `MessageSource` and provides special support for loading messages and for making them available in your environment. The automatic loading of messages is available in any environment, but automatic access is provided only in certain Spring-managed scenarios, such as when you are using Spring's MVC framework to build a web application. Although any class can implement `ApplicationContextAware` and thus access the automatically loaded messages, we suggest a better solution later in this chapter in the section "Using MessageSource in Stand-Alone Applications."

Before we continue, if you are unfamiliar with i18n support in Java, we suggest that you at least check out the JavaDocs (http://download.oracle.com/javase/6/docs/api/index.html) for the `Locale` and `ResourceBundle` classes.

Using ApplicationContext and MessageSource

Aside from `ApplicationContext`, Spring provides three `MessageSource` implementations: `ResourceBundleMessageSource`, `ReloadableResourceBundleMessageSource`, and `StaticMessageSource`. The `StaticMessageSource` is not really meant to be used in a production application because you can't configure it externally, and this is generally one of the main requirements when you are adding i18n capabilities to your application. The `ResourceBundleMessageSource` loads messages using a Java `ResourceBundle`. `ReloadableResourceBundleMessageSource` is essentially the same, except it supports scheduled reloading of the underlying source files.

All of the three `MessageSource` implementations also implement another interface called `HierarchicalMessageSource`, which allows for many `MessageSource` instances to be nested. This is key to the way `ApplicationContext` works with `MessageSources`.

To take advantage of `ApplicationContext`'s support for `MessageSource`, you must define a bean in your configuration of type `MessageSource` and with the name `messageSource`. `ApplicationContext` takes this `MessageSource` and nests it within itself, allowing you to access the messages using the `ApplicationContext`. This can be hard to visualize, so take a look at the following example.

Listing 5-33 shows a simple application that accesses a set of messages for both the English and Czech locales.

Listing 5-33. Exploring MessageSource Usage

```
package com.apress.prospring3.ch5.context;

import java.util.Locale;

import org.springframework.context.support.GenericXmlApplicationContext;

public class MessageSourceDemo {
```

```
public static void main(String[] args) {

    GenericXmlApplicationContext ctx = new GenericXmlApplicationContext();
    ctx.load("classpath:appContext/messageSource.xml");
    ctx.refresh();

    Locale english = Locale.ENGLISH;
    Locale czech = new Locale("cs", "CZ");

    System.out.println(ctx.getMessage("msg", null, english));
    System.out.println(ctx.getMessage("msg", null, czech));

    System.out.println(ctx.getMessage("nameMsg", new Object[] { "Clarence",
            "Ho" }, english));
}
}
```

Don't worry about the calls to getMessage() just yet; we return to those shortly. For now, just know that they retrieve a keyed message for the locale specified. In Listing 5-34 you can see the configuration used by this application (appContext/messageSource.xml).

Listing 5-34. Configuring a MessageSource Bean

```
<?xml version="1.0" encoding="UTF-8"?>
<beans xmlns="http://www.springframework.org/schema/beans"
    xmlns:xsi="http://www.w3.org/2001/XMLSchema-instance"
    xsi:schemaLocation="http://www.springframework.org/schema/beans
        http://www.springframework.org/schema/beans/spring-beans-3.1.xsd">

    <bean id="messageSource"
class="org.springframework.context.support.ResourceBundleMessageSource">
        <property name="basenames">
            <list>
                <value>buttons</value>
                <value>labels</value>
            </list>
        </property>
    </bean>
</beans>
```

Here we are defining a ResourceBundleMessageSource bean with the name messageSource as required and configuring it with a set of names to form the base of its file set. A Java ResourceBundle, which is used by ResourceBundleMessageSource, works on a set of properties files that are identified by base names. When looking for a message for a particular Locale, the ResourceBundle looks for a file that is named as a combination of the base name and the locale name. For instance, if the base name is foo and we are looking for a message in the en-GB (British English) locale, then the ResourceBundle looks for a file called foo_en_GB.properties.

For the previous example, the content of the properties files for English (labels_en.properties) and Czech (labels_cs_CZ.properties) are shown in Listing 5-35 and Listing 5-36, respectively.

Listing 5-35. labels_en.properties File

```
msg=The quick brown fox jumped over the lazy dog
nameMsg=My name is {0} {1}
```

Listing 5-36. labels_cs_CZ.properties File

```
msg=Príšerne žlutoucký kun úpel dábelské ódy
```

Running the MessageSourceDemo class in Listing 5-33 yields the following output:

```
The quick brown fox jumped over the lazy dog
Príšerne žlutoucký kun úpel dábelské ódy
My name is Clarence Ho
```

■ **Note** The translation of the Czech is "Terribly yellow horse was groaning devilish odes."

Now this example just raises even more questions. What did those calls to getMessage() mean? Why did we use ApplicationContext.getMessage() rather than access the ResourceBundleMessageSource bean directly? We'll answer each of these questions in turn.

The getMessage() Method

The MessageSource interface defines three overloads for the getMessage() method. These are described in Table 5-2.

Table 5-2. Overloads for MessageSource.getMessage()

Method Signature	Description
getMessage (String, Object[], Locale)	This is the standard getMessage() method. The String argument is the key of the message corresponding to the key in the properties file. In Listing 5-33, the first call to getMessage() used msg as the key, and this corresponded to the following entry in the properties file for the en locale: msg=The quick brown fox jumped over the lazy dog. The Object[] array argument is used for replacements in the message. In the third call to getMessage() in Listing 5-33, we passed in an array of two Strings. The message that was keyed as nameMsg was My name is {0} {1}. The numbers surrounded by braces are placeholders, and each one is replaced with the corresponding entry in the argument array. The final argument, Locale, tells ResourceBundleMessageSource which properties file to look in. Even though the first and second calls to getMessage() in the example used the same key, they returned different messages that correspond to the Locale that was passed in to getMessage().
getMessage (String, Object[], String, Locale)	This overload works in the same way as getMessage(String, Object[], Locale), other than the second String argument, which allows you to pass in a default value in case a message for the supplied key is not available for the supplied Locale.
getMessage (MessageSourceResolvable, Locale)	This overload is a special case. We discuss it in further detail in the section "The MessageSourceResolvable Interface."

Why Use ApplicationContext As a MessageSource?

To answer this question, we need to jump a little ahead of ourselves and look at the web application support in Spring. The answer, in general, to this question is that you shouldn't use the ApplicationContext as a MessageSource when doing so couples your bean to the ApplicationContext unnecessarily (this is discussed in more detail in the next section). You should use the ApplicationContext when you are building a web application using Spring's MVC framework.

The core interface in Spring MVC is Controller. Unlike frameworks like Struts that require you to implement your controllers by inheriting from a concrete class, Spring simply requires that you implement the Controller interface (or annotate your controller class with the @Controller annotation). Having said that, Spring provides a collection of useful base classes that you will use to implement your own controllers. All of these base classes are themselves subclasses (directly or indirectly) of the ApplicationObjectSupport class, which is a convenient superclass for any application objects that want to be aware of the ApplicationContext.

Remember that in a web application setting, the ApplicationContext is loaded automatically. ApplicationObjectSupport accesses this ApplicationContext, wraps it in a MessageSourceAccessor object, and makes that available to your controller via the protected getMessageSourceAccessor() method. MessageSourceAccessor provides a wide array of convenient methods for working with MessageSources. This form of "auto injection" is quite beneficial; it removes the need for all of your controllers to expose a MessageSource property.

However, this is not the best reason for using ApplicationContext as a MessageSource in your web application. The main reason to use ApplicationContext rather than a manually defined MessageSource bean is that Spring does, where possible, expose ApplicationContext, as a MessageSource, to the view tier. This means that when you are using Spring's JSP tag library, the <spring:message> tag automatically reads messages from the ApplicationContext, and when you are using JSTL, the <fmt:message> tag does the same.

All of these benefits mean that it is better to use the MessageSource support in ApplicationContext when you are building a web application, rather than manage an instance of MessageSource separately. This is especially true when you consider that all you need to do to take advantage of this feature is configure a MessageSource bean with the name messageSource.

Using MessageSource in Stand-Alone Applications

When you are using MessageSources in stand-alone applications where Spring offers no additional support other than to nest the MessageSource bean automatically in the ApplicationContext, it is best to make the MessageSources available using Dependency Injection. You can opt to make your bean ApplicationContextAware, but doing so precludes their use in a BeanFactory context. Add to this the fact that you complicate testing without any discernible benefit, and it is clear that you should stick to using Dependency Injection to access MessageSource objects in a stand-alone setting.

The MessageSourceResolvable Interface

You can use an object that implements MessageSourceResolvable in place of a key and a set of arguments when you are looking up a message from a MessageSource. This interface is most widely used in the Spring validation libraries to link Error objects to their internationalized error messages. You will see an example of how to use MessageSourceResolvable in Chapter 17 when we look at error handling in the Spring MVC library.

Application Events

Another feature of the ApplicationContext not present in the BeanFactory is the ability to publish and receive events using the ApplicationContext as a broker. In this section we will take a look at its usage.

Using Application Events

An event is class-derived from ApplicationEvent, which itself derives from java.util.EventObject. Any bean can listen for events by implementing the ApplicationListener<T> interface; the ApplicationContext automatically registers any bean that implements this interface as a listener when it is configured. Events are published using the ApplicationEventPublisher.publishEvent() method, so the publishing class must have knowledge of the ApplicationContext (which extends the ApplicationEventPublisher interface). In a web application, this is simple because many of your classes are derived from Spring Framework classes that allow access to the ApplicationContext through a protected method. In a stand-alone application, you can have your publishing bean implement ApplicationContextAware to enable it to publish events.

Listing 5-37 shows an example of a basic event class.

Listing 5-37. *Creating an Event Class*

```
package com.apress.prospring3.ch5.event;

import org.springframework.context.ApplicationEvent;

public class MessageEvent extends ApplicationEvent {

    private String msg;

    public MessageEvent(Object source, String msg) {
        super(source);
        this.msg = msg;
    }

    public String getMessage() {
        return msg;
    }
}
```

This code is quite basic; the only point of note is that the ApplicationEvent has a single constructor that accepts a reference to the source of the event. This is reflected in the constructor for MessageEvent. In Listing 5-38 you can see the code for the listener.

Listing 5-38. *The* MessageEventListener *Class*

```
package com.apress.prospring3.ch5.event;

import org.springframework.context.ApplicationListener;

public class MessageEventListener implements ApplicationListener<MessageEvent> {

    public void onApplicationEvent(MessageEvent event) {
        MessageEvent msgEvt = (MessageEvent) event;
        System.out.println("Received: " + msgEvt.getMessage());
    }
}
```

The ApplicationListener interface defines a single method, onApplicationEvent, that is called by Spring when an event is raised. The MessageEventListener shows its interest only in events of type MessageEvent (or its subclasses) by implementing the strongly typed ApplicationListener interface. If a

MessageEvent was received, it writes the message to stdout. Publishing events is simple; it is just a matter of creating an instance of the event class and passing it to the ApplicationEventPublisher .publishEvent() method, as shown in Listing 5-39.

***Listing 5-39.** Publishing an Event*

```java
package com.apress.prospring3.ch5.event;

import org.springframework.beans.BeansException;
import org.springframework.context.ApplicationContext;
import org.springframework.context.ApplicationContextAware;
import org.springframework.context.support.ClassPathXmlApplicationContext;

public class Publisher implements ApplicationContextAware {

    private ApplicationContext ctx;

    public static void main(String[] args) {

        ApplicationContext ctx = new ClassPathXmlApplicationContext(
                "classpath:events/events.xml");

        Publisher pub = (Publisher) ctx.getBean("publisher");
        pub.publish("Hello World!");
        pub.publish("The quick brown fox jumped over the lazy dog");
    }

    public void setApplicationContext(ApplicationContext applicationContext)
            throws BeansException {
        this.ctx = applicationContext;

    }

    public void publish(String message) {
        ctx.publishEvent(new MessageEvent(this, message));
    }
}
```

Here you can see that the Publisher class retrieves an instance of itself from the ApplicationContext and then, using the publish() method, publishes two MessageEvents to the ApplicationContext. The Publisher bean instance accesses the ApplicationContext by implementing ApplicationContextAware. Listing 5-40 shows the configuration for this example (events/events.xml).

***Listing 5-40.** Configuring ApplicationListener Beans*

```xml
<?xml version="1.0" encoding="UTF-8"?>
<beans xmlns="http://www.springframework.org/schema/beans"
    xmlns:xsi="http://www.w3.org/2001/XMLSchema-instance"
    xsi:schemaLocation="http://www.springframework.org/schema/beans
        http://www.springframework.org/schema/beans/spring-beans-3.1.xsd">

    <bean id="publisher" class="com.apress.prospring3.ch5.event.Publisher"/>
    <bean id="messageEventListener"
        class="com.apress.prospring3.ch5.event.MessageEventListener"/>
</beans>
```

Notice that you do not need a special configuration to register the `MessageEventListener` with the `ApplicationContext`; it is picked up automatically by Spring. Running this example results in the following output:

```
Received: Hello World!
Received: The quick brown fox jumped over the lazy dog
```

Considerations for Event Usage

There are many cases in an application where certain components need to be notified of certain events. Often you do this by writing code to notify each component explicitly or by using a messaging technology such as JMS. The drawback of writing code to notify each component in turn is that you are coupling those components to the publisher, in many cases unnecessarily.

Consider a situation where you cache product details in your application to avoid trips to the database. Another component allows product details to be modified and persisted to the database. To avoid making the cache invalid, the update component explicitly notifies the cache that the user details have changed. In this example, the update component is coupled to a component that, really, has nothing to do with its business responsibility. A better solution would be to have the update component publish an event every time a product's details are modified and then have interested components, such as the cache, listen for that event. This has the benefit of keeping the components decoupled, which makes it simple to remove the cache if you need or to add another listener that is interested in knowing when a product's details change.

Using JMS in this case would be overkill, because the process of invalidating the product's entry in the cache is quick and is not business critical. The use of the Spring event infrastructure adds very little overhead to your application.

Typically, we use events for reactionary logic that executes quickly and is not part of the main application logic. In the previous example, the invalidation of a product in cache happens in reaction to the updating of product details, it executes quickly (or it should), and it is not part of the main function of the application. For processes that are long running and form part of the main business logic, it is recommended to use JMS or similar messaging systems such as RabbitMQ. The main benefits of using JMS is that it is more suited to long-running processes, and as the system grows, you can, if necessary, factor the JMS-driven processing of messages containing business information onto a separate machine.

Accessing Resources

Often an application needs to access a variety of resources in different forms. You might need to access some configuration data stored in a file in the file system, some image data stored in a JAR file on the classpath, or maybe some data on a server elsewhere. Spring provides a unified mechanism for accessing resources in a protocol-independent way. This means your application can access a file resource in the same way, whether it is stored in the file system, in the classpath, or on a remote server.

At the core of Spring's resource support is the `org.springframework.core.io.Resource` interface. The `Resource` interface defines ten self-explanatory methods: `contentLength()`, `exists()`, `getDescription()`, `getFile()`, `getFileName()`, `getURI()`, `getURL()`, `isOpen()`, `isReadable()`, and `lastModified()`. In addition to these ten methods, there is one that is not quite so self-explanatory: `createRelative()`. The `createRelative()` method creates a new `Resource` instance using a path that is relative to the instance on which it is invoked. You can provide your own `Resource` implementations, although that is outside the scope of this chapter, but in most cases, you use one of the built-in implementations for accessing file (the `FileSystemResource` class), classpath (the `ClassPathResource` class), or URL resources (the `UrlResource` class).

Internally, Spring uses another interface, ResourceLoader, and the default implementation, DefaultResourceLoader, to locate and create Resource instances. However, you generally won't interact with DefaultResourceLoader, instead using another ResourceLoader implementation— ApplicationContext.

Listing 5-41 shows a sample application that accesses three resources using ApplicationContext.

Listing 5-41. Accessing Resources

```
package com.apress.prospring3.ch5.resource;

import org.springframework.context.ApplicationContext;
import org.springframework.context.support.ClassPathXmlApplicationContext;
import org.springframework.core.io.Resource;

public class ResourceDemo {

    public static void main(String[] args) throws Exception{
        ApplicationContext ctx = new ClassPathXmlApplicationContext(
        "classpath:events/events.xml");

        Resource res1 = ctx.getResource("file:///d:/temp/test.txt");
        displayInfo(res1);
        Resource res2 = ctx.getResource("classpath:test.txt");
        displayInfo(res2);
        Resource res3 = ctx.getResource("http://www.google.co.uk");
        displayInfo(res3);
    }

    private static void displayInfo(Resource res) throws Exception{
        System.out.println(res.getClass());
        System.out.println(res.getURL().getContent());
        System.out.println("");
    }
}
```

You should note that the configuration file used in this example is unimportant. Notice that in each call to getResource() we pass in a URI for each resource. You will recognize the common file: and http: protocols that we pass in for res1 and res3. The classpath: protocol we use for res2 is Spring-specific and indicates that the ResourceLoader should look in the classpath for the resource. Running this example results in the following output:

```
class org.springframework.core.io.UrlResource
sun.net.www.content.text.PlainTextInputStream@709446e4

class org.springframework.core.io.ClassPathResource
sun.net.www.content.text.PlainTextInputStream@16ba5c7a

class org.springframework.core.io.UrlResource
sun.net.www.protocol.http.HttpURLConnection$HttpInputStream@6825c828
```

Notice that for both the file: and http: protocols, Spring returns a UrlResource instance. Spring does include a FileSystemResource class, but the DefaultResourceLoader does not use this class at all. It's because Spring's default resource-loading strategy treats the URL and file as the same type of resource with difference protocols (i.e., file: and http:). If an instance of FileSystemResource is required, use the FileSystemResourceLoader. Once a Resource instance is obtained, you are free to access the contents as you see fit, using getFile(), getInputStream(), or getURL(). In some cases, such as when you are using the http: protocol, the call to getFile() results in a FileNotFoundException. For this reason, we recommend that you use getInputStream() to access resource contents because it is likely to function for all possible resource types.

Configuration Using Java Classes

Besides XML configuration, you can also use Java classes to configure Spring's ApplicationContext. Spring JavaConfig used to be a separate project, but starting with Spring 3.0, its major features for configuration using Java classes was merged into the core Spring Framework.

In this section, we will take a look at how to use Java classes to configure a Spring's ApplicationContext and its equivalent when using XML configuration.

ApplicationContext Configuration in Java

Let's see how we can configure Spring's ApplicationContext using Java classes, by referring to the same example for message provider and renderer that we presented in Chapter 4. Listing 5-42 recaps the message provider interface and a configurable message provider.

Listing 5-42. MessageProvider and ConfigurableMessageProvider

```
package com.apress.prospring3.ch5.javaconfig;

public interface MessageProvider {

    public String getMessage();

}


package com.apress.prospring3.ch5.javaconfig;

public class ConfigurableMessageProvider implements MessageProvider {

    private String message = "Default message";

    public ConfigurableMessageProvider() {
    }

    public ConfigurableMessageProvider(String message) {
        this.message = message;
    }

    public void setMessage(String message) {
        this.message = message;
    }

    public String getMessage() {
        return message;
    }
}
```

Listing 5-43 shows the MessageRenderer interface and the StandardOutMessageRenderer implementation.

Listing 5-43. *MessageRenderer and StandardOutMessageRenderer*

```
package com.apress.prospring3.ch5.javaconfig;

public interface MessageRenderer {

    public void render();

    public void setMessageProvider(MessageProvider provider);

    public MessageProvider getMessageProvider();

}


package com.apress.prospring3.ch5.javaconfig;

public class StandardOutMessageRenderer implements MessageRenderer {

    private MessageProvider messageProvider = null;

    public void render() {
    if (messageProvider == null) {
                throw new RuntimeException(
                "You must set the property messageProvider of class:"
        + StandardOutMessageRenderer.class.getName());
            }
            System.out.println(messageProvider.getMessage());
    }

    public void setMessageProvider(MessageProvider provider){
        this.messageProvider = provider;
    }

    public MessageProvider getMessageProvider() {
        return this.messageProvider;
    }

}
```

Listing 5-44 shows the XML configuration for the Spring ApplicationContext (app-context.xml).

Listing 5-44. *XML Configuration*

```
<?xml version="1.0" encoding="UTF-8"?>
<beans xmlns="http://www.springframework.org/schema/beans"
    xmlns:xsi="http://www.w3.org/2001/XMLSchema-instance"
    xmlns:p="http://www.springframework.org/schema/p"
    xmlns:c="http://www.springframework.org/schema/c"
    xsi:schemaLocation="http://www.springframework.org/schema/beans
```

```
            http://www.springframework.org/schema/beans/spring-beans-3.1.xsd">

    <bean id="messageRenderer"
class="com.apress.prospring3.ch5.javaconfig.StandardOutMessageRenderer"
        p:messageProvider-ref="messageProvider"/>

    <bean id="messageProvider"
class="com.apress.prospring3.ch5.javaconfig.ConfigurableMessageProvider"
        c:message="This is a configurable message"/>

</beans>
```

Listing 5-45 shows the testing program.

Listing 5-45. *XML Configuration Testing Program*

```
package com.apress.prospring3.ch5.javaconfig;

import org.springframework.context.ApplicationContext;
import org.springframework.context.support.ClassPathXmlApplicationContext;

public class JavaConfigSimpleExample {

    public static void main(String[] args) {

        ApplicationContext ctx = new
            ClassPathXmlApplicationContext("classpath:app-context.xml");

        MessageRenderer renderer =
            ctx.getBean("messageRenderer", MessageRenderer.class);

        renderer.render();

    }

}
```

When using a Java class instead of XML to configure the previous message provider and renderer, we just need to implement a normal JavaBean as usual, with the appropriate annotations for Spring's Java configuration. Listing 5-46 shows the Java class, which is equivalent to the XML configuration shown in Listing 5-44.

Listing 5-46. *Java Configuration*

```
package com.apress.prospring3.ch5.javaconfig;

import org.springframework.context.annotation.Bean;
import org.springframework.context.annotation.Configuration;

@Configuration
public class AppConfig {

    // XML:
    // <bean id="messageProvider"
class="com.apress.prospring3.ch5.javaconfig.ConfigurableMessageProvider"/>
```

```
    @Bean
    public MessageProvider messageProvider() {
        return new ConfigurableMessageProvider();
    }

    // XML:
    // <bean id="messageRenderer"
class="com.apress.prospring3.ch5.javaconfig.StandardOutMessageRenderer"
    //          p:messageProvider-ref="messageProvider"/>
    @Bean
    public MessageRenderer messageRenderer() {
        MessageRenderer renderer = new StandardOutMessageRenderer();

        // Setter injection
        renderer.setMessageProvider(messageProvider());

        return renderer;
    }
}
```

In the previous AppConfig class, you can see that we first use the @Configuration annotation to inform Spring that this is a Java-based configuration file. Afterward, the @Bean annotation was used to declare a Spring bean and the DI requirements. To help you understand the XML equivalent of the Java annotation and code, we added comments to the corresponding method. So, you can see that @Bean is equivalent to the <bean> tag, the method name is equivalent to the id attribute within the <bean> tag, and when instantiating the MessageRender bean, setter injection was achieved by calling the corresponding method to get the message provider, which is the same as using the <ref> tag in the XML configuration. Listing 5-47 shows how to initialize the ApplicationContext from Java configuration file.

Listing 5-47. Java Configuration Testing

```
package com.apress.prospring3.ch5.javaconfig;

import org.springframework.context.ApplicationContext;
import org.springframework.context.annotationAnnotationConfigApplicationContext;

public class JavaConfigSimpleExample {

    public static void main(String[] args) {

        ApplicationContext ctx = new
            AnnotationConfigApplicationContext(AppConfig.class);

        MessageRenderer renderer =
            ctx.getBean("messageRenderer", MessageRenderer.class);

        renderer.render();

    }

}
```

From the previous listing, we use the AnnotationConfigApplicationContext class, passing in the configuration class as the constructor argument (you can pass multiple configuration classes to it via the JDK varargs feature). Afterward, you can use the ApplicationContext returned as usual.

Note that Spring requires CGLIB to support Java configuration classes. Add the dependency in Table 5-3 to the project in STS.

Table 5-3. Dependency for Java Configuration

Group ID	Artifact ID	Version	Description
cglib	cglib	2.2.2	Code generation library required by Spring for Java configuration

Running the program will give the following result:

```
Default message
```

Having seen the basic usage of Java configuration class, let's proceed to more configuration options and their XML equivalents. For the message provider, let's say we want to externalize the message into a properties file (message.properties) and then inject it into the ConfigurableMessageProvider using Constructor Injection. The content of the message.properties is as follows:

```
message=Spring 3 Java Configuration Rocks!
```

Let's see the revised testing program, which loads the properties files by using the @PropertySource annotation and then injects them into the message provider implementation. In Listing 5-48, we also added a lot of various annotations that Spring supports for a base Java configuration and their XML equivalents. Note that for the @EnableTransactionManagement annotation to work, we need to add the dependency on the spring-tx module to the project (see Table 5-4).

Table 5-4. Dependency for Spring Transaction Support

Group ID	Artifact ID	Version	Description
org.springframework	spring-tx	3.1.0.RELEASE	Spring module for transaction support

Listing 5-48. Java Configuration Class (Revised)

```
package com.apress.prospring3.ch5.javaconfig;

import org.springframework.beans.factory.annotation.Autowired;
import org.springframework.context.annotation.Bean;
import org.springframework.context.annotation.ComponentScan;
import org.springframework.context.annotation.Configuration;
import org.springframework.context.annotation.DependsOn;
import org.springframework.context.annotation.Import;
import org.springframework.context.annotation.ImportResource;
import org.springframework.context.annotation.Lazy;
import org.springframework.context.annotation.PropertySource;
import org.springframework.context.annotation.Scope;
import org.springframework.core.env.Environment;
import org.springframework.transaction.annotation.EnableTransactionManagement;

@Configuration
@Import(OtherConfig.class)
```

```
// XML: <import resource="classpath:events/events.xml")
@ImportResource(value="classpath:events/events.xml")
// XML: <context:property-placeholder location="classpath:message.properties"/>
@PropertySource(value="classpath:message.properties")
// XML: <context:component-scan base-package="com.apress.prospring3.ch5.context"/>
@ComponentScan(basePackages={"com.apress.prospring3.ch5.context"})
@EnableTransactionManagement
public class AppConfig {

    @Autowired
    Environment env;

    // XML:
    // <bean id="messageProvider"
class="com.apress.prospring3.ch5.javaconfig.ConfigurableMessageProvider"/>
    @Bean
    @Lazy(value=true)    //XML <bean .... lazy-init="true"/>
    public MessageProvider messageProvider() {
        // Constructor injection
        return new ConfigurableMessageProvider(env.getProperty("message"));
    }

    // XML:
    // <bean id="messageRenderer"
class="com.apress.prospring3.ch5.javaconfig.StandardOutMessageRenderer"
    //         p:messageProvider-ref="messageProvider"/>
    @Bean(name="messageRenderer")
    @Scope(value="prototype")  // XML: <bean ... scope="prototype"/>
    @DependsOn(value="messageProvider")  // XML: <bean ... depends-on="messageProvider"/>
    public MessageRenderer messageRenderer() {
        MessageRenderer renderer = new StandardOutMessageRenderer();

        // Setter injection
        renderer.setMessageProvider(messageProvider());

        return renderer;
    }
}
```

Note that in Listing 5-48, the OtherConfig class is just an empty class annotated with @Configuration. In the listing, you can see a lot of common annotations for configuration in Java classes; we also provided their XML tag equivalents for your easy reference. The following are some special points about Listing 5-48:

- The @PropertySource annotation is used to load properties files into the Spring ApplicationContext, which accepts the location as the argument (more than one location can be provided). For XML, the <context:property-placeholder> serves the same purpose.

- The @Import annotation can import other configuration classes, which means you can also have multiple Java configuration classes for various configurations (e.g., one class can be dedicated to DAO beans declaration, one for the Service beans declaration, etc.).

- Besides the @Import, the @ImportResource can also be used to import configuration from XML files, which means you can use XML and Java configuration classes in a mix-and-match way, although we do not recommend doing that. Mixing XML and Java configuration will make your application harder to maintain, because you need to scan through both XML files and Java classes to search for a specific bean.

- The @ComponentScan defines the packages that Spring should scan for annotations for bean definitions. It's the same as the <context:component-scan> tag in the XML configuration.

- The other annotations are quite self-explanatory. The @Lazy annotation instructs Spring to instantiate the bean only when requested (same as the lazy-init="true" in XML), and @DependsOn tells Spring that a certain bean depends on some other beans, so Spring will make sure that those beans will be instantiated first. The @Scope annotation is to define the bean's scope.

- Application infrastructure services can also be defined in Java classes. For example, the @EnableTransactionManagement defines that we will use Spring's transaction management feature, which will be discussed further in Chapter 12.

- You may also notice the @Autowired property of the env variable, which is of the Environment type. This is the Environment abstraction feature that Spring 3.1 provides. We will discuss it later in this chapter.

Running the testing program again yields the following output:

```
Spring 3 Java Configuration Rocks!
```

This is the message defined in the message.properties file.

Java or XML Configuration?

As you already saw, using Java classes can achieve the same level of ApplicationContext configuration as XML. So, which one should you use? The consideration is quite like the one of whether we should use XML or Java annotations for DI configuration. Each approach has its own pros and cons. However, the recommendation is the same; that is, when you and your team decide on the approach to use, stick to it and keep the configuration style persistent, instead of scattered around between Java class and XML files. This will make the maintenance work much more difficult.

Profiles

Another interesting feature that Spring 3.1 brings to us as developers is the concept of configuration profiles. Basically, a profile instructs Spring to configure only the ApplicationContext that was defined when the specified profile was active. In this section we'll demonstrate the usage of profiles in a simple program.

An Example of Using the Spring Profiles Feature

Let's say there is a service called FoodProviderService that is responsible for providing food to schools, including kindergarten and high school. The FoodProviderService interface has only one method called provideLunchSet(), which will produce the lunch set to each student for the calling school. A lunch set is a list of Food objects, which is very simple class that has only a name attribute. Listing 5-49 shows the Food class.

Listing 5-49. The Food Class

```
package com.apress.prospring3.ch5.profile;

public class Food {

    private String name;

    public Food() {
    }

    public Food(String name) {
        this.name = name;
    }

    public String getName() {
        return name;
    }

    public void setName(String name) {
        this.name = name;
    }
}
```

Listing 5-50 shows the FoodProviderService interface.

Listing 5-50. The FoodProviderService Interface

```
package com.apress.prospring3.ch5.profile;

import java.util.List;

public interface FoodProviderService {

    public List<Food> provideLunchSet();

}
```

Now suppose that there are two different providers for the lunch set, one for kindergarten and one for high school. The lunch set produced by them is different, although the service they provide is the same, that is, to provide lunch to school students. So, now let's create two different implementations of the FoodProviderService using the same name but put them into different packages to identify their target school. Listings 5-51 and 5-52 show the two classes.

Listing 5-51. The Kindergarten FoodProviderService Implementations

```
package com.apress.prospring3.ch5.profile.kindergarten;

import java.util.ArrayList;
import java.util.List;

import com.apress.prospring3.ch5.profile.Food;
import com.apress.prospring3.ch5.profile.FoodProviderService;
```

```
public class FoodProviderServiceImpl implements FoodProviderService {

    public List<Food> provideLunchSet() {
        List<Food> lunchSet = new ArrayList<Food>();
        lunchSet.add(new Food("Milk"));
        lunchSet.add(new Food("Biscuits"));

        return lunchSet;
    }
}
```

Listing 5-52. The High-School FoodProviderService Implementations

```
package com.apress.prospring3.ch5.profile.highschool;

import java.util.ArrayList;
import java.util.List;

import com.apress.prospring3.ch5.profile.Food;
import com.apress.prospring3.ch5.profile.FoodProviderService;

public class FoodProviderServiceImpl implements FoodProviderService {

    public List<Food> provideLunchSet() {
        List<Food> lunchSet = new ArrayList<Food>();
        lunchSet.add(new Food("Coke"));
        lunchSet.add(new Food("Hamburger"));
        lunchSet.add(new Food("French Fries"));

        return lunchSet;
    }
}
```

From the previous listings, you can see that the two different implementations provide the same FoodProviderService interface but produce different combinations of food in the lunch set. So, now suppose a kindergarten wants the provider to deliver the lunch set for their students; let's see how we can use Spring's profile configuration to achieve this. We will run through the XML configuration first.

We will create two different XML configuration files, one for the kindergarten profile and the other for the high-school profile. Listings 5-53 and 5-54 show the configuration for kindergarten and high-school food providers, respectively.

Listing 5-53. XML Configuration for Kindergarten (kindergarten-config.xml)

```
<?xml version="1.0" encoding="UTF-8"?>
<beans xmlns="http://www.springframework.org/schema/beans"
    xmlns:xsi="http://www.w3.org/2001/XMLSchema-instance"
    xsi:schemaLocation="http://www.springframework.org/schema/beans
        http://www.springframework.org/schema/beans/spring-beans-3.1.xsd"
        profile="kindergarten">

    <bean id="foodProviderService"
class="com.apress.prospring3.ch5.profile.kindergarten.FoodProviderServiceImpl"/>

</beans>
```

Listing 5-54. XML Configuration for High School (highschool-config.xml)

```
<?xml version="1.0" encoding="UTF-8"?>
<beans xmlns="http://www.springframework.org/schema/beans"
    xmlns:xsi="http://www.w3.org/2001/XMLSchema-instance"
    xsi:schemaLocation="http://www.springframework.org/schema/beans
        http://www.springframework.org/schema/beans/spring-beans-3.1.xsd"
        profile="highschool">

    <bean id="foodProviderService"
class="com.apress.prospring3.ch5.profile.highschool.FoodProviderServiceImpl"/>

</beans>
```

From the previous two configurations, notice the usage of profile="kindergarten" and profile="highschool", respectively, within the <beans> tag. It actually tells Spring that those beans in the file should be instantiated only when the specified profile is active. Now let's see how to activate the correct profile when using Spring's ApplicationContext in a stand-alone application. Listing 5-55 shows the testing program.

Listing 5-55. Profile XML Configuration Example

```
package com.apress.prospring3.ch5.profile;

import java.util.List;

import org.springframework.context.support.GenericXmlApplicationContext;

public class ProfileXmlConfigExample {

    public static void main(String[] args) {

        GenericXmlApplicationContext ctx = new GenericXmlApplicationContext();
        ctx.getEnvironment().setActiveProfiles("kindergarten");
        ctx.load("classpath:profile/*-config.xml");
        ctx.refresh();

        FoodProviderService foodProviderService =
            ctx.getBean("foodProviderService", FoodProviderService.class);
        List<Food> lunchSet = foodProviderService.provideLunchSet();

        for (Food food: lunchSet) {
            System.out.println("Food: " + food.getName());
        }

    }
}
```

In the previous listing, we use the ctx.getEnvironment().setActiveProfiles() method to activate a certain profile. Note that multiple profiles can be activated for the same context (i.e., you can pass multiple profile names into the setActiveProfile() method via its varargs support). The previous listing will have the kindergarten profile activated. Afterward, the ctx.load() method will load both kindergarten-config.xml and highschool-config.xml, since we pass the method the wildcard as the prefix. In this case, only the beans in the file kindergarten-config.xml will be instantiated by the Spring base on the profile attribute. Running the program will produce the following output:

Food: Milk
Food: Biscuits

This is exactly what the implementation of the kindergarten provider will produce for the lunch set. Now change the profile string in the previous listing to "highschool", and the output will change to the following:

Food: Coke
Food: Hamburger
Food: French Fries

So, now you see the usage. Another interesting thing is that instead of programmatically activating a profile, you can also specify it by passing in the following JVM argument:

-Dspring.profiles.active="kindergarten"

Figure 5-2 shows how to configure the JVM argument in STS.

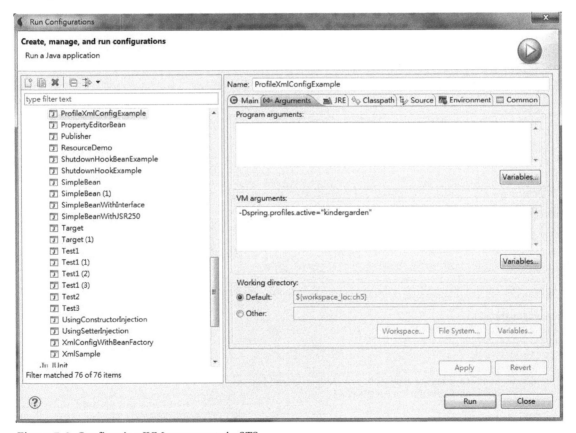

Figure 5-2. Configuring JVM arguments in STS

By passing this argument in, we can take away the line that sets the active profile and runs the program. The results are the same as the programmatic way. You can change the JVM argument to "highschool" and run the program again.

In Chapter 21, we will discuss how to use and activate profiles in web applications.

You can also use profiles when using a Java configuration instead of XML. Let's see how to do it. Like with the XML version, we develop two different Java configuration classes and define the profile by using the @Profile annotation. Listings 5-56 and 5-57 show the Java configuration file for the kindergarten and high school profiles, respectively.

Listing 5-56. Profile Java Configuration for Kindergarten

```
package com.apress.prospring3.ch5.profile;

import org.springframework.context.annotation.Bean;
import org.springframework.context.annotation.Configuration;
import org.springframework.context.annotation.Profile;

import com.apress.prospring3.ch5.profile.kindergarten.FoodProviderServiceImpl;

@Configuration
@Profile(value="kindergarten")
public class KindergartenConfig {

    @Bean
    public FoodProviderService foodProviderService() {
        return new FoodProviderServiceImpl();
    }
}
```

Listing 5-57. Profile Java Configuration for High School

```
package com.apress.prospring3.ch5.profile;

import org.springframework.context.annotation.Bean;
import org.springframework.context.annotation.Configuration;
import org.springframework.context.annotation.Profile;

import com.apress.prospring3.ch5.profile.highschool.FoodProviderServiceImpl;

@Configuration
@Profile(value="highschool")
public class HighschoolConfig {

    @Bean
    public FoodProviderService foodProviderService() {
    return new FoodProviderServiceImpl();
    }
}
```

You can see the two classes just mimic the two XML files that we presented earlier, with the @Profile annotation specifying the corresponding application profile to which it belongs. Let's implement another testing program to see the Java profile configuration in action. Listing 5-58 shows the testing program.

Listing 5-58. Profile Java Configuration Example

```
package com.apress.prospring3.ch5.profile;

import java.util.List;

import org.springframework.context.annotation.AnnotationConfigApplicationContext;

public class ProfileJavaConfigExample {

    public static void main(String[] args) {

        AnnotationConfigApplicationContext ctx = new AnnotationConfigApplicationContext();
        ctx.getEnvironment().setActiveProfiles("kindergarten");
        ctx.register(KindergartenConfig.class, HighschoolConfig.class);
        ctx.refresh();

        FoodProviderService foodProviderService =
            ctx.getBean("foodProviderService", FoodProviderService.class);
        List<Food> lunchSet = foodProviderService.provideLunchSet();

        for (Food food: lunchSet) {
            System.out.println("Food: " + food.getName());
        }

    }
}
```

In Listing 5-58, we used the AnnotationConfigApplicationContext implementation and its register() method to register the bean definitions from both the KindergartenConfig and HighschoolConfig classes. The other code remains the same. Run the program, and you will see the lunch set for kindergarten.

Using the JVM argument spring.profiles.active is the same as the XML example. I'll leave it to you to try it. The sample source code is included with the book's source code.

Considerations for Using Profiles

The profiles feature in Spring 3.1 creates another way for developers to manage the application's running configuration, which used to be done in build tools (e.g., Maven's profile support). Build tools rely on the arguments passed into the tool to pack the correct configuration/property files into the Java archive (JAR or WAR depends on the application type) and then deploy to the target environment. Spring's profile feature lets us as application developers define the profiles by ourselves and activate them either programmatically or by passing in the JVM argument. By using Spring's profile support, you can now use the same application archive and deploy to all different environments, by passing in the correct profiles as an argument during JVM startup. For example, you can have applications with different profiles such as (dev, hibernate), (prd, jdbc), and so on, with each different combination representing the running environment (development or production) and the data access library to use (Hibernate or JDBC). It brings application profile management into the programming side.

But this approach also has its drawbacks. For example, some may argue that putting all the configuration for different environments into application configuration files or Java classes and bundling them together will be error prone if not handled carefully (e.g., the administrator forgot to set the correct JVM argument in their application server environment). Packing files for all profiles together will also make the package a bit larger than usual. Again, let the application and configuration requirements drive you to select the approach that best fits your project.

Environment and PropertySource Abstraction

From the previous section, you already saw the usage of Spring's profile feature. To set the active profile, we need to access the Environment interface. The Environment interface is a new abstraction layer introduced in Spring 3.1; it serves to encapsulate the environment of the running Spring application.

Besides the profile, other key pieces of information encapsulated by the Environment interface are properties. Properties are used to store the application's underlying environment configuration, such as the location of the application folder, database connection information, and so on.

The Environment and PropertySource abstraction features in Spring 3.1 assist us as developers in accessing various configuration information from the running platform. Under the abstraction, all system properties, environment variables, and application properties are served by the Environment interface, which Spring populates when bootstrapping the ApplicationContext. Listing 5-59 shows a simple example.

Listing 5-59. *Spring Environment Abstraction Example*

```
package com.apress.prospring3.ch5.env;

import java.util.HashMap;
import java.util.Map;

import org.springframework.context.support.GenericXmlApplicationContext;
import org.springframework.core.env.ConfigurableEnvironment;
import org.springframework.core.env.MapPropertySource;
import org.springframework.core.env.MutablePropertySources;

public class EnvironmentSample {

    public static void main(String[] args) {

        GenericXmlApplicationContext ctx = new GenericXmlApplicationContext();
        ctx.refresh();

        ConfigurableEnvironment env = ctx.getEnvironment();
        MutablePropertySources propertySources = env.getPropertySources();
        Map appMap = new HashMap();
        appMap.put("application.home", "/etc/prospring3/home");
        propertySources.addLast(new MapPropertySource("PROSPRING3_MAP", appMap));

        System.out.println("user.home: " + System.getProperty("user.home"));
        System.out.println("JAVA_HOME: " + System.getenv("JAVA_HOME"));

        System.out.println("user.home: " + env.getProperty("user.home"));
        System.out.println("JAVA_HOME: " + env.getProperty("JAVA_HOME"));
        System.out.println("application.home: " + env.getProperty("application.home"));
    }
}
```

From Listing 5-59, after the ApplicationContext initialization, we get a reference to the ConfigurableEnvironment interface. Via the interface, a handle to the MutablePropertySources (a default implementation of the PropertySources interface, which allows manipulation of the contained property sources) was obtained. Afterward, we construct a map, put the application properties into the map, and then construct a MapPropertySource class (a PropertySource subclass that reads keys and values from a

Map instance) with the map. Finally, the MapPropertySource class was added to the MutablePropertySources via the addLast() method.

Let's run the program, and the following will be printed:

```
user.home: C:\Users\Clarence
JAVA_HOME: C: \Program Files\Java\jdk1.6.0_27
user.home: C: \Users\Clarence
JAVA_HOME: C: \Program Files\Java\jdk1.6.0_27
application.home: /etc/prospring3/home
```

For the first two lines, the JVM system property user.home and the environment variable JAVA_HOME was retrieved as we did before (by using the JVM's System class). However, for the last three lines, you can see that all the system properties, environment variables, and application properties can all be accessed via the Environment interface. You can see how the Environment abstraction can help us manage and access all the various properties within the application's running environment.

For the PropertySource abstraction, Spring will access the properties in the following default order:

- System properties for the running JVM

- Environment variables

- Application-defined properties

So, for example, suppose we defined the same application property, user.home, and added it to the Environment interface via the MutablePropertySources class. If you run the program, you will still see that the user.home was still retrieved from the JVM properties, not yours. However, Spring allows you to control the order of how the Environment should retrieve the properties. Let's revise Listing 5-59 a bit and see how it works. Listing 5-60 shows the revised version (the differences are highlighted in bold).

Listing 5-60. *Spring Environment Abstraction Example (Revised)*

```
// Codes omitted
public class EnvironmentSample {

    public static void main(String[] args) {

        GenericXmlApplicationContext ctx = new GenericXmlApplicationContext();
        ctx.refresh();

        ConfigurableEnvironment env = ctx.getEnvironment();
        MutablePropertySources propertySources = env.getPropertySources();
        Map appMap = new HashMap();
        appMap.put("user.home", "/etc/prospring3/home");
        propertySources.addFirst(new MapPropertySource("PROSPRING3_MAP", appMap));

        System.out.println("user.home: " + System.getProperty("user.home"));
        System.out.println("JAVA_HOME: " + System.getenv("JAVA_HOME"));

        System.out.println("user.home: " + env.getProperty("user.home"));
        System.out.println("JAVA_HOME: " + env.getProperty("JAVA_HOME"));
    }
}
```

For Listing 5-60, we have defined an application property also called user.home and added it as the first one to search for via the addFirst() method of the MutablePropertySources class. When you run the program, you will see the following output:

```
user.home: C:\Users\Clarence
JAVA_HOME: C:\Program Files\Java\jdk1.6.0_27
user.home: /etc/prospring3/home
JAVA_HOME: C:\Program Files\Java\jdk1.6.0_27
```

The first two lines remain the same because we still use the getProperty() and getenv() methods of the JVM System class to retrieve them. However, when using the Environment interface, you will see that the user.home property we defined takes precedence, since we defined it as the first one to search for property values.

In real life, you seldom need to interact directly with the Environment interface but will use a property placeholder in the form of ${} (e.g., ${application.home}) and inject the resolved value into Spring beans. Let's see this in action.

Suppose we had a class to store all the application properties loaded from a property file. Listing 5-61 shows the AppProperty class.

Listing 5-61. Spring Property Placeholder Example

```
package com.apress.prospring3.ch5.env;

public class AppProperty {

    private String applicationHome;

    private String userHome;

    public String getApplicationHome() {
        return applicationHome;
    }

    public void setApplicationHome(String applicationHome) {
        this.applicationHome = applicationHome;
    }

    public String getUserHome() {
        return userHome;
    }

    public void setUserHome(String userHome) {
        this.userHome = userHome;
    }
}
```

There's nothing interesting about the class. Listing 5-62 is the application.properties file that stores the running application's properties.

Listing 5-62. application.properties File

```
application.home=/etc/prospring3/home
user.home=/clarence/home
```

Note that the property file also declared the user.home property. Let's take a look at the Spring XML configuration (see Listing 5-63, the env/env.xml file).

Listing 5-63. *Spring Property Placeholder Configuration*

```xml
<?xml version="1.0" encoding="UTF-8"?>
<beans xmlns="http://www.springframework.org/schema/beans"
    xmlns:xsi="http://www.w3.org/2001/XMLSchema-instance"
    xmlns:context="http://www.springframework.org/schema/context"
    xsi:schemaLocation="http://www.springframework.org/schema/beans
        http://www.springframework.org/schema/beans/spring-beans-3.1.xsd
        http://www.springframework.org/schema/context
        http://www.springframework.org/schema/context/spring-context-3.1.xsd">

    <context:property-placeholder location="classpath:env/application.properties"/>

    <bean id="appProperty" class="com.apress.prospring3.ch5.env.AppProperty">
        <property name="applicationHome" value="${application.home}"/>
        <property name="userHome" value="${user.home}"></property>
    </bean>

</beans>
```

We used the `<context:property-placeholder>` tag to load the properties into Spring's Environment, which is wrapped into the ApplicationContext interface. We also use the placeholders to inject the values into the AppProperty bean. Listing 5-64 shows the testing program.

Listing 5-64. *Spring Property Placeholder Testing*

```java
package com.apress.prospring3.ch5.env;

import org.springframework.context.support.GenericXmlApplicationContext;

public class PlaceHolderSample {

    public static void main(String[] args) {

        GenericXmlApplicationContext ctx = new GenericXmlApplicationContext();
        ctx.load("classpath:env/env.xml");
        ctx.refresh();

        AppProperty appProperty = ctx.getBean("appProperty", AppProperty.class);

        System.out.println("application.home: " + appProperty.getApplicationHome());
        System.out.println("user.home: " + appProperty.getUserHome());
    }
}
```

Let's run the program, and you will see the following output:

```
application.home: /etc/prospring3/home
user.home: C:\Users\Clarence
```

You will see the application.home placeholder was properly resolved, while the user.home property was still retrieved from the JVM properties, which is correct because it's the default behavior for the PropertySource abstraction. To instruct Spring to give precedence for the values in the application.properties file, we add the attribute local-override="true" to the <context:property-placeholder> tag.

```
<context:property-placeholder local-override="true"
    location="classpath:env/application.properties"/>
```

The local-override attribute instructs Spring to override the existing properties with the properties defined in this placeholder. Run the program, and you will see that now the user.home property from the application.properties file was retrieved.

```
application.home: /etc/prospring3/home
user.home: /clarence/home
```

From the previous two sections, you can see that profiles and property source abstraction by the Environment interface in Spring 3.1 give us a powerful and centralized way to manage the configurations of the application environment.

Configuration Using JSR-330 Annotations

As we discussed in Chapter 1, JEE 6 provides support for JSR-330 (Dependency Injection for Java), which is a collection of annotations for expressing an application's DI configuration within a JEE container or other compatible IoC framework. Spring also supports and recognizes those annotations, so although you're not running your application in a JEE 6 container, you can still use JSR-330 annotations within Spring. Using JSR-330 annotations can help you ease the migration to the JEE 6 container or other compatible IoC container (e.g., Google Guice) away from Spring.

Again, let's take the message renderer and message provider as an example and implement it using JSR-330 annotations.

To support JSR-330 annotations, you need to add a dependency to the project, as shown in Table 5-5.

Table 5-5. Dependency for JSR-330 Support

Group ID	Artifact ID	Version	Description
javax.inject	javax.inject	1	JSR-330 standard library

The interface classes (MessageRenderer and MessageProvider) are the same, so we'll save some space and not list them. Listing 5-65 shows the implementation of ConfigurableMessageProvider.

Listing 5-65. ConfigurableMessageProvider (JSR-330)

```
package com.apress.prospring3.ch5.jsr330;

import javax.inject.Inject;
import javax.inject.Named;

@Named("messageProvider")
public class ConfigurableMessageProvider implements MessageProvider {

    private String message = "Default message";

    public ConfigurableMessageProvider() {
```

```
    }

    @Inject
    @Named("message")
    public ConfigurableMessageProvider(String message) {
        this.message = message;
    }

    public void setMessage(String message) {
        this.message = message;
    }

    public String getMessage() {
        return message;
    }
}
```

You will notice that all annotations belong to the javax.inject package, which is the JSR-330 standard. This class used @Named in two places. First, it can be used to declare an injectable bean (the same as the @Component or @Service annotation in Spring). In the listing, the @Named("messageProvider") annotation specifies that the ConfigurableMessageProvider is an injectable bean and gives it the name messageProvider, which is the same as the name attribute in Spring's <bean> tag. Second, we use constructor injection by using the @Inject annotation before the constructor that accepts a string value. Then, we use @Named to specify that we want to inject the value that had the name message assigned. Let's move on to see the StandardOutMessageRenderer class in Listing 5-66.

Listing 5-66. StandardOutMessageRenderer (JSR-330)

```
package com.apress.prospring3.ch5.jsr330;

import javax.inject.Inject;
import javax.inject.Named;
import javax.inject.Singleton;

@Named("messageRenderer")
@Singleton
public class StandardOutMessageRenderer implements MessageRenderer {

    @Inject
    @Named("messageProvider")
    private MessageProvider messageProvider = null;

    public void render() {
        if (messageProvider == null) {
            throw new RuntimeException(
                "You must set the property messageProvider of class:"
                + StandardOutMessageRenderer.class.getName());
        }

        System.out.println(messageProvider.getMessage());
    }

    public void setMessageProvider(MessageProvider provider) {
```

```
            this.messageProvider = provider;
    }

    public MessageProvider getMessageProvider() {
        return this.messageProvider;
    }
}
```

In Listing 5-66, we used @Named to define that it's an injectable bean. Notice the @Singleton annotation. It's worth noting that in the JSR-330 standard, a bean's default scope is nonsingleton, which is like Spring's prototype scope. So, in a JSR-330 environment, if you want your bean to be a singleton, you need to use the @Singleton annotation. However, using this annotation in Spring actually doesn't have any effect, because Spring's default scope for bean instantiation is already singleton. We just put it here for demonstration, and it's worth noting the difference between Spring and other JSR-330 compatible containers.

For the messageProvider property, we use @Inject for setter injection this time and specify that a bean with the name messageProvider should be used for injection.

Listing 5-67 defines a simple Spring XML configuration for the application (jsr330/jsr330.xml).

Listing 5-67. *Spring XML Configuration (JSR-330)*

```xml
<?xml version="1.0" encoding="UTF-8"?>
<beans xmlns="http://www.springframework.org/schema/beans"
    xmlns:xsi="http://www.w3.org/2001/XMLSchema-instance"
    xmlns:context="http://www.springframework.org/schema/context"
    xsi:schemaLocation="http://www.springframework.org/schema/beans
    http://www.springframework.org/schema/beans/spring-beans-3.1.xsd
    http://www.springframework.org/schema/context
    http://www.springframework.org/schema/context/spring-context-3.1.xsd">

    <context:component-scan base-package="com.apress.prospring3.ch5.jsr330"/>

    <bean id="message" class="java.lang.String">
        <constructor-arg value="You are running JSR330!"/>
    </bean>

</beans>
```

You don't need any special tags to use JSR-330; just configure your application like a normal Spring application. We use <context:component-scan> to instruct Spring to scan for the DI-related annotations, and Spring will recognize those JSR-330 annotations. We also declared a Spring bean called message for Constructor Injection into the ConfigurableMessageProvider class. Listing 5-68 shows the testing program.

Listing 5-68. *JSR-330 Example*

```java
package com.apress.prospring3.ch5.jsr330;

import org.springframework.context.support.GenericXmlApplicationContext;

public class Jsr330Example {

    public static void main(String[] args) {
```

```
        GenericXmlApplicationContext ctx = new GenericXmlApplicationContext();
        ctx.load("classpath:jsr330/jsr330.xml");
        ctx.refresh();

        MessageRenderer renderer = ctx.getBean("messageRenderer", MessageRenderer.class);
        renderer.render();
    }
}
```

It's the same as the previous samples. Running the program will yield the following output:

```
You are running JSR330!
```

By using JSR-330, you can ease the migration into other JSR-330 compatible IoC containers (e.g., JEE–6 compatible application servers, other DI containers such as Google Guice, etc.). However, Spring's annotations are much more feature rich and flexible than JSR-330 annotations. Some main differences are highlighted here:

- When using Spring's @Autowired annotation, you can specify a required attribute to indicate that the DI must be fulfilled (you can also use Spring's @Required annotation to declare this requirement), while for JSR-330's @Inject annotation, there is no such equivalent. Moreover, Spring provides the @Qualifier annotation, which allows more fine-grained control for Spring to perform autowiring of dependencies based on qualifier name.

- JSR-330 supports only singleton and nonsingleton bean scopes, while Spring supports more scopes, which is very useful for web applications.

- In Spring, you can use the @Lazy annotation to instruct Spring to instantiate the bean only when requested by the application. There's no such equivalent in JSR-330.

You can also mix and match Spring and JSR-330 annotations in the same application. However, it is recommended that you settle on either one to maintain a consistent style for your application. One possible way is to use JSR-330 annotations as much as possible and use Spring annotations when required. However, this brings you fewer benefits because you still need to do quite a bit of work in migrating to another DI container. In conclusion, Spring's annotations approach is recommended over JSR-330 annotations given the fact that Spring's annotations are much more powerful, unless there is a requirement that your application should be IoC container independent.

Summary

In this chapter, you saw a wide range of Spring-specific features that complement the core IoC capabilities. You saw how to hook into the life cycle of a bean and to make it aware of the Spring environment. We introduced FactoryBeans as a solution for IoC-enabling a wider set of classes. We also looked at how you can use PropertyEditors to simplify application configuration and to remove the need for artificial String-typed properties. Moreover, we finished with an in-depth look at some additional features offered by the ApplicationContext including i18n, event publication, and resource access.

We also covered some latest features that were introduced into Spring 3.0 and 3.1, such as using Java classes instead of XML configuration, profiles support, and the environment and property source abstraction layer. Finally, we discussed using JSR-330 standard annotations in Spring.

So far, we have covered the main concepts of the Spring Framework and its features as a DI container as well as other services that the core Spring Framework provides. In the next chapter and onward, we will discuss using Spring in different specific areas such as AOP, data access, transaction support, web application support, and so on.

CHAPTER 6

Introducing Spring AOP

Besides Dependency Injection (DI), another core feature that the Spring Framework brings to the developer community is Aspect-Oriented Programming (AOP). Although it used to be difficult to learn, understand, and implement, thanks to Spring's intensive use of AOP within the framework and a simplified AOP programming model that Spring provides, AOP has become a technique that developers use on day-to-day development, especially when developing Spring-based applications. AOP is often referred to as a tool for implementing crosscutting concerns. When you "cut through" the unfamiliar terminology, you use AOP for modularizing individual pieces of logic, known as *concerns*, and you apply these concerns to many parts of an application. Logging and security are typical examples of crosscutting concerns that are present in many applications. Consider an application that logs the start and end of every method for debugging purposes. You will probably refactor the logging code into a special class, but you still have to call methods on that class twice per method in your application in order to perform the logging. Using AOP, you can simply specify that you want the methods on your logging class to be invoked before and after each method call in your application.

It is important that you understand that AOP complements OOP, rather than competes with it. OOP is very good at solving a wide variety of problems that we, as programmers, encounter. However, if you look at the logging example again, it is quite plain to see that OOP is lacking when it comes to implementing crosscutting logic on a large scale. Using AOP on its own to develop an entire application is practically impossible, given that AOP functions on top of OOP. Likewise, although it is certainly possible to develop entire applications using OOP, you can work smarter by employing AOP to solve certain problems that involve crosscutting logic.

We are going to cover AOP in this chapter and the next. In particular, this chapter covers the following topics:

- *AOP basics*: Before we begin discussing Spring's AOP implementation, we cover the basics of AOP as a technology. Most of the concepts covered in this section are not specific to Spring and can be found in any AOP implementation. If you are already familiar with another AOP implementation, then feel free to skip this section.

- *Types of AOP*: There are two distinct types of AOP: static and dynamic. In static AOP, like that provided by AspectJ's (http://eclipse.org/aspectj/) compile-time weaving mechanisms, the crosscutting logic is applied to your code at compile time, and you cannot change it without modifying the code and recompiling. With dynamic AOP, like Spring AOP, crosscutting logic is applied dynamically, at runtime. This allows you to make changes in the distribution of crosscutting without recompiling the application. These types of AOP are complementary, and, when used together, they form a powerful combination that you can use in your applications.

■ **Note** Static and dynamic AOP are distinct from the static and dynamic crosscutting concepts. The differentiation between static and dynamic crosscutting is largely academic and is of no relevance to Spring AOP. For more information on this topic and on AOP as a whole, we recommend you read *AspectJ in Action: Enterprise AOP with Spring Applications*, second edition, by Ramnivas Laddad (Manning, 2010).

- *Spring AOP architecture*: In this section, we get down to the nitty-gritty of Spring's AOP implementation. Spring AOP is only a subset of the full AOP feature set found in other implementations like AspectJ. In this section, we take a high-level look at which features are present in Spring, how they are implemented, and why some features are excluded from the Spring implementation.

- *Proxies in Spring AOP*: Proxies are a huge part of how Spring AOP works, and you must understand them to get the most out of Spring AOP. In this section, we look at the two kinds of proxy: the JDK dynamic proxy and the CGLIB proxy. In particular, we look at the different scenarios in which Spring uses each proxy, the performance of the two proxy types, and some simple guidelines to follow in your application to get the most from Spring AOP.

- *Using Spring AOP*: In this section, we present some practical examples of AOP usage. We start off with a simple "Hello World" example to ease you into Spring's AOP code, and we continue with a detailed description of the different AOP features that are available in Spring, complete with examples.

In this chapter, we cover Spring AOP in isolation from much of the rest of the framework. In Chapter 7, we take a much more framework-oriented view of Spring AOP, including how to configure AOP using `ApplicationContext`.

AOP Concepts

As with most technologies, AOP comes with its own specific set of concepts and terms. It is important that you understand what these terms mean before we explain how to use AOP in an application. The following list explains the core concepts of AOP:

- *Joinpoints*: A joinpoint is a well-defined point during the execution of your application. Typical examples of joinpoints include a call to a method, the Method Invocation itself, class initialization, and object instantiation. Joinpoints are a core concept of AOP and define the points in your application at which you can insert additional logic using AOP.

- *Advice*: The code that is executed at a particular joinpoint is the advice. There are many different types of advice, such as *before*, which executes before the joinpoint, and *after*, which executes after it. In OOP, an advice comes in the form of a method within a class.

- *Pointcuts*: A pointcut is a collection of joinpoints that you use to define when advice should be executed. By creating pointcuts, you gain fine-grained control over how you apply advice to the components in your application. As mentioned previously, a typical joinpoint is a Method Invocation. A typical pointcut is the collection of all Method Invocations in a particular class. Often you can compose pointcuts in complex relationships to further constrain when advice is executed. We discuss pointcut composition in more detail in the next chapter.

- *Aspects*: An aspect is the combination of advice and pointcuts. This combination results in a definition of the logic that should be included in the application and where it should execute.

- *Weaving*: This is the process of actually inserting aspects into the application code at the appropriate point. For compile-time AOP solutions, this is, unsurprisingly, done at compile time, usually as an extra step in the build process. Likewise, for runtime AOP solutions, the weaving process is executed dynamically at runtime. AspectJ supports another weaving mechanism called *load-time weaving* (LTW), in which it intercepts the underlying JVM class loader and provides weaving to the bytecode when it is being loaded by the class loader.

- *Target*: An object whose execution flow is modified by some AOP process is referred to as the target object. Often you see the target object referred to as the advised object.

- *Introduction*: This is the process by which you can modify the structure of an object by introducing additional methods or fields to it. You can use introduction to make any object implement a specific interface without needing the object's class to implement that interface explicitly.

Don't worry if you find these concepts confusing; this will all become clear when you see some examples. Also, be aware that you are shielded from many of these concepts in Spring AOP, and some are not relevant because of Spring's choice of implementation. We will discuss each of these features in the context of Spring as we progress through the chapter.

Types of AOP

As we mentioned earlier, there are two distinct types of AOP: static and dynamic. The difference between them is really the point at which the weaving process occurs and how this process is achieved.

Static AOP

Many of the first AOP implementations were static. In static AOP, the weaving process forms another step in the build process for an application. In Java terms, you achieve the weaving process in a static AOP implementation by modifying the actual bytecode of your application, changing and extending the application code as necessary. Clearly, this is a well-performing way of achieving the weaving process because the end result is just Java bytecode, and you do not perform any special tricks at runtime to determine when advice should be executed.

The drawback of this mechanism is that any modifications you make to the aspects, even if you simply want to add another joinpoint, require you to recompile the entire application. AspectJ's compile-time weaving is an excellent example of a static AOP implementation.

Dynamic AOP

Dynamic AOP implementations, like Spring AOP, differ from static AOP implementations in that the weaving process is performed dynamically at runtime. How this is achieved is implementation-dependent, but as you will see, Spring's adopted approach is to create proxies for all advised objects, allowing for advice to be invoked as required. The slight drawback of dynamic AOP is that, typically, it does not perform as well as static AOP, but the performance is steadily increasing. The major benefit of dynamic AOP implementations is the ease with which you can modify the entire aspect set of an application without needing to recompile the main application code.

Choosing an AOP Type

Choosing whether to use static or dynamic AOP is actually quite a hard decision. There is no reason for you to choose a single implementation exclusively, because both have their benefits. As a matter of fact, starting from version 2.0, Spring already provided a tight integration with AspectJ, allowing you to use both types of AOP with ease. In general, the static AOP implementations have been around longer, and they tend to have more feature-rich implementations, with a greater number of available joinpoints. Indeed, Spring supports only a subset of the features available with AspectJ. Typically, if performance is absolutely critical or you need an AOP feature that is not implemented in Spring, then you will want to use AspectJ. In most other cases, Spring AOP is ideal for what you are trying to achieve. Make sure you are aware that many AOP-based features are already available in Spring, such as declarative transaction management. Reimplementing these using AspectJ is a waste of time and effort, especially since Spring has tried-and-tested implementations ready for you to use.

Most importantly, let the requirements of your application drive your choice of AOP implementation, and don't restrict yourself to a single implementation if a combination of implementations would better suit your application. In general, we have found that Spring AOP is less complex than AspectJ, so it tends to be our first choice. If we find that Spring AOP won't do what we want it to do or we discover during application tuning that performance is poor (for example, when profiling the application using a Java profiler, the profiling result indicates that much time was spent in Spring in generating the dynamic proxy for the defined aspects), then we move to AspectJ instead.

AOP in Spring

You can think of Spring's AOP implementation as coming in two logical parts. The first part is the AOP core, which provides fully decoupled, purely programmatic AOP functionality (Spring called it the Spring AOP API). The second part of the AOP implementation is the set of framework services that make AOP easier to use in your applications. On top of this, other components of Spring, such as the transaction manager and EJB helper classes, provide AOP-based services to simplify the development of your application. In this chapter, we focus solely on the basics of the AOP core. The framework services and the advanced functionality of the core are covered in Chapter 7.

Spring AOP is really a subset of the full AOP feature set, implementing only a handful of the constructs available in implementations like AspectJ. Don't be fooled into thinking Spring AOP is not useful, however. Indeed, one of the most powerful aspects of Spring AOP is that it is so simple to use because it is unencumbered with extraneous features that you often do not need. The implementation of only a subset of the AOP feature set is a specific design goal of Spring, allowing Spring to focus on simple access to the most common features of AOP. To make sure you are not left without the AOP features you need, Spring's designers designed Spring to fully integrate with AspectJ.

The AOP Alliance

The AOP Alliance (http://aopalliance.sourceforge.net/) is a joint effort between representatives of many open source AOP projects, including Rod Johnson of Spring, to define a standard set of interfaces for AOP implementations. The AOP Alliance is being very conservative, resisting the temptation to over-constrain AOP while it is still growing, and as a result, it has defined interfaces for only a subset of AOP features. Wherever applicable, Spring uses the AOP Alliance interfaces rather than defining its own. This allows you to reuse certain advice across multiple AOP implementations that support the AOP Alliance interfaces.

"Hello World!" in AOP

Before we dive into discussing the Spring AOP implementation in detail, we want to present a simple example to provide some context for these discussions. In this example, we take a simple class that outputs the message "World," and then using AOP, we transform an instance of this class at runtime to output "Hello World!" instead. Listing 6-1 shows the basic MessageWriter class.

Listing 6-1. The MessageWriter Class

```
package com.apress.prospring3.ch6;

public class MessageWriter {

    public void writeMessage() {
        System.out.print("World");
    }
}
```

The MessageWriter class is nothing special; it has just one method that writes the message "World" to console output. We want to advise—that is, add some advice to—this class so that the writeMessage() method actually writes "Hello World!" instead.

To do this, we need to execute some code before the method body executes to write "Hello," and we need to execute some code after the method body executes to write "!" to this. In AOP terms, what we need is an *around* advice—that is, advice that executes around a joinpoint. In this case, the joinpoint is the invocation of the writeMessage() method. Listing 6-2 shows the implementation of the around advice, the MessageDecorator class.

Listing 6-2. Implementing Around Advice

```
package com.apress.prospring3.ch6;

import org.aopalliance.intercept.MethodInterceptor;
import org.aopalliance.intercept.MethodInvocation;

public class MessageDecorator implements MethodInterceptor {

    public Object invoke(MethodInvocation invocation) throws Throwable {
        System.out.print("Hello ");
        Object retVal = invocation.proceed();
        System.out.println("!");
        return retVal;
    }
}
```

The MethodInterceptor interface is the AOP Alliance standard interface for implementing around advice for Method Invocation joinpoints. The MethodInvocation object represents the Method Invocation that is being advised, and using this object, we control when the Method Invocation is actually allowed to proceed. Because this is around advice, we are essentially capable of performing some actions before the method is invoked and some actions after it is invoked but before it returns. In

Listing 6-2, we simply write "Hello" to console output, invoke the method with a call to MethodInvocation.proceed(), and then write "!" to console output.

The final step in this sample is to weave the MessageDecorator advice (more specifically, the invoke() method) into the code. To do this, we create an instance of MessageWriter, the target, and then create a proxy of this instance, instructing the proxy factory to weave in the MessageDecorator advice. This is shown in Listing 6-3.

Listing 6-3. *Weaving the MessageDecorator Advice*

```java
package com.apress.prospring3.ch6;

import org.springframework.aop.framework.ProxyFactory;

public class HelloWorldAOPExample {

    public static void main(String[] args) {
        MessageWriter target = new MessageWriter();

        // create the proxy
        ProxyFactory pf = new ProxyFactory();

        pf.addAdvice(new MessageDecorator());
        pf.setTarget(target);

        MessageWriter proxy = (MessageWriter) pf.getProxy();

        // write the messages target.writeMessage();
        target.writeMessage();
        System.out.println("");
        proxy.writeMessage();
    }
}
```

The important part here is that we use the ProxyFactory class to create the proxy of the target object, weaving in the advice at the same time. We pass the MessageDecorator advice to the ProxyFactory with a call to addAdvice() and specify the target for weaving with a call to setTarget(). Once the target is set and some advice is added to the ProxyFactory, we generate the proxy with a call to getProxy(). Finally, we call writeMessage() on both the original target object and the proxy object. Before we run the program, we need to add the dependency on CGLIB into the project, as shown in Table 6-1.

Table 6-1. *Dependency for CGLIB*

Group ID	Artifact ID	Version	Description
cglib	cglib	2.2.2	Code generation library required by Spring AOP

After the dependency is added, we can now run the program in Listing 6-3. Here are the results of running this example:

```
World
Hello World!
```

As you can see, calling writeMessage() on the untouched target object resulted in a standard Method Invocation, and no extra content is written to console output. However, the invocation of the proxy caused the code in the MessageDecorator to execute, creating the desired output of "Hello World!" From this example, you can see that the advised class had no dependencies on Spring or the AOP Alliance interfaces; the beauty of Spring AOP, and indeed AOP in general, is that you can advise almost any class, even if that class was created without AOP in mind. The only restriction, in Spring AOP at least, is that you can't advise final classes, because they cannot be overridden and therefore cannot be proxied.

Spring AOP Architecture

The core architecture of Spring AOP is based around proxies. When you want to create an advised instance of a class, you must use the ProxyFactory class to create a proxy of an instance of that class, first providing the ProxyFactory with all the aspects that you want to be woven into the proxy. Using ProxyFactory is a purely programmatic approach to creating AOP proxies. For the most part, you don't need to use this in your application; instead, you can rely on the declarative AOP configuration mechanisms provided by Spring (the ProxyFactoryBean class, the aop namespace, and @AspectJ-style annotations) to provide declarative proxy creation. However, it is important to understand how proxy creation works. For the rest of this chapter, we will use the programmatic approach to proxy creation. In the next chapter, we discuss using Spring's declarative AOP configurations.

At runtime, Spring will analyze the cross-cutting concerns defined for the beans in the ApplicationContext and generate proxy beans (which wraps the underlying target bean) dynamically. Instead of calling the target bean directly, callers are injected with the proxied bean, and any calls to the target are received by the proxy bean. The proxy bean will then analyze the running condition (i.e., joinpoint, pointcut, advice, etc.) and weave in the appropriate advice accordingly. Figure 6-1 shows a high-level view of a Spring AOP proxy in action.

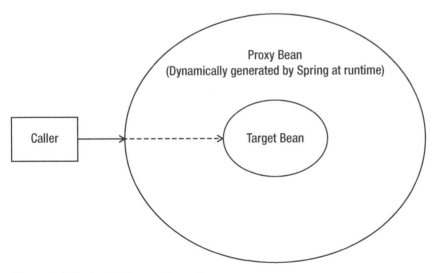

Figure 6-1. Spring AOP proxy in action

Internally, Spring has two proxy implementations: the JDK dynamic proxy and the CGLIB proxy. By default, when the target object to be advised implements some sort of an interface, Spring will use a JDK dynamic proxy to create proxy instances of the target. However, when the advised target object doesn't implement an interface (e.g., it's a concrete class), CGLIB will be used for proxy instance creation. One major reason is that JDK dynamic proxy only supports proxying of interfaces. We will discuss proxies in detail in the section "Understanding Proxies."

Joinpoints in Spring

One of the more noticeable simplifications in Spring AOP is that it supports only one joinpoint type: Method Invocation. At first glance, this might seem like a severe limitation if you are familiar with other AOP implementations like AspectJ, which supports many more joinpoints, but in fact this actually makes Spring more accessible.

The Method Invocation joinpoint is by far the most useful joinpoint available, and using it, you can achieve many of the tasks that make AOP useful in day-to-day programming. Remember that if you need to advise some code at a joinpoint other than a Method Invocation, you can always use Spring and AspectJ together.

Aspects in Spring

In Spring AOP, an aspect is represented by an instance of a class that implements the `Advisor` interface. Spring provides a selection of convenience `Advisor` implementations that you can use in your applications, thus removing the need for you to create lots of different `Advisor` implementations for your example. There are two subinterfaces of `Advisor`: `IntroductionAdvisor` and `PointcutAdvisor`. The `PointcutAdvisor` interface is implemented by all `Advisors` that use pointcuts to control the applicability of advice to joinpoints.

In Spring, introductions are treated as special kinds of advice. Using the `IntroductionAdvisor` interface, you can control those classes to which an introduction applies. We cover this in more detail in the next chapter.

We discuss the different `PointcutAdvisor` implementations in detail later in this chapter in the section "Advisors and Pointcuts in Spring."

About the ProxyFactory Class

The `ProxyFactory` class controls the weaving and proxy creation process in Spring AOP. Before you can actually create a proxy, you must specify the advised or target object. You can do this, as you saw earlier, using the `setTarget()` method. Internally, `ProxyFactory` delegates the proxy creation process to an instance of `DefaultAopProxyFactory`, which in turn delegates to either `Cglib2AopProxy` or `JdkDynamicAopProxy`, depending on the settings of your application. We discuss proxy creation in more detail later in this chapter.

Using the `ProxyFactory` class, you control which aspects you want to weave into the proxy. As mentioned earlier, you can weave only an aspect—that is, advice combined with a pointcut—into advised code. However, in some cases you want an advice to apply to the invocation of all methods in a class, not just a selection. For this reason, the `ProxyFactory` class provides the `addAdvice()` method that you saw in Listing 6-3. Internally, `addAdvice()` wraps the advice you pass it in an instance of `DefaultPointcutAdvisor`, which is the standard implementation of `PointcutAdvisor`, and configures it with a pointcut that includes all methods by default. When you want more control over the `Advisor` that is created, or when you want to add an introduction to the proxy, create the `Advisor` yourself and use the `addAdvisor()` method of the `ProxyFactory()`.

You can use the same `ProxyFactory` instance to create many different proxies, each with different aspects. To help with this, `ProxyFactory` has `removeAdvice()` and `removeAdvisor()` methods, which allow you to remove any advice or `Advisors` from the `ProxyFactory` that you previously passed to it. To check whether a `ProxyFactory` has a particular advice attached to it, call `adviceIncluded()`, passing in the advice object for which you want to check.

Creating Advice in Spring

Spring supports six different flavors of advice, described in Table 6-2.

Table 6-2. *Advice Types in Spring*

Advice Name	Interface	Description
Before	`org.springframework.aop` `.MethodBeforeAdvice`	Using before advice, you can perform custom processing before a joinpoint executes. Because a joinpoint in Spring is always a Method Invocation, this essentially allows you to perform preprocessing before the method executes. A before advice has full access to the target of the Method Invocation as well as the arguments passed to the method, but it has no control over the execution of the method itself. In case a before advice throws an exception, further execution of the interceptor chain (as well as the target method) will be aborted, and the exception will propagate back up the interceptor chain.
After returning	`org.springframework.aop` `.AfterReturningAdvice`	After-returning advice is executed after the Method Invocation at the joinpoint has finished executing and has returned a value. The after-returning advice has access to the target of the Method Invocation, the arguments passed to the method, and the return value as well. Because the method has already executed when the after-returning advice is invoked, it has no control over the Method Invocation at all. In case the target method throws an exception, the after-returning advice will not be run, and the exception will be propagated up to the call stack as usual.
After (finally)	`org.springframework.aop` `.AfterAdvice`	After-returning advice is executed only when the advised method completes normally. However, the after (finally) advice will be executed no matter the result of the advised method. The advice is executed even when the advised method fails and an exception is thrown.
Around	`org.aopalliance.intercept` `.MethodInterceptor`	In Spring, around advice is modeled using the AOP Alliance standard of a method interceptor. Your advice is allowed to execute before and after the Method Invocation, and you can control the point at which the Method Invocation is allowed to proceed. You can choose to bypass the method altogether if you want, providing your own implementation of the logic.
Throws	`org.springframework.aop` `.ThrowsAdvice`	Throws advice is executed after a Method Invocation returns, but only if that invocation threw an exception. It is possible for a throws advice to catch only specific exceptions, and if you choose to do so, you can access the method that threw the exception, the arguments passed into the invocation, and the target of the invocation.

Advice Name	Interface	Description
Introduction	`org.springframework.aop` `.IntroductionInterceptor`	Spring models introductions as special types of interceptors. Using an introduction interceptor, you can specify the implementation for methods that are being introduced by the advice. Introductions are covered in more detail in the next chapter.

We have found that these advice types, coupled with the Method Invocation joinpoint, allow us to perform about 90 percent of the tasks we want to perform with AOP. For the other 10 percent, which we use only rarely, we fall back on AspectJ.

Interfaces for Advice

From our previous discussion of the ProxyFactory class, recall that advice is added to a proxy either directly, using the addAdvice() method, or indirectly by using an Advisor, with the addAdvisor() method. The main difference between Advice and Advisor is that an Advisor carries an Advice with the associated Pointcut, which provides more fine-grained control on which joinpoints the Advice will intercept. With regard to advice, Spring created a well-defined hierarchy for advice interfaces. This hierarchy is based on the AOP Alliance interfaces and is shown in detail in Figure 6-2.

This kind of hierarchy has the benefit of not only being sound OO design but also that you can deal with advice types generically, such as by using a single addAdvice() method on the ProxyFactory, and you can add new advice types easily without having to modify the ProxyFactory class.

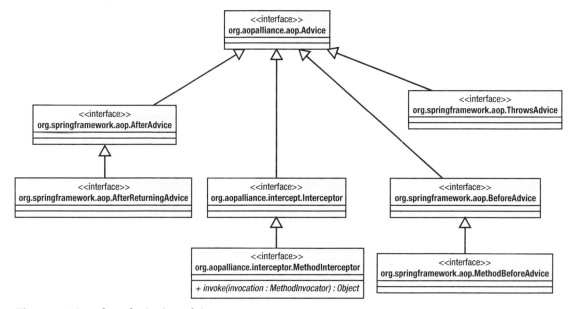

Figure 6-2. Interfaces for Spring advice types

Create Before Advice

Before advice is one of the most useful advice types available in Spring. A before advice can modify the arguments passed to a method and can prevent the method from executing by raising an exception. In the next chapter, you will see before advice used frequently when we look at how AOP is used in the SpringBlog application. In this section, we show you two examples of using before advice: a simple example that writes a message to console output containing the name of the method before the method executes and a simple security advice that you can use to restrict access to methods on an object.

In Listing 6-4, you can see the code for the SimpleBeforeAdvice class.

Listing 6-4. The SimpleBeforeAdvice Class

```
package com.apress.prospring3.ch6;

import java.lang.reflect.Method;

import org.springframework.aop.MethodBeforeAdvice;
import org.springframework.aop.framework.ProxyFactory;

public class SimpleBeforeAdvice implements MethodBeforeAdvice {

    public static void main(String[] args) {
        MessageWriter target = new MessageWriter();

        // create the proxy
        ProxyFactory pf = new ProxyFactory();

        pf.addAdvice(new SimpleBeforeAdvice());
        pf.setTarget(target);

        MessageWriter proxy = (MessageWriter) pf.getProxy();

        // write the messages
        proxy.writeMessage();
    }

    public void before(Method method, Object[] args, Object target)
            throws Throwable {
        System.out.println("Before method: " + method.getName());
    }
}
```

In this code, you can see that we have advised an instance of the MessageWriter class that we created earlier with an instance of the SimpleBeforeAdvice class. The MethodBeforeAdvice interface, which is implemented by SimpleBeforeAdvice, defines a single method, before(), which the AOP framework calls before the method at the joinpoint is invoked. Remember that, for now, we are using the default pointcut provided by the addAdvice() method, which matches all methods in a class. The before() method is passed three arguments: the method that is to be invoked, the arguments that will be passed to that method, and the Object that is the target of the invocation. The SimpleBeforeAdvice class uses the Method argument of the before() method to write a message to console output containing the name of the method to be invoked. Running this example gives us the following output:

```
Before method: writeMessage
World
```

As you can see, the output from the call to writeMessage() is shown, but just before it, you can see the output generated by the SimpleBeforeAdvice.

Securing Method Access Using Before Advice

The previous example was fairly trivial and didn't really show the power of AOP. In this section, we are going to build a before advice that checks user credentials before allowing the Method Invocation to proceed. If the user credentials are invalid, an exception is thrown by the advice, thus preventing the method from executing. The example in this section is simplistic. It allows users to authenticate with any password, and it also allows only a single, hard-coded user access to the secured methods. However, it does illustrate how easy it is to use AOP to implement a crosscutting concern such as security.

■ **Note** This is just an example of demonstrating the usage of before advice. For securing the method execution of Spring beans, the Spring Security project already provides comprehensive support; you don't need to implement the features by yourself.

Listing 6-5 shows the SecureBean class. This is the class that we will be securing using AOP.

Listing 6-5. The SecureBean Class

```
package com.apress.prospring3.ch6.security;

public class SecureBean {

    public void writeSecureMessage() {
        System.out.println("Every time I learn something new, "
            + "it pushes some old stuff out of my brain");
    }
}
```

The SecureBean class imparts a small pearl of wisdom from Homer Simpson, wisdom that we don't want everyone to see. Because this example requires users to authenticate, we are somehow going to need to store their details. Listing 6-6 shows the UserInfo class we use to store a user's credentials.

Listing 6-6. The UserInfo Class

```
package com.apress.prospring3.ch6.security;

public class UserInfo {
    private String userName;

    private String password;

    public UserInfo(String userName, String password) {
        this.userName = userName;
        this.password = password;
    }
```

```
    public String getPassword() {
        return password;
    }

    public String getUserName() {
        return userName;
    }
}
```

There is nothing really of interest in this class; it simply holds data about the user so that we can do something useful with it. Listing 6-7 shows the SecurityManager class, which is responsible for authenticating users and storing their credentials for later retrieval.

Listing 6-7. The SecurityManager Class

```
package com.apress.prospring3.ch6.security;

public class SecurityManager {

    private static ThreadLocal<UserInfo> threadLocal = new ThreadLocal<UserInfo>();

    public void login(String userName, String password) {
        // assumes that all credentials
        // are valid for a login
        threadLocal.set(new UserInfo(userName, password));
    }

    public void logout() {
        threadLocal.set(null);
    }

    public UserInfo getLoggedOnUser() {
        return threadLocal.get();
    }
}
```

The application uses the SecurityManager class to authenticate a user and, later, to retrieve the details of the currently authenticated user. The application authenticates a user using the login() method. In a real application, the login() method would probably check the supplied application against a database or LDAP directory, but here we assume all users are allowed to authenticate. The login() method creates a UserInfo object for the user and stores it on the current thread using a ThreadLocal. The logout() method sets any value that might be stored in the ThreadLocal to null. Finally, the getLoggedOnUser() method returns the UserInfo object for the currently authenticated user. This method returns null if no user is authenticated.

To check whether a user is authenticated and, if so, whether the user is permitted to access the methods on SecureBean, we need to create an advice that executes before the method and checks the UserInfo object returned by SecurityManager.getLoggedOnUser() against the set of credentials for allowed users. The code for this advice, SecurityAdvice, is shown in Listing 6-8.

Listing 6-8. The SecurityAdvice Class

```
package com.apress.prospring3.ch6.security;

import java.lang.reflect.Method;
```

```
import org.springframework.aop.MethodBeforeAdvice;

public class SecurityAdvice implements MethodBeforeAdvice {

    private SecurityManager securityManager;

    public SecurityAdvice() {
        this.securityManager = new SecurityManager();
    }

    public void before(Method method, Object[] args, Object target)
            throws Throwable {
        UserInfo user = securityManager.getLoggedOnUser();

        if (user == null) {
            System.out.println("No user authenticated");
            throw new SecurityException(
                "You must login before attempting to invoke the method: "
                + method.getName());
        } else if ("clarence".equals(user.getUserName())) {
            System.out.println("Logged in user is clarence - OKAY!");
        } else {
            System.out.println("Logged in user is " + user.getUserName()
                + " NOT GOOD :(");
            throw new SecurityException("User " + user.getUserName()
                + " is not allowed access to method " + method.getName());
        }
    }
}
```

The SecurityAdvice class creates an instance of SecurityManager in its constructor and then stores this instance in a field. You should note that the application and the SecurityAdvice don't need to share the same SecurityManager instance, because all data is stored with the current thread using ThreadLocal. In the before() method, we perform a simple check to see whether the user name of the authenticated user is clarence. If so, we allow the user access; otherwise, an exception is raised. Also notice that we check for a null UserInfo object, which indicates that the current user is not authenticated.

In Listing 6-9, you can see a sample application that uses the SecurityAdvice class to secure the SecureBean class.

Listing 6-9. The SecurityExample Class

```
package com.apress.prospring3.ch6.security;

import org.springframework.aop.framework.ProxyFactory;

public class SecurityExample {

    public static void main(String[] args) {
        // get the security manager
        SecurityManager mgr = new SecurityManager();

        // get the bean
        SecureBean bean = getSecureBean();

        // try as clarence
```

```
        mgr.login("clarence", "pwd");
        bean.writeSecureMessage();
        mgr.logout();

        // try as janm
        try {
            mgr.login("janm", "pwd");
            bean.writeSecureMessage();
        } catch(SecurityException ex) {
            System.out.println("Exception Caught: " + ex.getMessage());
        } finally {
            mgr.logout();
        }

        // try with no credentials
        try {
            bean.writeSecureMessage();
        } catch(SecurityException ex) {
            System.out.println("Exception Caught: " + ex.getMessage());
        }
    }

    private static SecureBean getSecureBean() {
        // create the target
        SecureBean target = new SecureBean();

        // create the advice
        SecurityAdvice advice = new SecurityAdvice();

        // get the proxy
        ProxyFactory factory = new ProxyFactory();
        factory.setTarget(target);
        factory.addAdvice(advice);
        SecureBean proxy = (SecureBean)factory.getProxy();

        return proxy;

    }
}
```

In the getSecureBean() method, we create a proxy of the SecureBean class that is advised using an instance of SecurityAdvice. This proxy is returned to the caller. When the caller invokes any method on this proxy, the call is first routed to the instance of SecurityAdvice for a security check. In the main() method, we test three different scenarios, invoking the SecureBean.writeSecureMessage() method with two different sets of user credentials and then no user credentials at all. Because the SecurityAdvice allows method calls to proceed only if the currently authenticated user is clarence, we expect that the only successful scenario in Listing 6-9 is the first of these scenarios. Running this example gives the following output:

```
Logged in user is clarence - OKAY!
Every time I learn something new, it pushes some old stuff out my brain
Logged in user is janm NOT GOOD :(
Exception Caught: User janm is not allowed access to method writeSecureMessage
No user authenticated
```

```
Exception Caught: You must login before attempting to invoke the method: writeSecureMessage
```

As you can see, only the first invocation of `SecureBean.writeSecureMessage()` was allowed to proceed. The remaining invocations were prevented by the `SecurityException` thrown by the `SecurityAdvice`.

This example is simple, but it does highlight the usefulness of the before advice. Security is a typical example of before advice, but we also find it useful when a scenario demands the modification of arguments going into the method. In Chapter 7, we show you how to use before advice to create an obscenity filter for the SpringBlog application.

Creating After-Returning Advice

As its name implies, after-returning advice is executed after the Method Invocation at the joinpoint returns. Given that the method has already executed, you can't change the arguments that are passed to it. Although you can read these arguments, you can't change the execution path, and you can't prevent the method from executing. These restrictions are expected; what is not expected, however, is the fact that you cannot modify the return value in the after-returning advice. You are simply restricted to performing some additional processing. Although after-returning advice cannot modify the return value of a Method Invocation, it can throw an exception that can be sent up the stack instead of the return value.

In this section, we look at two examples of using after-returning advice in an application. The first example simply writes a message to console output after the method has been invoked. The second example shows how you can use after-returning advice to add additional error checking to a method. Consider a class, KeyGenerator, that generates keys for cryptographic purposes. Many cryptographic algorithms suffer from the problem that a small number of keys in the keyspace are considered weak. A weak key is any key whose characteristics make it significantly easier to derive the original message without knowing the key. For the DES algorithm, there are a total of 256 possible keys. From this keyspace, 4 keys are considered weak, and another 12 are considered semi-weak. Although the chance of one of these keys being generated randomly is ridiculously small (1 in 252), testing for the keys is so simple that it seems almost lax to ignore the test. In the second example of this section, we build an after-returning advice that checks for weak keys generated by the KeyGenerator and raises an exception if one is found.

■ **Note** For more information on weak keys and cryptography at large, we recommend you read *Applied Cryptography* by Bruce Schneier (Wiley, 1995).

In Listing 6-10, you can see the `SimpleAfterReturningAdvice` class, which demonstrates the use of after-returning advice by writing a message to console output after a method has returned.

Listing 6-10. The SimpleAfterReturningAdvice Class

```
package com.apress.prospring3.ch6;

import java.lang.reflect.Method;

import org.springframework.aop.AfterReturningAdvice;
import org.springframework.aop.framework.ProxyFactory;

public class SimpleAfterReturningAdvice implements AfterReturningAdvice {
```

```
    public static void main(String[] args) {
        MessageWriter target = new MessageWriter();

        // create the proxy
        ProxyFactory pf = new ProxyFactory();

        pf.addAdvice(new SimpleAfterReturningAdvice());
        pf.setTarget(target);

        MessageWriter proxy = (MessageWriter) pf.getProxy();

        // write the messages
        proxy.writeMessage();
    }

    public void afterReturning(Object returnValue, Method method,
            Object[] args, Object target) throws Throwable {
        System.out.println("");
        System.out.println("After method: " + method.getName());
    }
}
```

This example is really not that different from the SimpleBeforeAdvice class you saw earlier. Notice that the AfterReturningAdvice interface declares a single method, afterReturning(), which is passed the return value of Method Invocation, a reference to the method that was invoked, the arguments that were passed to the method, and the target of the invocation. Running this example results in the following output:

```
World
After method: writeMessage
```

The output is very similar to that of the before advice example except that, as expected, the message written by the advice appears after the message written by the writeMessage() method.

A good use of after-returning advice is to perform some additional error checking when it is possible for a method to return an invalid value. In the scenario we described earlier, it is possible for a cryptographic key generator to generate a key that is considered weak for a particular algorithm. Ideally, the key generator would check for these weak keys, but since the chance of these keys arising is often very small, many generators do not check. By using an after-returning advice, we can advise the method that generates the key and performs this additional check. Listing 6-11 shows an extremely primitive key generator.

Listing 6-11. The KeyGenerator Class

```
package com.apress.prospring3.ch6.crypto;

import java.util.Random;

public class KeyGenerator {

    public static final long WEAK_KEY = 0xFFFFFFFF0000000L;
    public static final long STRONG_KEY = 0xACDF03F590AE56L;

    private Random rand = new Random();

    public long getKey() {
```

197

```
        int x = rand.nextInt(3);

        if(x == 1) {
            return WEAK_KEY;
        } else {
            return STRONG_KEY;
        }
    }
}
```

It is plain to see that this key generator is ridiculously insecure, but we didn't want you to have to wait around for years while a real key generator produced a weak key, so we created this generator, which has a one-in-three chance of producing a weak key. In Listing 6-12, you can see the WeakKeyCheckAdvice that checks to see whether the result of the getKey() method is a weak key.

Listing 6-12. *Checking for Weak Keys*

```
package com.apress.prospring3.ch6.crypto;

import java.lang.reflect.Method;

import org.springframework.aop.AfterReturningAdvice;

public class WeakKeyCheckAdvice implements AfterReturningAdvice {

    public void afterReturning(Object returnValue, Method method,
            Object[] args,Object target) throws Throwable {

        if ((target instanceof KeyGenerator)
                && ("getKey".equals(method.getName()))) {
            long key = ((Long) returnValue).longValue();

            if (key == KeyGenerator.WEAK_KEY) {
                throw new SecurityException(
                    "Key Generator generated a weak key. Try again");
            }
        }
    }
}
```

In the afterReturning() method, we check first to see whether the method that was executed at the joinpoint was the getKey() method. If so, we then check the result value to see whether it was the weak key. If we find that the result of the getKey() method was a weak key, then we throw a SecurityException to inform the calling code of this. Listing 6-13 shows a simple application that demonstrates the use of this advice.

Listing 6-13. *Testing the WeakKeyCheckAdvice Class*

```
package com.apress.prospring3.ch6.crypto;

import org.springframework.aop.framework.ProxyFactory;

public class AfterAdviceExample {

    public static void main(String[] args) {
```

```
        KeyGenerator keyGen = getKeyGenerator();

        for(int x = 0; x < 10; x++) {
            try {
                long key = keyGen.getKey();
                System.out.println("Key: " + key);
            } catch(SecurityException ex) {
                System.out.println("Weak Key Generated!");
            }
        }
    }

    private static KeyGenerator getKeyGenerator() {

        KeyGenerator target = new KeyGenerator();

        ProxyFactory factory = new ProxyFactory();
        Factory.setTarget(target);
        factory.addAdvice(new WeakKeyCheckAdvice());

        return (KeyGenerator)factory.getProxy();
    }
}
```

After creating an advised proxy of a KeyGenerator target, the AfterAdviceExample class attempts to generate ten keys. If a SecurityException is thrown during a single generation, then a message is written to console output informing the user that a weak key was generated; otherwise, the generated key is displayed. A single run of this on our machine generated the following output:

```
Key: 48658904092028502
Key: 48658904092028502
Weak Key Generated!
Key: 48658904092028502
Key: 48658904092028502
Key: 48658904092028502
Weak Key Generated!
Key: 48658904092028502
Key: 48658904092028502
Key: 48658904092028502
```

As you can see, the KeyGenerator class sometimes generates weak keys, as expected, and the WeakKeyCheckAdvice ensures that a SecurityException is raised whenever a weak key is encountered.

Creating Around Advice

Around advice functions like a combination of before and after advice, with one big difference—you can modify the return value. Not only that, but you can prevent the method from actually executing. This means that using around advice, you can essentially replace the entire implementation of a method with new code. Around advice in Spring is modeled as an interceptor using the MethodInterceptor interface. There are many uses for around advice, and you will find that many features of Spring are created using method interceptors, such as the remote proxy support and the transaction management features. Method interception is also a good mechanism for profiling the execution of your application, and it forms the basis of the example in this section.

We are not going to build a simple example for method interception; instead, we refer to the first example in Listing 6-2, which shows how to use a basic method interceptor to write a message on either side of a Method Invocation. Notice from this earlier example that the invoke() method of the MethodInterceptor class does not provide the same set of arguments as the MethodBeforeAdvice and AfterReturningAdvice—that is, the method is not passed the target of the invocation, the method that was invoked, or the arguments used. However, you can get access to this data using the MethodInvocation object that is passed to invoke(). You will see a demonstration of this in the following example.

For this example, we want to achieve some way to advise a class so that we get basic information about the runtime performance of its methods. Specifically, we want to know how long the method took to execute. To achieve this, we can use the StopWatch class included in Spring, and we clearly need a MethodInterceptor, because we need to start the StopWatch before the Method Invocation and stop it right afterward.

Listing 6-14 shows the WorkerBean class that we are going to profile using the StopWatch class and an around advice.

Listing 6-14. The WorkerBean Class

```
package com.apress.prospring3.ch6.profiling;

public class WorkerBean {

    public void doSomeWork(int noOfTimes) {
        for(int x = 0; x < noOfTimes; x++) {
            work();
        }
    }

    private void work() {
        System.out.print("");
    }
}
```

This is a very simple class. The doSomeWork() method accepts a single argument, noOfTimes, and calls the work() method exactly the number of times specified by this method. The work() method simply has a dummy call to System.out.print(), which passes in an empty String. This prevents the compiler from optimizing out the work() method and thus the call to work().

In Listing 6-15, you can see the ProfilingInterceptor class that uses the StopWatch class to profile Method Invocation times. We use this interceptor to profile the WorkerBean class shown in Listing 6-14.

Listing 6-15. The ProfilingInterceptor Class

```
package com.apress.prospring3.ch6.profiling;

import java.lang.reflect.Method;

import org.aopalliance.intercept.MethodInterceptor;
import org.aopalliance.intercept.MethodInvocation;
import org.springframework.util.StopWatch;

public class ProfilingInterceptor implements MethodInterceptor {

    public Object invoke(MethodInvocation invocation) throws Throwable {
        // start the stop watch
```

```
        StopWatch sw = new StopWatch();
        sw.start(invocation.getMethod().getName());

        Object returnValue = invocation.proceed();

        sw.stop();
        dumpInfo(invocation, sw.getTotalTimeMillis());
        return returnValue;
    }

    private void dumpInfo(MethodInvocation invocation, long ms) {
        Method m = invocation.getMethod();
        Object target = invocation.getThis();
        Object[] args = invocation.getArguments();

        System.out.println("Executed method: " + m.getName());
        System.out.println("On object of type: " +
                target.getClass().getName());

        System.out.println("With arguments:");
        for (int x = 0; x < args.length; x++) {
            System.out.print("        > " + args[x]);
        }
        System.out.print("\n");

        System.out.println("Took: " + ms + " ms");
    }
}
```

In the invoke() method, which is the only method in the MethodInterceptor interface, we create an instance of StopWatch and then start it running immediately, allowing the Method Invocation to proceed with a call to MethodInvocation.proceed(). As soon as the Method Invocation has ended and the return value has been captured, we stop the StopWatch and pass the total number of milliseconds taken, along with the MethodInvocation object, to the dumpInfo() method. Finally, we return the Object returned by MethodInvocation.proceed() so that the caller obtains the correct return value. In this case, we did not want to disrupt the call stack in any way; we were simply acting as an eavesdropper on the Method Invocation. If we had wanted, we could have changed the call stack completely, redirecting the method call to another object or a remote service, or we could simply have reimplemented the method logic inside the interceptor and returned a different return value.

The dumpInfo() method simply writes some information about the method call to console output, along with the time taken for the method to execute. In the first three lines of dumpInfo(), you can see how you can use the MethodInvocation object to determine the method that was invoked, the original target of the invocation, and the arguments used.

Listing 6-16 shows the ProfilingExample class that first advises an instance of WorkerBean with a ProfilingInterceptor and then profiles the doSomeWork() method.

Listing 6-16. The ProfilingExample Class

```
package com.apress.prospring3.ch6.profiling;

import org.springframework.aop.framework.ProxyFactory;

public class ProfilingExample {
```

```
public static void main(String[] args) {
    WorkerBean bean = getWorkerBean();
    bean.doSomeWork(10000000);
}

private static WorkerBean getWorkerBean() {
    WorkerBean target = new WorkerBean();

    ProxyFactory factory = new ProxyFactory();
    factory.setTarget(target);
    factory.addAdvice(new ProfilingInterceptor());

    return (WorkerBean)factory.getProxy();
}
}
```

You should be more than familiar with this code by now. Running this example on our machine produces the following output:

```
Executed method: doSomeWork
On object of type: com.apress.prospring3.ch6.profiling.WorkerBean
With arguments:
    > 10000000
Took: 874 ms
```

From this output, you can see which method was executed, what the class of the target was, what arguments were passed in, and how long the invocation took.

Creating Throws Advice

Throws advice is similar to after-returning advice in that it executes after the joinpoint, which is always a Method Invocation, but throws advice executes only if the method throws an exception. Throws advice is also similar to after-returning advice in that it has little control over program execution. If you are using a throws advice, you can't choose to ignore the exception that was raised and return a value for the method instead. The only modification you can make to the program flow is to change the type of exception that is thrown. This is actually quite a powerful idea and can make application development much simpler. Consider a situation where you have an API that throws an array of poorly defined exceptions. Using a throws advice, you can advise all classes in that API and reclassify the exception hierarchy into something more manageable and descriptive. Of course, you can also use throws advice to provide centralized error logging across your application, thus reducing the amount of error logging code that is spread across your application.

As you saw from the diagram in Figure 6-1, throws advice is implemented by the ThrowsAdvice interface. Unlike the interfaces you have seen so far, ThrowsAdvice does not define any methods; instead, it is simply a marker interface used by Spring. The reason for this is that Spring allows typed throws advice, which allows you to define exactly which Exception types your throws advice should catch. Spring achieves this by detecting methods with certain signatures using reflection. Spring looks for two distinct method signatures. This is best demonstrated with a simple example. Listing 6-17 shows a simple bean with two methods that both simply throw exceptions of different types.

Listing 6-17. The ErrorBean Class

```
package com.apress.prospring3.ch6;

public class ErrorBean {
```

```
    public void errorProneMethod() throws Exception {
        throw new Exception("Foo");
    }

    public void otherErrorProneMethod() throws IllegalArgumentException {
        throw new IllegalArgumentException("Bar");
    }
}
```

In Listing 6-18, you can see the SimpleThrowsAdvice class that demonstrates both of the method signatures that Spring looks for on a throws advice.

Listing 6-18. The SimpleThrowsAdvice Class

```
package com.apress.prospring3.ch6;

import java.lang.reflect.Method;

import org.springframework.aop.ThrowsAdvice;
import org.springframework.aop.framework.ProxyFactory;

public class SimpleThrowsAdvice implements ThrowsAdvice {

    public static void main(String[] args) throws Exception {
        ErrorBean errorBean = new ErrorBean();

        ProxyFactory pf = new ProxyFactory();
        pf.setTarget(errorBean);
        pf.addAdvice(new SimpleThrowsAdvice());

        ErrorBean proxy = (ErrorBean) pf.getProxy();

        try {
            proxy.errorProneMethod();
        } catch (Exception ignored) {

        }

        try {
            proxy.otherErrorProneMethod();
        } catch (Exception ignored) {
        }
    }

    public void afterThrowing(Exception ex) throws Throwable {
        System.out.println("***");
        System.out.println("Generic Exception Capture");
        System.out.println("Caught: " + ex.getClass().getName());
        System.out.println("***\n");
    }

    public void afterThrowing(Method method, Object[] args, Object target,
            IllegalArgumentException ex) throws Throwable {
        System.out.println("***");
```

```
        System.out.println("IllegalArgumentException Capture");
        System.out.println("Caught: " + ex.getClass().getName());
        System.out.println("Method: " + method.getName());
        System.out.println("***\n");
    }
}
```

We are sure that you understand the code in the main() method, so now we will just focus on the two afterThrowing() methods. The first thing Spring looks for in a throws advice is one or more public methods called afterThrowing(). The return type of the methods is unimportant, although we find it best to stick with void because this method can't return any meaningful value. The first afterThrowing() method in the SimpleThrowsAdvice class has a single argument of type Exception. You can specify any type of Exception as the argument, and this method is ideal when you are not concerned about the method that threw the exception or the arguments that were passed to it. Note that this method catches Exception and any subtypes of Exception unless the type in question has its own afterThrowing() method.

In the second afterThrowing() method, we declared four arguments to catch the Method that threw the exception, the arguments that were passed to the method, and the target of the Method Invocation. The order of the arguments in this method is important, and you must specify all four. Notice that the second afterThrowing() method catches exceptions of type IllegalArgumentException (or its subtype). Running this example produces the following output:

```
***
Generic Exception Capture
Caught: java.lang.Exception
***


***
IllegalArgumentException Capture
Caught: java.lang.IllegalArgumentException
Method: otherErrorProneMethod
***
```

As you can see, when a plain old Exception is thrown, the first afterThrowing() method is invoked, but when an IllegalArgumentException is thrown, the second afterThrowing() method is invoked. Spring invokes a single afterThrowing() method only for each Exception, and as you saw from the example in Listing 6-18, Spring uses the method whose signature contains the best match for the Exception type. In the situation where your after-throwing advice has two afterThrowing() methods, both declared with the same Exception type but one with a single argument and the other with four arguments, Spring invokes the four-argument afterThrowing() method.

As we mentioned earlier, after-throwing advice is useful in a variety of situations; it allows you to reclassify entire Exception hierarchies as well as build centralized Exception logging for your application. We have found that after-throwing advice is particularly useful when we are debugging a live application, because it allows us to add extra logging code without needing to modify the application's code.

Choosing an Advice Type

In general, the choice of which advice type you want to use is driven by the requirements of your application, but you should choose the most specific advice type for your need. That is to say, don't use an around advice when a before advice will do. In most cases, an around advice can accomplish everything that the other three advice types can, but it may be overkill for what you are trying to achieve. By using the most specific type of advice, you are making the intention of your code clearer, and you are also reducing the possibility of errors. Consider an advice that counts method calls. When you are using before advice, all you need to code is the counter, but with an around advice, you need to remember to invoke the method and return the value to the caller. These small things can allow spurious errors to creep into your application. By keeping the advice type as focused as possible, you reduce the scope for errors.

Advisors and Pointcuts in Spring

Thus far, all the examples you have seen have used the `ProxyFactory.addAdvice()` method to configure advice for a proxy. As we mentioned earlier, this method delegates to `addAdvisor()` behind the scenes, creating an instance of `DefaultPointcutAdvisor` and configuring it with a pointcut that points to all methods. In this way, the advice is deemed to apply to all methods on the target. In some cases, such as when you are using AOP for logging purposes, this may be desirable, but in other cases you may want to limit the methods to which an advice applies.

Of course, you could simply perform the checking in the advice itself that the method being advised is the correct one, but this approach has several drawbacks. First, hard-coding the list of acceptable methods into the advice reduces the advice's reusability. By using pointcuts, you can configure the methods to which an advice applies, without needing to put this code inside the advice; this clearly increases the reuse value of the advice. The second and third drawbacks with hard-coding the list of methods into the advice are performance related. To check the method being advised in the advice, you need to perform the check each time any method on the target is invoked. This clearly reduces the performance of your application. When you use pointcuts, the check is performed once for each method, and the results are cached for later use. The other performance-related drawback of not using pointcuts to restrict the list-advised methods is that Spring can make optimizations for nonadvised methods when creating a proxy, which results in faster invocations on nonadvised methods. These optimizations are covered in greater detail when we discuss proxies later in the chapter.

We strongly recommend that you avoid the temptation to hard-code method checks into your advice and instead use pointcuts wherever possible to govern the applicability of advice to methods on the target. That said, in some cases it is necessary to hard-code the checks into your advice. Consider the earlier example of the after-returning advice designed to catch weak keys generated by the `KeyGenerator` class. This kind of advice is closely coupled to the class it is advising, and it is wise to check inside the advice to ensure that it is applied to the correct type. We refer to this coupling between advice and target as *target affinity*. In general, you should use pointcuts when your advice has little or no target affinity—that is, it can apply to any type or a wide range of types. When your advice has strong target affinity, try to check that the advice is being used correctly in the advice itself; this helps reduce head-scratching errors when an advice is misused. We also recommend you avoid advising methods needlessly. As you will see, this results in a noticeable drop in invocation speed that can have a large impact on the overall performance of your application.

The Pointcut Interface

Pointcuts in Spring are created by implementing the `Pointcut` interface, as shown in Listing 6-19.

Listing 6-19. The Pointcut Interface

```
package org.springframework.aop;

public interface Pointcut {

    ClassFilter getClassFilter ();

    MethodMatcher getMethodMatcher();
}
```

As you can see from this code, the `Pointcut` interface defines two methods, `getClassFilter()` and `getMethodMatcher()`, which return instances of `ClassFilter` and `MethodMatcher`, respectively. When creating your own pointcuts from scratch, you must implement both the `ClassFilter` and `MethodMatcher` interfaces as well. Thankfully, as you will see in the next section, this is usually unnecessary because Spring provides a selection of `Pointcut` implementations that cover almost if not all of your use cases.

When determining whether a `Pointcut` applies to a particular method, Spring first checks to see whether the `Pointcut` applies to the method's class using the `ClassFilter` instance returned by `Pointcut.getClassFilter()`. Listing 6-20 shows the `ClassFilter` interface.

Listing 6-20. The `ClassFilter` Interface

```
org.springframework.aop;

public interface ClassFilter {

    boolean matches(Class<?> clazz);
}
```

As you can see, the `ClassFilter` interface defines a single method, `matches()`, that is passed an instance of `Class` that represents the class to be checked. As you have no doubt determined, the `matches()` method returns true if the pointcut applies to the class and false otherwise.

The `MethodMatcher` interface is more complex than the `ClassFilter` interface, as shown in Listing 6-21.

Listing 6-21. The `MethodMatcher` Interface

```
package org.springframework.aop;

public interface MethodMatcher {

    boolean matches(Method m, Class<?> targetClass);

    boolean isRuntime();

    boolean matches(Method m, Class<?> targetClass, Object[] args);
}
```

Spring supports two different types of `MethodMatcher`, static and dynamic, determined by the return value of `isRuntime()`. Before using a `MethodMatcher`, Spring calls `isRuntime()` to determine whether the `MethodMatcher` is static, indicated by a return value of false, or dynamic, indicated by a return value of true.

For a static pointcut, Spring calls the `matches(Method, Class<T>)` method of the `MethodMatcher` once for every method on the target, caching the return value for subsequent invocations of those methods. In this way, the check for method applicability is performed only once for each method, and subsequent invocations of a method do not result in an invocation of `matches()`.

With dynamic pointcuts, Spring still performs a static check using `matches(Method, Class<T>)` the first time a method is invoked to determine the overall applicability of a method. However, in addition to this and provided that the static check returned true, Spring performs a further check for each invocation of a method using the `matches(Method, Class<T>, Object[])` method. In this way, a dynamic `MethodMatcher` can determine whether a pointcut should apply based on a particular invocation of a method, not just on the method itself. For example, a pointcut needs to be applied only when the argument is an `Integer` with a value larger than 100. In this case, the `matches(Method, Class<T>, Object[])` method can be coded to perform further checking on the argument for each invocation.

Clearly, static pointcuts—that is, pointcuts whose `MethodMatcher` is static—perform much better than dynamic pointcuts because they avoid the need for an additional check per invocation. That said, dynamic pointcuts provide a greater level of flexibility for deciding whether to apply an advice. In general, we recommend you use static pointcuts wherever you can. However, in cases where your advice adds substantial overhead, it may be wise to avoid any unnecessary invocations of your advice by using a dynamic pointcut.

In general, you rarely create your own `Pointcut` implementations from scratch because Spring provides abstract base classes for both static and dynamic pointcuts. We look at these base classes, along with other `Pointcut` implementations, over the next few sections.

Available Pointcut Implementations

As of version 3.1, Spring provides eight implementations of the `Pointcut` interface: two abstract classes intended as convenience classes for creating static and dynamic pointcuts, and six concrete classes, one for each of the following:

- Composing multiple pointcuts together
- Handling control flow pointcuts
- Performing simple name-based matching
- Defining pointcuts using regular expressions
- Defining pointcuts using AspectJ expressions
- Defining pointcuts that look for specific annotations at the class or method level

Table 6-3 summarizes the eight `Pointcut` interface implementations.

Table 6-3. Summary of Spring Pointcut Implementations

Implementation Class	Description
`org.springframework.aop.support` `.annotation.AnnotationMatchingPointcut`	Pointcut that looks for specific Java annotation on a class or method. This class requires JDK 5 or higher.
`org.springframework.aop` `.aspectj.AspectJExpressionPointcut`	Pointcut that uses AspectJ weaver to evaluate a pointcut expression in AspectJ syntax.
`org.springframework.aop` `.support.ComposablePointcut`	The `ComposablePointcut` class is used to compose two or more pointcuts together with operations such as `union()` and `intersection()`. This class is covered in more detail in the next chapter.
`org.springframework.aop.support` `.ControlFlowPointcut`	The `ControlFlowPointcut` is a special case pointcut that matches all methods within the control flow of another method—that is, any method that is invoked either directly or indirectly as the result of another method being invoked. We cover `ControlFlowPointcut` in more detail in the next chapter.
`org.springframework.aop.support` `.DynamicMethodMatcherPointcut`	The `DynamicMethodMatcherPointcut` is intended as a base class for building dynamic pointcuts.

Implementation Class	Description
org.springframework.aop.support .JdkRegexpMethodPointcut	The JdkRexepMethodPointcut allows you to define pointcuts using JDK 1.4 regular expression support. This class requires JDK 1.4 or newer.
org.springframework.aop.support .NameMatchMethodPointcut	Using the NameMatchMethodPointcut, you can create a pointcut that performs simple matching against a list of method names.
org.springframework.aop.support .StaticMethodMatcherPointcut	The StaticMethodMatcherPointcut class is intended as a base for building static pointcuts.

Figure 6-3 shows the UML diagram for the Pointcut implementation classes.

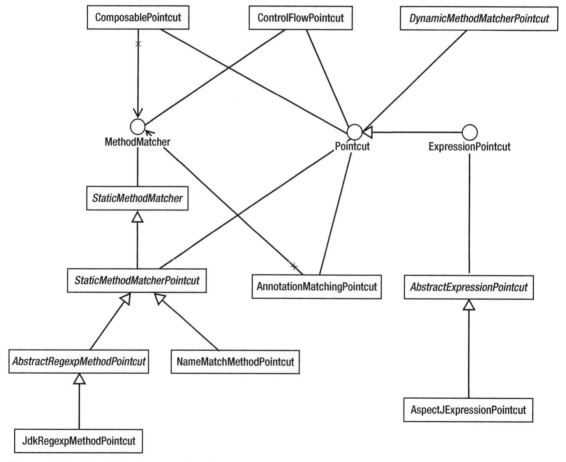

Figure 6-3. Pointcut implementation classes

We cover the six basic implementations in detail in the following sections. We leave discussions of the ComposablePointcut and ControlFlowPointcut classes until the next chapter.

Using DefaultPointcutAdvisor

Before you can use any Pointcut implementation, you must first create an instance of the Advisor interface, or more specifically a PointcutAdvisor interface. Remember from our earlier discussions that an Advisor is Spring's representation of an aspect (in the section "Aspects in Spring" in this chapter), a coupling of advice and pointcuts that governs which methods should be advised and how they should be advised. Spring provides a number of implementations of PointcutAdvisor, but for now we concern ourselves with just one—DefaultPointcutAdvisor (this class extends the AbstractGenericPointcut Advisor abstract class, which implements PointcutAdvisor). DefaultPointcutAdvisor is a simple PointcutAdvisor for associating a single Pointcut with a single Advice.

Creating a Static Pointcut Using StaticMethodMatcherPointcut

In this section, we will create a simple static pointcut by extending the abstract StaticMethodMatcherPointcut class. Since the StaticMethodMatcherPointcut class extends the StaticMethodMatcher class (an abstract class too), which implements the MethodMatcher interface, you are required to implement the method matches(Method, Class<?>); the rest of the Pointcut implementation is handled automatically. Although this is the only method you are required to implement (when extending the StaticMethodMatcherPointcut class), you may also want to override the getClassFilter() method as we do in this example to ensure that only methods of the correct type get advised.

For this example, we have two classes, BeanOne and BeanTwo, with identical methods defined in both. Listing 6-22 shows the BeanOne class.

Listing 6-22. *The BeanOne Class*

```
package com.apress.prospring3.ch6.staticpc;

public class BeanOne {

    public void foo() {
        System.out.println("foo");
    }

    public void bar() {
        System.out.println("bar");
    }
}
```

The BeanTwo class has identical methods to BeanOne. With this example, we want to be able to create a proxy of both classes using the same DefaultPointcutAdvisor but have the advice apply only to the foo() method of the BeanOne class. To do this, we created the SimpleStaticPointcut class, as shown in Listing 6-23.

Listing 6-23. *The SimpleStaticPointcut Class*

```
package com.apress.prospring3.ch6.staticpc;

import java.lang.reflect.Method;

import org.springframework.aop.ClassFilter;
```

```
import org.springframework.aop.support.StaticMethodMatcherPointcut;

public class SimpleStaticPointcut extends StaticMethodMatcherPointcut {

    public boolean matches(Method method, Class<?> cls) {
        return ("foo".equals(method.getName()));
    }

    public ClassFilter getClassFilter() {
        return new ClassFilter() {
            public boolean matches(Class<?> cls) {
                return (cls == BeanOne.class);
            }
        };
    }
}
```

Here you can see that we implemented the matches(Method, Class<?>) method as required by the StaticMethodMatcher abstract class. The implementation simply returns true if the name of the method is foo; otherwise, it returns false. Notice that we have also overridden the getClassFilter() method to return a ClassFilter instance whose matches() method returns true only for the BeanOne class. With this static pointcut, we are saying that only methods of the BeanOne class will be matched, and furthermore, only the foo() method of that class will be matched.

Listing 6-24 shows the SimpleAdvice class that simply writes out a message on either side of the Method Invocation.

Listing 6-24. *The SimpleAdvice Class*

```
package com.apress.prospring3.ch6.staticpc;

import org.aopalliance.intercept.MethodInterceptor;
import org.aopalliance.intercept.MethodInvocation;

public class SimpleAdvice implements MethodInterceptor {

    public Object invoke(MethodInvocation invocation) throws Throwable {
        System.out.println(">> Invoking " + invocation.getMethod().getName());
        Object retVal = invocation.proceed();
        System.out.println(">> Done");
        return retVal;
    }
}
```

In Listing 6-25, you can see a simple driver application for this example that creates an instance of DefaultPointcutAdvisor using the SimpleAdvice and SimpleStaticPointcut classes.

Listing 6-25. *The StaticPointcutExample Class*

```
package com.apress.prospring3.ch6.staticpc;

import org.aopalliance.aop.Advice;
import org.springframework.aop.Advisor;
import org.springframework.aop.Pointcut;
import org.springframework.aop.framework.ProxyFactory;
```

```java
import org.springframework.aop.support.DefaultPointcutAdvisor;

public class StaticPointcutExample {

    public static void main(String[] args) {
        BeanOne one = new BeanOne();
        BeanTwo two = new BeanTwo();

        BeanOne proxyOne;
        BeanTwo proxyTwo;

        // create pointcut, advice and advisor
        Pointcut pc = new SimpleStaticPointcut();
        Advice advice = new SimpleAdvice();
        Advisor advisor = new DefaultPointcutAdvisor(pc, advice);

        // create BeanOne proxy
        ProxyFactory pf = new ProxyFactory();
        pf.addAdvisor(advisor);
        pf.setTarget(one);
        proxyOne = (BeanOne)pf.getProxy();

        // create BeanTwo proxy
        pf = new ProxyFactory();
        pf.addAdvisor(advisor);
        pf.setTarget(two);
        proxyTwo = (BeanTwo)pf.getProxy();

        proxyOne.foo();
        proxyTwo.foo();

        proxyOne.bar();
        proxyTwo.bar();
    }
}
```

Notice that the DefaultPointcutAdvisor instance is then used to create two proxies: one for an instance of BeanOne and one for an instance of BeanTwo. Finally, both the foo() and bar() methods are invoked on the two proxies.

Running this example results in the following output:

```
>> Invoking foo
foo
>> Done
foo
bar
bar
```

As you can see, the only method for which the SimpleAdvice was actually invoked was the foo() method for the BeanOne class, exactly as expected. Restricting the methods that an advice applies is quite simple and, as you will see when we discuss the different proxy options, is key to getting the best performance out of your application.

211

Creating a Dynamic Pointcut Using DyanmicMethodMatcherPointcut

As we will demonstrate in this section, creating a dynamic pointcut is not much different from creating a static one. For this example, we create a dynamic pointcut for the class shown in Listing 6-26.

Listing 6-26. The SampleBean Class

```
package com.apress.prospring3.ch6.dynamicpc;

public class SampleBean {

    public void foo(int x) {
        System.out.println("Invoked foo() with: " + x);
    }

    public void bar() {
        System.out.println("Invoked bar()");
    }
}
```

For this example, we want to advise only the foo() method, but unlike the previous example, we want to advise this method only if the int argument passed to it is greater or less than 100.

As with static pointcuts, Spring provides a convenient base class for creating dynamic pointcuts—DynamicMethodMatcherPointcut. The DynamicMethodMatcherPointcut class has a single abstract method, matches(Method, Class<?>, Object[]) (via the MethodMatcher interface that it implements), that you must implement, but as you will see, it is also prudent to implement the matches(Method, Class<?>) method to control the behavior of the static checks. Listing 6-27 shows the SimpleDynamicPointcut class.

Listing 6-27. The SimpleDynamicPointcut Class

```
package com.apress.prospring3.ch6.dynamicpc;

import java.lang.reflect.Method;

import org.springframework.aop.ClassFilter;
import org.springframework.aop.support.DynamicMethodMatcherPointcut;

public class SimpleDynamicPointcut extends DynamicMethodMatcherPointcut {

    public boolean matches(Method method, Class<?> cls) {
        System.out.println("Static check for " + method.getName());
        return ("foo".equals(method.getName()));
    }

    public boolean matches(Method method, Class<?> cls, Object[] args) {
        System.out.println("Dynamic check for " + method.getName());

        int x = ((Integer) args[0]).intValue();

        return (x != 100);
    }

    public ClassFilter getClassFilter() {
        return new ClassFilter() {
```

```
        public boolean matches(Class<?> cls) {
            return (cls == SampleBean.class);
        }
    };
    }
}
```

As you can see from the code in Listing 6-27, we override the getClassFilter() method in a similar manner to the previous example shown in Listing 6-23. This removes the need to check the class in the method-matching methods—something that is especially important for the dynamic check. Although we are required to implement only the dynamic check, we implement the static check as well. The reason for this is that we know the bar() method will never be advised. By indicating this using the static check, Spring makes it so it never has to perform a dynamic check for this method. This is because when a static check method was implemented, Spring will first check against it, and if the checking result is a not a match, Spring will just stop the further dynamic checking. Moreover, the result of static check will be cached for better performance. But if we neglect the static check, Spring performs a dynamic check each time the bar() method is invoked. As a recommended practice, perform the class checking in the getClassFilter() method, method checking in the matches(Method, Class<?>) method, and argument checking in the matches(Method, Class<?>, Object[]) method. This will make your pointcut much easier to understand and maintain, and performance will be better too.

In the matches(Method, Class<?>, Object[]) method, you can see that we return false if the value of the int argument passed to the foo() method is not equal to 100; otherwise, we return true. Note that in the dynamic check, we know that we are dealing with the foo() method, because no other method makes it past the static check.

In Listing 6-28, you can see an example of this pointcut in action.

Listing 6-28. The DynamicPointcutExample Class

```
package com.apress.prospring3.ch6.dynamicpc;

import org.springframework.aop.Advisor;
import org.springframework.aop.framework.ProxyFactory;
import org.springframework.aop.support.DefaultPointcutAdvisor;

import com.apress.prospring3.ch6.staticpc.SimpleAdvice;

public class DynamicPointcutExample {

    public static void main(String[] args) {
        SampleBean target = new SampleBean();

        // create advisor
        Advisor advisor = new DefaultPointcutAdvisor(
            new SimpleDynamicPointcut(), new SimpleAdvice());

        // create proxy
        ProxyFactory pf = new ProxyFactory();
        pf.setTarget(target);
        pf.addAdvisor(advisor);
        SampleBean proxy = (SampleBean)pf.getProxy();

        proxy.foo(1);
        proxy.foo(10);
        proxy.foo(100);
```

```
        proxy.bar();
        proxy.bar();
        proxy.bar();
    }
}
```

Notice that we have used the same advice class as in the static pointcut example. However, in this example, only the first two calls to foo() should be advised. The dynamic check prevents the third call to foo() from being advised, and the static check prevents the bar() method from being advised. Running this example yields the following output:

```
Static check for foo
Static check for bar
Static check for toString
Static check for clone
Static check for foo
Dynamic check for foo
>> Invoking foo
Invoked foo() with: 1
>> Done
Dynamic check for foo
>> Invoking foo
Invoked foo() with: 10
>> Done
Dynamic check for foo
Invoked foo() with: 100
Static check for bar
Invoked bar()
Invoked bar()
Invoked bar()
```

As we expected, only the first two invocations of the foo() method were advised. Notice that none of the bar() invocations is subject to a dynamic check, thanks to the static check on bar(). An interesting point to note here is that the foo() method is actually subject to two static checks: one during the initial phase when all methods are checked and another when it is first invoked.

As you can see, dynamic pointcuts offer a greater degree of flexibility than static pointcuts, but because of the additional runtime overhead they require, you should use a dynamic pointcut only when absolutely necessary.

Using Simple Name Matching

Often when creating a pointcut, you want to match based on just the name of the method, ignoring method signature and return type. In this case, you can avoid needing to create a subclass of StaticMethodMatcherPointcut and use the NameMatchMethodPointcut (which is a subclass of StaticMethodMatcherPointcut) to match against a list of method names instead. When you are using NameMatchMethodPointcut, no consideration is given to the signature of the method, so if you have methods foo() and foo(int), they are both matched for the name foo.

Now for a demonstration. Listing 6-29 shows a simple class with four methods.

Listing 6-29. The NameBean Class

```
package com.apress.prospring3.ch6.namepc;

public class NameBean {
```

```
    public void foo() {
        System.out.println("foo");
    }

    public void foo(int x) {
        System.out.println("foo " + x);
    }

    public void bar() {
        System.out.println("bar");
    }

    public void yup() {
        System.out.println("yup");
    }
}
```

For this example, we want to match the foo(), foo(int), and bar() methods using the
NameMatchMethodPointcut; this translates to matching the names foo and bar. This is shown in Listing 6-30.

Listing 6-30. Using the NameMatchMethodPointcut

```
package com.apress.prospring3.ch6.namepc;

import org.springframework.aop.Advisor;
import org.springframework.aop.framework.ProxyFactory;
import org.springframework.aop.support.DefaultPointcutAdvisor;
import org.springframework.aop.support.NameMatchMethodPointcut;

import com.apress.prospring3.ch6.staticpc.SimpleAdvice;

public class NamePointcutExample {

    public static void main(String[] args) {
        NameBean target = new NameBean();

        // create advisor
        NameMatchMethodPointcut pc = new NameMatchMethodPointcut();
        pc.addMethodName("foo");
        pc.addMethodName("bar");
        Advisor advisor = new DefaultPointcutAdvisor(pc, new SimpleAdvice());

        // create the proxy
        ProxyFactory pf = new ProxyFactory();
        pf.setTarget(target);
        pf.addAdvisor(advisor);
        NameBean proxy = (NameBean)pf.getProxy();

        proxy.foo();
        proxy.foo(999);
        proxy.bar();
        proxy.yup();
    }
}
```

There is no need to create a class for the pointcut; you can simply create an instance of NameMatchMethodPointcut, and you are on your way. Notice that we have added two names to the pointcut, foo and bar, using the addMethodName() method. Running this example results in the following output:

```
>> Invoking foo
foo
>> Done
>> Invoking foo
foo 999
>> Done
>> Invoking bar
bar
>> Done
yup
```

As expected, the foo(), foo(int), and bar() methods are advised, thanks to the pointcut, but the yup() method is left unadvised.

Creating Pointcuts with Regular Expression

In the previous section, we discussed how to perform simple matching against a predefined list of methods. But what if you don't know all of the methods' names in advance, and instead you know the pattern that the names follow? For instance, what if you want to match all methods whose names starts with get? In this case, you can use one the regular expression pointcut JdkRegexpMethodPointcut to match a method name based on a regular expression.

The code in Listing 6-31 shows a simple class with three methods.

Listing 6-31. The RegexpBean Class

```java
package com.apress.prospring3.ch6.regexppc;

public class RegexpBean {

    public void foo1() {
        System.out.println("foo1");
    }

    public void foo2() {
        System.out.println("foo2");
    }

    public void bar() {
        System.out.println("bar");
    }
}
```

Using a regular expression-based pointcut, we can match all methods in this class whose name starts with foo. This is shown in Listing 6-32.

Listing 6-32. Using Regular Expressions for Pointcuts

```java
package com.apress.prospring3.ch6.regexppc;

import org.springframework.aop.Advisor;
import org.springframework.aop.framework.ProxyFactory;
import org.springframework.aop.support.DefaultPointcutAdvisor;
import org.springframework.aop.support.JdkRegexpMethodPointcut;

import com.apress.prospring3.ch6.staticpc.SimpleAdvice;

public class RegexpPointcutExample {

    public static void main(String[] args) {
        RegexpBean target = new RegexpBean();

        // create the advisor
        JdkRegexpMethodPointcut pc = new JdkRegexpMethodPointcut();
        pc.setPattern(".*foo.*");
        Advisor advisor = new DefaultPointcutAdvisor(pc, new SimpleAdvice());

        // create the proxy
        ProxyFactory pf = new ProxyFactory();
        pf.setTarget(target);
        pf.addAdvisor(advisor);
        RegexpBean proxy = (RegexpBean)pf.getProxy();

        proxy.foo1();
        proxy.foo2();
        proxy.bar();
    }
}
```

Notice we do not need to create a class for the pointcut; instead, we just create an instance of JdkRegexpMethodPointcut and specify the pattern to match, and we are done. The interesting thing to note is the pattern. When matching method names, Spring matches the fully qualified name of the method, so for foo1(), Spring is matching against com.apress.prospring3.ch6.regexppc.RegexpBean.foo1, which is why there's the leading .* in the pattern. This is a powerful concept because it allows you to match all methods within a given package, without needing to know exactly which classes are in that package and what the names of the methods are. Running this example yields the following output:

```
>> Invoking foo1
foo1
>> Done
>> Invoking foo2
foo2
>> Done
bar
```

As you would expect, only the foo1() and foo2() methods have been advised, because the bar() method does not match the regular expression pattern.

Creating Pointcuts with AspectJ Pointcut Expression

Besides JDK regular expressions, you can also use AspectJ's pointcut expression language for pointcut declaration. In the next chapter, you will see that when we declare the pointcut in XML configuration using the aop namespace, Spring defaults to use AspectJ's pointcut language. Moreover, when using Spring's @AspectJ annotation-style AOP support, you also need to use AspectJ's pointcut language. So when declaring pointcuts using expression language, using AspectJ pointcut expression is the best way to go. Spring provides the class AspectJExpressionPointcut for defining pointcuts using AspectJ's expression language. To use AspectJ pointcut expression with Spring, you need to include two AspectJ library files, aspectjrt.jar and aspectjweaver.jar, in your project's classpath. In STS, you can simply add the dependencies shown in Table 6-4 to your project.

Table 6-4. Maven Dependencies for AspectJ

Group ID	Artifact ID	Version	Description
org.aspectj	aspectjrt	1.6.11	AspectJ runtime library
org.aspectj	aspectjweaver	1.6.11	AspectJ weaving library

Let's take the previous example using JDK regular expression again and see how to use AspectJ expression to achieve the same result. Listing 6-33 shows the bean that was the same as the one in Listing 6-31; just the class name is different.

Listing 6-33. The AspectjexpBean Class

```
package com.apress.prospring3.ch6.aspectjexppc;

public class AspectjexpBean {

    public void foo1() {
        System.out.println("foo1");
    }

    public void foo2() {
        System.out.println("foo2");
    }

    public void bar() {
        System.out.println("bar");
    }
}
```

Using an AspectJ expression-based pointcut, we also can easily match all methods in this class whose names start with foo. This is shown in Listing 6-34.

Listing 6-34. Using AspectJ Expressions for Pointcuts

```
package com.apress.prospring3.ch6.aspectjexppc;

import org.springframework.aop.Advisor;
import org.springframework.aop.aspectj.AspectJExpressionPointcut;
```

```
import org.springframework.aop.framework.ProxyFactory;
import org.springframework.aop.support.DefaultPointcutAdvisor;

import com.apress.prospring3.ch6.staticpc.SimpleAdvice;

public class AspectjexpPointcutExample {

    public static void main(String[] args) {
        AspectjexpBean target = new AspectjexpBean();

        // create the advisor
        AspectJExpressionPointcut pc = new AspectJExpressionPointcut();
        pc.setExpression("execution(* foo*(..))");
        Advisor advisor = new DefaultPointcutAdvisor(pc, new SimpleAdvice());

        // create the proxy
        ProxyFactory pf = new ProxyFactory();
        pf.setTarget(target);
        pf.addAdvisor(advisor);
        AspectjexpBean proxy = (AspectjexpBean) pf.getProxy();

        proxy.foo1();
        proxy.foo2();
        proxy.bar();
    }
}
```

Note that we use the `AspectJExpressionPointcut`'s `setExpression()` method to set the matching criteria. The expression `"execution(* foo*(..))"` means that the advice should apply to the execution of any methods that start with foo, with any arguments, and return any types. Running the program will get the same result as the previous example using JDK regular expressions.

Creating Annotation Matching Pointcuts

If your application is annotation-based, you may want to use your own specified annotations for defining pointcuts, that is, apply the advice logic to all methods or types with specific annotations. Spring provides the class `AnnotationMatchingPointcut` for defining pointcuts using annotations. Again, let's reuse the previous example and see how we did it when using an annotation as a pointcut.

Let's define an annotation interface called `AdviceRequired`, which is an annotation that we will use for declaring a pointcut. Listing 6-35 shows the annotation class.

Listing 6-35. Using an Annotation for Pointcuts

```
package com.apress.prospring3.ch6.annotationpc;

import java.lang.annotation.ElementType;
import java.lang.annotation.Retention;
import java.lang.annotation.RetentionPolicy;
import java.lang.annotation.Target;

@Retention(RetentionPolicy.RUNTIME)
@Target({ElementType.TYPE, ElementType.METHOD})
```

```
public @interface AdviceRequired {
}
```

In the previous listing, you can see that we declare the interface as an annotation by using @interface as the type, and the @Target annotation defines that the annotation can apply at either the type or method level.

Listing 6-36 shows a simple bean with annotations in it.

Listing 6-36. *The SampleAnnotationBean Class*

```
package com.apress.prospring3.ch6.annotationpc;

public class SampleAnnotationBean {

    @AdviceRequired
    public void foo(int x) {
        System.out.println("Invoked foo() with: " +x);
    }

    public void bar() {
        System.out.println("Invoked bar()");
    }
}
```

For the previous bean, the foo() method was annotated with @AdviceRequired, to which we want the advice to be applied.

Listing 6-37 shows the testing program.

Listing 6-37. *Testing Pointcut by Using Annotation*

```
package com.apress.prospring3.ch6.annotationpc;

import org.springframework.aop.Advisor;
import org.springframework.aop.framework.ProxyFactory;
import org.springframework.aop.support.DefaultPointcutAdvisor;
import org.springframework.aop.support.annotation.AnnotationMatchingPointcut;

import com.apress.prospring3.ch6.staticpc.SimpleAdvice;

public class AnnotationPointcutExample {

    public static void main(String[] args) {
        SampleAnnotationBean target = new SampleAnnotationBean();

        // create the advisor
        AnnotationMatchingPointcut pc = AnnotationMatchingPointcut
            .forMethodAnnotation(AdviceRequired.class);
        Advisor advisor = new DefaultPointcutAdvisor(pc, new SimpleAdvice());

        // create the proxy
        ProxyFactory pf = new ProxyFactory();
        pf.setTarget(target);
        pf.addAdvisor(advisor);
        SampleAnnotationBean proxy = (SampleAnnotationBean) pf.getProxy();
```

```
        proxy.foo(100);
        proxy.bar();
    }
}
```

In the previous listing, an instance of AnnotationMatchingPointcut is acquired by calling its static method forMethodAnnotation() and passing in the annotation type. This indicates that we want to apply the advice to all the methods annotated with the given annotation. It's also possible to specify annotations applied at the type level by calling the forClassAnnotation() method. The following shows the output when the program runs:

```
>> Invoking foo
Invoked foo() with: 100
>> Done
Invoked bar()
```

As you can see, since we annotated the foo() method, only that method was advised.

Convenience Advisor Implementations

For many of the Pointcut implementations, Spring also provides a convenience Advisor implementation that acts as the Pointcut. For instance, instead of using the NameMatchMethodPointcut coupled with a DefaultPointcutAdvisor in the previous example, we could simply have used a NameMatchMethodPointcutAdvisor, as shown in Listing 6-38.

Listing 6-38. Using NameMatchMethodPointcutAdvisor

```
package com.apress.prospring3.ch6.namepc;

import org.springframework.aop.framework.ProxyFactory;
import org.springframework.aop.support.NameMatchMethodPointcutAdvisor;

import com.apress.prospring3.ch6.staticpc.SimpleAdvice;

public class NamePointcutUsingAdvisor {

    public static void main(String[] args) {
        NameBean target = new NameBean();

        // create advisor
        NameMatchMethodPointcutAdvisor advisor = new
            NameMatchMethodPointcutAdvisor(new SimpleAdvice());
        advisor.addMethodName("foo");
        advisor.addMethodName("bar");

        // create the proxy
        ProxyFactory pf = new ProxyFactory();
        pf.setTarget(target);
        pf.addAdvisor(advisor);
        NameBean proxy = (NameBean) pf.getProxy();

        proxy.foo();
        proxy.foo(999);
        proxy.bar();
```

```
        proxy.yup();
    }
}
```

Notice in Listing 6-38 that rather than creating an instance of `NameMatchMethodPointcut`, we configure the pointcut details on the instance of `NameMatchMethodPointcutAdvisor`. In this way, the `NameMatchMethodPointcutAdvisor` is acting as both the `Advisor` and the `Pointcut`.

You can find full details of the different convenient `Advisor` implementations by exploring the JavaDoc for the `org.springframework.aop.support` package. There is no noticeable performance difference between the two approaches, and aside from there being slightly less code in the second approach, there is very little difference in the actual coding approach. We prefer to stick with the first approach because we feel the intent is slightly clearer in the code. At the end of the day, the style you choose comes down to personal preference.

Understanding Proxies

So far, we have taken only a cursory look at the proxies generated by `ProxyFactory`. We mentioned that two types of proxy are available in Spring: JDK proxies created using the JDK `Proxy` class and CGLIB-based proxies created using the CGLIB `Enhancer` class. You may be wondering exactly what the difference between the two proxies is and why Spring needs two different types of proxy. In this section, we take a detailed look at the differences between the proxies.

The core goal of a proxy is to intercept Method Invocations and, where necessary, execute chains of advice that apply to a particular method. The management and invocation of advice is largely proxy independent and is managed by the Spring AOP framework. However, the proxy is responsible for intercepting calls to all methods and passing them as necessary to the AOP framework for the advice to be applied.

In addition to this core functionality, the proxy must also support a set of additional features. It is possible to configure the proxy to expose itself via the `AopContext` class (which is an abstract class) so that you can retrieve the proxy and invoke advised methods on the proxy from the target object. The proxy is responsible for ensuring that when this option is enabled via `ProxyFactory.setExposeProxy()`, the proxy class is appropriately exposed. In addition to this, all proxy classes implement the `Advised` interface by default, which allows for, among other things, the advice chain to be changed after the proxy has been created. A proxy must also ensure that any methods that return this—that is, return the proxied target—do in fact return the proxy and not the target.

As you can see, a typical proxy has quite a lot of work to perform, and all of this logic is implemented in both the JDK and CGLIB proxies.

Using JDK Dynamic Proxies

JDK proxies are the most basic type of proxy available in Spring. Unlike the CGLIB proxy, the JDK proxy can generate proxies only of interfaces, not classes. In this way, any object you want to proxy must implement at least one interface. In general, it is good design to use interfaces for your classes, but it is not always possible, especially when you are working with third-party or legacy code. In this case, you must use the CGLIB proxy.

When you are using the JDK proxy, all method calls are intercepted by the JVM and routed to the `invoke()` method of the proxy. This method then determines whether the method in question is advised (by the rules defined by the pointcut), and if so, it invokes the advice chain and then the method itself using reflection. In addition to this, the `invoke()` method performs all the logic discussed in the previous section.

The JDK proxy makes no determination between methods that are advised and unadvised until it is in the `invoke()` method. This means that for unadvised methods on the proxy, the `invoke()` method is still called, all the checks are still performed, and the method is still invoked using reflection. Obviously, this incurs runtime overhead each time the method is invoked, even though the proxy often performs no additional processing other than to invoke the unadvised method via reflection.

You can instruct the ProxyFactory to use a JDK proxy by specifying the list of interfaces to proxy using setInterfaces() (in the AdvisedSupport class that the ProxyFactory class extends indirectly).

Using CGLIB Proxies

With the JDK proxy, all decisions about how to handle a particular Method Invocation are handled at runtime each time the method is invoked. When you use CGLIB, CGLIB dynamically generates the bytecode for a new class on the fly for each proxy, reusing already generated classes wherever possible.

When a CGLIB proxy is first created, CGLIB asks Spring how it wants to handle each method. This means that many of the decisions that are performed in each call to invoke() on the JDK proxy are performed just once for the CGLIB proxy. Because CGLIB generates actual bytecode, there is also a lot more flexibility in the way you can handle methods. For instance, the CGLIB proxy generates the appropriate bytecode to invoke any unadvised methods directly, reducing the overhead introduced by the proxy. In addition to this, the CGLIB proxy determines whether it is possible for a method to return this; if not, it allows the method call to be invoked directly, again reducing the runtime overhead.

The CGLIB proxy also handles fixed advice chains differently than the JDK proxy. A fixed-advice chain is one that you guarantee will not change after the proxy has been generated. By default, you are able to change the advisors and advice on a proxy even after it is created, although this is rarely a requirement. The CGLIB proxy handles fixed advice chains in a particular way, reducing the runtime overhead for executing an advice chain.

Comparing Proxy Performance

So far, all we have done is discuss in loose terms the differences in implementation between the different proxy types. In this section, we are going to run a simple performance test to compare the performance of the CGLIB proxy with the JDK proxy.

Let's create an ISimpleBean interface and its implementation class, SimpleBean, which we will use as the target object for proxying. Listing 6-39 and Listing 6-40 show the ISimpleBean interface and SimpleBean class, respectively.

Listing 6-39. *The ISimpleBean Interface*

```
package com.apress.prospring3.ch6.proxies;

public interface ISimpleBean {

    public void advised();
    public void unadvised();

}
```

Listing 6-40. *The SimpleBean Class*

```
package com.apress.prospring3.ch6.proxies;

public class SimpleBean implements ISimpleBean {

    private long dummy = 0;
```

```
    public void advised() {
        dummy = System.currentTimeMillis();
    }

    public void unadvised() {
        dummy = System.currentTimeMillis();
    }
}
```

Listing 6-41 shows the TestPointcut class, which provides static checking on the method under advise.

Listing 6-41. *The TestPointcut Class*

```
package com.apress.prospring3.ch6.proxies;

import java.lang.reflect.Method;

import org.springframework.aop.support.StaticMethodMatcherPointcut;

public class TestPointcut extends StaticMethodMatcherPointcut {

    public boolean matches(Method method, Class cls) {
        return ("advised".equals(method.getName()));
    }
}
```

Listing 6-42 shows the NoOpBeforeAdvice class, which is just a simple before advice without any operation.

Listing 6-42. *The NoOpBeforeAdvice Class*

```
package com.apress.prospring3.ch6.proxies;

import java.lang.reflect.Method;

import org.springframework.aop.MethodBeforeAdvice;

public class NoOpBeforeAdvice implements MethodBeforeAdvice {

    public void before(Method method, Object[] args, Object target)
      throws Throwable {
        // no-op
    }
}
```

Listing 6-43 shows the code for the performance test.

Listing 6-43. *Testing Proxy Performance*

```
package com.apress.prospring3.ch6.proxies;

import org.springframework.aop.Advisor;
import org.springframework.aop.framework.Advised;
import org.springframework.aop.framework.ProxyFactory;
```

```java
import org.springframework.aop.support.DefaultPointcutAdvisor;

public class ProxyPerfTest {

    public static void main(String[] args) {
        ISimpleBean target = new SimpleBean();

        Advisor advisor = new DefaultPointcutAdvisor(new TestPointcut(),
                new NoOpBeforeAdvice());

        runCglibTests(advisor, target);
        runCglibFrozenTests(advisor, target);
        runJdkTests(advisor, target);
    }

    private static void runCglibTests(Advisor advisor, ISimpleBean target) {
        ProxyFactory pf = new ProxyFactory();
        pf.setProxyTargetClass(true);
        pf.setTarget(target);
        pf.addAdvisor(advisor);

        ISimpleBean proxy = (ISimpleBean)pf.getProxy();
        System.out.println("Running CGLIB (Standard) Tests");
        test(proxy);
    }

    private static void runCglibFrozenTests(Advisor advisor, ISimpleBean target) {
        ProxyFactory pf = new ProxyFactory();
        pf.setProxyTargetClass(true);
        pf.setTarget(target);
        pf.addAdvisor(advisor);
        pf.setFrozen(true);

        ISimpleBean proxy = (ISimpleBean)pf.getProxy();
        System.out.println("Running CGLIB (Frozen) Tests");
        test(proxy);
    }

    private static void runJdkTests(Advisor advisor, ISimpleBean target) {
        ProxyFactory pf = new ProxyFactory();
        pf.setTarget(target);
        pf.addAdvisor(advisor);
        pf.setInterfaces(new Class[]{ISimpleBean.class});

        ISimpleBean proxy = (ISimpleBean)pf.getProxy();
        System.out.println("Running JDK Tests");
        test(proxy);
    }

    private static void test(ISimpleBean bean) {
        long before = 0;
        long after = 0;

        // Test 1: test advised method
```

```
    System.out.println("Testing Advised Method");
    before = System.currentTimeMillis();
    for(int x = 0; x < 500000; x++) {
        bean.advised();
    }
    after = System.currentTimeMillis();;

    System.out.println("Took " + (after - before) + " ms");

    // Test 2: testing unadvised method
    System.out.println("Testing Unadvised Method");
    before = System.currentTimeMillis();
    for(int x = 0; x < 500000; x++) {
        bean.unadvised();
    }
    after = System.currentTimeMillis();;

    System.out.println("Took " + (after - before) + " ms");

    // Test 3: testing equals() method
    System.out.println("Testing equals() Method");
    before = System.currentTimeMillis();
    for(int x = 0; x < 500000; x++) {
        bean.equals(bean);
    }
    after = System.currentTimeMillis();;

    System.out.println("Took " + (after - before) + " ms");

    // Test 4: testing hashCode() method
    System.out.println("Testing hashCode() Method");
    before = System.currentTimeMillis();
    for(int x = 0; x < 500000; x++) {
        bean.hashCode();
    }
    after = System.currentTimeMillis();;

    System.out.println("Took " + (after - before) + " ms");

    // Test 5: testing method on Advised
    Advised advised = (Advised)bean;

    System.out.println("Testing Advised.getProxyTargetClass() Method");
    before = System.currentTimeMillis();
    for(int x = 0; x < 500000; x++) {
        advised.getTargetClass();
    }
    after = System.currentTimeMillis();;

    System.out.println("Took " + (after - before) + " ms");

    System.out.println(">>>\n");
    }
}
```

In this code, you can see that we are testing three kinds of proxy: a standard CGLIB proxy, a CGLIB proxy with a frozen advice chain (i.e., when a proxy is frozen by calling the setFrozen() method in the ProxyConfig class that ProxyFactory extends indirectly, CGLIB will perform further optimization; however, further advice change will not be allowed), and a JDK proxy. For each proxy type, we run the following five test cases:

- *Advised method (test 1)*: A method that is advised. The advice type used in the test is a before advice that performs no processing, so it reduces the effects of the advice on the performance tests.

- *Unadvised method (test 2)*: A method on the proxy that is unadvised. Often your proxy has many methods that are not advised. This test looks at how well unadvised methods perform for the different proxies.

- *The equals() method (test 3)*: This test looks at the overhead of invoking the equals() method. This is especially important when you use proxies as keys in a HashMap or similar collection.

- *The hashcode() method (test 4)*: As with the equals() method, the hashCode() method is important when you are using HashMaps or similar collections.

- *Executing methods on the Advised interface (test 5)*: As we mentioned earlier, a proxy implements the Advised interface by default, allowing you to modify the proxy after creation and to query information about the proxy. This test looks at how quick methods on the Advised interface can be accessed using the different proxy types.

We ran the test on an Intel Core i7 2.8GHz machine with 8GB of RAM. When running the test, we set the initial heap size of the JVM to 2048MB to reduce the effects of heap resizing on test results. The results are shown in Table 6-5.

Table 6-5. Proxy Performance Test Results (ms)

	CGLIB (Standard)	CGLIB (Frozen)	JDK
Advised method	148	67	129
Unadvised method	41	22	50
equals()	9	24	63
hashCode()	16	13	30
Advised.getProxyTargetClass()	7	14	15

From the results in this table, you can see that the performance between standard CGLIB and JDK dynamic proxy for both advised and unadvised methods don't have much difference. If you read the previous version of this book, you will find that the performance of JDK proxy was much slower for unadvised methods. This was because in the previous version of this book, the tests were run on JDK 1.4, and at that time, the performance of reflection was still very poor. This time the previous tests were run under JDK 6, for which the performance of the reflection mechanism is greatly improved.

However, there is a noticeable difference when you are using a CGLIB proxy with a frozen advice chain. Similar figures apply to the equals() and hashCode() methods, which are noticeably faster when you are using the CGLIB proxy. For methods on the Advised interface, you will notice that they are also faster on the CGLIB proxy. The reason for this is that Advised methods are handled early on in the intercept() method so they avoid much of the logic that is required for other methods.

Which Proxy to Use?

Deciding which proxy to use is typically an easy decision. The CGLIB proxy can proxy both classes and interfaces, whereas the JDK proxy can proxy only interfaces. In terms of performance, there is no significant difference between JDK and CGLIB standard mode (at least in running both advised and unadvised methods), unless you use CGLIB in frozen mode, in which case the advice chain can't be changed and CGLIB performs further optimization when in frozen mode. When proxying a class, the CGLIB proxy is the default choice because it is the only proxy capable of generating a proxy of a class. To use the CGLIB proxy when proxying an interface, you must set the value of the optimize flag in the ProxyFactory to true using the setOptimize() method.

■ **Note** Besides CGLIB, there is another bytecode manipulation library called Javassist, which is being used by some other popular projects (e.g., Hibernate). Some developers prefer Javassist over CGLIB and have raised a JIRA issue (http://jira.springsource.org/browse/SPR-5654) requesting the migration of the Spring AOP proxy from CGLIB to Javassist. The Spring development team is considering it during the Spring 3.2 timeline. There also exists an intermediate solution provided by the community. For those who interested in details about using Javassist with Spring AOP, please refer to the JIRA issue for details.

Summary

In this chapter, we introduced the core concepts of AOP and then looked at how these concepts translate into the Spring AOP implementation. We discussed the features that are and are not implemented in Spring AOP, and we pointed to AspectJ as an AOP solution for those features that Spring does not implement. We spent some time explaining the details of the advice types available in Spring, and you saw examples of the four types in action. We also looked at how you limit the methods to which an advice applies using pointcuts. In particular, we looked at the six basic pointcut implementations available with Spring. Finally, we covered the details of how the AOP proxies are constructed, the different options, and what makes them different. We concluded the discussion of proxies with a comparison of the performance between three different proxy types and highlighted some major differences and restrictions for choosing between a JDK vs. CGLIB proxy.

In Chapter 7, we will complete our discussion of the pointcuts available in Spring by looking at ComposablePointcut and ControlFlowPointcut in detail. We will spend some time looking at how you utilize Spring's AspectJ integration to extend the AOP feature set available to your application. We will also look at how AOP is supported by Spring Framework services, which means you can define and configure advice declaratively rather than programmatically.

CHAPTER 7

More Spring AOP and Annotations

In this chapter, we go into more detail about the AOP features available in Spring. In particular, we look at the topic in a much more real-world light: we explore the framework services in Spring that allow for transparent application of AOP, we cover real-world usage of AOP in the context of the sample application, and we also discuss overcoming the limitations of Spring AOP using Spring/AspectJ integration. More specifically, this chapter covers the following:

- *Advanced use of pointcuts:* This chapter finishes discussing pointcutting by looking at both `ComposablePointcut` and `ControlFlowPointcut`. This section also summarizes the whole pointcut discussion and looks at the appropriate techniques you should employ when you are using pointcuts in your application.

- *Introductions:* Mentioned briefly in the previous chapter, introductions allow you to add interface implementations dynamically to any object on the fly using the familiar interceptor concept.

- *AOP framework services:* We skipped over this topic completely in the previous chapter and focused solely on assembling AOP proxies and advice chains manually. However, in true Spring fashion, the framework fully supports configuring AOP transparently and declaratively. In this section, we look at three ways (the `ProxyFactoryBean` class, the `aop` namespace, and `@AspectJ`-style annotations) to inject declaratively defined AOP proxies into your application objects as collaborators, thus making your application completely unaware that it is working with advised objects.

- *Integrating AspectJ:* AspectJ is a fully featured AOP implementation. The main difference between AspectJ and Spring AOP is that AspectJ applies advice to target objects via weaving (either compile-time or load-time weaving), while as discussed in the previous chapter, Spring AOP is based on a proxy. The feature set of AspectJ is much greater than that of Spring AOP, but it is much more complicated to use than Spring. AspectJ is a good solution when you find that Spring AOP lacks a feature you need. Starting from version 2.0, you can take full advantage of Spring features when configuring your AspectJ aspects.

To run some of the examples in this chapter, you need to obtain AspectJ. You can download it from http://eclipse.org/aspectj. We used version 1.6.11 of AspectJ for the examples in this chapter. You can also add the Maven dependencies in Table 7-1 into your STS project.

Table 7-1. Maven Dependencies for AspectJ

Group ID	Artifact ID	Version	Description
org.aspectj	aspectjrt	1.6.11	AspectJ runtime library
org.aspectj	aspectjweaver	1.6.11	AspectJ weaving library

Advanced Use of Pointcuts

In the previous chapter, we looked at six basic Pointcut implementations Spring provides; for the most part, we found that these meet the needs of our applications. However, sometimes you need more flexibility when defining pointcuts. Spring provides two additional Pointcut implementations, ComposablePointcut and ControlFlowPointcut, that provide exactly the flexibility you need.

Use Control Flow Pointcuts

Spring control flow pointcuts, implemented by the ControlFlowPointcut class, are similar to the cflow construct available in many other AOP implementations, although they are not quite as powerful. Essentially, a control flow pointcut in Spring pointcuts all method calls below a given method or below all methods in a class. This is quite hard to visualize and is better explained using an example.

Listing 7-1 shows a SimpleBeforeAdvice that writes a message out describing the method it is advising.

Listing 7-1. The SimpleBeforeAdvice Class

```
package com.apress.prospring3.ch7.cflow;

import java.lang.reflect.Method;

import org.springframework.aop.MethodBeforeAdvice;

public class SimpleBeforcAdvice implements MethodBeforeAdvice {

    public void before(Method method, Object[] args, Object target)
            throws Throwable {
        System.out.println("Before method: " + method);
    }
}
```

This advice class allows us to see which methods are being pointcut by the ControlFlowPointcut. In Listing 7-2, you can see a simple class with one method—the method that we want to advise.

Listing 7-2. The TestBean Class

```
package com.apress.prospring3.ch7.cflow;

public class TestBean {

    public void foo() {
```

```
        System.out.println("foo()");
    }
}
```

In Listing 7-2, you can see the simple foo() method that we want to advise. We have, however, a special requirement—we want to advise this method only when it is called from another, specific method. Listing 7-3 shows a simple driver program for this example.

Listing 7-3. Using the ControlFlowPointcut Class

```
package com.apress.prospring3.ch7.cflow;

import org.springframework.aop.Advisor;
import org.springframework.aop.Pointcut;
import org.springframework.aop.framework.ProxyFactory;
import org.springframework.aop.support.ControlFlowPointcut;
import org.springframework.aop.support.DefaultPointcutAdvisor;

public class ControlFlowExample {

    public static void main(String[] args) {
        ControlFlowExample ex = new ControlFlowExample();
        ex.run();
    }

    public void run() {
        TestBean target = new TestBean();

        // create advisor
        Pointcut pc = new ControlFlowPointcut(ControlFlowExample.class,
            "test");
        Advisor advisor = new DefaultPointcutAdvisor(pc,
            new SimpleBeforeAdvice());

        // create proxy
        ProxyFactory pf = new ProxyFactory();
        pf.setTarget(target);
        pf.addAdvisor(advisor);

        TestBean proxy = (TestBean) pf.getProxy();

        System.out.println("Trying normal invoke");
        proxy.foo();
        System.out.println("Trying under ControlFlowExample.test()");
        test(proxy);
    }

    private void test(TestBean bean) {
        bean.foo();
    }
}
```

In Listing 7-3, the advised proxy is assembled with `ControlFlowPointcut` and then the `foo()` method is invoked twice: once directly from the `run()` method and once from the `test()` method. Here is the line of particular interest:

```
Pointcut pc = new ControlFlowPointcut(ControlFlowExample.class, "test");
```

In this line, we are creating a `ControlFlowPointcut` instance for the `test()` method of the `ControlFlowExample` class. Essentially, this says, "Pointcut all methods that are called from the `ControlFlowExample.test()` method." Note that although we said "Pointcut all methods," in fact, this really means "Pointcut all methods on the proxy object that is advised using the `Advisor` corresponding to this instance of `ControlFlowPointcut`."

You also need to add the dependency for CGLIB into your project, which was shown in Table 7-2.

Table 7-2. Dependency for CGLIB

Group ID	Artifact ID	Version	Description
cglib	cglib	2.2.2	Code generation library required by Spring AOP

Running the example in Listing 7-3 yields the following output:

```
Trying normal invoke
foo()
Trying under ControlFlowExample.test()
Before method: public void com.apress.prospring3.ch7.cflow.TestBean.foo()
foo()
```

As you can see, when the `foo()` method is first invoked outside of the control flow of the `test()` method, it is unadvised. When it executes for a second time, this time inside the control flow of the `test()` method, the `ControlFlowPointcut` indicates that its associated advice applies to the method, and thus the method is advised. Note that if we had called another method from within the `test()` method, one that was not on the advised proxy, it would not have been advised.

Control flow pointcuts can be extremely useful, allowing you to advise an object selectively only when it is executed in the context of another. However, be aware that you take a substantial performance hit for using control flow pointcut over other pointcuts. Figures from the Spring documentation indicate that a control flow pointcut is typically five times slower than other pointcuts on a 1.4 JVM.

Let's consider an example. Suppose we have a transaction processing system, which contains a `TransactionService` interface as well as an `AccountService` interface. We would like to apply an after advice so that when the `AccountService.updateBalance()` method is called by `TransactionService.reverseTransaction()`, an e-mail notification is sent to the customer, after the account balance is updated. However, e-mail will not be sent under any other circumstances. In this case, the control flow pointcut will be useful. Figure 7-1 shows the UML sequence diagram for this scenario.

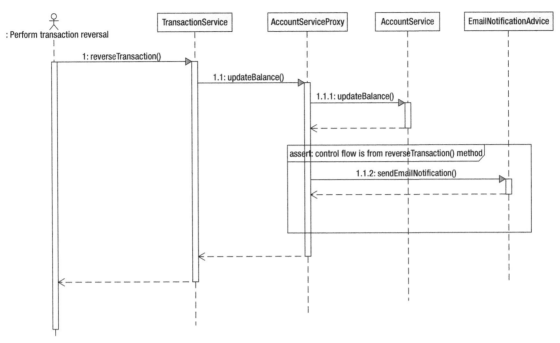

Figure 7-1. *UML sequence diagram for a control flow pointcut*

Using Composable Pointcut

In previous pointcutting examples, we used just a single pointcut for each Advisor. In most cases, this is usually enough, but in some cases, you may need to compose two or more pointcuts together to achieve the desired goal. Consider the situation where you want to pointcut all getter and setter methods on a bean. You have a pointcut for getters and a pointcut for setters, but you don't have one for both. Of course, you could just create another pointcut with the new logic, but a better approach is to combine the two pointcuts into a single pointcut using ComposablePointcut.

The ComposablePointcut supports two methods: union() and intersection(). By default, ComposablePointcut is created with a ClassFilter that matches all classes and a MethodMatcher that matches all methods, although you can supply your own initial ClassFilter and MethodMatcher during construction. The union() and intersection() methods are both overloaded to accept ClassFilter and MethodMatcher arguments.

The ComposablePointcut.union() method can be called by passing in an instance of either the ClassFilter, MethodMatcher, or Pointcut interface. The result of an union operation is that the ComposablePointcut will add an "or" condition into its call chain for matching with the joinpoints. It's the same for the ComposablePointcut.intersection() method, but this time an "and" condition will be added instead, which means that all ClassFilter, MethodMatcher, and Pointcut definitions within the ComposablePointcut should be match for applying an advice. You can imagine it as the "where" clause in a SQL query, with the union() method like the "or" operator and the intersection() method like the "and" operator.

As with control flow pointcuts, this is quite difficult to visualize, and it is much easier to understand with an example. Listing 7-4 shows a simple bean with three methods.

233

Listing 7-4. The SampleBean Class

```
package com.apress.prospring3.ch7.composable;

public class SampleBean {

    public String getName() {
        return "Clarence Ho";
    }

    public void setName(String name) {
    }

    public int getAge() {
        return 100;
    }
}
```

With this example, we are going to generate three different proxies using the same ComposablePointcut instance, but each time, we are going to modify the ComposablePointcut using either the union() or intersection() method. Following this, we will invoke all three methods on the SampleBean proxy and look at which ones have been advised. Listing 7-5 shows the code for this.

Listing 7-5. Investigating ComposablePointcut

```
package com.apress.prospring3.ch7.composable;

import java.lang.reflect.Method;

import org.springframework.aop.Advisor;
import org.springframework.aop.ClassFilter;
import org.springframework.aop.framework.ProxyFactory;
import org.springframework.aop.support.ComposablePointcut;
import org.springframework.aop.support.DefaultPointcutAdvisor;
import org.springframework.aop.support.StaticMethodMatcher;

import com.apress.prospring3.ch7.cflow.SimpleBeforeAdvice;

public class ComposablePointcutExample {

    public static void main(String[] args) {
        // create target
        SampleBean target = new SampleBean();

        ComposablePointcut pc = new ComposablePointcut(ClassFilter.TRUE,
            new GetterMethodMatcher());

        System.out.println("Test 1");
        SampleBean proxy = getProxy(pc, target);
        testInvoke(proxy);

        System.out.println("Test 2");
        pc.union(new SetterMethodMatcher());
        proxy = getProxy(pc, target);
```

```java
        testInvoke(proxy);

        System.out.println("Test 3");
        pc.intersection(new GetAgeMethodMatcher());
        proxy = getProxy(pc, target);
        testInvoke(proxy);
    }

    private static SampleBean getProxy(ComposablePointcut pc,
            SampleBean target) {
        // create the advisor
        Advisor advisor = new DefaultPointcutAdvisor(pc,
            new SimpleBeforeAdvice());

        // create the proxy
        ProxyFactory pf = new ProxyFactory();
        pf.setTarget(target);
        pf.addAdvisor(advisor);
        return (SampleBean) pf.getProxy();
    }

    private static void testInvoke(SampleBean proxy) {
        proxy.getAge();
        proxy.getName();
        proxy.setName("Clarence Ho");
    }

    private static class GetterMethodMatcher extends StaticMethodMatcher {

        public boolean matches(Method method, Class<?> cls) {
            return (method.getName().startsWith("get"));
        }
    }

    private static class GetAgeMethodMatcher extends StaticMethodMatcher {

        public boolean matches(Method method, Class<?> cls) {
            return "getAge".equals(method.getName());
        }
    }

    private static class SetterMethodMatcher extends StaticMethodMatcher {

        public boolean matches(Method method, Class<?> cls) {
            return (method.getName().startsWith("set"));
        }
    }

    }
}
```

The first thing to notice in this example is the set of three private MethodMatcher implementations. The GetterMethodMatcher matches all methods that start with get. This is the default MethodMatcher that we use to assemble the ComposablePointcut. Because of this, we expect that the first round of invocations on the SampleBean methods will result in only the getAge() and getName() methods being advised.

The SetterMethodMatcher matches all methods that start with set, and it is combined with the ComposablePointcut using union() for the second round of invocations. At this point, we have a union of two MethodMatchers: one that matches all methods starting with get and one that matches all methods starting with set. To this end, we expect that all invocations during the second round will be advised.

The GetAgeMethodMatcher is very specific and matches only the getAge() method. This MethodMatcher is combined with the ComposablePointcut using intersection() for the third round for invocations. Because the GetAgeMethodMatcher is being composed using intersection(), the only method that we expect to be advised in the third round of invocations is getAge(), because this is the only method that matches all the composed MethodMatchers.

Running this example results in the following output:

```
Test 1
Before method: public int com.apress.prospring3.ch7.composable.SampleBean.getAge()
Before method: public java.lang.String com.apress.prospring3.ch7⤸
.composable.SampleBean.getName()
Test 2
Before method: public int com.apress.prospring3.ch7.composable.SampleBean.getAge()
Before method: public java.lang.String com.apress.prospring3.ch7⤸
.composable.SampleBean.getName()
Before method: public void com.apress.prospring3.ch7⤸
.composable.SampleBean.setName(java.lang.String)
Test 3
Before method: public int com.apress.prospring3.ch7.composable.SampleBean.getAge()
```

As expected, the first round of invocations on the proxy saw only the getAge() and getName() methods being advised. For the second round, when the SetterMethodMatcher had been composed with the union() method, all methods were advised. In the final round, as a result of the intersection of the GetAgeMethodMatcher, only the getAge() method was advised.

Although this example demonstrated the use of MethodMatchers only in the composition process, it is just as simple to use ClassFilter when you are building the pointcut. Indeed, you can use a combination of MethodMatchers and ClassFilters when building your composite pointcut.

Composition and the Pointcut Interface

In the previous section, you saw how to create a composite pointcut using multiple MethodMatchers and ClassFilters. You can also create composite pointcuts using other objects that implement the Pointcut interface.

Another way for constructing a composite pointcut is to use the org.springframework.aop.support.Pointcuts class. The class provides three static methods. The intersection() and union() methods both take two pointcuts as arguments to construct a composite pointcut. On the other hand, a matches(Pointcut, Method, Class, Object[]) method also is provided for performing a quick check on whether a pointcut matches with the provided method, class, and method arguments.

The Pointcuts class supports operations on only two pointcuts. So, if you need to combine MethodMatcher and ClassFilter with Pointcut, you need to use the ComposablePointcut class. However, when you just need to combine two pointcuts, the Pointcuts class will be more convenient.

Pointcutting Summary

From the discussions in this chapter and in the previous chapter, you can see that Spring offers a powerful set of Pointcut implementations that should meet most, if not all, of your application's requirements. Remember that if you can't find a pointcut to suit your needs, you can create your own implementation from scratch by implementing Pointcut, MethodMatcher, and ClassFilter.

You use two patterns to combine pointcuts and advisors. The first pattern, the one we have used so far, involves having the pointcut implementation decoupled from the advisor. In the code we have seen up to this point, we created instances of Pointcut implementations and then used the DefaultPointcutAdvisor to add advice along with the Pointcut to the proxy.

The second option, one that is adopted by many of the examples in the Spring documentation, is to encapsulate the Pointcut inside your own Advisor implementation. This way, you have a class that implements both Pointcut and PointcutAdvisor, with the PointcutAdvisor.getPointcut() method simply returning this. This is an approach many classes, such as StaticMethodMatcherPointcutAdvisor, use in Spring.

We find that the first approach is the most flexible, allowing you to use different Pointcut implementations with different Advisor implementations. However, the second approach is useful in situations where you are going to be using the same combination of Pointcut and Advisor in different parts of your application, or, indeed, across many different applications. The second approach is useful when each Advisor must have a separate instance of a Pointcut; by making the Advisor responsible for creating the Pointcut, you can ensure that this is the case.

If you recall the discussion on proxy performance from the previous chapter, you will remember that unadvised methods perform much better than methods that are advised. For this reason, you should ensure that, by using Pointcuts, you only advise the methods that are absolutely necessary. This way, you reduce the amount of unnecessary overhead added to your application by using AOP.

Getting Started with Introductions

Introductions are an important part of the AOP feature set available in Spring. By using introductions, you can introduce new functionality to an existing object dynamically. In Spring, you can introduce an implementation of any interface to an existing object. You may well be wondering exactly why this is useful—why would you want to add functionality dynamically at runtime when you can simply add that functionality at development time? The answer to this question is easy. You add functionality dynamically when the functionality is crosscutting and is not easily implemented using traditional advice.

Introduction Basics

Spring treats introductions as a special type of advice, more specifically, as a special type of around advice. Because introductions apply solely at the class level, you cannot use pointcuts with introductions; semantically, the two don't match. An introduction adds new interface implementations to a class, and a pointcut defines which methods an advice applies. You create an introduction by implementing the IntroductionInterceptor interface, which extends the MethodInterceptor and the DynamicIntroductionAdvice interfaces. Figure 7-2 shows this structure along with the methods of both interfaces.

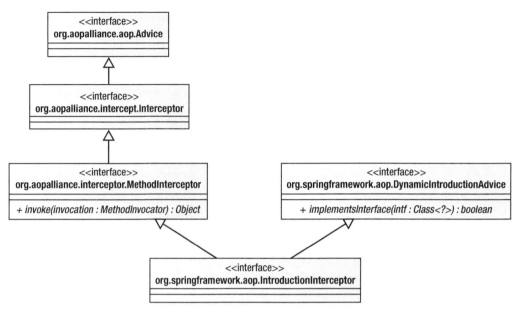

Figure 7-2. *Interface structure for introductions*

As you can see, the MethodInterceptor interface defines an invoke() method. Using this method, you provide the implementation for the interfaces that you are introducing and perform interception for any additional methods as required. Implementing all methods for an interface inside a single method can prove troublesome, and it is likely to result in an awful lot of code that you will have to wade through just to decide which method to invoke. Thankfully, Spring provides a default implementation of IntroductionInterceptor, DelegatingIntroductionInterceptor, which makes creating introductions much simpler. To build an introduction using DelegatingIntroductionInterceptor, you create a class that both inherits from DelegatingIntroductionInterceptor and implements the interfaces you want to introduce. The DelegatingIntroductionInterceptor then simply delegates all calls to introduced methods to the corresponding method on itself. Don't worry if this seems a little unclear; you will see an example of it in the next section.

Just as you need to use a PointcutAdvisor when you are working with pointcut advice, you need to use an IntroductionAdvisor to add introductions to a proxy. The default implementation of IntroductionAdvisor is DefaultIntroductionAdvisor, which should suffice for most, if not all, of your introduction needs. You should be aware that adding an introduction using ProxyFactory.addAdvice() is not permitted and results in an AopConfigException being thrown. Instead, you should use the addAdvisor() method and pass in an instance of the IntroductionAdvisor interface.

When using standard advice—that is, not introductions—it is possible for the same advice instance to be used for many different objects. The Spring documentation refers to this as the per-class life cycle, although you can use a single advice instance for many different classes. For introductions, the introduction advice forms part of the state of the advised object, and as a result, you must have a distinct advice instance for every advised object. This is called the per-instance life cycle. Because you must ensure that each advised object has a distinct instance of the introduction, it is often preferable to create a subclass of DefaultIntroductionAdvisor that is responsible for creating the introduction advice. This way, you only need to ensure that a new instance of your advisor class is created for each object, because it will automatically create a new instance of the introduction.

For example, we want to apply a before advice to the setFirstName() method on all instances of the Contact class. Figure 7-3 shows the same advice that applies to all objects of the Contact type.

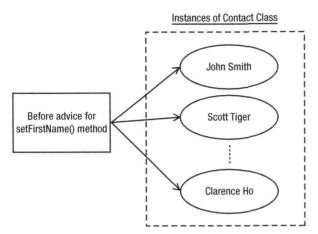

Figure 7-3. *Per-class life cycle of advice*

Now let's say we want to mix an introduction into all instances of Contact class, and the introduction will carry information for each Contact instance (e.g., an attribute isModified that indicates whether the specific instance was modified). In this case, the introduction will be created for each instance of Contact class and tied to that specific instance, as shown in Figure 7-4.

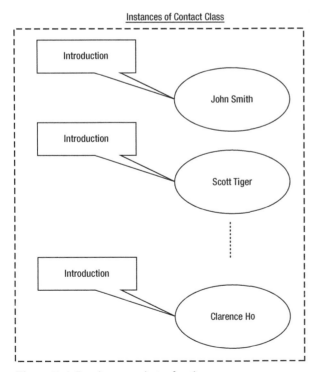

Figure 7-4. *Per-instance introduction*

That covers the basics of introduction creation. We will now discuss how you can use introductions to solve the problem of object modification detection.

Object Modification Detection with Introductions

Object modification detection is a useful technique for many reasons. Typically you apply modification detection to prevent unnecessary database access when you are persisting object data. If an object is passed to a method for modification but it comes back unmodified, there is little point in issuing an update statement to the database. Using a modification check in this way can really increase application throughput, especially when the database is already under a substantial load or is located on some remote network making communication an expensive operation.

Unfortunately, this kind of functionality is difficult to implement by hand because it requires you to add to every method that can modify object state to check whether the object state is actually being modified. When you consider all the null checks that have to be made and the checks to see whether the value is actually changing, you are looking at around eight lines of code per method. You could refactor this into a single method, but you still have to call this method every time you need to perform the check. Spread this across a typical application with many different classes that require modification checks, and you have a disaster waiting to happen.

This is clearly a place where introductions will help. We do not want to have to make it so each class that requires modification checks inherits from some base implementation, losing its only chance for inheritance as a result, nor do we really want to be adding checking code to each and every state-changing method. Using introductions, we can provide a flexible solution to the modification detection problem without having to write a bunch of repetitive, error-prone code.

In this example, we are going to build a full modification check framework using introductions. The modification check logic is encapsulated by the IsModified interface, an implementation of which will be introduced into the appropriate objects, along with interception logic to perform modification checks automatically. For the purposes of this example, we use JavaBeans conventions, in that we consider a modification to be any call to a setter method. Of course, we don't just treat all calls to a setter method as a modification—we check to see whether the value being passed to the setter is different from the one currently stored in the object. The only flaw with this solution is that setting an object back to its original state will still reflect a modification if any one of the values on the object changed. For example, you have a Contact object with the firstName attribute. Let's say that during processing the firstName attribute was changed from Peter to John. As a result, the object was marked as modified. However, it will still be marked as modified, even if the value is then changed back from John to its original value Peter in later processing. One way to keep track of such changes is to store the full history of changes in the object's entire life cycle. However, the implementation here is nontrivial and suffices for most requirements. Implementing the more complete solution would result in an overly complex example.

The IsModified Interface

Central to the modification check solution is the IsModified interface, which our fictional application uses to make intelligent decisions about object persistence. We do not look at how the application would use IsModified; instead, we focus on the implementation of the introduction. Listing 7-6 shows the IsModified interface.

Listing 7-6. The IsModified Interface

```
package com.apress.prospring3.ch7.introductions;

public interface IsModified {

    public boolean isModified();
}
```

There's nothing special here—just a single method, isModified(), indicating whether an object has been modified.

Creating a Mixin

The next step is to create the code that implements IsModified and that is introduced to the objects; this is referred to as a mixin. As we mentioned earlier, it is much simpler to create mixins by subclassing DelegatingIntroductionInterceptor than to create one by directly implementing the IntroductionInterceptor interface. Our mixin class, IsModifiedMixin, subclasses DelegatingIntroductionInterceptor and also implements the IsModified interface. This is shown in Listing 7-7.

Listing 7-7. The IsModifiedMixin Class

```
package com.apress.prospring3.ch7.introductions;

import java.lang.reflect.Method;
import java.util.HashMap;
import java.util.Map;

import org.aopalliance.intercept.MethodInvocation;
import org.springframework.aop.support.DelegatingIntroductionInterceptor;

public class IsModifiedMixin extends DelegatingIntroductionInterceptor
        implements IsModified {

    private boolean isModified = false;

    private Map<Method, Method> methodCache = new HashMap<Method, Method>();

    public boolean isModified() {
        return isModified;
    }

    public Object invoke(MethodInvocation invocation) throws Throwable {

        if (!isModified) {
            if ((invocation.getMethod().getName().startsWith("set"))
                && (invocation.getArguments().length == 1)) {

                // invoke the corresponding get method to see
                // if the value has actually changed
                Method getter = getGetter(invocation.getMethod());

                if (getter != null) {
                    // modification check is unimportant
                    // for write only methods
                    Object newVal = invocation.getArguments()[0];
                    Object oldVal = getter.invoke(invocation.getThis(), null);

                    if((newVal == null) && (oldVal == null)) {
                        isModified = false;
                    } else if((newVal == null) && (oldVal != null)) {
```

```
                                isModified = true;
                    } else if((newVal != null) && (oldVal == null)) {
                        isModified = true;
                    } else {
                        isModified = (!newVal.equals(oldVal));
                    }
                }
            }
        }
    }

    return super.invoke(invocation);
}

private Method getGetter(Method setter) {
    Method getter = null;

    // attempt cache retrieval.
    getter = (Method) methodCache.get(setter);

    if (getter != null) {
        return getter;
    }

    String getterName = setter.getName().replaceFirst("set", "get");
    try {
        getter = setter.getDeclaringClass().getMethod(getterName, null);

        // cache getter
        synchronized (methodCache) {
            methodCache.put(setter, getter);
        }

        return getter;
    } catch (NoSuchMethodException ex) {
        // must be write only
        return null;
    }
}
}
```

The first thing to notice here is the implementation of IsModified, which consists of the private modified field and the isModified() method. This example highlights why you must have one mixin instance per advised object—the mixin introduces not only methods to the object but also state. If you share a single instance of this mixin across many different objects, then you are also sharing the state, which means all objects show as modified the first time a single object becomes modified.

You do not actually have to implement the invoke() method for a mixin, but in this case, doing so allows us to detect automatically when a modification occurs. The implementation for the modification check is fairly trivial. We start by performing the check only if the object is still unmodified; we do not need to check for modifications once we know that the object has been modified. Next, we check to see whether the method is a setter, and if it is, we retrieve the corresponding getter method. Note that we cache the getter/setter pairs for quicker future retrieval. Finally, we compare the value returned by the getter with that passed to the setter to determine whether a modification has occurred. Notice that we check for the different possible combinations of null and set the modifications appropriately. It is important to remember that when you are using DelegatingIntroductionInterceptor, you must call super.invoke()

when overriding invoke() because it is the DelegatingIntroductionInterceptor that actually dispatches the invocation to the correct location, either the advised object or the mixin itself.

You can implement as many interfaces as you like in your mixin, each of which is automatically introduced into the advised object.

Creating an Advisor

The next step is to create an Advisor to wrap the creation of the mixin class. This step is optional, but it does help ensure that a new instance of the mixin is being used for each advised object. Listing 7-8 shows the IsModifiedAdvisor class.

Listing 7-8. Creating an Advisor for Your Mixin

```
package com.apress.prospring3.ch7.introductions;

import org.springframework.aop.support.DefaultIntroductionAdvisor;

public class IsModifiedAdvisor extends DefaultIntroductionAdvisor {

    public IsModifiedAdvisor() {
        super(new IsModifiedMixin());
    }
}
```

Notice that we have extended the DefaultIntroductionAdvisor to create our IsModifiedAdvisor. The implementation of this advisor is trivial and self-explanatory.

Putting It All Together

Now that we have a mixin class and an Advisor class, we can test the modification check framework. Listing 7-9 shows a simple class that we use to test the IsModifiedMixin.

Listing 7-9. The TargetBean Class

```
package com.apress.prospring3.ch7.introductions;

public class TargetBean {

    private String name;

    public void setName(String name) {
        this.name = name;
    }

    public String getName() {
        return name;
    }
}
```

This bean has a single property, name, that we use when we are testing the modification check mixin. Listing 7-10 shows how to assemble the advised proxy and then tests the modification check code.

Listing 7-10. Using the IsModifiedMixin

```
package com.apress.prospring3.ch7.introductions;

import org.springframework.aop.IntroductionAdvisor;
import org.springframework.aop.framework.ProxyFactory;

public class IntroductionExample {

    public static void main(String[] args) {
        // create the target
        TargetBean target = new TargetBean();
        target.setName("Clarence Ho");

        // create the advisor
        IntroductionAdvisor advisor = new IsModifiedAdvisor();

        // create the proxy
        ProxyFactory pf = new ProxyFactory();
        pf.setTarget(target);
        pf.addAdvisor(advisor);
        pf.setOptimize(true);

        TargetBean proxy = (TargetBean)pf.getProxy();
        IsModified proxyInterface = (IsModified)proxy;

        // test interfaces
        System.out.println("Is TargetBean?: " + (proxy instanceof TargetBean));
        System.out.println("Is IsModified?: " + (proxy instanceof IsModified));

        // test is modified implementation
        System.out.println("Has been modified?: " +
            proxyInterface.isModified());
        proxy.setName("Clarence Ho");
        System.out.println("Has been modified?: " +
            proxyInterface.isModified());
        proxy.setName("Rob Harrop");
        System.out.println("Has been modified?: " +
            proxyInterface.isModified());

    }
}
```

Notice that when we are creating the proxy, we set the optimize flag to true to force the use of the CGLIB proxy. The reason for this is that when you are using the JDK proxy to introduce a mixin, the resulting proxy will not be an instance of the object class (in this case TargetBean); the proxy implements only the mixin interfaces, not the original class. With the CGLIB proxy, the original class is implemented by the proxy along with the mixin interfaces.

Notice in the code that we test first to see whether the proxy is an instance of TargetBean and then to see whether it is an instance of IsModified. Both tests return true when you are using the CGLIB proxy, but only the IsModified test returns true for the JDK proxy. Finally, we test the modification check code by first setting the name property to its current value and then to a new value, checking the value of the isModified flag each time. Running this example results in the following output:

```
Is TargetBean?: true
Is IsModified?: true
Has been modified?: false
Has been modified?: false
Has been modified?: true
```

As expected, both instanceof tests return true. Notice that the first call to isModified(), before any modification occurred, returns false. The next call, after we set the value of name to the same value, also returns false. For the final call, however, after we set the value of name to a new value, the isModified() method returns true, indicating that the object has in fact been modified.

Introduction Summary

Introductions are one of the most powerful features of Spring AOP; they allow you not only to extend the functionality of existing methods but also to extend the set of interfaces and object implements dynamically. Using introductions is the perfect way to implement crosscutting logic that your application interacts with through well-defined interfaces. In general, this is the kind of logic that you want to apply declaratively rather than programmatically. By using the IsModifiedMixin defined in this example and the framework services discussed in the next section, we can declaratively define which objects are capable of modification checks, without needing to modify the implementations of those objects.

Obviously, because introductions work via proxies, they add a certain amount of overhead, and all methods on the proxy are considered to be advised, because you cannot use pointcuts in conjunction with introductions. However, in the case of many of the services that you can implement using introductions such as the object modification check, this performance overhead is a small price to pay for the reduction in code required to implement the service, as well the increase in stability and maintainability that comes from fully centralizing the service logic.

Framework Services for AOP

Up to now, we have had to write a lot of code to advise objects and generate the proxies for them. Although this in itself is not a huge problem, it does mean that all advice configuration is hard-coded into your application, removing some of the benefits of being able to advise a method implementation transparently. Thankfully, Spring provides additional framework services that allow you to create an advised proxy in your application configuration and then inject this proxy into a target bean just like any other dependencies.

Using the declarative approach to AOP configuration is preferable to the manual, programmatic mechanism. When you use the declarative mechanism, not only do you externalize the configuration of advice, but you also reduce the chance of coding errors. You can also take advantage of DI and AOP combined to enable AOP so it can be used in a completely transparent environment.

Configuring AOP Declaratively

When using declarative configuration of Spring AOP, three options exist.

- *Using ProxyFactoryBean:* In Spring AOP, the ProxyFactoryBean provides a declarative way for configuring Spring's ApplicationContext (and hence the underlying BeanFactory) in creating AOP proxies based on defined Spring beans.

- *Using Spring aop namespace:* Introduced in Spring 2.0, the aop namespace provides a simplified way (when compared to the ProxyFactoryBean) for defining aspects and their DI requirements in Spring applications. However, the aop namespace also uses the ProxyFactoryBean behind the scenes.

- • *Using @AspectJ-style annotations:* Besides the XML-based aop namespace, you can also use the @AspectJ-style annotations within your classes for configuring Spring AOP. Although the syntax it uses is based on AspectJ and you need to include some AspectJ libraries when using this option, Spring still uses the proxy mechanism, i.e., creates proxied objects for the targets, when bootstrapping the ApplicationContext.

Let's go through the option one by one in the following sections.

Using ProxyFactoryBean

The ProxyFactoryBean class is an implementation of FactoryBean that allows you to specify a bean to target, and it provides a set of advice and advisors for that bean that are eventually merged into an AOP proxy. Because you can use both advisor and advice with the ProxyFactoryBean, you can configure not only the advice declaratively but the pointcuts as well.

ProxyFactoryBean shares a common interface (the org.springframework.aop.framework.Advised interface) with ProxyFactory (both classes extend the org.springframework.aop.framework .AdvisedSupport class indirectly, which implements the Advised interface), and as a result, it exposes many of the same flags such as frozen, optimize, and exposeProxy. The values for these flags are passed directly to the underlying ProxyFactory, which allows you to configure the factory declaratively as well.

ProxyFactoryBean in Action

Using ProxyFactoryBean is actually very simple. You define a bean that will be the target bean, and then using ProxyFactoryBean, you define the bean that your application will actually access, using the target bean as the proxy target. Where possible, define the target bean as an anonymous bean inside the proxy bean declaration. This prevents your application from accidentally accessing the unadvised bean. However, in some cases, such as the sample we are about to show you, you may want to create more than one proxy for the same bean, so you should use a normal top-level bean for this case.

Listings 7-11 and 7-12 show two classes, one of which has a dependency on the other.

Listing 7-11. The MyDependency Class

```
package com.apress.prospring3.ch7.pfb;

public class MyDependency {

    public void foo() {
        System.out.println("foo()");
    }

    public void bar() {
        System.out.println("bar()");
    }
}
```

Listing 7-12. The MyBean Class

```
package com.apress.prospring3.ch7.pfb;

public class MyBean {
```

```
    private MyDependency dep;

    public void execute() {
        dep.foo();
        dep.bar();
    }

    public void setDep(MyDependency dep) {
        this.dep = dep;
    }
}
```

For this example, we are going to create two proxies for a single MyDependency instance, both with the same basic advice shown in Listing 7-13.

Listing 7-13. The MyAdvice Class

```
package com.apress.prospring3.ch7.pfb;

import java.lang.reflect.Method;
import org.springframework.aop.MethodBeforeAdvice;

public class MyAdvice implements MethodBeforeAdvice {

    public void before(Method method, Object[] args, Object target)
            throws Throwable {
        System.out.println("Executing: " + method);
    }
}
```

The first proxy will just advise the target using the advice directly; thus, all methods will be advised. For the second proxy, we will configure a AspectJExpressionPointcut and a DefaultPointcutAdvisor so that only the foo() method of the MyDependency class is advised. To test the advice, we will create two bean definitions of type MyBean, each of which will be injected with a different proxy. Then we will invoke the execute() method on each of these beans and observe what happens when the advised methods on the dependency are invoked.

Listing 7-14 shows the configuration for this example (pfb.xml).

Listing 7-14. Declarative AOP Configuration

```
<?xml version="1.0" encoding="UTF-8"?>
<beans xmlns="http://www.springframework.org/schema/beans"
      xmlns:xsi="http://www.w3.org/2001/XMLSchema-instance"
      xsi:schemaLocation="http://www.springframework.org/schema/beans
      http://www.springframework.org/schema/beans/spring-beans-3.1.xsd">

    <bean id="myBean1" class="com.apress.prospring3.ch7.pfb.MyBean">
        <property name="dep">
            <ref local="myDependency1"/>
        </property>
    </bean>

    <bean id="myBean2" class="com.apress.prospring3.ch7.pfb.MyBean">
        <property name="dep">
            <ref local="myDependency2"/>
```

```xml
            </property>
        </bean>

        <bean id="myDependencyTarget" class="com.apress.prospring3.ch7.pfb.MyDependency"/>

        <bean id="myDependency1" class="org.springframework.aop.framework.ProxyFactoryBean">
            <property name="target">
                <ref local="myDependencyTarget"/>
            </property>
            <property name="interceptorNames">
                <list>
                    <value>advice</value>
                </list>
            </property>
        </bean>

        <bean id="myDependency2" class="org.springframework.aop.framework.ProxyFactoryBean">
            <property name="target">
                <ref local="myDependencyTarget"/>
            </property>
            <property name="interceptorNames">
                <list>
                    <value>advisor</value>
                </list>
            </property>
        </bean>

        <bean id="advice" class="com.apress.prospring3.ch7.pfb.MyAdvice"/>

        <bean id="advisor" class="org.springframework.aop.support.DefaultPointcutAdvisor">
            <property name="advice">
                <ref local="advice"/>
            </property>
            <property name="pointcut">
                <bean class="org.springframework.aop.aspectj.AspectJExpressionPointcut">
                    <property name="expression">
                        <value>execution(* foo*(..))</value>
                    </property>
                </bean>
            </property>
        </bean>
    </bean>
</beans>
```

This code should be familiar to you. Notice that we are not really doing anything special; we are simply setting the properties that we set in code using Spring's DI capabilities. The only points of interest are that we use an anonymous bean for the pointcut and we use the ProxyFactoryBean class. We prefer to use anonymous beans for pointcuts when they are not being shared because it keeps the set of beans that are directly accessible as small and as application-relevant as possible. The important point to realize when you are using ProxyFactoryBean is that the ProxyFactoryBean declaration is the one to expose to your application and the one to use when you are fulfilling dependencies. The underlying target bean declaration is not advised, so you should use this bean only when you want to bypass the AOP framework, although in general, your application should not be aware of the AOP framework and thus should not want to bypass it. For this reason, you should use anonymous beans wherever possible to avoid accidental access from the application.

Listing 7-15 shows a simple class that grabs the two MyBean instances from the ApplicationContext and then runs the execute() method for each one.

Listing 7-15. The ProxyFactoryBeanExample Class

```
package com.apress.prospring3.ch7.pfb;

import org.springframework.context.support.GenericXmlApplicationContext;

public class ProxyFactoryBeanExample {

    public static void main(String[] args) {
        GenericXmlApplicationContext ctx = new GenericXmlApplicationContext();
        ctx.load("classpath:pfb.xml");
        ctx.refresh();

        MyBean bean1 = (MyBean)ctx.getBean("myBean1");
        MyBean bean2 = (MyBean)ctx.getBean("myBean2");

        System.out.println("Bean 1");
        bean1.execute();

        System.out.println("\nBean 2");
        bean2.execute();
    }
}
```

Running the example in Listing 7-15 results in the following output:

```
Bean 1
Executing: public void com.apress.prospring3.ch7.pfb.MyDependency.foo()
foo()
Executing: public void com.apress.prospring3.ch7.pfb.MyDependency.bar()
bar()

Bean 2
Executing: public void com.apress.prospring3.ch7.pfb.MyDependency.foo()
foo()
bar()
```

As expected, both the foo() and bar() methods in the first proxy are advised, because no pointcut was used in its configuration. For the second proxy, however, only the foo() method was advised because of the pointcut used in the configuration.

Using ProxyFactoryBean for Introductions

You are not limited in using the ProxyFactoryBean class for just advising an object but also for introducing mixins to your objects. Remember from our earlier discussion on introductions that you must use an IntroductionAdvisor to add an introduction; you cannot add an introduction directly. The same rule applies when you are using ProxyFactoryBean with introductions. When you are using ProxyFactoryBean, it becomes much easier to configure your proxies if you created a custom Advisor for your mixin as discussed earlier. Listing 7-16 shows a sample configuration for the IsModifiedMixin introduction we discussed earlier (introductions.xml).

Listing 7-16. Configuring Introductions with ProxyFactoryBean

```xml
<?xml version="1.0" encoding="UTF-8"?>
<beans xmlns="http://www.springframework.org/schema/beans"
    xmlns:xsi="http://www.w3.org/2001/XMLSchema-instance"
    xsi:schemaLocation="http://www.springframework.org/schema/beans
    http://www.springframework.org/schema/beans/spring-beans-3.1.xsd">

    <bean id="bean" class="org.springframework.aop.framework.ProxyFactoryBean">
        <property name="target">
            <bean  class="com.apress.prospring3.ch7.introductions.TargetBean">
                <property name="name">
                    <value>Clarence Ho</value>
                </property>
            </bean>
        </property>
        <property name="interceptorNames">
            <list>
                <value>advisor</value>
            </list>
        </property>
        <property name="proxyTargetClass">
            <value>true</value>
        </property>
    </bean>

    <bean id="advisor" class="com.apress.prospring3.ch7.introductions.IsModifiedAdvisor"/>
</beans>
```

As you can see from the configuration, we use the IsModifiedAdvisor class as the advisor for the ProxyFactoryBean, and because we do not need to create another proxy of the same target object, we use an anonymous declaration for the target bean. Listing 7-17 shows a modification of the previous introduction example that obtains the proxy from the ApplicationContext.

Listing 7-17. The IntroductionConfigExample Class

```java
package com.apress.prospring3.ch7.introductions;

import org.springframework.context.support.GenericXmlApplicationContext;

public class IntroductionConfigExample {

    public static void main(String[] args) {
        GenericXmlApplicationContext ctx = new GenericXmlApplicationContext();
        ctx.load("classpath:introductions.xml");
        ctx.refresh();

        TargetBean bean = (TargetBean) ctx.getBean("bean");
        IsModified mod = (IsModified) bean;

        // test interfaces
        System.out.println("Is TargetBean?: " + (bean instanceof TargetBean));
        System.out.println("Is IsModified?: " + (bean instanceof IsModified));
```

```
        // test is modified implementation
        System.out.println("Has been modified?: " + mod.isModified());
        bean.setName("Clarence Ho");
        System.out.println("Has been modified?: " + mod.isModified());
        bean.setName("Rob Harrop");
        System.out.println("Has been modified?: " + mod.isModified());
    }
}
```

Running this example yields exactly the same output as the previous introduction example, but this time the proxy is obtained from the ApplicationContext and no configuration is present in the application code.

ProxyFactoryBean Summary

When you use ProxyFactoryBean, you can configure AOP proxies that provide all the flexibility of the programmatic method without needing to couple your application to the AOP configuration. Unless you need to perform decisions at runtime as to how your proxies should be created, it is best to use the declarative method of proxy configuration over the programmatic method. Let's move on to see the other two options for declarative Spring AOP, which are both preferred options for applications based on Spring 2.0 or newer with JDK 5 or newer.

Using the aop Namespace

The aop namespace provides a greatly simplified syntax for declarative Spring AOP configurations. To show you how it works, let's reuse the previous example on using ProxyFactoryBean, with a slightly modified version in order to demonstrate its usage.

Listings 7-18 and 7-19 show the MyDependency and MyBean class, with some modifications.

Listing 7-18. The MyDependency Class

```
package com.apress.prospring3.ch7.aopns;

public class MyDependency {

    public void foo(int intValue) {
        System.out.println("foo(int): " + intValue);
    }

    public void bar() {
        System.out.println("bar()");
    }
}
```

Listing 7-19. The MyBean Class

```
package com.apress.prospring3.ch7.aopns;

public class MyBean {

    private MyDependency dep;
```

```
    public void execute() {
        dep.foo(100);
        dep.foo(101);
        dep.bar();
    }

    public void setDep(MyDependency dep) {
        this.dep = dep;
    }
}
```

In the previous listing, we modified the foo() method of the MyDependency class to accept an integer value as an argument. And in the MyBean class, the foo() method was called twice with different parameters.

Let's see what the advice class looks like. Listing 7-20 shows the revised MyAdvice class.

Listing 7-20. The MyAdvice Class

```
package com.apress.prospring3.ch7.aopns;

import org.aspectj.lang.JoinPoint;

public class MyAdvice {

    public void simpleBeforeAdvice(JoinPoint joinPoint) {
        System.out.println("Executing: " +
                joinPoint.getSignature().getDeclaringTypeName() + " "
                + joinPoint.getSignature().getName());
    }
}
```

You will see that the advice class no longer needs to implement the MethodBeforeAdvice interface. Also, the before advice accepts the JoinPoint as an argument but not the method, object, and arguments. Actually, for the advice class, this argument is optional, so you can leave the method with no argument. However, if in the advice you need to access the information of the joinpoint being advised (in this case we want to dump the information of the calling type and method name), then we need to define the acceptance of the argument. When the argument is defined for the method, Spring will automatically pass the joinpoint into the method for your processing.

Listing 7-21 shows the Spring XML configuration with the aop namespace (aopns.xml).

Listing 7-21. Configuring Spring AOP with the aop Namespace

```
<?xml version="1.0" encoding="UTF-8"?>
<beans xmlns="http://www.springframework.org/schema/beans"
    xmlns:xsi="http://www.w3.org/2001/XMLSchema-instance"
    xmlns:aop="http://www.springframework.org/schema/aop"
    xsi:schemaLocation="http://www.springframework.org/schema/beans
        http://www.springframework.org/schema/beans/spring-beans-3.1.xsd
        http://www.springframework.org/schema/aop
        http://www.springframework.org/schema/aop/spring-aop-3.1.xsd">

    <aop:config>

        <aop:pointcut id="fooExecution"
```

```
                expression="execution(* com.apress.prospring3.ch7..foo*(int))"/>

        <aop:aspect ref="advice">
            <aop:before pointcut-ref="fooExecution"
                method="simpleBeforeAdvice"/>
        </aop:aspect>

    </aop:config>

    <bean id="advice" class="com.apress.prospring3.ch7.aopns.MyAdvice"/>

    <bean id="myDependency"
        class="com.apress.prospring3.ch7.aopns.MyDependency"/>

    <bean id="myBean" class="com.apress.prospring3.ch7.aopns.MyBean">
        <property name="dep" ref="myDependency"/>
    </bean>
</beans>
```

First, we need to declare the aop namespace in the <beans> tags. Second, all the Spring AOP configuration was put under the tag <aop:config>. Under <aop:config>, you can then define the pointcut, aspects, advisors, and so on, and reference other Spring beans as usual.

From the previous configuration, we defined a pointcut with the ID fooExecution. The expression "execution(* com.apress.prospring3.ch7..foo*(int))" means that we want to advise all methods with the prefix foo, and the classes are defined under the package com.apress.prospring3.ch7 (including all the subpackages). Also, the foo() method should receive one argument with the integer type. Afterward, for the aspect, it was declared by using the <aop:aspect> tag, and the advice class is referencing the Spring bean with the ID "advice", which is the MyAdvice class. The pointcut-ref is referencing the defined pointcut with the ID fooExecution, and the before advice (declared by using the <aop:before> tag) is the method simpleBeforeAdvice() within the advice bean.

Listing 7-22 shows the testing program.

Listing 7-22. The AopNamespaceExample Class

```
package com.apress.prospring3.ch7.aopns;

import org.springframework.context.support.GenericXmlApplicationContext;

public class AopNamespaceExample {

    public static void main(String[] args) {

        GenericXmlApplicationContext ctx = new GenericXmlApplicationContext();
        ctx.load("classpath:aopns.xml");
        ctx.refresh();

        MyBean myBean = (MyBean) ctx.getBean("myBean");
        myBean.execute();
    }
}
```

There is nothing interesting here for the class. Just initialize the ApplicationContext as usual, retrieve the bean, and call its execute() method. Running the program will yield the following output:

```
Executing: com.apress.prospring3.ch7.aopns.MyDependency foo
foo(int): 100
Executing: com.apress.prospring3.ch7.aopns.MyDependency foo
foo(int): 101
bar()
```

As you can see, the two calls to the foo() method were advised but not the bar() method. It exactly works as we expected, and you can see the configuration was greatly simplified when compared to the ProxyFactoryBean configuration.

Let's further revise the previous sample into a bit more complicated case. Suppose now we want to advise only those methods with Spring beans with an ID starting with myDependency and an integer argument that is not equal to 100.

To runs the advice only when the argument is not 100, we need to modify the advice. Listing 7-23 shows the revised MyAdvice class.

Listing 7-23. The MyAdvice Class (Revised for Argument Checking)

```
package com.apress.prospring3.ch7.aopns;

import org.aspectj.lang.JoinPoint;

public class MyAdvice {

    // For both joinpoint and argument retrieval
    public void simpleBeforeAdvice(JoinPoint joinPoint, int intValue) {

        // Execute only when intValue is not 100
        if (intValue != 100) {
            System.out.println("Executing: " +
                joinPoint.getSignature().getDeclaringTypeName() + " "
                + joinPoint.getSignature().getName()
                + " argument: " + intValue);
        }
    }
}
```

Two places were modified. First, the argument intValue was added into the signature of the before advice. Second, in the advice, we check and exccute the logic only when the argument does not equal 100.

To pass the argument to the advice, we also need to revise the XML configuration a bit. In this case, we need to modify the point expression. The modified pointcut expression is shown here:

```
<aop:pointcut id="fooExecution" expression="execution(* foo*(int))
    and args(intValue) and bean(myDependency*)"/>
```

Two more directives were added to the pointcut expression. First, the args(intValue) instructs Spring to also pass the argument with the name intValue into the before advice. Second, the bean(myDependency*) directive instructs Spring to advise only the beans with an ID that has myDependency as the prefix. This is a powerful feature; if you have a well-defined structure of Spring beans naming, you can easily advise the objects that you want. For example, you can have advise that applies to all DAO beans by using bean(*DAO*) or all service layer beans using bean(*Service*), instead of using the fully qualified class name for matching.

Running the same testing program (AopNamespaceExample) will produce the following output:

```
foo(int): 100
Executing: com.apress.prospring3.ch7.aopns.MyDependency foo argument: 101
foo(int): 101
bar()
```

You can see that only the foo() with arguments not equal to 100 are advised.

Let's see one more example of using the aop namespace for around advice. Instead of creating another class to implement the MethodInterceptor interface, we can simply add a new method to the MyAdvice class. Listing 7-24 shows the new method, simpleAroundAdvice(), in the revised MyAdvice class.

Listing 7-24. The MyAdvice Class (Revised for Argument Checking)

```java
package com.apress.prospring3.ch7.aopns;

import org.aspectj.lang.JoinPoint;
import org.aspectj.lang.ProceedingJoinPoint;

public class MyAdvice {

    // For both joinpoint and argument retrieval
    public void simpleBeforeAdvice(JoinPoint joinPoint, int intValue) {

        // Execute only when intValue is not 100
        if (intValue != 100) {
        System.out.println("Executing: " +
            joinPoint.getSignature().getDeclaringTypeName() + " "
            + joinPoint.getSignature().getName()
            + " argument: " + intValue);
        }
    }

    public Object simpleAroundAdvice(ProceedingJoinPoint pjp, int intValue)
            throws Throwable {

        System.out.println("Before execution: " +
            pjp.getSignature().getDeclaringTypeName() + " "
            + pjp.getSignature().getName()
            + " argument: " + intValue);

        Object retVal = pjp.proceed();

        System.out.println("After execution: " +
            pjp.getSignature().getDeclaringTypeName() + " "
            + pjp.getSignature().getName() + " argument: " + intValue);

        return retVal;
    }
}
```

The newly added simpleAroundAdvice() method needs to take at least one argument of type ProceedingJoinPoint so that it can proceed with the invocation of the target object. We also added the intValue argument to display the value in the advice.

For the XML configuration, we just need to add one line to it. Listing 7-25 shows the code snippet.

Listing 7-25. Configuring Spring AOP with the aop Namespace (Around Advice)

```
...
        <aop:aspect ref="advice">
            <aop:before pointcut-ref="fooExecution"
                method="simpleBeforeAdvice"/>
            <aop:around pointcut-ref="fooExecution"
                method="simpleAroundAdvice"/>
        </aop:aspect>
...
```

We just added a new tag `<aop:around>` to declare the around advice and reference the same pointcut. Run the testing program again, and you will have the following output:

```
Before execution: com.apress.prospring3.ch7.aopns.MyDependency foo argument: 100
foo(int): 100
After execution: com.apress.prospring3.ch7.aopns.MyDependency foo argument: 100
Executing: com.apress.prospring3.ch7.aopns.MyDependency foo argument: 101
Before execution: com.apress.prospring3.ch7.aopns.MyDependency foo argument: 101
foo(int): 101
After execution: com.apress.prospring3.ch7.aopns.MyDependency foo argument: 101
bar()
```

There are two interesting points here. First, you see that the around advice was applied to both invocations of the foo() method, since it doesn't check the argument. Second, for the foo() method with 101 as an argument, both the before and around advice were executed, and by default the before advice takes precedence.

■ **Note** When using the aop namespace or the @AspectJ style, there are two types of after advice. The "after-returning" advice (using the `<aop:after-returning>` tag) applies only when the target method is completed normally. Another one is the "after" advice (using the `<aop:after>` tag), which takes place whether the method was completed normally or the method runs into an error and an exception is thrown. If you need an advice that executes regardless of the execution result of the target method, you should use the after advice.

Using @AspectJ-Style Annotations

As you might expect, when using Spring AOP with JDK 5 or above, you can also use annotation to declare your advice. Spring supports the @AspectJ style annotations that make use of the annotations and syntax provided by @AspectJ. However, as stated before, Spring still uses its own proxying mechanism for advising the target methods, not AspectJ's weaving mechanism.

In this section, we will go through how to implement the same aspects like the one in aop-namespace, by using @AspectJ style annotations. For the examples in this section, we will also use annotation for other Spring beans as well.

Listings 7-26 and 7-27 shows the MyDependency and MyBean classes with Spring's DI annotations.

Listing 7-26. The MyDependency Class

```java
package com.apress.prospring3.ch7.aspectjannotation;

import org.springframework.stereotype.Component;

@Component("myDependency")
public class MyDependency {

    public void foo(int intValue) {
        System.out.println("foo(int): " + intValue);
    }

    public void bar() {
        System.out.println("bar()");
    }
}
```

Listing 7-27. The MyBean Class

```java
package com.apress.prospring3.ch7.aspectjannotation;

import org.springframework.beans.factory.annotation.Autowired;
import org.springframework.stereotype.Component;

@Component("myBean")
public class MyBean {

    private MyDependency myDependency;

    public void execute() {
        myDependency.foo(100);
        myDependency.foo(101);
        myDependency.bar();
    }

    @Autowired
    public void setDep(MyDependency myDependency) {
        this.myDependency = myDependency;
    }
}
```

We annotate both classes with the @Component annotation and assign them with the corresponding name. In the MyBean class, the setter method of the property myDependency was annotated with @Autowired for automatic injection by Spring.

Now let's see the MyAdvice class using @AspectJ-style annotations. We will implement the pointcuts and the before and around advice altogether in one shot. Listing 7-28 shows the MyAdvice class.

Listing 7-28. The MyAdvice Class

```java
package com.apress.prospring3.ch7.aspectjannotation;

import org.aspectj.lang.JoinPoint;
import org.aspectj.lang.ProceedingJoinPoint;
import org.aspectj.lang.annotation.Around;
```

```java
import org.aspectj.lang.annotation.Aspect;
import org.aspectj.lang.annotation.Before;
import org.aspectj.lang.annotation.Pointcut;
import org.springframework.stereotype.Component;

@Component
@Aspect
public class MyAdvice {

    @Pointcut("execution(* com.apress.prospring3.ch7..foo*(int)) && args(intValue)")
    public void fooExecution(int intValue) {
    }

    @Pointcut("bean(myDependency*)")
    public void inMyDependency() {
    }

    @Before("fooExecution(intValue) && inMyDependency()")
    public void simpleBeforeAdvice(JoinPoint joinPoint, int intValue) {
        // Execute only when intValue is not 100
        if (intValue != 100) {
        System.out.println("Executing: " +
            joinPoint.getSignature().getDeclaringTypeName() + " "
            + joinPoint.getSignature().getName() + " argument: " + intValue);
        }
    }

    @Around("fooExecution(intValue) && inMyDependency()")
    public Object simpleAroundAdvice(ProceedingJoinPoint pjp, int intValue) throws Throwable {

        System.out.println("Before execution: " +
            pjp.getSignature().getDeclaringTypeName() + " "
            + pjp.getSignature().getName()
            + " argument: " + intValue);

        Object retVal = pjp.proceed();

        System.out.println("After execution: " +
            pjp.getSignature().getDeclaringTypeName() + " "
            + pjp.getSignature().getName()
            + " argument: " + intValue);

        return retVal;
    }
}
```

You will notice that the code structure is quite like the one we used in the aop namespace, just in this case we used annotations instead. However, there are still a few points worth noting:

- We used both the @Component and @Aspect to annotate the MyAdvice class. The @Aspect is to declare that it's an aspect class. To allow Spring to scan the component when we use the <context:component-scan> tag in the XML configuration, we also need to annotate the class with @Component.

- The pointcuts were defined as methods that returns void. In the class, we defined two pointcuts; both are annotated with @Pointcut. We intentionally split the pointcut expression in the aop namespace example into two. The first one (indicated by the method fooExecution(int intValue)) defines the pointcut for execution of foo*() methods within all classes under the package com.apress.prospring3.ch7 with an integer argument, and the argument (intValue) will also be passed into the advice. The other one (indicated by the method inMyDependency()) is to define another pointcut that defines all method executions with Spring beans' names prefixed by myDependency. Also note that we need to use && to define the "and" condition in the pointcut expression, while for the aop namespace, we need to use the and operator.

- The before advice method was annotated with @Before, while the around advice was annotated with @Around. For both advice, we pass in the value that uses the two pointcuts defined in the class. The value "fooExecution(intValue) && inMyDependency()" means the condition of both pointcuts should be matched for applying the advice, which is the same as the "intersection" operation in the ComposablePointcut.

- The before advice and around advice logic is the same as the one in the aop namespace example.

With all the annotations in place, the XML configuration becomes very simple. Listing 7-29 shows the configuration for this example (aspectjannotation.xml).

Listing 7-29. Configuring Spring AOP with @AspectJ Annotations

```
<?xml version="1.0" encoding="UTF-8"?>
<beans xmlns="http://www.springframework.org/schema/beans"
    xmlns:xsi="http://www.w3.org/2001/XMLSchema-instance"
    xmlns:aop="http://www.springframework.org/schema/aop"
    xmlns:context="http://www.springframework.org/schema/context"
    xsi:schemaLocation="http://www.springframework.org/schema/aop
      http://www.springframework.org/schema/aop/spring-aop-3.1.xsd
      http://www.springframework.org/schema/beans
      http://www.springframework.org/schema/beans/spring-beans-3.1.xsd
      http://www.springframework.org/schema/context
      http://www.springframework.org/schema/context/spring-context-3.1.xsd">

    <aop:aspectj-autoproxy/>

    <context:component-scan base-package="com.apress.prospring3.ch7.aspectjannotation"/>
</beans>
```

Only two tags were declared. The <aop:aspect-autorpoxy> is to inform Spring to scan for @AspectJ-style annotations, while the <context:component-scan> was still required for Spring to scan for Spring beans within the package that the advice resides. We also need to annotate the advice class with @Component to indicate that it's a Spring component.

The <aop:aspectj-autoproxy> tag carries an attribute called proxy-target-class. The default is false, which means that Spring will create standard interface-based proxies using a JDK dynamic proxy. If set to true, Spring will use CGLIB to create class-based proxies.

Listing 7-30 shows the testing program, the AspectJAnnotationExample class.

Listing 7-30. Testing AspectJ Annotation

```
package com.apress.prospring3.ch7.aspectjannotation;

import org.springframework.context.support.GenericXmlApplicationContext;

public class AspectJAnnotationExample {

    public static void main(String[] args) {

        GenericXmlApplicationContext ctx = new GenericXmlApplicationContext();
        ctx.load("classpath:aspectjannotation.xml");
        ctx.refresh();

        MyBean myBean = (MyBean) ctx.getBean("myBean");
        myBean.execute();

    }
}
```

Running the program will yield the same results as the aop namespace example:

```
Before execution: com.apress.prospring3.ch7.aspectjannotation.MyDependency foo argument: 100
foo(int): 100
After execution: com.apress.prospring3.ch7.aspectjannotation.MyDependency foo argument: 100
Executing: com.apress.prospring3.ch7.aspectjannotation.MyDependency foo argument: 101
Before execution: com.apress.prospring3.ch7.aspectjannotation.MyDependency foo argument: 101
foo(int): 101
After execution: com.apress.prospring3.ch7.aspectjannotation.MyDependency foo argument: 101
bar()
```

Considerations for Declarative Spring AOP Configuration

So far, we have discussed three different ways of declaring Spring AOP configuration, including the ProxyFactoryBean, the aop namespace, and @AspectJ-style annotations. We believe you will agree that the aop namespace is much simpler than the ProxyFactoryBean. So, the general question is, do you use aop namespace or @AspectJ-style annotations?

If your Spring application is XML configuration based, then using the aop namespace approach is a natural choice, because it keeps the AOP and DI configuration styles consistent. On the other hand, if your application is mainly annotation based, then use the @AspectJ annotation. The @AspectJ annotation approach also has the advantage that all the aspect-related information is encapsulated in one module, which is easier to manage.

Moreover, there are some other differences between the aop namespace and @AspectJ annotation approaches:

- The pointcut expression syntax has some minor differences (e.g., in the previous discussions, we need to use and in the aop namespace, but && in @AspectJ annotation).

- The aop namespace approach supports only the "singleton" aspect instantiation model.

- In the aop namespace, you can't "combine" multiple pointcut expressions. For example, in the example using @AspectJ, we can combine the two pointcut definitions (i.e., fooExecution(intValue) && inMyDependency()) in the before and around advice. But you can't do this when using the aop namespace, and you need to create a new pointcut expression that combines the matching conditions.

■ **Note** When you refer to Spring's reference manual, you will also see another mechanism called *automatic proxying*. Basically, it provides a few ways for you to define and apply the advice to a number of Spring beans within the `ApplicationContext`. For example, the `BeanNameAutoProxyCreator` class allows you to advise a number of Spring beans by the name, while the `DefaultAdvisorAutoProxyCreator` class allows you to apply an advisor to the beans within the `ApplicationContext` with the pointcut logic defined in the `Advisor` implementation class. However, both mechanisms can now be easily handled by the powerful pointcut expression support in both the `aop` namespace and @AspectJ-style annotations. So, we decided to skip the discussion of the automatic proxying here, but if you are interested, you can refer to Spring's reference manual for details.

AspectJ Integration

AOP provides a powerful solution to many of the common problems that arise with OOP-based applications. When using Spring AOP, you can take advantage of a select subset of AOP functionality that, in most cases, allows you to solve problems you encounter in your application. However, in some cases, you may want to use some AOP features that are outside the scope of Spring AOP.

From the joinpoint perspective, Spring AOP only supports pointcuts matching on the execution of public nonstatic methods. However, in some cases, you may need to apply advice to protected/private methods, during object construction or field access, and so on.

In those cases, you need to look at an AOP implementation with a fuller feature set. Our preference, in this case, is to use AspectJ, and because you can now configure AspectJ aspects using Spring, AspectJ forms the perfect complement to Spring AOP.

About AspectJ

AspectJ is a fully featured AOP implementation that uses a weaving process (either compile-time or load-time weaving) to introduce aspects into your code. In AspectJ, aspects and pointcuts are built using a Java-like syntax, which reduces the learning curve for Java developers. We are not going to spend too much time looking at AspectJ and how it works because that is outside the scope of this book. Instead, we present some simple AspectJ examples and show you how to configure them using Spring. For more information on AspectJ, you should definitely read *AspectJ in Action: Enterprise AOP with Spring Applications,* 2nd Edition, by Ramnivas Laddad (Manning, 2010).

■ **Note** We are not going to cover how to weave AspectJ aspects into your application. Refer to the AspectJ documentation for details on how to achieve this. Alternatively, Eclipse users can download the Eclipse AspectJ Development Tools (AJDT) and take advantage of full IDE integration and autocompilation. AJDT was also bundled with SpringSource Tool Suite (STS), so you don't need to download it separately when using STS.

Using Singleton Aspects

By default, AspectJ aspects are singletons, in that you get a single instance per classloader. The problem Spring faces with any AspectJ aspect is that it cannot create the aspect instance because that is handled by AspectJ itself. However, each aspect exposes a method, aspectOf() (which is from the org.aspectj.lang.Aspects class within the aspectjrt jar library), which can be used to access the aspect instance. Using the aspectOf() method and a special feature of Spring configuration, you can have Spring configure the aspect for you. The benefits of this cannot be understated. You can take full advantage of AspectJ's powerful AOP feature set without losing out on Spring's excellent DI and configuration abilities. This also means you do not need two separate configuration methods for your application; you can use the same Spring ApplicationContext approach for all your Spring-managed beans and for your AspectJ aspects.

There is actually nothing particularly special or difficult about configuring AspectJ aspects using Spring, as the following example shows. In Listing 7-31, you can see a basic class, MessageWriter, that we will advise using AspectJ.

Listing 7-31. The MessageWriter Class

```
package com.apress.prospring3.ch7.aspectj;

public class MessageWriter {

    public void writeMessage() {
        System.out.println("foobar!");
    }

    public void foo() {
        System.out.println("foo");
    }
}
```

For this example, we are going to use AspectJ to advise the writeMessage() method and write out a message before and after the method invocation. These messages will be configurable using Spring.

STS bundled the AspectJ Development Tools, which is an Eclipse plug-in for AspectJ development. We will use it to develop the example AspectJ aspect. To enable AspectJ support for the project, right-click the project and select Configure ➤ Convert to AspectJ Project. Figure 7-5 shows the STS menus.

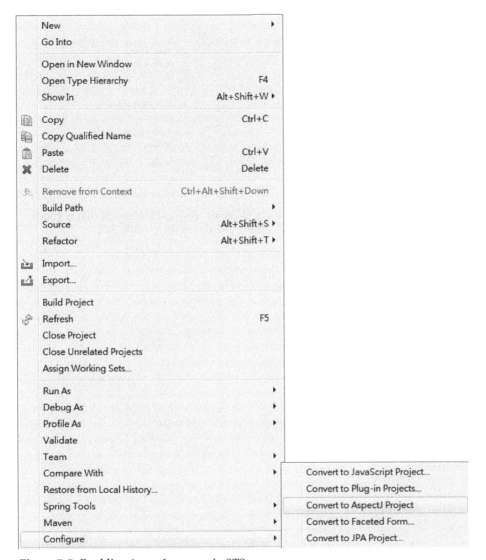

Figure 7-5. Enabling AspectJ support in STS

Afterward, we can then create an aspect by right-clicking the package name com.apress.prospring3.ch7.aspectj and selecting New ➤ Aspect, as shown in Figure 7-6.

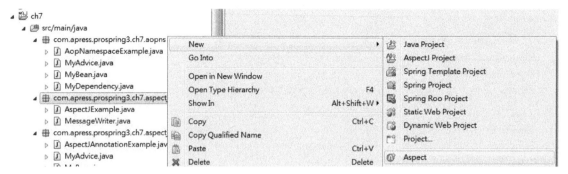

Figure 7-6. *Creating a new aspect*

However, if you now build the project, there will be a build error reported by AspectJ that is about the previous example, the MyAdvice class in Listing 7-28. Figure 7-7 shows the error in STS.

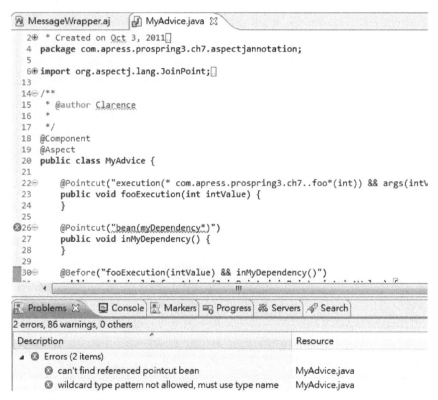

Figure 7-7. *AspectJ problem with the MyAdvice class*

The error is that in the @AspectJ annotation support example, we use the bean() pointcut designator, which is not supported by AspectJ. The bean() pointcut designator is a Spring extension added to AspectJ, and the purpose is to support providing bean name as the pointcut for @AspectJ-style annotation. So, if we enable AspectJ for the project, an error will be reported by the AspectJ tool. To have AspectJ tooling and the bean() pointcut designator coexist, there are two options:

- For the bean() pointcut designator, use the aop namespace in the XML configuration for declaration instead of the @AspectJ-style annotation.

- Do not use bean() pointcut designator when you want to use AspectJ in your project.

To get rid of the error, just delete the MyAdvice class at the moment.

Listing 7-32 shows the MessageWrapper aspect (the filename is MessageWrapper.aj, which is an AspectJ file instead of a standard Java class). The aspect was created using the New ➤ Aspect option in STS, as indicated in Figure 7-6.

Listing 7-32. MessageWrapper Aspect

```
package com.apress.prospring3.ch7.aspectj;

public aspect MessageWrapper {

    private String prefix;
    private String suffix;

    public void setPrefix(String prefix) {
        this.prefix = prefix;
    }

    public void setSuffix(String suffix) {
        this.suffix = suffix;
    }

    pointcut doWriting() :
        execution(*
            com.apress.prospring3.ch7.aspectj.MessageWriter.writeMessage());

    before() : doWriting() {
        System.out.println(prefix);
    }

    after() : doWriting() {
        System.out.println(suffix);
    }
}
```

Much of this code should look familiar. Essentially we create an aspect called MessageWrapper, and, just like a normal Java class, we give the aspect two properties, suffix and prefix, which we will use when advising the writeMessage() method. Next, we define a named pointcut, doWriting(), for a single joinpoint, in this case, the execution of the writeMessage() method. (AspectJ has a huge number of joinpoints, but coverage of those is outside the scope of this example.) Finally, we define two lots of advice: one that executes before the doWriting() pointcut and one that executes after it. The before advice writes a line containing the prefix, and the after advice writes a line containing the suffix. Listing 7-33 shows how this aspect is configured in Spring (aspectj.xml).

Listing 7-33. Configuring an AspectJ Aspect

```xml
<?xml version="1.0" encoding="UTF-8"?>
<beans xmlns="http://www.springframework.org/schema/beans
    xmlns:xsi="http://www.w3.org/2001/XMLSchema-instance"
    xsi:schemaLocation="http://www.springframework.org/schema/beans
      http://www.springframework.org/schema/beans/spring-beans-3.1.xsd">

    <bean id="aspect" class="com.apress.prospring3.ch7.aspectj.MessageWrapper"
        factory-method="aspectOf">
        <property name="prefix">
            <value>Ha Ha!</value>
        </property>
        <property name="suffix">
            <value>Ho Ho!</value>
        </property>
    </bean>
</beans>
```

As you can see, much of the configuration of the aspect bean is very similar to standard bean configuration. The only difference is the use of the `factory-method` attribute of the `<bean>` tag. The `factory-method` attribute is intended to allow classes that follow a traditional Factory pattern to be integrated seamlessly into Spring. For instance, if you have a class Foo with a private constructor and then a static factory method, `getInstance()`, using `factory-method` allows a bean of this class to be managed by Spring. The `aspectOf()` method exposed by every AspectJ aspect allows you to access the instance of the aspect and thus allows Spring to set the properties of the aspect. Listing 7-34 shows a simple driver application for this example.

Listing 7-34. AspectJ Configuration in Action

```java
package com.apress.prospring3.ch7.aspectj;

import org.springframework.context.support.GenericXmlApplicationContext;

public class AspectJExample {

    public static void main(String[] args) {
        GenericXmlApplicationContext ctx = new GenericXmlApplicationContext();
        ctx.load("classpath:aspectj.xml");
        ctx.refresh();

        MessageWriter writer = new MessageWriter();
        writer.writeMessage();
        writer.foo();
    }
}
```

Notice that first we load the `ApplicationContext` to allow Spring to configure the aspect. Next we create an instance of `MessageWriter` and then invoke the `writeMessage()` and `foo()` methods. The output from this example is as follows:

```
Ha Ha!
foobar!
Ho Ho!
foo
```

As you can see, the advice in the `MessageWrapper` aspect was applied to the `writeMessage()` method, and the prefix and suffix values specified in the `ApplicationContext` configuration were used by the advice when writing out the before and after messages.

AOP in the Sample Application

So far, you have seen lots of small examples of how to use the Spring AOP features, but as of yet, we have not looked at some practical uses of AOP in an application. Typical examples in this field are logging and security, and we have looked at these, albeit briefly, over the course of this chapter and the last. However, AOP is not just limited to use in logging and security, and it can be put to great use when you are implementing any application-specific logic that is crosscutting—that is, any logic in your application that needs to be called from a large number of separate components. In this section, we will give you an overview about how we use Spring AOP in the sample SpringBlog application to solve a problem involving crosscutting logic.

Filtering Obscenities in SpringBlog

One of the problems we faced when building the SpringBlog application was how to filter obscenities uniformly out of postings on the blog. This includes top-level blog entries as well as any comments made about a particular entry. We needed to ensure that neither an entry nor a comment could be created containing obscenities and that existing entries and comments could not be modified to contain obscenities. Specifically, we wanted the ability to obfuscate obscenities contained in postings automatically with inoffensive alternatives. Taking this further, we decided that in some cases, the blog owner might actually want to be able to add obscenities to their entries, acting as their own moderator, but want to restrict blog readers from posting comments containing obscenities.

The traditional approach to this problem would be to define an interface (for example, an `ObscenityFilter` interface) and then build an implementation of this interface and make it accessible through some factory class. Then, in each method where an entry or comment is created or modified, you invoke the `ObscenityFilter` to remove obscenities from the posting. However, the main problem with this approach is that all business logic that involves processing of blog entries and comments are going to have to remember to implement this check.

Using Spring AOP, we can create a much more elegant solution to this problem by factoring the obscenity check into a before advice that we can apply to any method that accepts a blog entry or comment domain object as an argument. An interesting point about this implementation is that, for the most part, we just followed good OOP practice as suggested in the traditional approach. We defined an interface, `ObscenityFilter`, and then built an implementation. Thanks to Spring DI, we were able to avoid the need to create a factory class, but by following good practices, we were able to build an obscenity filter that can be used equally well in both AOP and non-AOP settings.

The BlogPosting Interface

Within the blog, there are two distinct types of postings: a main blog entry, represented by an `Entry` object, and a comment about an entry, represented by a `Comment` object. Although these two objects represent different kinds of posting, they do share similar characteristics, such as body, subject, attachments, and date of posting. For this reason, we created an interface, `BlogPosting`, that allows `Comments` and `Entries` to be manipulated at the same time. Because all the String-typed properties of `Comment` and `Entry` are exposed on the `BlogPosting` interface, we use the `BlogPosting` interface in our obscenity filter advice.

Implementing ObscenityFilter

For the SpringBlog application, we decided to create an implementation of ObscenityFilter that allows the list of obscenities to filter to be specified as a List and that replaces the obscenities using the ROT13 algorithm. With the implementation of the ObscenityFilter interface finished (the ListBasedObscenityFilter class), an advice (the ObscenityFilterAdvice) was then created, which allows obscenity filter capabilities to be applied declaratively to any method that accepts Entry or Comment arguments. The basis of the ObscenityFilterAdvice is to modify the arguments passed to the method so that any String properties of the Entry or Comment objects are replaced with their obfuscated alternatives. Because we only need to look at the arguments passed to a method and perhaps modify them, a before advice is ideal for this. In addition, we decided to use the @AspectJ-style annotations to implement the advice.

Obscenity Filter Summary

As you can see from the example in this section, AOP has plenty of practical uses in a real application. We found that by using AOP for the obscenity filter, we were able to keep the code for the service layer of the SpringBlog application much cleaner and were also able to reduce the amount of code duplication within the application. When you build your own applications with Spring, it is worth it to take the time to identify crosscutting logic. Once you have done this, define the interfaces to interact with it, build the implementations, and then instead of using a factory and embedding calls against your interfaces throughout your code, use Spring AOP to weave the logic into your application transparently. For a detailed explanation on the implementation of the obscenity filter and its source code, please refer to the section "Obscenity Filter Using AOP" in Chapter 21.

Summary

In this chapter, we concluded our discussion on AOP. We looked at the advanced options for pointcutting, as well as how to extend the set of interfaces implemented by an object using introductions. A large part of this chapter focused on using Spring framework services to configure AOP declaratively, thus avoiding the need to hard-code AOP proxy construction logic into your code. We spent some time looking at how Spring and AspectJ are integrated to allow you to use the added power of AspectJ without losing any of the flexibility of Spring. In the next chapter, we move on to a completely different topic—how we can use Spring's JDBC support to radically simplify the creation of JDBC-based data access code.

CHAPTER 8

Spring JDBC Support

In the previous chapters, you saw how easy it is to build a fully Spring-managed application. You now have a solid understanding of bean configuration and Aspect-Oriented Programming (AOP)—in other words, you know how to wire up the entire application using Spring. However, one of the parts of the puzzle is missing: how do you get the data that drives the application?

Apart from simple throwaway command-line utilities, almost every application needs to persist data to some kind of data store. The most usual and convenient data store is a relational database.

The most notable open source relational databases are perhaps MySQL (www.mysql.com) and PostgreSQL (www.postgresql.org). In terms of RDBMS features being provided, both databases are about the same. MySQL is generally more widely used for web application development, especially on the Linux platform. On the other side, PostgreSQL is friendlier to Oracle developers, because its procedural language, PL/pgSQL, is very close to Oracle's PL/SQL language.

Even if you choose the fastest and most reliable database, you cannot afford to lose the offered speed and flexibility by using a poorly designed and implemented data access layer. Applications tend to use the data access layer very frequently; thus, any unnecessary bottlenecks in the data access code impact the entire application, no matter how well-designed it is.

In this chapter, we show you how you can use Spring to simplify the implementation of data access code using JDBC. We start by looking at the horrendous amount of code you would normally need to write without Spring and then compare it to a data access class implemented using Spring's data access classes. The result is truly amazing—Spring allows you to use the full power of human-tuned SQL queries while minimizing the amount of support code you need to implement. Specifically, we will discuss the following:

- *Comparing traditional JDBC code and Spring JDBC support*: We explore how Spring simplifies the old-style JDBC code while keeping the same functionality. You will also see how Spring accesses the low-level JDBC API and how this low-level API is mapped into convenient classes such as JdbcTemplate.

- *Connecting to the database*: Even though we do not go into every little detail of database connection management, we do show you the fundamental differences between a simple Connection and a DataSource. Naturally, we discuss how Spring manages the DataSources and which data sources you can use in your applications.

- *Retrieving and mapping the data to Java objects*: We show you how to retrieve data and then effectively map the selected data to Java objects. You also learn that Spring JDBC is a viable alternative to object-relational mapping (ORM) tools.

- *Inserting, updating, and deleting data:* Finally, we discuss how you can implement the insert, update, and delete operations so that any changes to the database you are using do not have a devastating impact on the code you have written.

269

WHAT IS A DATABASE?

Developers sometimes struggle to describe what a database is. In one case, a database represents the actual data, and in other cases, it may represent a piece of software that manages the data, an instance of a process of this software, or even the physical machine that runs the manager process. Formally, a database is a collection of data; the database software (such as Oracle, PostgreSQL, MySQL, and so on) is called *database management software* or, more specifically, a *relational database management system* (RDBMS); the instance of RDBMS is called a *database engine*; and finally, the machine that runs the database engine is called the *database server*. However, most developers immediately understand the meaning of the term *database* from the context in which it is used. This is why we use this term to represent all four meanings just described.

In recent years, because of the explosive growth of the Internet and cloud computing technologies, a lot of purpose-specific web applications such as social networks, search engine, maps, video, and so on, have arisen. To serve those applications' specific data access requirements, a lot of different categories of "databases" have also been developed. Some examples include key-value pair databases (generally referred to as NoSQL databases), graphics databases, document-centric databases, and so on. So, *database* is now a much broader term. However, a discussion of those nonrelational databases is not within the scope of this book, and we are referring to RDBMSs when we mention databases throughout this book.

Sample Data Model for Example Code

Before proceeding with the discussion, we would like to introduce a very simple data model that will be used for the examples throughout this chapter, as well as the next few chapters when discussing other data-accessing techniques (we will expand the model accordingly to fulfill the needs of each topic as we go).

The model is a very simple contact database. There are two tables. The first one is the CONTACT table, which stores a contact person's information, and the other table is CONTACT_TEL_DETAIL, which stores the telephone details of a contact. Each contact can have zero or more telephone numbers; in other words, it's a one-to-many relationship between CONTACT and CONTACT_TEL_DETAIL. A contact's information includes their first name, last name, and date of birth, while a piece of telephone detail information includes the telephone type (mobile, home, and so on) and the corresponding phone number. Figure 8-1 shows the entity-relationship (ER) diagram of the database.

Figure 8-1. Simple data model for example code

As you can see, both tables have an ID column that will be automatically assigned by the database during insert. For the CONTACT_TEL_DETAIL table, there is a foreign key relation to the CONTACT table, which is linked by the column CONTACT_ID with the primary key of the CONTACT table (i.e., the ID column).

■ **Note** The data model was created using an Eclipse plug-in called Clay Mark II. The unlicensed version can be used freely to create data models for free and open source databases including MySQL, PostgreSQL, HSQL, Derby, and so on. You don't need the plug-in to run the sample code, because the table creation scripts were provided with the sample code. However, the model diagram file (placed in ch8/data-model/prospring3-ch8-datamodel.clay) was included in the sample code, and if you are interested, you can install the plug-in and view the diagram (please refer to www.azzurri.co.jp for details).

Listing 8-1 shows the database creation script (which is MySQL compatible).

Listing 8-1. Simple Data Model Creation Script (schema.sql)

```
CREATE TABLE CONTACT (
        ID INT NOT NULL AUTO_INCREMENT
    , FIRST_NAME VARCHAR(60) NOT NULL
    , LAST_NAME VARCHAR(40) NOT NULL
    , BIRTH_DATE DATE
    , UNIQUE UQ_CONTACT_1 (FIRST_NAME, LAST_NAME)
    , PRIMARY KEY (ID)
);

CREATE TABLE CONTACT_TEL_DETAIL (
        ID INT NOT NULL AUTO_INCREMENT
    , CONTACT_ID INT NOT NULL
    , TEL_TYPE VARCHAR(20) NOT NULL
    , TEL_NUMBER VARCHAR(20) NOT NULL
    , UNIQUE UQ_CONTACT_TEL_DETAIL_1 (CONTACT_ID, TEL_TYPE)
    , PRIMARY KEY (ID)
    , CONSTRAINT FK_CONTACT_TEL_DETAIL_1 FOREIGN KEY (CONTACT_ID)
                    REFERENCES CONTACT (ID)
);
```

Listing 8-2 shows the script that populates some sample data into the CONTACT and CONTACT_TEL_DETAIL tables.

Listing 8-2. Simple Data Population Script (test-data.sql)

```
insert into contact (first_name, last_name, birth_date) values ('Clarence', 'Ho',↩
 '1980-07-30');
insert into contact (first_name, last_name, birth_date) values ('Scott', 'Tiger',↩
 '1990-11-02');
insert into contact (first_name, last_name, birth_date) values ('John', 'Smith',↩
 '1964-02-28');
insert into contact_tel_detail (contact_id, tel_type, tel_number) values (1, 'Mobile',↩
 '1234567890');
insert into contact_tel_detail (contact_id, tel_type, tel_number) values (1, 'Home',↩
 '1234567890');
insert into contact_tel_detail (contact_id, tel_type, tel_number) values (2, 'Home',↩
 '1234567890');
```

In later sections of this chapter, you will see examples to retrieve the data via JDBC from the database and directly map the resultset into Java objects (i.e., POJOs). Listings 8-3 and 8-4 show the Contact and ContactTelDetail domain classes, respectively.

Listing 8-3. The Contact Domain Object

```
package com.apress.prospring3.ch8.domain;

import java.io.Serializable;
import java.sql.Date;
import java.util.List;

public class Contact implements Serializable {

    private Long id;

    private String firstName;

    private String lastName;

    private Date birthDate;

    private List<ContactTelDetail> contactTelDetails;

    // Getter and setter method omitted

    public String toString() {
        return "Contact - Id: " + id + ", First name: " + firstName
            + ", Last name: " + lastName + ", Birthday: " + birthDate;
    }
}
```

Listing 8-4. The ContactTelDetail Domain Object

```
package com.apress.prospring3.ch8.domain;

import java.io.Serializable;

public class ContactTelDetail implements Serializable {

    private Long id;

    private Long contactId;

    private String telType;

    private String telNumber;

    // Getter and setter method omitted

    public String toString() {
        return "Contact Tel Detail - Id: " + id + ", Contact id: " + contactId
```

```
                        + ", Type: " + telType + ", Number: " + telNumber;
    }
}
```

Let's start with a very simple interface for ContactDao that encapsulates all the data access services for contact information. Listing 8-5 shows the ContactDao interface.

Listing 8-5. *The ContactDao Interface*

```
package com.apress.prospring3.ch8.dao;

import java.util.List;

import com.apress.prospring3.ch8.domain.Contact;

public interface ContactDao {

    public List<Contact> findAll();

    public List<Contact> findByFirstName(String firstName);

    public void insert(Contact contact);

    public void update(Contact contact);

    public void delete(Long contactId);
}
```

In the previous interface, we define two finder methods and the insert, update, and delete methods, respectively. They correspond to the CRUD terms (Create, Read, Update, Delete).

Finally, to facilitate testing, let's modify the log4j properties to turn the log level to DEBUG for all classes. At the DEBUG level, the Spring JDBC module will output all the underlying SQL statements being fired to database so you know what is exactly going on; it is especially useful for troubleshooting SQL statement syntax errors. Listing 8-6 shows the log4j.properties file (residing under /src/main/resources with the source code files for the Chapter 8 project) with the DEBUG level turned on.

Listing 8-6. *The log4j.properties File*

```
log4j.rootCategory=DEBUG, stdout

log4j.appender.stdout=org.apache.log4j.ConsoleAppender
log4j.appender.stdout.layout=org.apache.log4j.PatternLayout
log4j.appender.stdout.layout.ConversionPattern=%d{ABSOLUTE} %5p %40.40c:%4L - %m%n
```

■ **Note** In STS, after a Spring template project is created, STS will generate a log4j.properties file in the folder src/test/resources. You can simply move the file into the folder src/main/resources and modify it, or you can delete the one in src/test/resources and create the log4j.properties file in the /src/main/resources folder.

Exploring the JDBC Infrastructure

JDBC provides a standard way for Java applications to access data stored in a database. The core of the JDBC infrastructure is a driver that is specific to each database; it is this driver that allows Java code to access the database.

Once a driver is loaded, it registers itself with a java.sql.DriverManager class. This class manages a list of drivers and provides static methods for establishing connections to the database. The DriverManager's getConnection() method returns a driver-implemented java.sql.Connection interface. This interface allows you to run SQL statements against the database.

The JDBC framework is quite complex and well-tested; however, with this complexity comes difficulty in development. The first level of complexity lies in making sure your code manages the connections to the database. A connection is a scarce resource and is very expensive to establish. Generally, the database creates a thread or spawns a child process for each connection. Also, the number of concurrent connections is usually limited, and an excessive number of open connections slows down the database.

We will show you how Spring helps manage this complexity, but before we can proceed any further, we need to show you how to select, delete, and update data in pure JDBC.

Let's create a plain form of implementation of the ContactDao interface for interacting with the database via pure JDBC. Keeping in mind what we already know about database connections, we take the cautious and expensive (in terms of performance) approach of creating a connection for each statement. This greatly degrades the performance of Java and adds extra stress to the database because a connection has to be established for each query. However, if we kept a connection open, we could bring the database server to a halt. Listing 8-7 shows the code required for managing a JDBC connection, using MySQL as an example.

Listing 8-7. *Managing a JDBC Connection*

```java
public class PlainContactDao implements ContactDao {

    static {
        try {
            Class.forName("com.mysql.jdbc.Driver");
        } catch (ClassNotFoundException ex) {
            // noop
        }
    }

    private Connection getConnection() throws SQLException {
        return DriverManager.getConnection(
            "jdbc:mysql://localhost:3306/prospring3_ch8",
            "prospring3", "prospring3");
    }

    private void closeConnection(Connection connection) {
        if (connection == null) return;

        try {
            connection.close();
        } catch (SQLException ex) {
            // noop
        }
    }

    ...
```

This code is far from complete, but it gives you an idea of the steps you need in order to manage a JDBC connection. This code does not even deal with connection pooling, which is a common technique for managing connections to the database more effectively. We do not discuss connection pooling at this point (connection pooling is discussed in the "Database Connections and DataSources" section later in this chapter); instead, in Listing 8-8, we show an implementation of the findAll(), insert(), and delete() methods of the ContactDao interface using plain JDBC.

Listing 8-8. *Plain JDBC DAO Implementation*

```java
package com.apress.prospring3.ch8.dao.plain;

import java.sql.Connection;
import java.sql.DriverManager;
import java.sql.PreparedStatement;
import java.sql.ResultSet;
import java.sql.SQLException;
import java.sql.Statement;
import java.util.ArrayList;
import java.util.List;

import com.apress.prospring3.ch8.dao.ContactDao;
import com.apress.prospring3.ch8.domain.Contact;

public class PlainContactDao implements ContactDao {

    static {
        try {
            Class.forName("com.mysql.jdbc.Driver");
        } catch (ClassNotFoundException ex) {
            // noop
        }
    }

    private Connection getConnection() throws SQLException {
        return DriverManager.getConnection(
            "jdbc:mysql://localhost:3306/prospring3_ch8",
            "prospring3", "prospring3");
    }

    private void closeConnection(Connection connection) {
        if (connection == null) return;

        try {
            connection.close();
        } catch (SQLException ex) {
            // noop
        }
    }

    public List<Contact> findAll() {
        List<Contact> result = new ArrayList<Contact>();

        Connection connection = null;
```

```
        try {
            connection = getConnection();
            PreparedStatement statement =
                connection.prepareStatement("select * from contact");
            ResultSet resultSet = statement.executeQuery();
            while (resultSet.next()) {
                Contact contact = new Contact();
                contact.setId(resultSet.getLong("id"));
                contact.setFirstName(resultSet.getString("first_name"));
                contact.setLastName(resultSet.getString("last_name"));
                contact.setBirthDate(resultSet.getDate("birth_date"));
                result.add(contact);
            }
        } catch (SQLException ex) {
            ex.printStackTrace();
        } finally {
            closeConnection(connection);
        }

        return result;
    }

    public List<Contact> findByFirstName(String firstName) {
        return null;
    }

    public void insert(Contact contact) {
        Connection connection = null;
        try {
            connection = getConnection();
            PreparedStatement statement = connection.prepareStatement(
"insert into Contact (first_name, last_name, birth_date) values (?, ?, ?)"
, Statement.RETURN_GENERATED_KEYS);
            statement.setString(1, contact.getFirstName());
            statement.setString(2, contact.getLastName());
            statement.setDate(3, contact.getBirthDate());
            statement.execute();

            ResultSet generatedKeys = statement.getGeneratedKeys();
            if (generatedKeys.next()) {
                contact.setId(generatedKeys.getLong(1));
            }
        } catch (SQLException ex) {
            ex.printStackTrace();
        } finally {
            closeConnection(connection);
        }
    }

    public void update(Contact contact) {
    }

    public void delete(Long contactId) {
        Connection connection = null;
```

```
        try {
            connection = getConnection();
            PreparedStatement statement = connection.prepareStatement("delete from contact
where id=?");
            statement.setLong(1, contactId);
            statement.execute();
        } catch (SQLException ex) {
            ex.printStackTrace();
        } finally {
            closeConnection(connection);
        }
    }
}
```

Listing 8-9 shows a main testing program with the previous DAO implementation in action.

Listing 8-9. Pure JDBC Implementation Testing

```
package com.apress.prospring3.ch8;

import java.sql.Date;
import java.util.GregorianCalendar;
import java.util.List;

import com.apress.prospring3.ch8.dao.ContactDao;
import com.apress.prospring3.ch8.dao.plain.PlainContactDao;
import com.apress.prospring3.ch8.domain.Contact;

public class PlainJdbcSample {

    private static ContactDao contactDao = new PlainContactDao();

    public static void main(String[] args) {

        // List all contacts
        System.out.println("Listing initial contact data:");
        listAllContacts();

        System.out.println();

        // Insert a new contact
        System.out.println("Insert a new contact");
        Contact contact = new Contact();
        contact.setFirstName("Jacky");
        contact.setLastName("Chan");
        contact.setBirthDate(new Date((new GregorianCalendar(2001, 10,
1)).getTime().getTime())));
        contactDao.insert(contact);
        System.out.println("Listing contact data after new contact created:");
        listAllContacts();

        System.out.println();

        // Delete the above newly created contact
```

```
        System.out.println("Deleting the previous created contact");
        contactDao.delete(contact.getId());
        System.out.println("Listing contact data after new contact deleted:");
        listAllContacts();

    }

    private static void listAllContacts() {

        List<Contact> contacts = contactDao.findAll();

        for (Contact contact: contacts) {
            System.out.println(contact);
        }
    }
}
```

To run the program, you need to add the dependency for MySQL Java into your project, as shown in Table 8-1.

Table 8-1. Dependency for MySQL

Group ID	Artifact ID	Version	Description
mysql	mysql-connector-java	5.1.18	MySQL Java driver library

Running the program in Listing 8-9 will yield the following result (assuming you have a locally installed MySQL database, with a database called prospring3_ch8 that has a user name and password set to prospring3; it should be able to access the database schema, and you should run the scripts schema.sql and test-data.sql against the database to create the tables and populated the initial data):

```
Listing initial contact data:
Contact - Id: 1, First name: Clarence, Last name: Ho, Birthday: 1980-07-30
Contact - Id: 2, First name: Scott, Last name: Tiger, Birthday: 1990-11-02
Contact - Id: 3, First name: John, Last name: Smith, Birthday: 1964-02-28

Insert a new contact
Listing contact data after new contact created:
Contact - Id: 1, First name: Clarence, Last name: Ho, Birthday: 1980-07-30
Contact - Id: 2, First name: Scott, Last name: Tiger, Birthday: 1990-11-02
Contact - Id: 3, First name: John, Last name: Smith, Birthday: 1964-02-28
Contact - Id: 4, First name: Jacky, Last name: Chan, Birthday: 2001-11-01

Deleting the previous created contact
Listing contact data after new contact deleted:
Contact - Id: 1, First name: Clarence, Last name: Ho, Birthday: 1980-07-30
Contact - Id: 2, First name: Scott, Last name: Tiger, Birthday: 1990-11-02
Contact - Id: 3, First name: John, Last name: Smith, Birthday: 1964-02-28
```

As shown in the output, the first block of lines shows the initial data. The second block of lines shows that the new record was added. The final block of lines shows that the newly created contact was deleted.

As you can see from Listing 8-8, a lot of code needs to be moved to a helper class or—even worse—duplicated in each DAO class. This is the main disadvantage of JDBC from the application programmer's point of view—you just do not have time to code repetitive code in every DAO class. Instead, you want to concentrate on writing code that actually does what you need the DAO class to do: select, update, and delete the data. The more helper code you need to write, the more checked exceptions you need to handle, and the more bugs you may introduce in your code.

This is where a DAO framework and Spring come in. A framework eliminates the code that does not actually perform any custom logic and allows you to forget about all the housekeeping that needs to be performed. In addition, Spring's extensive JDBC support makes your life a lot easier.

Spring JDBC Infrastructure

The code we discussed in the first part of the chapter is not very complex, but it is annoying to write, and because there is so much of it to write, the likelihood of coding errors is quite high. It is time to take a look at how Spring makes things easier and more elegant.

Overview and Used Packages

JDBC support in Spring is divided into the five packages detailed in Table 8-2; each handles different aspects of JDBC access.

Table 8-2. Spring JDBC Packages

Package	Description
org.springframework.jdbc.core	Contains the foundations of JDBC classes in Spring. It includes the core JDBC class, JdbcTemplate, which simplifies programming database operations with JDBC. Several subpackages provide support of JDBC data access with more specific purposes (e.g., a JdbcTemplate class that supports named parameters) and related support classes as well.
org.springframework.jdbc.datasource	Contains helper classes and DataSource implementations that you can use to run JDBC code outside a JEE container. Several subpackages provide support for embedded databases, database initialization, and various datasource lookup mechanisms.
org.springframework.jdbc.object	Contains classes that help convert the data returned from the database into objects or lists of objects. These objects and lists are plain Java objects and therefore are disconnected from the database.
org.springframework.jdbc.support	The most important class in this package is SQLException translation support. This allows Spring to recognize error codes used by the database and map them to higher-level exceptions.
org.springframework.jdbc.config	Contains classes that supports JDBC configuration within Spring's ApplicationContext. For example, it contains handler class for the jdbc namespace (e.g., <jdbc:embedded-database> tags).

Let's start the discussion of Spring JDBC support by looking at the lowest-level functionality. The first thing you need to do before you can even think about running SQL queries is establish a connection to the database.

Database Connections and DataSources

You can use Spring to manage the database connection for you by providing a bean that implements javax.sql.DataSource. The difference between a DataSource and a Connection is that a DataSource provides and manages Connections.

DriverManagerDataSource (under the package org.springframework.jdbc.datasource) is the simplest implementation of a DataSource. By looking at the class name, you can guess that it simply calls the DriverManager to obtain a connection. The fact that DriverManagerDataSource doesn't support database connection pooling makes this class unsuitable for anything other than testing. The configuration of DriverManagerDataSource is quite simple, as you can see in Listing 8-10; you just need to supply the driver class name, a connection URL, a user name, and a password (datasource-drivermanager.xml).

Listing 8-10. *Spring-Managed DriverManagerDataSource dataSource Bean*

```xml
<?xml version="1.0" encoding="UTF-8"?>
<beans xmlns="http://www.springframework.org/schema/beans"
    xmlns:xsi="http://www.w3.org/2001/XMLSchema-instance"
    xmlns:context="http://www.springframework.org/schema/context"
    xsi:schemaLocation="http://www.springframework.org/schema/beans
        http://www.springframework.org/schema/beans/spring-beans-3.1.xsd
        http://www.springframework.org/schema/context
        http://www.springframework.org/schema/context/spring-context-3.1.xsd">

    <bean id="dataSource"
        class="org.springframework.jdbc.datasource.DriverManagerDataSource">
        <property name="driverClassName">
            <value>${jdbc.driverClassName}</value>
        </property>
        <property name="url">
            <value>${jdbc.url}</value>
        </property>
        <property name="username">
            <value>${jdbc.username}</value>
        </property>
        <property name="password">
            <value>${jdbc.password}</value>
        </property>
    </bean>

    <context:property-placeholder location="jdbc.properties"/>
</beans>
```

You most likely recognize the bold properties in the listing. They represent the values you normally pass to JDBC to obtain a Connection interface. The database connection information typically is stored in a properties file for easy maintenance and substitution in different deployment environments. Listing 8-11 shows a sample jdbc.properties from which Spring's property placeholder will load the connection information.

Listing 8-11. The jdbc.properties File

```
jdbc.driverClassName=com.mysql.jdbc.Driver
jdbc.url=jdbc:mysql://localhost:3306/prospring3_ch8
jdbc.username=prospring3
jdbc.password=prospring3
```

In real-world applications, you can use Apache Commons `BasicDataSource` (http://commons.apache.org/dbcp/) or a DataSource implemented by a JEE application server (e.g., JBoss, WebSphere, WebLogic, GlassFish, etc.), which may further increase the performance of the application. You could use a DataSource in the plain JDBC code and get the same pooling benefits; however, in most cases, you would still miss a central place to configure the datasource. Spring, on the other hand, allows you to declare a dataSource bean and set the connection properties in the ApplicationContext definition files (see Listing 8-12; the file name is `datasource-dbcp.xml`).

■ **Note** Besides Apache Commons `BasicDataSource`, other popular open source database connection pool libraries include the C3P0 (www.mchange.com/projects/c3p0/index.html) and BoneCP (http://jolbox.com/).

Listing 8-12. Spring-Managed dataSource Bean

```xml
<?xml version="1.0" encoding="UTF-8"?>
<beans xmlns="http://www.springframework.org/schema/beans"
    xmlns:xsi="http://www.w3.org/2001/XMLSchema-instance"
    xmlns:context="http://www.springframework.org/schema/context"
    xsi:schemaLocation="http://www.springframework.org/schema/beans
        http://www.springframework.org/schema/beans/spring-beans-3.1.xsd
        http://www.springframework.org/schema/context
        http://www.springframework.org/schema/context/spring-context-3.1.xsd">

    <bean id="dataSource"
        class="org.apache.commons.dbcp.BasicDataSource"
        destroy-method="close">
        <property name="driverClassName">
            <value>${jdbc.driverClassName}</value>
        </property>
        <property name="url">
            <value>${jdbc.url}</value>
        </property>
        <property name="username">
            <value>${jdbc.username}</value>
        </property>
        <property name="password">
            <value>${jdbc.password}</value>
        </property>
    </bean>

    <context:property-placeholder location="jdbc.properties"/>
</beans>
```

This particular Spring-managed DataSource is implemented in org.apache.commons.dbcp .BasicDataSource. The most important bit is that the dataSource bean implements javax.sql.DataSource, and you can immediately start using it in your data access classes.

Another way to configure a dataSource bean is to use JNDI. If the application you are developing is going to run in a JEE container, you can take advantage of the container-managed connection pooling. To use a JNDI-based data source, you need to change the dataSource bean declaration, as shown in Listing 8-13 (datasource-jndi.xml).

Listing 8-13. Spring-Managed JNDI dataSource Bean

```xml
<?xml version="1.0" encoding="UTF-8"?>
<beans xmlns="http://www.springframework.org/schema/beans"
    xmlns:xsi="http://www.w3.org/2001/XMLSchema-instance"
    xsi:schemaLocation="http://www.springframework.org/schema/beans
        http://www.springframework.org/schema/beans/spring-beans-3.1.xsd">

    <bean id="dataSource" class="org.springframework.jndi.JndiObjectFactoryBean">
        <property name="jndiName">
            <value>java:comp/env/jdbc/prospring3ch8</value>
        </property>
    </bean>
</beans>
```

In the previous example, we use Spring's JndiObjectFactoryBean to obtain the data source by JNDI lookup. Starting from version 2.5, Spring provides the jee namespace, which further simplifies the configuration. Listing 8-14 shows the same JNDI datasource configuration using the jee namespace (datasource-jee.xml).

Listing 8-14. Spring-Managed JNDI dataSource Bean (Using the jee Namespace)

```xml
<?xml version="1.0" encoding="UTF-8"?>
<beans xmlns="http://www.springframework.org/schema/beans"
    xmlns:xsi="http://www.w3.org/2001/XMLSchema-instance"
    xmlns:jee="http://www.springframework.org/schema/jee"
    xsi:schemaLocation="http://www.springframework.org/schema/beans
        http://www.springframework.org/schema/beans/spring-beans-3.1.xsd
        http://www.springframework.org/schema/jee
        http://www.springframework.org/schema/jee/spring-jee-3.1.xsd">

    <jee:jndi-lookup jndi-name="java:comp/env/jdbc/prospring3ch8"/>

</beans>
```

In the previous listing, we declare the jee namespace in the <beans> tag and then the <jee:jndi-lookup> tag to declare the data source.

If you take the JNDI approach, you must not forget to add a resource reference (resource-ref) in the application descriptor file (see Listing 8-15).

Listing 8-15. A Resource Reference in Descriptor Files

```xml
<root-node>
    <resource-ref>
        <res-ref-name>jdbc/prospring3ch8</res-ref-name>
```

```
        <res-type>javax.sql.DataSource</res-type>
        <res-auth>Container</res-auth>
    </resource-ref>
</root-node>
```

The `<root-node>` is a placeholder value; you need to change it depending on how your module is packaged. For example, it becomes `<web-app>` in the web deployment descriptor (`WEB-INF/web.xml`) if the application is a web module. Most likely, you will need to configure the `resource-ref` in an application server–specific descriptor file as well. However, notice that the `resource-ref` element configures the `jdbc/prospring3ch8` reference name and that the `dataSource` bean's `jndiName` is set to `java:comp/env/jdbc/prospring3ch8`.

As you can see, Spring allows you to configure the `DataSource` in almost any way you like, and it hides the actual implementation or location of the datasource from the rest of the application's code. In other words, your DAO classes do not know and do not need to know where the `DataSource` points.

The connection management is also delegated to the `dataSource` bean, which in turn performs the management itself or uses the JEE container to do all the work.

Embedded Database Support

Starting from version 3.0, Spring also offers embedded database support, which automatically starts an embedded database and exposes it as a `DataSource` for the application. Listing 8-16 shows the configuration of an embedded database (`app-context-xml.xml`).

Listing 8-16. *Spring Embedded Database Support*

```
<?xml version="1.0" encoding="UTF-8"?>
<beans xmlns="http://www.springframework.org/schema/beans"
    xmlns:xsi="http://www.w3.org/2001/XMLSchema-instance"
    xmlns:jdbc="http://www.springframework.org/schema/jdbc"
    xsi:schemaLocation="http://www.springframework.org/schema/beans
        http://www.springframework.org/schema/beans/spring-beans-3.1.xsd
        http://www.springframework.org/schema/jdbc
        http://www.springframework.org/schema/jdbc/spring-jdbc-3.1.xsd">

    <jdbc:embedded-database id="dataSource" type="H2">
        <jdbc:script location="classpath:schema.sql"/>
        <jdbc:script location="classpath:test-data.sql"/>
    </jdbc:embedded-database>

</beans>
```

In the previous listing, we first declared the `jdbc` namespace in the `<beans>` tag. Afterward, we use the `<jdbc:embedded-database>` to declare the embedded database and assign it with an ID of `dataSource`. Within the tag, we also instruct Spring to execute the scripts specified to create the database schema and populate testing data accordingly. Note that the order of the scripts is important, and the file that contains Data Definition Language (DDL) should always appears first, followed by the file with Data Manipulation Language (DML). For the type attribute, we specify the type of embedded database to use. As of version 3.1, Spring supports HSQL (default), H2, and DERBY.

The embedded database support is extremely useful for local development or unit testing. Throughout the rest of this chapter, we will use the embedded database to run the sample code, so your machine doesn't require a database to be installed in order to run the samples.

Using DataSources in DAO Classes

Let's restart with an empty ContactDao interface and a simple implementation of it. We will add more features as we go along and explain the Spring JDBC classes as we do so. Listing 8-17 shows the empty ContactDao interface.

Listing 8-17. ContactDao Interface and Implementation

```
public interface ContactDao { }
public class JdbcContactDao implements ContactDao { }
```

For the simple implementation, first we will add a dataSource property to it. The reason we want to add the dataSource property to the implementation class rather than the interface should be quite obvious: the interface does not need to know how the data is going to be retrieved and updated. By adding get/setDataSource methods to the interface, we—in the best-case scenario—force the implementations to declare the getter and setter stubs. Clearly, this is not a very good design practice. Take a look at the simple JdbcContactDao class in Listing 8-18.

Listing 8-18. JdbcUserDao with dataSource Property

```
package com.apress.prospring3.ch8.dao.jdbc.xml;

import javax.sql.DataSource;

import com.apress.prospring3.ch8.dao.ContactDao;

public class JdbcContactDao implements ContactDao {

    private DataSource dataSource;

    public void setDataSource(DataSource dataSource) {
        this.dataSource = dataSource;
    }
}
```

We can now instruct Spring to configure our contactDao bean using the JdbcContactDao implementation and set the dataSource property (see Listing 8-19; the file name is app-context-xml.xml).

Listing 8-19. Spring Application Context File with dataSource and contactDao Beans

```
// Namespace declaration omitted

<jdbc:embedded-database id="dataSource" type="H2">
    <jdbc:script location="classpath:schema.sql"/>
    <jdbc:script location="classpath:test-data.sql"/>
</jdbc:embedded-database>

<bean id="contactDao" class="com.apress.prospring3.ch8.dao.jdbc.xml.JdbcContactDao">
    <property name="dataSource">
        <ref local="dataSource"/>
    </property>
</bean>
```

To support the H2 database, we need to add the dependency on the H2 database into the project, as shown in Table 8-3.

Table 8-3. Dependency for the H2 Database

Group ID	Artifact ID	Version	Description
com.h2database	h2	1.3.160	H2 database Java library

Spring now creates the contactDao bean by instantiating the JdbcContactDao class with the dataSource property set to the dataSource bean.

It is good practice to make sure that all required properties on a bean have been set. The easiest way to do this is to implement the InitializingBean interface and provide an implementation for the afterPropertiesSet() method (see Listing 8-20). This way, you make sure that all required properties have been set on your JdbcContactDao. For further discussion of bean initialization, refer to Chapter 5.

Listing 8-20. JdbcContactDao Implementation with InitializingBean

```
package com.apress.prospring3.ch8.dao.jdbc.xml;

import javax.sql.DataSource;

import org.springframework.beans.factory.BeanCreationException;
import org.springframework.beans.factory.InitializingBean;

import com.apress.prospring3.ch8.dao.ContactDao;

public class JdbcContactDao implements ContactDao, InitializingBean {

    private DataSource dataSource;

    public void setDataSource(DataSource dataSource) {
        this.dataSource = dataSource;
    }

    public void afterPropertiesSet() throws Exception {
        if (dataSource == null) {
            throw new BeanCreationException("Must set dataSource on ContactDao");
        }
    }
}
```

The code we have looked at so far uses Spring to manage the data source and introduces the ContactDao interface and its JDBC implementation. We also set the dataSource property on the JdbcContactDao class in the Spring ApplicationContext file. Now we expand the code by adding the actual DAO operations to the interface and implementation.

Exception Handling

Because Spring advocates using runtime exceptions rather than checked exceptions, you need a mechanism to translate the checked SQLException into a runtime Spring JDBC exception. Because

Spring's SQL exceptions are runtime exceptions, they can be much more granular than checked exceptions. (By definition, this is not a feature of runtime exceptions, but it is very inconvenient to have to declare a long list of checked exceptions in the throws clause; hence, checked exceptions tend to be much more coarse-grained than their runtime equivalents.)

Spring provides a default implementation of the SQLExceptionTranslator interface, which takes care of translating the generic SQL error codes into Spring JDBC exceptions. In most cases, this implementation is sufficient enough, but we can extend Spring's default implementation and set our new SQLExceptionTranslator implementation to be used in JdbcTemplate, as shown in Listing 8-21.

At the same time, we need to add the dependency on spring-jdbc into the project, as shown in Table 8-4.

Table 8-4. Dependency for spring-jdbc

Group ID	Artifact ID	Version	Description
org.springframework	spring-jdbc	3.1.0.RELEASE	Spring JDBC module

Listing 8-21. Custom SQLExceptionTranslator

```
package com.apress.prospring3.ch8.exception.translator;

import java.sql.SQLException;

import org.springframework.dao.DataAccessException;
import org.springframework.dao.DeadlockLoserDataAccessException;
import org.springframework.jdbc.support.SQLErrorCodeSQLExceptionTranslator;

public class MySQLErrorCodesTranslator extends
    SQLErrorCodeSQLExceptionTranslator {

    protected DataAccessException customTranslate(String task,
            String sql, SQLException sqlex) {
        if (sqlex.getErrorCode() == -12345)
            return new DeadlockLoserDataAccessException(task, sqlex);
        return null;
    }
}
```

To use the custom translator, we need to pass it into JdbcTemplate in the DAO classes. Listing 8-22 shows a sample code snippet for this purpose.

Listing 8-22. Using Custom SQLExceptionTranslator in Spring Jdbc

```
// Within any DAO class

JdbcTemplate jdbcTemplate = new JdbcTemplate();
jdbcTemplate.setDataSource(dataSource);

// create a custom translator and set the datasource
// for the default translation lookup
MySQLErrorCodesTranslator errorTranslator =
    new MySQLErrorCodesTranslator();
```

```
errorTranslator.setDataSource(dataSource);
jdbcTemplate.setExceptionTranslator(errorTranslator);

// use the JdbcTemplate for this SqlUpdate
SqlUpdate sqlUpdate = new SqlUpdate();
sqlUpdate.setJdbcTemplate(jdbcTemplate);
sqlUpdate.setSql("update contact set first_name = 'Clarence'");
sqlUpdate.compile();
sqlUpdate.update();
```

Having the custom SQL exception translator in place, Spring will invoke it upon SQL exceptions detected when executing SQL statements against the database, and custom exception translation will happen when the error code is -12345. For other errors, Spring will fall back to its default mechanism for exception translation.

Obviously, nothing can stop you from creating the SQLExceptionTranslator as a Spring-managed bean and using the JdbcTemplate bean in your DAO classes. Don't worry if you don't remember reading about the JdbcTemplate class; we are going to discuss it in more detail.

The JdbcTemplate Class

This class represents the core of Spring's JDBC support. It can execute all types of SQL statements. In the most simplistic view, you can classify the data definition and data manipulation statements. Data definition statements cover creating various database objects (tables, views, stored procedures, and so on). Data manipulation statements manipulate the data and can be classified as select and update statements. A select statement generally returns a set of rows; each row has the same set of columns. An update statement modifies the data in the database but does not return any results.

The JdbcTemplate class allows you to issue any type of SQL statement to the database and return any type of result.

In this section, we will go through several common use cases for JDBC programming in Spring with the JdbcTemplate class.

Initializing JdbcTemplate in a DAO Class

Before we discuss how to use JdbcTemplate, let's take a look at how to prepare JdbcTemplate for use in the DAO class. It's very straightforward; most of the time you just need to construct the class by passing in the data source object (which should be injected by Spring into the DAO class). Listing 8-23 shows the code snippet that will initialize the JdbcTemplate object.

Listing 8-23. Initialize JdbcTemplate

```
private JdbcTemplate jdbcTemplate;

private DataSource dataSource;

public void setDataSource(DataSource dataSource) {
    this.dataSource = dataSource;
    this.jdbcTemplate = new JdbcTemplate(dataSource);
}
```

The general practice is to initialize the JdbcTemplate within the set data source method so that once the data source was injected by Spring, the JdbcTemplate will also be initialized and ready for use.

Once configured, the JdbcTemplate is thread safe. That means you can also choose to initialize a single instance of JdbcTemplate in Spring's XML configuration and have it inject into all DAO beans.

> ■ **Note** In the Spring `Jdbc` module, there is a class called `JdbcDaoSupport`. It wraps the `JdbcTemplate` class, and you can have your DAO classes extend the `JdbcDaoSupport` class. In this case, when the DAO class is injected with the data source, the `JdbcTemplate` will be initialized automatically.

Retrieving Single-Value-Use JdbcTemplate Class

Let's start with a simple query that returns a single value. For example, we want to be able to retrieve the first name of a contact by its ID. Let's add the method into the `ContactDao` interface first:

```
public String findFirstNameById(Long id);
```

Using `JdbcTemplate`, we can retrieve the value easily. Listing 8-24 shows the implementation of the `findFirstNameById()` method in the `JdbcContactDao` class. For other methods, empty implementations were created.

Listing 8-24. *Using JdbcTemplate to Retrieve a Single Value*

```
package com.apress.prospring3.ch8.dao.jdbc.xml;

// Import statement omitted

public class JdbcContactDao implements ContactDao, InitializingBean {

    public String findFirstNameById(Long id) {
        String firstName = jdbcTemplate.queryForObject(
            "select first_name from contact where id = ?",
            new Object[]{id}, String.class);
        return firstName;
    }

    public List<Contact> findAll() {
        return null;
    }

    public List<Contact> findByFirstName(String firstName) {
        return null;
    }

    public void insert(Contact contact) {
    }

    public void update(Contact contact) {
    }

    public void delete(Long contactId) {
    }

}
```

In the previous listing, we use the queryForObject() method of JdbcTemplate to retrieve the value of the first name. The first argument is the SQL string, and the second argument consists of the parameters to be passed to the SQL for parameter binding in object array format. The last argument is the type to be returned, which is String in this case. Besides Object, you can also query for other types like Long and Integer. Let's take a look at the outcome. Listing 8-25 shows the testing program.

Listing 8-25. Using JdbcTemplate

```
package com.apress.prospring3.ch8;

import org.springframework.context.support.GenericXmlApplicationContext;

import com.apress.prospring3.ch8.dao.ContactDao;

public class JdbcContactDaoSample {

    public static void main(String[] args) {

        GenericXmlApplicationContext ctx = new GenericXmlApplicationContext();
        ctx.load("classpath:app-context-xml.xml");
        ctx.refresh();

        ContactDao contactDao = ctx.getBean("contactDao", ContactDao.class);

        // Find first name by id
        System.out.println("First name for contact id 1 is: " +
            contactDao.findFirstNameById(1l));

    }
}
```

As expected, running the program yields the following output:

```
First name for contact id 1 is: Clarence
```

Using Named Parameters with NamedParameterJdbcTemplate

In the previous example, we are using the normal placeholder (the ? character) as query parameters. As you also see, we need to pass the parameters as an Object array. When using a normal placeholder, the order is very important, and the order that you put the parameters into the array should be the same as the order of the parameters in the query.

Some developers (like me) prefer to use named parameters to ensure that the parameter is being bound exactly as wanted. In Spring, a variant of JdbcTemplate, called NamedParameterJdbcTemplate (under the package org.springframework.jdbc.core.namedparam), provides supports for this. Let's see how it works.

For example, this time we want to add another method to find the last name by ID, so let's add the method to the ContactDao interface:

```
public String findLastNameById(Long id);
```

The initialization of the NamedParameterJdbcTemplate is the same as JdbcTemplate, so we just need to declare a variable with type NamedParameterJdbcTemplate and add the following line into the DAO class's setDataSource() method:

```
this.namedParameterJdbcTemplate = new NamedParameterJdbcTemplate(dataSource);
```

Now let's see how to implement the method. Listing 8-26 shows the implementation.

Listing 8-26. *Using NamedParameterJdbcTemplate to Retrieve a Single Value*

```
package com.apress.prospring3.ch8.dao.jdbc.xml;

// Import statement omitted

public class JdbcContactDao implements ContactDao, InitializingBean {

    // Other methods omitted

    public String findLastNameById(Long id) {
        String sql = "select last_name from contact where id = :contactId";

        SqlParameterSource namedParameters =
            new MapSqlParameterSource("contactId", id);
        return namedParameterJdbcTemplate.queryForObject(sql,
            namedParameters, String.class);
    }
}
```

First, you will see that instead of the ? placeholder, the named parameter (prefix by a semicolon) was used instead. Second, a SqlParameterSource was initialized, which is a Map-based SQL parameter source with the key as the named parameter's name and the value as the value of the parameter. Instead of SqlParameterSource, you can also simply construct a map for storing named parameters. Listing 8-27 is a variant of the previous method.

Listing 8-27. *Using NamedParameterJdbcTemplate to Retreive a Single Value*

```
package com.apress.prospring3.ch8.dao.jdbc.xml;

// Import statement omitted

public class JdbcContactDao implements ContactDao, InitializingBean {

    // Other methods omitted

    public String findLastNameById(Long id) {
    String sql = "select last_name from contact where id = :contactId";

    Map<String, Object> namedParameters = new HashMap<String, Object>();
    namedParameters.put("contactId", id);
    return namedParameterJdbcTemplate.queryForObject(sql,
        namedParameters, String.class);
    }
}
```

To test the code, just add the method into the main testing class in Listing 8-25 and run it. I will skip it here.

Retrieving Domain Objects with RowMapper<T>

Rather than retrieving a single value, most of the time you will want to query one or more rows and then transform each row into the corresponding domain object.

Spring's RowMapper<T> interface (under the package org.springframework.jdbc.core) provides a simple way for you to perform mapping from a JDBC resultset to POJOs. Let's see it in action by implementing the findAll() method of the ContactDao interface using the RowMapper<T> interface. Listing 8-28 shows the implementation of the findAll() method.

Listing 8-28. *Use RowMapper<T> to Query Domain Objects*

```
package com.apress.prospring3.ch8.dao.jdbc.xml;

// Import statements omitted
public class JdbcContactDao implements ContactDao, InitializingBean {

    // Other methods omitted

    public List<Contact> findAll() {
        String sql = "select id, first_name, last_name, birth_date from contact";
        return jdbcTemplate.query(sql, new ContactMapper());
    }

    private static final class ContactMapper implements RowMapper<Contact> {

        public Contact mapRow(ResultSet rs, int rowNum) throws SQLException {

            Contact contact = new Contact();
            contact.setId(rs.getLong("id"));
            contact.setFirstName(rs.getString("first_name"));
            contact.setLastName(rs.getString("last_name"));
            contact.setBirthDate(rs.getDate("birth_date"));
            return contact;
        }

    }
}
```

In the previous listing, we define a static inner class called ContactMapper that implements the RowMapper<T> interface. The class needs to provide the mapRow() implementation, which transforms the values in a specific record of the resultset into the domain object you want. Making it a static inner class allows you to share the RowMapper<T> among multiple finder methods.

Afterward, the findAll() method just needs to invoke the query method and pass in the query string and the row mapper. In case the query requires parameters, the query() method provides a overload that accepts the query parameters.

Let's add the following code snippet (Listing 8-29) into the testing program (the JdbcContactDaoSample class).

Listing 8-29. *Code Snippet for Listing Contacts*

```
    // Find and list all contacts
    List<Contact> contacts = contactDao.findAll();
    for (Contact contact: contacts) {
```

```
        System.out.println(contact);
        if (contact.getContactTelDetails() != null) {
            for (ContactTelDetail contactTelDetail:
                contact.getContactTelDetails()) {
                System.out.println("---" + contactTelDetail);
            }
        }
        System.out.println();
    }
```

Running the program yields the following result (other outputs were omitted):

```
Contact - Id: 1, First name: Clarence, Last name: Ho, Birthday: 1980-07-30

Contact - Id: 2, First name: Scott, Last name: Tiger, Birthday: 1990-11-02

Contact - Id: 3, First name: John, Last name: Smith, Birthday: 1964-02-28
```

Retrieving Nested Domain Objects with ResultSetExtractor

Let's proceed to a bit more complicated example, in which we need to retrieve the data from the parent (CONTACT) and child (CONTACT_TEL_DETAIL) table with a join and transform the data back into the nested object (ContactTelDetail within Contact) accordingly.

The previously mentioned RowMapper<T> is suitable only for row base mapping to a single domain object. For a more complicated object structure, we need to use the ResultSetExtractor interface. To demonstrate its use, let's add one more method, findAllWithDetail(), into the ContactDao interface. The method should populate the list of contacts with their telephone details.

```
public List<Contact> findAllWithDetail();
```

Listing 8-30 shows the implementation of the findAllWithDetail() method using ResultSetExtractor.

Listing 8-30. Use ResultSetExtractor to Query Domain Objects

```
package com.apress.prospring3.ch8.dao.jdbc.xml;

// Import statements omitted
public class JdbcContactDao implements ContactDao, InitializingBean {

    public List<Contact> findAllWithDetail() {
        String sql = "select c.id, c.first_name, c.last_name, c.birth_date" +
", t.id as contact_tel_id, t.tel_type, t.tel_number from contact c " +
"left join contact_tel_detail t on c.id = t.contact_id";
        return jdbcTemplate.query(sql, new ContactWithDetailExtractor());
    }

    private static final class ContactWithDetailExtractor implements
ResultSetExtractor<List<Contact>> {

        public List<Contact> extractData(ResultSet rs) throws SQLException,
DataAccessException {

            Map<Long, Contact> map = new HashMap<Long, Contact>();
```

```
            Contact contact = null;
            while (rs.next()) {
                Long id = rs.getLong("id");
                contact = map.get(id);
                if (contact == null) {   // new contact record
                    contact = new Contact();
                    contact.setId(id);
                    contact.setFirstName(rs.getString("first_name"));
                    contact.setLastName(rs.getString("last_name"));
                    contact.setBirthDate(rs.getDate("birth_date"));
                    contact.setContactTelDetails(new ArrayList<ContactTelDetail>());
                    map.put(id, contact);
                }
                // Process contact tel. detail (if exists)
                Long contactTelDetailId = rs.getLong("contact_tel_id");
                if (contactTelDetailId > 0) {
                    ContactTelDetail contactTelDetail = new ContactTelDetail();
                    contactTelDetail.setId(contactTelDetailId);
                    contactTelDetail.setContactId(id);
                    contactTelDetail.setTelType(rs.getString("tel_type"));
                    contactTelDetail.setTelNumber(rs.getString("tel_number"));
                    contact.getContactTelDetails().add(contactTelDetail);
                }
            }
            return new ArrayList<Contact> (map.values());
        }
    }
}
```

The code looks quite like the RowMapper sample, but this time we declare an inner class that implements ResultSetExtractor. Then we implement the extractData() method to transform the resultset into a list of Contact objects accordingly. For the findAllWithDetail() method, the query uses a left join to join the two tables so that contacts with no telephones will also be retrieved. The result is a Cartesian product of the two tables. Finally, we use the JdbcTemplate.query() method, passing in the query string and the resultset extractor.

Let's add the following code snippet (Listing 8-31) into the testing program (the JdbcContactDaoSample class).

Listing 8-31. Code Snippet for Listing Contacts

```
        // Find and list all contacts with details
        List<Contact> contactsWithDetail = contactDao.findAllWithDetail();
        for (Contact contact: contactsWithDetail) {
            System.out.println(contact);
            if (contact.getContactTelDetails() != null) {
                for (ContactTelDetail contactTelDetail: contact.getContactTelDetails()) {
                    System.out.println("---" + contactTelDetail);
                }
            }
            System.out.println();
        }
```

Run the testing program again, and it will yield the following output (other outputs were omitted):

```
Contact - Id: 1, First name: Clarence, Last name: Ho, Birthday: 1980-07-30
---Contact Tel Detail - Id: 2, Contact id: 1, Type: Home, Number: 1234567890
---Contact Tel Detail - Id: 1, Contact id: 1, Type: Mobile, Number: 1234567890

Contact - Id: 2, First name: Scott, Last name: Tiger, Birthday: 1990-11-02
---Contact Tel Detail - Id: 3, Contact id: 2, Type: Home, Number: 1234567890

Contact - Id: 3, First name: John, Last name: Smith, Birthday: 1964-02-28
```

You can see the contacts and their telephone details were listed accordingly. The data is based on the data population scripts in Listing 8-2.

So far, you have seen how to use JdbcTemplate to perform some common query operations. JdbcTemplate (and the NamedParameterJdbcTemplate class too) also provides a number of overloading update() methods that support data update operations, including insert, update, delete, and so on. However, the update() method is quite self-explanatory, so we decide not to cover it in this section.

On the other side, as you will see in later sections, we will use the Spring-provided SqlUpdate class to perform data update operations.

Spring Classes That Model JDBC Operations

In the preceding section, you saw how JdbcTemplate and the related data mapper utility classes had greatly simplified the programming model in developing data access logic with JDBC. Built on top of JdbcTemplate, Spring also provides a number of useful classes that model JDBC data operations and let developers maintain the query and transformation logic from resultset to domain objects in a more object-oriented fashion. As mentioned, those class are packaged under org.springframework.jdbc.object. Specifically, we will discuss the following classes:

MappingSqlQuery<T>: The MappingSqlQuery<T> class allows you to wrap the query string together with the mapRow() method into a single class.

SqlUpdate: The SqlUpdate class allows you to wrap any SQL update statement into it. It also provides a lot of useful functions for you to bind SQL parameters, retrieve the RDBMS-generated key after a new record is inserted, and so on.

BatchSqlUpdate: As the name implies, the class allows you to perform batch update operations. For example, you can loop through a Java List object and have the BatchSqlUpdate queue up the records and submit the update statements for you in a batch. You can set the batch size and flush the operation anytime as you want.

SqlFunction<T>: The SqlFunction<T> class allows you to call stored functions in the database with argument and return types. Another class, StoredProcedure, also exists that helps you invoke stored procedures.

■ **Note** In previous sections, all the sample code uses the XML type configuration. So, in the following sections, we will use Spring annotations for ApplicationContext configuration. In case you decide to adopt XML configuration in your application, we believe you will have a good idea of how to do it.

Setting Up JDBC DAO Using Annotations

First let's take a look on how to set up the DAO implementation class using annotations first. Listing 8-32 shows the ContactDao interface class with a more complete listing of the data access services it provides.

Listing 8-32. ContactDao Interface

```
package com.apress.prospring3.ch8.dao;

// Import statements omitted
public interface ContactDao {

    public List<Contact> findAll();

    public List<Contact> findAllWithDetail();

    public List<Contact> findByFirstName(String firstName);

    public String findFirstNameById(Long id);

    public String findLastNameById(Long id);

    public void insert(Contact contact);

    public void update(Contact contact);

    public void delete(Long contactId);

}
```

In Listing 8-33, the initial declaration and injection of the data source property using the JSR-250 annotation was shown. The class name is JdbcContactDao, but this time we put it under the package com.apress.prospring3.ch8.dao.jdbc.annotation.

Listing 8-33. Declaring JdbcContactDao Using Annotations

```
package com.apress.prospring3.ch8.dao.jdbc.annotation;

import javax.annotation.Resource;
import javax.sql.DataSource;

import org.apache.commons.logging.Log;
import org.apache.commons.logging.LogFactory;
import org.springframework.stereotype.Repository;
```

```
import com.apress.prospring3.ch8.dao.ContactDao;

@Repository("contactDao")
public class JdbcContactDao implements ContactDao {

    private Log log = LogFactory.getLog(JdbcContactDao.class);

    private DataSource dataSource;

    @Resource(name="dataSource")
    public void setDataSource(DataSource dataSource) {
        this.dataSource = dataSource;
    }

    public DataSource getDataSource() {
        return dataSource;
    }
}
```

In the previous listing, we use the @Repository to declare the Spring bean with a name of contactDao, and since the class contains data access code, the @Repository also instructs Spring to perform database-specific SQL exceptions to the more application-friendly DataAccessException hierarchy in Spring.

We also declare the log variable using Apache commons-logging to log the message within the program. And for the datasource property, we use JSR-250's @Resource to let Spring inject the data source with a name of dataSource.

We are going to implement the methods in the ContactDao interface one by one. In the meantime, let's first create an empty implementation of all the methods in the JdbcContactDao class. An easy way to do this is using STS to generate empty implementations on our behalf. In STS, right-click the class and select Source ➤ Override/Implement Methods (see Figure 8-2).

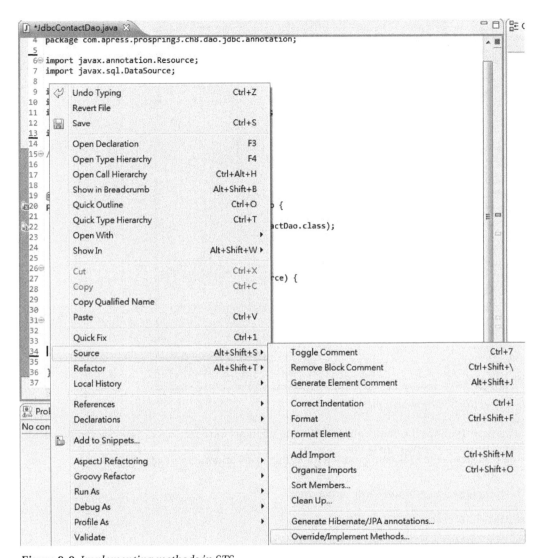

Figure 8-2. Implementing methods in STS

In the next screen, all methods under the ContactDao interface should be already checked, as shown in Figure 8-3. Just click OK, and an empty implementation of all the selected methods will be created automatically.

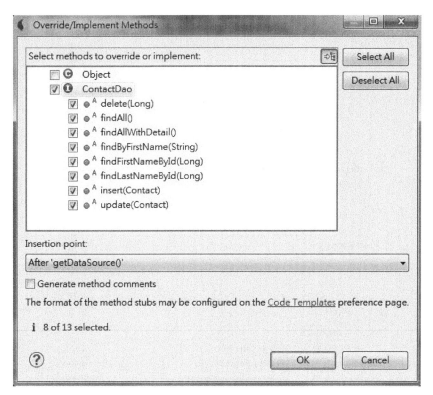

Figure 8-3. *Selecting to implement methods in STS*

Afterward, you will see the empty implementation methods were generated. Then we can proceed to implement the methods incrementally.

Listing 8-34 shows the XML configuration for Spring using annotations (app-context-annotation.xml).

Listing 8-34. *Spring Configuration Using Annotations*

```
<?xml version="1.0" encoding="UTF-8"?>
<beans xmlns="http://www.springframework.org/schema/beans"
    xmlns:xsi="http://www.w3.org/2001/XMLSchema-instance"
    xmlns:context="http://www.springframework.org/schema/context"
    xmlns:jdbc="http://www.springframework.org/schema/jdbc"
    xmlns:jee="http://www.springframework.org/schema/jee"
    xsi:schemaLocation="http://www.springframework.org/schema/beans
        http://www.springframework.org/schema/beans/spring-beans-3.1.xsd
        http://www.springframework.org/schema/context
        http://www.springframework.org/schema/context/spring-context-3.1.xsd
        http://www.springframework.org/schema/jdbc
        http://www.springframework.org/schema/jdbc/spring-jdbc-3.1.xsd
        http://www.springframework.org/schema/jee
        http://www.springframework.org/schema/jee/spring-jee-3.1.xsd">
```

```
<context:component-scan base-package="com.apress.prospring3.ch8.dao.jdbc.annotation"/>

<context:annotation-config/>

<jdbc:embedded-database id="dataSource" type="H2">
    <jdbc:script location="classpath:schema.sql"/>
    <jdbc:script location="classpath:test-data.sql"/>
</jdbc:embedded-database>
```

```
</beans>
```

There's nothing special about the configuration; we just declare the embedded database using H2 and use <context:component-scan> for automatic Spring bean discovery. Having the infrastructure in place, we can now proceed to the implementation of JDBC operations.

Querying Data Using MappingSqlQuery<T>

Spring provides the MappingSqlQuery<T> class for modeling query operations. Basically, we construct a MappingSqlQuery<T> class using the data source and the query string. On the other hand, we implement the mapRow() method to map each resultset record into the corresponding domain object.

Let's implement the findAll() method first. We begin by creating the SelectAllContacts class (which represents the query operation for selecting all contacts) that extends the MappingSqlQuery<T> abstract class. Listing 8-35 shows the SelectAllContacts class.

Listing 8-35. The SelectAllContacts Class

```
package com.apress.prospring3.ch8.dao.jdbc.annotation;

import java.sql.ResultSet;
import java.sql.SQLException;

import javax.sql.DataSource;

import org.springframework.jdbc.object.MappingSqlQuery;

import com.apress.prospring3.ch8.domain.Contact;

public class SelectAllContacts extends MappingSqlQuery<Contact> {

    private static final String SQL_SELECT_ALL_CONTACT =
        "select id, first_name, last_name, birth_date from contact";

    public SelectAllContacts(DataSource dataSource) {
        super(dataSource, SQL_SELECT_ALL_CONTACT);
    }

    protected Contact mapRow(ResultSet rs, int rowNum) throws SQLException {
        Contact contact = new Contact();

        contact.setId(rs.getLong("id"));
        contact.setFirstName(rs.getString("first_name"));
        contact.setLastName(rs.getString("last_name"));
```

```
            contact.setBirthDate(rs.getDate("birth_date"));

            return contact;
        }
    }
```

In Listing 8-35, within the SelectAllContacts class, the SQL for selecting all contacts is declared. In the class constructor, the super() method is called to construct the class, using the DataSource as well as the SQL statement. Moreover, the MappingSqlQuery<T>.mapRow() method is implemented to provide the mapping of the resultset to the Contact domain object.

Having the SelectAllContacts class in place, we can implement the findAll() method in the JdbcContactDao class. Listing 8-36 shows the class.

Listing 8-36. Implementing the findAll() Method

```
package com.apress.prospring3.ch8.dao.jdbc.annotation;

import java.util.List;

import javax.annotation.Resource;
import javax.sql.DataSource;

import org.apache.commons.logging.Log;
import org.apache.commons.logging.LogFactory;

import org.springframework.stereotype.Repository;

import com.apress.prospring3.ch8.dao.ContactDao;
import com.apress.prospring3.ch8.domain.Contact;

@Repository("contactDao")
public class JdbcContactDao implements ContactDao {

    private Log log = LogFactory.getLog(JdbcContactDao.class);

    private DataSource dataSource;

    private SelectAllContacts selectAllContacts;

    @Resource(name="dataSource")
    public void setDataSource(DataSource dataSource) {
        this.dataSource = dataSource;

        selectAllContacts = new SelectAllContacts(dataSource);
    }

    public DataSource getDataSource() {
        return dataSource;
    }

    public List<Contact> findAll() {
        return selectAllContacts.execute();
    }
```

```
        // Other empty implementation methods omitted
}
```

In Listing 8-36, in the setDataSource() method, upon the injection of the DataSource, an instance of the SelectAllContacts class is constructed. In the findAll() method, we simply invoke the SelectAllContacts.execute() method, which is inherited from the SqlQuery<T> abstract class indirectly. That's all we need to do. Listing 8-37 shows the sample program to test the logic.

Listing 8-37. Testing MappingSqlQuery

```java
package com.apress.prospring3.ch8;

// Import statements omitted
public class AnnotationJdbcDaoSample {

    public static void main(String[] args) {

        GenericXmlApplicationContext ctx = new GenericXmlApplicationContext();
        ctx.load("classpath:app-context-annotation.xml");
        ctx.refresh();

        ContactDao contactDao = ctx.getBean("contactDao", ContactDao.class);

        // Find and list all contacts
        List<Contact> contacts = contactDao.findAll();
        listContacts(contacts);

    }

    private static void listContacts(List<Contact> contacts) {
        for (Contact contact: contacts) {
            System.out.println(contact);
            if (contact.getContactTelDetails() != null) {
                for (ContactTelDetail contactTelDetail: contact.getContactTelDetails()) {
                    System.out.println("---" + contactTelDetail);
                }
            }
            System.out.println();
        }
    }
}
```

Running the testing program yields the following output:

```
Contact - Id: 1, First name: Clarence, Last name: Ho, Birthday: 1980-07-30

Contact - Id: 2, First name: Scott, Last name: Tiger, Birthday: 1990-11-02

Contact - Id: 3, First name: John, Last name: Smith, Birthday: 1964-02-28
```

In STS, since we set the logging properties to the DEBUG level, from the console output, you will also see the query that was submitted by Spring (see Figure 8-4).

```
JdbcTemplate: 635 - Executing prepared SQL query
JdbcTemplate: 570 - Executing prepared SQL statement [select id, first_name, last_name, birth_date from contact
```

Figure 8-4. Output in STS with debug logging level turned on

Let's proceed to implement the findByFirstName() method, which takes one named parameter. Like the previous sample, we create the class SelectContactByFirstName for the operation, which was shown in Listing 8-38.

Listing 8-38. The SelectContactByFirstName Class

```
package com.apress.prospring3.ch8.dao.jdbc.annotation;

// Import statements omitted

public class SelectContactByFirstName extends MappingSqlQuery<Contact> {

    private static final String SQL_FIND_BY_FIRST_NAME =
        "select id, first_name, last_name, birth_date from contact where first_name =
:first_name";

    public SelectContactByFirstName(DataSource dataSource) {
        super(dataSource, SQL_FIND_BY_FIRST_NAME);
        super.declareParameter(new SqlParameter("first_name", Types.VARCHAR));
    }

    protected Contact mapRow(ResultSet rs, int rowNum) throws SQLException {
        Contact contact = new Contact();

        contact.setId(rs.getLong("id"));
        contact.setFirstName(rs.getString("first_name"));
        contact.setLastName(rs.getString("last_name"));
        contact.setBirthDate(rs.getDate("birth_date"));

        return contact;
    }
}
```

The SelectContactByFirstName class is similar to the SelectAllContacts class (the differences are highlighted in bold). First, the SQL statement is different and carries a named parameter called first_name. In the constructor method, the declareParameter() method is called (which is inherited from the org.springframework.jdbc.object.RdbmsOperation abstract class indirectly). Let's proceed to implement the findByFirstName() method in the JdbcContactDao class. Listing 8-39 shows the code snippet.

Listing 8-39. Implementing the findByFirstName() Method

```
package com.apress.prospring3.ch8.dao.jdbc.annotation;

// Import statements omitted
@Repository("contactDao")
public class JdbcContactDao implements ContactDao {
```

```
    private SelectContactByFirstName selectContactByFirstName;

    @Resource(name="dataSource")
    public void setDataSource(DataSource dataSource) {
        this.dataSource = dataSource;

        selectAllContacts = new SelectAllContacts(dataSource);
        selectContactByFirstName = new SelectContactByFirstName(dataSource);
    }

    public List<Contact> findByFirstName(String firstName) {
        Map<String, Object> paramMap = new HashMap<String, Object>();
        paramMap.put("first_name", firstName);
        return selectContactByFirstName.executeByNamedParam(paramMap);
    }

    // Other code omitted

}
```

In Listing 8-39, upon data source injection, an instance of SelectContactByFirstName is constructed (note the lines in bold). Afterward, in the findByFirstName() method, a HashMap is constructed with the named parameters and values. Finally, the executeByNamedParam() method (inherited from SqlQuery<T> abstract class indirectly) is called. To test the method, add the code snippet in Listing 8-40 into the AnnotationJdbcDaoSample class.

Listing 8-40. Testing the findByFirstName() Method

```
        // Find contacts by first name
        contacts = contactDao.findByFirstName("Clarence");
        listContacts(contacts);
```

Running the program will produce the following output from the findByFirstName() method:

```
Contact - Id: 1, First name: Clarence, Last name: Ho, Birthday: 1980-07-30
```

One point worth noting here is that MappingSqlQuery<T> is suitable only for mapping a single row to a domain object. For a nested object, you still need to use JdbcTemplate with ResultSetExtractor like the example method findAllWithDetail() presented in the JdbcTemplate class section.

Updating Data Using SqlUpdate

For updating data, Spring provides the SqlUpdate class. Listing 8-41 shows the UpdateContact class that extends the SqlUpdate class for update operation.

Listing 8-41. The UpdateContact Class

```
package com.apress.prospring3.ch8.dao.jdbc.annotation;

import java.sql.Types;

import javax.sql.DataSource;

import org.springframework.jdbc.core.SqlParameter;
```

```
import org.springframework.jdbc.object.SqlUpdate;

public class UpdateContact extends SqlUpdate {

    private static final String SQL_UPDATE_CONTACT =
        "update contact set first_name=:first_name, last_name=:last_name,
birth_date=:birth_date where id=:id";

    public UpdateContact(DataSource dataSource) {
        super(dataSource, SQL_UPDATE_CONTACT);
        super.declareParameter(new SqlParameter("first_name", Types.VARCHAR));
        super.declareParameter(new SqlParameter("last_name", Types.VARCHAR));
        super.declareParameter(new SqlParameter("birth_date", Types.DATE));
        super.declareParameter(new SqlParameter("id", Types.INTEGER));
    }

}
```

Listing 8-41 should be familiar to you now. An instance of SqlUpdate class is constructed with the query, and the named parameters are declared too.

Listing 8-42 shows the implementation of the update() method in the JdbcContactDao class.

Listing 8-42. Using SqlUpdate

```
package com.apress.prospring3.ch8.dao.jdbc.annotation;

// Import statements omitted
@Repository("contactDao")
public class JdbcContactDao implements ContactDao {

    private UpdateContact updateContact;

    @Resource(name="dataSource")
    public void setDataSource(DataSource dataSource) {
        this.dataSource = dataSource;

        selectAllContacts = new SelectAllContacts(dataSource);
        selectContactByFirstName = new SelectContactByFirstName(dataSource);
        updateContact = new UpdateContact(dataSource);
    }

    public void update(Contact contact) {
        Map<String, Object> paramMap = new HashMap<String, Object>();
        paramMap.put("first_name", contact.getFirstName());
        paramMap.put("last_name", contact.getLastName());
        paramMap.put("birth_date", contact.getBirthDate());
        paramMap.put("id", contact.getId());
        updateContact.updateByNamedParam(paramMap);
        log.info("Existing contact updated with id: " + contact.getId());
    }

    // Other code omitted

}
```

In Listing 8-42, upon data source injection, an instance of UpdateContact is constructed (note the lines in bold). In the update() method, a HashMap of named parameters is constructed from the pass in Contact object, and then the updateByNamedParam() is called to update the contact record. To test the operation, add the code snippet in Listing 8-43 into the AnnotationJdbcDaoSample class.

Listing 8-43. Testing the update() Method

```
Contact contact;

// Update contact
contact = new Contact();
contact.setId(1l);
contact.setFirstName("Clarence");
contact.setLastName("Peter");
contact.setBirthDate(new Date((new GregorianCalendar(1977, 10,
1)).getTime().getTime())));
contactDao.update(contact);
contacts = contactDao.findAll();
listContacts(contacts);
```

In Listing 8-43, we simply construct a Contact object and then invoke the update() method. Running the program will produce the following output from the last listContacts() method:

```
11:12:27,020  INFO 3.ch8.dao.jdbc.annotation.JdbcContactDao:  87 - Existing contact updated
with id: 1
Contact - Id: 1, First name: Clarence, Last name: Peter, Birthday: 1977-11-01

Contact - Id: 2, First name: Scott, Last name: Tiger, Birthday: 1990-11-02

Contact - Id: 3, First name: John, Last name: Smith, Birthday: 1964-02-28
```

In the output, you can see that the contact with an ID of 1 was updated accordingly.

Inserting Data and Retrieving the Generated Key

For inserting data, we also use the SqlUpdate class. However, one interesting point here is about the primary key, the id column, which will be available only after the insert statement has completed, while the RDBMS generated the identity value for the record. The column ID was declared with the attribute AUTO_INCREMENT and is the primary key, which means the value was assigned by the RDBMS during the insert operation.

If you are using Oracle, you will probably get an unique ID first from an Oracle sequence and then fire the insert statement with the query. However, for our case, how can we retrieve the key generated by the RDBMS after the record is inserted?

In old versions of JDBC, the method is a bit tricky. For example, if we are using MySQL, we need to fire the SQL select last_insert_id() and select @@IDENTITY for Microsoft SQL Server.

Luckily, starting from JDBC version 3.0, a new feature was added that allows the retrieval of a RDBMS-generated key in a unified fashion. Listing 8-37 shows the implementation of the insert() method, which also retrieves the generated key for the inserted contact record. It will work in most databases (if not all); just make sure you are using a JDBC driver that is compatible with JDBC 3.0 or newer.

We start by creating the InsertContact class for the insert operation, which extends the SqlUpdate class. Listing 8-44 shows the class.

Listing 8-44. The InsertContact Class

```java
package com.apress.prospring3.ch8.dao.jdbc.annotation;

import java.sql.Types;

import javax.sql.DataSource;


import org.springframework.jdbc.core.SqlParameter;
import org.springframework.jdbc.object.SqlUpdate;

public class InsertContact extends SqlUpdate {

    private static final String SQL_INSERT_CONTACT =
        "insert into contact (first_name, last_name, birth_date) values (:first_name,
:last_name, :birth_date)";

    public InsertContact(DataSource dataSource) {
        super(dataSource, SQL_INSERT_CONTACT);
        super.declareParameter(new SqlParameter("first_name", Types.VARCHAR));
        super.declareParameter(new SqlParameter("last_name", Types.VARCHAR));
        super.declareParameter(new SqlParameter("birth_date", Types.DATE));
        super.setGeneratedKeysColumnNames(new String[] {"id"});
        super.setReturnGeneratedKeys(true);
    }

}
```

The InsertContact class is almost the same as the UpdateContact class. We just need to do two more things. When constructing the InsertContact class, we call the method SqlUpdate.setGeneratedKeysColumnNames() to declare the name of the ID column. The method SqlUpdate.setReturnGeneratedKeys() instructs the underlying JDBC driver to retrieve the generated key.

Listing 8-45 shows the implementation of the insert() method in the JdbcContactDao class.

Listing 8-45. Using SqlUpdate for Insert Operation

```java
package com.apress.prospring3.ch8.dao.jdbc.annotation;

// Import statements omitted
@Repository("contactDao")
public class JdbcContactDao implements ContactDao {
    private InsertContact insertContact;

    @Resource(name="dataSource")
    public void setDataSource(DataSource dataSource) {
        this.dataSource = dataSource;

        selectAllContacts = new SelectAllContacts(dataSource);
        selectContactByFirstName = new SelectContactByFirstName(dataSource);
        updateContact = new UpdateContact(dataSource);
        insertContact = new InsertContact(dataSource);
    }
```

```
    public void insert(Contact contact) {
        Map<String, Object> paramMap = new HashMap<String, Object>();
        paramMap.put("first_name", contact.getFirstName());
        paramMap.put("last_name", contact.getLastName());
        paramMap.put("birth_date", contact.getBirthDate());
        KeyHolder keyHolder = new GeneratedKeyHolder();
        insertContact.updateByNamedParam(paramMap, keyHolder);
        contact.setId(keyHolder.getKey().longValue());
        log.info("New contact inserted with id: " + contact.getId());
    }

// Other code omitted
}
```

From Listing 8-45, upon data source injection, an instance of InsertContact was constructed (note the lines in bold). In the insert() method, we also use the SqlUpdate.updateByNamedParam() method. However, we also pass in an instance of KeyHolder to the method, which will have the generated ID stored. After the data is inserted, we can then retrieve the generated key from the KeyHolder.

To test the operation, add the code snippet in Listing 8-46 into the AnnotationJdbcDaoSample class.

Listing 8-46. *Testing the insert() Method*

```
        // Insert contact
        contact = new Contact();
        contact.setFirstName("Rod");
        contact.setLastName("Johnson");
        contact.setBirthDate(new Date((new GregorianCalendar(2001, 10,
1)).getTime().getTime()));
        contactDao.insert(contact);
        contacts = contactDao.findAll();
        listContacts(contacts);
```

Running the program will produce the following output from the last listContacts() method:

```
11:36:08,871  INFO 3.ch8.dao.jdbc.annotation.JdbcContactDao:  88 - New contact inserted with
id: 4
Contact - Id: 1, First name: Clarence, Last name: Peter, Birthday: 1977-11-01

Contact - Id: 2, First name: Scott, Last name: Tiger, Birthday: 1990-11-02

Contact - Id: 3, First name: John, Last name: Smith, Birthday: 1964-02-28

Contact - Id: 4, First name: Rod, Last name: Johnson, Birthday: 2001-11-01
```

You can see that the new contact was inserted with an ID of 4 and retrieved correctly.

Batching Operations with BatchSqlUpdate

For batch operation, we use the BatchSqlUpdate class. The use is basically the same as the SqlUpdate class; we just need to do a few more things. To demonstrate its usage, let's add a new method into the ContactDao interface:

```
public void insertWithDetail(Contact contact);
```

The new insertWithDetail() method will insert both the contact and its telephone details into the database.

To be able to insert the telephone detail record, we need to create the InsertContactTelDetail class, which was shown in Listing 8-47. :InsertContactTelDetail class

Listing 8-47. The InsertContactTelDetail Class

```
package com.apress.prospring3.ch8.dao.jdbc.annotation;

import java.sql.Types;

import javax.sql.DataSource;

import org.springframework.jdbc.core.SqlParameter;
import org.springframework.jdbc.object.BatchSqlUpdate;

public class InsertContactTelDetail extends BatchSqlUpdate {

    private static final String SQL_INSERT_CONTACT_TEL =
        "insert into contact_tel_detail (contact_id, tel_type, tel_number) values
(:contact_id, :tel_type, :tel_number)";

    private static final int BATCH_SIZE = 10;

    public InsertContactTelDetail(DataSource dataSource) {
        super(dataSource, SQL_INSERT_CONTACT_TEL);
        declareParameter(new SqlParameter("contact_id", Types.INTEGER));
        declareParameter(new SqlParameter("tel_type", Types.VARCHAR));
        declareParameter(new SqlParameter("tel_number", Types.VARCHAR));
        setBatchSize(BATCH_SIZE);
    }
}
```

Note that in the constructor, we called the BatchSqlUpdate.setBatchSize() method to set the batch size for the JDBC insert operation.

Listing 8-48 shows the implementation of the insertWithDetail() method in the JdbcContactDao class.

Listing 8-48. Batch SQL Update Operation

```
package com.apress.prospring3.ch8.dao.jdbc.annotation;

// Import statements omitted
@Repository("contactDao")
public class JdbcContactDao implements ContactDao {

    private InsertContactTelDetail insertContactTelDetail;

    public void insertWithDetail(Contact contact) {

        insertContactTelDetail = new InsertContactTelDetail(dataSource);

        // Insert contact
        Map<String, Object> paramMap = new HashMap<String, Object>();
```

```
            paramMap.put("first_name", contact.getFirstName());
            paramMap.put("last_name", contact.getLastName());
            paramMap.put("birth_date", contact.getBirthDate());
            KeyHolder keyHolder = new GeneratedKeyHolder();
            insertContact.updateByNamedParam(paramMap, keyHolder);
            contact.setId(keyHolder.getKey().longValue());
            log.info("New contact inserted with id: " + contact.getId());

            // Batch insert contact tel. details
            List<ContactTelDetail> contactTelDetails =
                contact.getContactTelDetails();
            if (contactTelDetails != null) {
                for (ContactTelDetail contactTelDetail: contactTelDetails) {
                    paramMap = new HashMap<String, Object>();
                    paramMap.put("contact_id", contact.getId());
                    paramMap.put("tel_type", contactTelDetail.getTelType());
                    paramMap.put("tel_number", contactTelDetail.getTelNumber());
                    insertContactTelDetail.updateByNamedParam(paramMap);
                }
            }
            insertContactTelDetail.flush();
    }

    public List<Contact> findAllWithDetail() {
        JdbcTemplate jdbcTemplate = new JdbcTemplate(getDataSource());
        String sql = "select c.id, c.first_name, c.last_name, c.birth_date" +
", t.id as contact_tel_id, t.tel_type, t.tel_number from contact c " +
"left join contact_tel_detail t on c.id = t.contact_id";
        return jdbcTemplate.query(sql, new ContactWithDetailExtractor());
    }

    private static final class ContactWithDetailExtractor
        implements ResultSetExtractor<List<Contact>> {

        public List<Contact> extractData(ResultSet rs) throws
            SQLException, DataAccessException {

            Map<Long, Contact> map = new HashMap<Long, Contact>();
            Contact contact = null;
            while (rs.next()) {
                Long id = rs.getLong("id");
                contact = map.get(id);
                if (contact == null) {  // new contact record
                    contact = new Contact();
                    contact.setId(id);
                    contact.setFirstName(rs.getString("first_name"));
                    contact.setLastName(rs.getString("last_name"));
                    contact.setBirthDate(rs.getDate("birth_date"));
                    contact.setContactTelDetails(new ArrayList<ContactTelDetail>());
                    map.put(id, contact);
                }

                // Process contact tel. detail (if exists)
                Long contactTelDetailId = rs.getLong("contact_tel_id");
```

```
            if (contactTelDetailId > 0) {
                ContactTelDetail contactTelDetail = new ContactTelDetail();
                contactTelDetail.setId(contactTelDetailId);
                contactTelDetail.setContactId(id);
                contactTelDetail.setTelType(rs.getString("tel_type"));
                contactTelDetail.setTelNumber(rs.getString("tel_number"));
                contact.getContactTelDetails().add(contactTelDetail);
            }
        }
        return new ArrayList<Contact> (map.values());
    }
}

// Other code omitted

}
```

From Listing 8-48, each time the insertWithDetail() method is being called, a new instance of InsertContactTelDetail is constructed. The reason is that the BatchSqlUpdate class is not thread safe. Then we use it just like SqlUpdate. However, the BatchSqlUpdate class will queue up the insert operations and submit to the database in batch. Every time the number of records equals the batch size, Spring will fire a bulk insert operation to the database for the pending records. On the other hand, upon completion, we call the BatchSqlUpdate.flush() method to instruct Spring to flush all pending operations (i.e., the insert operations being queued that still haven't reached the batch size yet). Finally, we loop through the list of ContactTelDetail objects in the Contact object and invoke the BatchSqlUpdate.updateByNamedParam() method.

To facilitate testing, the findAllWithDetail() method was also implemented. Listing 8-49 shows the code snippet to add to the AnnotationJdbcDaoSample class for testing the batch insert operation.

Listing 8-49. *Testing the insertWithDetail() Method*

```
        // Insert contact with details
        contact = new Contact();
        contact.setFirstName("Michael");
        contact.setLastName("Jackson");
        contact.setBirthDate(new Date((new GregorianCalendar(1964, 10,
1)).getTime().getTime())));
        List<ContactTelDetail> contactTelDetails - new ArrayList<ContactTelDetail>();
        ContactTelDetail contactTelDetail = new ContactTelDetail();
        contactTelDetail.setTelType("Home");
        contactTelDetail.setTelNumber("11111111");
        contactTelDetails.add(contactTelDetail);
        contactTelDetail = new ContactTelDetail();
        contactTelDetail.setTelType("Mobile");
        contactTelDetail.setTelNumber("22222222");
        contactTelDetails.add(contactTelDetail);
        contact.setContactTelDetails(contactTelDetails);
        contactDao.insertWithDetail(contact);
        contacts = contactDao.findAllWithDetail();
        listContacts(contacts);
```

Running the program will produce the following output from the last listContacts() method:

```
Contact - Id: 1, First name: Clarence, Last name: Peter, Birthday: 1977-11-01
---Contact Tel Detail - Id: 2, Contact id: 1, Type: Home, Number: 1234567890
```

```
---Contact Tel Detail - Id: 1, Contact id: 1, Type: Mobile, Number: 1234567890

Contact - Id: 2, First name: Scott, Last name: Tiger, Birthday: 1990-11-02
---Contact Tel Detail - Id: 3, Contact id: 2, Type: Home, Number: 1234567890

Contact - Id: 3, First name: John, Last name: Smith, Birthday: 1964-02-28

Contact - Id: 4, First name: Rod, Last name: Johnson, Birthday: 2001-11-01

Contact - Id: 5, First name: Michael, Last name: Jackson, Birthday: 1964-11-01
---Contact Tel Detail - Id: 4, Contact id: 5, Type: Home, Number: 11111111
---Contact Tel Detail - Id: 5, Contact id: 5, Type: Mobile, Number: 22222222
```

You can see that the new contacts with the telephone details were all inserted into the database.

Calling Stored Functions Using SqlFunction

Spring also provides a number of classes to simplify the execution of stored procedures/functions using JDBC. In this section, we will show you a simple function using the SqlFunction class to call a SQL function in the database. We will use MySQL as an example, create a stored function, and call it using the SqlFunction<T> class.

We're assuming you have a MySQL database with a schema called prospring3_ch8, with a user name and password both equaling prospring3 (the same as the example in the section "Exploring the JDBC Infrastructure"). Let's create a stored function called getFirstNameById(), which accepts the contact's ID and returns the first name of the contact. Listing 8-50 shows the script to create the stored function in MySQL (store-function.sql). Run the script against the MySQL database.

Listing 8-50. Store Function for MySQL

```
DELIMITER //
CREATE FUNCTION getFirstNameById(in_id INT)
    RETURNS VARCHAR(60)
BEGIN
    RETURN (SELECT first_name FROM contact WHERE id = in_id);
END //
DELIMITER ;
```

The stored function should be self-explanatory. It simply accepts the ID and returns the first name of the contact record with the ID.

Let's create a new interface called ContactSfDao for this example. Listing 8-51 shows the interface.

Listing 8-51. The ContactSfDao Interface

```
package com.apress.prospring3.ch8.dao;

public interface ContactSfDao {

    public String getFirstNameById(Long id);

}
```

The second step is to create the SfFirstNameById class to represent the stored function operation, which extends the SqlFunction<T> class. Listing 8-52 shows the class.

Listing 8-52. The SfFirstNameById Interface

```
package com.apress.prospring3.ch8.dao.jdbc.annotation;

import java.sql.Types;

import javax.sql.DataSource;

import org.springframework.jdbc.core.SqlParameter;
import org.springframework.jdbc.object.SqlFunction;


public class SfFirstNameById extends SqlFunction<String> {

    private static final String SQL = "select getfirstnamebyid(?)";

    public SfFirstNameById(DataSource dataSource) {
        super(dataSource, SQL);
        declareParameter(new SqlParameter(Types.INTEGER));
        compile();
    }
}
```

In Listing 8-52, the class extends SqlFunction<T> and passes in the type String, which indicates the return type of the function. Then we declare the SQL to call the stored function in MySQL. Afterward, in the constructor, the parameter is declared, and then we compile the operation. Now the class is ready for our use in the implementation class. Listing 8-53 shows the JdbcContactSfDao class, which implements the ContactSfDao interface.

Listing 8-53. The JdbcContactSfDao Class

```
package com.apress.prospring3.ch8.dao.jdbc.annotation;

import java.util.List;

import javax.annotation.Resource;
import javax.sql.DataSource;

import org.springframework.stereotype.Repository;

import com.apress.prospring3.ch8.dao.ContactSfDao;

@Repository("contactSfDao")
public class JdbcContactSfDao implements ContactSfDao {

    private DataSource dataSource;

    private SfFirstNameById sfFirstNameById;

    @Resource(name="dataSource")
    public void setDataSource(DataSource dataSource) {
        this.dataSource = dataSource;

        sfFirstNameById = new SfFirstNameById(dataSource);
```

```
    }

    public DataSource getDataSource() {
        return dataSource;
    }

    public String getFirstNameById(Long id) {
        List<String> result = sfFirstNameById.execute(id);
        return result.get(0);
    }
}
```

In Listing 8-53, upon data source injection, an instance of SfFirstNameById is constructed. Then in the getFirstNameById() method, its execute() method was called, passing in the contact ID. The method will return a list of Strings, and we need only the first one, because there should be only one record returned in the resultset.

Listing 8-54 shows the Spring configuration file for connecting to MySQL (app-context-sf.xml).

Listing 8-54. *Spring Configuration for MySQL*

```xml
<?xml version="1.0" encoding="UTF-8"?>
<beans xmlns="http://www.springframework.org/schema/beans"
    xmlns:xsi="http://www.w3.org/2001/XMLSchema-instance"
    xmlns:context="http://www.springframework.org/schema/context"
    xsi:schemaLocation="http://www.springframework.org/schema/beans
        http://www.springframework.org/schema/beans/spring-beans-3.1.xsd
        http://www.springframework.org/schema/context
        http://www.springframework.org/schema/context/spring-context-3.1.xsd">

    <import resource="datasource-dbcp.xml"/>

    <context:component-scan base-package="com.apress.prospring3.ch8.dao.jdbc.annotation"/>

    <context:annotation-config/>
</beans>
```

In Listing 8-54, the file datasource-dbcp.xml is imported, which holds the datasource configuration to the MySQL database. To run the program, the dependency on commons-dbcp should be added to the project, as shown in Table 8-5.

Table 8-5. *Dependency for commons-dbcp*

Group ID	Artifact ID	Version	Description
commons-dbcp	commons-dbcp	1.4	Apache commons-dbcp database connection pool library

Listing 8-55 shows the testing program.

Listing 8-55. *Testing Stored Function in MySQL*

```java
package com.apress.prospring3.ch8;

import org.springframework.context.support.GenericXmlApplicationContext;
```

```
import com.apress.prospring3.ch8.dao.ContactSfDao;

public class JdbcContactSfDaoSample {

    public static void main(String[] args) {

        GenericXmlApplicationContext ctx = new GenericXmlApplicationContext();
        ctx.load("classpath:app-context-sf.xml");
        ctx.refresh();

        ContactSfDao contactSfDao = ctx.getBean("contactSfDao", ContactSfDao.class);

        System.out.println(contactSfDao.getFirstNameById(11));
    }
}
```

In the program, we pass an ID of 1 into the stored function. This will return Clarence as the first name if you ran the test-data.sql against the MySQL database. Running the program produces the following output:

```
15:16:11,990 DEBUG g.springframework.jdbc.core.JdbcTemplate: 635 - Executing prepared SQL
query
15:16:11,991 DEBUG g.springframework.jdbc.core.JdbcTemplate: 570 - Executing prepared SQL
statement [select firstnamebyid(?)]
15:16:11,998 DEBUG ramework.jdbc.datasource.DataSourceUtils: 110 - Fetching JDBC Connection
from DataSource
15:16:12,289 DEBUG ramework.jdbc.datasource.DataSourceUtils: 332 - Returning JDBC Connection
to DataSource
Clarence
```

You can see that the first name was retrieved correctly.

What is presented here is just a simple sample to demonstrate Spring JDBC module's functions. Spring also provides other classes (e.g., StoredProcedure) for you to invoke complex stored procedures that return complex data types. We recommend you refer to Spring's reference manual in case you need to access stored procedures using JDBC.

Using the Java Configuration

In case you prefer using the Java configuration class instead of the XML configuration, Listing 8-56 shows the Spring configuration class.

Listing 8-56. Using the Java Configuration

```
package com.apress.prospring3.ch8.javaconfig;

import javax.sql.DataSource;

import org.springframework.context.annotation.Bean;
import org.springframework.context.annotation.ComponentScan;
import org.springframework.context.annotation.Configuration;
import org.springframework.jdbc.datasource.embedded.EmbeddedDatabase;
import org.springframework.jdbc.datasource.embedded.EmbeddedDatabaseBuilder;
import org.springframework.jdbc.datasource.embedded.EmbeddedDatabaseType;
```

```
@Configuration
@ComponentScan(basePackages="com.apress.prospring3.ch8.dao.jdbc.annotation")
public class AppConfig {

    @Bean
    public DataSource dataSource() {
        EmbeddedDatabaseBuilder builder = new EmbeddedDatabaseBuilder();
        EmbeddedDatabase db = builder.setType(EmbeddedDatabaseType.H2).
            addScript("schema.sql").
            addScript("test-data.sql").build();
        return db;
    }
}
```

In the previous listing, we use EmbeddedDatabaseBuilder to construct the embedded H2 database; the effect is the same as using the <jdbc:embedded-database> tag in XML configuration. You can also use the @Profile feature to specify that the configuration is the target only for a specific environment (for example, dev).

Spring Data Project: JDBC Extensions

As mentioned at the beginning of this chapter, in recent years database technology has evolved so quickly with the rise of so many purpose-specific databases, nowadays RDBMS is not the only choice as an application's backend database management system. To respond to this database technology evolution and the developer community's need, Spring created the Spring Data project (*www.springsource.org/spring-data*). The major objective of the project is to provide useful extensions on top of Spring's core data access functionality to address the needs of Spring developers who are interacting with database backends other than RDBMSs. Advanced features to data access standards (e.g., JDBC, JPA) are also provided.

The Spring Data project comes with a lot of extensions. One extension that we would like to mention here is the JDBC Extensions (*www.springsource.org/spring-data/jdbc-extensions*). As its name implies, the extension provides some advanced features to facilitate the development of JDBC applications using Spring.

At the time of writing, the first release (version 1.0.0) is still in its milestone stage. The main features that the extension provides are listed here:

> *QueryDSL support:* QueryDSL (*www.querydsl.com*) is a domain-specific language that provides a framework for developing type-safe queries. Spring Data's JDBC Extensions provides QueryDslJdbcTemplate to facilitate the development of JDBC applications using QueryDSL instead of SQL statements.

> *Advanced support for Oracle Database:* The extension provides a lot of advanced features for Oracle Database users. On the database connection side, it supports Oracle-specific session settings, as well as Fast Connection Failover technology when working with Oracle RAC. Also, classes that integrate with Oracle Advanced Queueing are provided. On the data-type side, native support for Oracle's XML types, STRUCT and ARRAY, and so on, are provided.

If you are developing JDBC applications using Spring with Oracle Database, the JDBC Extensions is really worth a look.

Considerations for Using JDBC

From the previous discussions, you can see how Spring can make your life much easier when using JDBC to interact with the underlying RDBMS. However, there is still quite a lot of code you need to develop, especially when transforming the resultset into the corresponding domain objects.

On top of JDBC, a lot of open source libraries have been developed to help close the gap between the relational data structure and Java's OO model. For example, MyBatis (formerly known as iBATIS) is a popular DataMapper framework that is also based on SQL mapping. MyBatis lets you map objects with stored procedures or queries to an XML descriptor file (Java annotation is supported too). Like Spring, MyBatis provides a declarative way to query object mapping, greatly saving you the time it takes to maintain SQL queries that may be scattered around various DAO classes.

There are also many other ORM frameworks that focus on the object model, rather than the query. Popular ones include Hibernate, EclipseLink (also known as TopLink), and OpenJPA. All of them comply with the JCP's JPA specification.

In recent years, those ORM tools and mapping frameworks have become much more mature so that most developers will settle on one of them, instead of using JDBC directly. However, in cases where you need to have absolute control over the query that will be submitted to the database for performance purposes (e.g., using a hierarchical query in Oracle), Spring JDBC is really a viable option. And when using Spring, one great advantage is that you can mix and match different data access technologies. For example, you can use Hibernate as the main ORM and then JDBC as a supplement for some of the complex query logic or batch operations; you can mix and match them in a single business operation and then wrap them under the same database transaction. Spring will help you handle those situations easily.

Summary

This chapter showed you how to use Spring to simplify JDBC programming. You learned how to connect to a database and perform selects, updates, deletes, and inserts, as well as call stored functions. How to use the core Spring JDBC class, JdbcTemplate, was discussed in detail. In addition, we covered other Spring classes that are built on top of JdbcTemplate and that help you model various JDBC operations.

In the next few chapters, we will discuss how to use Spring with popular ORM technologies when developing data access logic.

CHAPTER 9

Using Hibernate in Spring

In the previous chapter, you saw how to use JDBC in Spring applications. However, even though Spring goes a long way toward simplifying JDBC development, you still have a lot of code to write.

In this chapter, we cover one of the object-relational mapping (ORM) libraries that has wide support in Spring—Hibernate.

If you have experience developing data access applications using EJB entity beans (prior to EJB 3.0), you may remember the painful process. Tedious configuration of mappings, transaction demarcation, and much boilerplate code in each bean to manage its life cycle greatly reduced the productivity when developing enterprise Java applications.

Just like Spring was developed to embrace POJO base development and declarative configuration management rather than EJB's heavy and clumsy setup, the developer community realize that a simpler, lightweight, and POJO base framework could ease the development of data access logic. Since then, many different libraries have appeared; they are generally referred to as *ORM libraries*. The main objective of an ORM library is to close the gap between the relational data structure in the RDBMS and the OO model in Java so that developers can focus on programming with the object model and at the same time easily perform actions related to persistence.

Of the ORM libraries available in the open source community, Hibernate is one of the most successful. Its features, such as POJO base approach, ease of development, and support of sophisticated relationship definitions, have won the heart of the mainstream Java developer community.

Hibernate's popularity has also affected the JCP, which developed the Java Data Objects (JDO) specification as one of the standard ORM technologies in Java EE. Starting from EJB 3.0, the EJB entity bean was even replaced with the Java Persistence API (JPA), within which a lot of the ideas were influenced by popular ORM libraries such as Hibernate, TopLink, and JDO.

The relationship between Hibernate and JPA is very close. Gavin King, the founder of Hibernate, represented JBoss as one of the JCP expert group members in defining the JPA specification. Starting from version 3.2, Hibernate has provided an implementation of JPA. So, when you develop applications with Hibernate, you can choose to use either Hibernate's own API or the JPA with Hibernate as the persistence service provider.

Having discussed a rough history of Hibernate, this chapter will cover how to use Spring with Hibernate when developing data access logic. Hibernate is such an extensive ORM library, so covering every aspect of Hibernate in just one chapter is simply not possible, and numerous books are dedicated to discussing Hibernate.

This chapter will cover the basic ideas and main use cases of using Hibernate in Spring. In particular, we are going to discuss the following topics:

- *Configuring the Hibernate SessionFactory*: The core concept of Hibernate revolves around the `Session` interface, which is managed by the `SessionFactory`. We will discuss how to configure Hibernate's session factory to work in a Spring application.

- *Major concepts of ORMs using Hibernate*: We will go through the major concepts of how to use Hibernate to map a POJO to the underlying relational database structure. Some commonly used relationships, including one-to-many and many-to-many, will also be discussed.

- *Data operations*: We will go through a number of examples of how to perform data operations (query, insert, update, delete) using Hibernate in the Spring environment. When working with Hibernate, its Session interface is the major interface that we will interact with.

■ **Note** When defining object-to-relational mappings, Hibernate supports two configuration styles. One is putting the mapping information in XML files, and the other is using Java annotations within the entity classes (in the ORM or JPA world, a Java class that is mapped to the underlying relational database structure is called an *entity class*). Nowadays, the annotation approach is a much more popular one. So, in this chapter, we will focus on using the annotation approach for object-relational mapping. For the mapping annotation, we will use the JPA standards (e.g., under the javax.persistence package), because they are interchangeable with Hibernate's own annotations and will help you with future migrations to a JPA environment.

Create a Hibernate Utility Project in STS

Just like Spring, Hibernate is a big library and is packaged into a number of modules (such as Hibernate Core, Entity Manager, and so on). Sometimes you may find it difficult to identify which Hibernate modules are required in your application. Fortunately, STS provides a simple way for you to create common types of projects based on Spring, and a template project with Hibernate is also provided.

To create a project using Spring with Hibernate support, in STS simply create a new project using the Simple Spring Hibernate Utility Project template, which you can find by selecting New Project ➤ Spring Template Project (see Figure 9-1).

Figure 9-1. Creating a project based on the Spring Hibernate Utility Project template in STS

Then, enter the project name and top-level package name, as in Figure 9-2.

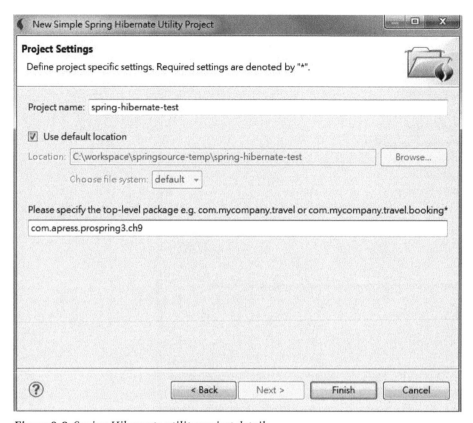

Figure 9-2. Spring Hibernate utility project details

Upon completion, STS will create a Maven-based project with the required dependencies. When you take a look at the file pom.xml (which is the Maven's project object model file) in the project's root folder, you will see Spring has added a dependency to the project. Listing 9-1 shows the code snippet.

Listing 9-1. Hibernate Dependency

```
<dependencies>

    <dependency>
        <groupId>org.hibernate</groupId>
        <artifactId>hibernate-entitymanager</artifactId>
        <version>3.6.0.Final</version>
    </dependency>
...
```

When compared to a simple Spring utility project, just one dependency is added. However, thanks to Maven's transitive dependencies feature, all the other required dependencies will be discovered and added by Maven into the project automatically. In STS, if you open pom.xml, the POM file editor will be displayed, and when you click the tab Dependencies Hierarchy, you will see the rest of the dependencies required by Hibernate (see Figure 9-3).

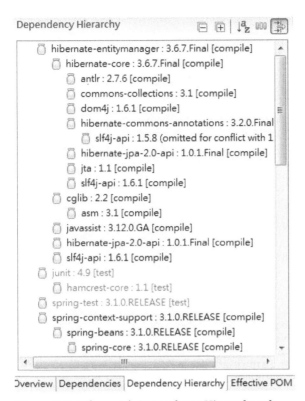

Figure 9-3. Hibernate's Dependency Hierarchy tab

As you can see in Figure 9-3, the hibernate-entitymanager module requires the hibernate-core module and in turn requires the hibernate-commons-annotations module, and so on. So, you will have a quick understanding of what is being included in your project.

However, for a production application, you may still need to fine-tune the pom.xml file to make sure that only the libraries and their correct versions were included.

Sample Data Model for Example Code

In Chapter 8, you saw a simple data model for demonstrating the code samples. In this chapter, in order to demonstrate some of the more complicate relationships, we will extend the data model a bit. Figure 9-4 shows the data model that will be used in this chapter.

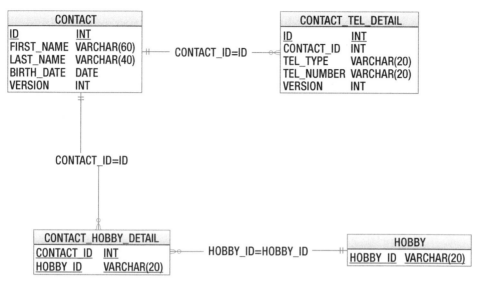

Figure 9-4. Sample data model for Hibernate

As shown in this data model, two new tables were added, namely, HOBBY and CONTACT_HOBBY_DETAIL (the join table), which models the many-to-many relationships between the CONTACT and HOBBY tables. On the other hand, a VERSION column was added to the CONTACT and CONTACT_TEL_DETAIL tables for optimistic locking, which we will discuss in detail later. In the examples in this chapter, we will use the embedded H2 database, so the database name is not required.

Listings 9-2 and 9-3 show the scripts for schema creation and sample data population.

Listing 9-2. Sample Data Model Creation Script (`schema.sql`)

```
CREATE TABLE CONTACT (
    ID INT NOT NULL AUTO_INCREMENT
    , FIRST_NAME VARCHAR(60) NOT NULL
    , LAST_NAME VARCHAR(40) NOT NULL
    , BIRTH_DATE DATE
    , VERSION INT NOT NULL DEFAULT 0
    , UNIQUE UQ_CONTACT_1 (FIRST_NAME, LAST_NAME)
    , PRIMARY KEY (ID)
);


CREATE TABLE HOBBY (
    HOBBY_ID VARCHAR(20) NOT NULL
    , PRIMARY KEY (HOBBY_ID)
);

CREATE TABLE CONTACT_TEL_DETAIL (
ID INT NOT NULL AUTO_INCREMENT
    , CONTACT_ID INT NOT NULL
    , TEL_TYPE VARCHAR(20) NOT NULL
    , TEL_NUMBER VARCHAR(20) NOT NULL
```

```
    , VERSION INT NOT NULL DEFAULT 0
    , UNIQUE UQ_CONTACT_TEL_DETAIL_1 (CONTACT_ID, TEL_TYPE)
    , PRIMARY KEY (ID)
    , CONSTRAINT FK_CONTACT_TEL_DETAIL_1 FOREIGN KEY (CONTACT_ID)
        REFERENCES CONTACT (ID)
);


CREATE TABLE CONTACT_HOBBY_DETAIL (
    CONTACT_ID INT NOT NULL
    , HOBBY_ID VARCHAR(20) NOT NULL
    , PRIMARY KEY (CONTACT_ID, HOBBY_ID)
    , CONSTRAINT FK_CONTACT_HOBBY_DETAIL_1 FOREIGN KEY (CONTACT_ID)
        REFERENCES CONTACT (ID) ON DELETE CASCADE
    , CONSTRAINT FK_CONTACT_HOBBY_DETAIL_2 FOREIGN KEY (HOBBY_ID)
    REFERENCES HOBBY (HOBBY_ID)
);
```

Listing 9-3. Data Population Script(test-data.sql)

```
insert into contact (first_name, last_name, birth_date) values↵
('Clarence', 'Ho', '1980-07-30');
insert into contact (first_name, last_name, birth_date) values↵
('Scott', 'Tiger', '1990-11-02');
insert into contact (first_name, last_name, birth_date) values↵
('John', 'Smith', '1964-02-28');

insert into contact_tel_detail (contact_id, tel_type, tel_number) values↵
(1, 'Mobile', '1234567890');
insert into contact_tel_detail (contact_id, tel_type, tel_number) values↵
(1, 'Home', '1234567890');
insert into contact_tel_detail (contact_id, tel_type, tel_number) values↵
(2, 'Home', '1234567890');

insert into hobby (hobby_id) values ('Swimming');
insert into hobby (hobby_id) values ('Jogging');
insert into hobby (hobby_id) values ('Programming');
insert into hobby (hobby_id) values ('Movies');
insert into hobby (hobby_id) values ('Reading');

insert into contact_hobby_detail(contact_id, hobby_id) values (1, 'Swimming');
insert into contact_hobby_detail(contact_id, hobby_id) values (1, 'Movies');
insert into contact_hobby_detail(contact_id, hobby_id) values (2, 'Swimming');
```

Configuring Hibernate SessionFactory

As mentioned earlier in this chapter, the core concept of Hibernate is based on the Session interface, which is obtained from the SessionFactory. Spring provides a number of classes to support the configuration of Hibernate's session factory as a Spring bean with the desired properties. Since we are going to use the annotation style, we will use the class AnnotationSessionFactoryBean. Listing 9-4 shows the corresponding XML configuration file (app-context.xml).

Listing 9-4. Spring Configuration for Hibernate's AnnotationSessionFactoryBean

```xml
<?xml version="1.0" encoding="UTF-8"?>
<beans xmlns="http://www.springframework.org/schema/beans"
    xmlns:xsi="http://www.w3.org/2001/XMLSchema-instance"
    xmlns:context="http://www.springframework.org/schema/context"
    xmlns:tx="http://www.springframework.org/schema/tx"
    xmlns:jdbc="http://www.springframework.org/schema/jdbc"
    xsi:schemaLocation="
      http://www.springframework.org/schema/jdbc
      http://www.springframework.org/schema/jdbc/spring-jdbc-3.1.xsd
      http://www.springframework.org/schema/beans
      http://www.springframework.org/schema/beans/spring-beans-3.1.xsd
      http://www.springframework.org/schema/tx
      http://www.springframework.org/schema/tx/spring-tx-3.1.xsd
      http://www.springframework.org/schema/context
      http://www.springframework.org/schema/context/spring-context-3.1.xsd">

    <jdbc:embedded-database id="dataSource" type="H2">
        <jdbc:script location="classpath:schema.sql"/>
        <jdbc:script location="classpath:test-data.sql"/>
    </jdbc:embedded-database>

    <bean id="transactionManager"
      class="org.springframework.orm.hibernate3.HibernateTransactionManager">
        <property name="sessionFactory" ref="sessionFactory"/>
    </bean>

    <tx:annotation-driven/>

    <context:component-scan base-package="com.apress.prospring3.ch9" />

    <bean id="sessionFactory"
class="org.springframework.orm.hibernate3.annotation.AnnotationSessionFactoryBean">
        <property name="dataSource" ref="dataSource"/>
        <property name="packagesToScan"
            value="com.apress.prospring3.ch9.domain"/>
        <property name="hibernateProperties">
            <props>
                <prop key="hibernate.dialect">org.hibernate.dialect.H2Dialect</prop>
                <prop key="hibernate.max_fetch_depth">3</prop>
                <prop key="hibernate.jdbc.fetch_size">50</prop>
                <prop key="hibernate.jdbc.batch_size">10</prop>
                <prop key="hibernate.show_sql">true</prop>
            </props>
        </property>
    </bean>
</beans>
```

In the previous configuration, several beans were declared in order to be able to support Hibernate's session factory. The main configurations are listed here:

- *The dataSource bean*: We declared the data source with an embedded database using H2.

- *The transactionManager bean*: The Hibernate session factory requires a transaction manager for transactional data access. Spring provides a transaction manager specifically for Hibernate 3 (`org.springframework.orm.hibernate3.HibernateTransactionManager`). The bean was declared with the ID `transactionManager` assigned. By default, Spring will look up the bean with the name `transactionManager` within its `ApplicationContext` whenever transaction management is required. We will discuss transactions in detail in Chapter 13. In addition, we declare the tag `<tx:annotation-driven>` to support the declaration of transaction demarcation requirements using annotations.

- *Component scan*: This tag should be familiar to you. We instruct Spring to scan the components under the package `com.apress.prospring3.ch9`.

- *Hibernate SessionFactory bean*: The `sessionFactory` bean is the most important part. Because we are using the Hibernate's annotation support, we use the `AnnotationSessionFactoryBean`. Within the bean, several properties are provided. First, as you might expected, we need to inject the data source bean into the session factory. Second, we instruct Hibernate to scan for the domain objects with the ORM annotation under the package `com.apress.prospring3.ch9.domain`. Finally, the `hibernateProperties` property provides configuration details for Hibernate. There are many configuration parameters, and we define only several important properties that should be provided for every application. Table 9-1 lists the major configuration parameters for the Hibernate session factory.

Table 9-1. Major Hibernate Configurations

Property	Description
`hibernate.dialect`	The database dialect for the queries that Hibernate should use. Hibernate supports the SQL dialects for many databases. Those dialects are subclasses of `org.hibernate.dialect.Dialect`. Major dialects include `H2Dialect`, `Oracle10gDialect`, `PostgreSQLDialect`, `MySQLDialect`, `SQLServerDialect`, and so on.
`hibernate.max_fetch_depth`	Declares the "depth" for outer joins when the mapping objects have associations with other mapped objects. This setting prevents Hibernate from fetching too much data with a lot of nested associations. A commonly used value is 3.
`hibernate.jdbc.fetch_size`	The number of records from the underlying JDBC resultset that Hibernate should use to retrieve the records from the database for each fetch. For example, a query was submitted to the database, and the resultset contains 500 records. If the fetch size is 50, then Hibernate will need to fetch 10 times to get all the data.
`hibernate.jdbc.batch_size`	Instructs Hibernate on the number of update operations that should be grouped together into a batch. This is very useful for performing batch job operations in Hibernate. Obviously, when we are doing a batch job updating hundreds of thousands of records, we would like Hibernate to group the queries in batches, rather than submit the updates one by one.

Property	Description
hibernate.show_sql	Indicates whether Hibernate should output the SQL queries to the log file or console. You should turn this on in a development environment, which can greatly help in the testing and troubleshooting process.

For the full list of properties that Hibernate supports, please refer to Hibernate's reference manual (http://docs.jboss.org/hibernate/core/3.6/reference/en-US/html/session-configuration.html).

ORM Mapping Using Hibernate Annotations

Having the configurations in place, the next step is to model the Java POJO entity classes and their mapping to the underlying relational data structure.

There are two approaches to the mapping. The first one is to design the object model first and then generate the DB scripts based on the object model. For example, for the session factory configuration, you can pass in the Hibernate property hibernate.hbm2ddl.auto to have Hibernate automatically export the schema DDL to the database. The second approach is to start with the data model first and then model the POJOs with the desired mappings. We prefer the latter approach, because we can have more control on the data model, which is very useful in optimizing the performance of data access. Based on the data model, Figure 9-5 shows the corresponding OO model with a class diagram.

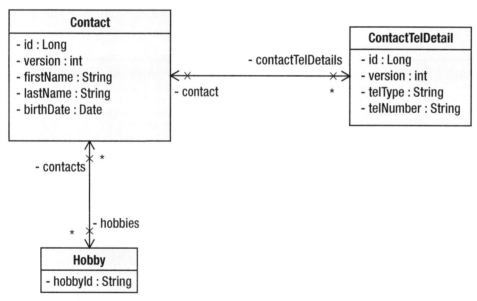

Figure 9-5. *Class diagram for the sample data model*

You can see there is a one-to-many relationship between Contact and ContactTelDetail, while there's a many-to-many relationship between the Contact and Hobby objects.

Simple Mappings

Let's begin with the mapping of simple attributes first. From the class diagram, there exists simple attributes in all three classes. Let's go through them one by one. Listing 9-5 shows the Contact class with the mapping annotations.

Listing 9-5. The Contact Class

```
package com.apress.prospring3.ch9.domain;

import static javax.persistence.GenerationType.IDENTITY;

import java.io.Serializable;
import java.util.Date;
import java.util.HashSet;
import java.util.Set;
import javax.persistence.*;

@Entity
@Table(name = "contact")
public class Contact implements Serializable {

    private Long id;
    private int version;
    private String firstName;
    private String lastName;
    private Date birthDate;

    @Id
    @GeneratedValue(strategy = IDENTITY)
    @Column(name = "ID")
    public Long getId() {
        return this.id;
    }

    public void setId(Long id) {
        this.id = id;
    }

    @Version
    @Column(name = "VERSION")
    public int getVersion() {
        return this.version;
    }

    public void setVersion(int version) {
        this.version = version;
    }

    @Column(name = "FIRST_NAME")
    public String getFirstName() {
        return this.firstName;
    }
```

```java
    public void setFirstName(String firstName) {
        this.firstName = firstName;
    }

    @Column(name = "LAST_NAME")
    public String getLastName() {
        return this.lastName;
    }

    public void setLastName(String lastName) {
        this.lastName = lastName;
    }

    @Temporal(TemporalType.DATE)
    @Column(name = "BIRTH_DATE")
    public Date getBirthDate() {
        return this.birthDate;
    }

    public void setBirthDate(Date birthDate) {
        this.birthDate = birthDate;
    }

    public String toString() {
        return "Contact - Id: " + id + ", First name: " + firstName
            + ", Last name: " + lastName + ", Birthday: " + birthDate;
    }
}
```

First, we annotate the type with @Entity, which means that this is a mapped entity class. The @Table annotation defines the table name in the database that this entity was being mapped to. For each mapped attribute, we annotate with the @Column annotation, with the column names provided. You can skip the table and column names in case the type and attribute names are exactly the same as the table and column names.

About the mappings, we would like to highlight a few points:

- For the birth date attribute, we annotate it with @Temporal, with the TemporalType DATE assigned. This means we would like to map the data type from the Java date type (java.util.Date) to the SQL data type (java.sql.Date). So, we can access the attribute birthDate in Contact object using java.util.Date as usual in our application.

- For the id attribute, we annotate it with @Id. This means it's the primary key of the object. Hibernate will use it as the unique identifier when managing the contact entity instances within its session. On the other hand, the @GeneratedValue annotation tells Hibernate how the id value was generated. The IDENTITY (we can use it directly within the annotation because of the import static statement) strategy means that the id was generated by the backend (the ID column of the CONTACT table is the primary key, with AUTO_INCREMENT specified, which means that the value will be generated and assigned by the database during insert operation) during insert.

- For the version attribute, we annotate it with @Version. This instructs Hibernate that we would like to use an optimistic locking mechanism, using the version attribute as a control. Every time Hibernate updates a record, it will compare the version of the entity instance to that of the record in the database. If both versions are the same, it means that no one updated the data before, and Hibernate will update the data and increment the version column. However, if the version is not the same, it means that someone has updated the record before, and Hibernate will throw a StaleObjectStateException exception, which Spring will translate to HibernateOptimisticLockingFailureException. In the example, we used an integer for version control. Instead of an integer, Hibernate supports using a timestamp as well. However, using an integer for version control is recommended because when using an integer, Hibernate will always increment the version number by 1 after each update. When using timestamp, Hibernate will update the latest timestamp after each update. A timestamp is slightly less safe, because two concurrent transactions may both load and update the same item in the same millisecond.

Another mapped object is ContactTelDetail, which is shown in Listing 9-6.

Listing 9-6. *The* ContactTelDetail *Class*

```
package com.apress.prospring3.ch9.domain;

// Import statements omitted
@Entity
@Table(name = "contact_tel_detail")
public class ContactTelDetail implements Serializable {

    private Long id;
    private int version;
    private String telType;
    private String telNumber;

    public ContactTelDetail() {
    }

    public ContactTelDetail(String telType, String telNumber) {
        this.telType = telType;
        this.telNumber = telNumber;
    }

    @Id
    @GeneratedValue(strategy = IDENTITY)
    @Column(name = "ID")
    public Long getId() {
        return this.id;
    }

    public void setId(Long id) {
        this.id = id;
    }

    @Version
    @Column(name = "VERSION")
    public int getVersion() {
        return this.version;
    }
```

```java
    public void setVersion(int version) {
        this.version = version;
    }

    @Column(name = "TEL_TYPE")
    public String getTelType() {
        return this.telType;
    }

    public void setTelType(String telType) {
        this.telType = telType;
    }

    @Column(name = "TEL_NUMBER")
    public String getTelNumber() {
        return this.telNumber;
    }

    public void setTelNumber(String telNumber) {
        this.telNumber = telNumber;
    }

}
```

There's nothing new for this class. Listing 9-7 shows the Hobby class.

***Listing 9-7.** The Hobby Class*

```java
package com.apress.prospring3.ch9.domain;

// Import statements omitted
@Entity
@Table(name = "hobby")
public class Hobby implements Serializable {

    private String hobbyId;

    @Id
    @Column(name = "HOBBY_ID")
    public String getHobbyId() {
        return this.hobbyId;
    }

    public void setHobbyId(String hobbyId) {
        this.hobbyId = hobbyId;
    }

    public String toString() {
        return "Hobby :" + getHobbyId();
    }
}
```

Again, there's nothing new for this mapping. Let's proceed to see how we model the associations between the Contact and ContactTelDetail classes.

One-to-Many Mappings

Hibernate has the capability to model a lot of different kinds of associations. The most common associations are one-to-many and many-to-many. For each Contact, they will have zero or more telephone numbers, so it's a one-to-many association (in ORM terms, the one-to-many association is used to model both zero-to-many and one-to-many relationships within the data structure). Listing 9-8 shows the code snippet for the Contact class for mapping with the ContactTelDetail class.

Listing 9-8. One-to-Many Association

```
package com.apress.prospring3.ch9.domain;

// Import statements omitted
@Entity
@Table(name = "contact")
public class Contact implements Serializable {

    // Other code omitted
    private Set<ContactTelDetail> contactTelDetails =
        new HashSet<ContactTelDetail>();

    @OneToMany(mappedBy = "contact", cascade=CascadeType.ALL,
        orphanRemoval=true)
    public Set<ContactTelDetail> getContactTelDetails() {
        return this.contactTelDetails;
    }

    public void setContactTelDetails(Set<ContactTelDetail> contactTelDetails) {
     this.contactTelDetails = contactTelDetails;
    }

    public void addContactTelDetail(ContactTelDetail contactTelDetail) {
        contactTelDetail.setContact(this);
        getContactTelDetails().add(contactTelDetail);
    }

    public void removeContactTelDetail(ContactTelDetail contactTelDetail) {
        getContactTelDetails().remove(contactTelDetail);
    }

}
```

As shown in Listing 9-8, the getter method of the attribute contactTelDetails is annotated with @OneToMany, which indicates the one-to-many relationship with the ContactTelDetail class. Several attributes are passed to the annotation. The mappedBy attribute indicates the property in the ContactTelDetail class that provides the association (i.e., linked up by the foreign key definition in the CONTACT_TEL_DETAIL table). The cascade attribute means that update operation should cascade to the child. The orphanRemoval means that after the contact telephone details have been updated, those entries that no longer exist in the set should be deleted from the database. Listing 9-9 shows the corresponding code snippet in the ContactTelDetail class for the association mapping.

Listing 9-9. One-to-Many Mapping in `ContactTelDetail`

```
package com.apress.prospring3.ch9.domain;

// Import statements omitted
@Entity
@Table(name = "contact_tel_detail")
public class ContactTelDetail implements Serializable {

    // Other code omitted
    private Contact contact;

    @ManyToOne
    @JoinColumn(name = "CONTACT_ID")
    public Contact getContact() {
        return this.contact;
    }

    public void setContact(Contact contact) {
        this.contact = contact;
    }

    public String toString() {
        return "Contact Tel Detail - Id: " + id + ", Contact id: "
            + getContact().getId() + ", Type: "
            + telType + ", Number: " + telNumber;
    }
}
```

From the previous listing, we annotated the getter method of the contact attribute with @ManyToOne, which indicates it's the other side of the association from Contact. We also specified the @JoinColumn annotation for the underlying foreign key column name. Finally, the toString() method was overridden to facilitate testing the example code later.

Many-to-Many Mappings

Let's move on to see the many-to-many mapping between the Contact and Hobby classes. Every contact has zero or more hobbies, and each hobby will also be linked up with zero or more contacts. So, it's a many-to-many mapping. A many-to-many mapping requires a join table, which is the CONTACT_HOBBY_DETAIL table in Figure 9-4. Listing 9-10 shows the code snippet in the Contact class to model the relationship.

Listing 9-10. Many-to-Many Association

```
package com.apress.prospring3.ch9.domain;

// Import statements omitted
@Entity
@Table(name = "contact")
public class Contact implements Serializable {

    // Rest of code omitted
    private Set<Hobby> hobbies = new HashSet<Hobby>();
```

```
@ManyToMany
@JoinTable(name = "contact_hobby_detail",
    joinColumns = @JoinColumn(name = "CONTACT_ID"),
    inverseJoinColumns = @JoinColumn(name = "HOBBY_ID"))
public Set<Hobby> getHobbies() {
    return this.hobbies;
}

public void setHobbies(Set<Hobby> hobbies) {
    this.hobbies = hobbies;
}
}
```

As shown in Listing 9-10, the getter method of the attribute hobbies in the Contact class are annotated with @ManyToMany. We also provide the @JoinTable to indicate the underlying join table that Hibernate should look for. The name is the join table's name, the joinColumns defines the column that is the FK to CONTACT table, and the inverseJoinColumns defines the column that is the FK to the other side of the association, i.e., the HOBBY table. Listing 9-11 shows the corresponding code snippet in the Hobby class.

Listing 9-11. Many-to-Many Mapping in the Hobby Class

```
package com.apress.prospring3.ch9.domain;

// Import statements omitted

@Entity
@Table(name = "hobby")
public class Hobby implements Serializable {

    // Other code omitted

    private Set<Contact> contacts = new HashSet<Contact>();

    @ManyToMany
    @JoinTable(name = "contact_hobby_detail",
        joinColumns = @JoinColumn(name = "HOBBY_ID"),
        inverseJoinColumns = @JoinColumn(name = "CONTACT_ID"))
    public Set<Contact> getContacts() {
        return this.contacts;
    }

    public void setContacts(Set<Contact> contacts) {
        this.contacts = contacts;
    }
}
```

The mapping is more or less the same as Listing 9-10, but the joinColumns and inverseJoinColumns attributes are reversed to reflect the association.

The Hibernate Session Interface

In Hibernate, when interacting with the database, the major interface you need to deal with is the Session interface, which is obtained from the SessionFactory.

Listing 9-12 shows that the ContactDaoImpl class contains the samples in this chapter. The configured Hibernate SessionFactory was injected into the class.

Listing 9-12. *Injecting Hibernate SessionFactory*

```
package com.apress.prospring3.ch9.dao.hibernate;

// Import statements omitted
@Repository("contactDao")
@Transactional
public class ContactDaoImpl implements ContactDao {

    // Other code omitted
    private Log log = LogFactory.getLog(ContactDaoImpl.class);

    private SessionFactory sessionFactory;

    public SessionFactory getSessionFactory() {
        return sessionFactory;
    }

    @Resource(name="sessionFactory")
    public void setSessionFactory(SessionFactory sessionFactory) {
        this.sessionFactory = sessionFactory;
    }
}
```

As usual, we declare the DAO class as a Spring bean with data access logic using the @Repository annotation. The @Transactional annotation defines the transaction requirements that we will discuss in Chapter 13. The sessionFactory attribute was set to be injected by using the @Resource annotation.

Database Operations with Hibernate

In this section, we will discuss how to perform database operations in Hibernate. Listing 9-13 shows the ContactDao interface, which indicates the contact data access services we are going to provide.

Listing 9-13. *The ContactDao Interface*

```
package com.apress.prospring3.ch9.dao;

import java.util.List;

import com.apress.prospring3.ch9.domain.Contact;

public interface ContactDao {

    // Find all contacts
    public List<Contact> findAll();

    // Find all contacts with telephone and hobbies
    public List<Contact> findAllWithDetail();

    // Find a contact with details by id
```

```
    public Contact findById(Long id);

    // Insert or update a contact
    public Contact save(Contact contact);

    // Delete a contact
    public void delete(Contact contact);
}
```

The interface is very simple; it has just three finder methods, one save method, and one delete method. The save() method will perform both the insert and update operations.

For the implementation class, the com.apress.prospring3.ch9.dao.hibernate.ContactDaoImpl class, we begin with creating the class with an empty implementation of all the methods in the ContactDao interface. In STS, it's very easy to do it. For details, please see the section "Setting UP JDBC DAO Using Annotations" in Chapter 8.

Query Data Using Hibernate Query Language

Hibernate, together with other ORM tools such as JDO and JPA, is engineered around the object model. So, after the mappings are defined, we don't need to construct SQL to interact with the database. Instead, for Hibernate, we use the Hibernate Query Language (HQL) to define our queries. When interacting with the database, Hibernate will translate the queries into SQL statements on our behalf.

When coding HQL queries, the syntax is quite like SQL. However, you need to think on the object side rather than data side. We will go through several examples in the following sections.

Simple Query with Lazy Fetching

Let's begin with the findAll() method, which simply retrieves all the contacts from the database. Listing 9-14 shows the code snippet.

Listing 9-14. Implementing the findAll Method

```
package com.apress.prospring3.ch9.dao.hibernate;

// Import statements omitted
@Repository("contactDao")
@Transactional
public class ContactDaoImpl implements ContactDao {

    // Other code omitted
    @Transactional(readOnly=true)
    public List<Contact> findAll() {
        return sessionFactory.getCurrentSession().
        createQuery("from Contact c").list();
    }
}
```

As shown in Listing 9-14, the method SessionFactory.getCurrentSession() gets hold of Hibernate's Session interface. Then, the Session.createQuery() method is called, passing in the HQL statement. The statement from Contact c simply retrieves all contacts from the database. An alternative syntax for the statement is select c from Contact c. The @Transactional(readOnly=true), which means we want the transaction to be set as read-only. Setting that attribute for finder methods will result in better performance.

Listing 9-15 shows a simple testing program for ContactDaoImpl.

Listing 9-15. *Testing the ContactDaoImpl Class*

```
package com.apress.prospring3.ch9;

import java.util.List;

import org.springframework.context.support.GenericXmlApplicationContext;

import com.apress.prospring3.ch9.dao.ContactDao;
import com.apress.prospring3.ch9.domain.Contact;

public class SpringHibernateSample {

    public static void main(String[] args) {

        GenericXmlApplicationContext ctx = new GenericXmlApplicationContext();
        ctx.load("classpath:app-context.xml");
        ctx.refresh();

        ContactDao contactDao = ctx.getBean("contactDao", ContactDao.class);
        List<Contact> contacts = contactDao.findAll();
        listContacts(contacts);

    }

    private static void listContacts(List<Contact> contacts) {
        System.out.println("");
        System.out.println("Listing contacts without details:");
        for (Contact contact: contacts) {
            System.out.println(contact);
            System.out.println();
        }
    }
}
```

Running the previous class will yield the following output:

```
Listing contacts without details:
Contact - Id: 1, First name: Clarence, Last name: Ho, Birthday: 1980-07-30

Contact - Id: 2, First name: Scott, Last name: Tiger, Birthday: 1990-11-02

Contact - Id: 3, First name: John, Last name: Smith, Birthday: 1964-02-28
```

The contact records were retrieved. However, what about the telephone and hobby details? Let's create a new method in the testing class to dump the details information. Listing 9-16 shows the code snippet.

Listing 9-16. *Testing the ContactDaoImpl Class*

```
// Other code omitted
public class SpringHibernateSample {
```

```java
public static void main(String[] args) {

    GenericXmlApplicationContext ctx = new GenericXmlApplicationContext();
    ctx.load("classpath:app-context.xml");
    ctx.refresh();

    ContactDao contactDao = ctx.getBean("contactDao", ContactDao.class);
    List<Contact> contacts = contactDao.findAll();
    listContactsWithDetail (contacts);

}

private static void listContactsWithDetail(List<Contact> contacts) {
    System.out.println("");
    System.out.println("Listing contacts with details:");
    for (Contact contact: contacts) {
        System.out.println(contact);
        if (contact.getContactTelDetails() != null) {
            for (ContactTelDetail contactTelDetail:
                    contact.getContactTelDetails()) {
                System.out.println(contactTelDetail);
            }
        }
        if (contact.getHobbies() != null) {
            for (Hobby hobby: contact.getHobbies()) {
                System.out.println(hobby);
            }
        }
        System.out.println();
    }
}
}
```

If you run the program again, you will see the following exception:

```
Listing contacts with details:
Contact - Id: 1, First name: Clarence, Last name: Ho, Birthday: 1980-07-30
Exception in thread "main" org.hibernate.LazyInitializationException:
…
```

You will see Hibernate throw the LazyInitializationException when you try to access the associations. It's because, by default, Hibernate will fetch the associations "lazily," which means that Hibernate will not join the association tables (i.e., CONTACT_TEL_DETAIL) for records. The rationale behind this is for performance consideration, since as you can imagine, if a query is retrieving thousands of records and all the associations were retrieved, there will be a massive amount of data transfer.

Query with Associations Fetching

To have Hibernate fetch the data from associations, there are two options. First, you can define the association with the fetch mode EAGER. The following is an example annotation:

```java
@ManyToMany(fetch=FetchType.EAGER)
```

This tells Hibernate to fetch the associated records in every query. However, as discussed, this will impact data retrieval performance.

The other option is to force Hibernate to fetch the associated records in the query when required. If you use Criteria query, you can call the function Criteria.setFetchMode() to instruct Hibernate to eagerly fetch the association. When using NamedQuery, you can use the "fetch" operator to instruct Hibernate to fetch the association eagerly.

Let's take a look at the implementation of the findAllWithDetail() method, which will retrieve all contact information together with their telephone details and hobbies. We will use the NamedQuery approach. The NamedQuery can be externalized into an XML file or declared using annotation in the entity class. Listing 9-17 shows the revised Contact domain object with the named query defined using annotations.

Listing 9-17. Using NamedQuery

```
@Entity
@Table(name = "contact")
@NamedQueries({
@NamedQuery(name="Contact.findAllWithDetail",
query="select distinct c from Contact c left join fetch c.contactTelDetails t left join fetch c.hobbies h")
})
public class Contact implements Serializable {
    // Other code omitted
}
```

From Listing 9-17, a NamedQuery called Contact.findAllWithDetail was defined. Then we define the query in HQL. Pay attention to the left join fetch clause, which instructs Hibernate to fetch the association eagerly. You also need to use select distinct; otherwise, Hibernate will return duplicate objects (e.g. , two contact objects will be returned if a single contact has two telephone details).

Listing 9-18 shows the implementation of the findAllWithDetail() method.

Listing 9-18. Implementing the findAllWithDetail Method

```
package com.apress.prospring3.ch9.dao.hibernate;

// Import statements omitted
@Repository("contactDao")
@Transactional
public class ContactDaoImpl implements ContactDao {

    // Other code omitted
    @Transactional(readOnly=true)
    public List<Contact> findAllWithDetail() {
        return sessionFactory.getCurrentSession().
        getNamedQuery("Contact.findAllWithDetail").list();
    }
}
```

This time we use the Session.getNamedQuery() method, passing in the name of the NamedQuery. Modifying the testing program to call ContactDao.findAllWithDetail() will yield the following output:

```
Listing contacts with details:
Contact - Id: 1, First name: Clarence, Last name: Ho, Birthday: 1980-07-30
Contact Tel Detail - Id: 2, Contact id: 1, Type: Home, Number: 1234567890
Contact Tel Detail - Id: 1, Contact id: 1, Type: Mobile, Number: 1234567890
```

```
Hobby :Swimming
Hobby :Movies

Contact - Id: 2, First name: Scott, Last name: Tiger, Birthday: 1990-11-02
Contact Tel Detail - Id: 3, Contact id: 2, Type: Home, Number: 1234567890
Hobby :Swimming

Contact - Id: 3, First name: John, Last name: Smith, Birthday: 1964-02-28
```

Now all the contacts with details were retrieved correctly.

Let's see another example with NamedQuery with parameters. This time, we will implement the findById() method and would like to fetch the associations as well. Listing 9-19 shows the Contact class with the new named query added.

Listing 9-19. Using NamedQuery with Parameters

```
@Entity
@Table(name = "contact")
@NamedQueries({
@NamedQuery(name="Contact.findById",
query="select distinct c from Contact c left join fetch c.contactTelDetails t
left join fetch c.hobbies h where c.id = :id"),
@NamedQuery(name="Contact.findAllWithDetail",
query="select distinct c from Contact c left join fetch c.contactTelDetails t left join  fetch
c.hobbies h")
})
public class Contact implements Serializable {
    // Other code omitted
}
```

From the named query with the name Contact.findById, we declare a named parameter :id. Listing 9-20 shows the implementation of the findById() in ContactDaoImpl.

Listing 9-20. Implementing the findById Method

```
package com.apress.prospring3.ch9.dao.hibernate;

// Import statements omitted
@Repository("contactDao")
@Transactional
public class ContactDaoImpl implements ContactDao {

    // Other code omitted
    @Transactional(readOnly=true)
    public Contact findById(Long id) {
        return (Contact) sessionFactory.getCurrentSession().
            getNamedQuery("Contact.findById").
            setParameter("id", id).uniqueResult();
    }
}
```

From Listing 9-20, we use the same Session.getNameQuery() method. But then we also call the setParameter() method, passing in the named parameter with its value. For multiple parameters, you can use the setParameterList() or setParameters() method of the Query interface.

There also exists some more advanced query methods, like native query and criteria query, which we will discuss in the next chapter when we talk about JPA.

To test the method, add the code snippet in Listing 9-21 into the `SpringHibernateSample` class.

Listing 9-21. Testing the findById Method

```
Contact contact;

// Find contact by ID
contact = contactDao.findById(1l);
System.out.println("");
System.out.println("Contact with id 1:" + contact);
System.out.println("");
```

Running the program will produce the following output (other output was omitted):

```
Contact with id 1:Contact - Id: 1, First name: Clarence, Last name: Ho, Birthday: 1980-07-30
```

Inserting Data

Inserting data in Hibernate is very simple. One other fancy thing is retrieving the database-generated primary key. In the previous chapter on JDBC, we needed to explicitly declare that we wanted to retrieve the generated key, pass in the KeyHolder, and get the key back from it after executing the insert statement. With Hibernate, all those actions are not required. Hibernate will cleverly retrieve the generated key and populate the domain object after insert. Listing 9-22 shows the implementation of the save() method.

Listing 9-22. Implementing the save Method

```
package com.apress.prospring3.ch9.dao.hibernate;

// Import statements omitted
@Repository("contactDao")
@Transactional
public class ContactDaoImpl implements ContactDao {

    // Other code omitted
    public Contact save(Contact contact) {
        sessionFactory.getCurrentSession().saveOrUpdate(contact);
        log.info("Contact saved with id: " + contact.getId());
        return contact;
    }
}
```

We just need to invoke the `Session.saveOrUpdate()` method, which can be used for both insert and update operations. We also log the ID of the saved contact object that will be populated by Hibernate after the object is persisted. Let's test the insert operation. Listing 9-23 shows the code snippet for inserting a new contact record. Add the code snippet into the `SpringHibernateSample` class.

Listing 9-23. Testing Insert Operation

```
// Add new contact
contact = new Contact();
contact.setFirstName("Michael");
```

```
contact.setLastName("Jackson");
contact.setBirthDate(new Date());
ContactTelDetail contactTelDetail =
    new ContactTelDetail("Home", "1111111111");
contact.addContactTelDetail(contactTelDetail);
contactTelDetail = new ContactTelDetail("Mobile", "2222222222");
contact.addContactTelDetail(contactTelDetail);
contactDao.save(contact);
contacts = contactDao.findAllWithDetail();
listContactsWithDetail(contacts);
```

As shown in Listing 9-23, we create a new contact, add two telephone details, and save the object. Afterward, we list all the contacts again. Running the program yields the following output:

```
Hibernate: insert into contact_tel_detail (ID, CONTACT_ID, TEL_NUMBER, TEL_TYPE, VERSION)
values (null, ?, ?, ?, ?)
2011-10-13 15:25:52,405 INFO [com.apress.prospring3.ch9.dao.hibernate.ContactDaoImpl] -
<Contact saved with id: 4>

Listing contacts with details:
Contact - Id: 1, First name: Clarence, Last name: Ho, Birthday: 1980-07-30
Contact Tel Detail - Id: 1, Contact id: 1, Type: Mobile, Number: 1234567890
Contact Tel Detail - Id: 2, Contact id: 1, Type: Home, Number: 1234567890
Hobby :Swimming
Hobby :Movies

Contact - Id: 4, First name: Michael, Last name: Jackson, Birthday: 2011-10-13
Contact Tel Detail - Id: 4, Contact id: 4, Type: Mobile, Number: 2222222222
Contact Tel Detail - Id: 5, Contact id: 4, Type: Home, Number: 1111111111

Contact - Id: 3, First name: John, Last name: Smith, Birthday: 1964-02-28

Contact - Id: 2, First name: Scott, Last name: Tiger, Birthday: 1990-11-02
Contact Tel Detail - Id: 3, Contact id: 2, Type: Home, Number: 1234567890
Hobby :Swimming
```

From the INFO log record, you can see that the id of the newly saved contact was populated correctly. Hibernate will also show all the SQL statements being fired to the database so you know what is actually happening behind the scenes.

Updating Data

Updating a contact is as easy as inserting data. Let's go through an example. Suppose for the contact with an ID of 1, we want to update its first name and remove the home telephone record. To test the update operation, add the code snippet in Listing 9-24 into the SpringHibernateSample class.

Listing 9-24. Testing Update Operation

```
// Update contact
contact = contactDao.findById(1l);
contact.setFirstName("Kim Fung");
Set<ContactTelDetail> contactTels = contact.getContactTelDetails();
ContactTelDetail toDeleteContactTel = null;
for (ContactTelDetail contactTel: contactTels) {
```

```
        if (contactTel.getTelType().equals("Home")) {
            toDeleteContactTel = contactTel;
        }
    }

    contact.removeContactTelDetail(toDeleteContactTel);
    contactDao.save(contact);
    contacts = contactDao.findAllWithDetail();
    listContactsWithDetail(contacts);
```

As shown in the previous listing, we first retrieve the record with an ID of 1. Afterward, the first name is changed. Then we loop through the telephone objects, retrieve the one with type "Home", and remove it from the contact's telephone detail property. Finally, we call the ContactDao.save() method again. When you run the program, you will see the following output (the other output was omitted):

```
Contact - Id: 1, First name: Kim Fung, Last name: Ho, Birthday: 1980-07-30
Contact Tel Detail - Id: 1, Contact id: 1, Type: Mobile, Number: 1234567890
Hobby :Movies
Hobby :Swimming
```

You will see the first name was updated, and the home telephone was removed. The telephone can be removed because of the orphanRemoval=true attribute we pass into the one-to-many association, which instructs Hibernate to remove all orphan records that exist in the database but are no longer found in the object when persisted.

```
@OneToMany(mappedBy = "contact", cascade=CascadeType.ALL, orphanRemoval=true)
```

Deleting Data

Deleting data is simple as well. Just call the Session.delete() method and pass in the contact object. Listing 9-25 shows the code snippet.

Listing 9-25. Implementing the delete Method

```
package com.apress.prospring3.ch9.dao.hibernate;

// Import statements omitted
@Repository("contactDao")
@Transactional
public class ContactDaoImpl implements ContactDao {

    // Other code omitted
    public void delete(Contact contact) {
        sessionFactory.getCurrentSession().delete(contact);
        log.info("Contact deleted with id: " + contact.getId());
    }
}
```

The delete operation will delete the contact record, together with all its associated information, including telephone details and hobbies, as we defined cascade=CascadeType.ALL in the mapping. Listing 9-26 shows the code snippet for testing the delete method. Add it into the SpringHibernateSample class for testing.

Listing 9-26. Testing Delete Operation

```
// Delete contact
contact = contactDao.findById(1l);
contactDao.delete(contact);
contacts = contactDao.findAllWithDetail();
listContactsWithDetail(contacts);
```

The previous listing retrieves the contact with an ID of 1 and then calls the delete method to delete the contact information. Running the program will produce the following output (other output was omitted):

```
Listing contacts with details:
Contact - Id: 4, First name: Michael, Last name: Jackson, Birthday: 2011-10-13
Contact Tel Detail - Id: 4, Contact id: 4, Type: Home, Number: 1111111111
Contact Tel Detail - Id: 5, Contact id: 4, Type: Mobile, Number: 2222222222

Contact - Id: 3, First name: John, Last name: Smith, Birthday: 1964-02-28

Contact - Id: 2, First name: Scott, Last name: Tiger, Birthday: 1990-11-02
Contact Tel Detail - Id: 3, Contact id: 2, Type: Home, Number: 1234567890
Hobby :Swimming
```

You can see that the contact with an ID of 1 was deleted.

Considerations of Using Hibernate

As you saw in the examples in this chapter, once all the object-to-relational mapping, associations, and queries are properly defined, Hibernate can provide an environment for you to focus on programming with the object model, rather than composing SQL statements for each operation. In the past few years, Hibernate has been evolving quickly and has been widely adopted by Java developers as the data access layer library, both in the open source community and in enterprises.

However, there are some points you need to bear in mind. First, because you don't have control over the generated SQL, you should be very careful when defining the mappings, especially the associations and their fetching strategy. Then observe the SQL statements generated by Hibernate to verify that all perform as you expect.

Understanding the internal mechanism of how Hibernate manages its session is also very important, especially in batch job operations. Hibernate will keep the managed objects in session and will flush and clear them regularly. Poorly designed data access logic may cause Hibernate to flush the session too frequently and greatly impact the performance. If you want absolute control over the query, you can use a native query, which we will discuss in next chapter.

Finally, the settings (batch size, fetch size, etc.) also play an important role in tuning Hibernate's performance. You should define them in your session factory and adjust them while load testing your application to identify the optimal value.

After all, Hibernate, and its excellent JPA support that we will discuss in next chapter, is a natural decision for Java developers looking for an OO way to implement data access logic.

Summary

In this chapter, we discussed the basic concepts of Hibernate and how to configure it within a Spring application. Then we covered common techniques for defining ORM mappings, and we covered associations and how to use the `HibernateTemplate` class to perform various database operations.

With regarding to Hibernate, we covered only a small piece of its functionalities and features. For those interested in using Hibernate with Spring, we highly recommend you study Hibernate's standard documentation. Also, numerous books discuss Hibernate in detail. I recommend *Beginning Hibernate*, Second Edition, and *Pro JPA 2: Mastering the Java Persistence API* (2009), both from Apress.

In the next chapter, we will take a look at the Java Persistence API (JPA) and how to use it when using Spring. Hibernate provides excellent support for JPA, and we will continue to use Hibernate as the persistence provider for the examples in next chapter. For query and update operations, JPA act likes Hibernate. So, in the next chapter, we will discuss some advanced topics including native and criteria query and how we use Hibernate and its JPA support in the sample application.

Data Access in Spring with JPA2

In the previous chapter, we discussed how to use Hibernate in Spring applications when implementing data access logic with the ORM approach. We demonstrated how to configure Hibernate's SessionFactory in Spring's configuration and how to use Hibernate's Session interface for various data access operations.

However, what we discussed in the previous chapter was just one aspect of Hibernate's usage. Another way of adopting Hibernate in a Spring application is to use Hibernate as a persistence provider of the JCP standard, the Java Persistence API (JPA).

As discussed earlier, Hibernate's POJO base mapping and its powerful query language (HQL) have gained great success and have influenced the development of data access technology standards in the Java world. After Hibernate, the JCP developed the Java Data Objects (JDO) standard and then JPA.

At the time of this writing, JPA has reached 2.0 (which is part of the JEE 6 technology stack); it is a much more mature technology and is being widely adopted by developers as the data access API standard. This is because JPA has standardized the ORM programming model with concepts such as PersistenceContext, EntityManager, and the Java Persistence Query Language (JPQL). These standardizations provide a way for developers to switch between JPA persistence providers such as Hibernate, EclipseLink, Oracle TopLink, OpenJPA, and so on. As a result, most new JEE applications are now adopting JPA as the data access layer.

Spring also provides intensive support for JPA. For example, a number of EntityManagerFactoryBeans are provided for bootstrapping a JPA entity manager in a Spring application, with support for all of the JPA providers mentioned earlier. The Spring Data project also provides a subproject called Spring Data JPA, which provides advanced support for using JPA in Spring applications. The main features of the Spring Data JPA project include the concepts of Repository and Specification, support for the Query Domain Specific Language (QueryDSL), and so on.

In this chapter, we will discuss how to use JPA (specifically JPA 2) with Spring, using Hibernate as the underlying persistence provider. You will learn how to implement the various database operations using JPA's EntityManager interface and JPQL (which is similar to HQL). Then we will discuss how Spring Data JPA can further help simplify JPA development. Finally, we will discuss some advanced topics related to ORM, including native queries and criteria queries.

Specifically, we will discuss the following topics:

- *Core concepts of JPA:* We will cover some of the major concepts of JPA.

- *Creating a simple Spring JPA utility project:* We will go through the steps for creating a Spring-based JPA project using STS. Although STS creates the project with required dependencies, we still need to fine-tune the project configurations in order to support all the features discussed in this chapter. As we move on to more advanced topics, additional third-party libraries will be required, so we will demonstrate how to add them in STS.

- *Configuring the JPA entity manager:* We will discuss the types of
  EntityManagerFactorys that Spring supports and how to configure the most
  commonly used one, LocalContainerEntityManagerFactoryBean, in Spring's XML
  configuration.

- *Data operations:* We will go through how to implement basic database operations
  in JPA. The concepts are quite like Hibernate. We will also discuss eliminating the
  DAO layer in JPA applications.

- *Advanced query operations:* We will discuss how to use native queries in JPA and
  the strongly typed criteria API in JPA for more flexible query operations.

- *Introducing Spring Data JPA:* We will discuss the Spring Data JPA project and
  demonstrate how it can help simplify the development of data access logic.

- *Tracking entity changes and auditing:* In database update operations, it's a
  common requirement in keep track of the date an entity was created or last
  updated and who made the change. Also, for critical information such as a
  customer, a history table that stores each version of the entity is always required.
  We will discuss how Spring Data JPA and Hibernate Envers (Hibernate Entity
  Versioning System) can help ease the development of such logic.

- *Using JPA with Hibernate in the sample application:* In the sample application, for
  the JPA implementation, we have chosen to eliminate the DAO layer and inject the
  entity manager directly into the service layer for executing the business logic. We
  will discuss how JPA will be adopted in the sample application.

■ **Note** Like Hibernate, JPA supports the definition of mappings either in XML or in Java annotations. In this
chapter, we will focus on the annotation type of mapping, because its usage is much more popular than the
XML style.

Introducing JPA 2

Like many other Java specification requests (JSRs), the objective of the JPA 2.0 specification (JSR-317) is
to standardize the ORM programming model in both the JSE and JEE environments. It defines a
common set of concepts, annotations, interfaces, and other services that a JPA persistence provider
should implement (all of them are put under the javax.persistence package). When programming to
the JPA standard, developers have the option of switching the underlying provider at will, just like
switching to another JEE-compliant application server for applications developed on the JEE standards.

Within JPA, the core concept is the EntityManager interface, which comes from factories of type
EntityManagerFactory. The main job of EntityManager is to maintain a persistence context, in which all
the entity instances under management will be stored. The configuration of an EntityManager is defined
as a persistence unit, and there can be more than one persistence unit in an application. If you are using
Hibernate, you can think of the persistence context as the same as the Session interface, while the
EntityManagerFactory is the same as the SessionFactory. In Hibernate, the managed entities are stored
in the session, which you can directly interact with via Hibernate's SessionFactory or Session interface.
However, in JPA, you can't interact with the persistence context directly. Instead, you need to rely on
EntityManager to do the work for you.

JPQL is very similar to HQL, so if you have used HQL before, it shouldn't be difficult for you to
manage JPQL. However, in JPA 2, a strongly typed criteria API was introduced, which relies on the

mapped entities' metadata to construct the query, so any errors will be discovered at compile time rather than runtime.

For a detailed discussion of JPA 2, we recommend the book *Pro JPA 2: Mastering the Java Persistence API* (Apress, 2009).

In this section, we will discuss the basic concepts of JPA, the sample data model that will be used in this chapter, and how to configure Spring's `ApplicationContext` to support JPA.

Creating a Simple Spring JPA Utility Project in STS

Let's create a JPA project in STS first. STS provides a template project called Simple Spring JPA Utility Project. To create such a project in STS, simply select New Project ➤ Spring Template Project, choose Simple Spring JPA Utility Project, and then enter the details for the project. Figure 10-1 shows the New Template Project dialog box, and Figure 10-2 shows the project settings.

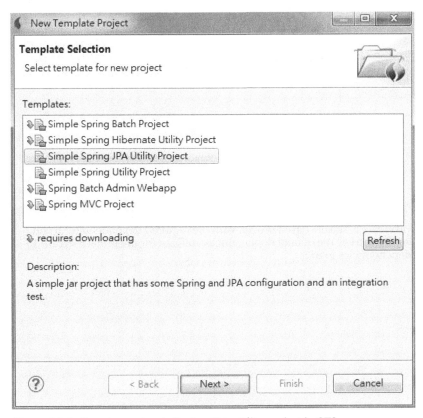

Figure 10-1. Creating a simple Spring JPA utility project in STS

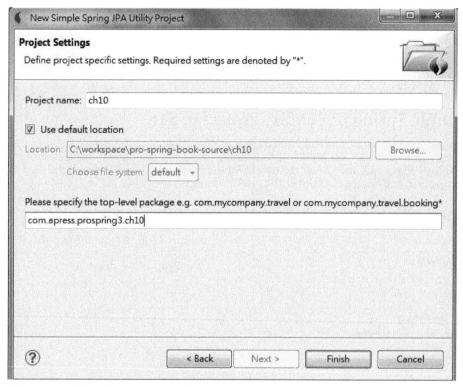

Figure 10-2. Simple Spring JPA utility project details

Upon completion, STS will create a Maven-based project with the required dependencies. If you open the project's pom.xml file, you will see the default dependencies defined for the project. Figure 10-3 shows a partial listing of the dependencies in STS.

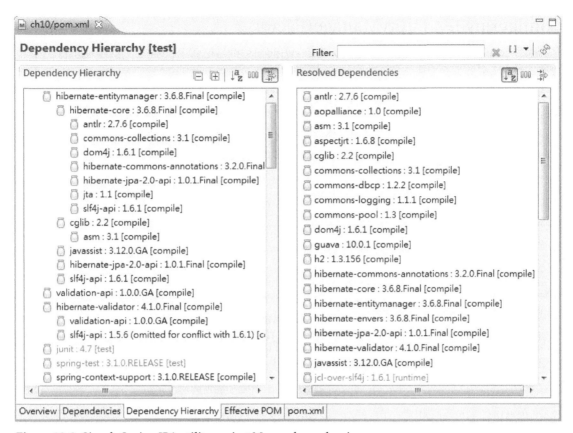

Figure 10-3. Simple Spring JPA utility project Maven dependencies

As you can see from Figure 10-3, Spring defaults to using Hibernate as the JPA provider for the JPA template project. Another step you need to take is to update the pom.xml file to use JDK 6 as the target runtime and update the project's configuration. Make sure the project is using Spring 3.1.

At the time of this writing, the JPA template project will add Hibernate version 3.6.0.Final as the dependency. Please change it to 3.6.8.Final within the pom.xml file, since the newer version provides bug fixes to the samples discussed in this chapter.

Sample Data Model for Example Code

In this chapter, we will use the same data model as Chapter 9. However, when we discuss how to implement the auditing features, we will add a few columns and a history table for demonstration. So, we will start with the same database creation scripts used in the previous chapter.

If you skipped Chapter 9, take a look at the data model presented in that chapter's "Sample Data Model for Example Code" section, which can help you understand the sample code in this chapter.

Configuring JPA EntityManagerFactory

As mentioned earlier in this chapter, to use JPA in Spring, we need to configure an EntityManagerFactory in Spring, just like the SessionFactory in Hibernate. Spring supports three types of EntityManagerFactory configuration.

The first one is using the LocalEntityManagerFactoryBean class. It's the simplest one, which requires only the persistence unit name. However, since it doesn't support the injection of a datasource and hence isn't able to participate in global transactions, it's suitable only for simple deployment.

The second option is for use in a JEE 6–compliant container, in which the application server bootstraps the JPA persistence unit based on the information in the deployment descriptors, so Spring will be able to look up the entity manager via JNDI lookup. Listing 10-1 shows a code snippet for looking up an entity manager via JNDI.

Listing 10-1. Looking Up Entity Manager via JNDI

```
<beans>
    <jee:jndi-lookup id="prospring3Emf"
        jndi-name="persistence/prospring3PersistenceUnit"/>
</beans>
```

In the JPA specification, a persistence unit should be defined in the configuration file META-INF/persistence.xml. However, Spring 3.1 provides a new feature that eliminates this need. We will show you that feature in this section.

The third option, which is the most common and will be used in this chapter as well as in the sample application, is the LocalContainerEntityManagerFactoryBean class. It supports the injection of a datasource and can participate in both local and global transactions. Listing 10-2 shows the corresponding XML configuration file (app-context.xml).

Listing 10-2. Spring Configuration for LocalContainerEntityManagerFactoryBean

```
<?xml version="1.0" encoding="UTF-8"?>
<beans xmlns="http://www.springframework.org/schema/beans"
    xmlns:xsi=http://www.w3.org/2001/XMLSchema-instance
    xmlns:context="http://www.springframework.org/schema/context"
    xmlns:jdbc=http://www.springframework.org/schema/jdbc
    xmlns:tx="http://www.springframework.org/schema/tx"
    xsi:schemaLocation="http://www.springframework.org/schema/jdbc
        http://www.springframework.org/schema/jdbc/spring-jdbc-3.1.xsd
        http://www.springframework.org/schema/beans
        http://www.springframework.org/schema/beans/spring-beans-3.1.xsd
        http://www.springframework.org/schema/tx
        http://www.springframework.org/schema/tx/spring-tx-3.1.xsd
        http://www.springframework.org/schema/context
        http://www.springframework.org/schema/context/spring-context-3.1.xsd">

    <description>Example configuration to get you started.</description>

    <jdbc:embedded-database id="dataSource" type="H2">
        <jdbc:script location="classpath:schema.sql"/>
        <jdbc:script location="classpath:test-data.sql"/>
    </jdbc:embedded-database>

    <bean id="transactionManager"
```

```
        class="org.springframework.orm.jpa.JpaTransactionManager">
        <property name="entityManagerFactory" ref="emf"/>
    </bean>

    <tx:annotation-driven transaction-manager="transactionManager" />

    <bean id="emf" class="org.springframework.orm.jpa.LocalContainerEntityManagerFactoryBean">
        <property name="dataSource" ref="dataSource" />
        <property name="jpaVendorAdapter">
            <bean class="org.springframework.orm.jpa.vendor.HibernateJpaVendorAdapter" />
        </property>
        <property name="packagesToScan"
            value="com.apress.prospring3.ch10.domain"/>
        <property name="jpaProperties">
            <props>
                <prop key="hibernate.dialect">
                    org.hibernate.dialect.H2Dialect
                </prop>
                <prop key="hibernate.max_fetch_depth">3</prop>
                <prop key="hibernate.jdbc.fetch_size">50</prop>
                <prop key="hibernate.jdbc.batch_size">10</prop>
                <prop key="hibernate.show_sql">true</prop>
            </props>
        </property>
    </bean>

    <context:annotation-config/>

    <context:component-scan
        base-package="com.apress.prospring3.ch10.service.jpa" />
</beans>
```

In the previous configuration, several beans are declared in order to be able to support the configuration of LocalContainerEntityManagerFactoryBean with Hibernate as the persistence provider. The main configurations are as follows:

- *The dataSource bean:* We declared the datasource with an embedded database using H2. Because it's an embedded database, the database name is not required.

- *The transactionManager bean:* The entity manager factory requires a transaction manager for transactional data access. Spring provides a transaction manager specifically for JPA (org.springframework.orm.jpa.JpaTransactionManager). The bean is declared with an ID of transactionManager assigned. We will discuss transactions in detail in Chapter 13. We declare the tag <tx:annotation-driven> to support a declaration of the transaction demarcation requirements using annotations.

- *Component scan:* The tag should be familiar to you. We instruct Spring to scan the components under the package com.apress.prospring3.ch10.service.jpa.

- *JPA EntityManagerFactory bean (emf):* The emf bean is the most important part. First, we declare the bean to use the LocalContainerEntityManagerFactoryBean. Within the bean, several properties are provided. First, as you might expected, we need to inject the datasource bean. Second, we configure the property jpaVendorAdapter with the class HibernateJpaVendorAdapter, because we are using

Hibernate. Third, we instruct the entity factory to scan for the domain objects with ORM annotations under the package `com.apress.prospring3.ch10.domain` (specified by the `<property name="packagesToScan">` tag). Note that this feature has been available only since Spring 3.1, and with the support of domain class scanning, you can skip the definition of the persistence unit in the `META-INF/persistence.xml` file. Finally, the `jpaProperties` property provides configuration details for the persistence provider, Hibernate. You will see that the configuration is just the same as those we used in Chapter 9. So, we will skip the explanation here.

ORM Mapping Using JPA Annotations

As mentioned, Hibernate influenced the design of JPA a lot. For the mapping annotations, they are so close that the annotations we used in Chapter 9 for mapping the domain objects to the database are the same in JPA.

If you take a look at the domain classes source code in Chapter 9, you will see that all mapping annotations are under the package `javax.persistence`, which means those annotations are already JPA compatible. So, we didn't repeat the code in this chapter. Please refer to Chapter 9 for the mappings and explanations.

Eliminating the DAO Layer

As you already saw in Chapter 8 and Chapter 9, when we use JDBC and Hibernate for programming data access logic, we use the DAO pattern. The intention of the DAO pattern is to wrap the different implementations of data access logic into its own layer so that those details are totally hidden from the service layer and the service layer is not aware of whether we are using JDBC or Hibernate in getting the data access job done.

However, after JPA was born, the justification of the existence of a DAO layer for data access logic becomes questionable. Because JPA was designed to be a standard in which the underlying persistence provider can be switched easily, there's simply no strong reason to maintain the data access logic in a separate DAO layer. So, nowadays, many JEE developers who standardized on JPA as the data access layer have chosen to eliminate the DAO layer and have the `EntityManager` directly injected into the service layer.

The justification of the existence of a DAO layer in JEE applications is still under hot debate, but one fact is that getting rid of the DAO layer simplifies the application architecture a lot, which is one of the main benefits. In this chapter and in the sample application, we have chosen to eliminate the DAO layer for the JPA implementation and instead provide the implementation of service layer by directly injecting the entity manager into the service layer classes.

However, it will not make a big difference if you or your development team still prefer the existence of the DAO layer. You can still program all the JPA logic into a separate DAO layer and have it injected into the service layer.

Injecting EntityManager into Service Layer Classes

For JDBC and Hibernate support, Spring provides the corresponding template classes `JdbcTemplate` and `HibernateTemplate` (although they are explicitly deprecated in favor of using Hibernate's `Session` interface directly, as we discussed in Chapter 9), which greatly simplifies the code we need to develop. For JPA, Spring also used to provide the `JpaTemplate` class. However, as JPA 2 has become much more mature, the Spring development team has found that it is unnecessary to provide such a template. If you refer to Spring Framework 3.1's JavaDoc, you will see that the class `JpaTemplate` is deprecated, and for JPA 2, Spring recommends that you use the `EntityManager` directly.

Once the EntityManagerFactory had been properly configured, injecting it into your service layer classes is very simple. Listing 10-3 shows the code snippet for the ContactServiceImpl class, which we will use as the sample for performing database operations using JPA.

Listing 10-3. Injection of EntityManager

```
package com.apress.prospring3.ch10.service.jpa;

// Import statements omitted
@Service("jpaContactService")
@Repository
@Transactional
public class ContactServiceImpl implements ContactService {

    private Log log = LogFactory.getLog(ContactServiceImpl.class);

    @PersistenceContext
    private EntityManager em;

    // Other code omitted
}
```

As shown in Listing 10-3, several annotations were applied to the class. The @Service annotation is to identify that it's a Spring component that provides business services to another layer and assigns the Spring bean the name jpaContactService. The @Repository annotation indicates that the class contains data access logic and instructs Spring to translate the vendor-specific exceptions to Spring's DataAccessException hierarchy. Actually, you can use @Repository("jpaContactService") and get rid of the @Service annotation; the effect is the same. Here we just use the @Service annotation to indicate it belongs to the service layer (like @Controller indicates the component is in the web layer) because it is more developer-friendly. As you will be already familiar, the @Transactional annotation is for defining transaction requirements.

To inject the EntityManager, we use the @PersistenceContext annotation, which is the standard JPA annotation for entity manager injection. You may wonder why we're using the different name (@PersistenceContext) to inject the entity manager, but if you consider that the persistence context is managed by EntityManager, the annotation makes perfect sense. If you have multiple persistence units in your application, you can also add the unitName attribute to the annotation to specify which persistence unit you want to be injected. Typically, a persistence unit represents an individual backend datasource.

Upon the injection of EntityManager, we are now ready to perform database operations, which will be discussed in the next section.

Database Operations with JPA

In this section, we will discuss how to perform database operations in JPA.

Listing 10-4 shows the ContactService interface, which indicates the contact information services we are going to provide.

Listing 10-4. The ContactService Interface

```
package com.apress.prospring3.ch10.service;

import java.util.List;
```

```
import com.apress.prospring3.ch10.domain.Contact;

public interface ContactService {

    // Find all contacts
    public List<Contact> findAll();

    // Find all contacts with telephone and hobbies
    public List<Contact> findAllWithDetail();

    // Find a contact with details by id
    public Contact findById(Long id);

    // Insert or update a contact
    public Contact save(Contact contact);

    // Delete a contact
    public void delete(Contact contact);
}
```

The interface is very simple; it has just three finder methods, one save method, and one delete method. The save method will serve both the insert and update operations.

Query Data Using the Java Persistence Query Language

The syntax for JPQL and HQL is very similar, and in fact, all the HQL queries that we used in Chapter 9 are reusable to implement the three finder methods within the ContactService interface.

Let's recap the named queries defined for the Contact entity class. Listing 10-5 shows the code snippet.

Listing 10-5. Named Queries for the Contact Domain Object

```
package com.apress.prospring3.ch10.domain;

import java.io.Serializable;
import javax.persistence.*;

@Entity
@Table(name = "contact")
@NamedQueries({
    @NamedQuery(name="Contact.findAll", query="select c from Contact c"),
    @NamedQuery(name="Contact.findById",
        query="select distinct c from Contact c left join fetch c.contactTelDetails t left
join fetch c.hobbies h where c.id = :id"),
    @NamedQuery(name="Contact.findAllWithDetail",
        query="select distinct c from Contact c left join fetch c.contactTelDetails t left
join fetch c.hobbies h")
})

public class Contact implements Serializable {

    // Other code omitted

}
```

When you compare the queries with those in Chapter 9, you will find no difference at all. So, if you are using Hibernate, migrating to JPA is relatively easy.

For the implementation class, com.apress.prospring3.ch10.service.jpa.ContactServiceImpl, we begin by creating the class with an empty implementation of all the methods in the ContactService interface. In STS, it's very easy to do it. For details, please see the section "Setting Up the JDBC DAO Using Annotations" in Chapter 8.

Let's begin with the findAll() method, which simply retrieves all the contacts from the database. Listing 10-6 shows the code snippet.

Listing 10-6. *Implementing the findAll() Method*

```
package com.apress.prospring3.ch10.service.jpa;

// Import statements omitted
@Service("jpaContactService")
@Repository
@Transactional
public class ContactServiceImpl implements ContactService {

    // Other code omitted
    @Transactional(readOnly=true)
    public List<Contact> findAll() {
        List<Contact> contacts = em.createNamedQuery("Contact.findAll",
            Contact.class).getResultList();
        return contacts;
    }
}
```

As shown in this listing, we use the EntityManager.createNamedQuery() method, passing in the name of the query and the expected return type. In this case, EntityManager will return a TypedQuery<X> interface. The method TypedQuery.getResultList() is then called to retrieve the contacts.

Listing 10-7 shows a simple testing program for ContactServiceImpl.

Listing 10-7. *Testing the ContactServiceImpl Class*

```
package com.apress.prospring3.ch10;

import java.util.List;

import org.springframework.context.support.GenericXmlApplicationContext;

import com.apress.prospring3.ch10.domain.Contact;
import com.apress.prospring3.ch10.domain.ContactTelDetail;
import com.apress.prospring3.ch10.domain.Hobby;
import com.apress.prospring3.ch10.service.ContactService;

public class JpaSample {

    public static void main(String[] args) {

        GenericXmlApplicationContext ctx = new GenericXmlApplicationContext();
        ctx.load("classpath:app-context.xml");
        ctx.refresh();
```

```
        ContactService contactService = ctx.getBean(
            "jpaContactService", ContactService.class);

        // List contacts without details
        List<Contact> contacts = contactService.findAll();
        listContacts(contacts);
    }

    private static void listContacts(List<Contact> contacts) {
        System.out.println("");
        System.out.println("Listing contacts without details:");
        for (Contact contact: contacts) {
            System.out.println(contact);
            System.out.println();
        }
    }
}
```

Running the previous class will yield the following output:

```
Listing contacts without details:
Contact - Id: 1, First name: Clarence, Last name: Ho, Birthday: 1980-07-30

Contact - Id: 2, First name: Scott, Last name: Tiger, Birthday: 1990-11-02

Contact - Id: 3, First name: John, Last name: Smith, Birthday: 1964-02-28
```

■ **Note** For associations, the JPA specification states that, by default, the persistence providers must fetch the association eagerly. However, for Hibernate's JPA implementation, the default fetching strategy is still lazy. So, when using Hibernate's JPA implementation, you don't need to explicitly define an association as lazy fetching. The default fetching strategy of Hibernate is different from the JPA specification.

Let's proceed to the findAllWithDetail() method, which will fetch all the associated telephone details and hobbies. Listing 10-8 shows the implementation.

Listing 10-8. Implementing the FindAllWithDetail() Method

```
package com.apress.prospring3.ch10.service.jpa;

// Import statements omitted
@Service("jpaContactService")
@Repository
@Transactional
public class ContactServiceImpl implements ContactService {

    // Other code omitted
    @Transactional(readOnly=true)
    public List<Contact> findAllWithDetail() {
```

```
        List<Contact> contacts = em.createNamedQuery(
            "Contact.findAllWithDetail", Contact.class).getResultList();
        return contacts;
    }
}
```

It's the same as the findAll() method, but it uses a different named query with left join fetch enabled. Listing 10-9 shows the revised testing program to list the contact details.

Listing 10-9. Testing the ContactServiceImpl Class

```
package com.apress.prospring3.ch10;

// Import statements omitted
public class JpaSample {

    public static void main(String[] args) {

        GenericXmlApplicationContext ctx = new GenericXmlApplicationContext();
        ctx.load("classpath:app-context.xml");
        ctx.refresh();

        ContactService contactService = ctx.getBean(
            "jpaContactService", ContactService.class);
        List<Contact> contacts = contactService.findAllWithDetail();
        listContactsWithDetail (contacts);

    }

    private static void listContactsWithDetail(List<Contact> contacts) {
        System.out.println("");
        System.out.println("Listing contacts with details:");
        for (Contact contact: contacts) {
            System.out.println(contact);
            if (contact.getContactTelDetails() != null) {
                for (ContactTelDetail contactTelDetail:
                        contact.getContactTelDetails()) {
                    System.out.println(contactTelDetail);
                }
            }
            if (contact.getHobbies() != null) {
                for (Hobby hobby: contact.getHobbies()) {
                    System.out.println(hobby);
                }
            }
            System.out.println();
        }
    }
}
```

If you run the program again, you will see the following output:

```
Listing contacts with details:
Contact - Id: 1, First name: Clarence, Last name: Ho, Birthday: 1980-07-30
Contact Tel Detail - Id: 2, Contact id: 1, Type: Home, Number: 1234567890
```

```
Contact Tel Detail - Id: 1, Contact id: 1, Type: Mobile, Number: 1234567890
Hobby :Swimming
Hobby :Movies

Contact - Id: 2, First name: Scott, Last name: Tiger, Birthday: 1990-11-02
Contact Tel Detail - Id: 3, Contact id: 2, Type: Home, Number: 1234567890
Hobby :Swimming

Contact - Id: 3, First name: John, Last name: Smith, Birthday: 1964-02-28
```

Let's see the findById() method, which demonstrates how to use a named query with named parameters in JPA. The associations will be fetched as well. Listing 10-10 shows the implementation.

Listing 10-10. *Implementing the findById() Method*

```java
package com.apress.prospring3.ch10.service.jpa;

// Import statements omitted
@Service("jpaContactService")
@Repository
@Transactional
public class ContactServiceImpl implements ContactService {

    // Other code omitted
    @Transactional(readOnly=true)
    public Contact findById(Long id) {
        TypedQuery<Contact> query = em.createNamedQuery(
            "Contact.findById", Contact.class);
        query.setParameter("id", id);
        return query.getSingleResult();
    }
}
```

As shown in Listing 10-10, EntityManager.createNamedQuery(java.lang.String name, java.lang.Class<T> resultClass) was called to get an instance of the TypedQuery<T> interface, which ensures that the result of the query must be of type Contact. Then the TypedQuery<T>.setParameter() method was used to set the values of the named parameters within the query and then to invoke the getSingleResult() method, since the result should contain only a single Contact object with the specified ID. We will leave the testing of the method as an exercise for you.

Query with Untyped Results

In many cases, you would like to submit a query to the database and manipulate the results at will, instead of storing them in a mapped entity class. One typical example is a web-based report that lists only a certain number of columns across multiple tables.

For example, say you have a web page that shows the summary information of all the contact information. The summary information contains each contact's first name, last name, and home telephone number only. Those contacts without home telephone numbers will not be listed. In this case, we can implement the function with a query and manually manipulate the resultset.

Let's name the method displayAllContactSummary(). Listing 10-11 shows a typical implementation of the method.

Listing 10-11. Implementing the displayAllContactSummary() Method

```
package com.apress.prospring3.ch10.service.jpa;

// Import statements omitted
@Service("contactSummaryUntype")
@Repository
@Transactional
public class ContactSummaryUntypeImpl {

    @PersistenceContext
    private EntityManager em;

    @Transactional(readOnly=true)
    public void displayAllContactSummary() {

        List result = em
            .createQuery("select c.firstName, c.lastName, t.telNumber "
                + "from Contact c left join c.contactTelDetails t "
                + " where t.telType='Home'").getResultList();
        int count = 0;
        for (Iterator i = result.iterator(); i.hasNext();) {
            Object[] values = (Object[]) i.next();
            System.out.println(++count + ": " + values[0] + ", "
                + values[1] + ", " + values[2]);
        }
    }
}
```

As shown in Listing 10-11, we use the EntityManager.createQuery() method to create a Query, passing in the JPQL statement, and then get the result list.

When we explicitly specify the columns to be selected within JPQL, JPA will return an iterator, and each item within the iterator is an array of objects. Then we loop through the iterator, and for each value in the object array, the value is displayed. Each object array corresponds to a record within the resultset. Listing 10-12 shows the testing program.

Listing 10-12. Testing the displayAllContactSummary() Method

```
package com.apress.prospring3.ch10;

import org.springframework.context.support.GenericXmlApplicationContext;

import com.apress.prospring3.ch10.service.jpa.ContactSummaryUntypeImpl;

public class ContactSummarySample {

    public static void main(String[] args) {

        GenericXmlApplicationContext ctx = new GenericXmlApplicationContext();
        ctx.load("classpath:app-context.xml");
        ctx.refresh();

        // Contact summary with untype result
        ContactSummaryUntypeImpl contactSummaryUntype =
```

```
            ctx.getBean("contactSummaryUntype",
                ContactSummaryUntypeImpl.class);
        contactSummaryUntype.displayAllContactSummary();

    }
}
```

Running the testing program will produce the following output:

```
1: Clarence, Ho, 1234567890
2: Scott, Tiger, 1234567890
```

In JPA, there is a more elegant solution rather than playing around with the object array returned from the query, which will be discussed in next section.

Query for a Custom Result Type with a Constructor Expression

In JPA, when querying for a custom result like the one in the previous section, you can instruct JPA to directly construct a POJO from each record for you. For the example in the previous section, let's create a POJO called ContactSummary that stores the results of the query for the contact summary. Listing 10-13 shows the class.

Listing 10-13. The ContactSummary Class

```
package com.apress.prospring3.ch10.domain;

import java.io.Serializable;

public class ContactSummary implements Serializable {

    private String firstName;

    private String lastName;

    private String homeTelNumber;

    public ContactSummary(String firstName, String lastName,
            String homeTelNumber) {
        this.firstName = firstName;
        this.lastName = lastName;
        this.homeTelNumber = homeTelNumber;
    }

    //Getter/setter methods omitted

    public String toString() {
        return "First name: " + firstName + " Last Name: " + lastName
            + " Home Phone: " + homeTelNumber;
    }
}
```

The previous ContactSummary class has the properties for each contact summary, with a constructor method that accepts all the properties.

Having the ContactSummary class in place, we can revise the method and use a constructor expression within the query to instruct the JPA provider to map the resultset to the ContactSummary class. Let's create an interface for the ContactSummary service first. Listing 10-14 shows the interface.

Listing 10-14. The ContactSummaryService Interface

```
package com.apress.prospring3.ch10.service;

import java.util.List;

import com.apress.prospring3.ch10.domain.ContactSummary;

public interface ContactSummaryService {

    public List<ContactSummary> findAll();

}
```

Listing 10-15 shows the implementation of the ContactSummaryService.findAll() method using the constructor expression for resultset mapping.

Listing 10-15. Implementation of the findAll() Method Using the Constructor Expression

```
package com.apress.prospring3.ch10.service.jpa;

// Import statements omitted
@Service("contactSummaryService")
@Repository
@Transactional
public class ContactSummaryServiceImpl implements ContactSummaryService {

    @PersistenceContext
    private EntityManager em;

    @Transactional(readOnly=true)
    public List<ContactSummary> findAll() {

    List<ContactSummary> result = em.createQuery(
        "select new com.apress.prospring3.ch10.domain.ContactSummary("
        + "c.firstName, c.lastName, t.telNumber) "
        + "from Contact c left join c.contactTelDetails t "
        + "where t.telType='Home'",
        ContactSummary.class).getResultList();
        return result;
    }
}
```

As shown in Listing 10-15, in the JPQL statement, the new keyword was specified, together with the fully qualified name of the POJO class that will store the results and pass in the selected attributes as the constructor argument of each ContactSummary class. Finally, the ContactSummary class was passed into the createQuery() method to indicate the result type.

To test the findAll() method, add the code snippet in Listing 10-16 into the main() method of the ContactSummarySample class.

Listing 10-16. Testing the findAll() Method Using the Constructor Expression

```
// Contact summary with constructor expression
ContactSummaryService contactSummaryService =
    ctx.getBean("contactSummaryService",ContactSummaryService.class);
List<ContactSummary> contacts = contactSummaryService.findAll();

for (ContactSummary contactSummary: contacts) {
    System.out.println(contactSummary);
}
```

Executing the ContactSummarySample class again will produce the output for each ContactSummary object within the list, as shown here (other output was omitted):

```
First name: Clarence Last Name: Ho Home Phone: 1234567890
First name: Scott Last Name: Tiger Home Phone: 1234567890
```

As you can see, the constructor expression is very useful for mapping the result of a custom query into POJOs for further application processing.

Inserting Data

Insert data in JPA is very simple. Like Hibernate, JPA also supports retrieving a database-generated primary key. Listing 10-17 shows the implementation of the save() method.

Listing 10-17. Implementing the save() Method

```
package com.apress.prospring3.ch10.service.jpa;

// Import statements omitted
@Service("jpaContactService")
@Repository
@Transactional
public class ContactServiceImpl implements ContactService {

    // Other code omitted
    public Contact save(Contact contact) {
        if (contact.getId() == null) { // Insert Contact
            log.info("Inserting new contact");
            em.persist(contact);
        } else {                        // Update Contact
            em.merge(contact);
            log.info("Updating existing contact");
        }
        log.info("Contact saved with id: " + contact.getId());
        return contact;
    }
}
```

As shown in Listing 10-17, the save() method first checks whether the object is a new entity instance, by checking the id value. If id is null (i.e., not yet assigned), then it's a new entity instance, and the EntityManager.persist() method will be invoked. When calling the persist() method, the EntityManager will persist the entity and make it a managed instance within the current persistence context. If the id value exists, then it's an update, and the EntityManager.merge() method will be called instead. When the merge() method is called, the EntityManager will merge the state of the entity into the current persistence context.

Let's test the insert operation. Listing 10-18 shows the code snippet for insert a new contact record.

Listing 10-18. Testing Insert Operation

```
// Other code omitted
public class JpaSample {

    public static void main(String[] args) {

        GenericXmlApplicationContext ctx = new GenericXmlApplicationContext();
        ctx.load("classpath:app-context.xml");
        ctx.refresh();

        ContactService contactService = ctx.getBean(
            "jpaContactService", ContactService.class);

        // Add new contact
        Contact contact = new Contact();
        contact.setFirstName("Michael");
        contact.setLastName("Jackson");
        contact.setBirthDate(new Date());
        ContactTelDetail contactTelDetail =
            new ContactTelDetail("Home", "1111111111");
        contact.addContactTelDetail(contactTelDetail);
        contactTelDetail = new ContactTelDetail("Mobile", "2222222222");
        contact.addContactTelDetail(contactTelDetail);
        contactService.save(contact);
        List<Contact> contacts = contactService.findAllWithDetail();
        listContactsWithDetail(contacts);
    }

    private static void listContactsWithDetail(List<Contact> contacts) {
        System.out.println("");
        System.out.println("Listing contacts with details:");
        for (Contact contact: contacts) {
            System.out.println(contact);
            if (contact.getContactTelDetails() != null) {
                for (ContactTelDetail contactTelDetail:
                    contact.getContactTelDetails()) {
                    System.out.println(contactTelDetail);
                }
            }
            if (contact.getHobbies() != null) {
                for (Hobby hobby: contact.getHobbies()) {
                    System.out.println(hobby);
                }
            }
            System.out.println();
        }
    }

}
```

As shown in Listing 10-18, we create a new contact, add two telephone details, and save the object. Then we list all the contacts again. Running the program yields the following output (the output of existing contacts was omitted):

```
2011-10-19 19:35:54,968 INFO [com.apress.prospring3.ch10.service.jpa.ContactServiceImpl]
<Inserting new contact>
Hibernate: insert into contact (ID, BIRTH_DATE, FIRST_NAME, LAST_NAME, VERSION) values (null,
?, ?, ?, ?)
Hibernate: insert into contact_tel_detail (ID, CONTACT_ID, TEL_NUMBER, TEL_TYPE, VERSION)
values(null, ?, ?, ?, ?)
Hibernate: insert into contact_tel_detail (ID, CONTACT_ID, TEL_NUMBER, TEL_TYPE, VERSION)
values (null, ?, ?, ?, ?)
2011-10-19 19:35:54,992 INFO [com.apress.prospring3.ch10.service.jpa.ContactServiceImpl]
<Contact saved with id: 4>

Listing contacts with details:
...
Contact - Id: 4, First name: Michael, Last name: Jackson, Birthday: 2011-10-19
Contact Tel Detail - Id: 5, Contact id: 4, Type: Mobile, Number: 2222222222
Contact Tel Detail - Id: 4, Contact id: 4, Type: Home, Number: 1111111111
```

From the INFO log record, you can see that the id of the newly saved contact was populated correctly. Hibernate will also show all the SQL statement being fired to the database.

Updating Data

Updating contacts is as easy as inserting data. Let's go through an example. Suppose for a contact with an ID of 1, we want to update its first name and remove the home telephone record. To test the update operation, add the code snippet in Listing 10-19 into the main() method of the JpaSample class.

Listing 10-19. Testing Update Operation

```
        // Other code omitted

        // Find contact by ID
        contact = contactService.findById(1l);
        System.out.println("");
        System.out.println("Contact with id 1:" + contact);
        System.out.println("");

        // Update contact
        contact.setFirstName("Kim Fung");
        Set<ContactTelDetail> contactTels = contact.getContactTelDetails();
        ContactTelDetail toDeleteContactTel = null;
        for (ContactTelDetail contactTel: contactTels) {
            if (contactTel.getTelType().equals("Home")) {
                toDeleteContactTel = contactTel;
            }
        }
        contactTels.remove(toDeleteContactTel);
        contactService.save(contact);
        contacts = contactService.findAllWithDetail();
        listContactsWithDetail(contacts);
```

As shown in Listing 10-19, we first retrieve the record with an ID of 1. Then we change the first name. Then we loop through the telephone objects and retrieve the one with type "Home" and remove it from the contact's telephone detail property. Finally, we call the ContactService.save() method again. When you run the program, you will see the following output (other output was omitted):

```
Contact - Id: 1, First name: Kim Fung, Last name: Ho, Birthday: 1980-07-30
Contact Tel Detail - Id: 1, Contact id: 1, Type: Mobile, Number: 1234567890
Hobby :Movies
Hobby :Swimming
```

You will see the first name was updated, and the home telephone was removed. The telephone can be removed because of the orphanRemoval=true attribute that was defined in the one-to-many association, which instructs the JPA provider (i.e., Hibernate) to remove all orphan records that exist in database but are no longer found in the object when persisted.

```
@OneToMany(mappedBy = "contact", cascade=CascadeType.ALL, orphanRemoval=true)
```

Deleting Data

Deleting data is simple. Just call the EntityManager.remove() method and pass in the contact object. Listing 10-20 shows the code snippet.

Listing 10-20. *Implementing the delete() Method*

```
package com.apress.prospring3.ch10.service.jpa;

// Import statements omitted
@Service("jpaContactService")
@Repository
@Transactional
public class ContactServiceImpl implements ContactService {

    private Log log = LogFactory.getLog(ContactServiceImpl.class);

    // Other code omitted
    public void delete(Contact contact) {
        Contact mergedContact = em.merge(contact);
        em.remove(mergedContact);
        log.info("Contact with id: " + contact.getId()
            + " deleted successfully");
    }
}
```

As shown in Listing 10-20, first the EntityManager.merge() method is invoked to merge the state of the entity into the current persistence context. The merge() method will return the managed entity instance. Then the EntityManager.remove() is called, passing in the managed contact entity instance. The remove operation will delete the contact record, together with all its associated information, including telephone details and hobbies, as we defined the cascade=CascadeType.ALL in the mapping. To test the delete operation, add the code snippet in Listing 10-21 into the main() method of the JpaSample class.

Listing 10-21. *Testing Delete Operation*

```
        // Delete contact
        contact = contactService.findById(1l);
```

```
        contactService.delete(contact);
        contacts = contactService.findAllWithDetail();
        listContactsWithDetail(contacts);
```

The previous listing retrieves the contact with an ID of 1 and then calls the delete() method to delete the contact information. Running the program will produce the following output (other output was omitted):

```
Listing contacts with details:
Contact - Id: 4, First name: Michael, Last name: Jackson, Birthday: 2011-10-13
Contact Tel Detail - Id: 4, Contact id: 4, Type: Home, Number: 1111111111
Contact Tel Detail - Id: 5, Contact id: 4, Type: Mobile, Number: 2222222222

Contact - Id: 3, First name: John, Last name: Smith, Birthday: 1964-02-28

Contact - Id: 2, First name: Scott, Last name: Tiger, Birthday: 1990-11-02
Contact Tel Detail - Id: 3, Contact id: 2, Type: Home, Number: 1234567890
Hobby :Swimming
```

You can see that the contact with an ID of 1 was deleted.

Native Query

Having discussed performing trivial database operations using JPA, now let's proceed to some more advanced topics. Sometimes you may want to have absolute control over the query that will be submitted to the database. One example is using a hierarchical query in an Oracle database. This kind of query is database-specific and referred to as a *native query*.

JPA supports the execution of native queries; the EntityManager will submit the query to the database as is, without any mapping or transformation performed. You may wonder why we don't use JDBC directly if JDBC supports direct submission of queries to the database. Spring also provides nice support for programming JDBC access logic and performs row mapping back to Java POJOs.

One main benefit of using JPA native queries is the mapping of the resultset back to the ORM-mapped entity classes. The following two sections discuss how to use a native query to retrieve all contacts and directly map the resultset back to the Contact objects.

Simple Native Query

To demonstrate how to use a native query, let's implement a new method to retrieve all the contacts from the database using a native query. Listing 10-22 shows the new method in the ContactService interface.

Listing 10-22. The findAllByNativeQuery() Method

```
package com.apress.prospring3.ch10.service;

// Other code omitted
public interface ContactService {

    // Other code omitted

    // Find all contacts by native query
    public List<Contact> findAllByNativeQuery();
}
```

Listing 10-23 shows the implementation of the findAllByNativeQuery() method.

Listing 10-23. Implementing the findAllByNativeQuery() Method

```
package com.apress.prospring3.ch10.service.jpa;

// Import statements omitted
@Service("jpaContactService")
@Repository
@Transactional
public class ContactServiceImpl implements ContactService {

    private Log log = LogFactory.getLog(ContactServiceImpl.class);

    // Other code omitted
    final static String ALL_CONTACT_NATIVE_QUERY =
        "select id, first_name, last_name, birth_date, version from contact";

    @Transactional(readOnly=true)
    public List<Contact> findAllByNativeQuery() {
        return em.createNativeQuery(ALL_CONTACT_NATIVE_QUERY,
            Contact.class).getResultList();
    }
}
```

As shown in Listing 10-23, you can see the native query is just a simple SQL statement to retrieve all the columns from the CONTACT table. To create and execute the query, the EntityManager.createNativeQuery() was first called, passing in the query string as well as the result type. The result type should be a mapped entity class (in this case the Contact class). The createNativeQuery() method returns a Query interface, which provides the getResultList() operation to get the result list. The JPA provider will execute the query and transform the resultset into the entity instances, based on the JPA mappings defined in the entity class. Executing the previous method produces the same result as the findAll() method.

Native Query with SQL Resultset Mapping

In the previous section, for EntityManager.createNativeQuery(), besides the mapped domain object, you can also pass in a string, which indicates the name of a SQL resultset mapping. A SQL resultset mapping is defined at the entity class level using the @SqlResultSetMapping annotation. A SQL resultset mapping can have one or more entity and column mappings.

Let's define a simple SQL resultset mapping in the Contact entity class (see Listing 10-24).

Listing 10-24. Using SQL Resultset Mapping

```
package com.apress.prospring3.ch10.domain;

// Other code omitted
@SqlResultSetMapping(
    name="contactResult",
    entities=@EntityResult(entityClass=Contact.class)
)
public class Contact implements Serializable {
...
```

A SQL resultset mapping called contactResult was defined for the entity class, with the entityClass attribute in the Contact class itself. JPA supports more complex mapping for multiple entities and supports mapping down to column-level mapping.

After the SQL resultset mapping is defined, the findAllByNativeQuery() method can be invoked using the resultset mapping's name. Listing 10-25 shows the code snippet.

Listing 10-25. *Implementing the findAllByNativeQuery() Method Using SQL Resultset Mapping*

```
package com.apress.prospring3.ch10.service.jpa;

// Other code omitted
public class ContactServiceImpl implements ContactService {

    // Other code omitted

    @Transactional(readOnly=true)
    public List<Contact> findAllByNativeQuery() {
        return em.createNativeQuery(ALL_CONTACT_NATIVE_QUERY,
            "contactResult").getResultList();
    }
}
```

As you can see, JPA also provides strong support for executing native queries, with a flexible SQL resultset mapping facility provided.

Criteria Query Using the JPA 2 Criteria API

Most applications will provide a frontend for users to search for information. Most likely a large number of searchable fields will be displayed, and the users will enter only some of them and do the search. It's very difficult to prepare a large number of queries with each possible combination of the parameters that users may choose to enter. In this situation, the criteria API query feature comes to the rescue.

In JPA 2, one major new feature introduced was a strongly typed criteria API query. In this new criteria API, the criteria being passed into the query is based on the mapped entity classes' metamodel. As a result, each criteria specified is strongly typed, and errors will be discovered at compile time, rather than runtime.

In the JPA criteria API, an entity class's metamodel is represented by the entity class name with a suffix of an underscore (_). For example, the metamodel class for the Contact entity class will be Contact_. Listing 10-26 shows the Contact_ class.

Listing 10-26. *JPA 2 Strongly Typed Criteria API: Metamodel*

```
package com.apress.prospring3.ch10.domain;

import java.util.Date;
import javax.persistence.metamodel.SetAttribute;
import javax.persistence.metamodel.SingularAttribute;
import javax.persistence.metamodel.StaticMetamodel;

@StaticMetamodel(Contact.class)
public abstract class Contact_ {

public static volatile SingularAttribute<Contact, Long> id;
    public static volatile SetAttribute<Contact, ContactTelDetail>
        contactTelDetails;
```

```
public static volatile SingularAttribute<Contact, String> lastName;
public static volatile SingularAttribute<Contact, Date> birthDate;
public static volatile SetAttribute<Contact, Hobby> hobbies;
public static volatile SingularAttribute<Contact, String> firstName;
public static volatile SingularAttribute<Contact, Integer> version;

}
```

As shown in Listing 10-26, the metamodel class is annotated with @StaticMetamodel, and the attribute is the mapped entity class. Within the class are the declaration of each attribute and its related types.

It would be tedious to code and maintain those metamodel classes. However, tools can help generate those metamodel classes automatically based on the JPA mappings within the entity classes. The one provided by Hibernate is called Hibernate Metamodel Generator (www.hibernate.org/subprojects/jpamodelgen.html). Using the tool with some configurations in STS, the metamodel classes will be generated/updated automatically every time your project is built.

Let's go through the procedure to enable the autogeneration of metamodel classes for your JPA entity classes. First, we need to have the JAR files in Table 10-1 ready for our project. Both JAR files can be found in the download package from the previously mentioned web site. The version we are using is 1.1.1.

Table 10-1. JAR Files for Metamodel Class Generation

JAR File	Description
hibernate-jpamodelgen-1.1.1.Final.jar	This is the main library for generating metamodel classes. You can locate the file at hibernate-jpamodelgen-1.1.1.Final after extracting the downloaded package.
hibernate-jpa-2.0-api-1.0.0.Final.jar	The is the JPA standard library provided by Hibernate. You can locate the file at hibernate-jpamodelgen-1.1.1.Final\lib after extracting the download package.

Second, copy the files into your project. For example, I put the JAR files into the folder named metamodel-generator-lib in the root folder of my project, as shown in Figure 10-4.

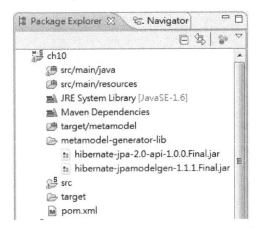

Figure 10-4. Hibernate metamodel generator library in STS

After the JAR files are in place, right-click the project name and choose Properties. Select Java Compiler ➤ Annotation Processing, select "Enable project specific settings," and then select "Enable annotation processing." Enter the folder name **target/metamodel** in the field "Generated source directory." Figure 10-5 shows the properties details.

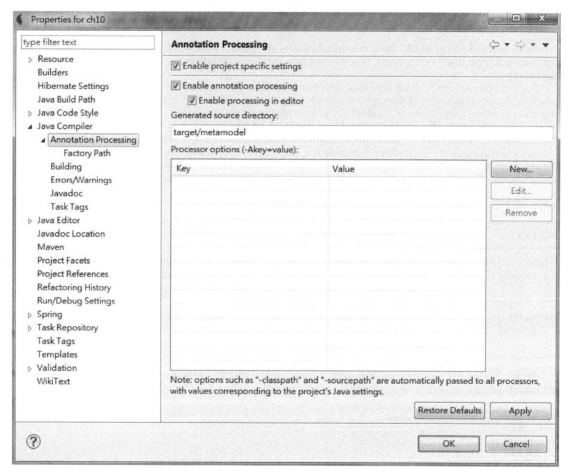

Figure 10-5. Enabling annotation processing in STS

Then click the option Factory Path (on the left-side menu), select "Enable project specific settings," then click the Add JARs button, and choose the two JAR files mentioned earlier into the factory path. Figure 10-6 shows the files selected.

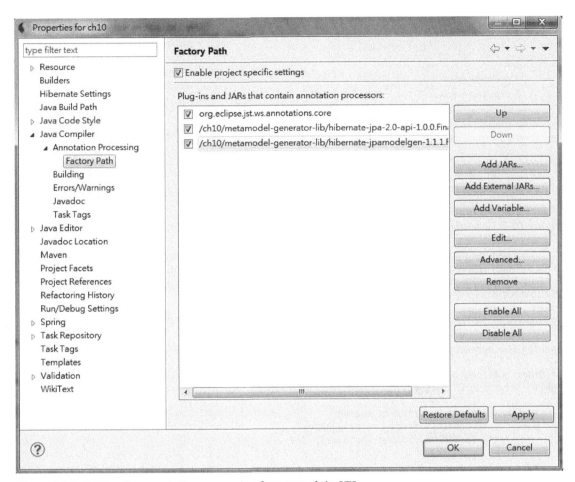

Figure 10-6. Setting the annotation processing factory path in STS

After completion, click the OK button, and STS will prompt you whether to rebuild the project. Clicking Yes will rebuild the project, and annotation processing will generate the metamodel classes. Figure 10-7 shows the generated metamodel classes.

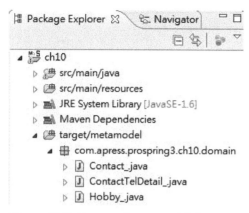

Figure 10-7. Generated metamodel classes

After generating the metamodel classes, we can proceed to implement more flexible queries using a JPA 2 strongly typed criteria API query. Let's define a query that accepts both the first name and last name for searching contacts. Listing 10-27 shows the definition of the new method findByCriteriaQuery() in the ContactService interface.

Listing 10-27. The findByCriteriaQuery() Method

```
package com.apress.prospring3.ch10.service;

// Other code omitted
public interface ContactService {

    // Find contacts by criteria query
    public List<Contact> findByCriteriaQuery(
        String firstName, String lastName);
}
```

Listing 10-28 shows the implementation of the findByCriteriaQuery() method using a JPA 2 criteria API query.

Listing 10-28. Implementing the findByCriteriaQuery() Method

```
package com.apress.prospring3.ch10.service.jpa;

// Other code omitted
public class ContactServiceImpl implements ContactService {

    @Transactional(readOnly=true)
    public List<Contact> findByCriteriaQuery(
        String firstName, String lastName) {

        log.info("Finding contact for firstName: " + firstName
                + " and lastName: " + lastName);

        CriteriaBuilder cb = em.getCriteriaBuilder();
```

```
        CriteriaQuery<Contact> criteriaQuery = cb.createQuery(Contact.class);
        Root<Contact> contactRoot = criteriaQuery.from(Contact.class);
        contactRoot.fetch(Contact_.contactTelDetails, JoinType.LEFT);
        contactRoot.fetch(Contact_.hobbies, JoinType.LEFT);

        criteriaQuery.select(contactRoot).distinct(true);

        Predicate criteria = cb.conjunction();

        // First Name
        if (firstName != null) {
            Predicate p = cb.equal(contactRoot.get(Contact_.firstName),
                firstName);
             criteria = cb.and(criteria, p);
        }

        // Last Name
        if (lastName != null) {
            Predicate p = cb.equal(contactRoot.get(Contact_.lastName),
                lastName);
            criteria = cb.and(criteria, p);
        }
    }

        criteriaQuery.where(criteria);
        List<Contact> result = em.createQuery(criteriaQuery).getResultList();
        return result;
    }
}
```

Listing 10-28 is elaborated on here:

- EntityManager.getCriteriaBuilder() was called to retrieve an instance of
  CriteriaBuilder.

- A typed query was created using CriteriaBuilder.createQuery(), passing in
  Contact as the result type.

- The CriteriaQuery.from() method was invoked, passing in the entity class. The
  result is a query root object (i.e., the Root<Contact> interface) corresponding to the
  specified entity. The query root object forms the basis for path expressions within
  the query.

- The two Root.fetch() method calls enforce the eager fetching of the associations
  relating to telephone details and hobbies. The JoinType.LEFT argument specifies
  an outer join. Calling the Root.fetch() method with JoinType.LEFT as the second
  argument is equivalent to specifying the left join fetch join operation in JPQL.

- The CriteriaQuery.select() method is called and passes the root query object as
  the result type. The distinct() method with true means that duplicate records
  should be eliminated.

- A Predicate instance was obtained by calling the CriteriaBuilder.conjunction()
  method, which means that a conjunction of one or more restrictions is about to be
  made. A Predicate can be a simple or compound predicate, and a predicate is a
  restriction that indicates the selection criteria defined by an expression.

- The first name and last name arguments are checked. If the argument is not null, a new Predicate will be constructed using the CriteriaBuilder() method (i.e., the CriteriaBuilder.and() method). The method equal() is to specify an equal restriction, within which the Root.get() was called, passing in the corresponding attribute of the entity class's metamodel to which the restriction applies. The constructed predicate was then "conjunct" with the existing predicate (stored by the variable criteria) by calling the CriteriaBuilder.and() method.

- The Predicate is constructed with all the criteria and restrictions and passed as the where clause to the query by calling the CriteriaQuery.where() method.

- Finally, CriteriaQuery was passed to the EntityManager. The EntityManager will then construct the query based on the CriteriaQuery passed in, execute the query, and return the result.

To test the criteria query operation, add the code snippet in Listing 10-29 to the main() method of the JpaSample class.

Listing 10-29. Testing the findByCriteriaQuery() Method

```
// Find contact by criteria query
contacts = contactService.findByCriteriaQuery("John", "Smith");
listContactsWithDetail(contacts);
```

Running the program will produce the following output (other output was omitted):

```
2011-10-20 18:42:34,411 INFO [com.apress.prospring3.ch10.service.jpa.ContactServiceImpl] -
<Finding contact for firstName: John and lastName: Smith>
...

Listing contacts with details:
Contact - Id: 3, First name: John, Last name: Smith, Birthday: 1964-02-28
```

You can try a different combination or pass null value to either of the arguments to observe the output.

Introducing Spring Data JPA

The Spring Data JPA project is a subproject under the Spring Data umbrella project. The main objective of the Spring Data JPA project is to provide additional features for simplifying application development with JPA.

Spring Data JPA provides several main features. In this section, we will discuss two main features. The first one is the Repository abstraction, while the other one is the entity listener for keeping track of basic audit information of entity classes.

Adding Spring Data JPA Library Dependencies

To use Spring Data JPA, we need to add several dependencies to the project. Table 10-2 describes the Maven dependencies required.

Table 10-2. Maven Dependencies for Spring Data JPA

Group ID	Artifact ID	Version	Description
org.springframework.data	spring-data-jpa	1.0.1.RELEASE	This is the Spring Data JPA library.
org.springframework	spring-aspects	3.1.0.RELEASE	These are Spring advanced AOP features that Spring Data JPA depends on.
joda-time	joda-time	2.0	Joda-time (http://joda-time.sourceforge.net/) is a date-time API that Spring Data JPA uses.
joda-time	joda-time-hibernate	1.3	This is a Joda-time library for integration with Hibernate for date-time type data persistence.
com.google.guava	guava	10.0.1	This contains useful helper classes.

In STS, you can use the POM editor to add the dependencies easily. Just double-click the file pom.xml in the package explorer. In the POM editor, click the Dependencies tab and enter the additional dependencies. Figure 10-8 shows an example for adding spring-data-jpa.

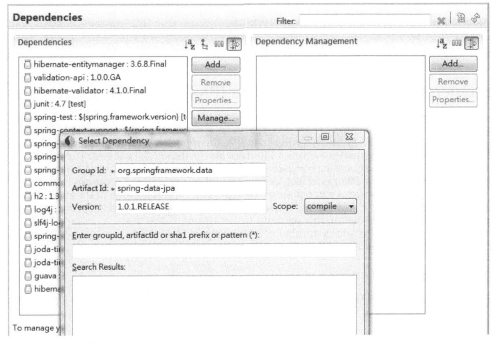

Figure 10-8. Adding dependencies to the Spring project

Figure 10-9 shows the list in STS after all the dependencies were added.

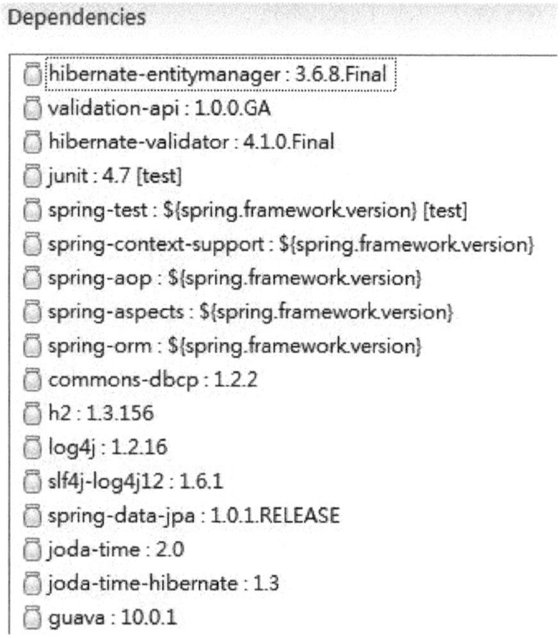

Dependencies

- hibernate-entitymanager : 3.6.8.Final
- validation-api : 1.0.0.GA
- hibernate-validator : 4.1.0.Final
- junit : 4.7 [test]
- spring-test : ${spring.framework.version} [test]
- spring-context-support : ${spring.framework.version}
- spring-aop : ${spring.framework.version}
- spring-aspects : ${spring.framework.version}
- spring-orm : ${spring.framework.version}
- commons-dbcp : 1.2.2
- h2 : 1.3.156
- log4j : 1.2.16
- slf4j-log4j12 : 1.6.1
- spring-data-jpa : 1.0.1.RELEASE
- joda-time : 2.0
- joda-time-hibernate : 1.3
- guava : 10.0.1

Figure 10-9. Maven dependencies for the Spring Data JPA project

After adding the dependencies, we can proceed to explore Spring Data JPA's features.

Database Operations Using Spring Data JPA Repository Abstraction

One of the main concepts of Spring Data and its all subprojects is the Repository abstraction, which belongs to the Spring Data Commons project (www.springsource.org/spring-data/commons). At the time of this writing, it's at version 1.1.0.RELEASE. In Spring Data JPA, the repository abstraction wraps the underlying JPA EntityManager and provides a simpler interface for JPA-based data access. The central interface within Spring Data is the org.springframework.data.repository.Repository<T,ID extends Serializable> interface, which is a marker interface belonging to the Spring Data Commons distribution. Spring Data provides various extensions of the Repository interface; one of them is the org.springframework.data.repository.CrudRepository interface (which also belongs to Spring Data Commons project), which we will discuss in this section.

The CrudRepository interface provides a number of commonly used methods. Listing 10-30 shows the interface declaration, which is extracted from Spring Data Commons project source code.

Listing 10-30. The CrudRepository Interface

```
package org.springframework.data.repository;

import java.io.Serializable;

@NoRepositoryBean
```

```java
public interface CrudRepository<T, ID extends Serializable> extends Repository<T, ID> {

    T save(T entity);

    Iterable<T> save(Iterable<? extends T> entities);

    T findOne(ID id);

    boolean exists(ID id);

    Iterable<T> findAll();

    long count();

    void delete(ID id);

    void delete(T entity);

    void delete(Iterable<? extends T> entities);

    void deleteAll();
}
```

The method name is quite self-explanatory. It's better to show how the Repository abstraction works by going through a simple example. Let's revise the ContactService interface a bit, down to just three finder methods. Listing 10-31 shows the revised ContactService interface. After the ContactService interface is revised, the com.apress.prospring3.ch10.JpaSample and com.apress.prospring3.ch10.service.jpa.ContactServiceImpl classes will have errors. Just delete these two classes and proceed with the implementation of the interface using Spring Data JPA.

Listing 10-31. The Revised ContactService Interface

```java
package com.apress.prospring3.ch10.service;

import java.util.List;
import com.apress.prospring3.ch10.domain.Contact;

public interface ContactService {

    // Find all contacts
    public List<Contact> findAll();

    // Find contacts by first name
    public List<Contact> findByFirstName(String firstName);

    // Find contacts by first name and last name
    public List<Contact> findByFirstNameAndLastName(
        String firstName, String lastName);
}
```

The next step is to prepare the ContactRepository interface, which extends the CrudRepository interface. Listing 10-32 shows the ContactRepository interface.

Listing 10-32. *The* ContactRepository *Interface*

```
package com.apress.prospring3.ch10.repository;

import java.util.List;

import org.springframework.data.repository.CrudRepository;

import com.apress.prospring3.ch10.domain.Contact;

public interface ContactRepository extends CrudRepository<Contact, Long> {

    public List<Contact> findByFirstName(String firstName);

    public List<Contact> findByFirstNameAndLastName(
        String firstName, String lastName);

}
```

We just need to declare two methods in this interface, because the findAll() method is already provided by the CrudRepository.findAll() method. As shown in Listing 10-32, the ContactRepository interface extends the CrudRepository interface, passing in the entity class (Contact) and the ID type (Long). One fancy aspect of Spring Data's Repository abstraction is that when you use the common naming convention such as findByFirstName and findByFirstNameAndLastName, you don't need to provide Spring Data JPA with the named query. Instead, Spring Data JPA will "infer" and construct the query for you based on the method name. For example, for the findByFirstName() method, Spring Data JPA will automatically prepare the query select c from Contact c where c.firstName = :firstName for you and set the named parameter firstName from the argument.

To use the Repository abstraction, we have to define it in Spring's configuration. Listing 10-33 shows the configuration file (spring-data-app-context.xml).

Listing 10-33. JPA Repository Configuration in Spring

```
<?xml version="1.0" encoding="UTF-8"?>
<beans xmlns="http://www.springframework.org/schema/beans"
    xmlns:xsi="http://www.w3.org/2001/XMLSchema-instance"
    xmlns:context="http://www.springframework.org/schema/context"
    xmlns:jdbc="http://www.springframework.org/schema/jdbc"
    xmlns:jpa="http://www.springframework.org/schema/data/jpa"
    xmlns:tx="http://www.springframework.org/schema/tx"
    xsi:schemaLocation="http://www.springframework.org/schema/beans
        http://www.springframework.org/schema/beans/spring-beans-3.1.xsd
        http://www.springframework.org/schema/context
        http://www.springframework.org/schema/context/spring-context-3.1.xsd
        http://www.springframework.org/schema/jdbc
        http://www.springframework.org/schema/jdbc/spring-jdbc-3.1.xsd
        http://www.springframework.org/schema/data/jpa
        http://www.springframework.org/schema/data/jpa/spring-jpa-1.0.xsd
        http://www.springframework.org/schema/tx
        http://www.springframework.org/schema/tx/spring-tx-3.1.xsd">

    <jdbc:embedded-database id="dataSource" type="H2">
        <jdbc:script location="classpath:schema.sql"/>
        <jdbc:script location="classpath:test-data.sql"/>
```

```
    </jdbc:embedded-database>

    <bean id="transactionManager"
        class="org.springframework.orm.jpa.JpaTransactionManager">
        <property name="entityManagerFactory" ref="emf"/>
    </bean>

    <tx:annotation-driven transaction-manager="transactionManager" />

    <bean id="emf" class="org.springframework.orm.jpa.LocalContainerEntityManagerFactoryBean">
        <property name="dataSource" ref="dataSource" />
        <property name="jpaVendorAdapter">
            <bean class="org.springframework.orm.jpa.vendor.HibernateJpaVendorAdapter" />
        </property>
        <property name="packagesToScan"
            value="com.apress.prospring3.ch10.domain"/>
        <property name="jpaProperties">
            <props>
                <prop key="hibernate.dialect">
                    org.hibernate.dialect.H2Dialect
                </prop>
                <prop key="hibernate.max_fetch_depth">3</prop>
                <prop key="hibernate.jdbc.fetch_size">50</prop>
                <prop key="hibernate.jdbc.batch_size">10</prop>
                <prop key="hibernate.show_sql">true</prop>
            </props>
        </property>
    </bean>

    <context:annotation-config/>

    <context:component-scan
        base-package="com.apress.prospring3.ch10.service.springjpa"/>

    <jpa:repositories base-package="com.apress.prospring3.ch10.repository"
                      entity-manager-factory-ref="emf"
                      transaction-manager-ref="transactionManager"/>
</beans>
```

First, we need to add the jpa namespace in the configuration file. Then, the `<jpa:repositories>` tag was used to configure Spring Data JPA's Repository abstraction. We instruct Spring to scan the package com.apress.prospring3.ch10.repository for repository interfaces and to pass in the EntityManagerFactory and transaction manager, respectively.

We can now proceed to the implementation. Listing 10-34 shows the implementation of the three finder methods of the ContactService interface.

Listing 10-34. The ContactServiceImpl Class

```
package com.apress.prospring3.ch10.service.springjpa;

// Import statements omitted
@Service("springJpaContactService")
@Repository
@Transactional
```

```
public class ContactServiceImpl implements ContactService {

    @Autowired
    private ContactRepository contactRepository;

    @Transactional(readOnly=true)
    public List<Contact> findAll() {
        return Lists.newArrayList(contactRepository.findAll());
    }

    @Transactional(readOnly=true)
    public List<Contact> findByFirstName(String firstName) {
        return contactRepository.findByFirstName(firstName);
    }

    @Transactional(readOnly=true)
    public List<Contact> findByFirstNameAndLastName(
        String firstName, String lastName) {
        return contactRepository.findByFirstNameAndLastName(
            firstName, lastName);
    }
}
```

You can see that instead of the EntityManager, we just need to inject the ContactRepository interface into the service class, and Spring Data JPA will do all the dirty work for us. Listing 10-35 shows the testing program.

Listing 10-35. The SpringJpaSample Class

```
package com.apress.prospring3.ch10;

// Import statements omitted
public class SpringJpaSample {

    public static void main(String[] args) {

        GenericXmlApplicationContext ctx = new GenericXmlApplicationContext();
        ctx.load("classpath:spring-data-app-context.xml");
        ctx.refresh();

        ContactService contactService = ctx.getBean(
            "springJpaContactService", ContactService.class);

        // Find all contacts
        List<Contact> contacts = contactService.findAll();
        listContacts(contacts);

        // Find contacts by first name
        contacts = contactService.findByFirstName("Clarence");
        listContacts(contacts);

        // Find contacts by first name and last name
        contacts = contactService.findByFirstNameAndLastName("Clarence", "Ho");
```

```
        listContacts(contacts);

    }

    private static void listContacts(List<Contact> contacts) {
        System.out.println("");
        System.out.println("Listing contacts without details:");
        for (Contact contact: contacts) {
            System.out.println(contact);
            System.out.println();
        }
    }
}
```

There's nothing special about the class. Running the program will yield the contact listing as expected. We leave it to you for testing it.

You have seen how Spring Data JPA can help simplify the development. We don't need to prepare a named query, don't need to call the `EntityManager.createQuery()` method, and so on.

What we covered were only the simplest examples. The `Repository` abstraction supports a lot of features, including defining custom queries with the `@Query` annotation, the `Specification` feature (belong to the Spring Data JPA project as of version 1.0.1.RELEASE), and so on. For more information, please refer to SpringSource's reference documentation listed here:

- Spring Data Commons Project: `http://static.springsource.org/spring-data/data-commons/docs/current/reference/html/`

- Spring Data JPA Project: `http://static.springsource.org/spring-data/data-jpa/docs/current/reference/html/`

Keeping Track of Changes on the Entity Class

In most applications, we need to keep track of basic audit activities for the business data being maintained by users. The audit information typically includes the user who creates the data, the date it was created, the date it was last modified, and the user who last modified it.

The Spring Data JPA provides a function in the form of a JPA entity listener, which helps you keep track of those audit information automatically. To use the feature, the entity class needs to implement the `org.springframework.data.domain.Auditable<U,ID extends Serializable>` interface (belonging to Spring Data Commons) or extend any class that implemented the interface. Listing 10-36 shows the `Auditable` interface that was extracted from Spring Data's reference documentation.

Listing 10-36. The Auditable Interface

```
package org.springframework.data.domain;

import java.io.Serializable;

import org.joda.time.DateTime;

public interface Auditable<U, ID extends Serializable>
    extends Persistable<ID> {

    U getCreatedBy();
    void setCreatedBy(final U createdBy);
```

```
DateTime getCreatedDate();
void setCreated(final DateTime creationDate);

U getLastModifiedBy();
void setLastModifiedBy(final U lastModifiedBy);

DateTime getLastModifiedDate();
void setLastModified(final DateTime lastModifiedDate);
}
```

To show how it works, let's create a new table called CONTACT_AUDIT in our database schema, which is based on the CONTACT table, with four audit-related columns added. Listing 10-37 shows the table creation script (schema.sql).

Listing 10-37. *The CONTACT_AUDIT Table*

```
CREATE TABLE CONTACT_AUDIT (
      ID INT NOT NULL AUTO_INCREMENT
    , FIRST_NAME VARCHAR(60) NOT NULL
    , LAST_NAME VARCHAR(40) NOT NULL
    , BIRTH_DATE DATE
    , VERSION INT NOT NULL DEFAULT 0
    , CREATED_BY VARCHAR(20)
    , CREATED_DATE TIMESTAMP
    , LAST_MODIFIED_BY VARCHAR(20)
    , LAST_MODIFIED_DATE TIMESTAMP
    , UNIQUE UQ_CONTACT_AUDIT_1 (FIRST_NAME, LAST_NAME)
    , PRIMARY KEY (ID)
);
```

In Listing 10-37, the four columns with bold characters indicate the audit-related columns. The next step is to create the entity class called ContactAudit. It's basically the same as the Contact entity class; we just added the mapping for the four audit columns. Also, the class implements the Auditable interface. Listing 10-38 shows the code snippet that was added on top of the Contact class.

Listing 10-38. *The ContactAudit Class*

```
package com.apress.prospring3.ch10.domain;

// Import statements omitted
@Entity
@Table(name = "contact_audit")
public class ContactAudit implements Auditable<String, Long>, Serializable {

    // other declaration mapping properties omitted

    // Audit fields
    private String createdBy;
    private DateTime createdDate;
    private String lastModifiedBy;
    private DateTime lastModifiedDate;

    @Column(name="CREATED_BY")
    public String getCreatedBy() {
```

```java
        return createdBy;
    }

    public void setCreatedBy(String createdBy) {
        this.createdBy = createdBy;
    }

    @Column(name="CREATED_DATE")
    @Type(type="org.joda.time.contrib.hibernate.PersistentDateTime")
    public DateTime getCreatedDate() {
        return createdDate;
    }

    public void setCreatedDate(DateTime createdDate) {
        this.createdDate = createdDate;
    }

    @Column(name="LAST_MODIFIED_BY")
    public String getLastModifiedBy() {
        return lastModifiedBy;
    }

    public void setLastModifiedBy(String lastModifiedBy) {
        this.lastModifiedBy = lastModifiedBy;
    }

    @Column(name="LAST_MODIFIED_DATE")
    @Type(type="org.joda.time.contrib.hibernate.PersistentDateTime")
    public DateTime getLastModifiedDate() {
        return lastModifiedDate;
    }

    public void setLastModifiedDate(DateTime lastModifiedDate) {
        this.lastModifiedDate = lastModifiedDate;
    }

    @Transient
    public boolean isNew() {
        if (id == null) {
            return true;
        } else {
            return false;
        }
    }

    public String toString() {
        return "Contact - Id: " + id + ", First name: " + firstName
                    + ", Last name: " + lastName + ", Birthday: " + birthDate
            + ", Create by: " + createdBy + ", Create date: " + createdDate
            + ", Modified by: " + lastModifiedBy + ", Modified date: "
            + lastModifiedDate;
    }
}
```

In Listing 10-38, the ContactAudit entity class implements the Auditable interface and implements the methods by mapping the four auditing columns. The @Column annotations were applied to map to the actual column in the table. For the two date attributes (createdDate, lastModifiedDate), the Hibernate custom user type annotation @Type was applied with the implementation class set to org.joda.time.contrib.hibernate.PersistentDateTime. Like how the Spring Data JPA's Auditable interface uses Joda-time library's DateTime type, the joda-time-hibernate library provides this custom user type for use with Hibernate when persisting the attribute into the TIMESTAMP column in the database. The isNew() method of the Auditable interface (inherited from the org.springframework.data.domain.Persistable<ID extends Serializable> interface) is also implemented. The annotation @Transient means that the field doesn't need to persist. Spring Data JPA uses this function to identify whether it's a new entity in order to determine whether we need to set the createdBy and createdDate attribute. In the implementation, we just check the ID, and if the value is null, then we return true, it means it's a new entity instance.

Listing 10-39 shows the ContactAuditService interface, where we define only a few methods to demonstrate the auditing feature.

Listing 10-39. *The ContactAuditService Interface*

```
package com.apress.prospring3.ch10.service;

import java.util.List;

import com.apress.prospring3.ch10.domain.ContactAudit;

public interface ContactAuditService {

        public List<ContactAudit> findAll();

        public ContactAudit findById(Long id);

        public ContactAudit save(ContactAudit contact);

}
```

The next step is to create the ContactAuditRepository interface, which is shown in Listing 10-40.

Listing 10-40. *The ContactAuditRepository Interface*

```
package com.apress.prospring3.ch10.repository;

import org.springframework.data.repository.CrudRepository;

import com.apress.prospring3.ch10.domain.ContactAudit;

public interface ContactAuditRepository extends
    CrudRepository<ContactAudit, Long> {

}
```

The ContactAuditRepository interface just extended the CrudRepository, which already implemented all the methods that we are going to implement for ContactAuditService. The findById() method was implemented by the CrudRepository.findOne() method.

Listing 10-41 shows the service implementation class ContactAuditServiceImpl.

Listing 10-41. The ContactAuditServiceImpl Class

```
package com.apress.prospring3.ch10.service.springjpa;

// Import statements omitted
@Service("contactAuditService")
@Repository
@Transactional
public class ContactAuditServiceImpl implements ContactAuditService {

    @Autowired
    private ContactAuditRepository contactAuditRepository;

    @Transactional(readOnly=true)
    public List<ContactAudit> findAll() {
        return Lists.newArrayList(contactAuditRepository.findAll());
    }

    public ContactAudit findById(Long id) {
        return contactAuditRepository.findOne(id);
    }

    public ContactAudit save(ContactAudit contact) {
        return contactAuditRepository.save(contact);
    }

}
```

You may be familiar with the code now. The ContactAuditRepository interface is autowired, and all the methods in the ContactAuditService interface are implemented.

We also need to add a few configurations. The first one to add is to declare the AuditingEntityListener<T>, which is a JPA entity listener that provides the auditing service. To declare the listener, create a file called /src/main/resources/META-INF/orm.xml (it's mandatory to use this file name, which is specified by JPA specification) under the project root folder and declare the listener, like the one in Listing 10-42.

Listing 10-42. Declaring the Entity Listener

```
<?xml version="1.0" encoding="UTF-8" ?>
<entity-mappings xmlns="http://java.sun.com/xml/ns/persistence/orm"
    xmlns:xsi="http://www.w3.org/2001/XMLSchema-instance"
    xsi:schemaLocation="http://java.sun.com/xml/ns/persistence/orm
        http://java.sun.com/xml/ns/persistence/orm_2_0.xsd"
        version="2.0">
    <description>JPA</description>

    <persistence-unit-metadata>
        <persistence-unit-defaults>
            <entity-listeners>
                <entity-listener
class="org.springframework.data.jpa.domain.support.AuditingEntityListener" />
        </entity-listeners>
        </persistence-unit-defaults>
```

```
    </persistence-unit-metadata>
```

```
</entity-mappings>
```

The listener will be picked by the JPA provider during persistence (i.e., save and update events) for audit fields processing.

We also need to define the listener in Spring's configuration. Listing 10-43 shows the code snippet (in the file spring-data-app-context.xml).

Listing 10-43. *Declaring the Entity Listener in Spring*

```
    <!-- Other definitions omitted -->
    <jpa:auditing auditor-aware-ref="auditorAwareBean"/>

    <bean id="auditorAwareBean"
class="com.apress.prospring3.ch10.springjpa.auditor.AuditorAwareBean"/>
```

The tag `<jpa:auditing>` is to enable the Spring Data JPA auditing feature, while the bean auditorAwareBean is the bean providing the user information. Listing 10-44 shows the AuditorAwareBean class.

Listing 10-44. *The AuditorAwareBean Class*

```
package com.apress.prospring3.ch10.springjpa.auditor;

import org.springframework.data.domain.AuditorAware;

public class AuditorAwareBean implements AuditorAware<String> {

    public String getCurrentAuditor() {
        return "prospring3";
    }

}
```

The AuditorAwareBean implements the AuditorAware<T> interface, passing in the type String. In real situations, this should be an instance of user information, for example, a User class, which represents the logged-in user who is performing the data update action. We use String here just for simplicity. In the AuditorAwareBean class, the method getCurrentAuditor() was implemented, and the value is hard-coded to prospring3. In real situations, the user should be obtained from the underlying security infrastructure. For example, in Spring Security, the user information can be retrieved from the SecurityContextHolder class.

Now all the implementation work is completed. Listing 10-45 shows the testing program.

Listing 10-45. *Testing the Spring Data JPA Auditing Feature*

```
package com.apress.prospring3.ch10;

// Import statements omitted
public class SpringJpaAuditSample {

    public static void main(String[] args) {

        GenericXmlApplicationContext ctx = new GenericXmlApplicationContext();
        ctx.load("classpath:spring-data-app-context.xml");
```

```
        ctx.refresh();

        ContactAuditService contactService = ctx.getBean(
            "contactAuditService", ContactAuditService.class);

        List<ContactAudit> contacts = contactService.findAll();
        listContacts(contacts);

        // Add new contact
        System.out.println("Add new contact");
        ContactAudit contact = new ContactAudit();
        contact.setFirstName("Michael");
        contact.setLastName("Jackson");
        contact.setBirthDate(new Date());
        contactService.save(contact);
        contacts = contactService.findAll();
        listContacts(contacts);

        // Find by id
        contact = contactService.findById(1l);
        System.out.println("");
        System.out.println("Contact with id 1:" + contact);
        System.out.println("");

        // Update contact
        System.out.println("Update contact");
        contact.setFirstName("Tom");
        contactService.save(contact);
        contacts = contactService.findAll();
        listContacts(contacts);
    }

    private static void listContacts(List<ContactAudit> contacts) {
        System.out.println("");
        System.out.println("Listing contacts without details:");
        for (ContactAudit contact: contacts) {
            System.out.println(contact);
            System.out.println();
        }
    }
}
```

In Listing 10-45, we list the contact audit information both after a new contact was inserted and after it's later updated. Running the program will produce the following output:

```
Add new contact
Listing contacts without details:
Contact - Id: 1, First name: Michael, Last name: Jackson, Birthday: 2011-10-21, Create by:
prospring3,
Create date: 2011-10-21T10:45:52.483+08:00, Modified by: prospring3, Modified date: 2011-10-
21T10:45:52.483+08:00

Update contact
Listing contacts without details:
```

```
Contact - Id: 1, First name: Tom, Last name: Jackson, Birthday: 2011-10-21, Create by:
prospring3,
Create date: 2011-10-21T10:45:52.483+08:00, Modified by: prospring3, Modified date: 2011-10-
21T10:45:52.596+08:00
```

In the previous output, you can see that after the new contact is created, the create date and last modify dates are the same. However, after the update, the last modified date is updated. Auditing is another handy feature that Spring Data JPA provides so that you don't need to implement the logic yourself.

This wraps up our discussion of Spring Data JPA. Let's move on to see another useful function that Hibernate provides for keeping entity versions.

Keeping Entity Versions by Using Hibernate Envers

In an enterprise application, for business-critical data, it is always a requirement to keep "versions" of each entity. For example, in a customer relationship management (CRM) system, each time a customer record is inserted, updated, or deleted, the previous version should be kept in a history or auditing table to fulfill the firm's auditing or other compliance requirements.

To accomplish this, there are two common options. The first one is to create database triggers that will clone the pre-update record into the history table before any update operations, and the second is to develop the logic in the data access layer (e.g., by using AOP). However, both options have their drawbacks. The trigger approach is tied to the database platform, while implementing the logic manually is quite clumsy and error prone.

Hibernate Envers (Entity Versioning System) is a Hibernate module specifically designed to automate the versioning of entities. In this section, we will discuss how to use Envers to implement the versioning of the ContactAudit entity.

■ **Note** Hibernate Envers is not a feature of JPA. We mention it here because we believe it's more appropriate to cover this after we have discussed some basic auditing feature that you can do with Spring Data JPA. As a matter of fact, maintaining history records of critical business data (e.g., customer, transaction, and so on) is a basic feature in an enterprise application.

Envers supports two different auditing strategies, which are shown in Table 10-3.

Table 10-3. Envers Auditing Strategies

Auditing Strategy	Description
Default	Envers will maintain a column for the revision of the record. Every time a record is inserted or updated, a new record will be inserted into the history table with the revision number retrieved from a database sequence or table.
Validity Audit	This strategy stores both the start and end revisions of each history record. Every time a record is inserted or updated, a new record will be inserted into the history table with the start revision number. At the same time, the previous record will be updated with the end revision number. It's also possible to configure Envers to record the timestamp at which the end revision was updated into the previous history record.

In this section, we will demonstrate the validity audit strategy. Although it will trigger more database updates, retrieving the history records becomes much faster. Because the end revision timestamp is also written to the history records, it will be easier to identify the image of a record at a specific point of time when querying the data.

Adding Hibernate Envers Dependencies

We need to add the Maven dependency listed in Table 10-4 to our project.

Table 10-4. Hibernate Envers Dependencies

Group ID	Artifact ID	Version	Description
org.hibernate	hibernate-envers	3.6.8.Final	Hibernate Envers module library

Adding Tables for Entity Versioning

To support entity versioning, we need to add a few tables. First, for each table that the entity (in this case, it's the ContactAudit entity class) will be versioning, we need to create the corresponding history table. For the versioning of records in the CONTACT_AUDIT table, let's create a history table called CONTACT_AUDIT_H. Listing 10-46 shows the table creation script (schema.sql).

Listing 10-46. The CONTACT_AUDIT_H Table

```
CREATE TABLE CONTACT_AUDIT_H (
        ID INT NOT NULL
    , FIRST_NAME VARCHAR(60) NOT NULL
    , LAST_NAME VARCHAR(40) NOT NULL
    , BIRTH_DATE DATE
    , VERSION INT NOT NULL DEFAULT 0
    , CREATED_BY VARCHAR(20)
    , CREATED_DATE TIMESTAMP
    , LAST_MODIFIED_BY VARCHAR(20)
    , LAST_MODIFIED_DATE TIMESTAMP
    , AUDIT_REVISION INT NOT NULL
    , ACTION_TYPE INT
    , AUDIT_REVISION_END INT
    , AUDIT_REVISION_END_TS TIMESTAMP
    , UNIQUE UQ_CONTACT_AUDIT_H_1 (FIRST_NAME, LAST_NAME)
    , PRIMARY KEY (ID, AUDIT_REVISION)
);
```

To support the validity audit strategy, we need to add four columns for each history table (the bold columns in Listing 10-46). Table 10-5 shows the columns and their purposes.

Table 10-5. Columns Required for History Table

Column Type	Data Type	Description
AUDIT_REVISION	INT	The start revision of the history record
AUDIT_TYPE	INT	The action type. Possible values: 0 – Add, 1 – Modify, 2 – Delete
AUDIT_REVISION_END	INT	The end revision of the history record
AUDIT_REVISION_END_TS	TIMESTAMP	The timestamp at which the end revision was updated

Hibernate Envers requires another table for keeping track of the revision number and the timestamp at which each revision was created. The table name should be REVINFO. Listing 10-47 shows the table creation script (schema.sql).

Listing 10-47. The REVINFO Table

```
CREATE TABLE REVINFO (
     REVTSTMP BIGINT NOT NULL
  , REV INT NOT NULL AUTO_INCREMENT
  , PRIMARY KEY (REVTSTMP, REV)
);
```

The REV column is for storing each revision number, which will be autoincremented when a new history record is created. The REVTSTMP column stores the timestamp (in a number format) when the revision was created.

Configuring EntityManagerFactory for Entity Versioning

Hibernate Envers is implemented in the form of EJB listeners. We can configure those listeners in the LocalContainerEntityManagerFactory bean. Listing 10-48 shows the revised bean configuration (in the file spring-data-app-context.xml).

Listing 10-48. Configuring Hibernate Envers in Spring

```
<bean id="emf" class="org.springframework.orm.jpa.LocalContainerEntityManagerFactoryBean">
    <!-- Other settings omitted -->
    <property name="jpaProperties">
        <props>

            <!-- Other properties omitted -->

            <!-- Listeners for Hibernate Envers -->
            <prop key="hibernate.ejb.event.post-insert">
                org.hibernate.ejb.event.EJB3PostInsertEventListener,
                org.hibernate.envers.event.AuditEventListener
            </prop>
            <prop key="hibernate.ejb.event.post-update">
```

```
                    org.hibernate.ejb.event.EJB3PostUpdateEventListener,
                    org.hibernate.envers.event.AuditEventListener
                </prop>
                <prop key="hibernate.ejb.event.post-delete">
                    org.hibernate.ejb.event.EJB3PostDeleteEventListener,
                    org.hibernate.envers.event.AuditEventListener
                </prop>
                <prop key="hibernate.ejb.event.pre-collection-update">
                    org.hibernate.envers.event.AuditEventListener
                </prop>
                <prop key="hibernate.ejb.event.pre-collection-remove">
                    org.hibernate.envers.event.AuditEventListener
                </prop>
                <prop key="hibernate.ejb.event.post-collection-recreate">
                    org.hibernate.envers.event.AuditEventListener
                </prop>

                <!-- Properties for Hibernate Envers -->
                <prop key="org.hibernate.envers.audit_table_suffix">_H</prop>
                <prop key="org.hibernate.envers.revision_field_name">
                    AUDIT_REVISION
                </prop>
                <prop key="org.hibernate.envers.revision_type_field_name">
                    ACTION_TYPE
                </prop>
                <prop key="org.hibernate.envers.audit_strategy">
                    org.hibernate.envers.strategy.ValidityAuditStrategy
                </prop>
                <prop key="org.hibernate.envers.audit_strategy_validity_end_rev_field_name">
                    AUDIT_REVISION_END
                </prop>
                <prop
key="org.hibernate.envers.audit_strategy_validity_store_revend_timestamp">
                    True
                </prop>
                <prop
key="org.hibernate.envers.audit_strategy_validity_revend_timestamp_field_name">
                    AUDIT_REVISION_END_TS
                </prop>
            </props>
        </property>
    </bean>
```

As shown in Listing 10-48, the Envers audit event listener
(org.hibernate.envers.event.AuditEventListener) is attached to various persistence events. The
listener intercepts the events post-insert, post-update, or post-delete and clones the pre-update image
of the entity class into the history table. The listener is also attached to those association update events
pre-collection-update, pre-collection-remove, and pre-collection-recreate for handling the update
operations of the entity class's associations. Envers is capable of keeping the history of the entities
within an association (e.g., one-to-many, many-to-many, and so on).

A few properties are also defined for Hibernate Envers, which are summarized in Table 10-6 (the
prefix of the properties, org.hibernate.envers, was omitted for clarity).

Table 10-6. Properties for Hibernate Envers

Column Type	Description
audit_table_suffix	The table name suffix for the versioned entity. For example, for the entity class ContactAudit, which is mapped to the CONTACT_AUDIT table, Envers will keep the history in the table CONTACT_AUDIT_H, since we defined the value _H for the property.
revision_field_name	The history table's column for storing the revision number for each history record.
revision_type_field_name	The history table's column for storing the update action type.
audit_strategy	The audit strategy to use for entity versioning.
audit_strategy_validity_end_↵rev_field_name	The history table's column for storing the end revision number for each history record. Required only when using the validity audit strategy.
audit_strategy_validity_store_↵revend_timestamp	Whether to store the timestamp when the end revision number for each history record is updated. Required only when using the validity audit strategy.
audit_strategy_validity_revend_↵timestamp_field_name	The history table's column for storing the timestamp when the end revision number for each history record is updated. Required only when using the validity audit strategy and the previous property is set to true.

Coding Changes for Entity Versioning and History Retrieval

To enable the versioning of an entity, just annotate the entity class with @Audited. Listing 10-49 shows the ContactAudit entity class with the annotation applied.

Listing 10-49. The Revised ContactAudit Class

```
package com.apress.prospring3.ch10.domain;

// Import statements omitted

import org.hibernate.envers.Audited;
import org.hibernate.envers.NotAudited;

@Entity
@Audited
@Table(name = "contact_audit")
public class ContactAudit implements Auditable<String, Long>, Serializable {

    // Other code omitted
    @ManyToMany
```

```
@NotAudited
// Other mapping annotations omitted
public Set<Hobby> getHobbies() {
    return this.hobbies;
}

@OneToMany(mappedBy = "contact", cascade=CascadeType.ALL,
    orphanRemoval=true)
@NotAudited
public Set<ContactTelDetail> getContactTelDetails() {
    return this.contactTelDetails;
}
}
```

As shown in Listing 10-49, the entity class is annotated with @Audited, which Envers listeners will check for and perform versioning of the updated entities. By default, Envers will also try to keep a history of the associations. So, it also will try to keep the history of the contact's telephone details and hobbies. In case we don't want to keep versions of the association entities, we need to annotate them with the @NotAudited annotation.

To retrieve the history records, Envers provides the org.hibernate.envers.AuditReader interface, which can be obtained from the AuditReaderFactory class. Let's add a new method called findAuditByRevision() into the ContactAuditService interface for the retrieving the ContactAudit history record by the revision number. Listing 10-50 shows the code snippet.

Listing 10-50. The findAuditByRevision() Method

```
package com.apress.prospring3.ch10.service;

public interface ContactAuditService {

    public ContactAudit findAuditByRevision(Long id, int revision);
    ...
}
```

To retrieve a history record, one option is to pass in the entity's ID and the revision number. Envers also provides other methods for retrieving history records (for details, please refer to docs.jboss.org/hibernate/envers/3.6/reference/en-US/html/queries.html). Listing 10-51 shows the implementation of the method.

Listing 10-51. Implementing the findAuditByRevision() Method

```
package com.apress.prospring3.ch10.service.springjpa;

// Import statements omitted

import org.hibernate.envers.AuditReader;
import org.hibernate.envers.AuditReaderFactory;

@Service("contactAuditService")
@Repository
@Transactional
public class ContactAuditServiceImpl implements ContactAuditService {
```

```
// Other code omitted
@PersistenceContext
private EntityManager entityManager;

@Transactional(readOnly=true)
public ContactAudit findAuditByRevision(Long id, int revision) {
        AuditReader auditReader = AuditReaderFactory.get(entityManager);
        return auditReader.find(ContactAudit.class, id, revision);
}

}
```

As shown in Listing 10-51, the EntityManager was injected into the class, which was passed to the AuditReaderFactory to retrieve an instance of AuditReader. Then we can then call the AuditReader.find() method to retrieve the instance of the ContactAudit entity at a particular revision.

Testing Entity Versioning

Let's take a look at how entity versioning works. Listing 10-52 shows the testing code snippet. In Listing 10-52, the code for bootstrapping ApplicationContext and the listContacts() function is the same as the one in the SpringJpaSample class.

Listing 10-52. Testing Entity Versioning

```
package com.apress.prospring3.ch10;

// Import statements omitted

public class SpringJpaAuditSample {

    public static void main(String[] args) {

            // Other code omitted
            // Add new contact
            System.out.println("Add new contact");
            ContactAudit contact - new ContactAudit();
            contact.setFirstName("Michael");
            contact.setLastName("Jackson");
            contact.setBirthDate(new Date());
            contactService.save(contact);
            contacts = contactService.findAll();
            listContacts(contacts);

            // Update contact
            System.out.println("Update contact");
            contact.setFirstName("Tom");
            contactService.save(contact);
            contacts = contactService.findAll();
            listContacts(contacts);

            // Find audit record by revision
            ContactAudit oldContact = contactService.findAuditByRevision(1l, 1);
            System.out.println("");
```

```
            System.out.println("Old Contact with id 1 and rev 1:" + oldContact);
            System.out.println("");
            oldContact = contactService.findAuditByRevision(1l, 2);
            System.out.println("");
            System.out.println("Old Contact with id 1 and rev 2:" + oldContact);
            System.out.println("");
        }

}
```

From Listing 10-52, we first create a new contact and then update it. Then we retrieve the ContactAudit entities with revisions 1 and 2, respectively. Running the code will produce the following output:

```
Listing contacts without details:
Contact - Id: 1, First name: Tom, Last name: Jackson, Birthday: 2011-10-21, Create by:
prospring3, Create date: 2011-10-21T13:54:24.242+08:00, Modified by: prospring3, Modified
date: 2011-10-21T13:54:24.360+08:00

Old Contact with id 1 and rev 1:Contact - Id: 1, First name: Michael, Last name: Jackson,
Birthday: 2011-10-21, Create by: prospring3, Create date: 2011-10-21T13:54:24.242+08:00,
Modified by: prospring3, Modified date: 2011-10-21T13:54:24.242+08:00

Old Contact with id 1 and rev 2:Contact - Id: 1, First name: Tom, Last name: Jackson,
Birthday: 2011-10-21, Create by: prospring3, Create date: 2011-10-21T13:54:24.242+08:00,
Modified by: prospring3, Modified date: 2011-10-21T13:54:24.360+08:00
```

From the previous output, you can see that after the update operation, the ContactAudit's first name was changed to Tom. However, when looking at the history, at revision 1, the first name is Michael. At revision 2, the first name becomes Tom. Also notice that the last modified date of revision 2 reflects the updated date-time correctly.

Considerations When Using JPA

Although this chapter is long, it covered only a small portion of JPA. For example, using JPA to call database stored procedures was not covered. JPA is a complete and powerful ORM data access standard, and with the help of third-party libraries like Spring Data JPA and Hibernate Envers, you can implement various cross-cutting concerns relatively easily.

JPA is a JEE standard that is supported by most major open source communities as well as commercial vendors (e.g., JBoss, GlassFish, WebSphere, WebLogic, and so on). So, it's a compelling choice for adopting JPA as the data access standard. If you require absolute control over the query, you can use JPA's native query support, instead of using JDBC directly.

In conclusion, for developing JEE applications with Spring, we recommend using JPA to implement the data access layer. When desired, you can still mix in JDBC for some special data access needs. Always remember that Spring allows you to mix and match different data access technologies easily with the transaction management transparently handled for you.

Using JPA in the Sample Application

In this section, we will discuss the relationships between the topics discussed in this chapter and the sample application that we will develop. Topics include the backend database and the JPA implementation for various database operations.

We will also highlight how we adopt the features in Spring Data JPA to help simplify the data access logic and keep track of the basic audit information.

Finally, we will discuss how the entity versioning feature of the sample application was implemented using Hibernate's Envers module.

Database Backend

For database backend, the JDBC embedded database with H2 will be used. However, the scripts (database creation script, initial data population script) will be designed to be compatible with MySQL too. So, when desired, the application is able to use MySQL as the backend database.

For Spring's ApplicationContext configuration, we will simply use the <jdbc:embedded-database> tag to declare an embedded database. Two SQL scripts will be developed. One (called schema.sql) is for database creation, and the other (called initial-data.sql) is for initial data population (e.g., initial users, categories and subcategories, sample blog entries, etc.).

Using JPA for Persistence Layer Implementation

As mentioned in Chapter 3, for the persistence layer, two different implementations will be provided. One will use JPA, while the other will use MyBatis.

For the JPA implementation, we will use JPA 2, with Hibernate as the persistence provider. All the entity classes will be placed under the package com.apress.prospring3.springblog.domain, and the object-to-relational mapping properties will be defined by using standard JPA 2 annotations (under the javax.persistence package).

In addition, we will use Spring Data JPA to simplify the various database operations. All the repository interfaces (e.g., the EntryRepository interface for supporting the Entry entity class) will be placed under the package com.apress.prospring3.springblog.repository. Moreover, in order to support browsing blog entries in the web application frontend, pagination support will be implemented.

In terms of database operations, querying is the most complicated part. In the frontend, users can choose to filter entries by posting dates, categories, and subcategories, and so on. To fulfill this requirement, we will use JPA 2's strongly typed criteria query API.

Auditing and Entity Versioning

In the sample application, all blog entries and comments will have auditing features enabled.

With the help of Spring Data JPA's auditing feature, we will keep track of basic audit information (created by, created date, last modified by, last modified date) for blog posting and comments.

When a blog posting entry or comment is updated, Hibernate's Envers module will be used for keeping versions of each record. History tables will be created for blog posting and comment tables to keep the history records.

For details, please refer to Chapter 21.

Summary

In this chapter, we covered the basic concepts of JPA and how to configure JPA's EntityManagerFactory in Spring, using Hibernate as the persistence service provider.

Then, we discussed using JPA to perform basic database operations. Advanced topics included native queries and the strongly typed JPA criteria API.

Then we demonstrated how Spring Data JPA's Repository abstraction can help simplify JPA application development, as well as how to use its entity listener to keep track of basic auditing information for entity classes. For full versioning of entity classes, using Hibernate Envers to fulfill the requirement was also covered.

In the next chapter, we will discuss another popular data access library: MyBatis (formerly known as iBATIS).

CHAPTER 11

Using MyBatis in Spring

In the previous three chapters, you saw how Spring supports seamless integration with different libraries and techniques for implementing data access logic, from the traditional JDBC approach to ORM solutions including Hibernate and the JEE standard JPA. In this chapter, we will discuss another popular data access library: MyBatis (www.mybatis.org).

Formerly known as iBATIS (which was hosted on the Apache Software Foundation and was retired), MyBatis is a Java library (a .NET version is also available) that provides a data mapper framework for mapping the database relational structure into Java's OO model. However, instead of focusing on programming to the OO model like ORM does, MyBatis is more focused on the SQL side. You can think of MyBatis as the hybrid approach between JDBC and ORM. The MyBatis development team classifies MyBatis as a SQL-based data mapping solution for object-oriented software development.

In this chapter, we are going to focus on implementing the data access layer of a Spring application using MyBatis. Specifically, we will cover the following:

- *Configuration*: We will discuss how to configure MyBatis with Spring, including the Maven dependencies required and the configuration of MyBatis's SqlSessionFactory in Spring's ApplicationContext.

- *MyBatis SQL mapping*: In this section, you will learn how to define SQL mappings with MyBatis for transforming the resultset of SQL queries into the properties of the corresponding Java domain objects.

- *CRUD operations*: You will learn how to implement select, update, and delete operations using MyBatis. You will also learn how to implement select operations that represent major types of data relationships.

- *Using MyBatis in the sample application*: In the sample application, for the MyBatis implementation, we will eliminate the DAO layer and have the MyBatis mappers being directly injected into the service layer for executing business logic. We will discuss how MyBatis will be adopted in the sample application.

Getting Started with MyBatis in Spring

In this section, we will cover how to set up MyBatis to work with Spring. First we will provide a brief introduction to MyBatis, and then we will demonstrate how to create a project in STS for working with MyBatis. Also, we will present the data model that will be used for implementing the samples in this chapter. Finally, we will discuss the Spring configuration required for working with MyBatis.

Introducing MyBatis

iBATIS, the old name of MyBatis, was started by Clinton Begin in 2001, with the project code donated to Apache Software Foundation (ASF) in 2004. Based on its SQL mapping focus, simple infrastructure, and easy-to-understand mapping definitions from SQL queries to the Java OO model, iBATIS gained popularity quickly and became one of the most used data access libraries in the Java developer community.

After staying in ASF for six years, the iBATIS development team realized that data-accessing technologies in the open source world had changed dramatically. Consequently, the team decided to introduce numerous significant changes into the library. Starting with version 3, the project also changed its name to MyBatis, left ASF, and became an independent open source framework. The iBATIS project at ASF was also retired. At the time of this writing, the current version of MyBatis is 3.0.6.

Before Spring 3.0, Spring had out-of-the-box support for iBATIS version 2. However, because of the difficulties in synchronizing the massive changes from iBATIS 2 to MyBatis 3 with the Spring framework, Spring's development team decided to drop the built-in support of MyBatis.

To deal with this situation, the MyBatis team has started the MyBatis Spring Integration Project (called mybatis-spring). At the time of this writing, the current version of mybatis-spring is 1.0.2.

Creating a Simple Utility Project with MyBatis Support in STS

In STS, there is no template project provided for using Spring with MyBatis, so we need to create a simple Spring utility project in STS and then add the required dependencies manually. First create a simple Spring utility project in STS (please refer to Appendix A for details). Double-check that the project is using JSE 6 and Spring 3.1.

Upon project creation, open the pom.xml file in the POM editor and add the dependencies listed in Table 11-1.

Table 11-1. Maven Dependencies for Spring with MyBatis

Group ID	Artifact ID	Version	Description
org.springframework	spring-jdbc	3.1.0.RELEASE	Spring library for JDBC access, which is required by all applications with data access logic
org.springframework	spring-tx	3.1.0.RELEASE	Spring library required for transaction support.
com.h2database	h2	1.3.160	H2 database library for embedded database support
org.mybatis	mybatis	3.0.6	MyBatis core library
org.mybatis	mybatis-spring	1.0.2	MyBatis with Spring integration library

Figure 11-1 shows STS with the Maven dependencies after all the dependencies have been defined.

```
Dependency Hierarchy                                         日 田 | ↓ᵃ_z 000 ⬚

    🗋 junit : 4.7 [test]
    🗋 spring-test : 3.1.0.RELEASE [test]
 ◢ 🗋 spring-context : 3.1.0.RELEASE [compile]
    ◢ 🗋 spring-aop : 3.1.0.RELEASE [compile]
       🗋 aopalliance : 1.0 [compile]
       🗋 spring-asm : 3.1.0.RELEASE [compile]
       🗋 spring-beans : 3.1.0.RELEASE [compile]
       🗋 spring-core : 3.1.0.RELEASE [compile]
    ◢ 🗋 spring-beans : 3.1.0.RELEASE [compile]
       🗋 spring-core : 3.1.0.RELEASE [compile]
    ◢ 🗋 spring-core : 3.1.0.RELEASE [compile]
       🗋 spring-asm : 3.1.0.RELEASE [compile]
       🗋 commons-logging : 1.1.1 [compile]
    ◢ 🗋 spring-expression : 3.1.0.RELEASE [compile]
       🗋 spring-core : 3.1.0.RELEASE [compile]
       🗋 spring-asm : 3.1.0.RELEASE [compile]
 ◢ 🗋 spring-jdbc : 3.1.0.RELEASE [compile]
       🗋 spring-beans : 3.1.0.RELEASE [compile]
       🗋 spring-core : 3.1.0.RELEASE [compile]
       🗋 spring-tx : 3.1.0.RELEASE [compile]
 ◢ 🗋 spring-tx : 3.1.0.RELEASE [compile]
       🗋 aopalliance : 1.0 [compile]
       🗋 spring-aop : 3.1.0.RELEASE [compile]
       🗋 spring-beans : 3.1.0.RELEASE [compile]
       🗋 spring-context : 3.1.0.RELEASE [compile]
       🗋 spring-core : 3.1.0.RELEASE [compile]
    🗋 log4j : 1.2.14 [compile]
    🗋 h2 : 1.3.160 [compile]
    🗋 mybatis : 3.0.6 [compile]
 ◢ 🗋 mybatis-spring : 1.0.2 [compile]
       🗋 mybatis : 3.0.6 [compile]
       🗋 spring-core : 3.0.6.RELEASE (omitted for conflict with 3.1.0.RELEASE) [compile]
       🗋 spring-tx : 3.0.6.RELEASE (omitted for conflict with 3.1.0.RELEASE) [compile]
       🗋 spring-jdbc : 3.0.6.RELEASE (omitted for conflict with 3.1.0.RELEASE) [compile]
       🗋 spring-context : 3.0.6.RELEASE (omitted for conflict with 3.1.0.RELEASE) [compile]
```

Figure 11-1. Maven dependencies for Spring with MyBatis

To have MyBatis display all the SQL queries fired to the database, we need to turn on the DEBUG log level. Let's put the log4j properties file into the folder src/main/resources with the root logger level set to DEBUG. Listing 11-1 shows the log4j.properties file content.

■ **Note**   In STS, after a Spring template project is created, STS will generate a log4j.properties file in the folder src/test/resources. You can simply move the file into the folder src/main/resources and modify it, or you can delete the one in src/test/resources and create the log4j.properties file in the /src/main/resources folder.

Listing 11-1. log4j.properties File

```
log4j.rootCategory=DEBUG, stdout
log4j.appender.stdout=org.apache.log4j.ConsoleAppender
log4j.appender.stdout.layout=org.apache.log4j.PatternLayout
log4j.appender.stdout.layout.ConversionPattern=%d{ABSOLUTE} %5p %40.40c:%4L - %m%n
```

Sample Data Model for Example Code

For the sample data model for the examples in this chapter, we will use the same model as presented in Chapter 9, when we discussed using Hibernate with Spring, with some minor modifications. Figure 11-2 shows the sample data model.

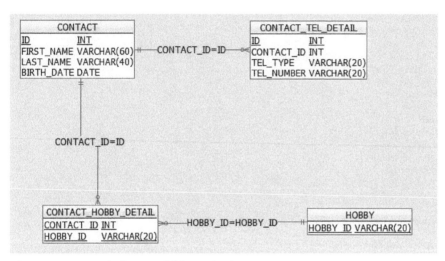

Figure 11-2. Sample data model for MyBatis

The main difference between this model and the one in Chapter 9 is that the VERSION column of the CONTACT and CONTACT_TEL_DETAIL tables are removed. The main reason for this is that MyBatis doesn't provide optimistic locking support with the VERSION column like Hibernate does. However, you will be able to see in the sample application how to implement optimistic locking using MyBatis.

Listings 11-2 and 11-3 show the scripts for schema creation (schema.sql) and sample data population (test-data.sql), respectively.

Listing 11-2. Sample Data Model Creation Script

```
CREATE TABLE CONTACT (
    ID INT NOT NULL AUTO_INCREMENT
    , FIRST_NAME VARCHAR(60) NOT NULL
    , LAST_NAME VARCHAR(40) NOT NULL
    , BIRTH_DATE DATE
    , UNIQUE UQ_CONTACT_1 (FIRST_NAME, LAST_NAME)
    , PRIMARY KEY (ID)
);
```

```
CREATE TABLE HOBBY (
    HOBBY_ID VARCHAR(20) NOT NULL
    , PRIMARY KEY (HOBBY_ID)
);

CREATE TABLE CONTACT_TEL_DETAIL (
    ID INT NOT NULL AUTO_INCREMENT
    , CONTACT_ID INT NOT NULL
    , TEL_TYPE VARCHAR(20) NOT NULL
    , TEL_NUMBER VARCHAR(20) NOT NULL
    , UNIQUE UQ_CONTACT_TEL_DETAIL_1 (CONTACT_ID, TEL_TYPE)
    , PRIMARY KEY (ID)
    , CONSTRAINT FK_CONTACT_TEL_DETAIL_1 FOREIGN KEY (CONTACT_ID)
      REFERENCES CONTACT (ID)
);

CREATE TABLE CONTACT_HOBBY_DETAIL (
    CONTACT_ID INT NOT NULL
    , HOBBY_ID VARCHAR(20) NOT NULL
    , PRIMARY KEY (CONTACT_ID, HOBBY_ID)
    , CONSTRAINT FK_CONTACT_HOBBY_DETAIL_1 FOREIGN KEY (CONTACT_ID)
      REFERENCES CONTACT (ID) ON DELETE CASCADE
    , CONSTRAINT FK_CONTACT_HOBBY_DETAIL_2 FOREIGN KEY (HOBBY_ID)
      REFERENCES HOBBY (HOBBY_ID)
);
```

Listing 11-3. *Data Population Script*

```
insert into contact (first_name, last_name, birth_date)
    values ('Clarence', 'Ho', '1980-07-30');
insert into contact (first_name, last_name, birth_date)
    values ('Scott', 'Tiger', '1990-11-02');
insert into contact (first_name, last_name, birth_date)
    values ('John', 'Smith', '1964-02-28');

insert into contact_tel_detail (contact_id, tel_type, tel_number)
    values (1, 'Mobile', '1234567890');
insert into contact_tel_detail (contact_id, tel_type, tel_number)
    values (1, 'Home', '1234567890');
insert into contact_tel_detail (contact_id, tel_type, tel_number)
    values (2, 'Home', '1234567890');

insert into hobby (hobby_id) values ('Swimming');
insert into hobby (hobby_id) values ('Jogging');
insert into hobby (hobby_id) values ('Programming');
insert into hobby (hobby_id) values ('Movies');
insert into hobby (hobby_id) values ('Reading');

insert into contact_hobby_detail(contact_id, hobby_id) values (1, 'Swimming');
insert into contact_hobby_detail(contact_id, hobby_id) values (1, 'Movies');
insert into contact_hobby_detail(contact_id, hobby_id) values (2, 'Swimming');
```

Configuring MyBatis SqlSessionFactory and MapperScannerConfigurer

The core concept of MyBatis surrounds the SqlSession interface (under the package org.apache.ibatis.session), which was obtained from the SqlSessionFactory interface (under the package org.apache.ibatis.session). Both the SqlSession and SqlSessionFactory interfaces belong to the mybatis-3.0.6 library. To configure the factory in Spring, we use the SqlSessionFactoryBean class (under the package org.mybatis.spring), which belongs to the mybatis-spring module (mybatis-spring-1.0.2 library).

Another important concept in MyBatis is the mapper interfaces, which are simple Java interface classes, that will be processed by MyBatis for mapping configuration between SQL queries and domain object properties. The mapping can be defined in either XML files (having the same name as the interface class) or annotations within the mapper interface. The mybatis-spring module provides another class, called MapperScannerConfigurer (under the package org.mybatis.spring.mapper), which supports a convenient way to instruct MyBatis to scan for mapper interface classes and register them as MapperFactoryBean<T> (under the package org.mybatis.spring.mapper and belonging to the mybatis-spring module), which enables injection of MyBatis mapper interfaces into other Spring beans.

The mapper interfaces will be discussed in detail later, and you will see how it can help simplify the development of database operations without the need to interact with the SqlSession interface directly.

Listing 11-4 shows the Spring application context configuration (app-context.xml).

Listing 11-4. Spring Configuration for MyBatis

```xml
<?xml version="1.0" encoding="UTF-8"?>
<beans xmlns="http://www.springframework.org/schema/beans"
    xmlns:xsi="http://www.w3.org/2001/XMLSchema-instance"
    xmlns:context="http://www.springframework.org/schema/context"
    xmlns:jdbc="http://www.springframework.org/schema/jdbc"
    xmlns:tx="http://www.springframework.org/schema/tx"
    xsi:schemaLocation="http://www.springframework.org/schema/beans
        http://www.springframework.org/schema/beans/spring-beans-3.1.xsd
        http://www.springframework.org/schema/context
        http://www.springframework.org/schema/context/spring-context-3.1.xsd
        http://www.springframework.org/schema/jdbc
        http://www.springframework.org/schema/jdbc/spring-jdbc-3.1.xsd
        http://www.springframework.org/schema/tx
        http://www.springframework.org/schema/tx/spring-tx-3.1.xsd">

    <jdbc:embedded-database id="dataSource" type="H2">
        <jdbc:script location="classpath:schema.sql" />
        <jdbc:script location="classpath:test-data.sql" />
    </jdbc:embedded-database>

    <bean id="transactionManager"
class="org.springframework.jdbc.datasource.DataSourceTransactionManager">
        <property name="dataSource" ref="dataSource" />
    </bean>

    <tx:annotation-driven />

    <context:component-scan
        base-package="com.apress.prospring3.ch11.service.mybatis" />
```

```
<!-- Define the SqlSessionFactory -->
<bean id="sqlSessionFactory"
    class="org.mybatis.spring.SqlSessionFactoryBean">
    <property name="dataSource" ref="dataSource" />
    <property name="typeAliasesPackage"
        value="com.apress.prospring3.ch11.domain" />
</bean>

<!-- Scan for mappers and let them be autowired -->
<bean class="org.mybatis.spring.mapper.MapperScannerConfigurer">
    <property name="basePackage"
        value="com.apress.prospring3.ch11.persistence" />
</bean>
```

```
</beans>
```

Most of the beans should be familiar to you; let's focus our attention on the beans sqlSessionFactory and org.mybatis.spring.mapper.MapperScannerConfigurer.

The sqlSessionFactory is implemented by the mybatis-spring provided class org.mybatis.spring.SqlSessionFactoryBean. As you might expect, the factory requires the data source bean. Also, the property typeAliasesPackage defines the packages storing the domain objects that MyBatis should look for when perform mapping from SQL resultset into POJOs. It's similar to the mapped entity classes in Hibernate and JPA.

Note that, in the configuration, the same instance of the dataSource bean is being injected into both Spring's transactionManager bean and MyBatis's sqlSessionFactory bean. This is because the SqlSessionFactoryBean class is designed specifically to leverage the existing DataSourceTransactionManager in Spring. Once a Spring transaction manager is configured, you can configure transactions in Spring as you normally would. Both @Transactional annotations and AOP-style configurations are supported. The mybatis-spring module will transparently manage transactions once they are set up. You just need to ensure that the same instance of dataSource was injected into both the transactionManager and SqlSessionFactory beans.

The class org.mybatis.spring.mapper.MapperScannerConfigurer is also provided by the mybatis-spring module. The class accepts the package name, from which MyBatis will scan for mapper interfaces. Also, the MapperScannerConfigurer bean also needs an instance of SqlSessionFactory to be injected. If there is only one SqlSessionFactory bean in the ApplicationContext, it will be autowired into the MapperScannerConfigurer bean. However, if your application contains multiple SqlSessionFactory beans (for example, in a multiple data source application, you have sqlSessionFactoryA bean for data source A and another sqlSessionFactoryB bean for data source B), then you will need to explicitly pass the reference to the corresponding SqlSessionFactory bean into each MapperScannerConfigurer bean.

Having the configuration in place, we can proceed to the next step, which is to define the SQL mapping in MyBatis between queries and the POJO model.

SQL Mapping in MyBatis

When implementing data access logic using MyBatis, the most important and time-consuming step is to define the mappings between the queries for various database operations and the corresponding domain objects. The mapping is closely related to what operations are required and their underlying queries. So, for the contact information service, let's define the ContactService interface that we will implement first. Listing 11-5 shows the interface.

Listing 11-5. The ContactService *Interface*

```
package com.apress.prospring3.ch11.service;

import java.util.List;

import com.apress.prospring3.ch11.domain.Contact;

public interface ContactService {

    // Find all contacts - without details
    public List<Contact> findAll();

    // Find all contacts - with tels and hobbies
    public List<Contact> findAllWithDetail();

    // Find by ID - with tels and hobbies
    public Contact findById(Long id);

    // Create a new or save an existing contact
    public Contact save(Contact contact);

    // Delete a contact
    public void delete(Contact contact);

    // Find a contact by first name and last name
    public List<Contact> findByFirstNameAndLastName(String firstName,
        String lastName);

}
```

The interface should be self-explanatory. It consists of a few finder methods for retrieving summary or detail contact information, within which some accept parameters as searching criteria, while other methods include insert, update, and delete operations. Later we will implement the service in the class ContactServiceImpl.

Mapper Interfaces and SQL Mapping Files

The mapper interfaces and the mapping files make up the heart of how MyBatis works. They work together with the domain objects to perform mapping between query results to domain objects, and vice versa. For mapping each domain object, three main files are involved. Table 11-2 describes the files and shows an example of each.

Table 11-2. MyBatis Mapper Interface and Mapping File

File Type	Purpose	Example
Domain object	The POJO that queries will be mapped to.	The Contact class (under the package com.apress.prospring3.ch11.domain) that holds the information of a contact
Mapper interface	The Java interfaces that MyBatis will scan for and register as MapperFactoryBeans. All the database operations supported for the relating domain object will be defined here.	The ContactMapper interface (under the package com.apress.prospring3.ch11.persistence) for the Contact domain object
SQL mapping configuration file	The XML configuration file that stores the details of mapping between SQL queries and domain objects. The file should be in the project's classpath and have the same name as the mapper interface.	The ContactMapper.xml file (under the folder src/main/resources with the package name com.apress.prospring3.ch11.persistence)

A diagram can help in understanding the structure better. For example, to implement the findAll() method of the ContactService interface, the files and their content will look like the one in Figure 11-3.

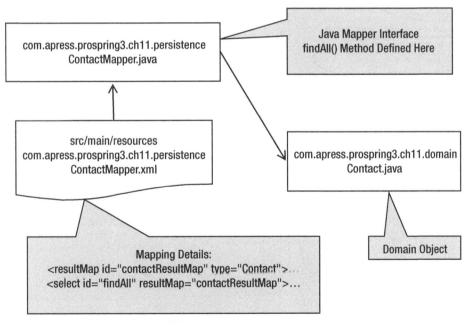

Figure 11-3. MyBatis mapping files structure

As Figure 11-3 shows, the mapper interface class has a corresponding XML file with the same name (ContactMapper.java and ContactMapper.xml), supporting the operations on the domain object Contact.java.

Upon the completion of all mappings, the project structure will look like the STS screen shown in Figure 11-4.

Figure 11-4. *MyBatis mapping files structure in STS*

SQL Mapping XML Configuration

In the mapper XML configuration files, MyBatis provides numerous tags for performing mapping operations. Table 11-3 highlights some of the most frequently used tags.

Table 11-3. Major Tags in MyBatis XML Mapping File

Tag Name	Description
resultMap	Maps the resultset of select operations into the domain objects. A lot of subtags (for example, <id>, <result>, <association>, <collection>, and so on) were provided for data type definitions, mapping associations, and so on.
select	Defines a select operation. The query to be submitted, named parameters, and which result map to use are defined here.
insert	Defines an insert operation. The domain object properties will be mapped to the insert statement's named parameters. A database-generated key can be set to be retrieved by MyBatis after the insert statement.
update	Defines an update operation.
delete	Defines a delete operation.

Database Operations with MyBatis

In this section, we discuss how to perform various CRUD operations with MyBatis in Spring.

For querying data, we will discuss how to perform mappings from SQL to POJOs, as well as model the relationships between domain objects. Moreover, topics including named parameters and dynamic SQL support in MyBatis will also be covered.

Finally, we will also discuss how to use MyBatis to implement insert/update/delete operations.

Querying Data

MyBatis provides intensive support for querying data in a database. Basically, for each select operation, we will define the SQL statement, the parameters, the result type (Java type), and the result mapping to use. Various relationships (one-to-one, one-to-many, and many-to-many) can be mapped easily. Another powerful feature in MyBatis is the support of dynamic SQL, which we will discuss in the following sections.

Simple Selects

Let's start with the simplest method of ContactService, the findAll() method. The method simply retrieves all contact information from the database, without their telephone and hobby details.

Let's begin with a Contact domain object without any association first. Listing 11-6 shows the class content.

Listing 11-6. The Contact Domain Object

```
package com.apress.prospring3.ch11.domain;

import java.io.Serializable;
import java.util.Date;
```

```
public class Contact implements Serializable {

    private Long id;
    private String firstName;
    private String lastName;
    private Date birthDate;

    // Getter/setter methods omitted

    public String toString() {
        return "Contact - Id: " + id + ", First name: " + firstName
            + ", Last name: " + lastName + ", Birthday: " + birthDate;
    }
}
```

The class is a simple POJO, with nothing we need to specify here. The next step is to define the contact's mapper interface (and the findAll() method), which was shown in Listing 11-7.

Listing 11-7. The ContactMapper Interface

```
package com.apress.prospring3.ch11.persistence;

import java.util.List;

import com.apress.prospring3.ch11.domain.Contact;

public interface ContactMapper {

    public List<Contact> findAll();

}
```

There's nothing special for the interface either. We just need to define the database operations supported by the mapper, which will be scanned by the MapperScannerConfigurer class and can be autowired into Spring beans.

The next step is the most important part, the XML mapping file. Listing 11-8 shows the content for mapping the findAll() operation (ContactMapper.xml).

Listing 11-8. The Mapping of the findAll Operation

```
<?xml version="1.0" encoding="UTF-8"?>
<!DOCTYPE mapper PUBLIC "-//mybatis.org//DTD Mapper 3.0//EN"
"http://mybatis.org/dtd/mybatis-3-mapper.dtd">

<mapper namespace="com.apress.prospring3.ch11.persistence.ContactMapper">

    <resultMap id="contactResultMap" type="Contact">
        <id property="id" column="ID" />
        <result property="firstName" column="FIRST_NAME" />
        <result property="lastName" column="LAST_NAME" />
        <result property="birthDate" column="BIRTH_DATE" />
    </resultMap>

    <select id="findAll" resultMap="contactResultMap">
```

```
        SELECT
        ID,
        FIRST_NAME,
        LAST_NAME,
        BIRTH_DATE
        FROM CONTACT
    </select>

</mapper>
```

The following are the main points for the mapping configuration:

- The file begins with a <mapper> tag with a namespace attribute defined. The namespace attribute (i.e., com.apress.prospring3.ch11.persistence.ContactMapper) indicates the name of the file and the interface (i.e., ContactMapper.xml and ContactMapper.java), which should be the same (in this case, com.apress.prospring3.ch11.persistence.ContactMapper).

- The <resultMap> defines a unique result mapping of a select operation. Depending on an application's needs, many result maps can be defined. As shown in Listing 11-8, we specify that the domain object to be mapped is the Contact object. Here we don't need to provide the package name of the domain object, because it was already provided in the sqlSessionFactory bean's typeAliasesPackage property in Spring ApplicationContext (see app-context.xml in Listing 11-4). Then we use the <id> tag to define the property for the id field and the corresponding column name in the query. Afterward, we use a number of <result> tags to map the domain object property to the selected columns.

- The <select> tag defines the query operation. Note that the id attribute should be in line with the method name defined in the ContactMapper interface. Then, the attribute resultMap specifies the mapping to use for transforming the resultset to a Contact domain object. The body of the tag is the SQL statement to use.

After defining the mapping, we can proceed with the implementation. For the implementation class, com.apress.prospring3.ch11.service.mybatis.ContactServiceImpl, we begin with creating the class with an empty implementation of all the methods in the ContactService interface. In STS, it's very easy to do it. For details, please refer to Chapter 8.

Listing 11-9 shows the implementation of the findAll() ContactService interface.

Listing 11-9. Implementing the findAll() Method

```
package com.apress.prospring3.ch11.service.mybatis;

// Import statements omitted

@Service("contactService")
@Repository
@Transactional
public class ContactServiceImpl implements ContactService {

    private Log log = LogFactory.getLog(ContactServiceImpl.class);

    @Autowired
    private ContactMapper contactMapper;
```

```
@Transactional(readOnly=true)
public List<Contact> findAll() {
    List<Contact> contacts = contactMapper.findAll();
    return contacts;
}

// Other code omitted
}
```

As shown in Listing 11-9, the mapper interface is injected into the service class, and the findAll() method simply calls the corresponding method in the ContactMapper interface. MyBatis will perform all the underlying work.

That's all for the findAll() method implementation. Listing 11-10 shows the testing program.

Listing 11-10. Testing the findAll() Method

```
package com.apress.prospring3.ch11;

import java.util.List;

import org.springframework.context.support.GenericXmlApplicationContext;

import com.apress.prospring3.ch11.domain.Contact;
import com.apress.prospring3.ch11.service.ContactService;

public class MyBatisSample {

    public static void main(String[] args) {

        GenericXmlApplicationContext ctx = new GenericXmlApplicationContext();
        ctx.load("classpath:app-context.xml");
        ctx.refresh();

        ContactService contactService = ctx.getBean("contactService",
            ContactService.class);

        List<Contact> contacts;

        // Find all contacts
        contacts = contactService.findAll();
        listContacts(contacts);

    }

    private static void listContacts(List<Contact> contacts) {
        System.out.println("");
        System.out.println("Listing contacts without details:");
        for (Contact contact: contacts) {
            System.out.println(contact);
            System.out.println();
        }
    }

}
```

Running the program will yield the output in STS shown in Figure 11-5.

```
11:22:22,733 DEBUG      org.mybatis.spring.SqlSessionUtils:  27 - Registering transaction synchronization for SqlSession [org.apache.ibatis.
11:22:22,784 DEBUG           java.sql.PreparedStatement:  27 - ==> Executing: SELECT ID, FIRST_NAME, LAST_NAME, BIRTH_DATE FROM CONTACT
11:22:22,785 DEBUG           java.sql.PreparedStatement:  27 - ==> Parameters:
11:22:22,802 DEBUG                   java.sql.ResultSet:  27 - <==    Columns: ID, FIRST_NAME, LAST_NAME, BIRTH_DATE
11:22:22,802 DEBUG                   java.sql.ResultSet:  27 - <==        Row: 1, Clarence, Ho, 1980-07-30
11:22:22,803 DEBUG                   java.sql.ResultSet:  27 - <==        Row: 2, Scott, Tiger, 1990-11-02
11:22:22,804 DEBUG                   java.sql.ResultSet:  27 - <==        Row: 3, John, Smith, 1964-02-28
11:22:22,807 DEBUG      org.mybatis.spring.SqlSessionUtils:  27 - Releasing transactional SqlSession [org.apache.ibatis.session.defaults.Def
11:22:22,807 DEBUG      org.mybatis.spring.SqlSessionUtils:  27 - Transaction synchronization committing SqlSession [org.apache.ibatis.sessi
11:22:22,807 DEBUG .datasource.DataSourceTransactionManager: 752 - Initiating transaction commit
11:22:22,807 DEBUG .datasource.DataSourceTransactionManager: 264 - Committing JDBC transaction on Connection [conn2: url=jdbc:h2:mem:dataSour
11:22:22,808 DEBUG      org.mybatis.spring.SqlSessionUtils:  27 - Transaction synchronization closing SqlSession [org.apache.ibatis.session.
11:22:22,808 DEBUG .datasource.DataSourceTransactionManager: 322 - Releasing JDBC Connection [conn2: url=jdbc:h2:mem:dataSource user=SA] afte
11:22:22,809 DEBUG ramework.jdbc.datasource.DataSourceUtils: 332 - Returning JDBC Connection to DataSource

Listing contacts without details:
Contact - Id: 1, First name: Clarence, Last name: Ho, Birthday: Wed Jul 30 00:00:00 CST 1980

Contact - Id: 2, First name: Scott, Last name: Tiger, Birthday: Fri Nov 02 00:00:00 CST 1990

Contact - Id: 3, First name: John, Last name: Smith, Birthday: Fri Feb 28 00:00:00 CST 1964
```

Figure 11-5. Output of findAll() method in STS

As shown in Figure 11-5, we turned the DEBUG log on, so besides the contact information, the select statement that was submitted by MyBatis to the database was also displayed. This is very useful for development purposes.

Defining the Mapping Using MyBatis Annotations

In addition to XML-based configuration, MyBatis also supports mapping definitions using Java annotations, just as many other tools do.

When using annotations, they should apply to the mapper interface. Listing 11-11 shows the ContactMapper interface with annotations used for the mapping definition.

Listing 11-11. Mappings Using MyBatis Annotation Support

```java
package com.apress.prospring3.ch11.persistence;

import java.util.List;

import org.apache.ibatis.annotations.*;

import com.apress.prospring3.ch11.domain.Contact;

public interface ContactMapperAnnotation {

    @Select(value="SELECT ID,FIRST_NAME,LAST_NAME,BIRTH_DATE FROM CONTACT")
    @Results(value={
        @Result(javaType=Contact.class),
        @Result(property="id", column="ID"),
        @Result(property="firstName", column="FIRST_NAME"),
        @Result(property="lastName", column="LAST_NAME"),
        @Result(property="birthDate", column="BIRTH_DATE")
    })
    List<Contact> findAll();

}
```

As shown in Listing 11-11, you can see that the findAll() method is annotated with @Select, which specifies the query, and the @Results and nested @Result annotations define the mapping details. You can see the annotation structure is quite like the XML style in Listing 11-8. (In this case, the method name findAll becomes the id attribute within the <select> tag.)

Basically, MyBatis provides annotation equivalents for all XML configurations. So, you can choose the annotation approach and totally get rid of the XML mapper files. However, for complex queries and mappings, a lot of code will be embedded into the interface class.

So, in this chapter, we will focus on the XML-style mapping definition in MyBatis.

One-to-Many and Many-to-Many Selects in MyBatis

Let's proceed to see the mapping of associations in MyBatis by looking at the relationships within the Contact domain object. For the association with the ContactTelDetail domain object, it's a one-to-many association. For the association with the Hobby domain object, it's a many-to-many association.

We begin with the one-to-many association. Listings 11-12 and 11-13 show the contactTelDetails property added into the Contact class and show the ContactTelDetail class, respectively.

Listing 11-12. The contactTelDetails Property in the Contact Class

```
package com.apress.prospring3.ch11.domain;

import java.io.Serializable;
import java.util.*;

public class Contact implements Serializable {

    // Other code omitted

    private Set<ContactTelDetail> contactTelDetails =
        new HashSet<ContactTelDetail>();
}
```

Listing 11-13. The ContactTelDetail Class

```
package com.apress.prospring3.ch11.domain;

import java.io.Serializable;

public class ContactTelDetail implements Serializable {

    private Long id;
    private Contact contact;
    private String telType;
    private String telNumber;

    // Getter/setter methods omitted

    public String toString() {
        return "Contact Tel Detail - Id: " + id + ", Contact id: "
            + contact.getId() + ", Type: " + telType
            + ", Number: " + telNumber;
    }
}
```

In MyBatis, for one-to-many (and many-to-many too) collection-type mapping, we use the `<collection>` tag (MyBatis provides the `<association>` tag for a one-to-one relationship). For mapping associations, MyBatis provides two options: *nested selects* and *nested results*. Let's take a look at both options and see their differences.

Select Associations with Nested Select

As you might be able to guess from the name, the nested select approach mean firing additional queries for each contact to retrieve the telephone details. So, when there are five contacts selected by the contact query, five more queries will be sent to the database for each contact to retrieve the telephone details, resulting in 5 + 1 = 6 queries fired. This is well-known as the *N+1* query condition. Let's see the nested select in action by implementing the `findAllWithDetail()` method in the `ContactService` interface. Listing 11-14 shows the `findAllWithDetail()` method declared in the `ContactMapper` interface.

Listing 11-14. *The findAllWithDetail Method*

```
package com.apress.prospring3.ch11.persistence;

import java.util.List;

import com.apress.prospring3.ch11.domain.Contact;

public interface ContactMapper {

    public List<Contact> findAll();

    public List<Contact> findAllWithDetail();

}
```

Listing 11-15 shows the `ContactMapper.xml` file, with the one-to-many association between `Contact` and `ContactTelDetail` objects defined using a nested select.

Listing 11-15. *Nested Select in MyBatis XML Mapping Definition*

```xml
<mapper namespace="com.apress.prospring3.ch11.persistence.ContactMapper">

    <!-- Other code omitted -->

    <resultMap id="contactResultDetailMap" type="Contact">
        <id property="id" column="ID" />
        <result property="firstName" column="FIRST_NAME" />
        <result property="lastName" column="LAST_NAME" />
        <result property="birthDate" column="BIRTH_DATE" />
        <collection property="contactTelDetails" ofType="ContactTelDetail"
            column="id" select="selectTelDetailsForContact">
        </collection>
    </resultMap>

    <resultMap id="contactTelDetailResultMap" type="ContactTelDetail" >
        <id property="id" column="ID" />
        <result property="telType" column="TEL_TYPE"/>
        <result property="telNumber" column="TEL_NUMBER"/>
```

413

```
    </resultMap>

    <select id="findAllWithDetail" resultMap="contactResultDetailMap">
        SELECT
        C.ID,
        C.FIRST_NAME,
        C.LAST_NAME,
        C.BIRTH_DATE
        FROM CONTACT C
    </select>

    <select id="selectTelDetailsForContact" parameterType="long"
        resultType="ContactTelDetail" resultMap="contactTelDetailResultMap">
        SELECT
        ID,
        TEL_TYPE,
        TEL_NUMBER
        FROM CONTACT_TEL_DETAIL WHERE CONTACT_ID = #{id}
    </select>

</mapper>
```

The following are the main points for the mapping configuration in Listing 11-15:

- A new <resultMap> with an ID of contactResultDetailMap is defined. In this result map, a <collection> tag is added and mapped to the contactTelDetails property of the Contact class. The type is ContactTelDetail, the corresponding statement for selecting the telephone for each details is selectTelDetailsForContact, and the value that needs to be passed to the select statement is the ID column of the CONTACT table.

- A new <resultMap> with an ID of contactTelDetailResultMap is added, which performs mapping from the selectTelDetailsForContact operation into the ContactTelDetail objects.

- A new <select> operation called selectTelDetailsForContact is added that will be used by the findAllWithDetail operation. This statement receives a parameter ID, which indicates the ID of each contact record.

Listing 11-16 shows the implementation of the findAllWithDetail() method in the ContactServiceImpl class.

Listing 11-16. *Implementation of the findAllWithDetail() Method*

```
package com.apress.prospring3.ch11.service.mybatis;

// Import statements omitted

@Service("contactService")
@Repository
@Transactional
public class ContactServiceImpl implements ContactService {


    // Other code omitted
```

```
@Transactional(readOnly=true)
public List<Contact> findAllWithDetail() {
    List<Contact> contacts = contactMapper.findAllWithDetail();
    for (Contact contact: contacts) {
        populateContactTelDetail(contact);
    }
    return contacts;
}

private void populateContactTelDetail(Contact contact) {
    if (contact.getContactTelDetails() != null) {
        for (ContactTelDetail contactTelDetail:
            contact.getContactTelDetails()) {
            contactTelDetail.setContact(contact);
        }
    }
}
}
```

The findAllWithDetail() will invoke the method with the same name in the ContactMapper interface. Then the private method populateContactTelDetail() is called to populate the Contact object reference for each ContactTelDetail object obtained for each contact.

To test the findAllWithDetail() method, add the code snippet in Listing 11-17 into the main() method of the MyBatisSample class.

Listing 11-17. Testing MyBatis Nested Select

```
// Find all contacts with details
contacts = contactService.findAllWithDetail();
listContactsWithDetail(contacts);
```

Then, add the listContactsWithDetail() method in Listing 11-18 into the MyBatisSample class.

Listing 11-18. The listContactsWithDetail() Method

```
private static void listContactsWithDetail(List<Contact> contacts) {
    System.out.println("");
    System.out.println("Listing contacts with details:");
    for (Contact contact: contacts) {
        System.out.println(contact);
        if (contact.getContactTelDetails() != null) {
            for (ContactTelDetail contactTelDetail:
                contact.getContactTelDetails()) {
                System.out.println(contactTelDetail);
            }
        }
        System.out.println();
    }
}
```

Running the MyBatisSample program will produce the following output (the other output was omitted):

```
==>  Executing: SELECT C.ID, C.FIRST_NAME, C.LAST_NAME, C.BIRTH_DATE FROM CONTACT C
==> Parameters:
```

415

```
<==     Columns: ID, FIRST_NAME, LAST_NAME, BIRTH_DATE
<==         Row: 1, Clarence, Ho, 1980-07-30
==>  Executing: SELECT ID, TEL_TYPE, TEL_NUMBER FROM CONTACT_TEL_DETAIL WHERE CONTACT_ID = ?
==> Parameters: 1(Long)
<==     Columns: ID, TEL_TYPE, TEL_NUMBER
<==         Row: 2, Home, 1234567890
<==         Row: 1, Mobile, 1234567890
<==         Row: 2, Scott, Tiger, 1990-11-02
==>  Executing: SELECT ID, TEL_TYPE, TEL_NUMBER FROM CONTACT_TEL_DETAIL WHERE CONTACT_ID = ?
==> Parameters: 2(Long)
<==     Columns: ID, TEL_TYPE, TEL_NUMBER
<==         Row: 3, Home, 1234567890
<==         Row: 3, John, Smith, 1964-02-28
==>  Executing: SELECT ID, TEL_TYPE, TEL_NUMBER FROM CONTACT_TEL_DETAIL WHERE CONTACT_ID = ?
==> Parameters: 3(Long)

Listing contacts with details:
Contact - Id: 1, First name: Clarence, Last name: Ho, Birthday: Wed Jul 30 00:00:00 CST 1980
Contact Tel Detail - Id: 1, Contact id: 1, Type: Mobile, Number: 1234567890
Contact Tel Detail - Id: 2, Contact id: 1, Type: Home, Number: 1234567890

Contact - Id: 2, First name: Scott, Last name: Tiger, Birthday: Fri Nov 02 00:00:00 CST 1990
Contact Tel Detail - Id: 3, Contact id: 2, Type: Home, Number: 1234567890

Contact - Id: 3, First name: John, Last name: Smith, Birthday: Fri Feb 28 00:00:00 CST 1964
```

As shown in the output (the other DEBUG messages were removed), you will see that four select statements were fired: one for the contact and one for each of the three selected contacts. If the resultset contains 1,000 records, then 1,001 statements will be fired separately, which will produce a massive data load on the database server and data traffic between the application container and database.

Another, more elegant way is to use a nested result, which we will discuss in next section.

Select Associations with Nested Results

Another way to model associations in MyBatis is to use nested results. Basically, instead of submitting separate queries for each parent object, the query was rewritten to join the tables. Then, in the result map, the properties of the nested objects are mapped accordingly, and MyBatis will populate the object graph properly for you.

To save a little space, let's also model the many-to-many relationship between the Contact and Hobby objects. Listings 11-19 and 11-20 show the revised Contact and Hobby domain objects.

Listing 11-19. The hobbies Property in the Contact Class

```
package com.apress.prospring3.ch11.domain;

import java.io.Serializable;
import java.util.*;

public class Contact implements Serializable {

    // Other code omitted

    private Set<Hobby> hobbies = new HashSet<Hobby>();
}
```

Listing 11-20. The Hobby Class

```
package com.apress.prospring3.ch11.domain;

import java.io.Serializable;

public class Hobby implements Serializable {

    private String hobbyId;

    // Getter/setter methods omitted

    public String toString() {
        return "Hobby :" + getHobbyId();
    }
}
```

Listing 11-21 shows the revised ContactMapper.xml file, with the one-to-many association between the Contact and ContactTelDetail objects, as well as the many-to-many association to the Hobby object defined using nested results.

Listing 11-21. Nested Results in MyBatis XML Mapping Definition

```
<mapper namespace="com.apress.prospring3.ch11.persistence.ContactMapper">

    <!-- Other code omitted -->

    <resultMap id="contactResultDetailMap" type="Contact">
        <id property="id" column="ID" />
        <result property="firstName" column="FIRST_NAME" />
        <result property="lastName" column="LAST_NAME" />
        <result property="birthDate" column="BIRTH_DATE" />
        <collection property="contactTelDetails" ofType="ContactTelDetail">
            <id property="id" column="CONTACT_TEL_ID"/>
            <result property="telType" column="TEL_TYPE"/>
            <result property="telNumber" column="TEL_NUMBER"/>
        </collection>
        <collection property="hobbies" ofType="Hobby">
            <result property="hobbyId" column="HOBBY_ID"/>
        </collection>
    </resultMap>

    <select id="findAllWithDetail" resultMap="contactResultDetailMap">
        SELECT
        C.ID,
        C.FIRST_NAME,
        C.LAST_NAME,
        C.BIRTH_DATE,
        T.ID AS CONTACT_TEL_ID,
        T.TEL_TYPE,
        T.TEL_NUMBER,
        H.HOBBY_ID
        FROM CONTACT C
        LEFT OUTER JOIN CONTACT_TEL_DETAIL T ON C.ID = T.CONTACT_ID
```

```
        LEFT OUTER JOIN CONTACT_HOBBY_DETAIL H ON C.ID = H.CONTACT_ID
    </select>
<mapper>
```

As shown in Listing 11-21, the select query for findAllWithDetail was first revised to an outer join of the CONTACT_TEL_DETAIL and CONTACT_HOBBY_DETAIL tables to retrieve the detail information.

Then, the result map contactResultDetailMap was also revised to directly map the resultset columns into properties of the nested objects within the associations. For example, for the contactTelDetails property, each property of the corresponding ContactTelDetail object was mapped to the corresponding column within the select statement. Similarly, the many-to-many mapping for the property hobbies is just the same. However, the query joins the CONTACT_HOBBY_DETAIL table (which stores the mapping between the CONTACT and HOBBY tables), and the results are mapped to the underlying Hobby object of the hobbies property.

To test the findAllWithDetail() method again, we need to revise the listContactsWithDetail() method to also display the hobbies attribute. Listing 11-22 shows the revised method in the MyBatisSample class.

Listing 11-22. The Revised listContactsWithDetail() Method

```java
    private static void listContactsWithDetail(List<Contact> contacts) {
        System.out.println("");
        System.out.println("Listing contacts with details:");
        for (Contact contact: contacts) {
            System.out.println(contact);
            if (contact.getContactTelDetails() != null) {
                for (ContactTelDetail contactTelDetail:
                    contact.getContactTelDetails()) {
                    System.out.println(contactTelDetail);
                }
            }
            if (contact.getHobbies() != null) {
                for (Hobby hobby: contact.getHobbies()) {
                    System.out.println(hobby);
                }
            }
            System.out.println();
        }
    }
```

The difference with the previous version is highlighted in bold. Running the MyBatisSample class again will produce the following output (other output was omitted):

```
==>  Executing: SELECT C.ID, C.FIRST_NAME, C.LAST_NAME, C.BIRTH_DATE, T.ID AS CONTACT_TEL_ID,
T.TEL_TYPE, T.TEL_NUMBER, H.HOBBY_ID FROM CONTACT C LEFT OUTER JOIN CONTACT_TEL_DETAIL T ON
C.ID = T.CONTACT_ID LEFT OUTER JOIN CONTACT_HOBBY_DETAIL H ON C.ID = H.CONTACT_ID
==>  Parameters:
<==    Columns: ID, FIRST_NAME, LAST_NAME, BIRTH_DATE, ID, TEL_TYPE, TEL_NUMBER, HOBBY_ID
<==        Row: 1, Clarence, Ho, 1980-07-30, 2, Home, 1234567890, Movies
<==        Row: 1, Clarence, Ho, 1980-07-30, 2, Home, 1234567890, Swimming
<==        Row: 1, Clarence, Ho, 1980-07-30, 1, Mobile, 1234567890, Movies
<==        Row: 1, Clarence, Ho, 1980-07-30, 1, Mobile, 1234567890, Swimming
<==        Row: 2, Scott, Tiger, 1990-11-02, 3, Home, 1234567890, Swimming
<==        Row: 3, John, Smith, 1964-02-28, null, null, null, null
```

```
Listing contacts with details:
Contact - Id: 1, First name: Clarence, Last name: Ho, Birthday: Wed Jul 30 00:00:00 CST 1980
Contact Tel Detail - Id: 1, Contact id: 1, Type: Mobile, Number: 1234567890
Contact Tel Detail - Id: 2, Contact id: 1, Type: Home, Number: 1234567890
Hobby :Movies
Hobby :Swimming

Contact - Id: 2, First name: Scott, Last name: Tiger, Birthday: Fri Nov 02 00:00:00 CST 1990
Contact Tel Detail - Id: 3, Contact id: 2, Type: Home, Number: 1234567890
Hobby :Swimming

Contact - Id: 3, First name: John, Last name: Smith, Birthday: Fri Feb 28 00:00:00 CST 1964
```

In the output, you can see that only one query is fired and six records are returned, while MyBatis will map the object graph properly, and the contact with detail information is displayed correctly.

Selects in MyBatis with Named Parameters

Let's see another select example with a named parameter, which is the findById() method. The method accepts a named parameter called id and needs to pass it to the query in MyBatis.

Listing 11-23 shows the method added to the ContactMapper interface.

Listing 11-23. The findById() Method

```java
package com.apress.prospring3.ch11.persistence;

import java.util.List;

import com.apress.prospring3.ch11.domain.Contact;

public interface ContactMapper {

    public List<Contact> findAll();

    public List<Contact> findAllWithDetail();

    public Contact findById(Long id);

}
```

The method accepts the ID and returns the contact record found. Listing 11-24 shows the mapping defined in the ContactMapper.xml file.

Listing 11-24. The Mapping of the findById Select Operation

```xml
<!-- Other code omitted -->

<select id="findById" parameterType="long"
    resultMap="contactResultDetailMap">
    SELECT
    C.ID,
    C.FIRST_NAME,
    C.LAST_NAME,
```

```
        C.BIRTH_DATE,
        T.ID AS CONTACT_TEL_ID,
        T.TEL_TYPE,
        T.TEL_NUMBER,
        H.HOBBY_ID
        FROM CONTACT C
        LEFT OUTER JOIN CONTACT_TEL_DETAIL T ON C.ID = T.CONTACT_ID
        LEFT OUTER JOIN CONTACT_HOBBY_DETAIL H ON C.ID = H.CONTACT_ID
        WHERE C.ID = #{id}
    </select>
```

The select operation uses the same result map as the previous findAllWithDetail operation, which populates the Contact object graph. The query is the same too; just a named parameter called id was added to the query. When we call the method ContactMapper.findById() and pass in the id, MyBatis will pass the named parameter into the select operation.

Listing 11-25 shows the implementation of the findById() method in the ContactServiceImpl class.

Listing 11-25. Implementation of the findById() Method

```
package com.apress.prospring3.ch11.service.mybatis;

// Import statements omitted

@Service("contactService")
@Repository
@Transactional
public class ContactServiceImpl implements ContactService {


    // Other code omitted
    @Transactional(readOnly=true)
    public Contact findById(Long id) {
        Contact contact = contactMapper.findById(id);
        populateContactTelDetail(contact);
        return contact;
    }

    // Other code omitted

}
```

To test the findById() method, add the code snippet in Listing 11-26 into the main() method of the MyBatisSample class.

Listing 11-26. Testing the findById() Method

```
        // Find contact by id
        contacts = new ArrayList<Contact>();
        System.out.println("Finding contact with id 1");
        Contact contact = contactService.findById(1l);
        contacts.add(contact);
        listContactsWithDetail(contacts);
```

Running the program will produce the result for a contact with an ID of 1.

Selects in MyBatis Using Dynamic SQL

One powerful feature in MyBatis for programming select operations is dynamic SQL, which eases the development of more complex queries a lot. To demonstrate its use, let's add the method findByFirstNameAndLastName() into the ContactMapper interface, as in Listing 11-27.

Listing 11-27. The findByFirstNameAndLastName() Method

```
package com.apress.prospring3.ch11.persistence;

import java.util.List;

import com.apress.prospring3.ch11.domain.*;

public interface ContactMapper {

    public List<Contact> findAll();

    public List<Contact> findAllWithDetail();

    public Contact findById(Long id);

    public List<Contact> findByFirstNameAndLastName(SearchCriteria criteria);
}
```

From Listing 11-27, instead of accepting two parameters (first name and last name), we defined a Java class to store the searching criteria. Listing 11-28 shows the SearchCriteria class.

Listing 11-28. The SearchCriteria Class

```
package com.apress.prospring3.ch11.domain;

public class SearchCriteria {

    private String firstName;
    private String lastName;

    // Getter/setter method omitted
}
```

The class simply stores the possible search criteria into the attributes. Let's see how the search criteria were substituted into the dynamic SQL in MyBatis. Listing 11-29 shows the mapping of the findByFirstNameAndLastName operation.

Listing 11-29. Mapping of the findByFirstNameAndLastName Operation

```
<!-- Other code omitted -->

<select id="findByFirstNameAndLastName" parameterType="SearchCriteria"
    resultMap="contactResultDetailMap">
    SELECT
    C.ID,
    C.FIRST_NAME,
```

```
            C.LAST_NAME,
            C.BIRTH_DATE,
            T.ID AS CONTACT_TEL_ID,
            T.TEL_TYPE,
            T.TEL_NUMBER,
            H.HOBBY_ID
        FROM CONTACT C
        LEFT OUTER JOIN CONTACT_TEL_DETAIL T ON C.ID = T.CONTACT_ID
        LEFT OUTER JOIN CONTACT_HOBBY_DETAIL H ON C.ID = H.CONTACT_ID
        <where>
            <if test="firstName != null">
                first_name = #{firstName}
            </if>
            <if test="lastName != null">
                AND last_name = #{lastName}
            </if>
        </where>
    </select>
```

From Listing 11-29, the magic happens in the <where> tag, which will be handled by MyBatis in composing the dynamic SQL intelligently. For example, it will first test whether the firstName attribute in the SearchCriteria being passed in is null. If not, it will add the clause WHERE FIRST_NAME = and the attribute into the query accordingly. The same thing happens for the attribute lastName. One fancy thing is that if you do not provide the first name, MyBatis will intelligent remove the AND operator from the WHERE clause using the last name. If both attributes are null, MyBatis will simply drop the WHERE clause entirely. Listing 11-30 shows the implementation of the findByFirstNameAndLastName() method in the ContactServiceImpl class.

Listing 11-30. Implementing the findByFirstNameAndLastName() Method

```java
package com.apress.prospring3.ch11.service.mybatis;

// Import statements omitted

@Service("contactService")
@Repository
@Transactional
public class ContactServiceImpl implements ContactService {

    // Other code omitted
    @Transactional(readOnly=true)
    public List<Contact> findByFirstNameAndLastName(String firstName,
        String lastName) {
        log.info("Finding contact with first name: " + firstName
            + " and last name: " + lastName);
        Contact contact = new Contact();
        contact.setFirstName(firstName);
        contact.setLastName(lastName);
        SearchCriteria criteria = new SearchCriteria();
        criteria.setFirstName(firstName);
        criteria.setLastName(lastName);

        List<Contact> contacts = contactMapper.findByFirstNameAndLastName(criteria);
        for (Contact contactTemp: contacts) {
```

```
            populateContactTelDetail(contactTemp);
        }

        return contacts;
    }
}
```

As shown in Listing 11-30, the method is still accepting the first name and last name as the parameters. However, it will construct the SearchCriteria instance and pass to the ContactMapper for data retrieval. To test the findByFirstNameAndLastName() method, add the code snippet in Listing 11-31 into the main() method of the MyBatisSample class.

Listing 11-31. Testing the findByFirstNameAndLastName() Method

```
        // Find contact by first name and last name
        contacts = contactService.findByFirstNameAndLastName("Clarence", "Ho");
        listContactsWithDetail(contacts);
```

Running the code will output the corresponding contact information. You can try different combinations and observe the SQL statement being generated by MyBatis.

Besides <where>, MyBatis provides a lot of different tags for building very flexible dynamic SQL statements. Also, for constructing dynamic SQL within Java code, MyBatis provides classes like SqlBuilder and SelectBuilder. Please refer to the official documentation at the MyBatis web site for details.

Inserting Data

Let's see how we insert new contact information into the database using MyBatis. From the select operations, we defined only the mapper interface ContactMapper. However, to support the insert operation of the associations (i.e., ContactTelDetail and Hobby), we also need to define the mapper interface and XML configuration files for them. Listings 11-32 and 11-33 show the new method insertContact() for the ContactMapper interface and the corresponding query mapping in the ContactMapper.xml file.

Listing 11-32. insertContact Operation for ContactMapper

```
package com.apress.prospring3.ch11.persistence;

import java.util.List;

import com.apress.prospring3.ch11.domain.*;
public interface ContactMapper {

    public List<Contact> findAll();

    public List<Contact> findAllWithDetail();

    public Contact findById(Long id);

    public List<Contact> findByFirstNameAndLastName(SearchCriteria criteria);

    public void insertContact(Contact contact);

}
```

Listing 11-33. insertContact Operation for ContactMapper.xml File

```
<insert id="insertContact" parameterType="Contact" useGeneratedKeys="true"
    keyProperty="id">
    INSERT INTO CONTACT (FIRST_NAME, LAST_NAME, BIRTH_DATE)
    VALUES (#{firstName}, #{lastName}, #{birthDate})
</insert>
```

From Listing 11-33, we use the <insert> tag to define a mapping for the insert operation. The attribute parameterType is of course the Contact object. Also, the attribute useGeneratedKeys instructs MyBatis to retrieve the record key generated by the database during insert, and the property for the key value should be stored back in the id attribute of the Contact object.

Listings 11-34 and 11-35 show the ContactTelDetailMapper interface (with the insertContactTelDetail() method) and the ContactTelDetailMapper.xml mapping file, respectively.

Listing 11-34. The ContactTelDetailMapper Interface

```
package com.apress.prospring3.ch11.persistence;


import com.apress.prospring3.ch11.domain.ContactTelDetail;

public interface ContactTelDetailMapper {

    public void insertContactTelDetail(ContactTelDetail contactTelDetail);

}
```

Listing 11-35. The ContactTelDetailMapper.xml Mapping File

```
<?xml version="1.0" encoding="UTF-8"?>
<!DOCTYPE mapper PUBLIC "-//mybatis.org//DTD Mapper 3.0//EN"
"http://mybatis.org/dtd/mybatis-3-mapper.dtd">

<!-- Contact Tel Detail Mapper -->
<mapper namespace="com.apress.prospring3.ch11.persistence.ContactTelDetailMapper">

    <insert id="insertContactTelDetail" parameterType="ContactTelDetail"
        useGeneratedKeys="true" keyProperty="id">
        INSERT INTO CONTACT_TEL_DETAIL (CONTACT_ID, TEL_TYPE, TEL_NUMBER)
        VALUES (#{contact.id}, #{telType}, #{telNumber})
    </insert>

</mapper>
```

The many-to-many association between the Contact and Hobby objects relies on the mapping table CONTACT_HOBBY_DETAIL, so we need to define the domain object, mapper interface, and mapping XML configuration for the mapping table too. Listing 11-36 shows the ContactHobbyDetail object.

Listing 11-36. The ContactHobbyDetail Domain Object

```
package com.apress.prospring3.ch11.domain;

public class ContactHobbyDetail {
```

```
    private Long contactId;
    private String hobbyId;

    // Getter/setter methods omitted
}
```

Listings 11-37 and 11-38 show the ContactHobbyDetailMapper interface (with the insertContactHobbyDetail() method) and the ContactHobbyDetailMapper.xml mapping file, respectively.

Listing 11-37. The ContactHobbyDetailMapper Interface

```
package com.apress.prospring3.ch11.persistence;

import com.apress.prospring3.ch11.domain.ContactHobbyDetail;

public interface ContactHobbyDetailMapper {

    void insertContactHobbyDetail(ContactHobbyDetail contactHobbyDetail);

}
```

Listing 11-38. The ContactHobbyDetailMapper.xml Mapping File

```
<?xml version="1.0" encoding="UTF-8"?>
<!DOCTYPE mapper PUBLIC "-//mybatis.org//DTD Mapper 3.0//EN"
"http://mybatis.org/dtd/mybatis-3-mapper.dtd">

<!-- Contact Hobby Detail Mapper -->
<mapper namespace="com.apress.prospring3.ch11.persistence.ContactHobbyDetailMapper">

    <insert id="insertContactHobbyDetail" parameterType="ContactHobbyDetail">
        INSERT INTO CONTACT_HOBBY_DETAIL (CONTACT_ID, HOBBY_ID)
        VALUES (#{contactId}, #{hobbyId})
    </insert>

</mapper>
```

Now we can implement the save() method in the ContactServiceImpl class. Listing 11-39 shows the code snippet.

Listing 11-39. Implementing the insert Operation

```
package com.apress.prospring3.ch11.service.mybatis;

// Import statements omitted
@Service("contactService")
@Repository
@Transactional
public class ContactServiceImpl implements ContactService {

    // Other code omitted

    @Autowired
```

```
    private ContactTelDetailMapper contactTelDetailMapper;

    @Autowired
    private ContactHobbyDetailMapper contactHobbyDetailMapper;

    public Contact save(Contact contact) {
        if (contact.getId() == null) {
            insert(contact);
        }
        return contact;
    }

    private Contact insert(Contact contact) {
        contactMapper.insertContact(contact);
        Long contactId = contact.getId();
        ContactHobbyDetail contactHobbyDetail;
        if (contact.getContactTelDetails() != null) {
            for (ContactTelDetail contactTelDetail:
                contact.getContactTelDetails()) {
                contactTelDetail.setContact(contact);
                contactTelDetailMapper.insertContactTelDetail(contactTelDetail);
            }
        }
        if (contact.getHobbies() != null) {
            for (Hobby hobby: contact.getHobbies()) {
                contactHobbyDetail = new ContactHobbyDetail();
                contactHobbyDetail.setContactId(contactId);
                contactHobbyDetail.setHobbyId(hobby.getHobbyId());
                contactHobbyDetailMapper.insertContactHobbyDetail(
                    contactHobbyDetail);
            }
        }
        return contact;
    }
}
```

As shown in Listing 11-39, the mapper for the associations is autowired into the service class. In addition, the save() method will check for the existence of the id attribute within the Contact instance. If it does not exist, then it's an insert operation, and the private insert() method will be called. In the insert() method, first the contact record is saved with the ID retrieved into the Contact object. The ID is then used for insert operations of the corresponding telephone and hobby details. To test the insert operation, add the code snippet in Listing 11-40 to the main() method of the MyBatisSample class.

Listing 11-40. Testing the save() Method Implementation

```
    // Add new contact
    System.out.println("Add new contact");
    contact = new Contact();
    contact.setFirstName("Michael");
    contact.setLastName("Jackson");
    contact.setBirthDate(new Date());
    Set<ContactTelDetail> contactTelDetails =
        new HashSet<ContactTelDetail>();
    ContactTelDetail contactTelDetail = new ContactTelDetail();
```

```
contactTelDetail.setTelType("Home");
contactTelDetail.setTelNumber("111111");
contactTelDetails.add(contactTelDetail);
contactTelDetail = new ContactTelDetail();
contactTelDetail.setTelType("Mobile");
contactTelDetail.setTelNumber("222222");
contactTelDetails.add(contactTelDetail);
contact.setContactTelDetails(contactTelDetails);
Set<Hobby> hobbies = new HashSet<Hobby>();
Hobby hobby = new Hobby();
hobby.setHobbyId("Jogging");
hobbies.add(hobby);
contact.setHobbies(hobbies);
contactService.save(contact);
contacts = contactService.findAllWithDetail();
listContactsWithDetail(contacts);
```

In Listing 11-40, a new contact is constructed, and two telephone records and one hobby record are created too. Then the save() method of ContactService is invoked. Running the program will produce the following output (other output was omitted):

```
Contact - Id: 4, First name: Michael, Last name: Jackson, Birthday: Wed Oct 26 00:00:00 CST
2011
Contact Tel Detail - Id: 4, Contact id: 4, Type: Home, Number: 111111
Contact Tel Detail - Id: 5, Contact id: 4, Type: Mobile, Number: 222222
Hobby :Jogging
```

You can see that a new contact with an ID of 4 was created, and the data was populated correctly.

Updating Data

Updating contact data is a bit complicated, mostly for the one-to-many telephone and many-to-many hobby associations. Let's implement the update method with the following sequence of operations:

1. Update the contact record.

2. Before updating the telephone details, retrieve the existing telephone details for the contact, and store the list of IDs for removing orphan records.

3. For each telephone detail, check whether the ID exists. If it does not exist, insert a new one. Otherwise, update the existing one. Also, remove the ID from the list of orphan records. After updating all the telephone details, check the list of IDs for any orphan telephone detail records. If any orphan telephone records exist, delete them.

4. For hobbies, first delete all the existing mappings from the CONTACT_HOBBY_DETAIL table and then insert the ones within the updated Contact object.

This sequence is just a typical handling mechanism; you can fine-tune it to suit your specific needs. First we need to add the update operation in the ContactMapper interface and XML file. Listings 11-41 and 11-42 show the respective code snippets.

Listing 11-41. updateContact Operation for ContactMapper

```
package com.apress.prospring3.ch11.persistence;

import java.util.List;

import com.apress.prospring3.ch11.domain.*;

public interface ContactMapper {

    public List<Contact> findAll();

    public List<Contact> findAllWithDetail();

    public Contact findById(Long id);

    public List<Contact> findByFirstNameAndLastName(SearchCriteria criteria);

    public void insertContact(Contact contact);

    public void updateContact(Contact contact);

}
```

Listing 11-42. updateContact Operation for the ContactMapper.xml File

```
<update id="updateContact" parameterType="Contact">
    UPDATE CONTACT SET
    FIRST_NAME = #{firstName},
    LAST_NAME = #{lastName},
    BIRTH_DATE = #{birthDate}
    WHERE ID = #{id}
</update>
```

There's just one new thing for Listing 11-42: the <update> tag is used for the update operation.

For the ContactTelDetailMapper interface and XML file, we need to add three operations. The first one is to retrieve the existing telephones by contact ID. The second one is to update an existing telephone detail, and the third one is to remove orphan telephone records by a list of IDs. Listings 11-43 and 11-44 show the code snippets for the ContactTelDetailMapper interface (with the new selectTelDetailForContact(), updateContactTelDetail(), and deleteOrphanContactTelDetail() methods) and the ContactTelDetailMapper.xml file, respectively.

Listing 11-43. The ContactTelDetailMapper Interface

```
package com.apress.prospring3.ch11.persistence;

import java.util.List;

import com.apress.prospring3.ch11.domain.ContactTelDetail;

public interface ContactTelDetailMapper {
```

```
    public void insertContactTelDetail(ContactTelDetail contactTelDetail);

    public List<ContactTelDetail> selectTelDetailForContact(Long contactId);

    public void updateContactTelDetail(ContactTelDetail contactTelDetail);

    public void deleteOrphanContactTelDetail(List<Long> ids);

}
```

Listing 11-44. *The* ContactTelDetailMapper.xml *Mapping File*

```xml
<!-- Contact Tel Detail Mapper -->
<mapper namespace="com.apress.prospring3.ch11.persistence.ContactTelDetailMapper">

    <!--  Other mappings omitted  -->

    <resultMap id="contactTelDetailResultMap" type="ContactTelDetail">
        <id property="id" column="id" />
        <result property="telType" column="tel_type" />
        <result property="telNumber" column="tel_number" />
    </resultMap>

    <select id="selectTelDetailForContact" parameterType="long"
        resultMap="contactTelDetailResultMap">
        SELECT
        ID,
        TEL_TYPE,
        TEL_NUMBER
        FROM CONTACT_TEL_DETAIL WHERE CONTACT_ID = #{contactId}
    </select>

    <update id="updateContactTelDetail" parameterType="ContactTelDetail">
        UPDATE CONTACT_TEL_DETAIL SET
        TEL_TYPE = #{telType},
        TEL_NUMBER = #{telNumber}
        WHERE ID = #{id}
    </update>

    <delete id="deleteOrphanContactTelDetail">
        DELETE FROM CONTACT_TEL_DETAIL
        WHERE ID IN
        <foreach item="item" index="index" collection="list"
            open="(" separator="," close=")">
            #{item}
        </foreach>
    </delete>
</mapper>
```

As shown in Listing 11-44, the select operation selectTelDetailForContact selects the telephone details by contact ID and returns a list of ContactTelDetail objects. The updateContactTelDetail operation is for updating an existing telephone record, while the operation deleteOrphanContactTelDetail is for deleting orphan telephone records. We use the <foreach> tag provided by MyBatis and pass in a List of IDs to delete from. MyBatis will construct the delete statement DELETE FROM CONTACT_TEL_DETAIL WHERE ID IN (…) intelligently. This is another useful tag.

For the ContactHobbyDetailMapper interface and XML file, we need to add just one more operation, which is the deleteHobbyDetailForContact() method for removing all mappings for a contact.

Listings 11-45 and 11-46 show the ContactHobbyDetailMapper interface (with the new deleteHobbyDetailForContact() method) and the ContactHobbyDetailMapper.xml mapping file for an update operation, respectively.

Listing 11-45. *The ContactHobbyDetailMapper Interface*

```
package com.apress.prospring3.ch11.persistence;

import com.apress.prospring3.ch11.domain.ContactHobbyDetail;

public interface ContactHobbyDetailMapper {

    public void insertContactHobbyDetail(ContactHobbyDetail contactHobbyDetail);

    public void deleteHobbyDetailForContact(Long contactId);

}
```

Listing 11-46. *The ContactHobbyDetailMapper.xml Mapping File*

```
<!-- Other code omitted -->

<delete id="deleteHobbyDetailForContact" parameterType="long">
    DELETE FROM CONTACT_HOBBY_DETAIL WHERE CONTACT_ID = #{contactId}
</delete>
```

Now we can proceed to implement the update() method in the ContactServiceImpl class. Listing 11-47 shows the code snippet.

Listing 11-47. *Implementing the update Operation*

```
// Other codes omitted
public Contact save(Contact contact) {
    if (contact.getId() == null) {
        insert(contact);
    } else {
        update(contact);
    }
    return contact;
}

private Contact update(Contact contact) {
    contactMapper.updateContact(contact);
    Long contactId = contact.getId();
    ContactHobbyDetail contactHobbyDetail;

    // List storing orphan ids of contact tel details
    List<Long> ids = new ArrayList<Long>();
```

```
    // Retrieve existing telephones for contact
    List<ContactTelDetail> oldContactTelDetails =
        contactTelDetailMapper.selectTelDetailForContact(contactId);
    for (ContactTelDetail contactTelDetail: oldContactTelDetails) {
        ids.add(contactTelDetail.getId());
    }

    // Update telephone details
    if (contact.getContactTelDetails() != null) {
        for (ContactTelDetail contactTelDetail:
            contact.getContactTelDetails()) {
            if (contactTelDetail.getId() == null) {
                contactTelDetailMapper.insertContactTelDetail(contactTelDetail);
            } else {
                contactTelDetailMapper.updateContactTelDetail(contactTelDetail);
                ids.remove(contactTelDetail.getId());
            }
        }
        if (ids.size() > 0) {
            contactTelDetailMapper.deleteOrphanContactTelDetail(ids);
        }
    }

    // Update hobby details
    contactHobbyDetailMapper.deleteHobbyDetailForContact(contact.getId());
    if (contact.getHobbies() != null) {
        for (Hobby hobby: contact.getHobbies()) {
            contactHobbyDetail = new ContactHobbyDetail();
            contactHobbyDetail.setContactId(contactId);
            contactHobbyDetail.setHobbyId(hobby.getHobbyId());
            contactHobbyDetailMapper.insertContactHobbyDetail(contactHobbyDetail);
        }
    }

    return contact;
}
```

In Listing 11-47, the update logic was implemented in the sequence as described in the beginning of this section. To test the update operation, add the code snippet in Listing 11-48 to the main() method of the MyBatisSample class.

Listing 11-48. Testing the save() Method Implementation for the Update Operation

```
    // Update contact
    System.out.println("Update contact with id 1");
    contact = contactService.findById(1l);
    contact.setFirstName("Kim Fung");
    Set<ContactTelDetail> contactTels = contact.getContactTelDetails();
    ContactTelDetail toDeleteContactTel = null;
    for (ContactTelDetail contactTel: contactTels) {
        if (contactTel.getTelType().equals("Home")) {
            toDeleteContactTel = contactTel;
        }
    }
```

```
        contactTels.remove(toDeleteContactTel);
        hobby = new Hobby();
        hobby.setHobbyId("Jogging");
        contact.getHobbies().add(hobby);
        contactService.save(contact);
        contacts = contactService.findAllWithDetail();
        listContactsWithDetail(contacts);
```

In Listing 11-48, the contact with an ID of 1 is first retrieved. Then, the first name is updated, the home telephone record is removed, and a new hobby is added. Next, the save() method is called to save the contact. Running the program will produce the following output (other output was omitted):

```
Contact - Id: 1, First name: Kim Fung, Last name: Ho, Birthday: Wed Jul 30 00:00:00 CST 1980
Contact Tel Detail - Id: 1, Contact id: 1, Type: Mobile, Number: 1234567890
Hobby :Movies
Hobby :Swimming
Hobby :Jogging
```

You can see that the contact was updated correctly.

Deleting Data

Deleting data is much easier. We just need to implement operations to delete the contact in the CONTACT table, as well as the underlying records in the CONTACT_TEL_DETAIL and CONTACT_HOBBY_DETAIL tables, respectively. Listings 11-49 and 11-50 show the new method deleteContact() for the ContactMapper interface and the corresponding query mapping in the ContactMapper.xml file.

Listing 11-49. deleteContact Operation for ContactMapper

```
package com.apress.prospring3.ch11.persistence;

import java.util.List;

import com.apress.prospring3.ch11.domain.*;

public interface ContactMapper {

    public List<Contact> findAll();

    public List<Contact> findAllWithDetail();

    public Contact findById(Long id);

    public List<Contact> findByFirstNameAndLastName(SearchCriteria criteria);

    public void insertContact(Contact contact);

    public void updateContact(Contact contact);

    void deleteContact(Long id);

}
```

Listing 11-50. deleteContact Operation for ContactMapper.xml File

```
<delete id="deleteContact" parameterType="long">
    DELETE FROM CONTACT WHERE ID = #{id}
</delete>
```

There's just one thing new here, where the `<delete>` tag was used to indicate a delete operation.
Listings 11-51 and 11-52 show the ContactTelDetailMapper interface (with the new
deleteTelDetailForContact() method) and the ContactTelDetailMapper.xml mapping file, respectively.

Listing 11-51. The ContactTelDetailMapper Interface

```
package com.apress.prospring3.ch11.persistence;

import java.util.List;

import com.apress.prospring3.ch11.domain.ContactTelDetail;

public interface ContactTelDetailMapper {

    public List<ContactTelDetail> selectTelDetailForContact(Long contactId);

    public void insertContactTelDetail(ContactTelDetail contactTelDetail);

    public void updateContactTelDetail(ContactTelDetail contactTelDetail);

    public void deleteOrphanContactTelDetail(List<Long> ids);

    void deleteTelDetailForContact(Long contactId);

}
```

Listing 11-52. The ContactTelDetailMapper.xml Mapping File

```
<delete id="deleteTelDetailForContact" parameterType="long">
    DELETE FROM CONTACT_TEL_DETAIL WHERE CONTACT_ID = #{contactId}
</delete>
```

For the ContactHobbyDetailMapper interface, we don't need to add new operation, because the
operation for deleting the hobby mappings for a contact was already implemented in the update
operation.
Now we can proceed to implement the delete() method in the ContactServiceImpl class. Listing
11-53 shows the code snippet.

Listing 11-53. Implementing the Delete Operation

```
// Other codes omitted
public void delete(Contact contact) {
    Long contactId = contact.getId();
    contactTelDetailMapper.deleteTelDetailForContact(contactId);
    contactHobbyDetailMapper.deleteHobbyDetailForContact(contactId);
    contactMapper.deleteContact(contactId);
}
```

The delete method is very simple. First we delete the child records, including the telephone and hobby details. Then we delete the contact record.

To test the delete operation, add the code snippet in Listing 11-54 to the main() method of the MyBatisSample class.

Listing 11-54. Testing the delete() Method Implementation

```
// Delete contact
System.out.println("Delete contact with id 1");
contact = contactService.findById(1l);
contactService.delete(contact);
contacts = contactService.findAllWithDetail();
listContactsWithDetail(contacts);
```

Running the program will delete the contact with an ID of 1.

Considerations When Using MyBatis

As you can see from the samples presented in this chapter, MyBatis is an excellent data access library focused on SQL mapping. When developing applications with MyBatis, most of the time you will be focused on the design and mapping of the result maps and various select, insert, update, and delete operations.

In terms of mapping, MyBatis provides a rich set of tags that can help you build dynamic and complicated queries and map to the corresponding domain objects easily. As you also saw from the samples, we don't need to directly interact with the SqlSession interface. Most of the time the mapper interfaces will be able to fulfill your needs.

However, if you want, you can choose to interact with the SqlSession interface and construct the queries in a programmatic way.

In conclusion, if you prefer to have more control over the SQL statements being submitted to the database and want a flexible and easy way to define the mapping of the resultset to the domain objects, MyBatis provides a much more elegant solution than JDBC.

However, when using MyBatis, there are some considerations too. For example, you need to implement the record locking mechanism (for example, a VERSION column for optimistic locking) and keep versions of history records manually. Also, if the data model changes frequently, you will need to review all those queries that will be affected by the change. In terms of ongoing maintenance, the effort of using MyBatis will be higher than that of using ORM libraries such as Hibernate and JPA.

Using MyBatis in the Sample Application

In this section, we will discuss the topics in this chapter in relation to the sample application that we will develop. Topics include the backend database and the MyBatis implementation for various database operations.

We will also highlight how we adopt the features in MyBatis to help us simplify the data access logic.

Finally, we will discuss how we keep track of the basic audit information and how the entity versioning feature is implemented, even though MyBatis doesn't provide out-of-the-box support for these features.

Database Backend

For the database backend, the JDBC embedded database with H2 will be used. However, the scripts (database creation script, initial data population script) will be designed to be compatible with MySQL too. So, when desired, the application is able to use MySQL as the backend database.

For Spring's `ApplicationContext` configuration, we will simply use the `<jdbc:embedded-database>` tag to declare an embedded database. Two SQL scripts will be developed. One is for database creation (called `schema.sql`), and the other is for initial data (for example, initial users, categories and subcategories, sample blog entries, and so on) population (called `initial-data.sql`).

Using MyBatis for Persistence Layer Implementation

As mentioned in Chapter 3, for the persistence layer, two different implementations will be provided. One will use JPA, while the other will use MyBatis.

For the MyBatis implementation, we will use MyBatis 3. More specifically, the MyBatis mapper interfaces and XML-style mapping configurations will be adopted. All the entity classes will be placed under the package `com.apress.prospring3.springblog.domain` (actually the same set of domain objects will be used by both JPA and MyBatis for mapping).

In addition, all the MyBatis mapper interfaces (for example, the `EntryMapper` interface for supporting the `Entry` entity class) will be placed under the package `com.apress.prospring3.springblog.persistence`. Moreover, to support browsing blog posting entries in the web application frontend, pagination support will be implemented as well.

In terms of database operations, query is the most complicated part since in the frontend users can choose to filter posting entries by posting dates, categories and subcategories, and so on. To fulfill this requirement, we will use MyBatis's dynamic SQL feature.

Auditing and Entity Versioning

In the sample application, all blog posting entries and comments will have auditing features enabled.

For keeping track of basic audit information (created by, created date, last modified by, last modified date) for blog posting and comments, as well as keeping versions of each record, we will utilize MyBatis's plug-in mechanism to intercept the calls to the update operation and populate the basic audit information (created by, created date, last modified by, last modified date) accordingly. On the other hand, a copy of the preupdate record will be saved into the history table.

For details, please refer to the section "MyBatis Service Implementation" in Chapter 21.

Summary

In this chapter, we discussed how Spring integrates with MyBatis (formerly iBATIS) when developing data access logic. Topics included the core concepts, configuration, and mapping definition, and so on.

Then, we discussed how to perform various database operations using MyBatis. We covered various techniques in retrieving data with different associations and how to use dynamic SQL.

In this chapter, we covered only a small portion of the features available in MyBatis when implementing most common database operations. For detailed information about MyBatis and its documentation, please refer to the project web site (`www.mybatis.org`).

CHAPTER 12

Designing and Implementing Spring-Based Applications

In previous chapters, we discussed various topics related to application development with Spring, including Spring's `ApplicationContext` configuration, various DI mechanisms, AOP support for cross-cutting concerns, and how Spring integrates with different data access technologies for interacting with backend relational databases.

When discussing implementations of data access logic, you saw how to use different implementation patterns. For example, in Chapter 8, which covered data access with JDBC, the data access logic was encapsulated in DAOs. In Chapters 10 and 11, when discussing JPA and MyBatis, we eliminated the DAO layer and had the JPA's `EntityManager` and MyBatis's mapper interfaces injected into the service layer directly. In those chapters, we also mentioned the design of domain objects (or the entity classes, in JPA terms) and showed how their attributes and relationships were modeled and mapped to the database structure.

Before we proceed, let's take a short break from programming topics and discuss some of the main principles in designing and implementing Spring-based applications. We believe that taking a step back and revisiting the application design practice for JEE applications here will help you better correlate the topics as we proceed with the overall application architecture.

Application design is a big topic, and we do not intend to cover all aspects of it. In this chapter, we will discuss some tried-and-tested OOP practices that result in applications that have clearly defined component responsibilities and that are also easy to test and maintain. This chapter looks at the impact Spring has on application design, paying particular attention to patterns and practices that you will find easy to apply when you are building your application with Spring. Much of this chapter focuses on the design decisions we made when building the SpringBlog application, and we use that application as the basis for our examples and discussions. In addition to the application design principles, we will discuss how you can use many of the Spring technologies covered so far to implement the data access and service layers of the SpringBlog application.

Specifically, in this chapter we look at the following:

- *Interface-driven design*: Interface-driven design is a traditional OOP best practice. When you use interface-driven design, the main components of your application are defined in terms of interfaces rather than concrete classes. Java offers first-class support for this kind of design with its notion of interfaces separate from classes. In this section of the chapter, we discuss interface-driven design in general terms and why you should use it in your applications.

- *Building a Domain Object Model*: In this section of the chapter, we look at the notion of a Domain Object Model (DOM), a collection of objects that provides an abstract model of the data in an application's problem domain. By creating a DOM for your application, you are creating a set of objects for modeling application data and behavior that matches some abstract ideas of your problem domain.

- *The data access layer*: Most applications nowadays need to access some kind of persistent data store, typically a relational database. Chapters 8 through 11 discussed Spring's support for a variety of different data access methods. In this section of the chapter, we look at the design issues related to building a data access layer to service the rest of your application.

- *Building the service layer*: An application's service layer is where all of the business logic that makes up the application is encapsulated. In this section, we look at how the service layer interacts with the Domain Object Model and data access layer to provide a unified interface to access application functionality. We also look at the business requirements of the SpringBlog application and how this translates into an interface design and an implementation of that interface.

You should note that this chapter does not cover the design or implementation of the application's web tier; that is covered in greater detail in Chapters 17 and 18. In particular, we do not cover how the SpringBlog service layer is utilized by the web frontend, nor do we explore how Spring uses the validation logic to support data validation and error reporting in the frontend. Both of these topics are covered in Chapters 17 and 18.

Designing to Interfaces

Designing to interfaces is a common practice when architecting and implementing an application, no matter which framework or standard (Spring, JBoss Seam, Guice, EJB, and so on) you are working on. One of the main design goals of Spring is to further ease the development of applications that are designed and implemented around a set of well-defined interfaces. Before we can look at designing a Spring-based application in any detail, we should explore exactly why designing to interfaces is such a big thing and how Spring goes about making it easier.

Why Design to Interfaces

There are many reasons you should design and code your applications to interfaces rather than to a concrete class hierarchy, but perhaps the biggest reason is to reduce coupling. If components in your application communicate with each other in terms of interfaces rather than concrete types, it becomes very easy to swap out a component if it becomes problematic. This capability allows you to switch from one implementation to another, without having to touch the rest of the application code; indeed, it is possible for your application to work with many different implementations of the same interface without even being aware that it is doing so. For example, when using profile support in Spring, you can provide different concrete implementations of the same interface, without any impact on the rest of the application.

Remember also that, in Java, a class has only one shot at concrete inheritance but can implement as many interfaces as necessary. By defining application components in terms of interfaces rather than classes, you are not going to constrain an implementing class to a particular base class unnecessarily. One other benefit, as we discussed in Chapter 7, is that using interfaces makes it possible to adopt AOP's introduction support to "mix in" specific interfaces into target beans when addressing cross-cutting concerns, without introducing additional complexity into the source code of the target components.

On the testing side, one of the main benefits gained by this loose coupling is the increase in testability. As the heads of a busy development team, we are constantly seeking new ways to improve the test coverage in the applications we produce as a direct way of improving the quality of the product we send to the customer. By designing to interfaces, we can swap out an implementation of an interface for a mock implementation, which allows us more flexibility when testing. For example, when unit testing a web controller, we definitely want to focus on whether the controller is behaving correctly, assuming that the service classes it depends on are working properly. In this case, it will be very useful to provide a "mocked" version of the service class that always return the expected results to the web controller under test.

The Factory Pattern

One of the key problems you will encounter when implementing an application where all the components are defined in terms of interfaces is how your application goes about locating instances of classes that implement the interfaces. A traditional solution to this is to use the Factory Pattern. The Factory Pattern defines a class whose responsibility is to provide application components with implementations of other application components; in this case, the available components are defined in terms of interfaces, not concrete implementations. Consider a system that has a business interface called OrderService. Other components in the system want to obtain implementations of this interface without knowing ahead of time which implementation they need. To implement such a system, we can build a Factory class like the one shown in Listing 12-1. Note that the OrderService interface and the DefaultOrderServiceImpl implementation class (which implements the OrderService interface) are empty, without any methods defined.

Listing 12-1. A Basic Factory Class Implementation

```
package com.apress.prospring3.ch12.factory;

import com.apress.prospring3.ch12.service.OrderService;
import com.apress.prospring3.ch12.service.impl.DefaultOrderServiceImpl;

public class BasicFactory {
    private static final BasicFactory instance;
    private OrderService orderService;

    static {
        instance = new BasicFactory();
    }

    public static BasicFactory getInstance() {
        return instance;
    }

    public BasicFactory() {
        this.orderService = new DefaultOrderServiceImpl();
    }

    public OrderService getOrderService() {
        return this.orderService;
    }
}
```

This is a simplistic Factory implementation, but it does illustrate the basic Factory Pattern approach. Now any application that wants to get access to an implementation of OrderService simply uses the getOrderService() method of the BasicFactory class.

Drawbacks of the Basic Factory Pattern

In its basic form, the Factory Pattern has three main drawbacks:

- There is no way to change an implementing class without a recompile.

- There is no way to make multiple implementations available transparently to different components. This is part of a larger problem in that the Factory class requires each component to have some knowledge of the Factory and which method on the Factory to invoke.

- There is no way simply to switch instantiation models. In Listing 12-1, we maintained a singleton instance of DefaultOrderServiceImpl, but if we wanted to return many instances, we would have to recompile the Factory class.

These drawbacks are discussed in detail in the next three sections.

Externally Configurable Factories

From the example in Listing 12-1, you can see that changing the implementation class means changing the BasicFactory class and recompiling. One of the benefits of interface-based design is that you can swap out implementations for new ones very easily. However, having to recompile the Factory removes some of the ease with which this can be done. In many projects in the past, before Spring was available, we created factories that allowed the implementation class for interfaces to be specified in an external configuration file (as you already saw in Chapter 2, when implementing the MessageSupportFactory class). This solved the initial problem, but it added more development burden to our project, and it did not really help out with the two remaining problems.

Supporting Multiple Implementations Transparently

Supporting multiple implementations transparently is perhaps the biggest drawback of the traditional Factory Pattern. The basic method on the BasicFactory class, getOrderService(), can return only one particular implementation (or a random choice), but it cannot choose which implementation to return based on the caller. This leads, naturally, to an implementation such as that shown in Listing 12-2. Note that the SuperOrderServiceImpl is also an empty class, which implements the OrderService interface.

Listing 12-2. Basic Support for Multiple Implementations

```
package com.apress.prospring3.ch12.factory;

import com.apress.prospring3.ch12.service.OrderService;
import com.apress.prospring3.ch12.service.impl.DefaultOrderServiceImpl;
import com.apress.prospring3.ch12.service.impl.SuperOrderServiceImpl;

public class MultiFactory {
    private static final BasicFactory instance;
    private OrderService orderService;
    private OrderService superOrderService;
    static {
        instance = new BasicFactory();
    }
```

```
    public static BasicFactory getInstance() {
        return instance;
    }

    public MultiFactory() {
        this.orderService = new DefaultOrderServiceImpl();
        this.superOrderService = new SuperOrderServiceImpl();
    }

    public OrderService getOrderService() {
        return this.orderService;
    }

    public OrderService getSuperOrderService() {
        return this.superOrderService;
    }
}
```

With this implementation, components that need to access the SuperOrderServiceImpl implementation class can call the getSuperOrderService() method. However, this approach just negates the benefit of a factory. Although the components are not coupled by class to a particular implementation, they are coupled by the method they call on the factory. Another drawback to this approach is that each new implementation requires a change to the Factory code and a change to the component that needs the new implementation. Having to add a new method for each new implementation makes this approach very difficult to configure externally.

Another implementation that tries to solve the problem of transparent support for multiple implementations requires components that invoke the getOrderService() method to pass in their class to the getOrderService() method so that the factory can decide, based on the class of the caller, which implementation to return. This implementation suffers from numerous problems, not least of which is that it works only with classes, meaning two instances of the same class cannot have different implementations of the OrderService. You will also find that the implementation of the getOrderService() method quickly becomes messy when you have many components that need an OrderService implementation.

A little more elegant approach to this problem is to use a lookup-style approach by having each component look up the implementation with a key. So, instead of calling getOrderService(), a component calls getOrderService("someKey"). The drawback of this approach is that in order to maintain full flexibility, each component must use a separate key so that its implementation can be changed separately from the others. When the dependent object wants a different implementation of the same business service, it still needs to change the code to use the key of the corresponding implementation.

The root of this problem lies in the fact that a component actively has to ask for an implementation class, and to gain full flexibility and ensure that each component can get the appropriate concrete implementation class that it needs, the request has to be completely unique. This is a problem that is not solved using the traditional Factory Pattern.

Supporting Multiple Instantiation Modes

Another problem is supporting multiple instantiation modes of an implementation class for different components. This problem suffers from many of the issues discussed in the preceding section, and again, the core of this problem is that a component actively has to ask for an implementation class. This problem is also not solved using the traditional Factory Pattern. Thankfully, Spring solves all of these problems; we discuss how in the next section.

Impact of Spring on Interface-Based Design

Spring has a huge impact on applications that are designed using interfaces. Because Spring takes care of wiring all the components together, you no longer have to worry about creating Factory classes that consider every possible situation.

On the surface, when you are building interface-based applications, the biggest benefit from Spring is the reduction in glue code that you have to write. This benefit is further enhanced by the excellent out-of-the-box support for external configuration of component dependencies. However, the biggest benefit comes from Spring's use of Dependency Injection. Because Spring removes the responsibility for dependency location from the components themselves and simply asks that components allow it to provide them with the dependencies, Spring is able to solve the last two of the three problems discussed previously.

Dependency Injection means that Spring can provide any instance of any implementation class to any instance of any application component without requiring any special coding in the application component whatsoever. This is coupled with the fact that Spring can freely manage the life cycle of any instance of any dependency that it is managing for an application component.

Basically, this means that Spring has all the features that we need to design interface-based applications, and we don't have to worry about how we are going to glue the components together during implementation.

Building a Domain Object Model

A Domain Object Model (DOM) is a set of classes that model concepts from the problem domain. Again, the DOM is a big topic, and we will just cover the main concepts of the DOM in this section. For a more complete description of the DOM Pattern, we recommend you read *Patterns of Enterprise Application Architecture* by Martin Fowler (Addison-Wesley, 2002) or *Domain-Driven Design: Tackling Complexity in the Heart of Software* by Eric Evans (Addison-Wesley, 2003). Although we do not go into great detail on this pattern, we do show you why we chose to create a DOM for the SpringBlog application and how we built our DOM.

Spring and the Domain Object Model

Given that this is a book on Spring, you might find it strange that we dedicate considerable space to a topic that is not directly related to Spring in any way. Of the applications that we have built using Spring, the only objects that are consistently not managed by Spring are domain objects. (Even though in Spring it's possible to have Spring manage domain objects by applying the @Component annotation to the classes and assigning them with prototype scope, most of the time we will choose to manage domain objects within the application.) The reason for this is that, practically, Spring does not need to be involved with domain objects. Generally, you create many instances of your domain objects using the new() operator and perform processing either in the service or data access layer. Although Spring also supports the injection of new instance of domain objects every time it was requested (by using the bean scope prototype), generally developers will not adopt this approach since typically domain objects do not take advantage of Dependency Injection, because they generally have few dependencies outside of the DOM itself, and they don't require much configuration.

You might well be wondering, then, why so much attention is paid to the DOM. The answer is simple. The DOM is the most critical area that affects so many other parts of the application, parts that are managed by Spring, that getting it right is very important to getting your whole application right.

The DOM Is Not the Same As a Value Object

The important thing to understand about the DOM Pattern is that it is not the same as the Value Object (often called Data Transfer Object) Pattern. The Value Object Pattern was created to overcome a shortcoming in the original EJB specification that meant that all calls to an EJB were remote. Configuring the state of an EJB typically means many calls, all of which are remote. Using a value object, object state is transferred in bulk using a single remote call, thus reducing the performance hit of making many remote calls.

■ **Note** Officially the Value Object Pattern is not the same as the Data Transfer Object Pattern. Martin Fowler defines a value object as "a small simple object, like money or a date range, whose equality isn't based on identity." You can find details at `http://martinfowler.com/bliki/ValueObject.html`. The confusion arises, however, from the Core J2EE Patterns catalog that uses the term *value object* for many of the examples of the Data Transfer Object Pattern. (For details, please refer to "Core J2EE Patterns: Transfer Object" and the Transfer Object class diagram in the online catalog at `http://java.sun.com/blueprints/corej2eepatterns/Patterns /TransferObject.html`.) In this section, we use the terms *value object* and *data transfer object* interchangeably, but we are talking about the Data Transfer Object Pattern.

A DOM is an object-based representation of the application problem domain, intended to allow the programmer to code in terms of objects that exist in the problem domain. While a value object purely encompasses state, it is perfectly acceptable for a domain object to encompass both state and behavior (although you may choose not to encapsulate behavior inside domain objects).

Another key difference between domain objects and value objects is that a value object's structure is driven by the need to transfer data remotely, whereas a domain object is modeled to represent a real-world concept and is not driven by some need of the application infrastructure. As we discuss later, we believe there are no hard-and-fast rules for modeling domain objects; you have to choose a level of granularity that matches your application and the functions it will perform.

It is possible for an application to have both domain objects and value objects. In this approach, value objects are used by the service layer to communicate with other layers, such as the presentation layer and the data access layer. These value objects are then converted as appropriate into domain objects and passed into the presentation layer for rendering. In general, this approach is not recommended. One reason is that maintenance will be complicated, because changes to domain objects also mean changes to the related value objects. The other reason is that with Spring, the data access and web framework is so powerful that it is simple to map data directly to domain objects, both for processing and for presentation.

Why Create a Domain Object Model

Creating a DOM requires some up-front effort in order to identify domain objects and then create an in-code representation of these objects. However, this up-front effort is far outweighed by the time you will save and the bugs you will avoid when it comes to implementing business logic to do something with your domain objects. We find that using a good DOM makes creating the code to solve business problems much easier, since you are able to code in terms of the problem rather than in terms of the machine the application runs on. A good DOM makes it easier for developers to transform application requirements into application features.

Modeling Domain Objects

There are a great many different methodologies and approaches to domain object modeling. Some practices advocate letting the underlying data store drive your object model, whereas some practices say, "Let the business domain drive the object model." In practice, we have found that a happy medium between these two approaches results in a DOM that is both easy to work with and well-performing.

For small applications with only five or six database tables, it is often easier just to create one domain object that corresponds to each database table. Although these objects are not strictly domain objects—in that their creation is not driven by the problem domain but rather the data structure—they are close enough for the purposes of such a simple application. Indeed, in many small applications, the result of an extensive domain modeling process is an object model that matches the database structure entirely.

For larger applications, much more attention has to be put into the real-world problem domain and the underlying data store. When we are building a DOM for an application, we usually focus on three main points:

- How the problem domain is structured

- How the domain objects will be used

- How the underlying data store is constructed

What we are looking for is a DOM that is as close to the ideal model as possible without affecting the performance of the data store too much and without having too great an impact on code that has to use the domain objects.

Typically, a DOM is quite granular, and you might end up with more than one class for a single logical concept. For instance, consider the concept of an order in a purchasing system. Typically an order is modeled as a single Order object with one or more OrderLine objects that represent each line item of the order. Trying to model an order using a single object leads to an object model that is unnecessarily coarse and unwieldy and difficult to implement and maintain. You should always look for opportunities to increase the granularity of your domain objects when it makes working with the DOM easier.

You will also find that your DOM contains objects that do not exist in your datastore. For instance, a typical purchasing system has some notion of a shopping cart, perhaps represented by Cart and CartItem objects. Unless you are required to persist content across user sessions, chances are these domain objects do not have corresponding tables for data storage. Remember, you are not simply building an object-oriented representation of your database; you are modeling the business domain. This point cannot be stressed enough. We have seen plenty of projects that created a pseudo-DOM derived directly from the datastore, and inevitably these projects suffered from the lack of abstraction that can be gained from a well-defined DOM.

We have found that a solid DOM comes from taking the time to look at your problem domain, identifying the objects in the domain, and then looking at how the natural granularity of these objects fits into the requirements of your application. Although we take both the utilization of the domain objects and the underlying data store into consideration, we don't like to let these have undue influence on our DOM.

It is important to remember that the goal of building a DOM is to create a set of classes that help you and other developers build the application at a level of abstraction that is closer to the application's problem domain. In general, we consider all other concerns secondary when building a DOM. For example, if you find that performance is suffering because of the design of your DOM, feel free to fine-tune the model. However, make sure that the problem is caused by the design of the DOM (e.g., a single domain object was found containing a large number of long text fields like CLOB or TEXT, which impact the performance of data retrieval). You don't want to reduce the benefits of your DOM out of the mistaken belief that it is performing badly.

Database Modeling and Domain Object Modeling

Although database modeling and domain object modeling are quite similar, the results you get from each are rarely the same, and indeed, you rarely want them to be. When modeling a database, you are looking for the structure that allows you to store and retrieve data in the most efficient and consistent manner. When you are building a DOM, performance is obviously important, but so is building an application on top of an object-oriented model that is easy to work with and makes assembling your business logic simple. In general, we have found that it is best to model the database in the way that is best for the database and to model the DOM, initially at least, in a way that is best for the DOM. You can make any changes later, if and when you identify performance bottlenecks.

Modeling Domain Object Relationships

The most common mistake we see in a DOM, especially when the DOM is driven by the design of the database, is that domain objects are created to represent relationships among table entities. This comes from the fact that a many-to-many relationship between two tables in a database must have a join table to construct the relationship. Relationships in a DOM should be modeled in a much more OOP-style way, with domain objects maintaining references to other domain objects or lists of domain objects.

A common mistake when populating domain object data from a database, such as what would be done in the data access layer of an application, is to assume that all related domain objects (e.g., when retrieving data from the ORDER table into the Order domain object, the list of Item objects within the Order object should be retrieved from the ORDER_ITEM table together) must be loaded from the database as well—this is not so. See the section "Domain Object Relationships" for a more detailed discussion of this problem.

To Encapsulate Behavior or Not?

You are not forced to have your domain objects encapsulate any behavior at all; indeed, you can choose to have your domain objects represent just the state of your problem domain. In most cases, we have found that it is better to factor out much of the business logic into a set of service objects that work with domain objects rather than encapsulate this logic inside the domain objects. Typically, we place all logic that interacts with components outside of the DOM into the service objects. In this way, we are reducing the coupling between the DOM and components involved in application logic. This allows the DOM to be used in a wider variety of scenarios, and often, you will find that the DOM can be reused in other applications that solve problems in the same domain.

Where we like to encapsulate behavior in the DOM is in situations where the logic is implemented purely in interactions between domain objects. The JPetStore sample application included with Spring provides a great example of this that can be mapped to our purchasing system example. In this scenario, a user has a shopping cart, represented by a Cart object, and a list of CartItem objects. When the user is ready to purchase the items in her cart and create an order, the application has to create an Order object along with a list of OrderLine objects that corresponds to the data modeled by the Cart and CartItem objects. This is a perfect example of when behavior should be encapsulated inside the DOM. The conversion from Cart to Order is coded purely in terms of domain objects with no dependencies on other components in your application. In JPetStore, the Order class has an initOrder() method that accepts two arguments, Account and Cart. All the logic required to create an Order based on the Cart object for the user represented by the Account object is represented in this method.

As with most things related to modeling, there are no hard-and-fast rules about when to put logic inside a domain object and when to factor it out into a service object. You should avoid placing logic inside your domain objects when it causes your domain objects to depend on other application components outside of the DOM. In this way, you are ensuring that your DOM is as reusable as possible.

On the flipside of this, logic that involves only domain objects is ideally placed in the DOM, which allows it to be used wherever the DOM is used.

The SpringBlog Domain Object Model

Let's take a look at the DOM for the sample application. Figure 12-1 shows the SpringBlog DOM for blog posting–related domain objects, while Figure 12-2 shows the DOM for blog users and their granted roles.

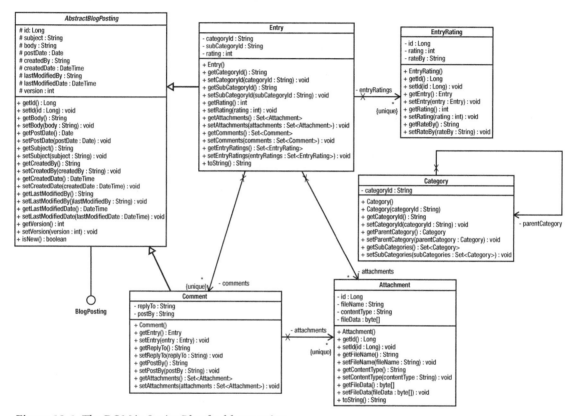

Figure 12-1. The DOM in SpringBlog for blog posting

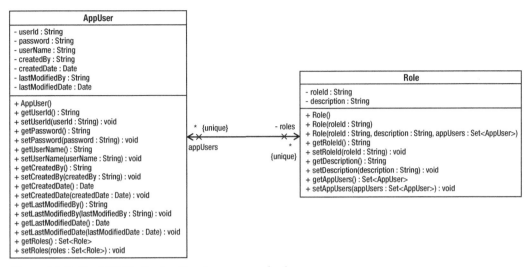

Figure 12-2. The DOM in SpringBlog for users and roles

Although the DOM is not very complicated, it does highlight some of the points we have been talking about. They are discussed in the next three sections.

Inheritance in the SpringBlog DOM

Central to the SpringBlog application is the concept of a posting. Postings come in two types: entries, which are top-level postings to the blog, and comments, which are comments about a particular blog entry. We have decided to define common posting characteristics in an interface, BlogPosting, shown in Listing 12-3, and have both Entry and Comment implement this interface.

Listing 12-3. The BlogPosting Interface

```
package com.apress.prospring3.springblog.domain;

import java.util.Date;
import java.util.Set;

import com.apress.prospring3.springblog.domain.Attachment;

public interface BlogPosting {
    public String getBody();
    public void setBody(String body);

    public Date getPostDate();
    public void setPostDate(Date postDate);

    public String getSubject();
    public void setSubject(String subject);
}
```

However, this results in undue code duplication, with both Entry and Comment having their own implementations of BlogPosting. To get around this, we introduce the AbstractBlogPosting class and have Entry and Comment extend this class. Listing 12-4 shows AbstractBlogPosting.

Listing 12-4. The AbstractBlogPosting Class

```
package com.apress.prospring3.springblog.domain;

// Import statements omitted
public abstract class AbstractBlogPosting implements BlogPosting {

    protected Long id;
    protected String subject;
    protected String body;
    protected Date postDate;
    protected String createdBy;
    protected DateTime createdDate;
    protected String lastModifiedBy;
    protected DateTime lastModifiedDate;
    protected int version;

    public String getBody() {
        return body;
    }

    public void setBody(String body) {
        this.body = body;
    }

    public Date getPostDate() {
        return postDate;
    }

    public void setPostDate(Date postDate) {
        this.postDate = postDate;
    }

    public String getSubject() {
        return subject;
    }

    public void setSubject(String subject) {
        this.subject = subject;
    }

    // Other setter/getter methods omitted
}
```

By extending this base class, we move all the BlogPosting implementation details out of Entry and Comment, reducing code duplication. As an example of this, Listing 12-5 shows the code for the Entry class.

Listing 12-5. The Entry Class

```java
package com.apress.prospring3.springblog.domain;

// Import statements omitted
public class Entry extends AbstractBlogPosting {

    private static final int MAX_BODY_LENGTH = 80;
    private static final String THREE_DOTS = "...";

    private String categoryId;
    private String subCategoryId;
    private Set<EntryAttachment> attachments = new HashSet<EntryAttachment>();
    private Set<Comment> comments = new HashSet<Comment>();


    public Entry() {
    }

    public String getShortBody() {
        if (body.length() <= MAX_BODY_LENGTH)
            return body;
        StringBuffer result = new StringBuffer(MAX_BODY_LENGTH + 3);
        result.append(body.substring(0, MAX_BODY_LENGTH));
        result.append(THREE_DOTS);

        return result.toString();
    }

    public String getCategoryId() {
        return this.categoryId;
    }

    public void setCategoryId(String categoryId) {
        this.categoryId = categoryId;
    }

    public String getSubCategoryId() {
        return this.subCategoryId;
    }

    public void setSubCategoryId(String subCategoryId) {
        this.subCategoryId = subCategoryId;
    }

    public Set<EntryAttachment> getAttachments() {
        return this.attachments;
    }

    public void setAttachments(Set<EntryAttachment> attachments) {
        this.attachments = attachments;
    }

    public Set<Comment> getComments() {
```

449

```
        return this.comments;
    }

    public void setComments(Set<Comment> comments) {
        this.comments = comments;
    }

}
```

This is a pattern that is used extensively in Spring and throughout the SpringBlog application. Common functionality is defined in interfaces rather than abstract classes, but we provide a default implementation of the interface as an abstract class. The reason for this is that, where possible, we can take advantage of the abstract base class as with Entry and Comment, thus removing the need for each class to implement the BlogPosting interface directly. However, should a requirement arise for the Entry class to extend the Foo class, then we can simply implement the BlogPosting interface directly in Entry. The main point to remember here is that you do not define common functionality in terms of abstract classes because doing so restricts you to a set an inheritance hierarchy. Instead, you define common functionality in terms of interfaces, along with default implementations of these interfaces as abstract base classes. This way, you can take advantage of the inherited implementation wherever possible, but you are not artificially constraining your inheritance hierarchy.

A point worth noting here is that we did not reflect this inheritance tree in the database. That is to say, we didn't create a BLOG_POSTING table to store the shared data and then two tables, ENTRY and COMMENT, to store the entity-specific data. The main reason for this is that we didn't think that an application the size of SpringBlog warranted the complexity of that structure; plus, this example highlights our point about having a DOM that is different in structure than the database. The main reason for defining this inheritance hierarchy, besides that it is a good design, is to allow the SpringBlog application to work with the common data in the Entry and Comment objects, without having to differentiate between the two. A good example of this is the obscenity filter that was introduced in Chapter 7 and is covered in detail in Chapter 21.

Domain Behavior in SpringBlog

Although the SpringBlog domain model is simplistic, we still need to encapsulate some logic in the domain model. Because the body of a blog posting could potentially be very long, we wanted a mechanism to get a snippet of the body to use when it displays a list of blog postings. For this reason, we create the Entry.getShortBody() method (note that this method was not defined in neither the BlogPosting interface nor the AbstractBlogPosting class) shown in Listing 12-6.

Listing 12-6. Behavior in the Entry Class

```
package com.apress.prospring3.springblog.domain;

// Import statements omitted
public class Entry extends AbstractBlogPosting {

    private static final int MAX_BODY_LENGTH = 80;
    private static final String THREE_DOTS = "...";

    public String getShortBody() {
        if (body.length() <= MAX_BODY_LENGTH)
            return body;
        StringBuffer result = new StringBuffer(MAX_BODY_LENGTH + 3);
```

```
        result.append(body.substring(0, MAX_BODY_LENGTH));
        result.append(THREE_DOTS);

        return result.toString();
    }

// Codes omitted
}
```

Here you can see that to build the short body, we take the first 80 characters of the body and simply append three dots to the end. This is a simplistic implementation, but it does highlight a typical scenario for encapsulating logic in the DOM.

Domain Object Relationships

In the DOM represented in Figure 12-1, notice that we defined an association between Entry and Attachment and between Comment and Attachment. As part of the SpringBlog requirements, we want to be able to upload and store files with both types of posting. In the database, we have a table to store the attachments called ATTACHMENT. Then to associate attachments with an entry or a comment, we have two other tables: ENTRY_ATTACHMENT_DETAIL and COMMENT_ATTACHMENT_DETAIL. A common mistake we see is that people create domain objects to model these relationships, rather than using standard Java features to relate the objects together. When you have a one-to-one relationship in your database, you can model this in the DOM by having one object maintain a reference to the other. For one-to-many or many-to-many relationships, using Java collections makes it simple to represent these complex relationships in a familiar manner that is simple to work with in code. Listing 12-7, a snippet from the Entry class, shows how we use a Set to store the Attachment objects for each posting.

Listing 12-7. Using Set for Domain Object Relationships

```
package com.apress.prospring3.springblog.domain;

// Import statements omitted
public class Entry extends AbstractBlogPosting {

    private Set<Attachment> attachments = new HashSet<Attachment>(0);

    public Set<Attachment> getAttachments() {
        return this.attachments;
    }

    public void setAttachments(Set<Attachment> attachments) {
        this.attachments = attachments;
    }

    // Codes omitted
}
```

Rather than using additional objects to model relationships, we use a simple Set to model the one-to-many relationship. Aside from reducing the amount of code we need to type, this method prevents the DOM from becoming polluted with needless classes and allows familiar Java concepts such as Iterator to be used when navigating relationships.

Domain Object Model Summary

In this section, we looked at the DOM for the SpringBlog application, and we spent some time discussing the basics of domain object modeling and implementation. There is no doubt that the scope of this topic is much broader than what we have covered here. Indeed, a whole range of books is available that discusses the topic in detail (one excellent book about this topic is *Domain-Driven Design: Tackling Complexity in the Heart of Software*, Addison-Wesley Professional). We only scratched the surface here, and we focused on why you want to build a DOM, what the focus is when building one, and some general topics related to the SpringBlog application.

Although it is certainly possible to build applications without defining and building a DOM, it is our experience that taking the time to do so pays off in reduced complexity, lower maintenance costs, and fewer bugs.

Designing and Building the Data Access Layer

Having discussed the DOM, let's proceed to the layer that is dedicated to performing the interaction between the database and transforming the retrieved data to the DOM for processing by the service layer.

No one will question the need for a data access layer, because data access logic is always complex and performance-critical. For example, in some cases where the performance of data access is critical, the data access layer should be capable of firing tuned native queries to the database to maximize the performance on data retrieval. Moreover, issues such as concurrency control (e.g., optimistic/pessimistic locking), caching, data auditing, and security requirements should be addressed by the data access layer.

Typically, when implementing the data access layer, the DAO Pattern is widely adopted in JEE applications, in which the responsibility of the DAO is to encapsulate the underlying persistence technologies (e.g., JDBC, Hibernate, etc.). However, because today the persistence frameworks have become much more mature and the rise of adopting JPA and its EntityManager that already hides the persistence provider from the developer, it is a common practice to eliminate the DAO layer. Instead, the persistence provider Service Provider Interface (SPI) will be injected into the service layer directly when retrieving data. Figure 12-3 shows a diagram that uses DAO. (For example, for JDBC, the access logic still involves writing a lot of queries within the code, and for this case, it's still better to put that code in the DAO class to hide the service layer from those SQL statements.) Figure 12-4 shows another diagram within which the persistence providers (e.g., EntityManager in JPA, mapper interfaces in MyBatis) are injected into the service layer directly.

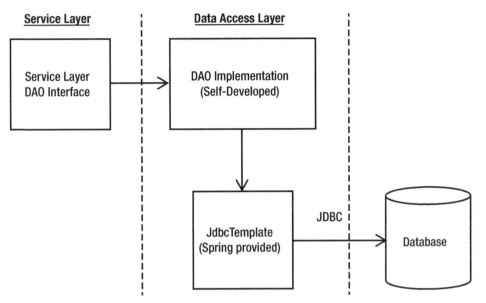

Figure 12-3. Application design with DAO Pattern

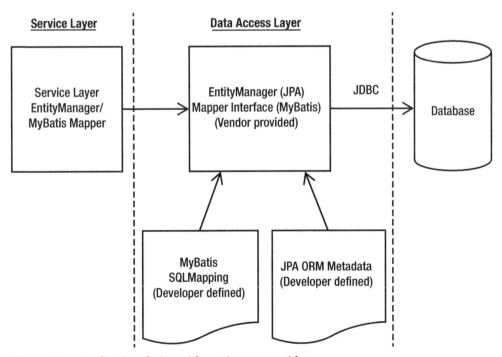

Figure 12-4. Application design with persistence providers

Practical Design Considerations

Thanks to the evolution and maturity of various persistence technologies and Spring's flexibility in integrating with those technologies, the task of designing and building a data access layer is much simpler these days. Practically, the most difficult and time-consuming task is to perform mapping between the underlying database structure and the DOM in the application. However, you should bear in mind a few practical considerations when creating your data access layer that will help you build data access logic that is simpler to use and easier to extend.

Domain Objects or Data Transfer Objects?

Most of the time you don't need to rely on DTO for shipping data between different layers. As discussed earlier this chapter, nowadays all popular persistence technologies and JEE itself supports using POJO as the underlying DOM, making it possible for the service layer, presentation layer only, and data access layer to communicate using domain objects directly.

Since all domain objects are now POJOs, they can be easily supported by frontend presentation frameworks (e.g., Spring MVC, JSF, Adobe Flex, to name a few) to directly interact with the service layer via domain objects.

However, in some cases, the DTO Pattern is still worth considering. For example, a domain object contains many long text data attributes that may not be required to send to the frontend for every request. In this case, it is worth considering whether to create a value object that stores only the exact attributes required by the corresponding frontend in order to minimize the data transfer between the presentation layer and service layer.

DAO Interfaces

As a rule of thumb, always define your DAOs (if you decided to go for the DAO Pattern) in terms of interfaces, not classes. When writing code in your service objects to work with your DAOs, code to the interfaces, not the implementation classes. Remember that when you are using Spring, it is a trivial job to pass an instance of the appropriate DAO implementation to your service layer, so using interfaces for your DAOs places very little additional coding burden on you.

DAO Granularity

When deciding how to structure your DAO interfaces, definitely avoid creating one DAO per domain object and one DAO per table. Sometimes, these structures appear naturally after thoughtful design, but don't assume that either one of these structures is necessarily the best.

A big problem we often see with projects is the "one DAO per table" problem. When you define a structure like this, you end up with DAOs representing join tables that serve no purpose other than to join two other tables in a many-to-many relationship. Plus, you often find that you have to pass a single domain object to lots of different DAOs to have the data persisted.

This is a classic example of letting the database drive the design of your DAO layer. This is something that, in practice, we have found to be a bad idea. The purpose of a DAO is to map domain objects to the database, and vice versa. Because the bulk of your application is interacting with the domain objects, not the database, it makes sense to let the DOM drive database design. Let your DAOs hide the complexity of mapping the data in your domain objects to the database; that is their job. You are trying to avoid the situation where persisting a domain object requires you to interact with many different DAOs. Situations like this arise naturally, such as when a domain object has a reference to another domain object of a different type and both have been modified and thus need to be persisted. In this case, you can encapsulate that logic in your service layer, but you do not need to create this problem artificially.

So, then you might wonder if you should let the DOM drive the design of the DAOs. Well, yes and no. Yes, in that the purpose of the DAO is to get DOM data into and out of the persistent data store, so it makes sense to let the DOM act as the driver. No, in that blindly creating one DAO per domain object leads to a situation where the persistence of one logical unit of data leads to calls to many different DAOs. Consider the earlier example of the Order and OrderLine objects that are created from the Cart and CartItem objects. Because it is unlikely that you are going to want to save or retrieve OrderLine objects without doing the same to an Order object, it makes sense to encapsulate persistence logic for both domain objects in a single OrderDao, rather than create OrderDao and OrderLineDao.

Data Access Layer Summary

Creating a data access layer for your application provides the rest of your application components with a standard mechanism for storing and retrieving data. Without a data access layer, you will find that data access code becomes spread out through your application, often resulting in code duplication that is hard to maintain. In the long term, this poorly managed code inevitably leads to bugs and developer headaches.

Depending on the technology decision of implementing the data access layer, most of the time you won't need to adopt the DAO Pattern anymore. Many popular persistence technologies and standards already do a very good job of hiding all the database access details for you. So, it's recommended that you inject those persistence providers to the service layer directly. This will simplify the application architecture, as well as result in code that is easier to trace and maintain.

In case you decided to use DAO or it's the standard that your team or company has standardized on, you should always define DAOs as interfaces and then implement these interfaces using your chosen data access technology. When you are using Spring, working with interfaces is trivial, and you can easily provide concrete implementations of your DAO interfaces to other components in your application.

In this section, we looked at some of the main design-related issues that are present when you are building a data access layer for your application. In reality, much of the complexity in a data access layer comes from implementation, not design. You can find more details on data access in Chapter 8 through Chapter 11.

Designing the Service Layer

At this point in our application design discussion, we have a way of representing the data in our problem domain so that we can manipulate it in code, and we have a way of storing this data in a database and then getting it back out later. However, currently we are not doing much with this data. Unless your application is especially simplistic, chances are some kind of logic needs to be implemented. Earlier, we discussed cases where you should encapsulate logic inside your domain objects. In this section, we look at providing a layer of service objects to provide a standard interface to the rest of your application logic.

Why Have a Service Layer

As with the question as to why you should have a data access layer, the answer to this question is plain and simple once you have implemented a few applications without one. If you do not bring together all the business logic in a single place, it ends up spread out through your presentation code, typically resulting in lots of code duplication, not to mention creating code that lacks clearly defined boundaries for responsibilities. Code duplication issues aside, failing to define clear boundaries between code with different responsibilities often results in code that is difficult to trace and maintain, because it becomes hard to pinpoint the location of a given function.

A well-defined service layer acts as a sort of gateway into your application, providing your presentation code with a simple, unified way to get at business logic. A good service layer also serves as a definition of what your application can actually perform and what logic is available to be presented to the user.

A significant drawback of not having a service layer comes about when you decide to have two kinds of user interface for the same logic. Perhaps you built a web application, but now you want to provide a desktop-based application for users who use the application often. If your business logic code is embedded within your web presentation code, you are going to have to either refactor the code out of the presentation layer, which requires a significant amount of effort in rework and testing, or simply reproduce the business logic code again, this time embedded within the code of the rich client (e.g., Swing, RCP, and so on).

Nowadays, besides various frontends, your business services will also probably be accessible from other systems. For example, your application may provide real-time stock quote information to some other third-party business partners. Mostly likely, you will need to support the access by those partners to your real-time data via web services (e.g., web services, RESTful-WS, and so on). Also, when processing data in batches (e.g., from a file), the data manipulation logic should not have much difference from that of a user entering the data via the web interface. A centralized service layer as the entry point for data coming from all possible sources becomes a critical part in keeping your application maintainable.

Designing Business Interfaces

As with most components in your application, you should start by defining a set of interfaces for the service objects in your application. Any code that interacts with your service layer should do so through these interfaces. For components that Spring manages, you can supply implementations using DI. If you have to support components that Spring does not manage, you may want to supply a simple Factory class to allow for implementation lookup.

Service Layer Dependencies

As with all the interfaces we have talked about, you should avoid defining dependencies in the interfaces of your service objects. The service object should be completely implementation-independent. A well-defined service object interface has only those methods that serve business functions. Avoid exposing types from your data access layer through your service objects. Your service objects should insulate the presentation code from the underlying data access layer completely. For example, one of your service objects might access all its data using web services or via a JMS queue. A good way to ensure that your service object interface is as accessible as possible is to ensure that return and argument types do not couple the presentation code to anything other than the DOM. You are going to be passing domain objects through all the layers of your application, but other components such as DAOs should stay well within their own layer.

Service Object Granularity

When designing the objects required in the service layer, try to relate them with the possible use cases in the business requirements.

A common practice is to group the logic that manipulates highly related domain objects into the same service object interface. For example, in the SpringBlog application, the design of the service layer is composed of the interfaces listed in Table 12-1.

Table 12-1. Spring JDBC Packages

Service Interface	Purpose	Related Domain Objects
EntryService	Provide services for blog entry posting: • Various searching function • Retrieve a particular entry • Update operations • Attachment-related operations	Entry Attachment
CommentService	Provide services for comment posting: • Retrieve all attachments for a particular entry • Update operations • Attachment-related operations	Comment Attachment
UserService	Provide services for security: • User maintenance • Role assignment	AppUser Role
HousekeepingService	Provide housekeeping services: • Purging of old entry and comment history records	Histories of Entry and Comment objects

Bear in mind that in application design, there is no definitely right or wrong approach. However, there are better and worse designs. A good design should be easy to document and understandable by both the technical team as well as the business analyst. Moreover, always think about flexibility, maintainability, and trackability. Finally, make sure your service layer doesn't couple to any special type of consumer.

Service Layer Summary

In this section, we discussed the issues you should consider when designing and building a service layer for your Spring application. Then, by looking at the SpringBlog's service layer, we demonstrated how to design the interfaces within the service layer by grouping operations for closely related domain objects into the same service interface.

Summary

In this chapter, we looked at a lot of problems associated with traditional applications, and you saw how Spring can help you solve these problems. We discussed a variety of problems that occur during application development, and we looked at sensible ways in which these problems can be solved effectively. Throughout the chapter, we examined how the practices we discussed were used when we design the SpringBlog application.

This chapter only scratched the surface of application design as a whole, but we covered some major considerations that are specific to Spring-based applications and problems that you can fix easily when using Spring. For a fuller discussion of application design for SpringBlog, refer to Chapter 23.

In the next chapter, we present a detailed look at transaction support, including full examples of both local and distributed transactions and some useful tips for testing transactional methods.

CHAPTER 13

Transaction Management

Transactions are one of the most critical parts of building a reliable enterprise application. The most common type of transaction is a database operation. In a typical database update operation, a database transaction begins, data is updated, and then the transaction is committed or rolled back, depending on the result of the database operation. However, in many cases, depending on the application requirements and the backend resources that the application needs to interact with (such as an RDBMS, message-oriented middleware, an ERP system, and so on), transaction management can be much more complicated.

In the early days of Java application development (after JDBC was created but before the JEE standard or an application framework like Spring was available), developers programmatically controlled and managed transactions within application code. When JEE and, more specifically, the EJB standard became available, developers were able to use container-managed transactions (CMTs) to manage transactions in a declarative way. But the complicated transaction declaration in the EJB deployment descriptor was difficult to maintain and introduced unnecessary complexity for transaction processing. Some developers favored having more control over the transaction and chose bean-managed transactions (BMT) to manage transactions in a programmatic way. However, the complexity of programming with the Java Transaction API (JTA) also hindered developers' productivity.

As discussed in Chapters 6 and 7 on AOP, transaction management is a cross-cutting concern and should not be coded within the business logic. The most appropriate way to implement transaction management is to allow developers to define transaction requirements in a declarative way and have frameworks such as Spring, JEE, or AOP weave in the transaction processing logic on our behalf. In this chapter, we will discuss how Spring helps simplify the implementation of transaction-processing logic. Spring provides support for both declarative and programmatic transaction management.

Spring offers excellent support for declarative transactions, which means you do not need to clutter your business logic with transaction management code. All you have to do is declare those methods (within classes or which layers) that must participate in a transaction, together with the details of transaction configuration details, and Spring will take care of handling the transaction management. To be more specific, in this chapter we look at the following:

- *Spring transaction abstraction layer:* We discuss the base components of Spring transaction abstraction classes and explain how to use these classes to control the properties of the transactions.

- *Declarative transaction management:* We show you how to use Spring to implement declarative transactional management using just plain Java objects. We offer examples for declarative transaction management using the XML configuration files as well as Java annotations.

- *Programmatic transaction management:* Even though programmatic transaction management is not used very often, we explain how to use the Spring-provided `TransactionTemplate` class, which gives you full control over the transaction management code.

- *Global transactions with JTA:* For global transactions that need to span multiple backend resources, we will show an example of how to configure and implement global transactions in Spring using JTA.

Exploring the Spring Transaction Abstraction Layer

When developing your applications, no matter whether you choose to use Spring or not, you have to make a fundamental choice when you use transactions about whether to use global or local transactions. Local transactions are specific to a single transactional resource (a JDBC connection, for example), whereas global transactions are managed by the container and can span multiple transactional resources.

Transaction Types

Local transactions are easy to manage, and if all operations in your application need to interact with just one transactional resource (such as a JDBC transaction), using local transactions will be sufficient. However, if you are not using an application framework such as Spring, you have a lot of transaction management code to write, and if in the future the scope of the transaction needs to be extended across multiple transactional resources, you have to drop the local transaction management code and rewrite it to use global transactions.

In the Java world, global transactions were implemented with the Java Transaction API (JTA). In this scenario, a JTA-compatible transaction manager connects to multiple transactional resources via respective resource managers, which are capable of communicating with the transaction manager over the XA protocol (an open standard defining distributed transactions), and the 2 Phase Commit (2PC) mechanism was used to ensure that all backend datasources were updated or rolled back altogether. If either of the backend resources fails, the entire transaction will roll back, and hence the updates to other resources will be rolled back too.

Figure 13-1 shows a high-level view of global transactions with JTA.

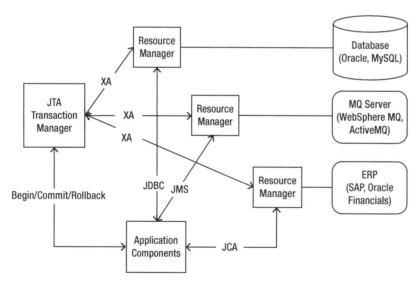

Figure 13-1. *Overview of global transactions with JTA*

As shown in Figure 13-1, four main parties participate in a global transaction (also generally referred to as *distributed transactions*). The first party is the backend resource, such as an RDBMS, messaging middleware, an enterprise resource planning (ERP) system, and so on.

The second party is the resource manager, which was generally provided by the backend resource vendor and is responsible for interacting with the backend resource. For example, when connecting to a MySQL database, we will need to interact with the MysqlXADataSource class provided by MySQL's Java connector. Other backend resources (e.g., MQ, ERP, and so on) will provide their resource managers too.

The third party is the JTA transaction manager, which is responsible for managing, coordinating, and synchronizing the transaction status with all resource managers that are participating in the transaction. The XA protocol will be used, which is an open standard widely used for distributed transaction processing. The JTA transaction manager also supports 2PC so that all changes will be committed together, and if any resource update fails, the entire transaction will be rolled back, resulting in none of the resources being updated. The entire mechanism was specified by the Java Transaction Service (JTS) specification.

The final component is the application. Either the application itself or the underlying container or Spring framework that the application runs on will manage the transaction (begin, commit, roll back a transaction, and so on). At the same time, the application will interact with the underlying backend resources via various standards defined by JEE. As shown in Figure 13-1, the application connects to the RDBMS via JDBC, MQ via JMS, and an ERP system via Java Connector Architecture (JCA).

JTA is supported by all full-blown JEE-compliant application servers (e.g., JBoss, WebSphere, WebLogic, GlassFish, and so on), within which the transaction is available via JNDI lookup. As for stand-alone applications or web containers (e.g., Tomcat, Jetty, and so on), there also exists open source and commercial solutions that provide support for JTA/XA in those environments (e.g., Atomikos, JOTM, Bitronix, and so on).

Implementations of the PlatformTransactionManager

In Spring, the PlatformTransactionManager interface uses the TransactionDefinition and TransactionStatus interfaces to create and manage transactions. The actual implementation of these interfaces must have detailed knowledge of the transaction manager. Figure 13-2 shows the implementations of PlatformTransactionManager in Spring as of version 3.1.

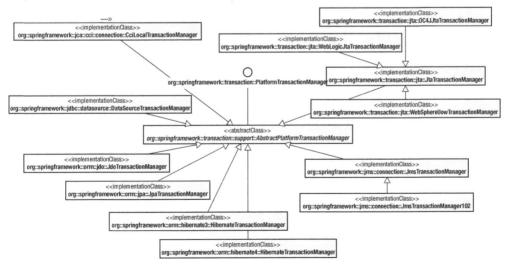

Figure 13-2. PlatformTransactionManager implementations as of Spring 3.1

Spring provides a rich set of implementations for the PlatformTransactionManager interface. The CciLocalTransactionManager class supports JEE JCA and the Common Client Interface (CCI). The DataSourceTransactionManager class is for generic JDBC connections. For the ORM side, there are a number of implementations, including JDO (JdoTransactionManager class), JPA (JpaTransactionManager class), and Hibernate 3 and Hibernate 4 (HibernateTransactionManager with different package names). For JMS, the implementations include JMS 1.1 or newer (JmsTransactionManager class) and JMS 1.0.2 (JmsTransactionManager102 class). For JTA, the generic implementation class is the JtaTransactionManager class. Spring also provides several JTA transaction manager classes that are specific to particular application servers. Those classes provide native support for WebSphere (WebSphereUowTransactionManager class), WebLogic (WebLogicJtaTransactionManager class), and Oracle OC4J (OC4JJtaTransactionManager class).

Analyzing Transaction Properties

In this section, we will discuss the transaction properties that Spring supports, focusing on interacting with RDBMS as the backend resource.

Transactions have the four notoriously known ACID properties—atomicity, consistency, isolation, and durability—and it is up to the transactional resources to maintain these aspects of a transaction. You cannot control the atomicity, consistency, and durability of a transaction, but you can control the transaction propagation and timeout, as well as configure whether the transaction should be read-only and specify the isolation level.

Spring encapsulates all these settings in a TransactionDefinition interface. This interface is used in the core interface of the transaction support in Spring, the PlatformTransactionManager interface, whose implementations perform transaction management on a specific platform, such as JDBC or JTA. The core method, PlatformTransactionManager.getTransaction(), takes a TransactionDefinition interface as an argument and returns a TransactionStatus interface. The TransactionStatus interface is used to control the transaction execution, more specifically to set the transaction result and to check whether the transaction is completed or whether it is a new transaction.

The TransactionDefinition Interface

As we mentioned earlier, the TransactionDefinition interface controls the properties of a transaction. Let's take a more detailed look at the TransactionDefinition interface (see Listing 13-1) and describe its methods.

Listing 13-1. TransactionDefinition Interface

```
package org.springframework.transaction;

import java.sql.Connection;

public interface TransactionDefinition {

    // Variable declaration statements omitted

    int getPropagationBehavior();

    int getIsolationLevel();

    int getTimeout();
```

```
boolean isReadOnly();

String getName();
```

}

The simple and obvious methods of this interface are getTimeout(), which returns the time (in seconds) in which the transaction must complete, and isReadOnly(), which indicates whether the transaction is read-only. The transaction manager implementation can use this value to optimize the execution and check to make sure that the transaction is performing only read operations. The getName() method returns the name of the transaction.

The other two methods, getPropagationBehavior() and getIsolationLevel(), need to be discussed in more detail. We begin with getIsolationLevel(), which controls what changes to the data other transactions see. Table 13-1 lists the transaction isolation levels you can use and explains what changes made in the current transaction other transactions can access.

Table 13-1. *Transaction Isolation Levels*

Isolation Level	Description
TransactionDefinition.ISOLATION_DEFAULT	Default isolation level of the underlying datastore.
TransactionDefinition.ISOLATION_READ_UNCOMMITTED	Lowest level of isolation; it is barely a transaction at all because it allows this transaction to see data modified by other uncommitted transactions.
TransactionDefinition.ISOLATION_READ_COMMITTED	Default level in most databases; it ensures that other transactions are not able to read data that has not been committed by other transactions. However, the data that was read by one transaction can be updated by other transactions.
TransactionDefinition.ISOLATION_REPEATABLE_READ	Stricter than ISOLATION_READ_COMMITED; it ensures that once you select data, you can select at least the same set again. However, if other transactions insert new data, you can still select the newly inserted data.
TransactionDefinition.ISOLATION_SERIALIZABLE	The most expensive and reliable isolation level; all transactions are treated as if they were executed one after another.

Choosing the appropriate isolation level is very important for the consistency of the data, but making these choices can have a great impact on performance. The highest isolation level, TransactionDefinition.ISOLATION_SERIALIZABLE, is particularly expensive to maintain.

The getPropagationBehavior() method specifies what happens to a transactional call depending on whether there is an active transaction. Table 13-2 describes the values for this method.

Table 13-2. Propagation Behavior Values

Isolation Level	Description
TransactionDefinition.PROPAGATION_REQUIRED	Supports a transaction if one already exists. If there is no transaction, it starts a new one.
TransactionDefinition.PROPAGATION_SUPPORTS	Supports a transaction if one already exists. If there is no transaction, it executes nontransactionally.
TransactionDefinition.PROPAGATION_MANDATORY	Supports a transaction if one already exists. Throws an exception if there is no active transaction.
TransactionDefinition.PROPAGATION_REQUIRES_NEW	Always starts a new transaction. If an active transaction already exists, it is suspended.
TransactionDefinition.PROPAGATION_NOT_SUPPORTED	Does not support execution with an active transaction. Always executes nontransactionally and suspends any existing transaction.
TransactionDefinition.PROPAGATION_NEVER	Always executes nontransactionally even if an active transaction exists. Throws an exception if an active transaction exists.
TransactionDefinition.PROPAGATION_NESTED	Runs in a nested transaction if an active transaction exists. If there is no active transaction, the execution is executed as if Transaction Definition.PROPAGATION_REQUIRED is set.

The TransactionStatus Interface

The TransactionStatus interface, shown in Listing 13-2, allows a transactional manager to control the transaction execution. The code can check whether the transaction is a new one or whether it is a read-only transaction and it can initiate a rollback.

Listing 13-2. TransactionStatus Declaration

```
package org.springframework.transaction;

public interface TransactionStatus extends SavepointManager {

    boolean isNewTransaction();

    boolean hasSavepoint();

    void setRollbackOnly();

    boolean isRollbackOnly();
```

```
    void flush();

    boolean isCompleted();

}
```

The methods of the `TransactionStatus` interface are fairly self-explanatory; the most notable one is `setRollbackOnly()`, which causes a rollback and ends the active transaction.

The `hasSavePoint()` method returns whether the transaction internally carries a save point (i.e., that transaction was created as a nested transaction based on a save point). The `flush()` method flushes the underlying session to a datastore if applicable (e.g., when using with Hibernate). The `isCompleted()` method returns whether the transaction has ended (i.e., committed or rolled back).

Sample Data Model and Infrastructure for Example Code

This section provides an overview of the data model and the infrastructure that will be used in the examples of transaction management.

In this chapter, we will use JPA with Hibernate as the persistence layer for implementing data access logic. In addition, the Spring Data JPA and its repository abstraction will also be used to simplify basic database operations development.

Creating a Simple Spring JPA Utility Project with Dependencies

Let's start by creating the project first. Because we are using JPA, create a new Spring template project and choose Simple Spring JPA Utility Project. Then, enter the project details, as shown in Figure 13-3.

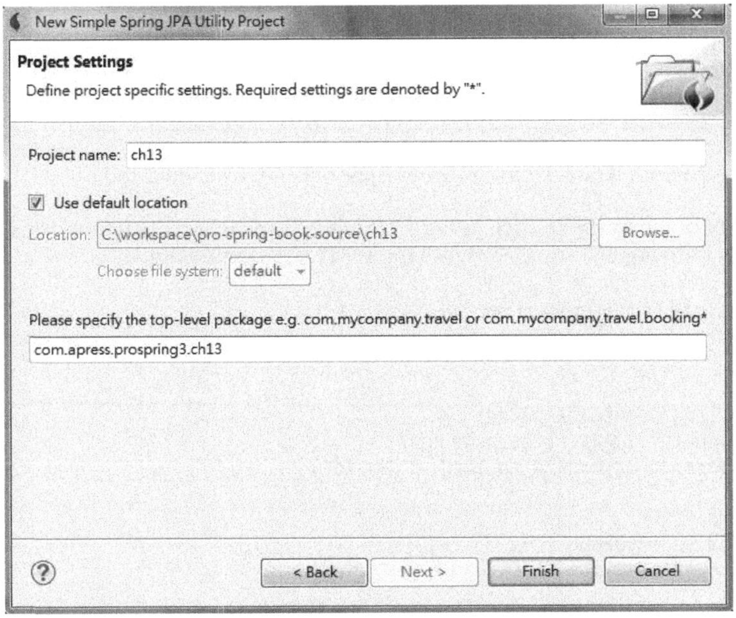

Figure 13-3. Creating a simple Spring JPA utility project in STS

Upon project creation, we also need to add the required dependencies to the project for the examples in this chapter. Table 13-3 shows the additional dependencies required.

Table 13-3. Maven Dependencies for Spring Data JPA

Group ID	Artifact ID	Version	Description
org.springframework.data	spring-data-jpa	1.0.1.RELEASE	Spring Data JPA library.
org.springframework	spring-aspects	3.1.0.RELEASE	Spring advanced AOP features that Spring Data JPA depends on.
joda-time	joda-time	2.0	Joda-time (http://joda-time.sourceforge.net/) is a date-time API that Spring Data JPA uses.
joda-time	joda-time-hibernate	1.3	Joda-time library for integration with Hibernate for date-time data persistence.
com.google.guava	guava	10.0.1	Contains useful helper classes.
org.aspectj	aspectjrt	1.6.11	AspectJ library. Required for the example of the aop-namespace for transaction declaration.
org.aspectj	aspectjweaver	1.6.11	AspectJ weaving library.
org.slf4j	slf4j-log4j12	1.6.1	The library that bridges the SLF4J logging to log4j library.

Make sure you are using Spring 3.1 with JDK 6. Please refer to Appendix A for the detailed procedure.

To observe the detailed behavior of the example code as we modify the transaction attributes, let's also turn on the DEBUG-level logging in log4j. Listing 13-3 shows the log4j.properties file.

Listing 13-3. Turning on DEBUG Logging in log4j.properties

```
log4j.rootCategory=DEBUG, stdout

log4j.appender.stdout=org.apache.log4j.ConsoleAppender
log4j.appender.stdout.layout=org.apache.log4j.PatternLayout
log4j.appender.stdout.layout.ConversionPattern=%d %p [%c] - <%m>%n

log4j.category.org.apache.activemq=ERROR
log4j.category.org.springframework.batch=DEBUG
log4j.category.org.springframework.transaction=INFO

log4j.category.org.hibernate.SQL=DEBUG
```

Sample Data Model and Common Classes

To keep things simple, we will use just one table, the CONTACT table, that we used throughout the chapters about data access. Listings 13-4 and 13-5 show the data creation script (schema.sql) and test data population script, respectively (test-data.sql).

Listing 13-4. Table Creation Script

```
DROP TABLE IF EXISTS CONTACT;

CREATE TABLE CONTACT (
    ID INT NOT NULL AUTO_INCREMENT
    , FIRST_NAME VARCHAR(60) NOT NULL
    , LAST_NAME VARCHAR(40) NOT NULL
    , BIRTH_DATE DATE
    , VERSION INT NOT NULL DEFAULT 0
    , UNIQUE UQ_CONTACT_1 (FIRST_NAME, LAST_NAME)
    , PRIMARY KEY (ID)
);
```

Listing 13-5. Test Data Population Script

```
insert into contact (first_name, last_name, birth_date)
    values ('Clarence', 'Ho', '1980-07-30');
insert into contact (first_name, last_name, birth_date)
    values ('Scott', 'Tiger', '1990-11-02');
insert into contact (first_name, last_name, birth_date)
    values ('John', 'Smith', '1964-02-28');
```

The entity class is simple too; Listing 13-6 shows the Contact class.

Listing 13-6. The Contact Class

```
package com.apress.prospring3.ch13.domain;

// Import statements omitted
@Entity
@Table(name = "contact")
@NamedQueries({
@NamedQuery(name="Contact.findAll", query="select c from Contact c"),
@NamedQuery(name="Contact.countAll", query="select count(c) from Contact c")
})
public class Contact implements Serializable {

    private Long id;
    private int version;
    private String firstName;
    private String lastName;
    private Date birthDate;

    public Contact() {
    }
```

```java
    @Id
    @GeneratedValue(strategy = IDENTITY)
    @Column(name = "ID")
    public Long getId() {
        return this.id;
    }

    public void setId(Long id) {
        this.id = id;
    }

    @Version
    @Column(name = "VERSION")
    public int getVersion() {
        return this.version;
    }

    public void setVersion(int version) {
        this.version = version;
    }

    @Column(name = "FIRST_NAME")
    public String getFirstName() {
        return this.firstName;
    }

    public void setFirstName(String firstName) {
        this.firstName = firstName;
    }

    @Column(name = "LAST_NAME")
    public String getLastName() {
        return this.lastName;
    }

    public void setLastName(String lastName) {
        this.lastName = lastName;
    }

    @Temporal(TemporalType.DATE)
    @Column(name = "BIRTH_DATE")
    public Date getBirthDate() {
        return this.birthDate;
    }

    public void setBirthDate(Date birthDate) {
        this.birthDate = birthDate;
    }

    public String toString() {
        return "Contact - Id: " + id + ", First name: " + firstName
            + ", Last name: " + lastName + ", Birthday: " + birthDate;
    }
}
```

To use Spring Data JPA's repository abstraction, we also need to define the ContactRepository interface, which extends Spring Data Common's CrudRepository<T,ID extends Serializable> interface. Listing 13-7 shows the ContactRepository interface.

Listing 13-7. The ContactRepository Class

```
package com.apress.prospring3.ch13.repository;

import org.springframework.data.repository.CrudRepository;

import com.apress.prospring3.ch13.domain.Contact;

public interface ContactRepository extends CrudRepository<Contact, Long> {

}
```

As shown in Listing 13-7, no additional method is required, because those methods provided by the CrudRepositoy interface already are sufficient for the examples in this chapter.

Finally, let's take a look at the ContactService interface, which defines all the business logic in relation to the Contact entity class. Listing 13-8 shows the ContactService interface.

Listing 13-8. The ContactService Interface

```
package com.apress.prospring3.ch13.service;

import java.util.List;

import com.apress.prospring3.ch13.domain.Contact;

public interface ContactService {

    public List<Contact> findAll();

    public Contact findById(Long id);

    public Contact save(Contact contact);

    public long countAll();
}
```

All methods are self-explanatory. In the next section, we will discuss how to implement transaction management in various ways by implementing the ContactService interface.

Declarative and Programmatic Transactions with Spring

In Spring, there are three options for transaction management. Two of them are for declarative transaction management, with one using Java annotations and the other using XML configuration. The third option is managing transactions programmatically. We will go through the three of them one by one in the following sections.

Using Annotations for Transaction Management

Currently, using annotations is the most common way to define transaction requirements in Spring. The main benefit is that the transaction requirement, together with the detail transaction properties (timeout, isolation level, propagation behavior, and so on), were defined within the code itself, which makes the application easier to trace and maintain.

To enable annotation support for transaction management in Spring, we need to add the `<tx:annotation-driven>` tag in the XML configuration file. Listing 13-9 shows the configuration file (`tx-annotation-app-context.xml`).

Listing 13-9. Spring Configuration for Annotation Transaction Support

```
<?xml version="1.0" encoding="UTF-8"?>
<beans xmlns="http://www.springframework.org/schema/beans"
    xmlns:xsi="http://www.w3.org/2001/XMLSchema-instance"
    xmlns:context="http://www.springframework.org/schema/context"
    xmlns:jdbc="http://www.springframework.org/schema/jdbc"
    xmlns:tx="http://www.springframework.org/schema/tx"
    xmlns:jpa="http://www.springframework.org/schema/data/jpa"
    xsi:schemaLocation="http://www.springframework.org/schema/jdbc
        http://www.springframework.org/schema/jdbc/spring-jdbc-3.1.xsd
        http://www.springframework.org/schema/beans
        http://www.springframework.org/schema/beans/spring-beans-3.1.xsd
        http://www.springframework.org/schema/tx
        http://www.springframework.org/schema/tx/spring-tx-3.1.xsd
        http://www.springframework.org/schema/data/jpa
        http://www.springframework.org/schema/data/jpa/spring-jpa-1.0.xsd
        http://www.springframework.org/schema/context
        http://www.springframework.org/schema/context/spring-context-3.1.xsd">

    <jdbc:embedded-database id="dataSource" type="H2">
        <jdbc:script location="classpath:schema.sql"/>
        <jdbc:script location="classpath:test-data.sql"/>
    </jdbc:embedded-database>

    <bean id="transactionManager" class="org.springframework.orm.jpa.JpaTransactionManager">
        <property name="entityManagerFactory" ref="emf"/>
    </bean>

    <tx:annotation-driven/>

    <bean id="emf" class="org.springframework.orm.jpa.LocalContainerEntityManagerFactoryBean">
        <property name="dataSource" ref="dataSource" />
        <property name="jpaVendorAdapter">
            <bean class="org.springframework.orm.jpa.vendor.HibernateJpaVendorAdapter" />
        </property>
        <property name="packagesToScan" value="com.apress.prospring3.ch13.domain"/>
        <property name="jpaProperties">
            <props>
                <prop key="hibernate.dialect">
                    org.hibernate.dialect.H2Dialect
                </prop>
                <prop key="hibernate.max_fetch_depth">3</prop>
                <prop key="hibernate.jdbc.fetch_size">50</prop>
```

```
                <prop key="hibernate.jdbc.batch_size">10</prop>
                <prop key="hibernate.show_sql">true</prop>
            </props>
        </property>
    </bean>

    <context:component-scan
        base-package="com.apress.prospring3.ch13.service.annotation" />

    <jpa:repositories base-package="com.apress.prospring3.ch13.repository"
        entity-manager-factory-ref="emf"
        transaction-manager-ref="transactionManager"/>

</beans>
```

If you have read Chapter 10, the previous configuration should be familiar to you. First, an embedded H2 database was defined with the database creation and data population scripts. Then, because we are using JPA, the JpaTransactionManager bean was defined. The <tx:annotation-driven> specifies that we are using annotations for transaction management. The EntityManagerFactory bean was then defined, followed by the <context:component-scan> to scan the service layer classes. Finally, the <jpa:repositories> tag was used to enable Spring Data JPA's repository abstraction.

For the implementation class of the ContactService interface, the com.apress.prospring3.ch13.service.annotation.ContactServiceImpl class, we begin by creating the class with an empty implementation of all the methods in the ContactService interface. In STS, it's very easy to do it. For details, please refer to Chapter 8.

Let's implement the ContactService.findAll() method first. Listing 13-10 shows the ContactServiceImpl class with the findAll() method implemented.

Listing 13-10. *The ContactServiceImpl Class with the findAll() Method Implemented*

```java
package com.apress.prospring3.ch13.service.annotation;

// Import statement omitted
@Service("contactService")
@Repository
@Transactional
public class ContactServiceImpl implements ContactService {

    @Autowired
    private ContactRepository contactRepository;

    @Transactional(readOnly=true)
    public List<Contact> findAll() {
        return Lists.newArrayList(contactRepository.findAll());
    }

}
```

When using annotation-based transaction management, the only annotation that we need to deal with is the @Transactional annotation. From Listing 13-10, the @Transactional annotation was applied at the class level, which means that, by default, Spring will ensure that a transaction is present before the execution of each method within the class. The @Transactional annotation supports a number of attributes that you can provide to override the default behavior. Table 13-4 shows the available attributes, together with the possible and default values.

Table 13-4. Attributes for the @Transactional Annotation

Attribute Name	Default Value	Possible Values
propagation	Propagation.REQUIRED	Propagation.REQUIRED Propagation.SUPPORTS Propagation.MANDATORY Propagation.REQUIRES_NEW Propagation.NOT_SUPPORTED Propagation.NEVER Propagation.NESTED
isolation	Isolation.DEFAULT (Default isolation level of the underlying resource)	Isolation.DEFAULT Isolation.READ_UNCOMMITTED Isolation.READ_COMMITTED Isolation.REPEATABLE_READ Isolation.SERIALIZABLE
timeout	TransactionDefinition.TIMEOUT_DEFAULT (Default transaction timeout in seconds of the underlying resource)	An integer value larger than zero; indicates the number in seconds for transaction timeout
readOnly	false	True false
rollbackFor	Exception classes for which transaction will be rolled back	N/A
rollbackForClassName	Exception class names for which transaction will be rolled back	N/A
noRollbackFor	Exception classes for which transaction will not be rolled back	N/A
noRollbackForClassName	Exception class names for which transaction will not be rolled back	N/A
value	"" (A qualifier value for the specified transaction)	N/A

As a result, based on Table 13-4, the @Transactional annotation without any attribute means that the transaction propagation is required, the isolation is the default, the timeout is the default, and the mode is read-write.

For the findAll() method in Listing 13-10, the method was annotated with @Transactional(readOnly=true). This will override the default annotation applied at the class level, with all other attributes unchanged, but the transaction is set to read-only.

Listing 13-11 shows the testing program for the findAll() method.

Listing 13-11. Testing the findAll() Method

```
package com.apress.prospring3.ch13;

import java.util.List;

import org.springframework.context.support.GenericXmlApplicationContext;

import com.apress.prospring3.ch13.domain.Contact;
import com.apress.prospring3.ch13.service.ContactService;

public class TxAnnotationSample {

    public static void main(String[] args) {

        GenericXmlApplicationContext ctx = new GenericXmlApplicationContext();
        ctx.load("classpath:tx-annotation-app-context.xml");
        ctx.refresh();

        ContactService contactService = ctx.getBean("contactService",
            ContactService.class);

        List<Contact> contacts = contactService.findAll();

        for (Contact contactTemp: contacts) {
            System.out.println(contactTemp);
        }
    }
}
```

Running the program will produce the following output:

```
DEBUG [org.springframework.orm.jpa.JpaTransactionManager] - <Creating new transaction with
name [com.apress.prospring3.ch13.service.annotation.ContactServiceImpl.findAll]:
PROPAGATION_REQUIRED,ISOLATION_DEFAULT,readOnly; ''>
DEBUG [org.hibernate.transaction.JDBCTransaction] - <begin>
Hibernate: select contact0_.ID as ID0_, contact0_.BIRTH_DATE as BIRTH2_0_,
contact0_.FIRST_NAME as FIRST3_0_, contact0_.LAST_NAME as LAST4_0_, contact0_.VERSION as
VERSION0_ from contact contact0_
DEBUG [org.springframework.orm.jpa.JpaTransactionManager] - <Initiating transaction commit>
DEBUG [org.springframework.orm.jpa.JpaTransactionManager] - <Committing JPA transaction on
EntityManagerÉ
[org.hibernate.ejb.EntityManagerImpl@5b62f030]>
DEBUG [org.hibernate.transaction.JDBCTransaction] - <commit>
DEBUG [org.hibernate.transaction.JDBCTransaction] - <re-enabling autocommit>
DEBUG [org.hibernate.transaction.JDBCTransaction] - <committed JDBC Connection>
DEBUG [org.hibernate.jdbc.ConnectionManager] - <aggressively releasing JDBC connection>
DEBUG [org.hibernate.jdbc.ConnectionManager] - <releasing JDBC connection [ (open
PreparedStatements: 0, globally: 0) (open ResultSets: 0, globally: 0)]>
DEBUG [org.springframework.orm.jpa.JpaTransactionManager] - <Closing JPA EntityManager
[org.hibernate.ejb.EntityManagerImpl@5b62f030] after transaction>
Contact - Id: 1, First name: Clarence, Last name: Ho, Birthday: 1980-07-30
Contact - Id: 2, First name: Scott, Last name: Tiger, Birthday: 1990-11-02
Contact - Id: 3, First name: John, Last name: Smith, Birthday: 1964-02-28
```

As shown in the previous output, the irrelevant output statements were removed for clarity. The notable log messages relating to transaction processing are in bold. In the first line, before the findAll() method is run, Spring's JpaTransactionManager creates a new transaction (the name is equal to the fully qualified class name with the method name) with default attributes, but the transaction is set to read-only, as defined at the method-level @Transactional annotation. Then, the query is submitted, and upon completion and without any errors, the transaction is committed. The creation and commit operations of the transaction are handled by the JpaTransactionManager.

Let's proceed to the implementation of the update operation. We need to implement both the findById() and save() methods in the ContactService interface. Listing 13-12 shows the implementation.

Listing 13-12. The ContactServiceImpl Class with the findById() and save() Methods Implemented

```
package com.apress.prospring3.ch13.service.annotation;

// Import statement omitted
@Service("contactService")
@Repository
@Transactional
public class ContactServiceImpl implements ContactService {

    // Codes omitted
    @Transactional(readOnly=true)
    public Contact findById(Long id) {
        return contactRepository.findOne(id);
    }

    public Contact save(Contact contact) {
        return contactRepository.save(contact);
    }
}
```

As shown in Listing 13-12, the findById() method is also annotated with @Transactional(readOnly=true). Generally, the readOnly=true attribute should be applied to all finder methods. The main reason is that most persistence providers will perform a certain level of optimization on read-only transactions. For example, Hibernate will not maintain the snapshots of the managed instances retrieved from the database with read-only turned on.

For the save() method, we simply invoke the CrudRepository.save() method and don't provide any annotation. This means the class-level annotation will be used, which is a read-write transaction.

Let's modify the TxAnnotationSample class for testing the save() method, as shown in Listing 13-13.

Listing 13-13. Testing the save() Method

```
package com.apress.prospring3.ch13;

// Import statements omitted
public class TxAnnotationSample {

    public static void main(String[] args) {

        GenericXmlApplicationContext ctx = new GenericXmlApplicationContext();
        ctx.load("classpath:tx-annotation-app-context.xml");
        ctx.refresh();
```

```
    ContactService contactService = ctx.getBean("contactService",
        ContactService.class);

    Contact contact = contactService.findById(1l);
    contact.setFirstName("Peter");
    contactService.save(contact);
    System.out.println("Contact saved successfully");
    }

}
```

As shown in Listing 13-13, the Contact object with id 1 is retrieved, and then the first name is updated and saved to the database. Running the code produces the following output:

```
DEBUG [org.springframework.orm.jpa.JpaTransactionManager] –<Creating new transaction with name
[com.apress.prospring3.ch13.service.annotation.ContactServiceImpl.findById]
:PROPAGATION_REQUIRED,ISOLATION_DEFAULT,readOnly; ''>
DEBUG [org.hibernate.transaction.JDBCTransaction] - <begin>
Hibernate: select contact0_.ID as ID0_0_, contact0_.BIRTH_DATE as BIRTH2_0_0_,
contact0_.FIRST_NAME as FIRST3_0_0_, contact0_.LAST_NAME as LAST4_0_0_, contact0_.VERSION as
VERSION0_0_ from contact contact0_ where contact0_.ID=?
DEBUG [org.springframework.orm.jpa.JpaTransactionManager] - <Creating new transaction with
name [com.apress.prospring3.ch13.service.annotation.ContactServiceImpl.save]:
PROPAGATION_REQUIRED,ISOLATION_DEFAULT; ''>
DEBUG [org.hibernate.transaction.JDBCTransaction] - <begin>
DEBUG [org.springframework.orm.jpa.JpaTransactionManager] - <Initiating transaction commit>
DEBUG [org.springframework.orm.jpa.JpaTransactionManager] –É
<Committing JPA transaction on EntityManager [org.hibernate.ejb.EntityManagerImpl@396c75ed]>
DEBUG [org.hibernate.transaction.JDBCTransaction] - <commit>
DEBUG [org.hibernate.event.def.AbstractFlushingEventListener] - <processing flush-time
cascades>
DEBUG [org.hibernate.event.def.AbstractFlushingEventListener] - <dirty checking collections>
DEBUG [org.hibernate.event.def.AbstractFlushingEventListener] - <Flushed: 0 insertions, 1
updates, 0 deletions to 1 objects>
DEBUG [org.hibernate.event.def.AbstractFlushingEventListener] - <Flushed: 0 (re)creations, 0
updates, 0 removals to 0 collections>
Hibernate: update contact set BIRTH_DATE=?, FIRST_NAME=?, LAST_NAME=?, VERSION=? where ID=?
and VERSION=?
DEBUG [org.hibernate.transaction.JDBCTransaction] - <re-enabling autocommit>
DEBUG [org.hibernate.transaction.JDBCTransaction] - <committed JDBC Connection>
DEBUG [org.hibernate.jdbc.ConnectionManager] –<aggressively releasing JDBC connection>
DEBUG [org.hibernate.jdbc.ConnectionManager] - <releasing JDBC connection [ (open
PreparedStatements: 0, globally: 0) (open ResultSets: 0, globally: 0)]>
DEBUG [org.springframework.orm.jpa.JpaTransactionManager] - <Closing JPA EntityManager
[org.hibernate.ejb.EntityManagerImpl@396c75ed] after transaction>
DEBUG [org.springframework.orm.jpa.EntityManagerFactoryUtils] –<Closing JPA EntityManager>
Contact saved successfully
```

The main log messages are in bold. You can see that for the transaction for the save() method, the default attributes are inherited from the class-level @Transactional annotation. Upon completion of the update operation, Spring's JpaTransactionManager fires a transaction commit, which causes Hibernate to flush the persistence context and commit the underlying JDBC connection to the database.

Finally, let's take a look at the countAll() method. We will investigate two different transaction configurations for this method. Although the CrudRepository.count() method can fulfill the purpose, we will not use that method. Instead, we will implement another method for demonstration purposes. It's mainly because the methods defined by the CrudRepository interface in Spring Data were already marked with the appropriate transaction attributes.

Listing 13-14 shows the new method countAllContacts() defined in the ContactRepository interface.

Listing 13-14. *The ContactRepository Interface with the countAllContacts() Method*

```
package com.apress.prospring3.ch13.repository;

import org.springframework.data.jpa.repository.Query;
import org.springframework.data.repository.CrudRepository;

import com.apress.prospring3.ch13.domain.Contact;

public interface ContactRepository extends CrudRepository<Contact, Long> {

    @Query("select count(c) from Contact c")
    public Long countAllContacts();
}
```

As shown in Listing 13-14, for the new countAllContacts() method, the @Query annotation is applied, with the value equaling the JPQL statement that counts the number of contacts. Listing 13-15 shows the implementation of the countAll() method in the ContactServiceImpl class.

Listing 13-15. *The ContactServiceImpl Class with the countAll() Method Implemented*

```
package com.apress.prospring3.ch13.service.annotation;

// Import statement omitted
@Service("contactService")
@Repository
@Transactional
public class ContactServiceImpl implements ContactService {

    // Codes omitted
    @Transactional(readOnly=true)
    public long countAll() {
        return contactRepository.countAllContacts();
    }
}
```

The annotation is the same as other finder methods. Listing 13-16 shows the testing code snippet.

Listing 13-16. *Testing the countAll() Method*

```
package com.apress.prospring3.ch13;

public class TxAnnotationSample {

    public static void main(String[] args) {

        GenericXmlApplicationContext ctx = new GenericXmlApplicationContext();
```

```
        ctx.load("classpath:tx-annotation-app-context.xml");
        ctx.refresh();

        ContactService contactService = ctx.getBean("contactService",
            ContactService.class);

        // Testing countAll() method
        System.out.println("Contact count: " + contactService.countAll());
    }
}
```

Running the program will produce the following output:

```
DEBUG [org.springframework.orm.jpa.JpaTransactionManager] -↵
<Creating new transaction with name ↵
[com.apress.prospring3.ch13.service.annotation.ContactServiceImpl.countAll]:
PROPAGATION_REQUIRED,ISOLATION_DEFAULT,readOnly; ''>
DEBUG [org.hibernate.transaction.JDBCTransaction] - <begin>
Hibernate: select count(*) as col_0_0_ from contact contact0_ limit ?
DEBUG [org.hibernate.transaction.JDBCTransaction] - <commit>
DEBUG [org.hibernate.transaction.JDBCTransaction] - <re-enabling autocommit>
DEBUG [org.hibernate.transaction.JDBCTransaction] - <committed JDBC Connection>
DEBUG [org.springframework.orm.jpa.JpaTransactionManager] - <Closing JPA EntityManager
[org.hibernate.ejb.EntityManagerImpl@4a005364] after transaction>
DEBUG [org.springframework.orm.jpa.EntityManagerFactoryUtils] - <Closing JPA EntityManager>
Contact count: 3
```

As shown in the previous output, you can see that the transaction for the countAll() was created with read-only equaling true as expected.

But for the countAll() function, we don't want it to be enlisted in a transaction at all. The reason is that we don't need the result to be managed by the underlying JPA EntityManager. Instead, we just want to get the count and forget about it. In this case, we can override the transaction propagation behavior to Propagation.NEVER. Listing 13-17 shows the revised countAll() method.

Listing 13-17. The ContactServiceImpl Class with Revised countAll() Implemented

```
package com.apress.prospring3.ch13.service.annotation;

// Import statement omitted
@Service("contactService")
@Repository
@Transactional
public class ContactServiceImpl implements ContactService {

    // Codes omitted
    @Transactional(propagation=Propagation.NEVER)
    public long countAll() {
        return contactRepository.count();
    }
}
```

Run the testing code in Listing 13-16 again, and you will find that the transaction will not be created for the countAll() method.

This section covered some major configurations that you will deal with when processing transactions on a day-to-day basis. For special cases, you may need to define the timeout, isolation level, rollback (or not) for specific exceptions, and so on.

■ **Note** Spring's `JpaTransactionManager` doesn't support a custom isolation level. Instead, it will always use the default isolation level for the underlying datastore. If you are using Hibernate as the JPA service provider, there is a workaround when supporting a custom isolation level by extending the `HibernateJpaDialect` class (for details, please refer to the article at http://amitstechblog.wordpress.com/2011/05/31/supporting-custom-isolation-levels-with-jpa).

Using XML Configuration for Transaction Management

Another common approach of declarative transaction management is to use Spring's AOP support. Before Spring version 2, we needed to use the `TransactionProxyFactoryBean` class to define transaction requirements for Spring beans. However, ever since version 2, Spring provides a much simpler way by introducing aop-namespace and using the common AOP configuration technique for defining transaction requirements.

In this section, the example we will use is the same as the annotation one. We will just modify it to the XML configuration style. Listing 13-18 shows the XML configuration file for transaction management (tx-declarative-app-context.xml).

Listing 13-18. XML Configuration for Transaction Management

```
<?xml version="1.0" encoding="UTF-8"?>
<beans xmlns="http://www.springframework.org/schema/beans"
    xmlns:xsi="http://www.w3.org/2001/XMLSchema-instance"
    xmlns:context="http://www.springframework.org/schema/context"
    xmlns:jdbc="http://www.springframework.org/schema/jdbc"
    xmlns:tx="http://www.springframework.org/schema/tx"
    xmlns:jpa="http://www.springframework.org/schema/data/jpa"
    xmlns:aop="http://www.springframework.org/schema/aop"
    xsi:schemaLocation="http://www.springframework.org/schema/jdbc
        http://www.springframework.org/schema/jdbc/spring-jdbc-3.1.xsd
        http://www.springframework.org/schema/beans
        http://www.springframework.org/schema/beans/spring-beans-3.1.xsd
        http://www.springframework.org/schema/tx
        http://www.springframework.org/schema/tx/spring-tx-3.1.xsd
        http://www.springframework.org/schema/data/jpa
        http://www.springframework.org/schema/data/jpa/spring-jpa-1.0.xsd
        http://www.springframework.org/schema/context
        http://www.springframework.org/schema/context/spring-context-3.1.xsd
        http://www.springframework.org/schema/aop
        http://www.springframework.org/schema/aop/spring-aop-3.1.xsd">

    <aop:config>
        <aop:pointcut id="serviceOperation" expression=
```

```xml
            "execution(* com.apress.prospring3.ch13.service.declarative.*ServiceImpl.*(..))"/>
        <aop:advisor pointcut-ref="serviceOperation" advice-ref="txAdvice"/>
    </aop:config>

    <tx:advice id="txAdvice">
        <tx:attributes>
            <tx:method name="find*" read-only="true"/>
            <tx:method name="count*" propagation="NEVER"/>
            <tx:method name="*"/>
        </tx:attributes>
    </tx:advice>

    <jdbc:embedded-database id="dataSource" type="H2">
        <jdbc:script location="classpath:schema.sql"/>
        <jdbc:script location="classpath:test-data.sql"/>
    </jdbc:embedded-database>

    <bean id="transactionManager" class="org.springframework.orm.jpa.JpaTransactionManager">
        <property name="entityManagerFactory" ref="emf"/>
    </bean>

    <bean id="emf" class="org.springframework.orm.jpa.LocalContainerEntityManagerFactoryBean">
        <property name="dataSource" ref="dataSource" />
        <property name="jpaVendorAdapter">
            <bean class="org.springframework.orm.jpa.vendor.HibernateJpaVendorAdapter" />
        </property>
        <property name="packagesToScan" value="com.apress.prospring3.ch13.domain"/>
        <property name="jpaProperties">
            <props>
                <prop key="hibernate.dialect">
                    org.hibernate.dialect.H2Dialect
                </prop>
                <prop key="hibernate.max_fetch_depth">3</prop>
                <prop key="hibernate.jdbc.fetch_size">50</prop>
                <prop key="hibernate.jdbc.batch_size">10</prop>
                <prop key="hibernate.show_sql">true</prop>
            </props>
        </property>
    </bean>

    <context:component-scan
        base-package="com.apress.prospring3.ch13.service.declarative" />

    <jpa:repositories base-package="com.apress.prospring3.ch13.repository"
        entity-manager-factory-ref="emf"
        transaction-manager-ref="transactionManager"/>

</beans>
```

The configuration is quite similar to the annotation one in Listing 13-9 (the differences are in bold). Basically, the <tx:annotation-driven> tag was removed, and the <context:component-scan> tag was modified for the package name we used for declarative transaction management. The most important tags are <aop:config> and <tx:advice>.

Under the <aop:config> tag, a pointcut was defined for all operations within the service layer (i.e., all implementation classes under the com.apress.prospring3.ch13.service.declarative package). The advice is referencing the bean with an ID of txAdvice, which is defined by the <tx:advice> tag. In the <tx:advice> tag, we configure the transaction attributes for various methods that we want to participate in a transaction. As shown in the tag, we specify that all finder methods (i.e., methods with the prefix find) will be read-only, and we specify that the count methods (i.e., methods with the prefix count) will not participate in transaction. For the rest of the methods, the default transaction behavior will be applied. This configuration is the same as the one we did in the annotation example. Listing 13-19 shows the implementation class for XML declarative transaction management.

Listing 13-19. ContactServiceImpl Class for XML Transaction Configuration

```
package com.apress.prospring3.ch13.service.declarative;

// Import statements omitted

@Service("contactService")
@Repository
public class ContactServiceImpl implements ContactService {

    @Autowired
    private ContactRepository contactRepository;

    public List<Contact> findAll() {
        return Lists.newArrayList(contactRepository.findAll());
    }

    public Contact findById(Long id) {
        return contactRepository.findOne(id);
    }

    public Contact save(Contact contact) {
        return contactRepository.save(contact);
    }

    public long countAll() {
        return contactRepository.countAllContacts ();
    }
}
```

Listing 13-19 is basically the same as the annotation example, but just the @Transactional annotations were removed, because now the weaving of transactions will be done by Spring AOP based on the XML configuration. Listing 13-20 shows the testing program.

Listing 13-20. Testing the XML Transaction Configuration

```
package com.apress.prospring3.ch13;

import java.util.List;

import org.springframework.context.support.GenericXmlApplicationContext;

import com.apress.prospring3.ch13.domain.Contact;
```

```
import com.apress.prospring3.ch13.service.ContactService;

public class TxDeclarativeSample {

    public static void main(String[] args) {

        GenericXmlApplicationContext ctx = new GenericXmlApplicationContext();
        ctx.load("classpath:tx-declarative-app-context.xml");
        ctx.refresh();

        ContactService contactService = ctx.getBean("contactService",
            ContactService.class);

        // Testing findAll() method
        List<Contact> contacts = contactService.findAll();

        for (Contact contact: contacts) {
            System.out.println(contact);
        }

        // Testing save() method
        Contact contact = contactService.findById(1l);
        contact.setFirstName("Peter");
        contactService.save(contact);
        System.out.println("Contact saved successfully");

        // Testing countAll() method
        System.out.println("Contact count: " + contactService.countAll());

    }

}
```

We will leave you to test the program and observe the output for transaction-related operations that Spring and Hibernate has performed. Basically, they are the same as the annotation example.

Using Programmatic Transactions

The third option is to control the transaction behavior programmatically. In this case, we have two options. The first one is to inject an instance of PlatformTransactionManager into the bean and interact with the transaction manager directly. Another option is to use the Spring-provided TransactionTemplate class, which simplifies your work a lot. In this section, we will demonstrate using the TransactionTemplate class. To make it simple, we will just focus on implementing the ContactService.countAll() method.

Listing 13-21 shows the XML configuration for using programmatic transaction (tx-programmatic-app-context.xml).

Listing 13-21. Spring Configuration for Programmtic Transaction Management

```
<?xml version="1.0" encoding="UTF-8"?>
<beans xmlns="http://www.springframework.org/schema/beans"
    xmlns:xsi="http://www.w3.org/2001/XMLSchema-instance"
    xmlns:context="http://www.springframework.org/schema/context"
```

```xml
    xmlns:jdbc="http://www.springframework.org/schema/jdbc"
    xmlns:tx="http://www.springframework.org/schema/tx"
    xmlns:jpa="http://www.springframework.org/schema/data/jpa"
    xsi:schemaLocation="http://www.springframework.org/schema/jdbc
        http://www.springframework.org/schema/jdbc/spring-jdbc-3.1.xsd
        http://www.springframework.org/schema/beans
        http://www.springframework.org/schema/beans/spring-beans-3.1.xsd
        http://www.springframework.org/schema/tx
        http://www.springframework.org/schema/tx/spring-tx-3.1.xsd
        http://www.springframework.org/schema/data/jpa
        http://www.springframework.org/schema/data/jpa/spring-jpa-1.0.xsd
        http://www.springframework.org/schema/context
        http://www.springframework.org/schema/context/spring-context-3.1.xsd">

<jdbc:embedded-database id="dataSource" type="H2">
    <jdbc:script location="classpath:schema.sql"/>
    <jdbc:script location="classpath:test-data.sql"/>
</jdbc:embedded-database>

<bean id="transactionTemplate"
    class="org.springframework.transaction.support.TransactionTemplate">
    <property name="propagationBehaviorName" value="PROPAGATION_NEVER"/>
    <property name="timeout" value="30"/>
    <property name="transactionManager" ref="transactionManager"/>
</bean>

<bean id="transactionManager" class="org.springframework.orm.jpa.JpaTransactionManager">
    <property name="entityManagerFactory" ref="emf"/>
</bean>

<bean id="emf" class="org.springframework.orm.jpa.LocalContainerEntityManagerFactoryBean">
    <property name="dataSource" ref="dataSource" />
    <property name="jpaVendorAdapter">
        <bean class="org.springframework.orm.jpa.vendor.HibernateJpaVendorAdapter" />
    </property>
    <property name="packagesToScan"
        value="com.apress.prospring3.ch13.domain"/>
    <property name="jpaProperties">
        <props>
            <prop key="hibernate.dialect">
                org.hibernate.dialect.H2Dialect
            </prop>
            <prop key="hibernate.max_fetch_depth">3</prop>
            <prop key="hibernate.jdbc.fetch_size">50</prop>
            <prop key="hibernate.jdbc.batch_size">10</prop>
            <prop key="hibernate.show_sql">true</prop>
        </props>
    </property>
</bean>

<context:component-scan
    base-package="com.apress.prospring3.ch13.service.programmatic" />
```

```
<jpa:repositories base-package="com.apress.prospring3.ch13.repository"
    entity-manager-factory-ref="emf"
    transaction-manager-ref="transactionManager"/>

</beans>
```

As shown in Listing 13-21, the AOP transaction advice was removed. In addition, a transactionTemplate bean was defined using the org.springframework.transaction.support.TransactionTemplate class, with the transaction attributes defined in the properties section. Let's take a look on the implementation of the countAll() method, which is shown in Listing 13-22.

Listing 13-22. Programmatic Transaction Management Implementation

```
package com.apress.prospring3.ch13.service.programmatic;

// Import statements omitted
@Service("contactService")
@Repository
public class ContactServiceImpl implements ContactService {

    @Autowired
    private TransactionTemplate transactionTemplate;

    @PersistenceContext
    private EntityManager em;
    // Other methods not implemented

    public long countAll() {
        return transactionTemplate.execute(new TransactionCallback<Long>() {
            public Long doInTransaction(TransactionStatus transactionStatus) {
                return em.createNamedQuery("Contact.countAll",
                    Long.class).getSingleResult();
            }

        });
    }
}
```

In Listing 13-22, the TransactionTemplate class was injected from Spring. And then in the countAll() method, the TransactionTemplate.execute() method was invoked, passing in a declaration of an inner class that implements the TransactionCallback<T> interface. Then the doInTransaction() was overridden with the desired logic. The logic will run within the attributes as defined by the transactionTemplate bean. Listing 13-23 shows the testing program.

Listing 13-23. Testing Programmatic Transaction

```
package com.apress.prospring3.ch13;

import org.springframework.context.support.GenericXmlApplicationContext;

import com.apress.prospring3.ch13.service.ContactService;
```

```
public class TxProgrammaticSample {

    public static void main(String[] args) {

        GenericXmlApplicationContext ctx = new GenericXmlApplicationContext();
        ctx.load("classpath:tx-programmatic-app-context.xml");
        ctx.refresh();

        ContactService contactService = ctx.getBean("contactService",
            ContactService.class);

        System.out.println("Contact count: " + contactService.countAll());

    }
}
```

We will leave it to you to run the program and observe the result. Try to tweak the transaction attributes and see what happens in the transaction processing of the countAll() method.

Considerations on Transaction Management

So, having discussed the various ways for implementing transaction management, which one should you use? The declarative approach is recommended in all cases, and you should avoid implementing transaction management within your code as far as possible. Most of the time when you find it necessary to code transaction control logic in the application, it is because of bad design, and in this case, you should consider refactoring your logic into manageable pieces and have the transaction requirements defined on those pieces declaratively.

For the declarative approach, using XML and using annotations both have their own pros and cons. Some developers prefer not to declare transaction requirements in code, while others prefer using annotations for easy maintenance, because you can see all the transaction requirement declaration within the code. Again, let the application requirements drive your decision, and once your team or company has standardized on the approach, stay consistent with the configuration style.

Global Transactions with Spring

Many enterprise Java applications will need to access multiple backend resources. For example, a piece of customer information received from an external business partner will need to update the databases for multiple systems (CRM, ERP, and so on). Some will even need to produce a message and send it to an MQ server via JMS for all other applications within the company that are interested in customer information. Transactions that span multiple backend resources are referred to as *global* (or distributed) transactions.

A main characteristic of a global transaction is the guarantee of atomicity, which means that involved resources are all updated or none is updated. This includes complex coordination and synchronization logic that should be handled by the transaction manager. In the Java world, JTA is the de facto standard for implementing global transactions.

Spring supports JTA transactions equally well as local transactions and hides that logic from the business code. In this section, we will demonstrate how to implement global transactions by using JTA with Spring.

Infrastructure for Implementing the JTA Sample

We are using the same table as the previous samples in this chapter. However, the embedded H2 database doesn't fully support XA (at least at the time of writing), so in this example, we will use MySQL as the backend database.

We also want to show how to implement global transactions with JTA in a stand-alone application or web container environment. So, in this example, we will use Atomikos (www.atomikos.com/Main/TransactionsEssentials), which is a widely used open source JTA transaction manager for use in a non-JEE environment.

To show how global transactions work, we need at least two different backend resources. To make things simple, we will use one MySQL database but two JPA entity managers to simulate the use case. The effect is the same because you have multiple JPA persistence units to distinct backend databases. The version we are using in developing this sample is the MySQL 5.1.58 Community Server edition.

In the MySQL database, we will create two schemas, as shown in Table 13-5.

Table 13-5. *MySQL Database Schemas*

Schema Name	Connection Information	Data Population Scripts
prospring3_ch13a	User: prospring3_ch13a Password: prospring3_ch13a	schema.sql test-data.sql
prospring3_ch13b	User: prospring3_ch13b Password: prospring3_ch13b	schema.sql test-data.sql

I am using phpMyAdmin (www.phpmyadmin.net) to set up the schema and scripts. However, you can use whatever tools you feel familiar with to set up the schemas and users.

Then, we will need to add the required dependencies on MySQL and Atomikos to the project. Table 13-6 shows the dependencies required.

Table 13-6. *Maven Dependencies for MySQL and Atomikos*

Group ID	Artifact ID	Version	Description
mysql	mysql-connector-java	5.1.18	The Java library for MySQL 5
com.atomikos	transactions-jdbc	3.7.0	The JTA transaction library for Atomikos
com.atomikos	transactions-hibernate3	3.7.0	The library for Atomikos integration with Hibernate 3

After the setup has completed, we can proceed to the Spring configuration and implementation.

Implementing Global Transactions with JTA

First let's take a look at Spring's configuration. Listing 13-24 shows the file content (tx-jta-app-context.xml).

Listing 13-24. Spring Configuration with JTA

```xml
<?xml version="1.0" encoding="UTF-8"?>
<beans xmlns="http://www.springframework.org/schema/beans"
    xmlns:xsi="http://www.w3.org/2001/XMLSchema-instance"
    xmlns:context="http://www.springframework.org/schema/context"
    xmlns:jdbc="http://www.springframework.org/schema/jdbc"
    xmlns:tx="http://www.springframework.org/schema/tx"
    xsi:schemaLocation="http://www.springframework.org/schema/jdbc
        http://www.springframework.org/schema/jdbc/spring-jdbc-3.1.xsd
        http://www.springframework.org/schema/beans
        http://www.springframework.org/schema/beans/spring-beans-3.1.xsd
        http://www.springframework.org/schema/tx
        http://www.springframework.org/schema/tx/spring-tx-3.1.xsd
        http://www.springframework.org/schema/context
        http://www.springframework.org/schema/context/spring-context-3.1.xsd">

    <bean id="dataSourceA"
        class="com.atomikos.jdbc.AtomikosDataSourceBean"
        init-method="init" destroy-method="close">
        <property name="uniqueResourceName"><value>XADBMSA</value></property>
        <property name="xaDataSourceClassName">
            <value>com.mysql.jdbc.jdbc2.optional.MysqlXADataSource</value>
        </property>
        <property name="xaProperties">
            <props>
                <prop key="databaseName">prospring3_ch13a</prop>
                <prop key="user">prospring3_ch13a</prop>
                <prop key="password">prospring3_ch13a</prop>
            </props>
        </property>
        <property name="poolSize"><value>1</value></property>
    </bean>

    <bean id="dataSourceB"
        class="com.atomikos.jdbc.AtomikosDataSourceBean"
        init-method="init" destroy-method="close">
        <property name="uniqueResourceName"><value>XADBMSB</value></property>
        <property name="xaDataSourceClassName">
            <value>com.mysql.jdbc.jdbc2.optional.MysqlXADataSource</value>
        </property>
        <property name="xaProperties">
            <props>
                <prop key="databaseName">prospring3_ch13b</prop>
                <prop key="user">prospring3_ch13b</prop>
                <prop key="password">prospring3_ch13b</prop>
            </props>
        </property>
        <property name="poolSize"><value>1</value></property>
    </bean>

    <!-- Construct Atomikos UserTransactionManager, needed to configure Spring -->
    <bean id="atomikosTransactionManager"
        class="com.atomikos.icatch.jta.UserTransactionManager"
```

```
        init-method="init" destroy-method="close">
        <!--  when close is called, should we force transactions
            to terminate or not? -->
        <property name="forceShutdown">
            <value>true</value>
        </property>
    </bean>

    <!-- Also use Atomikos UserTransactionImp, needed to configure Spring  -->
    <bean id="atomikosUserTransaction"
        class="com.atomikos.icatch.jta.UserTransactionImp">
        <property name="transactionTimeout"><value>300</value></property>
    </bean>

    <!-- Configure the Spring framework to use JTA transactions
        from Atomikos -->
    <bean id="transactionManager"
        class="org.springframework.transaction.jta.JtaTransactionManager">
        <property name="transactionManager">
            <ref bean="atomikosTransactionManager"/>
        </property>
        <property name="userTransaction">
            <ref bean="atomikosUserTransaction"/>
        </property>
    </bean>

    <tx:annotation-driven transaction-manager="transactionManager" />

    <bean id="emfBase"
class="org.springframework.orm.jpa.LocalContainerEntityManagerFactoryBean"
abstract="true">
        <property name="jpaVendorAdapter">
            <bean
class="org.springframework.orm.jpa.vendor.HibernateJpaVendorAdapter"
/>
        </property>
        <property name="packagesToScan"
            value="com.apress.prospring3.ch13.domain"/>
        <property name="jpaProperties">
            <props>
                <prop key="hibernate.transaction.factory_class">
com.atomikos.icatch.jta.hibernate3.AtomikosJTATransactionFactory
                </prop>
                <prop key="hibernate.transaction.manager_lookup_class">
com.atomikos.icatch.jta.hibernate3.TransactionManagerLookup</prop>
                <prop key="hibernate.dialect">
                    org.hibernate.dialect.MySQL5Dialect
                </prop>
                <prop key="hibernate.max_fetch_depth">3</prop>
                <prop key="hibernate.jdbc.fetch_size">50</prop>
                <prop key="hibernate.jdbc.batch_size">10</prop>
                <prop key="hibernate.show_sql">true</prop>
            </props>
        </property>
```

```
    </bean>

    <bean id="emfA" parent="emfBase">
        <property name="dataSource" ref="dataSourceA" />
    </bean>

    <bean id="emfB" parent="emfBase">
        <property name="dataSource" ref="dataSourceB" />
    </bean>

    <context:component-scan
        base-package="com.apress.prospring3.ch13.service.jta" />

</beans>
```

The configuration is quite long but not too complex. First, two datasource beans are defined to indicate the two different database resources. The beans names are dataSourceA and dataSourceB, which connect to the schemas prospring3_ch13a and prospring3_ch13b, respectively. Both datasource beans use the class com.atomikos.jdbc.AtomikosDataSourceBean, which supports an XA-compliant datasource, and within the two beans' definitions, MySQL's XA datasource implementation class was defined (com.mysql.jdbc.jdbc2.optional.MysqlXADataSource), which is the resource manager for MySQL. Then, the database connection information is provided. Note that the poolSize attribute defines the number of connections within the connection pool that Atomikos need to maintain. It's not mandatory. However, if the attribute is not provided, Atomikos will use the default value 1.

For the Atomikos part, two beans, the atomikosTransactionManager and atomikosUserTransaction beans, are defined. The implementation classes are provided by Atomikos, which implements the standard JEE's TransactionManager and UserTransaction interfaces, respectively. Those beans provide the transaction coordination and synchronization services required by JTA and communicate with the resource managers over the XA protocol in supporting 2PC. Then, Spring's transactionManager bean (with JtaTransactionManager as the implementation class) was defined, injecting the two transaction beans provided by Atomikos. This instructs Spring to use Atomikos JTA for transaction management.

Then, three EntityManagerFactory beans are defined, named emfBase, emfA, and emfB. The emfBase bean is an abstract parent bean, which wraps the common JPA properties. The emfBase bean is implemented with Spring's LocalContainerEntityManagerFactoryBean class. The emfA and emfB beans both inherit the configuration from the parent bean emfBase, and the only difference between the two beans is that they were injected with the corresponding datasource (i.e., dataSourceA injected into emfA, and dataSourceB injected into emfB). Consequently, emfA will connect to MySQL's prospring3_ch13a schema via the dataSourceA bean, while emfB will connect to the prospring3_ch13b schema via the dataSourceB bean. Take a look at the properties hibernate.transaction.factory_class and hibernate.transaction.manager_lookup_class in the emfBase bean. These two properties are very important, because they are used by Hibernate to look up the underlying UserTransaction and TransactionManager interfaces in order to participate in the persistence context that it's managing into the global transaction. The classes are provided by the Atomikos transactions-hibernate3 module.

Listing 13-25 shows the ContactServiceImpl class for JTA. Note that for simplicity only the save() method is implemented.

Listing 13-25. JTA ContactService Implementation Class

```
package com.apress.prospring3.ch13.service.jta;

import java.util.List;

import javax.persistence.EntityManager;
```

```
import javax.persistence.PersistenceContext;
import javax.persistence.PersistenceException;

import org.springframework.orm.jpa.JpaSystemException;
import org.springframework.stereotype.Repository;
import org.springframework.stereotype.Service;
import org.springframework.transaction.annotation.Transactional;

import com.apress.prospring3.ch13.domain.Contact;
import com.apress.prospring3.ch13.service.ContactService;

@Service("contactService")
@Repository
@Transactional
public class ContactServiceImpl implements ContactService {

    @PersistenceContext(unitName="emfA")
    private EntityManager emA;

    @PersistenceContext(unitName="emfB")
    private EntityManager emB;

    @Transactional(readOnly=true)
    public List<Contact> findAll() {
        return null;
    }

    @Transactional(readOnly=true)
    public Contact findById(Long id) {
        return null;
    }

    public Contact save(Contact contact) {
        Contact contactB = new Contact();
        contactB.setFirstName(contact.getFirstName());
        contactB.setLastName(contact.getLastName());
        if (contact.getId() == null) {
            emA.persist(contact);
            emB.persist(contactB);
            //throw new JpaSystemException(new PersistenceException());
        } else {
            emA.merge(contact);
            emB.merge(contact);
        }

        return contact;
    }

    public long countAll() {
        return 0;
    }
}
```

From Listing 13-25, the two entity managers defined are injected into the ContactServiceImpl class. In the save() method, we will persist the contact object to the two different schemas, respectively. Ignore the throw exception statement at the moment; we will use it later to verify that the transaction was rolled back when saving to the schema prospring3_ch13b fails. Listing 13-26 shows the testing program.

Listing 13-26. Testing JTA

```
package com.apress.prospring3.ch13;

import org.springframework.context.support.GenericXmlApplicationContext;

import com.apress.prospring3.ch13.domain.Contact;
import com.apress.prospring3.ch13.service.ContactService;

public class TxJtaSample {

    public static void main(String[] args) {

        GenericXmlApplicationContext ctx = new GenericXmlApplicationContext();
        ctx.load("classpath:tx-jta-app-context.xml");
        ctx.refresh();

        ContactService contactService = ctx.getBean("contactService",
            ContactService.class);

        Contact contact = new Contact();
        contact.setFirstName("Jta");
        contact.setLastName("Manager");
        contactService.save(contact);
        System.out.println("Contact saved successfully");

    }
}
```

The program creates a new contact object and calls the ContactService.save() method. The implementation will try to persist the same object to two databases. Running the program will produce the following output (the other output was omitted):

```
INFO [atomikos] - <createCompositeTransaction ( 300000 ): created new ROOT transaction with id
192.168.11.8.tm0000100001>
DEBUG [org.springframework.orm.jpa.EntityManagerFactoryUtils] - <Opening JPA EntityManager>
DEBUG [org.hibernate.impl.SessionImpl] - <opened session at timestamp: 13208330451>
DEBUG [atomikos] - <getCompositeTransaction()  returning instance with id
192.168.11.8.tm0000100001>
INFO [atomikos] - <registerSynchronization ( com.atomikos.icatch.jta.Sync2Sync@380199d8 ) for
transaction 192.168.11.8.tm0000100001>
DEBUG [org.hibernate.jdbc.JDBCContext] - <successfully registered Synchronization>
DEBUG [org.springframework.orm.jpa.EntityManagerFactoryUtils] - <Registering transaction
synchronization for JPA EntityManager>
DEBUG [org.hibernate.jdbc.ConnectionManager] - <opening JDBC connection>
Hibernate: insert into contact (BIRTH_DATE, FIRST_NAME, LAST_NAME, VERSION) values (?, ?, ?, ?)
INFO [atomikos] - <addParticipant ( XAResourceTransaction:
3139322E3136382E31312E382E746D30303030313030303031:3139322E3136382E31312E382E746D31 ) for
transaction 192.168.11.8.tm0000100001>
```

```
INFO [atomikos] - <XAResource.start (
3139322E3136382E31312E382E746D3030303031303030303031:3139322E3136382E31312E382E746D31 ,
XAResource.TMNOFLAGS ) on resource XADBMSA represented by XAResource instance
com.mysql.jdbc.jdbc2.optional.JDBC4MysqlXAConnection@49b29f80>
INFO [atomikos] - <XAResource.end (
3139322E3136382E31312E382E746D3030303031303030303031:3139322E3136382E31312E382E746D31 ,
XAResource.TMSUCCESS ) on resource XADBMSA represented by XAResource instance
com.mysql.jdbc.jdbc2.optional.JDBC4MysqlXAConnection@49b29f80>
DEBUG [org.springframework.orm.jpa.EntityManagerFactoryUtils] - <Opening JPA EntityManager>
DEBUG [org.hibernate.impl.SessionImpl] - <opened session at timestamp: 13208330452>
DEBUG [atomikos] - <getCompositeTransaction()  returning instance with id
192.168.11.8.tm0000100001>
DEBUG [org.hibernate.jdbc.ConnectionManager] - <opening JDBC connection>
DEBUG [atomikos] - <getCompositeTransaction()  returning instance with id
192.168.11.8.tm0000100001>
Hibernate: insert into contact (BIRTH_DATE, FIRST_NAME, LAST_NAME, VERSION) values (?, ?, ?,
?)
DEBUG [atomikos] - <getCompositeTransaction()  returning instance with id
192.168.11.8.tm0000100001>
DEBUG [atomikos] - <getCompositeTransaction()  returning instance with id
192.168.11.8.tm0000100001>
INFO [atomikos] - <registerSynchronization ( com.atomikos.icatch.jta.Sync2Sync@45b2b450 ) for
transaction 192.168.11.8.tm0000100001>
DEBUG [org.hibernate.jdbc.JDBCContext] - <successfully registered Synchronization>
DEBUG [org.springframework.orm.jpa.EntityManagerFactoryUtils] - <Registering transaction
synchronization for JPA EntityManager>
INFO [atomikos] - <addParticipant ( XAResourceTransaction:
3139322E3136382E31312E382E746D3030303031303030303031:3139322E3136382E31312E382E746D32 ) for
transaction 192.168.11.8.tm0000100001>
INFO [atomikos] - <XAResource.start (
3139322E3136382E31312E382E746D3030303031303030303031:3139322E3136382E31312E382E746D32 ,
XAResource.TMNOFLAGS ) on resource XADBMSB represented by XAResource instance
com.mysql.jdbc.jdbc2.optional.JDBC4MysqlXAConnection@3f7aa2a8>
INFO [atomikos] - <XAResource.end (
3139322E3136382E31312E382E746D3030303031303030303031:3139322E3136382E31312E382E746D32 ,
XAResource.TMSUCCESS ) on resource XADBMSB represented by XAResource instance
com.mysql.jdbc.jdbc2.optional.JDBC4MysqlXAConnection@3f7aa2a8>
DEBUG [org.springframework.orm.jpa.EntityManagerFactoryUtils] - <Closing JPA EntityManager>
DEBUG [org.springframework.orm.jpa.EntityManagerFactoryUtils] - <Closing JPA EntityManager>
INFO [atomikos] - <commit() done (by application) of transaction 192.168.11.8.tm0000100001>
DEBUG [atomikos] - <About to call prepare on XAResource instance:
com.mysql.jdbc.jdbc2.optional.JDBC4MysqlXAConnection@49b29f80>
INFO [atomikos] - <XAResource.prepare (
3139322E3136382E31312E382E746D3030303031303030303031:3139322E3136382E31312E382E746D32 )
returning OK on resource XADBMSB represented by XAResource instance
com.mysql.jdbc.jdbc2.optional.JDBC4MysqlXAConnection@3f7aa2a8>
INFO [atomikos] - <XAResource.commit (
3139322E3136382E31312E382E746D3030303031303030303031:3139322E3136382E31312E382E746D31 , false)
on resource XADBMSA represented by XAResource instance
com.mysql.jdbc.jdbc2.optional.JDBC4MysqlXAConnection@49b29f80>
Contact saved successfully
```

From the output, you will see that Atomikos creates a composite transaction, communicates with the XA datasource (MySQL in this case), performs synchronization, commits the transaction, and so on.

From the database, you will see that the new contact is persisted to both schemas of the database, respectively.

Now let's see how the rollback works. As shown in the code in Listing 13-25, instead of calling emB.persist(), we just throw an exception. Listing 13-27 shows the code snippet.

Listing 13-27. *Testing JTA Transaction Rollback*

```
//emB.persist(contactB);
throw new JpaSystemException(new PersistenceException());
```

To test the rollback scenario, delete the new records inserted by the previous example from the two MySQL databases first (i.e., the contact record with FIRST_NAME Jta and LAST_NAME Manager). Running the program again will produce the following results:

```
Hibernate: insert into contact (BIRTH_DATE, FIRST_NAME, LAST_NAME, VERSION) values (?, ?, ?,
?)
INFO [atomikos] - <afterCompletion ( STATUS_ROLLEDBACK ) called  on Synchronization:
org.hibernate.transaction.synchronization.HibernateSynchronizationImpl@45c81ac0>
INFO [atomikos] - <rollback() done of transaction 192.168.11.8.tm0000100002>
Exception in thread "main" org.springframework.orm.jpa.JpaSystemException: nested exception is
javax.persistence.PersistenceException
...
Caused by: javax.persistence.PersistenceException
```

As shown in the previous output, the first contact is persisted (note the insert statement). However, when saving to the second datasource, because an exception is thrown, Atomikos will roll back the entire transaction. You can take a look at the schema prospring3_ch13a to check that the new contact was not saved.

Considerations on Using JTA Transaction Manager

Whether to use JTA for global transaction management is under hot debate. For example, the Spring development team generally does not recommend using JTA for global transactions, and SpringSource's Dr. David Syer has posted an article describing seven ways to implement distributed transactions, four of them without using JTA (www.javaworld.com/javaworld/jw-01-2009/jw-01-spring-transactions.html).

As a general principle, when your application is deployed to a full-blown JEE application server, there is no point not using JTA because all the vendors of the popular JEE application servers have optimized their JTA implementation for their platforms. That's one major feature that you are paying for.

For stand-alone or web container deployment, let the application requirements drive your decision and perform load testing as early as possible to verify that the performance is not being impacted by using JTA.

One piece of good news is that Spring works seamlessly with both local and global transactions in most major web and JEE containers, so code modification is generally not required when you switch from one transaction management strategy to another.

In case you decide to use JTA within your application, make sure you use Spring's JtaTransactionManager. There is another excellent article from Spring's team discussing using Spring with JTA (http://blog.springsource.org/2011/08/15/configuring-spring-and-jta-without-full-java-ee).

Summary

Transaction management is a key part of ensuring data integrity in almost any type of application. In this chapter, we discussed how to use Spring to manage transactions with almost no impact on your source code. You also learned how to use local and global transactions.

We provided various examples of transaction implementation, including declarative ways of using XML configuration and annotation, as well as the programmatic approach.

Local transactions are supported inside/outside of a JEE application server, and only simple configuration is required to enable local transaction support in Spring. However, setting up a global transaction environment involves more work and greatly depends on which JTA provider and corresponding backend resources your application needs to interact with.

CHAPTER 14

Validation with Type Conversion and Formatting

In an enterprise application, validation is critical. The purpose of validation is to verify that the data being processed fulfills all predefined business requirements as well as to ensure the data integrity and usefulness in other layers of the application.

In application development, data validation is always mentioned along with conversion and formatting. The reason is that most likely the format of the source of data is different from the format being used in the application server. For example, in a web application, a user enters information in the web browser frontend. When the user saves the data, the data is sent to the server (after the local validation has completed). On the server side, a data-binding process will be performed, in which the data from the HTTP request will be extracted, converted, and bound to the corresponding domain objects (for example, users enter contact information in an HTML form that will be bound to a Contact object in the server), based on the formatting rules defined for each attribute (for example, the date format pattern is yyyy-MM-dd). When the data binding is complete, the validation rules are applied to the domain object to check for any constraint violation. If everything runs fine, the data is persisted, and a success message is displayed to the user. Otherwise, validation error messages are populated and displayed to the user.

In the first part of this chapter, you will learn how Spring provides sophisticated support for type conversion, field formatting, and validation. Specifically, this chapter will cover the following topics:

- *The Spring type conversion system and the formatter service provider interface (SPI)*: We will discuss the new generic type conversion system and formatter SPI introduced in Spring 3. We will show you how the new services can be used to replace the previous PropertyEditor support and how they convert between any Java types.

- *Validation in Spring*: We will discuss how Spring supports domain object validation. First, we will provide a short introduction to Spring's own Validator interface. Then, we will focus on the JSR-303 Bean Validation support offered since Spring 3.

Creating a Project in STS for Samples

Let's create the project for the samples in this chapter. In STS, create a new Spring template project and choose Simple Spring Utility Project.

In addition, upon project creation, add the other required dependencies , as shown in Table 14-1. Also, verify that the project is using Spring 3.1 and JDK 6.

Table 14-1. Maven Dependencies for Validation

Group ID	Artifact ID	Version	Description
javax.validation	validation-api	1.0.0.GA	JSR-303 API library.
org.hibernate	hibernate-validator	4.2.0.Final	Hibernate Validator library that supports JSR-303 Bean Validation.
joda-time	joda-time	2.0	Joda-time (joda-time.sourceforge.net/) is a date-time API that Spring Data JPA uses. In this chapter, we will use it in our domain objects.
org.slf4j	slf4j-log4j12	1.6.1	The SLF4J logging library (www.slf4j.org) will be used as the logging library for the samples in this chapter. This library will help chain the SLF4J logger to the underlying log4j library for logging purposes.

Spring Type Conversion System

In Spring 3, a new type conversion system was introduced, providing a powerful way to convert between any Java types within Spring-powered applications. In this section, we will discuss how this new service can perform the same functionality provided by the previous PropertyEditor support, as well as how it supports the conversion between any Java types. We will also demonstrate how to implement a custom type converter using the Converter SPI.

Conversion from a String Using PropertyEditors

In Chapter 5, we covered how Spring handles the conversion from a String in the properties files into the properties of POJOs by supporting PropertyEditors. Let's do a quick review here, and then we will cover how Spring's Converter SPI (available since 3.0) provides a more powerful alternative.

Consider a Contact class with a couple of attributes, as in Listing 14-1.

Listing 14-1. The Contact Class

```
package com.apress.prospring3.ch14.domain;

import java.net.URL;

import org.joda.time.DateTime;

public class Contact {

    private String firstName;

    private String lastName;

    private DateTime birthDate;
```

```
    private URL personalSite;

    // Getter/setter methods omitted

    public String toString() {
        return "First name: " + getFirstName()
            + " - Last name: " + getLastName()
            + " - Birth date: " + getBirthDate()
            + " - Personal site: " + getPersonalSite();
    }
}
```

As shown in Listing 14-1, for the birth date attribute, we use JodaTime's DateTime class. In addition, there is a URL type field that indicates the contact's personal web site if applicable.

Now suppose we want to construct Contact objects in Spring's ApplicationContext, with values stored either in Spring's configuration file or in a properties file. Listing 14-2 shows the Spring XML configuration file (prop-editor-app-context.xml).

Listing 14-2. Spring Configuration for Property Editor

```
<?xml version="1.0" encoding="UTF-8"?>
<beans xmlns="http://www.springframework.org/schema/beans"
    xmlns:xsi="http://www.w3.org/2001/XMLSchema-instance"
    xmlns:context="http://www.springframework.org/schema/context"
    xmlns:p="http://www.springframework.org/schema/p"
    xsi:schemaLocation="http://www.springframework.org/schema/beans
        http://www.springframework.org/schema/beans/spring-beans-3.1.xsd
        http://www.springframework.org/schema/context
        http://www.springframework.org/schema/context/spring-context-3.1.xsd">

    <context:annotation-config/>

    <context:property-placeholder
        location="classpath:application.properties"/>

    <bean id="dateTimeEditor"
        class="com.apress.prospring3.ch14.pe.editor.DateTimeEditor">
        <constructor-arg value="${date.format.pattern}"/>
    </bean>

    <bean class="org.springframework.beans.factory.config.CustomEditorConfigurer">
        <property name="customEditors">
            <map>
                <entry key="org.joda.time.DateTime">
                    <ref local="dateTimeEditor" />
                </entry>
            </map>
        </property>
    </bean>

    <bean id="clarence" class="com.apress.prospring3.ch14.domain.Contact"
        p:firstName="Clarence"
        p:lastName="Ho"
        p:birthDate="1970-12-31"
```

```
            p:personalSite="http://www.clarence.com"
    />

    <bean id="myContact" class="com.apress.prospring3.ch14.domain.Contact"
        p:firstName="${myContact.firstName}"
        p:lastName="${myContact.lastName}"
        p:birthDate="${myContact.birthDate}"
        p:personalSite="${myContact.personalSite}"
    />

</beans>
```

As shown in Listing 14-2, we construct two different beans of the Contact class. The clarence bean is constructed with values provided in the configuration file, while for the myContact bean, the attributes are externalized into a properties file. In addition, a custom editor is defined for converting from a String to JodaTime's DateTime type, and the date-time format pattern is externalized in the properties file too. Listing 14-3 shows the properties file (application.properties).

Listing 14-3. The application.properties File

```
date.format.pattern=yyyy-MM-dd

myContact.firstName=Scott
myContact.lastName=Tiger
myContact.birthDate=1984-6-30
myContact.personalSite=http://www.somedomain.com
```

Listing 14-4 shows the custom editor for converting String values into the JodaTime DateTime type.

Listing 14-4. Custom Editor for JodaTime DateTime

```
package com.apress.prospring3.ch14.pe.editor;

import java.beans.PropertyEditorSupport;

import org.joda.time.DateTime;
import org.joda.time.format.DateTimeFormat;
import org.joda.time.format.DateTimeFormatter;

public class DateTimeEditor extends PropertyEditorSupport {

    private DateTimeFormatter dateTimeFormatter;

    public DateTimeEditor(String dateFormatPattern) {
        dateTimeFormatter = DateTimeFormat.forPattern(dateFormatPattern);
    }

    public void setAsText(String text) throws IllegalArgumentException {
        setValue(DateTime.parse(text, dateTimeFormatter));
    }
}
```

Listing 14-4 should be self-explanatory. Let's test it. Listing 14-5 shows the testing program.

Listing 14-5. Testing Property Editor

```
package com.apress.prospring3.ch14.pe;

import org.springframework.context.support.GenericXmlApplicationContext;

import com.apress.prospring3.ch14.domain.Contact;

public class PropEditorExample {

    public static void main(String[] args) {

        GenericXmlApplicationContext ctx = new GenericXmlApplicationContext();
        ctx.load("classpath:prop-editor-app-context.xml");
        ctx.refresh();

        Contact clarence = ctx.getBean("clarence", Contact.class);
        System.out.println("Clarence info: " + clarence);

        Contact myContact = ctx.getBean("myContact", Contact.class);
        System.out.println("My contact info: " + myContact);
    }
}
```

As shown in Listing 14-5, the two different Contact beans are retrieved from ApplicationContext and printed. Running the program will produce the following output:

```
Clarence info: First name: Clarence - Last name: Ho - Birth date: 1970-12-
31T00:00:00.000+08:00 - Personal site: http://www.clarence.com
My contact info: First name: Scott - Last name: Tiger - Birth date: 1984-06-
30T00:00:00.000+08:00 - Personal site: http://www.somedomain.com
```

As shown in the output, the properties are converted and applied to the Contact beans. Figure 14-1 shows the logical view on how the conversion by PropertyEditors was done.

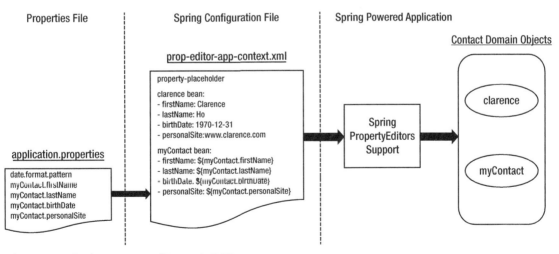

Figure 14-1. Spring support of PropertyEditors

Introducing Spring 3 Type Conversion

In Spring 3.0, a general type conversion system was introduced, which resides under the package org.springframework.core.convert. In addition to providing an alternative to PropertyEditor support, the type conversion system can also be configured to convert between any Java types and POJOs (while PropertyEditor is focused on converting String representations in the properties file into Java types).

Implementing a Custom Converter

To see the type conversion system in action, let's revisit the previous example and use the same Contact class. Suppose this time we want to use the type conversion system to convert the date in String format into the Contact's birthDate property, which is of JodaTime's DateTime type. To support the conversion, instead of creating a custom PropertyEditor, we create a custom converter by implementing the org.springframework.core.convert.converter.Converter<S,T> interface. Listing 14-6 shows the custom converter.

Listing 14-6. Custom DateTime Converter

```
package com.apress.prospring3.ch14.converter;

import javax.annotation.PostConstruct;

import org.joda.time.DateTime;
import org.joda.time.format.DateTimeFormat;
import org.joda.time.format.DateTimeFormatter;
import org.springframework.beans.factory.annotation.Autowired;
import org.springframework.core.convert.converter.Converter;

public class StringToDateTimeConverter
    implements Converter<String, DateTime> {

    private static final String DEFAULT_DATE_PATTERN = "yyyy-MM-dd";

    private DateTimeFormatter dateFormat;

    private String datePattern = DEFAULT_DATE_PATTERN;

    public String getDatePattern() {
        return datePattern;
    }

    @Autowired(required=false)
    public void setDatePattern(String datePattern) {
        this.datePattern = datePattern;
    }

    @PostConstruct
    public void init() {
        dateFormat = DateTimeFormat.forPattern(datePattern);
    }

    public DateTime convert(String dateString) {
```

```
        return dateFormat.parseDateTime(dateString);
    }
}
```

As shown in Listing 14-6, we implement the interface Converter<String, DateTime>, which means the converter is responsible for converting a String (the source type S) to a DateTime type (the target type T). The injection of the date-time pattern is optional, by annotating it with @Autowired(required=false). If not injected, the default pattern yyyy-MM-dd is used. Then, in the initialization method (the init() method annotated with @PostConstruct), an instance of JodaTime's DateTimeFormat class is constructed, which will perform the conversion based on the specified pattern. Finally, the convert() method is implemented to provide the conversion logic.

Configuring ConversionService

To use the conversion service instead of PropertyEditor, we need to configure an instance of the org.springframework.core.convert.ConversionService interface in Spring's ApplicationContext. Listing 14-7 shows the configuration file (conv-service-app-context.xml).

Listing 14-7. Configuration of ConversionService

```xml
<?xml version="1.0" encoding="UTF-8"?>
<beans xmlns="http://www.springframework.org/schema/beans"
    xmlns:xsi="http://www.w3.org/2001/XMLSchema-instance"
    xmlns:context="http://www.springframework.org/schema/context"
    xmlns:p="http://www.springframework.org/schema/p"
    xsi:schemaLocation="http://www.springframework.org/schema/beans
        http://www.springframework.org/schema/beans/spring-beans-3.1.xsd
        http://www.springframework.org/schema/context
        http://www.springframework.org/schema/context/spring-context-3.1.xsd">

    <context:annotation-config/>

    <bean id="conversionService"
class="org.springframework.context.support.ConversionServiceFactoryBean">
        <property name="converters">
            <list>
                <bean class="com.apress.prospring3.ch14.converter.StringToDateTimeConverter"/>
            </list>
        </property>
    </bean>

    <bean id="clarence" class="com.apress.prospring3.ch14.domain.Contact"
        p:firstName="Clarence"
        p:lastName="Ho"
        p:birthDate="1978-08-09"
        p:personalSite="http://www.clarence.com"
    />
</beans>
```

As shown in Listing 14-7, we instruct Spring to use the type conversion system by declaring a conversionService bean with the class ConversionServiceFactoryBean. If no conversion service bean is defined, Spring will use the PropertyEditor-based system.

By default, the type conversion service supports conversion between common types including strings, numbers, enums, collections, maps, and so on. In addition, the conversion from Strings to Java types within the PropertyEditor-based system is supported.

For the conversionService bean, a custom converter is configured for conversion from a String to DateTime. Listing 14-8 shows a testing program.

Listing 14-8. Testing ConversionService

```
package com.apress.prospring3.ch14.convserv;

import org.springframework.context.support.GenericXmlApplicationContext;

import com.apress.prospring3.ch14.domain.Contact;

public class ConvServExample {

    public static void main(String[] args) {

        GenericXmlApplicationContext ctx = new GenericXmlApplicationContext();
        ctx.load("classpath:conv-service-app-context.xml");
        ctx.refresh();

        Contact clarence = ctx.getBean("clarence", Contact.class);

        System.out.println("Contact info: " + clarence);

    }
}
```

Running the testing program produces the following output:

```
Contact info: First name: Clarence - Last name: Ho - Birth date: 1978-08-09T00:00:00.000+08:00
- Personal site: http://www.clarence.com
```

As you can see, the clarence bean's property conversion result is the same as when we use PropertyEditors.

Converting Between Arbitrary Types

The real strength of the type conversion system is the ability to convert between arbitrary types. To see it in action, suppose we have another class, called AnotherContact, that is the same as the Contact class. Listing 14-9 shows the class.

Listing 14-9. The AnotherContact Class

```
package com.apress.prospring3.ch14.domain;

import java.net.URL;

import org.joda.time.DateTime;

public class AnotherContact {
```

```
    private String firstName;

    private String lastName;

    private DateTime birthDate;

    private URL personalSite;

    // Other code omitted
}
```

We want to be able to convert any instance of the Contact class to the AnotherContact class, but the firstName and lastName of Contact will become lastName and firstName of AnotherContact, respectively. Let's implement another custom converter to perform the conversion. Listing 14-10 shows the custom converter.

Listing 14-10. The AnotherContact Class

```
package com.apress.prospring3.ch14.converter;

import org.springframework.core.convert.converter.Converter;

import com.apress.prospring3.ch14.domain.AnotherContact;
import com.apress.prospring3.ch14.domain.Contact;

public class ContactToAnotherContactConverter
    implements Converter<Contact, AnotherContact> {

    public AnotherContact convert(Contact contact) {
        AnotherContact anotherContact = new AnotherContact();
        anotherContact.setFirstName(contact.getLastName());
        anotherContact.setLastName(contact.getFirstName());
        anotherContact.setBirthDate(contact.getBirthDate());
        anotherContact.setPersonalSite(contact.getPersonalSite());

        return anotherContact;
    }
}
```

The class is simple; just swap the firstName and lastName attributes between the Contact and AnotherContact classes. To register the custom converter into ApplicationContext, replace the definition of the conversionService bean definition in the file (conv-service-app-context.xml) with the code snippet in Listing 14-11.

Listing 14-11. Adding the Converter to the Conversion Service

```
    <bean id="conversionService"
class="org.springframework.context.support.ConversionServiceFactoryBean">
        <property name="converters">
            <list>
                <bean class="com.apress.prospring3.ch14.converter.StringToDateTimeConverter"/>
                <bean
class="com.apress.prospring3.ch14.converter.ContactToAnotherContactConverter"/>
            </list>
```

```
        </property>
    </bean>
```

The order of the beans within the converters property is not important.

To test the conversion, we use the same testing program as the previous sample, which is the ConvServExample class. Listing 14-12 shows the revised main() method.

Listing 14-12. Testing Conversion Service

```
package com.apress.prospring3.ch14.convserv;

// Import statements omitted
public class ConvServExample {

    public static void main(String[] args) {

        GenericXmlApplicationContext ctx = new GenericXmlApplicationContext();
        ctx.load("classpath:conv-service-app-context.xml");
        ctx.refresh();

        Contact clarence = ctx.getBean("clarence", Contact.class);

        System.out.println("Contact info: " + clarence);

        ConversionService conversionService = ctx.getBean(ConversionService.class);

        // Convert from Contact to AnotherContact
        AnotherContact anotherContact =
            conversionService.convert(clarence, AnotherContact.class);
        System.out.println("Another contact info: " + anotherContact);

        // Conversion from String to Array
        String[] stringArray = conversionService.convert(
            "a,b,c", String[].class);
        System.out.println("String array: " + stringArray[0] +
            stringArray[1] + stringArray[2]);

        // Conversion from List to Set
        List<String> listString = new ArrayList<String>();
        listString.add("a");
        listString.add("b");
        listString.add("c");
        Set<String> setString = conversionService.convert(
            listString, HashSet.class);
        for (String string: setString)
            System.out.println("Set: " + string);
    }
}
```

In Listing 14-12, look at the bold line, in which a handle to the ConversionService interface is obtained from the ApplicationContext. Because we already registered the ConversionService in ApplicationContext with our custom converters, we can use it to convert the Contact object, as well as convert between other types that the conversion service already supports. As shown in the listing, examples of converting from a String (delimited by a comma character) to an Array and from a List to a Set were also added for demonstration purposes.

Running the program produces the following output:

```
Contact info: First name: Clarence - Last name: Ho - Birth date: 1978-08-09T00:00:00.000+08:00
- Personal site: http://www.clarence.com
Another contact info: First name: Ho - Last name: Clarence - Birth date: 1978-08-
09T00:00:00.000+08:00 - Personal site: http://www.clarence.com
String array: abc
Set: b
Set: c
Set: a
```

As shown in the output, you will see that Contact and AnotherContact are converted correctly, as well as the String to Array and the List to Set. With Spring's type conversion service, you can create custom converters easily and perform conversion at any layer within your application. One possible use case is that you have two different systems with the same contact information that you need to update. However, the database structure is different (for example, the last name in system A means the first name in system B, and so on). You can use the type conversion system to convert the objects before persisting to each individual system.

Starting with Spring 3.0, Spring MVC makes heavy use of the conversion service (as well as the formatter SPI that we will discuss in the next section). In the web application context configuration, the declaration of the tag <mvc:annotation-driven/> will automatically register all default converters (for example, StringToArrayConverter, StringToBooleanConverter, and StringToLocaleConverter, all residing under the org.springframework.core.convert.support package) and formatters (for example, CurrencyFormatter, DateFormatter, and NumberFormatter, all residing under various subpackages within the org.springframework.format package). More will be covered in Chapters 17 and 18, when we discuss web application development in Spring.

Field Formatting in Spring 3

Besides the type conversion system, another great feature that Spring brings to developers is the Formatter SPI. As you might expect, this SPI can help configure the field-formatting aspects.

In the Formatter SPI, the main interface for implementing a formatter is the org.springframework.format.Formatter<T> interface. Spring provides a few implementations of commonly used types, including CurrencyFormatter, DateFormatter, NumberFormatter, and PercentFormatter.

Implementing a Custom Formatter

Implementing a custom formatter is easy too. We will use the same Contact class and implement a custom formatter for converting the DateTime type of the birthDate attribute to and from a String.

However, this time we will take a different approach; we will extend Spring's org.springframework.format.support.FormattingConversionServiceFactoryBean class and provide our custom formatter. The FormattingConversionServiceFactoryBean class is a factory class that provides convenient access to the underlying FormattingConversionService class, which supports the type conversion system, as well as field formatting according to the formatting rules defined for each field type.

Listing 14-13 shows a custom class that extends the FormattingConversionServiceFactoryBean class, with a custom formatter defined for formatting JodaTime's DateTime type.

Listing 14-13. The ApplicationConversionServiceFactoryBean Class

```
package com.apress.prospring3.ch14.convserv.factory;

import java.text.ParseException;
import java.util.HashSet;
import java.util.Locale;
import java.util.Set;

import javax.annotation.PostConstruct;

import org.joda.time.DateTime;
import org.joda.time.format.DateTimeFormat;
import org.joda.time.format.DateTimeFormatter;
import org.slf4j.Logger;
import org.slf4j.LoggerFactory;
import org.springframework.beans.factory.annotation.Autowired;
import org.springframework.format.Formatter;
import org.springframework.format.support.FormattingConversionServiceFactoryBean;

public class ApplicationConversionServiceFactoryBean extends
    FormattingConversionServiceFactoryBean {

    final Logger logger =
        LoggerFactory.getLogger(ApplicationConversionServiceFactoryBean.class);

    private static final String DEFAULT_DATE_PATTERN = "yyyy-MM-dd";

    private DateTimeFormatter dateFormat;

    private String datePattern = DEFAULT_DATE_PATTERN;

    private Set<Formatter<?>> formatters = new HashSet<Formatter<?>>();

    public String getDatePattern() {
        return datePattern;
    }

    @Autowired(required=false)
    public void setDatePattern(String datePattern) {
        this.datePattern = datePattern;
    }

    @PostConstruct
    public void init() {
        dateFormat = DateTimeFormat.forPattern(datePattern);
        formatters.add(getDateTimeFormatter());
        setFormatters(formatters);
    }

    public Formatter<DateTime> getDateTimeFormatter() {
        return new Formatter<DateTime>() {
            public DateTime parse(String dateTimeString, Locale locale) throws ParseException {
```

```
            logger.info("Parsing date string: " + dateTimeString);
            return dateFormat.parseDateTime(dateTimeString);
        }
        public String print(DateTime dateTime, Locale locale) {
            logger.info("Formatting datetime: " + dateTime);
            return dateFormat.print(dateTime);
        }
    };
    }
}
```

In Listing 14-13, the custom formatter is in bold. It implements the Formatter<DateTime> interface and implements two methods defined by the interface. The parse() method parses the String format into the DateTime type (the locale was also passed for localization support), while the print() method is to format a DateTime instance into a String. The date pattern can be injected into the bean (or the default will be yyyy-MM-dd). Also, in the init() method, the custom formatter is registered by calling the setFormatters() method. You can add as many formatters as required.

Configuring ConversionServiceFactoryBean

To configure the ApplicationConversionServiceFactoryBean in Spring's ApplicationContext, we just need to declare a bean with that class as the provider. Listing 14-14 shows the configuration (conv-format-service-app-context.xml).

Listing 14-14. The conv-format-service-app-context.xml File

```xml
<?xml version="1.0" encoding="UTF-8"?>
<beans xmlns="http://www.springframework.org/schema/beans"
    xmlns:xsi="http://www.w3.org/2001/XMLSchema-instance"
    xmlns:context="http://www.springframework.org/schema/context"
    xmlns:p="http://www.springframework.org/schema/p"
    xsi:schemaLocation="http://www.springframework.org/schema/beans
        http://www.springframework.org/schema/beans/spring-beans-3.1.xsd
        http://www.springframework.org/schema/context
        http://www.springframework.org/schema/context/spring-context-3.1.xsd">

    <context:annotation-config/>

    <bean id="conversionService"
class="com.apress.prospring3.ch14.convserv.factory.ApplicationConversionServiceFactoryBean"/>

    <bean id="clarence" class="com.apress.prospring3.ch14.domain.Contact"
        p:firstName="Clarence"
        p:lastName="Ho"
        p:birthDate="1978-08-09"
        p:personalSite="http://www.clarence.com"
    />
</beans>
```

Listing 14-15 shows the testing program.

Listing 14-15. Testing Custom Formatter

```
package com.apress.prospring3.ch14.convserv;

import org.springframework.context.support.GenericXmlApplicationContext;
import org.springframework.core.convert.ConversionService;

import com.apress.prospring3.ch14.domain.Contact;

public class ConvFormatServExample {

    public static void main(String[] args) {

        GenericXmlApplicationContext ctx = new GenericXmlApplicationContext();
        ctx.load("classpath:conv-format-service-app-context.xml");
        ctx.refresh();

        Contact clarence = ctx.getBean("clarence", Contact.class);

        System.out.println("Contact info: " + clarence);

        ConversionService conversionService = ctx.getBean(
            "conversionService", ConversionService.class);
        System.out.println("Birthdate of contact is : " +
            conversionService.convert(clarence.getBirthDate(), String.class));
    }
}
```

Running the program produces the following output:

```
INFO [com.apress.prospring3.ch14.convserv.factory.ApplicationConversionServiceFactoryBean] –
<Parsing date string: 1978-08-09>
Contact info: First name: Clarence - Last name: Ho - Birth date: 1978-08-09T00:00:00.000+08:00
- Personal site: http://www.clarence.com
INFO [com.apress.prospring3.ch14.convserv.factory.ApplicationConversionServiceFactoryBean] –
<Formatting datetime: 1978-08-09T00:00:00.000+08:00>
Birthdate of contact is : 1978-08-09
```

In the output, you can see Spring uses our custom formatter's parse() method to convert the property from a String to the DateTime type of the birthDate attribute. When we call the ConversionService.convert() method and pass in the birthDate attribute, Spring will call the print() method to format the output.

Validation in Spring

Validation is a critical part of any application. Validation rules applied on domain objects ensure that all business data is well structured and fulfills all the business definitions. The ideal case is that all validation rules are maintained in a centralized location and the same set of rules are applied to the same type of data, no matter which source the data comes from (for example, user input via a web application, from a remote application via web services, from a JMS message, from a file, and so on).

When talking about validation, conversion and formatting are important too, because before a piece of data can be validated, it should be converted to the desired POJO according to the formatting rules defined for each type.

For example, a user enters some contact information via the web application within the browser and then submits the data to the server. On the server side, if the web application was developed in Spring MVC, Spring will extract the data from the HTTP request and perform the conversion from a String to the desired type based on the formatting rule (for example, a String representing a date will be converted into a Date field, with the formatting rule yyyy-MM-dd). The process is called *data binding*. When the data binding is complete and the domain object constructed, validation will then be applied to the object, and any errors will be returned and displayed to the user. If validation succeeds, the object will be persisted to the database.

Figure 14-2 shows the process.

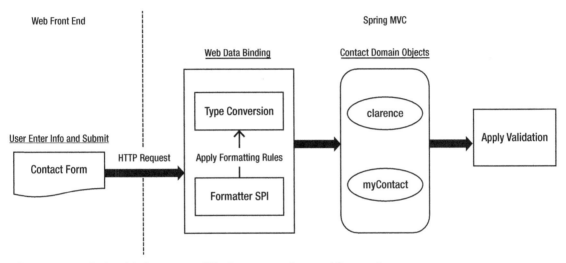

***Figure 14-2.** Relationship between validation, conversion, and formatting*

Spring supports two main types of validation. The first one is provided by Spring, within which custom validators can be created by implementing the org.springframework.validation.Validator interface. The other one is via Spring's support of JSR-303, the Bean Validation API. We will go through both of them in the coming sections.

Using Spring Validator Interface

Using Spring's Validator interface, we can develop some validation logic by creating a class to implement the interface.

Let's see how it works. For the Contact class that we've worked with so far, suppose the first name cannot be empty. To validate Contact objects against this rule, we can create a custom validator. Listing 14-16 shows the validator class.

***Listing 14-16.** The ContactValidator Class*

```
package com.apress.prospring3.ch14.validator;

import org.springframework.stereotype.Component;
import org.springframework.validation.Errors;
import org.springframework.validation.ValidationUtils;
```

```java
import org.springframework.validation.Validator;

import com.apress.prospring3.ch14.domain.Contact;

@Component("contactValidator")
public class ContactValidator implements Validator {

    public boolean supports(Class<?> clazz) {
        return Contact.class.equals(clazz);
    }

    public void validate(Object obj, Errors e) {
        ValidationUtils.rejectIfEmpty(e, "firstName", "firstName.empty");
    }
}
```

As shown in Listing 14-16, the validator class implements the Validator interface and implements two methods. The supports() method indicates whether validation of the passed-in class type is supported by the validator. The validate() method performs validation on the passed-in object. The result will be stored in an instance of the org.springframework.validation.Errors interface. In the validate() method, we perform a check only on the firstName attribute and use the convenient ValidationUtils.rejectIfEmpty() method to ensure that the first name of contact is not empty. The last argument is the error code, which can be used for looking up validation messages from resource bundles for displaying localized error messages.

Listing 14-17 shows the Spring configuration file (spring-validator-app-context.xml).

Listing 14-17. Configuration for Spring Validator

```xml
<?xml version="1.0" encoding="UTF-8"?>
<beans xmlns="http://www.springframework.org/schema/beans"
    xmlns:xsi="http://www.w3.org/2001/XMLSchema-instance"
    xmlns:context="http://www.springframework.org/schema/context"
    xsi:schemaLocation="http://www.springframework.org/schema/beans
        http://www.springframework.org/schema/beans/spring-beans-3.1.xsd
        http://www.springframework.org/schema/context
        http://www.springframework.org/schema/context/spring-context-3.1.xsd">

    <context:annotation-config/>

    <context:component-scan base-package="com.apress.prospring3.ch14.validator"/>
</beans>
```

Listing 14-18 shows the testing program for the validator class.

Listing 14-18. Testing Spring Validator

```java
package com.apress.prospring3.ch14.validator;

import java.util.List;

import org.springframework.context.support.GenericXmlApplicationContext;
import org.springframework.validation.BeanPropertyBindingResult;
import org.springframework.validation.ObjectError;
import org.springframework.validation.ValidationUtils;
```

```
import org.springframework.validation.Validator;

import com.apress.prospring3.ch14.domain.Contact;

public class SpringValidatorSample {

    public static void main(String[] args) {

        GenericXmlApplicationContext ctx = new GenericXmlApplicationContext();
        ctx.load("classpath:spring-validator-app-context.xml");
        ctx.refresh();

        Contact contact = new Contact();
        contact.setFirstName(null);
        contact.setLastName("Ho");

        Validator contactValidator = ctx.getBean(
            "contactValidator", Validator.class);

        BeanPropertyBindingResult result =
            new BeanPropertyBindingResult(contact, "Clarence");

        ValidationUtils.invokeValidator(contactValidator, contact, result);

        List<ObjectError> errors = result.getAllErrors();
        System.out.println("No of validation errors: " + errors.size());

        for (ObjectError error: errors) {
            System.out.println(error.getCode());
        }
    }
}
```

As shown in Listing 14-18, a Contact object is constructed with first name set to null. Then, the validator is retrieved from the ApplicationContext. To store the validation result, an instance of BeanPropertyBindingResult class is constructed. To perform the validation, the ValidationUtils.invokeValidator() method is called. Then we check for validation errors.

Running the program produces the following output:

```
No of validation errors: 1
firstName.empty
```

The validation produces one error, and the error code is displayed correctly.

Using JSR-303 Bean Validation

In Spring 3, full support for the JSR-303 Bean Validation API was introduced. The Bean Validation API defines a set of constraints in the form of Java annotations (for example, @NotNull) under the package javax.validation.constraints that can be applied to the domain objects. In addition, custom validators (for example, class-level validators) can be developed and applied using annotation.

Using the Bean Validation API frees you from coupling to a specific validation service provider. By using the Bean Validation API, you can use standard annotations and the API for implementing validation logic to your domain objects, without knowing the underlying validation service provider. For example, the Hibernate Validator (http://hibernate.org/subprojects/validator) is a popular JSR-303

511

compliant validation service provider. If you created the simple Spring JPA utility project in Chapter 10, the dependency on Hibernate Validator was already added for you.

Spring provides seamless support for the Bean Validation API. The main features include support for JSR-303 standard annotations for defining validation constraints, custom validators, and configuration of JSR-303 validation within Spring's ApplicationContext. Let's go through them one by one in the following sections.

Defining Validation Constraints on Object Properties

Let's begin with applying validation constraints to domain object properties. Listing 14-19 shows a Customer class with validation constraints applied to the firstName and customerType attributes.

Listing 14-19. The Customer Class

```
package com.apress.prospring3.ch14.domain;

import javax.validation.constraints.NotNull;
import javax.validation.constraints.Size;

public class Customer {

    @NotNull
    @Size(min=2, max=60)
    private String firstName;

    private String lastName;

    @NotNull
    private CustomerType customerType;

    private Gender gender;

    // Getter/setter methods omitted

    public boolean isIndividualCustomer() {
        return this.customerType.equals(CustomerType.INDIVIDUAL);
    }
}
```

In Listing 14-19, the validation constraints applied are shown in bold. For the firstName attribute, two constraints are applied. The first one is governed by the @NotNull annotation, which indicates that the value should not be null. Moreover, the @Size annotation governs the length of the firstName attribute. The @NotNull constraint is applied to the customerType attribute too. Listings 14-20 and 14-21 show the CustomerType and Gender classes, respectively.

Listing 14-20. The CustomerType Class

```
package com.apress.prospring3.ch14.domain;

public enum CustomerType {

    INDIVIDUAL("I"), CORPORATE("C");
```

```
    private String code;

    private CustomerType(String code) {
        this.code = code;
    }

    public String toString() {
        return this.code;
    }
}
```

Listing 14-21. The Gender Class

```
package com.apress.prospring3.ch14.domain;

public enum Gender {

    MALE("M"), FEMALE("F");

    private String code;

    private Gender(String code) {
        this.code = code;
    }

    public String toString() {
        return this.code;
    }
}
```

The customer type indicates whether a customer is an individual or a company, while the gender should be applied for only individual customers. For companies, the gender should be null.

Configuring Bean Validation Support in Spring

To configure the support of the Bean Validation API in Spring ApplicationContext, we define an instance of the class org.springframework.validation.beanvalidation.LocalValidatorFactoryBean in Spring's configuration. Listing 14-22 shows the configuration (jsr303-app-context.xml).

Listing 14-22. Configuring Bean Validation API in Spring

```
<?xml version="1.0" encoding="UTF-8"?>
<beans xmlns="http://www.springframework.org/schema/beans"
    xmlns:xsi="http://www.w3.org/2001/XMLSchema-instance"
    xmlns:context="http://www.springframework.org/schema/context"
    xsi:schemaLocation="http://www.springframework.org/schema/beans
        http://www.springframework.org/schema/beans/spring-beans-3.1.xsd
        http://www.springframework.org/schema/context
        http://www.springframework.org/schema/context/spring-context-3.1.xsd">

    <context:annotation-config/>
```

```
<context:component-scan
    base-package="com.apress.prospring3.ch14.jsr303.service"/>

<bean id="validator"
class="org.springframework.validation.beanvalidation.LocalValidatorFactoryBean"/>

</beans>
```

As shown in Listing 14-22, the declaration of a bean with the class LocalValidatorFactoryBean is all that is required. By default, Spring will search for the existence of the Hibernate Validator library in the classpath. Now, let's create a service class that provides a validation service for the Customer class. Listing 14-23 shows the content.

Listing 14-23. *The MyBeanValidationService Class*

```
package com.apress.prospring3.ch14.jsr303.service;

import java.util.Set;

import javax.validation.ConstraintViolation;
import javax.validation.Validator;

import org.springframework.beans.factory.annotation.Autowired;
import org.springframework.stereotype.Service;

import com.apress.prospring3.ch14.domain.Customer;

@Service("myBeanValidationService")
public class MyBeanValidationService {

    @Autowired
    private Validator validator;

    public Set<ConstraintViolation<Customer>> validateCustomer(Customer customer) {
        return validator.validate(customer);
    }
}
```

As shown in Listing 14-23, an instance of the javax.validation.Validator was injected (note the difference from the Spring-provided Validator interface, which is org.springframework.validation.Validator). Once the LocalValidatorFactoryBean is defined, you can create a handle to the Validator interface anywhere in your application. To perform validation on a POJO, the Validator.validate() method is called. The validation results will be returned as a List of the ConstraintViolation<T> interface.

Listing 14-24 shows the testing program.

Listing 14-24. *The Jsr303Sample Class*

```
package com.apress.prospring3.ch14.jsr303;

import java.util.HashSet;
import java.util.Set;
```

```java
import javax.validation.ConstraintViolation;

import org.springframework.context.support.GenericXmlApplicationContext;

import com.apress.prospring3.ch14.domain.Customer;
import com.apress.prospring3.ch14.domain.CustomerType;
import com.apress.prospring3.ch14.jsr303.service.MyBeanValidationService;

public class Jsr303Sample {

    public static void main(String[] args) {

        GenericXmlApplicationContext ctx = new GenericXmlApplicationContext();
        ctx.load("classpath:jsr303-app-context.xml");
        ctx.refresh();

        MyBeanValidationService myBeanValidationService =
            ctx.getBean("myBeanValidationService",
                MyBeanValidationService.class);

        Customer customer = new Customer();

        // Test basic constraints
        customer.setFirstName("C");
        customer.setLastName("Ho");
        customer.setCustomerType(null);
        customer.setGender(null);

        validateCustomer(customer, myBeanValidationService);

    }

    private static void validateCustomer(Customer customer,
        MyBeanValidationService myBeanValidationService) {

        Set<ConstraintViolation<Customer>> violations =
            new HashSet<ConstraintViolation<Customer>>();
        violations = myBeanValidationService.validateCustomer(customer);

        listViolations(violations);
    }

    private static void listViolations(Set<ConstraintViolation<Customer>> violations) {

        System.out.println("No. of violations: " + violations.size());

        for (ConstraintViolation<Customer> violation: violations) {
            System.out.println("Validation error for property: " +
                violation.getPropertyPath()
                + " with value: " + violation.getInvalidValue()
                + " with error message: " + violation.getMessage());
        }
    }
}
```

As shown in Listing 14-24, a Customer object is constructed with firstName and customerType violating the constraints. In the validateCustomer() method, the MyBeanValidationService.validateCustomer() method is called, which in turn will invoke the JSR-303 Bean Valiadation API.

Running the program will produce the following output:

```
No. of violations: 2
Validation error for property: firstName with value: C with error message: size must be
between 2 and 60
Validation error for property: customerType with value: null with error message: may not be
null
```

As you can see, there are two violations, and the messages are shown. In the output, you will also see that Hibernate Validator had already constructed default validation error messages based on the annotation. You can also provide your own validation error message, which we will demonstrate in the next section.

Creating a Custom Validator

Besides attribute-level validation, we can apply class-level validation. For example, for the Customer class, for individual customers, we want to make sure that the lastName and gender attributes are not null. In this case, we can develop a custom validator to perform the check. In the Bean Validation API, developing a custom validator is a two-step process. First create an Annotation type for the validator, as shown in Listing 14-25. The second step is to develop the class that implements the validation logic.

Listing 14-25. *The CheckIndividualCustomer Annotation*

```
package com.apress.prospring3.ch14.jsr303.validator;

import java.lang.annotation.Documented;
import java.lang.annotation.ElementType;
import java.lang.annotation.Retention;
import java.lang.annotation.RetentionPolicy;
import java.lang.annotation.Target;

import javax.validation.Constraint;
import javax.validation.Payload;

@Retention(RetentionPolicy.RUNTIME)
@Target(ElementType.TYPE)
@Constraint(validatedBy=IndividualCustomerValidator.class)
@Documented
public @interface CheckIndividualCustomer {

    String message() default "Individual customer should have gender and last name defined";
    Class<?>[] groups() default {};
    Class<? extends Payload>[] payload() default {};

}
```

In Listing 14-25, the @Target(ElementType.TYPE) means that the annotation should be applied only at the class level. The @Constraint annotation indicates that it's a validator, and the validatedBy attribute specifies the class providing the validation logic. Within the body, three attributes are defined (in the form of a method), as follows:

- The message attribute defines the message (or error code) to return when the constraint is violated. Default message can also be provided in the annotation.

- The groups attribute specifies the validation group if applicable. It's possible to assign validators to different groups and perform validation on a specific group.

- The payload attribute specifies additional payload objects (of the class implementing the javax.validation.Payload interface). It allows you to attach additional information to the constraint (for example, a payload object can indicate the severity of a constraint violation).

Listing 14-26 shows the IndividualCustomerValidator class that provides the validation logic.

Listing 14-26. The IndividualCustomerValidator Class

```
package com.apress.prospring3.ch14.jsr303.validator;

import javax.validation.ConstraintValidator;
import javax.validation.ConstraintValidatorContext;

import com.apress.prospring3.ch14.domain.Customer;

public class IndividualCustomerValidator implements
    ConstraintValidator<CheckIndividualCustomer, Customer> {

    public void initialize(CheckIndividualCustomer constraintAnnotation) {
    }

    public boolean isValid(Customer customer,
        ConstraintValidatorContext context) {

        boolean result = true;

        if (customer.getCustomerType() != null &&
            (customer.isIndividualCustomer()
            && (customer.getLastName() == null ||
                customer.getGender() == null))
        ) {
            result = false;
        }

        return result;
    }

}
```

In Listing 14-26, the IndividualCustomerValidator implements the ConstraintValidator<CheckIndividualCustomer, Customer> interface, which means that the validator checks the CheckIndividualCustomer annotation on the Customer classes. The isValid() method is implemented, and the underlying validation service provider (for example, Hibernate Validator) will pass the instance under validation to the method. In the method, we verify that if the customer is an individual, then the lastName and gender properties should not be null. The result is a boolean value that indicates the validation result.

To enable the validation, apply the @CheckIndividualCustomer annotation to the Customer class, as shown in Listing 14-27.

Listing 14-27. Applying Custom Validation to the Customer Class

```
package com.apress.prospring3.ch14.domain;

// Import statements omitted
@CheckIndividualCustomer
public class Customer {

    // Other code omitted
}
```

To test the custom validation, add the code snippet in Listing 14-28 to the main() method of the testing class (Jsr303Sample) in Listing 14-24.

Listing 14-28. Applying Custom Validation to the Customer Class

```
        // Test custom constraints
        customer.setFirstName("Clarence");
        customer.setLastName("Ho");
        customer.setCustomerType(CustomerType.INDIVIDUAL);
        customer.setGender(null);

        validateCustomer(customer, myBeanValidationService);
```

Running the program produces the following output (the other output was omitted):

```
No. of violations: 1
Validation error for property:  with value: com.apress.prospring3.ch14.domain.Customer@d3f136e
with error message: Individual customer should have gender and last name defined
```

In the output, you can see that the value under check (which is the Customer object) violates the validation rule for individual customers, because the gender attribute is null. Note also that in the output, the property path is empty, because it's a class-level validation error.

Using AssertTrue for Custom Validation

Besides implementing a custom validator, another way to apply custom validation in the Bean Validation API is using the @AssertTrue annotation. Let's see how it works.

For the Customer class, remove the @CheckIndividualCustomer annotation and add the code snippet in Listing 14-29 to the Customer class.

Listing 14-29. Applying @AssertTrue to the Customer Class

```
package com.apress.prospring3.ch14.domain;

// Import statements omitted
public class Customer {

    // Codes omitted
    @AssertTrue(message="Individual customer should have gender and last name defined")
    private boolean isValidIndividualCustomer() {

        boolean result = true;
```

```
        if (getCustomerType() != null &&
            (isIndividualCustomer() && (gender == null || lastName == null)))
            result = false;

        return result;
    }
}
```

As shown in Listing 14-29, the isValidIndividualCustomer() method is added to the Customer class and annotated with @AssertTrue (which is under the package javax.validation.constraints). When invoking validation, the provider will invoke the checking and make sure that the result is true. JSR-303 also provides the @AssertFalse annotation to check for some condition that should be false. Now run the testing program (Jsr303Sample) again, and you will get the same output as produced by the custom validator.

Considerations for Custom Validation

So, for custom validation in JSR-303, which approach should you use? The custom validator or the @AssertTrue annotation? Generally, the @AssertTrue method is simpler to implement, and you can see the validation rules right in the code of the domain objects.

However, for validators with more complicated logic (for example, you need to inject a service class, access a database, and check for some valid values), then implementing a custom validator is the way to go, because you never want to inject service-layer objects into your domain objects. Also, custom validators can be reused across similar domain objects.

Which Validation API to Use?

Having discussed Spring's own Validator interface and the Bean Validation API, which one should you use in your application? JSR-303 is definitely the way to go. The following are the major reasons:

- JSR-303 is a JEE standard and is broadly supported by many frontend/backend frameworks (for example, Spring, JPA 2, Spring MVC, GWT, and so on).

- JSR-303 provides a standard validation API that hides the underlying provider, so you are not tied to a specific provider.

- Spring tightly integrates with JSR-303 starting with version 3. For example, in the Spring MVC web controller, you can annotate the argument in a method with the @Valid (under the package javax.validation) annotation, and Spring will invoke JSR-303 validation automatically during the data-binding process. Moreover, in a Spring MVC web application context configuration, a simple tag called <mvc:annotation-driven/> will configure Spring to automatically enable the Spring 3 type conversion system and field formatting, as well as support of JSR-303 Bean Validation.

- If you are using JPA 2, the provider will automatically perform JSR-303 validation to the entity before persisting, providing another layer of protection.

For detailed information about using JSR-303 Bean Validation with Hibernate Validator as the implementation provider, please refer to Hibernate Validator's documentation page (http://docs.jboss.org/hibernate/validator/4.2/reference/en-US/html).

Validation with Type Conversion and Formatting in the Sample Application

In the SpringBlog application, Spring 3's new type conversion and formatting system will be adopted. For validation, the JSR-303 Bean Validation API will be used, with Hibernate Validator as the underlying validation service provider.

To see how these techniques are adopted, let's take the major entity class, the AbstractBlogPosting class, which is the base class for both blog posting entries and comments, as an example. The class stores the common properties such as the subject, body, and post date, among others.

The main validation and formatting rules of the properties within the AbstractBlogPosting entity class are as follows:

- The subject field is mandatory, and the number of characters should be between 10 and 50.

- The body field is mandatory, and the number of characters should be between 10 and 200.

- The postDate field will be automatically populated by the application, and when it is displayed to the frontend, we will use the format yyyy-MM-dd (the default date pattern defined by ISO).

- The creation date and last-modified date will be automatically populated by the application, and when it is displayed to the frontend, we will use the format yyyy-MM-dd'T'HH:mm:ss.SSSZZ (the default date-time pattern defined by ISO).

To define the validation and formatting rule in the AbstractBlogPosting class, standard JSR-303 annotations will be used and applied to the corresponding properties. Listing 14-30 shows the code snippet of the AbstractBlogPosting class with validation and formatting annotations applied.

Listing 14-30. The AbstractBlogPosting Class

```
package com.apress.prospring3.springblog.domain;

import static javax.persistence.GenerationType.IDENTITY;

import java.io.Serializable;

import javax.persistence.*;
import javax.validation.constraints.*;

import org.hibernate.annotations.Type;
import org.joda.time.DateTime;
import org.springframework.data.domain.Auditable;
import org.springframework.format.annotation.DateTimeFormat;
import org.springframework.format.annotation.DateTimeFormat.ISO;

@MappedSuperclass
public abstract class AbstractBlogPosting
    implements BlogPosting, Auditable<String, Long>, Serializable {

    // Other code omitted
```

```
@NotNull
@Size(min=10, max=2000, message="{validation.posting.body.Size.message}")
@Column(name = "BODY")
public String getBody() {
    return body;
}

@Column(name = "POST_DATE")
@Type(type="org.joda.time.contrib.hibernate.PersistentDateTime")
@DateTimeFormat(iso=ISO.DATE)
public DateTime getPostDate() {
    return postDate;
}

@NotNull
@Size(min=10, max=50, message="{validation.posting.subject.Size.message}")
@Column(name = "SUBJECT")
public String getSubject() {
    return subject;
}

@Column(name = "CREATED_DATE")
@Type(type="org.joda.time.contrib.hibernate.PersistentDateTime")
@DateTimeFormat(iso=ISO.DATE_TIME)
public DateTime getCreatedDate() {
    return this.createdDate;
}

@Column(name = "LAST_MODIFIED_DATE")
@Type(type="org.joda.time.contrib.hibernate.PersistentDateTime")
@DateTimeFormat(iso=ISO.DATE_TIME)
public DateTime getLastModifiedDate() {
    return this.lastModifiedDate;
}
}
```

In Listing 14-30, you can see that the @NotNull and @Size JSR-303 annotations are applied to both the body and subject properties. For the @Size annotation, instead of hard-coding the message text into the message attribute, we provided the key of the message, and Hibernate Validator will retrieve the corresponding message template text from the message resource bundle (the default name of the message bundle properties file is ValidationMessages.properties), so as to support i18n (internationalization). Listing 14-31 shows the two messages defined in Listing 14-30.

Listing 14-31. The ValidationMessages.properties File

```
validation.posting.body.Size.message=body must be between {min} and {max} characters
validation.posting.subject.Size.message=subject must be between {min} and {max} characters
```

In Listing 14-31, you can see that the variables min and max are defined in the message template, which will be automatically substituted with the corresponding attributes within the @Size annotation. By defining the message this way, i18n can be implemented easily. For example, to support Hong Kong's traditional Chinese (with locale code zh_HK), we just need to prepare a ValidationMessages_zh_HK.properties file with the messages in traditional Chinese.

In addition, as shown in Listing 14-30, the @DateTimeFormat annotation is applied to the postDate, createdDate, and lastModifiedDate properties. Those annotations belong to Spring 3's type conversion and formatting system. For postDate, the pattern is defined as ISO.DATE, which stands for the pattern yyyy-MM-dd. For createdDate and LastModifiedDate, the pattern is defined as ISO.DATE_TIME, which stands for the pattern yyyy-MM-dd'T'HH:mm:ss.SSSZZ.

Enabling the validation, type conversion, and formatting support for Spring 3 is very easy. In the sample application, we will use Spring MVC in the presentation layer, namely, in the dispatcher servlet's WebApplicationContext, so we just need to define <mvc:annotation-driven>, and Spring will do the rest for us. You'll learn more about this in Chapter 17, when we discuss data validation in developing web applications.

For more details for the usage of validation, type conversion and formatting in the sample application, please refer to Chapter 21.

Summary

In this chapter, we covered the Spring 3 type conversion system as well as the field formatter SPI. You saw how the new type conversion system can be used for arbitrary type conversion, in addition to the PropertyEditors support.

In addition, we covered validation support in Spring, Spring's Validator interface, and the recommended JSR-303 Bean Validation support in Spring 3.

Task Scheduling in Spring

Task scheduling is a common feature in enterprise applications. Task scheduling mainly is composed of three parts: the task (which is the piece of business logic needed to run at a specific time or on a regular basis), the trigger (which specifies the condition under which the task should be executed), and the scheduler (which executes the task based on the information from the trigger).

Specifically, this chapter will cover the following topics:

- *Task scheduling in Spring:* We will discuss how Spring supports task scheduling, focusing on the TaskScheduler abstraction introduced in Spring 3. We'll also cover scheduling scenarios such as fixed-interval scheduling and cron expressions.

- *Asynchronous task execution:* We will discuss how to use the new @Async annotation in Spring 3 to execute tasks asynchronously.

Create a Project in STS for the Sample Projects

Let's create the sample project for this chapter. In STS, create a new Spring template project by choosing Simple Spring JPA Utility Project. The reason of choosing this project template is that we will develop a sample job that will update the data in the backend RDBMS.

Upon project creation, other dependencies are required, as shown in Table 15-1. Add them into your project. Also, verify that the project is using Spring 3.1 and JDK 6.

Table 15-1. Maven Dependencies for Task Scheduling

Group ID	Artifact ID	Version	Description
org.springframework.data	spring-data-jpa	1.0.1.RELEASE	Spring Data JPA library.
joda-time	joda-time	2.0	Joda-time (http://joda-time.sourceforge.net/) is a date-time API that Spring Data JPA uses. In this chapter, we will use it in our domain objects too.
joda-time	joda-time-hibernate	1.3	Joda-time library for integration with Hibernate for date-time data persistence.

Group ID	Artifact ID	Version	Description
com.google.guava	guava	10.0.1	Contains useful helper classes.
org.slf4j	slf4j-log4j12	1.6.1	The SLF4J logging library (www.slf4j.org) will be used as the logging library for the samples in this chapter. This library will help chain the SLF4J logger to the underlying log4j library for logging purposes.

Task Scheduling in Spring

Enterprise applications often need to schedule tasks. In many applications, various tasks (such as sending e-mail notifications to customers, running day-end jobs, doing data housekeeping, updating data in batches, and so on) need to be scheduled to run on a regular basis, either in a fixed interval (e.g., every hour) or at a specific schedule (e.g., at 8 p.m. every night, from Monday to Friday). As mentioned, task scheduling consists of three parts: the schedule definition (trigger), the task execution (scheduler), and the task itself.

There are many different ways to trigger the execution of a task in a Spring application. One way is to trigger a job externally from a scheduling system that already exists in the application deployment environment. For example, many enterprises use commercial systems, such as Ctrl-M or CA Autosys, for scheduling tasks. If the application is running on a Linux/Unix platform, the crontab scheduler can be used. The job triggering can be done by sending a RESTful-WS request to the Spring application and having Spring's MVC controller trigger the task.

Another way is to use the task scheduling support in Spring. Spring provides three options in terms of task scheduling:

- *Support of JDK Timer*: Spring supports JDK's Timer object for task scheduling.

- *Integrates with Quartz*: The Quartz Scheduler (www.quartz-scheduler.org) is a popular open source scheduling library.

- *Spring's own TaskScheduler abstraction*: Spring 3 introduces the TaskScheduler abstraction, which provides a simple way to schedule tasks and supports most typical requirements.

In this section, we will focus on using Spring's TaskScheduler abstraction for task scheduling.

Introducing Spring TaskScheduler Abstraction

In Spring's TaskScheduler abstraction, there are mainly three participants:

- *The Trigger interface*: The org.springframework.scheduling.Trigger interface provides support for defining the triggering mechanism. Spring provides two Trigger implementations. The CronTrigger class supports triggering based on a cron expression, while the PeriodicTrigger class supports triggering based on an initial delay and then a fixed interval.

- *The task*: The task is the piece of business logic that needs to be scheduled. In Spring, a task can be specified as a method within any Spring bean.

- *The TaskScheduler interface*: The org.springframework.scheduling.TaskScheduler interface provides support for task scheduling. Spring provides three implementation classes of the TaskScheduler interface. The TimerManagerTaskScheduler class (under the package org.springframework.scheduling.commonj) wraps CommonJ's commonj.timers.TimerManager interface, which is commonly used in commercial JEE application servers such as WebSphere, WebLogic, and so on. The ConcurrentTaskScheduler and ThreadPoolTaskScheduler (both under the package org.springframework.scheduling.concurrent) classes wrap the java.util.concurrent.ScheduledThreadPoolExecutor class. Both classes support task execution from a shared thread pool.

Figure 15-1 shows the relationships between the Trigger interface, the TaskScheduler interface, and the task (that implements the java.lang.Runnable interface).

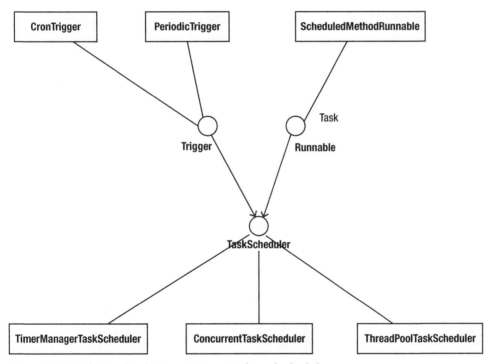

Figure 15-1. *Relationship between trigger, task, and scheduler*

To schedule tasks using Spring's TaskScheduler abstraction, you have two options. One is to use the task-namespace in Spring's XML configuration, and the other is to use annotations. Let's go through each of them.

Sample Task

To demonstrate task scheduling in Spring, let's implement a simple job first, namely, an application maintaining a database of car information. Listing 15-1 shows the Car class, which is implemented as a JPA entity class.

Listing 15-1. The Car Class

```
package com.apress.prospring3.ch15.domain;

import static javax.persistence.GenerationType.IDENTITY;

import javax.persistence.Column;
import javax.persistence.Entity;
import javax.persistence.GeneratedValue;
import javax.persistence.Id;
import javax.persistence.Table;
import javax.persistence.Version;

import org.hibernate.annotations.Type;
import org.joda.time.DateTime;

@Entity
@Table(name="car")
public class Car {

    private Long id;

    private String licensePlate;

    private String manufacturer;

    private DateTime manufactureDate;

    private int age;

    private int version;

    @Id
    @GeneratedValue(strategy = IDENTITY)
    @Column(name = "ID")
    public Long getId() {
        return id;
    }

    @Column(name="LICENSE_PLATE")
    public String getLicensePlate() {
        return licensePlate;
    }

    @Column(name="MANUFACTURER")
    public String getManufacturer() {
        return manufacturer;
```

```
    }

    @Column(name="MANUFACTURE_DATE")
    @Type(type="org.joda.time.contrib.hibernate.PersistentDateTime")
    public DateTime getManufactureDate() {
        return manufactureDate;
    }

    @Column(name="AGE")
    public int getAge() {
        return age;
    }

    @Version
    public int getVersion() {
        return version;
    }

    // Setter method omitted

    public String toString() {
        return "License: " + licensePlate + " - Manufacturer: " + manufacturer
            + " - Manufacture Date: " + manufactureDate + " - Age: " + age;
    }
}
```

Listings 15-2 and 15-3 shows the table creation script (schema.sql) and testing data population script (test-data.sql) for the Car entity class, respectively.

Listing 15-2. *The Table Creation Script*

```
DROP TABLE IF EXISTS CONTACT;

CREATE TABLE CAR (
    ID INT NOT NULL AUTO_INCREMENT
    , LICENSE_PLATE VARCHAR(20) NOT NULL
    , MANUFACTURER VARCHAR(20) NOT NULL
    , MANUFACTURE_DATE DATE NOT NULL
    , AGE INT NOT NULL DEFAULT 0
    , VERSION INT NOT NULL DEFAULT 0
    , UNIQUE UQ_CAR_1 (LICENSE_PLATE)
    , PRIMARY KEY (ID)
);
```

Listing 15-3. *The Testing Data Population Script*

```
insert into car (license_plate, manufacturer, manufacture_date) values↵
  ('LICENSE-1001', 'Ford', '1980-07-30');
insert into car (license_plate, manufacturer, manufacture_date) values↵
  ('LICENSE-1002', 'Toyota', '1992-12-30');
insert into car (license_plate, manufacturer, manufacture_date) values↵
  ('LICENSE-1003', 'BMW', '2003-1-6');
```

Let's define a service layer for the Car entity. We will use Spring Data's JPA and its repository abstraction support. Listing 15-4 shows the CarRepository interface.

Listing 15-4. The CarRepository Interface

```
package com.apress.prospring3.ch15.repository;

import org.springframework.data.repository.CrudRepository;

import com.apress.prospring3.ch15.domain.Car;

public interface CarRepository extends CrudRepository<Car, Long> {
}
```

It's nothing special; we just implemented the CrudRepository<Car,Long> interface. Listings 15-5 and 15-6 shows the CarService interface and the implementation CarServiceImpl class, respectively.

Listing 15-5. The CarService Interface

```
package com.apress.prospring3.ch15.service;

import java.util.List;

import com.apress.prospring3.ch15.domain.Car;

public interface CarService {

    public List<Car> findAll();

    public Car save(Car car);

    public void updateCarAgeJob();
}
```

Listing 15-6. The CarServiceImpl Class

```
package com.apress.prospring3.ch15.service.jpa;

// Import statements omitted
@Service("carService")
@Repository
@Transactional
public class CarServiceImpl implements CarService {

    final Logger logger = LoggerFactory.getLogger(CarServiceImpl.class);

    @Autowired
    CarRepository carRepository;

    @Transactional(readOnly=true)
    public List<Car> findAll() {
        return Lists.newArrayList(carRepository.findAll());
    }
```

```
    public Car save(Car car) {
        return carRepository.save(car);
    }

    public void updateCarAgeJob() {

        // Update age of cars
        List<Car> cars = findAll();

        DateTime currentDate = DateTime.now();
        int age;

        logger.info("");
        logger.info("Car age update job started");
        for (Car car: cars) {
            age = new Period(car.getManufactureDate(), currentDate,
                    PeriodType.years()).getYears();
            car.setAge(age);
            save(car);
            logger.info("Car age update--- " + car);
        }
        logger.info("Car age update job completed successfully");
        logger.info("");

    }
}
```

Two methods were provided; one retrieves information about all cars, and the other persists an updated Car object. The third method, updateCarAgeJob(), is the job that needs to be run regularly to update the age of the car based on the manufacture date of the car and the current date.

Listing 15-7 shows the Spring configuration to support the car application (car-job-app-context.xml).

Listing 15-7. The car-job-app-context.xml File

```
<?xml version="1.0" encoding="UTF-8"?>
<beans xmlns=http://www.springframework.org/schema/beans
    xmlns:context="http://www.springframework.org/schema/context"
    xmlns:jdbc="http://www.springframework.org/schema/jdbc"
    xmlns:tx="http://www.springframework.org/schema/tx"
    xmlns:jpa="http://www.springframework.org/schema/data/jpa"
    xmlns:repository="http://www.springframework.org/schema/data/repository"
    xmlns:xsi="http://www.w3.org/2001/XMLSchema-instance"
    xsi:schemaLocation="http://www.springframework.org/schema/beans
        http://www.springframework.org/schema/beans/spring-beans-3.1.xsd
        http://www.springframework.org/schema/context
        http://www.springframework.org/schema/context/spring-context-3.1.xsd
        http://www.springframework.org/schema/jdbc
        http://www.springframework.org/schema/jdbc/spring-jdbc-3.1.xsd
        http://www.springframework.org/schema/tx
        http://www.springframework.org/schema/tx/spring-tx-3.1.xsd
        http://www.springframework.org/schema/data/jpa
        http://www.springframework.org/schema/data/jpa/spring-jpa-1.0.xsd
        http://www.springframework.org/schema/data/repository
```

```
                http://www.springframework.org/schema/data/repository/spring-repository-1.0.xsd"
    >

        <jdbc:embedded-database id="dataSource" type="H2">
            <jdbc:script location="classpath:schema.sql"/>
            <jdbc:script location="classpath:test-data.sql"/>
        </jdbc:embedded-database>

        <bean id="transactionManager"
            class="org.springframework.orm.jpa.JpaTransactionManager">
            <property name="entityManagerFactory" ref="emf"/>
        </bean>

        <tx:annotation-driven transaction-manager="transactionManager" />

        <bean id="emf" class="org.springframework.orm.jpa.LocalContainerEntityManagerFactoryBean">
            <property name="dataSource" ref="dataSource" />
            <property name="jpaVendorAdapter">
                <bean class="org.springframework.orm.jpa.vendor.HibernateJpaVendorAdapter" />
            </property>
            <property name="packagesToScan"
                value="com.apress.prospring3.ch15.domain"/>
            <property name="jpaProperties">
                <props>
                    <prop key="hibernate.dialect">
                        org.hibernate.dialect.H2Dialect
                    </prop>
                    <prop key="hibernate.max_fetch_depth">3</prop>
                    <prop key="hibernate.jdbc.fetch_size">50</prop>
                    <prop key="hibernate.jdbc.batch_size">10</prop>
                    <prop key="hibernate.show_sql">true</prop>
                </props>
            </property>
        </bean>

        <context:annotation-config/>

        <jpa:repositories base-package="com.apress.prospring3.ch15.repository"
            entity-manager-factory-ref="emf"
            transaction-manager-ref="transactionManager"/>

        <context:component-scan
            base-package="com.apress.prospring3.ch15.service.jpa" />

</beans>
```

The configuration should be familiar to you. Now let's proceed to schedule the car age update job in Spring.

Task Scheduling Using task-namespace

Like the support for other namespaces in Spring, task-namespace provides a simplified configuration for scheduling tasks using Spring's TaskScheduler abstraction.

Using task-namespace for task scheduling is very simple. Listing 15-8 shows the configuration file (task-namespace-app-context.xml).

Listing 15-8. Spring Configuration Using task-namespace

```
<?xml version="1.0" encoding="UTF-8"?>
<beans xmlns=http://www.springframework.org/schema/beans
    xmlns:task="http://www.springframework.org/schema/task"
    xmlns:xsi="http://www.w3.org/2001/XMLSchema-instance"
    xsi:schemaLocation="http://www.springframework.org/schema/beans
        http://www.springframework.org/schema/beans/spring-beans-3.1.xsd
        http://www.springframework.org/schema/task
        http://www.springframework.org/schema/task/spring-task-3.1.xsd"
>

    <import resource="car-job-app-context.xml"/>

    <task:scheduler id="myScheduler" pool-size="10"/>

    <task:scheduled-tasks scheduler="myScheduler">
        <task:scheduled ref="carService" method="updateCarAgeJob"
            fixed-delay="10000"/>
    </task:scheduled-tasks>

</beans>
```

As shown in Listing 15-8, the context for the car application was imported. When it encounters the <task:scheduler> tag, Spring will instantiate an instance of the ThreadPoolTaskScheduler class, while the attribute pool-size specifies the size of the thread pool that the scheduler can use. Within the <task:scheduled-tasks> tag, one or more tasks can be scheduled. In the <task:scheduled> tag, a task can reference a Spring bean (the carService bean in this case) and a specific method within the bean (in this case the updateCarAgeJob() method). The attribute fixed-delay will instruct Spring to instantiate a PeriodicTrigger as the Trigger implementation for the TaskScheduler.

Listing 15-9 shows the testing program for task scheduling.

Listing 15-9. Testing Task Scheduling in Spring

```
package com.apress.prospring3.ch15.schedule;

import org.springframework.context.support.GenericXmlApplicationContext;

public class ScheduleTaskSample {

    public static void main(String[] args) {

        GenericXmlApplicationContext ctx = new GenericXmlApplicationContext();
        ctx.load("classpath:task-namespace-app-context.xml");
        ctx.refresh();

        while (true) {
        }
    }
}
```

The class is simple; just bootstrap the ApplicationContext and then keep looping. If the application is deployed to an application server environment, the scheduler will keep running.

Running the program will produce the following batch job output every ten seconds:

```
INFO [com.apress.prospring3.ch15.service.jpa.CarServiceImpl] - <>
INFO [com.apress.prospring3.ch15.service.jpa.CarServiceImpl] - <Car age update job started>
INFO [com.apress.prospring3.ch15.service.jpa.CarServiceImpl] - <Car age update--- License:
LICENSE-1001 - Manufacturer: Ford - Manufacture Date: 1980-07-30T00:00:00.000+08:00 - Age: 31>
INFO [com.apress.prospring3.ch15.service.jpa.CarServiceImpl] - <Car age update--- License:
LICENSE-1002 - Manufacturer: Toyota - Manufacture Date: 1992-12-30T00:00:00.000+08:00 - Age:
18>
INFO [com.apress.prospring3.ch15.service.jpa.CarServiceImpl] - <Car age update--- License:
LICENSE-1003 - Manufacturer: BMW - Manufacture Date: 2003-01-06T00:00:00.000+08:00 - Age: 8>
INFO [com.apress.prospring3.ch15.service.jpa.CarServiceImpl] - <Car age update job completed
successfully>
INFO [com.apress.prospring3.ch15.service.jpa.CarServiceImpl] - <>
```

From the output, you can see the cars' age attributes were updated.

Besides a fixed interval, a more flexible scheduling mechanism is to use a cron expression. In Listing 15-8, change the line from this:

```
<task:scheduled ref="carService" method="updateCarAgeJob" fixed-delay="10000"/>
```

to the following:

```
<task:scheduled ref="carService" method="updateCarAgeJob" cron="0 * * * * *"/>
```

After the change, run the ScheduleTaskSample class again, and you will see the job will run every minute. The Quartz's CronTrigger tutorial page (e.g., www.quartz-scheduler.org/documentation/quartz-2.1.x/tutorials/crontrigger) provides a detailed description of the structure and gives examples of cron expressions.

Task Scheduling Using Annotation

Another option for scheduling tasks using Spring's TaskScheduler abstraction is to use an annotation. Spring provides the @Scheduled annotation for this purpose.

To enable annotation support for task scheduling, we need to provide the <task:annotation-driven> tag in Spring's XML configuration. Listing 15-10 shows the configuration (task-annotation-app-context.xml).

Listing 15-10. *Spring Configuration for Annotation-Based Scheduling*

```
<?xml version="1.0" encoding="UTF-8"?>
<beans xmlns=http://www.springframework.org/schema/beans
    xmlns:task="http://www.springframework.org/schema/task"
    xmlns:xsi="http://www.w3.org/2001/XMLSchema-instance"
    xsi:schemaLocation="http://www.springframework.org/schema/beans
        http://www.springframework.org/schema/beans/spring-beans-3.1.xsd
        http://www.springframework.org/schema/task
        http://www.springframework.org/schema/task/spring-task-3.1.xsd"
>

    <import resource="car-job-app-context.xml"/>
```

```
<task:scheduler id="myScheduler" pool-size="10"/>

<task:annotation-driven scheduler="myScheduler"/>
```

```
</beans>
```

As shown in Listing 15-10, the `<task:annotation-driven>` tag enables support for annotation-based scheduling, with the scheduler attribute referencing the myScheduler bean.

To schedule a specific method in a Spring bean, just annotate the method with @Scheduled and pass in the scheduling requirements. Listing 15-11 shows the code snippet of the revised CarServiceImpl class.

Listing 15-11. *Revised CarServiceImpl Class*

```
package com.apress.prospring3.ch15.service.jpa;

import org.springframework.scheduling.annotation.Scheduled;

// Other code omitted
public class CarServiceImpl implements CarService {

    @Scheduled(fixedDelay=10000)
    //@Scheduled(fixedRate=10000)
    //@Scheduled(cron="0 * * * * *")
    public void updateCarAgeJob() {

        // Other code omitted
    }
}
```

Listing 15-12 shows the testing program.

Listing 15-12. *Testing Annotation-Based Scheduling*

```
package com.apress.prospring3.ch15.schedule;

import org.springframework.context.support.GenericXmlApplicationContext;

public class ScheduleTaskAnnotationSample {

    public static void main(String[] args) {

        GenericXmlApplicationContext ctx = new GenericXmlApplicationContext();
        ctx.load("classpath:task-annotation-app-context.xml");
        ctx.refresh();

        while (true) {
        }
    }
}
```

Running the program will produce the same output as using task-namespace. You can try different triggering mechanisms by changing the attribute within the @Scheduled annotation (i.e., fixedDelay, fixedRate, cron). Feel free to test it yourself.

Asynchronous Task Execution in Spring

In version 3.0, Spring also supports using annotations to execute a task asynchronously. To use it, you just need to annotate the method with @Async.

Let's go through a simple example to see it in action. Listing 15-13 and Listing 15-14 show the AsyncService interface and its implementation class AsyncServiceImpl, respectively.

Listing 15-13. The AsyncService Interface

```
package com.apress.prospring3.ch15.service;

import java.util.concurrent.Future;

public interface AsyncService {

    public void asyncTask();

    public Future<String> asyncWithReturn(String name);

}
```

Listing 15-14. The AsyncServiceImpl Class

```
package com.apress.prospring3.ch15.service.async;

import java.util.concurrent.Future;

import org.slf4j.Logger;
import org.slf4j.LoggerFactory;
import org.springframework.scheduling.annotation.Async;
import org.springframework.scheduling.annotation.AsyncResult;
import org.springframework.stereotype.Service;

import com.apress.prospring3.ch15.service.AsyncService;

@Service("asyncService")
public class AsyncServiceImpl implements AsyncService {

    final Logger logger = LoggerFactory.getLogger(AsyncServiceImpl.class);

    @Async
    public void asyncTask() {

        logger.info("Start execution of async. task");

        try {
            Thread.sleep(10000);
        } catch (Exception ex) {
            ex.printStackTrace();
        }

        logger.info("Complete execution of async. task");
```

```
    }

    @Async
    public Future<String> asyncWithReturn(String name) {

        logger.info("Start execution of async. task with return");

        try {
            Thread.sleep(5000);
        } catch (Exception ex) {
            ex.printStackTrace();
        }

        logger.info("Complete execution of async. task with return");

        return new AsyncResult<String>("Hello: " + name);
    }
}
```

The AsyncService defines two methods. The asyncTask() is a simple task that logs information to the logger. The method asyncWithReturn() accepts a String argument and returns an instance of the java.util.concurrent.Future<V> interface. Note the code in bold; upon completion of the asyncWithReturn(), the result is stored in an instance of the org.springframework.scheduling.annotation.AsyncResult<V> class, which implements the Future<V> interface and can be used by the caller to retrieve the result of the execution later.

Listing 15-15 shows the Spring configuration file (async-app-context.xml).

Listing 15-15. Spring Configuration for Async Task

```
<?xml version="1.0" encoding="UTF-8"?>
<beans xmlns="http://www.springframework.org/schema/beans"
    xmlns:xsi="http://www.w3.org/2001/XMLSchema-instance"
    xmlns:context="http://www.springframework.org/schema/context"
    xmlns:task="http://www.springframework.org/schema/task"
    xsi:schemaLocation="http://www.springframework.org/schema/beans
        http://www.springframework.org/schema/beans/spring-beans-3.1.xsd
        http://www.springframework.org/schema/context
        http://www.springframework.org/schema/context/spring-context-3.1.xsd
        http://www.springframework.org/schema/task
        http://www.springframework.org/schema/task/spring-task-3.1.xsd">

    <context:annotation-config/>

    <context:component-scan
        base-package="com.apress.prospring3.ch15.service.async"/>

    <task:annotation-driven />

</beans>
```

From Listing 15-15, we need the <task:annotation-driven /> tag for support of the @Async annotation. Listing 15-16 shows the testing program.

Listing 15-16. Testing Async Task

```
package com.apress.prospring3.ch15.schedule;

import java.util.concurrent.Future;

import org.springframework.context.support.GenericXmlApplicationContext;

import com.apress.prospring3.ch15.service.AsyncService;

public class AsyncTaskSample {

    public static void main(String[] args) {

        GenericXmlApplicationContext ctx = new GenericXmlApplicationContext();
        ctx.load("classpath:async-app-context.xml");
        ctx.refresh();

        AsyncService asyncService = ctx.getBean(
            "asyncService", AsyncService.class);

        for (int i = 0; i < 5; i++)
            asyncService.asyncTask();

        Future<String> result1 = asyncService.asyncWithReturn("Clarence");
        Future<String> result2 = asyncService.asyncWithReturn("John");
        Future<String> result3 = asyncService.asyncWithReturn("Robert");

        try {
            Thread.sleep(6000);

            System.out.println("Result1: " + result1.get());
            System.out.println("Result2: " + result2.get());
            System.out.println("Result3: " + result3.get());
        } catch (Exception ex) {
            ex.printStackTrace();
        }
    }
}
```

From Listing 15-16, we call the asyncTask() method five times and then the asyncWithReturn() three times with different arguments, and then we retrieve the result after sleeping for six seconds.

Running the program will produce the following output:

```
2011-11-23 17:46:16,276 INFO [com.apress.prospring3.ch15.service.async.AsyncServiceImpl] -
<Start execution of async. task>
2011-11-23 17:46:16,277 INFO [com.apress.prospring3.ch15.service.async.AsyncServiceImpl] -
<Start execution of async. task>
2011-11-23 17:46:16,277 INFO [com.apress.prospring3.ch15.service.async.AsyncServiceImpl] -
<Start execution of async. task>
2011-11-23 17:46:16,277 INFO [com.apress.prospring3.ch15.service.async.AsyncServiceImpl] -
<Start execution of async. task>
2011-11-23 17:46:16,277 INFO [com.apress.prospring3.ch15.service.async.AsyncServiceImpl] -
<Start execution of async. task>
```

```
2011-11-23 17:46:16,277 INFO [com.apress.prospring3.ch15.service.async.AsyncServiceImpl] -
<Start execution of async. task with return>
2011-11-23 17:46:16,277 INFO [com.apress.prospring3.ch15.service.async.AsyncServiceImpl] -
<Start execution of async. task with return>
2011-11-23 17:46:16,277 INFO [com.apress.prospring3.ch15.service.async.AsyncServiceImpl] -
<Start execution of async. task with return>
2011-11-23 17:46:21,278 INFO [com.apress.prospring3.ch15.service.async.AsyncServiceImpl] -
<Complete execution of async. task with return>
2011-11-23 17:46:21,278 INFO [com.apress.prospring3.ch15.service.async.AsyncServiceImpl] -
<Complete execution of async. task with return>
2011-11-23 17:46:21,278 INFO [com.apress.prospring3.ch15.service.async.AsyncServiceImpl] -
<Complete execution of async. task with return>
Result1: Hello: Clarence
Result2: Hello: John
Result3: Hello: Robert
2011-11-23 17:46:26,277 INFO [com.apress.prospring3.ch15.service.async.AsyncServiceImpl] -
<Complete execution of async. task>
2011-11-23 17:46:26,278 INFO [com.apress.prospring3.ch15.service.async.AsyncServiceImpl] -
<Complete execution of async. task>
2011-11-23 17:46:26,278 INFO [com.apress.prospring3.ch15.service.async.AsyncServiceImpl] -
<Complete execution of async. task>
2011-11-23 17:46:26,278 INFO [com.apress.prospring3.ch15.service.async.AsyncServiceImpl] -
<Complete execution of async. task>
2011-11-23 17:46:26,278 INFO [com.apress.prospring3.ch15.service.async.AsyncServiceImpl] -
<Complete execution of async. task>
```

From the output, you can see that all the calls were started at the same time. The three calling with return values complete first and are displayed on the console output. Finally, the five asyncTask() methods called were completed too.

Task Scheduling in the Sample Application

In the SpringBlog application, we will store the history records for both blog posting entries and comments for auditing purposes. However, we also decided to keep only those history records for 30 days in order not to consume too much database storage. To fulfill the requirement, we will adopt Spring 3's TaskScheduler abstraction support to implement a schedule job to purge the audit records older than 30 days. The job will run every day at midnight.

We will use the annotation style for task scheduling. First we will define an interface for the housekeeping job. Listing 15-17 shows the interface.

Listing 15-17. The HousekeepingService Interface

```
package com.apress.prospring3.springblog.service;

public interface HousekeepingService {

    /**
    * Scheduled job to purge audit records.
    */
    public void auditPurgeJob();

}
```

The interface defines the auditPurgeJob() method for the audit record housekeeping task. Listing 15-18 shows the implementation class with the @Scheduled annotation applied.

Listing 15-18. The HousekeepingServiceImpl Class

```
package com.apress.prospring3.springblog.service.jpa;

import org.springframework.beans.factory.annotation.Value;
import org.springframework.scheduling.annotation.Scheduled;
import org.springframework.stereotype.Repository;
import org.springframework.stereotype.Service;
import org.springframework.transaction.annotation.Transactional;

import com.apress.prospring3.springblog.service.HousekeepingService;

@Service("housekeepingService")
@Repository
@Transactional
public class HousekeepingServiceImpl implements HousekeepingService {

    @Value("${audit.record.history.days}")
    private int auditHistoryDays;

    @Scheduled(cron="0 0 0 * * ?")
    public void auditPurgeJob() {
        // Purge audit record logic goes here
    }
}
```

From Listing 15-18, the @Scheduled annotation was applied to the auditPurgeJob() method with a cron expression. The cron expression means that the job should run at midnight every day. For the number of days that the audit records will be kept, we will externalize it into a properties file for easy maintenance. To enable the annotation-style task scheduling, we will define the <task:annotation-driven> tag in the root WebApplicationContext.

For more details, please refer to Chapter 21.

Summary

In this chapter, we covered Spring's support for task scheduling. We focused on Spring's built-in TaskScheduler abstraction and demonstrated how to use it to fulfill task scheduling needs with a sample batch data update job. We also covered how Spring 3 supports annotation for executing tasks asynchronously.

CHAPTER 16

Using Spring Remoting

An enterprise application typically needs to communicate with other applications. Take, for example, for a company selling products; when a customer places an order, an order-processing system processes the order and generates a transaction. During the order processing, an inquiry is made to the inventory system to check whether the product is available in stock. Upon order confirmation, a notification is sent to the fulfillment system to deliver the product to the customer. Finally, the information is sent to the accounting system; an invoice is generated and the payment is processed.

Most of the time, this business process is not fulfilled by a single application but a number of applications working together. Some of the applications may be developed in-house, and others may be purchased from external vendors. Moreover, the applications may be running on different machines in different locations and implemented with different technologies and programming languages (for example, Java, .NET, C++, and so on). Performing the handshaking between applications in order to build an efficient business process is always a critical task when architecting and implementing an application. As a result, remoting support via various protocols and technologies is needed for an application to participate well in an enterprise environment.

In the Java world, remoting support has existed since it was first created. In early days (Java 1.*x*), most remoting requirements were implemented using traditional TCP sockets or Java Remote Method Invocation (RMI). After J2EE came on the scene, EJB and JMS became common choices for interapplication server communications. The rapid evolution of XML and the Internet gave rise to remote support using XML over HTTP , including the Java API for XML-based RPC (JAX-RPC), the Java API for XML Web Services (JAX-RPC), and HTTP-based technologies (for example, Hessian, Burlap, and so on). Spring also offers its own HTTP-based remoting support, called the Spring HTTP invoker. In recent years, to cope with the explosive growth of the Internet and more responsive web application requirements (for example, via Ajax), more lightweight and efficient remoting support of applications has become critical for the success of an enterprise. Consequently, the Java API for RESTful Web Services (JAX-RS) was created and quickly gained popularity. Other protocols, such as Comet and HTML5 WebSocket, also attracted a lot of developers. Needless to say, remoting technologies keep evolving at a rapid pace.

In terms of remoting, as mentioned, Spring provides its own support (for example, the Spring HTTP invoker), as well as supports a lot of technologies mentioned earlier (for example, RMI, EJB, JMS, Hessian, Burlap, JAX-RPC, JAX-WS, JAX-RS, and so on). It's not possible to cover all of them in this chapter. So, here we will focus on those that are most commonly used. Specifically, this chapter will cover the following topics:

- *Spring HTTP invoker*: If both applications that need to communicate are Spring based, the Spring HTTP invoker provides a simple and efficient way for invoking the services exposed by other applications. We will show you how to use the Spring HTTP invoker to expose a service within its service layer, as well as invoking the services provided by a remote application.

- *Using JMS in Spring*: The Java Messaging Service (JMS) provides another asynchronous and loosely coupled way of exchanging messages between applications. We will show you how Spring simplifies application development with JMS.

- *Using RESTful web services in Spring*: Designed specifically around the HTTP protocol, RESTful web services are the most commonly used technology for providing remote support for an application, as well as supporting highly interactive web application frontends using Ajax. We will show you how Spring 3 MVC provides comprehensive support for exposing services using JAX-RS and how to invoke services using the RestTemplate class. We will also discuss how to secure the services for protecting unauthorized access to the services.

Creating the Project in STS for the Samples

Let's create the project for the samples in this chapter. Since we will expose the developed services via HTTP, we need to create a web-based project with Spring MVC. In STS, create a new Spring template project and choose Spring MVC Project, as shown in Figure 16-1.

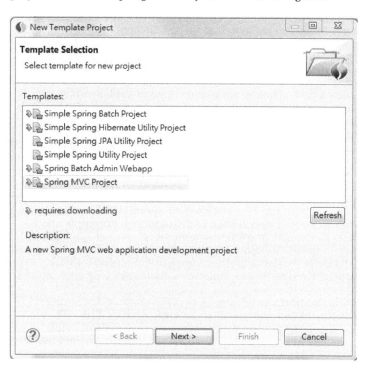

Figure 16-1. *Creating a Spring MVC project in STS*

On the next screen, enter the information for the project for the samples in this chapter, as shown in Figure 16-2.

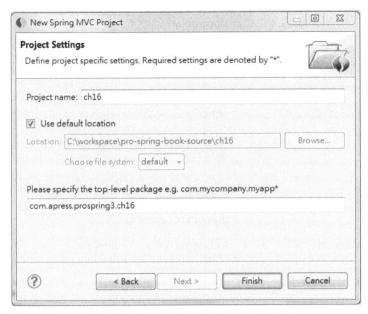

Figure 16-2. Entering details for a Spring MVC project

Upon completion, STS will create a web project with the required dependencies, including the Spring MVC module.

Implementing the Service Layer for the Samples

We want to show you some more practical samples instead of a simple "Hello World" application. So, we will implement a simple contact information service (like the one in previous chapters) using JPA and then expose its services to remote clients. This section discusses how to implement the service layer.

Adding Required Dependencies for the JPA Backend

We need to add the required dependencies to the project. Table 16-1 shows the dependencies required for implementing a service layer with JPA 2 and Hibernate as the persistence provider. Also, Spring Data JPA will be used. In addition, verify that the project is using Spring 3.1.

Table 16-1. Maven Dependencies for Service Layer

Group ID	Artifact ID	Version	Description
org.springframework	spring-jdbc	3.1.0.RELEASE	Spring JDBC module.
org.springframework	spring-orm	3.1.0.RELEASE	Spring ORM module.
org.springframework	spring-tx	3.1.0.RELEASE	Spring transaction support module.
org.springframework.data	spring-data-jpa	1.0.1.RELEASE	Spring Data JPA library.

Group ID	Artifact ID	Version	Description
org.hibernate	hibernate-entitymanager	3.6.8.Final	Hibernate entity manager with JPA 2 support.
javax.validation	validation-api	1.0.0.GA	The JSR-303 Bean Validation API library.
org.hibernate	hibernate-validator	4.2.0.Final	Hibernate's implementation of JSR-303.
com.h2database	h2	1.3.160	H2 database for embedded JDBC database.
joda-time	joda-time	2.0	Joda-time (joda-time.sourceforge.net/) is a date-time API that Spring Data JPA uses. In this chapter, we will use it in our domain objects too.
joda-time	joda-time-hibernate	1.3	Joda-time library for integration with Hibernate for date-time data persistence.
com.google.guava	guava	10.0.1	Contains useful helper classes.

Figure 16-3 shows the dependencies in STS upon completion.

Figure 16-3. Maven dependencies for a Spring MVC project with JPA backend

Verifying the Project

Let's verify that the application is working before we proceed. In STS, in the Servers view, verify that a tc Server instance (a specialized version of Tomcat provided by VMware SpringSource) exists, as shown in Figure 16-4.

Figure 16-4. tc Server in STS

If you don't see it, then you will need to create one. Please refer to Appendix A for details.

We can now configure the project to run on the server and deploy and test it. Right-click the project, choose Run As, and then choose Run on Server, as shown in Figure 16-5.

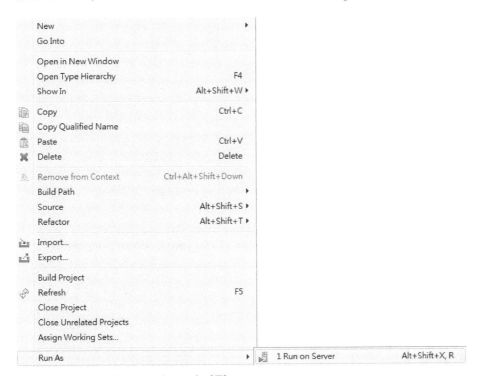

Figure 16-5. Running on tc Server in STS

Choose the tc Server (if it's not the only one you see on the screen), as shown in Figure 16-6.

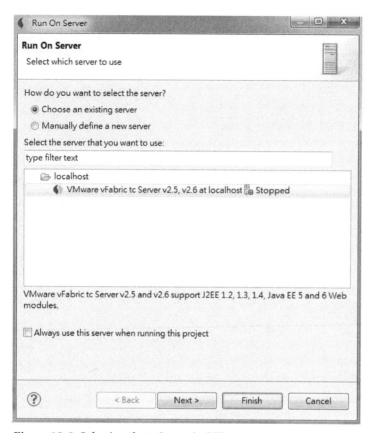

Figure 16-6. Selecting the tc Server in STS

On the next screen, the project should have been added by STS for you, as shown in Figure 16-7.

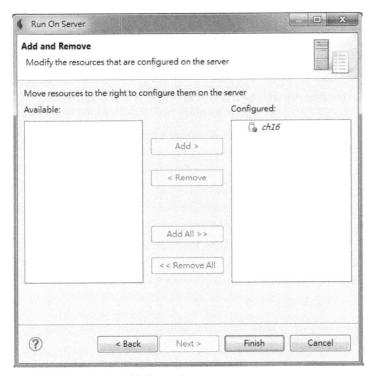

Figure 16-7. Project added to tc Server

Click Finish, and STS will build the project, deploy to the server, and then bring up the welcome page that was automatically created with the template project, as shown in Figure 16-8.

Figure 16-8. Default welcome page of Spring MVC project

It's a simple JSP page that shows the "Hello World" message and the server time. Don't worry about the question marks; they are because of the developer machine's locale setup (mine is zh_HK for Hong Kong). If your machine is running English as the locale, then you should see the time format correctly.

This page indicates that the project was created normally, and we can now proceed to implement the service layer and expose it for remote access.

Data Model for Samples

For the data model in the samples in this chapter, we will use a very simple one, which contains only a single CONTACT table for storing contact information. Listing 16-1 shows the script for schema creation (schema.sql in the /src/main/resources folder).

Listing 16-1. Sample Database Schema

```
DROP TABLE IF EXISTS CONTACT;

CREATE TABLE CONTACT (
    ID INT NOT NULL AUTO_INCREMENT
    , FIRST_NAME VARCHAR(60) NOT NULL
    , LAST_NAME VARCHAR(40) NOT NULL
    , BIRTH_DATE DATE
    , VERSION INT NOT NULL DEFAULT 0
    , UNIQUE UQ_CONTACT_1 (FIRST_NAME, LAST_NAME)
    , PRIMARY KEY (ID)
);
```

As you can see, the CONTACT table stores only a few basic fields of a contact's information. Listing 16-2 shows the testing data population script (test-data.sql).

Listing 16-2. Sample Data Population Script

```
insert into contact (first_name, last_name, birth_date) values
    ('Clarence', 'Ho', '1980-07-30');
insert into contact (first_name, last_name, birth_date) values
    ('Scott', 'Tiger', '1990-11-02');
insert into contact (first_name, last_name, birth_date) values
    ('John', 'Smith', '1964-02-28');
```

Implementing and Configuring ContactService

Having the template project created and sample data model and scripts ready, we can start to implement and configure the service layer for our samples in this chapter.

In the following sections, we will discuss the implementation of the ContactService using JPA 2, Spring Data JPA, and Hibernate as the persistence service provider. Then, we will cover how to configure the service layer in the Spring project.

Implementing ContactService

In the samples, we will expose the services for various operations on the contact information to remote clients. First we need to create the Contact entity class, which is shown in Listing 16-3.

Listing 16-3. The Contact Entity Class

```
package com.apress.prospring3.ch16.domain;

import static javax.persistence.GenerationType.IDENTITY;

import java.io.Serializable;

import javax.persistence.*;

import org.hibernate.annotations.Type;
import org.joda.time.DateTime;

@Entity
@Table(name = "contact")
public class Contact implements Serializable {

    private Long id;
    private int version;
    private String firstName;
    private String lastName;
    private DateTime birthDate;

    @Id
    @GeneratedValue(strategy = IDENTITY)
    @Column(name = "ID")
    public Long getId() {
        return id;
    }

    @Version
    @Column(name = "VERSION")
    public int getVersion() {
        return version;
    }

    @Column(name = "FIRST_NAME")
    public String getFirstName() {
        return firstName;
    }

    @Column(name = "LAST_NAME")
    public String getLastName() {
        return lastName;
    }

    @Column(name = "BIRTH_DATE")
    @Type(type="org.joda.time.contrib.hibernate.PersistentDateTime")
    public DateTime getBirthDate() {
        return birthDate;
    }

    // Setter methods omitted
```

```
    public String toString() {
        return "Contact - Id: " + id + ", First name: " + firstName
            + ", Last name: " + lastName + ", Birthday: " + birthDate;
    }
}
```

As shown in Listing 16-3, standard JPA annotations are used. We also use JodaTime's DateTime class for the birthDate attribute.

Let's proceed to the service layer; Listing 16-4 shows the ContactService interface, with the services we want to expose.

Listing 16-4. The ContactService Interface

```
package com.apress.prospring3.ch16.service;

import java.util.List;

import com.apress.prospring3.ch16.domain.Contact;

public interface ContactService {

    public List<Contact> findAll();

    public List<Contact> findByFirstName(String firstName);

    public Contact findById(Long id);

    public Contact save(Contact contact);

    public void delete(Contact contact);
}
```

The methods should be self-explanatory. Because we will use Spring Data JPA's repository support, we will implement the ContactRepository interface, as shown in Listing 16-5.

Listing 16-5. The ContactRepository Interface

```
package com.apress.prospring3.ch16.repository;

import java.util.List;

import org.springframework.data.repository.CrudRepository;

import com.apress.prospring3.ch16.domain.Contact;

public interface ContactRepository extends CrudRepository<Contact, Long> {

    public List<Contact> findByFirstName(String firstName);
}
```

As discussed in Chapter 10, by extending the CrudRepository<T,ID extends Serializable> interface, for the methods in ContactService, we only need to explicitly declare the findByFirstName() method.

Listing 16-6 shows the implementation class of the ContactService interface.

Listing 16-6. The ContactServiceImpl Class

```
package com.apress.prospring3.ch16.service.jpa;

import java.util.List;

import org.springframework.beans.factory.annotation.Autowired;
import org.springframework.stereotype.Repository;
import org.springframework.stereotype.Service;
import org.springframework.transaction.annotation.Transactional;

import com.apress.prospring3.ch16.domain.Contact;
import com.apress.prospring3.ch16.repository.ContactRepository;
import com.apress.prospring3.ch16.service.ContactService;
import com.google.common.collect.Lists;

@Service("contactService")
@Repository
@Transactional
public class ContactServiceImpl implements ContactService {

    @Autowired
    private ContactRepository contactRepository;

    @Transactional(readOnly=true)
    public List<Contact> findAll() {
        return Lists.newArrayList(contactRepository.findAll());
    }

    @Transactional(readOnly=true)
    public List<Contact> findByFirstName(String firstName) {
        return contactRepository.findByFirstName(firstName);
    }

    @Transactional(readOnly=true)
    public Contact findById(Long id) {
        return contactRepository.findOne(id);
    }

    public Contact save(Contact contact) {
        return contactRepository.save(contact);
    }

    public void delete(Contact contact) {
        contactRepository.delete(contact);
    }
}
```

If you have any problems understanding Listing 16-6, please refer to Chapter 10 for a detailed description of implementing a service layer using JPA as the persistence provider. The implementation is basically completed, and the next step is to configure the service in Spring's ApplicationContext within the web project, which will be discussed in the next section.

Configuring ContactService

To set up the service layer within the Spring MVC project, we create an individual configuration file called datasource-tx-jpa.xml under the folder /src/main/resource. Listing 16-7 shows the configuration file.

Listing 16-7. The datasource-tx-jpa.xml Configuration File

```xml
<?xml version="1.0" encoding="UTF-8"?>
<beans xmlns="http://www.springframework.org/schema/beans"
    xmlns:xsi="http://www.w3.org/2001/XMLSchema-instance"
    xmlns:context="http://www.springframework.org/schema/context"
    xmlns:jdbc="http://www.springframework.org/schema/jdbc"
    xmlns:jpa="http://www.springframework.org/schema/data/jpa"
    xmlns:tx="http://www.springframework.org/schema/tx"
    xsi:schemaLocation="http://www.springframework.org/schema/beans
        http://www.springframework.org/schema/beans/spring-beans-3.1.xsd
        http://www.springframework.org/schema/context
        http://www.springframework.org/schema/context/spring-context-3.1.xsd
        http://www.springframework.org/schema/jdbc
        http://www.springframework.org/schema/jdbc/spring-jdbc-3.1.xsd
        http://www.springframework.org/schema/data/jpa
        http://www.springframework.org/schema/data/jpa/spring-jpa-1.0.xsd
        http://www.springframework.org/schema/tx
        http://www.springframework.org/schema/tx/spring-tx-3.1.xsd">

    <jdbc:embedded-database id="dataSource" type="H2">
        <jdbc:script location="classpath:schema.sql"/>
        <jdbc:script location="classpath:test-data.sql"/>
    </jdbc:embedded-database>

    <bean id="transactionManager" class="org.springframework.orm.jpa.JpaTransactionManager">
        <property name="entityManagerFactory" ref="emf"/>
    </bean>

    <tx:annotation-driven transaction-manager="transactionManager" />

    <bean id="emf" class="org.springframework.orm.jpa.LocalContainerEntityManagerFactoryBean">
        <property name="dataSource" ref="dataSource" />
        <property name="jpaVendorAdapter">
            <bean class="org.springframework.orm.jpa.vendor.HibernateJpaVendorAdapter" />
        </property>
        <property name="packagesToScan" value="com.apress.prospring3.ch16.domain"/>
        <property name="jpaProperties">
            <props>
                <prop key="hibernate.dialect">
                        org.hibernate.dialect.H2Dialect
                </prop>
                <prop key="hibernate.max_fetch_depth">3</prop>
                <prop key="hibernate.jdbc.fetch_size">50</prop>
                <prop key="hibernate.jdbc.batch_size">10</prop>
                <prop key="hibernate.show_sql">true</prop>
            </props>
        </property>
```

```
    </bean>

    <context:annotation-config/>

    <jpa:repositories base-package="com.apress.prospring3.ch16.repository"
                       entity-manager-factory-ref="emf"
                       transaction-manager-ref="transactionManager"/>
</beans>
```

For details on the definition of each bean, please refer to Chapter 10. Then, we need to import the configuration into Spring's root WebApplicationContext. For a Spring MVC template project, the file is located at /src/main/webapp/WEB-INF/spring/root-context.xml. Listing 16-8 shows the revised file.

Listing 16-8. The root-context.xml File

```
<?xml version="1.0" encoding="UTF-8"?>
<beans xmlns="http://www.springframework.org/schema/beans"
    xmlns:xsi="http://www.w3.org/2001/XMLSchema-instance"
    xmlns:context="http://www.springframework.org/schema/context"
    xsi:schemaLocation="http://www.springframework.org/schema/beans
        http://www.springframework.org/schema/beans/spring-beans-3.1.xsd
        http://www.springframework.org/schema/context
        http://www.springframework.org/schema/context/spring-context-3.1.xsd">

    <import resource="classpath:datasource-tx-jpa.xml" />

    <context:component-scan
        base-package="com.apress.prospring3.ch16.service.jpa" />
</beans>
```

First the context namespace is added to the configuration file. Then, the file datasource-tx-jpa.xml was imported into the WebApplicationContext, and finally, we instruct Spring to scan for the specified package for Spring beans.

Now, the service layer is completed and ready to be exposed and used by remote clients.

Using the Spring HTTP Invoker

If the application you are going to communicate with is also Spring-powered, using the Spring HTTP invoker is a good choice. It provides an extremely simple way to expose the services within the Spring WebApplicationContext to remote clients also using the Spring HTTP invoker to invoke the service. The procedures for exposing and accessing the service are elaborated in the following sections.

Exposing the Service

To expose the service, in the root-context.xml configuration file, add the bean definition in Listing 16-9.

Listing 16-9. Bean for Exposing Contact Service Using HTTP Invoker

```
    <bean name="contactExporter"
class="org.springframework.remoting.httpinvoker.HttpInvokerServiceExporter">
        <property name="service" ref="contactService" />
```

```
    <property name="serviceInterface"
        value="com.apress.prospring3.ch16.service.ContactService" />
</bean>
```

As shown in Listing 16-9, a contactExporter bean was defined with the HttpInvokerServiceExporter class, which is for exporting any Spring bean as a service via the HTTP invoker. Within the bean, two properties are defined. The first one is the service property, indicating the bean providing the service. For this property, the contactService bean is injected. The second property is the interface type to expose, which is the com.apress.prospring3.ch16.service.ContactService interface.

Next, we need to define a servlet within the web deployment descriptor (/src/main/webapp/WEB-INF/web.xml) for the service. Listing 16-10 shows the code snippet to add into the web.xml file.

Listing 16-10. *Servlet Definition for the HTTP Invoker*

```
<!-- Spring Remoting with HTTP Invoker -->
<servlet>
    <servlet-name>contactExporter</servlet-name>
    <servlet-class>
        org.springframework.web.context.support.HttpRequestHandlerServlet
    </servlet-class>
</servlet>

<servlet-mapping>
    <servlet-name>contactExporter</servlet-name>
    <url-pattern>/remoting/ContactService</url-pattern>
</servlet-mapping>
```

As shown in Listing 16-10, a servlet with the class HttpRequestHandlerServlet is defined, which is used to expose the Spring exporter defined in the WebApplicationContext. Note the servlet name (contactExporter) should match with the bean name of the exporter (see Listing 16-9; the bean name is also contactExporter). Then, the servlet is mapped to the URL /remoting/ContactService under the web context (i.e., http://localhost:8080/ch16) of the application.

Until now, if you are using the STS project's default setting, the project should have been rebuilt and deployed to the tc Server. Now we can proceed to develop the client to invoke the service.

Invoking the Service

Invoking a service via the Spring HTTP invoker is very simple. First we configure a Spring ApplicationContext, as shown in Listing 16-11 (http-invoker-app-context.xml).

Listing 16-11. *Spring ApplicationContext for HTTP Invoker Client*

```
<?xml version="1.0" encoding="UTF-8"?>
<beans xmlns="http://www.springframework.org/schema/beans"
    xmlns:xsi="http://www.w3.org/2001/XMLSchema-instance"
    xsi:schemaLocation="http://www.springframework.org/schema/beans
        http://www.springframework.org/schema/beans/spring-beans-3.1.xsd">

    <bean id="remoteContactService"
class="org.springframework.remoting.httpinvoker.HttpInvokerProxyFactoryBean">
        <property name="serviceUrl"
            value="http://localhost:8080/ch16/remoting/ContactService" />
        <property name="serviceInterface"
```

```
                    value="com.apress.prospring3.ch16.service.ContactService" />
    </bean>
```

```
</beans>
```

As shown in Listing 16-11, for the client side, a bean of type HttpInvokerProxyFactoryBean is declared. Two properties are set. The serviceUrl specifies the location of the remote service, which is http://localhost:8080/ch16/remoting/ContactService. The second property is the interface of the service (i.e., ContactService interface). If you are developing another project for the client, you need to have the ContactService interface and the Contact entity class within your client application's classpath.

Listing 16-12 shows a main class for invoking the remote service.

Listing 16-12. The HttpInvokerClientSample Class

```java
package com.apress.prospring3.ch16.remoting;

import java.util.List;

import org.springframework.context.support.GenericXmlApplicationContext;

import com.apress.prospring3.ch16.domain.Contact;
import com.apress.prospring3.ch16.service.ContactService;

public class HttpInvokerClientSample {

    public static void main(String[] args) {

        GenericXmlApplicationContext ctx = new GenericXmlApplicationContext();
        ctx.load("classpath:http-invoker-app-context.xml");
        ctx.refresh();

        ContactService contactService =
            ctx.getBean("remoteContactService", ContactService.class);

        // Find all contacts
        System.out.println("Finding all contacts");
        List<Contact> contacts = contactService.findAll();
        listContacts(contacts);

        // Find contacts by first name
        System.out.println("Finding contact with first name equals Clarence");
        contacts = contactService.findByFirstName("Clarence");
        listContacts(contacts);

    }

    private static void listContacts(List<Contact> contacts) {

        for (Contact contact: contacts) {
            System.out.println(contact);
        }
        System.out.println("");

    }
}
```

As shown in Listing 16-12, the program is just like any other stand-alone Spring application. The ApplicationContext is initialized, and then the contactService bean is retrieved. Then we just call its methods like a local application. Running the program produces the following output:

```
Finding all contacts
Contact - Id: 1, First name: Clarence, Last name: Ho, Birthday: 1980-07-30T00:00:00.000+08:00
Contact - Id: 2, First name: Scott, Last name: Tiger, Birthday: 1990-11-02T00:00:00.000+08:00
Contact - Id: 3, First name: John, Last name: Smith, Birthday: 1964-02-28T00:00:00.000+08:00

Finding contact with first name equals Clarence
Contact - Id: 1, First name: Clarence, Last name: Ho, Birthday: 1980-07-30T00:00:00.000+08:00
```

In the previous output, you can see the findAll() and findByFirstName() methods are called, and the results are returned.

Using JMS in Spring

Using message-oriented middleware (generally referred to as an *MQ server*) is another popular way to support communication between applications. The main benefits of a message queue (MQ) server is that it provides an asynchronous and loosely coupled way for application integration. In the Java world, JMS is the standard for connecting to an MQ server for sending or receive messages.

An MQ server maintains a list of queues and topics for which applications can connect to and send and receive messages. The following is a brief description of the difference between a queue and a topic:

- *Queue*: A queue is used to support a point-to-point message exchange model. When a producer sends a message to a queue, the MQ server keeps the message within the queue and delivers it to one and only one consumer the next time the consumer connects.

- *Topic*: A topic is used to support the publish-subscribe model. Any number of clients can subscribe to the message within a topic. When a message arrives for that topic, the MQ server delivers it it to all clients that have subscribed to the message. This model is particularly useful when you have multiple applications that will be interested in the same piece of information (for example, a news feed).

In JMS, a producer connects to an MQ server and sends a message to a queue or topic. A consumer also connects to the MQ server and listens to a queue or topics for messages of interest. In JMS 1.1, the API was unified so the producer and consumer don't need to deal with different APIs for interacting with queues and topics. In this section, we will focus on the point-to-point style for using queues, which is a more commonly used pattern within an enterprise.

To develop and test a JMS application, an MQ server is required. In this section, we will use the Apache ActiveMQ server (activemq.apache.org), which is a very popular open source MQ server.

To prepare for the sample, several new Maven dependencies are required, as listed in Table 16-2. Please add them into your project.

Table 16-2. Maven Dependencies for JMS and ActiveMQ

Group ID	Artifact ID	Version	Description
org.springframework	spring-jms	3.1.0.RELEASE	Spring JMS module
org.apache.activemq	activemq-core	5.5.1	ActiveMQ Java library
javax.jms	jms-api	1.1-rev-1	JMS 1.1 API

Setting up an ActiveMQ server and using JMS with Spring are discussed in the following sections.

Setting Up ActiveMQ

Setting up ActiveMQ for development use is easy. First, download the latest release from ActiveMQ web site (activemq.apache.org/download.html) and extract the archive into a folder on your computer. At the time of this writing, the latest release is 5.5.1.

Upon extraction, navigate to the bin folder, and run the activemq command (for Windows, it's activemq.bat, while for Unix/Linux, it's activemq). The server will be started, and upon completion, you will see the output like the one in Figure 16-9.

```
C:\apache-activemq-5.5.1\bin>activemq
Java Runtime: Sun Microsystems Inc. 1.6.0_29 C:\Program Files\Java\jdk1.6.0_29\jre
  Heap sizes: current=125056k free=122439k max=466048k
    JVM args: -Dcom.sun.management.jmxremote -Xmx512M -Dorg.apache.activemq.UseDedicatedTaskRunner=true -Djava.util.logg
ing.config.file=logging.properties -Dactivemq.classpath=C:\apache-activemq-5.5.1\bin\../conf;C:\apache-activemq-5.5.1\bi
n\../conf; -Dactivemq.home=C:\apache-activemq-5.5.1\bin\.. -Dactivemq.base=C:\apache-activemq-5.5.1\bin\..
ACTIVEMQ_HOME: C:\apache-activemq-5.5.1\bin\..
ACTIVEMQ_BASE: C:\apache-activemq-5.5.1\bin\..
Loading message broker from: xbean:activemq.xml
 INFO | Refreshing org.apache.activemq.xbean.XBeanBrokerFactory$1@6c4fc156: startup date [Wed Nov 30 14:48:35 CST 2011];
 root of context hierarchy
 WARN | destroyApplicationContextOnStop parameter is deprecated, please use shutdown hooks instead
 INFO | PListStore:C:\apache-activemq-5.5.1\bin\..\data\localhost\tmp_storage started
 INFO | Using Persistence Adapter: KahaDBPersistenceAdapter[C:\apache-activemq-5.5.1\bin\..\data\kahadb]
 INFO | KahaDB is version 3
 INFO | Recovering from the journal ...
 INFO | Recovery replayed 1 operations from the journal in 0.015 seconds.
 INFO | ActiveMQ 5.5.1 JMS Message Broker (localhost) is starting
 INFO | For help or more information please see: http://activemq.apache.org/
 INFO | Listening for connections at: tcp://Clarence-PC:61616
 INFO | Connector openwire Started
 INFO | ActiveMQ JMS Message Broker (localhost, ID:Clarence-PC-63489-1322635717052-0:1) started
 INFO | jetty-7.1.6.v20100715
 INFO | ActiveMQ WebConsole initialized.
 INFO | Initializing Spring FrameworkServlet 'dispatcher'
 INFO | ActiveMQ Console at http://0.0.0.0:8161/admin
 INFO | ActiveMQ Web Demos at http://0.0.0.0:8161/demo
 INFO | RESTful file access application at http://0.0.0.0:8161/fileserver
 INFO | Started SelectChannelConnector@0.0.0.0:8161
■
```

Figure 16-9. Starting the ActiveMQ server

On the screen, you will see that the ActiveMQ server is listening to port 61616 for a JMS connection. In addition, an embedded web server was also started for administration, which is at localhost:8161/admin. Open a web browser and access the administration web site. The first page you see will be like the one in Figure 16-10.

Figure 16-10. *ActiveMQ Server Admin web site*

Let's create a queue for testing. In the top menu, click Queues; then in the text box, enter **prospring3** as the queue name and click the Create button. Upon completion, the queue will be created, as shown in Figure 16-11.

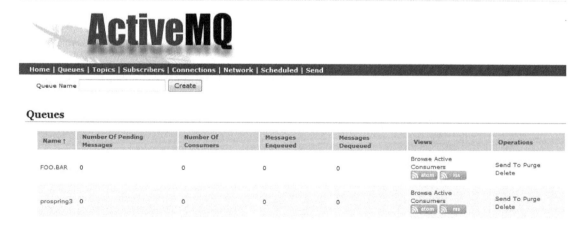

Figure 16-11. *Creating a queue in ActiveMQ*

Up to this point, the setup of ActiveMQ server has been completed, and we can proceed to develop a JMS client using Spring to connect to the server and receive messages.

Implementing a JMS Listener in Spring

To develop a message listener, we need to create a class that implements the javax.jms.MessageListener interface and implements its onMessage() method. Listing 16-13 shows the class.

Listing 16-13. A JMS Message Listener Class

```
package com.apress.prospring3.ch16.jms.listener;

import javax.jms.JMSException;
import javax.jms.Message;
import javax.jms.MessageListener;
import javax.jms.TextMessage;

import org.slf4j.Logger;
import org.slf4j.LoggerFactory;

public class SimpleMessageListener implements MessageListener {

    private static final Logger logger =
    LoggerFactory.getLogger(SimpleMessageListener.class);

    public void onMessage(Message message) {

        TextMessage textMessage = (TextMessage) message;

        try {
            logger.info("Message received: " + textMessage.getText());
        } catch (JMSException ex) {
            logger.error("JMS error", ex);
        }

    }
}
```

As shown in Listing 16-13, in the onMessage() method, an instance of the javax.jms.Message interface will be passed upon message arrival. Within the method, the message was cast to an instance of the javax.jms.TextMessage interface, and the message body in text was retrieved using the TextMessage.getText() method. For a list of possible message formats, please refer to JEE's online documentation (http://docs.oracle.com/javaee/6/api/javax/jms/Message.html).

Having the message listener in place, the next step is to define the Spring ApplicationContext configuration. Listing 16-14 shows the file (jms-listener-app-context.xml).

Listing 16-14. JMS Message Listener Configuration

```
<?xml version="1.0" encoding="UTF-8"?>
<beans xmlns="http://www.springframework.org/schema/beans"
    xmlns:xsi="http://www.w3.org/2001/XMLSchema-instance"
    xmlns:jms="http://www.springframework.org/schema/jms"
```

```
    xmlns:p="http://www.springframework.org/schema/p"
    xsi:schemaLocation="http://www.springframework.org/schema/beans
        http://www.springframework.org/schema/beans/spring-beans-3.1.xsd
        http://www.springframework.org/schema/jms
        http://www.springframework.org/schema/jms/spring-jms-3.1.xsd">

    <bean id="connectionFactory"
        class="org.apache.activemq.ActiveMQConnectionFactory"
        p:brokerURL="tcp://localhost:61616" />

    <bean id="simpleMessageListener"
class="com.apress.prospring3.ch16.jms.listener.SimpleMessageListener"/>

    <jms:listener-container container-type="default"
        connection-factory="connectionFactory" acknowledge="auto">
        <jms:listener destination="prospring3" ref="simpleMessageListener"
            method="onMessage" />
    </jms:listener-container>

</beans>
```

As shown in Listing 16-14, we first declare a javax.jms.ConnectionFactory interface provided by the ActiveMQ Java library (the ActiveMQConnectionFactory class). Note that the property brokerURL should be the same as the one when you start up ActiveMQ, as shown in Figure 16-9. Then, a bean of type SimpleMessageListener is declared. Finally, we use the handy <jms:listener-container> tag provided by Spring's jms namespace to declare a message listener, providing the destination (i.e., the prospring3 queue), the bean reference, and the method to invoke on message arrival.

Listing 16-15 shows the main testing program to test the receiving message.

Listing 16-15. Testing JMS Message Listener

```
package com.apress.prospring3.ch16.jms;

import org.springframework.context.support.GenericXmlApplicationContext;

public class JmsListenerSample {

    public static void main(String[] args) {

        GenericXmlApplicationContext ctx = new GenericXmlApplicationContext();
        ctx.load("classpath:jms-listener-app-context.xml");
        ctx.refresh();

        while (true) {
        }

    }
}
```

There is nothing special about the program. It just initializes the ApplicationContext and then loops indefinitely. Just run the program, and it will connect to ActiveMQ and wait for messages to arrive in the prospring3 queue. Now let's try to send a message to the prospring3 queue. In ActiveMQ admin web site, click the Send option in the top menu, enter the queue name and message body, and then click Send, as shown in Figure 16-12.

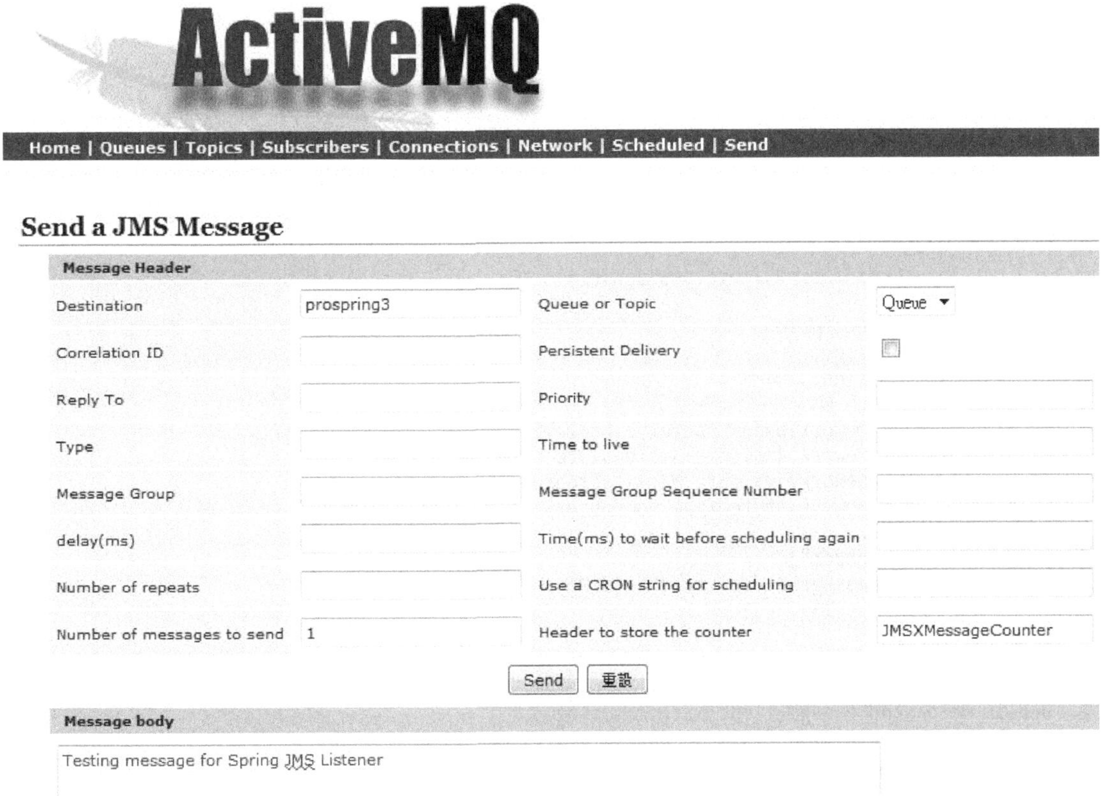

Figure 16-12. Sending a message in ActiveMQ

After the Send button is clicked, you will see the message output by the listener in STS's output console:

```
INFO : com.apress.prospring3.ch16.jms.listener.SimpleMessageListener – Message received:
Testing message for Spring JMS Listener
```

You can see how easy it is to set up a JMS listener in Spring for remote communication. In a JEE application server environment, you just need to configure the connection factory using JNDI lookup within the Spring configuration file. No other code change is required.

Sending JMS Messages in Spring

Let's see how to send messages using JMS in Spring. We will use the handy `org.springframework.jms.core.JmsTemplate` class for the purpose. First we will develop a `MessageSender` interface and its implementation class, `SimpleMessageSender`. Listings 16-16 and 16-17 show the interface and the class, respectively.

Listing 16-16. The MessageSender Interface

```
package com.apress.prospring3.ch16.jms.sender;

public interface MessageSender {

    public void sendMessage(String message);
}
```

Listing 16-17. The SimpleMessageSender Class

```
package com.apress.prospring3.ch16.jms.sender;

import javax.jms.JMSException;
import javax.jms.Message;
import javax.jms.Session;

import org.springframework.beans.factory.annotation.Autowired;
import org.springframework.jms.core.JmsTemplate;
import org.springframework.jms.core.MessageCreator;
import org.springframework.stereotype.Component;

@Component("messageSender")
public class SimpleMessageSender implements MessageSender {

    @Autowired
    private JmsTemplate jmsTemplate;

    public void sendMessage(final String message) {
        this.jmsTemplate.send(new MessageCreator() {
            public Message createMessage(Session session)
                throws JMSException {
                return session.createTextMessage(message);
            }
        });
    }
}
```

As shown in Listing 16-17, an instance of JmsTemplate is injected. In the sendMessage() method, we call the JmsTemplate.send() method, with an in-place construction of an instance of the org.springframework.jms.core.MessageCreator interface. In the MessageCreator instance, the createMessage() method is implemented to create a new instance of TextMessage that will be sent to ActiveMQ.

Listing 16-18 shows the Spring configuration of the JMS sender (jms-sender-app-context.xml).

Listing 16-18. Spring Configuration for Sending Messages

```
<?xml version="1.0" encoding="UTF-8"?>
<beans xmlns="http://www.springframework.org/schema/beans"
    xmlns:xsi="http://www.w3.org/2001/XMLSchema-instance"
    xmlns:context="http://www.springframework.org/schema/context"
    xmlns:jms="http://www.springframework.org/schema/jms"
    xmlns:p="http://www.springframework.org/schema/p"
```

```
    xsi:schemaLocation="http://www.springframework.org/schema/beans
        http://www.springframework.org/schema/beans/spring-beans-3.1.xsd
        http://www.springframework.org/schema/context
        http://www.springframework.org/schema/context/spring-context-3.1.xsd
        http://www.springframework.org/schema/jms
        http://www.springframework.org/schema/jms/spring-jms-3.1.xsd">

    <context:annotation-config/>

    <bean id="connectionFactory"
        class="org.apache.activemq.ActiveMQConnectionFactory"
        p:brokerURL="tcp://localhost:61616" />

    <bean id="jmsTemplate" class="org.springframework.jms.core.JmsTemplate">
        <constructor-arg name="connectionFactory" ref="connectionFactory"/>
        <property name="defaultDestinationName" value="prospring3"/>
    </bean>

    <context:component-scan
        base-package="com.apress.prospring3.ch16.jms.sender"/>

</beans>
```

As shown in Listing 16-18, the connectionFactory bean is defined as usual. In addition, an instance of JmsTemplate is declared, with the connectionFactory as the constructor argument, and the defaultDestinationName is set to the prospring3 queue.

Listing 16-19 shows the main testing program for sending messages.

Listing 16-19. Test Sending Messages

```java
package com.apress.prospring3.ch16.jms;

import org.springframework.context.support.GenericXmlApplicationContext;

import com.apress.prospring3.ch16.jms.sender.MessageSender;

public class JmsSenderSample {

    public static void main(String[] args) {

        GenericXmlApplicationContext ctx = new GenericXmlApplicationContext();
        ctx.load("classpath:jms-sender-app-context.xml");
        ctx.refresh();

        // Send message
        MessageSender messageSender = ctx.getBean("messageSender",
            MessageSender.class);

        messageSender.sendMessage("Clarence testing JMS message");
    }

}
```

The program is simple. Running the program will send the message to the queue. If the JmsListenerSample class is still running (or you can run it now), you will get the message with the following output:

```
INFO : com.apress.prospring3.ch16.jms.listener.SimpleMessageListener - Message received:
Clarence testing JMS message
```

In real life, the message will most likely be in XML format, representing a piece of business information (for example, an online order, transaction, booking, and so on).

This section covers only the basic usage scenarios of JMS. For details, please refer to the online JEE tutorial at http://docs.oracle.com/javaee/5/tutorial/doc/bncdq.html.

Using RESTful-WS in Spring

Nowadays, RESTful-WS is perhaps the most widely used technology for remote access. From remote service invocation via HTTP to supporting an Ajax-style interactive web frontend, RESTful-WS is being adopted intensively.

There are a number of reasons for the popularity of RESTful web services:

- *Easy to understand*: RESTful web services are designed around the HTTP protocol. The URL, together with the HTTP method, specifies the intention of the request. For example, the URL http://somedomain.com/restful/customer/1 with an HTTP method of GET means that the client wants to retrieve the customer information where the customer ID equals 1.

- *Lightweight*: RESTful is much more lightweight when compared to SOAP-based web services, which include a large amount of metadata to describe which service the client wants to invoke. For a RESTful request and response, it's simply an HTTP request and response like any other web application.

- *Firewall friendly*: Because RESTful web services are designed to be accessed via HTTP (or HTTPS), the application becomes much more firewall friendly and easily accessed by remote clients.

In this section, we will discuss the basic concepts of RESTful-WS and Spring's support of RESTful-WS through its Spring MVC module.

Introducing RESTful Web Services

The REST in RESTful-WS is short for REpresentational State Transfer, which is an architectural style. REST defines a set of architectural constraints that together describe a "uniform interface" for accessing resources.

The main concepts of the "uniform interface" include the identification of resources and the manipulation of resources through representations.

For the identification of resources, a piece of information should be accessible via a Uniform Resource Identifier (URI). For example, the URL http://www.somedomain.com/api/contact/1 is a URI that represents a resource, which is a piece of contact information with an identifier of 1. If the contact with an identifier of 1 does not exist, the client will get a 404 HTTP error, just like a page not found in a web site. Another example, http://www.somedomain.com/api/contacts, is a URI that represents a resourcethat is a list of contact information.

Those identifiable resources will be able to be managed through various representations, as shown in Table 16-3.

Table 16-3. Representations for Manipulating Resources

Representation	Description
GET	GET retrieves a representation of a resource.
HEAD	Identical to GET, without response body. Typically used for getting a header.
POST	POST creates a new resource.
PUT	PUT updates a resource.
DELETE	DELETE deletes a resource.
OPTIONS	OPTIONS retrieves allowed HTTP methods.

For a detail description of RESTful web services, we recommend the book *Ajax and REST Recipes, A Problem-Solution Approach* (Apress, 2006).

Adding Required Dependencies for Samples

To develop the samples in this section, a number of dependencies are required, as listed in Table 16-4. Add them into your project.

Table 16-4. Maven Dependencies for RESTful Web Services

Group ID	Artifact ID	Version	Description
org.springframework	spring-oxm	3.1.0.RELEASE	Spring object-to-XML mapping module.
org.codehaus.jackson	jackson-mapper-lgpl	1.9.2	Jackson JSON processor to support data in JSON format.
org.codehaus.castor	castor-xml	1.3.2	The Castor XML library will be used for marshaling and unmarshaling of XML data.
org.springframework.security	spring-security-core	3.1.0.RELEASE	Spring Security core module.
org.springframework.security	spring-security-web	3.1.0.RELEASE	Spring Security web module for securing RESTful-WS.
org.springframework.security	spring-security-config	3.1.0.RELEASE	Spring Security configuration module.
org.apache.httpcomponents	httpclient	4.1.2	Apache HTTP Components project. The HTTP client library will be used for RESTful-WS invocation.

The Contact RESTful Web Service

When developing a RESTful-WS application, the first step is to design the service structure, which includes what HTTP methods will be supported, together with the target URLs for different operations.

For our contact RESTful web services, we want to support query, create, update, and delete operations. For querying, we want to support retrieving all contacts or a single contact by ID.

The services will be implemented as a Spring MVC controller. The name is the `ContactController` class, under the package `com.apress.prospring3.ch16.web.restful.controller`. The URL pattern, HTTP method, description, and corresponding controller methods are shown in Table 16-5. For the URLs, they all use the prefix `http://localhost:8080/ch16/restful`. In terms of data format, both XML and JSON will be supported. The corresponding format will be provided according to the accept media type of the client's HTTP request header.

Table 16-5. Design of RESTful Web Services

URL	HTTP Method	Description	Controller Method
/contact/listdata	GET	To retrieve all contacts	listData(…)
/contact/{id}	GET	To retrieve a single contact with the specified ID	findContactById(…)
/contact	POST	To create a new contact	create(…)
/contact/{id}	PUT	To update an existing contact with the specified ID	update(…)
/contact	DELETE	To delete a contact with ID	delete(…)

Using Spring MVC to Expose RESTful Web Services

In this section, we will show you how to use Spring MVC to expose the contact services as RESTful web services as designed in the previous section.

First we will create another domain object, the `Contacts` class. Listing 16-20 shows the `Contacts` class.

Listing 16-20. The Contacts Class

```
package com.apress.prospring3.ch16.domain;

import java.io.Serializable;
import java.util.List;

public class Contacts implements Serializable {

    private List<Contact> contacts;

    public Contacts() {
    }

    public Contacts(List<Contact> contacts) {
        this.contacts = contacts;
```

```
    }

    // Getter/setter methods omitted
}
```

As shown in Listing 16-20, the Contacts class has a single property, which is a list of Contact objects. The purpose is to support the transformation from a list of contacts (returned by the listData() method within the ContactController class) into XML or JSON format.

Configuring Castor XML

To support the transformation of the returned contact information into XML format, we will use the Castor XML library (http://castor.codehaus.org). Castor supports several modes between POJO and XML transformation, and in this sample, we will use an XML file to define the mapping. Listing 16-21 shows the mapping file (/src/main/resources/oxm-mapping.xml).

Listing 16-21. Defining Castor XML Mapping

```
<mapping>

    <class name="com.apress.prospring3.ch16.domain.Contacts">
        <field name="contacts" type="com.apress.prospring3.ch16.domain.Contact"↵
collection="arraylist">
            <bind-xml name="contact"/>
        </field>
    </class>

    <class name="com.apress.prospring3.ch16.domain.Contact" identity="id">

        <map-to xml="contact" />

        <field name="id" type="long">
            <bind-xml name="id" node="element"/>
        </field>
        <field name="firstName" type="string">
            <bind-xml name="firstName" node="element" />
        </field>
        <field name="lastName" type="string">
            <bind-xml name="lastName" node="element" />
        </field>
        <field name="birthDate" type="string" handler="dateHandler">
            <bind-xml name="birthDate" node="element" />
        </field>
        <field name="version" type="integer">
            <bind-xml name="version" node="element" />
        </field>

    </class>

    <field-handler name="dateHandler" class="com.apress.prospring3.ch16↵
.xml.handler.DateTimeFieldHandler">
        <param name="date-format" value="yyyy-MM-dd"/>
    </field-handler>
</mapping>
```

As shown in Listing 16-21, two mappings are defined. The first <class> tag maps the Contacts class, within which its contacts property (a List of Contact objects) is mapped using the <bind-xml name="contact"/> tag (note the characters in bold). The Contact object is then mapped (with the <map-to xml="contact" /> tag within the second <class> tag). In addition, to support the transformation from JodaTime's DateTime type (for Contact's birthDate attribute), we implement a custom Castor field handler. Listing 16-22 shows the field handler.

Listing 16-22. Custom Field Handler for DateTime Type in Castor

```
package com.apress.prospring3.ch16.xml.handler;

import java.util.Properties;

import org.exolab.castor.mapping.GeneralizedFieldHandler;
import org.exolab.castor.mapping.ValidityException;
import org.joda.time.DateTime;
import org.joda.time.format.DateTimeFormat;
import org.joda.time.format.DateTimeFormatter;

public class DateTimeFieldHandler extends GeneralizedFieldHandler {

    private static String dateFormatPattern;

    public void setConfiguration(Properties config) throws ValidityException {
        dateFormatPattern = config.getProperty("date-format");
    }

    public Object convertUponGet(Object value) {

        DateTime dateTime = (DateTime) value;

        return format(dateTime);
    }

    public Object convertUponSet(Object value) {

        String dateTimeString = (String) value;

        return parse(dateTimeString);
    }

    public Class<DateTime> getFieldType() {
        return DateTime.class;
    }

    protected static String format(final DateTime dateTime) {

        String dateTimeString = "";

        if (dateTime != null) {
            DateTimeFormatter dateTimeFormatter =
                DateTimeFormat.forPattern(dateFormatPattern);
            dateTimeString = dateTimeFormatter.print(dateTime);
```

```
        }

        return dateTimeString;

    }

    protected static DateTime parse(final String dateTimeString) {

        DateTime dateTime = new DateTime();

        if (dateTimeString != null) {
            DateTimeFormatter dateTimeFormatter =
            DateTimeFormat.forPattern(dateFormatPattern);
            dateTime = dateTimeFormatter.parseDateTime(dateTimeString);
        }

        return dateTime;

    }
}
```

As shown in Listing 16-22, we extend Castor's org.exolab.castor.mapping.GeneralizedFieldHandler class and implement the convertUponGet(), convertUponSet(), and getFieldType() methods. Within the methods, we implement the logic to perform the transformation between DateTime and String for use by Castor.

In addition, we also define a properties file for use with Castor. Listing 16-23 shows the file (src/main/resources/castor.properties).

Listing 16-23. The castor.properties File

```
org.exolab.castor.indent=true
```

As shown in Listing 16-23, the property instructs Castor to generate XML with an indent, which is much easier to read when testing.

Implementing the ContactController

The next step is to implement the controller class, ContactController. Listing 16-24 shows the ContactController class, which has all the methods in Table 16-5 implemented.

Listing 16-24. The ContactController Class

```
package com.apress.prospring3.ch16.web.restful.controller;

import org.slf4j.Logger;
import org.slf4j.LoggerFactory;
import org.springframework.beans.factory.annotation.Autowired;
import org.springframework.stereotype.Controller;
import org.springframework.web.bind.annotation.PathVariable;
import org.springframework.web.bind.annotation.RequestBody;
import org.springframework.web.bind.annotation.RequestMapping;
import org.springframework.web.bind.annotation.RequestMethod;
import org.springframework.web.bind.annotation.ResponseBody;
```

```
import com.apress.prospring3.ch16.domain.Contact;
import com.apress.prospring3.ch16.domain.Contacts;
import com.apress.prospring3.ch16.service.ContactService;

@Controller
@RequestMapping(value="/contact")
public class ContactController {

    final Logger logger = LoggerFactory.getLogger(ContactController.class);

    @Autowired
    private ContactService contactService;

    @RequestMapping(value = "/listdata", method = RequestMethod.GET)
    @ResponseBody
    public Contacts listData() {
        return new Contacts(contactService.findAll());
    }

    @RequestMapping(value="/{id}", method=RequestMethod.GET)
    @ResponseBody
    public Contact findContactById(@PathVariable Long id) {
        return contactService.findById(id);
    }

    @RequestMapping(value="/", method=RequestMethod.POST)
    @ResponseBody
    public Contact create(@RequestBody Contact contact) {
        logger.info("Creating contact: " + contact);
        contactService.save(contact);
        logger.info("Contact created successfully with info: " + contact);
        return contact;
    }

    @RequestMapping(value="/{id}", method=RequestMethod.PUT)
    @ResponseBody
    public void update(@RequestBody Contact contact,
        @PathVariable Long id) {
        logger.info("Updating contact: " + contact);
        contactService.save(contact);
        logger.info("Contact updated successfully with info: " + contact);
    }

    @RequestMapping(value="/{id}", method=RequestMethod.DELETE)
    @ResponseBody
    public void delete(@PathVariable Long id) {
        logger.info("Deleting contact with id: " + id);
        Contact contact = contactService.findById(id);
        contactService.delete(contact);
        logger.info("Contact deleted successfully");
    }
}
```

The main points about Listing 16-24 are as follows:

- The class is annotated with @Controller, indicating that it's a Spring MVC controller.

- The class-level annotation @RequestMapping(value="/contact") indicates that this controller will be mapped to all URLs under the main web context. In this sample, all URLs under http://localhost:8080/ch16/contact will be handled by this controller.

- The ContactService within the service layer implemented earlier this chapter is autowired into the controller.

- The @RequestMapping annotation for each method indicates the URL pattern and the corresponding HTTP method that it will be mapped to. For example, the listData() method will be mapped to the http://localhost:8080/ch16/contact/listdata URL, with an HTTP GET method. For the update() method, it will be mapped to the URL http://localhost:8080/ch16/contact/{id}, with an HTTP PUT method.

- The @ResponseBody annotation is applied to all methods. This instructs that all the return value from the methods should be written to the HTTP response stream directly.

- For methods that accept path variables (for example, the findContactById() method), the path variable is annotated with @PathVariable. This instructs Spring MVC to bind the path variable within the URL (for example, http://localhost:8080/ch16/contact/1) into the id argument of the findContactById() method. Note that for the id argument, the type is Long, while Spring 3's type conversion system will automatically handle the conversion from String to Long for us.

- For the create() and update() method, the Contact argument is annotated with @RequestBody. This instructs Spring to automatically bind the content within the HTTP request body into the Contact domain object. The conversion will be done by the declared instances of the HttpMessageConverter<Object> interface (under the package org.springframework.http.converter) for supporting formats, which will be discussed later in this chapter.

Configuring the RESTful Servlet

After the controller is completed, we can define it in Spring MVC. First we need to define a DispatcherServlet (under the package org.springframework.web.servlet) to instruct Spring MVC to dispatch all RESTful requests to the ContactController.

To declare the servlet, add the code snippet in Listing 16-25 into the web deployment descriptor file (src/main/webapp/WEB-INF/web.xml).

Listing 16-25. The Dispatcher Servlet for RESTful-WS

```
<!-- RESTful Servlet -->
<servlet>
    <servlet-name>restful</servlet-name>
    <servlet-class>
        org.springframework.web.servlet.DispatcherServlet
    </servlet-class>
    <init-param>
```

```
            <param-name>contextConfigLocation</param-name>
            <param-value>
                /WEB-INF/spring/appServlet/restful-context.xml
            </param-value>
        </init-param>
        <load-on-startup>1</load-on-startup>
    </servlet>

    <servlet-mapping>
        <servlet-name>restful</servlet-name>
        <url-pattern>/restful/*</url-pattern>
    </servlet-mapping>
```

As shown in Listing 16-25, a servlet named restful is declared, which is of type DispatcherServlet (details for the DispatcherServlet will be discussed in Chapters 17 and 18). In Spring MVC, each DispatchServlet will have its own WebApplicationContext (however, all service-layer beans defined in the root-context.xml file, which called the root WebApplicationContext, will be available for each servlet's own WebApplicationContext too).

The <servlet-mapping> tag instructs the web container (for example, Tomcat) that all URLs under the pattern /restful/* (for example, http://localhost:8080/ch16/restful/contact) will be handled by the restful servlet.

As shown in Listing 16-25, for the restful servlet, we also specify that the Spring WebApplicationContext for this DispatcherServlet should be loaded from /WEB-INF/spring/appServlet/restful-context.xml. Listing 16-26 shows the configuration file.

Listing 16-26. The Spring WebApplicationContext for RESTful-WS

```
<?xml version="1.0" encoding="UTF-8"?>
<beans xmlns="http://www.springframework.org/schema/beans"
    xmlns:xsi="http://www.w3.org/2001/XMLSchema-instance"
    xmlns:context="http://www.springframework.org/schema/context"
    xmlns:mvc="http://www.springframework.org/schema/mvc"
    xsi:schemaLocation="http://www.springframework.org/schema/beans
        http://www.springframework.org/schema/beans/spring-beans-3.1.xsd
        http://www.springframework.org/schema/context
        http://www.springframework.org/schema/context/spring-context-3.1.xsd
        http://www.springframework.org/schema/mvc
        http://www.springframework.org/schema/mvc/spring-mvc-3.1.xsd">

    <mvc:annotation-driven>
        <mvc:message-converters>
            <bean
class="org.springframework.http.converter.json.MappingJacksonHttpMessageConverter"/>
            <bean
class="org.springframework.http.converter.xml.MarshallingHttpMessageConverter">
                <property name="marshaller" ref="castorMarshaller"/>
                <property name="unmarshaller" ref="castorMarshaller"/>
            </bean>
        </mvc:message-converters>
    </mvc:annotation-driven>

    <context:component-scan
        base-package="com.apress.prospring3.ch16.web.restful.controller"/>
```

```
<bean id="castorMarshaller"
    class="org.springframework.oxm.castor.CastorMarshaller">
    <property name="mappingLocation" value="classpath:oxm-mapping.xml"/>
</bean>
```

```
</beans>
```

The important points for Listing 16-26 are as follows:

- The `<mvc:annotation-driven>` tag enables the annotation support for Spring MVC (i.e., the `@Controller` annotation), as well as registers Spring 3's type conversion and formatting system. In addition, JSR-303 validation support is also enabled under the definition of this tag.

- Under `<mvc:annotation-driven>`, the `<mvc:message-converters>` tag declares the instances of `HttpMessageConverter` that will be used for media conversion for supported formats. Note that the `<mvc:message-converters>` tag was introduced in Spring 3.1. Because we will support both JSON and XML as the data format, two converters are declared. The first one is `MappingJacksonHttpMessageConverter`, which is Spring's support for the Jackson JSON library (http://jackson.codehaus.org). The other one is `MarshallingHttpMessageConverter`, which is provided by the `spring-oxm` module for XML marshaling/unmarshaling. Within the `MarshallingHttpMessageConverter`, we need to define the marshaler and unmarshaler to use, which is the one provided by Castor in our case.

- For the `castorMarshaller` bean, we use the Spring-provided class `org.springframework.oxm.castor.CastorMarshaller`, which integrates with Castor, and we provide the mapping location that Castor required for its processing.

- The `<context:component-scan>` tag instructs Spring to scan for the specified package for controller classes.

Now, the server-side service is complete. If your tc Server is on, the project would have been built and deployed to the server automatically. If not, rebuild the project and start the server.

You may find that while starting the web application, errors will be reported by Spring, because of the previous implemented samples. To fix this, do the following:

1. Move the controller class `HomeController` from the package `com.apress.prospring3` to a new package called `com.apress.prospring3.ch16.web.app.controller`.

2. In the file src/main/webapp/WEB-INF/spring/appServlet/servlet-context.xml, change the line from `<context:component-scan base-package="com.apress.prospring3" />` to `<context:component-scan base-package="com.apress.prospring3.ch16.web.app.controller" />`.

Using curl to Test RESTful-WS

Let's do a quick test of the RESTful web services that we implemented. One easy way is to use `curl` (http://curl.haxx.se), which is a command-line tool for transporting data with URL syntax. To use the tool, just download it from the web site and extract in onto your computer.

For example, to test the retrieval of all contacts, open a command prompt in Windows or a terminal in Unix/Linux, and fire the command shown in Listing 16-27.

Listing 16-27. *curl Command for Testing RESTful-WS*

```
curl -v -H "Accept: application/json" http://localhost:8080/ch16/restful/contact/listdata
```

The command in Listing 16-27 will send an HTTP request to the server's RESTful web service; in this case, it will invoke the listData() method in ContactController to retrieve and return all contact information. Also, the –H option declares an HTTP header attribute, meaning that the client wants to receive data in JSON format. Running the command will produce the output shown in Figure 16-13.

```
C:\Users\Clarence>curl -v -H "Accept: application/json" http://localhost:8080/ch16/restful/contact/listdata
* About to connect() to localhost port 8080 (#0)
* connected
* Connected to localhost () port 8080 (#0)
> GET /ch16/restful/contact/listdata HTTP/1.1
> User-Agent: curl/7.21.0 (amd64-pc-win32) libcurl/7.21.0 OpenSSL/0.9.8o zlib/1.2.3
> Host: localhost:8080
> Accept: application/json
>
< HTTP/1.1 200 OK
< Server: Apache-Coyote/1.1
< Content-Type: application/json
< Transfer-Encoding: chunked
< Date: Thu, 01 Dec 2011 03:42:24 GMT
<
{"contacts":[{"id":1,"version":0,"firstName":"Clarence","lastName":"Ho","birthDate":333734400000},{"id":2,"version":0,"f
irstName":"Scott","lastName":"Tiger","birthDate":657475200000},{"id":3,"version":0,"firstName":"John","lastName":"Smith"
,"birthDate":-184406400000}]}* Connection #0 to host localhost left intact
* Closing connection #0
```

Figure 16-13. *Testing RESTful-WS using curl with the JSON format*

In Figure 16-13, you can see that the data in JSON format for the initially populated contact information was returned. Now let's take a look at the XML format; the command is shown in Listing 16-28.

Listing 16-28. *curl Command for Testing RESTful-WS*

```
curl -v -H "Accept: application/xml" http://localhost:8080/ch16/restful/contact/listdata
```

As shown in Listing 16-28, there is only one difference compared to Listing 16-27. The accept media was changed from JSON to XML. Running the command will produce the output shown in Figure 16-14.

```
C:\Users\Clarence>curl -v -H "Accept: application/xml" http://localhost:8080/ch16/restful/contact/listdata
* About to connect() to localhost port 8080 (#0)
* connected
* Connected to localhost () port 8080 (#0)
> GET /ch16/restful/contact/listdata HTTP/1.1
> User-Agent: curl/7.21.0 (amd64-pc-win32) libcurl/7.21.0 OpenSSL/0.9.8o zlib/1.2.3
> Host: localhost:8080
> Accept: application/xml
>
< HTTP/1.1 200 OK
< Server: Apache-Coyote/1.1
< Content-Type: application/xml
< Transfer-Encoding: chunked
< Date: Thu, 01 Dec 2011 03:42:55 GMT
<
<?xml version="1.0" encoding="UTF-8"?>
<contacts>
    <contact>
        <id>1</id>
        <firstName>Clarence</firstName>
        <lastName>Ho</lastName>
        <birthDate>1980-07-30</birthDate>
        <version>0</version>
    </contact>
    <contact>
        <id>2</id>
        <firstName>Scott</firstName>
        <lastName>Tiger</lastName>
        <birthDate>1990-11-02</birthDate>
        <version>0</version>
    </contact>
    <contact>
        <id>3</id>
        <firstName>John</firstName>
        <lastName>Smith</lastName>
        <birthDate>1964-02-28</birthDate>
        <version>0</version>
    </contact>
</contacts>
* Connection #0 to host localhost left intact
```

Figure 16-14. Testing RESTful-WS using curl with the XML format

As shown in Figure 16-14, the data in XML format was correctly returned. This is because of the HttpMessageConverters that were defined in the RESTful servlet's WebApplicationContext, while Spring MVC will invoke the corresponding message converter based on the client's HTTP header's accept media information and will write to the HTTP response accordingly.

Using RestTemplate to Access RESTful-WS

For Spring-based applications, the RestTemplate class is designed for accessing RESTful web services. In this section, we will discuss how to use the class to access the contact service on the server.

First let's take a look at the basic ApplicationContext configuration for Spring RestTemplate, as shown in Listing 16-29 (restful-client-app-context.xml).

Listing 16-29. The restful-client-app-context.xml File

```xml
<?xml version="1.0" encoding="UTF-8"?>
<beans xmlns="http://www.springframework.org/schema/beans"
    xmlns:xsi="http://www.w3.org/2001/XMLSchema-instance"
```

```
        xsi:schemaLocation="http://www.springframework.org/schema/beans
            http://www.springframework.org/schema/beans/spring-beans-3.1.xsd">

    <bean id="restTemplate"
        class="org.springframework.web.client.RestTemplate">
        <property name="messageConverters">
            <list>
                <bean
class="org.springframework.http.converter.xml.MarshallingHttpMessageConverter">
                    <property name="marshaller" ref="castorMarshaller"/>
                    <property name="unmarshaller" ref="castorMarshaller"/>
                    <property name="supportedMediaTypes">
                        <list>
                            <bean class="org.springframework.http.MediaType">
                                <constructor-arg index="0" value="application"/>
                                <constructor-arg index="1" value="xml"/>
                            </bean>
                        </list>
                    </property>
                </bean>
            </list>
        </property>
    </bean>

    <bean id="castorMarshaller"
        class="org.springframework.oxm.castor.CastorMarshaller">
        <property name="mappingLocation" value="classpath:oxm-mapping.xml"/>
    </bean>
</beans>
```

As shown in Listing 16-29, a restTemplate bean is declared using the RestTemplate class. With the class, the property messageConverters is injected with an instance of MarshallingHttpMessageConverter using Castor, the same as the one on the server side. The mapping file will be shared among both the server and client sides. In addition, for the restTemplate bean, within the anonymous class MarshallingHttpMessageConverter, the property supportedMediaTypes is injected with an anonymous bean declaration of an MediaType instance, indicating that the only supported media is XML. As a result, the client is always expecting XML as the return data format, and Castor will help perform the conversion between POJO and XML.

Let's try the service to get all contacts first. Listing 16-30 shows the main testing program.

Listing 16-30. Testing RestTemplate

```
package com.apress.prospring3.ch16.restful;

import org.springframework.context.support.GenericXmlApplicationContext;
import org.springframework.web.client.RestTemplate;

import com.apress.prospring3.ch16.domain.Contact;
import com.apress.prospring3.ch16.domain.Contacts;

public class RestfulClientSample {

    private static final String URL_GET_ALL_CONTACTS =
        "http://localhost:8080/ch16/restful/contact/listdata";
```

```
    private static final String URL_GET_CONTACT_BY_ID =
        "http://localhost:8080/ch16/restful/contact/{id}";
    private static final String URL_CREATE_CONTACT =
        "http://localhost:8080/ch16/restful/contact/";
    private static final String URL_UPDATE_CONTACT =
        "http://localhost:8080/ch16/restful/contact/{id}";
    private static final String URL_DELETE_CONTACT =
        "http://localhost:8080/ch16/restful/contact/{id}";

    public static void main(String[] args) {

        GenericXmlApplicationContext ctx = new GenericXmlApplicationContext();
        ctx.load("classpath:restful-client-app-context.xml");
        ctx.refresh();

        Contacts contacts;
        Contact contact;

        RestTemplate restTemplate = ctx.getBean(
            "restTemplate", RestTemplate.class);

        // Test retrieve all contacts
        System.out.println("Testing retrieve all contacts:");
        contacts = restTemplate.getForObject(
            URL_GET_ALL_CONTACTS, Contacts.class);
        listContacts(contacts);

    }

    private static void listContacts(Contacts contacts) {
        for (Contact contact: contacts.getContacts()) {
            System.out.println(contact);
        }
        System.out.println("");
    }
}
```

As shown in Listing 16-30, the URLs for accessing various operations are declared, which will be used in later samples. In the main() method, the instance of RestTemplate is retrieved, and then the RestTemplate.getForObject() is called (which corresponds to the HTTP GET method), passing in the URL and the expected return type, which is the Contacts class that contains the full list of contacts.

Make sure the tc Server is running. Running the program will produce the following output:

```
Testing retrieve all contacts:
Contact - Id: 1, First name: Clarence, Last name: Ho, Birthday: 1980-07-30T00:00:00.000+08:00
Contact - Id: 2, First name: Scott, Last name: Tiger, Birthday: 1990-11-02T00:00:00.000+08:00
Contact - Id: 3, First name: John, Last name: Smith, Birthday: 1964-02-28T00:00:00.000+08:00
```

As you can see, the MarshallingHttpMessageConverter registered within the RestTemplate will convert the message into a POJO automatically.

Next, let's try to retrieve a contact by ID. Add the code snippet in Listing 16-31 into the main() method of the RestfulClientSample class.

Listing 16-31. Testing RestTemplate

```
// Test retrieve contact by id
System.out.println("Testing retrieve a contact by id :");
contact = restTemplate.getForObject(
    URL_GET_CONTACT_BY_ID, Contact.class, 1);
System.out.println(contact);
System.out.println("");
```

As shown in Listing 16-31, we use a variant of the RestTemplate.getForObject() method, which also passes in the ID of the contact we want to retrieve as the path variable within the URL (the {id} path variable in the URL_GET_CONTACT_BY_ID). If the URL has more than one path variable, you can use an instance of Map<String,Object> or use the varargs support of the method to pass in the path variables. For the case of varargs, you need to follow the order of the path variable as declared in the URL. Running the program again will produce the following output (other output was omitted):

```
Testing retrieve all contact by id :
Contact - Id: 1, First name: Clarence, Last name: Ho, Birthday: 1980-07-30T00:00:00.000+08:00
```

As you can see, the correct contact was retrieved.

Now it's update's turn. Add the code snippet in Listing 16-32 into the main() method of the RestfulClientSample class.

Listing 16-32. Testing RestTemplate for Update Operation

```
// Test update contact
contact = restTemplate.getForObject(
    URL_UPDATE_CONTACT, Contact.class, 1);
contact.setFirstName("Kim Fung");
System.out.println("Testing update contact by id :");
restTemplate.put(URL_UPDATE_CONTACT, contact, 1);
System.out.println("Contact update successfully: " + contact);
System.out.println("");
```

As shown in Listing 16-32, first we retrieve the contact we want to update. After the contact object is updated, we then use the RestTemplate.put() method, which corresponds to the HTTP PUT method, passing in the update URL, the updated contact object, and the ID of the contact to update. Running the program again produces the following output (other output was omitted):

```
Testing update contact by id :
Contact update successfully: Contact - Id: 1, First name: Kim Fung, Last name: Ho, Birthday:
1980-07-30T00:00:00.000+08:00
```

If now you take a look at tc Server's console output, since we set Hibernate to show SQL and log the information during update, you will also see the following output:

```
Hibernate: update contact set BIRTH_DATE=?, FIRST_NAME=?, LAST_NAME=?, VERSION=? where ID=?
and VERSION=?
INFO : com.apress.prospring3.ch16.web.restful.controller.ContactController - Contact updated
successfully with info: Contact - Id: 1, First name: Kim Fung, Last name: Ho, Birthday: 1980-
07-30T00:00:00.000+08:00
```

Next is the delete operation. Add the code snippet in Listing 16-33 into the main() method of the RestfulClientSample class.

Listing 16-33. Testing RestTemplate for the Delete Operation

```
// Testing delete contact
restTemplate.delete(URL_DELETE_CONTACT, 1);
System.out.println("Testing delete contact by id :");
contacts = restTemplate.getForObject(
    URL_GET_ALL_CONTACTS, Contacts.class);
listContacts(contacts);
```

As shown in Listing 16-33, the RestTemplate.delete() method is called, which corresponds to the HTTP DELETE method, passing in the URL and the ID. Then, all contacts are retrieved and displayed again to verify the deletion. Running the program again produces the following output (other output was omitted):

```
Testing delete contact by id :
Contact - Id: 2, First name: Scott, Last name: Tiger, Birthday: 1990-11-02T00:00:00.000+08:00
Contact - Id: 3, First name: John, Last name: Smith, Birthday: 1964-02-28T00:00:00.000+08:00
```

As you can see, the contact with an ID of 1 was deleted.

Finally, let's try the insert operation. Add the code snippet in Listing 16-34 into the main() method of the RestfulClientSample class.

Listing 16-34. Testing RestTemplate for Insert Operation

```
// Testing create contact
System.out.println("Testing create contact :");
Contact contactNew = new Contact();
contactNew.setFirstName("James");
contactNew.setLastName("Gosling");
contactNew.setBirthDate(new DateTime());
contactNew = restTemplate.postForObject(
    URL_CREATE_CONTACT, contactNew, Contact.class);
System.out.println("Contact created successfully: " + contactNew);
```

As shown in Listing 16-34, a new instance of the Contact object was constructed. Then the RestTemplate.postForObject() method was called, which corresponds to the HTTP POST method, passing in the URL, the Contact object we want to create, and the class type. Running the program again (please restart tc Server first to reinitialize the contact data) will produce the following output:

```
Testing create contact :
Contact created successfully: Contact - Id: 4, First name: James, Last name: Gosling,
Birthday: 2011-12-01T00:00:00.000+08:00
```

The contact was created on the server and returned to the client.

Securing RESTful-WS with Spring Security

Any remoting service requires security to restrict unauthorized parties from accessing the service and retrieving business information or acting on it. RESTful-WS is no exception. In this section, we will demonstrate how to use the Spring Security project (http://static.springsource.org/spring-security/site/index.html) to secure the RESTful-WS on the server. In the sample in this section, we will use Spring Security 3.1 (as of this writing, the latest release is 3.1.0.RELEASE), which provides some useful support for RESTful-WS.

Using Spring Security to secure RESTful-WS is a three-step process. First, in the web application deployment descriptor (web.xml), we need to declare a filter; the code snippet is shown in Listing 16-35.

Listing 16-35. Declaring Spring Security Filter in web.xml

```
<!-- Spring Security Configuration -->
<filter>
    <filter-name>springSecurityFilterChain</filter-name>
    <filter-class>
        org.springframework.web.filter.DelegatingFilterProxy
    </filter-class>
</filter>

<filter-mapping>
    <filter-name>springSecurityFilterChain</filter-name>
    <url-pattern>/restful/*</url-pattern>
</filter-mapping>
```

As shown in Listing 16-35, a filter is declared to enable Spring Security to intercept the HTTP request for an authentication and authorization check. Because we only want to secure RESTful-WS, the filter is applied only to the URL pattern /restful/* (see the <filter-mapping> tag).

The next step is to create the Spring Security configuration, which will reside in the root WebApplicationContext. Listing 16-36 shows the file (src/main/webapp/WEB-INF/spring/web-security.xml).

Listing 16-36. Spring Security Configuration

```
<?xml version="1.0" encoding="UTF-8"?>
<beans:beans xmlns="http://www.springframework.org/schema/security"
    xmlns:beans="http://www.springframework.org/schema/beans"
    xmlns:xsi="http://www.w3.org/2001/XMLSchema-instance"
    xsi:schemaLocation="http://www.springframework.org/schema/beans
        http://www.springframework.org/schema/beans/spring-beans-3.1.xsd
        http://www.springframework.org/schema/security
        http://www.springframework.org/schema/security/spring-security-3.1.xsd">

    <!-- Stateless RESTful service using Basic authentication -->
    <http pattern="/restful/**" create-session="stateless">
        <intercept-url pattern='/**' access='ROLE_REMOTE' />
        <http-basic />
    </http>

    <authentication-manager>
        <authentication-provider>
            <user-service>
                <user name="remote" password="remote"
                    authorities="ROLE_REMOTE" />
            </user-service>
        </authentication-provider>
    </authentication-manager>

</beans:beans>
```

In Listing 16-36, we declare the security namespace (note the line xmlns="http://www.springframework.org/schema/security") and use it as the default namespace for

the configuration file. In the <http> tag, we declared that the resources under the URL /restful/**
should be protected. The attribute create-session, which was new in Spring Security 3.1.0, was
introduced to allow us to configure whether the HTTP session will be created upon authentication.
Since the RESTful-WS we are using is stateless, we set the value to stateless, which instructs Spring
Security not to create an HTTP session for all RESTful requests. This can help improve the performance
of the RESTful services.

Next, in the <intercept-url> tag, we set that only users with the ROLE_REMOTE role assigned can
access the RESTful service. The <http-basic/> specifies that only HTTP Basic Authentication is
supported for RESTful services.

The <authentication-manager> tag defines the authentication information. Here we define a simple
authentication provider with a hard-coded user and password (both set to remote) with the ROLE_REMOTE
role assigned. In an enterprise environment, most likely the authentication will be done by either a
database or an LDAP lookup. Finally, we import the Spring Security configuration in the root
WebApplicationContext. Add the following line into the file src/main/webapp/WEB-INF/spring/root-
context.xml:

```
<import resource="web-security.xml" />
```

Now the security setup is complete. The project should have been rebuilt and deployed. If you run
the RestfulClientSample class again, you will have the following output (other output was omitted):

```
Exception in thread "main" org.springframework.web.cient.HttpClientErrorException: 401
Unauthorized
```

You will get the HTTP status code 401, which means you are not authorized to access the service.
Now let's config the client's RestTemplate to provide the credential information to the server.

First the configuration for the RESTful client program needs to be revised. Listing 16-37 shows the
revised configuration file (restful-client-app-context.xml).

Listing 16-37. Revised restful-client-app-context.xml File

```
<?xml version="1.0" encoding="UTF-8"?>
<beans xmlns="http://www.springframework.org/schema/beans"
    xmlns:xsi="http://www.w3.org/2001/XMLSchema-instance"
    xsi:schemaLocation="http://www.springframework.org/schema/beans
        http://www.springframework.org/schema/beans/spring-beans-3.1.xsd">

    <bean id="restTemplate"
        class="org.springframework.web.client.RestTemplate">
        <constructor-arg ref="httpRequestFactory"/>
        <property name="messageConverters">
            <!-- Setting same as before and omitted here -->
        </property>
    </bean>

    <bean id="castorMarshaller"
        class="org.springframework.oxm.castor.CastorMarshaller">
        <property name="mappingLocation" value="classpath:oxm mapping.xml"/>
    </bean>

    <bean id="httpRequestFactory"
        class="org.springframework.http.client.HttpComponentsClientHttpRequestFactory">
        <constructor-arg>
            <bean class="org.apache.http.impl.client.DefaultHttpClient">
```

```
                  <property name="credentialsProvider">
                      <bean
class="com.apress.prospring3.ch16.restful.support.CustomCredentialsProvider">
                          <property name="credentials">
                              <bean class="org.apache.http.auth.UsernamePasswordCredentials">
                                  <constructor-arg name="userName" value="remote"/>
                                  <constructor-arg name="password" value="remote"/>
                              </bean>
                          </property>
                      </bean>
                  </property>
              </bean>
          </constructor-arg>
      </bean>

</beans>
```

The differences from the previous version are in bold. First, in the restTemplate bean, a constructor argument with a reference to the httpRequestFactory bean is injected. For the httpRequestFactory bean, the HttpComponentsClientHttpRequestFactory class is used, which is Spring's support for Apache HttpComponents' HttpClient library, and we need the library to construct an instance of DefaultHttpClient that stores the credentials for our client. To support the injection of credentials, we implement a simple CustomCredentialsProvider class, as shown in Listing 16-38.

Listing 16-38. The CustomCredentialsProvider Class

```
package com.apress.prospring3.ch16.restful.support;

import org.apache.http.auth.AuthScope;
import org.apache.http.auth.Credentials;
import org.apache.http.impl.client.BasicCredentialsProvider;

public class CustomCredentialsProvider extends BasicCredentialsProvider {

    public void setCredentials(Credentials credentials) {
        this.setCredentials(AuthScope.ANY, credentials);
    }

}
```

As shown in Listing 16-38, the class extends the BasicCredentialsProvider class within the HttpComponents library, and a new setter method is implemented to support the injection of a credential. Looking back at Listing 16-37, you will see that the credential is injected into this class using an instance of UsernamePasswordCredentials class. The UsernamePasswordCredentials class is constructed with the remote user name and password. With the httpRequestFactory constructed and injected into the RestTemplate, all RESTful requests fired using this template will carry the credential provided. Now we can simply run the RestfulClientSample class again, and you will see that the services are invoked as usual.

Using JSR-303 with RESTful Web Services

The final topic we will discuss is the seamless support of Spring MVC with the JSR-303 Bean Validation API. When using RESTful-WS, we can also apply the defined validation rule to the request arguments.

Let's revisit the Contact entity class and define a constraint on the firstName attribute. Listing 16-39 shows the code snippet of the revised getFirstName() method.

Listing 16-39. *Revised getFirstName() Method of Contact Class*

```
@NotNull
@Size(min=3, max=60)
@Column(name = "FIRST_NAME")
public String getFirstName() {
    return firstName;
}
```

Then, in the ContactController class, in the create() method, add the @Valid annotation (javax.validation.Valid) before the contact argument. Listing 16-40 shows the code snippet of the revised create() method of the ContactController class.

Listing 16-40. *Revised create() Method of ContactController Class*

```
@RequestMapping(value="/", method=RequestMethod.POST)
@ResponseBody
public Contact create(@RequestBody @Valid Contact contact) {
    logger.info("Creating contact: " + contact);
    contactService.save(contact);
    logger.info("Contact created successfully with info: " + contact);
    return contact;
}
```

The differences from the previous version are in bold. The support of the @Valid annotation for the argument was also introduced in Spring 3.1. With the annotation in place, Spring will perform JSR-303 validation to the Contact domain object after data binding, and exceptions will be thrown if violations are found.

To see it in action, let's modified the insert operation of the RestfulClientSample class. Listing 16-41 shows the revised code snippet in the RestfulClientSample class for testing the insert operation.

Listing 16-41. *Revised insert Operation of RestfulClientSample Class*

```
    // Testing create contact
    System.out.println("Testing create contact :");
    Contact contactNew = new Contact();
    contactNew.setFirstName("JJ");
    contactNew.setLastName("Gosling");
    contactNew.setBirthDate(new DateTime());
    contactNew = restTemplate.postForObject(
        URL_CREATE_CONTACT, contactNew, Contact.class);
    System.out.println("Contact created successfully: " + contactNew);
```

In Listing 16-41, the differences from the previous version are in bold. When setting the first name, we intentionally set it to two characters only, which violates the rule (minimum three characters) defined for the attribute.

To also see the violations logged at the server, we need to turn on the log level of the package `org.springframework.web` to debug. To do this, locate the code snippet in the file `src/main/resources/log4j.xml` and change the log level from `info` to `debug`, as shown in Listing 16-42.

Listing 16-42. Changing Log4j Log Level

```
<logger name="org.springframework.web">
    <level value="debug" />
</logger>
```

Rebuild the project and deploy to tc Server. Now run the `RestfulClientSample` class again, and you will see the following output (other output was omitted):

```
Exception in thread "main" org.springframework.web.client.HttpClientErrorException: 400 Bad
Request
```

When it fails validation, Spring MVC will return the HTTP status code 400 automatically, which indicates that the data in the request body is getting an error. If you take a look at the server output console, you will see the following output (other output was omitted):

```
DEBUG: org.springframework.web.servlet.mvc.support.DefaultHandlerExceptionResolver - Resolving
exception from handler [public com.apress.prospring3.ch16.domain.Contact
com.apress.prospring3.ch16.web.restful.controller.ContactController.create
(com.apress.prospring3.ch16.domain.Contact)]:
org.springframework.web.method.annotation.support.
MethodArgumentNotValidException: Validation failed for argument at index [0] in method: public
com.apress.prospring3.ch16.domain.Contact
com.apress.prospring3.ch16.web.restful.controller.ContactController.  create(com.apress.prospr
ing3.ch16.domain.Contact), with 1 error(s): [Field error in object 'contact' on field
'firstName': rejected value [JJ]; codes
[Size.contact.firstName,Size.firstName,Size.java.lang.String,Size];
arguments[org.springframework.context.support.DefaultMessageSourceResolvable: codes
[contact.firstName,firstName]; arguments []; default message [firstName],60,3]; default
message [size must be between 3 and 60]]
```

In the previous output, you can see the JSR-303 validation error message is displayed. In real life, you should let the client know this error. This can be done by designing a POJO that stores the errors and then returns them to the client so the client knows what's wrong within the request. We will leave it to you as an exercise.

Remoting in the Sample Application

In the SpringBlog application, the main remoting functionality is the retrieval of blog posting entries by the clients. To fulfill the requirement, we will use Spring MVC's comprehensive RESTful-WS support.

The main highlights of the implementation of the blog feed service are as follows:

- A RESTful servlet will be defined for remote retrieval of blog posting entries via RESTful-WS.

- A controller will be implemented in the web layer to accept requests (with a predefined URL and HTTP GET method) and return the most recent blog posting entries to the client.

- In terms of data formats, JSON and XML will be supported, and the techniques discussed in this chapter will be used in the sample application.

For details, please refer to the section " RESTful-WS for RSS Feed of Blog Post Entries" in Chapter 21.

Summary

In this chapter, we covered the most commonly used remoting techniques in Spring-based applications.

If both applications are running Spring, then using the Spring HTTP invoker is a viable option. If an asynchronous mode or loosely coupled mode of integration is required, then JMS is a commonly used approach. Finally, we discussed how to use RESTful-WS in Spring for exposing services or accessing services using the `RestTemplate` class.

In the next chapter, we will discuss using Spring to implement the web layer.

CHAPTER 17

Web Applications with Spring

In an enterprise application, the presentation layer is a critical layer that significantly affects the acceptance level of the application by the users. The presentation layer is the front door into your application. It lets the users perform business functions provided by the application, as well as provides a visual view of the information that is being maintained by the application. How the user interface performs greatly contributes to the success of the application.

Because of the explosive growth of the Internet (especially via cloud computing these days and the rise of different kinds of devices that people are using), developing an application's presentation layer is a very challenging task. The following are some of the major considerations when developing web applications:

- *Performance*: Performance is always the top requirement of a web application. If users choose a function or click a link and it takes a long time to execute (in the world of Internet, ten seconds is like a century), users will definitely not be happy with the application.

- *User-friendly*: The application should be easy to use and easy to navigate with clear instructions without confusing the user.

- *Interactive and richness*: The user interface should be highly interactive and responsive. In addition, the presentation should be rich in terms of visual presentation, such as charting, dashboard type of interface, and so on.

- *Accessibility*: Nowadays, users require that the application is accessible from anywhere via any device. In the office, they will use their desktop for accessing the application. On the road, users will use various mobile devices including laptops, tablets, smartphones, and so on, to access the application.

Developing a web application to fulfill the previous requirements is not easy, but they are considered mandatory for business users. Fortunately, many new technologies and frameworks have also been developed to address those needs. Recently, many web application frameworks and libraries—such as Spring MVC, Struts, Tapestry, Java Server Faces (JSF), Adobe Flex, Google Web Toolkit (GWT), jQuery, and Dojo, to name a few—provide tools and rich component libraries that can help you develop highly interactive web frontends. In addition, many frameworks provide tools or corresponding widget libraries targeting mobile device including smartphones and tablets. In addition, the rise of the HTML5 and CSS3 standards and the support of these latest standards by most web browsers and mobile device manufacturers help ease the development of web applications that need to be available anywhere from any device.

In terms of web application development, Spring provides comprehensive and intensive support. The Spring MVC module provides a solid infrastructure and Model View Controller (MVC) framework for web application development. When using Spring MVC, you can use various view technologies (for example, JSP, Velocity, and so on). In addition, Spring MVC integrates with many common web frameworks and toolkits (for example, Struts, Adobe Flex, GWT, and so on). Other Spring projects help address specific needs for web applications. For example, Spring MVC, when combined with the Spring Web Flow project and its Spring Faces module, provides comprehensive support for developing web applications with complex flows and using JSF as the view technology. Simply speaking, there are so many choices out there in terms of presentation layer development.

This chapter will focus on Spring MVC and will discuss how we can use the powerful features provided by Spring MVC to develop highly performing web applications. Specifically, this chapter will cover the following topics:

- *Spring MVC*: We will discuss the main concepts of the MVC pattern and introduce Spring MVC. For Spring MVC, we will go through its core concepts, including its WebApplicationContext hierarchy and the request-handling life cycle.

- *i18n, locale, and theming*: Spring MVC provides comprehensive support for common web application requirements including i18n (internationalization), locale, and theming. We will discuss how to use Spring MVC to develop web applications that support those requirements.

- *View and Ajax support*: Spring MVC supports many view technologies. In this chapter, we will focus on using JavaServer Pages (JSP) as the view part of the web application. On top of JSP, JavaScript will be used to provide the richness part. There are many outstanding and popular JavaScript libraries such as jQuery, Dojo, and so on. In this chapter, we will focus on using jQuery, with its subproject jQuery UI library that supports the development of highly interactive web applications.

- *Pagination and file upload support*: When developing the samples in this chapter, we will discuss how we can use Spring Data JPA and the frontend jQuery component to provide pagination support when browsing grid-based data. In addition, how to implement file upload in Spring MVC will be covered. Instead of integration with Apache Commons File Upload, we will discuss how we can use Spring MVC with the Servlet 3.0 container's built-in multipart support for file upload.

- *Security*: Security is a big topic in web applications. We will discuss how we can use Spring Security to help protect the application and handle logins and logouts.

- *Spring MVC and the sample application*: Many topics discussed in this chapter will be used in developing the sample application for this book. We will give a high-level overview of the relationship between the topics in this chapter and the sample application.

Create Project in STS for Samples

As usual, the first step is to create the project for the samples in this chapter. Because we are discussing web applications, we need to create a Spring MVC project. In addition, we will create a service layer using JPA 2 with Hibernate and Spring Data JPA as the persistence service provider. To create the project in STS, please refer to Chapter 16, which also details the required dependencies. Make sure to change the project name and all package names to use "ch17" instead of "ch16" for this chapter. After you have created the project, verify that you can see the default home page created by the template project, which indicates that the initial project works correctly.

Implement the Service Layer for Samples

In the service layer for this chapter, we will still use the contact application as the sample, like the one in Chapter 16. However, the service layer and the data model will be a bit more complicated than the one we developed in Chapter 16 in order to show you some web application features such as file upload support. In this section, we will discuss the data model and the implementation of the service layer that will be used throughout this chapter.

Data Model for Samples

For the data model in the samples in this chapter, we will use a very simple one, which contains only a single CONTACT table for storing contact information. Listing 17-1 shows the script for schema creation (schema.sql in the /src/main/resources folder).

Listing 17-1. Sample Database Schema

```
DROP TABLE IF EXISTS CONTACT;

CREATE TABLE CONTACT (
        ID INT NOT NULL AUTO_INCREMENT
    , FIRST_NAME VARCHAR(60) NOT NULL
    , LAST_NAME VARCHAR(40) NOT NULL
    , BIRTH_DATE DATE
    , DESCRIPTION VARCHAR(2000)
    , PHOTO BLOB
    , VERSION INT NOT NULL DEFAULT 0
    , UNIQUE UQ_CONTACT_1 (FIRST_NAME, LAST_NAME)
    , PRIMARY KEY (ID)
);
```

As you can see, the CONTACT table stores only a few basic fields of a contact's information. One thing worth mentioning is the PHOTO column, of the BLOB (binary large object) data type, which will be used to store the photo of a contact using file upload. Listing 17-2 shows the testing data population script (/src/main/resources/test-data.sql).

Listing 17-2. Sample Data Population Script

```
insert into contact (first_name, last_name, birth_date) values ('Clarence', 'Ho', '1980-07-30');
insert into contact (first_name, last_name, birth_date) values ('Scott', 'Tiger', '1990-11-02');
insert into contact (first_name, last_name, birth_date) values ('John', 'Smith', '1964-02-28');
insert into contact (first_name, last_name, birth_date) values ('Peter', 'Jackson', '1944-1-
10');
insert into contact (first_name, last_name, birth_date) values ('Jacky', 'Chan', '1955-10-31');
insert into contact (first_name, last_name, birth_date) values ('Susan', 'Boyle', '1970-05-06');
insert into contact (first_name, last_name, birth_date) values ('Tinner', 'Turner', '1967-04-
30');
insert into contact (first_name, last_name, birth_date) values ('Lotus', 'Notes', '1990-02-28');
insert into contact (first_name, last_name, birth_date) values ('Henry', 'Dickson', '1997-06-
30');
insert into contact (first_name, last_name, birth_date) values ('Sam', 'Davis', '2001-01-31');
insert into contact (first_name, last_name, birth_date) values ('Max', 'Beckham', '2002-02-01');
insert into contact (first_name, last_name, birth_date) values ('Paul', 'Simon', '2002-02-28');
```

This time, more testing data was populated in order to show you the pagination support later.

Implementing and Configuring ContactService

Having the project created and sample data model and scripts ready, we can start to implement and configure the service layer for our samples in this chapter.

In the following sections, we will first discuss the implementation of the ContactService using JPA 2, Spring Data JPA, and Hibernate as the persistence service provider. Then we will cover the configuration of the service layer in the Spring project.

Implementing ContactService

In the samples, we will expose the services for various operations on the contact information to the presentation layer. First we need to create the Contact entity class, which is shown in Listing 17-3.

Listing 17-3. The Contact Entity Class

```java
package com.apress.prospring3.ch17.domain;

import static javax.persistence.GenerationType.IDENTITY;

import java.io.Serializable;

import javax.persistence.*;

import org.hibernate.annotations.Type;
import org.joda.time.DateTime;
import org.springframework.format.annotation.DateTimeFormat;
import org.springframework.format.annotation.DateTimeFormat.ISO;

@Entity
@Table(name = "contact")
public class Contact implements Serializable {

    private Long id;
    private int version;
    private String firstName;
    private String lastName;
    private DateTime birthDate;
    private String description;
    private byte[] photo;

    @Id
    @GeneratedValue(strategy = IDENTITY)
    @Column(name = "ID")
    public Long getId() {
        return id;
    }

    @Version
    @Column(name = "VERSION")
    public int getVersion() {
```

```
        return version;
    }

    @Column(name = "FIRST_NAME")
    public String getFirstName() {
        return firstName;
    }

    @Column(name = "LAST_NAME")
    public String getLastName() {
        return lastName;
    }

    @Column(name = "BIRTH_DATE")
    @Type(type="org.joda.time.contrib.hibernate.PersistentDateTime")
    @DateTimeFormat(iso=ISO.DATE)
    public DateTime getBirthDate() {
        return birthDate;
    }

    @Column(name = "DESCRIPTION")
    public String getDescription() {
        return description;
    }

    @Basic(fetch=FetchType.LAZY)
    @Lob @Column(name = "PHOTO")
    public byte[] getPhoto() {
        return photo;
    }

    @Transient
    public String getBirthDateString() {
        String birthDateString = "";
        if (birthDate != null)
            birthDateString = org.joda.time.format.DateTimeFormat.forPattern("yyyy-MM-↵
dd").print(birthDate);
            return birthDateString;
        }

    public String toString() {
        return "Contact - Id: " + id + ", First name: " + firstName
            + ", Last name: " + lastName + ", Birthday: " + birthDate
            + ", Description: " + description;
    }

    // Setter methods omitted
}
```

As shown in Listing 17-3, standard JPA annotations are used. We also use JodaTime's DateTime class for the birthDate attribute. Please also note the following:

- A new transient property (by applying the @Transient annotation to the getter method) called birthDateString is added, which will be used for frontend presentation in later samples.

- For the photo attribute, we use a byte array as the Java data type, which corresponds to the BLOB data type in the RDBMS. In addition, the getter method is annotated with @Lob and @Basic(fetch=FetchType.LAZY). The former annotation indicates to JPA provider that it's a large object column, while the latter indicates that the attribute should be fetched lazily in order to avoid a performance impact when loading a class that does not require photo information.

Let's proceed to the service layer. Listing 17-4 shows the ContactService interface with the services we would like to expose.

Listing 17-4. The ContactService Interface

```
package com.apress.prospring3.ch17.service;

import java.util.List;

import com.apress.prospring3.ch17.domain.Contact;

public interface ContactService {

    public List<Contact> findAll();

    public Contact findById(Long id);

    public Contact save(Contact contact);
}
```

The methods should be self-explanatory. Because we will use Spring Data JPA's repository support, we will implement the ContactRepository interface, as shown in Listing 17-5.

Listing 17-5. The ContactRepository Interface

```
package com.apress.prospring3.ch17.repository;

import org.springframework.data.repository.CrudRepository;

import com.apress.prospring3.ch17.domain.Contact;

public interface ContactRepository extends CrudRepository<Contact, Long> {
}
```

As discussed in Chapter 10, the ContactRepository interface extends the CrudRepository<T,ID extends Serializable> interface from the Spring Data Commons module, which already provides the basic methods required by the samples.

Listing 17-6 shows the implementation class of the ContactService interface.

Listing 17-6. The ContactServiceImpl Class

```
package com.apress.prospring3.ch17.service.jpa;
```

```
import java.util.List;

import org.springframework.beans.factory.annotation.Autowired;
import org.springframework.stereotype.Repository;
import org.springframework.stereotype.Service;
import org.springframework.transaction.annotation.Transactional;

import com.apress.prospring3.ch17.domain.Contact;
import com.apress.prospring3.ch17.repository.ContactRepository;
import com.apress.prospring3.ch17.service.ContactService;
import com.google.common.collect.Lists;

@Service("contactService")
@Repository
@Transactional
public class ContactServiceImpl implements ContactService {

    @Autowired
    private ContactRepository contactRepository;

    @Transactional(readOnly=true)
    public List<Contact> findAll() {
        return Lists.newArrayList(contactRepository.findAll());
    }

    @Transactional(readOnly=true)
    public Contact findById(Long id) {
        return contactRepository.findOne(id);
    }

    public Contact save(Contact contact) {
        return contactRepository.save(contact);
    }
}
```

If you have any problems understanding Listing 17-6, please refer to Chapter 10 for a detailed description of implementing a service layer using JPA as the persistence provider. The implementation is basically completed, and the next step is to configure the service in Spring's ApplicationContext within the web project, which will be discussed in next section.

Configuring ContactService

To set up the service layer within the Spring MVC project, first we create an individual configuration file called datasource-tx-jpa.xml under the folder /src/main/resources. Listing 17-7 shows the configuration file.

Listing 17-7. The datasource-tx-jpa.xml Configuration File

```
<?xml version="1.0" encoding="UTF-8"?>
<beans xmlns="http://www.springframework.org/schema/beans"
    xmlns:xsi="http://www.w3.org/2001/XMLSchema-instance"
    xmlns:context="http://www.springframework.org/schema/context"
    xmlns:jdbc="http://www.springframework.org/schema/jdbc"
```

```xml
    xmlns:jpa="http://www.springframework.org/schema/data/jpa"
    xmlns:tx="http://www.springframework.org/schema/tx"
    xsi:schemaLocation="http://www.springframework.org/schema/beans
        http://www.springframework.org/schema/beans/spring-beans-3.1.xsd
        http://www.springframework.org/schema/context
        http://www.springframework.org/schema/context/spring-context-3.1.xsd
        http://www.springframework.org/schema/jdbc
        http://www.springframework.org/schema/jdbc/spring-jdbc-3.1.xsd
        http://www.springframework.org/schema/data/jpa
        http://www.springframework.org/schema/data/jpa/spring-jpa-1.0.xsd
        http://www.springframework.org/schema/tx
        http://www.springframework.org/schema/tx/spring-tx-3.1.xsd">

<jdbc:embedded-database id="dataSource" type="H2">
    <jdbc:script location="classpath:schema.sql"/>
    <jdbc:script location="classpath:test-data.sql"/>
</jdbc:embedded-database>

<bean id="transactionManager" class="org.springframework.orm.jpa.JpaTransactionManager">
    <property name="entityManagerFactory" ref="emf"/>
</bean>

<tx:annotation-driven transaction-manager="transactionManager" />

<bean id="emf" class="org.springframework.orm.jpa.LocalContainerEntityManagerFactoryBean">
    <property name="dataSource" ref="dataSource" />
    <property name="jpaVendorAdapter">
        <bean class="org.springframework.orm.jpa.vendor.HibernateJpaVendorAdapter" />
    </property>
    <property name="packagesToScan" value="com.apress.prospring3.ch17.domain"/>
    <property name="jpaProperties">
        <props>
            <prop key="hibernate.dialect">
                    org.hibernate.dialect.H2Dialect
            </prop>
            <prop key="hibernate.max_fetch_depth">3</prop>
            <prop key="hibernate.jdbc.fetch_size">50</prop>
            <prop key="hibernate.jdbc.batch_size">10</prop>
            <prop key="hibernate.show_sql">true</prop>
        </props>
    </property>
</bean>

<context:annotation-config/>

<jpa:repositories base-package="com.apress.prospring3.ch17.repository"
                  entity-manager-factory-ref="emf"
                  transaction-manager-ref="transactionManager"/>
</beans>
```

For details on the definition of each bean, please refer to Chapter 10. Next we need to import the configuration into Spring's root `WebApplicationContext`. For a Spring MVC template project, the file is located at `/src/main/webapp/WEB-INF/spring/root-context.xml`. Listing 17-8 shows the revised file.

Listing 17-8. The root-context.xml File

```
<?xml version="1.0" encoding="UTF-8"?>
<beans xmlns="http://www.springframework.org/schema/beans"
    xmlns:xsi="http://www.w3.org/2001/XMLSchema-instance"
    xmlns:context="http://www.springframework.org/schema/context"
    xsi:schemaLocation="http://www.springframework.org/schema/beans
        http://www.springframework.org/schema/beans/spring-beans-3.1.xsd
        http://www.springframework.org/schema/context
        http://www.springframework.org/schema/context/spring-context-3.1.xsd">

    <import resource="classpath:datasource-tx-jpa.xml" />

    <context:component-scan
        base-package="com.apress.prospring3.ch17.service.jpa" />
</beans>
```

First the `context` namespace is added to the configuration file. Then the file `datasource-tx-jpa.xml` is imported into the `WebApplicationContext`, and finally, we instruct Spring to scan for the specified package for Spring beans.

Now the service layer is completed and ready to be exposed and used by remote clients.

Introducing MVC and Spring MVC

Before we move on to implement the presentation layer, let's go through some major concepts of MVC as a pattern in web applications and how Spring MVC provides comprehensive support in this area.

In the following sections, we will discuss these high-level concepts one by one. First, we will give a brief introduction to MVC. Second, we will present a high-level view of Spring MVC and its `WebApplicationContext` hierarchy. Finally, we will discuss the request life cycle within Spring MVC.

Introducing MVC

MVC is a commonly used pattern in implementing the presentation layer of an application. The main principle of the MVC pattern is to define an architecture with clear responsibilities for different components. As its name implies, there are three participants within the MVC pattern:

- *Model*: A model represents the business data as well as the "state" of the application within the context of the user. For example, in an e-commerce web site, the model will include the user profile information, shopping cart data, and order data if users purchase goods on the site.

- *View*: This presents the data to the user in the desired format, supports interaction with users, and supports client-side validation, i18n, styles, and so on.

- *Controller*: The controller handles requests for actions performed by users in the frontend, interacting with the service layer, updating the model, and directing users to the appropriate view based on the result of execution.

Because of the rise of Ajax-based web applications, the MVC pattern has been enhanced to provide a more responsive and rich user experience. For example, when using JavaScript, the view can "listen" to events or actions performed by the user and then submit an `XMLHttpRequest` to the server. On the controller side, instead of returning the view, the raw data (for example, in XML or JSON format) is returned, and the JavaScript application performs "partial" updates of the view with the received data. Figure 17-1 shows this concept.

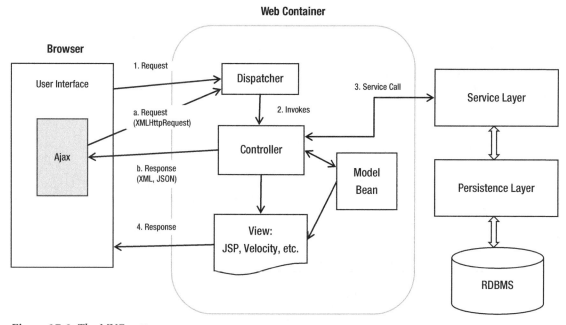

Figure 17-1. The MVC pattern

Figure 17-1 illustrates a commonly used web application pattern, which can be treated as an enhancement to the traditional MVC pattern. A normal view request is handled as follows:

1. *Request*: A request is submitted to the server. On the server side, most frameworks (for example, Spring MVC, Struts, and so on) will have a dispatcher (in the form of a servlet) to handle the request.

2. *Invokes*: The dispatcher dispatches the request to the appropriate controller based on the HTTP request information and the web application configuration.

3. *Service Call*: The controller interacts with the service layer.

4. *Response*: The controller updates the model and, based on the execution result, returns the corresponding view to the user.

In addition, within a view, Ajax calls will happen. For example, say the user is browsing data within a grid. When the user clicks the next page, instead of a full page refresh, the following flow will happen:

1. *Request*: An XMLHttpRequest is prepared and submitted to the server. The dispatcher will dispatch the request to the corresponding controller.

2. *Response*: The controller interacts with the service layer, and the response data will be formatted and sent to the browser. No view is involved in this case. The browser receives the data and performs a partial update of the existing view.

Introducing Spring MVC

In the Spring Framework, the Spring MVC module provides comprehensive support for the MVC pattern, with support for other features (for example, theming, i18n, validation, type conversion and formatting, and so on) that ease the implementation of the presentation layer.

In the following sections, we will discuss the main concepts of Spring MVC. Topics include Spring MVC's WebApplicationContext hierarchy, a typical request-handling life cycle, and configuration.

Spring MVC WebApplicationContext Hierarchy

In Spring MVC, the DispatcherServlet is the central servlet that receives requests and dispatches them to the appropriate controllers. In a Spring MVC application, there can be any number of DispatcherServlets for various purposes (for example, handling user interface requests, RESTful-WS requests, and so on), and each DispatcherServlet has its own WebApplicationContext configuration, which defines the servlet-level characteristics, such as controllers supporting the servlet, handler mapping, view resolving, i18n, theming, validation, type conversion and formatting, and so on.

Underneath the servlet-level WebApplicationContext configurations, Spring MVC also maintains a root WebApplicationContext, which includes the application-level configurations such as backend data source, security, service and persistence layer configuration, and so on. The root WebApplicationContext will be available to all servlet-level WebApplicationContext.

Let's look at an example. Let's say in an application we have two DispatcherServlets. One servlet is to support the user interface (we call it the application servlet), and the other is to provide services in the form of RESTful-WS to other applications (we call it the RESTful servlet). In Spring MVC, we will define the configurations for both the root WebApplicationContext and the WebApplicationContext for the two DispatcherServlets. Figure 17-2 shows the WebApplicationContext hierarchy that will be maintained by Spring MVC for this scenario.

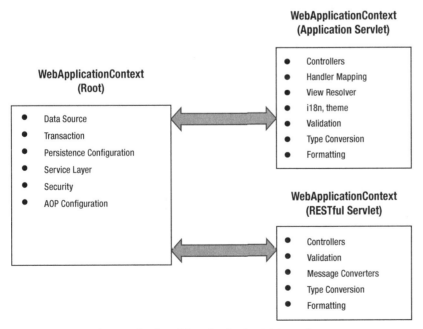

Figure 17-2. Spring MVC WebApplicationContext hierarchy

Spring MVC Request Life Cycle

Let's see how Spring MVC handles a request. Figure 17-3 shows the main components involved in handling a request in Spring MVC. The figure is based on the one described in the Spring Framework forum (http://forum.springsource.org/showthread.php?21639-Spring-MVC-Request-Lifecycle-Diagram), with modifications.

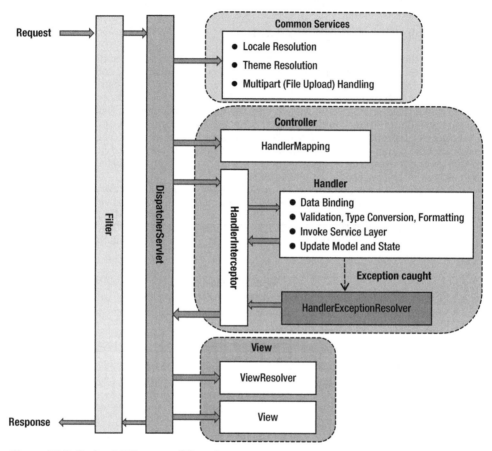

Figure 17-3. Spring MVC request life cycle

The main components and their purposes are as follows:

- *Filter*: The filter applies to every request. Several commonly used filters and their purposes are described in the next section.

- *Dispatcher servlet*: The servlet analyzes the requests and dispatches them to the appropriate controller for processing.

- *Common services*: The common services will apply to every request to provide supports including i18n, theme, file upload, and so on. Their configuration is defined in the DispatcherServlet's WebApplicationContext.

- *Handler mapping*: This maps the request to the handler (a method within a Spring MVC controller class). Since Spring 2.5, in most situations the configuration is not required because Spring MVC will automatically register the org.springframework.web.servlet.mvc.annotation.DefaultAnnotationHandlerMap ping class that maps handlers based on HTTP paths expressed through the @RequestMapping annotation at the type or method level within controller classes.

- *Handler interceptor*: In Spring MVC, you can register interceptors for the handlers for implementing common checking or logic. For example, a handler interceptor can check and ensure that only the handlers can be invoked during office hours.

- *Handler exception resolver*: In Spring MVC, the HandlerExceptionResolver interface (under the package org.springframework.web.servlet) is designed to deal with unexpected exceptions thrown during request processing by handlers. By default, the DispatcherServlet registers the DefaultHandlerExceptionResolver class (under the package org.springframework.web.servlet.mvc.support). This resolver handles certain standard Spring MVC exceptions by setting a specific response status code. You can also implement your own exception handler by annotating a controller method with the @ExceptionHandler annotation and passing in the exception type as the attribute.

- *View Resolver*: Spring MVC's ViewResolver interface (under the package org.springframework.web.servlet) supports view resolution based on a logical name returned by the controller. There are many implementation classes to support various view resolving mechanisms. For example, the UrlBasedViewResolver class supports direct resolution of logical names to URLs. The ContentNegotiatingViewResolver class supports dynamic resolving of views depending on the media type supported by the client (such as XML, PDF, JSON, and so on). There also exists a number of implementations to integrate with different view technologies, such as FreeMarker (FreeMarkerViewResolver), Velocity (VelocityViewResolver), and JasperReports (JasperReportsViewResolver).

These descriptions cover only a few commonly used handlers and resolvers. For a full description, please refer to the Spring Framework reference documentation and its Javadoc.

Spring MVC Configuration

To enable Spring MVC within a web application, some initial configuration is required, especially for the web deployment descriptor web.xml, residing in the folder /src/main/webapp/WEB-INF (Spring 3.1 introduced a new feature that supports code-based configuration within a Servlet 3.0 web container, which we will discuss in "Support for Servlet 3 Code-Based Configuration" in this chapter).

To configure Spring MVC support for web applications, we need to perform the following configurations in the web deployment descriptor:

- Configuring the root WebApplicationContext
- Configuring the servlet filters required by Spring MVC
- Configuring the dispatcher servlets within the application

In the Spring MVC template project, the web.xml file it generates supports Servlet 2.5. In this chapter, we will use Servlet 3.0 (the tcServer that comes with STS is built on top of Apache Tomcat 7, which already supports Servlet 3.0), so we need to change the XML header from 2.5 to 3.0 too. Listing 17-9 shows the revised web.xml file.

Listing 17-9. The Web Deployment Description for Spring MVC

```xml
<?xml version="1.0" encoding="UTF-8"?>
<web-app version="3.0" xmlns="http://java.sun.com/xml/ns/javaee"
    xmlns:xsi="http://www.w3.org/2001/XMLSchema-instance"
    xsi:schemaLocation="http://java.sun.com/xml/ns/javaee
        http://java.sun.com/xml/ns/javaee/web-app_3_0.xsd">

    <!-- The definition of the Root Spring Container shared by all Servlets and Filters -->
    <context-param>
        <param-name>contextConfigLocation</param-name>
        <param-value>/WEB-INF/spring/root-context.xml</param-value>
    </context-param>

    <!-- Spring MVC filters -->
    <filter>
        <filter-name>CharacterEncodingFilter</filter-name>
        <filter-class>
            org.springframework.web.filter.CharacterEncodingFilter
        </filter-class>
        <init-param>
            <param-name>encoding</param-name>
            <param-value>UTF-8</param-value>
        </init-param>
        <init-param>
            <param-name>forceEncoding</param-name>
            <param-value>true</param-value>
        </init-param>
    </filter>

    <filter>
        <filter-name>HttpMethodFilter</filter-name>
        <filter-class>
            org.springframework.web.filter.HiddenHttpMethodFilter
        </filter-class>
    </filter>

    <filter>
        <filter-name>Spring OpenEntityManagerInViewFilter</filter-name>
        <filter-class>
            org.springframework.orm.jpa.support.OpenEntityManagerInViewFilter
        </filter-class>
    </filter>

    <filter-mapping>
        <filter-name>CharacterEncodingFilter</filter-name>
        <url-pattern>/*</url-pattern>
    </filter-mapping>

    <filter-mapping>
        <filter-name>HttpMethodFilter</filter-name>
        <url-pattern>/*</url-pattern>
    </filter-mapping>
```

```
<filter-mapping>
    <filter-name>Spring OpenEntityManagerInViewFilter</filter-name>
    <url-pattern>/*</url-pattern>
</filter-mapping>

<!-- Creates the Spring Container shared by all Servlets and Filters -->
<listener>
    <listener-class>
        org.springframework.web.context.ContextLoaderListener
    </listener-class>
 </listener>

<!-- Processes application requests -->
<servlet>
    <servlet-name>appServlet</servlet-name>
    <servlet-class>
        org.springframework.web.servlet.DispatcherServlet
    </servlet-class>
    <init-param>
        <param-name>contextConfigLocation</param-name>
        <param-value>
            /WEB-INF/spring/appServlet/servlet-context.xml
        </param-value>
    </init-param>
    <load-on-startup>1</load-on-startup>
</servlet>

<servlet-mapping>
    <servlet-name>appServlet</servlet-name>
    <url-pattern>/</url-pattern>
</servlet-mapping>

</web-app>
```

The main points for Listing 17-9 are as follows:

- In the <web-app> tag, the version attribute and the corresponding URL are changed to version 3.0 to indicate to the web container that the web application will use Servlet 3.0.

- In the <context-param> tag, the contextConfigLocation param is provided, which defines the location of Spring's root WebApplicationContext configuration file.

- A number of servlet filters provided by Spring MVC are defined, and all filters are mapped to the web application root context URL. Those filters are commonly used in web applications. Table 17-1 shows the filters configured and their purpose.

- A listener of class org.springframework.web.context.ContextLoaderListener is defined. This is for Spring to bootstrap and shut down the root WebApplicationContext.

- One dispatcher servlet (called appServlet) is defined. We use the one generated by the template project for the contact application's presentation layer. The WebApplicationContext for the dispatcher servlet is located at /src/main/webapp/WEB-INF/spring/appServlet/servlet-context.xml.

599

Table 17-1. Commonly used Spring MVC Servlet Filters

Filter Class Name	Description
`org.springframework.web.filter.CharacterEncodingFilter`	This filter is used to specify the character encoding for request.
`org.springframework.web.filter.HiddenHttpMethodFilter`	This filter provides support for HTTP methods other than GET and POST (for example, PUT).
`org.springframework.orm.jpa.support.OpenEntityManagerInViewFilter`	This filter binds the JPA `EntityManager` to the thread for the entire processing of the request. It can help restore the same `EntityManager` for subsequent requests of the same user so that JPA features such as lazy fetching will be able to work.

Create the First View in Spring MVC

Having the service layer and Spring MVC configuration in place, we can start to implement our first view. In this section, we will implement a simple view to display all contacts that were initially populated by the script `test-data.sql`.

As mentioned earlier, we will use JSPX to implement the view. JSPX is JSP in well-formed XML format. The main advantages of JSPX over JSP are as follows:

- JPSX forces the separation of code from the view layer more strictly. For example, you can't place Java scriptlets in JSPX document.

- Tools might perform instant validation (on the XML syntax), so mistakes can be caught earlier.

- JSPX is the recommended format when using JSP with Spring MVC, as well as other Spring projects (Spring Web Flow, Spring Roo, and so on).

To prepare for the first view, one new Maven dependency is required, as listed in Table 17-2. Please add it to your project.

Table 17-2. Maven Dependencies for Spring MVC View

Group ID	Artifact ID	Version	Description
joda-time	joda-time-jsptags	1.1.1	JSP tag library that support formatting of Joda Time types in views

Configure the DispatcherServlet

The next step is to configure the `DispatcherServlet`. To implement this simple view, we need to make some minor modifications to the default configuration file generated by Spring template project. Listing 17-10 shows the revised configuration (`/src/main/webapp/WEB-INF/spring/appServlet/servlet-context.xml`).

Listing 17-10. The DispatcherServlet Configuration

```xml
<?xml version="1.0" encoding="UTF-8"?>
<beans:beans xmlns="http://www.springframework.org/schema/mvc"
    xmlns:xsi="http://www.w3.org/2001/XMLSchema-instance"
    xmlns:beans="http://www.springframework.org/schema/beans"
    xmlns:context="http://www.springframework.org/schema/context"
    xsi:schemaLocation="http://www.springframework.org/schema/mvc
        http://www.springframework.org/schema/mvc/spring-mvc-3.1.xsd
        http://www.springframework.org/schema/beans
        http://www.springframework.org/schema/beans/spring-beans-3.1.xsd
        http://www.springframework.org/schema/context
        http://www.springframework.org/schema/context/spring-context-3.1.xsd">

    <annotation-driven />

    <resources mapping="/resources/**" location="/resources/" />

    <beans:bean class="org.springframework.web.servlet.view.InternalResourceViewResolver">
        <beans:property name="prefix" value="/WEB-INF/views/" />
        <beans:property name="suffix" value=".jspx" />
    </beans:bean>

    <context:component-scan
        base-package="com.apress.prospring3.ch17.web.controller" />

</beans:beans>
```

As shown in Listing 17-10, the mvc namespace is declared as the default namespace. The
<annotation-driven> tag enables the support of annotation configuration for Spring MVC controllers, as
well as enabling Spring 3 type conversion and formatting support. Also, support for JSR-303 Bean
Validation is enabled by this tag. The <resources> tag defines the static resources (for example, CSS,
JavaScript, images, and so on) and their locations so Spring MVC can improve the performance in
serving those files. The <context:component-scan> tag should be familiar to you.

For the ViewResolver interface, we will keep on using the InternalResourceViewResolver class as the
implementation. However, for the suffix, we will change it to .jspx.

Implement the ContactController

Having the DispatherServlet's WebApplicationContext configured, the next step is to implement the
controller class. Listing 17-11 shows the ContactController class.

Listing 17-11. The ContactController Class

```java
package com.apress.prospring3.ch17.web.controller;

import java.util.List;

import org.slf4j.Logger;
import org.slf4j.LoggerFactory;
import org.springframework.beans.factory.annotation.Autowired;
import org.springframework.stereotype.Controller;
```

601

```
import org.springframework.ui.Model;
import org.springframework.web.bind.annotation.RequestMapping;
import org.springframework.web.bind.annotation.RequestMethod;

import com.apress.prospring3.ch17.domain.Contact;
import com.apress.prospring3.ch17.service.ContactService;

@RequestMapping("/contacts")
@Controller
public class ContactController {

    final Logger logger = LoggerFactory.getLogger(ContactController.class);

    @Autowired
    private ContactService contactService;

    @RequestMapping(method = RequestMethod.GET)
    public String list(Model uiModel) {
        logger.info("Listing contacts");

        List<Contact> contacts = contactService.findAll();
        uiModel.addAttribute("contacts", contacts);

        logger.info("No. of contacts: " + contacts.size());

        return "contacts/list";
    }
}
```

As shown in Listing 17-11, the annotation @Controller is applied to the class, indicating that it's a
Spring MVC controller. The @RequestMapping annotation at the class level indicates the root URL that will
be handled by the controller. In this case, all URLs with the prefix /ch17/contacts will be dispatched to
this controller. In the list() method, the @RequestMapping annotation is also applied, but this time the
method is mapped to the HTTP GET method. This means that the URL /ch17/contacts with the HTTP
GET method will be handled by this method. Within the list() method, the list of contacts are retrieved
and saved into the Model interface passed in to the method by Spring MVC. Finally, the logical view name
contacts/list is returned. In the DispatcherServlet configuration, the InternalResourceViewResolver is
configured as the view resolver, and the file has the prefix /WEB-INF/views/ and the suffix .jspx. As a
result, Spring MVC will pick up the file /WEB-INF/views/contacts/list.jspx as the view.

Implement the Contact List View

The next step is to implement the view page for displaying the contact information, which is the file
/src/main/webapp/WEB-INF/views/contacts/list.jspx. Listing 17-12 shows the page content.

Listing 17-12. The Contact List View

```
<?xml version="1.0" encoding="UTF-8" standalone="no"?>
<div xmlns:jsp="http://java.sun.com/JSP/Page"
    xmlns:c="http://java.sun.com/jsp/jstl/core"
    xmlns:joda="http://www.joda.org/joda/time/tags"
    version="2.0">
```

```
<jsp:directive.page contentType="text/html;charset=UTF-8"/>
<jsp:output omit-xml-declaration="yes"/>

<h1>Contact Listing</h1>

<c:if test="${not empty contacts}">
    <table>
        <thead>
            <tr>
                <th>First Name</th>
                <th>Last Name</th>
                <th>Birth Date</th>
            </tr>
        </thead>
        <tbody>
            <c:forEach items="${contacts}" var="contact">
                <tr>
                    <td>${contact.firstName}</td>
                    <td>${contact.lastName}</td>
                    <td><joda:format value="${contact.birthDate}" pattern="yyyy-MM-↵
dd"/></td>
                </tr>
            </c:forEach>
        </tbody>
    </table>

</c:if>

</div>
```

If you have developed JSP before, Listing 17-12 should be familiar to you. But since this is a JSPX page, the page content is embedded under the <div> tag. In addition, the tag libraries being used are declared as XML namespaces.

First, the <jsp:directive.page> tag defines the attributes that apply to the entire JSPX page, while the <jsp:output> tag controls the properties of the output of the JSPX document.

Second, the tag <c:if> detects whether the model attribute contacts is empty. Because we already populated some contact information in the database, the contacts attribute should contain data. As a result, the <c:forEach> tag will render the contact information in the table within the page. Note the use of the <joda:format> tag to format the birthDate attribute, which is of JodaTime's DateTime type.

Testing the Contact List View

Now we are ready to test the contact list view. First verify that the context root of the web application is ch17. To do this, select the project, right-click, and select Properties. Then in the left menu, click the option Web Project Settings and verify that the "Context root" setting is ch17, as shown in Figure 17-4.

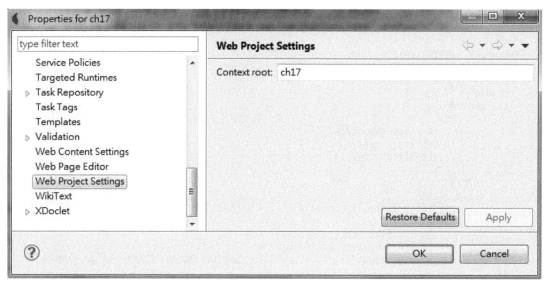

Figure 17-4. *Web project settings in STS*

If you are using the default setting within your STS workspace, the project should be built automatically and published to the target tc Server. To test the contact list view, open a web browser and visit the URL http://localhost:8080/ch17/contacts. You should be able to see the contact listing page, as shown in Figure 17-5.

Figure 17-5. *The contact list view*

Now we have our first view working. In the upcoming sections, we will enrich the application with more views and enable support of i18n, themes, and so on.

Spring MVC Project Structure Overview

Before we dive into the implementation of the various aspects of a web application, let's take a look at what the project structure in our sample web application developed in this chapter looks like.

Typically, in a web application, a lot of files are required to support various features. For example, there are a lot of static resource files, such as style sheets, JavaScript files, images, component libraries, and so on. Then there are files that support presenting the interface in various languages. And of course, there are the view pages that will be parsed and rendered by the web container, as well as the layout and definition files that will be used by templating framework (for example, Apache Tiles) for providing a consistent look and feel of the application.

It's always a good practice to store files that serve different purposes in a well-structured folder hierarchy to give you a clear picture of the various resources being used by the application and ease ongoing maintenance work.

Figure 17-6 shows the folder structure of the sample web application that will be developed in this chapter. The purpose of each folder (under the root folder /src/main/webapp) is listed in Table 17-3. Note that the structure presented here is not mandatory but is commonly used in the developer community for web application development.

In the upcoming sections, we will need various files (for example, CSS files, JavaScript files, images, and so on) to support the implementation. The source code of the CSS and JavaScript will not be shown here. So, we recommend you download a copy of the source code for this chapter and extract it to a temporary folder so that you can copy the files required into the project directly.

Figure 17-6. Sample web project folder structure

Table 17-3. Sample Web Project Folder Structure Description

Folder Name	Purpose	Note
ckeditor	CKEditor (http://ckeditor.com) is a JavaScript component library that provides a rich-text editor in input form. We will use it to enable rich-text editing of a contact's description.	Copy the folder from the sample source code into the folder of your project.
images	Stores the images for the application.	
jqgrid	jqGrid(www.trirand.com/blog) is a component built on top of jQuery that provides various grid-based components for data presentation. We will use this library for implementing the grid in order to display contacts, as well as to support Ajax-style pagination.	Copy the folder from the sample source code into the folder of your project.
scripts	This is the folder for all generic JavaScript files. For the samples in this chapter, jQuery (http://jquery.org) and jQuery UI (http://jqueryui.com) JavaScript libraries will be used to implement a rich user interface. The scripts will be placed in this folder. In-house JavaScript libraries should be put here too.	Copy the folder from the sample source code into the folder of your project.
styles	Stores the style sheet files and related images in supporting the styles.	Copy the folder from the sample source code into the folder of your project.
WEB-INF/i18n	Files for supporting i18n. In Figure 17-6, the file application*.properties stores the layout-related text (for example, page titles, field labels, menu titles, and so on). The message*.properties file stores various messages (for example, success and error messages, validation messages, and so on). In the sample, we will support both English (US) and Chinese (HK).	Copy the folder from the sample source code into the folder of your project.
WEB-INF/layouts	This folder stores the layout view and definitions. Those files will be used by the Apache Tiles (http://tiles.apache.org) templating framework.	
WEB-INF/spring	This folder stores the Spring MVC WebApplicationContext configurations. Both the root-level and dispatcher servlet–level context configurations are stored here.	
WEB-INF/views	This folder stores the views (in our case, JSPX files) that will be used by the application.	

i18n (Internationalization)

When developing web applications, it's always good practice to enable i18n in the early stage. The main work is to externalize the user interface text and messages into properties files.

Even though you won't have i18n requirements on day one, it's good to externalize the language-related settings so that it will be easier later when you need to support more languages.

With Spring MVC, enabling i18n is very simple. First, externalize the language-related user interface settings into various properties files within the /WEB-INF/i18n folder, as described in Table 17-3. Because we will support both English (US) and Chinese (HK), we will need four files. The application.properties and message.properties files store the settings for the default locale, which in our case is English (US). In addition, the application_zh_HK.properties message_zh_HK.properties file stores the settings in the Chinese (HK) language.

Configure i18n in DispatcherServlet Configuration

Having the language settings in place, the next step is to configure the DispatcherServlet's WebApplicationContext for i18n support.

Listing 17-13 shows the revised configuration file with i18n support (servlet-context.xml).

Listing 17-13. Revised Servlet Context Configuration

```xml
<?xml version="1.0" encoding="UTF-8"?>
<beans:beans xmlns="http://www.springframework.org/schema/mvc"
    xmlns:xsi="http://www.w3.org/2001/XMLSchema-instance"
    xmlns:beans="http://www.springframework.org/schema/beans"
    xmlns:p="http://www.springframework.org/schema/p"
    xmlns:context="http://www.springframework.org/schema/context"
    xsi:schemaLocation="http://www.springframework.org/schema/mvc
        http://www.springframework.org/schema/mvc/spring-mvc-3.1.xsd
        http://www.springframework.org/schema/beans
        http://www.springframework.org/schema/beans/spring-beans-3.1.xsd
        http://www.springframework.org/schema/context
        http://www.springframework.org/schema/context/spring-context-3.1.xsd">

    <annotation-driven />

    <resources location="/, classpath:/META-INF/web-resources/" mapping="/resources/**"/>

    <default-servlet-handler/>

    <beans:bean class="org.springframework.web.servlet.view.InternalResourceViewResolver">
        <beans:property name="prefix" value="/WEB-INF/views/" />
        <beans:property name="suffix" value=".jspx" />
    </beans:bean>

    <context:component-scan
        base-package="com.apress.prospring3.ch17.web.controller" />

    <interceptors>
        <beans:bean class="org.springframework.web.servlet.i18n.LocaleChangeInterceptor"
            p:paramName="lang"/>
```

```
</interceptors>

<beans:bean
class="org.springframework.context.support.ReloadableResourceBundleMessageSource"
    id="messageSource" p:basenames="WEB-INF/i18n/messages,WEB-INF/i18n/application"
    p:fallbackToSystemLocale="false"/>

<beans:bean class="org.springframework.web.servlet.i18n.CookieLocaleResolver"
    id="localeResolver" p:cookieName="locale"/>

</beans:beans>
```

In Listing 17-13, the differences from the previous version are highlighted in bold. First, the p namespace is added, and the resource definition is revised to reflect the new folder structure as presented in Table 17-3. The <resources> tag belongs to the mvc namespace and was introduced in Spring 3. This tag defines the locations of the static resource files, which enable Spring MVC to handle the files within those folders efficiently. Within the tag, the location attribute defines the folders for the static resources. The first path, /, indicates the root folder for the web application, which is /src/main/webapp, while the second path, classpath:/META-INF/web-resources/, indicates the resource files for the included library. It will be useful if you include the Spring JavaScript module, which includes the supporting resource files within the /META-INF/web-resources folder. The mapping attribute defines the URL for mapping to static resources; as an example, for the URL http://localhost:8080/ch17/resources/styles/standard.css, Spring MVC will retrieve the file standard.css from the folder /src/main/webapp/styles. The <default-servlet-handler/> tag enables the mapping of the DispatcherServlet to the web application's root context URL, while still allowing static resource requests to be handled by the container's default servlet.

Second, a Spring MVC interceptor with class LocaleChangeInterceptor is defined, which intercepts all the requests to the DispatcherServlet. The interceptor supports locale switching with a configurable request parameter. From the interceptor configuration, the URL param with the name lang is defined for changing the locale for the application.

Then, a bean with class ReloadableResourceBundleMessageSource is defined. As explained in Chapter 5, the ReloadableResourceBundleMessageSource class implements the MessageSource interface, which loads the messages from the defined files (in this case, it's the messages*.properties and application*.properties in the /WEB-INF/i18n folder) in supporting i18n. Note the property fallbackToSystemLocale. This property instructs Spring MVC whether to fall back to the locale of the system that the application is running on when a special resource bundle for the client locale isn't found.

Finally, a bean with the CookieLocaleResolver class is defined. This class supports the storage and retrieval of locale settings from the user browser's cookie.

Modify the Contact List View for i18n Support

Now we can change the JSPX page to display i18n messages. Listing 17-14 shows the revised contact list view (list.jspx).

Listing 17-14. Revised Contact List View for i18n

```
<?xml version="1.0" encoding="UTF-8" standalone="no"?>
<div xmlns:jsp="http://java.sun.com/JSP/Page"
    xmlns:c="http://java.sun.com/jsp/jstl/core"
    xmlns:joda="http://www.joda.org/joda/time/tags"
    xmlns:spring="http://www.springframework.org/tags"
```

```
version="2.0">
<jsp:directive.page contentType="text/html;charset=UTF-8"/>
<jsp:output omit-xml-declaration="yes"/>

<spring:message code="label_contact_list" var="labelContactList"/>
<spring:message code="label_contact_first_name" var="labelContactFirstName"/>
<spring:message code="label_contact_last_name" var="labelContactLastName"/>
<spring:message code="label_contact_birth_date" var="labelContactBirthDate"/>

<h1>${labelContactList}</h1>

<c:if test="${not empty contacts}">
    <table>
        <thead>
            <tr>
                <th>${labelContactFirstName}</th>
                <th>${labelContactLastName}</th>
                <th>${labelContactBirthDate}</th>
            </tr>
        </thead>
        <tbody>
            <c:forEach items="${contacts}" var="contact">
                <tr>
                    <td>${contact.firstName}</td>
                    <td>${contact.lastName}</td>
                    <td><joda:format value="${contact.birthDate}" pattern="yyyy-MM-dd"/></td>
                </tr>
            </c:forEach>
        </tbody>
    </table>

</c:if>

</div>
```

As shown in Listing 17-14, the differences from the previous version are highlighted in bold. First, the spring namespace is added into the page. Then, the <spring:message> tag is used to load the messages required by the view in the corresponding variables. Finally, the page title and the labels are changed to use the i18n messages.

After the project is built and redeployed, open the browser and point to the URL http://localhost:8080/ch17/contacts?lang=zh_HK; you will see the page in Chinese (HK) locale, like the one in Figure 17-7.

Figure 17-7. *The contact list view in the Chinese (HK) language*

Because we defined `localeResolver` in the `DispatcherServlet`'s `WebApplicationContext`, Spring MVC will store the locale setting in your browser's cookie (with the name `locale`), and by default, the cookie will be kept for the user session. If you want to persist the cookie for a longer time, in the `localeResolver` bean definition in Listing 17-13, you can override the property `cookieMaxAge`, which is inherited from the class `org.springframework.web.util.CookieGenerator`.

To switch to English (US), you can append the URL in your browser with `?lang=en_US`, and the page will switch back to English (US). Although we don't provide the properties file named `application_en_US.properties`, Spring MVC will fall back to use the file `application.properties`, which stores the properties in default language of English.

Theming and Templating

Besides i18n, a web application requires an appropriate look and feel (for example, a business web site needs a professional look and feel, while a social web site needs a more vivid style), as well as a consistent layout so that users will not get confused while using the web application.

In a web application, the styles should be externalized in style sheets, instead of hard-coded into the view page. In addition, the style names should be consistent so that various "themes" can be prepared by simply switching the style sheet file. Spring MVC provides comprehensive support for the theming of web applications.

In addition, in order to provide a consistent layout, a templating framework is required. In this section, we will use Apache Tiles (http://tiles.apache.org), a popular page templating framework, for view templating support. Spring MVC tightly integrates with Apache Tiles in this aspect.

In the following sections, we will discuss how to enable theming support in Spring MVC, as well as how to use Apache Tiles to define our page layout.

Theming Support

Spring MVC provides comprehensive support for theming, and enabling it in web applications is easy. For example, in the sample contact application in this chapter, we want to create a theme and name it standard. First, in the folder /src/main/webapp/WEB-INF/classes, create a file named standard.properties with the content in Listing 17-15.

Listing 17-15. The standard.properties File

```
styleSheet=resources/styles/standard.css
```

As shown in Listing 17-15, the properties file contains a property named styleSheet, which points to the style sheet to use for the standard theme. This properties file is the ResourceBundle for the theme, and you can add as many components for your theme as you want (for example, the logo image location, background image location, and so on).

The next step is to configure the DispatcherServlet's WebApplicationContext for theming support by modifying the configuration file (servlet-context.xml). First, with in the <interceptors> definition, we need to add one more interceptor bean, as shown in Listing 17-16.

Listing 17-16. Configure the Theme Interceptor

```
<interceptors>
    <beans:bean class="org.springframework.web.servlet.theme.ThemeChangeInterceptor"/>
    <beans:bean class="org.springframework.web.servlet.i18n.LocaleChangeInterceptor"
p:paramName="lang"/>
</interceptors>
```

As shown in Listing 17-16, the new interceptor is highlighted in bold (the order is not important). The ThemeChangeInterceptor class intercepts every request for changing the theme.

Second, add the bean definitions in Listing 17-17 into the configuration file (servlet-context.xml).

Listing 17-17. Configure Theme Support

```
<beans:bean class="org.springframework.ui.context.support.ResourceBundleThemeSource"
id="themeSource"/>

<beans:bean class="org.springframework.web.servlet.theme.CookieThemeResolver"
id="themeResolver" p:cookieName="theme" p:defaultThemeName="standard"/>
```

As shown in Listing 17-17, two beans are defined. The first bean, implemented by the ResourceBundleThemeSource class, is responsible for loading the ResourceBundle of the active theme. For example, if the active theme is called standard, the bean will look for the file standard.properties as the ResourceBundle of the theme. The second bean, implemented by the CookieThemeResolver class, is used to resolve the active theme for users. The property defaultThemeName defines the default theme to use, which is the standard theme. Note that as its name implies, the CookieThemeResolver class uses cookies to store the theme for the user. There also exists the SessionThemeResolver class that stores the theme attribute in a user's session.

Now the standard theme is configured and ready for use in our views. Listing 17-18 shows the revised contact list view (/WEB-INF/views/contacts/list.jspx) with theme support.

Listing 17-18. Contact List View with Theme Support

```
<?xml version="1.0" encoding="UTF-8" standalone="no"?>

    <!-- Other code omitted -->
```

```
    <spring:message code="label_contact_birth_date" var="labelContactBirthDate"/>

  <head>
     <spring:theme code="styleSheet" var="app_css" />
     <spring:url value="/${app_css}" var="app_css_url" />
     <link rel="stylesheet" type="text/css" media="screen" href="${app_css_url}" />
  </head>

  <h1>${labelContactList}</h1>

  <!-- Other code omitted -->

</div>
```

In Listing 17-18, the new code is highlighted in bold. A <head> section is added in the view, and the <spring:theme> tag is used to retrieve the styleSheet property from the theme's ResourceBundle, which is the style sheet file standard.css. Finally, the link to the style sheet is added into the view.

After rebuilding and redeploying the application to the server, open the browser and point to the contact list view's URL again (http://localhost:8080/ch17/contacts), and you will see that the style defined in standard.css file was applied, as shown in Figure 17-8.

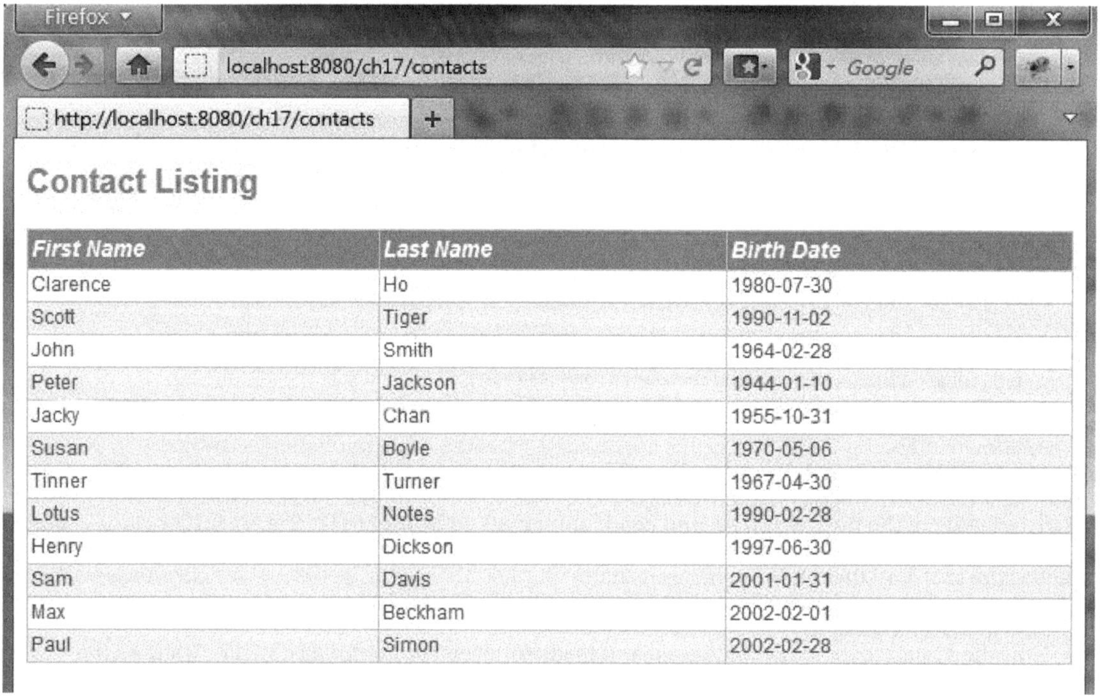

Figure 17-8. The contact list view with theme support enabled

Using Spring MVC's theme support, you can easily add new themes or change the existing theme within your application.

View Templating with Apache Tiles

For view templating using JSP technology, Apache Tiles (http://tiles.apache.org) is the most popular framework in use. Spring MVC tightly integrates with Tiles.

In order to use Tiles, we need to add the required dependencies in the project, as shown in Table 17-4.

Table 17-4. Maven Dependencies for Apache Tiles

Group ID	Artifact ID	Version	Description
org.apache.tiles	tiles-core	2.2.2	The core library for Apache Tiles
org.apache.tiles	tiles-jsp	2.2.2	Apache Tiles support for JSP view files

In the following sections, we will discuss how to implement page templates, including page layout design, definition, and implementation of the components within the layout.

Template Layout Design

First we need to define how many templates are required in our application and, for each different template, what the layout looks like.

In the contact sample in this chapter, we require only one template. The layout is rather trivial, as shown in Figure 17-9.

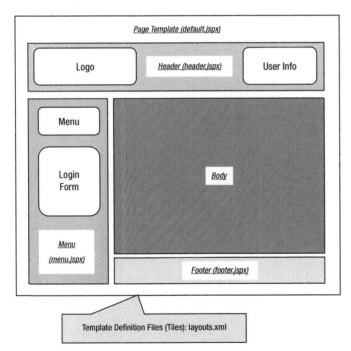

Figure 17-9. Page template with layout components

As you can see from Figure 17-9, the template requires the following page components:

- /WEB-INF/views/header.jspx: This page provides the header area.

- /WEB-INF/views/menu.jspx: This page provides the left menu area, as well as the login form that will be implemented later in this chapter.

- /WEB-INF/views/footer.jspx: This page provides the footer area.

We will use Apache Tiles to define the template, and we need to develop the page template file as well as the layout definitions file, as listed here:

- /WEB-INF/layouts/default.jspx: This page provides the overall page layout for a specific template.

- /WEB-INF/layouts/layouts.xml: This file stores the page layout definitions required by Apache Tiles.

Implement Page Layout Components

Having the layout defined, we can implement the page components. First we will develop the page template file and the layout definition files required by Apache Tiles.

Listing 17-19 shows the Apache Tiles definition file (src/main/webapp/WEB-INF/layouts.xml).

Listing 17-19. Apache Tiles Definition File

```
<?xml version="1.0" encoding="UTF-8"?>
<!DOCTYPE tiles-definitions PUBLIC
    "-//Apache Software Foundation//DTD Tiles Configuration 2.1//EN"
    "http://tiles.apache.org/dtds/tiles-config_2_1.dtd">

<tiles-definitions>

  <definition name="default" template="/WEB-INF/layouts/default.jspx">
    <put-attribute name="header" value="/WEB-INF/views/header.jspx" />
    <put-attribute name="menu" value="/WEB-INF/views/menu.jspx" />
    <put-attribute name="footer" value="/WEB-INF/views/footer.jspx" />
  </definition>

</tiles-definitions>
```

The file should be easy to understand. There is one page template definition, with the name default. The template code is in the file default.jspx. Within the page, three components are defined, named header, menu, and footer. The content of the components will be loaded from the file provided by the value attribute. For a detailed description of the Tiles definition, please refer to the project documentation page (http://tiles.apache.org/2.2/framework/tiles-core/dtddoc/index.html).

Listing 17-20 shows the default page template (default.jspx).

Listing 17-20. The Default Template File

```
<html xmlns:jsp="http://java.sun.com/JSP/Page"
      xmlns:c="http://java.sun.com/jsp/jstl/core"
      xmlns:fn="http://java.sun.com/jsp/jstl/functions"
      xmlns:tiles="http://tiles.apache.org/tags-tiles"
```

```
    xmlns:spring="http://www.springframework.org/tags">

<jsp:output doctype-root-element="HTML" doctype-system="about:legacy-compat" />

<jsp:directive.page contentType="text/html;charset=UTF-8" />
<jsp:directive.page pageEncoding="UTF-8" />

<head>
    <meta http-equiv="Content-Type" content="text/html; charset=UTF-8" />
    <meta http-equiv="X-UA-Compatible" content="IE=8" />

    <spring:theme code="styleSheet" var="app_css" />
    <spring:url value="/${app_css}" var="app_css_url" />
    <link rel="stylesheet" type="text/css" media="screen" href="${app_css_url}" />

    <!-- Get the user locale from the page context (it was set by Spring MVC's locale
resolver) -->
    <c:set var="userLocale">
        <c:set var="plocale">${pageContext.response.locale}</c:set>
        <c:out value="${fn:replace(plocale, '_', '-')}" default="en" />
    </c:set>

    <spring:message code="application_name" var="app_name" htmlEscape="false"/>
    <title><spring:message code="welcome_h3" arguments="${app_name}" /></title>
</head>

<body class="tundra spring">
    <div id="headerWrapper">
        <tiles:insertAttribute name="header" ignore="true" />
    </div>
    <div id="wrapper">
        <tiles:insertAttribute name="menu" ignore="true" />
        <div id="main">
            <tiles:insertAttribute name="body"/>
            <tiles:insertAttribute name="footer" ignore="true"/>
        </div>
    </div>
</body>
</html>
```

The page is basically a JSP page. The highlights are as follows:

- The <spring:theme> tag is placed in the template, which supports theming at the template level.

- The <tiles:insertAttribute> tag is used to indicate the page components that need to be loaded from other files, as indicated in the layouts.xml file.

Now let's implement the header, menu, and footer components. The contents are shown in Listings 17-21, 17-22, and 17-23, respectively.

Listing 17-21. The Header Component (header.jspx)

```
<div id="header" xmlns:jsp="http://java.sun.com/JSP/Page"
    xmlns:spring="http://www.springframework.org/tags"
```

```
    version="2.0">
    <jsp:directive.page contentType="text/html;charset=UTF-8" />
    <jsp:output omit-xml-declaration="yes" />

    <spring:message code="header_text" var="headerText"/>

    <div id="appname">
        <h1>${headerText}</h1>
    </div>

</div>
```

Listing 17-22. The Menu Component (menu.jspx)

```
<?xml version="1.0" encoding="UTF-8" standalone="no"?>
<div id="menu" xmlns:jsp="http://java.sun.com/JSP/Page"
    xmlns:c="http://java.sun.com/jsp/jstl/core"
    xmlns:spring="http://www.springframework.org/tags"
    version="2.0">
        <jsp:directive.page contentType="text/html;charset=UTF-8" />
        <jsp:output omit-xml-declaration="yes" />

        <spring:message code="menu_header_text" var="menuHeaderText"/>
        <spring:message code="menu_add_contact" var="menuAddContact"/>
        <spring:url value="/contacts?form" var="addContactUrl"/>

    <h3>${menuHeaderText}</h3>
    <a href="${addContactUrl}"><h3>${menuAddContact}</h3></a>

</div>
```

Listing 17-23. The Footer Component (footer.jspx)

```
<?xml version="1.0" encoding="UTF-8" standalone="no"?>
<div id="footer" xmlns:jsp="http://java.sun.com/JSP/Page"
    xmlns:spring="http://www.springframework.org/tags" version="2.0">
    <jsp:directive.page contentType="text/html;charset=UTF-8" />
    <jsp:output omit-xml-declaration="yes" />

    <spring:message code="home_text" var="homeText"/>
    <spring:message code="label_en_US" var="labelEnUs"/>
    <spring:message code="label_zh_HK" var="labelZhHk"/>
    <spring:url value="/contacts" var="homeUrl"/>

    <a href="${homeUrl}">${homeText}</a> |
    <a href="${homeUrl}?lang=en_US">${labelEnUs}</a> |
    <a href="${homeUrl}?lang=zh_HK">${labelZhHk}</a>

</div>
```

Now for contact list view, we can modify it to fit into the template. Basically, we just need to remove the <head> section, because it's now in the template page (default.jspx). Listing 17-24 shows the revised contact list view.

Listing 17-24. The Revised Contact List View (/views/contacts/list.jspx)

```
<?xml version="1.0" encoding="UTF-8" standalone="no"?>
<div xmlns:jsp="http://java.sun.com/JSP/Page"
    xmlns:c="http://java.sun.com/jsp/jstl/core"
    xmlns:joda="http://www.joda.org/joda/time/tags"
    xmlns:spring="http://www.springframework.org/tags"
    version="2.0">
    <jsp:directive.page contentType="text/html;charset=UTF-8"/>
    <jsp:output omit-xml-declaration="yes"/>

    <spring:message code="label_contact_list" var="labelContactList"/>
    <spring:message code="label_contact_first_name" var="labelContactFirstName"/>
    <spring:message code="label_contact_last_name" var="labelContactLastName"/>
    <spring:message code="label_contact_birth_date" var="labelContactBirthDate"/>

    <h1>${labelContactList}</h1>

    <c:if test="${not empty contacts}">
        <table>
            <thead>
                <tr>
                    <th>${labelContactFirstName}</th>
                    <th>${labelContactLastName}</th>
                    <th>${labelContactBirthDate}</th>
                </tr>
            </thead>
            <tbody>
                <c:forEach items="${contacts}" var="contact">
                    <tr>
                        <td>${contact.firstName}</td>
                        <td>${contact.lastName}</td>
                        <td><joda:format value="${contact.birthDate}" pattern="yyyy-MM-dd"/></td>
                    </tr>
                </c:forEach>
            </tbody>
        </table>

    </c:if>

</div>
```

Now the template, definition, and components are ready; the next step is to configure Spring MVC to integrate with Apache Tiles.

Configure Tiles in Spring MVC

Configure Tiles support in Spring MVC is simple. In the DispatcherServlet configuration (servlet-context.xml), we need to make a modification to replace the InternalResourceViewResolver with the UrlBasedViewResolver class. Listing 17-25 shows the revisions that need to be made to the configuration file.

Listing 17-25. Configure Tiles Support in Spring MVC

```
<?xml version="1.0" encoding="UTF-8"?>

    <!-- Other code omitted -->
    <!-- Remove the following bean -->
    <beans:bean class="org.springframework.web.servlet.view.InternalResourceViewResolver">
        <beans:property name="prefix" value="/WEB-INF/views/" />
        <beans:property name="suffix" value=".jspx" />
    </beans:bean>

    <!-- Other code omitted -->

    <!-- Add the following beans -->
    <!-- Tiles Configuration -->
    <beans:bean class="org.springframework.web.servlet.view.UrlBasedViewResolver"
        id="tilesViewResolver">
        <beans:property name="viewClass"
value="org.springframework.web.servlet.view.tiles2.TilesView"/>
    </beans:bean>

    <beans:bean class="org.springframework.web.servlet.view.tiles2.TilesConfigurer"
id="tilesConfigurer">
        <beans:property name="definitions">
            <beans:list>
                <beans:value>/WEB-INF/layouts/layouts.xml</beans:value>
                <!-- Scan views directory for Tiles configurations -->
                <beans:value>/WEB-INF/views/**/views.xml</beans:value>
            </beans:list>
        </beans:property>
    </beans:bean>

</beans:beans>
```

In Listing 17-25, the bean you need to remove is in italics, while the new bean definitions are in bold. First, the original ViewResolver bean (with the InternalResourceViewResolver class) is removed. Then, a ViewResolver bean with the class UrlBasedViewResolver is defined, with the property viewClass set to the TilesView class, which is Spring MVC's support for Tiles. Finally, a tilesConfigurer bean is defined that provides the layout configurations required by Tiles.

One final configuration file we need to prepare is the /WEB-INF/views/contacts/views.xml file, which defines the views for the contact application in our sample. Listing 17-26 shows the file content.

Listing 17-26. The views.xml File

```
<?xml version="1.0" encoding="UTF-8" standalone="no"?>
<!DOCTYPE tiles-definitions PUBLIC "-//Apache Software Foundation//DTD Tiles Configuration
2.1//EN" "http://tiles.apache.org/dtds/tiles-config_2_1.dtd">
<tiles-definitions>
    <definition extends="default" name="contacts/list">
        <put-attribute name="body"
            value="/WEB-INF/views/contacts/list.jspx" />
    </definition>
</tiles-definitions>
```

As shown in Listing 17-26, the logical view name is mapped to the corresponding body attribute of the view to display. As in the ContactController class in Listing 17-11, the list() method returns the logical view name contacts/list, so Tiles will be able to map the view name to the correct template and the view body to display.

We can now test the page. Make sure that the project was rebuilt and deployed to the server. Load the contact list view again (http://localhost:8080/ch17/contacts), and the view based on the template will be displayed, like the one shown in Figure 17-10.

Figure 17-10. Contact list view with Apache Tiles

Implement the Views for Contact Information

Now we can proceed to implement the views that allow users to view the details of a contact, create new contacts, or update existing contact information.

In the following sections, we will discuss the mapping of URLs to the various views, as well as how the views are implemented. We will also discuss how to enable JSR-303 validation support in Spring MVC for the edit view.

Mapping of URLs to the Views

First we need to design how the various URLs are to be mapped to the corresponding views. In Spring MVC, one of the best practices is to follow the RESTful-style URL for mapping views. Table 17-5 shows the URLs-to-views mapping, as well as the controller method name that will handle the action.

Table 17-5. Mapping of URLs to Views

URL	HTTP Method	Controller Method	Description
/contacts	GET	list()	List the contact information.
/contacts/{id}	GET	show()	Display a single contact's information.
/contacts/{id}?form	GET	updateForm()	Display the edit form for updating an existing contact.
/contacts/{id}?form	POST	update()	Users update the contact information and submit the form. Data will be processed here.
/contacts?form	GET	createForm()	Display the edit form for creating a new contact.
/contacts?form	POST	create()	Users enter contact information and submit the form. Data will be processed here.
/contacts/photo/{id}	GET	downloadPhoto()	Download the photo of a contact.

Implementing the Show Contact View

Now we implement the view for showing a contact's information. Implementing the show view is a three-step process:

1. Implement the controller method.
2. Implement the show contact view (/views/contacts/show.jspx).
3. Modify the view definition file for the view (/views/contacts/views.xml).

Listing 17-27 shows the show() method implementation of the ContactController class for displaying a contact's information.

Listing 17-27. The show() Method of the ContactController Class

```
package com.apress.prospring3.ch17.web.controller;

// Import statements omitted
@RequestMapping("/contacts")
@Controller
public class ContactController {

    // Other code omitted
```

```
    @RequestMapping(value = "/{id}", method = RequestMethod.GET)
    public String show(@PathVariable("id") Long id, Model uiModel) {
        Contact contact = contactService.findById(id);
        uiModel.addAttribute("contact", contact);
        return "contacts/show";
    }
}
```

In Listing 17-27, in the show() method, the @RequestMapping annotation applied to the method indicates that the method is to handle the URL /contacts/{id} with the HTTP GET method. In the method, the @PathVariable annotation was applied to the argument id, which instructs Spring MVC to extract the id from the URL into the argument. Then the contact is retrieved and added to the Model, and the logical view name contacts/show is returned. The next step is to implement the show contact view (/views/contacts/show.jspx), which is shown in Listing 17-28.

Listing 17-28. The Show Contact View

```
<?xml version="1.0" encoding="UTF-8" standalone="no"?>
<div xmlns:jsp="http://java.sun.com/JSP/Page"
    xmlns:c="http://java.sun.com/jsp/jstl/core"
    xmlns:spring="http://www.springframework.org/tags"
    xmlns:form="http://www.springframework.org/tags/form"
    xmlns:joda="http://www.joda.org/joda/time/tags"
    version="2.0">
    <jsp:directive.page contentType="text/html;charset=UTF-8"/>
    <jsp:output omit-xml-declaration="yes"/>

    <spring:message code="label_contact_info" var="labelContactInfo"/>
    <spring:message code="label_contact_first_name" var="labelContactFirstName"/>
    <spring:message code="label_contact_last_name" var="labelContactLastName"/>
    <spring:message code="label_contact_birth_date" var="labelContactBirthDate"/>
    <spring:message code="label_contact_description" var="labelContactDescription"/>
    <spring:message code="label_contact_update" var="labelContactUpdate"/>
    <spring:message code="date_format_pattern" var="dateFormatPattern"/>

    <spring:url value="/contacts" var="editContactUrl"/>

    <h1>${labelContactInfo}</h1>

    <div id="contactInfo">

        <c:if test="${not empty message}">
            <div id="message" class="${message.type}">${message.message}</div>
        </c:if>

        <table>
            <tr>
                <td>${labelContactFirstName}</td>
                <td>${contact.firstName}</td>
            </tr>
            <tr>
                <td>${labelContactLastName}</td>
                <td>${contact.lastName}</td>
            </tr>
```

```
        <tr>
            <td>${labelContactBirthDate}</td>
            <td><joda:format value="${contact.birthDate}"
pattern="${dateFormatPattern}"/></td>
        </tr>
        <tr>
            <td>${labelContactDescription}</td>
            <td>${contact.description}</td>
        </tr>
    </table>

    <a href="${editContactUrl}/${contact.id}?form">${labelContactUpdate}</a>

    </div>

</div>
```

The page is simple; it simply displays the model attribute contact within the page.

The final step is to modify the view definition file (/views/contacts/views.xml) for mapping the logical view name contacts/show. Simply append the code snippet in Listing 17-29 into the file, under the <tiles-definitions> tag.

Listing 17-29. The Show Contact View Mapping

```
<definition extends="default" name="contacts/show">
    <put-attribute name="body"
        value="/WEB-INF/views/contacts/show.jspx" />
</definition>
```

The show contact view is complete. Now we need to add an anchor link into the contact list view (/views/contacts/list.jspx) for each contact to the show contact view. Listing 17-30 shows the modification required.

Listing 17-30. Add the Anchor Link in the List Contact View

```
<spring:url value="/contacts/" var="showContactUrl"/>


<!-- Other code omitted -->
                <td>
                    <a href="${showContactUrl}/${contact.id}">${contact.firstName}</a>
                </td>
```

As shown in Listing 17-30, we declare an URL variable using the <spring:url> tag and add an anchor link for the firstName attribute. To test the show contact view, upon rebuild and deploy, open the contact list view again. The list should now include the hyperlink to the show contact view, as shown in Figure 17-11.

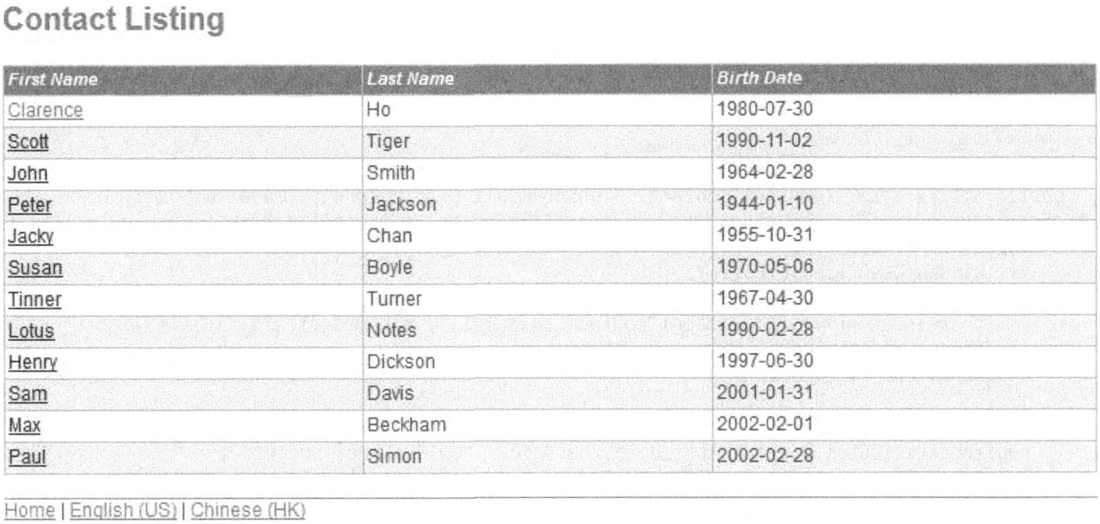

Contact Listing

First Name	Last Name	Birth Date
Clarence	Ho	1980-07-30
Scott	Tiger	1990-11-02
John	Smith	1964-02-28
Peter	Jackson	1944-01-10
Jacky	Chan	1955-10-31
Susan	Boyle	1970-05-06
Tinner	Turner	1967-04-30
Lotus	Notes	1990-02-28
Henry	Dickson	1997-06-30
Sam	Davis	2001-01-31
Max	Beckham	2002-02-01
Paul	Simon	2002-02-28

Home | English (US) | Chinese (HK)

Figure 17-11. Contact list view with link to show contact view

Clicking any link will bring you to the show contact view. Figure 17-12 shows the screen after clicking the first link.

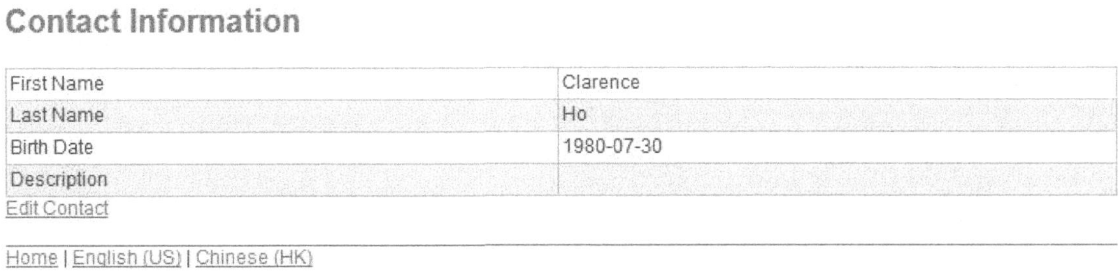

Contact Information

First Name	Clarence
Last Name	Ho
Birth Date	1980-07-30
Description	

Edit Contact

Home | English (US) | Chinese (HK)

Figure 17-12. Show contact view

Implementing the Edit Contact View

Let's implement the view for editing a contact. It's the same as the show view; first we add the methods updateForm() and update() to the ContactController class. Listing 17-31 shows the code snippet for the two methods.

Listing 17-31. Code Snippet for Update Contact

```
package com.apress.prospring3.ch17.web.controller;

// Import statements omitted
@RequestMapping("/contacts")
@Controller
```

```
public class ContactController {

    // Other code omitted
    @Autowired
    MessageSource messageSource;

    @RequestMapping(value = "/{id}", params = "form", method = RequestMethod.POST)
    public String update(Contact contact, BindingResult bindingResult, Model uiModel,
HttpServletRequest httpServletRequest, RedirectAttributes redirectAttributes, Locale locale) {
        logger.info("Updating contact");
        if (bindingResult.hasErrors()) {
            uiModel.addAttribute("message", new Message("error",
                messageSource.getMessage("contact_save_fail", new Object[]{}, locale)));
            uiModel.addAttribute("contact", contact);
            return "contacts/update";
        }
        uiModel.asMap().clear();
        redirectAttributes.addFlashAttribute("message", new Message("success",
            messageSource.getMessage("contact_save_success", new Object[]{}, locale)));
        contactService.save(contact);
        return "redirect:/contacts/" + UrlUtil.encodeUrlPathSegment(contact.getId().toString(),
            httpServletRequest);
    }

    @RequestMapping(value = "/{id}", params = "form", method = RequestMethod.GET)
    public String updateForm(@PathVariable("id") Long id, Model uiModel) {
        uiModel.addAttribute("contact", contactService.findById(id));
        return "contacts/update";
    }

}
```

In Listing 17-31, the highlights are as follows:

- The MessageSource interface is autowired into the controller for retrieving messages with i18n support.

- For the updateForm() method, the contact is retrieved and saved into the Model, and then the logical view contacts/update is returned, which will display the edit contact view.

- The update() method will be triggered when user updates contact information and clicks the Save button. This method needs a bit of explanation. First, Spring MVC will try to bind the submitted data to the Contact domain object and perform the type conversion and formatting automatically. If binding errors are found (for example, the birth date was entered in the wrong format), the errors will be saved into the BindingResult interface (under the package org.springframework.validation), and an error message will be saved into the Model, redisplaying the edit view. If the binding is successful, the data will be saved, and the logical view name will be returned for the display contact view by using redirect: as the prefix. Note that we want to display the message after the redirect, so we need to use the RedirectAttributes.addFlashAttribute() method (an interface under the package org.springframework.web.servlet.mvc.support) for displaying the success message in the show contact view. In Spring MVC, flash

attributes are saved temporarily before the redirect (typically in the session) to be
made available to the request after the redirect and removed immediately.

- The Message class is a custom class that stores the message retrieved from
  MessageSource and the type of message (i.e., success or error) for the view to
  display in the message area. Listing 17-32 shows the content of the Message class.

- The UrlUtil is a utility class for encoding the URL for redirect. Listing 17-33 shows
  its content.

Listing 17-32. *The Message Class*

```
package com.apress.prospring3.ch17.web.form;

public class Message {

    private String type;

    private String message;

    public Message() {
    }

    public Message(String type, String message) {
        this.type = type;
        this.message = message;
    }

    // Getter/setter method omitted
}
```

Listing 17-33. *The UrlUtil Class*

```
package com.apress.prospring3.ch17.web.util;

import java.io.UnsupportedEncodingException;

import javax.servlet.http.HttpServletRequest;

import org.springframework.web.util.UriUtils;
import org.springframework.web.util.WebUtils;

public class UrlUtil {

    public static String encodeUrlPathSegment(String pathSegment, HttpServletRequest
httpServletRequest) {
        String enc = httpServletRequest.getCharacterEncoding();
        if (enc == null) {
            enc = WebUtils.DEFAULT_CHARACTER_ENCODING;
        }
        try {
            pathSegment = UriUtils.encodePathSegment(pathSegment, enc);
        }
        catch (UnsupportedEncodingException uee) {}
```

```
        return pathSegment;
    }
}
```

Next is the edit contact view (/views/contacts/edit.jspx), and we will use it for both updating and creating new contact. Listing 17-34 shows the content.

Listing 17-34. *The Edit Contact View*

```
<?xml version="1.0" encoding="UTF-8" standalone="no"?>
<div xmlns:jsp="http://java.sun.com/JSP/Page"
    xmlns:c="http://java.sun.com/jsp/jstl/core"
    xmlns:spring="http://www.springframework.org/tags"
    xmlns:form="http://www.springframework.org/tags/form"
    version="2.0">
    <jsp:directive.page contentType="text/html;charset=UTF-8"/>
    <jsp:output omit-xml-declaration="yes"/>

    <spring:message code="label_contact_new" var="labelContactNew"/>
    <spring:message code="label_contact_update" var="labelContactUpdate"/>
    <spring:message code="label_contact_first_name" var="labelContactFirstName"/>
    <spring:message code="label_contact_last_name" var="labelContactLastName"/>
    <spring:message code="label_contact_birth_date" var="labelContactBirthDate"/>
    <spring:message code="label_contact_description" var="labelContactDescription"/>
    <spring:message code="label_contact_photo" var="labelContactPhoto"/>

    <spring:eval expression="contact.id == null ? labelContactNew:labelContactUpdate"
        var="formTitle"/>

    <h1>${formTitle}</h1>

    <div id="contactUpdate">
    <form:form modelAttribute="contact" id="contactUpdateForm" method="post">

        <c:if test="${not empty message}">
            <div id="message" class="${message.type}">${message.message}</div>
        </c:if>

        <form:label path="firstName">
            ${labelContactFirstName}*
        </form:label>
        <form:input path="firstName" />
        <div>
            <form:errors path="firstName" cssClass="error" />
        </div>
        <p/>

        <form:label path="lastName">
            ${labelContactLastName}*
        </form:label>
        <form:input path="lastName" />
        <div>
            <form:errors path="lastName" cssClass="error" />
        </div>
```

```
        <p/>

        <form:label path="birthDate">
            ${labelContactBirthDate}
        </form:label>
        <form:input path="birthDate" id="birthDate"/>
        <div>
            <form:errors path="birthDate" cssClass="error" />
        </div>
        <p/>

        <form:label path="description">
            ${labelContactDescription}
        </form:label>
        <form:textarea cols="60" rows="8" path="description" id="contactDescription"/>
        <div>
            <form:errors path="description" cssClass="error" />
        </div>
        <p/>

        <form:hidden path="version" />

        <button type="submit">Save</button>
        <button type="reset">Reset</button>

    </form:form>
    </div>

</div>
```

The highlights for Listing 17-34 are as follows:

- The `<spring:eval>` tag is used, which uses the Spring Expression Language to test whether the contact id is null. If yes, then it's a new contact; otherwise, it's an update. The corresponding form title will be displayed.

- Various Spring MVC `<form>` tags are used within the form for displaying the label, the input field, and errors in case binding was not successful on form submission.

Next, add the view mapping to the view definition file (/views/contacts/views.xml). Listing 17-35 shows the code snippet.

Listing 17-35. *The Edit Contact View Mapping*

```
<definition extends="default" name="contacts/update">
    <put-attribute name="body"
        value="/WEB-INF/views/contacts/edit.jspx" />
</definition>
```

The edit view is completed. Then rebuild and deploy the project. Click the edit link in Figure 17-12. The edit view will be displayed, as shown in Figure 17-13.

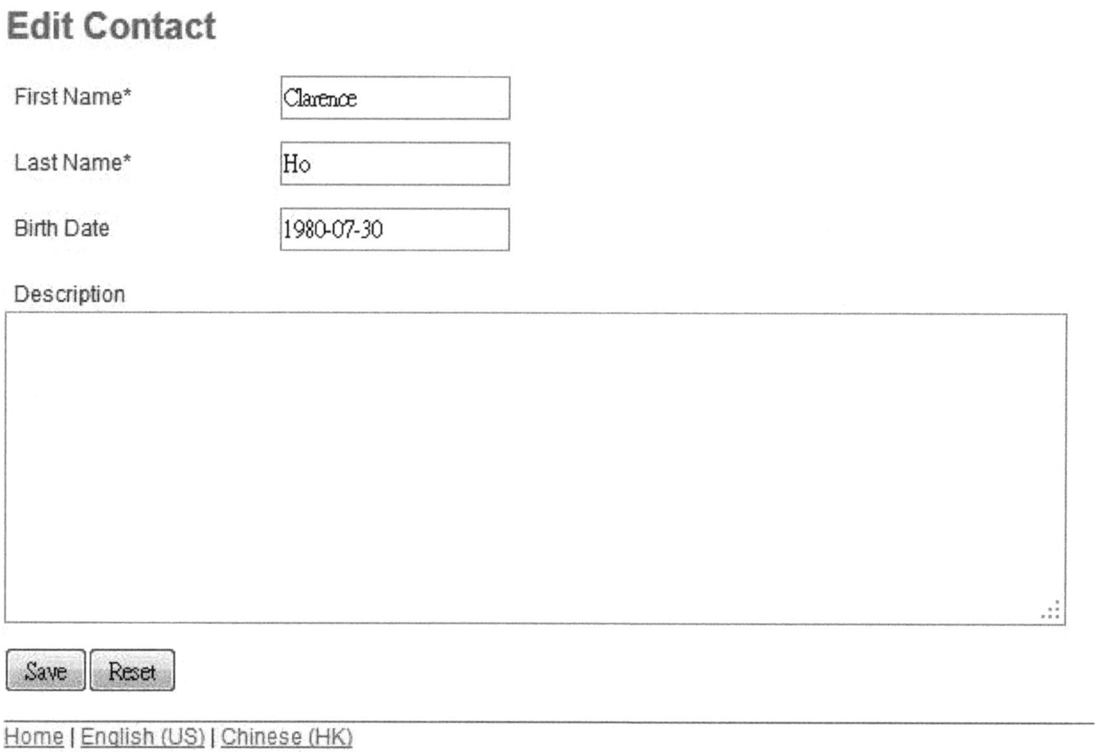

Edit Contact
First Name*
Clarence
Last Name*
Ho
Birth Date
1980-07-30
Description
Save
Reset
Home | English (US) | Chinese (HK)

Figure 17-13. *Edit contact view*

Update the information and click the Save button. If binding was success, then you will see the success message, and the show contact view will be displayed, as shown in Figure 17-14.

Contact Information
Contact saved successfully
First Name
Kim Fung
Last Name
Ho
Birth Date
1980-07-30
Description
Edit Contact
Home | English (US) | Chinese (HK)

Figure 17-14. *Show contact view (after contact update successful)*

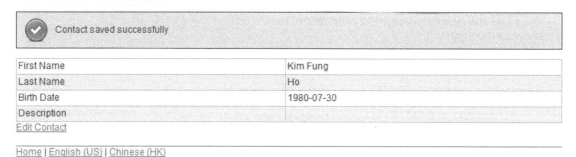

Implementing the Add Contact View

Implementing the add contact view is much like the edit view. Because we will reuse the edit.jspx page, we only need to add the methods in the ContactController class and the view definition.

Listing 17-36 shows the code snippet for the two new methods for the add contact function in the ContactController class.

Listing 17-36. The Add Contact Methods

```
package com.apress.prospring3.ch17.web.controller;

// Import statements omitted
@RequestMapping("/contacts")
@Controller
public class ContactController {

    // Other code omitted
    @RequestMapping(params = "form", method = RequestMethod.POST)
    public String create(Contact contact, BindingResult bindingResult, Model uiModel,
HttpServletRequest httpServletRequest, RedirectAttributes redirectAttributes, Locale locale) {

        logger.info("Creating contact");
        if (bindingResult.hasErrors()) {
            uiModel.addAttribute("message", new Message("error",
                messageSource.getMessage("contact_save_fail", new Object[]{}, locale)));
            uiModel.addAttribute("contact", contact);
            return "contacts/create";
        }

        uiModel.asMap().clear();
        redirectAttributes.addFlashAttribute("message", new Message("success",
            messageSource.getMessage("contact_save_success", new Object[]{}, locale)));

        logger.info("Contact id: " + contact.getId());

        contactService.save(contact);
        return "redirect:/contacts/" + UrlUtil.encodeUrlPathSegment(contact.getId().toString(),
            httpServletRequest);
    }

    @RequestMapping(params = "form", method = RequestMethod.GET)
    public String createForm(Model uiModel) {
        Contact contact = new Contact();
        uiModel.addAttribute("contact", contact);
        return "contacts/create";
    }
}
```

Next, add the view mapping to the view definition file (/views/contacts/views.xml). Listing 17-37 shows the code snippet.

Listing 17-37. The Add Contact View Mapping

```
<definition extends="default" name="contacts/create">
    <put-attribute name="body"
        value="/WEB-INF/views/contacts/edit.jspx" />
</definition>
```

The add view is now complete. After you rebuild and deploy the project, click the New Contact link in the menu area in Figure 17-10. The add contact view will be displayed, as shown in Figure 17-15.

Add Contact

First Name*

Last Name*

Birth Date

Description

Save   Reset

Home | English (US) | Chinese (HK)

Figure 17-15. Add contact view

Enable JSR-303 Bean Validation

Let's configure JSR-303 Bean Validation support for the create and update contact actions. First, apply the validation constraints to the Contact domain object. In this sample, we define constraints only for the firstName and lastName attributes. Listing 17-38 shows the code snippet for the annotations applied to the firstName and lastName attributes.

Listing 17-38. Applying Constraints to the Contact Domain Object

```
package com.apress.prospring3.ch17.domain;

// Import statements omitted
@Entity
@Table(name = "contact")
public class Contact implements Serializable {
```

```
// Other code omitted

@NotEmpty(message="{validation.firstname.NotEmpty.message}")
@Size(min=3, max=60, message="{validation.firstname.Size.message}")
@Column(name = "FIRST_NAME")
public String getFirstName() {
    return firstName;
}

@NotEmpty(message="{validation.lastname.NotEmpty.message}")
@Size(min=1, max=40, message="{validation.lastname.Size.message}")
@Column(name = "LAST_NAME")
public String getLastName() {
    return lastName;
}
}
```

In Listing 17-38, the constraints applied are highlighted in bold. Note that for the validation message, we use a code by using the curly braces. This will cause the validation messages to retrieve from the ResourceBundle and hence support i18n.

To enable JSR-303 validation during the web data binding process, we just need to apply the @Valid annotation to the argument of the create() and update() methods in the ContactController class. Listing 17-39 shows the code snippet.

Listing 17-39. Enable JSR-303 Validation in Controller

```
public String update(@Valid Contact contact, …

public String create(@Valid Contact contact, …
```

We also want the JSR-303 validation message to use the same ResourceBundle as for the views. To do this, we need to configure the validator in the DispatcherServlet configuration (servlet-context.xml). Listing 17-40 shows the code snippet for the change.

Listing 17-40. Configure JSR-303 Support in Spring MVC

```
<?xml version="1.0" encoding="UTF-8"?>

    <!-- Other code omitted -->

    <annotation-driven validator="validator"/>
    <!-- Other code omitted -->

    <beans:bean id="validator"
class="org.springframework.validation.beanvalidation.LocalValidatorFactoryBean">
        <beans:property name="validationMessageSource" ref="messageSource"/>
    </beans:bean>
</beans:beans>
```

The changes are highlighted in bold. First, a validator bean is defined, with the class LocalValidatorFactoryBean, for JSR-303 support. Note that we set the validationMessageSource property to reference the messageSource bean defined, which instructs the JSR-303 validator to look up the messages by the codes from the messageSource bean. Then for the <annotation-driven> tag, the validator attribute is explicitly defined to reference the validator bean we defined.

That's all, and we can test the validation now. Bring up the add contact view, and just click the Save button. The validation messages will be displayed, as shown in Figure 17-16.

Add Contact

⊗ Failed saving contact

First Name*   [   ]

First name must be between 3 and 60
First name is required

Last Name*   [   ]

Last name must be between 1 and 40
Last name is required

Birth Date   [   ]

Description

[   ]

[Save] [Reset]

Home | English (US) | Chinese (HK)

Figure 17-16. JSR-303 validation error messages

Switch to the Chinese (HK) language, and do the same thing. This time, the messages will be displayed in Chinese, as shown in Figure 17-17.

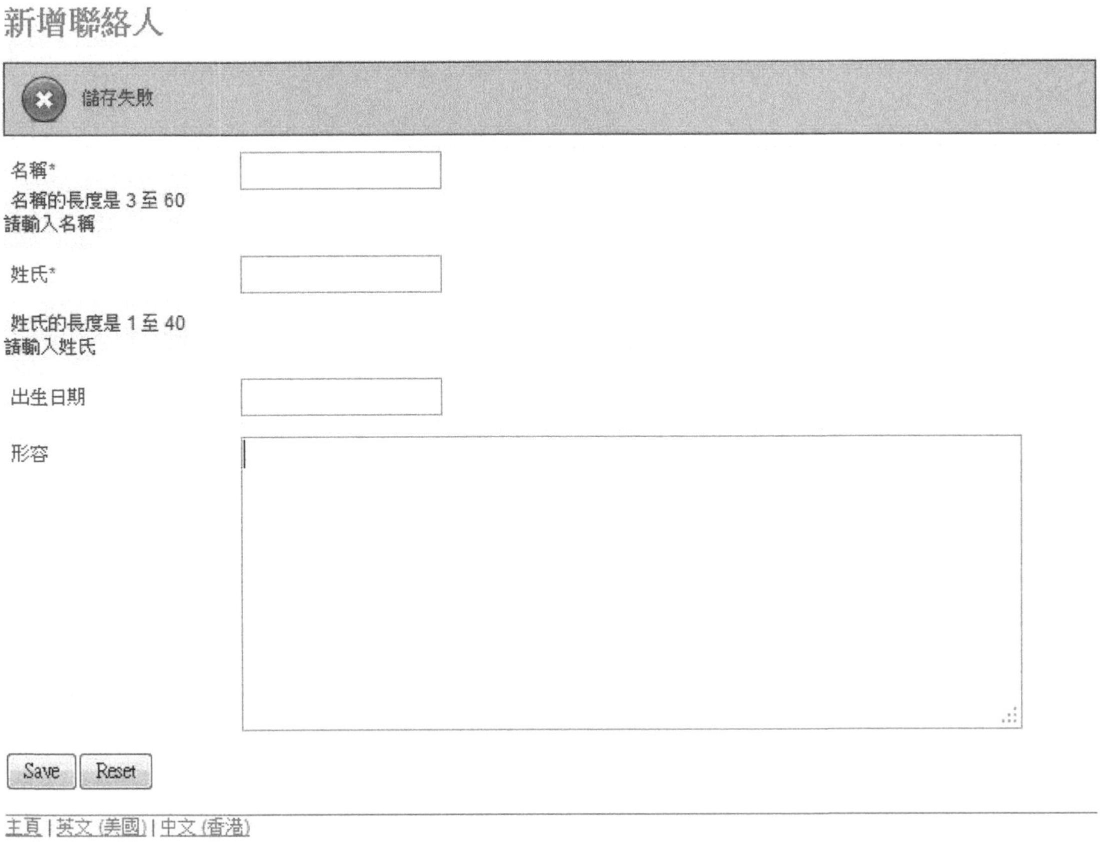

新增聯絡人

❌ 儲存失敗

名稱*
名稱的長度是 3 至 60
請輸入名稱

姓氏*

姓氏的長度是 1 至 40
請輸入姓氏

出生日期

形容

| Save | Reset |

主頁 | 英文 (美國) | 中文 (香港)

Figure 17-17. *JSR-303 validation error messages (i18n)*

Now the views are basically complete, except the delete action. We will leave that one to you as an exercise. Next, we will start to give our application more richness.

Using jQuery and jQuery UI

Although the views for our contact application work well, the user interface is quite raw. For example, for the birth date field, it would be much better if we could add a date picker when the user enters the birth date of the contact, instead of inputting the date string manually.

To provide a richer interface to the users of a web application, unless you are using rich Internet application (RIA) technologies that require special runtimes on the web browser client (for example, Adobe Flex requires Flash, JavaFX requires JRE, Microsoft Silverlight requires Silverlight, and so on), you need to use JavaScript to implement the features.

However, developing web frontends with raw JavaScript is not easy. The syntax is very different from Java, and you also need to deal with cross-browser compatibility issues. As a result, a lot of open source JavaScript libraries are available that can make the process easier, such as jQuery, Dojo Toolkit, and so on.

In the following sections, we will discuss how to use jQuery and jQuery UI to develop more responsive and interactive user interfaces. We will also discuss some commonly used jQuery plug-ins for specific purposes, such as rich-text editing support, and discuss some grid-based components for browsing data.

Introducing jQuery and jQuery UI

jQuery (http://jquery.org) is one of the most popular JavaScript libraries being used for web frontend development. jQuery provides comprehensive support for main features including a robust "selector" syntax for selecting DOM elements within the document, a sophisticated event model, powerful Ajax support, and so on.

Built on top of jQuery, the jQuery UI library (http://jqueryui.com) provides a rich set of widgets and effects. Main features include widgets for commonly used user interface components (a date picker, autocomplete, accordion, and so on), drag and drop, effects and animation, theming, and so on.

There also are a lot of jQuery plug-ins developed by the jQuery community for specific purposes, and we will discuss two of them in this chapter.

What we cover here only scratches the surface of jQuery. For more details on using jQuery, we recommend the books *jQuery Recipes: A Problem-Solution Approach* (Apress, 2010) and *jQuery in Action*, Second Edition (Manning, 2010).

Enable jQuery and jQuery UI in a View

To be able to use jQuery and jQuery UI components in our view, we need to include the required style sheets and JavaScript files.

If you read the section "Spring MVC Project Structure Overview" earlier in this chapter, the required files should have been already copied into the project. The main files that we need to include in our view are as follows:

- /src/main/webapp/scripts/jquery-1.7.1.js: This is the core jQuery JavaScript library. The version we use in this chapter is 1.7.1. Note that it's the full source version. In production, you should use the minified version (that is, jquery-1.7.1.min.js), which is optimized and compressed to improve download and execution performance.

- /src/main/webapp/scripts/jquery-ui-1.8.16.custom.min.js: This is the jQuery UI library bundled with a theme style sheet that can be customized and downloaded from the jQuery UI Themeroller page (http://jqueryui.com/themeroller). The jQuery UI version we are using is 1.8.16. Note that it's the minified version of JavaScript.

- /src/main/webapp/styles/custom-theme/jquery-ui-1.8.16.custom.css: This is the style sheet for the custom theme that will be used by jQuery UI for theming support.

To include the previous files, we only need to include them in our template page (i.e., /layouts/default.jspx). Listing 17-41 shows the code snippet that needs to be added to the page.

Listing 17-41. Include jQuery in Template Page

```
<html xmlns:jsp="http://java.sun.com/JSP/Page"

    <!-- Other code omitted -->
```

```
<head>
    <meta http-equiv="Content-Type" content="text/html; charset=UTF-8" />
    <meta http-equiv="X-UA-Compatible" content="IE=8" />

    <spring:theme code="styleSheet" var="app_css" />
    <spring:url value="/${app_css}" var="app_css_url" />
    <link rel="stylesheet" type="text/css" media="screen" href="${app_css_url}" />

    <!-- jQuery and jQuery UI -->
    <spring:url value="/resources/scripts/jquery-1.7.1.js" var="jquery_url" />
    <spring:url value="/resources/scripts/jquery-ui-1.8.16.custom.min.js"
        var="jquery_ui_url" />
    <spring:url value="/resources/styles/custom-theme/jquery-ui-1.8.16.custom.css"
        var="jquery_ui_theme_css" />
    <link rel="stylesheet" type="text/css" media="screen" href="${jquery_ui_theme_css}" />
    <script src="${jquery_url}" type="text/javascript"><jsp:text/></script>
    <script src="${jquery_ui_url}" type="text/javascript"><jsp:text/></script>

<!-- Other code omitted -->
</html>
```

In Listing 17-41, the code that needs to be added is highlighted in bold. First, the <spring:url> tag is used to define the URLs for the files and store them in variables. Then, in the <head> section, the reference to the CSS and JavaScript files is added. Note the use of the <jsp:text/> tag within the <script> tag. This is because JSPX will autocollapse tags without a body. So, the tag <script …></script> in the file will end up as <script …/> in the browser, which will cause undetermined behavior in the page. The addition of the <jsp:text/> ensures that the <script> tag will not render in the page because it avoids unexpected issues.

With these scripts included, we can add some fancier stuff into our view. For the edit contact view, let's make our buttons looks a bit better and enable the date picker component for the birth date field. Listing 17-42 shows the change that we need to add to the view (/views/contacts/edit.jspx) for the button and date field.

Listing 17-42. Decorate the Button and Date Picker in the Edit Contact View

```
<?xml version="1.0" encoding="UTF-8" standalone="no"?>

<!-- Other code omitted -->

<script type="text/javascript">
$(function(){
    $('#birthDate').datepicker({
        dateFormat: 'yy-mm-dd',
        changeYear: true
    });
});
</script>

<!-- Other code omitted -->

    <button type="submit" class="ui-button ui-widget ui-state-default ui-corner-all ui-↵
button-text-only">
        <span class="ui-button-text">Save</span>
```

```
            </button>
            <button type="reset" class="ui-button ui-widget ui-state-default ui-corner-all ui-↵
button-text-only">
                <span class="ui-button-text">Reset</span>
            </button>

    <!-- Other code omitted -->

</div>
```

In Listing 17-42, the changes required are highlighted in bold. First, the $(function(){}) syntax instructs jQuery to execute the script when the document is ready. Within the function, the birth date input field (with id birthDate) is decorated using jQuery UI's datepicker() function. Second, various style class are added to the buttons.

Now reload the page, and you will see the new button style, and when you click the birth date field, the date picker component will be displayed, as shown in Figure 17-18.

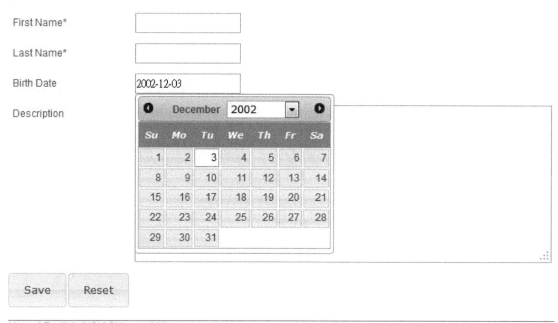

Figure 17-18. Enable jQuery in view

Rich-Text Editing with CKEditor

For the description field of the contact information, we use the Spring MVC's <form:textarea> tag to support multiline input. Suppose we want to enable rich-text editing, which is a common requirement for long text inputs such as user comments.

To support this feature, we will use the rich-text component library CKEditor
(http://ckeditor.com), which is a common rich-text JavaScript component, with integration with jQuery
UI. The files are in the folder /src/main/webapp/ckeditor of the sample source code.

First we need to include the required JavaScript files into the template page (default.jspx). Listing
17-43 shows the code snippet you need to add to the page.

Listing 17-43. Add CKEditor to Page Template

```
<html xmlns:jsp="http://java.sun.com/JSP/Page"

    <!-- Other code omitted -->

      <!-- jQuery and jQuery UI -->
      <spring:url value="/resources/scripts/jquery-1.7.1.js" var="jquery_url" />
      <spring:url value="/resources/scripts/jquery-ui-1.8.16.custom.min.js"
          var="jquery_ui_url" />
      <spring:url value="/resources/styles/custom-theme/jquery-ui-1.8.16.custom.css"
          var="jquery_ui_theme_css" />
      <link rel="stylesheet" type="text/css" media="screen" href="${jquery_ui_theme_css}" />
      <script src="${jquery_url}" type="text/javascript"><jsp:text/></script>
      <script src="${jquery_ui_url}" type="text/javascript"><jsp:text/></script>

      <!-- CKEditor -->
      <spring:url value="/resources/ckeditor/ckeditor.js" var="ckeditor_url" />
      <spring:url value="/resources/ckeditor/adapters/jquery.js" var="ckeditor_jquery_url" />
      <script type="text/javascript" src="${ckeditor_url}"><jsp:text/></script>
      <script type="text/javascript" src="${ckeditor_jquery_url}"><jsp:text/></script>

    <!-- Other code omitted -->
</html>
```

In Listing 17-43, the code to be added is highlighted in bold. We included two scripts, the core
CKEditor script and the adapter with jQuery.

The next step is to enable the CKEditor in the edit contact view. Listing 17-44 shows the change
required for the page (edit.jspx).

Listing 17-44. Add CKEditor to Edit Contact View

```
<?xml version="1.0" encoding="UTF-8" standalone="no"?>

    <!-- Other code omitted -->

    <script type="text/javascript">
    $(function(){
        $('#birthDate').datepicker({
            dateFormat: 'yy-mm-dd',
            changeYear: true
        });

        $("#contactDescription").ckeditor(
            {
                toolbar : 'Basic',
                uiColor : '#CCCCCC'
```

```
            }
        );
    });
    </script>

    <!-- Other code omitted -->

</div>
```

In Listing 17-44, the change is highlighted in bold. The contact description field is decorated with CKEditor when the document is ready. Reload the add contact page, and the description field will be enabled with rich-text editing support, as shown in Figure 17-19.

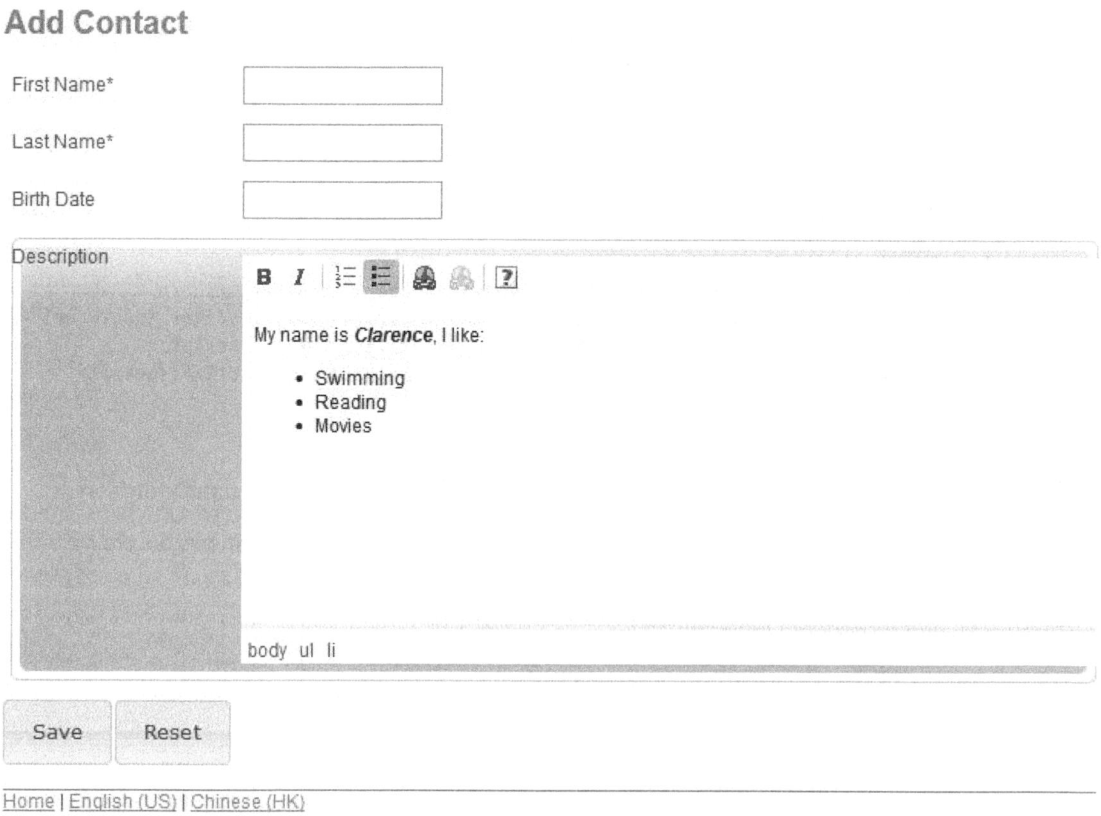

Add Contact

First Name*

Last Name*

Birth Date

Description

B *I* | ≡ | ≡ | 🖼 🔍 | ❓

My name is *Clarence*, I like:

- Swimming
- Reading
- Movies

body ul li

Save   Reset

Figure 17-19. *Use CKEditor for rich-text editing.*

For complete documentation on using and configuring CKEditor, please refer to the project documentation site (http://docs.cksource.com/CKEditor_3.x/Developers_Guide).

Data Grid with Pagination using jqGrid

The current contact list view is fine if only a few contacts exist in the system. However, as the data grows to thousands and even more records, performance will become a problem.

A common solution is to implement a data grid component, with pagination support, for data browsing so that the user just browses a certain number of records, which avoids a large amount of data transfer between the browser and the web container. In this section, we will demonstrate the implementation of a data grid with jqGrid (http://www.trirand.com/blog), a popular JavaScript-based data grid component. The version we are using is 4.3.1.

For the pagination support, we will use jqGrid's built-in Ajax pagination support, which fires an XMLHttpRequest for each page and accepts JSON data format for page data. So, we need to add the JSON library dependency into our project, as shown in Table 17-6.

Table 17-6. Maven Dependencies for JSON

Group ID	Artifact ID	Version	Description
org.codehaus.jackson	jackson-mapper-lgpl	1.9.2	Jackson JSON processor to support data in JSON format

In the following sections, we will discuss how to implement the pagination support on both the server and client sides. First, we will cover implementing the jqGrid component in the contact list view. Then, we will discuss how to implement pagination on the server side by using Spring Data Commons module's comprehensive pagination support.

Enable jqGrid in the Contact List View

To enable jqGrid in our views, first we need to include the required JavaScript and style sheet files in the template page (default.jspx). Listing 17-45 shows the code snippet required.

Listing 17-45. Add jqGrid to Page Template

```
<html xmlns:jsp="http://java.sun.com/JSP/Page"

    <!-- Other code omitted -->

        <!-- CKEditor -->
        <spring:url value="/resources/ckeditor/ckeditor.js" var="ckeditor_url" />
        <spring:url value="/resources/ckeditor/adapters/jquery.js" var="ckeditor_jquery_url" />
        <script type="text/javascript" src="${ckeditor_url}"><jsp:text/></script>
        <script type="text/javascript" src="${ckeditor_jquery_url}"><jsp:text/></script>

        <!-- jqGrid -->
        <spring:url value="/resources/jqgrid/css/ui.jqgrid.css" var="jqgrid_css" />
        <spring:url value="/resources/jqgrid/js/i18n/grid.locale-en.js"
            var="jqgrid_locale_url" />
        <spring:url value="/resources/jqgrid/js/jquery.jqGrid.min.js" var="jqgrid_url" />
        <link rel="stylesheet" type="text/css" media="screen" href="${jqgrid_css}" />
        <script type="text/javascript" src="${jqgrid_locale_url}"> <jsp:text/></script>
```

```
<script type="text/javascript" src="${jqgrid_url}"><jsp:text/></script>
```

```
<!-- Other code omitted -->
```

```
</html>
```

In Listing 17-45, the new code is highlighted in bold. First, the grid-specific CSS file is loaded. Then, two JavaScript files are required. The first one is the locale script (in this case, we use English), and the second one is the jqGrid core library file (jquery.jqGrid.min.js).

The next step is to modify the contact list view (list.jspx) to use jqGrid. Listing 17-46 shows the revised page.

Listing 17-46. Contact List Page with jqGrid

```xml
<?xml version="1.0" encoding="UTF-8" standalone="no"?>
<div xmlns:jsp="http://java.sun.com/JSP/Page"
    xmlns:c="http://java.sun.com/jsp/jstl/core"
    xmlns:spring="http://www.springframework.org/tags"
    version="2.0">
<jsp:directive.page contentType="text/html;charset=UTF-8"/>
<jsp:output omit-xml-declaration="yes"/>

<spring:message code="label_contact_list" var="labelContactList"/>
<spring:message code="label_contact_first_name" var="labelContactFirstName"/>
<spring:message code="label_contact_last_name" var="labelContactLastName"/>
<spring:message code="label_contact_birth_date" var="labelContactBirthDate"/>
<spring:url value="/contacts/" var="showContactUrl"/>

<script type="text/javascript">
$(function(){
  $("#list").jqGrid({
    url:'${showContactUrl}/listgrid',
    datatype: 'json',
    mtype: 'GET',
    colNames:['${labelContactFirstName}', '${labelContactLastName}',
        '${labelContactBirthDate}'],
    colModel :[
      {name:'firstName', index:'firstName', width:150},
      {name:'lastName', index:'lastName', width:100},
      {name:'birthDateString', index:'birthDate', width:100}
    ],
    jsonReader : {
        root:"contactData",
        page: "currentPage",
        total: "totalPages",
        records: "totalRecords",
        repeatitems: false,
        id: "id"
    },
    pager: '#pager',
    rowNum:10,
    rowList:[10,20,30],
    sortname: 'firstName',
    sortorder: 'asc',
```

```
        viewrecords: true,
        gridview: true,
        height: 250,
        width: 500,
        caption: '${labelContactList}',
        onSelectRow: function(id){
            document.location.href ="${showContactUrl}/" + id;
        }
    });
});
</script>

<c:if test="${not empty message}">
    <div id="message" class="${message.type}">${message.message}</div>
</c:if>

<h2>${labelContactList}</h2>

<div>
<table id="list"><tr><td/></tr></table>
</div>
<div id="pager"></div>
</div>
```

As shown in Listing 17-46, we declare a `<table>` tag with an ID of `list` for displaying the grid data. Under the table, a `<div>` section with an ID of `pager` is defined, which is the pagination part for jqGrid.

Within the JavaScript, when the document is ready, we instruct jqGrid to decorate the table with an ID of `list` into a grid and provide detail configuration information. Some main highlights of the scripts are as follows:

- The `url` attribute specifies the link for sending `XMLHttpRequest`, which gets the data for the current page.

- The `datatype` attribute specifies the data format, in this case JSON. jqGrid also supports XML format.

- The `mtype` attribute defines the HTTP method to use, which is GET.

- The `colNames` attribute defines the column header for the data to be displayed in the grid, while the `colModel` attribute defines the detail for each data column.

- The `jsonReader` attribute defines the JSON data format that the server will be returning.

- The `pager` attribute enables pagination support.

- The `onSelectRow` attribute defines the action to take when a row was selected. In our case, we will direct the user to the show contact view with the contact ID.

For a detailed description on the configuration and usage of jqGrid, please refer to the project's documentation site (www.trirand.com/jqgridwiki/doku.php?id=wiki:jqgriddocs).

Enable Pagination on the Server Side

On the server side, there are several steps to take to implement pagination. First we will use the Spring Data Commons module's pagination support. To enable this, we need only to modify the

ContactRepository interface to extend the PagingAndSortingRepository<T,ID extends Serializable> interface instead of the CrudRepository<T,ID extends Serializable> interface. Listing 17-47 shows the revised interface.

Listing 17-47. The Revised ContactRepository Interface

```
package com.apress.prospring3.ch17.repository;

import org.springframework.data.repository.PagingAndSortingRepository;

import com.apress.prospring3.ch17.domain.Contact;

public interface ContactRepository extends PagingAndSortingRepository<Contact, Long> {

}
```

The next step is to add a new method in the ContactService interface to support retrieving the data by page. Listing 17-48 shows the revised interface.

Listing 17-48. The Revised ContactService Interface

```
package com.apress.prospring3.ch17.service;

import java.util.List;

import org.springframework.data.domain.Page;
import org.springframework.data.domain.Pageable;

import com.apress.prospring3.ch17.domain.Contact;

public interface ContactService {

    public List<Contact> findAll();

    public Contact findById(Long id);

    public Contact save(Contact contact);

    public Page<Contact> findAllByPage(Pageable pageable);

}
```

As shown in Listing 17-48, a new method findAllByPage() is added, taking an instance of the Pageable interface as an argument. Listing 17-49 shows the implementation of the findAllByPage() method in the ContactServiceImpl class. The method returns an instance of the Page<T> interface (belonging to Spring Data Commons and under the package org.springframework.data.domain).

Listing 17-49. The Revised ContactServiceImpl Class

```
package com.apress.prospring3.ch17.service.jpa;

// Import statements omitted
```

```
@Service("contactService")
@Repository
@Transactional
public class ContactServiceImpl implements ContactService {

    // Other code omitted

    @Transactional(readOnly=true)
    public Page<Contact> findAllByPage(Pageable pageable) {
        return contactRepository.findAll(pageable);
    }

}
```

In Listing 17-49, the method implementation is highlighted in bold. In the method, we simply call the findAll(Pageable) method, which was provided by the PagingAndSortingRepository<T,ID extends Serializable> interface.

The next step is to implement the method in the ContactController class to take the Ajax request from jqGrid for page data. Listing 17-50 shows the implementation.

Listing 17-50. The Revised ContactController Class

```
package com.apress.prospring3.ch17.web.controller;

// Import statements omitted

@RequestMapping("/contacts")
@Controller
public class ContactController {

    // Other code omitted

    @RequestMapping(value = "/listgrid", method = RequestMethod.GET,
        produces="application/json")
    @ResponseBody
    public ContactGrid listGrid(@RequestParam(value = "page", required = false) Integer page,
        @RequestParam(value = "rows", required = false) Integer rows,
        @RequestParam(value = "sidx", required = false) String sortBy,
        @RequestParam(value = "sord", required = false) String order) {

        logger.info("Listing contacts for grid with page: {}, rows: {}", page, rows);
        logger.info("Listing contacts for grid with sort: {}, order: {}", sortBy, order);

        // Process order by
        Sort sort = null;
        String orderBy = sortBy;
        if (orderBy != null && orderBy.equals("birthDateString"))
            orderBy = "birthDate";

        if (orderBy != null && order != null) {
            if (order.equals("desc")) {
                sort = new Sort(Sort.Direction.DESC, orderBy);
```

```
        } else
            sort = new Sort(Sort.Direction.ASC, orderBy);
    }

    // Constructs page request for current page
    // Note: page number for Spring Data JPA starts with 0, while jqGrid starts with 1
    PageRequest pageRequest = null;

    if (sort != null) {
        pageRequest = new PageRequest(page - 1, rows, sort);
    } else {
        pageRequest = new PageRequest(page - 1, rows);
    }

    Page<Contact> contactPage = contactService.findAllByPage(pageRequest);

    // Construct the grid data that will return as JSON data
    ContactGrid contactGrid = new ContactGrid();

    contactGrid.setCurrentPage(contactPage.getNumber() + 1);
    contactGrid.setTotalPages(contactPage.getTotalPages());
    contactGrid.setTotalRecords(contactPage.getTotalElements());

    contactGrid.setContactData(Lists.newArrayList(contactPage.iterator()));

    return contactGrid;
    }
}
```

In Listing 17-50, the new method listGrid() is highlighted in bold. Basically, the method handles the Ajax request, reads the parameters (page number, records per page, sort by, sort order) from the request (the parameter names in the code sample are jqGrid's defaults), constructs an instance of the PageRequest class that implements the Pageable interface, and then invokes the ContactService.findAllByPage() method to get the page data. Then, an instance of the ContactGrid class is constructed and returned to jqGrid in JSON format. Listing 17-51 shows the ContactGrid class.

Listing 17-51. The ContactGrid Class

```
package com.apress.prospring3.ch17.web.form;

import java.util.List;

import com.apress.prospring3.ch17.domain.Contact;

public class ContactGrid {

    private int totalPages;

    private int currentPage;

    private long totalRecords;
```

```
        private List<Contact> contactData;

        // Getter/setter methods omitted
}
```

Now we are ready to test the new contact list view. Make sure the project is rebuilt and deployed, and then invoke the contact list view. You should see a view like the one shown in Figure 17-20.

Contact Listing

Contact Listing			▲
First Name ⬍	Last Name	Birth Date	
Clarence	Ho	1980-07-30	
Henry	Dickson	1997-06-30	
Jacky	Chan	1955-10-31	
John	Smith	1964-02-28	
Lotus	Notes	1990-02-28	
Max	Beckham	2002-02-01	
Paul	Simon	2002-02-28	
Peter	Jackson	1944-01-10	
Sam	Davis	2001-01-31	
Scott	Tiger	1990-11-02	

⬛◀ ◀◀ Page `1` of 2 ▶▶ ▶⬛ `10` ▼   View 1 - 10 of 12

Home | English (US) | Chinese (HK)

Figure 17-20. Contact list view with jgGrid

You can play around with the grid, browse the pages, change the number of records per page, change the sort order by clicking the column headers, and so on. i18n is also supported, and you can try to see the grid with Chinese labels.

jqGrid also supports data filtering. For example, we can filter data by first names containing "clarence" or when the birth date is between a date range. We will use filtering in the sample application and will discuss it in Chapter 21.

File Upload Handling

The contact information has a field of BLOB type to store a photo, which can be uploaded from the client. In this section, we will discuss how to implement file upload in Spring MVC.

For a long time, the standard servlet specification didn't support file upload. As a result, Spring MVC worked with other libraries (the most common one being the Apache Commons FileUpload library, http://commons.apache.org/fileupload) to serve this purpose. Spring MVC has built-in support for Commons FileUpload. However, from Servlet 3.0, file upload has become a built-in feature of the web container. Tomcat 7 supports Servlet 3.0, and Spring 3.1 also added support for Servlet 3.0 file upload.

In the following sections, we will discuss how to implement the file upload using Spring MVC 3.1 and Servlet 3.0.

To support file upload, we need one more dependency, and we also need to revise the dependency for Servlet API versions 2.5 to 3.0. Table 17-7 shows the dependency that requires deletion and the two new dependencies we need to add.

Table 17-7. Maven Dependencies for File Upload

Group ID	Artifact ID	Version	Description
javax.servlet	servlet-api	2.5	Delete this dependency.
javax	javaee-web-api	6.0	JEE 6.0 Web Profile API, which contains the library for Servlet 3.0. Please use the provided scope for this dependency.
commons-io	commons-io	2.1	The Apache Commons IO module provides a lot of useful functions to ease I/O handling in Java.

Configuring File Upload Support

In a Servlet 3.0–compatible web container with Spring MVC, configuring file upload support is a two-step process.

First, in the web deployment descriptor (web.xml) for the DispatchServlet definition, we need to add a <multipart-config> section. Listing 17-52 shows the code snippet for this change.

Listing 17-52. Add File Upload Support in web.xml

```
<?xml version="1.0" encoding="UTF-8"?>
<web-app version="3.0" xmlns="http://java.sun.com/xml/ns/javaee"

    <!-- Other code omitted -->

    <!-- Processes application requests -->
    <servlet>
        <servlet-name>appServlet</servlet-name>
        <servlet-class>org.springframework.web.servlet.DispatcherServlet</servlet-class>
        <init-param>
            <param-name>contextConfigLocation</param-name>
            <param-value>/WEB-INF/spring/appServlet/servlet-context.xml</param-value>
        </init-param>
        <load-on-startup>1</load-on-startup>
        <multipart-config>
            <max-file-size>5000000</max-file-size>
        </multipart-config>
    </servlet>
```

```
<!-- Other code omitted -->
```

```
</web-app>
```

The change is highlighted in bold. In Servlet 3.0, the servlet that supports file upload should be provided with a `<multipart-config>` tag to configure the support. The `<max-file-size>` tag controls the maximum file size allowed for upload, which is 5MB.

Second, we need to configure a bean that implements the `MultipartResolver` interface in the `DispatcherServlet`'s `WebApplicationContext`. Listing 17-53 shows the bean definition that you need to add to the file (`servlet-context.xml`).

Listing 17-53. Configure the MultipartResolver Support in Spring MVC

```
<beans:bean
    class="org.springframework.web.multipart.support.StandardServletMultipartResolver"
    id="multipartResolver"/>
```

Note the implementation class `StandardServletMultipartResolver`, which is new in Spring 3.1 for supportinging native file upload in the Servlet 3.0 container.

Modify Views for File Upload Support

We need to modify two views for file upload support. The first one is the edit view (`edit.jspx`) to support photo upload for a contact, and the second one is the show view (`show.jspx`) for displaying the photo.

Listing 17-54 shows the changes required for the edit view.

Listing 17-54. Edit Contact View for File Upload Support

```
<?xml version="1.0" encoding="UTF-8" standalone="no"?>

    <!-- Other code omitted -->

    <form:form modelAttribute="contact" id="contactUpdateForm" method="post"
        enctype="multipart/form-data">

        <!-- Other code omitted -->

        <form:label path="description">
            ${labelContactDescription}
        </form:label>
        <form:textarea cols="60" rows="8" path="description" id="contactDescription"/>
        <div>
            <form:errors path="description" cssClass="error" />
        </div>
        <p/>

        <label for="file">
            ${labelContactPhoto}
        </label>
        <input name="file" type="file"/>
        <p/>
```

```
<!-- Other code omitted -->
```

```
</div>
```

In Listing 17-54, the changes are highlighted in bold. In the `<form:form>` tag, we need to enable the multipart file upload support by specifying the attribute enctype. Next, the file upload field is added to the form.

We also need to modify the show view to display the photo for a contact. Listing 17-55 shows the changes required to the view (`show.jspx`).

Listing 17-55. Show Contact View for Display File

```
<?xml version="1.0" encoding="UTF-8" standalone="no"?>

    <!-- Other code omitted -->

    <spring:message code="label_contact_photo" var="labelContactPhoto"/>
    <spring:url value="/contacts/photo" var="contactPhotoUrl"/>

    <!-- Other code omitted -->
            <tr>
                <td>${labelContactDescription}</td>
                <td>${contact.description}</td>
            </tr>
            <tr>
                <td>${labelContactPhoto}</td>
                <td><img src="${contactPhotoUrl}/${contact.id}"></img></td>
            </tr>
    <!-- Other code omitted -->
</div>
```

In Listing 17-55, the changes are highlighted in bold. A new row is added to the table for displaying the photo by pointing to the URL for photo download, as specified in Table 17-5.

Modify Controller for File Upload Support

The final step is to modify the controller. We need to make two changes. The first change is to the `create()` method to accept the upload file as a request parameter. The second change is to implement a new method for photo download based on the supplied contact ID. Listing 17-56 shows the revised ContactController class.

Listing 17-56. Revised Controller Class with File Upload and Download Support

```
package com.apress.prospring3.ch17.web.controller;

import javax.servlet.http.Part;

// Other import statements omitted
@RequestMapping("/contacts")
@Controller
public class ContactController {

    @RequestMapping(method = RequestMethod.POST)
```

```
    public String create(@Valid Contact contact, BindingResult bindingResult, Model uiModel,
HttpServletRequest httpServletRequest, RedirectAttributes redirectAttributes, Locale locale,
@RequestParam(value="file", required=false) Part file) {
        logger.info("Creating contact");
        if (bindingResult.hasErrors()) {
            uiModel.addAttribute("message", new Message("error",
                messageSource.getMessage("contact_save_fail", new Object[]{}, locale)));
            uiModel.addAttribute("contact", contact);
            return "contacts/create";
        }
        uiModel.asMap().clear();
        redirectAttributes.addFlashAttribute("message", new Message("success",
            messageSource.getMessage("contact_save_success", new Object[]{}, locale)));

        logger.info("Contact id: " + contact.getId());

        // Process upload file
        if (file != null) {
            logger.info("File name: " + file.getName());
            logger.info("File size: " + file.getSize());
            logger.info("File content type: " + file.getContentType());
            byte[] fileContent = null;
            try {
                InputStream inputStream = file.getInputStream();
                if (inputStream == null) logger.info("File inputstream is null");
                    fileContent = IOUtils.toByteArray(inputStream);
                    contact.setPhoto(fileContent);
                } catch (IOException ex) {
                    logger.error("Error saving uploaded file");
                }
            contact.setPhoto(fileContent);
        }

        contactService.save(contact);
        return "redirect:/contacts/" +
UrlUtil.encodeUrlPathSegment(contact.getId().toString(), httpServletRequest);
    }

    @RequestMapping(value = "/photo/{id}", method = RequestMethod.GET)
    @ResponseBody
    public byte[] downloadPhoto(@PathVariable("id") Long id) {

        Contact contact = contactService.findById(id);

        if (contact.getPhoto() != null) {
            logger.info("Downloading photo for id: {} with size: {}", contact.getId(),
                contact.getPhoto().length);
        }

        return contact.getPhoto();
    }

}
```

In Listing 17-56, the changes are highlighted in bold. In the create() method, a new request parameter of interface type javax.servlet.http.Part is added as an argument, which Spring MVC will provide based on the uploaded content in the request. Then the method will get the content saved into the photo property of the Contact object.

Then, a new method downloadPhoto() is added to handle the file download. The method just retrieves the photo field from the contact object and directly writes into the response stream, which corresponds to the <img> tag in the show view.

To test the file upload function, reload the page and add a new contact with photo, as shown in Figure 17-21.

Add Contact

Figure 17-21. Upload photo for contact

Upon completion, you will be able to see the photo in the show view, as shown in Figure 17-22.

Contact Information

Figure 17-22. Show contact view with photo

We also need to modify the edit function for changing the photo, but we will skip it here. You can refer to the sample source code.

Securing a Web Application with Spring Security

Suppose now we want to secure our contact application. Only those users who logged into the application with a valid user ID can add a new contact or update existing contacts. Other users, known as anonymous users, can only view contact information.

Spring Security is the best choice for securing Spring-based applications. Although mostly used in the presentation layer, Spring Security can help secure all layers within the application, including the service layer. In the following sections, we will demonstrate how to use Spring Security to secure the contact application.

Table 17-8 lists the dependencies required for Spring Security.

Table 17-8. Maven Dependencies for Spring Security

Group ID	Artifact ID	Version	Description
org.springframework.security	spring-security-core	3.1.0.RELEASE	Spring Security core module
org.springframework.security	spring-security-web	3.1.0.RELEASE	Spring Security web module
org.springframework.security	spring-security-config	3.1.0.RELEASE	Spring Security configuration module
org.springframework.security	spring-security-taglibs	3.1.0.RELEASE	Spring Security JSP tag library

651

Configuring Spring Security

To configure Spring Security, first we need to configure a filter in the web deployment descriptor (web.xml). Listing 17-57 shows the code snippet you need to add to the web.xml file.

Listing 17-57. Configure Spring Security Filter

```
<?xml version="1.0" encoding="UTF-8"?>
<web-app version="3.0" xmlns="http://java.sun.com/xml/ns/javaee"

    <!-- Other code omitted -->

    <!-- Spring Security Configuration -->
    <filter>
        <filter-name>springSecurityFilterChain</filter-name>
        <filter-class>org.springframework.web.filter.DelegatingFilterProxy</filter-class>
    </filter>

    <filter-mapping>
        <filter-name>springSecurityFilterChain</filter-name>
        <url-pattern>/*</url-pattern>
    </filter-mapping>

    <!-- Other code omitted -->
</web-app>
```

In Listing 17-57, the filter for Spring Security is highlighted in bold. The next step is to define the Spring Security context, which will be imported by the root WebApplicationContext configuration file. Listing 17-58 shows the configuration file (/WEB-INF/spring/security-context.xml).

Listing 17-58. Spring Security Context Configuration

```
<?xml version="1.0" encoding="UTF-8"?>
<beans:beans xmlns="http://www.springframework.org/schema/security"
    xmlns:beans="http://www.springframework.org/schema/beans"
    xmlns:xsi="http://www.w3.org/2001/XMLSchema-instance"
    xsi:schemaLocation="http://www.springframework.org/schema/beans
        http://www.springframework.org/schema/beans/spring-beans-3.1.xsd
        http://www.springframework.org/schema/security
        http://www.springframework.org/schema/security/spring-security-3.1.xsd">

    <http use-expressions="true">
        <intercept-url pattern='/*' access='permitAll' />
        <form-login login-page="/contacts" authentication-failure-url="/security/loginfail"
            default-target-url="/contacts" />
        <logout logout-success-url="/contacts"/>
    </http>

    <authentication-manager>
        <authentication-provider>
            <user-service>
                <user name="user" password="user" authorities="ROLE_USER" />
            </user-service>
```

```
        </authentication-provider>
    </authentication-manager>

</beans:beans>
```

Since our requirement is simple, the configuration is simple too. First, the `<http>` tag defines the security configuration for HTTP requests. The attribute `use-expressions` means that we want to use Spring Expression Language (SpEL) for the expressions. The `<intercept-url>` tag specifies that all users are allowed to enter the application. We will see how we can protect the function by hiding the editing options in the view using Spring Security's tag library and controller method security. Then the `<form-login>` defines the support for form login. As we discussed in the layout, the login form will display on the left. We provide a logout link as well.

The `<authentication-manager>` tag defines the authentication mechanism. In the configuration, we hard-code a single user with the role `ROLE_USER` assigned. In a production environment, the user should be authenticated against the database, LDAP, or an SSO mechanism.

Listing 17-59 shows the revised `root-context.xml` file to import the security configuration file.

Listing 17-59. *Spring Security Context Configuration*

```
<?xml version="1.0" encoding="UTF-8"?>
<beans xmlns="http://www.springframework.org/schema/beans"

    <!-- Other code omitted -->

    <import resource="classpath:datasource-tx-jpa.xml" />

    <import resource="security-context.xml"/>

    <context:component-scan base-package="com.apress.prospring3.ch17.service.jpa"/>

</beans>
```

The import statement is highlighted in bold.

Adding Login Functions to the Application

We need to modify two page components: the header (`header.jspx`) and the menu (`menu.jspx`).

Listing 17-60 shows the revised `header.jspx` file to display the user information if the user is logged in.

Listing 17-60. *Display Login User Information*

```
<div id="header" xmlns:jsp="http://java.sun.com/JSP/Page"
        xmlns:spring="http://www.springframework.org/tags"
        xmlns:sec="http://www.springframework.org/security/tags"
        version="2.0">
        <jsp:directive.page contentType="text/html;charset=UTF-8" />
        <jsp:output omit-xml-declaration="yes" />

    <spring:message code="header_text" var="headerText"/>
    <spring:message code="label_logout" var="labelLogout"/>
    <spring:message code="label_welcome" var="labelWelcome"/>
    <spring:url var="logoutUrl" value="/j_spring_security_logout" />
```

```
    <div id="appname">
        <h1>${headerText}</h1>
    </div>

    <div id="userinfo">
        <sec:authorize access="isAuthenticated()">${labelWelcome}
            <sec:authentication property="principal.username" />
            <br/>
            <a href="${logoutUrl}">${labelLogout}</a>
        </sec:authorize>
    </div>

</div>
```

In Listing 17-60, the changes from the previous version are highlighted in bold. First, the tag library with the prefix sec is added for Spring Security tag library. Then, a <div> section with the <sec:authorize> tag is added to detect whether the user is logged in. If yes (i.e., the isAuthenticated() expression returns true), the user name will be displayed, as well as a logout link.

Listing 17-61 shows the revised menu.jspx file, which has the login form added; the New Contact option will display only if the user is logged in.

Listing 17-61. Display Login Form

```
<?xml version="1.0" encoding="UTF-8" standalone="no"?>
<div id="menu" xmlns:jsp="http://java.sun.com/JSP/Page"
    xmlns:c="http://java.sun.com/jsp/jstl/core"
    xmlns:spring="http://www.springframework.org/tags"
    xmlns:sec="http://www.springframework.org/security/tags"
    version="2.0">
        <jsp:directive.page contentType="text/html;charset=UTF-8" />
        <jsp:output omit-xml-declaration="yes" />

        <spring:message code="menu_header_text" var="menuHeaderText"/>
        <spring:message code="menu_add_contact" var="menuAddContact"/>
        <spring:url value="/contacts?form" var="addContactUrl"/>

    <spring:message code="label_login" var="labelLogin"/>
    <spring:url var="loginUrl" value="/j_spring_security_check" />

    <h3>${menuHeaderText}</h3>
    <sec:authorize access="hasRole('ROLE_USER')">
        <a href="${addContactUrl}"><h3>${menuAddContact}</h3></a>
    </sec:authorize>

    <sec:authorize access="isAnonymous()">
    <div id="login">
        <form name="loginForm" action="${loginUrl}" method="post">
            <table>
                <caption align="left">Login:</caption>
                <tr>
                    <td>User Name:</td>
                    <td><input type="text" name="j_username"/></td>
```

```
            </tr>
            <tr>
                <td>Password:</td>
                <td><input type="password" name="j_password"/></td>
            </tr>
            <tr>
                <td colspan="2" align="center"><input name="submit" type="submit"
                    value="Login"/></td>
            </tr>
        </table>
    </form>
</div>
</sec:authorize>

</div>
```

In Listing 17-61, the changes from the previous version are highlighted in bold. First, the add contact menu item will render only when the user is logged in and has the role ROLE_USER granted (as specified in the <sec:authorized> tag). Second, if the user is not logged in (the second <sec:authorized> tag, when the expression isAnonymous() returns true), then the login form will be displayed.

Reload the page, and it will display the login form, as shown in Figure 17-23. Note the new contact link is shown.

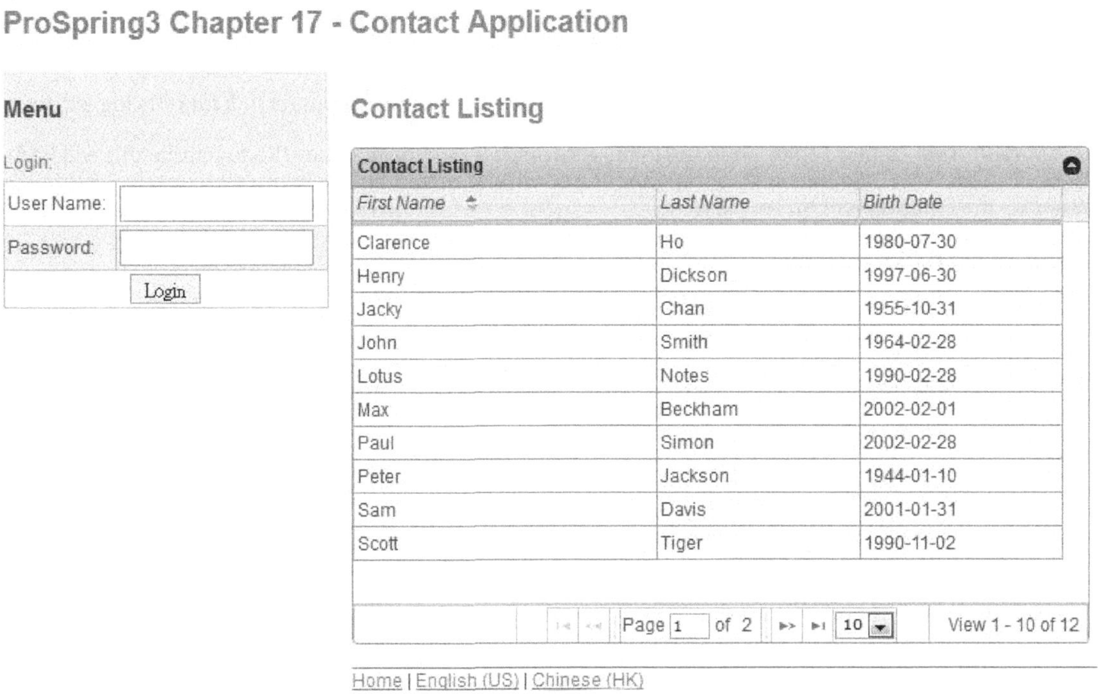

ProSpring3 Chapter 17 - Contact Application

Menu

Login:

User Name:	
Password:	
	Login

Contact Listing

Contact Listing			⊙
First Name ⇕	Last Name	Birth Date	
Clarence	Ho	1980-07-30	
Henry	Dickson	1997-06-30	
Jacky	Chan	1955-10-31	
John	Smith	1964-02-28	
Lotus	Notes	1990-02-28	
Max	Beckham	2002-02-01	
Paul	Simon	2002-02-28	
Peter	Jackson	1944-01-10	
Sam	Davis	2001-01-31	
Scott	Tiger	1990-11-02	

|◄ ◄◄ Page 1 of 2 ►► ►| 10 ▼   View 1 - 10 of 12

Home | English (US) | Chinese (HK)

Figure 17-23. The login form

Enter **user** in both the user name and password fields and click Login button. The user information will be displayed in the header area, as shown in Figure 17-24. The new contact link is also shown.

Figure 17-24. The login user information in header area

We also need to modify the show view (show.jspx) to show the edit contact link for only logged-in users, but we will skip that here.

As defined in Listing 17-58, when the login information is incorrect, the URL to handle this will be at /security/loginfail. So, we need to implement a controller to handle this login fail scenario. Listing 17-62 shows the SecurityController class.

Listing 17-62. The SecurityController Class

```
package com.apress.prospring3.ch17.web.controller;

// Import statements omitted
@RequestMapping("/security")
@Controller
public class SecurityController {

    final Logger logger = LoggerFactory.getLogger(SecurityController.class);
    @Autowired
    private MessageSource messageSource;

    @RequestMapping("/loginfail")
    public String loginFail(Model uiModel, Locale locale) {
        logger.info("Login failed detected");
        uiModel.addAttribute("message", new Message("error",
            messageSource.getMessage("message_login_fail", new Object[]{}, locale)));
        return "contacts/list";
    }
}
```

The controller class will handle all URLs with the prefix security, while the method loginFail() will handle the login fail scenario. In the method, we store the login fail message in the Model and then redirect to the home page. Now reload the page and enter the wrong user information; the home page will be displayed again with the login fail message, as shown in Figure 17-25.

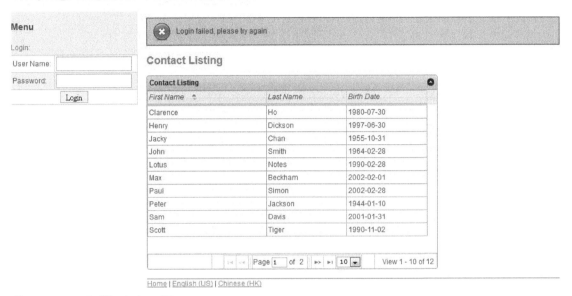

Figure 17-25. Fail login handling

Using Annotations to Secure Controller Methods

Hiding the new contact link in the menu is not enough. For example, if you enter the URL in the browser directly (http://localhost:8080/ch17/contacts?form), you can still see the add contact page, even though you are not logged in yet. The reason is that we haven't protected the application at the URL level. One method for protecting the page is to configure the Spring Security filter chain (in the file security-context.xml) to intercept the URL for only authenticated users. However, doing this will block all other users from seeing the contact list view.

An alternative for solving the problem is to apply security at the controller method level, using Spring Security's annotation support.

To enable method-level security, we need to modify the DispatcherServlet configuration (servlet-context.xml), as shown in Listing 17-63.

Listing 17-63. Enable Method-Level Security

```xml
<?xml version="1.0" encoding="UTF-8"?>
<beans:beans xmlns="http://www.springframework.org/schema/mvc"
    xmlns:xsi="http://www.w3.org/2001/XMLSchema-instance"
    xmlns:beans="http://www.springframework.org/schema/beans"
    xmlns:p="http://www.springframework.org/schema/p"
    xmlns:context="http://www.springframework.org/schema/context"
```

```
xmlns:security="http://www.springframework.org/schema/security"
xsi:schemaLocation="http://www.springframework.org/schema/mvc
    http://www.springframework.org/schema/mvc/spring-mvc-3.1.xsd
    http://www.springframework.org/schema/beans
    http://www.springframework.org/schema/beans/spring-beans-3.1.xsd
    http://www.springframework.org/schema/context
    http://www.springframework.org/schema/context/spring-context-3.1.xsd
    http://www.springframework.org/schema/security
    http://www.springframework.org/schema/security/spring-security-3.1.xsd">

    <!-- DispatcherServlet Context: defines this servlet's request-processing infrastructure -
->

    <!-- Enables the Spring MVC @Controller programming model -->
    <annotation-driven validator="validator"/>

    <!-- Enable controller method level security -->
    <security:global-method-security pre-post-annotations="enabled"/>

    <!-- Other code omitted -->

</beans:beans>
```

As shown in Listing 17-63, the security namespace is added. Then, the <security:global-method-security> tag is used to enable Spring Security's method-level security, and the pre-post-annotations attribute enables the support of annotations.

Now we can use the @PreAuthorize annotation for the controller method we want to protect. Listing 17-64 shows an example of protecting the createForm() method.

Listing 17-64. Applying Spring Security Annotations

```
@PreAuthorize("isAuthenticated()")
@RequestMapping(params = "form", method = RequestMethod.GET)
public String createForm(Model uiModel) {
    Contact contact = new Contact();
    uiModel.addAttribute("contact", contact);
    return "contacts/create";
}
```

As shown in Listing 17-64, we use the @PreAuthorize annotation (under the package org.springframework.security.access.prepost) to secure the createForm() method, with an argument being the expression for security requirements.

Now you can try to directly enter the new contact URL in the browser, and if you are not logged in, Spring Security will redirect you to the login page, which is the contact list view as configured in the security-context.xml file.

Support for Servlet 3 Code-Based Configuration

Another new feature in Spring 3.1 relating to the web layer is the support of Servlet 3's code-based configuration, which provides an alternative to the XML configuration required in the web deployment descriptor file (web.xml). In this section, we will show you how to use Java code to bootstrap the DispatcherServlet WebApplicationContext instead of configuring it in the web.xml file.

To use code-based configuration, we just need to develop a class that implements the org.springframework.web.WebApplicationInitializer interface. The WebApplicationInitializer interface was introduced in Spring 3.1, and all classes implementing this interface will be automatically detected by the org.springframework.web.SpringServletContainerInitializer class (which implements Servlet 3's javax.servlet.ServletContainerInitializer interface), which bootstraps automatically in any Servlet 3.0 containers.

Let's see a simple example of using code-based configuration to bootstrap the DispatcherServlet WebApplicationContext, instead of declaring it in the web.xml file.

First, remove the following servlet and servlet mapping definition in Listing 17-65 from the web.xml file.

Listing 17-65. Remove the Following Servlet Definition from web.xml

```
<servlet>
    <servlet-name>appServlet</servlet-name>
    <servlet-class>org.springframework.web.servlet.DispatcherServlet</servlet-class>
    <init-param>
        <param-name>contextConfigLocation</param-name>
        <param-value>/WEB-INF/spring/appServlet/servlet-context.xml</param-value>
    </init-param>
    <load-on-startup>1</load-on-startup>
    <multipart-config>
        <max-file-size>5000000</max-file-size>
    </multipart-config>
</servlet>

<servlet-mapping>
    <servlet-name>appServlet</servlet-name>
    <url-pattern>/</url-pattern>
</servlet-mapping>
```

Second, create a class that implements the WebApplicationInitializer interface. Here we called it MyWebAppInitializer, and its content is shown in Listing 17-66.

Listing 17-66. The MyWebAppInitializer Class

```
package com.apress.prospring3.ch17.web.init;

import javax.servlet.MultipartConfigElement;
import javax.servlet.ServletContext;
import javax.servlet.ServletException;
import javax.servlet.ServletRegistration;

import org.springframework.web.WebApplicationInitializer;
import org.springframework.web.context.support.XmlWebApplicationContext;
import org.springframework.web.servlet.DispatcherServlet;

public class MyWebAppInitializer implements WebApplicationInitializer {

    @Override
    public void onStartup(ServletContext container) throws ServletException {

        XmlWebApplicationContext appContext = new XmlWebApplicationContext();
```

```
    appContext.setConfigLocation("/WEB-INF/spring/appServlet/servlet-context.xml");

    ServletRegistration.Dynamic dispatcher =
        container.addServlet("appServlet", new DispatcherServlet(appContext));

    MultipartConfigElement multipartConfigElement =
        new MultipartConfigElement(null, 5000000, 5000000, 0);
    dispatcher.setMultipartConfig(multipartConfigElement);

    dispatcher.setLoadOnStartup(1);
    dispatcher.addMapping("/");
    }
}
```

As shown in Listing 17-66, the `WebApplicationInitializer.onStartup()` method is overridden, with the logic to load the `WebApplicationContext` for the `DispatcherServlet` implemented. By calling the method `ServletContext.addServlet()`, we can add the servlet to the underlying web container. The method will return an instance of the `javax.servlet.ServletRegistration.Dynamic` interface, and via this interface, we can configure various attributes for the servlet, such as the `loadOnStartup` servlet-to-URL mapping, as well as the multipart support for file uploading, and so on. Rebuild and deploy the project, and the `DispatcherServlet`'s `WebApplicationContext` will be bootstrapped like the one defined in the `web.xml` file.

Using this approach, when combined with the Java code-based configuration of Spring, it's possible to implement a pure Java code-based configuration of a Spring-based web application, without the need to declare any Spring configuration in `web.xml` or other Spring XML configuration files. For a more detailed description of this feature, please refer to Spring Framework's online documentation for the `WebApplicationInitializer` interface (http://static.springsource.org/spring/docs/3.1.x/javadoc-api/org/springframework/web/WebApplicationInitializer.html).

Spring MVC in the Sample Application

Many topics discussed in this chapter will be adopted in the sample application for implementing the presentation layer, and their relationships will be covered in this section.

MVC Implementation for SpringBlog

For the presentation layer of the SpringBlog application, Spring MVC will be used for implementing the MVC pattern, and JSPX will be used as the view technology. The usage of Spring MVC and related libraries are as follows:

- *Internationalization*: Spring MVC's built-in support for i18n will be used to support various languages in the SpringBlog application. In SpringBlog, support of English (US) and Chinese (HK) will be provided.

- *Theming*: We will use the theming support in Spring MVC. For example, the `<spring:theme>` tag will be used in a page template to load the active theme being used.

- *Page templating*: In the SpringBlog application, Apache Tiles will be used for page templating. The page layout will be much like the one we presented in this chapter, with standard components including a header, menu, footer, body, and so on. Spring MVC's built-in support for using Tiles as the view resolver will be used also.

- *Validation, type conversion, and formatting*: All frontend validation in the SpringBlog application will rely on JSR-303 Bean Validation. Spring 3's new type conversion and formatting support will be used too. All the JSR-303 validation messages will also support i18n as discussed in this chapter.

Rich User Interface and Ajax

All JavaScript libraries discussed in this chapter will be used to provide richness to the SpringBlog application. Highlights are as follows:

- *User interface*: jQuery and jQuery UI will be used for implementing SpringBlog's user interface. For example, when searching blog entries by a date range, the date picker widget will be used.

- *Rich-text editing*: CKEditor will be used to provide rich-text editing support for users when posting blog entries and comments.

- *Data grid with pagination*: jqGrid will be used for browsing the blog entries in a grid-based interface. Pagination support will be provided, and users will be able to sort the entries by various attributes, as well as change the number of records displayed per page. Moreover, we will use jqGrid's filter support to allow users to search for entries by subject, post date range, and so on.

Security Support

In SpringBlog, Spring Security will be used to protect the functions. Highlights are as follows:

- *User and role*: The SpringBlog database will have tables to store the defined users and roles. For each user, roles granted will also be stored for authentication and authorization. Users can only act on what they were allowed to do based on the roles granted. For example, only the user who posted the entry can modify the entry. In addition, only users with the administrator role granted can view the audit history of an entry.

- *User interface*: The user interface will be rendered based on the roles using the techniques demonstrated in this chapter. In the views, Spring Security's JSP tag library will be used to display user information, as well as display the functions that the users are allowed to do. In addition, method-level security will applied at the controller level wherever required, using Spring Security's annotation support.

Servlet 3.0 Support

The latest support of Spring 3.1 MVC with a Servlet 3.0–compatible web container will also be used in the SpringBlog application. Highlights are as follows:

- *File upload*: One feature in SpringBlog is that users can upload attachments to their blog entries or comments. We will use Spring MVC 3.1 multipart support for Servlet 3.0 to implement this feature.

For details, please refer to Chapter 21.

Summary

In this chapter, we covered many topics related to web frontend development using Spring MVC.

First we discussed the high-level concepts of the MVC pattern. Then we covered Spring MVC's architecture, including its WebApplicationContext hierarchy, request-handling life cycle, and configuration.

Next we developed a sample contact application using Spring MVC, with JSPX as the view technology. During the course of developing the samples, different areas were elaborated on. Main topics included i18n, theming, and template support with Apache Tiles. Moreover, we used jQuery, jQuery UI, and other JavaScript libraries to enrich the interface. Samples included the date picker, rich-text editor, data grid with pagination support, and so on. How to secure a web application with Spring Security was discussed too.

We also went through some new features brought to us by Spring 3.1 for supporting Servlet 3.0–compatible web containers. We demonstrated how to handle file upload by using Spring 3.1 MVC within a Servlet 3.0 environment. Also, the new support for code-based configuration instead of configuration in web.xml file was covered.

In the next chapter, we will discuss more features that Spring brings us in terms of web application development.

Spring Web Flow and JSF

In the previous chapter, we discussed developing web application with Spring MVC, using JSPX and JavaScript as the view technologies.

In terms of web application development, there are numerous options, including native clients (for example, Adobe Flex, JavaFX, Microsoft Silverlight, and so on), MVC frameworks (for example, Spring MVC, JBoss Seam, Struts, and so on), and view technologies (for example, JSP, Velocity, JavaScript, JSF, and so on).

Besides Spring MVC, Spring provides a project called Spring Web Flow (`www.springsource.org/webflow`), which supports the development of flow-based web applications; it also has tight integration with view technologies such as the Dojo Toolkit and JSF. Moreover, Spring Web Flow tightly integrates with Spring MVC for supporting web application features such as i18n, theming, and validation.

In this chapter, we will discuss how the Spring Web Flow project can help you develop a flow-based web application. Moreover, we will demonstrate how Spring Web Flow works with JSF (a component-based view technology, which is also the standard view technology within the JEE stack) using the Spring Faces module (under Spring Web Flow) and PrimeFaces (`http://primefaces.org`), a popular JSF component library. Specifically, this chapter will cover the following topics:

- *Spring Web Flow*: We will introduce Spring Web Flow and the main features that it provides, including its support for developing flow-based application, its more fine-grained scope of Java beans, and the view technologies that Spring Web Flow integrates with.

- *JSF*: We will present a high-level description of JSF (specifically, JSF 2). Its main concepts, including the component-based model, view-handling life cycle, templating support, and so on, will be discussed. In addition, we will also briefly describe some commonly used JSF component libraries.

- *Spring Web Flow and PrimeFaces*: We will demonstrate how to use Spring Web Flow and PrimeFaces to develop a flow-based web application.

Project for Sample Backend

It's always better to develop a web application with a concrete backend, other than some simple "Hello World" examples. As a result, a sample backend project was prepared in the sample source code so that you can just import the project and the backend will be ready. We then can focus on frontend development. In the following sections, we will briefly describe the sample backend and how to import the project for developing the frontend samples in this chapter.

The Sample Backend Service Layer

The backend for the samples in this chapter is a simple contact application. Each contact has basic information, including first name, last name, and date of birth. In addition, a contact also has zero or more hobbies. Figure 18-1 shows the domain object model.

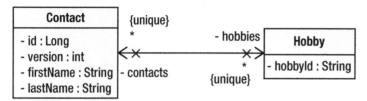

Figure 18-1. *Domain object model for backend sample*

For the backend, we will use JPA 2 and Hibernate as the persistence service provider. Also, Spring Data JPA's repository abstraction will be used. Figure 18-2 shows a class diagram of the service layer.

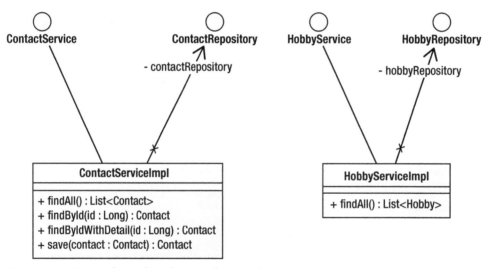

Figure 18-2. *Service layer class diagram for samples*

Import the Sample Backend in STS

Because this chapter focuses on the frontend development, we have prepared a project with the service layer implemented so that you can just import it and then proceed to implement the frontend.

From the sample code, extract the file ch18-backend.zip into your STS workspace. Then import the project in STS.

To import the project, in STS choose the menu option File ➤ Import, and in the Select dialog choose Existing Projects into Workspace under the General category, as shown in Figure 18-3; then click Next.

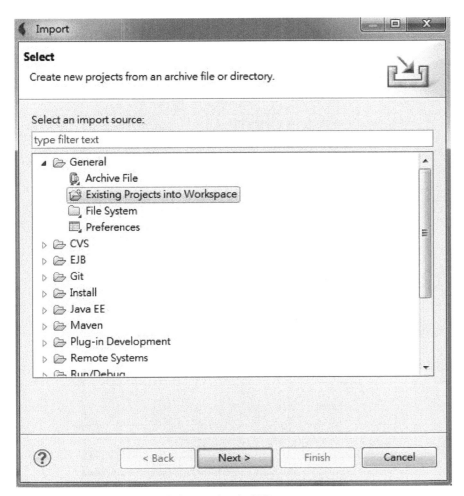

Figure 18-3. Importing an existing project in STS

Then, in the Import Projects dialog, choose the project extracted from the sample source code, and then click Finish (see Figure 18-4).

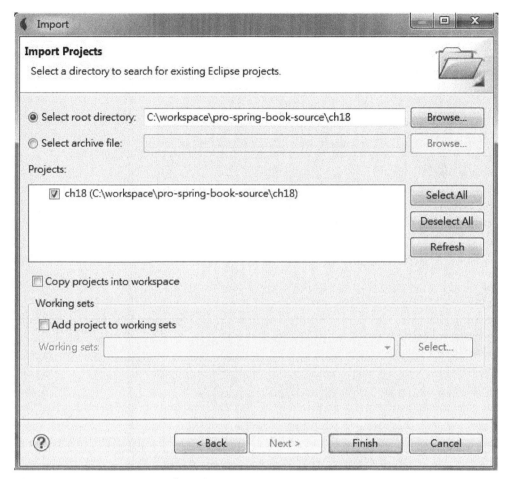

Figure 18-4. Importing a sample project

Up to this point, the project setup is complete, and we are ready to start to implement the frontend using Spring Web Flow and PrimeFaces. Before that, though, let's take a look at the high-level concepts of Spring Web Flow and JSF.

Introducing Spring Web Flow

Building on top of Spring MVC's foundation, Spring Web Flow was designed to provide advanced support for organizing the flows inside a web application. Additionally, extended functionalities are provided in various web application areas.

In the following sections, we will present a high-level overview of Spring Web Flow. The main features, modules, integration with view technologies such as JavaScript libraries and JSF, and so on, will be discussed.

Spring Web Flow Modules

There are several modules within the Spring Web Flow distribution. For example, in this chapter, we will discuss using Spring Faces (a module within Spring Web Flow) with the JSF component library PrimeFaces to develop a flow-based web application. Later we will add the dependency of Spring Faces into the project. Figure 18-5 shows the dependency hierarchy after importing the Spring Faces module in the project in STS.

Figure 18-5. Dependency hierarchy of Spring Web Flow

As you can see from Figure 18-5, Spring Faces depends on other Spring Web Flow modules like Spring Web Flow, which is the core module; Spring Web Flow in turn depends on other Spring projects like Spring MVC, Spring Expression, and so on. The modules in the Spring Web Flow distribution (as of version 2.3.0.RELEASE) are as follows:

- *Spring Web Flow (*`spring-webflow`*)*: This is the core module in Spring Web Flow; it provides the infrastructure for managing flows and, for each flow, its conversation, state, and views.

- *Spring Faces (*`spring-faces`*)*: Spring Web Flow provides first-class support for JSF, and the supporting components are packaged within the Spring Faces module. Starting from version 2.2, Spring Web Flow supports core JSF 2 features including partial state saving, resource request and handling, Ajax support, and so on. Spring Web Flow also integrates tightly with common JSF component libraries including JBoss RichFaces (`www.jboss.org/richfaces`) and PrimeFaces (`www.primefaces.org`).

- *Spring JavaScript (*`spring-js, spring-js-resources`*)*: The Spring JavaScript module provides support for view development with JavaScript. For example, in the rendered HTML view, JavaScript can be used for Ajax communication with servers and partial view updates. Moreover, the Spring JavaScript Resources bundle (`spring-js-resources.jar`) includes the Dojo Toolkit (a popular JavaScript library) as well as the Spring-provided JavaScript library that supports integration with the Dojo Toolkit.

- *Spring Binding (*`spring-binding`*)*: As its name implies, the Spring Binding module is responsible for binding the view state to the underlying model. Starting from version 2.1, Spring Web Flow uses Spring 3's type conversion and formatting system in the process of binding. In addition, Spring Web Flow 2.3 also added support for JSR-303 Bean Validation.

Spring Web Flow Features

Spring Web Flow is an extension to the MVC pattern; it provides support for developing flow-based applications and supports more fine-grained bean scopes. The architecture of Spring Web Flow is built around the following three main concepts:

- *Flow*: A flow is a business process representing a use case. In Spring Web Flow, a flow consists of a series of steps called *states*. Each state is typically presented to the user within a view (there are also other states that are not view related; for example, the decision state determines the next state of the flow depending on the runtime condition). Within the view, user events occur that are handled by the state. These events can trigger transitions to other states that result in view navigation within the entire flow. Spring Web Flow provides a domain-specific language (DSL) that can be used to implement very complex flows for your application.

- *View*: The same as in the MVC pattern, a view is a user interface that presents the state of the model to the user and provides user interaction with Ajax support and partial view updates.

- *Conversation*: In a web application, in terms of bean scopes, there are three types, namely, request, session, and application. The request and session scopes are used intensively for the presentation layer. However, in many web applications, especially flow-based, the model beans should maintain their state across multiple requests until the flow is finished. In this case, the request scope is not enough. However, using session scope would be overkill, because the state would be kept in the user's `HttpSession` for the entire session. To address this, Spring Web Flow introduces the concept of a conversation, which holds the data until a flow is completed. The main purpose of this is to avoid putting too much data into the session scope, which will cause memory consumption issues when there a lot of concurrent users. When using Spring Web Flow, understanding the scopes of beans and variables that it maintains is very important. Table 18-1 shows the available scopes and their purposes.

Table 18-1. Available Bean Scopes in Spring Web Flow

Scope	Purpose
Flow	The variables with flow scope are allocated when the flow starts and are destroyed when the flow ends. It's the scope to use if you want the variable, which usually stores the interaction state as well as the underlying model, to be maintained during the entire flow. A flow scope bean should implement the java.io.Serializable interface. A flow scope variable is not accessible in its subflows.
View	The variables with view scope are allocated when the flow enters a view (called the view-state) and destroyed when the state exits. In other words, view scope variables survive only within a view. When you need to display information (for example, a list of contacts) that is required only within a certain view within the flow, you should use the view scope to minimize the memory consumption.
Request	Variables with request scope are created when the flow is called and destroyed when the flow returns.
Flash	Variables with flash scope are allocated when the flow starts. Then, they will be cleared after each view is rendered and destroyed when the flow completes. It's useful for those variables that exist in every view, but the value will be different in each view. One example is the status message that will be displayed in every step of the flow to indicate the flow status or display messages to users.
Conversation	The conversation scope is the same as the flow scope. The only difference with flow scope is that the variables with the conversation scope will be available for its flows. For example, an order application provides a flow for entering order information. Within the flow, one step is to invoke a flow called *select-customer* to select the customer who places the order. However, in the subflow, when selecting the customer, the information about the order should be available because it contains some filter criteria (for example, an international order can be placed only by customers living in certain countries). For this case, the order should be placed under the conversation scope.

For a detailed description of Spring Web Flow, please refer to the project documentation site (http://static.springsource.org/spring-webflow/docs/2.3.x/reference/html/index.html) and the book *Pro Spring MVC with Web Flow* (Apress, 2012).

Introducing JSF

JavaServer Faces (JSF) is another popular view technology used for developing the presentation layer of an enterprise application. Generally speaking, JSF is a request-driven MVC web framework based on a component-driven UI design model.

However, the first generation of JSF (called JSF 1) has been criticized for its steep learning curve, complexity in building custom components, and lack of support for Ajax. JSF 2 greatly simplifies the model, as well as provides out-of-the-box support for Ajax.

JSF is the standard view technology within the JEE stack, so every major JEE application server vendor (for example, JBoss, IBM, Oracle, and so on) supports JSF and ships with its own JSF component library. Furthermore, there are a lot of open source and commercial projects that provide JSF component libraries, such as JBoss RichFaces, PrimeFaces, ICEfaces, and so on.

JSF mainly consists of four components: the view, model interaction, navigation, and life cycle. These four components will be discussed in the following sections.

View

In JSF, as with the MVC pattern, a view is a page that presents data to the user. However, because JSF is a component-based framework, a view is represented by a tree of UI components, which are exposed in the view as markup tags. The UI component hierarchy is represented by nesting tags.

As of JSF 2, Facelets is the standard technology for all JSF pages. Facelets, which adopts the XHTML syntax, provides built-in support of page templating, without the need of other templating frameworks like Apache Tiles.

Model Interaction

In JSF, the view stores a tree of UI components with values and provides user interactions. When a user takes an action, the request will be submitted to the server for processing. On the server side, the values in the UI component tree will be transformed back into the model for processing. This process represents the action between the UI components and the underlying model.

In JSF 2, the JSF 2.0 Expression Language (EL) is used for referencing model objects from UI components. When the response is rendered to the user, the UI components get their values from the associated model properties. During the interaction, type-safe conversion and server-side validation occur automatically.

To support highly interactive web pages in JSF, model objects are usually implemented as "backing beans" on a page basis. In this case, the model object represents the state of the model properties stored by the view. In managing those beans, JSF also adopts the concept of IoC, and they are called JSF Managed Beans, which can be defined in the JSF config files (called faces-config.xml) or by using annotations. However, JSF's EL allows integration with technologies outside JSF. For example, when using JSF with Spring Web Flow, the standard Spring beans can be used as JSF managed beans, using the standard DI mechanism provided by the Spring Framework.

Navigation

JSF provides a framework for defining page navigation rules. For example, in a view, when a user performs an action, the request is submitted to the server. On the server side, an "action controller" will process the request by interacting with the service layer, and then depending on the outcome and the navigation rules defined in the faces-config.xml file, the corresponding view will be displayed to the user.

However, when using Spring Web Flow, the JSF navigation mechanism is not required. As described in the section "Spring Web Flow Features" earlier in this chapter, Spring Web Flow provides built-in support for flow definition, which can replace the navigation model provided by JSF.

Application Life Cycle

The most critical part of JSF to understand is its application life cycle. The entire life cycle starts when the web application running JSF receives a request, runs through six phases, and then renders a response and displays it to the user. The six phases are listed here:

1. *Restore view*: In a JSF application, every view is associated with a view ID and is stored in the FacesContext's (under package javax.faces.context) session object. In JSF, a view is a collection of components associated with its current state, which can be stored in either the server or client side (controlled by the parameter javax.faces.STATE_SAVING_METHOD) in a web deployment descriptor. When a user takes an action in the view and sends a request to the server, the first phase in JSF is to restore the view back from its state.

2. *Apply requests*: After the component tree is restored, each component in the tree extracts its new value from the request parameters by using its decode method.

3. *Process validations*: In this phase, the JSF implementation processes all validators registered on the components in the tree. It examines the component attributes that specify the rules for the validation and compares these rules to the local value stored for the component. JSF 2 fully supports validation with JSR-303 Bean Validation.

4. *Update model values*: Upon validation completion, the JSF implementation will walk through the component tree and set the corresponding server-side object properties to the components' local values. Only the bean properties pointed at by an input component's value attribute will be updated. In this binding process, type conversion and formatting also occurs, and in case the conversion failed, the life cycle advances directly to the render response phase so that the page is rerendered with errors displayed.

5. *Invoke application*: In this phase, the JSF implementation invokes the application to handle form submissions. At this point, the component values will have been converted, validated, and applied to the model objects, so they can be used to execute the application's business logic. During the execution, the JSF implementation will handle any application-level events, such as submitting a form or linking to another page. In addition, if the view being processed was reconstructed from state information from a previous request, and if a component has fired an event, these events are broadcast to interested listeners.

6. *Render response*: In this final phase, the resulting view is displayed with all of its components in their current state.

You can install your own phase listeners by creating a class that implements the javax.faces.event.PhaseListener interface into the life cycle to do whatever you want before or after each or every phase. A phase listener has full access to the entire JSF framework, including manipulating the view.

Figure 18-6 shows the life cycle.

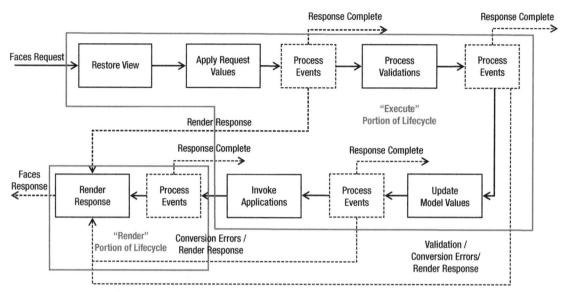

Figure 18-6. *JSF application life cycle with the execution and render portions highlighted*

This description covers only the very basics of JSF. For a more detailed description, an excellent JSF 2 online tutorial is available at `www.coreservlets.com/JSF-Tutorial/jsf2`.

The Sample Spring Web Flow Application

In this chapter, to demonstrate using the combination of Spring Web Flow and JSF for flow-based applications, we will develop a simple flow to implement a function for creating new contacts.

In the following sections, we will discuss the design of the overall flow for creating new contacts and the project structure for the sample in this chapter.

Design of the Sample Flow

As described earlier in this chapter, a contact consists of basic information about a user (first name, last name, date of birth), as well as their hobbies. When creating new contacts, a wizard-like approach will be used, which allows the users to enter the information in different pages, review the overall information, and then confirm by submitting the information for processing. The process is much like registering on many web sites.

Figure 18-7 shows the overall flow of creating contacts and their associated views that we need to implement. In the figure, the arrow labels represent buttons on the pages. For example, each page has a Back button, and the pages in the Add process all have an Exit button.

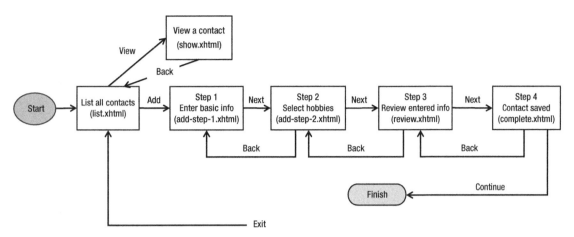

Figure 18-7. *The flow for new contact creation*

As shown in Figure 18-7, the first page that users will see is a list of all contacts. When a user selects a row and clicks the View Selected button, the show contact view will be displayed. In the show contact view, the user can navigate back to the list contact page by clicking the Back button.

When a user clicks the Add Contact button, it triggers the add contact flow. The first step is to enter basic information. Clicking the Next button will navigate to the view for selecting hobbies. The next step is the review page where the user reviews all the information entered. When the user confirms the information, the contact is persisted, and the complete view is displayed.

At any page within the flow, the user can navigate to the previous page by clicking the Back button or end the flow and return to the list contact view by clicking the Exit button.

Project Structure

Before we implement the add contact flow, let's take a look at the project folder structure.

Figure 18-8 shows the folder structure of the sample web flow application that will be developed in this chapter. Table 18-2 lists the purpose of each folder (under the root folder /src/main/webapp).

Figure 18-8. Spring Web Flow project structure

Table 18-2. Spring Web Flow Project Folder Structure Description

Folder Name	Purpose
styles	Stores all the required style sheets. We will use the theming support of PrimeFaces for this sample.
WEB-INF/flows	This folder stores all the flows within the application. Each flow folder stores the files required for supporting that particular flow. For example, the contacts folder stores the files for the add contact flow. All the view files, together with the flow definition file, will be stored in this folder.

Folder Name	Purpose
WEB-INF/i18n	Files for supporting i18n messages.
WEB-INF/layouts	This folder stores the layout template that will be used by Facelets.
WEB-INF/spring	This folder stores the Spring MVC WebApplicationContext configurations. Both the root-level and dispatcher servlet–level context configurations are stored here. Spring Web Flow configuration will be stored in this folder too.

Spring Web Flow and JSF Configuration

This section discusses the necessary configurations required for a web application running on Spring Web Flow, JSF 2, and PrimeFaces.

Adding Required Dependencies

For developing applications using Spring Web Flow and JSF 2 with PrimeFaces, the required corresponding dependencies are shown in Table 18-3. Add them into your project.

Table 18-3. Maven Dependencies for Spring Web Flow, JSF 2, and PrimeFaces

Group ID	Artifact ID	Version	Description
org.springframework.webflow	spring-faces	2.3.0.RELEASE	Spring Faces module within Spring Web Flow; supports integration with JSF 2.
com.sun.faces	jsf-api	2.0.7	JSF 2 API. Note that there is a compatibility issue between JSF 2.1 with Spring Web Flow 2.3 at the time of writing.
com.sun.faces	jsf-impl	2.0.7	Oracle Sun's reference implementation of JSF 2.
org.primefaces	primefaces	3.0.1	PrimeFaces component library that supports JSF 2.

Configuring JSF

For a JSF application, we need to specify a JSF-dedicated configuration file (the faces-config.xml file under the /WEB-INF folder). This file typically stores the general JSF configurations, information on the managed beans (not required if you use the annotation style), and the navigation rules. However, we will use Spring Web Flow, which integrates with Spring Framework's IoC for DI, so the configuration required in this file is minimal. Listing 18-1 shows the content of the file (WEB-INF/faces-config.xml).

Listing 18-1. JSF Configuration File

```xml
<?xml version='1.0' encoding='UTF-8'?>
<faces-config xmlns="http://java.sun.com/xml/ns/javaee"
    xmlns:xsi="http://www.w3.org/2001/XMLSchema-instance"
    xsi:schemaLocation="http://java.sun.com/xml/ns/javaee
        http://java.sun.com/xml/ns/javaee/web-facesconfig_2_0.xsd"
        version="2.0">

    <application>
        <locale-config>
            <default-locale>en</default-locale>
            <supported-locale>en</supported-locale>
        </locale-config>
        <message-bundle>MessageResources</message-bundle>
        <resource-bundle>
            <base-name>MessageResources</base-name>
            <var>msg</var>
        </resource-bundle>
    </application>

</faces-config>
```

As shown in Listing 18-1, the only configuration required is for i18n. We will support only English for this sample, and the message bundle is stored in the MessageResources.properties file (under the class path at the /src/main/resources folder). The <var> tag specifies that the messages will be available to the EL under the variable name msg, which we will see in action when developing the views.

Configuring Web Deployment Descriptor

The next step is to configure the web.xml file for JSF support. Listing 18-2 shows the revised web deployment descriptor.

Listing 18-2. Revised Web Deployment Descriptor

```xml
<?xml version="1.0" encoding="UTF-8"?>
<web-app version="2.5" xmlns="http://java.sun.com/xml/ns/javaee"
    xmlns:xsi="http://www.w3.org/2001/XMLSchema-instance"
    xsi:schemaLocation="http://java.sun.com/xml/ns/javaee
    http://java.sun.com/xml/ns/javaee/web-app_2_5.xsd">

    <context-param>
        <param-name>contextConfigLocation</param-name>
        <param-value>/WEB-INF/spring/root-context.xml</param-value>
    </context-param>

    <listener>
        <listener-class>
            org.springframework.web.context.ContextLoaderListener
        </listener-class>
    </listener>
```

```
<!-- JSF 2 -->
<!-- Use JSF view templates saved as *.xhtml, for use with Facelets -->
<context-param>
    <param-name>javax.faces.DEFAULT_SUFFIX</param-name>
    <param-value>.xhtml</param-value>
</context-param>

<!-- Enables special Facelets debug output during development -->
<context-param>
    <param-name>javax.faces.PROJECT_STAGE</param-name>
    <param-value>Development </param-value>
</context-param>

<!-- Causes Facelets to refresh templates during development -->
<context-param>
    <param-name>javax.faces.FACELETS_REFRESH_PERIOD</param-name>
    <param-value>1</param-value>
</context-param>

<!-- Just here so the JSF implementation can initialize, *not* used at runtime -->
<servlet>
    <servlet-name>Faces Servlet</servlet-name>
    <servlet-class>javax.faces.webapp.FacesServlet</servlet-class>
    <load-on-startup>1</load-on-startup>
</servlet>

<!-- Just here so the JSF implementation can initialize -->
<servlet-mapping>
    <servlet-name>Faces Servlet</servlet-name>
    <url-pattern>*.faces</url-pattern>
</servlet-mapping>

<servlet>
   <servlet-name>appServlet</servlet-name>
   <servlet-class>org.springframework.web.servlet.DispatcherServlet</servlet-class>
   <init-param>
      <param-name>contextConfigLocation</param-name>
      <param-value>/WEB-INF/spring/appServlet/servlet-context.xml</param-value>
   </init-param>
   <load-on-startup>1</load-on-startup>
</servlet>

<servlet-mapping>
   <servlet-name>appServlet</servlet-name>
   <url-pattern>/app/*</url-pattern>
</servlet-mapping>

</web-app>
```

In Listing 18-2, the JSF-related configurations are highlighted in bold. First, several JSF configuration parameters are provided. The javax.faces.DEFAULT_SUFFIX parameter defines the file suffix for JSF view files, which should be xhtml so as to work with Facelets. The javax.faces.PROJECT_STAGE parameter defines the project stage. The value of Development causes more output messages to be displayed to the web browser to facilitate troubleshooting. In production, the value Production should be used. The parameter javax.faces.FACELETS_REFRESH_PERIOD defines the interval in seconds for the Facelets compiler to check for changes made to the page template. Setting the value to 1 means the change will be checked every second, so when we make frequent changes to the page templates during development, each change can be detected immediately. In the production environment, set the value to -1 so that all compiled templates will not be checked for changes.

Second, a servlet with class javax.faces.webapp.FacesServlet is declared. The servlet is used only to bootstrap the JSF environment.

You will also see the definition of a DispatcherServlet for the contact application that was mapped to the URL pattern /app/*. Since Spring Web Flow tightly integrates with Spring MVC, we use the DispatcherServlet to dispatch the request to the underlying Spring Web Flow executor for request processing.

Configuring Spring Web Flow and Spring MVC

The final step in configuration relates to Spring Web Flow and Spring MVC. For Spring Web Flow, we will prepare an individual configuration file. When using Spring MVC, the configuration file usually resides in the same folder as the DispatcherServlet configuration file. Listing 18-3 shows the configuration file (/WEB-INF/spring/appServlet/webflow.xml).

Listing 18-3. Spring Web Flow Configuration File

```xml
<?xml version="1.0" encoding="UTF-8"?>
<beans:beans xmlns="http://www.springframework.org/schema/webflow-config"
    xmlns:xsi="http://www.w3.org/2001/XMLSchema-instance"
    xmlns:beans="http://www.springframework.org/schema/beans"
    xmlns:faces="http://www.springframework.org/schema/faces"
    xsi:schemaLocation="http://www.springframework.org/schema/webflow-config
        http://www.springframework.org/schema/webflow-config/spring-webflow-config-2.0.xsd
        http://www.springframework.org/schema/beans
        http://www.springframework.org/schema/beans/spring-beans-3.1.xsd
        http://www.springframework.org/schema/faces
        http://www.springframework.org/schema/faces/spring-faces-2.0.xsd">

    <!-- Executes flows: the central entry point into the Spring Web Flow system -->
    <flow-executor id="flowExecutor">
        <flow-execution-listeners>
            <listener ref="facesContextListener"/>
        </flow-execution-listeners>
    </flow-executor>

    <!-- The registry of executable flow definitions -->
    <flow-registry id="flowRegistry"
        flow-builder-services="flowBuilderServices"
        base-path="/WEB-INF/flows">
        <flow-location-pattern value="/**/flow.xml" />
    </flow-registry>

    <!-- Configures the Spring Web Flow JSF integration -->
    <faces:flow-builder-services id="flowBuilderServices"/>
```

```
    <!-- A listener to create and release a FacesContext -->
    <beans:bean id="facesContextListener"
class="org.springframework.faces.webflow.FlowFacesContextLifecycleListener"/>

</beans:beans>
```

In Listing 18-3, the webflow-config-namespace is declared as the default namespace. Also, the faces namespace is defined for JSF-related configurations.

First, the <flow-executor> tag defines an instance of the org.springframework.webflow.executor.FlowExecutor interface, which is the central façade and entry-point service interface into the Spring Web Flow system for driving the executions of flow definitions.

Second, the <flow-registry> tag defines a registry for the flow definitions within the application. From the listing, the flow definitions are stored in files named flow.xml, under the parent folder /WEB-INF/flows. For example, the file /WEB-INF/flows/contacts/flow.xml will store the flow definition for the contact application.

The <faces:flow-builder-services> tag defines an instance of the org.springframework.webflow.engine.builder.support.FlowBuilderServices class, with JSF integration, which is required for Spring Web Flow when building the flows within the flow registry.

Finally, the bean with an ID of facesContextListener and the implementation class FlowFacesContextLifecycleListener defines an instance of the org.springframework.webflow.execution.FlowExecutionListener interface, which creates an instance of the org.springframework.faces.webflow.FlowFacesContext class. The FlowFacesContext class extends JSF's FacesContext abstract class (under the package javax.faces.context), which provides the context for the underlying JSF 2 runtime environment.

Listing 18-4 shows the Spring MVC DispatcherServlet WebApplicationContext (/WEB-INF/spring/appServlet/servlet-context.xml.

Listing 18-4. *Spring MVC Configuration File*

```xml
<?xml version="1.0" encoding="UTF-8"?>
<beans:beans xmlns="http://www.springframework.org/schema/mvc"
    xmlns:xsi="http://www.w3.org/2001/XMLSchema-instance"
    xmlns:beans="http://www.springframework.org/schema/beans"
    xmlns:p="http://www.springframework.org/schema/p"
    xmlns:context="http://www.springframework.org/schema/context"
    xmlns:faces="http://www.springframework.org/schema/faces"
    xsi:schemaLocation="http://www.springframework.org/schema/mvc
        http://www.springframework.org/schema/mvc/spring-mvc-3.1.xsd
        http://www.springframework.org/schema/beans
        http://www.springframework.org/schema/beans/spring-beans-3.1.xsd
        http://www.springframework.org/schema/context
        http://www.springframework.org/schema/context/spring-context-3.1.xsd
        http://www.springframework.org/schema/faces
        http://www.springframework.org/schema/faces/spring-faces.xsd">

    <beans:import resource="webflow.xml" />

    <annotation-driven />

    <resources location="/" mapping="/resources/**"/>

    <faces:resources/>
```

```
<context:component-scan base-package="com.apress.prospring3.ch18.web" />

<beans:bean class="org.springframework.webflow.mvc.servlet.FlowHandlerMapping">
    <beans:property name="flowRegistry" ref="flowRegistry" />
</beans:bean>

<beans:bean class="org.springframework.web.servlet.view.UrlBasedViewResolver">
    <beans:property name="viewClass"
        value="org.springframework.faces.mvc.JsfView" />
    <beans:property name="prefix" value="/WEB-INF/views/" />
    <beans:property name="suffix" value=".xhtml" />
</beans:bean>

<beans:bean class="org.springframework.faces.webflow.JsfFlowHandlerAdapter">
    <beans:property name="flowExecutor" ref="flowExecutor" />
</beans:bean>

<beans:bean
class="org.springframework.context.support.ReloadableResourceBundleMessageSource"
    id="messageSource"
    p:basenames="WEB-INF/i18n/messages,WEB-INF/i18n/application"
    p:fallbackToSystemLocale="false"/>

</beans:beans>
```

In Listing 18-4, most of the beans should be familiar to you. First, the configuration in webflow.xml is imported. The <faces:resources/> tag is to enable the support of JSF 2 resource requests. The anonymous bean with class FlowHandlerMapping implements Spring MVC's HandlerMapping interface for integration with Spring MVC in the Spring Web Flow environment. It maps the URL path to the id of the registered flow definitions.

For the view resolver, we use the same UrlBasedViewResolver in Spring MVC, with the suffix changed to xhtml. The anonymous bean with the implementation class JsfFlowHandlerAdapter replaces the instance of the default AjaxHandler interface (under the package org.springframework.js.ajax of the spring-js module) with a JsfAjaxHandler class (under the package org.springframework.faces.webflow in the spring-faces module) when JSF 2 is the runtime environment.

Finally, the bean with ID messageSource is the same as the one for Spring MVC.

Implementing the Sample Flow

Now the infrastructure and configurations are complete, and we can start to implement the add contact flow. In the following sections, we will go through the steps to implement the flow. Various steps, including the flow definition, template view, various contact views, controller class, backing bean classes, and so on, will be discussed.

Define the Flow Definition

Let's begin with defining the contact application flow, which was illustrated in Figure 18-7. As discussed in the configuration section, the flow definition file is /WEB-INF/flows/contacts/flow.xml. There is a convenient way to create a web flow definition file in STS. Just right-click the contacts folder, choose New, and then choose Spring Web Flow Definition File. Listing 18-5 shows the flow definition.

Listing 18-5. A Web Flow Definition

```xml
<?xml version="1.0" encoding="UTF-8"?>
<flow xmlns=http://www.springframework.org/schema/webflow
    xmlns:xsi="http://www.w3.org/2001/XMLSchema-instance"
    xsi:schemaLocation="http://www.springframework.org/schema/webflow
        http://www.springframework.org/schema/webflow/spring-webflow-2.0.xsd"
        start-state="start">

    <view-state id="start" view="list.xhtml">
        <on-entry>
            <evaluate expression="contactController.newContactListBean()"
                result="viewScope.contactListBean"/>
        </on-entry>
        <transition on="view" to="show">
            <set name="requestScope.contactId" value="contactListBean.selectedContact.id"/>
        </transition>
        <transition on="add" to="add-step-1">
            <evaluate expression="contactController.newContactBean()"
                result="flowScope.contactBean"/>
        </transition>
    </view-state>

    <view-state id="add-step-1" view="add-step-1.xhtml">
        <transition on="next" to="add-step-2"/>
    </view-state>

    <view-state id="add-step-2" view="add-step-2.xhtml">
        <transition on="next" to="review"/>
        <transition on="back" to="add-step-1"/>
    </view-state>

    <view-state id="review" view="review.xhtml">
        <transition on ="next" to="complete">
            <evaluate expression="contactController.saveContact(flowRequestContext)"/>
        </transition>
        <transition on="back" to="add-step-2"/>
    </view-state>

    <view-state id="complete" view="complete.xhtml">
        <transition on="continue" to="finish"/>
    </view-state>

    <end-state id="finish"/>

    <view-state id="show" view="show.xhtml">
        <on-entry>
            <evaluate expression="contactController.showContact(flowRequestContext)"
                result="viewScope.contact"/>
        </on-entry>
        <transition on ="back" to="start"/>
    </view-state>

    <global-transitions>
```

```
            <transition on="exit" to="start"/>
        </global-transitions>

</flow>
```

Listing 18-5 reflects the complete flow of the contact application. The corresponding views, controller methods, and backing beans will be developed later. The flow is defined using Spring Web Flow's DSL. As in the webflow.xml configuration, the flow registry bean is configured with the base path /WEB-INF/flows, and this flow definition file resides under the folder contacts. This flow will be automatically registered in Spring Web Flow with the ID contacts, accessible via the URL /ch18/app/contacts.

In the flow definition, besides the namespace declarations, a start-state attribute is also provided with the value start, which indicates the state of the flow when this flow starts. In our case, the start state is the state with the ID start. The start state specifies the view attribute with list.xhtml, which indicates the file to render for this state. Then, within the <view-state> tag, in the <on-entry> tag (which means when the flow enters this state), the newContactListBean() method of the Spring bean with name contactController will be executed. This retrieves the list of contacts. The resulting contact list (stored in the ContactListBean class, to be implemented later) is stored as a view scope variable. The <transition> tags defines the possible navigation paths within the flow based on the action taken by the user. For the start state in the contact list view, when a user selects a contact and clicks the View Selected button, it will navigate to the show contact view. When the Add Contact button is clicked, it will navigate to the first step of the add contact flow.

The other <view-state> tags are defined according to the designed add contact flow. Within each state, the user can choose to proceed or step backward. The <global-transitions> tag defines a global transition rule. In this case, a global rule is specified so that whenever the user clicks the Exit button, the exit transition will be triggered, and the flow will always navigate back to the start state, which is the contact list view.

For the view state with the IDs review and show, note that an argument called flowRequestContext was passed into the corresponding methods. The flowRequestContext argument is an implicit EL variable within Spring Web Flow, which enables access to the RequestContext API, a representation of the current flow request.

The <end-state> tag indicates the end of a flow. By default, when a flow ends, a new flow will be created, and Spring Web Flow will navigate to the start state of the flow. If the end state happens in a subflow, it will return to the parent flow.

Spring Web Flow supports a lot of other features, such as many other states (for example, decision-state, action-state, and so on) and the definition of subflows, with input/output parameters passing between the flows. For a full description, please refer to Spring Web Flow's online documentation (http://static.springsource.org/spring-webflow/docs/2.3.x/reference/html/index.html).

In STS, it's also possible to view the flow in a graphical format. First make sure that the Spring Project nature is active for the project and the flow.xml file is added as a flow definition within the project. You can then right-click the flow.xml file, choose Open With, and then choose Spring Web Flow XML Editor, as shown in Figure 18-9.

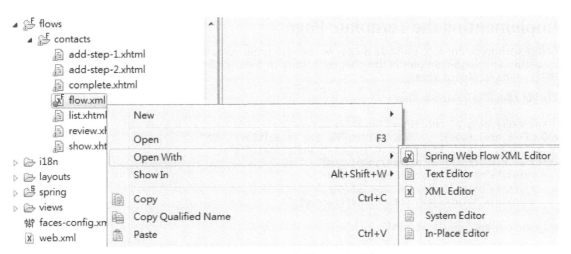

Figure 18-9. Opening a flow definition with Spring Web Flow XML Editor

Then, click the flow-graph tab, and the flow definition will be presented in the editor area with a graphical format, giving you a more user-friendly view of the flow definition, as shown in Figure 18-10.

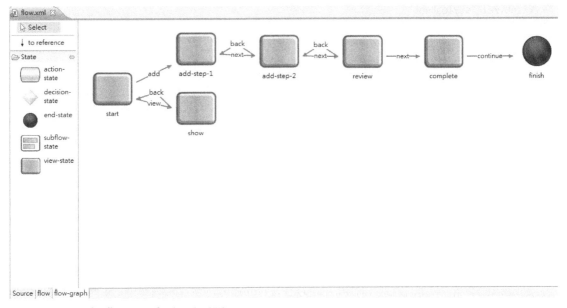

Figure 18-10. The flow-graph view in STS

Implementing the Template Page

Before we implement each individual view, we need to implement the template page, which will be used by all the views in the samples in this chapter. Listing 18-6 shows the template page (/WEB-INF/layouts/standard.xhtml).

Listing 18-6. The Template Page

```
<?xml version="1.0" encoding="UTF-8" ?>
<!DOCTYPE html PUBLIC "-//W3C//DTD XHTML 1.0 Transitional//EN"
"http://www.w3.org/TR/xhtml1/DTD/xhtml1-transitional.dtd">
<html xmlns="http://www.w3.org/1999/xhtml"
    xmlns:h="http://java.sun.com/jsf/html"
    xmlns:f="http://java.sun.com/jsf/core"
    xmlns:ui="http://java.sun.com/jsf/facelets">

<f:view contentType="text/html">

<h:head>
    <meta http-equiv="Content-Type" content="text/html; charset=UTF-8" />
    <title>JSF 2, Spring Web Flow, and PrimeFaces</title>
    <link rel="stylesheet"
href="${request.contextPath}/app/resources/styles/blueprint/screen.css" type="text/css"
media="screen, projection" />
    <link rel="stylesheet"
href="${request.contextPath}/app/resources/styles/blueprint/print.css" type="text/css"
media="print" />
    <!--[if lt IE 8]>
        <link rel="stylesheet" href="${request.servletPath}/styles/blueprint/ie.css"
type="text/css" media="screen, projection" />
    <![endif]-->
</h:head>

<h:body>
    <div class="container">
        <div>
            <h1>JSF 2, PrimeFaces, and Spring Web Flow</h1>
            <h3 class="alt">
                <ui:insert name="title"/>
            </h3>
            <hr/>
        </div>

        <div>
            <ui:insert name="content"/>
        </div>
    </div>
</h:body>

</f:view>
</html>
```

In Listing 18-6, the layout of the template page is quite simple. In JSF, there are three main tag libraries: h-namespace, f-namespace, and ui-namespace:

- The h-namespace library corresponds to the HTML components. For example, the
  <h:body> tag corresponds to the HTML <BODY> tag.

- The f-namespace corresponds to the JSF-specific features. For example, the
  <f:view> tag defines the JSF view. Within this tag, all the UI components,
  including their hierarchy and state, will be stored by the JSF runtime environment.

- The ui-namespace is used by Facelets to define the elements within the template.
  For example, the <ui:insert> tag specifies that content should be inserted here.
  The views using this template should provide the content for this template to
  include.

Implementing a Custom Converter

For a contact's date of birth attribute, we use JodaTime. However, JSF and PrimeFaces don't support the
display of JodaTime natively. As a result, we need to implement a custom JSF converter to serve the
purpose of displaying the date of birth of a contact in the frontend.

In JSF, implementing a custom converter is quite easy. All we need to do is to implement the
javax.faces.convert.Converter interface. Listing 18-7 shows the class content.

Listing 18-7. A JSF Custom Converter

```
package com.apress.prospring3.ch18.web.converter;

import javax.faces.component.UIComponent;
import javax.faces.context.FacesContext;
import javax.faces.convert.Converter;
import javax.faces.convert.FacesConverter;

import org.joda.time.DateTime;
import org.joda.time.format.DateTimeFormat;

@FacesConverter("jodaDataTimeConverter")
public class JodaDateTimeConverter implements Converter {

    private static final String PATTERN = "yyyy-MM-dd";

    @Override
    public Object getAsObject(FacesContext ctx, UIComponent component, String value) {
        return DateTimeFormat.forPattern(PATTERN).parseDateTime(value);
    }

    @Override
    public String getAsString(FacesContext ctx, UIComponent component, Object value) {

        DateTime dateTime = (DateTime) value;

        return DateTimeFormat.forPattern(PATTERN).print(dateTime);
    }
}
```

In Listing 18-7, the JodaDateTimeConverter class implements JSF's Converter interface and overrides
the two methods getAsObject() (converts from String to JodaTime) and getAsString() (converts from
JodaTime to String). Also note that the class is annotated with @FacesConverter to indicate to the JSF

runtime that it's a JSF converter. The attribute defined within the annotation is the ID of the converter. We will see how to use it when we implement the list contact view.

Implementing the Controller and Backing Bean

The next step is to implement the controller class, as well as the backing bean for the list contact view.

First let's implement the backing bean, the ContactListBean class. This class is used to store the list of contacts, as well as the selected contact when a user clicks a row in the data table. Listing 18-8 shows its content.

Listing 18-8. *The ContactListBean Class*

```
package com.apress.prospring3.ch18.web.view;

import java.io.Serializable;
import java.util.List;

import com.apress.prospring3.ch18.domain.Contact;

public class ContactListBean implements Serializable {

    private List<Contact> contacts;

    private Contact selectedContact;

    // Getter/setter methods omitted
}
```

The bean is a simple POJO bean, with the attributes to store the list of retrieved contacts and the contact selected by the user in the frontend. Note that the backing bean should implement the Serializable interface.

Listing 18-9 shows the ContactController class.

Listing 18-9. *The ContactController Class*

```
package com.apress.prospring3.ch18.web.controller;

import org.slf4j.Logger;
import org.slf4j.LoggerFactory;
import org.springframework.beans.factory.annotation.Autowired;
import org.springframework.stereotype.Component;

import com.apress.prospring3.ch18.service.ContactService;
import com.apress.prospring3.ch18.web.view.ContactListBean;

@Component("contactController")
public class ContactController {

    private static final Logger logger = LoggerFactory.getLogger(ContactController.class);

    @Autowired
    private ContactService contactService;
```

```
    public ContactListBean newContactListBean() {

        ContactListBean contactListBean = new ContactListBean();

        contactListBean.setContacts(contactService.findAll());

        return contactListBean;

    }
}
```

The class is a simple POJO, too. We just define it as a Spring bean (by using the @Component annotation), and Spring Web Flow will be able to locate it and execute the method when entering the start state. As you can see, the method simply invokes the method from the service layer, stores the contact lists into a new instance of the ContactListBean class, and then returns the instance. In the flow definition, the returned object will be stored in the view scope variable, available to JSF when rendering the response.

■ **Note** In Listing 18-9, the @Component annotation, rather than the @Controller annotation, is used. This is because in this chapter we use Spring Web Flow to control the application flow, not Spring MVC's controller classes. So, we just need to declare it as a trivial Spring bean implementing the list contact view.

Now we can implement the list contact view, which is the start state of the flow. Listing 18-10 shows the code of the view (/WEB-INF/flows/contacts/list.xhtml).

Listing 18-10. The List Contact View

```
<!DOCTYPE composition PUBLIC "-//W3C//DTD XHTML 1.0 Transitional//EN"
"http://www.w3.org/TR/xhtml1/DTD/xhtml1-transitional.dtd">
<ui:composition xmlns="http://www.w3.org/1999/xhtml"
    xmlns:ui="http://java.sun.com/jsf/facelets"
    xmlns:h="http://java.sun.com/jsf/html"
    xmlns:f="http://java.sun.com/jsf/core"
    xmlns:p="http://primefaces.org/ui"
    template="/WEB-INF/layouts/standard.xhtml">

<ui:define name="title">#{msg['application_name']}</ui:define>

<ui:define name="content">

<h:form>
    <h:panelGrid columns="1">

    <p:commandButton value="#{msg['label_contact_new']}" action="add"/>

    <p:dataTable var="contact" value="#{contactListBean.contacts}"
                paginator="true" rows="10"
                paginatorTemplate="{CurrentPageReport} {FirstPageLink} {PreviousPageLink} ↵
{PageLinks} {NextPageLink} {LastPageLink} {RowsPerPageDropdown}"
```

```
                    rowsPerPageTemplate="5,10,15"
                    rowKey="#{contact.id}"
                    selectionMode="single"
                    selection="#{contactListBean.selectedContact}">
            <f:facet name="header">
                #{msg['label_contact_list']}
            </f:facet>

            <p:column sortBy="#{contact.firstName}">
                <f:facet name="header">
                    <h:outputText value="#{msg['label_contact_first_name']}" />
                </f:facet>
                <h:outputText value="#{contact.firstName}" />
            </p:column>

            <p:column sortBy="#{contact.lastName}">
                <f:facet name="header">
                    <h:outputText value="#{msg['label_contact_last_name']}" />
                </f:facet>
                <h:outputText value="#{contact.lastName}" />
            </p:column>

            <p:column sortBy="#{contact.birthDate}">
                <f:facet name="header">
                    <h:outputText value="#{msg['label_contact_birth_date']}" />
                </f:facet>
                <h:outputText value="#{contact.birthDate}">
                    <f:converter converterId="jodaDataTimeConverter" />
                </h:outputText>
            </p:column>

            <f:facet name="footer">
                <p:commandButton value="View Selected" icon="ui-icon-search"
                        update="form:display" action="view"/>
            </f:facet>
        </p:dataTable>

        </h:panelGrid>

    </h:form>
    </ui:define>

</ui:composition>
```

In Listing 18-10, one new namespace (the p-namespace) was defined, which corresponds to the PrimeFaces JSF components. The Facelets' <ui:composition> tag is used to define a composition of view components, using standard.xhtml as the template file.

The <ui:define> tags define the contents for including in the template. You can see that the two variables (title and content) required by the template (specified by the <ui:insert> tag in standard.xhtml) are provided.

For the content area, we use PrimeFaces' DataTable component to display the list of contacts in a table format. EL expressions were used to access the model attributes in the underlying backing beans, which are maintained by Spring Web Flow based on the flow definition. In the <p:dataTable> tag, configuration parameters are provided, such as the support of pagination, rows per page, selection mode, and so on. Within the table, the `<p:column>` tags define each contact property to display. Note that for the `birthDate` attribute, we use the `<f:converter>` tag with the `id` attribute referencing the custom converter implemented for the JodaTime's `DateTime` type. In the footer of the table, a View Selected button is defined for viewing the selected contact's information.

The PrimeFaces web site provides a user guide that you can download freely (`www.primefaces.org/documentation.html`), as well as a comprehensive showcase that includes the appearance, description, and source code for each component (`www.primefaces.org/showcase-labs/ui/home.jsf`).

You can also enable a code-assist feature when developing the view with JSF and PrimeFaces tags. The procedure is easy in STS; you just right-click the project and select Properties. Then in the left menu, select the option Project Facets. Then, on the right, check the Project Facet option JavaServer Faces, as shown in Figure 18-11.

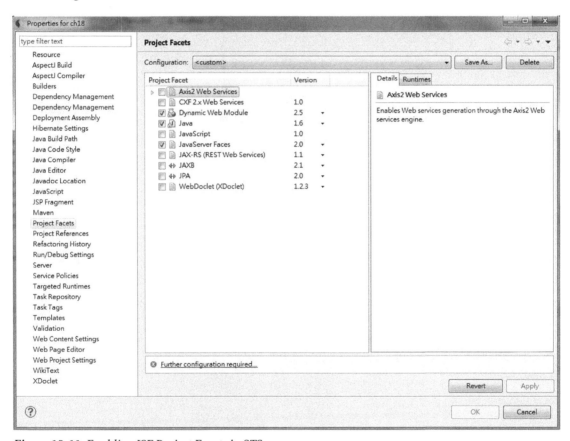

Figure 18-11. Enabling JSF Project Facets in STS

At the bottom, you will notice that there is a notification that indicates that further configuration is required. Clicking the link will invoke the dialog for JSF configuration. Because we already added the dependencies for JSF and defined the `faces-config.xml` file, we don't need to define anything here. Just uncheck all the options, as shown in Figure 18-12.

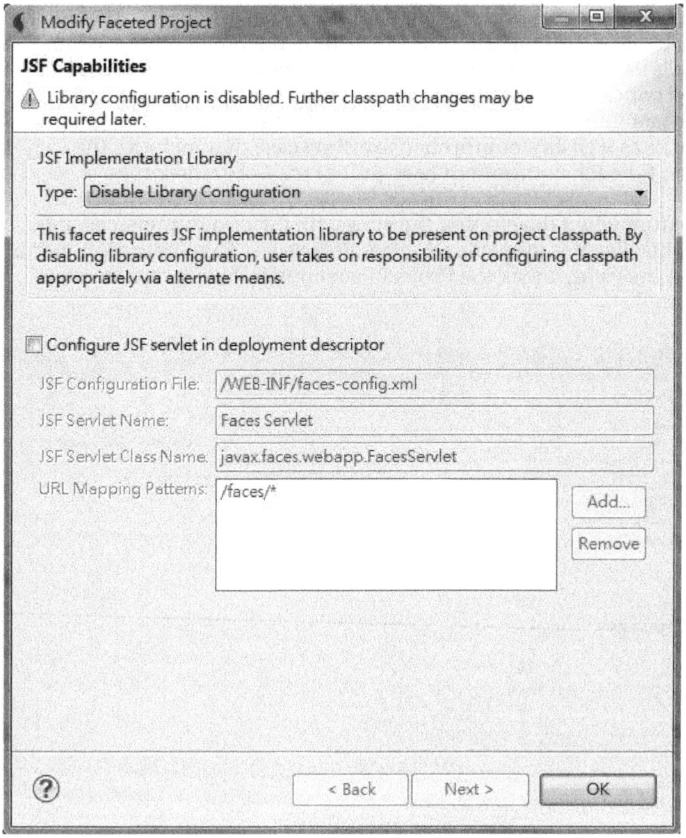

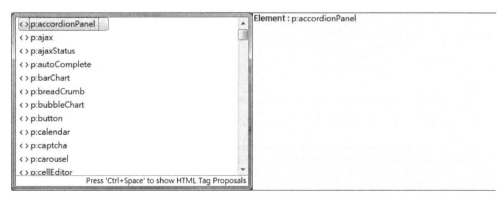

Figure 18-12. The JSF project configuration in STS

Now the code-assist feature for the JSF view is enabled. In the XHTML editor page, when you press Ctrl+spacebar or type the tag library prefix, a code-assist dialog will be displayed, as shown in Figure 18-13.

Figure 18-13. JSF code-assist in STS

Before we can test the view, we also need to update the project settings for the web project properties. To do this, right-click the project and select Properties. Then click the item Web Project Settings. In the right side of the dialog, set the "Context root" value to ch18, as shown in Figure 18-14.

Figure 18-14. Web project settings in STS

Now we are ready to test the list contact view, although the other components of the flow are still not implemented. After the project is built and deployed, open a browser and enter the URL http://localhost:8080/ch18/app/contacts. The list contact view (which is the start state of the flow) will be displayed, as shown in Figure 18-15.

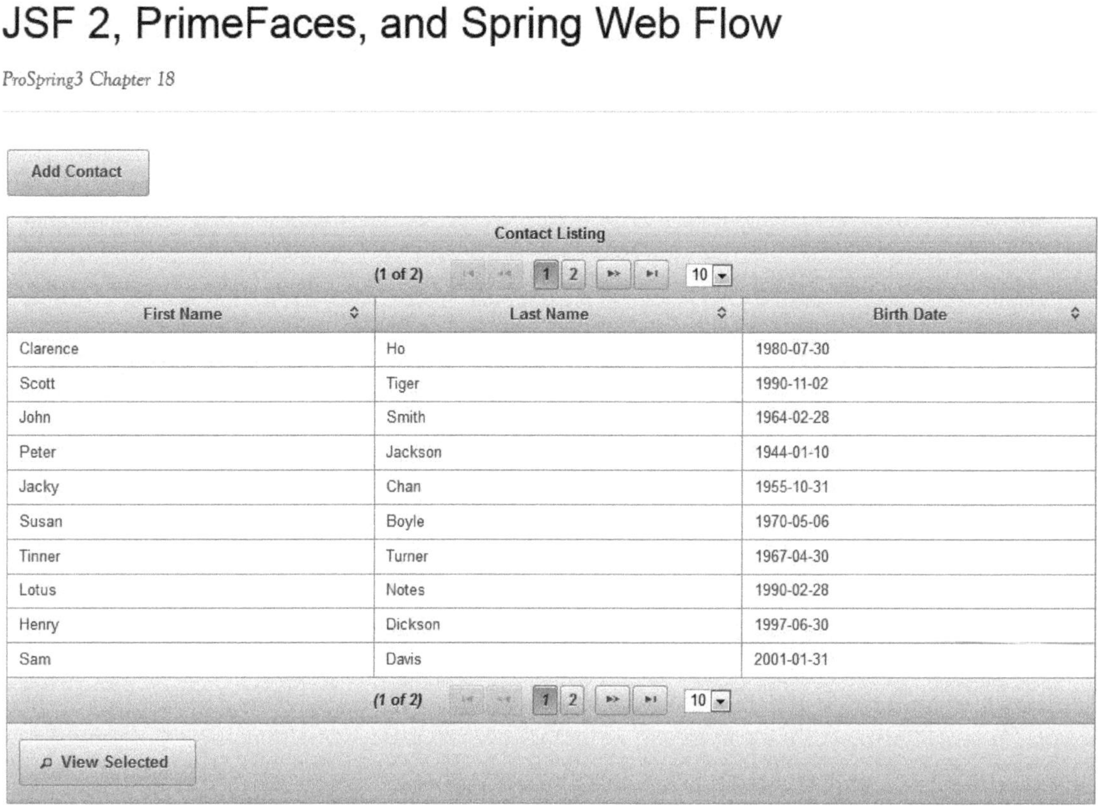

JSF 2, PrimeFaces, and Spring Web Flow

ProSpring3 Chapter 18

Add Contact

Contact Listing		
(1 of 2) 1 2 10 ▾		
First Name ⇕	Last Name ⇕	Birth Date ⇕
Clarence	Ho	1980-07-30
Scott	Tiger	1990-11-02
John	Smith	1964-02-28
Peter	Jackson	1944-01-10
Jacky	Chan	1955-10-31
Susan	Boyle	1970-05-06
Tinner	Turner	1967-04-30
Lotus	Notes	1990-02-28
Henry	Dickson	1997-06-30
Sam	Davis	2001-01-31
(1 of 2) 1 2 10 ▾		

◢ View Selected

Figure 18-15. *The list contact view*

Implementing the Show Contact View

Let's implement the show contact view, which will be displayed when the user selects a row and clicks the View Selected button.

Take a look at the code snippet in Listing 18-11, which was extracted from the start state in the flow definition in Listing 18-5 (flow.xml).

Listing 18-11. *Navigate from List Contact to Show Contact View*

```
<view-state id="start" view="list.xhtml">
    <on-entry>
        <evaluate expression="contactController.newContactListBean()"
            result="viewScope.contactListBean"/>
    </on-entry>
    <transition on="view" to="show">
        <set name="requestScope.contactId" value="contactListBean.selectedContact.id"/>
    </transition>
    <transition on="add" to="add-step-1">
```

```
            <evaluate expression="contactController.newContactBean()"
                result="flowScope.contactBean"/>
        </transition>
    </view-state>
    ...
    <view-state id="show" view="show.xhtml">
        <on-entry>
            <evaluate expression="contactController.showContact(flowRequestContext)"
                result="viewScope.contact"/>
        </on-entry>
        <transition on ="back" to="start"/>
    </view-state>
```

In Listing 18-11, the navigation to the contact show view and the show state was highlighted in bold. Within the <transition> tag in the start state, a variable called contactId with the request scope was set (based on the id of the contact of the selected row) and then transitioned to the show state.

In the show state, the ContactController.showContact() method is called, passing in an instance of the org.springframework.webflow.execution.RequestContext interface; the result (the contact object with the selected ID) is stored in a view scope variable called contact, and then the view (show.xhtml) is rendered.

Listing 18-12 shows the implementation of the showContact() method.

Listing 18-12. *Implementing the showContact() Method*

```
package com.apress.prospring3.ch18.web.controller;

// Import statements omitted
@Component("contactController")
public class ContactController {

    // Other code omitted

    public Contact showContact(RequestContext context) {

        Long id = context.getRequestScope().getLong("contactId");

        logger.info("Selected contact id: {}", id);

        return contactService.findByIdWithDetail(id);

    }
}
```

In Listing 18-12, the method RequestContext.getRequestScope().getLong() is called to retrieve the contactId variable, and then the method ContactService.findByIdWithDetail() is called, which will load the contact with the hobbies for the contact. The returned Contact object is stored as a view scope variable for rendering the show contact view.

Listing 18-13 shows the show contact view (webapp/WEB-INF/flows/contacts/show.xhtml).

Listing 18-13. *The Show Contact View*

```
<!DOCTYPE composition PUBLIC "-//W3C//DTD XHTML 1.0 Transitional//EN"
"http://www.w3.org/TR/xhtml1/DTD/xhtml1-transitional.dtd">
<ui:composition xmlns="http://www.w3.org/1999/xhtml"
```

```
    xmlns:ui="http://java.sun.com/jsf/facelets"
    xmlns:h="http://java.sun.com/jsf/html"
    xmlns:f="http://java.sun.com/jsf/core"
    xmlns:p="http://primefaces.org/ui"
    template="/WEB-INF/layouts/standard.xhtml">

<ui:define name="title">#{msg['application_name']}</ui:define>

<ui:define name="content">

<h1>Contact</h1>

<h:form >

    <h3>
        <h:outputText value="#{msg['label_contact_first_name']}: "/>
        <h:outputText value="#{contact.firstName}"/>
        <br/>
        <h:outputText value="#{msg['label_contact_last_name']}: "/>
        <h:outputText value="#{contact.lastName}"/>
        <br/>
        <h:outputText value="#{msg['label_contact_birth_date']}: "/>
        <h:outputText value="#{contact.birthDate}">
            <f:converter converterId="jodaDataTimeConverter" />
        </h:outputText>
    </h3>
    <h3>#{msg['label_contact_hobbies']}</h3>
    <p:dataList value="#{contact.hobbiesAsList}" var="hobby">
        #{hobby.hobbyId}
    </p:dataList>
    <br/>

    <p:toolbar>
        <p:toolbarGroup align="left">
            <p:commandButton value="Back" action="back"/>
        </p:toolbarGroup>
    </p:toolbar>
</h:form>

</ui:define>

</ui:composition>
```

In Listing 18-13, the contact information is rendered based on the properties stored in the contact variable. Note that for rendering the hobbies information, the Contact object's transient method getHobbiesAsList() is called. The reason is that JSF is not able to render detail information stored in a Set. So, the helper method getHobbiesAsList() is implemented to return the hobbies as a List.

To test the show contact view, select a row and then click the View Selected button. Then the contact information will be displayed, as shown in Figure 18-16.

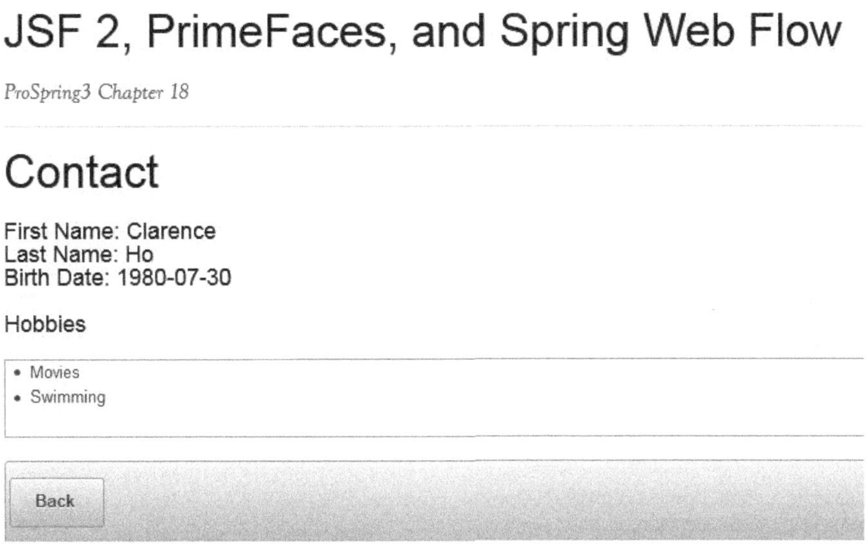

JSF 2, PrimeFaces, and Spring Web Flow

ProSpring3 Chapter 18

Contact

First Name: Clarence
Last Name: Ho
Birth Date: 1980-07-30

Hobbies

- Movies
- Swimming

Back

Figure 18-16. *The show contact view*

Implement the Add Contact Flow

Having the contact list view and show contact view ready, we can proceed to implement the add contact flow. In the following sections, we will discuss the implementation of the views in the add contact flow.

Step 1: Enter Basic Information

The add contact flow will be started when the user clicks the Add Contact button in the list contact view. The first state is step 1, in which the user will enter the basic information of a contact, including the first name, last name, and date of birth.

Take a look on the code snippet in Listing 18-14, which was extracted from the start state in the flow definition in Listing 18-5 (flow.xml).

Listing 18-14. *Navigate from List Contact to Step 1 of Add Contact*

```
<view-state id="start" view="list.xhtml">
    <on-entry>
        <evaluate expression="contactController.newContactListBean()"
            result="viewScope.contactListBean"/>
    </on-entry>
    <transition on="view" to="show">
        <set name="requestScope.contactId" value="contactListBean.selectedContact.id"/>
    </transition>
    <transition on="add" to="add-step-1">
        <evaluate expression="contactController.newContactBean()"
            result="flowScope.contactBean"/>
    </transition>
</view-state>
```

```
<view-state id="add-step-1" view="add-step-1.xhtml">
    <transition on="next" to="add-step-2"/>
</view-state>
```

In Listing 18-14, the transition and the add-step-1 state are highlighted in bold. Before the transition, the method ContactController.newContactBean() is called, which creates a new instance of the ContactBean class and stores it as a flow scope variable. This makes the variable available to all the steps within the add contact flow.

Listing 18-15 shows the ContactBean class, which stores the entered information across the flow and contains properties that facilitates user interaction by using PrimeFaces components.

Listing 18-15. The ContactBean Class

```
package com.apress.prospring3.ch18.web.view;

import java.io.Serializable;

import org.primefaces.model.DualListModel;

import com.apress.prospring3.ch18.domain.Contact;
import com.apress.prospring3.ch18.domain.Hobby;

public class ContactBean implements Serializable {

    private Contact contact;

    private DualListModel<Hobby> hobbies;

    // Getter/setter methods omitted
}
```

In Listing 18-15, the ContactBean class contains two properties. One is the contact property, which stores the contact information. The second one, the hobbies property, is of type DualListModel, which is used by PrimeFaces' PickList component for step 2.

Listing 18-16 shows the implementation of the newContactBean() method in the ContactController class.

Listing 18-16. The newContactBean() Method

```
package com.apress.prospring3.ch18.web.controller;

// Import statements omitted
@Component("contactController")
public class ContactController {

    // Other code omitted

    @Autowired
    private HobbyService hobbyService;

    public ContactBean newContactBean() {

        logger.info("Creating new contact bean");
        ContactBean contactBean = new ContactBean();
```

```
        Contact contact = new Contact();
        contactBean.setContact(contact);

        List<Hobby> hobbiesSource = new ArrayList<Hobby>();
        List<Hobby> hobbiesTarget = new ArrayList<Hobby>();

        for (Hobby hobby: hobbyService.findAll()) {
            hobbiesSource.add(hobby);
        }

        DualListModel<Hobby> hobbies = new DualListModel<Hobby>(hobbiesSource, hobbiesTarget);

        contactBean.setHobbies(hobbies);

        return contactBean;
    }
}
```

In Listing 18-16, the newContactBean() method will create an instance of ContactBean, and the hobbies property is also instantiated and stored into the ContactBean object for use in step 2.

Listing 18-17 shows the step 1 view (webapp/WEB-INF/flows/contacts/add-step-1.xhtml).

Listing 18-17. *The Add Contact Step 1 View*

```
<!DOCTYPE composition PUBLIC "-//W3C//DTD XHTML 1.0 Transitional//EN"
"http://www.w3.org/TR/xhtml1/DTD/xhtml1-transitional.dtd">
<ui:composition xmlns="http://www.w3.org/1999/xhtml"
    xmlns:ui="http://java.sun.com/jsf/facelets"
    xmlns:h="http://java.sun.com/jsf/html"
    xmlns:f="http://java.sun.com/jsf/core"
    xmlns:p="http://primefaces.org/ui"
    template="/WEB-INF/layouts/standard.xhtml">

<ui:define name="title">#{msg['application_name']}</ui:define>

<ui:define name="content">

<h1>#{msg['title_contact_add_step_1']}</h1>

<h:form >

    <p:messages/>
    <h:panelGrid columns="2">
        <h:outputLabel for="firstName">#{msg['label_contact_first_name']}</h:outputLabel>
        <p:inputText id="firstName" value="#{contactBean.contact.firstName}"/>
        <h:outputLabel for="lastName">#{msg['label_contact_last_name']}</h:outputLabel>
        <p:inputText id="lastName" value="#{contactBean.contact.lastName}"/>
        <h:outputLabel for="birthDate">#{msg['label_contact_birth_date']}</h:outputLabel>
        <p:calendar id="birthDate" value="#{contactBean.contact.birthDate}" pattern="yyyy-MM-dd">
            <f:converter converterId="jodaDataTimeConverter" />
        </p:calendar>
    </h:panelGrid>

    <p:toolbar>
```

697

```
            <p:toolbarGroup align="left">
                <p:commandButton value="Next" action="next" execute="@form" update="@form"/>
                <p:commandButton value="Exit" action="exit" immediate="true"/>
            </p:toolbarGroup>
        </p:toolbar>

    </h:form>

</ui:define>

</ui:composition>
```

In Listing 18-17, fields are provided with PrimeFaces' input components. Note the use of the `<p:calendar>` tag, which uses PrimeFaces' Calendar component and supports a pop-up date picker.

After the project is built and deployed, test the view by clicking the Add Contact button in the list contact view. Step 1 view will be created, as shown in Figure 18-17.

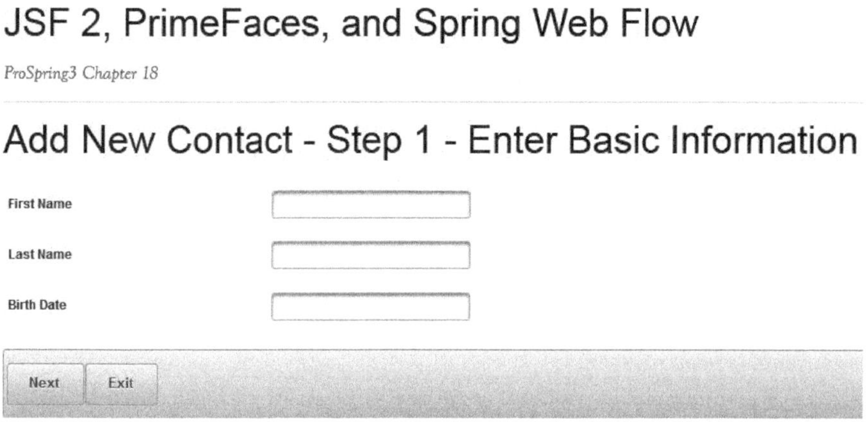

JSF 2, PrimeFaces, and Spring Web Flow

ProSpring3 Chapter 18

Add New Contact - Step 1 - Enter Basic Information

First Name	[ ]
Last Name	[ ]
Birth Date	[ ]

Next	Exit

Figure 18-17. Add contact : step 1

Support of JSR-303 Bean Validation

JSF 2 supports JSR-303 Bean Validation natively. The Contact class already is annotated with constraints on both the firstName and lastName properties. The file /src/main/resources/ValidationMessages.properties stores the validation messages. Note the use of the @form in the PrimeFaces' CommandButton component in Listing 18-17, which is a keyword in PrimeFaces that triggers the update of the form. During the update process, JSR-303 validation will be triggered automatically during the JSF application life cycle. To see it in action, in the step 1 view, click the Next button without having entered anything. The same view will be displayed again but with the validation messages displayed, as shown in Figure 18-18.

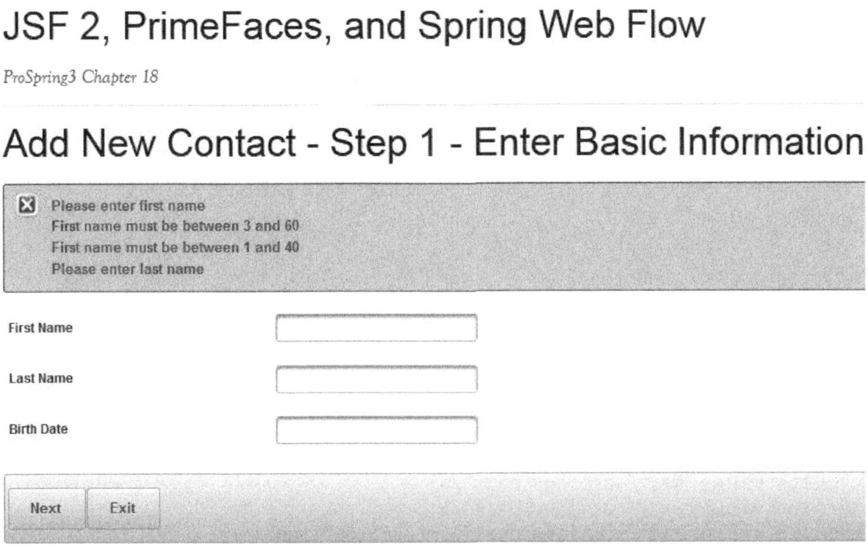

JSF 2, PrimeFaces, and Spring Web Flow

ProSpring3 Chapter 18

Add New Contact - Step 1 - Enter Basic Information

⊠ Please enter first name
First name must be between 3 and 60
First name must be between 1 and 40
Please enter last name

First Name

Last Name

Birth Date

Next   Exit

Figure 18-18. *JSF support of JSR-303 Bean Validation*

Step 2: Select Hobbies

Let's proceed to implement step 2, which is to select the hobbies for the contact. Listing 18-18 shows the view file (`webapp/WEB-INF/flows/contacts/add-step-2.xhtml`).

Listing 18-18. *The Add Contact Step 2 View*

```
<!DOCTYPE composition PUBLIC "-//W3C//DTD XHTML 1.0 Transitional//EN"
"http://www.w3.org/TR/xhtml1/DTD/xhtml1-transitional.dtd">
<ui:composition xmlns="http://www.w3.org/1999/xhtml"
    xmlns:ui="http://java.sun.com/jsf/facelets"
    xmlns:h="http://java.sun.com/jsf/html"
    xmlns:f="http://java.sun.com/jsf/core"
    xmlns:p="http://primefaces.org/ui"
    template="/WEB-INF/layouts/standard.xhtml">

<ui:define name="title">#{msg['application_name']}</ui:define>

<ui:define name="content">

<h1>#{msg['title_contact_add_step_2']}</h1>

<h:form >

    <h3>

        <h:outputText value="#{msg['label_contact_first_name']}: "/>
        <h:outputText value="#{contactBean.contact.firstName}"/>
        <br/>
```

```
            <h:outputText value="#{msg['label_contact_last_name']}: "/>
            <h:outputText value="#{contactBean.contact.lastName}"/>
            <br/>
            <h:outputText value="#{msg['label_contact_birth_date']}: "/>
            <h:outputText value="#{contactBean.contact.birthDate}">
                <f:converter converterId="jodaDataTimeConverter" />
            </h:outputText>

        </h3>

        <p:pickList value="#{contactBean.hobbies}"
                    var="hobby"
                    itemLabel="#{hobby.hobbyId}"
                    itemValue="#{hobby.hobbyId}"
                    converter="hobby"/>

        <p:toolbar>
            <p:toolbarGroup align="left">
                <p:commandButton value="Next" action="next"/>
                <p:commandButton value="Back" action="back"/>
                <p:commandButton value="Exit" action="exit" immediate="true"/>
            </p:toolbarGroup>
        </p:toolbar>
    </h:form>

</ui:define>

</ui:composition>
```

In Listing 18-18, note the use of the PrimeFaces' PickList component for selecting hobbies. The PickList is bound to the hobbies property of the ContactBean class, which is of the DualListModel class. The available hobbies are stored in the source property, while the selected hobbies are stored in the target property. For the hobby property, we also need to implement a custom converter for transformation between the String and Hobby classes. Listing 18-19 shows the converter class.

Listing 18-19. *The Hobby Converter Class*

```
package com.apress.prospring3.ch18.web.converter;

import javax.faces.component.UIComponent;
import javax.faces.context.FacesContext;
import javax.faces.convert.Converter;
import javax.faces.convert.FacesConverter;

import com.apress.prospring3.ch18.domain.Hobby;

@FacesConverter("hobby")
public class HobbyConverter implements Converter {

    @Override
    public Object getAsObject(FacesContext ctx, UIComponent component, String value) {
        return new Hobby(value);
    }
```

```
    @Override
    public String getAsString(FacesContext ctx, UIComponent component, Object value) {
        return (String) value;
    }
}
```

Listing 18-19 should be self-explanatory. To test the view, enter information in step 1, and then click the Next button. Step 2 will be displayed, as shown in Figure 18-19.

JSF 2, PrimeFaces, and Spring Web Flow

ProSpring3 Chapter 18

Figure 18-19. *Add contact : step 2*

Step 3: Review Information

Step 3 of the add contact flow is to review the entered information so that the user can go back to modify the information or save the contact information. Listing 18-20 shows the step 3 view (webapp/WEB-INF/flows/contacts/review.xhtml).

Listing 18-20. *The Review Contact View*

```
<!DOCTYPE composition PUBLIC "-//W3C//DTD XHTML 1.0 Transitional//EN"
"http://www.w3.org/TR/xhtml1/DTD/xhtml1-transitional.dtd">
<ui:composition xmlns="http://www.w3.org/1999/xhtml"
    xmlns:ui="http://java.sun.com/jsf/facelets"
    xmlns:h="http://java.sun.com/jsf/html"
    xmlns:f="http://java.sun.com/jsf/core"
    xmlns:p="http://primefaces.org/ui"
    template="/WEB-INF/layouts/standard.xhtml">

<ui:define name="title">#{msg['application_name']}</ui:define>
```

```
<ui:define name="content">

<h1>#{msg['title_contact_add_review']}</h1>

<h:form >

    <h3>
        <h:outputText value="#{msg['label_contact_first_name']}: "/>
        <h:outputText value="#{contactBean.contact.firstName}"/>
        <br/>
        <h:outputText value="#{msg['label_contact_last_name']}: "/>
        <h:outputText value="#{contactBean.contact.lastName}"/>
        <br/>
        <h:outputText value="#{msg['label_contact_birth_date']}: "/>
        <h:outputText value="#{contactBean.contact.birthDate}">
            <f:converter converterId="jodaDataTimeConverter" />
        </h:outputText>
    </h3>
    <h3>#{msg['label_contact_hobbies']}</h3>
    <p:dataList value="#{contactBean.hobbies.target}" var="hobby">
        #{hobby.hobbyId}
    </p:dataList>
    <br/>

    <p:toolbar>
        <p:toolbarGroup align="left">
            <p:commandButton value="Save" action="next"/>
            <p:commandButton value="Back" action="back"/>
            <p:commandButton value="Exit" action="exit" immediate="true"/>
        </p:toolbarGroup>
    </p:toolbar>
</h:form>

</ui:define>

</ui:composition>
```

In Listing 18-20, the contact information is displayed. To test the view, select the hobbies for the contact, and then click the Next button. The review page will be displayed, as shown in Figure 18-20.

JSF 2, PrimeFaces, and Spring Web Flow

ProSpring3 Chapter 18

Add New Contact - Review Information

First Name: Andy
Last Name: Lau
Birth Date: 2012-01-01

Hobbies

- Swimming
- Jogging
- Programming
- Movies
- Reading

Figure 18-20. *Add contact : review information*

Step 4: Add Contact Complete

Take a look at the code snippet in Listing 18-21, which was extracted from the start state in the flow definition in Listing 18-5 (flow.xml).

Listing 18-21. Navigate from Review to Complete Add Contact

```
<view-state id="review" view="review.xhtml">
    <transition on ="next" to="complete">
        <evaluate expression="contactController.saveContact(flowRequestContext)"/>
    </transition>
    <transition on="back" to="add-step-2"/>
</view-state>

<view-state id="complete" view="complete.xhtml">
    <transition on="continue" to="finish"/>
</view-state>

<end-state id="finish"/>
```

In Listing 18-21, which enables the transition from review to complete state, the complete and end states are highlighted in bold. During the transition, the ContactController.saveContact() method will be called, which persists the Contact object, and then the complete view will be displayed. Listing 18-22 shows the implementation of the saveContact() method.

Listing 18-22. The saveContact() Method

```
package com.apress.prospring3.ch18.web.controller;

// Import statements omitted
@Component("contactController")
public class ContactController {

    // Other code omitted

    public void saveContact(RequestContext context) {

        // Retrieve contact bean
        ContactBean contactBean = (ContactBean) context.getFlowScope().get("contactBean");
        Contact contact = contactBean.getContact();

        Set<Hobby> hobbies = new HashSet<Hobby>(contactBean.getHobbies().getTarget());

        contact.setHobbies(hobbies);

        contactService.save(contact);

        logger.info("Contact {} {} saved successfully", contact.getFirstName(),
            contact.getLastName());

        context.getMessageContext().addMessage(new
            MessageBuilder().info().code("message_contact_save_success").build());
    }
}
```

In Listing 18-22, in the saveContact() method, the flow scope variable contactBean is retrieved from Spring Web Flow's RequestContext, the contact property is retrieved, the hobbies property is populated, and then the Contact object is persisted. Upon completion, a success message is constructed and put into the MessageContext, and the complete view is rendered. In Listing 18-4, in the Spring MVC configuration, we defined the messageSource bean with the message file paths specified. Let's create a folder called i18n under the WEB-INF folder and the file messages.properties for storing the success message. We just need to put the following line into the file for the success message:

```
message_contact_save_success=Contact saved successfully
```

Listing 18-23 shows the complete view (webapp/WEB-INF/flows/contacts/complete.xhtml).

Listing 18-23. The Complete View

```
<!DOCTYPE composition PUBLIC "-//W3C//DTD XHTML 1.0 Transitional//EN"
"http://www.w3.org/TR/xhtml1/DTD/xhtml1-transitional.dtd">
<ui:composition xmlns="http://www.w3.org/1999/xhtml"
    xmlns:ui="http://java.sun.com/jsf/facelets"
    xmlns:h="http://java.sun.com/jsf/html"
    xmlns:f="http://java.sun.com/jsf/core"
    xmlns:p="http://primefaces.org/ui"
    template="/WEB-INF/layouts/standard.xhtml">

<ui:define name="title">#{msg['application_name']}</ui:define>
```

```
<ui:define name="content">

<h1>#{msg['title_contact_add_complete']}</h1>

<p:messages/>

<h:form >

    <h3>
        <h:outputText value="#{msg['label_contact_first_name']}: "/>
        <h:outputText value="#{contactBean.contact.firstName}"/>
        <br/>
        <h:outputText value="#{msg['label_contact_last_name']}: "/>
        <h:outputText value="#{contactBean.contact.lastName}"/>
        <br/>
        <h:outputText value="#{msg['label_contact_birth_date']}: "/>
        <h:outputText value="#{contactBean.contact.birthDate}">
            <f:converter converterId="jodaDataTimeConverter" />
        </h:outputText>
    </h3>
    <h3>#{msg['label_contact_hobbies']}</h3>
    <p:dataList value="#{contactBean.hobbies.target}" var="hobby">
        #{hobby.hobbyId}
    </p:dataList>
    <br/>

    <p:toolbar>
        <p:toolbarGroup align="left">
            <p:commandButton value="Continue" action="continue"/>
        </p:toolbarGroup>
    </p:toolbar>
</h:form>

</ui:define>

</ui:composition>
```

At this point, the add contact flow is complete. After the project is built and deployed, you can try
the entire flow. Click the Next or Back button in any state, and you will see that the value was kept for the
entire flow. Figure 18-21 shows what it looks like after a contact is saved successfully.

JSF 2, PrimeFaces, and Spring Web Flow

ProSpring3 Chapter 18

Add New Contact - Complete

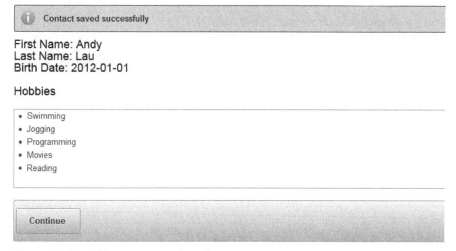

ⓘ Contact saved successfully

First Name: Andy
Last Name: Lau
Birth Date: 2012-01-01

Hobbies

- Swimming
- Jogging
- Programming
- Movies
- Reading

Continue

Figure 18-21. Add contact complete view

Summary

In this chapter, we covered using Spring Web Flow and JSF 2 when implementing a flow-based web application.

First we discussed the high-level concepts of both Spring Web Flow and JSF 2. Then, the first-class support of JSF in Spring Web Flow was covered, with the required dependencies and configurations.

Then we designed a sample flow for adding a contact. The design of the flow, including state transitions, views, variables, and so on, was elaborated on.

Finally, we went through the steps to implement the flow. Steps included the development of the flow definition, controller class, backing beans, custom converters, views using JSF, and PrimeFaces components.

CHAPTER 19

Spring Testing

When developing applications for enterprise use, testing is an important way to ensure that the completed application performs as expected and fulfills all kinds of requirements (architectural, security, user requirements, and so on).

Every time a change is made, you should ensure that the changes that were introduced don't impact the existing logic. Maintaining an ongoing build and test environment is critical for ensuring high-quality applications. Reproducible tests with high coverage for all your code allow you to deploy new applications and changes to applications with a high level of confidence.

In an enterprise development environment, there are many different kinds of testing that target each layer within an enterprise application, and each kind of testing has its own characteristics and requirements.

In this chapter, we will discuss the basic concepts involved in the testing of various application layers, especially in the testing of Spring-powered applications. We also will cover the ways in which Spring makes implementing the test cases of various layers easier for developers. Specifically, this chapter will cover the following topics:

- *Enterprise testing framework*: We will briefly describe an enterprise testing framework. We will discuss various kinds of testing and their purposes. In this chapter, we will focus on unit testing, targeting various application layers.

- *Logic unit test*: The finest unit test is to test only the logic of the methods within a class, with all other dependencies being "mocked" with the correct behavior. In this chapter, we will discuss the implementation of logic unit testing for the Spring MVC controller classes, with the help of a Java mock library to perform the mocking of a class's dependencies.

- *Integration unit test*: In an enterprise testing framework, integration testing refers to testing the interaction of a group of classes within different application layers for a specific piece of business logic. Typically, in an integration testing environment, the service layer should test with the persistence layer, with the backend database available. However, as application architecture evolves and the maturity of lightweight in-memory databases evolves, it's now a common practice to "unit test" the service layer with the persistence layer and backend database as a whole. For example, in this chapter, we will use JPA 2, with Hibernate and Spring Data JPA as the persistence provider and with H2 as the database. In this architecture, it's of less importance to "mock" Hibernate and Spring Data JPA when testing the service layer. As a result, in this chapter, we will discuss testing of the service layer together with the persistence layer and the H2 in-memory database. This kind of testing is generally referred to as *integration unit testing*, which sits in the middle of unit testing and full-blown integration testing.

- *Frontend unit test*: Even if we test every layer of the application, after the application is deployed, we still need to ensure that the entire application works as expected. More specifically, for a web application, upon deployment to the continuous build environment, we should run "frontend" testing to ensure that the user interface is working properly. For example, for a contact application, we should ensure that each step of the normal functionality works properly, and we also should test exceptional cases (e.g., how the application functions when information doesn't pass the validation phase). In this chapter, we will discuss how to use an open source framework to help automate the testing of the frontend of a web application.

Project for Sample Web Application

For the test cases in this chapter, we will take use contact web application that we implemented in Chapter 17 as the target application under test.

Import the Sample Backend in STS

Because this chapter focuses on unit test development, we have prepared a project for the sample web application so that you can just import it and then proceed to implement the test cases.

From the sample code, extract the file ch19-notest.zip into your STS workspace. Then you can then import the project into STS.

To import the project, in STS choose the menu option File ➤ Import, and in the Select dialog, choose Existing Projects into Workspace under the General category, as shown in Figure 19-1.

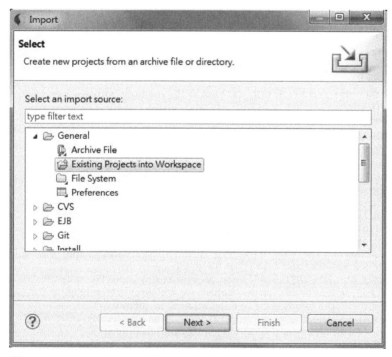

Figure 19-1. Importing existing project in STS

Then, in the Import Projects dialog, choose the project extracted from the sample source code, and then click Finish (see Figure 19-2).

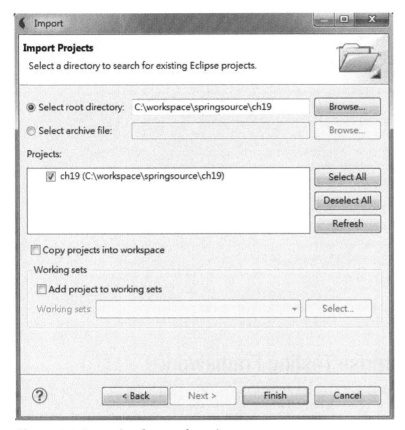

Figure 19-2. Importing the sample project

Upon project import completion, build and deploy to the tc Server in STS. Then, when the project is published and the tc Server is started, test the sample contact application by visiting the URL http://localhost:8080/ch19/contacts within your web browser, as shown in Figure 19-3.

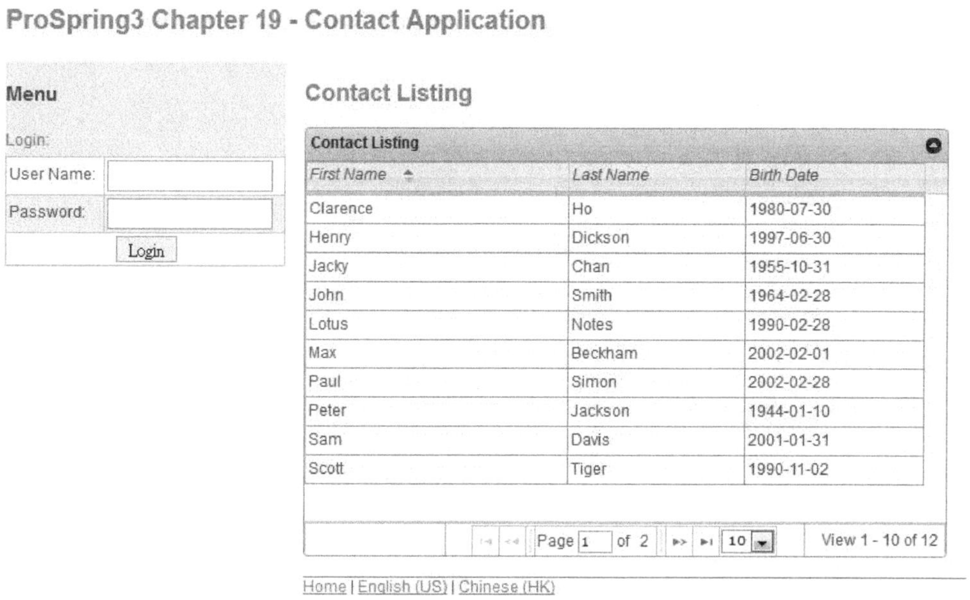

ProSpring3 Chapter 19 - Contact Application

Menu

Login:

User Name:	
Password:	
	Login

Contact Listing

Contact Listing			⊙
First Name ▲	Last Name	Birth Date	
Clarence	Ho	1980-07-30	
Henry	Dickson	1997-06-30	
Jacky	Chan	1955-10-31	
John	Smith	1964-02-28	
Lotus	Notes	1990-02-28	
Max	Beckham	2002-02-01	
Paul	Simon	2002-02-28	
Peter	Jackson	1944-01-10	
Sam	Davis	2001-01-31	
Scott	Tiger	1990-11-02	

|◄ ◄◄ Page 1 of 2 ►► ►| 10 ▼   View 1 - 10 of 12

Home | English (US) | Chinese (HK)

Figure 19-3. Sample contact web application

At this point, the sample application setup is complete, so we can proceed to implementing the test cases.

Introducing an Enterprise Testing Framework

An *enterprise testing framework* refers to the testing activities in the entire application's life cycle. In various phases, different testing activities will be performed to verify that the functionalities of the application are working as expected according to the defined business and technical requirements.

In each phase, different test cases will be executed. Some will be automated, while some will be performed manually. In each case, the result will be verified by the corresponding personnel (e.g., business analysts, application users, and so on).

Figure 19-4 shows a typical enterprise testing framework.

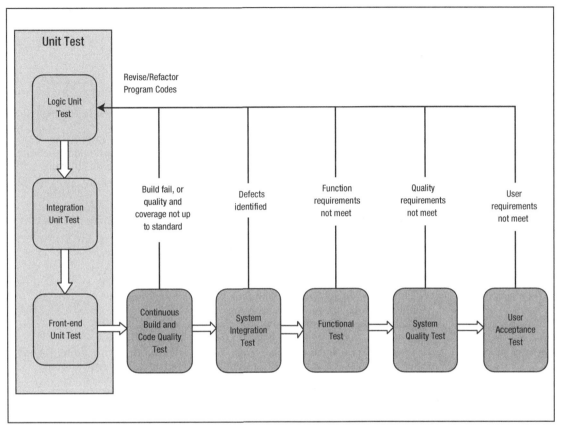

Figure 19-4. *An enterprise testing framework*

Table 19-1 describes the characteristics and objectives of each type of testing, as well as common tools and libraries that are used for implementing the test cases.

Table 19-1. *Description of Enterprise Testing Framework*

Test Category	Description	Common Tools
Logic unit test	A logic unit test takes a single object and tests it by itself, without worrying about the role it plays in the surrounding system.	Unit test: JUnit, TestNG Mock object: Mockito, EasyMock
Integration unit test	An integration unit test focuses on testing the interaction between components in a "near real" environment. These tests will exercise the interactions with the container (embedded DB, web container, and so on).	Embedded DB: H2Database DB testing: DBUnit In memory web container: Jetty

Test Category	Description	Common Tools
Frontend unit test	A frontend unit test focuses on testing the user interface. The objective is to ensure that each user interface reacts to users' actions and produces the output to the users as expected.	Selenium
Continuous build and code quality test	The application code base should be built on a regular basis to ensure that the code quality complies with the standard (e.g., comments were all in place, no empty exception catch block, and so on). Also, test coverage should be as high as possible to ensure that all developed lines of codes are tested.	Code Quality: PMD, CheckStyle, CodePro Analytix Test Coverage: Cobertura Build Tool: Gradle, Maven, Sonar Continuous Build: Hudson, Jenkins
System integration test	The system integration test verifies the accuracy of the communication among all programs in the new system and between the new system and all of the external interfaces. The integration test must also prove that the new system performs according to the functional specifications and functions effectively in the operating environment without adversely affecting other systems.	IBM Rational Systems Tester
Functional test	Use cases and business rules are tested by functional tests. The goals of these tests are to verify that inputs are accepted properly and outputs are generated properly, where "properly" means in accordance both with the use case specifications and with the business rules. This is black-box testing by interacting with the application via the GUI and analyzing the results.	IBM Rational Functional Tester, HP Quick Test Professional
System quality test	The system quality test is to ensure that the developed application meets those nonfunctional requirements. Most of the time, this tests the performance of the application to ensure that the target requirements for concurrent users of the system and workload are met. Other nonfunctional requirements include security, high availability features, and so on.	Apache JMeter, HP LoadRunner

Test Category	Description	Common Tools
User acceptance test	The user acceptance test simulates the actual working conditions of the new system, including the user manuals and procedures. Extensive user involvement in this stage of testing provides the user with invaluable training in operating the new system. It also benefits the programmer or designer to see the user experience with the new programs. This joint involvement encourages the user and operations personnel to approve the system conversion.	IBM Rational TestManager, HP Quality Center

In this chapter, we will focus on the implementation of the three kinds of unit test (logic unit test, integration unit test, and frontend unit test) and see how the Spring TestContext framework and other supporting tools and libraries can help in developing those test cases.

Instead of presenting the full details and list of classes that the Spring Framework provides in the testing area, we will discuss the usage of the most commonly used patterns and the supporting interfaces and classes within the Spring TestContext framework as we implement the sample test cases in this chapter.

Implementing Logic Unit Test

As previously discussed, a logic unit test is the finest level of testing. The objective is to verify the behavior of an individual class, with all the class's dependencies being "mocked" with expected behavior.

In this section, we will demonstrate a logic unit test by implementing the test cases for the ContactController class, with the service layer being "mocked" with expected behavior.

To help mock the behavior of the service layer, we will use Mockito (http://code.google.com/p/mockito), which is a popular mocking framework.

Adding Required Dependencies

First we need to add the dependency on Mockito into the project, as shown in Table 19-2.

Table 19-2. Maven Dependencies for Mockito

Group ID	Artifact ID	Version	Description
org.mockito	mockito-core	1.9.0	The core library of the Mockito mocking framework

Add the dependency in Table 19-2 to the project in STS.

Unit Testing Spring MVC Controller

In the contact web application we implemented in Chapter 17, Spring MVC was used as the presentation layer. In the presentation layer, controller classes provide the integration between the user interface and the service layer.

Methods in controller classes will be mapped to the HTTP requests. Within the method, the request will be processed, will bind to model objects, and will interact with the service layer (which was injected into the controller classes via Spring's DI) to process the data. Upon completion, depending on the result, the controller class will update the model and the view state (e.g., user messages, and so on) and return the logical view (or the model with the view together) for Spring MVC to resolve the view to be displayed to the user.

For unit testing controller classes, the main objective is to make sure that the controller methods update the model and other view states properly and return the correct view. In addition, when an error happens, testing ensures that the correct exception is thrown and the error messages are saved into the state for displaying to the user. As we only want to test the controller classes' behavior, we need to "mock" the service layer with the correct behavior.

For the ContactController class in the sample application, we would like to develop the test cases for the list() and create() methods. In the following sections, we will discuss the steps for this, including the development of some common infrastructure classes that support controller class testing and the implementation of the test cases.

Implement the Infrastructure Classes

For a group of common tests (e.g., test cases for controller classes, service layer testing classes, and so on), it's always a best practice to develop a common abstract parent class that has the mandatory testing infrastructure set up correctly.

In this chapter, we will use Java classes for configuring Spring's TestContext. In addition, we will use the profile feature in Spring 3.1 for configuring the components specific to the test environment.

Let's implement the Java class for Spring's ApplicationContext (the ControllerTestConfig class), which is shown in Listing 19-1. Note that testing classes and resource files should be placed in the folders /src/test/java and /src/test/resources, respectively.

Listing 19-1. The ControllerTestConfig Class

```
package com.apress.prospring3.ch19.test.config;

import org.springframework.context.annotation.Configuration;
import org.springframework.context.annotation.Profile;

@Configuration
@Profile("test")
public class ControllerTestConfig {

}
```

In Listing 19-1, we indicate to Spring that it's an ApplicationContext configuration class by applying the @Configuration annotation to the class. Then, the @Profile annotation was applied to the class to indicate the profile (in this case the test profile) that the beans configured in this class belong to.

We don't need any beans at the moment. However, it's always a good practice to maintain a configuration class so that when the need arises in future (e.g., the Spring MVC layer needs to integrate with an external FTP server), then the mocked bean for the FTP server can be defined in this configuration class.

The next step is to implement the abstract base class for controller class test cases (the AbstractControllerTest class), which is shown in Listing 19-2.

Listing 19-2. The AbstractControllerTest Class

```
package com.apress.prospring3.ch19.web.controller;

import org.junit.runner.RunWith;
import org.springframework.test.context.ActiveProfiles;
import org.springframework.test.context.ContextConfiguration;
import org.springframework.test.context.junit4.SpringJUnit4ClassRunner;

import com.apress.prospring3.ch19.test.config.ControllerTestConfig;

@RunWith(SpringJUnit4ClassRunner.class)
@ContextConfiguration(classes = {ControllerTestConfig.class})
@ActiveProfiles("test")
public class AbstractControllerTest {

}
```

In Listing 19-2, we applied several annotations to the abstract base class. First, the @RunWith annotation belongs to the JUnit library (in this chapter, we are using JUnit version 4.10), which indicates the runner classes used to execute the test case. Within the annotation, Spring's SpringJUnit4ClassRunner is provided, which is Spring's JUnit support class for running test cases within Spring's ApplicationContext environment.

Second, the @ContextConfiguration indicates to the Spring JUnit runner on the configuration to be loaded. Within the annotation, we specified the classes attribute, which indicates that configuration was defined in the provided Java classes. It's also possible to load the context from XML files by providing the locations attribute, but you can't provide both locations and classes attributes together.

Finally, the @ActiveProfiles annotation is applied, passing in the profile name test as the attribute. This indicates to Spring that beans belonging to the test profile should be loaded.

Testing the list() Method

Having the infrastructure classes in place, let's create our first test case for the ContactController.list() method. In this test case, we want to make sure that when the method is called, after the list of contacts is retrieved from the service layer, the information is saved correctly into the model, and the correct logical view name is returned. Listing 19-3 shows the test case.

Listing 19-3. Testing the list() Method

```
package com.apress.prospring3.ch19.web.controller;

import static org.junit.Assert.assertEquals;
import static org.junit.Assert.assertNotNull;
import static org.mockito.Mockito.mock;
import static org.mockito.Mockito.when;

import java.util.ArrayList;
import java.util.List;

import org.junit.Before;
import org.junit.Test;
import org.springframework.test.util.ReflectionTestUtils;
```

```java
import org.springframework.ui.ExtendedModelMap;

import com.apress.prospring3.ch19.domain.Contact;
import com.apress.prospring3.ch19.service.ContactService;

public class ContactControllerTest extends AbstractControllerTest {

    private final List<Contact> contacts = new ArrayList<Contact>();

    private ContactService contactService;

    @Before
    public void initContacts() {
        // Initialize list of contacts for mocked ContactService
        Contact contact = new Contact();
        contact.setId(1l);
        contact.setFirstName("Clarence");
        contact.setLastName("Ho");
        contacts.add(contact);
    }

    @Test
    public void testList() throws Exception {

        contactService = mock(ContactService.class);
        when(contactService.findAll()).thenReturn(contacts);

        ContactController contactController = new ContactController();

        ReflectionTestUtils.setField(contactController, "contactService",
            contactService);

        ExtendedModelMap uiModel = new ExtendedModelMap();

        String result = contactController.list(uiModel);

        assertNotNull(result);
        assertEquals(result, "contacts/list");

        List<Contact> modelContacts = (List<Contact>) uiModel.get("contacts");

        assertEquals(1, modelContacts.size());
    }
}
```

In Listing 19-3, first the class extends AbstractControllerTest, which inherits all the required infrastructure for testing the controller class. Then, in the test case, the initContacts() method is applied with the @Before annotation, which indicates to JUnit that the method should be run before running each test case (in case you want to run some logic before the entire test class, use the @BeforeClass annotation). In the method, a list of contacts is initialized with hard-coded information.

Second, the testList() method is applied with the @Test annotation, which indicates to JUnit that it's a test case that JUnit should run. Within the test case, the private variable contactService (of type ContactService) is mocked by using Mockito's Mockito.mock() method (note the import static statement). The when() method is also provided by Mockito to mock the ContactService.findAll() method, which will be used by the ContactController class.

Third, an instance of ContactController class is created, and then its contactService variable, which will be injected by Spring in normal situations, is set with the mocked instance by using the Spring-provided ReflectionTestUtils class's setField() method. ReflectionTestUtils provides a collection of reflection-based utility methods for use in unit and integration testing scenarios. In addition, an instance of the ExtendedModelMap class (which implements the org.springframework.ui.Model interface) is constructed.

Next, the ContactController.list() method is called, passing in the instance of the ExtendedModelMap class. Upon invocation, the result is verified by calling the various assert methods (provided by JUnit) to ensure that the correct logical view name is returned, and the list of contact information is saved correctly in the model for used by the view.

Now we can run the test case. To run it in STS, right-click the class and then choose Run As ➤ JUnit Test. The test case should run successfully, and you can verify it in the JUnit view, as shown in Figure 19-5.

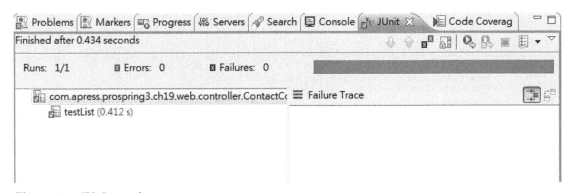

Figure 19-5. JUnit test view

Now let's proceed with the create() method.

Testing the create() Method

Listing 19-4 shows the code snippet for testing the create() method.

Listing 19-4. Testing the create() Method

```java
package com.apress.prospring3.ch19.web.controller;

import org.springframework.context.MessageSource;
import org.springframework.mock.web.MockHttpServletRequest;

import org.mockito.stubbing.Answer;
import org.mockito.invocation.InvocationOnMock;

// Other import statements omitted
public class ContactControllerTest extends AbstractControllerTest {

    // Other code omitted
```

```
    private MessageSource messageSource;

    @Test
    public void testCreate() {

        final Contact newContact = new Contact();
        newContact.setId(999l);
        newContact.setFirstName("Rod");
        newContact.setFirstName("Johnson");

        contactService = mock(ContactService.class);
        when(contactService.save(newContact)).thenAnswer(new Answer<Contact>() {
            public Contact answer(InvocationOnMock invocation) throws Throwable {
                contacts.add(newContact);
                return newContact;
            }
        });

        messageSource = mock(MessageSource.class);
        when(messageSource.getMessage("contact_save_success", new Object[]{},
            Locale.ENGLISH)).thenReturn("success");

        ContactController contactController = new ContactController();
        ReflectionTestUtils.setField(contactController, "contactService",
            contactService);
        ReflectionTestUtils.setField(contactController, "messageSource",
            messageSource);

        BindingResult bindingResult = new BeanPropertyBindingResult(
            newContact, "contact");
        ExtendedModelMap uiModel = new ExtendedModelMap();
        HttpServletRequest httpServletRequest = new MockHttpServletRequest();
        RedirectAttributes redirectAttributes =
            new RedirectAttributesModelMap();
        Locale locale = Locale.ENGLISH;

        String result = contactController.create(newContact, bindingResult,
            uiModel, httpServletRequest, redirectAttributes, locale, null);

        assertNotNull(result);
        assertEquals("redirect:/contacts/999", result);
        assertEquals(2, contacts.size());
    }
}
```

In Listing 19-4, the ContactService.save() method is mocked to simulate the addition of a new Contact object in the list of contacts. Note the use of the org.mockito.stubbing.Answer<T> interface, which mocks the method with the expected logic and returns a value.

Moreover, a mocked instance of the MessageSource interface is mocked with Mockito. Then an instance of ContactController class is constructed, and its dependencies to ContactService and MessageSource are set with the mocked implementation. In addition, besides ExtendedModelMap, instances of RedirectAttributes and HttpServletRequest are constructed. For the HttpServletRequest interface, note the use of the MockHttpServletRequest class, which is Spring's mocked implementation. There are also a number of mock classes within the org.springframework.mock.web package to help implement unit tests. For the `BindingResult` interface, an instance of the `BeanPropertyBindingResult` class was constructed that will perform the registration and evaluation of binding errors on JavaBean objects, by using standard JavaBean property access.

Then, the `ContactController.create()` method is called, and assert operations are invoked to verify the result. Run the result again, and note the result in the JUnit view.

For the `create()` method, we should create more test cases to test various scenarios. For example, we need to test when data access errors are encountered during the save operation.

Implementing an Integration Unit Test

In this section, we will implement the integration unit test for the service layer. In the contact application, the core service is the class `com.apress.prospring3.ch19.service.jpa.ContactServiceImpl`, which is the JPA implementation of the `com.apress.prospring3.ch19.service.ContactService` interface.

When unit testing the service layer, we will use the H2 in-memory database to host the data model and testing data, with the JPA providers (Hibernate and Spring Data JPA's repository abstraction) in place. The objective is to ensure that the `ContactServiceImpl` class is performing the business functions correctly.

In the following sections, we will show how to test some of the finder methods and the save operation of the `ContactServiceImpl` class.

Adding Required Dependencies

For implementing test cases with the database in place, we need a library that can help populate the desired testing data in the database before executing the test case and that can perform the necessary database operations easily. Moreover, in order to make it easier to prepare the test data, we will support the preparation of test data in Microsoft Excel format.

To fulfill these purposes, additional libraries are required. On the database side, DBUnit (`http://dbunit.sourceforge.net`) is a common library that can help implement database-related testing. In addition, the Apache POI (`http://poi.apache.org`) project's library will be used to help parse the test data that was prepared in Microsoft Excel. Table 19-3 shows the required dependencies.

Table 19-3. Maven Dependencies for Integration Unit Test

Group ID	Artifact ID	Version	Description
org.dbunit	dbunit	2.4.8	The DBUnit library
org.apache.poi	poi	3.2-FINAL	Apache POI library that supports reading and writing of files in Microsoft Office format

Add the dependencies in Table 19-3 into the project in STS.

Configuring the Profile for Service Layer Testing

The bean definition profiles feature introduced in Spring 3.1 is very useful for implementing a test case with the appropriate configuration of the testing components. To facilitate the testing of the service layer, we will also use the profile feature for the `ApplicationContext` configuration.

For the contact application, we would like to have two profiles, as follows:

- *Development profile ("dev")*: Profile with configuration for the development environment. For example, in the development system, the backend H2 database will have both the database creation and the initial data population scripts executed.

- *Testing profile ("test")*: Profile with configuration for the testing environment. For example, in the testing environment, the backend H2 database will have only the database creation script executed, while the data will be populated by the test case.

Let's configure the profile environment for the contact application. For the contact application, the backend configuration (i.e., data source, JPA, transaction, and so on) was defined in the configuration XML file /src/main/resources/datasource-tx-jpa.xml. We would like to configure the data source in the file for dev profile only. To do this, we need to wrap the data source bean with the profile configuration. Listing 19-5 shows the code snippet for the change required.

Listing 19-5. Configure Profile for Data Source

```xml
<?xml version="1.0" encoding="UTF-8"?>
<beans xmlns="http://www.springframework.org/schema/beans"

    <!-- Other code omitted -->

    <beans profile="dev">
        <jdbc:embedded-database id="dataSource" type="H2">
            <jdbc:script location="classpath:schema.sql"/>
            <jdbc:script location="classpath:test-data.sql"/>
        </jdbc:embedded-database>
    </beans>

</beans>
```

The change to apply is highlighted in bold. As shown in the code snippet, the dataSource bean is wrapped with the <beans> tag and given the profile attribute with the value dev, which indicates that the data source is applicable only for the development system.

To bootstrap the web application with the development profile, we add the parameter in the web deployment descriptor (another way is to modify the web container startup script). Listing 19-6 shows the code snippet.

Listing 19-6. Configure Profile in web.xml

```xml
<?xml version="1.0" encoding="UTF-8"?>
<web-app version="3.0" xmlns="http://java.sun.com/xml/ns/javaee"
    xmlns:xsi="http://www.w3.org/2001/XMLSchema-instance"
    xsi:schemaLocation="http://java.sun.com/xml/ns/javaee
    http://java.sun.com/xml/ns/javaee/web-app_3_0.xsd">

    <!-- The definition of the Root Spring Container shared by all Servlets and Filters -->
    <context-param>
        <param-name>contextConfigLocation</param-name>
        <param-value>/WEB-INF/spring/root-context.xml</param-value>
    </context-param>
    <context-param>
```

```
    <param-name>spring.profiles.active</param-name>
    <param-value>dev</param-value>
</context-param>

<!-- Other code omitted -->
```

```
</web-app>
```

The new parameter to apply is highlighted in bold. The parameter spring.profiles.active is given the value dev to indicate that Spring should bootstrap WebApplicationContext with the beans defined for the dev profile.

Implementing the Infrastructure Classes

Before implementing the individual test case, we need to implement the infrastructure classes, including the Java configuration class and the base class for service layer testing. In addition, we also need to implement some classes to support the population of test data in the Excel file. Moreover, to ease the development of the test case, we want to introduce a custom annotation called @DataSets, which accepts the Excel file name as the argument. We will develop a custom test execution listener (a feature supported by the Spring testing framework) to check for the existence of the annotation and load the data accordingly.

In the following sections, we will discuss how to implement the various infrastructure classes and the custom listener that loads data from the Excel file.

Implementing Custom TestExecutionListener

In the spring-test module, the org.springframework.test.context.TestExecutionListener interface defines a listener API that can intercept the events in the various phases of the test case execution (e.g., before and after the class under test, before and after the method under test, and so on). In testing the service layer, we will implement a custom listener for the newly introduced @DataSets annotation. The objective is to support the population of test data with a simple annotation on the test case. For example, to test the ContactService.findAll() method, we would like to have the code look like the code snippet in Listing 19-7.

Listing 19-7. Usage of the @DataSets Annotation

```
@DataSets(setUpDataSet="/com/apress/prospring3/ch19/service/jpa/ContactServiceImplTest.xls")
@Test
public void testFindAll() throws Exception {

    List<Contact> result = customerService.findAll();
    …
}
```

In Listing 19-7, the application of the @DataSets annotation to the test case indicates that before running the test, testing data needs to be loaded into the database from the specified Excel file.

First we need to define the custom annotation, which is shown in Listing 19-8.

Listing 19-8. *The Custom Annotation (@DataSets)*

```
package com.apress.prospring3.ch19.test.annotation;

import java.lang.annotation.ElementType;
import java.lang.annotation.Retention;
import java.lang.annotation.RetentionPolicy;
import java.lang.annotation.Target;

@Retention(RetentionPolicy.RUNTIME)
@Target(ElementType.METHOD)
public @interface DataSets {

    String setUpDataSet() default "";

}
```

In Listing 19-8, the custom annotation @DataSets is a method-level annotation. In addition, the custom test listener class will be developed by implementing the TestExecutionListener interface, which is shown in Listing 19-9.

Listing 19-9. *The Custom Test Execution Listener*

```
package com.apress.prospring3.ch19.test.listener;

import org.dbunit.IDatabaseTester;
import org.dbunit.dataset.IDataSet;
import org.dbunit.util.fileloader.XlsDataFileLoader;
import org.springframework.test.context.TestContext;
import org.springframework.test.context.TestExecutionListener;

import com.apress.prospring3.ch19.test.annotation.DataSets;

public class ServiceTestExecutionListener implements TestExecutionListener {

    private IDatabaseTester databaseTester;

    public void afterTestClass(TestContext arg0) throws Exception {
        // TODO Auto-generated method stub
    }

    public void afterTestMethod(TestContext arg0) throws Exception {
        // Clear up testing data if exists
        if (databaseTester != null) {
            databaseTester.onTearDown();
        }
    }

    public void beforeTestClass(TestContext arg0) throws Exception {
        // TODO Auto-generated method stub
    }

    public void beforeTestMethod(TestContext testCtx) throws Exception {
```

```
        // Check for existence of DataSets annotation for the method under testing
        DataSets dataSetAnnotation =
            testCtx.getTestMethod().getAnnotation(DataSets.class);

        if ( dataSetAnnotation == null ) {
            return;
        }

        String dataSetName = dataSetAnnotation.setUpDataSet();

        // Populate data set if data set name exists
        if ( ! dataSetName.equals("") ) {
            databaseTester = (IDatabaseTester)
                testCtx.getApplicationContext().getBean("databaseTester");
            XlsDataFileLoader xlsDataFileLoader = (XlsDataFileLoader)
                testCtx.getApplicationContext().getBean("xlsDataFileLoader");
            IDataSet dataSet = xlsDataFileLoader.load(dataSetName);

            databaseTester.setDataSet(dataSet);
            databaseTester.onSetup();
        }
    }

    public void prepareTestInstance(TestContext arg0) throws Exception {
        // TODO Auto-generated method stub
    }
}
```

In Listing 19-9, after implementing the TestExecutionListener interface, a number of methods need to be implemented. However, in our case, we are interested only in the methods beforeTestMethod() and afterTestMethod(), in which the population and cleanup of the testing data before and after the execution of each test method will be performed. Note that within each method, Spring will pass in an instance of the TestContext class so the method can access the underlying testing ApplicationContext bootstrapped by the Spring Framework.

The method beforeTestMethod() is of particular interest. First, it will check for the existence of the @DataSets annotation for the test method. If the annotation exists, the test data will be loaded from the specified Excel file. In this case, the IDatabaseTester interface (with the implementation class org.dbunit.DataSourceDatabaseTester, which we will discuss later) was obtained from the TestContext. The IDatabaseTester interface is provided by DBUnit and supports database operations based on a given database connection or data source.

Second, an instance of the XlsDataFileLoader class was obtained from the TestContext. The XlsDataFileLoader class is DBUnit's support of loading data from the Excel file. It uses the Apache POI library behind the scenes for reading file in Microsoft Office format. Then, the XlsDataFileLoader.load() method is called to load the data from file, which returns an instance of the IDataSet interface, representing the set of data loaded.

Finally, the IDatabaseTester.setDataSet() is called to set the testing data, and the IDatabaseTester.onSetup() method is called to trigger the population of data.

In the afterTestMethod() method, the IDatabaseTester.onTearDown() method is called to clean up the data.

Implementing the Configuration Class

Let's proceed to implement the configuration class for the testing environment. Listing 19-10 shows the code.

Listing 19-10. The ServiceTestConfig Class

```java
package com.apress.prospring3.ch19.test.config;

import javax.sql.DataSource;

import org.dbunit.DataSourceDatabaseTester;
import org.dbunit.util.fileloader.XlsDataFileLoader;
import org.springframework.context.annotation.Bean;
import org.springframework.context.annotation.ComponentScan;
import org.springframework.context.annotation.Configuration;
import org.springframework.context.annotation.ImportResource;
import org.springframework.context.annotation.Profile;
import org.springframework.jdbc.datasource.embedded.EmbeddedDatabaseBuilder;
import org.springframework.jdbc.datasource.embedded.EmbeddedDatabaseType;

@Configuration
@ImportResource("classpath:datasource-tx-jpa.xml")
@ComponentScan(basePackages={"com.apress.prospring3.ch19.service.jpa"})
@Profile("test")
public class ServiceTestConfig {

    @Bean
    public DataSource dataSource() {
        return new EmbeddedDatabaseBuilder().setType(EmbeddedDatabaseType.H2)
            .addScript("classpath:schema.sql").build();
    }

    @Bean(name="databaseTester")
        public DataSourceDatabaseTester dataSourceDatabaseTester() {
        DataSourceDatabaseTester databaseTester =
            new DataSourceDatabaseTester(dataSource());
        return databaseTester;
    }

    @Bean(name="xlsDataFileLoader")
    public XlsDataFileLoader xlsDataFileLoader() {
        return new XlsDataFileLoader();
    }
}
```

In Listing 19-10, the ServiceTestConfig class defines the ApplicationContext for service layer testing. First, the XML configuration file datasource-tx-jpa.xml is imported, which defines the transaction and JPA configuration that is reusable for testing. Then the @ComponentScan annotation is applied to instruct Spring to scan the service layer beans that we want to test. The @Profile annotation specifies that the beans defined in this class belong to the test profile.

Second, within the class, another dataSource bean was declared that executes only the schema.sql script to the H2 database without any data. The databaseTester and xlsDataFileLoader beans were used by the custom test execution listener for loading test data from the Excel file. Note that the dataSourceDatabaseTester bean was constructed using the dataSource bean defined for the testing environment.

Implementing the Base Test Class

Listing 19-11 shows the abstract base class for service layer testing.

Listing 19-11. The AbstractServiceImplTest Class

```
package com.apress.prospring3.ch19.service.jpa;

import javax.persistence.EntityManager;
import javax.persistence.PersistenceContext;

import org.junit.runner.RunWith;
import org.springframework.test.context.ActiveProfiles;
import org.springframework.test.context.ContextConfiguration;
import org.springframework.test.context.TestExecutionListeners;
import org.springframework.test.context.junit4.AbstractTransactionalJUnit4SpringContextTests;
import org.springframework.test.context.junit4.SpringJUnit4ClassRunner;

import com.apress.prospring3.ch19.test.config.ServiceTestConfig;
import com.apress.prospring3.ch19.test.listener.ServiceTestExecutionListener;

@RunWith(SpringJUnit4ClassRunner.class)
@ContextConfiguration(classes = {ServiceTestConfig.class})
@TestExecutionListeners({ServiceTestExecutionListener.class})
@ActiveProfiles("test")
public abstract class AbstractServiceImplTest extends
AbstractTransactionalJUnit4SpringContextTests {

    @PersistenceContext
    protected EntityManager em;
}
```

In Listing 19-11, the @RunWith annotation is the same as testing the controller class. The @ContextConfiguration specifies that the ApplicationContext configuration should be loaded from the ServiceTestConfig class. The @TestExecutionListeners annotation indicates that the ServiceTestExecutionListener class should be used for intercepting the test case execution life cycle. The @ActiveProfiles annotation specifies the profile to use. So, in this case, the dataSource bean defined in the ServiceTestConfig class will be loaded, instead of the one defined in the datasource-tx-jpa.xml file, since it belongs to the dev profile.

In addition, the class extends Spring's AbstractTransactionalJUnit4SpringContextTests class, which is Spring's support for JUnit, with Spring's DI and transaction management mechanism in place. Note that in Spring's testing environment, Spring will roll back the transaction upon execution of each test method so that all database update operations will be rolled back. To control the rollback behavior, you can use the @Rollback annotation at the method level.

Finally, within the abstract base class, the EntityManager is autowired, which can then be used within test cases.

Unit Testing Service Layer

Having the configuration and infrastructure classes in place, we can implement the unit test for the service layer.

Let's begin with unit testing the finder methods, including the ContactService.findAll() and ContactService.findByFirstNameAndLastName() methods. First we need to prepare the testing data in Excel format. A common practice is to put the file into the same folder as the test case class, with the same name. So, in this case, the file name is /src/test/java/com/apress/prospring3/ch19/service/jpa/ContactServiceImplTest.xls. Figure 19-6 shows the file content.

As shown in Figure 19-6, the testing data was prepared in a worksheet. The worksheet's name is the table's name, while the first row is the column name within the table. You can see that we specified the ID column, but no value was provided. This is because the ID will be populated by the database. We had only one contact record in the file, so the findAll() method should return one contact.

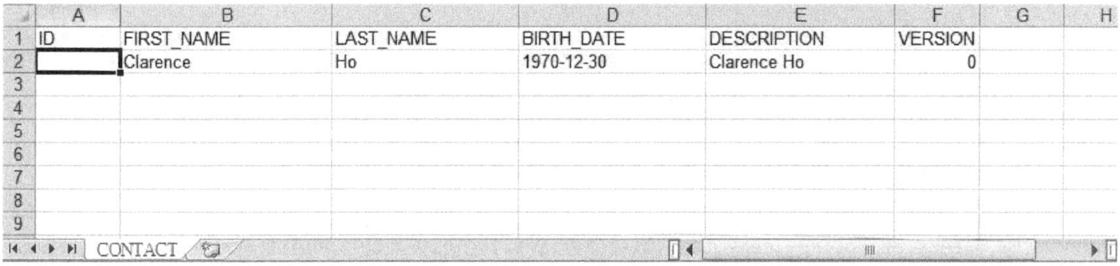

Figure 19-6. Test data in Excel format

Listing 19-12 shows the test class with test cases for the two finder methods.

Listing 19-12. Testing the Finder Methods

```
package com.apress.prospring3.ch19.service.jpa;

import static org.junit.Assert.assertEquals;
import static org.junit.Assert.assertNotNull;
import static org.junit.Assert.assertNull;

import java.util.List;

import org.junit.Test;
import org.springframework.beans.factory.annotation.Autowired;

import com.apress.prospring3.ch19.domain.Contact;
import com.apress.prospring3.ch19.service.ContactService;
import com.apress.prospring3.ch19.test.annotation.DataSets;

public class ContactServiceImplTest extends AbstractServiceImplTest {

    @Autowired
    ContactService customerService;

    @DataSets(
```

```
setUpDataSet="/com/apress/prospring3/ch19/service/jpa/ContactServiceImplTest.xls")
    @Test
    public void testFindAll() throws Exception {

        List<Contact> result = customerService.findAll();

        assertNotNull(result);
        assertEquals(1, result.size());
    }

    @DataSets(
setUpDataSet="/com/apress/prospring3/ch19/service/jpa/ContactServiceImplTest.xls")
    @Test
    public void testFindByFirstNameAndLastName_1() throws Exception {

        Contact result = customerService.findByFirstNameAndLastName("Clarence", "Ho");

        assertNotNull(result);
    }

    @DataSets(
setUpDataSet="/com/apress/prospring3/ch19/service/jpa/ContactServiceImplTest.xls")
    @Test
    public void testFindByFirstNameAndLastName_2() throws Exception {

        Contact result = customerService.findByFirstNameAndLastName("Peter", "Chan");

        assertNull(result);
    }
}
```

In Listing 19-12, the test case extends the base test class AbstractServiceImplTest, which contains all the required configuration for the test. There is one test case for the findAll() method and two test cases for the testFindByFirstNameAndLastName() method (one retrieves a result and one doesn't). All the finder methods are applied with the @DataSets annotation with the contact test data file in Excel. In addition, the ContactService is autowired into the test case from the ApplicationContext. The rest of the code should be self-explanatory. Various assert statements are applied in each test case to make sure that the result is as expected.

To run the test class, right-click it and choose Run As ➤ JUnit Test. Figure 19-7 shows STS.

Figure 19-7. JUnit test view for service layer testing

Next, let's test the save operation. In our case, we would like to test two scenarios. One is the normal situation in which a valid contact is saved successfully, and the other is a contact have an error that should cause the correct exception being thrown. Listing 19-13 shows the code snippet for the two test cases.

Listing 19-13. Testing the Save Operation

```java
package com.apress.prospring3.ch19.service.jpa;

import javax.validation.ConstraintViolationException;

// Other import statements omitted

public class ContactServiceImplTest extends AbstractServiceImplTest {

    // Other code omitted

    @Test
    public void testAddContact() throws Exception {

        // Clear all existing data in Contact table
        deleteFromTables("CONTACT");

        Contact contact = new Contact();
        contact.setFirstName("Rod");
        contact.setLastName("Johnson");

        contact = customerService.save(contact);
        em.flush();

        List<Contact> contacts = customerService.findAll();
        assertEquals(1, contacts.size());

    }

    @Test(expected=ConstraintViolationException.class)
    public void testAddContactWithJSR303Error() throws Exception {

        // Clear all existing data in Contact table
        deleteFromTables("CONTACT");

        Contact contact = new Contact();

        contact = customerService.save(contact);
        em.flush();

        List<Contact> contacts = customerService.findAll();
        assertEquals(0, contacts.size());

    }
}
```

In Listing 19-13, take a look at the testAddContact() method. Within the method, to ensure that no data exists in the CONTACT table, we call the convenient method deleteFromTables() provided by the

AbstractTransactionalJUnit4SpringContextTests class to clean up the table. Note that after calling the save operation, we need to explicitly call the EntityManager.flush() method to force Hibernate to flush the persistence context to the database so that the findAll() method can retrieve the information from the database correctly.

In the second test method, the testAddContactWithJSR303Error() method, we test the save operation of a contact with a validation error. Note that in the @Test annotation, an expected attribute is passed, which specifies that this test case is expected to throw an exception with the specified type, which in this case is the ConstraintViolationException class.

Run the test class again and verify the result in the JUnit view.

Note that we covered only the most commonly used classes within Spring's testing framework. Spring's testing framework provides a lot of support classes and annotations that allow us to apply fine control during the execution of the test case life cycle. For example, the @BeforeTransaction and @AfterTransaction annotations allow certain logic to be executed before Spring initiates a transaction or after a transaction is completed for the test case. For a more detailed description of the various aspects of Spring's testing framework, kindly refer to Spring's reference documentation.

Implementing a Frontend Unit Test

Another testing area of particular interest is testing the frontend behavior as a whole, upon the deployment of the web application to a web container like Apache Tomcat.

The main reason is that even though we test every layer within the application, we still need to make sure that the views behave correctly with different actions from users. Automating frontend testing is very important in saving time for developers and users when repeating the actions on the frontend for a test case.

However, developing a test case for a frontend is a challenging task, especially for those web applications with a lot of interactive, rich, and Ajax-based components.

In the following sections, we will discuss implementing frontend unit testing with Selenium (http://seleniumhq.org), a popular open source framework for automated frontend testing.

Adding Required Dependencies

To use Selenium, we need to add the dependency into our project, as shown in Table 19-4.

Table 19-4. Maven Dependencies for Selenium

Group ID	Artifact ID	Version	Description
org.seleniumhq.selenium	selenium-java	2.15.0	Selenium library for Java

Introducing Selenium

Selenium is a powerful and comprehensive tool and framework target for automating web-based frontend testing. The main feature is that by using Selenium, we can "drive" the browsers, simulating user interactions with the application, and perform verification of the view status.

Selenium supports common browsers including Firefox, IE, and Chrome. In terms of languages, Java, C#, PHP, Perl, Ruby, and Python are supported. Selenium is also designed with Ajax and rich Internet applications (RIAs) in mind, making automated testing of modern web applications possible.

In case your application has a lot of frontend user interfaces and needs to run a large number of frontend tests, the selenium-server module provides built-in grid functionality that supports the execution of frontend tests among a group of computers.

The Selenium IDE is a Firefox plug-in that can help "record" the user interactions with the web application. It also supports replay and exports the scripts into various formats that can help simplify the development of test cases.

Starting from version 2.0, Selenium integrates the WebDriver API, which addresses a number of limitations and provides an alternative, and simpler, programming interface. The result is a comprehensive object-oriented API that provides additional support for a larger number of browsers along with improved support for modern advanced web application testing problems.

In this sample, we will use Selenium with its WebDriver API support to implement the frontend test cases for the contact application.

Implementing a Test Case for a Frontend UI

For the frontend testing, we would like to develop the test case for the add contact interface. Both a normal scenario (i.e., a user enters information correctly and the contact is saved successfully) and an exceptional case (i.e., a validation error occurs, and the messages are displayed) will be implemented.

Implementing the simple test case in Selenium is pretty easy. Listing 19-14 shows the code of the test class.

Listing 19-14. Frontend Unit Testing with Selenium

```
package com.apress.prospring3.ch19.test.ui;

import org.junit.After;
import org.junit.Before;
import org.junit.Test;
import org.openqa.selenium.WebDriver;
import org.openqa.selenium.WebDriverBackedSelenium;
import org.openqa.selenium.firefox.FirefoxDriver;

import com.thoughtworks.selenium.SeleneseTestBase;

public class UIAddContactTest extends SeleneseTestBase {

    private static final String USERNAME = "user";
    private static final String PASSWORD = "user";

    @Before
    public void setUp() throws Exception {
        WebDriver driver = new FirefoxDriver();
        String baseUrl = "http://localhost:8080/";
        selenium = new WebDriverBackedSelenium(driver, baseUrl);
    }

    @Test
    public void testAddContact() {

        // Login
        loginAs(USERNAME, PASSWORD);
```

```
        // Enter add contact form
        selenium.open("/ch19/contacts?form");
        selenium.waitForPageToLoad("30000");

        // Fill in contact information
        selenium.type("firstName", "Andy");
        selenium.type("lastName", "Lau");
        selenium.click("name=submit");

        // Verification
        verifyTrue(selenium.isTextPresent("Andy"));
        verifyTrue(selenium.isTextPresent("Lau"));

        // Logout
        logout();
    }

    @Test
    public void testAddContactWithEmptyForm() {

        // Login
        loginAs(USERNAME, PASSWORD);

        // Enter add contact form
        selenium.open("/ch19/contacts?form");
        selenium.waitForPageToLoad("30000");

        // Submit form
        selenium.click("name=submit");

        // Verification
        verifyTrue(selenium.isTextPresent("Failed saving contact"));

        // Logout
        logout();
    }

    @After
    public void tearDown() throws Exception {
        selenium.stop();
    }

    private void loginAs(String userName, String password) {
        selenium.open("/ch19/contacts");
        selenium.type("j_username", userName);
        selenium.type("j_password", password);
        selenium.click("name=login");
        selenium.waitForPageToLoad("30000");
    }

    private void logout() {
        selenium.click("link=Logout");
    }
}
```

In Listing 19-14, the class extends the SeleneseTestBase class, which provides many handy methods to ease the implementation of a test case. In the setup() method, an instance of the WebDriver interface is prepared, with the FirefoxDriver class, which will invoke the Firefox browser installed on the testing machine for test case execution. Drivers also exist for Chrome, IE, HtmlUnit, and so on. If your web application needs cross-browser support, you can run the same test again with different web drivers to ensure the application behaves consistently across different browsers. Then, an instance of the WebDriverBackedSelenium class is constructed, which is Selenium's support for using WebDriver API to drive the browser interaction.

Next, take a look at the loginAs() and logout() methods, which will be reused by multiple test cases for login and logout actions. For example, in the loginAs() method, it will open the home page (i.e., http://localhost:8080/ch19/contacts), populate the form fields j_username and j_password, and then click the Login button. In the form, the elements should have the correct names assigned. For example, take a look at the login form in the view file menu.jspx in Listing 19-15.

Listing 19-15. *The Login Form*

```
<form name="loginForm" action="${loginUrl}" method="post">
    <table>
        <caption align="left">Login:</caption>
        <tr>
            <td>User Name:</td>
            <td><input type="text" name="j_username"/></td>
        </tr>
        <tr>
            <td>Password:</td>
            <td><input type="password" name="j_password"/></td>
        </tr>
        <tr>
            <td colspan="2" align="center"><input name="login" type="submit" value="Login"/>↵
</td>
        </tr>
    </table>
</form>
```

The form fields with names assigned are highlighted in bold. So, when the line selenium.type("j_username", userName) is executed, the form field with the name j_username will be populated with the supplied user name, and so on.

The testAddContact() method is the test case for a normal add contact operation. After login, the new contact URL is called (using the open() method), and then the contact information is entered, and the Save button is clicked. Afterward, the verifyTrue() method is called to verify that the add operation completed successfully with the contact information present on the page.

The testAddContactWithEmptyForm() simulates the case that a user clicks the Save button without entering any contact information. As a result, the save operation should fail, and the verifyTrue() method will be called to verify that the error message is displayed in the page.

To run the test, just right-click the test class and run it as a JUnit test. Make sure that the web application is deployed and the tc Server is up and running. Then you will see that the test cases will invoke a copy of Firefox automatically, and the login, contact information input, and verification logic will be executed accordingly.

From this simple example, you can see how Selenium can help automate the user interaction with the web application frontend with cross-browser compatibility. For more details, please refer to Selenium's online documentation (http://seleniumhq.org/docs).

Verifying Test Case Code Coverage

The test cases that we developed should cover most of the business logic and user interfaces that were developed, which is referred to as *code coverage*. In an ideal case, the code coverage percentage should be 100 percent, which means that each line of code written is tested thoroughly.

In Eclipse (which STS is running on), there are a lot of plug-ins that can help you in visualizing the code coverage of the test cases written. In this section, we will present you with a tool called CodePro Analytix (http://code.google.com/intl/en/javadevtools/codepro/doc/index.html).

CodePro Analytix used to be a commercial tool. Google acquired the parent company, however, and now the tool is distributed for free. CodePro Analytix provides a lot of code quality management features, such as code analysis, JUnit test generation, code coverage, and so on. To install CodePro Analytix in STS, choose Help ➤ Install New Software in STS, and then click the Add button. Enter the name CodePro Analytix and the updated site URL http://dl.google.com/eclipse/inst/codepro/latest/3.7. The components will then displayed for your selection, as shown in Figure 19-8.

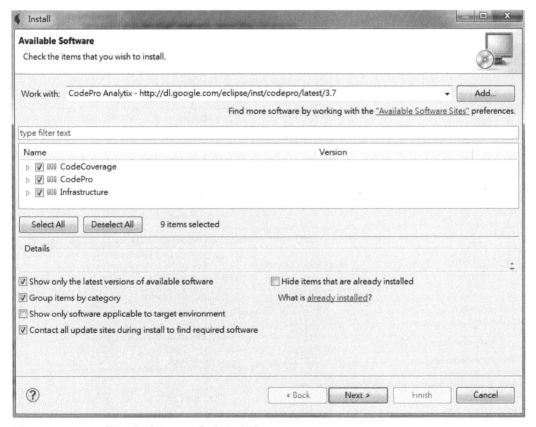

Figure 19-8. Installing CodePro Analytix in STS

Just choose all the components (although in this section, we use only the Code Coverage tool), and click the Next button to install the plug-in.

After the installation is completed and STS has restarted, we can start to measure the code coverage. First, we need to enable the instrument for code coverage testing. Right-click the project, select CodePro Tools, and then select Instrument for Code Coverage, as shown in Figure 19-9.

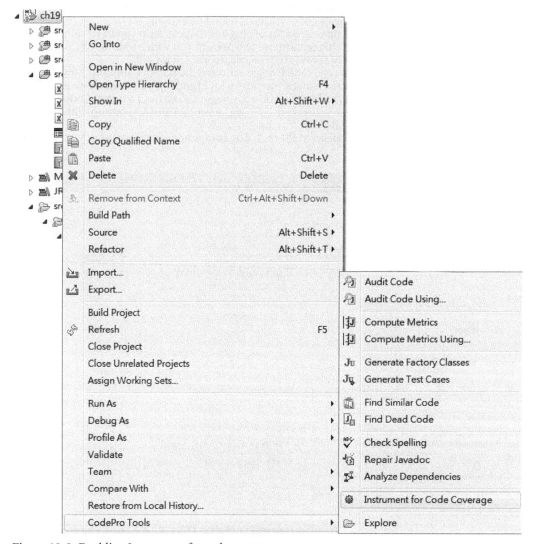

Figure 19-9. Enabling Instrument for code coverage

Then, run the unit test, and upon completion, CodePro tool will automatically bring up the Code Coverage view with the code coverage result presented. Figure 19-10 shows STS after the execution of the ContactServiceImplTest class.

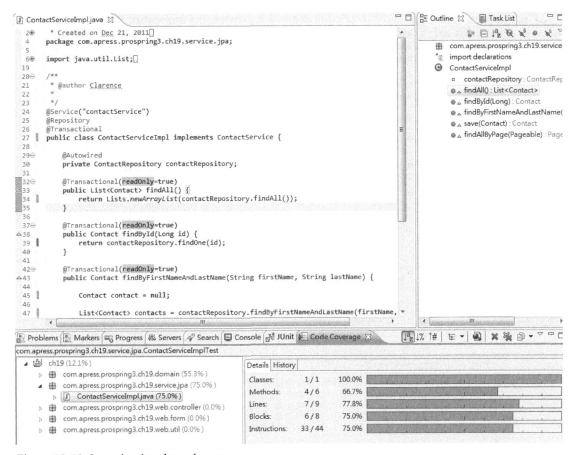

Figure 19-10. Investigating the code coverage

In the lower part, the Code Coverage view presents you with the code coverage of all the classes. Since the test class was testing the ContactServiceImpl class, we can click the class and verify the detailed code coverage information on the right side. In Figure 19-10 you can see that the code coverage for the class is 75 percent (shown after the class on the left side). Double-click the class, which will open it in the editor area. In the editor view, the tested code will have a green indicator on the left side, while red indicates that the code was not called during testing. Consequently, you can visualize how much code your test case has covered and see which methods or lines of code were not tested. It's a handy tool to help you increase your code coverage.

Summary

In this chapter, we covered how to develop various kinds of unit testing in Spring-based applications with the help of commonly used frameworks, libraries, and tools including JUnit, DBUnit, Mockito, Selenium, and so on.

First, we presented a high-level description of an enterprise testing framework, which shows what tests should be executed in each phase of the application development life cycle. Second, we developed three types of test, including the logic unit test, integration unit test, and frontend unit test, respectively.

Finally, we discussed how to use the CodePro Analytix tool to measure the code coverage of the test classes.

Testing an enterprise application is a huge topic, and if you want to have a more detailed understanding of the JUnit library, we recommend the book *JUnit in Action*, Second Edition (Manning, 2010).

CHAPTER 20

Spring Projects: Batch, Integration, and Roo

In previous chapters, we covered how the Spring Framework provides a solid framework with DI and AOP to help you develop enterprise Java applications. We also covered a few other Spring projects (for example, Spring Data JPA, Spring Security, Spring Web Flow, and so on) that can help further enhance the capability of Spring-based applications in specific areas.

As a matter of fact, the massive adoption of the Spring Framework in both open source and enterprise environments has created a huge development ecosystem, which has created a need for extensions to the Spring Framework. Consequently, on top of the Spring Framework, a lot of other Spring projects targeting more specific application aspects have been developed. For example, the Spring Social project supports the integration of Spring-based applications with popular social networks like Facebook and Twitter, while the Spring Mobile project aims to simplify the development of mobile web applications. You can find a full list of projects maintained by the SpringSource team at www.springsource.org/projects.

All Spring projects were designed with the same rationale, that is, to promote best practices in application development (in other words, programming to interfaces, DI, AOP, and so on) and to integrate seamlessly with the Spring Framework's ApplicationContext environment.

In this chapter, we will present a high-level discussion of a few popular Spring projects that can help you develop Spring-based applications. Specifically, this chapter will cover the following topics:

- *Spring Batch*: The Spring Batch project (http://static.springsource.org/spring-batch) provides a comprehensive framework and standard skeleton for developing batch jobs within Spring-powered applications. We will provide a high-level overview of the project, as well as demonstrate its usage by developing a simple contact-importing job.

- *Spring Integration*: The Spring Integration project (www.springsource.org/spring-integration) integrates Spring-based applications with other applications and data sources. It provides a lightweight messaging-based platform for implementing many typical enterprise integration patterns (EIPs). In this chapter, we will briefly describe this project and demonstrate how the Spring Integration and Spring Batch projects can join together to execute batch jobs with a simple EIP.

- *Spring Roo:* The Spring Roo project (www.springsource.org/spring-roo) provides a comprehensive tool that can help you build applications with simple commands. It's extremely useful for building application prototypes, and the underlying Java code generated by Spring Roo is fully customizable. In this chapter, we will give you a taste of what Spring Roo is by using it to generate a simple contact application.

Project for Chapter Samples

In this chapter, we will use the backend of the contact web application we implemented in Chapter 18 as the sample and build a batch job for importing contact information in XML format.

Import the Sample Backend in STS

The first part of this chapter focuses on integration and batch job development, so we have prepared a project for the sample backend that you can simply import and then proceed to implement the batch job.

From the sample code, we extract the file ch20-batch-backend.zip into your STS workspace. Then, we can import the project in STS.

To import the project, in STS, choose the menu option File ➤ Import, and in the Select dialog, choose Existing Projects into Workspace under the General category, as shown in Figure 20-1.

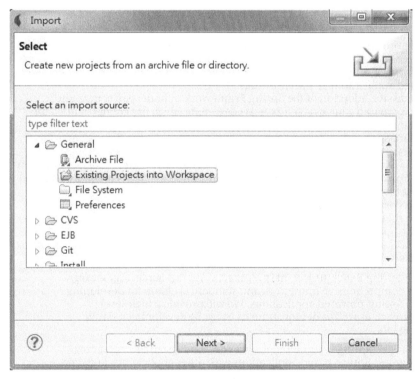

Figure 20-1. Importing an existing project in STS

Next, in the Import Projects dialog, choose the project extracted from the sample source code, and then click Finish, as shown in Figure 20-2.

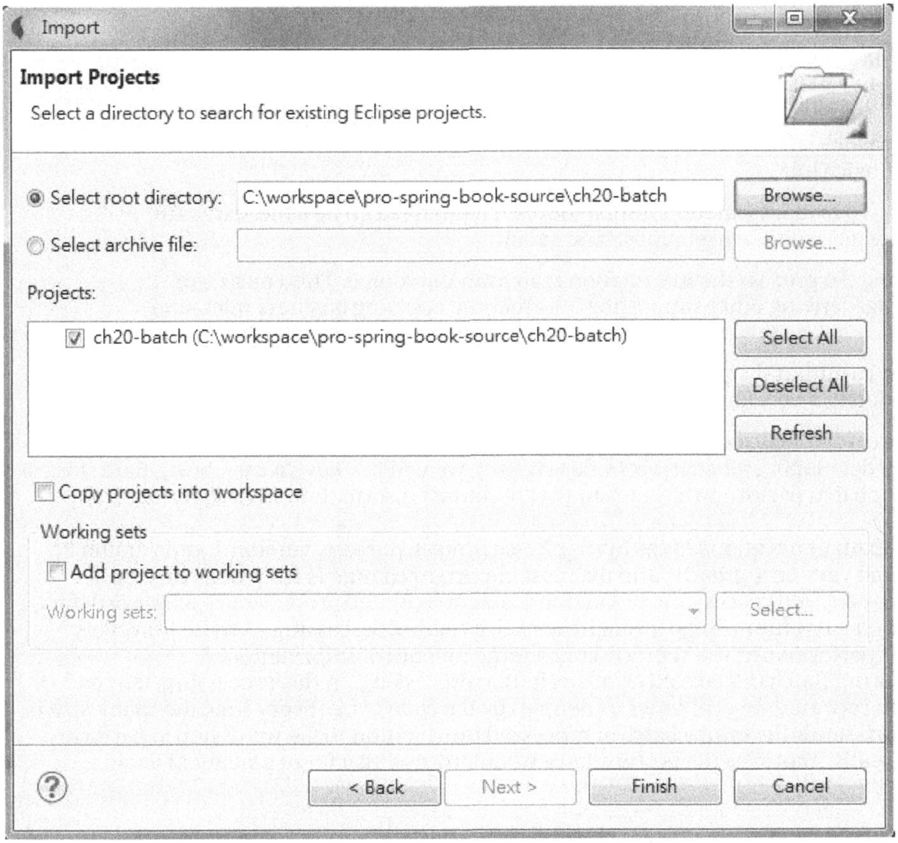

Figure 20-2. Importing the sample project

Introducing Spring Batch

Started in 2007, the Spring Batch project has become more and more popular for developing batch jobs in Spring applications. It's a collaborative effort between SpringSource and Accenture, and its initial objective was to develop a standard template and framework for implementing and executing various kinds of batch jobs in an enterprise environment. In version 2, Spring Batch became much more mature as changes were introduced to greatly improve the performance and support of many different kinds of policies (for example, skipping error records, retry, restart, parallel execution, and so on) in batch job execution. In the following sections, we will look at the fundamental concepts of the Spring Batch project, including the main flow and processing of a batch job, the infrastructure and metadata, and the main execution policies all provided by Spring Batch out of the box.

Batch Job Flow and Process

Every enterprise application requires some sort of batch processing that performs business logic on a large set of information. The following are some examples of batch jobs:

- Importing/exporting information from/to external systems

- End-of-day processing for transaction processing systems

- Generating external document (for example, monthly customer statements)

Although every batch job executes different logic, the high-level flow is similar. The following is the flow of a typical batch job:

1. *Reading*: To read information from a source. The source can be a file, database, JMS message, web service request, and so on.

2. *Processing*: To process the information read from the source. This consists of validating, deriving other supporting information, applying business rules, and so on.

3. *Writing*: To output the processed information into the destination. The destination can be a file, database, JMS message, web service response, and so on.

Spring Batch provides the execution infrastructure and many out-of-the-box classes that greatly simplify the work of developing a batch job. In this chapter, we will see how to use Spring Batch to implement a batch job that performs the batch import of contact information in XML format from a file.

There are two main generations of the Spring Batch project, namely, version 1 and version 2. Version 2 differs from version 1 greatly, and the most important change is from item-oriented processing to chunk-oriented processing. In version 1's item-oriented processing, each record (for example, a line within a flat file) will go through the entire read -> processing -> write flow. This proved to have poor performance when processing a large amount of information.

In version 2, Spring Batch introduced chunk-oriented processing. In this processing, the read -> processing steps are repeated several times as defined by the chunk size. Every time the chunk size is reached, Spring Batch sends the entire batch of processed information to the write step to perform a bulk update. This greatly improves the performance when processing a large amount of data.

Spring Batch Infrastructure Components

Table 20-1 lists the main runtime infrastructure components of Spring Batch. Note that all components are interfaces.

Table 20-1. Spring Batch Infrastructure Components

Component	Description
JobRepository	Provides data access operations (CRUD) to the underlying Spring Batch metadata.
JobLauncher	For launching a job. Responsible for starting a job execution based on a given job and parameters.
JobOperator (new in version 2)	Provides batch job operations (for example, stop a running job, restart a failed or stopped job).
JobExplorer (new in version 2)	Retrieves the job execution status information from metadata.

Figure 20-3 shows the high-level overview of the Spring Batch infrastructure components extracted from Spring Batch's reference documentation.

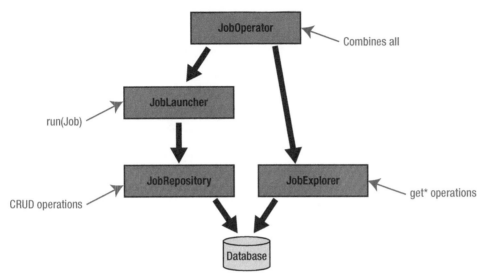

Figure 20-3. *Spring Batch infrastructure components*

Spring Batch Metadata

Spring Batch maintains all job execution information in its own metadata. Most likely, the metadata will be maintained in the same database as the enterprise application, although you can choose to have in-memory metadata (however, by using this, you lose the major benefits of Spring Batch, such as restarting a failed job, and so on). Spring Batch provides DDL scripts for creating the metadata structure in most commonly used RDBMSs. Figure 20-4 shows the data model of Spring Batch in an Oracle 11g database.

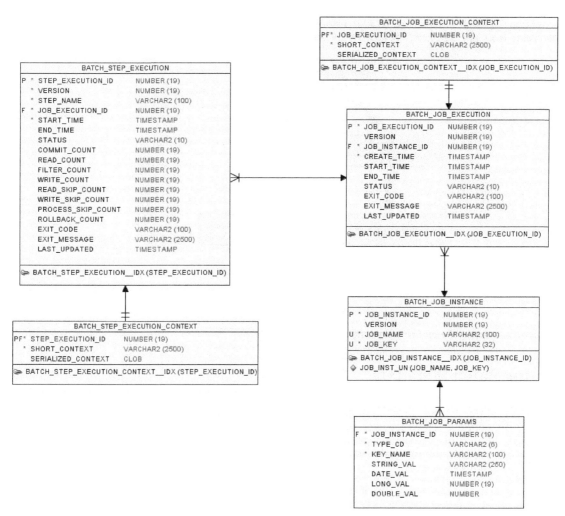

Figure 20-4. *Spring Batch metadata for Oracle 11g*

Table 20-2 describes the category and purpose of each table within Spring Batch's metadata.

Table 20-2. Spring Batch Metadata

Category	Table	Description
Job Instance	BATCH_JOB_INSTANCE	Every time the job launcher starts a job, a new batch job instance will be created, and the execution information (for example, job name, parameters, and so on) will be stored in the BATCH_JOB_INSTANCE table. In the BATCH_JOB_INSTANCE table, there is a column called JOB_KEY, which is generated based on the job parameters (for example, file name, date, and so on) for that specific job instance. One important concept is that there is a unique constraint in the BATCH_JOB_INSTANCE table, composed of the JOB_NAME and JOB_KEY columns. This means that the job together with the job parameters should be unique. For the contact import job, the name of the job is importContactJob, and the job parameter is the file name. In this case, for every import contact job, the file name should be unique. If you try to launch the job with the same file name, Spring Batch will complain that a job instance already exists (because the job parameter was repeated).
	BATCH_JOB_PARAMS	The parameters for the job instance will be stored into the BATCH_JOB_PARAMS table.
Job Execution	BATCH_JOB_EXECUTION	The BATCH_JOB_EXECUTION table stores the execution information of each job instance. A batch job instance can have more than one execution (for example, the first execution was failed, and then was restarted with success in the second execution).
	BATCH_JOB_EXECUTION_CONTEXT	Stores the batch job execution metadata.
Step Execution	BATCH_STEP_EXECUTION	Stores the execution information for each step (in other words, read, process, write, and custom tasks) within each job execution.
	BATCH_STEP_EXECUTION_CONTEXT	Stores the step execution meta data.

Job Execution Policies

Spring Batch supports a lot of different error handling and execution strategies that can fulfill almost any enterprise-level batch job requirements. Table 20-3 lists some of the commonly used policies.

Table 20-3. Job Execution Policies

Policy	Description
Skip failed records	It's possible to instruct Spring Batch to "skip" those problematic records (for example, one record doesn't pass validation), instead of rejecting the entire chunk of records or file.
Retry on error	Spring Batch supports retry policy when error occurs. For example, an item-processing step can retry a number of times (it may need to invoke some kind of external web service call to validate the data, but under heavy loading, the external service may not respond within a certain time occasionally) before it fails.
Multi-thread Step Processing	A step can be configured to run in a multithreaded environment to improve performance.
Parallel processing	Steps within a job can configure for parallel execution to further boost the performance.
Step Partitioning	Spring Batch provides an SPI that support the partitioning of a step. In this case, the step is called the *master*, while the partitioned steps are called the *slaves*. The slave steps can be executed either by local threads or remotely for better performance.
Remote chunking	In Spring Batch, it's possible to delegate chunk processing to multiple machines. For example, the master machine can perform the read process, while multiple slave machines perform chunk-based writing of data (via the ChunkProvider<T> interface). This provides a very flexible horizontal scaling solution for batch job execution.

Implementing a Batch Job

Let's see Spring Batch in action by implementing a simple batch job. In the contact application we developed in Chapter 18, each contact contains basic information including the first name, last name, and date of birth. In addition, each contact associates with zero or more hobbies. The backend for basic CRUD operations is already available after importing the sample project mentioned earlier in this chapter.

In this section, we will implement a batch job for importing contact information from an XML file into the database. Castor (http://castor.codehaus.org) will be used as the XML marshaller and unmarshaller.

In the following sections, we will go through the processing of implementing the batch job. Steps including the required dependencies, batch job configuration, file format, and so on, will be covered.

Adding Required Dependencies

First we need to add the dependencies for Spring Batch and Castor into the project, as shown in Table 20-4.

Table 20-4. Maven Dependencies for Spring Batch and Castor

Group ID	Artifact ID	Version	Description
org.springframework.batch	spring-batch-core	2.1.8.RELEASE	Spring Batch core library. Classes that support batch job configuration, job launchers, and so on, are packaged in this module.
org.springframework.batch	spring-batch-infrastructure	2.1.8.RELEASE	Spring Batch infrastructure library. For example, classes that support various readers and writers (for example, file, database, and so on) are packaged in this module.
org.springframework	spring-oxm	3.1.0.RELEASE	Spring OXM module for supporting transformation between POJOs and XML format.
org.codehaus.castor	castor-xml	1.3.2	Castor XML library.

Add the dependencies in Table 20-4 into the project in STS.

Spring Batch Infrastructure Configuration

To use Spring Batch, a few setup and configuration tasks are required. First, the schema for creating the metadata tables for storing Spring Batch operational data should be included during the database initialization process.

In the contact application, we are using the embedded H2 database, which is defined in the file /src/main/resources/datasource-tx-jpa.xml. Listing 20-1 shows the code snippet for the change required for the file.

Listing 20-1. Adding the Spring Batch Schema Script

```xml
<?xml version="1.0" encoding="UTF-8"?>
<beans xmlns="http://www.springframework.org/schema/beans"

    <!-- Other code omitted -->

    <jdbc:embedded-database id="dataSource" type="H2">
        <jdbc:script location="classpath:schema.sql"/>
        <jdbc:script location="classpath:/org/springframework/batch/core/schema-h2.sql"/>
        <jdbc:script location="classpath:test-data.sql"/>
    </jdbc:embedded-database>

    <!-- Other code omitted -->

</beans>
```

In Listing 20-1, the change made is highlighted in bold. In Spring Batch, the DDL for creating the metadata structure is stored in the spring-batch-core module, under the package org.springframework.batch.core. Because we are using H2, we use the schema-h2.sql file. There are also existing scripts for most commonly used databases.

Second, we need to configure Spring Batch infrastructure components. At a minimum, the job repository and job launcher beans are required. Listing 20-2 shows the configuration file (/src/main/resources/batch-context.xml).

Listing 20-2. *Spring Batch Configuration*

```xml
<?xml version="1.0" encoding="UTF-8"?>
<beans xmlns="http://www.springframework.org/schema/beans"
    xmlns:xsi=http://www.w3.org/2001/XMLSchema-instance
    xmlns:context="http://www.springframework.org/schema/context"
    xsi:schemaLocation="http://www.springframework.org/schema/beans
      http://www.springframework.org/schema/beans/spring-beans-3.1.xsd
      http://www.springframework.org/schema/context
      http://www.springframework.org/schema/context/spring-context-3.1.xsd">

    <bean id="jobRepository" class="org.springframework.batch.core.repository↵
.support.JobRepositoryFactoryBean">
        <property name="databaseType" value="h2" />
        <property name="dataSource" ref="dataSource" />
        <property name="transactionManager" ref="transactionManager" />
        <property name="isolationLevelForCreate" value="ISOLATION_DEFAULT"/>
    </bean>

    <bean id="jobLauncher" class="org.springframework.batch.core.launch↵
.support.SimpleJobLauncher">
        <property name="jobRepository" ref="jobRepository" />
    </bean>
</beans>
```

In Listing 20-2, 2 Spring Batch beans are defined. First, the jobRepository bean is defined with the JobRepositoryFactoryBean class, which will create an instance of the org.springframework.batch.core.repository.support.SimpleJobRepository class using Spring Batch's DAO implementations. The SimpleJobRepository class implements the org.springframework.batch.core.repository.JobRepository interface, which stores JobInstances, JobExecutions, and StepExecutions using the injected DAOs.

Second, the jobLauncher bean is defined with the SimpleJobLauncher implementation class, which implements the org.springframework.batch.core.launch.JobLauncher interface. The SimpleJobLauncher uses Spring Core's TaskExecutor interface for job launching. By default, a synchronized task executor (the SyncTaskExecutor class) will be instantiated for job launching. The jobRepository bean will be injected into the jobLauncher bean so that the job execution details can be updated to the underlying Spring Batch metadata storage.

Implementing the Import Contact Job

Now we can proceed to implement the batch job. Let's define the XML file format first. Listing 20-3 shows the sample XML file with a contact's information (the contacts.xml file in the project's root folder).

Listing 20-3. The `contacts.xml` *File*

```xml
<?xml version="1.0" encoding="UTF-8"?>
<contacts>
    <contact>
        <firstName>Kim Fung</firstName>
        <lastName>Ho</lastName>
        <birthDate>1980-07-30</birthDate>
        <hobby>
            <hobbyId>Swimming</hobbyId>
        </hobby>
        <hobby>
            <hobbyId>Movies</hobbyId>
        </hobby>
    </contact>
</contacts>
```

In Listing 20-3, a contact's information is wrapped under the `<contact>` tag. The root tag is the `<contacts>` tag, which can accommodate more contact information for import into the database.

We will use Castor to map the XML to the POJO. Listing 20-4 shows the mapping file (`/src/main/resources/oxm-mapping.xml`).

Listing 20-4. Castor XML Mapping Definition File

```xml
<mapping>

    <class name="com.apress.prospring3.ch20.domain.Contacts">
        <field name="contacts" type="com.apress.prospring3.ch20.domain.Contact"↵
 collection="arraylist">
            <bind-xml name="contact"/>
        </field>
    </class>

    <class name="com.apress.prospring3.ch20.domain.Contact" identity="id">

        <map-to xml="contact" />

        <field name="id" type="long">
            <bind-xml name="id" node="element"/>
        </field>
        <field name="firstName" type="string">
            <bind-xml name="firstName" node="element" />
        </field>
        <field name="lastName" type="string">
            <bind-xml name="lastName" node="element" />
        </field>
        <field name="birthDate" type="string" handler="dateHandler">
            <bind-xml name="birthDate" node="element" />
        </field>
        <field name="version" type="integer">
            <bind-xml name="version" node="element" />
        </field>
```

```xml
            <field name="hobbies" type="com.apress.prospring3.ch20.domain.Hobby" collection="set">
                <bind-xml name="hobby"/>
            </field>

    </class>

    <class name="com.apress.prospring3.ch20.domain.Hobby" identity="hobbyId">

        <map-to xml="hobby" />

        <field name="hobbyId" type="string">
            <bind-xml name="hobbyId" node="element" />
        </field>

    </class>

    <field-handler name="dateHandler" class="com.apress.prospring3.ch20.xml↵
.handler.DateTimeFieldHandler">
        <param name="date-format" value="yyyy-MM-dd"/>
    </field-handler>
</mapping>
```

If you followed the section "Using RESTful-WS in Spring" in Chapter 16, the mapping definition should be familiar to you. The domain objects Contacts, Contact, and Hobby are mapped. In addition, the hobbies property of the Contact class, which is a Set of Hobby object, is also mapped.

Since we use JodaTime's DateTime type for the date of birth property, we need to implement the custom handler, which is shown in Listing 20-5.

Listing 20-5. Castor XML Custom Field Handler Implementation Class

```java
package com.apress.prospring3.ch20.xml.handler;

import java.util.Properties;

import org.exolab.castor.mapping.*;
import org.joda.time.DateTime;
import org.joda.time.format.DateTimeFormat;
import org.joda.time.format.DateTimeFormatter;

public class DateTimeFieldHandler extends GeneralizedFieldHandler {

    private static String dateFormatPattern;

    public void setConfiguration(Properties config) throws ValidityException {
        dateFormatPattern = config.getProperty("date-format");
    }

    public Object convertUponGet(Object value) {
        DateTime dateTime = (DateTime) value;
        return format(dateTime);
    }

    public Object convertUponSet(Object value) {
        String dateTimeString = (String) value;
```

```
        return parse(dateTimeString);
    }

    public Class<DateTime> getFieldType() {
        return DateTime.class;
    }

    protected static String format(final DateTime dateTime) {

        String dateTimeString = "";

        if (dateTime != null) {
            DateTimeFormatter dateTimeFormatter = DateTimeFormat.forPattern(dateFormatPattern);
            dateTimeString = dateTimeFormatter.print(dateTime);
        }

        return dateTimeString;
    }

    protected static DateTime parse(final String dateTimeString) {

        DateTime dateTime = new DateTime();

        if (dateTimeString != null) {
            DateTimeFormatter dateTimeFormatter = DateTimeFormat.forPattern(dateFormatPattern);
            dateTime = dateTimeFormatter.parseDateTime(dateTimeString);
        }

        return dateTime;

    }

}
```

The custom field handler is basically the same as the one we implemented in Chapter 16, for supporting the RESTful-WS in XML format.

Next is the ApplicationContext configuration, which includes the import contact job. Listing 20-6 shows the configuration file (/src/main/resources/app-context.xml).

Listing 20-6. Spring Batch Job Configuration

```
<?xml version="1.0" encoding="UTF-8"?>
<beans xmlns="http://www.springframework.org/schema/beans"
    xmlns:xsi="http://www.w3.org/2001/XMLSchema-instance"
    xmlns:context="http://www.springframework.org/schema/context"
    xmlns:batch="http://www.springframework.org/schema/batch"
    xsi:schemaLocation="http://www.springframework.org/schema/beans
        http://www.springframework.org/schema/beans/spring-beans-3.1.xsd
        http://www.springframework.org/schema/context
        http://www.springframework.org/schema/context/spring-context-3.1.xsd
        http://www.springframework.org/schema/batch
        http://www.springframework.org/schema/batch/spring-batch-2.1.xsd">

    <import resource="classpath:datasource-tx-jpa.xml"/>
```

```xml
    <import resource="classpath:batch-context.xml"/>

    <context:component-scan base-package="com.apress.prospring3.ch20.service.jpa,
com.apress.prospring3.ch20.batch"/>

    <bean id="validator" class="org.springframework.validation
.beanvalidation.LocalValidatorFactoryBean"/>

    <!-- XML Marshaller -->
    <bean id="batchMarshaller" class="org.springframework.oxm.castor.CastorMarshaller">
        <property name="mappingLocation" value="classpath:oxm-mapping.xml"/>
    </bean>

    <!-- Batch job: Contact import -->
    <batch:job id="importContactsJob">
        <batch:step id="readWriteStep">
            <batch:tasklet transaction-manager="transactionManager">
                <batch:chunk
                    reader="contactItemReader"
                    processor="contactItemProcessor"
                    writer="contactItemWriter"
                    commit-interval="100"/>
            </batch:tasklet>
        </batch:step>
        <batch:listeners>
            <batch:listener ref="importContactJobListener"/>
        </batch:listeners>
    </batch:job>

    <bean id="contactItemReader" class="org.springframework.batch
.item.xml.StaxEventItemReader" scope="step">
        <property name="resource" value="file:///#{jobParameters['inputFile']}"/>
        <property name="fragmentRootElementName" value="contact"/>
        <property name="unmarshaller" ref="batchMarshaller"/>
    </bean>

    <bean id="contactItemWriter" class="org.springframework.batch
.item.adapter.ItemWriterAdapter">
        <property name="targetObject" ref="contactService" />
        <property name="targetMethod" value="save" />
    </bean>

    <bean id="batchValidator" class="com.apress.prospring3.ch20.
batch.validator.BeanValidationValidator" />

    <bean id="contactItemProcessor" class="org.springframework.
batch.item.validator.ValidatingItemProcessor">
        <property name="validator" ref="batchValidator" />
    </bean>

    <bean id="importContactJobListener" class="com.apress.prospring3.ch20.
batch.listener.ImportContactJobListener"/>

</beans>
```

In Listing 20-6, the batch-namespace is declared to facilitate the job definition. Within the configuration, the required files (datasource-tx-jpa.xml, batch-context.xml) are imported.

Then, the validator bean is defined, because we will use JSR-303 for data validation within the item processor (for details, please refer to Chapter 14). The batchMarshaller is declared for Castor to perform marshaling and unmarshalling between POJO and XML.

The importContactsJob bean defines the import contact batch job. In the job definition, only one step is defined, which contains one tasklet and chunk process. Within the chunk processing, the reader, processor, and writer properties are referencing the contactItemReader, contactItemProcessor, and contactItemWriter, respectively. The property commit-interval set the chunk size, which in our case is set to 100.

For the reader, which is the contactItemReader bean, the StaxEventItemReader<T> class is used, which is Spring Batch's support for reading data in XML format. For the resource property, the job parameter named inputFile (which is the name of the input file) is passed. The fragmentRootElementName property defines the tag corresponding to each contact's information, which is the <contact> tag. The unmarshaller property specifies the XML unmarshaller to use, which in our case is the Castor's batchMarshaller bean.

For the writer, which is the contactItemWriter bean, the ItemWriterAdapter<T> class is used, which is Spring Batch's support for calling an existing Spring bean's method for item writing. In the configuration, you can see the save() method of the contactService bean is used. You can see how Spring Batch can be seamlessly integrated with the existing ApplicationContext.

In STS, the Spring Config Editor also provides a graphical view of the batch job configuration. To see it, make sure you open the app-context.xml file with the Spring Config Editor, and click the tab batch-graph in the editor view. Figure 20-5 shows the tab for the import contacts job.

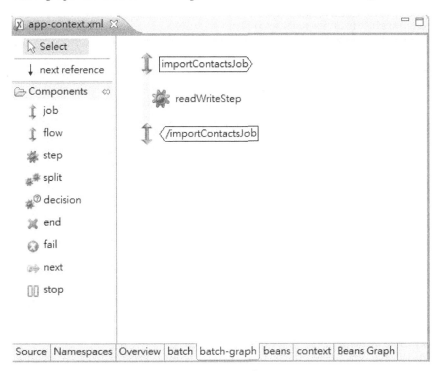

Figure 20-5. Graphical view of Spring batch job in STS

For the processor, which is the contactItemProcessor bean, we use the ValidatingItemProcessor<T> class, which is Spring Batch's support for item-level validation. In its configuration, the bean with BeanValidationValidator class is injected. Listing 20-7 shows the class content.

Listing 20-7. The BeanValidationValidator Class

```java
package com.apress.prospring3.ch20.batch.validator;

import java.util.HashSet;
import java.util.Set;

import javax.validation.ConstraintViolation;

import org.springframework.batch.item.validator.ValidationException;
import org.springframework.batch.item.validator.Validator;
import org.springframework.beans.factory.annotation.Autowired;

public class BeanValidationValidator<Contact> implements Validator<Contact> {

    @Autowired
    private javax.validation.Validator validator;

    public void validate(Contact value) throws ValidationException {

        Set<ConstraintViolation<Contact>> violations =
            new HashSet<ConstraintViolation<Contact>>();
        violations = validator.validate(value);
        if(!violations.isEmpty()) {
            throw new ValidationException("Validation failed for " + value
                + ": " + violationsToString(violations));
        }
    }

    private String violationsToString(Set<ConstraintViolation<Contact>> violations) {

        StringBuilder violationMessage = new StringBuilder();

        for (ConstraintViolation<Contact> violation: violations) {
            violationMessage.append(violation.getMessage() + "|");
        }

        return violationMessage.toString();
    }
}
```

In Listing 20-7, the class implements the org.springframework.batch.item.validator.Validator<T> interface, which is Spring Batch's support for item-level validation. Within the class, the JSR-303 validator bean is autowired. Within the validate() method, the item, which is of the Contact type, will be passed into the bean to perform validation. Then, the Contact object will be checked for constraint violations and in case violations exist, an instance of ValidationException class will be thrown.

Note that in Listing 20-6, in the importContactsJob bean, a job listener is provided too. The bean name is importContactJobListener. The job listener is a powerful feature provided by Spring Batch so that custom logic can be execute in every phase of the batch job processing life cycle. In this case, the job listener just lists all the contacts after the job was completed to see whether the contact was imported successfully. Listing 20-8 shows the listener class content.

Listing 20-8. The ImportContactJobListener Class

```
package com.apress.prospring3.ch20.batch.listener;

import java.util.List;

import org.slf4j.Logger;
import org.slf4j.LoggerFactory;
import org.springframework.batch.core.JobExecution;
import org.springframework.batch.core.JobExecutionListener;
import org.springframework.beans.factory.annotation.Autowired;

import com.apress.prospring3.ch20.domain.Contact;
import com.apress.prospring3.ch20.service.ContactService;

public class ImportContactJobListener implements JobExecutionListener {

    private static final Logger logger = LoggerFactory.getLogger(ImportContactJobListener.class);

    @Autowired
    private ContactService contactService;

    @Override
    public void afterJob(JobExecution arg0) {
        List<Contact> contacts = contactService.findAll();
        for (Contact contact: contacts) {
            logger.info("Contact: {}", contact);
        }
    }

    @Override
        public void beforeJob(JobExecution arg0) {
    }
}
```

In Listing 20-8, the class implements the JobExecutionListener interface. In the afterJob() method, the ContactService.findAll() method is called, and the list of contacts will be logged to the console output. Note that the JobExecution class is also passed into the listener so that all job execution information is available for processing.

Now we can execute the batch job. Listing 20-9 shows the class for launching the job.

Listing 20-9. Batch Job Execution

```
package com.apress.prospring3.ch20;

import java.util.HashMap;
import java.util.Map;

import org.springframework.batch.core.*;
```

```java
import org.springframework.batch.core.launch.*;
import org.springframework.context.support.GenericXmlApplicationContext;

public class ContactJobTest {

    public static void main(String[] args) {

        GenericXmlApplicationContext ctx = new GenericXmlApplicationContext();
        ctx.load("classpath:app-context.xml");
        ctx.refresh();

        JobLauncher jobLauncher = ctx.getBean("jobLauncher", JobLauncher.class);

        Job contactJob = ctx.getBean("importContactsJob", Job.class);

        Map<String, JobParameter> jobParamMap = new HashMap<String, JobParameter>();
        jobParamMap.put("inputFile", new JobParameter("C:/temp/contacts.xml"));

        try {
            jobLauncher.run(contactJob, new JobParameters(jobParamMap));
        } catch (Exception ex) {
            ex.printStackTrace();
        }

        System.out.println("Contact import job completed successfully");
    }
}
```

In Listing 20-9, the job launcher bean and the import contact job beans are obtained from ApplicationContext. Then, an instance of Map<String, JobParameter> is constructed, with the inputFile parameter populated. Finally, the batch job is launched with the job and job parameters. Before running the class, put a copy of the contacts.xml file into the folder C:/temp, as indicated in the job parameter. Upon running the class, the following output will be logged to the console output (the other, irrelevant output was omitted):

```
INFO : org.springframework.batch.core.launch.support.SimpleJobLauncher - No TaskExecutor has
been set, defaulting to synchronous executor.
INFO : org.springframework.oxm.castor.CastorMarshaller - Configured using [class path resource
[oxm-mapping.xml]]
INFO : org.springframework.batch.core.launch.support.SimpleJobLauncher - Job: [FlowJob:
[name=importContactsJob]] launched with the following parameters:
[{inputFile=C:/temp/contacts.xml}]
INFO : org.springframework.batch.core.job.SimpleStepHandler - Executing step: [readWriteStep]
Hibernate: insert into contact (ID, BIRTH_DATE, FIRST_NAME, LAST_NAME, VERSION) values (null,
?, ?, ?, ?)
Hibernate: insert into contact_hobby_detail (CONTACT_ID, HOBBY_ID) values (?, ?)
Hibernate: insert into contact_hobby_detail (CONTACT_ID, HOBBY_ID) values (?, ?)
INFO : com.apress.prospring3.ch20.service.jpa.ContactServiceImpl - Finding all contacts
Hibernate: select contact0_.ID as ID0_, contact0_.BIRTH_DATE as BIRTH2_0_,
contact0_.FIRST_NAME as FIRST3_0_, contact0_.LAST_NAME as LAST4_0_, contact0_.VERSION as
VERSION0_ from contact contact0_
INFO : com.apress.prospring3.ch20.batch.listener.ImportContactJobListener - Contact: Contact -
Id: 1, First name: Clarence, Last name: Ho, Birthday: 1980-07-30T00:00:00.000+08:00
```

```
INFO : com.apress.prospring3.ch20.batch.listener.ImportContactJobListener - Contact: Contact -
Id: 2, First name: Scott, Last name: Tiger, Birthday: 1990-11-02T00:00:00.000+08:00
INFO : com.apress.prospring3.ch20.batch.listener.ImportContactJobListener - Contact: Contact -
Id: 3, First name: Kim Fung, Last name: Ho, Birthday: 1980-07-30T00:00:00.000+08:00
INFO : org.springframework.batch.core.launch.support.SimpleJobLauncher - Job: [FlowJob:
[name=importContactsJob]] completed with the following parameters:
[{inputFile=C:/temp/contacts.xml}] and the following status: [COMPLETED]
Contact import job completed successfully
```

The testing data file (in test-data.sql) contains two contact records, and from the output, you can see that the contact (with id = 3) in the XML file was imported successfully.

Spring Batch provides a solid foundation that can help fulfill complex batch job requirements. For more details, we recommend the book *Pro Spring Batch* (Apress, 2011).

Using Spring Batch with Spring Integration

While Spring Batch provides a sophisticated batch job execution environment, Spring Integration provides an excellent integration environment for enterprise applications. With Spring Integration, information exchange with external systems becomes much easier, no matter where the information comes from or needs to be sent to. Out-of-the-box support for file, e-mail, and JMS-based integration is provided.

Even if your initial batch job execution requirements are very simple, we still recommend that you set up Spring Batch to integrate with Spring Integration to ensure that the application execution environment is flexible enough to cater to more complicated integration requirements in the future.

In the following sections, we will demonstrate how Spring Batch can work with Spring Integration to implement a file polling mechanism so that when a file arrives in a folder, Spring Integration will launch the import contact job automatically.

Introducing Spring Integration

Some core concepts of Spring Integration are as follows:

- *Channel*: Spring Integration is a message-based integration framework, and a channel is the placeholder for messages. Channels are the glue for linking up the various message producers and consumers within an application.

- *Message endpoint*: In Spring Integration, message endpoint comes in the form of adapters, which connect application components to various channels. In the import contact job, we will use the <inbound-channel-adapter> tag to connect the file polling component to the batch job request channel.

- *Transformer*: As the name implies, a transformer connects different channels and performs the necessary message transformation.

- *Service activator*: In Spring Integration, the service activator is an endpoint that invokes the business process of an application by passing in the appropriate message.

Figure 20-6 provides a graphical view of how the components in Spring Integration and Spring Batch work together to launch the import contact job by using a file polling mechanism.

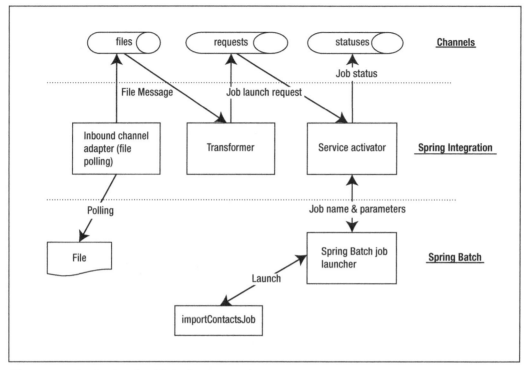

Figure 20-6. *Spring Batch with Spring Integration*

In Figure 20-6, at the top three channels are defined for storing message, namely, files, requests, and statuses.

First, the inbound channel adapter from Spring Integration's file support is used for file polling. When a file arrives, a file message will be created and stored in the files channel.

Second, the transformer will pick up the message from the files channel, perform the transformation (in this case, the file message will be transformed into a job launch request message), and output the transformed message into the requests channel. The service activator picks up the job launch request message from the requests channel and launches the job accordingly. The result of the job execution will be output into the statuses channel.

Adding Required Dependencies

Table 20-5 shows the required dependencies for Spring Integration and Spring Batch's support of Spring Integration.

Table 20-5. *Maven Dependencies for Spring Integration*

Group ID	Artifact ID	Version	Description
`org.springframework.integration`	spring-integration-core	2.1.0.RELEASE	Spring Integration's core library.
`org.springframework.integration`	spring-integration-file	2.1.0.RELEASE	Spring Integration's support for file-related I/O integration patterns.
`org.springframework.batch`	spring-batch-integration	1.2.1.RELEASE	Belongs to the Spring Batch Admin project, which provides classes for working with Spring Integration. For example, the classes for supporting job launching from Spring Integration are packaged into this library.

Add the dependencies in Table 20-5 into the project in STS.

Implementing the File Polling Mechanism

Implementing the file polling mechanism in Spring Integration for launching a Spring Batch job is pretty easy.

We need to configure the components in Figure 20-6 in Spring's ApplicationContext configuration (batch-context.xml). Listing 20-10 shows the changes that need to be made to the file.

Listing 20-10. *The Revised batch-context.xml File*

```
<?xml version="1.0" encoding="UTF-8"?>
<beans xmlns="http://www.springframework.org/schema/beans"
    xmlns:xsi="http://www.w3.org/2001/XMLSchema-instance"
    xmlns:integration="http://www.springframework.org/schema/integration"
    xmlns:file="http://www.springframework.org/schema/integration/file"
    xmlns:context="http://www.springframework.org/schema/context"
    xsi:schemaLocation="http://www.springframework.org/schema/beans
      http://www.springframework.org/schema/beans/spring-beans-3.1.xsd
      http://www.springframework.org/schema/integration
      http://www.springframework.org/schema/integration/spring-integration.xsd
      http://www.springframework.org/schema/integration/file
      http://www.springframework.org/schema/integration/file/spring-integration-file.xsd
      http://www.springframework.org/schema/context
      http://www.springframework.org/schema/context/spring-context-3.1.xsd">

    <!-- Other code omitted -->

    <!-- Spring Integration Configuration: Start -->
    <integration:channel id="files"/>
```

```xml
<integration:channel id="requests"/>

<integration:channel id="statuses">
    <integration:queue capacity="10"/>
</integration:channel>

<file:inbound-channel-adapter
    directory="file:C:/temp/contact"
    channel="files">
    <integration:poller id="poller" fixed-delay="5000"/>
</file:inbound-channel-adapter>

<integration:transformer input-channel="files" output-channel="requests">
    <bean class="com.apress.prospring3.ch20.batch.integration.FileMessageToJobRequest">
        <property name="job" ref="importContactsJob"/>
        <property name="fileParameterName" value="inputFile"/>
    </bean>
</integration:transformer>

<integration:service-activator method="launch" input-channel="requests"
    output-channel="statuses">
    <bean id="messageHandler"
        class="org.springframework.batch.integration.launch.JobLaunchingMessageHandler">
        <constructor-arg ref="jobLauncher"/>
    </bean>
</integration:service-activator>
<!-- Spring Integration Configuration: End -->
```

```xml
</beans>
```

In Listing 20-10, the required changes are highlighted in bold. First, the integration namespace and file namespace are declared, which belongs to Spring Integration's components. Second, the channels are declared.

Then, the <file:inbound-channel-adapter> tag is used to define the inbound channel adapter, which represents Spring Integration's support for file-based integration. The directory attribute defines the input folder, and the channel attribute defines the channel the message should be output to. The subtag <integration:poller> defines the polling mechanism, with a delay of 5000ms, which means the adapter will poll the folder for incoming files for every five seconds.

Next is the transformer part. The <integration:transformer> tag defines the transformer for the file message, with a custom implementation class (the FileMessageToJobRequest class) that performs the transformation from the file message into a job launch request message. Listing 20-11 shows the class.

Listing 20-11. The FileMessageToJobRequest Class

```java
package com.apress.prospring3.ch20.batch.integration;

import java.io.File;

import org.springframework.batch.core.Job;
import org.springframework.batch.core.JobParametersBuilder;
import org.springframework.batch.integration.launch.JobLaunchRequest;
import org.springframework.integration.Message;
```

```java
import org.springframework.integration.annotation.Transformer;

public class FileMessageToJobRequest {

    private Job job;
    private String fileParameterName;

    public void setFileParameterName(String fileParameterName) {
        this.fileParameterName = fileParameterName;
    }

    public void setJob(Job job) {
        this.job = job;
    }

    @Transformer
    public JobLaunchRequest toRequest(Message<File> message) {
        JobParametersBuilder jobParametersBuilder = new JobParametersBuilder();
        jobParametersBuilder.addString(fileParameterName,
            message.getPayload().getAbsolutePath());
        return new JobLaunchRequest(job, jobParametersBuilder.toJobParameters());
    }
}
```

In Listing 20-11, the toRequest() method is applied with the @Transformer annotation, which indicates to Spring Integration that this method should be executed for message transformation. The job (indicates the batch job to launch) and fileParameterName (indicates the name of the job parameter for the input file) properties are injected. Within the method, the passed-in File message is transformed into an instance of the JobLaunchRequest class and returned, which will then be output to the requests channel.

Finally, the <integration:service-activator> tag defines the service activator. Within the bean definition, a messageHandler bean with the JobLaunchingMessageHandler class is declared, which represents Spring Batch's support for launching jobs from Spring Integration.

In STS, the Spring Config Editor also supports visualizing the integration configuration. To see it, in the Spring Config Editor's view, click the tab integration-graph. Figure 20-7 shows the sample integration configuration.

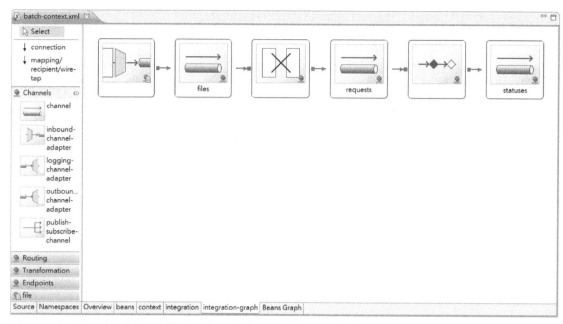

Figure 20-7. Graphical view of Spring Integration configuration in STS

Now we can test the file polling. Listing 20-12 shows the testing program.

Listing 20-12. Testing File Polling

```
package com.apress.prospring3.ch20;

import org.springframework.context.support.GenericXmlApplicationContext;

public class BatchIntegrationTest {

    public static void main(String[] args) {

        GenericXmlApplicationContext ctx = new GenericXmlApplicationContext();
        ctx.load("classpath:app-context.xml");
        ctx.refresh();

        System.out.println("App context initialized successfully");

        while (true) {
        }
    }
}
```

In Listing 20-12, we just need to bootstrap the ApplicationContext and then keep looping. Spring Integration will perform file polling within the C:/temp/contact folder, which is defined in the inbound channel adapter bean. To test it, put the file contacts.xml into the C:/temp/contact folder, and from the STS console output, you should see that the job will be launched automatically. Some sample output is shown here (the irrelevant output was omitted).

```
INFO : org.springframework.integration.file.FileReadingMessageSource - Created message:
[[Payload=\temp\contact\contacts.xml][Headers={timestamp=1326274023267, id=17cc6b63-5694-4160-
a2d6-a75430fa7515}]]
INFO : org.springframework.batch.core.launch.support.SimpleJobLauncher - Job: [FlowJob:
[name=importContactsJob]] launched with the following parameters:
[{inputFile=C:\temp\contact\contacts.xml}]
INFO : org.springframework.batch.core.job.SimpleStepHandler - Executing step: [readWriteStep]
Hibernate: insert into contact (ID, BIRTH_DATE, FIRST_NAME, LAST_NAME, VERSION) values (null,
?, ?, ?, ?)
Hibernate: insert into contact_hobby_detail (CONTACT_ID, HOBBY_ID) values (?, ?)
Hibernate: insert into contact_hobby_detail (CONTACT_ID, HOBBY_ID) values (?, ?)
INFO : com.apress.prospring3.ch20.service.jpa.ContactServiceImpl - Finding all contacts
Hibernate: select contact0_.ID as ID0_, contact0_.BIRTH_DATE as BIRTH2_0_,
contact0_.FIRST_NAME as FIRST3_0_, contact0_.LAST_NAME as LAST4_0_, contact0_.VERSION as
VERSION0_ from contact contact0_
INFO : com.apress.prospring3.ch20.batch.listener.ImportContactJobListener - Contact: Contact -
Id: 1, First name: Clarence, Last name: Ho, Birthday: 1980-07-30T00:00:00.000+08:00
INFO : com.apress.prospring3.ch20.batch.listener.ImportContactJobListener - Contact: Contact -
Id: 2, First name: Scott, Last name: Tiger, Birthday: 1990-11-02T00:00:00.000+08:00
INFO : com.apress.prospring3.ch20.batch.listener.ImportContactJobListener - Contact: Contact -
Id: 3, First name: Kim Fung, Last name: Ho, Birthday: 1980-07-30T00:00:00.000+08:00
INFO : org.springframework.batch.core.launch.support.SimpleJobLauncher - Job: [FlowJob:
[name=importContactsJob]] completed with the following parameters:
[{inputFile=C:\temp\contact\contacts.xml}] and the following status: [COMPLETED]
```

In the output, you can see that the message was created, the job was launched, and the import contact job completed successfully.

Spring Batch plus Spring Integration provides a powerful batch job execution and enterprise integration environment that integrates with Spring application's service layer for consistent business logic execution seamlessly.

For more details on Spring Integration, we recommend the book *Pro Spring Integration* (Apress, 2011).

Introducing Spring Roo

Another interesting project in Spring's portfolio is the Spring Roo project (www.springsource.org/spring-roo). Spring Roo provides a next-generation rapid application development platform that greatly enhances the productivity of developers of Spring-based applications.

Spring Roo provides an innovative command-line interface with useful hints that can help you define a Domain Object Model (DOM), persistence layer, service layer, and presentation layer quickly. In the persistence layer, Spring Roo provides first-class support on JPA 2, and with Spring Roo 1.2, Spring Data JPA's repository abstraction support was also added.

With Spring Roo, you have the option to have the persistence logic built into the JPA entity classes, or you can instruct Roo to generate a service layer to host your business logic. JSR-303 is supported out of the box.

On the presentation layer, Roo provides first-class support for Spring MVC and can generate a basic user interface automatically with templating support (with Apache Tiles), theming, i18n, validation, and so on, out of the box. You can also instruct Roo to generate the presentation layer using Spring Web Flow. For the view side, in version 1.2.0, when using Spring MVC, Roo will generate views in JSPX pages. JSF support with PrimeFaces as the component library is also provided.

Roo also supports the implementation of extensions via its add-on architecture. At the time of writing, there are many add-ons already (although some of the add-ons are still in the early development stage), including add-ons for GWT, Vaadin, Adobe Flex, jQuery, and so on. Add-ons that support other Spring projects, including Spring Security, Spring Integration, and so on, are also available.

STS also provides out-of-the-box support for Spring Roo. In STS, there is an option for you to create a Spring Roo project, and a Spring Roo Shell is provided for you in STS too.

Applications generated by Spring Roo are highly customizable. If you want to override the default behavior for any layer that was generated by Roo, take back the control on the logic you want to execute, or add your own logic on the classes generated by Roo, you can do so; Roo's design provides a clean separation of the logic that was generated by Roo and those implemented by developers.

In the following sections, we will present you with a high-level overview of Spring Roo and then see it in action by developing a simple contact application.

Configure Spring Roo in STS

At the time of writing, STS 2.8.1 comes bundled with Spring Roo version 1.1.5. However, version 1.2.0 brings a lot of exciting new features, and we will use it for this section. So, we need to download and install Spring Roo 1.2.0 and configure STS to use the new version of Spring Roo.

Download the Spring Roo 1.2.0 distribution from the URL `http://s3.amazonaws.com/dist.springframework.org/release/ROO/spring-roo-1.2.0.RELEASE.zip` (or from the SpringSource community project's download center at `www.springsource.org/spring-community-download`) and unzip the file into your PC. Then, in STS, choose Window ➤ Preferences and then the option Spring ➤ Roo Support. You will see the default version bundled is 1.1.5. Click the Add button to add version 1.2.0, and browse to the folder of your Roo installation, as shown in Figure 20-8.

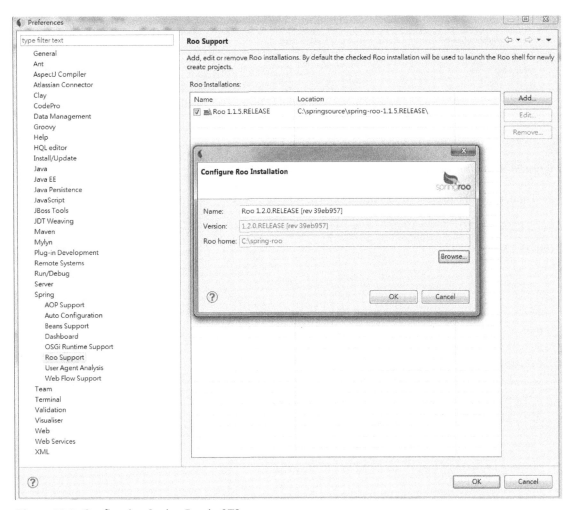

Figure 20-8. *Configuring Spring Roo in STS*

Upon completion, make sure that 1.2.0 is the default version and then click OK button. Now we are ready to create a Spring Roo project.

Create a Spring Roo Project

Creating a Spring Roo project in STS is extremely easy. In STS, choose File ➤ New ➤ Spring Roo Project, as shown in Figure 20-9.

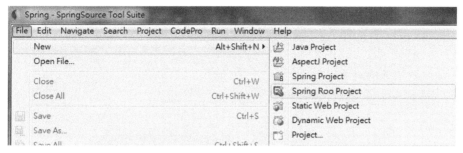

Figure 20-9. *Creating a Spring Roo project*

Then, enter the project information shown in Figure 20-10.

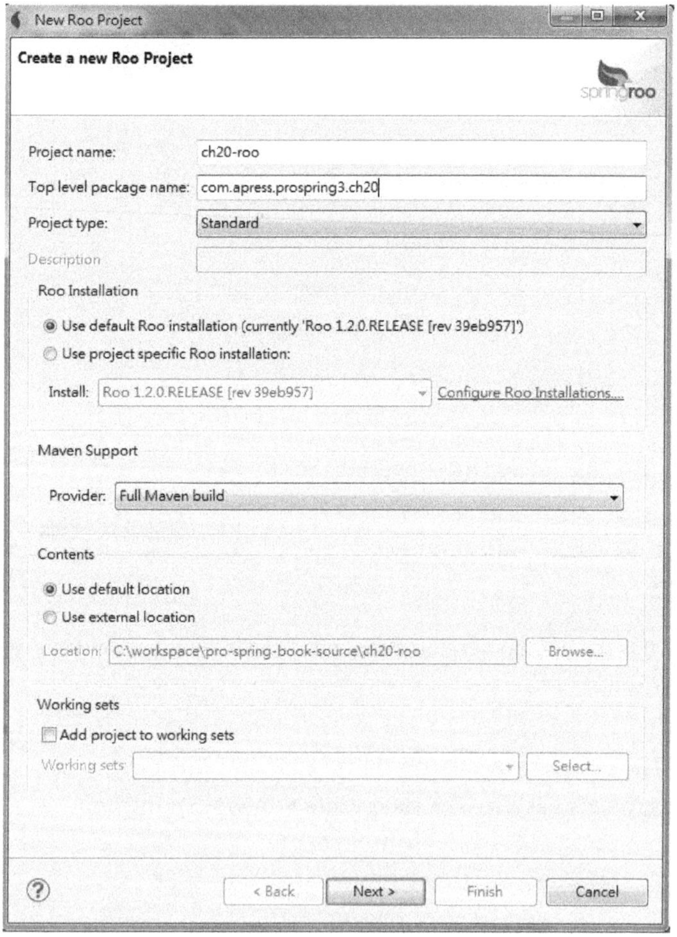

Figure 20-10. *Spring Roo project information*

Then click Next and Finish, and STS will create the project. STS will also open the Roo Shell view automatically, as shown in Figure 20-11.

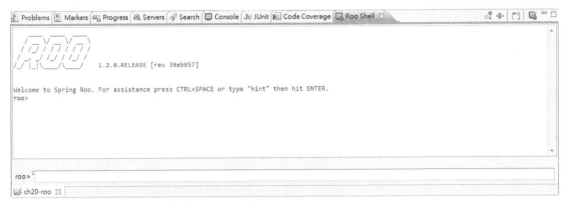

Figure 20-11. The Spring Roo Shell view in STS

Let's proceed to configure the DOM.

Set Up the Persistence Layer and Entity Class

For the DOM, Spring Roo provides first-class support for JPA entities. Setting up the persistence layer and the corresponding entity classes that are required for the application is the first step.

In this sample, we will set up the persistence layer using the H2 in-memory database as the backend and using Hibernate as the JPA persistence provider. To do this, enter the following command at the Roo prompt:

```
persistence setup --database H2_IN_MEMORY --provider HIBERNATE
```

The persistence setup command is to instruct Spring Roo to create the persistence layer for our application. The options specify the H2 database with Hibernate as the provider. In Roo Shell, all options are prefix with --, and you can always press Ctrl+spacebar for code assistance and hints. Press Enter, and then Roo will generate the persistence layer. Upon completion, in the Package Explorer, you will see the project structure, as shown in Figure 20-12.

Figure 20-12. The Spring Roo project with the persistence layer

What Spring Roo did was add the required Maven dependencies and configure the ApplicationContext with the required components, the database connection information (in the database.properties file), and the JPA persistence.xml file.

The next step is to create the Contact entity class. Enter the following command to create the class:

```
entity jpa --class ~.domain.Contact
```

The command indicates that we want to create a JPA entity class, with the package name com.apress.prospring3.ch20 (the ~ character indicates the base package we defined when creating the project), the subpackage name domain, and the class name Contact.

Then, Roo will generate the entity class, together with a number of AspectJ classes. Note that at the time of writing, the Roo Shell has a minor problem: it doesn't add the path /src/main/java to the source folder of the project, so we need to manually add it. To do this, in STS, right-click the project and select Properties ➤ Java Build Path; then click the Add Folder button and check the /src/main/java folder, as shown in Figure 20-13.

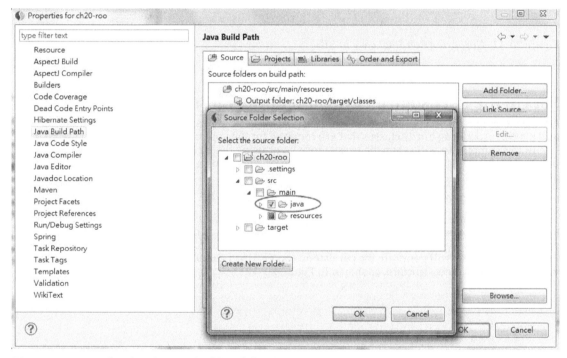

Figure 20-13. *Configuring the Java build path for the Spring Roo project*

Now when you look at the Package Explorer, you will see only the Contact class, not other AspectJ classes generated by Roo. The reason is that by default the Package Explorer view will filter out those classes from the view. To see it, in the Package Explorer view, click the View menu (the triangle symbol), and select Filters, as shown in Figure 20-14.

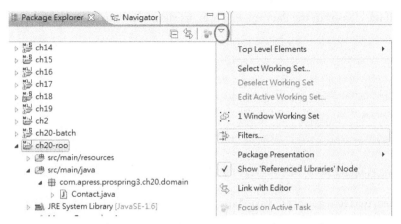

Figure 20-14. *Configuring the Filters option in Package Explorer*

In the Java Element Filters dialog, uncheck the option called Hide generated Spring Roo ITDs, as shown in Figure 20-15.

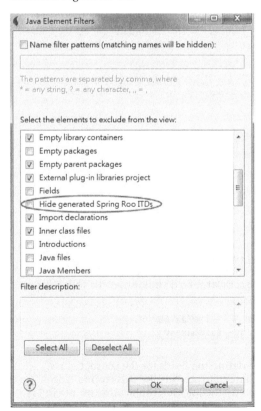

Figure 20-15. *Configuring Package Explorer to see Spring Roo–generated classes*

Then you will able to see all the classes in the Package Explorer, as shown in Figure 20-16.

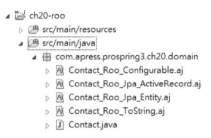

Figure 20-16. *Spring Roo–generated classes*

The AspectJ classes (*.aj files) that Roo generated are AspectJ intertype declarations (ITD) classes. These ITDs are the magic behind Spring Roo and store all the logic generated and maintained by Roo. For example, the ITDs will store the getter/setter methods, common properties for JPA (for example, the ID, version, and so on), the toString() method, and so on.

At this point, when you take a look at the Roo Shell view, you will see that the shell is "focused" on the Contact class, as shown in Figure 20-17.

```
Problems  Markers  Progress  Servers  Search  Console  JUnit  Code Coverage  Roo Shell

Created SPRING_CONFIG_ROOT\database.properties
Updated SPRING_CONFIG_ROOT\applicationContext.xml
Created SRC_MAIN_RESOURCES\META-INF\persistence.xml
Updated ROOT\pom.xml [added dependencies com.h2database:h2:1.3.161, org.hibernate:hibernate-core:3.6.8.Final,
org.hibernate:hibernate-entitymanager:3.6.8.Final, org.hibernate.javax.persistence:hibernate-jpa-2.0-api:1.0.1.Final,
org.hibernate:hibernate-validator:4.2.0.Final, javax.validation:validation-api:1.0.0.GA, cglib:cglib-nodep:2.2.2,
javax.transaction:jta:1.1, org.springframework:spring-jdbc:${spring.version}, org.springframework:spring-orm:${spring.version},
commons-pool:commons-pool:1.5.6, commons-dbcp:commons-dbcp:1.3]
roo> entity jpa --class ~.domain.Contact
Created SRC_MAIN_JAVA\com\apress\prospring3\ch20\domain
Created SRC_MAIN_JAVA\com\apress\prospring3\ch20\domain\Contact.java
Created SRC_MAIN_JAVA\com\apress\prospring3\ch20\domain\Contact_Roo_Configurable.aj
Created SRC_MAIN_JAVA\com\apress\prospring3\ch20\domain\Contact_Roo_ToString.aj
Created SRC_MAIN_JAVA\com\apress\prospring3\ch20\domain\Contact_Roo_Jpa_ActiveRecord.aj
Created SRC_MAIN_JAVA\com\apress\prospring3\ch20\domain\Contact_Roo_Jpa_Entity.aj
~.domain.Contact roo>

roo>

ch20-roo
```

Figure 20-17. *Roo Shell focus*

In Roo, *focus* means that all the subsequent class-level commands will be applied to the class that currently has the focus. The next step is to define the properties for the Contact class. We will need to create three properties, namely, firstName, lastName, and birthDate. To do this, enter the following commands one by one:

```
field string --fieldName firstName --notNull --sizeMin 3 --sizeMax 60
field string --fieldName lastName --notNull --sizeMin 1 --sizeMax 40
field date --fieldName birthDate --type java.util.Date
```

In the above commands, the field command is used to define the fields for the Contact class. Because we already focusing on the Contact class, we don't need to provide the class name. The attribute after the field is the type, and then the field name and the JSR-303 constraints for the fields appear.

After the field properties are generated, the next step is to configure Spring Data JPA repository abstraction for the Contact class. Enter the following command into the Roo prompt:

```
repository jpa --interface ~.repository.ContactRepository --entity ~.domain.Contact
```

The previous command instructs Roo to generate the JPA repository interface that uses Spring Data JPA. At this point, the persistence layer is basically complete.

Set Up the Service Layer

Starting with version 1.2.0, Roo added support for generating service-layer classes. To see this in action, let's create the ContactService interface like we did in previous chapters. To do this, enter the following command at the Roo prompt:

```
service --interface ~.service.ContactService --entity ~.domain.Contact
```

The service command is used to instruct Roo to create the ContactService interface, which will be used to manipulate the Contact entity class. Upon completion, in the Package Explorer, you will see that besides the interface class, Roo also generates the implementation class ContactServiceImpl. In addition, if you take a look at the ITD ContactServiceImpl_Roo_Service.aj file that Roo generates, the repository interface (ContactRepository) is autowired into the service class automatically.

At this point, a backend for the Contact entity class with basic CRUD operations support is created.

Set Up the Presentation Layer

In Spring Roo, generating a web application with Spring MVC is extremely easy. First we need to instruct Roo to set up Spring MVC for the application. Enter the following command at the Roo prompt:

```
web mvc setup
```

If you look at the Package Explorer now, you will see that Roo generated the web environment folder structure, the web deployment descriptor (web.xml), the DispatcherServlet WebApplicationContext configuration file (webmvc-config.xml), and so on.

The next step is to generate the controller class and view files for the Contact entity class. To do this, enter the following command at the Roo prompt:

```
web mvc all --package ~.web.controller
```

The command simply instructs Roo to generate scaffold Spring MVC controllers for all entities in the project without an existing controller class. Roo with then generate the controller class for the Contact entity, as well as the JSPX view files for maintaining contact information.

Now a basic application is generated, and after building and deploying to the tc Server in STS, start the server, and enter the URL http://localhost:8080/ch20-roo in the browser. The application will be displayed, as shown in Figure 20-18.

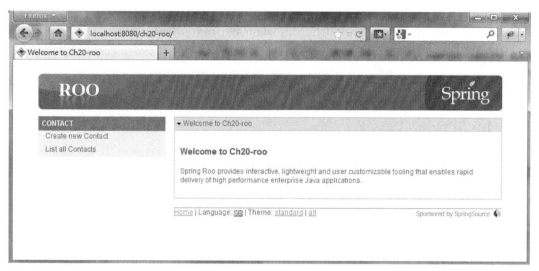

Figure 20-18. *Generated Spring Roo application*

Click the link Create new Contact to create a new contact, and you will see the form shown in Figure 20-19.

Figure 20-19. *Creating a new contact*

Note that the date field already has the date picker enabled. If you view the page source, you will notice that the generated view has the Dojo Toolkit JavaScript library included. The JSPX view with the Dojo Toolkit is the default that Roo will generate for a web application's frontend. After the new contact is saved, click the List all Contacts link, and you will see the added contact, as shown in Figure 20-20.

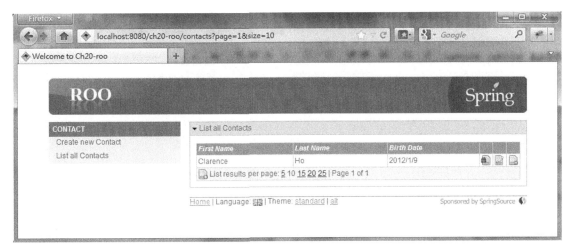

Figure 20-20. *Listing the contacts*

In Figure 20-20, you will see that the buttons for viewing, editing, and deleting the contact (the three buttons to the right of the contact) are already provided in the data table. Moreover, pagination support is enabled. In the footer, you can also see that support for theming and i18n are already there, too.

Roo allows you to take control of the logic in every class, context configuration, view file, and others whenever you want. For example, let's say now we want to have the Spring MVC controller class logic back into the Java class file and take control of it instead of leaving it under Roo's management. To do this, right-click the ITD class for the controller class (`ContactController_Roo_Controller.aj`), and then choose Refactor ➤ Push In, as shown in Figure 20-21.

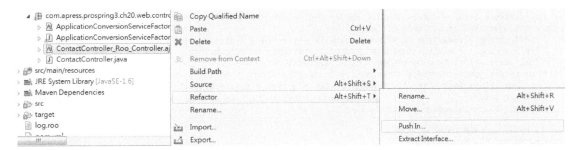

Figure 20-21. *Push In logic from Spring Roo*

The Push In Intertype Declaration dialog will be displayed, with all the methods generated by Roo. You can choose to "push in" only some of the methods (by expanding the class node and selecting the methods you want to push in) or all methods at once, as shown in Figure 20-22.

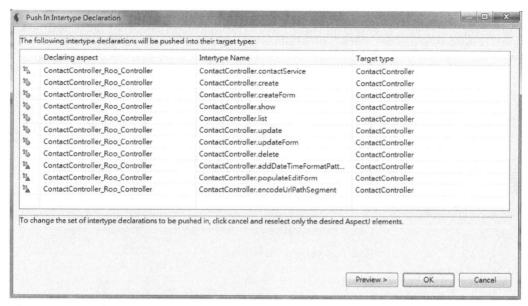

Figure 20-22. *Push In Intertype Declaration dialog*

Upon push in, the logic will be extracted into the `ContactController` class. You can then take a look at the `ContactController` class and the methods that were pushed in.

All the Roo commands that you entered will be stored in the file called `log.roo` (located in the project's root folder), so you can use it as the script for creating similar projects. It's a very convenient feature; Figure 20-23 shows the `log.roo` file for the contact application that we generated.

```
   log.roo ☒
 1 // Spring Roo 1.2.0.RELEASE [rev 39eb957] log opened at 2012-01-12 12:47:45
 2 project --topLevelPackage com.apress.prospring3.ch20 --projectName ch20-roo --java 6
 3 // Spring Roo 1.2.0.RELEASE [rev 39eb957] log closed at 2012-01-12 12:47:45
 4 // Spring Roo 1.2.0.RELEASE [rev 39eb957] log opened at 2012-01-12 12:47:47
 5 persistence setup --database H2_IN_MEMORY --provider HIBERNATE
 6 entity jpa --class ~.domain.Contact
 7 field string --fieldName firstName --notNull --sizeMin 3 --sizeMax 60
 8 field string --fieldName lastName --notNull --sizeMin 1 --sizeMax 40
 9 field date --fieldName birthDate --type java.util.Date
10 repository jpa --interface ~.repository.ContactRepository --entity ~.domain.Contact
11 service --interface ~.service.ContactService --entity ~.domain.Contact
12 web mvc setup
13 web mvc all --package ~.web.controller
14
```

Figure 20-23. *The Roo log file*

Spring Roo Add-on

Another powerful feature of Spring Roo is the add-on architecture, which allows you to create custom add-ons to Roo to fulfill your specific needs. There are a lot of add-ons already available; some were developed by the Roo team, some by open source communities, and others by developers of a specific tool or library who want to have their offering available to Roo applications.

From the Roo Shell, you can list, search, or install add-ons. At the Roo prompt, type **addon**, and then press Ctrl+spacebar; you will see the available commands relating to add-ons, as shown in Figure 20-24.

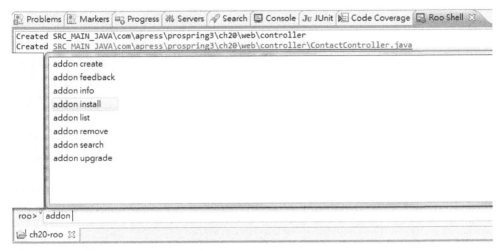

Figure 20-24. Roo add-on commands

For example, the addon list command lists the add-ons currently available for install and use in your Roo application. Figure 20-25 shows the output of the addon list command.

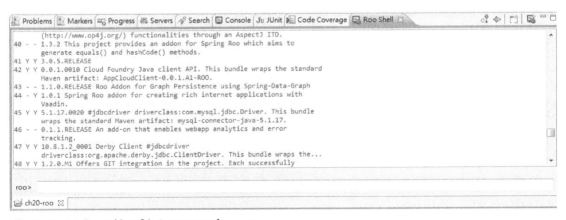

Figure 20-25. Roo addon list command output

In the figure, you can see the available add-ons and their descriptions. For example, you can see that the add-on with ID 44 enables you to develop RIAs in Spring Roo with Vaadin, which is a popular frontend library built on top of GWT.

Conclusion on Spring Roo

With the previous sample, you got a little taste of how Roo can help provide a rapid development environment. The Roo project is still evolving quickly, and many add-ons are being developed.

The Roo project has great potential, so it is worth keeping an eye on its development. Even though you may find it not good enough to have it generate your JEE application for production use, it is still very useful for generating application prototypes during the initial design phase. Also, the folder structure and classes that Roo generates are based on industry best practices, and the code style, context configuration, and so on, are all based on the SpringSource team's recommendations.

It's also worth taking a look at the application that Roo generates for you and using it as a learning tool to understand the best practices and coding style for Spring-based applications.

If you are interested in learning more about Spring Roo, please refer to the reference documentation (`http://static.springsource.org/spring-roo/reference/html/index.html`) and the book *Spring Roo in Action* (Manning, 2012).

Spring Batch and Spring Integration in the Sample Application

In the SpringBlog application, we will adopt Spring Batch and Spring Integration to implement the job of importing blog posting entries from an XML file.

The mechanism discussed in this chapter will be used in developing the batch job. First, the XML file format for blog posting will be defined, together with the corresponding Castor mapping definitions.

Second, Spring Integration's file polling support will be used for scanning the arrival of a file containing new blog postings. When a new file arrives, the inbound channel adapter will pick up the file, and then the file message will be output to the file's channel.

The same transformer developed in this chapter will be used to transform the file message into the job launch request message, and outputting it to the requests channel.

A batch job will be implemented for importing the blog posting entries, which use the same service layer to perform write processing. JSR-303 validation will be used for item processing too. The service activator will be used to launch the job.

For details, please refer to Chapter 21.

Summary

In this chapter, we covered several interesting and useful Spring projects that can help us fulfill common application requirements.

First, we discussed the Spring Batch project and its chunk-based processing architecture and saw it in action by implementing a contact import job. Then, we demonstrated how Spring Integration can help perform message-based integration, its support for file-related operations, and how it works with Spring Batch for job launching.

Finally, we discussed the interesting Spring Roo project for rapid application development and prototyping. We discussed its innovative command-line support for code generation of various application layers, flexibility in taking back the control from the generated code, and the add-on architecture that allows the addition of your preferred tools and libraries.

Sample Application in Detail

In Chapter 3, we presented you with an architectural overview of the sample application for this book, including the layered application architecture, main features, and screenshots of the completed application. Then, in Chapter 12, we discussed a few main topics with regard to designing and implementing Spring applications, with some reference to the sample application, too. As we have gone through each chapter, we covered the main relationships between the features and discussed their adoption in the sample application.

In this chapter, we will discuss the details of the sample application, called SpringBlog, that was developed for this book. The objective is to elaborate on the details of the application design and explain the implementation of the main features that were discussed within each relevant chapter, including how they work together in a complete JEE application. Specifically, in this chapter, we will look at the following:

- *Project setup*: We will discuss how to set up the project and STS so that you can build and get the sample application up and running on your machine. Instructions are provided on how to use Spring Framework's bean definition profiles feature to switch the backend RDBMS (between MySQL and H2) and service layer implementations (between Hibernate JPA 2 and MyBatis).

- *Application design*: We will discuss the main design elements of the application. The data model, domain object model, and UML model of the major use cases will be covered.

- *Implementation details*: We will discuss how the main features of the sample application are implemented in detail. Topics include using AOP for the obscenity filter, creating a service layer using Hibernate and JPA 2, implementing validation with conversion and formatting, creating the frontend, using RESTful-WS, creating batch jobs, scheduling a job for purging audit data, and so on.

Although all the SpringBlog features mentioned in the book have been incorporated into the implemented source code, some of those features are still under development as the book goes to print (for example, using the MyBatis implementation to handle comment posts, file uploads, and so on). We will update the sample application's source code periodically to implement these features, and that code will be hosted in a repository on GitHub. Also, as comments are received from readers, existing features may be enhanced and new features added. So, kindly check out the source code repository on a regular basis for any changes.

The following are the features within the sample application that are still under development at the time of writing:

- MyBatis implementations including entry updates, comment posts, file uploads, and maintaining entity versions

- The scheduled job for purging old history records for blog entries and comments
- User maintenance and role assignment
- Maintenance of categories and subcategories for blog entries
- Unit testing

Setting Up the Sample Application

Let's get the source code and set up the project in STS. Then, we'll set up tc Server and deploy the SpringBlog application to see it in action. It will be much easier to understand the source code when seeing how it works side by side with the text.

In the following sections, we will discuss how to set up the project in STS and get the SpringBlog application up and running. Topics include obtaining the source code, importing the project, setting up the server, and switching between different RDBMSs and service layer implementations.

To set up the project and run the sample application, you need JDK 6 or newer, SpringSource Tool Suite (2.8.1 or newer), and an Internet connection available on your development machine. To test the MySQL backend, a local instance of MySQL database with version 5.1 or newer and a basic knowledge of managing a MySQL database (for example, creating a user, running a script, and so on) are assumed.

Project Setup

To set up the project, we need to get the source code and import it into STS. There are two ways to obtain the source code. The first option is to get it from the sample source code for this book and extract the file `9781430241071_ch21.zip` into your STS workspace. Another option is to check out the latest source code from the SpringBlog repository on GitHub. The URL for the repository of the SpringBlog application is `https://github.com/prospring3/springblog`.

After the source code is available on your development machine, import the project into STS. To import the project in STS, choose the menu option File ➤ Import, and on the Select screen, choose Existing Projects into Workspace under the General category, as shown in Figure 21-1.

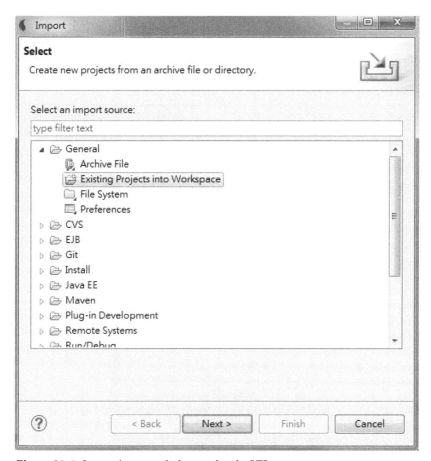

Figure 21-1. Importing an existing project in STS

Then, on the Import Projects screen, choose the project extracted from the sample source code, and then click Finish (see Figure 21-2).

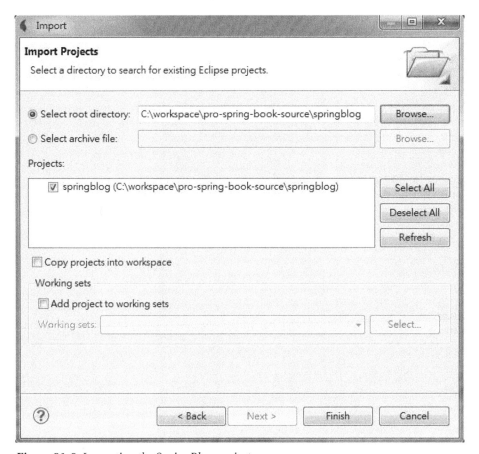

Figure 21-2. Importing the SpringBlog project

Then, you may need to wait for a while for the Maven plug-in to download the required dependencies and build the project.

Upon project import completion, define a tc Server instance for deploying the SpringBlog application. You can also choose to deploy on any existing tc Server instance in your STS. For detailed steps of creating a tc Server instance, please refer to Appendix A. Also make sure you add your project to the target tc Server and have the project classes and libraries published to the server (in other words, the project was built and deployed to the target tc Server). Figure 21-3 shows the Servers view in STS. For our case, the "base" template of a tc Server instance is good enough for the sample application.

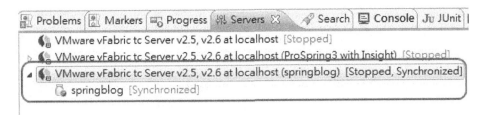

Figure 21-3. *Adding the SpringBlog project to tc Server in STS*

Start the tc Server. Then, open a browser and enter the URL
`http://localhost:8080/springblog/blogs`. You should see the initial page of the SpringBlog application,
like the one in Figure 21-4.

Figure 21-4. *The initial page of SpringBlog*

At this point, the project has been set up successfully. Note that, by default, the sample application doesn't include any sample blog entries. Please log in to the application (click the Hint button under the Login button for the default user accounts) and post some blog entries and comments to get some hands-on experience with the application.

Switching Between the MySQL and H2 Databases

By default, the SpringBlog application will initialize an embedded H2 database and run the required scripts accordingly, so no additional setup is required. However, the database scripts and application also work fine with MySQL. This section lists the procedure for setting up the application with a MySQL database so that you can keep track of the database records as you play around the application.

Listing 21-1 shows the content of the Spring configuration file /src/main/webapp/WEB-INF/spring /datasource.xml, which stores the datasource configuration for the SpringBlog application.

Listing 21-1. The Data Source Configuration File

```xml
<?xml version="1.0" encoding="UTF-8"?>
<beans xmlns="http://www.springframework.org/schema/beans"
    xmlns:xsi="http://www.w3.org/2001/XMLSchema-instance"
    xmlns:jdbc="http://www.springframework.org/schema/jdbc"
    xsi:schemaLocation="http://www.springframework.org/schema/beans
        http://www.springframework.org/schema/beans/spring-beans-3.1.xsd
        http://www.springframework.org/schema/jdbc
        http://www.springframework.org/schema/jdbc/spring-jdbc-3.1.xsd">

    <!-- For embedded JH2 database -->
    <beans profile="h2">
        <jdbc:embedded-database id="dataSource" type="H2">
            <jdbc:script location="classpath:sql/schema.sql"/>
            <jdbc:script location="classpath:/org/springframework/batch/core/schema-h2.sql"/>
            <jdbc:script location="classpath:sql/initial-data.sql"/>
        </jdbc:embedded-database>
    </beans>

    <!-- For MySQL database -->
    <beans profile="mysql">
        <bean id="dataSource" class="com.mchange.v2.c3p0.ComboPooledDataSource"
            destroy-method="close">
            <property name="driverClass" value="com.mysql.jdbc.Driver" />
            <property name="jdbcUrl" value="jdbc:mysql://localhost:3306/springblog" />
            <property name="user" value="springblog" />
            <property name="password" value="springblog" />
        </bean>
    </beans>

</beans>
```

In Listing 21-1, two different datasource beans are declared. Each bean is wrapped under the <beans> tag with a profile attribute provided. This is the new profile feature introduced in Spring Framework 3.1. So, depending on the active profile setting, Spring will initiate the dataSource bean accordingly.

When the profile is set to h2, the <jdbc:embedded-database> will initialize an embedded H2 database and run the scripts provided within the bean definition. We need to run three scripts (note that the order is important) for the SpringBlog application:

1. `schema.sql`: This is the data model for the SpringBlog application.

2. `schema-h2.sql`: This is the schema for the tables required by Spring Batch.

3. `initial-data.sql`: This is the initial data (users, roles, categories, and so on) for the SpringBlog application.

To set up MySQL, as shown in the `dataSource` bean definition for the `mysql` profile, in MySQL, set up a database called `springblog` and then a user with the user name and password both set to `springblog` (or you can change the datasource settings based on your preference). You then need to run the three scripts (`schema.sql`, `schema-mysql.sql`, `initial-data.sql`) in the folder `/src/main/resources/sql`, respectively. Note that the file `schema-mysql.sql` is for the creation of Spring Batch tables.

Next, we need to modify the active profile of Spring's `WebApplicationContext` to use the `dataSource` bean for MySQL. To change the active profile, we need to modify the setting in the web deployment descriptor file (`/WEB-INF/web.xml`), as in the code snippet shown in Listing 21-2.

Listing 21-2. Changing the Active Profile in the web.xml File

```xml
<?xml version="1.0" encoding="UTF-8"?>
<web-app version="2.5" xmlns="http://java.sun.com/xml/ns/javaee"
    xmlns:xsi="http://www.w3.org/2001/XMLSchema-instance"
    xsi:schemaLocation="http://java.sun.com/xml/ns/javaee
        http://java.sun.com/xml/ns/javaee/web-app_2_5.xsd">

    <!-- The definition of the Root Spring Container shared by all Servlets and Filters -->
    <!-- Enable escaping of form submission contents -->
    <context-param>
        <param-name>defaultHtmlEscape</param-name>
        <param-value>true</param-value>
    </context-param>
    <context-param>
        <param-name>spring.profiles.active</param-name>
        <!-- Spring profile parameters
            First profile: jpa - JPA implementation
                           mybatis - MyBatis implementation
            Second profile: mysql - MySQL DB
                            h2 - H2 database
        -->
        <param-value>jpa,h2</param-value>
    </context-param>
        <context-param>
            <param-name>contextConfigLocation</param-name>
            <param-value>
                /WEB-INF/spring/root-context.xml
                /WEB-INF/spring/datasource.xml
                /WEB-INF/spring/batch-context.xml
                /WEB-INF/spring/*-tx-config.xml
                /WEB-INF/spring/*-service-context.xml
            </param-value>
        </context-param>

    <!-- Other code omitted -->

</web-app>
```

In Listing 21-2, there are two profile values for the SpringBlog application. The first one controls the service layer implementation to use (jpa or mybatis), and the second (in bold) controls the datasource bean to initialize. To use MySQL, change the second profile value from h2 to mysql. When the project is rebuilt and deployed to tc Server, the application will run against the MySQL database.

Switching Between the JPA and MyBatis Implementations

As shown in the previous section, for the service layer, changing from an JPA 2 implementation to an MyBatis implementation is easy too. You just need to change the first profile value from jpa to mybatis. For example, for the parameter with the name spring.profiles.active, the value mybatis,mysql indicates to Spring to load the beans from the respective profiles, which will use the MyBatis implementation of the service layer and the dataSource bean for MySQL.

As mentioned in Chapter 5, one other method to set the active profile is using the launch configuration of tc Server. This will eliminate the need of modifying the web.xml file and repackaging the web application archive file.

To change the launch configuration, in STS's Servers view, double-click the tc Server that the SpringBlog application is running on, and click the link "Open launch configuration," as shown in Figure 21-5.

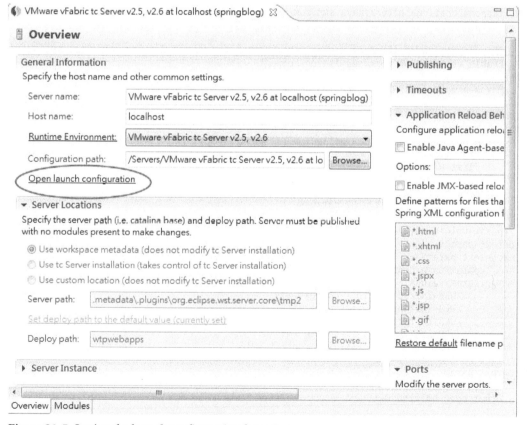

Figure 21-5. Setting the launch configuration for tc Server

Then in the dialog, click the Arguments tab, and add the parameter `-Dspring.profiles`
`.active="mybatis,mysql"` in the "VM arguments" text box, as shown in Figure 21-6.

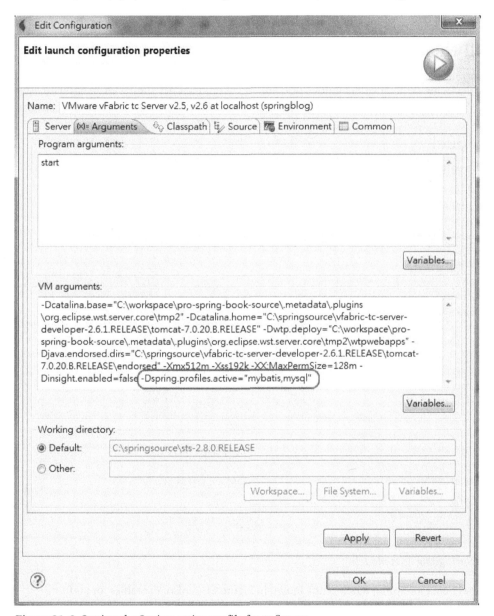

Figure 21-6. *Setting the Spring active profile for tc Server*

After changing the VM argument of the tc Server, the corresponding parameter can be removed from the web.xml file, and you can try the different combinations of service layer and backend RDBMS by simply changing the VM argument of the launch configuration of the tc Server.

Application Design

This section gives you an overview on the application design details. In the following sections, the various design aspects, including the data model, domain object model, UML model for major use cases, and so on, will be covered.

The Data Model

Let's start with the data model, shown in the entity-relationship diagram in Figure 21-7.

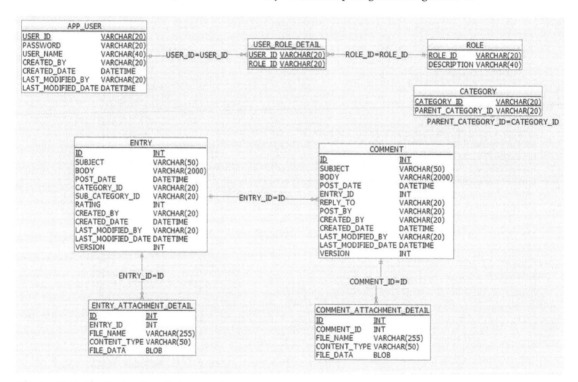

Figure 21-7. The SpringBlog data model

Note that the schema for Spring Batch is not shown in Figure 21-7. Also, the tables for auditing purposes (the ENTRY_H, COMMENT_H, and REVINFO tables, which will be populated by the Hibernate Envers module) are not shown here for clarity. For Figure 21-7, the table names and their purposes are listed in Table 21-1.

Table 21-1. SpringBlog Tables

Table Name	Purpose
APP_USER	This table stores the user information for security control with Spring Security. Users will be authenticated with the information in this table.
ROLE	This tables stores the available roles (in other words, normal user and administrator, as well as remote client) within the application.
USER_ROLE_DETAIL	This is the join table that stores the roles granted to each user.
CATEGORY	This tables stores the category for each blog post (for example, Java, JPA, Spring, and so on). A category can be a subcategory, and in this case, the column PARENT_CATEGORY_ID indicates the parent category.
ENTRY	This table stores the blog post entries.
ENTRY_ATTACHMENT_DETAIL	This table stores the attachments for blog post entries.
COMMENT	This table stores the comments to blog post entries. It has a many-to-one relationship to the ENTRY table.
COMMENT_ATTACHMENT_DETAIL	This table stores the attachments for comment entries.

Domain Object Model

Now let's proceed to the domain object model. As discussed in Chapter 12, the DOM is an object-based representation of the application problem domain. In SpringBlog, the domain is the information related to blog posts. The DOM is closely related to the data model, and in JEE applications, no matter whether you are using ORM or data mapping technology, there will be a "mapping" process in transforming the data model into Java's DOM. Figure 21-8 shows the DOM of the SpringBlog application.

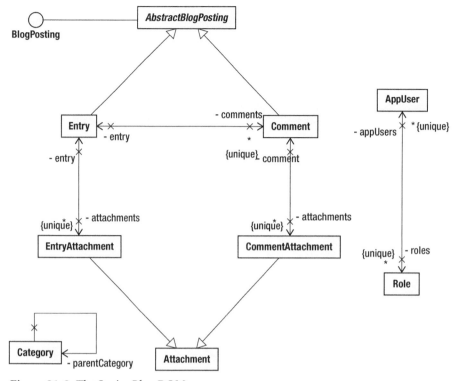

Figure 21-8. *The SpringBlog DOM*

As shown in Figure 21-8, there are some differences between the DOM and the data model in Figure 21-7:

- Both the Entry and Comment classes extend the AbstractBlogPosting class, which contains the common properties and behavior of an entry, whether it's a blog entry or comment. However, you will not see a table for the abstract class. It's the same case for the Attachment class. In addition, the AbstractBlogPosting class implements the BlogPosting interface, which the AOP obscenity filter will be based on whether or not the target object had this interface implemented to determine whether checking and obfuscation of obscenities are required.

- The relationship between the AppUser and Role classes is many-to-many, because an user can be granted multiple roles, and a role can be assigned to many users. From the data model, you will see a join table (USER_ROLE_DETAIL) that holds the relationship. While in the DOM, you will not see a class for the join table.

- The Category class has a self-referencing relationship to itself to indicate the hierarchy of the parent and subcategories.

The UML Model

The UML model contains various diagrams that reflect the behavior of the classes within the application. There are two main types of UML diagrams, namely, static and dynamic diagrams. A static diagram reflects the classes and their relationship from a design point of view, without indicating the interaction between the classes. Examples of static diagrams include use case diagrams and class diagrams. Dynamic diagrams indicate how the classes collaborate and interact with each other to complete a business flow. Examples include sequence diagrams, activity diagrams, collaboration diagrams, state diagrams, and so on.

In this section, we will focus on using sequence diagrams to reflect the flow and the interaction between the classes in the various application layers. In the following sections, we will discuss the sequence diagrams of three main use cases within the SpringBlog application, including creating a blog post entry, using RESTful-WS, and creating batch jobs.

Create Blog Post Entry

Let's take a look on the sequence diagram for creating a blog post entry, which is shown in Figure 21-9.

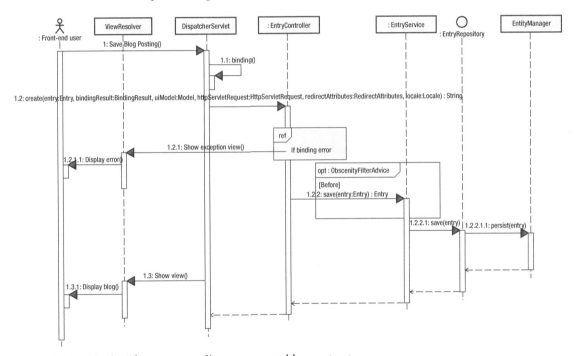

Figure 21-9. A SpringBlog sequence diagram: create blog post entry

In Figure 21-9, the sequence diagram shows the flow of the process of creating a blog post entry, as well as the interactions between the main classes within each layer, from the presentation layer down to the persistence layer. In this case, the JPA 2 implementation is used, and the flow is as follows:

1. The user logs into the SpringBlog application, creates a new entry, enters the information, and clicks the Save button. The browser will then submit a POST request to the server.

2. Spring MVC's DispatcherServlet receives the request, analyzes the details of the HTTP request, and identifies the controller method to invoke. In this case, the EntryController (under the package com.apress.prospring3.springblog

.web.blogapp.controller) class's create() method will be invoked. At the same time, binding for the request data into the corresponding domain object will be performed. The entire binding process includes validation, conversion, and formatting.

3. Within the EntryController.create() method, the BindingResult argument will be checked first to see whether there exists any error. If an error occurs, a message will be saved into the Model instance, and the edit page will be redisplayed with the error messages.

4. If the binding process succeeds, the controller will invoke the save() method of the EntryService interface (under the package com.apress.prospring3.springblog.service), passing in the Entry object as the argument. Note that since we are using the JPA 2 implementation, the implementation class EntryServiceImpl (under the package com.apress.prospring3.springblog.service.jpa) will be used. At the same time, a before advice will be applied (we will see the details later) to check for obscenities in the blog post.

5. The EntryServiceImpl class will persist the blog post entry by invoking the persistence provider. In the JPA 2 implementation, Spring Data JPA's repository abstraction will be used (the EntryRepository interface under the package com.apress.prospring3.springblog.repository), which will in turn invoke the underlying Hibernate EntityManager for persisting the data into the backend RDBMS.

6. After the saving operation succeeds, the controller will return the logical view (in this case in the show blog page). The DispatchServlet will pass the logical view name to the ViewResolver. The ViewResolver will resolve the corresponding view (based on the configuration) for displaying the frontend to the user.

Remember that for simplicity, the interactions with some of the components were skipped. For example, Spring Security's SecurityFilterChain will intercept each request for authorization purposes.

RESTful-WS for RSS Feed of Blog Post Entries

The second use case is the RSS feed that outputs the blog post entries in either XML or JSON format to the HTTP remote clients. Before we discuss the diagram, let's take a look at how the feed works first. To retrieve the RSS feed in XML format, submit the curl command in Listing 21-3 with the SpringBlog application up and running.

Listing 21-3. Command for the RSS Feed in XML Format

```
curl -v -u remote:remote -H "Accept: application/xml"↵
 http://localhost:8080/springblog/restful/blog/listdata
```

In Listing 21-3, the user name for remote access to SpringBlog's RESTful-WS is provided, together with the URL for the RSS feed. The request header is set to accept XML as the supported format. Figure 21-10 shows the output in XML format.

```
C:\  命令提示字元

* Connected to localhost () port 8080 (#0)
* Server auth using Basic with user 'remote'
> GET /springblog/restful/blog/listdata HTTP/1.1
> Authorization: Basic cmVtb3RlOnJlbW90ZQ==
> User-Agent: curl/7.21.0 (amd64-pc-win32) libcurl/7.21.0 OpenSSL/0.9.8o zlib/1.2.3
> Host: localhost:8080
> Accept: application/xml
>
< HTTP/1.1 200 OK
< Server: Apache-Coyote/1.1
< Content-Type: application/xml;charset=UTF-8
< Transfer-Encoding: chunked
< Date: Sat, 28 Jan 2012 05:40:36 GMT
<
<?xml version="1.0" encoding="UTF-8"?>
<entries>
    <entry>
        <id>1</id>
        <subject>Welcome to SpringBlog</subject>
        <category>Spring</category>
        <subCategory></subCategory>
        <body>&lt;p&gt;&#xd;
        Welcome to SpringBlog application!&lt;/p&gt;&#xd;
</body>
        <postDate>2012-01-28</postDate>
        <postBy>clarence</postBy>
        <lastModifiedDate>2012-01-28</lastModifiedDate>
        <lastModifiedBy>clarence</lastModifiedBy>
        <version>0</version>
    </entry>
    <entry>
        <id>2</id>
        <subject>Spring Framework 3.1</subject>
        <category>Spring</category>
        <subCategory></subCategory>
        <body>&lt;p&gt;&#xd;
        Spring Framework 3.1 rocks!&lt;/p&gt;&#xd;
</body>
        <postDate>2012-01-28</postDate>
        <postBy>clarence</postBy>
        <lastModifiedDate>2012-01-28</lastModifiedDate>
        <lastModifiedBy>clarence</lastModifiedBy>
        <version>0</version>
    </entry>
</entries>
```

Figure 21-10. The RSS feed in XML format

Listing 21-4 shows the command for requesting data in JSON format.

Listing 21-4. Command for the RSS Feed in JSON Format

```
curl -v -u remote:remote -H "Accept: application/json"↵
 http://localhost:8080/springblog/restful/blog/listdata
```

The only difference with the previous command is that the supported media of the request header is set to JSON format. Figure 21-11 shows the response in JSON format.

```
CM 命令提示字元

* About to connect() to localhost port 8080 (#0)
* connected
* Connected to localhost () port 8080 (#0)
* Server auth using Basic with user 'remote'
> GET /springblog/restful/blog/listdata HTTP/1.1
> Authorization: Basic cmVtb3RlOnJlbW90ZQ==
> User-Agent: curl/7.21.0 (amd64-pc-win32) libcurl/7.21.0 OpenSSL/0.9.8o zlib/1.2.3
> Host: localhost:8080
> Accept: application/json
>
< HTTP/1.1 200 OK
< Server: Apache-Coyote/1.1
< Content-Type: application/json;charset=UTF-8
< Transfer-Encoding: chunked
< Date: Sat, 28 Jan 2012 05:41:22 GMT
<
{"entries":[{"id":1,"subject":"Welcome to SpringBlog","postDate":1327680000000,"createdBy":"clarence","createdDate":
728026664,"lastModifiedBy":"clarence","lastModifiedDate":1327728026664,"version":0,"categoryId":"Spring","subCategor
:"","shortBody":"<p>\r\n\tWelcome to SpringBlog application!</p>\r\n","new":false,"postDateString":"2012-01-28","las
ifiedDateString":"2012-01-28 13:20:26"},{"id":2,"subject":"Spring Framework 3.1","postDate":1327680000000,"createdBy
larence","createdDate":1327728053036,"lastModifiedBy":"clarence","lastModifiedDate":1327728053036,"version":0,"categ
d":"Spring","subCategoryId":"","shortBody":"<p>\r\n\tSpring Framework 3.1 rocks!</p>\r\n","new":false,"postDateStrin
2012-01-28","lastModifiedDateString":"2012-01-28 13:20:53"}]}* Connection #0 to host localhost left intact
* Closing connection #0
```

Figure 21-11. The RSS feed in JSON format

Now let's see how RESTful-WS for the RSS feed works. Figure 21-12 shows the sequence diagram of the RESTful-WS feed in action.

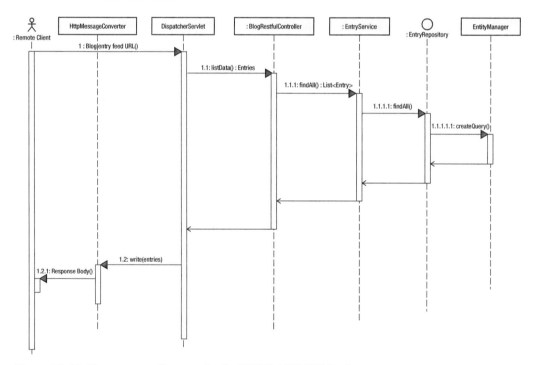

Figure 21-12. The sequence diagram for the RESTful-WS RSS feed

790

For the backend service interaction, the sequence diagram works the same as the use case for creating a blog post entry, as shown in Figure 21-9. The main difference is on the presentation layer. Based on the request URL, the DispatcherServlet will dispatch the request to the BlogRestfulController class's listData() method. In turn, the controller will invoke the service layer to retrieve the list of blog post entries.

Then, the resulting Entries class (which includes the listing Entry domain objects) will be returned by the controller. The result will be directly written to the response body. In Spring MVC, as you will see later in the configuration, the HttpMessageConverter<T> will be invoked to transform the object into the format requested by the client. Either the JSON converter (the org.springframework.http.converter .json.MappingJacksonHttpMessageConverter class) or the XML converter (org.springframework.http .converter.xml.MarshallingHttpMessageConverter) will be invoked, depending on the request header of the client.

The Batch Job for Importing Blog Posts from an XML File

Another use case is the batch import of blog post entries from XML files. Let's see it in action. First make sure that the SpringBlog application is up and running, and then place the file (with the name entries.xml; a copy of the file exists in the project's root folder) into the folder C:\temp\entries (configured in the <file:inbound-channel-adapter> bean in the file batch-context.xml). Listing 21-5 shows the content of entries.xml with a single blog post entry.

Listing 21-5. The XML File with Blog Post Entry

```
<?xml version="1.0" encoding="UTF-8"?>
<entries>
    <entry>
        <subject>SpringBlog by batch</subject>
        <category>Spring</category>
        <subCategory>Spring Batch</subCategory>
        <body>
            Testing SpringBlog posting entry by batch upload
        </body>
    </entry>
</entries>
```

By default, Spring Integration will poll for a file every five seconds (also defined in the file batch-context.xml). Then, when you visit the application frontend, you will notice that the entry was imported into SpringBlog, as shown in Figure 21-13.

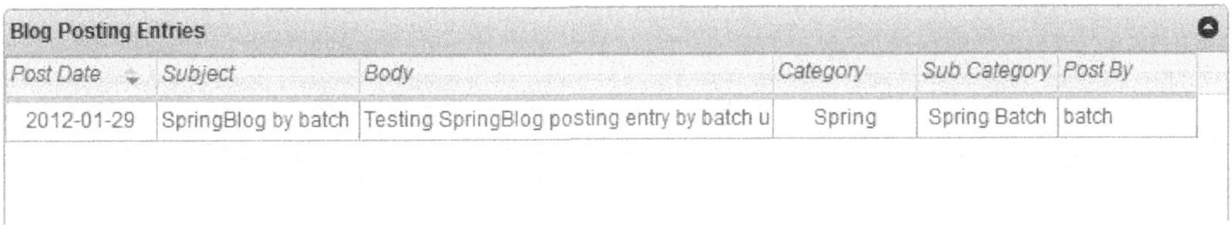

Blog Posting Entries					
Post Date ⏷	Subject	Body	Category	Sub Category	Post By
2012-01-29	SpringBlog by batch	Testing SpringBlog posting entry by batch u	Spring	Spring Batch	batch

Figure 21-13. The imported RSS feed in SpringBlog

The entire job import process is composed of two main parts, namely, job launching and job execution. Figure 21-14 shows the sequence diagram of the job launching process.

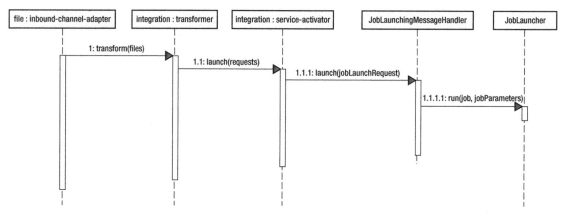

Figure 21-14. *The job launching process*

The main flow of the job launching process is as follows:

1. Spring Integration's inbound channel adapter polls the file for new entries.

2. Upon the arrival of a file, the transformer will transform the information into a job launch request message.

3. Spring Integration's service activator receives the job launch request message and passes it to the corresponding message handler. In our case, the message handler is the JobLaunchingMessageHandler class (under the package org.springframework.batch.integration.launch), which belongs to the Spring Batch Integration module within the Spring Batch Admin project.

4. When you look into the configuration of the messageHandler bean defined within the <integration:service-activator> bean in the batch-context.xml file, the constructor argument of the message handler is the job launcher (the JobLauncher interface under the package org.springframework.batch.core.launch, which belongs to Spring Batch). The message handler will run the job with the transformed job parameters.

The next phase is job execution, which is shown in Figure 21-15.

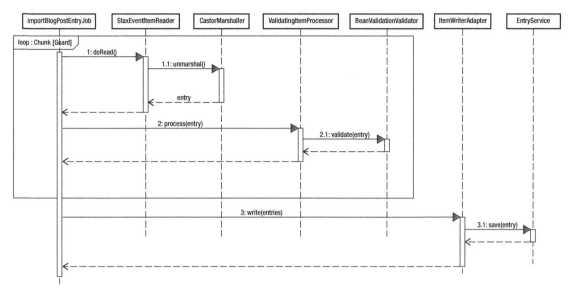

Figure 21-15. The job execution process

As you can see from Figure 21-15, Spring Batch will process each item on a chunk basis, which includes the following steps:

1.   Read in each item, and invoke Castor's marshaler to unmarshal the XML fragment into the corresponding Entry object.

2.   The Entry object is then passed to the item processor, which will perform JSR-303 Beans Validation on the Entry object.

After the items within a chunk are processed, the writer will be invoked to write the processed entries. In our case, the ItemWriterAdapter<T> class (under the package org.springframework.batch.item.adapter) will be invoked to dedicate the writing process to the SpringBlog's service layer for saving each entry.

Configuration Details

Having discussed the design details, let's proceed to the configuration of the SpringBlog application. In the following sections, we will discuss the various configurations of the application, from web deployment descriptor to Spring's WebApplicationContext hierarchy.

The Web Deployment Descriptor Configuration

Let's take a look on the web deployment descriptor (web.xml), which is shown in Listing 21-6.

Listing 21-6. The web.xml File

```
<?xml version="1.0" encoding="UTF-8"?>
<web-app version="2.5" xmlns="http://java.sun.com/xml/ns/javaee"
    xmlns:xsi="http://www.w3.org/2001/XMLSchema-instance"
```

```xml
    xsi:schemaLocation="http://java.sun.com/xml/ns/javaee
    http://java.sun.com/xml/ns/javaee/web-app_2_5.xsd">

<!-- The definition of the Root Spring Container shared by all Servlets and Filters -->
<!-- Enable escaping of form submission contents -->
<context-param>
    <param-name>defaultHtmlEscape</param-name>
    <param-value>true</param-value>
</context-param>
<context-param>
    <param-name>spring.profiles.active</param-name>
    <!-- Spring profile parameters
        First profile: jpa - JPA implementation
                       mybatis - MyBatis implementation
        Second profile: mysql - MySQL DB
                        h2 - H2 database
    -->
    <param-value>jpa,h2</param-value>
</context-param>
<context-param>
    <param-name>contextConfigLocation</param-name>
        <param-value>
            /WEB-INF/spring/root-context.xml
            /WEB-INF/spring/datasource.xml
            /WEB-INF/spring/batch-context.xml
            /WEB-INF/spring/*-tx-config.xml
            /WEB-INF/spring/*-service-context.xml
        </param-value>
    </context-param>

<!-- Spring Security Configuration -->
<filter>
    <filter-name>springSecurityFilterChain</filter-name>
    <filter-class>org.springframework.web.filter.DelegatingFilterProxy</filter-class>
</filter>

<filter-mapping>
    <filter-name>springSecurityFilterChain</filter-name>
    <url-pattern>/*</url-pattern>
</filter-mapping>

<filter>
    <filter-name>CharacterEncodingFilter</filter-name>
    <filter-class>org.springframework.web.filter.CharacterEncodingFilter</filter-class>
    <init-param>
        <param-name>encoding</param-name>
        <param-value>UTF-8</param-value>
    </init-param>
    <init-param>
        <param-name>forceEncoding</param-name>
        <param-value>true</param-value>
    </init-param>
</filter>
```

```xml
    <filter>
        <filter-name>HttpMethodFilter</filter-name>
        <filter-class>org.springframework.web.filter.HiddenHttpMethodFilter</filter-class>
    </filter>

    <!-- Need to comment out the following filter for MyBatis -->
    <filter>
        <filter-name>Spring OpenEntityManagerInViewFilter</filter-name>
        <filter-class>org.springframework.orm.jpa.support.OpenEntityManagerInViewFilter↵
</filter-class>
    </filter>

    <filter-mapping>
        <filter-name>CharacterEncodingFilter</filter-name>
        <url-pattern>/*</url-pattern>
    </filter-mapping>

    <filter-mapping>
        <filter-name>HttpMethodFilter</filter-name>
        <url-pattern>/*</url-pattern>
    </filter-mapping>

    <!-- Need to comment out the following filter for MyBatis -->
    <filter-mapping>
        <filter-name>Spring OpenEntityManagerInViewFilter</filter-name>
        <url-pattern>/*</url-pattern>
    </filter-mapping>

    <!-- Creates the Spring Container shared by all Servlets and Filters -->
    <listener>
        <listener-class>org.springframework.web.context.ContextLoaderListener</listener-class>
    </listener>

    <!-- Spring MVC Dispatcher Servlet for SpringBlog application -->
    <servlet>
        <servlet-name>blogAppServlet</servlet-name>
        <servlet-class>org.springframework.web.servlet.DispatcherServlet</servlet-class>
        <init-param>
            <param-name>contextConfigLocation</param-name>
            <param-value>/WEB-INF/spring/blogapp-webmvc-config.xml</param-value>
        </init-param>
        <load-on-startup>1</load-on-startup>
        <multipart-config>
            <max-file-size>5000000</max-file-size>
        </multipart-config>
    </servlet>

    <servlet-mapping>
        <servlet-name>blogAppServlet</servlet-name>
        <url-pattern>/</url-pattern>
    </servlet-mapping>

    <!-- Spring MVC Dispatcher Servlet for RESTful-WS -->
    <servlet>
```

```
        <servlet-name>restful</servlet-name>
        <servlet-class>org.springframework.web.servlet.DispatcherServlet</servlet-class>
        <init-param>
            <param-name>contextConfigLocation</param-name>
            <param-value>/WEB-INF/spring/restful-context.xml</param-value>
        </init-param>
        <load-on-startup>1</load-on-startup>
    </servlet>

    <servlet-mapping>
        <servlet-name>restful</servlet-name>
        <url-pattern>/restful/*</url-pattern>
    </servlet-mapping>

</web-app>
```

In Listing 21-6, first several context parameters (with the `<context-param>` tag) are defined. As discussed in previous section, the parameter `spring.profiles.active` defines the active profiles for Spring's `WebApplicationContext`, which can also be replaced with tc Server's launch configuration (by defining the active profile as JVM argument). Then, the `contextConfigLocation` parameter instructs Spring about the location of the configuration files to load from. Note the use of wildcards to load configurations from various profiles; the `WebApplicationContext` hierarchy will be described in next section.

Then a number of filters are declared. The filters are used by Spring Security and Spring MVC for processing incoming requests. For a detailed description, please refer to Chapter 17.

Finally, two Spring `DispatcherServlets` are defined. The `blogAppServlet` servlet defines the configuration for the web frontend, while the `restful` servlet is for the RESTful-WS configuration.

The Spring WebApplicationContext Hierarchy

For Spring's `WebApplicationContext` configuration, the files are all located under the folder `/WEB-INF/spring`. The file names and purposes are listed in Table 21-2.

Table 21-2. SpringBlog WebApplicationContext Configuration Files

Table Name	Purpose
root-context.xml	Defines the main configuration that should be available for the entire SpringBlog application.
security-context.xml	Defines the authentication and authorization configurations for the SpringBlog application. Role-based access rules to all protected resources (including web frontend and RESTful-WS) are defined here. It is imported by the root-context.xml file.
datasource.xml	Defines the backend RDBMS datasource configuration.
batch-context.xml	Defines the configuration for Spring Integration and Spring Batch. Used for the batch job for importing blog post entries from XML files.

Table Name	Purpose
jpa-tx-config.xml	Defines the transaction and JPA entity manager configuration for the JPA profile.
mybatis-tx-config.xml	Defines the transaction and MyBatis session factory configuration for the MyBatis profile.
jpa-service-context.xml	Defines the service layer configuration of JPA profile. For example, only the Spring beans for the JPA implementation will be scanned.
mybatis-service-context.xml	Defines the service layer configuration of the MyBatis profile. For example, only the Spring beans for the MyBatis implementation will be scanned.
blogapp-webmvc-config.xml	Defines the WebApplicationContext configuration for the blogAppServlet servlet.
restful-context.xml	Defines the WebApplicationContext configuration for the restful servlet.

Figure 21-16 shows the logical view of the WebApplicationContext hierarchy.

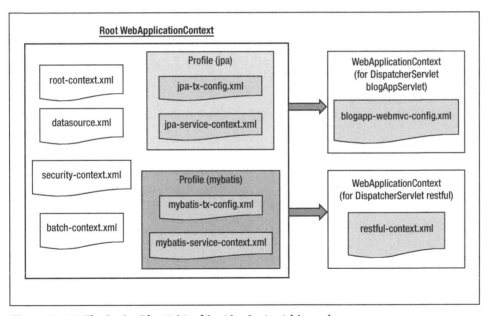

Figure 21-16. The SpringBlog WebApplicationContext hierarchy

In Figure 21-16, the root WebApplicationContext contains the Spring configuration for the components that will be shared by all of DispatcherServlet's WebApplicationContext. Within the root

WebApplicationContext, the security configuration, datasource setup (for both the MySQL and H2 database profiles), batch job configuration, and the service layer and persistence configurations (for both the JPA and MyBatis profiles) are defined.

You can find detailed descriptions of each configuration file by referring to the corresponding chapters. For example, the JPA-related configuration appears in Chapter 10, the MyBatis configuration is in Chapter 11, the Spring Batch and Integration configurations are in Chapter 20, and so on.

The AspectJ Load-Time Weaving Configuration

As mentioned in Chapter 7, for the obscenity filter feature, we will use Spring's AspectJ annotation style (for example, @Aspect, and so on) to implement a before advice for the implementation. To enable this support, we need to enable load-time weaving (LTW) support of the Spring Framework for AspectJ in the web container environment. Because we will use tc Server for running the SpringBlog application, this section will cover the procedure for setting up LTW support for an application in tc Server. However, the procedure is the same for Apache Tomcat.

First we need to configure LTW support in Spring's WebApplicationContext. In SpringBlog, the setting is defined in the root-context.xml file, which is shown in Listing 21-7.

Listing 21-7. The root-context.xml File

```xml
<?xml version="1.0" encoding="UTF-8"?>
<beans xmlns="http://www.springframework.org/schema/beans"
    xmlns:xsi="http://www.w3.org/2001/XMLSchema-instance"
    xmlns:context="http://www.springframework.org/schema/context"
    xmlns:aop="http://www.springframework.org/schema/aop"
    xmlns:util="http://www.springframework.org/schema/util"
    xmlns:task="http://www.springframework.org/schema/task"
    xsi:schemaLocation="http://www.springframework.org/schema/beans
      http://www.springframework.org/schema/beans/spring-beans-3.0.xsd
      http://www.springframework.org/schema/context
      http://www.springframework.org/schema/context/spring-context-3.1.xsd
      http://www.springframework.org/schema/task
      http://www.springframework.org/schema/task/spring-task-3.1.xsd
      http://www.springframework.org/schema/aop
      http://www.springframework.org/schema/aop/spring-aop-3.1.xsd
      http://www.springframework.org/schema/util
      http://www.springframework.org/schema/util/spring-util-3.1.xsd">

    <!-- Application properties -->
    <context:property-placeholder location="classpath:springblog.properties"/>

    <!-- Enable AspectJ Load Time Weaving -->
    <aop:aspectj-autoproxy/>
    <context:load-time-weaver/>

    <!-- Import security context -->
    <import resource="security-context.xml"/>

    <!-- Enable Task Scheduling support with annotation -->
    <task:scheduler id="myScheduler" pool-size="10"/>
    <task:annotation-driven scheduler="myScheduler"/>
```

```
<!-- Enable JSR-303 Bean Validation API -->
<bean id="validator" class="org.springframework.validation.beanvalidation↵
.LocalValidatorFactoryBean"/>

<!-- List of words to be replaced by Obscenities Filter -->
<util:list id="obscenities">
    <value>crap</value>
</util:list>

</beans>
```

In Listing 21-7, the LTW-related configuration is highlighted in bold. First, the `<aop:aspectj-autoproxy>` tag instructs Spring to support AspectJ-style AOP configuration and to create Spring-based AOP proxies behind the scene. Second, the `<context:load-time-weaver>` tag enables the LTW feature of the Spring Framework for weaving the classes with a special class loader.

Then, we need to copy the Spring Framework's instrument support of the Tomcat class loader to the web container's library folder. For Tomcat, the file name is `org.springframework.instrument.tomcat-3.1.0.RELEASE.jar`; it can be found either in the download package of the Spring Framework or at Maven Central. Obtain the library and copy it to the `lib` folder of the Tomcat server. For example, on my PC, Tomcat is located at `C:\apache-tomcat-7.0.25`, so I will copy the JAR file into the folder `C:\apache-tomcat-7.0.25\lib`.

One bit of good news for STS users is that for tc Server, the library will be there as you create new tc Server instances. Figure 21-17 shows the folder for the tc Server instance called `springblog`, which was created for deploying the sample application.

Figure 21-17. The Spring LTW library for Tomcat

Next, we need to provide information to Tomcat about the LTW mechanism we will use in the SpringBlog application. We can either do it in the tc Server's configuration or create related configuration files within the SpringBlog project. In the sample application, we created the related configuration files in the project so that we don't need to modify the server's configuration.

In the folder `/src/main/webapp/META-INF`, you will see the files `context.xml` and `aop.xml`, with the content shown in Listings 21-8 and 21-9, respectively.

Listing 21-8. The `context.xml` File

```
<Context path="/springblog">
<Loader
    loaderClass="org.springframework.instrument.classloading.tomcat↵
.TomcatInstrumentableClassLoader"
    useSystemClassLoaderAsParent="false" />
</Context>
```

Listing 21-9. The aop.xml File

```xml
<aspectj>
    <weaver>
        <!-- only weave classes in our application-specific packages -->
        <include within="com.apress.prospring3.springblog.*" />
    </weaver>
    <aspects>
        <aspect
            name="org.springframework.beans.factory.aspectj.AnnotationBeanConfigurerAspect" />
        <aspect
            name="org.springframework.transaction.aspectj.AnnotationTransactionAspect" />
    </aspects>
</aspectj>
```

In Listing 21-8, in the context.xml file, we instruct tc Server to use the class loader provided by the Spring Framework, which supports LTW of classes in Spring's WebApplicationContext. In Listing 21-9, the aop.xml file defines the LTW configuration for AspectJ. First, we provide the package under which Spring's AspectJ support should weave the classes. Second, the <aspects> tag defines the aspects to use. For the SpringBlog application, only two are required. The AnnotationBeanConfigurerAspect aspect (the suffix is .aj) supports the aspect class with the annotation @Configurable, which marks a class as being eligible for Spring-driven configuration. The AnnotationTransactionAspect aspect enables the support of @Transactional annotations in the service layer.

For the coding side, we will discuss the implementation of the obscenity filter in detail in a later section.

Implementation Details

Having discussed the design and configuration details, let's proceed to the implementation details. Since the code base is quite large, it's not possible to cover all the classes in detail. So, in the following sections, we will focus the discussion on the major implementation classes and a high-level overview of each layer. Topics include implementing the service layer, implementing AOP, scheduling jobs, implementing the presentation layer, and so on.

Service Layer Implementation

As mentioned in Chapter 3, for the service layer, implementations for using both JPA 2 (with Hibernate and Spring Data JPA) and MyBatis as the persistence provider will be developed. The details of the respective implementations will be covered in the following sections. In this section, we will focus the discussion on the services related to blog post entry.

Listing 21-10 shows the EntryService interface, which defines the services provided by SpringBlog for blog post entry and will be implemented by both the JPA 2 and MyBatis implementation classes.

Listing 21-10. The EntryService Interface

```java
package com.apress.prospring3.springblog.service;

import java.util.List;

import org.springframework.data.domain.Page;
```

```
import org.springframework.data.domain.Pageable;

import com.apress.prospring3.springblog.domain.Entry;
import com.apress.prospring3.springblog.domain.SearchCriteria;

public interface EntryService {

    public List<Entry> findAll();

    public Entry findById(Long id);

    public List<Entry> findByCategoryId(String categoryId);

    public Entry save(Entry entry);

    public void delete(Entry entry);

    public Page<Entry> findAllByPage(Pageable pageable);

    public Page<Entry> findEntryByCriteria(SearchCriteria searchCriteria, Pageable pageable);

}
```

In Listing 21-10, various finder methods, some with pagination support, and the data update (including insert, update, and delete operations) are defined. To keep the discussion simple, we will focus on the implementation of the save() method, which is highlighted in bold.

For the details about the design and implementation of the DOM for blog post entry, see Chapter 12. If you haven't read the chapter, it's time to take a look at it to understand the design of the domain object model.

JPA Service Implementation

For the JPA 2 implementation of the service layer, Hibernate will be used as the persistence provider. In addition, Spring Data JPA's repository abstraction will be used to simplify the development of persistence logic. As mentioned in the section "The Spring WebApplicationContext Hierarchy," the configuration for the JPA implementation is provided in the files jpa-tx-config.xml and jpa-service-context.xml files. For a detailed explanation of the configuration, please refer to Chapter 10.

Spring Data JPA's repository abstraction will be used for persistence logic, so we need to implement the repository interface for the Entry object. Listing 21-11 shows the EntryRepository interface.

Listing 21-11. The EntryRepository Interface

```
package com.apress.prospring3.springblog.repository;

import java.util.List;

import org.joda.time.DateTime;
import org.springframework.data.domain.Page;
import org.springframework.data.domain.Pageable;
import org.springframework.data.jpa.repository.Query;
import org.springframework.data.repository.PagingAndSortingRepository;
import org.springframework.data.repository.query.Param;
```

```
import com.apress.prospring3.springblog.domain.Entry;

public interface EntryRepository extends PagingAndSortingRepository<Entry, Long> {

    public List<Entry> findByCategoryId(String categoryId);

    @Query("select e from Entry e where e.subject like :subject and e.categoryId like↵
    :categoryId and e.postDate between :fromPostDate and :toPostDate")
    public Page<Entry> findEntryByCriteria(
        @Param("subject") String subject,
        @Param("categoryId") String categoryId,
        @Param("fromPostDate") DateTime fromPostDate,
        @Param("toPostDate") DateTime toPostDate, Pageable pageable);
}
```

In Listing 21-11, the EntryRespository interface extends Spring Data Commons' PagingAndSortingRepository<T,ID extends Serializable> interface in order to provide basic CRUD operation, as well as support the paging and sorting functions required by the presentation layer. Because PagingAndSortingRepository<T,ID extends Serializable> already provided the save() method, we don't need to define the method within the EntryRepository interface.

Listing 21-12 shows the code snippet for the implementation of the save() method.

Listing 21-12. The EntryServiceImpl Class for JPA 2 Implementation

```
package com.apress.prospring3.springblog.service.jpa;

// Import statements omitted

@Service("entryService")
@Repository
@Transactional
public class EntryServiceImpl implements EntryService{

    @Autowired
    private EntryRepository entryRepository;

    // Other code omitted

    @Override
    public Entry save(Entry entry) {
        // If new entry, set post date to current date
        if (entry.getId() == null) {
            entry.setPostDate(new DateTime());
        }
        return entryRepository.save(entry);
    }
}
```

In Listing 21-12, the class is located under the package com.apress.prospring3.springblog .service.jpa, which contains the JPA 2 implementation for all service layer interfaces. The EntryRepository interface is autowired into the class. The save() method will be used for both insert and update operations, and first, the id property will be checked. If it's null, then it's a new object, and the postDate property will be set as the current date. Then, the CrudRepository<T,ID extends

Serializable>.save() method (inherited from the PagingAndSortingRepository<T,ID extends Serializable> interface) will be invoked to persist the object via Hibernate.

MyBatis Service Implementation

For the MyBatis implementation of the service layer, the SQL mapping XML configuration will be used to define the mapping between SQL and the DOM. As mentioned in the section "The Spring WebApplicationContext Hierarchy," the configuration of the MyBatis implementation is provided in the files mybatis-tx-config.xml and mybatis-service-context.xml. For a detailed explanation of the configuration, please refer to Chapter 11.

Listing 21-12 shows the content of the mapper file for the Entry object (file name EntryMapper.xml, located in the folder /src/main/resources/com/apress/prospring3/springblog/persistence).

Listing 21-13. The EntryMapper.xml File

```xml
<?xml version="1.0" encoding="UTF-8"?>
<!DOCTYPE mapper PUBLIC "-//mybatis.org//DTD Mapper 3.0//EN"
"http://mybatis.org/dtd/mybatis-3-mapper.dtd">

<mapper namespace="com.apress.prospring3.springblog.persistence.EntryMapper">

    <!-- Other code omitted -->

    <insert id="insertEntry" parameterType="Entry" useGeneratedKeys="true" keyProperty="id">
        INSERT INTO ENTRY (SUBJECT, BODY, POST_DATE, CATEGORY_ID, SUB_CATEGORY_ID,
            CREATED_BY, CREATED_DATE, LAST_MODIFIED_BY, LAST_MODIFIED_DATE)
        VALUES (#{subject}, #{body}, #{postDate}, #{categoryId}, #{subCategoryId},
            #{createdBy}, #{createdDate}, #{lastModifiedBy}, #{lastModifiedDate})
    </insert>

</mapper>
```

If you read Chapter 11, Listing 21-13 should look familiar to you. The insertEntry mapping constructs the SQL INSERT statement based on the provided Entry object, the attribute useGeneratedKeys instructs MyBatis to use the key generated by the backend RDBMS (H2 or MySQL), and the keyProperty attribute indicates the property for the primary key column.

Listing 21-14 shows the code snippet for the implementation of the save() method.

Listing 21-14. The EntryServiceImpl Class for MyBatis Implementation

```java
package com.apress.prospring3.springblog.service.mybatis;

// Import statement omitted

@Service("entryService")
@Repository
@Transactional
public class EntryServiceImpl implements EntryService {

    @Autowired
    private EntryMapper entryMapper;
```

```
    // Other code omitted

    @Override
    public Entry save(Entry entry) {
        if (entry.getId() == null) {
            entryMapper.insertEntry(entry);
        } else {
            entryMapper.updateEntry(entry);
        }
        return entry;
    }
}
```

In Listing 21-14, the EntryMapper interface, which will be created dynamically based on the declaration of the anonymous bean with class org.mybatis.spring.mapper.MapperScannerConfigurer in the file mybatis-tx-config.xml, is autowired into the class. Then, in the save() method, the id property will be checked for whether it's a new object. If it's a new object, the insertEntry() method will be invoked, and MyBatis will use the mapping definition with an ID of insertEntry to construct the INSERT statement.

Remember that as mentioned in Chapter 10, for the JPA 2 implementation, the auditing feature of Spring Data JPA was used to populate the basic audit information, including the create date and creator, last modified date, and last modifier for each Entry object. In MyBatis, there is no such equivalent. As a result, the MyBatis plug-in feature is used to implement the logic to update the fields accordingly before the insert operation. Listing 21-15 shows the MyBatis plug-in class for updating basic audit information.

Listing 21-15. The MyBatisPlugin Class

```
package com.apress.prospring3.springblog.mybatis.plugin;

import java.util.Properties;

import org.apache.ibatis.executor.Executor;
import org.apache.ibatis.executor.parameter.DefaultParameterHandler;
import org.apache.ibatis.mapping.MappedStatement;
import org.apache.ibatis.plugin.Interceptor;
import org.apache.ibatis.plugin.Intercepts;
import org.apache.ibatis.plugin.Invocation;
import org.apache.ibatis.plugin.Signature;
import org.joda.time.DateTime;
import org.springframework.beans.factory.annotation.Autowired;
import org.springframework.data.domain.Auditable;

import com.apress.prospring3.springblog.auditor.AuditorAwareBean;

@Intercepts(
    {@Signature(type = Executor.class, method = "update",
        args = {MappedStatement.class, Object.class }) }
)
public class MyBatisPlugin implements Interceptor {

    @Autowired
    private AuditorAwareBean auditorAwareBean;

    @Override
```

```
    public Object intercept(Invocation invocation) throws Throwable {
        return invocation.proceed();
    }

    @Override
    public Object plugin(Object target) {

        if (target instanceof DefaultParameterHandler) {
            DefaultParameterHandler paramHandler = (DefaultParameterHandler) target;
            Object obj = paramHandler.getParameterObject();

            if (obj != null) {

                if (obj instanceof Auditable) {

                    DateTime currentTimeStamp = new DateTime();
                    String currentUser = auditorAwareBean.getCurrentAuditor();

                    Auditable auditable = (Auditable) obj;
                    if (auditable.getCreatedDate() == null) {
                        auditable.setCreatedDate(currentTimeStamp);
                        auditable.setCreatedBy(currentUser);
                    }
                    auditable.setLastModifiedBy(currentUser);
                    auditable.setLastModifiedDate(currentTimeStamp);

                }
            }
        }

        return target;
    }

    @Override
    public void setProperties(Properties properties) {
    }
}
```

In Listing 21-15, the MyBatis @Intercepts annotation is used to indicate to MyBatis that this class will intercept MyBatis operations. The nested @Signature annotation defines the class, method, and argument that we want to intercept. In our case, it's the update operation.

Within the class, the MyBatis Interceptor interface is implemented. The main logic for updating the audit properties of the domain object is in the plugin() method. In the method, we check whether the target object is of type DefaultParameterHandler, which MyBatis uses for mapping the domain object properties into the SQL statements. If that's the case, we will check whether the domain object contains auditable properties by checking whether the class is assignable to the Spring Data Commons Auditable interface, since all domain objects with those auditing properties implement that interface.

If all the conditions match, then the audit fields will be updated accordingly before MyBatis performs the mapping operation. As you saw, the MyBatis plug-in system is the trick for intercepting various mapping operations for custom logic.

For configuration of the plug-in, please refer to the sqlSessionFactory bean definition in the file mybatis-tx-config.xml.

Obscenity Filter Using AOP

In SpringBlog, the obscenity filter is the main feature to showcase the usage of Spring AOP in implementing cross-cutting concerns in an application. In this section, we will look into the details of its implementation. For Spring configuration and the corresponding setup in tc Server, please refer to the section "The AspectJ Load-Time Weaving Configuration" in this chapter.

Listing 21-16 shows the ObscenityFilter interface, which defines the methods for the obscenity filter feature.

Listing 21-16. The ObscenityFilter Interface

```
package com.apress.prospring3.springblog.common.aop;

public interface ObscenityFilter {

    public boolean containsObscenities(String data);

    public String obfuscateObscenities(String data);
}
```

For the obscenity filter, two methods are defined. The containsObscenities() method is to check for the existence of obscenities within the data, while the obfuscateObscenities() method is to transform the obscenities into random meaningless words, by using ROT13 algorithm.

Listing 21-17 shows the implementation class of the ObscenityFilter interface.

Listing 21-17. The ListBasedObscenityFilter Class

```
package com.apress.prospring3.springblog.common.aop;

import java.util.List;
import java.util.regex.Matcher;
import java.util.regex.Pattern;
import javax.annotation.Resource;
import org.springframework.stereotype.Service;

@Service("obscenityFilter")
public class ListBasedObscenityFilter implements ObscenityFilter {

    private List<String> obscenities = null;
    private Pattern obscenityPattern = null;

    @Resource(name="obscenities")
    public void setObscenities(List<String> obscenities) {
        this.obscenities = obscenities;
        buildRegex();
    }

    private void buildRegex() {
        StringBuffer sb = new StringBuffer();
        int size = obscenities.size();

        for (int x = 0; x < size; x++) {
            if (x != 0) {
                sb.append("|");
```

```
        }
        sb.append("(");
        sb.append(obscenities.get(x));
        sb.append(")");
    }

    obscenityPattern = Pattern.compile(sb.toString(), Pattern.CASE_INSENSITIVE);
}

/**
 * Returns true if the data contain an obscenity otherwise returns false
 */
public boolean containsObscenities(String data) {
    Matcher m = obscenityPattern.matcher(data);
    return m.find();
}

/**
 * Obfuscate all obscenities in a String
 */
public String obfuscateObscenities(String data) {
    Matcher m = obscenityPattern.matcher(data);
    StringBuffer out = new StringBuffer(data.length());

    while (m.find()) {
        if (m.group(0) != null) {
            m.appendReplacement(out, rot13(m.group(0)));
        }
    }

    m.appendTail(out);

    return out.toString();
}

/**
 * Rot13 encode a String value.
 * @param in
 * @return Encoded string
 */
private String rot13(String in) {
    char[] chars = in.toCharArray();

    for (int x = 0; x < chars.length; x++) {
        char c = chars[x];
        if (c >= 'a' && c <= 'm')
            c += 13;
        else if (c >= 'n' && c <= 'z')
            c -= 13;
        else if (c >= 'A' && c <= 'M')
            c += 13;
        else if (c >= 'A' && c <= 'Z') c -= 13;

        chars[x] = c;
    }
```

```
        }

        return new String(chars);
    }
}
```

In Listing 21-17, the ListBasedObscenityFilter class implements the obscenity filter with a list containing predefined obscenities, which is defined by the obscenities bean in the root-context.xml file and injected into the class via the @Resource annotation. Based on the list, a regular expression was constructed that will be used by the containsObscenities() method to check for the existence of obscenities. The obfuscateObscenities() method also uses the same regular expression constructed to scan for the obscenities and to perform obfuscation using the ROT13 algorithm.

Finally is the advice class, which is a before advice that will perform the filtering for all operations within the service layer with an argument that can be assigned to the BlogPosting interface. Listing 21-18 shows the advice class.

Listing 21-18. The ObscenityFilterAdvice Class

```
package com.apress.prospring3.springblog.common.aop;

import org.aspectj.lang.JoinPoint;
import org.aspectj.lang.annotation.Aspect;
import org.aspectj.lang.annotation.Before;
import org.springframework.beans.factory.annotation.Autowired;
import org.springframework.beans.factory.annotation.Configurable;
import org.springframework.stereotype.Component;

import com.apress.prospring3.springblog.domain.BlogPosting;

@Component
@Configurable
@Aspect
public class ObscenityFilterAdvice {

    @Autowired
    private ObscenityFilter obscenityFilter;

    public void setObscenityFilter(ObscenityFilter obscenityFilter) {
        this.obscenityFilter = obscenityFilter;
    }

    @Before("execution(* com.apress.prospring3.springblog.service..*(..))")
    public void filterObscenities(JoinPoint joinPoint)
            throws Throwable {
        Object[] args = joinPoint.getArgs();
        for (int x = 0; x < args.length; x++) {
            if (args[x] instanceof BlogPosting) {
                BlogPosting arg = (BlogPosting) args[x];
                if (obscenityFilter.containsObscenities(arg.getBody())) {
                    arg.setBody(obscenityFilter.obfuscateObscenities(arg.getBody()));
                }
                if (obscenityFilter.containsObscenities(arg.getSubject())) {
                    arg.setSubject(obscenityFilter
                            .obfuscateObscenities(arg.getSubject()));
```

```
            }
          }
        }
      }
    }
  }
}
```

In Listing 21-18, several annotations are applied at the class level. The @Component annotation indicates to Spring that it's a Spring bean, while the @Configurable annotation indicates that this advice should be configured by Spring, by which Spring will create Spring-based AOP proxies for the weaving classes. Finally, the AspectJ's @Aspect annotation indicates to Spring that it's an AOP advice and will trigger Spring's support of AspectJ's annotation style.

Within the advice, the ObscenityFilter interface is autowired. The filterObscenities() method is annotated with @Before along with the pointcut expression, which indicates that it's a before advice and should intercept all service layer methods. Within the method, the arguments will be checked to see whether they are assignable to the BlogPosting interface. If that's the case, then the argument should be either the Entry or Comment object, and the obscenity filter logic will be applied.

To see it in action, you can post a new entry that contains the word *crap* in either the subject or body field. Then after you save the entry, you will notice that the word has been translated into *penc*, which is the result of the ROT13 algorithm. See Figures 3-6 and 3-7 in Chapter 3.

Scheduling the Job for Purging Audit Data

Another feature that we demonstrated in the SpringBlog application is job scheduling, by which we use it to implement a daily job to purge the audit history data for Entry and Comment objects that are older than 30 days. In this section, we will see the implementation in detail.

As you already saw in Chapter 15, task scheduling in Spring is very easy, and in SpringBlog, we use the annotation style for scheduling the audit data purging job. Listing 21-19 shows the code snippet in the root-context.xml file that enables annotation-style scheduling support.

Listing 21-19. Configuring Annotation-Based Scheduling in Spring

```
<!-- Enable Task Scheduling support with annotation -->
<task:scheduler id="myScheduler" pool-size="10"/>
<task:annotation-driven scheduler="myScheduler"/>
```

In Listing 21-19, the <task:scheduler> tag will cause Spring to create a ThreadPoolTaskScheduler instance with the specified thread pool size. Then, the <task:annotation-driven> tag enables the annotation-style scheduling definition. Listing 21-20 shows the HousekeepingService interface, which defines the data housekeeping jobs that need to be performed by the SpringBlog application.

Listing 21-20. The HousekeepingService Interface

```
package com.apress.prospring3.springblog.service;

public interface HousekeepingService {

    /**
     * Scheduled job to purge audit records.
     */
    public void auditPurgeJob();

}
```

Only one auditPurgeJob() method is defined, which contains the logic to purge the old audit history data. Listing 21-21 shows the JPA 2 implementation class.

Listing 21-21. The HousekeepingServiceImpl Class

```
package com.apress.prospring3.springblog.service.jpa;

import org.springframework.beans.factory.annotation.Value;
import org.springframework.scheduling.annotation.Scheduled;
import org.springframework.stereotype.Repository;
import org.springframework.stereotype.Service;
import org.springframework.transaction.annotation.Transactional;

import com.apress.prospring3.springblog.service.HousekeepingService;

@Service("housekeepingService")
@Repository
@Transactional
public class HousekeepingServiceImpl implements HousekeepingService {

    @Value("${audit.record.history.days}")
    private int auditHistoryDays;

    @Scheduled(cron="0 0 0 * * ?")
    public void auditPurgeJob() {
        // Purge audit record logic goes here
    }
}
```

In Listing 21-21, the number of days for keeping the audit history is externalized into the /src/main/resources/springblog.properties file. The auditPurgeJob() is applied with the @Scheduled annotation to indicate to Spring that it's a scheduled task. The cron expression was used, which means that the job will run every day at midnight. We leave the logic empty here, but you can imagine it's very easy to implement. We just need to perform a batch update operation to delete the records from the ENTRY_H and COMMENT_H tables (in the file schema.sql) for which the create timestamp is older than the specified number of days.

Presentation Layer

For the presentation layer of the SpringBlog application, basically most of the topics discussed in Chapter 17 are applied here. Major highlights are summarized here:

- Spring MVC will be used for implementing the Model View Controller pattern for the presentation layer, with JSPX as the view technology.

- Spring MVC support for i18n, theming, and RESTful-WS (for Ajax-style interaction with jQuery) will be used throughout the presentation layer.

- Apache Tiles will be used as the page templating technology. Also, Spring's integration with Apache Tiles will be used for resolving the view to display based on the logical view names.

- Spring 3's support of JSR-303 Beans Validation, type conversion, and formatting will be used for binding the requests and for converting string formats into Java types.

- For the views, jQuery and jQuery UI will be used to enrich the user interactions. Moreover, various jQuery plug-ins will be used for specific purposes. For example, jqGrid will be used for grid-based display of blog entries, with support for page size, pagination, and sorting. The CKEditor was used for rich-text input.

- Spring Security will be used for the authentication and authorization of protected resources. For example, only logged-in users can post new blog entries or comment on existing blog posts, and the administrator can view the audit history of a blog post entry.

- For the file attachment upload feature, Spring Framework 3.1's support of the Servlet 3.0 file-uploading feature will be used.

Since most of the topics mentioned in Chapter 17 were applied to the presentation layer of the SpringBlog application, it's highly recommended you read Chapter 17 first, if you haven't done so. In the following sections, we will highlight some of the main implementation details of the SpringBlog presentation layer. In the following section, the main implementation details of the presentation layer will be provided.

Web Resource Files Folder Structure

In the SpringBlog presentation layer, all the resource files (JSPX view file, Apache Tiles layout template, CSS style sheets, JavaScripts, and related libraries, Spring WebApplicationContext configuration files) are stored under the folder /src/main/webapp. Figure 21-18 shows the folder structure for the SpringBlog application in STS.

The structure is basically the same as the sample application we developed in Chapter 17. The JavaScript resources (including jQuery, jQuery UI, jqGrid, CKEditor, and so on) are stored in the folders scripts, jqgrid, and ckeditor, respectively. The styles folder stores the CSS files that support theming of SpringBlog, and the images folder stores the images.

The layouts folder stores the page layout template for Apache Tiles. The spring folder stores the Spring WebApplicationContext configuration files. The views folder stores all the JSPX view files for the frontend. The views folder stores the template components, such as the header, menu, footer, and so on. The blogs and comments subfolders store the view files for listing, viewing, adding, and editing blog posts and comment entries, respectively.

Figure 21-18. The SpringBlog web resources folder structure

Controller Class

The controller classes are the central part of the frontend presentation logic. They handle the requests received from the DispatcherServlet, either from the frontend or from RESTful-WS clients. Then, the controller classes perform required processing logic based on the request, interact with the service layer, and return the logical view to the DispatcherServlet (or directly write to the response body). In this section, we will also focus on the EntryController class, which handles the requests with regard to the blog post entries. Specifically, we will discuss creating a new blog post entry.

Listing 21-22 shows the code snippet for the methods related to creating a new blog post within the EntryController class in the SpringBlog application.

Listing 21-22. The EntryController Class

```
package com.apress.prospring3.springblog.web.blogapp.controller;

// Import statements omitted

@RequestMapping("/blogs")
@Controller
public class EntryController {

    final Logger logger = LoggerFactory.getLogger(EntryController.class);

    @Autowired
    private MessageSource messageSource;

    @Autowired
    private EntryService entryService;

    @Autowired
    private CategoryService categoryService;

    @RequestMapping(method = RequestMethod.POST)
    public String create(@Valid Entry entry, BindingResult bindingResult, Model uiModel,
            HttpServletRequest httpServletRequest, RedirectAttributes redirectAttributes,
            Locale locale) {
        logger.info("Creating entry");
        if (bindingResult.hasErrors()) {
            uiModel.addAttribute("message", new Message("error",
                messageSource.getMessage("entry_save_fail", new Object[]{}, locale)));
            uiModel.addAttribute("entry", entry);
            populateSelectBox(uiModel, entry);
            return "blogs/create";
        }
        uiModel.asMap().clear();
        redirectAttributes.addFlashAttribute("message", new Message("success",
            messageSource.getMessage("entry_save_success", new Object[]{}, locale)));

        logger.info("Entry id: " + entry.getId());
        entryService.save(entry);
        return "redirect:/blogs/" + UrlUtil.encodeUrlPathSegment(entry.getId().toString(),
            httpServletRequest);
    }

    @PreAuthorize("isAuthenticated()")
    @RequestMapping(params = "form", method = RequestMethod.GET)
    public String createForm(Model uiModel) {
        Entry entry = new Entry();
        uiModel.addAttribute("entry", entry);
        populateSelectBox(uiModel, entry);
        return "blogs/create";
```

```
    }

    // Other code omitted
}
```

In Listing 21-22, two methods are related to the process of creating a new blog post. The createForm() method is responsible for creating a new Entry domain object, saving into the Model interface and returning the logical view for displaying the entry update view (defined by the logical view blogs/create). Note that the method was annotated with @PreAuthorize, which is Spring Security's support for method-level authorization, since only logged-in users are allowed to create blog posts.

The create() method handles the submission of the form after users enter the blog post entry details. The @Valid annotation to the Entry type argument instructs Spring MVC to perform JSR-303 validations on the submitted object. All constraint violations will be stored in the BindingResult, and if errors are found, a message will be stored into the Model interface and returned to the same view as when editing a blog post entry, with error messages displayed. Figure 21-19 shows sample validation messages displayed when the user simply clicks the Save button without entering any information.

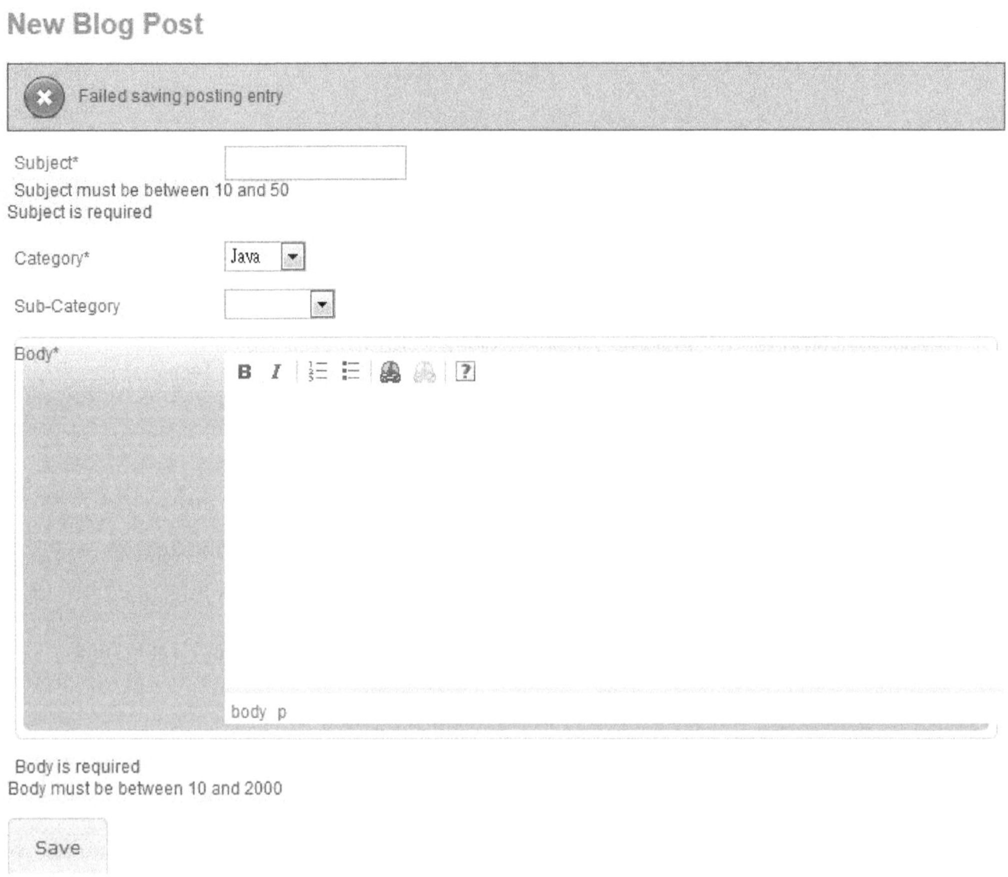

Figure 21-19. SpringBlog JSR-303 validation

Listing 21-23 shows the code snippet for the AbstractBlogPosting class (which was extended by the Entry class) with JSR-303 validation constraints defined on the subject property.

Listing 21-23. The AbstractBlogPosting Class

```
package com.apress.prospring3.springblog.domain;

// Import statements omitted

@MappedSuperclass
@Audited
public abstract class AbstractBlogPosting implements BlogPosting, Auditable<String, Long>,⏎
 Serializable {

    protected Long id;
    protected String subject;
    protected String body;
    protected DateTime postDate;
    protected String createdBy;
    protected DateTime createdDate;
    protected String lastModifiedBy;
    protected DateTime lastModifiedDate;
    protected int version;

    // Other code omitted

    @NotEmpty(message="{validation.posting.subject.NotEmpty.message}")
    @Size(min=10, max=50, message="{validation.posting.subject.Size.message}")
    @Column(name = "SUBJECT")
    public String getSubject() {
        return subject;
    }
}
```

In Listing 21-23, the @NotEmpty and the @Size annotations applied to the getSubject() method define the JSR-303 validation constraints for the subject property. The message is a code, and the message details are externalized into the message files to support i18n (for more details, please refer to Chapter 17). The bean declaration <mvc:annotation-driven validator="validator"/> in the blogapp-webmvc-config.xml file will turn on the validation automatically.

Type Conversion and Formatting

In the SpringBlog application, Spring Framework 3's new type conversion and formatting system was used for binding, converting, and formatting the data between the frontend views and the controller classes. The <mvc:annotation-driven> tag will also turn on the new type conversion and formatting system. After the feature is turned on, Spring will automatically convert between common Java types (for example, int/Integer, long/Long, and so on) to the String representations. In addition, annotations are provided for defining the desired format. In this section, we will discuss the use of the @DateTimeFormat annotation for controlling the format for JodaTime's DateTime type.

Listing 21-24 shows another code snippet of the AbstractBlogPosting class, which has the @DateTimeFormat annotation applied.

Listing 21-24. The AbstractBlogPosting Class

```
package com.apress.prospring3.springblog.domain;

// Import statements omitted

@MappedSuperclass
@Audited
public abstract class AbstractBlogPosting implements BlogPosting, Auditable<String, Long>,↵
 Serializable {

    protected Long id;
    protected String subject;
    protected String body;
    protected DateTime postDate;
    protected String createdBy;
    protected DateTime createdDate;
    protected String lastModifiedBy;
    protected DateTime lastModifiedDate;
    protected int version;

    @Column(name = "CREATED_DATE")
    @Type(type="org.joda.time.contrib.hibernate.PersistentDateTime")
    @DateTimeFormat(iso=ISO.DATE_TIME)
    public DateTime getCreatedDate() {
        return this.createdDate;
    }

    @Column(name = "LAST_MODIFIED_DATE")
    @Type(type="org.joda.time.contrib.hibernate.PersistentDateTime")
    @DateTimeFormat(iso=ISO.DATE_TIME)
    public DateTime getLastModifiedDate() {
        return this.lastModifiedDate;
    }

    // Other code omitted
}
```

In Listing 21-24, the date-time format annotations are highlighted in bold. For the createdDate and lastModifiedDate properties, the annotation is applied, and the type ISO.DATE_TIME format is used, which corresponds to the format yyyy-MM-dd'T'hh:mm:ss.SSSZ (for example, 2012-01-30T13:53:52.324+08:00). This is because for the create date and last modified date, we also want to know the time in addition to the date. Note that Spring supports the formatting of JodaTime's DateTime type out of the box.

Figure 21-20 shows the view page of a blog post entry in SpringBlog, and in the figure, you can see the conversion and formatting in action.

Blog Entry

Subject	Welcome to SpringBlog
Category	Java
Sub-Category	
Body	Welcome to SpringBlog
Post Date	2012-01-30
Post By	clarence
Create Date	2012-01-30T14:12:52.607+08:00
Last Modified Date	2012-01-30T14:12:52.607+08:00
Attachments	
0 comments	

Edit | Upload Attachment | Post a comment | View Audit History

Figure 21-20. SpringBlog type conversion and formatting

In Figure 21-20, the create date and last modified date are shown in the appropriate format.

There are still many other features that were implemented in the SpringBlog application, such as i18n, theming, jQuery, pagination, Ajax for dynamic update of category boxes (in other words, when the parent category is changed, the list box for the subcategory select box will refresh with the result from an Ajax call), file upload, and so on. However, the implementations were based on Ajax calls between jQuery and the Spring MVC layer, which are basically the same as the implementation of the pagination in the data table using jqGrid; therefore, they are detailed in Chapter 17, and we will skip the discussion here.

Summary

In this chapter, we discussed the details of the design and implementation of the sample application for this book, the SpringBlog application.

First, instructions were provided on how to set up the project, as well as switch between different datasources and implementations with Spring Framework 3.1's support of bean definition profiles.

Second, we elaborated on the design of the SpringBlog application. Topics included the data model, domain object model, and UML model of the main use cases within the application.

Then, we discussed the configuration of the SpringBlog application. Topics included the web deployment descriptor configuration, as well as the Spring's `WebApplicationContext` hierarchy.

Finally, the detailed implementation of the main features that showcase the Spring Framework's powerful features were discussed. The implementation of the service layer, AOP for obscenity filtering, task scheduling, and the presentation layer were discussed in detail.

CHAPTER 22

Scripting Support in Spring

In previous chapters, we saw how the Spring Framework can help Java developers create JEE applications. By using the Spring Framework's DI mechanism and its integration with each layer (via libraries within the Spring Framework's own modules or via integration with third-party libraries), you can simplify implementing and maintaining business logic.

However, all the logic we have developed so far was with the Java language. Although one of the most successful programming languages in history, Java is still criticized for some weaknesses, such as its language structure or its lack of comprehensive support in areas like massive parallel processing.

For example, one feature of the Java language is that all variables are statically typed. In other words, in a Java program, each variable declared should have a static type associated with it (in other words, String, int, Object, ArrayList, and so on). However, in some scenarios, dynamic typing may be preferred, which is supported by dynamic languages like JavaScript.

To address those requirements, many scripting languages have been developed. Some of the most popular ones include JavaScript, Groovy, Scala, Ruby, and Erlang. Almost all of those languages support dynamic typing and were designed to provide the features that are not available in Java, as well as targeting specific purposes. For example, Scala (www.scala-lang.org) combines functional programming patterns with OO patterns and supports a more comprehensive and scalable concurrent programming model with concepts of actors and message passing. In addition, Groovy (http://groovy.codehaus.org) provides a simplified programming model and supports the implementation of domain-specific languages (DSLs) that make the application code easier to read and maintain.

One other important concept that those scripting languages bring to Java developers is closures (which we will discuss in more detail later in this chapter). Simply speaking, a closure is a piece (or block) of code wrapped in an object. It's executable like a Java method and can receive parameters and return objects and values. In addition, it's also a normal object that can be passed with a reference around your application, like any POJO in Java.

In this chapter, we will discuss some main concepts behind scripting languages, with the main focus on Groovy; you'll see how the Spring Framework can work with scripting language seamlessly to provide specific functionality to Spring-based applications. Specifically, this chapter will cover the following topics:

- *Scripting support in Java*: In JCP, JSR-223 (the Scripting for the Java Platform API) enables the support of scripting languages in Java; it has been available in Java since JSE 6. We will provide an overview of scripting support in Java.

- *Groovy*: We will provide a high-level introduction to the Groovy language, which is one of the most popular scripting languages being used with Java, specifically using the Spring Framework.

- *Using Groovy with Spring:* The Spring Framework provides comprehensive support for scripting languages. As of version 3.1, out-of-the-box support for Groovy, JRuby, and BeanShell is provided. In this chapter, we will discuss how to use Groovy with Spring to implement a simple rule engine based on the DSL supported by Groovy.

This chapter is not intended to serve as a detailed reference on using scripting languages. Each language in books of their own that discuss their design and usage in detail. The main objective of this chapter is to give you an idea how the Spring Framework supports scripting languages, with a sound example on what the benefit are of using a scripting language in addition to Java in a Spring-based application.

Project for Chapter Samples

We will use a simple Spring utility project as our starting point for the samples that will be developed in this chapter. For using Groovy, an additional procedure is required to install the Groovy plug-in for Eclipse; the steps are detailed in the following sections.

Create a Simple Spring Utility Project

The first step is to create a simple Spring utility project. In STS, choose File ➤ New ➤ Spring Template Project, and then choose Simple Spring Utility Project, as shown in Figure 22-1.

Figure 22-1. Creating a simple Spring utility project in STS

Then, enter the project information, as shown in Figure 22-2.

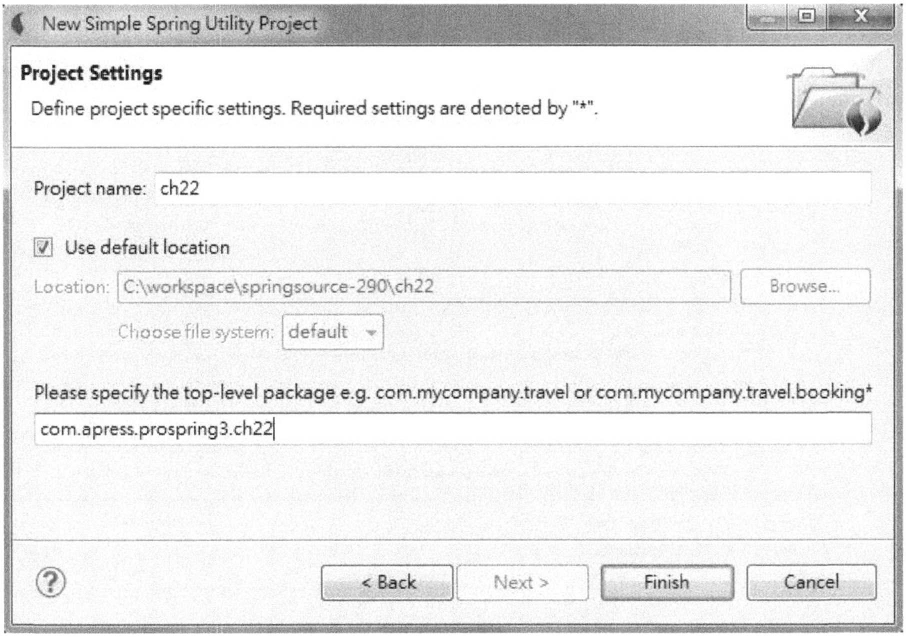

Figure 22-2. Entering project information

After you create the project, make sure that the project is using Spring 3.1 and JSE 6.

Installing the Groovy Plug-in for Eclipse

Groovy provides an Eclipse plug-in that can help manage the development of a project using pure Groovy or Java projects with Groovy classes. However, by default, the plug-in is not bundled with STS, so we need to install it.

To install the plug-in, in STS, open the Spring dashboard (by clicking the Spring Dashboard menu icon in the Spring perspective). In the dashboard view, click the tab Extensions, and select Groovy Eclipse. Then click the Install button, as shown in Figure 22-3.

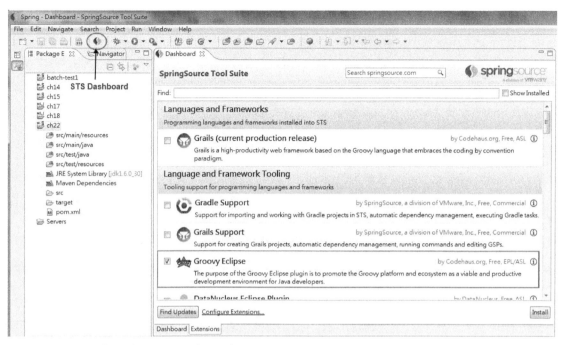

Figure 22-3. Installing the Groovy Eclipse plug-in

The Install dialog opens. Select all the items and click the Next button to install, as shown in Figure 22-4.

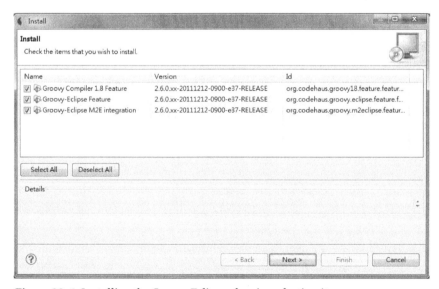

Figure 22-4. Installing the Groovy Eclipse plug-in: selecting items

After the installation completes and you restart STS, right-click the project in STS, and add the Groovy Project nature to the project, as shown in Figure 22-5.

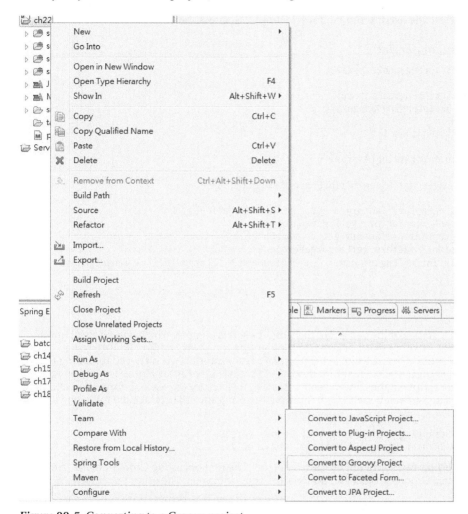

Figure 22-5. *Converting to a Groovy project*

At this point, the project setup is complete. However, we still need to add the relevant Maven dependencies so that the project can be built from Maven. (We will let you know when dependencies need to be added.)

Scripting Support in Java

Starting with JSE 6, the Scripting for the Java Platform API (JSR-223) is bundled into the JDK. Its objective is to provide a standard mechanism for running logic written in other scripting languages on the JVM.

Out of the box, JDK 6 comes bundled with the engine called Mozilla Rhino, which is able to evaluate JavaScript programs. This section will give you an introduction to the JSR-223 support in JDK 6.

In JDK 6, the scripting support classes reside in the package javax.script. First let's develop a simple program to retrieve the list of script engines. Listing 22-1 shows the class content.

Listing 22-1. *Listing Scripting Engines*

```
package com.apress.prospring3.ch22.jsr223;

import javax.script.ScriptEngineFactory;
import javax.script.ScriptEngineManager;

public class ListScriptEngines {

    public static void main(String[] args) {

        ScriptEngineManager mgr = new ScriptEngineManager();

        for (ScriptEngineFactory factory : mgr.getEngineFactories()) {
            String engineName= factory.getEngineName();
            String languageName = factory.getLanguageName();
            String version = factory.getLanguageVersion();
            System.out.println("Engine name: " + engineName + " Language: " + languageName + " ↵
version: " + version);
        }
    }
}
```

In Listing 22-1, an instance of the ScriptEngineManager class is created, which will discover and maintain a list of engines (in other words, classes implementing the javax.script.ScriptEngine interface) from the classpath. Then, a list of ScriptEngineFactory interfaces is retrieved by calling the ScriptEngineManager.getEngineFactories() method. The ScriptEngineFactory interface is used to describe and instantiate script engines. From each ScriptEngineFactory interface, information about the scripting language support can be retrieved. Running the program will produce the following output in the console:

```
Engine name: Groovy Scripting Engine Language: Groovy version: 1.8.4
Engine name: Mozilla Rhino Language: ECMAScript version: 1.6
```

As shown in the output, two script engines are detected. The first one is the Groovy engine, since we converted the project to a Groovy project and added the Groovy libraries. The other one is ECMAScript, which is JavaScript.

Let's write a simple program to evaluate a basic JavaScript expression. The program is shown in Listing 22-2.

Listing 22-2. *Evaluates a JavaScript Expression*

```
package com.apress.prospring3.ch22.jsr223;

import javax.script.ScriptEngine;
import javax.script.ScriptEngineManager;
import javax.script.ScriptException;

public class JavaScriptTest {
```

```
public static void main(String[] args) {

    ScriptEngineManager mgr = new ScriptEngineManager();

    ScriptEngine jsEngine = mgr.getEngineByName("JavaScript");

    try {
        jsEngine.eval("print('Hello JavaScript in Java')");
    } catch (ScriptException ex) {
        ex.printStackTrace();
    }
  }
}
```

In Listing 22-2, an instance of ScriptEngine interface is retrieved from the ScriptEngineManager class, using the name JavaScript. Then, the ScriptEngine.eval() method is called, passing in a String argument, which contains a JavaScript expression. Note that the argument can also be a java.io.Reader class, which can read JavaScript from a file. Running the program will produce the following result:

```
Hello JavaScript in Java
```

This should give you an idea of how to run scripts in Java. However, it's not of much interest to just dump some output using another language. In the next section, we will introduce Groovy, a powerful and comprehensive scripting language.

Introducing Groovy

Started by James Strachan in 2003, the main objective of Groovy is to provide an agile and dynamic language for the JVM, with features inspired from other popular scripting languages including Python, Ruby, and Smalltalk. Groovy is built on top of Java, extends Java, and addresses some of the shortcomings in Java.

In the following sections, we will discuss some main features and concepts behind Groovy and how it supplements Java to address specific application needs. Note that many features mentioned here also are available in other scripting languages (for example, Scala, Erlang, Python, and Clojure).

Dynamic Typing

One main difference between Groovy (and many other scripting languages) and Java is the support of dynamic typing of variables. In Java, all properties and variables should be statically typed. In other words, the type should be provided with the declare statement. However, Groovy supports the dynamic typing of variables. In Groovy, dynamic typing variables are declared with the keyword def.

Let's see this in action by developing a simple Groovy script. The file suffix of a Groovy class or script is groovy. In STS, in a project with Groovy enabled, you can create a Groovy class or script by right-clicking the package name, choosing New ➤ Other, and then selecting the Groovy class.

Listing 22-3 shows a simple Groovy script with dynamic typing in action (the file name is DynamicTyping.groovy).

Listing 22-3. Dynamic Typing in Groovy

```groovy
package com.apress.prospring3.ch22.groovy

class Contact {
    def firstName
    def lastName
    def birthDate

    String toString() { "($firstName,$lastName,$birthDate)" }
}

Contact contact = new Contact(firstName: 'Clarence', lastName: 'Ho', birthDate: new Date())
Contact anotherContact = new Contact(firstName: 20, lastName: 'Ho', birthDate: new Date())

println contact
println anotherContact

println contact.firstName + 20
println anotherContact.firstName + 20
```

Listing 22-3 shows a Groovy script, which can be run directly from within STS (right-click the file and choose Run As, and then choose either Groovy Script or Java Application). The main difference is that a Groovy script can be executed without compilation (Groovy provides a command-line tool called groovy that can execute Groovy scripts directly) or can be compiled to Java bytecode and then executed just like other Java classes. Groovy scripts don't require a main() method for execution. Also, a class declaration that matches the file name is not required.

In Listing 22-3, a class Contact is defined, with the properties set to dynamic typing with the def keyword. Three properties are declared. Then, the toString() method is overridden with a closure that returns a string.

Then, two instances of the Contact object are constructed, with shorthand syntax provided by Groovy to define the properties. For the first Contact object, the firstName attribute is supplied with a String, while an integer is provided for the second Contact object. Finally, the println statement (the same as calling System.out.println() method) is used for printing the two contact objects. To show how Groovy handles dynamic typing, two println statements are defined to print the output for the operation firstName + 20. Note that in Groovy, when passing an argument to a method, the parentheses are optional.

Running the program will produce the following output:

```
(Clarence,Ho,Mon Jan 16 17:14:50 CST 2012)
(20,Ho,Mon Jan 16 17:14:50 CST 2012)
Clarence20
40
```

From the output, you can see that since the firstName is defined with dynamic typing, the object constructs successfully when passing in either a String or an integer as the type. In addition, in the last two println statements, the add operation was correctly applied to the firstName property of both objects. In the first scenario, since firstName is a String, the string 20 is appended to it. For the second scenario, since firstName is an integer, integer 20 is added to it, resulting in 40.

Dynamic typing support of Groovy provides greater flexibility for manipulating class properties and variables in application logic.

Simplified Syntax

Groovy also provides simplified syntax so that the same logic in Java can be implemented in Groovy with less code. Some of the basic syntax is as follows:

- A semicolon is not required for ending a statement.

- In methods, the return keyword is optional.

- All methods and classes are public by default. So, unless required, you don't need to declare the public keyword for method declaration.

- Within a class, Groovy will automatically generate the getter/setter methods for the declared properties. So in a Groovy class, you just need to declare the type and name (for example, String firstName or def firstName), and you can access the properties in any other Groovy/Java classes by using the getter/setter methods automatically. In addition, you can also simply access the property without the get/set prefix (for example, contact.firstName = 'Clarence'). Groovy will handle them for you intelligently.

Groovy also provides simplified syntax and many useful methods to the Java Collection API. Listing 22-4 shows some of the commonly used Groovy operations for list manipulation (the file name is CollectionSample.groovy).

Listing 22-4. *Groovy for Managing List*

```groovy
package com.apress.prospring3.ch22.groovy

// Define a list as an ArrayList
def list = ['This', 'is', 'Clarence']
assert list.size() == 3
assert list.class == ArrayList

// Reverse a list
assert list.reverse() == ['Clarence', 'is', 'This']

// Sort a list by string size
assert list.sort{ it.size() } == ['is', 'This', 'Clarence']

// Sub list
assert list[0..1] == ['is', 'This']

// Use << for append item
assert list << 'Ho' == ['is', 'This', 'Clarence', 'Ho']
```

The listing shows only a very small portion of the features that Groovy offers. For a more detailed description, please refer to the Groovy online documentation at http://groovy.codehaus.org/JN1015-Collections.

Closure

One of the most important features that Groovy adds to Java is the support of closures. A closure allows a piece of code to be wrapped as an object and to be passed freely within the application. Closure is a very powerful feature that enables smart and dynamic behavior. The addition of closure support to the Java language has been requested for a long time. JSR-335, Lambda Expressions for the Java Programming Language, which aims to support programming in a multicore environment by adding closures and related features to the Java language, was scheduled to be included in JSE 8. However, if you want to enjoy the benefits that closures bring to your application, you need to use a scripting language like Groovy, Python, Scala, Ruby, Clojure, and so on.

Listing 22-5 shows a very simple example of using closures (the file name is SimpleClosure.groovy) in Groovy.

Listing 22-5. *A Simple Closure Example*

```
package com.apress.prospring3.ch22.groovy.closure

def names = ['Clarence', 'Johnny', 'Mary']

names.each {println 'Hello: ' + it}
```

In Listing 22-5, a list is declared. Then, the convenient each() method is used for an operation that will iterate through each item in the list. The argument to the each() method is a closure, which is enclosed in curly braces in Groovy. As a result, the logic in the closure will be applied to each item within the list. Within the closure, it is a special variable used by Groovy to represent the item currently in context. So, the closure will prefix each item in the list with the String "Hello: " and then print it. Running the script will produce the following output:

```
Hello: Clarence
Hello: Johnny
Hello: Mary
```

As mentioned, a closure can be declared as a variable and used when required. Another example is shown in Listing 22-6 (the file name is ClosureOnMap.groovy).

Listing 22-6. *Define a Closure as Variable*

```
package com.apress.prospring3.ch22.groovy.closure

def map = ['a': 10, 'b': 50]

Closure square = {key, value -> map[key] = value * value}

map.each square

println map
```

In Listing 22-6, a map is defined. Then, a variable of type Closure is declared. The closure accepts the key and value of a map's entry as its arguments, and the logic calculates the square of the value of the key. Running the program will produce the following output:

```
[a:100, b:2500]
```

This was just a simple introduction to closures. In the next section, we will develop a simple rule engine using Groovy and Spring. Closures will be used also. For a more detailed description of using closures in Groovy, please refer to the online documentation at http://groovy.codehaus.org/JN2515-Closures.

Using Groovy with Spring

The main benefit that Groovy and other scripting languages bring to Java-based applications is the support of dynamic behavior. By using a closure, business logic can be packaged as an object and passed around the application like any other variables.

Another main feature of Groovy is the support for developing DSLs by using its simplified syntax and closures. As the name implies, a DSL is a language targeted for a particular domain with very specific goals in design and implementation. The objective is to build a language that is understandable not only by the developers but the business analysts and users as well. Most of the time, the domain is a business area. For example, DSLs can be defined for customer classification, sales charge calculation, salary calculation, and so on.

In this section, we will demonstrate using Groovy to implement a simple rule engine with Groovy's DSL support. The implementation is referencing the sample from the excellent article on this topic at www.pleus.net/articles/grules/grules.pdf, with modifications. In addition, we will discuss how Spring's support of refreshable beans enables the update of the underlying rules on the fly without the need to compile, package, and deploy the application.

In this sample, we will implement a rule used for classifying a specific contact into different categories based on their age, which is calculated based on their date of birth property.

Adding Required Dependencies

In the sample, we will use Groovy and the JodaTime library, so we need to add the required dependencies in Table 22-1 to our project.

Table 22-1. Maven Dependencies for Groovy and JodaTime

Group ID	Artifact ID	Version	Description
org.codehaus.groovy	groovy	1.8.5	Groovy library
joda-time	joda-time	2.0	JodaTime date-time type library

The Contact Domain

As mentioned, a DSL targets a specific domain, and most of the time the domain is referring to some kind of business data. For the rule we are going to implement, it was designed to be applied to the domain of contact information.

So, the first step is to develop the domain object model we want the rule to apply to. In this sample, the DOM is very simple and contains only one Contact entity class, as shown in Listing 22-7. Note that it's a POJO class like what we did in previous chapters.

Listing 22-7. The Contact Domain

```
package com.apress.prospring3.ch22.domain;

import org.joda.time.DateTime;

public class Contact {
```

```
    private Long id;

    private String firstName;

    private String lastName;

    private DateTime birthDate;

    private String ageCategory;

    // Getter/setter methods omitted

    public String toString() {
        return "Contact - Id: " + id + ", First name: " + firstName
            + ", Last name: " + lastName + ", Birthday: " + birthDate
            + ", Age category: " + ageCategory;
    }
}
```

In Listing 22-7, the Contact class is a simple contact information. For the ageCategory property, we want to develop a dynamic rule that can be used to perform classification. The rule will calculate the age based on the birthDate property and then assign the ageCategory property (for example, kid, youth, adult, and so on) based on the rule.

Implementing the Rule Engine

The next step is to develop a simple rule engine for applying the rules on the domain object. First we need to define what information a rule needs to contain. Listing 22-8 shows the Rule class, which is a Groovy class (the file name is Rule.groovy).

Listing 22-8. The Rule Class

```
package com.apress.prospring3.ch22.rule.domain

class Rule {

    private boolean singlehit = true
    private conditions = new ArrayList()
    private actions = new ArrayList()
    private parameters = new ArrayList()

}
```

In Listing 22-8, each rule has several properties. The conditions property defines the various conditions that the rule engine should check for with the domain object under processing. The actions property defines the actions to take when a match on the condition is hit. The parameters property defines the behavior of the rule, which is the outcome of the action for different conditions. Finally, the singlehit property defines whether the rule should end its execution immediately whenever a match of condition is found.

The next step is the engine for rule execution. Listing 22-9 shows the RuleEngine interface (note it's a Java interface).

Listing 22-9. *The RuleEngine Interface*

```
package com.apress.prospring3.ch22.rule.engine;

import com.apress.prospring3.ch22.rule.domain.Rule;

public interface RuleEngine {

    public void run(Rule rule, Object object);

}
```

The interface defines only a method run(), which is to apply the rule to the domain object argument.

We will provide the implementation of the rule engine in Groovy. Listing 22-10 shows the Groovy class RuleEngineImpl (the file name is RuleEngineImpl.groovy).

Listing 22-10. *The RuleEngineImpl Groovy Class*

```
package com.apress.prospring3.ch22.rule.engine.impl

import org.springframework.stereotype.Component

import com.apress.prospring3.ch22.rule.domain.Rule
import com.apress.prospring3.ch22.rule.engine.RuleEngine

@Component("ruleEngine")
class RuleEngineImpl implements RuleEngine {

    public void run(Rule rule, Object object) {

        println "Executing rule"

        def exit=false // Exit flag for singlehit mode

        // Iterate over the parameter sets
        rule.parameters.each{ArrayList params ->
            def paramIndex=0 // Points to the current parameter
            def success=true

            if(!exit){
                // Check all conditions
                rule.conditions.each{
                    println "Condition Param index: " + paramIndex
                    success = success && it(object,params[paramIndex])
                    println "Condition success: " + success
                    paramIndex++
                }

                // If all conditions true, perform actions
                if(success && !exit){
                    rule.actions.each{
                        println "Action Param index: " + paramIndex
                        it(object,params[paramIndex])
                        paramIndex++
```

```
            }
            // If single hit, exit after first condition match
            if (rule.singlehit){
                exit=true
            }
        }
    }
  }
 }
}
```

In Listing 22-10, first the RuleEngineImpl implements the RuleEngine Java interface, and Spring's annotation is applied like any other POJO. Within the run() method, the parameters defined in the rule were passed into a closure for processing one by one. For each parameter (which is a list of values), the conditions (each condition is a closure) are checked one by one with the corresponding item within the parameter's list and the domain object. The success indicator becomes true only when all the conditions result in a positive match. In this case, the actions (each action is a closure too) defined in the rule will be performed on the object, with the corresponding value within the parameter's list. Finally, if a match is found for a specific parameter and the singlehit variable is true, the rule execution will be stopped and will exit immediately.

To allow the retrieval of a rule in a more flexible way, let's define a RuleFactory interface, as shown in Listing 22-11. Note that it's a Java interface.

Listing 22-11. The RuleFactory Interface

```
package com.apress.prospring3.ch22.rule.factory;

import com.apress.prospring3.ch22.rule.domain.Rule;

public interface RuleFactory {

    public Rule getAgeCategoryRule();

}
```

In Listing 22-11, since there is only one rule for an age category classification for contacts, the interface defines only a single method for retrieving the rule.

To make our rule engine transparent to the consumer, let's develop a simple service layer to wrap it up. Listing 22-12 and Listing 22-13 show the ContactService interface and the ContactServiceImpl class, respectively. Note that they are Java implementations.

Listing 22-12. The ContactService Interface

```
package com.apress.prospring3.ch22.service;

import com.apress.prospring3.ch22.domain.Contact;

public interface ContactService {

    public void applyRule(Contact contact);
}
```

Listing 22-13. The `ContactServiceImpl` *Class*

```
package com.apress.prospring3.ch22.service.impl;

import org.springframework.beans.factory.annotation.Autowired;
import org.springframework.context.ApplicationContext;
import org.springframework.stereotype.Service;

import com.apress.prospring3.ch22.domain.Contact;
import com.apress.prospring3.ch22.rule.domain.Rule;
import com.apress.prospring3.ch22.rule.engine.RuleEngine;
import com.apress.prospring3.ch22.rule.factory.RuleFactory;
import com.apress.prospring3.ch22.service.ContactService;

@Service("contactService")
public class ContactServiceImpl implements ContactService {

    @Autowired
    ApplicationContext ctx;

    @Autowired
    private RuleFactory ruleFactory;

    @Autowired
    private RuleEngine ruleEngine;

    public void applyRule(Contact contact) {

        // Apply ageCategory rule
        ruleFactory = ctx.getBean("ruleFactory", RuleFactory.class);
        Rule ageCategoryRule = ruleFactory.getAgeCategoryRule();
        ruleEngine.run(ageCategoryRule, contact);
    }
}
```

In Listing 22-13, the required Spring beans are autowired into the service implementation class. In the `applyRule()` method, the rule is obtained from the rule factory and then applied to the `Contact` object. The result is that the `ageCategory` property for the `Contact` will be derived based on the rule's defined conditions, actions, and parameters.

Implement the Rule Factory as a Spring Refreshable Bean

Now we can implement the rule factory and the rule for age category classification. We want to be able to update the rule on the fly and have Spring check for its changes and pick it up to apply the latest logic. The Spring Framework provides wonderful support for Spring beans written in scripting languages, called *refreshable beans*. We will see how to configure a Groovy script as a Spring bean and instruct Spring to refresh the bean on a regular interval later. First let's see the implementation of the rule factory in Groovy. To allow dynamic refresh, we put the class into an external folder. In the project root, create a folder called `resources`. The `RuleFactoryImpl` class (which is a Groovy class, with the name `RuleFactoryImpl.groovy`) will be placed into this folder. Listing 22-14 shows the class content.

Listing 22-14. The RuleFactoryImpl Class

```
import org.joda.time.DateTime
import org.joda.time.Years;

import com.apress.prospring3.ch22.rule.domain.Rule
import com.apress.prospring3.ch22.rule.factory.RuleFactory

class RuleFactoryImpl implements RuleFactory {

    Closure age = { birthDate -> return Years.yearsBetween(birthDate, new ↵
DateTime()).getYears() }

    public Rule getAgeCategoryRule() {

        // Rule definition
        Rule rule = new Rule()

        // ***************** CONFIGURATION *****************
        rule.singlehit=true

        // ************************************************
        rule.conditions=[
        // ***************** CONDITIONS ********************
        {object, param -> age(object.birthDate) >= param}, {object, param -> ↵
age(object.birthDate) <= param}
        // ************************************************
        ]

        rule.actions=[
        // ***************** ACTIONS **********************
        {object, param -> object.ageCategory = param}
        // ************************************************
        ]

        rule.parameters=[
        // *************** PARAMETERSETS *******************
        // Min age, Max age, ageCategory
        [0,10,'Kid'],
        [11,20,'Youth'],
        [21,40,'Adult'],
        [41,60,'Middle-aged'],
        [61,120,'Old']
        // ************************************************
        ]

        return rule
    }
}
```

In Listing 22-14, the class implements the RuleFactory interface, and the getAgeCategoryRule() method is implemented to provide the rule. Within the rule, a Closure called age is defined to calculate the age based on the birthDate property (which is of JodaTime's DateTime type) of a Contact object.

Within the rule, two conditions are defined. The first one is to check whether the age of a contact is larger than or equal to the provided parameter value, while the second check is for the smaller than or equal to condition.

Then, one action is defined to assign the value provided in the parameter to the ageCategory property of the Contact object.

The parameters define the values for both condition checking and action. For example, in the first parameter, it means that when the age is between 0 and 10, then the value Kid will be assigned to the ageCategory property of the Contact object, and so on. So, for each parameter, the first two values will be used by the two conditions to check for age range, while the last value will be used for assigning the ageCategory property.

The next step is to define the Spring ApplicationContext. Listing 22-15 shows the configuration file (/src/main/resources/app-context.xml).

Listing 22-15. The Spring Configuration

```
<?xml version="1.0" encoding="UTF-8"?>
<beans xmlns="http://www.springframework.org/schema/beans"
    xmlns:xsi="http://www.w3.org/2001/XMLSchema-instance"
    xmlns:context="http://www.springframework.org/schema/context"
    xmlns:lang="http://www.springframework.org/schema/lang"
    xsi:schemaLocation="http://www.springframework.org/schema/beans
        http://www.springframework.org/schema/beans/spring-beans-3.1.xsd
        http://www.springframework.org/schema/context
        http://www.springframework.org/schema/context/spring-context-3.1.xsd
        http://www.springframework.org/schema/lang
        http://www.springframework.org/schema/lang/spring-lang-3.1.xsd">

    <context:component-scan base-package="com.apress.prospring3.ch22" />

    <lang:groovy id="ruleFactory" refresh-check-delay="5000"
        script-source="file:resources/RuleFactoryImpl.groovy"/>

</beans>
```

The configuration is simple. For defining Spring beans in a scripting language, we need to use lang-namespace. Then, the <lang:groovy> tag is used to declare a Spring bean with a Groovy script. The script-source attribute defines the location of the Groovy script that Spring will load from. For the refreshable bean, the attribute refresh-check-delay should be provided. In this case, we supplied the value of 5000ms, which instructs Spring to check for file changes if the elapsed time from the last invocation is greater than five seconds. Note that Spring will not check the file every five seconds. Instead, it will check the file only when the corresponding bean is invoked.

Testing the Age Category Rule

Now we are ready to test the rule. The testing program is shown in Listing 22-16, which is a Java class.

Listing 22-16. Testing the Rule Engine

```
package com.apress.prospring3.ch22;

import org.joda.time.format.DateTimeFormat;
import org.springframework.context.support.GenericXmlApplicationContext;
```

```
import com.apress.prospring3.ch22.domain.Contact;
import com.apress.prospring3.ch22.service.ContactService;

public class RuleEngineTest {

    public static void main(String[] args) {

        GenericXmlApplicationContext ctx = new GenericXmlApplicationContext();
        ctx.load("classpath:app-context.xml");
        ctx.refresh();

        ContactService contactService = ctx.getBean("contactService", ContactService.class);

        // Construct Contact object
        Contact contact = new Contact();
        contact.setId(1l);
        contact.setFirstName("Clarence");
        contact.setLastName("Ho");
        contact.setBirthDate(DateTimeFormat.forPattern("yyyy-MM-dd").parseDateTime("1980-08-09"));

        // Apply rule to contact object
        contactService.applyRule(contact);
        System.out.println("Contact: " + contact);

        // Wait for rule to be updated
        try {
            System.in.read();
        } catch (Exception ex) {
            ex.printStackTrace();
        }

        // Apply the rule again
        contactService.applyRule(contact);
        System.out.println("Contact: " + contact);
    }
}
```

In Listing 22-16, upon initialization of Spring's GenericXmlApplicationContext, an instance of Contact object is constructed. Then, the instance of ContactService interface is obtained to apply the rule onto the Contact object and then output the result to the console. The program will be paused for user input, before the second application of the rule. During the pause, we can then modify the RuleFactoryImpl.groovy class so that Spring will refresh the bean and we can see the changed rule in action.

Running the testing program will produce the following output:

```
Executing rule
Condition Param index: 0
Condition success: true
Condition Param index: 1
Condition success: false
Condition Param index: 0
Condition success: true
Condition Param index: 1
Condition success: false
```

```
Condition Param index: 0
Condition success: true
Condition Param index: 1
Condition success: true
Action Param index: 2
Contact: Contact - Id: 1, First name: Clarence, Last name: Ho, Birthday: 1980-08-
09T00:00:00.000+08:00, Age category: Adult
```

From the logging statement in the output, since the age of the contact is 31, you can see that the rule will find a matching in the third parameter (in other words, [21,40,'Adult']). As a result, the ageCategory is set to Adult.

Now the program is paused, so let's change the parameters within the RuleFactoryImpl.groovy class. Listing 22-17 shows the code snippet.

Listing 22-17. *Modify Rule Parameters*

```
rule.parameters=[
// *************** PARAMETERSETS *******************
// Min age, Max age, ageCategory
[0,10,'Kid'],
[11,20,'Youth'],
[21,30,'Adult'],
[31,60,'Middle-aged'],
[61,120,'Old']
// *********************************************
]
```

In Listing 22-17, the changes are highlighted in bold. Change and save the file as indicated. Now press the Enter key in the console area to trigger the second application of the rule to the same object. After the program continues, the following output will be produced:

```
Executing rule
Condition Param index: 0
Condition success: true
Condition Param index: 1
Condition success: false
Condition Param index: 0
Condition success: true
Condition Param index: 1
Condition success: false
Condition Param index: 0
Condition success: true
Condition Param index: 1
Condition success: false
Condition Param index: 0
Condition success: true
Condition Param index: 1
Condition success: false
Condition Param index: 0
Condition success: true
Condition Param index: 1
Condition success: true
Action Param index: 2
Contact: Contact - Id: 1, First name: Clarence, Last name: Ho, Birthday: 1980-08-
09T00:00:00.000+08:00, Age category: Middle-aged
```

In the previous output, you can see the rule execution stops at the fourth parameter (in other words, [31,60,'Middle-aged']), and as a result, the value Middle-aged is assigned to the ageCategory property.

If you take a look at the article that was referred to when we prepared this sample (www.pleus.net/articles/grules/grules.pdf), it also shows how the rule parameter can be externalized into an Excel file, so users can prepare and update the parameter file by themselves.

Of course, this rule is a simple one, but you should have an idea of how a scripting language like Groovy can help supplement Spring-based Java EE applications in specific areas like rule engine with DSL.

You may be asking, "Is it possible to go one step further by storing the rule into the database and then have Spring's refreshable bean feature detect the change from the database?" This can help further simplify the maintenance of rule by providing a frontend for users (or administrator) to update the rule into the database on the fly, instead of uploading the file. Actually, there is a JIRA issue in the Spring Framework that discusses this (https://jira.springsource.org/browse/SPR-5106). Stay tuned with this feature. In the meantime, providing a user frontend to upload the rule class is also a workable solution. Of course, extreme care should be taken in this case, and the rule should be tested thoroughly before you upload it to the production environment.

Summary

In this chapter, we covered how to use scripting languages in Java applications and demonstrated how the Spring Framework's support of scripting language can help provide dynamic behavior to the application.

First we discussed JSR-223, the Scripting for the Java Platform API, which was built into JSE 6 and supports the execution of JavaScript out of the box. Then, we introduced Groovy, a popular scripting language within the Java developer communities. We also demonstrated some of its main features when compared to the traditional Java language.

Finally, we discussed the support of scripting languages in the Spring Framework. We saw it in action by designing and implementing a very simple rule engine using Groovy's DSL support. We also discussed how the rule can be modified and have the Spring Framework pick up the changes automatically by using its refreshable bean feature, without the need to compile, package, and deploy the application.

CHAPTER 23

Spring Application Monitoring

A typical JEE application contains a number of layers and components, such as the presentation layer, service layer, persistence layer, backend data source, and so on. During the development stage or after the application had been deployed to the quality assurance (QA) or production environment, we want to ensure that the application is in a healthy state without any potential problems or bottlenecks.

In a Java application, various areas may cause performance problems or overload server resources (such as CPU, memory, I/O, and so on). Examples are inefficient Java code, memory leaks (for example, Java code keeps allocating new objects without releasing the reference and prevents the underlying JVM from freeing up the memory during the garbage collection process), JVM parameters, thread pool parameters, data source configurations (for example, the number of concurrent database connections allowed), database setup, long-running SQL queries, and so on.

Consequently, there is a need to understand an application's runtime behavior and identify whether there are any potential bottlenecks or problems. In the Java world, a lot of tools can help monitor the detailed runtime behavior of JEE applications. Most of them are built on top of the Java Management Extensions (JMX) technology.

In this chapter, we will discuss several common techniques for monitoring Spring-based JEE applications. Specifically, this chapter will cover the following topics:

- *Spring support of JMX*: We will discuss Spring's comprehensive support of JMX and demonstrate how to expose Spring beans for monitoring with JMX tools. In this chapter, we will use VisualVM (http://visualvm.java.net/index.html) as the application monitoring tool.

- *Monitoring Hibernate statistics and Spring Batch:* Hibernate and Spring Batch also provide support classes and infrastructure for exposing the operational status and performance metrics using JMX. We will take a look at how to enable the JMX monitoring of those commonly used components in Spring-powered JEE applications.

- *Spring Insight*: Spring Insight (www.springsource.org/insight) is a technology developed by SpringSource that provides comprehensive support and a user interface that can help developers understand and visualize the behavior of any Spring-powered application. The tool is bundled with the tc Server Developer Edition in STS. We will discuss how to use Spring Insight to monitor Spring-based JEE applications.

Remember that this chapter is not intended to be an introduction to JMX, and a basic understanding of JMX is assumed. For detailed information, please refer to Oracle's online resource at www.oracle.com/technetwork/java/javase/tech/javamanagement-140525.html.

Project for Chapter Samples

In this chapter, we will use the web application we developed in Chapter 17 as the application to monitor. To show how to monitor Spring Batch jobs, a batch job was added to the application for importing contact information into the database from an XML file.

We prepared a project for the sample application that will be used for monitoring; you can simply import it and then proceed to implement the required classes.

From the sample code, extract the file ch23-nojmx.zip into your STS workspace. Then, import the project in STS.

To import the project, in STS choose the menu option File ➤ Import, and on the Select screen of the Import wizard, choose Existing Projects into Workspace under the General category, as shown in Figure 23-1.

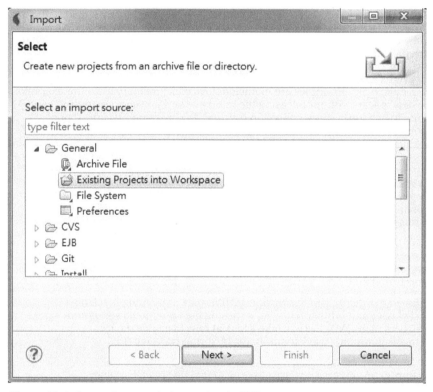

Figure 23-1. Importing an existing project in STS

Then, on the Import Projects screen, choose the project extracted from the sample source code, and click Finish (see Figure 23-2).

Figure 23-2. Importing a sample project

After completing the project import, build and deploy to tc Server in STS, and start the tc Server. After the web application starts up successfully, open a browser and enter the URL http://localhost:8080/ch23/contacts to verify the application. Figure 23-3 shows the sample application.

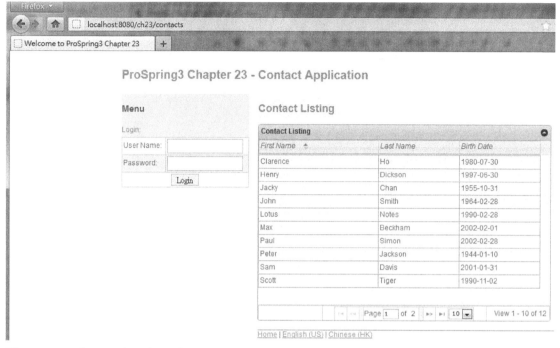

Figure 23-3. *The sample web application*

To reiterate, the sample application is the same as the web application developed in Chapter 17. In addition, a batch job was implemented that will poll the folder `C:\temp\contact\contacts.xml` for contact information in XML format for batch upload.

JMX Support in Spring

In JMX, the classes that are exposed for JMX monitoring and management are called *managed beans* (generally referred to as *MBeans*). The Spring Framework supports several mechanisms for exposing MBeans. In this chapter, we will focus on exposing Spring beans (which were developed as simple POJOs) as MBeans for JMX monitoring.

In the following sections, we will discuss the procedure for exposing a bean containing application-related statistics as an MBean for JMX monitoring. Topics include implementing the Spring bean, exposing the Spring bean as an MBean in Spring `ApplicationContext`, and using VisualVM to monitor the MBean. In addition, we will also discuss how some metrics relating to Spring Security can be exposed to JMX.

Exporting a Spring Bean to JMX

As an example, for the sample web application, which maintains a list of contact information, we would like to expose the count of the contacts in the database for JMX monitoring purposes. So, let's implement the interface and the class, which are shown in Listings 23-1 and 23-2, respectively.

Listing 23-1. The AppStatistics Interface

```
package com.apress.prospring3.ch23.jmx;

public interface AppStatistics {

    public int getTotalContactCount();
}
```

Listing 23-2. The AppStatisticsImpl Class

```
package com.apress.prospring3.ch23.jmx.impl;

import org.springframework.beans.factory.annotation.Autowired;

import com.apress.prospring3.ch23.jmx.AppStatistics;
import com.apress.prospring3.ch23.service.ContactService;

public class AppStatisticsImpl implements AppStatistics {

    @Autowired
    private ContactService contactService;

    public int getTotalContactCount() {
        return contactService.findAll().size();
    }
}
```

In Listing 23-2, a method is defined to retrieve the total count of contact records in the database. To expose the Spring bean as JMX, we need to add configuration in Spring's ApplicationContext. For simplicity, we will use the one already in the sample application, the /src/main/resources/batch-context.xml file, which stores the configuration for batch jobs. Listing 23-3 shows the code snippet needed to add to the file.

Listing 23-3. Expose Spring Bean to JMX

```
<?xml version="1.0" encoding="UTF-8"?>
<beans xmlns="http://www.springframework.org/schema/beans"

    <!-- Other code omitted -->

    <!-- Spring MBean for JMX Monitoring -->
    <bean id="appStatisticsBean" class="com.apress.prospring3.ch23.jmx.impl.AppStatisticsImpl"/>

    <bean id="jmxExporter" class="org.springframework.jmx.export.MBeanExporter">
        <property name="beans">
            <map>
                <entry key="bean:name=ProSpring3ContactApp" value-ref="appStatisticsBean"/>
            </map>
        </property>
    </bean>

</beans>
```

In Listing 23-3, the bean definition we need to add is highlighted in bold. First, the bean for the POJO with statistics we want to expose is declared. Second, the jmxExporter bean with the implementation class MBeanExporter is declared.

The MBeanExporter class is the core class within the Spring Framework's support for JMX. It's responsible for registering Spring beans with a JMX MBean server (a server that implements JDK's javax.management.MBeanServer interface, which exists in most commonly used web and JEE containers, like Tomcat and WebSphere). When exposing a Spring bean as an MBean, Spring will attempt to locate a running MBeanServer instance within the server and register the MBean with it. For the tc Server, which is bundled with STS and built on top of Tomcat, an MBeanServer will be created automatically, so no additional configuration is required.

Within the jmxExporter bean, the property beans defines the Spring beans we want to expose. It's a Map, and any number of MBeans can be specified here. In our case, we would like to expose the appStatisticsBean bean, which contains information about the contact application we want to show to administrators. For the MBean definition, the key will be used as the ObjectName (the javax.management.ObjectName class in JDK) for the Spring bean referenced by the corresponding entry value. In the previous configuration, the appStatisticsBean will be exposed under the ObjectName bean:name=ProSpring3ContactApp. By default, all public properties of the bean are exposed as attributes, and all public methods are exposed as operations.

Now the MBean is available for monitoring via JMX. Let's proceed to set up VisualVM and use its JMX client for monitoring purposes.

Setting Up VisualVM for JMX Monitoring

VisualVM is a very useful tool that can help in monitoring Java applications in various aspects. It's a free tool that bundles with JDK 6 (the jvisualvm.exe file under the bin folder in the JDK installation folder). A stand-alone version can also be downloaded from the project web site (http://visualvm.java.net/download.html). We will use the stand-alone version in this chapter; at the time of writing, the version is 1.3.3.

To install VisualVM, download the zip install file from the download site and extract it onto your local computer. Then, under the folder bin, execute the program visualvm.exe on Windows (or execute the visualvm script for Unix/Linux).

The VisualVM uses a plug-in system to support various monitoring functions. To support monitoring MBeans of Java applications, we need to install the MBeans plug-in. To install the plug-in, in VisualVM's menu, choose Tools ➤ Plug-ins, click the Available Plug-ins tab, check the plug-in VisualVM-MBeans, and click the Install button, as shown in Figure 23-4.

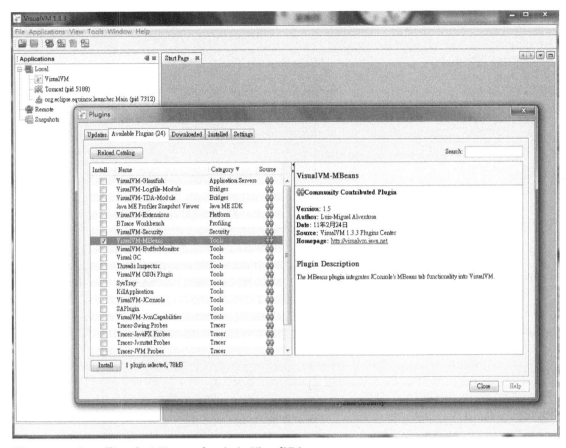

Figure 23-4. Installing the MBeans plug-in in VisualVM

After completing the installation, verify that the tc Server is up and the sample application is running. Then in VisualVM's left Applications view, you should be able to see that the Tomcat process is running, as shown in Figure 23-5.

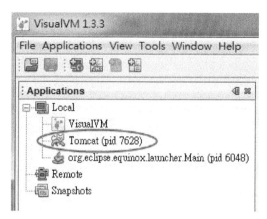

Figure 23-5. *VisualVM main screen showing the Tomcat process*

By default, VisualVM will scan for the Java applications that are running on the JDK 6 platform. (JSE 6 allows the creation of a JMX client that uses the Attach API to enable out-of-the-box monitoring and management of any applications that are started on the Java SE 6 platform.) In Figure 23-5, the Tomcat process is the tc Server that was running in STS. Double-clicking the node will bring up the monitoring screen, as shown in Figure 23-6.

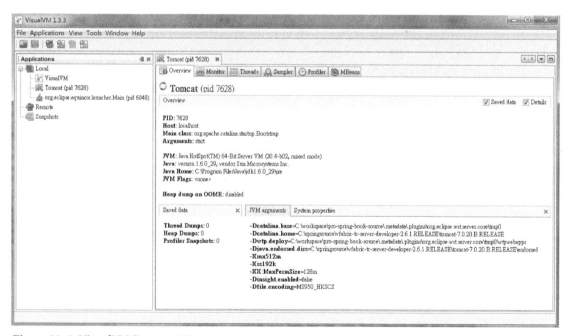

Figure 23-6. *VisualVM Tomcat JMX monitoring*

After the installation of the VisualVM-MBeans plug-in, you will able to see the MBeans tab. Clicking the tab will show the available MBeans. You should see the node called "bean." When you expand it, it will show the `ProSpring3ContactApp` MBean that was exposed, as shown in Figure 23-7.

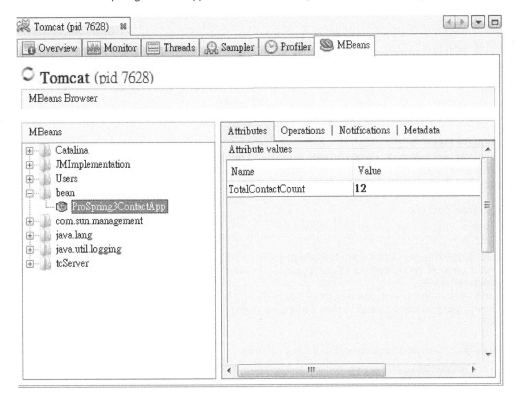

Figure 23-7. The `ProSpring3ContactApp` MBean

On the right side, you will see the method that we implemented in the bean, with the attribute `TotalContactCount` (which was automatically derived by the `getTotalContactCount()` method within the bean). Feel free to add a new contact in the sample application and refresh the view. The count will be revised accordingly.

Monitoring Logged-In Users

JMX is very useful for monitoring an application's status and metrics. One common use case is to expose the number of logged-in users for a web application. In this section, we will show you how to expose the number of logged-in users in the sample application to JMX.

As discussed in Chapter 17, we used Spring Security for application security management. Spring Security supports the configuration of a session registry, which can be injected into our Spring bean, and we retrieve the number of logged-in users. To do this, we need to enable concurrent session control in Spring Security. So, in the web deployment descriptor (the `web.xml` file), add a Spring Security listener. Listing 23-4 shows the listener declaration.

Listing 23-4. The Spring Security Concurrent Session Listener

```xml
<?xml version="1.0" encoding="UTF-8"?>
<web-app version="3.0" xmlns="http://java.sun.com/xml/ns/javaee"

    <!-- Other code omitted -->

    <!-- Creates the Spring Container shared by all Servlets and Filters -->
    <listener>
        <listener-class>org.springframework.web.context.ContextLoaderListener</listener-class>
    </listener>

    <!-- Spring Security concurrent session listener -->
    <listener>
        <listener-class>
            org.springframework.security.web.session.HttpSessionEventPublisher
        </listener-class>
    </listener>

    <!-- Other code omitted -->

</web-app>
```

In Listing 23-4, the listener declaration is highlighted in bold. Its Spring Security's listener implementation is created for publishing HTTP session-related events, such as a user logging in, and a new HTTP session is created.

Then we need to enable session management in the Spring Security configuration. Listing 23-5 shows the code snippet you need to add to the configuration file (the /WEB-INF/spring/security-context.xml file).

Listing 23-5. Configure Session Management in Spring Security

```xml
<?xml version="1.0" encoding="UTF-8"?>
<beans:beans xmlns="http://www.springframework.org/schema/security"

    <!-- Other code omitted -->

    <http use-expressions="true">
        <intercept-url pattern='/*' access='permitAll' />
        <form-login login-page="/contacts" authentication-failure-url="/security/loginfail"
            default-target-url="/contacts" />
        <logout logout-success-url="/contacts"/>
        <session-management>
            <concurrency-control max-sessions="1" session-registry-alias="sessionRegistry"/>
        </session-management>
    </http>

    <!-- Other code omitted -->

</beans:beans>
```

In Listing 23-5, the additional configuration is highlighted in bold. Under the <http> tag, the <session-management> tag defines the configuration related to session handling. Within the tag, the <concurrency-control> tag instructs Spring Security to perform concurrency control of user login sessions. The max-sessions attribute defines the maximum number of concurrent sessions allowed for each user, and the session-registry-alias attribute is to ask Spring Security to expose the session registry that it's managing as a Spring bean with the name sessionRegistry, for injection into our Spring MBean later.

Now we can modify the bean to autowire the session registry and expose the number of logged-in users to JMX. Let's add two methods to show the information of logged-in users. Listings 23-6 and 23-7 show the revised AppStatistics interface and AppStatisticsImpl class, respectively.

Listing 23-6. The Revised AppStatistics Interface

```
package com.apress.prospring3.ch23.jmx;

import java.util.List;

public interface AppStatistics {

    public int getTotalContactCount();

    public int getLoggedInUserCount();

    public List<Object> getLoggedInUsers();

}
```

Listing 23-7. The Revised AppStatisticsImpl Class

```
package com.apress.prospring3.ch23.jmx.impl;

import java.util.List;

import org.springframework.beans.factory.annotation.Autowired;
import org.springframework.security.core.session.SessionRegistry;

import com.apress.prospring3.ch23.jmx.AppStatistics;
import com.apress.prospring3.ch23.service.ContactService;

public class AppStatisticsImpl implements AppStatistics {

    @Autowired
    private ContactService contactService;

    @Autowired
    private SessionRegistry sessionRegistry;

    public int getTotalContactCount() {
        return contactService.findAll().size();
    }

    public int getLoggedInUserCount() {
        return sessionRegistry.getAllPrincipals().size();
    }
```

```
public List<Object> getLoggedInUsers() {
    return sessionRegistry.getAllPrincipals();
  }
}
```

In Listings 23-6 and 23-7, the changes are highlighted in bold. In the interface, two methods are added. The getLoggedInUserCount() method shows the number of logged-in users, while the getLoggedInUsers() method will return the list of the logged-in principals maintained by Spring Security. In the class, Spring Security's SessionRegistry interface is autowired, and in the methods, the SessionRegistry.getAllPrincipals() method is called to retrieve the logged-in users.

After the project is rebuilt and deployed and the application is reloaded, you will be able to see the two new metrics in the VisualVM screen, as shown in Figure 23-8.

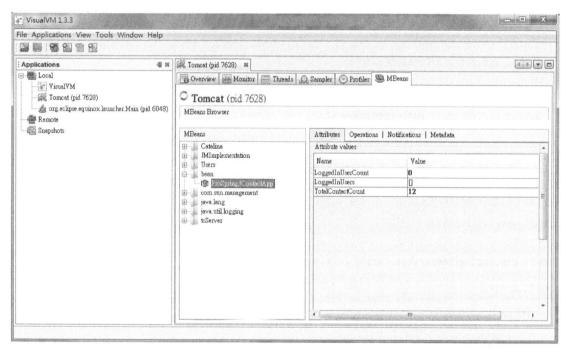

Figure 23-8. *Monitoring the logged-in users*

In Figure 23-8, you can see the two user-related metrics. The LoggedInUserCount metric shows the number of logged-in users, which is 0 at the moment. In addition, the LoggedInUsers metric shows the list of principals, which is currently empty.

Now log into the sample application (using "user" as both the user name and password). Then, in VisualVM, refresh the view (there is a Refresh button at the bottom), and you will see the login count incremented by one, as shown in Figure 23-9.

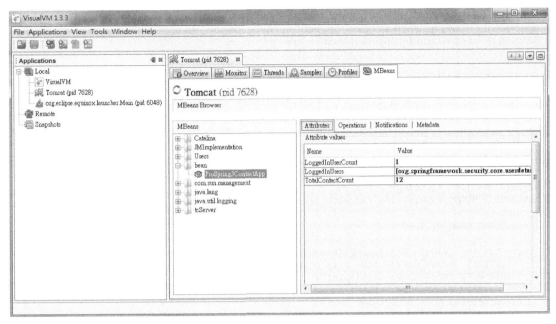

Figure 23-9. Showing the new logged-in user

You can see that the count is now 1. If you want to see who has logged in, you can click the Operations tab and then the operation getLoggedInUsers, and a pop-up dialog will show the content of the list, which contains the name of the logged-in user, as shown in Figure 23-10.

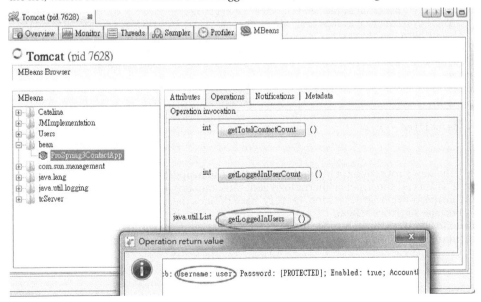

Figure 23-10. Showing the logged-in user name

In Figure 23-10, you can see the information of each logged-in user, including the user name. This is quite useful, for example, when an operator needs to check whether there are still users logging into the application before performing any maintenance actions.

Monitoring Hibernate Statistics

Hibernate also supports the maintenance and exposure of persistence-related metrics to JMX. To enable this, in the JPA configuration (the file /src/main/resources/datasource-tx-jpa.xml file), add two more Hibernate properties, as shown in Listing 23-8.

Listing 23-8. *Enable Hibernate Statistics*

```xml
<?xml version="1.0" encoding="UTF-8"?>
<beans xmlns="http://www.springframework.org/schema/beans"

    <!-- Other code omitted -->

    <bean id="emf" class="org.springframework.orm.jpa.LocalContainerEntityManagerFactoryBean">
        <property name="dataSource" ref="dataSource" />
        <property name="jpaVendorAdapter">
            <bean class="org.springframework.orm.jpa.vendor.HibernateJpaVendorAdapter" />
        </property>
        <property name="packagesToScan" value="com.apress.prospring3.ch23.domain"/>
        <property name="jpaProperties">
            <props>
                <prop key="hibernate.dialect">org.hibernate.dialect.H2Dialect</prop>
                <prop key="hibernate.max_fetch_depth">3</prop>
                <prop key="hibernate.jdbc.fetch_size">50</prop>
                <prop key="hibernate.jdbc.batch_size">10</prop>
                <prop key="hibernate.show_sql">true</prop>
                <!-- Hibernate statistics properties -->
                <prop key="hibernate.generate_statistics">true</prop>
                <prop key="hibernate.session_factory_name">sessionFactory</prop>
            </props>
        </property>
    </bean>

    <!-- Other code omitted -->

</beans>
```

In Listing 23-8, the new properties are highlighted in bold. The property hibernate.generate_statistics instructs Hibernate to generate statistics for its JPA persistence provider, while the property hibernate.session_factory_name defines the name of the session factory required by the Hibernate statistics MBean.

Finally, we need to add the MBean into Spring's MBeanExporter configuration. Listing 23-9 shows the code snippet you need to add to the configuration file (src/main/resources/batch-context.xml).

Listing 23-9. MBean for Hibernate Statistics

```xml
<?xml version="1.0" encoding="UTF-8"?>
<beans xmlns="http://www.springframework.org/schema/beans"

    <!-- Other code omitted -->

    <!-- Spring MBean for JMX Monitoring -->
    <bean id="appStatisticsBean" class="com.apress.prospring3.ch23.jmx.impl↩
.AppStatisticsImpl"/>

    <bean id="jmxExporter" class="org.springframework.jmx.export.MBeanExporter">
        <property name="beans">
            <map>
                <entry key="bean:name=ProSpring3ContactApp" value-ref="appStatisticsBean"/>
                <entry key="bean:name=ProSpring3ContactApp-hibernate" value-ref=↩
"statisticsBean"/>
            </map>
        </property>
    </bean>

    <bean id="statisticsBean" class="org.hibernate.jmx.StatisticsService">
        <property name="statisticsEnabled">
            <value>true</value>
        </property>
        <property name="sessionFactoryJNDIName">
            <value>sessionFactory</value>
        </property>
    </bean>

</beans>
```

In Listing 23-9, the changes are highlighted in bold. A new statisticsBean is declared, with Hibernate's StatisticsService class as the implementation. This is how Hibernate supports exposing statistics to JMX. Note the property sessionFactoryJNDIName, which should match the one defined in Listing 23-8 (hibernate.session_factory_name). Then within the jmxExporter bean, another bean with ObjectName bean:name=ProSpring3ContactApp-hibernate is declared that references the statisticsBean bean.

Now the Hibernate statistics are enabled and available via JMX. After the application is reloaded and the VisualVM is refreshed, you will be able to see the Hibernate statistics MBean. Clicking the node will display the detail statistics on the right side. Note that for the information that is not of Java primitive type (for example, a List), you can click in the field, which will expand the field to show the content. Figure 23-11 shows the MBeans tab, with the mapped entity classes and the executed queries fields expanded.

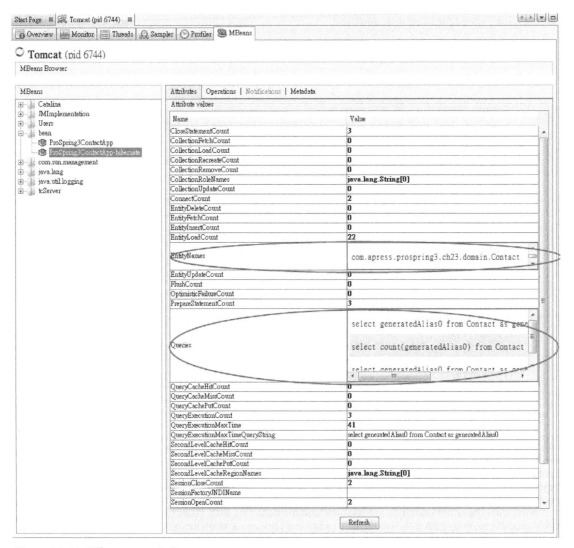

Figure 23-11. Hibernate statistics

In Figure 23-11, you can see many other metrics, such as ConnectCount, FlushCount, SecondLevelCacheHitCount, and so on. Those figures are very useful for you to understand the persistence behavior within your application and can assist you in troubleshooting and performance-tuning exercises.

Monitoring Spring Batch Jobs

If you are using Spring Batch for running batch jobs, you can also use Spring Batch's JMX support for batch job status monitoring. The Spring Batch Admin project is a subproject of Spring Batch that provides the class and infrastructure required for exposing job execution status to JMX. First, the dependency to Spring Batch Admin, as shown in Table 23-1, should be added to the project.

Table 23-1. Maven Dependencies for Spring Batch Admin

Group ID	Artifact ID	Version	Description
org.springframework.batch	spring-batch-admin-manager	1.2.1.RELEASE	Spring Batch Admin manager module that includes the classes required for exposing job status via JMX

The next step is to configure the required bean for Spring Batch and Spring Batch Admin to expose the metrics via JMX. Listing 23-10 shows the bean definitions that need to be added to the configuration file (batch-context.xml).

Listing 23-10. MBean for Spring Batch

```xml
<?xml version="1.0" encoding="UTF-8"?>
<beans xmlns="http://www.springframework.org/schema/beans"

    <!-- Other code omitted -->

    <!-- Spring Batch Admin for JMX -->
    <context:mbean-export default-domain="spring.application"/>

    <bean id="batchMBeanExporter" class="org.springframework.batch.admin.jmx
.BatchMBeanExporter">
        <property name="jobService">
            <bean class="org.springframework.aop.framework.ProxyFactoryBean">
                <property name="target" ref="jobService" />
                <property name="interceptorNames" value="cacheInterceptor" />
            </bean>
        </property>
        <property name="defaultDomain" value="spring.application" />
    </bean>

    <bean id="cacheInterceptor" class="org.springframework.batch.admin.util
.SimpleEhCacheInterceptor" />

    <bean id="jobService" class="org.springframework.batch.admin.service
.SimpleJobServiceFactoryBean">
        <property name="jobRepository" ref="jobRepository" />
        <property name="jobLauncher" ref="jobLauncher" />
        <property name="jobLocator" ref="jobRegistry" />
        <property name="dataSource" ref="dataSource" />
    </bean>
</beans>
```

In Listing 23-10, the new bean definitions are highlighted in bold. First, the <context:mbean-export> tag is defined to instruct Spring to scan for classes with related JMX annotations metadata. This is the mechanism that Spring Batch Admin uses for exposing its status via JMX.

Second, the `batchMBeanExporter` bean with the implementation class `BatchMBeanExporter` is declared. The class extends Spring's `MBeanExporter` class and references the bean with the implementation class `SimpleJobServiceFactoryBean` for retrieving batch job metrics.

After the application is rebuilt, redeployed, and reloaded, the metrics for Spring Batch will be available via JMX. In VisualVM, after the view was refreshed, you will see the node with name `spring.application`, which is the default MBean domain defined by the `<context:mbean-export>` tag. Click to expand it, and you will see the MBeans that are exposed via Spring Batch Admin. The one of particular interest is `JobExecution`, which shows the jobs defined and their related execution metrics. Figure 23-12 shows the application just started, without any job executed (the job name in the sample application is `importContactsJob`).

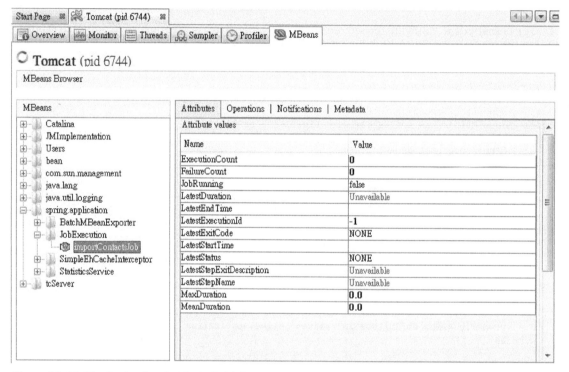

Figure 23-12. The Spring Batch Admin initial screen

Now trigger the batch job to run. Copy the file `contacts.xml` in the project's root folder into the folder `C:\temp\contact`. You will see from STS's tc Server console output that the job was triggered and the contact information in the file was uploaded. Then, the screen in VisualVM will be updated, as shown in Figure 23-13.

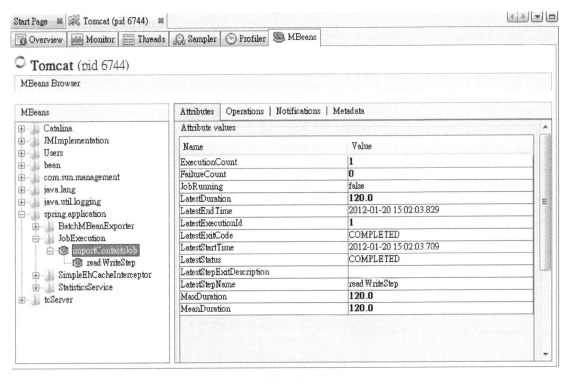

Figure 23-13. *The Spring Batch Admin screen with batch job run*

In the figure, you will see the execution count updated, together with the metrics of the last job execution. You will also notice that the step readWriteStep of the job has appeared. Clicking into it will show the details of the step execution metrics (note that this step is the only step in the job), as shown in Figure 23-14.

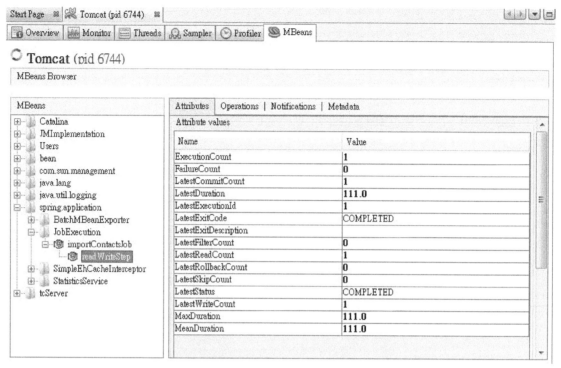

Figure 23-14. Spring Batch admin screen with the metrics for `readWriteStep`

Now you have an idea how Spring's JMX support can help you monitor many aspects of the application behavior and status, either by JMX MBeans already bundled with a third-party library or by implementing your custom MBean.

Monitoring an Application with Spring Insight

Spring Insight is another offering from SpringSource that supports comprehensive monitoring and visualization of Spring-based web applications.

In this section, we will demonstrate using Spring Insight Developer (an edition of Spring Insight targeted for developer use) to monitor the sample web application.

In the following sections, we will discuss the procedure required, including setting up a tc Server instance with Spring Insight enabled and using it to monitor the main aspects of a Spring-based JEE application.

Introducing Spring Insight

Spring Insight provides a number of features. The feature most relevant to application developers is the ability to trace and capture the statistics and performance figures across all layers of a web application. Some of the main information that Spring Insight can help to capture is as follows:

- The response time of various pages within a web application over a designated period of time
- Detailed description of each request, its parameters, and its headers
- The list of component method calls and their parameters
- A list of all database queries and their performance
- The interaction between Spring beans and their performance

Under the hood, Spring Insight use AspectJ to intercept operations in target web applications. Targeted web applications are loaded with a special classloader that dynamically instruments web applications during runtime.

Configuring Spring Insight

The easiest way to understand Spring Insight is to see it in action. In this section, we will demonstrate how to set up an environment with Spring Insight Developer for monitoring our sample application.

With STS, setting up Spring Insight Developer is easy. The tc Server Developer Edition that is bundled with STS already has Spring Insight Developer included. To use it, we just need to configure a tc Server instance with Spring Insight enabled.

To configure a tc Server with Spring Insight enabled, in STS's Servers view, right-click in any empty area and then select New ➤ Server. The New Server wizard will be displayed. Enter the server name, as shown in Figure 23-15.

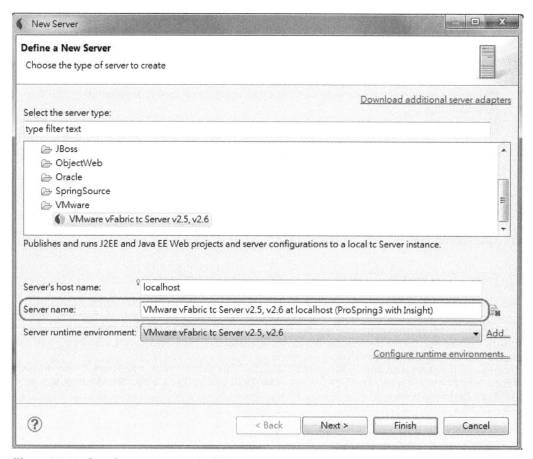

Figure 23-15. *Creating a new server in STS*

Click the Next button, and the tc Server Configuration screen will be displayed. Select "Create new instance," and click the Next button, as shown in Figure 23-16.

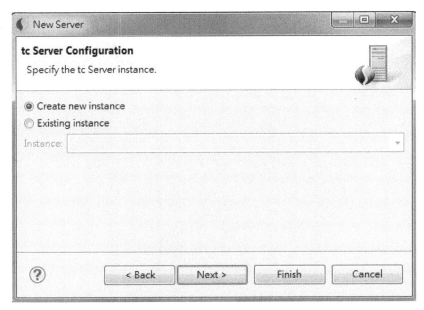

Figure 23-16. The tc Server Configuration dialog

In the Create tc Server Instance dialog that opens, enter a name for the tc Server instance (for example, prospring3-ch23-insight) and check "insight" in the Templates select box. This instructs tc Server to create a new instance with the Spring Insight template (see Figure 23-17).

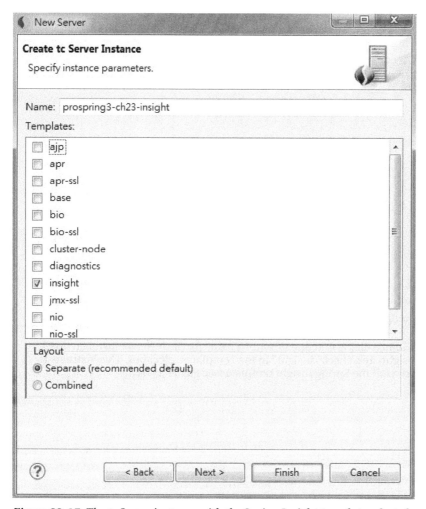

Figure 23-17. The tc Server instance with the Spring Insight template selected

Then, click Next to add the project into the server, as shown in Figure 23-18.

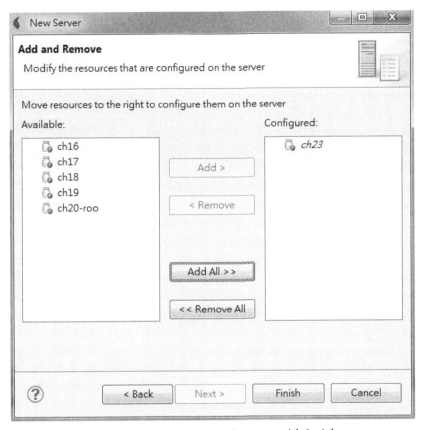

Figure 23-18. Adding a project to tc Server instance with Insight

Click the Finish button, and wait for the server instance creation to complete. You will then see the new server with the project added, as shown in Figure 23-19.

Figure 23-19. tc Server in the Servers view in STS

Now publish the project and start the server. After it has started, we can explore the web application's behavior with Spring Insight.

Using Spring Insight

Spring Insight provides a web application for visualizing the performance of the applications deployed to that server instance. To access Spring Insight on the tc Server, enter the URL `http://localhost:8080/insight` in your browser. The first page should look like Figure 23-20.

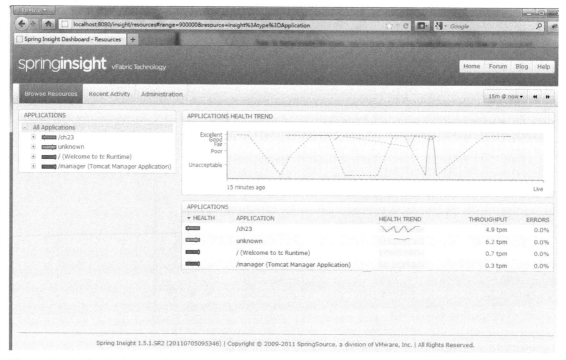

Figure 23-20. *The Spring Insight home page*

From the figure, you can see that one of the applications is our sample application, under the URL /ch23. Play around with the sample application (in another browser tab or window), and then click the item /ch23. The end points with their high-level throughput figures will be displayed, as shown in Figure 23-21.

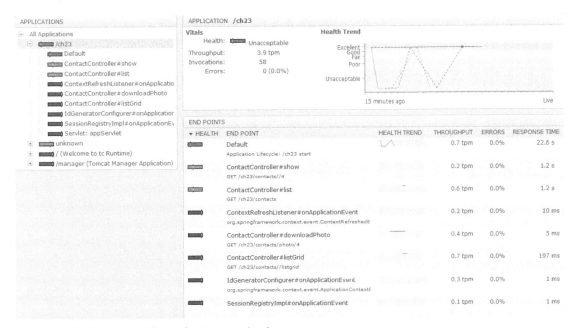

Figure 23-21. *Spring Insight: endpoints monitoring*

To see the details of an end point, click it on the left side, and the details will be shown on the right, as shown in Figure 23-22.

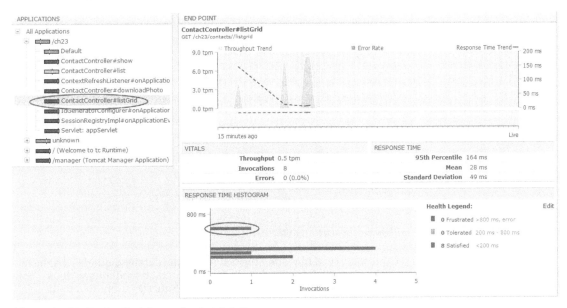

Figure 23-22. *Spring Insight: end point details*

Figure 23-22 shows the invocations for the end point `ContactController#listGrid` (which corresponds to the method `listGrid()` in the `ContactController` class, which will be invoked by the jQuery grid to retrieve the page of contact information for display). On the right side, you will see the response time histogram, which shows the various invocations during the monitoring period. Clicking into any invocation will cause the trace information to display below the histogram. Figure 23-23 shows an example.

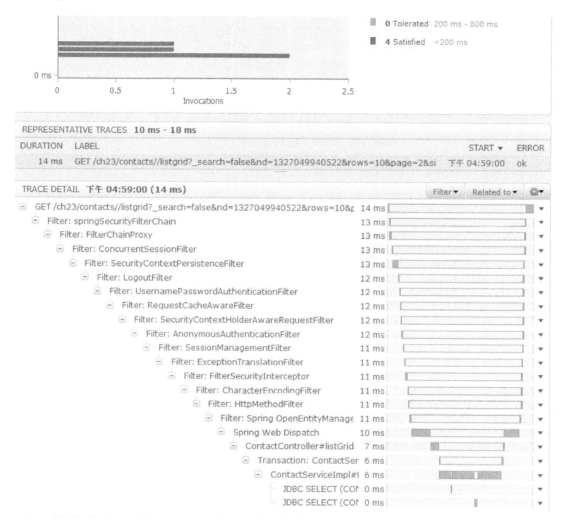

Figure 23-23. Spring Insight: end point invocation details

In Figure 23-23, you will see the details call tree, the time taken, and the database queries that have been fired to the database. So, you have a full picture of the application interaction among various Spring beans within your application, as well as the execution time for the queries submitted to the database. With the information, you will be able to identify the bottleneck of your application quickly and perform corresponding remedial actions.

This concludes our introduction to Spring Insight. Spring Insight is very useful tool that can help you analyze your application behavior in many different aspects. You can even use Spring Insight Developer Kit to develop plug-ins to extend Spring Insight for collecting specific metrics about your application. One example is to analyze traces from Spring Insight and produce new types of end points, such as a JMS message queue.

For details, please refer to SpringSource's online documentation at
`http://static.springsource.com/projects/tc-server/2.5/devedition/htmlsingle/devedition.html`.

Summary

In this chapter, we covered various topics of monitoring a Spring-powered JEE application.

First, we discussed Spring's support of JMX, the standard in monitoring Java applications. Topics included implementing custom MBeans for exposing application-related information, as well as exposing statistics of common components like Hibernate and Spring Batch.

Second, we covered using Spring Insight to visualize the application's performance on tc Server. Topics included setting up a tc Server instance with Spring Insight enabled, as well as some of the main metrics that can be seen from Spring Insight's web frontend.

SpringSource Tool Suite

The chapters in this book gave specific instructions on using STS when creating projects and implementing the sample code within each chapter. If you have gone through all the samples, you will already have a fair understanding of STS.

The objective of this appendix is to describe other basic topics when using STS that were not covered in the regular chapters. This appendix is intended for developers who are not familiar with STS. However, basic knowledge of using Eclipse for Java application development is assumed.

If you already are an Eclipse power user or are familiar with STS (or the Spring IDE), feel free to skip this appendix and use it for reference only when required.

In this appendix, we will discuss some basic topics related to STS. Specifically, the following topics will be covered:

- *Installation*: We will discuss how to install STS. Although STS also supports Mac OS X and Linux, we will focus on installing and using STS on the Windows platform.

- *Project setup and dependency management:* We will discuss how to create Spring projects in STS and manage the required dependencies within the project. We will focus on the Maven dependency management with the m2e plug-in (the official Maven plug-in for Eclipse IDE).

- *Using STS*: We will discuss installing extensions, managing tc Server, and so on.

Introducing STS

STS is the IDE tool offered by SpringSource for Spring application developers. It includes a number of plug-ins, which provide support for developing Spring-based applications, as well as integrates with other Eclipse plug-ins (such as m2e, AspectJ Development Tool, and so on). Some major features are highlighted here:

- It supports the creation and editing of Spring's `ApplicationContext` configuration XML files with code assistance and validation.

- It provides graphical views of Spring configuration such as the bean graph, Web Flow diagram, Spring Batch and Integration diagrams, and so on.

- It supports the installation of extensions for other features (for example, for the development of Groovy classes and scripts, Grails, and so on).

- It supports the management of tc Server Developer Edition for local web application development and testing.

STS Installation

STS can be installed in two ways. First, SpringSource has prepared a bundled version with Eclipse and the required plug-ins. Second, if you already have an Eclipse development environment, you can simply extend it with the plug-ins provided by STS. Either way, make sure you already have a JDK (version 6 or newer) installed in your PC.

Installing the Stand-Alone Version of STS

The simplest way to install STS is to download the bundle from the STS web site that has Eclipse bundled with it. So, you need to download the proper version for your development machine from the tools web site (`www.springsource.org/downloads/sts`). Figure A-1 shows the download site, with the versions available for the Windows platform (note that versions are also available for Mac OS X and Linux).

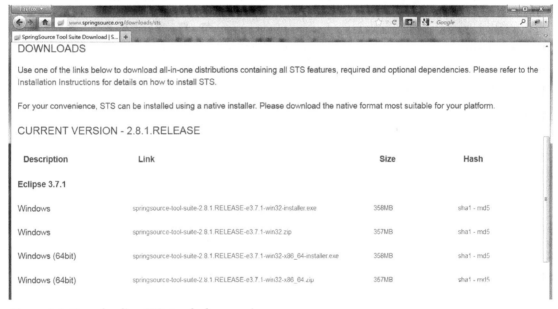

Figure A-1. *Downloading STS stand-alone version*

Select the correct version for your computer. For Windows, versions for both 32- and 64-bit Windows are available. In addition, there are two forms of distribution. One is in Windows installer format that you can simply click to install, and the other is a zip file that you can extract and use to set up STS yourself.

We will use the 64-bit Windows installer for our demonstration (the latest stable version at the time of writing is 2.8.1). It's very straightforward. Upon completing the download, click the executable file to start the installation. There are several steps for the installation; Figure A-2 shows step 1.

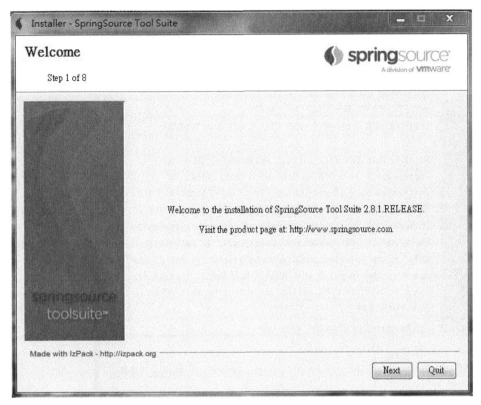

Figure A-2. STS installation: step 1

Click the Next button and proceed to step 2, as shown in Figure A-3.

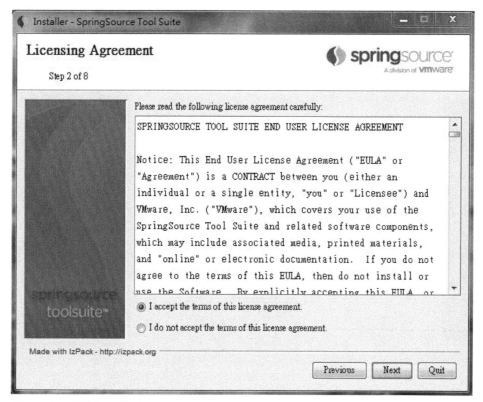

Figure A-3. *STS installation: step 2*

Accept the license agreement and click the Next button to proceed to the next step, as indicated in Figure A-4.

Figure A-4. STS installation: step 3

Select the folder in which you want to install STS. Then, click Next to proceed to the next step, as shown in Figure A-5.

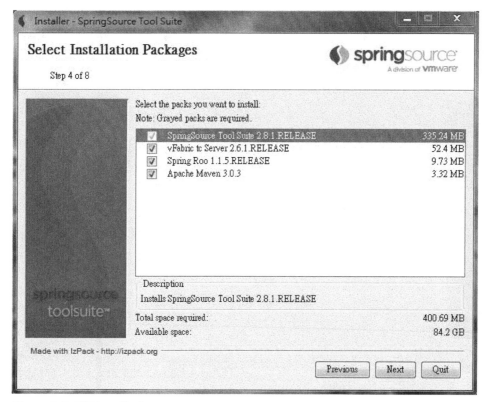

Figure A-5. STS installation: step 4

Step 4 will display the available optional items for your selection. Options include the tc Server Developer Edition, Spring Roo, and Apache Maven stand-alone version (based on version 3). Make sure all the options are selected, and then click Next to proceed to the next step, as shown in Figure A-6.

Figure A-6. *STS installation: step 5*

Select the JDK installation folder on your computer, and then click the Next button to proceed to the next step, as shown in Figure A-7.

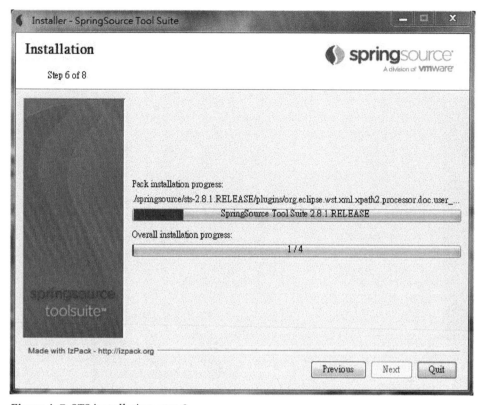

Figure A-7. *STS installation: step 6*

Wait until the installation is complete, and then choose whether to create a shortcut for STS, as shown in Figure A-8.

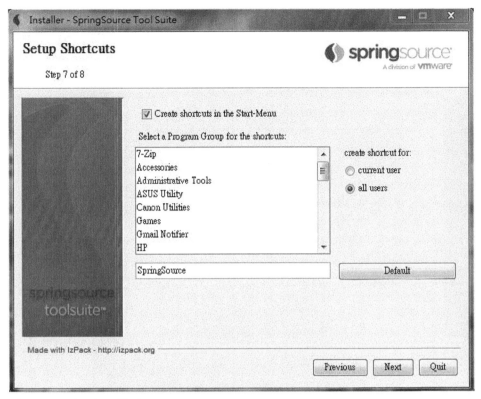

Figure A-8. *STS installation: step 7*

Click Next to complete the installation, as shown in Figure A-9.

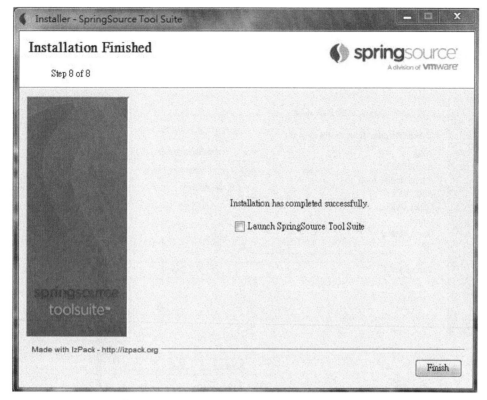

Figure A-9. STS installation: step 8

At this point, the installation of the stand-alone version of STS is complete. Click Finish.

Installing STS to an Existing Eclipse Environment

Another way to set up STS is to extend an existing Eclipse installation. In the following example, we will demonstrate installing STS onto an existing Eclipse (version 3.7.1) setup. Eclipse comes in various bundles. For this example, the Eclipse IDE for Java EE Developers version is used (please refer to the web site www.eclipse.org/downloads for the list of available bundles). Before we can install STS, we need to install some Eclipse plug-ins required by STS.

To install the Maven plug-in for Eclipse, choose the menu item Help ➤ Install New Software in Eclipse. Click the Add button, enter the name (**m2e**) and the update site URL http://download.eclipse.org/technology/m2e/releases, and click OK button. Then, choose the component to install, as shown in Figure A-10.

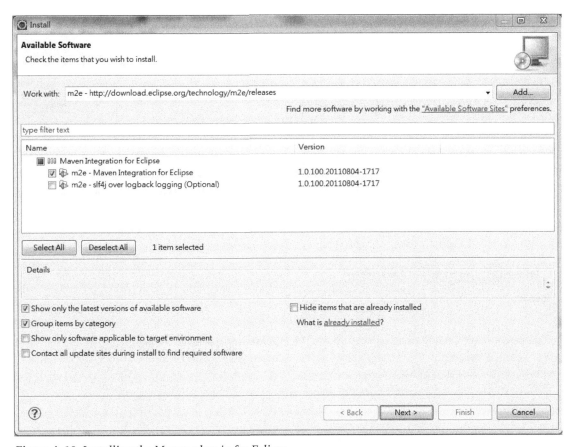

Figure A-10. Installing the Maven plug-in for Eclipse

The next plug-in we need to install is the Jetty runtime environment, which includes an update to the JSP plug-in that is required by STS. In the Install dialog, click the Add button to open the Add Repository dialog, and enter the name (**Jetty Runtime**) and the URL `http://download.eclipse.org/jetty/updates/3.7` for the update site information. After the repository is added, the available components will be displayed in the Install dialog. Choose the components to install, and click the Next button to continue the installation, as shown in Figure A-11.

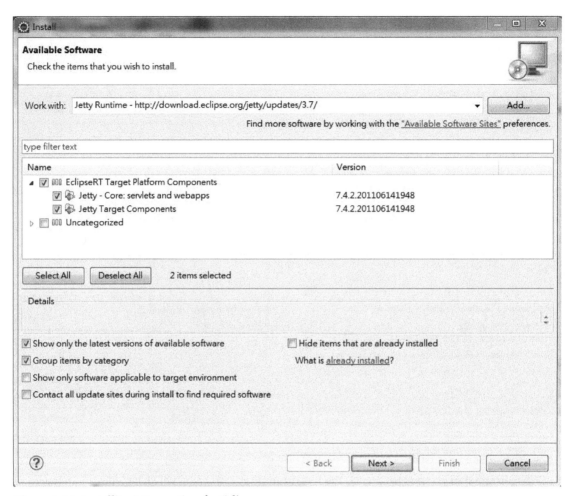

Figure A-11. Installing Jetty runtime for Eclipse

After that is complete, we can proceed to install the STS plug-ins. Prepare a file called bookmarks.xml with the content, as shown in Listing A-1.

Listing A-1. The bookmarks.xml File for STS

```xml
<?xml version="1.0" encoding="UTF-8"?>
<bookmarks>
    <site url="http://dist.springsource.com/release/TOOLS/update/e3.7" selected="true"↵
name="SpringSource Update Site for Eclipse 3.7"/>
    <site url="http://dist.springsource.com/release/TOOLS/composite/e3.7" selected="true"↵
name="SpringSource Update Site for Eclipse 3.7 (Dependencies)"/>
    <site url="http://download.eclipse.org/releases/indigo" selected="true" name="Indigo"/>
</bookmarks>
```

The file contains all the update sites required for installing STS. Then, open the Install dialog (by select Help ➤ Install New Software… in Eclipse top menu), as shown in Figure A-11. Click the link Available Software Sites, click the Import button, and select the file, as shown in Figure A-12.

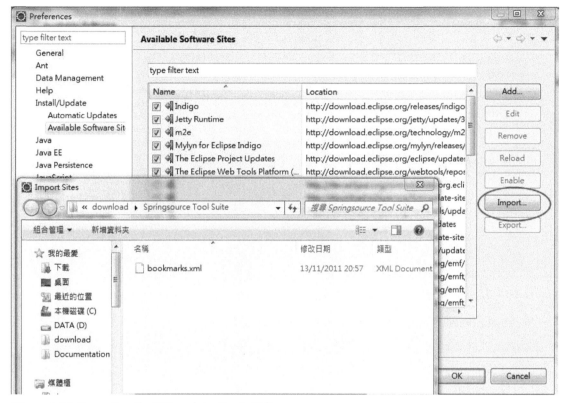

Figure A-12. Importing the STS update sites in Eclipse

Upon completion, you will see that the STS update sites are added, as shown in Figure A-13.

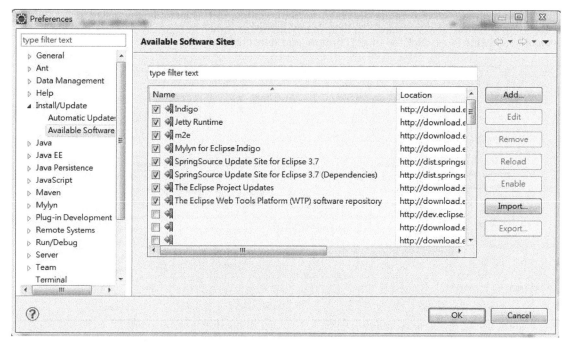

Figure A-13. *STS update sites in Eclipse*

Back in the Install dialog, select the components to install, as shown in Figure A-14.

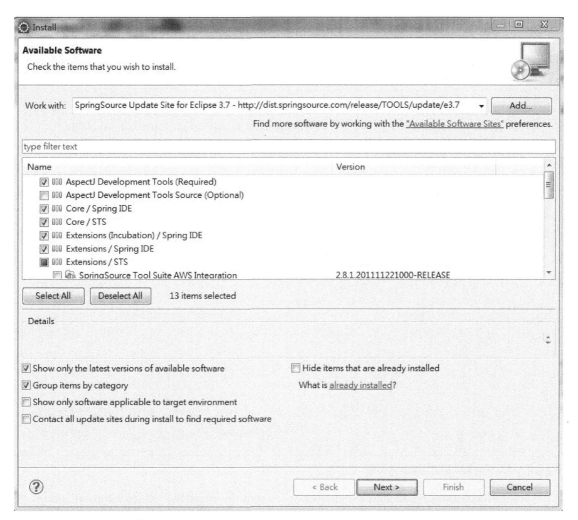

Figure A-14. Selecting STS components

We don't need all the components, and some components require additional plug-ins to be installed first. Select the components suitable for your environment; Figure A-15 shows the components selected in our sample.

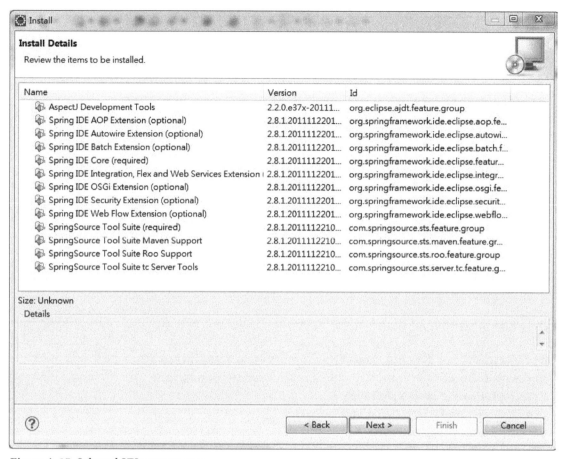

Figure A-15. Selected STS components

Click the Next button, and follow the instructions to start the installation. Once the installation is complete, the STS-related functions will be available.

Project Setup and Dependency Management

After STS is installed, we can create a project and start development. STS provides a number of template projects with preconfigured settings and dependencies. In STS, choose File ➤ New ➤ Spring Template Project, and a list of available template projects will be presented for your selection. Figure A-16 shows the available template projects as of version 2.8.1.

Figure A-16. Selecting a Spring project template

Clicking the project name presents you with a brief description of the purpose of the project.

Create a Simple Spring Utility Project

Let's create a simple project. Choose the Simple Spring Utility Project template, and click Next. Then enter the project information, as shown in Figure A-17.

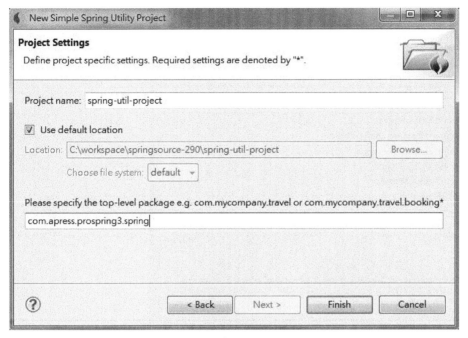

Figure A-17. Creating a simple Spring utility project

STS will create the project. STS template projects are all generated according to Maven's standard project folder structure, and they use Maven for dependency management. Spring and Maven natures are automatically added to the project, as shown in Figure A-18.

Figure A-18. A simple Spring utility project

After project creation, we need to update the configuration generated by STS. For example, at the time of this writing, the generated project will use Spring Framework 3.0.6.RELEASE and JDK 5 by default. Let's change the project to use Spring Framework 3.1.0.RELEASE and JDK 6, respectively. Double-click the pom.xml file, and in the editor, click the pom.xml tab and edit the configuration, as shown in Figure A-19.

```
 M  *spring-util-project/pom.xml  ✕
 6      <groupId>org.springframework.samples.spring</groupId>
 7      <artifactId>spring-utility</artifactId>
 8      <version>1.0.0.CI-SNAPSHOT</version>
 9      <packaging>jar</packaging>
10      <name>Spring Utility</name>
11      <url>http://www.springframework.org</url>
12⊖     <description>
13          <![CDATA[
14        This project is a minimal jar utility with Spring configuration.
15        ]]>
16      </description>
17⊖     <properties>
18          <maven.test.failure.ignore>true</maven.test.failure.ignore>
19          <spring.framework.version>3.1.0.RELEASE</spring.framework.version>
20⊖     </properties>    <dependencies>
21⊖         <dependency>
22              <groupId>junit</groupId>
23              <artifactId>junit</artifactId>
24              <version>4.7</version>
25              <scope>test</scope>
26          </dependency>
27⊖         <dependency>
28              <groupId>org.springframework</groupId>
29              <artifactId>spring-test</artifactId>
30              <version>${spring.framework.version}</version>
31              <scope>test</scope>
32          </dependency>
33⊖         <dependency>
34              <groupId>org.springframework</groupId>
35              <artifactId>spring-context</artifactId>
36              <version>${spring.framework.version}</version>
37          </dependency>
38⊖         <dependency>
39              <groupId>log4j</groupId>
40              <artifactId>log4j</artifactId>
41              <version>1.2.14</version>
42          </dependency>
43      </dependencies>
44
45⊖     <build>
46⊖         <plugins>
47⊖             <plugin>
48                  <groupId>org.apache.maven.plugins</groupId>
49                  <artifactId>maven-compiler-plugin</artifactId>
50⊖                 <configuration>
51                      <source>1.6</source>
52                      <target>1.6</target>
53                  </configuration>
54              </plugin>
55
56          </plugins>
57      </build>
58 </project>
59
```

Overview | Dependencies | Dependency Hierarchy | Effective POM | pom.xml

Figure A-19. Modifying the Maven configuration

However, just modifying the pom.xml file is not enough. For example, if you now right-click the project and select Properties ➤ Java Compiler, you will see that the project is still using JDK 5, as shown in Figure A-20.

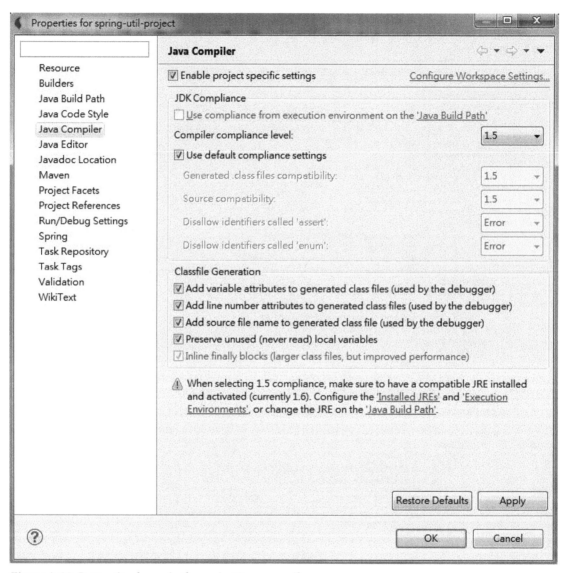

Figure A-20. Properties shown in the project Java compiler

This is because even though you modified the pom.xml file, the Maven plug-in will not update the project configuration automatically. You can update the project configuration either by changing the properties shown in Figure A-20 directly or by right-clicking the project and choosing Maven ➤ Update Project Configuration, as shown in Figure A-21.

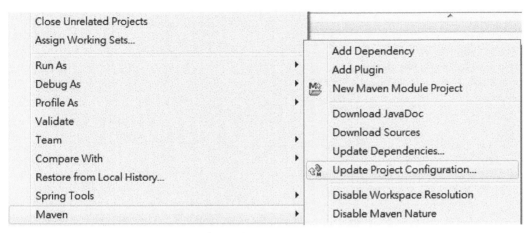

Figure A-21. Updating the project configuration

However, in STS 2.8.1 with the version of the m2e plug-in that we are using, one strange behavior is that after updating the project configuration with Maven, the Spring nature will then be removed. In this case, you can add it back by right-clicking the project and then choosing Spring Tools ➤ Add Spring Project Nature.

Dependency Management for a Project

With the Maven plug-in, managing the library dependencies for your project becomes much easier. For example, in the pom.xml file editor view, click the Dependencies tab, as shown in Figure A-22.

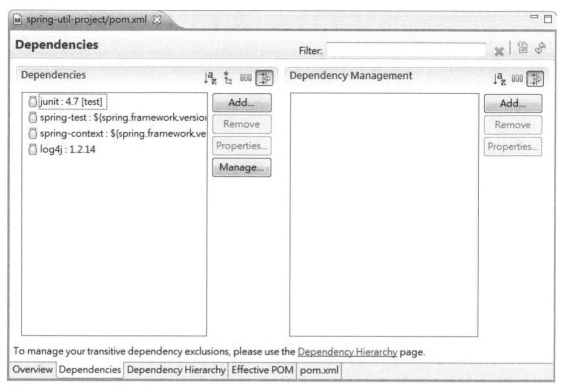

Figure A-22. Maven dependency management in the project

To add a dependency into your project, click the Add button on the left side to open the Select Dependency dialog. Then enter the information for the dependency. Figure A-23 shows the Select Dependency dialog with the information entered for adding the dependency in Hibernate Entity Manager, which includes the Hibernate library and its JPA support (they will appear in Figure A-24 after the dependency is added).

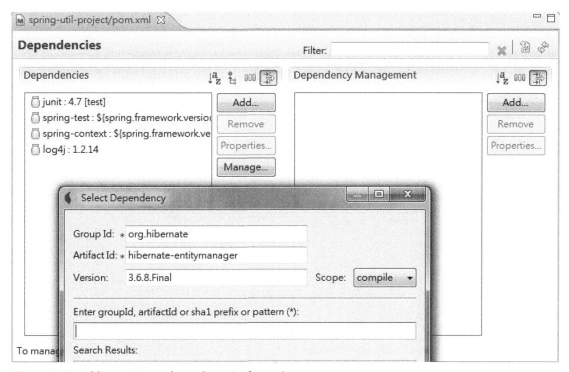

Figure A-23. Adding a Maven dependency in the project

After the dependency is added, save the file. The Maven dependencies for the project will be updated automatically. If you click the Dependency Hierarchy tab, you will see the entire dependency hierarchy, as shown in Figure A-24.

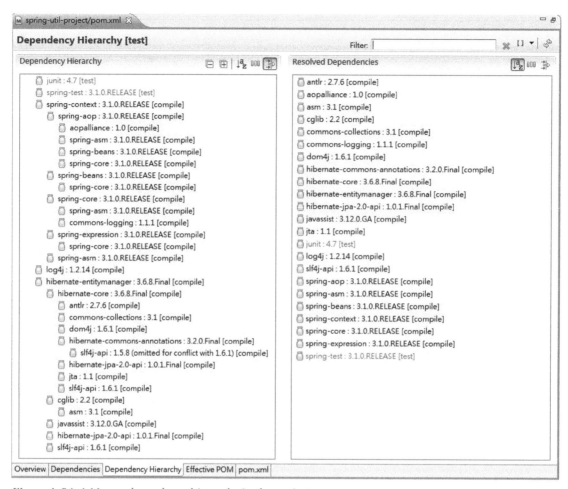

Figure A-24. A Maven dependency hierarchy in the project

In Figure A-24, you will notice that after the Hibernate Entity Manager dependency is added, the other required dependencies are also added (for example, the Hibernate Core library). This feature is called *transitive dependencies management* in Maven.

In various chapters, you will see that different dependencies are required. For all cases, you can simply follow the procedure here for managing the dependencies.

Using STS

Now you have a basic understanding of what STS can do for you. In this section, we will discuss some other areas of STS, such as installing extensions and managing tc Server.

Installing STS Extensions

STS comes with a basic set of plug-ins, including those for AOP, Spring Beans, Security, Web Flow support, and so on. On top of those plug-ins, STS also provides a lot of extensions that support the development of Spring-based applications or integration with other popular tools and frameworks.

To see the available extensions and install those you require, first open the Spring Dashboard view. A quick way to open the view is to click the Dashboard icon in the toolbar, as shown in Figure A-25.

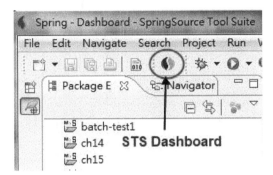

Figure A-25. The icon for opening the Dashboard view in STS

In the view, click the Extensions tab, and the list of available extensions will be displayed, as shown in Figure A-26.

Figure A-26. Installing extensions in STS

In Figure A-26, you will see a lot of extensions, such as the support for Grails, the Google plug-in for Eclipse, and so on. Simple check the extension you want, and then click the Install button to install it.

Configuring VMware tc Server in STS

STS comes bundled with tc Server Developer Edition, with Apache Tomcat 7 embedded, which is very useful for local web application development. tc Server supports the creation of instances with various capabilities. To create a new server instance, in the Servers view (you can open it by selecting Window ➤ Show View ➤ Servers in STS's top menu), right-click an empty area and choose New ➤ Server to display the dialog for creating a new server, as shown in Figure A-27.

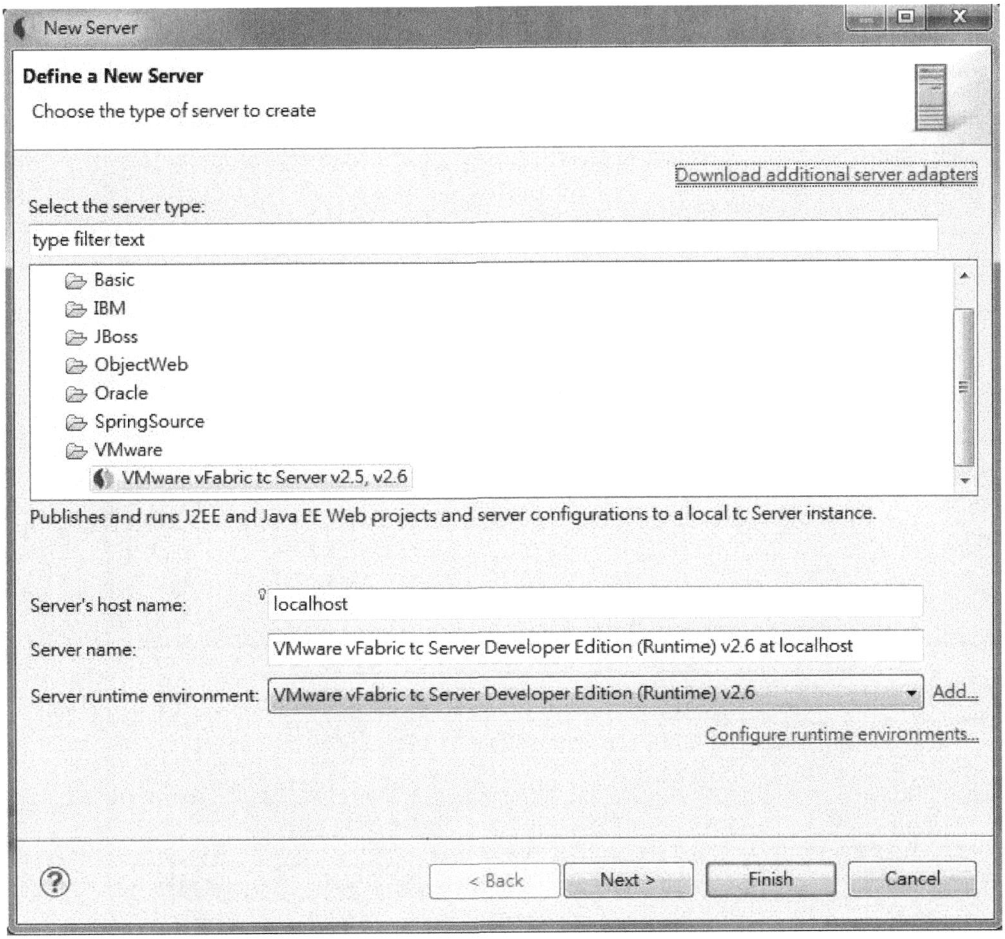

Figure A-27. Defining a new server

Click the Next button and choose the option Create New instance on the next screen. In the Create tc Server Instance dialog, enter the name of the instance; then select the template you want to use for the new instance (see Figure A-28).

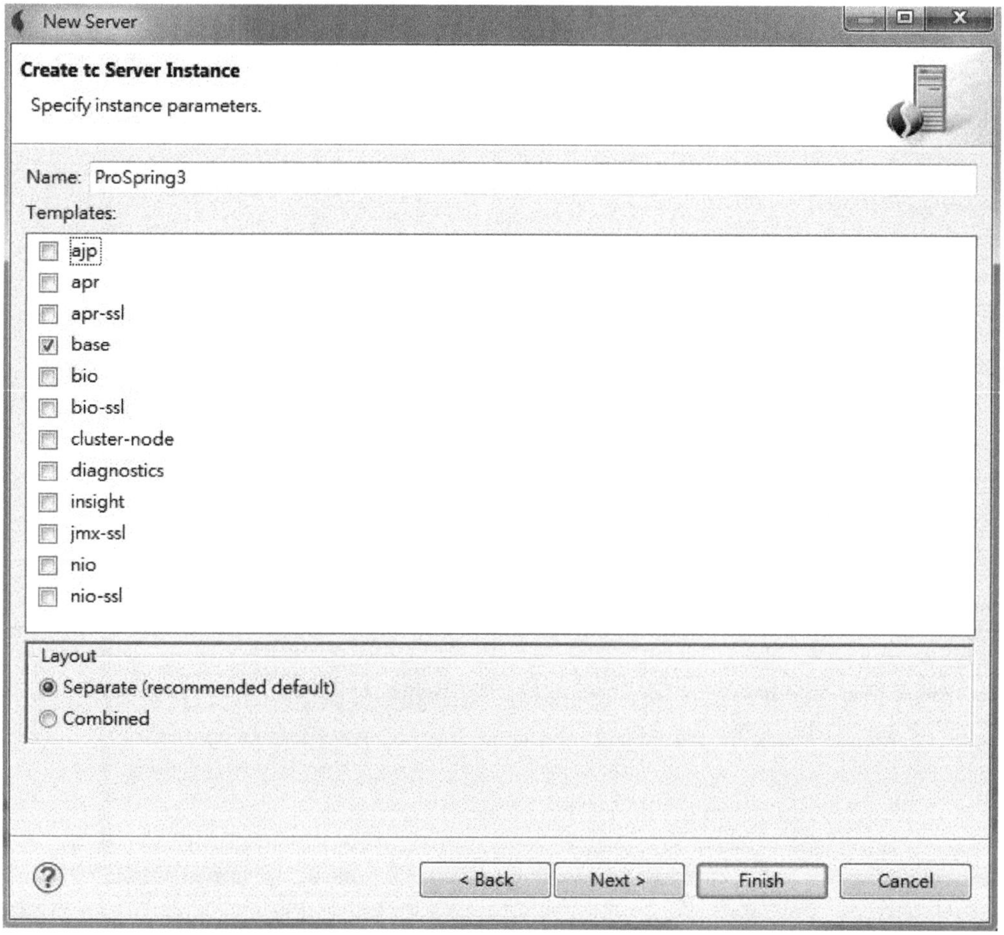

Figure A-28. Creating a new tc Server instance

As shown in Figure A-28, the selected base template instructs STS to create a tc Server instance based on Tomcat 7. For a detailed description of the meaning of each template, as well as coverage on how to use tc Server for your development, please refer to its online documentation at http://static.springsource.com/projects/tc-server/2.5/getting-started/htmlsingle/getting-started.html.

Summary

In this appendix, we showed you how to use STS. Topics included installing it, using Spring template projects, managing Maven dependencies, updating project configuration, and managing tc Server.

Index

S

Schedule tasks. *See also* Taskscheduler
    abstraction
    asynchronous task execution
        Async task, 535
        AsyncService interface, 534
        AsyncServiceImpl class, 534
        output, 536
        testing program, 535
    features, 523
    parts, 524
    SpringBlog application
        HousekeepingService interface, 537
        HousekeepingServiceImpl class, 538
    STS projects, 523–524
    task options, 524
Scripting languages
    closures, 819
    features, 819
    Groovy
        closure, 827–828
        contact domain, 829
        convertion, 823
        dependencies, 829
        dynamic type, 825–826
        Eclipse plug-in installation, 821–823
        ojectives, 825
        refreshable beans, 833–835
        rule engine, 830–833
        simplified syntax, 827
        Spring, 829
        testing program, 835–838
    JSR-223
        JavaScript expression, 824
        Mozilla Rhino, 824
        script engines, 824
        ScriptEngine.eval() method, 825
        ScriptEngineManager class, 824
    requirements, 819
    Spring utility project, 820–821
Service layer
    dependencies, 457
    drawbacks, 456
    service object granularity, 457
Spring
    alternatives
        Google Guice, 12
        JBoss Seam Framework, 12
        JEE 6 Container, 12
        PicoContainer, 12
    AOP (*see* Aspect-oriented
        programming (AOP))
    application portability, 114

applications, 23
    Ajax and MVC basic project, 26
    configuration-basic project, 25
    jPetStore, 25
    MVC Showcase project, 25
    petcare, 26
    petclinic, 24
    Petclinic Groovy, 24
    sample source code, 23
    task-basic project, 25
    Webflow, 26
definition, 1
dependency injection, 2
    AOP, 4–5
    benefits, 3
    data access, 6
    dependency management, 3
    dynamic scripting support, 9
    evolution, 3–4
    exception handling, 9
    features and bean factory, 18
    improved testability, 4
    injection-oriented application, 4
    interfaces, 2
    JavaBeans, 2
    JEE, simplification and integration, 7
    job scheduling support, 9
    mail support, 8
    MVC, 7
    Object/XML Mapping (OXM), 6–7
    reduced glue code, 3
    remote access mechanisms, 8
    simplified application configuration, 3
    SpEL, 5
    transactions, 7
    validation, 5–6
documentation, 27
Enterprise Bundle Repositories, 19
features, 113–114
framework, 14
Hello World application
    ApplicationContext interface, 33–34
    command-line arguments, 27–28
    execution output, 35
    HelloWorldMessageProvider class,
        28–29
    in Java version, 27
    MessageProvider interface, 28
    MessageRenderer interface, 28
    MessageSupportFactory, 30–31
    refactor, 29
    StandardOutMessageRenderer class, 29
    XML configuration, 34
Hibernate (*see* Hibernate)
IoC technique, 2

CPSIA information can be obtained at www.ICGtesting.com
Printed in the USA
LVOW010030250113

317172LV00010B/132/P